Archaeology of Prehistoric Native America

GARLAND REFERENCE LIBRARY OF THE HUMANITIES (VOL. 1537)

Archaeology of Prehistoric Native America

An Encyclopedia

Editor
Guy Gibbon

Associate Editors

Kenneth M. Ames
James A. Brown
Joseph L. Chartkoff
Patricia L. Crown
George C. Frison

Donald H. Mitchell
David Morrison
David L. Pokotylo
James D. Wilde
W. Raymond Wood

GARLAND PUBLISHING, INC.
A MEMBER OF THE TAYLOR & FRANCIS GROUP
New York & London
1998

Library of Congress Cataloging-in-Publication Data

Archaeology of prehistoric native America : an encyclopedia / general editor,
    Guy Gibbon ; with Kenneth M. Ames . . . [et al.].
            p.   cm. — (Garland reference library of the humanities ;
    vol. 1537)
        Includes bibliographical references and index.
        ISBN 0-8153-0725-X (hardcover)
        1. Indians of North America—Antiquities—Encyclopedias.   2. North
America—Antiquities—Encyclopedias.   3. Archaeology—North America—
Encyclopedias.   I. Gibbon, Guy E., 1939–   . II. Ames, Kenneth M.
III. Series.
E77.9.A72   1998
970.01'03—dc21   98-11443
                                                                      CIP

Cover photograph by Corson Hirschfeld
Cover design by Lawrence Wolfson Design, New York

Printed on acid-free, 250-year-life paper
Manufactured in the United States of America

In memory of Hillary Gibbon
(1969–1994)

Contents

Acknowledgments

A work of this magnitude is always the product of many people. Special thanks to the volume's associate editors, who brought a collective expertise to the project that no single archaeologist has as an individual in North American archaeology today. The Smithsonian Institution, American Museum of Natural History, Society for American Archaeology, Texas Department of State, Wilford Laboratory of Archaeology at the University of Minnesota, and many other institutions kindly granted permission to either publish illustrations or the results of work carried out under their jurisdiction. Kennie Lyman, Marianne Lown, Earl Roy, Jennifer Brosious, and Helga McCue at Garland Publishing brought professional publishing expertise to the product at various stages of its development. Extra special thanks to Mary Cooney, the volume's copy editor. Deb Dale Jones, Brad Johnson, and Sangwoo Han, graduate students in the Interdisciplinary Archaeological Studies program at the University of Minnesota, provided invaluable help in organizing the project, acquiring illustrations, and preparing the index. Finally, many thanks to my wife, Ann, for a high level of tolerance throughout the project.

Reader's Guide

When did people first enter North America? Where did they come from? Who were they? How did they spread throughout the continent and how long did it take them? *Archaeology of Prehistoric Native America: An Encyclopedia* provides answers to these and many other questions and a comprehensive introduction to the precontact cultures of continental North America. Organized by major culture areas (Arctic/Subarctic, California, Eastern Woodlands, Great Basin, Northwest Coast, Plateau, Plains, and Southwest) and two topical categories (Pre-Clovis/Paleoindian and General), the encyclopedia contains more than 750 entries and 400,000 words. Prepared by well-known regional specialists, the entries pertaining to each culture area describe the area, its major cultural complexes, and some of its more important archaeological sites, food resources, pioneer archaeologists, and unique features. The associate editors by culture area are David Morrison (Arctic/Subarctic), Joseph L. Chartkoff (California), James A. Brown (Eastern Woodlands), James D. Wilde (Great Basin), Donald H. Mitchell (Northwest Coast), David L. Pokotylo and Kenneth M. Ames (Plateau), W. Raymond Wood (Plains), and Patricia L. Crown (Southwest). The Pre-Clovis/Paleoindian entries, prepared by George C. Frison, include reviews of major cultural complexes (e.g., Clovis, Folsom, Gainey, Midland) and of many major sites (e.g., Hell Gap, Horner, Crowfield, Lubbock Lake) and issues (e.g., bone modification, taphonomy, pre-Clovis complexes). The General Category, prepared by Guy Gibbon, the volume editor, includes more than 140 entries concerning climatic episodes, resources, pioneer archaeologists, general tool types, and special topics such as archaeoastronomy, cultural-resource management, fire, and rock art. Maps, a list of entries by culture area and topical category at the end of this guide, and an extensive index make this a particularly user-friendly encyclopedia. Written for the informed lay person, college-level student, and professional, *Archaeology of Prehistoric Native America: An Encyclopedia* is an important resource for the study of the earliest North Americans.

North American Natural and Cultural Areas

Broad geographic patterns are visible in the distribution of the archaeological remains of prehistoric people in North America. These associations are thought to be the result of shared cultural solutions by hunter-gatherers and horticulturalists to problems they faced in adapting to the various natural environments of the continent. An essential element in learning about Precolumbian peoples in North America, then, is understanding better the natural environments to which they were adjusting.

In this volume, North America is considered that part of the Western Hemisphere bounded by Mexico and the Gulf of Mexico on the south and the Arctic Ocean on the north, and by the North Atlantic Ocean on the east and the North Pacific Ocean and the Bering Sea on the west. As thus defined, it is composed of the continental United States and Canada and covers ca.19.4 million km^2 (7.5 million square miles). It is ca. 4,830 km (3,000 miles) across at its widest point. As a physiographic province, North America is characterized by a relatively high cordillera that runs the length of its western edge and lesser mountain chains that run north-south along its eastern edge. In between these western and eastern mountain systems is a vast central lowland. The continent may be divided into five areas that are roughly homogeneous in their present appearance, geologic history, and types of rocks present. These are the Western Cordillera, the Appalachians, the Canadian Shield, the Central Lowlands, and the Coastal Plain (see Figure 1).

The most impressive physiographic feature of North America is a string of high, rugged mountains called the Western Cordillera that run the length of the continent. They have the greatest relief of this portion of the continent. The cordillera's diverse structure is exhibited by the nature of its components, which include the Rocky Mountains on the east, high intermontane plateaus, tablelands, and desert basins west of the Rockies, and the Pacific Mountains west of them. Like the mountains themselves, the valleys of the area also tend to run in a north-south direction. The eastern mountains, the Appalachians, are an ancient eroded mosaic of valleys and hills whose relief ranges from 90 to 460 m (300–1,500 feet). Still, the tallest peaks in the Appalachians are less than half the height of the highest peaks in the Western Cordillera. The steepest slopes and highest hills occur along the valleys of the many streams that run down these mountains. The highest summits are present in the Piedmont and the Blue Ridge mountains in the southern portion of the highlands, and in the mountains of eastern Canada and New England to the north. A northeast-southwest-trending string of lower ridges and valleys lies directly west of these mountains.

To the north in the interior lowlands is the glacial peneplain of the Canadian Shield. Now a vast region of irregular basins and rocky hills with an average relief of only 30 m (100 feet), this area once contained weathered mountain ranges that were scraped away by continental glaciers and deposited as debris in the Central Lowlands to the south. Swamp and water mostly fill the network of basins that course through the Canadian Shield. The Central Lowlands to the south and west are covered with glacial sediments of various ages. Debris from the most recent glaciers (23,050–8050 B.C., or 25,000–10,000 years B.P.) that were centered on the Canadian Shield was dumped east of the Missouri River and north of the Ohio River. Retreating lobes of ice left distinctive moraines 30–60 m (100–200 feet) high in this region. South of the boundary of these late glacial movements, older Paleozoic sediments form a hilly transition to the Appalachian highlands, and the Great Plains to the west are covered with old sediments from its bordering mountain chain. Only the Ozark-Ouachita upland in Arkansas and Missouri, a western extension of the Appalachians, towers above the broad expanse of these interior plains.

East and south of the Appalachians is the Coastal Plain, an area of relatively soft, young sediments. The simplest geological structure in North America, the plain dips toward the sea and widens southward as it encircles the Gulf of Mexico. Erosion has created flattish, low "vales" between hills that are 30–60 m (100–200 feet) high. Extensive marshes and swamps cover the young seaward margin of the plain.

Patterns of physiography form a palette on which other natural elements, such as climate, soils, vegetation, and animal life, were mixed. Together, they created the natural environmental zones in which Precolumbian people lived. Discrete environmental zones can be identified at many levels of scale. On a local scale, for example, archaeologists soon learn the importance to native peoples of slight variations in relief, distance to water sources, soil permeability, and duration of sunlight in winter months. On the scale of continents, six broad environmental zones may be recognized in North America. These are the Arctic, the Subarctic, the Eastern Forest and Coastal Plain, the grasslands, the deserts, and the Pacific Coast. Although conditioned by geological understructure and physiography, many of the natural elements that together constitute these zones, such as vegetation, animal life, and soils, generally correlate closely with climate, which itself is largely determined by latitude and by the clash of cold and warm air masses. North America's mid-latitude weather results from its position in regard to polar and tropical air masses. The storm tracks caused by their interaction generally move from west to east, with winter the time of greatest storminess. The nature of the climate of various areas of North America—and therefore of their vegetation and animal life—is determined primarily by the position of these storm tracks. Seasonal shifts in climate are also linked to the position of these tracks, for, as the sun rises in the sky in the summer, the Northern Hemisphere warms as the tracks shift northward.

The Arctic zone is crossed by polar tundra and polar ice caps from Greenland to Alaska. Because much of this zone is north of the storm tracks, it has long cold winters, short cool sum-

Figure 1. Physiographic areas of North America. (Drawn by Deborah Schoenholz)

mers, little precipitation in either season, and frozen soils. Only few trees and a narrow range of animal species are found in this harsh environment. Tundra vegetation consists in general of short herbaceous plants and lichens on better-drained uplands and mosses in the ample bogs. Many bird species nest there in warmer months, but few stay the winter. Among the larger animals are caribou, polar bear, musk-ox, and arctic fox. Mosquitoes and swarms of biting black flies can make life miserable for both people and animals in the summer. The Subarctic, or taiga, zone directly to the south covers the northern Plains, the northern section of the

Western Cordillera, and the southern portion of the Canadian Shield. Although it is a region of thin, infertile soils, its longer, milder summers support a northern coniferous forest (taiga) composed of stands of spruce, fir, and pine with some birch, poplar, larch, and willow. The scant undergrowth present is usually near streams. Typical large animals include moose, caribou, elk, deer, black bear, fox, lynx, wolves, beavers, porcupines, rabbits, and squirrels. As the summer becomes shorter and harsher to the north, the trees become smaller and rarer, and the taiga grades into tundra.

The Eastern Forest and Coastal Plain zone below the eastern Subarctic is crossed by humid continental climatic belts that become progressively subtropical to the south. Warm tropical air masses flow at times as far north as the Great Lakes. Mirroring the marked seasonal temperature changes, the vegetation cover gradually shifts from coniferous trees in the north to deciduous trees in the south. Typical northern trees are beech, birch, maple, and oak; walnut, hickory, tulip, and other species of oak are found to the south. The forests thin to the west as they approach the grasslands, with trees increasingly confined to river courses. Rich soils and sufficient rainfall make agriculture possible except along the northern fringe. The Coastal Plain is covered by sandy soils and open long-leaf pine forests. Swamp trees like cypress and gum are common along the more poorly drained stream valleys of this plain. Among the characteristic animal forms in the Eastern Forest and Coastal Plain are deer, fox, raccoons, muskrats, skunks, squirrels, and rabbits.

Between the eastern forests and the deserts and mountains of the West are vast grasslands that once held large numbers of wild animals, including antelope, coyote, jackrabbits, prairie dogs, ground squirrels, and huge herds of bison. Except for some cottonwoods and other deciduous trees along moister, perennial streams, the primary vegetation in this dry climate consists of grasses and herbaceous forms. In general, taller varieties of grass, often more than 2 m (6 feet) in height, are present in dense growths to the east. Less dense growths of shorter bunch grasses are present to the west. To the southwest, in the even more arid deserts, shrub forms, such as sagebrush, creosote bush, and greasewood, replace grasses as the dominant vegetation. Cacti flourish in the driest places, and the only perennial streams flow into the zone from more humid sources. Because of the harshness

of the environment, fox and rabbits are among the few larger animals that live permanently in the zone. Exceptions to these semiarid and arid climatic conditions in western North America are the mountain ranges. Although they have for the most part relatively low precipitation, they are not considered desert or steppe areas. In general, that portion of the desert zone north of latitude 35° is considered middle-latitude semiarid or steppe, and that portion to the south subtropical arid or semiarid. The final zone is the Pacific Coast, which may be divided into southern and northern sections. The southern, which includes most of California, has a warmer, drier "Mediterranean" climate, poorer soils, and scrub bush as the principal vegetation. With its humid marine climate, the rainy northern section has more fertile soils and more lush vegetation.

Recognizing that the broad ethnographic regions identified by early anthropologists in North America generally coincided with natural environmental zones, ethnologists began to organize cultural similarities and differences in terms of culture areas in the late nineteenth century. The traditional culture areas of North America are the Arctic, the Subarctic, the Great Plains or simply the Plains, the Eastern Woodlands, California, the Great Basin, the Southwest, the Northwest Coast, and the Plateau (see Figure 2). They are used as an aid in organizing this encyclopedia because archaeologists working within a culture area usually share common terminology, concepts, and research concerns, and many syntheses and annual conferences occur today at this level of organization. Separate entries for each of these culture areas, and for the concept of a culture area, are included in the encyclopedia. The reader should be aware, however, that archaeologists subdivide or lump these areas for various purposes and that their use tends to obscure interactions across their boundaries.

Although useful organizational devices, culture areas tend to lose their integrity when they are extended back 4,500 years or more. Before that time, the climate and vegetation of North America were significantly different from today. Between ca. 6050 and 3050 B.C. (8000–5000 years B.P.), a climatic episode called the Altithermal or Hypsithermal greatly extended the boundaries of grasslands and deserts. The hot, dry weather of this period influenced the natural environment of all areas of North America at least to some extent. Earlier, at the maximum of the last glacial period (16,050 B.C., or 18,000 years B.P.), the Wisconsin, ice sheets extended as far south as central Iowa and the Ohio Valley in the east and the Columbia River Basin in the west. Many areas were colder and wetter than they are today, and immense expanses of regions now arid or semiarid were then swamp and lake-filled grasslands. As the glaciers withdrew ca. 10,050 B.C. (12,000 years B.P.), environmental changes were rapid when storm tracks shifted northward bringing warm air with them. Vegetation zones, which had collapsed southward as ice lobes thrust down from the north, followed the warming climate northward until they reached their present positions. Perhaps paradoxically, some species of big animals, such as mammoths, mastodons, long-horned bison, camelids, horses, and giant ground sloths, became extinct early in this transition. An integral part of learning about the earliest Precolumbian North Americans involves, then, a study of these changes in the natural environment and of the many ways that

Figure 2. Culture Areas of prehistoric North America. (Drawn by Deborah Schoenholz)

people adjusted to them. Among the entries that contribute to an understanding of these natural changes are Climatic Episodes (Holocene); Holocene; Hypsithermal/Altithermal; Late Wisconsin; Laurentide Ice Sheet; and Mammoth/Mastodon.

Further Readings

Porter, S.C. (editor). 1983. *The Late Quaternary of the United States: 1. The Late Pleistocene.* University of Minnesota Press, Minneapolis.

Roberts, N. 1989. *The Holocene: An Environmental History.* Basil Blackwell, New York.

Ruddiman, W.F., and H.E. Wright, Jr. (editors). 1987. *North America and Adjacent Oceans During the Last Deglaciation.* Geology of North America, vol. K-3. Geological Society of America, Boulder.

Wright, H.E., Jr. (editor). 1984. *The Late Quaternary of the United States: 2. The Holocene.* University of Minnesota Press, Minneapolis.

Wright, H.E., Jr., J.E. Kutzbach, T. Webb III, W.F. Ruddiman, F.A. Street-Perrott, and P.J. Bartlein (editors). 1993. *Global Climates Since the Last Glacial Maximum.* University of Minnesota Press, Minneapolis.

North American Prehistory: An Outline

Most archaeologists agree that the first humans to enter North America came across the Bering Strait from Siberia sometime between 23,050 and 12,050 B.C. (25,000–14,000 years B.P.). This conclusion is supported by genetic and linguistic research, by comparative dental morphology, and by the presence in the small sample of early human skeletal remains of only anatomically modern individuals. The same archaeologists often strongly disagree, however, on exactly when in this interval people made the crossing. Their varied answers seem to depend on how they think the first people entered the continent, on what they believe their lifeway was, and on what they as archaeologists are willing to accept as confirming evidence of the presence of early North Americans. Although the first humans to enter North America could have paddled into Alaska and down the coast in boats, they are thought instead to have walked across a land bridge exposed by a lowering of world sea levels as much as 100 m (330 feet) during the height of the last, or Wisconsin, glaciation. While not proven beyond a doubt, this reconstruction seems to fit the facts best. People living in the northern steppe/tundra belt that stretched from Europe to Alaska were hunting the large, grass-eating game animals that were moving across the 1500-km (930-mile) -wide land bridge into the Americas at this time. Furthermore, the earliest well-documented archaeological remains in North America are those of big-game hunters rather than fisher folk. Presumably, small numbers of northeast Asians filtered into North America in pursuit of the mammoth, wild horses, and musk-oxen that lived in this harsh Arctic environment.

The land bridge, or Beringia as it is known, was exposed from ca. 23,050 to 12,050 B.C. (25,000–14,000 years B.P.), the coldest part of the last phase of the Wisconsin glacial period. This phase, the Late Wisconsin, extended from ca. 23,050 to 8050 B.C. (25,000–10,000 years B.P.). To the east and south, two great ice masses covered much of the northern half of the continent. In the west, the Cordilleran glacier complex was centered in southern Alaska and British Columbia. It spread at its maximum just south of Seattle. The much larger Laurentide ice sheet to the east stretched at its maximum (16,050 B.C., or 18,000 years B.P.) from the Atlantic Ocean into southeast Alberta.

As the ice sheets melted in their retreat, large areas of the north became strewn with the rocks and sediments the glaciers had swept up when they expanded southward. At the same time, most of Beringia and the Late Wisconsin coastline of Alaska were being submerged by the rising oceans. As a consequence, the great majority of the very earliest settlements are now likely underwater or tons of rock. The earliest dated human settlements in the Arctic are sites in the Yukon and Alaska, such as the Bluefish Caves, Dry Creek, Walker Road, Mesa, and Putu. While some like the Bluefish Caves could date to 12,050 B.C. (14,000 years B.P.), most seem to fall between 10,050 and 9050 B.C. (12,000–11,000 years B.P.). Most are also associated with wedge-shaped cores and microblades that resemble those in the Dyuktai tradition across the Bering Strait in Siberia. Apparently, the Dyuktai people were the first to enter this part of northeast Asia, ca. 28,050 B.C. (30,000 years B.P.). A few sites, like Dry Creek in the Alaska Range, contain cobbles, flakes, and thin bifacial knives but no microblades. After ca. 9050 B.C. (11,000 years B.P.), nearly all sites in this far northwestern region of North

America contain microblades and wedge-shaped cores. These early sites have been grouped into a Beringian tradition (ca. 9050–6550 B.C., or 11,000–8500 years B.P.) that may be the archaeological remains of the earliest ancestors of all Native Americans except the Aleut and Inuit (Eskimo), who entered at a later date.

The earliest widely accepted radiocarbon-dated cultural deposits south of the ice sheets are in the Meadowcroft Rock Shelter, a Miller-complex site in Pennsylvania. These deposits date to at least 10,850 and possibly 12,550 B.C. (12,800 and 14,500 years B.P.). Some underwater sites in the Aucilla River area of Florida, such as Page-Ladson, may be as old.

While the precise millennium when the first humans entered North America remains in dispute, the earliest firm archaeological evidence does not seem to date earlier than ca. 11,050 B.C. (13,000 years B.P.). It is possible that people had entered the continent and passed southward through an "ice-free corridor" between the two major ice masses into temperate latitudes by ca. 12,050 B.C. (14,000 years B.P.). The Pre-Clovis entry summarizes evidence that some archaeologists believe points to an even earlier settlement.

The first well-documented inhabitants of North America were Clovis big-game hunters in the Plains and Far West, whose remains date between 9250 and 8950 B.C. (11,200–10,900 years B.P.). Distinctive fluted Clovis projectile points have been found throughout much of the continent below the retreating ice sheets. However, this Paleoindian culture is best known from mammoth and bison kills on the Plains, such as Blackwater Draw, Lehner, Murray Springs, and Lindsay. At the end of the Wisconsin glaciation, herds of bison and mammoth roamed the great grasslands present at that time. In more mountainous or forested regions, Early Paleoindians seems to have had a more varied subsistence base, such as in the Crowfield and Gainey complexes and the Debert, Bull Brook, and Thunderbird sites in the Great Lakes and the Northeast.

By ca. 8950 B.C. (10,900 years B.P.), Clovis was replaced by increasingly distinctive regional hunting-and-gathering cultures that were adjusting to rapid changes in their local environments. Among the reasons for this diversification are a rapid warming of the climate and the extinction of many species of Ice Age big game, the wasting away of the massive continental ice sheets, rising sea levels, often radical changes in

the distribution of forests and grasslands, a growing human population, and increasingly restricted group mobility in many areas.

By ca. 3050 B.C. (5000 years B.P.), North America's Holocene (postglacial) climate, sea levels, and vegetation cover had assumed their approximate modern positions. The continent's natural areas as defined above developed during this process of drastic environmental change. They are used in this encyclopedia as "culture area" settings within which long-term historical and adaptive trends can be traced. The list of entries at the end of this guide is organized by these culture areas: the Arctic/Subarctic, the Plains, the Eastern Woodlands, California, the Great Basin, the Southwest, the Northwest Coast, and the Plateau.

Although the inhabitants of North America were still dependent on wild vegetable and animal foods, ease of living and natural-resource abundance varied widely among, and to a degree within, culture areas. By 2050 B.C. (4000 years B.P.), a few more favored localities were experiencing accelerating population growth. Accompanying this trend was an increasingly long-term occupation of base camps, or sedentism. And in the Southwest and the larger river valleys of the Southeast and the southern Midwest, some populations were already supplementing their wild-food supplies by the cultivation of native plant species. Because of the growing numbers of people, the presence of larger and more sedentary villages, a more varied and visible toolkit, and the repeated annual use of favored camping spots, the numbers of known sites for this period are greater than those for earlier periods. As a result, many of these more recent cultures are better documented than those of their more nomadic ancestors.

In the Aleutian Islands and Alaska in the Far North, specialized hunter-gatherer adaptations developed from the earlier Beringian tradition on the coast and in the diverse birch forest and tundra environments of the interior. Although the region's environmental diversity is already reflected in earlier toolkits, clearly separable cultural traditions become more clearly visible in the archaeological record after ca. 4050 B.C. (6000 years B.P.). An example is the Aleutian tradition (ca. 3050 B.C.–A.D. 1700, or 5000–250 years B.P.) in the eastern Aleutian Islands and on the Pacific Coast. Another is the Arctic Small Tool tradition, which appeared in Alaska ca. 2550 B.C. (4500 years B.P.). These latter peoples are thought to have been nomadic hunters who followed herds of caribou and musk-ox. Some became the first people to settle the eastern Arctic when they wandered as far east as Greenland ca. 2050 B.C. (4000 years B.P.). In Alaska, the Arctic Small Tool tradition was replaced ca. 1050 B.C. (3000 years B.P.) by the Norton tradition, a collection of peoples who intensively hunted both sea mammals and land animals. This transition has been traced in the Aleutians at sites like Anangula and Chaluka. These traditions are probably the archaeological remains of the early ancestors of the historic Aleut and Inuit people. Both the Norton and the eastern Arctic Small Tool traditions were replaced in the first millennium A.D. by the long-lived Thule culture. This culture's kayaks, toggled harpoons, and art-work are a familiar part of the distinctive early historic Inuit sea-mammal-hunting culture. The Thule became the first known Native Americans to encounter Europeans when they entered northwest Greenland and met the Norsemen, who were already living in the southern parts of the island.

In the arid West and Southwest, the disappearance of the rich Late Wisconsin grasslands and their big game meant a shift in subsistence emphasis to a wide variety of wild-plant foods, smaller animals like rabbit and deer, and fish where available. By 9050–8050 B.C. (11,000–10,000 years B.P.), a distinctive "Archaic" adaptation was developing in the Great Basin, Southwest, and large parts of California. In general, small bands of hunter-gatherers moved from one temporary shelter to another as they exploited seasonally available foods, with the coast and interior rivers, lakes, and swamps favored locations. This lifeway has been preserved in amazing detail by the arid climate in Utah, Nevada, and some bordering states at sites like Danger Cave, Lovelock Cave, Hogup Cave, and Gatecliff Shelter. Besides the plant and animal foods eaten by these early hunter-gatherers, many other types of organic artifacts have been preserved, including rope, baskets, sandals, and nets. While many of these people continued their mobile lifeway for thousands of years until historic contact, others in the Southwest and in favored coastal areas, such as southern California and the Pacific Northwest, were becoming increasingly sedentary. By ca. 6050 B.C. (8000 years B.P.), for example, people were already gathering land-based food resources and capturing fish and marine mammals in coastal southern California. Eventually in especially hospitable areas, like the Santa Barbara

Channel, fairly elaborate societies developed around a subsistence base focused on the gathering of tubers and plants, fishing, and the collection of shellfish.

By 8050 B.C. (10,000 years B.P.), Archaic cultures were widespread as well in the Eastern Woodlands. As in other areas of the temperate zone, the long Archaic period, which lasted to ca. 1050 B.C. (3000 years B.P.), is marked by the long-term development of increasingly more efficient ways of exploiting a broader variety of forest and river-valley food resources. This trend has been labeled "primary forest efficiency." Beginning with the Dalton tradition (ca. 8550 B.C., or 10,500 years B.P.) in the Southeast and the Midwest, the Archaic has been subdivided into Early, Middle, and Late periods. At least by 2050 B.C. (4000 years B.P.), evidence of increasing sedentism, a more intense exploitation of food resources, increased long-distance exchange and ceremonialism, and some cultivation of native plants is widespread in some southeastern and midwestern river-valley bottoms. These trends are documented at stratified sites, such as Koster and Modoc Rock Shelter in Illinois and Indian Knoll in Kentucky, and culminate in extraordinary Late Archaic cultures like Poverty Point in the Lower Mississippi Basin.

On the Plains, a long sequence of bison-hunting cultures can be traced from Clovis to the historic period. These include Late Paleo-indian complexes, such as Folsom, Agate Basin, Alberta, and Plainview, and Archaic cultures, such as Oxbow, Hanna, Pelican Lake, and Besant. Still later pottery-using Plains Woodland phases, such as Avonlea and Vickers, continued to be based on bison as a main food staple. This long tradition is well documented at sites like Olsen-Chubbuck and Lindenmeier in Colorado, Ventana Cave and Murray Springs in Arizona, Blackwater Draw and Folsom in New Mexico, Cherokee Sewer in Iowa, and Head-Smashed-In Buffalo Jump in Alberta.

Regional Archaic hunter-gatherer traditions were replaced by Woodland archaeological cultures in the Eastern Woodlands after 1050 B.C. (3000 years B.P.). The most intensely studied of these new cultures belong to the Early and Middle Woodland periods and are associated with often spectacular earthworks, huge burial mounds, and elaborate burial customs. Adena (ca. 500 B.C.–A.D. 200, or 2450–1750 years B.P.) and Hopewell (ca. 100 B.C.–A.D. 450, or 2050–1500 years B.P.), which are both centered in Ohio, are the best known of these.

Despite the richness of their remains, earlier Woodland people were not agriculturalists. Gourds had been cultivated in some parts of this culture area by 5050 B.C. (7000 years B.P.). And both later Archaic and Woodland people cultivated native plants, such as sumpweed and sunflowers. Maize (corn) was only an incidental and late addition to this suite of domesticates, which has been called the Eastern Agricultural complex. Maize and bean agriculture did not become important until the development after A.D. 900 (1050 years B.P.) of complex Mississippian chiefdoms in the Southeast and the southern Midwest. Cahokia in Illinois and Moundville in Alabama are among the many great Mississippian ceremonial centers. Early Spanish explorers walked through Mississippian towns in their journeys through the Southeast. An agricultural lifeway was adopted as well by Woodland-tradition societies in the Northeast, such as the Iroquoian, and by contemporary Upper Mississippian people (e.g., Fort Ancient, Oneota) in the Upper Mississippi River drainage and Plains Village people in the prairies and plains to the west.

Maize entered the Southwest by ca. 2050–1550 B.C. (4000–3500 years B.P.). Hundreds of years later, some groups of people had begun to farm and live in sedentary villages. The well-known cultural traditions of this culture area—Hohokam, Mogollon, and Anasazi—emerged from this base. Indian groups living in the Southwest today are considered descendants of the Anasazi and the Hohokam. Southwestern pueblos, such as Snaketown and Casa Grande in Arizona, Pecos in New Mexico, and Cliff Palace in Colorado, are among the most spectacular archaeological sites in North America.

In the list of entries at the end of this guide, the earliest archaeological complexes and sites are included under the Pre-Clovis/Paleoindian heading. This list also includes a number of special topics, ranging from Mammoth/Mastodon to the vexing problem of Bone Modification, that are of particular interest to this time period. Subsequent archaeological complexes are presented under specific culture-area headings. Each culture-area list includes a listing of important sites, the names of pioneer archaeologists, and various special topics. The General Category at the end has entries for other pioneer archaeologists, climatic and environmental terms, resources, general tool types, and many special topics, such as Archaeoastronomy, Demography, Language, the Reburial Issue, and Rock Art.

Further Readings

Fagan, B.M. 1995. *Ancient North America: The Archaeology of a Continent.* 2nd ed. Thames and Hudson, New York.

Jennings, J.D. 1987. *The Prehistory of North America.* 3rd ed. Mayfield, Palo Alto.

———. (editor). 1983. *Ancient North Americans.* W.H. Freeman, San Francisco.

Willey, G.R. 1966. *Introduction to American Archaeology: 1. North America.* Prentice-Hall, Englewood Cliffs.

History of North American Archaeology

The changing goals, concepts, and methods of prehistoric archaeology in North America reflect broad trends in the emergence of Canada and the United States as modern Euro-American nations. While many individual personalities and events shaped the growth of archaeology within this context, this outline necessarily concentrates on the structure of the drama within which these individuals and events played their role. Individual entries in the encyclopedia discuss in greater detail the motivation, setting, problem orientation, and procedures of pioneer archaeologists throughout this growth. The location of the founding European settlements in the east, regional environmental characteristics, and the visibility and "allure" of the archaeological record itself within each culture area were important elements in the pattern of development of archaeology on this continent. Most important, the pace of development until the twentieth century was quicker toward the east, the direction from which new peoples and ideas were moving westward across the continent. Since the tempo of development was not uniform throughout the continent, the periods used here refer to dominant interests, problems, and achievements rather than to the actual pace of change in an individual state or province.

Incidental Discovery and Speculation (A.D. 1492–1840). The earliest reports of archaeological features in North America were written by explorers and travelers whose observations were incidental to their travels. As a result, only the most conspicuous features were described. Still other incidental discoveries were made by government employees who, as part of their profession, kept records of interesting features. Examples are geological survey crews and land surveyors. Many other incidental recordings of prominent archaeological features were made by military officers and fur traders.

Speculation naturally arose concerning the origins and identities of the peoples responsible for these prehistoric earthworks and artifacts. Since extensive collections of artifacts, an understanding of the great time depth represented by these remains, and basic archaeological tools of excavation and interpretation were lacking, travelers, antiquarians, and armchair speculators fabricated a New World past woven from myths within their own European worldview. The lost continents of Atlantis and Mu were considered likely homelands of the Indians, as were the eastern Mediterranean and "Hindustan." However, the dominant myth of the times concerned a mysterious race of now vanished civilized people. It was these people, it was thought, who built the thousands of earthen mounds scattered across the eastern portion of the continent. The "Mound Builders" were supposedly vanquished by later waves of incoming Indians, whose cultures were considered not advanced enough to organize mound construction. Because the mounds were thought to contain treasures left by the Mound Builders, they bore the brunt of early archaeological explorations by antiquarians and pothunters. With rare exceptions, this amounted to plunder, for excavations were rarely systematic, notes were seldom taken, and only prized artifacts saved.

Systematic Survey and Testing (1840–1920). The long period of incidental discovery and speculation was brought to an end by the gradual emergence of systematically conducted surveys and excavations. The roots of the empirical orientation that has been a defining feature of North American archaeology ever since extends back to these first systematic explorations. Not surprisingly, they concentrated on the distribution, structure, origin, purpose, and content of the mounds that had attracted so much earlier attention. The initial field surveys were conducted for the most part by individuals undertaking large-scale "natural history" reconnaissance surveys of antiquities for national institutions. One of the first of these was led by Ephraim G. Squier and Edwin H. Davis in the 1840s for the newly founded Smithsonian Institution in Washington, D.C. Their *Ancient Monuments of the Mississippi Valley* (1848) was the first publication of the institution. Systematic survey and testing also began on a smaller scale within states and provinces, with their dates of origin generally earlier toward the east. Among the many other people who played

a prominent role in the development of archaeology at the time were Adolph Bandelier, Benjamin Smith Barton, William Bartram, Frank H. Cushing, William Henry Holmes, Clarence B. Moore, John Wesley Powell, Frederick Ward Putnam, and Cyrus Thomas.

Interpretation in the great majority of these reports was still profoundly influenced by the myths of the earlier period. Nonetheless, description eventually began to outweigh speculation, and further mound explorations eventually led to the shattering of the myth of the Mound Builders. Cyrus Thomas and others demonstrated not only that mounds were still being built in historic times by American Indians, but also that they had been built in the past by a variety of Indian societies. Near the turn of the century, syntheses of available archaeological and ethnographic information led to the formulation of archaeological culture areas, such as William H. Holmes's syntheses of pottery distributions and the historic distributions of ethnic groups. The period of systematic survey and testing was characterized, too, by the establishment of numerous societies and publications dedicated to archaeological pursuits and by the professionalization of the discipline. The local naturalist, historical, and scientific societies that emerged during this period were largely responsible for the early organization and advancement of archaeology. Most reports of the period were dedicated to the systematic collection and description of regional antiquities, for an urgent need was felt to record information that was rapidly disappearing before the advance of the North American settler.

The explorations carried out during this period resulted for the most part in a mass of unorganized descriptive data about the form, distribution, and content of mounds or of other highly visible archaeological features. The unraveling of this mass of information eventually led to the further professionalization of the discipline and a growing gap between professional and amateur interests in the following period. However, the state of affairs at the time was understandable, because conceptual schemes for organizing information and for reconstructing cultural contexts were either absent or too broad to be useful at the local level. What does characterize the period is the concern for careful description, advancement in field methods and reporting techniques, and increasing recognition of the great antiquity of the American Indian. In addition, there was a growing concern for the preservation of sites and artifacts and the integration of archaeology, ethnology, linguistics, and physical anthropology, first in the great museums and later in departments of anthropology. The period was characterized by the intellectual leadership of individuals associated with eastern institutions, such as the Smithsonian, the American Museum of Natural History in New York City, and Harvard University in Cambridge, Massachusetts. The most far-reaching advance of the period may have been the recognition among professionals that the Mound Builders were a myth. This realization made possible the exploration of a greater range of problems, even though the popular picture of North American prehistory remained distorted by images from the speculative period of incidental discoveries.

Syntheses, Taxonomies, and Chronologies (1920–1960). The 1920s and 1930s saw the emergence of many new trends that are still important in North American archaeology. The problem of organizing the mass of rapidly accumulating observations concerning archaeological features became even more severe in the 1930s with the launching of government-sponsored large-scale excavations and surveys. These federally funded relief projects were initiated to provide jobs during the Great Depression. Among the organizations involved were the Works Progress Administration (WPA) and the Civilian Conservation Corps (CCC), which are discussed in the entry titled Federally Funded Archaeology. Various taxonomic frameworks were suggested, including Will C. McKern's Midwestern Taxonomic System and the Gladwinian Classification. McKern's system was referred to in the late 1940s as "the single most constructive achievement in the eastern United States during the past twenty-five years in attacking the problem of the description and classification of archaeological evidence" (Guthe 1952:9).

By the end of the 1930s, a major shift was occurring in archaeology from an essentially antiquarian mound and ethnic approach to a taxonomic and historically oriented perspective. Although taxonomic studies dominated archaeology in many regions of North America for some time, accumulating information concerning trait clusters and culture areas eventually led in the 1940s to an increasing interest in the relative chronological positions of archaeological cultures, their origins, and their pattern of change through time. The relative ages of ar-

chaeological cultures were estimated primarily by stratigraphic position and by differential skeletal preservation. A number of competing regional chronologies and the first comprehensive culture histories of a number of large-scale regions appeared during this decade. By the end of the 1940s, a fairly accurate framework for the relative temporal positions of many archaeological cultures had been established. This achievement was a consequence in large part of the application of taxonomic systems, for the systems provided an objective method of expressing cultural relationships through descriptive classification. The application of taxonomic systems also led to the abandonment of many earlier hypotheses that had been based on inadequate information and spurious ethnographic and linguistic associations. Nevertheless, the taxonomic approach, with its failure to delineate among different time periods, had the effect of emphasizing the enumeration of detailed trait lists. This emphasis detracted from the study of cultural dynamics, although trait lists were occasionally used to reconstruct past lifeways.

Even though archaeologists of prehistoric North America were becoming increasingly concerned with establishing the chronological positions of their archaeological cultures, they still lacked the technical ability to measure absolute time depth. For this reason, many of their hypotheses concerning cultural development remained untestable speculation. This exasperating situation was profoundly modified in the 1950s with the invention of the radiocarbon dating method. The radiocarbon dating method provided the means of establishing firm chronological frameworks within which the dynamics of cultural change could be examined. The increasingly firm chronological framework provided not only a sound base for the transformation of older taxonomic systems, but also important new insights into the development of archaeological cultures throughout North America as well. A major revision was soon made in estimates of the antiquity of the American Indian in the New World. In addition, archaeologists became increasingly intrigued by the possible interrelationships between shifting environments and cultural adaptations. The innovations of this period eventually led to the transformation of the discipline and the emergence of contemporary archaeology.

This was the period, too, of the "founding fathers" of archaeology in most states and provinces. These pioneers of modern archaeology synthesized existing information, named most of the local archaeological cultures, often popularized archaeology for the lay public, and presented the broad outlines of archaeology in their area. Their main methodological tools included a taxonomic system, the "culture area" concept, the "direct historical" approach, and controlled survey and excavation. As a group, they were understandably more interested at the time in compiling and synthesizing information than in the development of anthropological or other kinds of theory. This interest is clearly reflected in their historical and chronological focus, which involved the construction of taxonomies, areal chronologies, and space-time charts, the refinement of stratigraphic and seriational procedures, and the rapid adoption of new absolute dating techniques.

It was also a critical period in North America for the exchange of information among archaeologists, for the myriad new excavations and surveys had produced a mountain of information. Annual regional conferences, such as the Plains Anthropological Conference (founded in 1931), and journals, like the *Plains Anthropologist* (first issued in 1954), appeared at this time. The Society for American Archaeology was created in 1934, and its quarterly journal, *American Antiquity,* in 1935.

Recent Trends (1960–). Since 1960, the concept of "archaeology as anthropology" has come to dominate North American archaeology. Archaeologists have increasingly focused on the organization of settlements and their dynamics in response to the triggering effects of changes in their cultural and natural environments. This increasing emphasis reflects the availability of more sophisticated dating techniques at the end of the last period and broader trends in the development of American anthropology and science. As archaeologists gradually shifted their focus to anthropologically oriented research, they began to tackle the interrelationship between culture and environment, cognitive studies that examine the past symbolic context of archaeological remains, and processual studies aimed at tracing out and explaining structural transformations in societal forms. Interdisciplinary and more technical approaches have been adopted, and the complexity of the archaeological record recognized. In general, then, the recent past of North American archaeology has been characterized by reconstructions of paleoenvironments, a focus on context and

function, settlement-pattern studies, the formulation of evolutionary stages, attempts to derive process, and the transformation of archaeological data into cultural data. Most fundamental, an effort has been made to explain human cultural and social behavior in the past.

Other recent trends in North American archaeology include: a massive growth in the number of professional archaeologists; an increased use of statistics and computers; the introduction of large-scale probability-based surveys; the refinement of excavation procedures with the introduction of electronic detecting, flotation, aerial photography, large earth moving equipment, and other devices; a tendency for journals to become more technical; a growing gap between amateur and professional archaeologists; a de-emphasis on mound research (discussed in the Reburial Issue entry); and the testing of hypotheses and the explanation of past events as a research ideal. However, the most profound influence in this period has been the rippling effect of laws enacted to protect archaeological resources from destruction. Federal, state, and provincial laws have been enacted in response to the widespread destruction of historic structures and archaeological sites in modern times. In the United States, examples of these laws include the National Historic Preservation Act of 1966, the National Environmental Policy Act of 1969, and Presidential Executive Order 11593, which was signed in 1971. These laws have resulted in the establishment of State Historic Preservation Offices, the National Register of Historic Places, park archaeologists, and massive increases in the number of archaeological surveys conducted across the country. State laws have led to the appointment of state archaeologists and the initiation of statewide conservation plans. One overriding result of these laws has been the rise to dominance of "cultural-resource management" over other archaeological pursuits within recent years. Undoubtedly, more archaeologists are involved in assessing the impact of impending construction projects on cultural resources than in problem-oriented research, although the two goals are not incompatible.

Summary. During each period of its development, North American archaeology has been motivated by special problems and interests. In the speculative period of incidental discoveries, the dominant problem was "who"—who were the Mound Builders? During the following period of systematic survey and excavation, the principle problem shifted to "what" and "where." In the period of synthesis and the construction of taxonomies and chronologies, the problem eventually became "when." In recent years, the problems that motivate much archaeological research are "how" and "why." North American prehistoric archaeology has followed the path of many other disciplines from initial speculation, to observation and classification, and, eventually, to explanation and the search for a deeper understanding of the subject matter. Like the pieces in a large and complex kaleidoscope, the material remains of the past can be viewed from many different perspectives.

Further Readings

Fitting, J.E. (editor). 1973. *The Development of North American Archaeology.* Anchor Books, Garden City.

Guthe, C.E. 1952. Twenty-Five Years of Archeology in the Eastern United States. In *Archeology of Eastern United States,* edited by J.B. Griffin, pp. 1–12. University of Chicago Press, Chicago.

Renfrew, C., and P. Bahn. 1991. *Archaeology: Theories, Methods and Practice.* Thames and Hudson, New York.

Trigger, B.G. 1989. *A History of Archaeological Thought.* Cambridge University Press, New York.

Willey, G.R., and J.A. Sabloff. 1993. *A History of American Archaeology.* 3rd ed. W.H. Freeman, New York.

Dating Conventions

Archaeologists employ a bewildering array of conventions in dating periods and events in precontact North America. A seemingly straightforward approach is to say that something happened "so many years ago," let us say, 10,000 years ago. Problems arise when the age is much more recent. An event that occurred 500 years ago for an archaeologist writing in A.D. 1900 will have happened 600 years ago for his great granddaughter writing in A.D. 2000. Archaeologists and other scientists have solved this problem by adopting A.D. 1950 as "present." The use of this convention is signaled by the initials B.P. (before present "1950"). Another seemingly straightforward convention is to label dates B.C. (before Christ) and A.D. (*anno Domini,* since the beginning of the Christian era). Although the Julian calendar is the basis of the civil calendar used throughout the world today, some people object to the use of culturally laden symbols like A.D. and B.C. in scientific discourse.

Whichever of these conventions is used, the interpretation of dates is complicated by problems inherent in radiocarbon dating, the primary means of assigning an age to prehistoric archaeological materials in North America today. Before the development of the radiocarbon dating method by J.R. Arnold and Willard F. Libby in the late 1940s, the actual ages of North America's oldest cultures were greatly underestimated, and an independent procedure for comparing the calendar ages of archaeological materials in distant areas, like Alaska and Florida, was unavailable. Radiocarbon dating is one of the most important contributions of the natural sciences to North American archaeology in the twentieth century, for it provides relatively inexpensive "absolute" age determinations of ancient organic material. In addition, its most effective age range, between about 50,000 and 500 years ago, easily spans what most archaeologists consider the bounds of the prehistoric period on the North American continent. Nonetheless, at least two sources of confusion exist in interpreting radiocarbon dates.

First, because of the variable decay rates of carbon 14 atoms, radiocarbon dates have an associated statistical error range that can span hundreds of years. Furthermore, the chances are only two out of three that the "correct" age is within this span. For example, a radiocarbon date of A.D. 450 ± 180 is read, "there is a two-out-of-three chance that the dated material falls within the A.D. 270–630 time span." Unlike this conventional radiocarbon dating method, which relies on measures of decay rates, the newer accelerator mass spectrometry (AMS) method actually counts the number of carbon 14 atoms present. Besides allowing the dating of very small samples, AMS dating provides a much shorter error range, often on the order of ± 20 or 30 years.

A second source of confusion in interpreting radiocarbon dates results from the uneven production rate of carbon 14 in the atmosphere in the past. In general, the older the true calendar age of dated material, the greater the discrepancy between radiocarbon and calendar dates. This means that radiocarbon dates have to be corrected, or "calibrated," to obtain calendar years. A typical adjustment used as an example by Brian Fagan in his *People of the Earth* (HarperCollins, 7th ed., 1992, p. 26) is a calibrated interval of 145 B.C. to A.D. 210 for a date of 10 B.C. ± 30. The accumulating discrepancy with time is evident in the following sequence of calibrated intervals: A.D. 500 (A.D. 265–640), 1000 B.C. (1530–905 B.C.), 3000 B.C. (3950–3640 B.C.), 5000 B.C. (6285–5445 B.C.).

Archaeologists have adopted certain conventions in publishing radiocarbon determinations to distinguish between uncalibrated and calibrated dates. In scientific publications, uncalibrated laboratory determinations are presented as, for instance, 1960 ± 65 B.P. (UGa-1622). Here, 1960 is the radiocarbon age before A.D. 1950, ± 65 is the associated probable error, 1622 is the laboratory analysis number, and UGa is the code for the laboratory where the sample was processed. The mean uncorrected date of this example sample is 10 B.C. Several different conventions are employed to signal presentation of a calibrated date. In one, the "scientific," uncalibrated dates are indicated by B.P. and the calibrated dates by cal B.C. (or A.D.). In the other, the "historical" b.c. (or a.d.) marks uncalibrated dates and B.C. (or A.D.) calibrated ones.

Because North American archaeologists use different calibration curves and because the degree of these calibrations will almost certainly shift in the future, all radiocarbon dates in this encyclopedia are uncalibrated unless stated otherwise. This means that dates in an entry are not equivalent to calendar years. An age estimate of 1250 B.C. (3200 years B.P.), for example, is most likely not exactly 200 years older than a date of 1050 B.C. (3000 years B.P.), and older samples actually date in most instances considerably earlier than their radiocarbon ages. While the actual calibration of radiocarbon dates is difficult, ballpark estimates of their calendar dates can be easily obtained from "approximate calibration" tables like the one in Table 1. Other easy conversion tables are present in most introductory archaeology textbooks. Finally, because the purpose of this encyclopedia is to provide an introductory overview of North American prehistory, the majority of the radiocarbon dates presented in the entries are in the form of mean uncorrected dates without laboratory citations.

TABLE I.

Approximate Equivalents of Uncalibrated and Calibrated Radiocarbon Dates.

Uncalibrated Radiocarbon Years B.P.	Calibrated Radiocarbon Years B.P.	Years B.C./A.D.
12,000	13,990	B.C. 12,040
11,500	13,420	11,470
11,000	12,920	10,970
10,500	12,420	10,470
10,000	11,160	9210
9500	10,510	8560
9000	9980	8030
8500	9500	7550
8000	8860	6910
7500	8270	6320
7000	7790	5840
6500	7380	5440
6000	6840	4880
5500	6300	4340
5000	5730	3780
4500	5150	3200
4000	4440	2490
3500	3770	1820
3000	3190	1240
2500	2610	B.C. 660
2000	1940	A.D. 10
1500	1350	600
1000	930	1020
500	520	A.D. 1430

Prepared by G. Gibbon

Further Readings

Bowman, S. 1990. *Radiocarbon Dating*. University of California Press, Berkeley.
Hedges, R.E.M., and J.A.J. Gowlett. 1986. Radiocarbon Dating by Accelerator Mass Spectrometry. *Scientific American* 254(1):100–107.
Taylor, R.E. 1987. *Radiocarbon Dating: An Archaeological Perspective*. Academic Press, New York.

Additional Sources of Information

Information about the archaeological record of the Precolumbian peoples of North America, which is already abundant, is accumulating at an accelerating pace and is available in an ever expanding variety of sources. Numerous journals exist at the continental, national, regional, and local levels. Most cited in this encyclopedia are listed in Table 2. Many museums, university

Table 2.

List of Journals, Bulletins, and Occasional Papers

A. Journals

American Anthropologist
American Antiquarian
American Antiquity
American Archeology
Anthropologia
Archaeology in Montana
Archaeology of Eastern North America
Archeologist
Arctic
Arctic Anthropology
B.C. Studies
Canadian Journal of Archaeology
Central Plains Archaeology
Central States Archaeological Journal
Current Research in the Pleistocene
Early Georgia
El Palacio
Florida Anthropologists
Idaho Archaeologist
Illinois Archaeology
Illinois State Archaeological Society Journal
Indian Notes
Journal of Alabama Archaeology
Journal of California and Great Basin Anthropology
Journal of California Anthropology
Journal of Cherokee Studies
Journal of Ethnobiology
Journal of Field Archaeology
Journal of Intermountain Archaeology
Journal of Middle Atlantic Archaeology
Journal of New World Archaeology
Journal of the Iowa Archaeological Society
Kiva
Lithic Technology

Louisiana Archaeology
Man in the Northeast
Manitoba Archaeological Newsletter
Masterkey
Michigan Archaeologist
Midcontinental Journal of Archaeology
Minnesota Archaeologist
Missouri Archaeologist
Muskox
North American Archaeologist
North Dakota Archaeologist
North Dakota History
Northwest Anthropological Research Notes
Ohio Archaeological and Historical Quarterly
Ohio Archaeologist
Ontario Archaeology
Pacific Coast Archaeological Society Quarterly
Pennsylvania Archaeologist
Plains Anthropologist
Plateau
Scientific American
South Carolina Antiquities
South Dakota Archaeology
Southeastern Archaeology
Southwestern Journal of Anthropology
Southwestern Lore
Syesis
Tebiwa
Tennessee Anthropologist
Tennessee Archaeologist
Utah Archaeology
West Virginia Archaeologist
Wisconsin Archeologist
Wyoming Archaeologist

B. Bulletins, Monographs, and Other Series

Anthropology in British Columbia
Anthropological Papers of the American Museum
  of Natural History
Anthropological Papers of the Archeological
  Society of New Mexico
Anthropological Papers of the University of Alaska
Anthropological Papers of the University of Arizona
Anthropological Papers of the University of
  Michigan
Archaeological Reports of the Mississippi
  Department of Archives and History
Archaeological Survey of Alberta Occasional Papers

Archaeology in Washington
Arizona State Museum Archaeological Series
Arkansas Archeological Survey Research Series
Association of Oregon Archaeologists Occasional
  Papers
Ballena Press Anthropological Papers
Brigham Young University Museum of Peoples and
  Cultures Occasional Papers
Bulletin of the Archaeological Society of Delaware
Bulletin of the Illinois Archaeological Survey
Bulletin of the Massachusetts Archaeological Society
Bulletin of the New York State Museum

(continued on next page)

Table 2. *(continued)*

Bulletin of the Oklahoma Anthropological Society
Bulletin of the Texas Anthropological Society
Bulletin of the Texas Archaeological and
Paleontological Society
Bulletin of the Texas Archaeological Society
Canadian Archaeological Association Bulletin
Canadian Archaeological Association Occasional
Papers
Center for Archaeological Research at Davis
Publications
Central Washington University Archaeological Reports
Chapters in Nebraska History
Cincinnati Museum of Natural History Occasional
Papers in Archaeology
Contract Abstracts and CRM Archeology
Contributions of the University of California
Archaeological Research Facility
Crow Canyon Archaeological Center Occasional
Papers
Eastern New Mexico Contributions
in Anthropology
Eastern Washington University Reports in
Archeology and History
Fieldiana: Anthropology
Illinois State Museum Reports of Investigations
Indian Notes and Monographs
Indiana Historical Society Prehistoric Research Series
Kampsville Seminars in Archeology
Kroeber Anthropological Society Papers
Medallion Papers
Memoirs of the Colorado Archaeological Society
Memoirs of the Society for American Archaeology
Milwaukee Public Museum Publications in
Anthropology
Milwaukee Public Museum Scientific Publications
Minnesota Prehistoric Archaeology Series
Nebraska State Historical Society Publications
in Anthropology
Nevada Archaeological Survey Research Papers
Nevada State Museum Anthropological Papers
Northern Arizona University Archaeological Series
Northwestern Archeological Program Scientific
Papers
Northwestern California Archaeological Society
Occasional Papers
Occasional Papers of the British Columbia
Provincial Museum
Occasional Papers on Wyoming Archaeology
Occasional Publications in Maine Archaeology
Occasional Publications in Minnesota Anthropology
Occasional Publications in Northeastern Anthropology
Ohio State University Occasional Papers in
Anthropology

Oklahoma Anthropological Society Memoirs
Papers of the Archaeology Institute of America
Papers of the Maxwell Museum of Anthropology
Papers of the Peabody Museum of American
Archaeology and Ethnology
Papers of the Robert S. Peabody Foundation for
Archaeology
Peabody Museum Monographs
Plains Anthropologist Memoirs
Prehistory Research Series of the Indiana Historical
Society
Proceedings of the Society for California Archaeology
Reports of the Office of the Iowa State Archaeologist
Researches and Transactions of the New York State
Archaeological Association
Royal Ontario Museum Art and Archaeology
Occasional Papers
San Diego Museum of Man Papers
Saskatchewan Museum of Natural History
Anthropological Series
School of American Research Monographs
Simon Fraser University Department of Archaeology
Publications
Society for American Archaeology Memoirs
Southeastern Archaeological Conference Bulletin
Southern Indian Studies
Southwest Museum Papers
Studies in Illinois Archaeology
Studies in Oklahoma's Past
Transactions and Collections of the American
Antiquity Society
UCLA Archaeological Survey Annual Report
University of California Anthropological Records
University of California Archaeological Survey
Reports
University of California Publications in American
Archaeology and Ethnology
University of Georgia Series in Anthropology
University of Idaho Anthropological Research
Manuscript Series
University of Kansas Publications in Anthropology
University of Kentucky Reports in Anthropology
and Archaeology
University of Minnesota Publications in Anthropology
University of Oregon Archaeological Papers
University of Tennessee Reports of Investigations
University of Utah Anthropological Papers
University of Washington Publications
in Anthropology
University of West Florida Reports of Investigations
Utah State University Contributions to Anthropology
Wichita State Publications in Anthropology
Wyoming Contributions to Anthropology

Prepared by G. Gibbon

anthropology departments, historical societies, and archaeological research centers also publish more occasional technical and popular series that summarize the results of site excavations, regional surveys and syntheses, and artifact studies. A warning, however. Some issues have a restricted distribution to protect site locations. The second part of Table 2 lists many of the series mentioned in the Further Readings section that follows most entries. While some of these journals and series are no longer being published, older issues remain an indispensable source of information.

The Archaeological Survey of Canada regularly publishes valuable archaeological reports, as does the National Park Service in the United States. University and college libraries often contain copies of Master's theses and Ph.D. dissertations that examine some aspect of North American archaeology. A relatively easy way to discover the titles of interesting dissertations is to scan issues of *University Microfilms*, a University of Michigan–based publication that provides the titles (with a brief abstract) of recent dissertations from all but a few North American universities and colleges. The proceedings of a state's Academy of Science often contain useful articles on North American archaeology, as do general history and science publications, such as state historical society proceedings, *Science*, and *Scientific American*. An increasingly popular resource is the Internet. This resource includes discussion groups, electronic journals and archives, and an ever increasing variety of other kinds of information. In the future, electronic information will become the single most efficient source of information for this and other topics. Most university and larger public libraries have electronic reference guides that can be easily searched using the name of an author, the title of a book, or keywords. National systems exist, too, that permit searches through journals for relevant

articles using a similar system. Most of these services are now available through the Internet.

Numerous books continue to be written on some aspect of North American archaeology. Besides the Internet, an efficient if tiresome way to discover interesting titles of contemporary books is to pore over the archaeology section of *Books in Print* (both hard- and soft-cover volumes), which is available for browsing at bookstores and in many libraries. Since the majority of these books are published by university and historical society presses, a telephone call to one or more of these presses in the region of interest might produce useful results. In the United States, the Smithsonian Institution in Washington, D.C., has published books and series on North American archaeology since the middle of the nineteenth century. A particularly valuable source is the institution's Handbook of North American Indians series, which is being published under the general editorship of W.C. Sturtevant. As of 1996, volumes existed for the Arctic, the Subarctic, the Northwest Coast, California, the Southwest, the Great Basin, and the Northeast.

Advice and often experience can be obtained from many regional institutions, such as province and state historical societies, amateur archaeological societies, and anthropology departments at local colleges and universities (ask to talk to a regional archaeologist). Nearly every state has a state archaeologist and a Historic Preservation Office. Increasingly, many areas have regional research institutions that provide educational opportunities. An example is the Institute for Minnesota Archaeology in Minneapolis, which offers laboratory and field training, lectures, and many other opportunities for the aspiring archaeologist. A few telephone calls—and some persistence—should result in helpful information about how people lived in Precolumbian North America.

Entries by Culture Area and Topical Category

Arctic/Subarctic

Areas/Regions
Far North
Arctic
Subarctic

Archaeological Units
Acasta Lake
Aishihik Phase
Aleutian Tradition
Arctic Small Tool Tradition
Arctic Woodland Culture
Birnirk Culture
Blackduck

British Mountain Tradition
Choris Culture
Denali Complex
Denbigh Flint Complex
Dorset Culture
Dorset/Thule Transition
Groswater Culture
Independence I and II
Inugsuk Culture
Ipiutak Culture
Kachemak Tradition
Klo-kut and Old Chief Phases
Koniag Culture

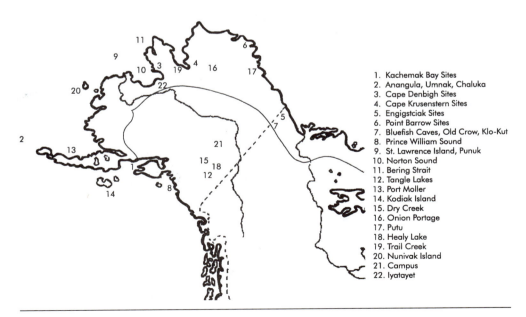

1. Kachemak Bay Sites
2. Anangula, Umnak, Chaluka
3. Cape Denbigh Sites
4. Cape Krusenstern Sites
5. Engigstciak Sites
6. Point Barrow Sites
7. Bluefish Caves, Old Crow, Klo-Kut
8. Prince William Sound
9. St. Lawrence Island, Punuk
10. Norton Sound
11. Bering Strait
12. Tangle Lakes
13. Port Moller
14. Kodiak Island
15. Dry Creek
16. Onion Portage
17. Putu
18. Healy Lake
19. Trail Creek
20. Nunivak Island
21. Campus
22. Iyatayet

Figure 3. Alaskan-Yukon region sites and areas. (Drawn by Deborah Schoenholz)

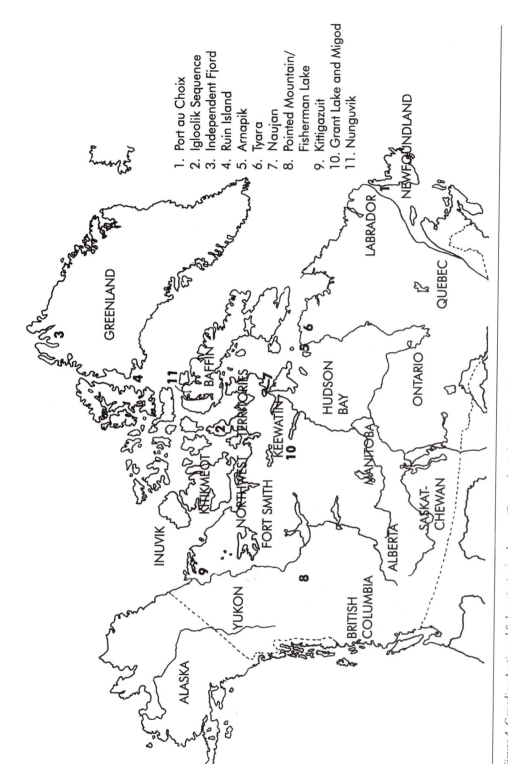

1. Port au Choix
2. Igloolik Sequence
3. Independent Fjord
4. Ruin Island
5. Arnapik
6. Tyara
7. Naujan
8. Pointed Mountain/
   Fisherman Lake
9. Kittigazuit
10. Grant Lake and Migod
11. Nunguvik

Figure 4. Canadian Arctic and Subarctic sites and areas. (Drawn by Deborah Schoenholz)

Lagoon Complex
Laurel Culture
Maritime Archaic Tradition
Northern Archaic Tradition

Northern Cordilleran Tradition
Northern Plano Culture
Northwest Microblade Tradition
Norton Culture

TABLES 3A–3F.

Arctic and Subarctic Chronological Tables.

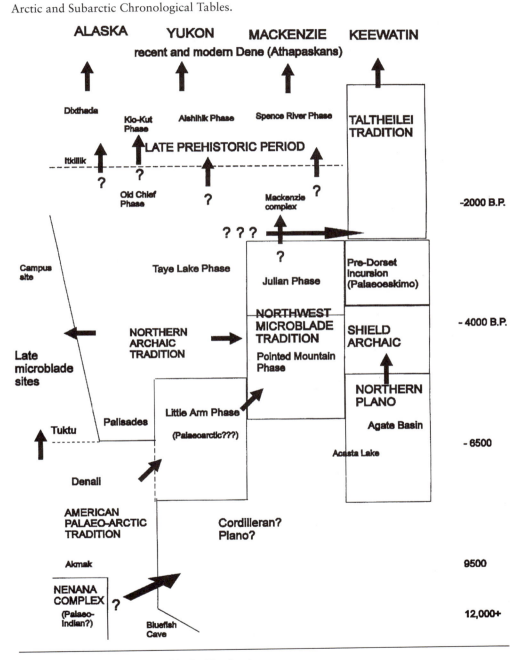

3A. Western Subarctic. (Prepared by D. Morrison)

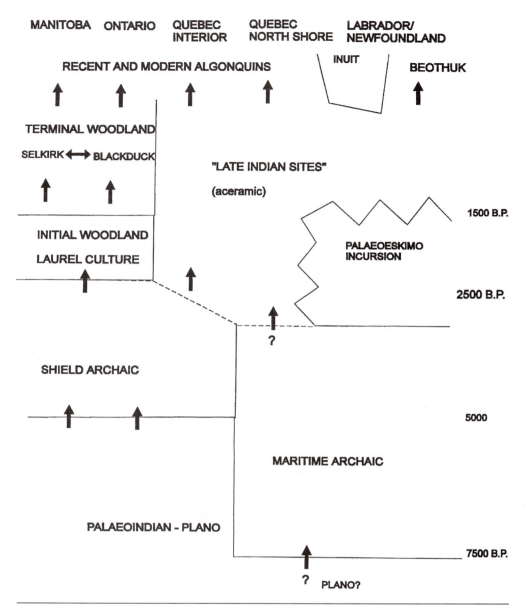

3B. Eastern Subarctic. (Prepared by D. Morrison)

Norton Tradition
Ocean Bay Tradition
Old Bering Sea/Okvik Culture
Pre-Dorset
Punuk Culture
Ruin Island Phase
Saqqaq Culture
Selkirk
Selkirk Composite
Shield Culture

Spence River Phase
Taltheilei Tradition
Thule Culture

Climate/Environment
Little Ice Age

Names
Collins, Henry B.
Giddings, James Louis

Jenness, Diamond
Mathiassen, Therkel

Sites
Anangula (Alaska)
Campus Site (Alaska)
Cape Krusenstern (Alaska)
Engigstciak (Yukon Territory)
Igloolik Sequence (Northwest Territories)
Iyatayet (Alaska)
Kittigazuit (Yukon Territory)
Migod (Northwest Territories)
Naujan (Northwest Territories)

Nunguvik and Saatut Sites (Northwest Territories)
Pointed Mountain/Fisherman Lake (Northwest Territories)
Port Moller (Alaska)
St. Lawrence Island Sites (Alaska)

Special Topics
Central Subarctic Woodland Culture
Hudson Bay Lowlands Prehistory
Norse in America
Quebec's Subarctic Region
Tangle Lakes District

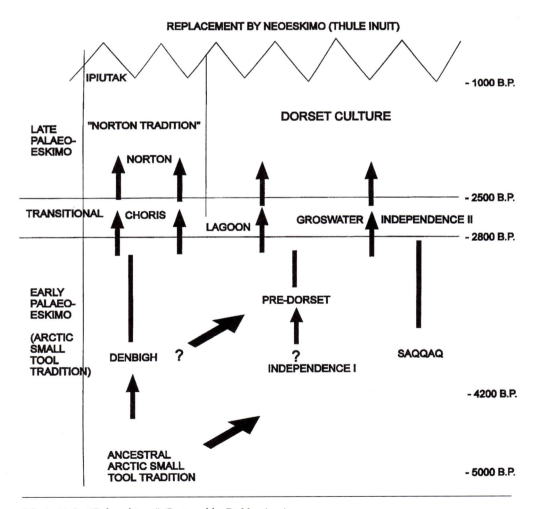

3C. Arctic I—"Paleoeskimo." (Prepared by D. Morrison)

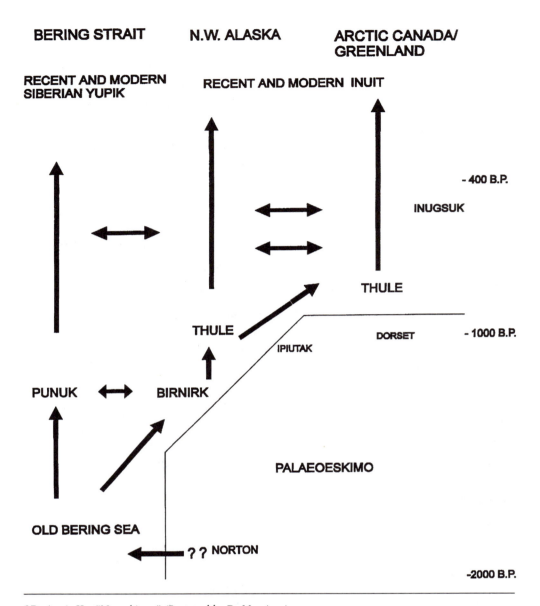

BERING STRAIT   **N.W. ALASKA**   **ARCTIC CANADA/ GREENLAND**

RECENT AND MODERN SIBERIAN YUPIK

RECENT AND MODERN INUIT

- 400 B.P.

INUGSUK

THULE

THULE

DORSET   - 1000 B.P.

IPIUTAK

PUNUK   ⟷   **BIRNIRK**

PALAEOESKIMO

OLD BERING SEA

? ? NORTON

-2000 B.P.

3D. Arctic II—"Neoeskimo." (Prepared by D. Morrison)

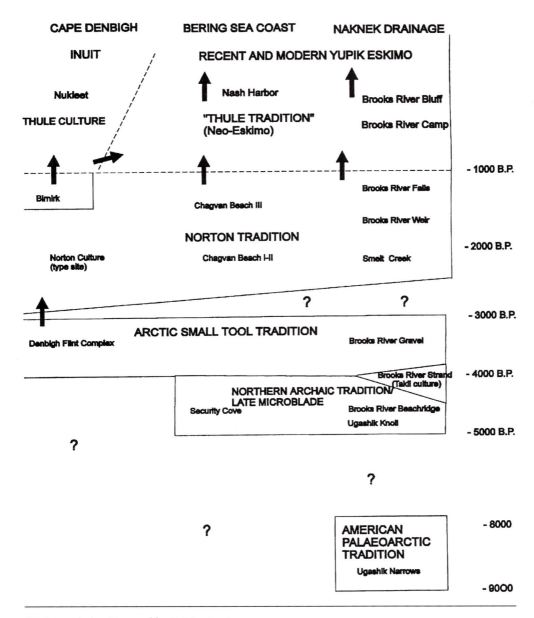

CAPE DENBIGH	BERING SEA COAST	NAKNEK DRAINAGE	
INUIT	**RECENT AND MODERN YUPIK ESKIMO**		
Nukleet	Nash Harbor	Brooks River Bluff	
THULE CULTURE	"THULE TRADITION" (Neo-Eskimo)	Brooks River Camp	
			— 1000 B.P.
Birnirk		Brooks River Falls	
	Chagvan Beach III	Brooks River Weir	
	NORTON TRADITION		— 2000 B.P.
Norton Culture (type site)	Chagvan Beach I-II	Smelt Creek	
	?	?	— 3000 B.P.
ARCTIC SMALL TOOL TRADITION		Brooks River Gravel	
Denbigh Flint Complex			— 4000 B.P.
		Brooks River Strand (Takli culture)	
	NORTHERN ARCHAIC TRADITION/ LATE MICROBLADE	Brooks River Beachridge	
	Security Cove	Ugashik Knoll	
?			— 5000 B.P.
	?		
?	AMERICAN PALAEOARCTIC TRADITION Ugashik Narrows		— 8000
			— 9000

3E. West Alaska. (Prepared by D. Morrison)

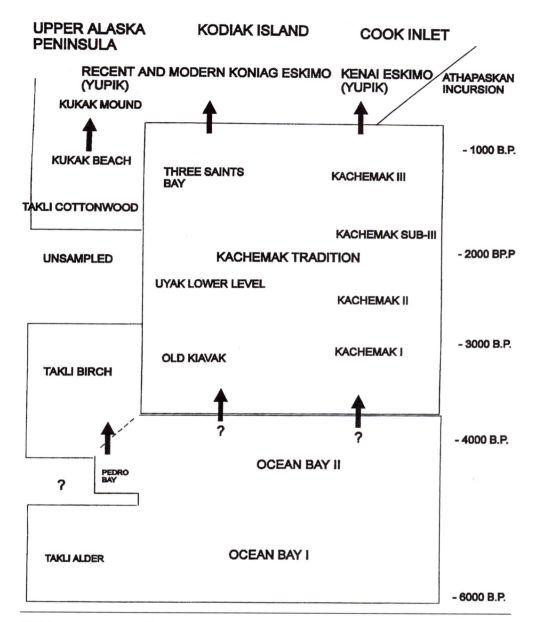

UPPER ALASKA PENINSULA   KODIAK ISLAND   COOK INLET

RECENT AND MODERN KONIAG ESKIMO   KENAI ESKIMO   ATHAPASKAN
(YUPIK)   (YUPIK)   INCURSION

KUKAK MOUND

- 1000 B.P.

KUKAK BEACH

THREE SAINTS BAY   KACHEMAK III

TAKLI COTTONWOOD

KACHEMAK SUB-III

UNSAMPLED   KACHEMAK TRADITION   - 2000 BP.P

UYAK LOWER LEVEL

KACHEMAK II

- 3000 B.P.

OLD KIAVAK   KACHEMAK I

TAKLI BIRCH

?   ?   - 4000 B.P.

PEDRO BAY   OCEAN BAY II

?

TAKLI ALDER   OCEAN BAY I

- 6000 B.P.

3F. *Eskimo Area. (Prepared by D. Morrison)*

California

Regional Prehistory
California Culture Area
Central California Prehistory
Eastern California

Northwestern California
Sierra Nevada and Cascade Ranges
Southern California Coast

1. Point St. George
2. Iron Gate Reservoir
3. Nightfire Island
4. Gunther Island,
    Humboldt Bay
5. Trinity Reservoir
6. Mendocino
7. Patrick Site
8. Oroville Reservoir
9. Borax Lake
10. Windmiller Mounds

11. Emeryville Shellmound
12. Hotchkiss Mound
13. Patterson Mound,
    University Village
14. Crane Flat,
    Yosemite District
15. Monterey
16. Tranquility Site
17. Rose Spring Site
18. Death Valley
19. Buena Vista Hills

20. Oak Grove Sites
21. Santa Rosa Island
22. Santa Cruz Island
23. Topanga Canyon
24. Encino
25. Malaga Cave
26. Santa Catalina Island
27. C.W. Harris Site
28. La Jolla Sites
29. Pinto Basin
30. Lake Mohave

Figure 5. California sites and areas. (Drawn by Deborah Schoenholz)

Table 4.
California
Chronological
Table.

BP	Major Subdivisions	Central California	San Francisco Bay Area	Southeastern Deserts	Northeastern California	North Coast Ranges	Northwestern California Coast	Central Sierra	Southern Cascades Northern Sierra	Coastal Southern California
150	Final Pacific	Hotchkiss	Patterson Mound	Shoshonean	Bidwell Phase	Clearwater, Shasta Complexes	Gunther Island, Patrick's Point, Point St. George II	Mariposa Complex	Oroville	Canaliño
500	Late Pacific	Hotchkiss	Lower Emeryville	Yuman	Alkali Phase			Tamarack Complex	Sweetwater	Canaliño
1500	Middle Pacific	Cosumnes	University Village Complex	Amargosa	Emerson Phase	Mendocino Complex	Point St. George I	Crane Flat Complex	Bidwell	Campbell
2500	Early Pacific	Windmiller	University Village Complex	Pinto Basin	Bare Creek Phase	Mendocino Complex			Mesilla	Campbell
4000	Late Archaic			Pinto Basin	Menlo Phase	Borax Lake				Encinitas (La Jolla, Topango Culture, Millingstone Horizon)
6000	Middle Archaic		Stanford	Lake Mohave		Borax Lake				Encinitas (La Jolla, Topango Culture, Millingstone Horizon)
8000	Early Archaic	Buena Vista, Tulare Lakes, Tranquility	Santa Clara Valley	Lake Mohave		Borax Lake Post Pattern				San Dieguito
10,000	Paleoindian								- - - Paleoindian - - -	
12,000										

Prepared by G. Gibbon

Animal and Plant Resources
Abalone
Acorns (California)
Olivella (California)
Pismo Clam

Artifacts
Beads (California)
Charmstones
Discoidal/Chunky Stone
Gaming Pieces (California)
Mano/Metate
Milling Tools
Mortar and Pestle
Pottery (California)
Shell Money (California)
Stone Disks (California)

Names
Campbell, Elizabeth
Curtis, Freddie
Davis, Emma Lou
Heizer, Robert Fleming
Meighan, Clement W.

Nelson, Nels C.
Rogers, David Banks
Rogers, Malcolm J.
Treganza, Adán
Uhle, Max
Wallace, William J.

Materials
Obsidian
Quartz Crystals
Steatite

Sites
Borax Lake Site
C.W. Harris Site
Gunther Island Site

Special Topics
Architecture (California)
Burials (California)
California (Space/Time Framework)
Rock Art (California)
Watercraft (California)

Eastern Woodlands

Areas/Regions
Eastern Woodlands Culture Area

Archaeological Units
Archaic Period
Eastern Woodlands Archaic
Eastern Woodlands Early Archaic
Eastern Woodlands Late Archaic
Eastern Woodlands Middle Archaic
Bifurcate Tradition
Central Riverine Archaic
Corner-Notched Tradition
Dalton
Gulf of Maine Archaic Tradition
Lake Forest Archaic
Laurentian Archaic
Mast Forest Archaic
Old Copper Culture
Poverty Point Culture
Red Paint Culture
Stallings Culture
Tellico Archaic

Woodland Period
Early Woodland
Late Woodland
Middle Woodland
Adena
Coles Creek Culture
Copena
Crab Orchard
Deptford Culture
Emergent Mississippian
Gulf Tradition
Havana Hopewell
Hopewell Interaction Sphere
Marksville
Miller Culture
Ohio Hopewell
Point Peninsula Culture
Swift Creek
Tchefuncte Culture
Weeden Island Culture

Mississippian Culture
Angel Site and Phase
Caborn-Welborn Phase
Caddoan Area Mississippian
Dallas Culture
Fort Ancient Culture
Iroquoian Culture
Oneota
Plaquemine Culture
St. Johns Tradition
Upper Mississippian Culture

Names
Chapman, Carl Haley
DeJarnette, David L.
Krieger, Alex D.
Wintemberg, William J.

Resources
Chenopodium
Copper
Eastern Agricultural Complex
Galena
Maple Surgaring
Mica (Eastern Woodlands)
Squash

Sumpweed
Sunflower

Sites
Angel Site and Phase (Indiana)
Aztalan (Wisconsin)
Boylston Street Fish Weirs (Massachusetts)
Brand Site (Arkansas)
Cahokia (Illinois)
Chauga (South Carolina)
Chota-Tanasee (Tennessee)
Chucalissa (Tennessee)
Crystal River Site (Florida)
Dickson Mounds (Illinois)
Doerschuk Site (North Carolina)
Dover Quarry (Tennessee)
Draper Site (Ontario)
Dust Cave (Alabama)
Etowah (Georgia)
Eva Site (Tennessee)
Fatherland Site (Mississippi)
Fort Ancient Site (Ohio)
Fort Center Site (Florida)
Fort Walton Site and Culture (Florida)
Frontenac Island Site (New York)
Garden Creek Site (North Carolina)

1. Glades Culture Area
2. Fort Center
3. Little Salt Springs
4. Weeden Island
5. St. Johns Culture Area
6. Crystal River
7. McKeithen
8. Aucilla River
9. Fort Walton Culture Area
10. Fort Walton Mound
11. Kolomoki
12. Mandeville
13. Swift Creek
14. Deptford
15. Stalling's Island
16. Ocmulgee
17. Etowah
18. Chauga
19. Doerschuck-Hardway
20. Tellico Reservoir
21. Eva
22. Miller
23. Dust Cave
24. Moundville
25. Tchefuncte
26. Plaquemine Culture Area
27. Marksville
28. Coles Creek
29. Poverty Point
30. Jaketown
31. Mound City
32. Brand
33. Toltec

34. Caddoan Culture Area
35. Spiro
36. Rogers Rockshelter
37. Graham Cave
38. Kimmswick
39. American Bottom
40. Koster
41. Illinois River Valley
42. Modoc Rockshelter
43. Kincaid
44. Indian Knoll
45. Serpent Mound
46. Hopewell Site
47. Ohio Adena-Hopewell Center
48. St. Albans
49. Williamson
50. Thunderbird, Flint Run Complex
51. Meadowcroft Rockshelter
52. Shoop
53. Bull Brook
54. Boylston Street Fish Weirs
55. Neville
56. Hathaway
57. Point Peninsula
58. Maxon-Derby
59. Lamoka Lake
60. Rice Lake, Ontario
61. Oconto
62. Aztalan
63. Trempealeau Mounds
64. Red Wing Locality
65. Cambria Phase
66. Laurel, Blackduck, Sandy Lake

Figure 6. Eastern Woodlands sites and areas. (Drawn by Deborah Schoenholz)

TABLE 5.

Eastern Woodlands Chronological Table.

BP	Major Subdivisions	Southeast	Midwest	Northeast
500				
1000	Late Woodland	— Mississippian —	Oneota Fort Ancient	Iroquoian
			Emergent Mississippian	
		Coles Creek		
1500		Weeden Island		Owasco
2000	Middle Woodland		—— Hopewellian ——	
3000	Early Woodland	Deptford	Adena	Middlesex
		Poverty Point		
			Lake Forest	Laurentian
4000	Late Archaic	Central Riverine and Mast Forest Archaic		Lamoka
5000		Indian Knoll		
6000	Middle Archaic	Eva		
7000				
8000		Icehouse Bottom	Koster	L'Anse Amour Neville
9000	Early Archaic	Corner-Notched and Bifurcate Traditions		
10,000		Dalton		
11,000	Paleoindian		--- Eastern Fluted Point ---	
---		Aucilla River		
14,000			Meadowcroft Rockshelter	

Prepared by G. Gibbon

George C. Davis Site (Texas)
Goforth-Saindon and Huntsville Mounds
   (Arkansas)
Gottschall Site (Wisconsin)
Graham Cave (Missouri)
Great Salt Spring (Illinois)

Hardaway Site (North Carolina)
Hawkshaw (Florida)
Hiwassee Island (Tennessee)
Hochelaga (Ontario)
Hopewell Site (Ohio)
Incinerator, or Sunwatch Village
  (Ohio)
Indian Knoll (Kentucky)
Key Marco (Florida)
King Site (Georgia)
Klunk-Gibson Mound Group
  (Illinois)
Kolomoki (Georgia)
Koster (Illinois)
Lamoka Lake Site (New York)
Madisonville (Ohio)
Mandeville (Georgia)
Mann Site (Indiana)
Maxon-Derby Site (New York)
McGraw (Ohio)
McKeithen Site (Florida)
Mill Creek Quarry (Illinois)
Modoc Rock Shelter (Illinois)
Monks Mound (Illinois)
Mound City (Ohio)
Moundville (Alabama)
Neville Site (New Hampshire)
Newark Earthworks (Ohio)
Ocmulgee Site (Georgia)
Parkin Site (Arkansas)
Phillips Spring (Missouri)
Pinson Mounds Site (Tennessee)
Poverty Point Site (Louisiana)

Range Site (Illinois)
Red Wing Locality (Minnesota)
Rice Lake Site (Ontario)
Rodgers Shelter (Missouri)
Sand Lake Site (Wisconsin)
Seip (Ohio)
Serpent Mound, Great (Ohio)
Spiro (Oklahoma)
Toltec Mounds Site (Arkansas)
Toqua (Tennessee)
Town Creek Site (North Carolina)
Trempealeau Locality (Wisconsin)
Turner Site (Ohio)
Warren Wilson Site (North Carolina)
Wickliffe Site (Kentucky)

Special Topics/Artifacts
Belle Glade Culture
Ceramics in the Far Northeast
Earspool
Earthworks (Eastern Woodlands)
Effigy Mounds
Fish Wiers and Traps (Eastern Woodlands)
Paddle-and-Anvil Technique
Panpipe
Platform Mounds (Southwest)
Platform Pipe
Poverty Point Objects
Primary Forest Efficiency
South Appalachian Tradition
Southeastern Ceremonial Complex
Wall-Trench Structures

Great Basin

Areas/Regions
Great Basin, The

Archaic
Great Basin Archaic

Formative
Fremont
Virgin Anasazi

Late Prehistoric
Eastern Great Basin Late Prehistoric Period
Southern Great Basin Late Prehistoric Period

Names
Antevs, Ernst
Cressman, Luther Sheeleigh
Heizer, Robert Fleming
Jennings, Jesse D.
Judd, Neil Merton
Steward, Julian H.

Sites
Catlow and Roaring Springs Caves
  (Oregon)
Danger Cave (Utah)
Hidden Cave (Nevada)

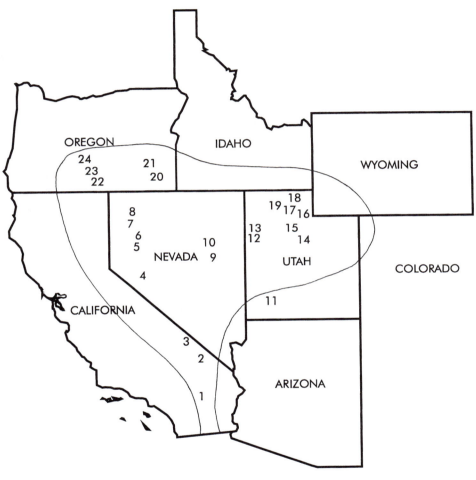

Figure 7. Great Basin sites and areas. (Drawn by Deborah Schoenholz)

TABLE 6.

Great Basin Chronological Table.

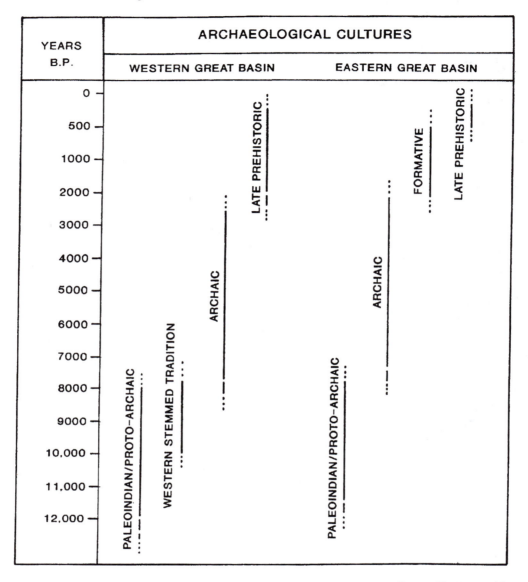

Prepared by J. D. Wilde

Northwest Coast

Areas/Regions
Northwest Coast Culture Area

Archaeological Units
Bella Bella Sequence
Bella Coola Area
Charles/St. Mungo Culture Type
Early Coast Microblade
Fraser River Canyon Sequence
Fraser River Stone Sculpture Complex
Graham Tradition
Gulf of Georgia Culture Type
Kitselas Canyon Sequence
Locarno Beach Culture
Lower Columbia River Valley Sequence
Marpole Culture Type
Moresby Tradition
Prince Rupert Harbor

Puget Lowland Sequence
Queen Charlotte Strait Sequence
Southeast Alaskan Sequence
Southern Northwest Coast
Transitional Complex
Washington Ocean Coast Sequence
West Coast Culture Type
Willamette Valley Sequence

Names
Borden, Charles E.
Laguna, Frederica de

Resources
Eulachon
Pacific Salmon
Western Red Cedar

TABLE 7.
Northwest Coast Chronological Table.

Time	Southeast Alaska	Kitselas Canyon	Queen Charlotte Islands	West Coast Vancouver Island	Queen Charlotte Strait	Strait of Georgia	Fraser River Canyon	Columbia River Estuary	Portland Basin	The Dalles	Willamette Valley	Southern Northwest Coast
CONTACT	LATE PERIOD	KLEANZA PHASE	GRAHAM TRADITION	WEST COAST CULTURE TYPE	QUEEN CHARLOTTE STRAIT CULTURE TYPE	GULF OF GEORGIA CULTURE TYPE	CANYON CULTURE TYPE	HISTORIC	MULTNOMAH 3	HISTORIC	LATE ARCHAIC PERIOD	FORMATIVE STAGE
1500								ILWACO 2	MULTNOMAH 2	FULL PROTO-HISTORIC		
1000									MULTNOMAH 1			
500	MIDDLE PERIOD	PAUL MASON PHASE				MARPOLE CULTURE TYPE	SKAMEL CULTURE TYPE	ILWACO 1			LATE ARCHAIC STAGE	
AD / BC		SKEENA PHASE			OBSIDIAN CULTURE TYPE				MERRYBELL			
500						LOCARNO BEACH CULTURE TYPE	BALDWIN CULTURE TYPE			INITIAL PROTO-HISTORIC	MIDDLE ARCHAIC PERIOD	MIDDLE ARCHAIC STAGE
1000		GITAUS PHASE										
1500								SEA ISLAND PHASE				
2000		BORNITE PHASE	TRANSITIONAL COMPLEX			CHARLES CULTURE TYPE						
2500												
3000												

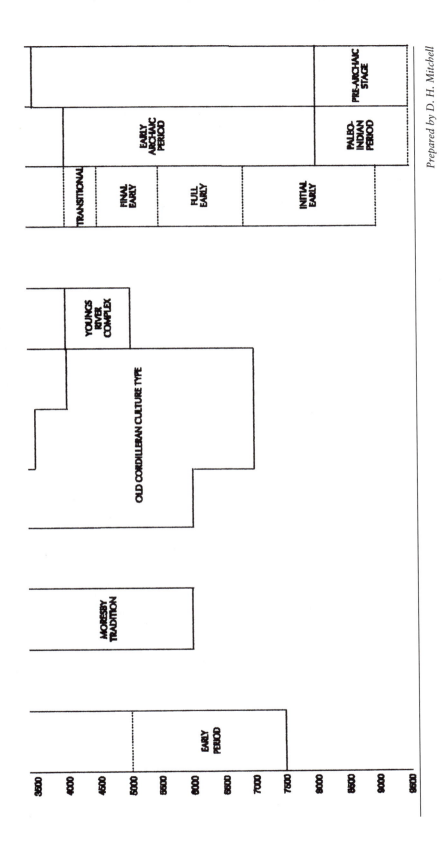

Prepared by D. H. Mitchell

Areas/Regions
Central Plains Tradition
Middle Missouri Tradition
Plains

Western Plains Late Archaic Regional
  Variant
Western Plains Middle Archaic Regional
  Variant
Yonkee

Archaeological Units
Plains Archaic
Albion Boardinghouse Phase
Apex Phase
Besant Phase
Front Range Phase
Logan Creek Complex
Magic Mountain Phase
McKean
Mortlach Aggregate
Mount Albion Phase
Munkers Creek Phase
Nebo Hill Phase
Oxbow Complex
Pelican Lake
Southern Rocky Mountain Early Archaic
  Regional Variant
Western Plains Early Archaic Regional
  Variant

Plains Woodland
Arkansas Phase
Avonlea
Colorado Plains Woodland Regional Variant
Kansas City Hopewell
Keith Variant
Killarney Focus
Loseke Creek Variant
Pomona Phase
Sandy Lake
Selkirk
Selkirk Composite
Sonota Burial Complex
South Platte Phase
Sterns Creek Variant
Valley Variant
Vickers Focus
Williams Complex

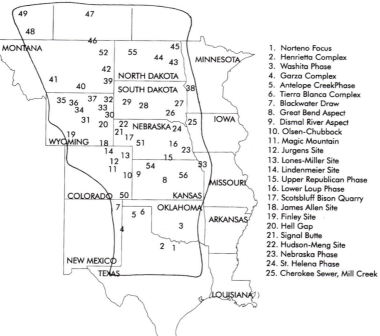

1. Norteno Focus
2. Henrietta Complex
3. Washita Phase
4. Garza Complex
5. Antelope CreekPhase
6. Tierra Blanca Complex
7. Blackwater Draw
8. Great Bend Aspect
9. Dismal River Aspect
10. Olsen-Chubbock
11. Magic Mountain
12. Jurgens Site
13. Lones-Miller Site
14. Lindenmeier Site
15. Upper Republican Phase
16. Lower Loup Phase
17. Scotsbluff Bison Quarry
18. James Allen Site
19. Finley Site
20. Hell Gap
21. Signal Butte
22. Hudson-Meng Site
23. Nebraska Phase
24. St. Helena Phase
25. Cherokee Sewer, Mill Creek

26. Anoka Phase
27. James River
28. Arzberger Site
29. Lange-Ferguson Site
30. Agate Basin
31. Casper Site
32. McKean
33. Carter/Kerr-McGee
34. Colby Site
35. Mummy Cave
36. Horner Site
37. Hanson Site
38. Cambria Phase
39. Horner Site
40. Pictograph Cave
41. Anzick Site
42. Lindsay Mammoth
43. Northeastern Plains
    Village Sites
44. Sonota
45. Devil's Lake-Sourisford
46. Avonlea
47. Mortlach
48. Heads-Smashed-In
49. Old Women's Jump
50. Apishapa Phase
51. Ashe Hollow
52. Hagen Site
53. Kansas City Hopewell
54. Keith Variant
55. Knife River NHS
56. Munkers Creek Phase

Figure 8. Plains sites and areas. (Drawn by Deborah Schoenholz.)

Plains Village Tradition
Middle Missouri Tradition:
Anderson Phase
Cambria
Fort Yates Phase
Grand Detour Phase
Great Oasis
Huff Phase
Mill Creek Quarry
Thomas Riggs Phase
Central Plains Tradition:
Itskari (formerly "Loup River") Phase
Lower Loup Phase
Nebraska Phase
Smoky Hill Phase
St. Helena Phase
Upper Republican Phase
Initial Coalescent (Campbell Creek Phase
    and/ or Arzberger Phase)
Coalescent Tradition:
Bad River Phase
Heart River Phase
Knife River Phase
Lower Loup Phase
Redbird Phase

Southern Plains Villagers
Antelope Creek Phase
Custer Phase
Garza Complex
Great Bend Aspect
Henrietta Focus
Little River Focus
Lower Walnut Focus
Norteño Focus
Pratt Complex
Tierra Blanca Complex
Uncas Complex
Upper Canark Regional Variant
Washita River Phase

Western Plains Villagers
Apishapa Phase
Dismal River Aspect
Purgatoire Phase
Upper Purgatoire Complex

Other Units
Intermountain Tradition
Old Women's Phase

One Gun Phase
Steed-Kisker Phase
White Rock/Glen Elder "Phase"

Climate/Environment
Hypsithermal/Altithermal

Names
Champe, John Leland
Lehmer, Donald Jayne
Mulloy, William Thomas
Strong, William Duncan
Wedel, Waldo R.

Sites
Antonsen Site (Montana)
Arzberger Site (South Dakota)
Ash Hollow Cave (Nebraska)
Biesterfeldt Site (North Dakota)
Big Horn Medicine Wheel (Wyoming)
"Big Village" Site of the Omahas (Nebraska)
Cherokee Sewer Site (Iowa)
Cluny Earthlodge Village (Alberta)
Crow Creek Site (South Dakota)
Grandmother's Lodge (North Dakota)
Hagen Site (Montana)
Head-Smashed-In Buffalo Jump (Alberta)
Knife River Indian Villages National
    Historic Site (North Dakota)
Lost Terrace Site (Montana)
Magic Mountain Site (Colorado)
Mummy Cave (Wyoming)
Obsidian Cliff Plateau Quarries
    (Wyoming)
Pictograph Cave (Montana)
Pilgrim Site (Montana)
Ponca Fort (Nebraska)
Schmitt Chert Mine (Montana)
Scott County Pueblo (Kansas)
Signal Butte (Nebraska)

Special Topics
Catlinite
Earthlodge
Knife River Flint
Linear Mounds (Plains)
Medicine Wheels
Pryor Stemmed-Lovell Constricted
Tipi Ring, Stone
Wascana Ware

TABLE 8. Plains Chronological Table.

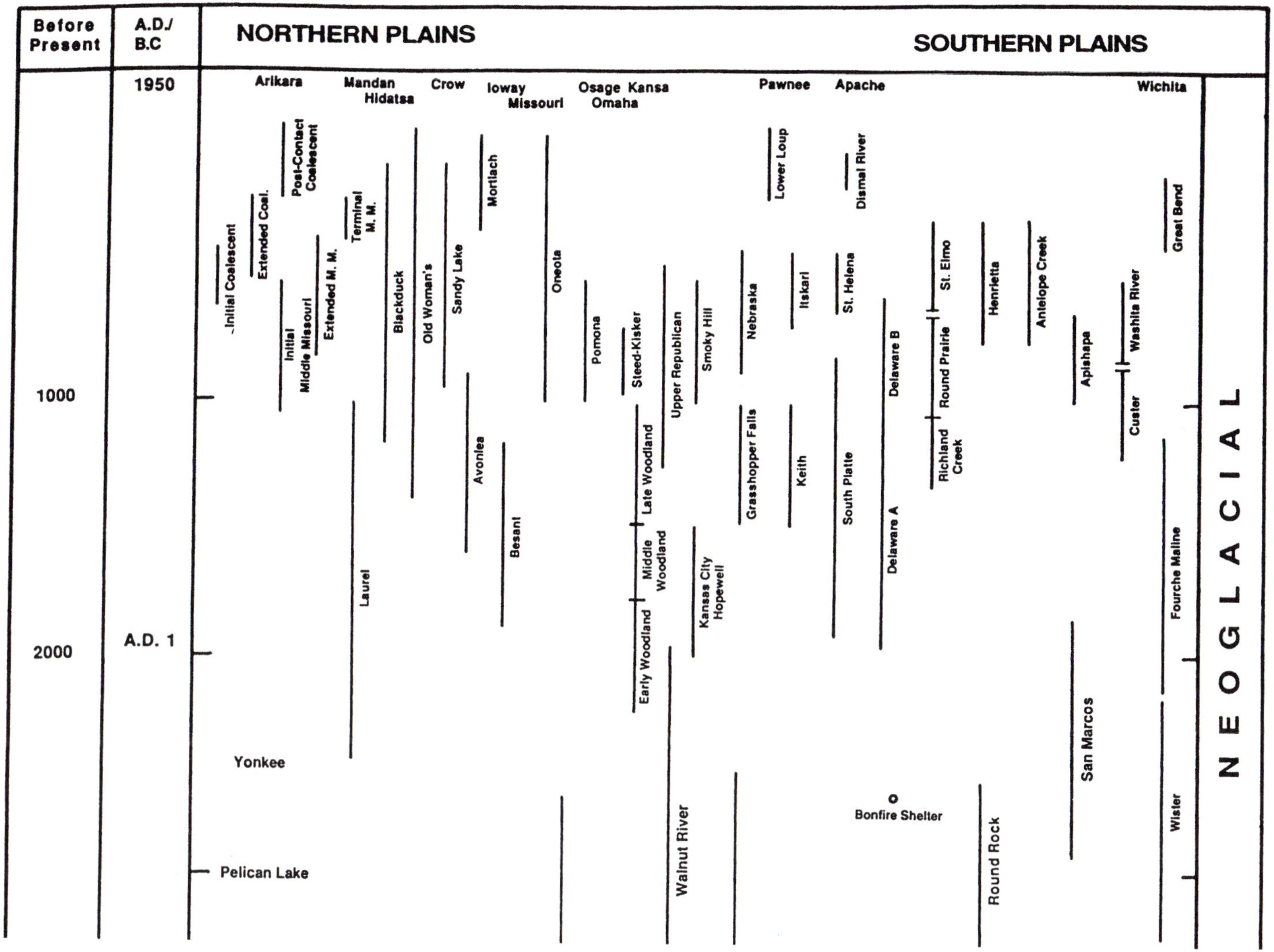

NORTHERN PLAINS — **SOUTHERN PLAINS**

NEOGLACIAL

Before Present	A.D./B.C													
	1950	Arikara	Mandan Hidatsa	Crow	Ioway Missouri	Osage Kansa Omaha		Pawnee	Apache				Wichita	

Columns (Northern Plains): Arikara, Mandan Hidatsa, Crow, Ioway Missouri, Osage Kansa Omaha, Missouri, Pawnee, Apache, Wichita

Time scale: 1950 (A.D./B.C), A.D. 1; Before Present: 1000, 2000

Entries (Northern Plains):
- Initial Coalescent
- Extended Coal.
- Post-Contact Coalescent
- Initial Middle Missouri
- Extended M. M.
- Terminal M. M.
- Laurel
- Blackduck
- Old Woman's
- Sandy Lake
- Mortlach
- Avonlea
- Besant
- Oneota
- Pomona
- Steed-Kisker
- Upper Republican
- Smoky Hill
- Kansas City Hopewell
- Early Woodland
- Middle Woodland
- Late Woodland
- Nebraska
- Grasshopper Falls
- Keith
- Itskari
- Lower Loup
- South Platte
- St. Helena
- Dismal River
- Yonkee
- Pelican Lake

Entries (Southern Plains):
- Great Bend
- Washita River
- Custer
- Apishapa
- Antelope Creek
- Henrietta
- Richland Creek
- Round Prairie
- St. Elmo
- Delaware A
- Delaware B
- Fourche Maline
- San Marcos
- Wister
- Round Rock
- Walnut River
- Bonfire Shelter

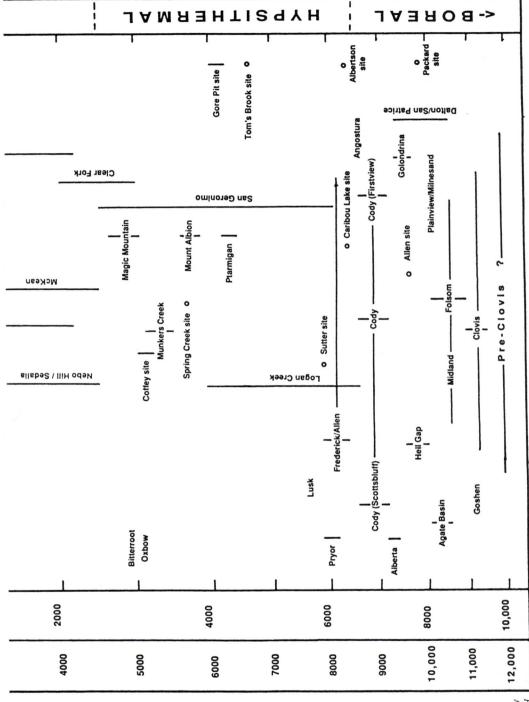

Prepared by
W. R. Wood

TABLE 9.
Plateau Chronological Table.

Years BP	Chilcotin	Fraser-Thompson	Okanagan	Arrow Lakes-Slocan	Kootenay Pend Oreille	Kettle Falls	Middle Columbia	Snake River	Clearwater River	Salmon River
0	Lulua Phase / Eagle Lake Phase / Kamloops Phase	Kamloops Horizon	Cassimer Bar Phase	Slocan Phase	Akanohonek Complex	Shwayip Period	Late Period	Numipu Phase	Kooskia Phase	Corn Creek Phase
1000						Sinaikst Period		Piqunin Phase		Owl Creek Phase
2000	Lillooet Phase	Thompson Horizon	Chiliwist Phase	Vallican Phase	?????	Takumakst Period		Harder Phase	Ahsahka Phase	Big Creek Phase
3000	?????	Shuswap Horizon		Deer Park Phase	Inissimi Complex	Skitak Period	Middle Period	Tucannon Phase		
4000	Chert Debitage Sites	Lochnore Phase	Indian Dan Phase			Ksunku Period		Hatwai Phase	Hatwai Phase	Shoup Phase
5000	?????	Lehman Phase								
6000		Early Nesikep Tradition	Okanagan Phase		Goatfell Complex	?????	Early Period	Cascade Phase		
7000						Slawntehus Period				Early Prehistoric Period
8000			?????		?????					
9000						Shonitkwu Period		Windust Phase		?????
10,000										
11,000							?????			

Plateau Pithouse Tradition; Nesikep Tradition; Early Period

Prepared by D. L. Pokotylo and K. M. Ames

Plateau

Areas/Regions
Northern (Canadian) Plateau
Plateau Culture Area
Southern (Columbia) Plateau

Archaeological Units
Arrow Lakes/Slocan Valley Sequence
Chilcotin Plateau
Classic Lillooet Culture

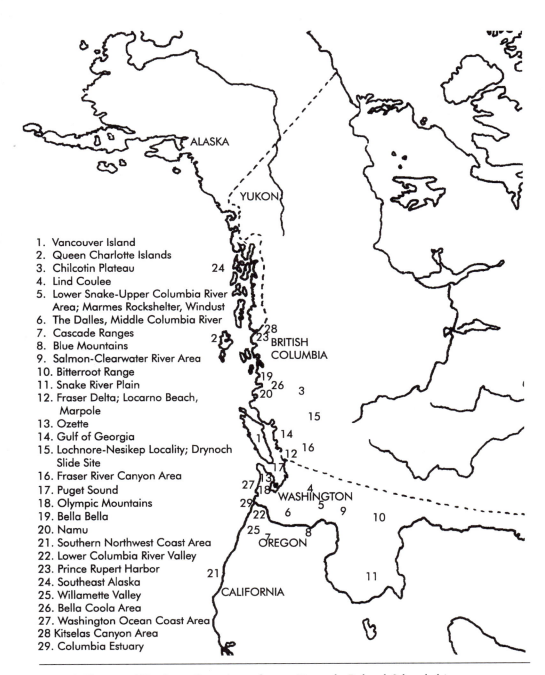

1. Vancouver Island
2. Queen Charlotte Islands
3. Chilcotin Plateau
4. Lind Coulee
5. Lower Snake-Upper Columbia River Area; Marmes Rockshelter, Windust
6. The Dalles, Middle Columbia River
7. Cascade Ranges
8. Blue Mountains
9. Salmon-Clearwater River Area
10. Bitterroot Range
11. Snake River Plain
12. Fraser Delta; Locarno Beach, Marpole
13. Ozette
14. Gulf of Georgia
15. Lochnore-Nesikep Locality; Drynoch Slide Site
16. Fraser River Canyon Area
17. Puget Sound
18. Olympic Mountains
19. Bella Bella
20. Namu
21. Southern Northwest Coast Area
22. Lower Columbia River Valley
23. Prince Rupert Harbor
24. Southeast Alaska
25. Willamette Valley
26. Bella Coola Area
27. Washington Ocean Coast Area
28 Kitselas Canyon Area
29. Columbia Estuary

Figure 9. Plateau and Northwest Coast sites and areas. (Drawn by Deborah Schoenholz)

Early Period (Plateau)
Kettle Falls Sequence
Kootenay-Pend d'Oreille Rivers Sequence
Lower Snake River Sequence
Mid-Columbia River Region Sequence
Nesikep Tradition
Okanagan Valley Sequence
Plateau Microblade Tradition
Plateau Pithouse Tradition
Salmon River–Clearwater River Sequences

Animal and Plant Resources
Freshwater Mussels (Plateau)
Plateau Root Foods
Plateau Ungulates
Salmon Pacific

Names
Borden, Charles E.
Cressman, Luther Sheeleigh
Leonhardy, Frank Clinton
Smith, Harlan Ingersoll

Special Topics/Artifacts
Cachepits (Plateau)
Earth Ovens
Longhouses (Plateau)
Mazama Tephra
Pithouse
Pithouses (Plateau)

Southwest

Areas/Regions
Anasazi Culture Area
Hohokam Culture Area
Mogollon Culture Area
Patayan Culture Area
Southwest Culture Area

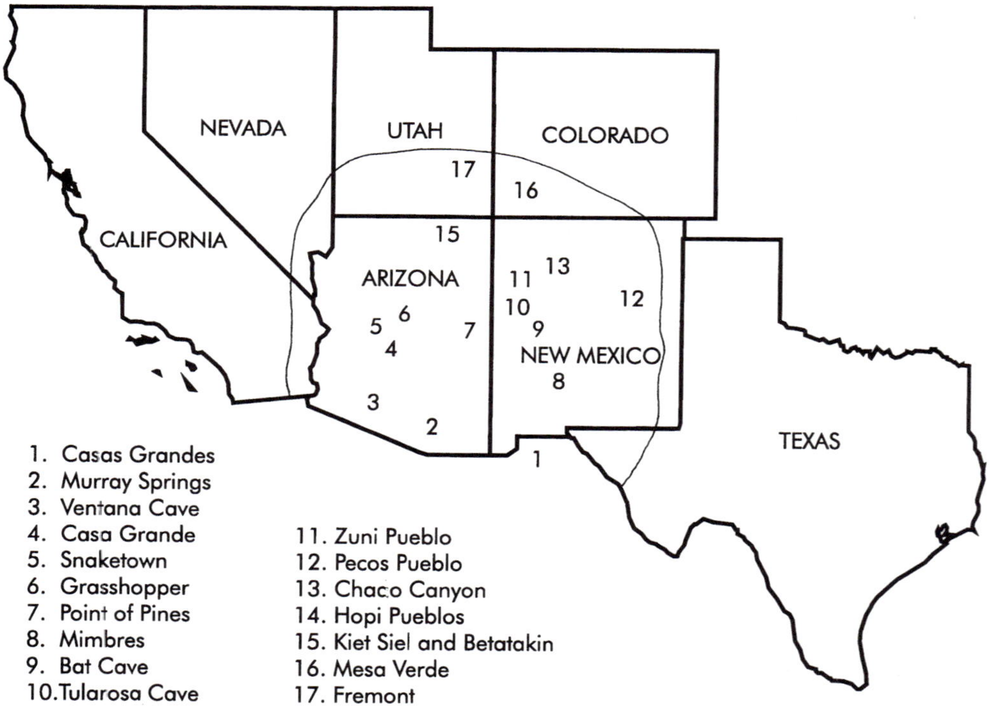
NEVADA
UTAH
COLORADO
CALIFORNIA
ARIZONA
NEW MEXICO
TEXAS
1. Casas Grandes
2. Murray Springs
3. Ventana Cave
4. Casa Grande
5. Snaketown
6. Grasshopper
7. Point of Pines
8. Mimbres
9. Bat Cave
10. Tularosa Cave
11. Zuni Pueblo
12. Pecos Pueblo
13. Chaco Canyon
14. Hopi Pueblos
15. Kiet Siel and Betatakin
16. Mesa Verde
17. Fremont

Figure 10. Southwest sites and areas. (Drawn by Deborah Schoenholz)

TABLE 10.

Southwest Chronological Table.

BP	ANASAZI	MOGOLLON	HOHOKAM	PATAYAN
500	Pueblo IV	Abandonment	El Polvoron Phase	
600			Civano Phase	Patayan II
700		Mogollon Pueblo		
800	Pueblo III		Soho Phase	
900				
1000	Pueblo II		Sacaton Phase	
1100			Santa Cruz Phase	Patayan I
1200	Pueblo I	Late Pithouse	Gila Butte Phase	
			Snaketown Phase	
1300			Sweetwater Phase	
1400	Basketmaker III		Estrella Phase	
1500				
1600			Vahki Phase	
1700	(Basketmaker II)			
1800		Early Pithouse	Red Mountain Phase	
1900				
2000				
2100				
Time Gap				
		LATE ARCHAIC		
3500		MIDDLE ARCHAIC		
7000		EARLY ARCHAIC		
9000		PALEOINDIAN		

Prepared by P. L. Crown

Culture/Archaeological Units
Cochise Culture
Oshara Tradition
Picosa
Southwestern Archaic

Anasazi:
   Chaco Branch
   Cibola Branch
   Kayenta Branch
   Largo-Gallina Branch

Little Colorado Branch
Mesa Verde Branch
Rio Grande Branch
Mogollon:
    Black River Branch
    Forestdale Branch
    Jornada Branch of the Mogollon Culture
    Mimbres Branch
    Pine Lawn Branch
    San Simon Branch of the Mogollon
Salado Horizon
Sinagua Tradition

Names
Brew, John Otis
Martin, Paul Sidney
Morris, Earl H.
Roberts, Frank H.H., Jr.
Spier, Leslie

Sites
Bandelier National Monument
    (New Mexico)
Bat Cave (New Mexico)
Bear Village (Arizona)
Betatakin (Arizona)
Bluff Village (Arizona)
Broken K Pueblo (Arizona)
Carter Ranch Pueblo (Arizona)
Casa Grande (Arizona)
Casa Rinconada (New Mexico)
Casas Grandes (Mexico)

Cliff Palace (Colorado)
Gran Quivira (New Mexico)
Grasshopper Pueblo (Arizona)
Hodges Ruin (Arizona)
Hovenweep (Colorado)
Kiet Siel (Arizona)
Papagueria (Arizona)
Pecos Pueblo (New Mexico)
Point of Pines Ruin (Arizona)
Pueblo Bonito (New Mexico)
Sand Canyon Pueblo (Colorado)
Snaketown (Arizona)
Tularosa Cave (New Mexico)
University Indian Ruin (Arizona)
Ventana Cave (Arizona)
Yellow Jacket Ruin (Colorado)
Zuni Pueblo (New Mexico)

Special Topics
Adobe
Ballcourt
Compound
Gladwinian Classification of Cultures
Jacal
Kiva
Lower Sonoran Agricultural Complex
Pecos Classification
Pithouse
Platform Mounds (Southwest)
Pueblo
Rancheria
Upper Sonoran Agricultural Complex

Pre-Clovis/Paleoindian

Archaeological Units
Agate Basin Complex
Alberta Complex
Alder Complex
Angostura Cultural Complex
Beringian Tradition
Clovis Cultural Complex
Cody
Crowfield Cultural Complex
Cumberland Cultural Complex
Dalton
Denali Complex
Early Coast Microblade
Flint Run Complex

Folsom Complex
Frederick Complex and Projectile
    Point Type
Gainey Complex
Goshen Complex
Hell Gap Complex
Lusk Complex and Projectile
    Point Type
Midland Complex
Miller Complex
Moresby Tradition
Nenana Complex
Paleoarctic Tradition
Parkhill Cultural Complex

General Category

Cushing, Frank H.
Davis, Edwin H.
Dawson, John W.
Douglass, Andrew Ellicott
Ford, James Alfred
Griffin, James B.
Haven, Samuel F.
Heizer, Robert Fleming
Holmes, William Henry
Hrdlicka, Ales
Jefferson, Thomas
Jennings, Jesse D.
Judd, Neil Merton
Keyes, Charles Reuben
Kidder, Alfred V.
Libby, Willard F.
McKern, Will C.
Moore, Clarence B.
Moorehead, Warren King
Nelson, Nels C.
Parker, Arthur Caswell
Powell, John Wesley
Putnam, Frederick Ward
Ritchie, William A.
Shetrone, Henry Clyde
Smith, Harlan Ingersoll
Squier, Ephraim G.
Steward, Julian H.
Strong, William Duncan
Taylor, Walter W.
Thomas, Cyrus
Uhle, Max
Webb, William Snyder
Wedel, Waldo R.
Willey, Gordon R.

Resources
Beans
Bison
Copper
Corn
Maple Sugaring
Nuts
Obsidian
River Snails
Salt
Shell Middens
Squash
Steatite
Tobacco

Special Topics
Archaeoastronomy
Archaeological Culture
Archaeometallurgy

Archaic
Complex
Component
Cultural Resource Management
Culture Areas
Demography
Federally Funded Archaeology
Fiber Artifacts and Ethnicity
Fire
Health and Disease
Horizon
Language
Lost Continent of Atlantis Theory
Lost Race Theory
Lost Tribe Theory
Midwestern Taxonomic System
   (Midwestern Taxonomic Method)
Mound Builder Myth
Period
Petroglyph
Phase
Reburial Issue
Ridged-Field Agriculture
Rock Art
Site
Stage
Tradition
World-Systems Approach

General Tool Types
Abrader
Anvil
Atlatl
Awl
Axe/Adze
Bannerstone
Biface
Billet
Bipolar Percussion
Blade/Bladelet
Bow and Arrow
Burin
Chert/Flint
Chopper
Core
Dart/Spear Points
Debitage/Debris
Denticulate
Disc
Discoidal/Chunky Stone
Drill
Earspool
Flake
Flaker
Flute

Gorget
Gouge
Graver
Hammerstone
Heat Treatment of Silicates
Hoe
Mace
Mano/Metate
Mortar and Pestle
Needle
Notched Piece
Paleolith

Pick
Pin
Pipe
Pitted Stone
Plummet
Rattle
Retouch
Retouched Piece
Scraper
Spud
Uniface

Contributors

Steven Acheson
Archaeology Branch
Government of British Columbia
Victoria, British Columbia
Graham Tradition

Robert E. Ackerman
Department of Anthropology
Washington State University
Pullman, Washington
*Birnirk Phase, Old Bering Sea/Okvik Culture,
St. Lawrence Island Sites*

Michael A. Adler
Department of Anthropology
Southern Methodist University
Dallas, Texas
*Cliff Palace, Mesa Verde Branch, Yellow
Jacket Ruin*

James M. Adovasio
Department of Anthropology
   and Archaeology
Mercyhurst College
Erie, Pennsylvania
Miller Culture

George A. Agogino
Department of Anthropology
Eastern New Mexico University
Portales, New Mexico
Blackwater Draw, Hell Gap Site, Sandia Cave

Steven R. Ahler
Research and Collections Center
Illinois State Museum
Springfield, Illinois
Modoc Rock Shelter

Richard Ahlstrom
SWCA Environmental Consultants
Tucson, Arizona
Pecos Classification

C. Melvin Aikens
Department of Anthropology
University of Oregon
Eugene, Oregon
Hogup Cave, Jesse D. Jennings

Kenneth M. Ames
Department of Anthropology
Portland State University
Portland, Oregon
*Frank Clinton Leonhardy, Longhouses (Plateau),
Lower Snake River Sequence, Plateau Culture
Area (with D. L. Pokotylo), Prince Rupert Harbor,
Southern (Columbia) Plateau, Windust Complex*

Daniel S. Amick
Department of Sociology and Anthropology
Loyola University
Chicago, Illinois
Folsom Site

David G. Anderson
Southeast Archeological Center
National Park Service
Tallahassee, Florida
*South Appalachian Tradition, Southeastern
Paleoindian, Swift Creek*

Douglas D. Anderson
Department of Anthropology
Brown University
Providence, Rhode Island
*Arctic Woodland Culture, Birnirk Culture, Cape
Krusenstern, James Louis Giddings, Iyatayet*

Duane Anderson
School of American Research
Santa Fe, New Mexico
Cherokee Sewer Site

Scott F. Anfinson
SHPO Office
Minnesota Historical Society
St. Paul, Minnesota
*Cambria, Cultural Resource Management,
Great Oasis*

Kurt F. Anschuetz
Rio Grande Foundation
Santa Fe, New Mexico
Largo-Gallina Branch

Constance Arzigian
Mississippi Valley Archaeology Center
University of Wisconsin-La Crosse
La Crosse, Wisconsin
Nuts

Arthur C. Aufderheide
Department of Pathology
University of Minnesota
Duluth, Minnesota
Health and Disease

Douglas B. Bamforth
Department of Anthropology
University of Colorado
Boulder, Colorado
Lime Creek

Frank E. Bayham
Department of Anthropology
California State University-Chico
Chico, California
Cochise Culture

Charlotte Beck
Department of Anthropology
Hamilton College
Clinton, New York
Western Stemmed Tradition (with G. T. Jones)

Judith A. Bense
Department of Sociology and Anthropology
University of West Florida
Pensacola, Florida
*Deptford Culture, Hawkshaw, Weeden Island
Culture*

Robert L. Bettinger
Department of Anthropology
University of California-Davis
Davis, California
*Great Basin High Altitude Adaptations,
Numic Expansion*

William T. Billeck
Smithsonian Institution
National Museum of Natural History
Washington, D.C
Catlinite, Knife River Flint

Astrida R. Blukis Onat
BOAS, Inc.
Seattle, Washington
Puget Lowland Sequence

Robson Bonnichsen
Center for the Study of the First Americans
Oregon State University
Corvallis, Oregon
*Anzick Clovis Burial (with S. Jones),
Bone Modification*

Bruce J. Bourque
Library/Archives Museum Building
Maine State Museum
Augusta, Maine
Red Paint Culture

John R. Bozell
Nebraska State Historical Society
Lincoln, Nebraska
*Ash Hollow Cave (with J. Ludwickson), Central
Plains Tradition (with J. Ludwickson), Itskari
Phase (formerly "Loup River"; with J. Lud-
wickson), Lower Loup Phase (with J. Ludwick-
son), Nebraska Phase (with J. Ludwickson),
Redbird Phase (with J. Ludwickson), Signal
Butte (with J. Ludwickson), Smoky Hill Phase
(with J. Ludwickson), Upper Republican Phase
(with J. Ludwickson)*

Bruce A. Bradley
Crow Canyon Archaeological Center
Cortez, Colorado
*Cody, Horner Site, Lithic Technology
(Paleoindian), Sand Canyon Pueblo*

Jack Brink
Provincial Museum of Alberta
Edmonton, Alberta
Head-Smashed-In Buffalo Jump

Richard H. Brooks
Department of Anthropology
University of Nevada
Las Vegas, Nevada
Tule Springs (with D. E. Tuohy)

Ian W. Brown
Alabama Museum of Natural History
University of Alabama
Tuscaloosa, Alabama
Fatherland Site, Plaquemine Culture

James A. Brown
Department of Anthropology
Northwestern University
Evanston, Illinois
Koster, Mississippian Culture, Southeastern Ceremonial Complex

John Brumley
Ethos Consultants
Havre, Montana
Medicine Wheels, Oxbow Complex, Tipi Ring, Stone

Vaughn M. Bryant, Jr
Department of Anthropology
Texas A&M University
College Station, Texas
Pre-Clovis

R.A. Bryson
Center for Climatic Research
University of Wisconsin-Madison
Madison, Wisconsin
Climatic Episodes (Holocene)

David V. Burley
Department of Archaeology
Simon Fraser University
Burnaby, British Columbia
Marpole Culture Type

Brian M. Butler
Center for Archaeological Investigations
Southern Illinois University
Carbondale, Illinois
Crab Orchard

William B. Butler
National Park Service
Rocky Mountain National Park
Estes Park, Colorado
Albion Boardinghouse Phase, Apex Phase, Arkansas Phase, Colorado Plains Woodland Regional Variant, Front Range Phase, Magic Mountain Phase, Magic Mountain Site, Mount Albion Phase, South Platte Phase, Southern Rocky Mountain Early Archaic Regional Variant, Upper Purgatoire Complex, Western Plains Early Archaic Regional Variant, Western Plains Late Archaic Regional Variant, Western Plains Middle Archaic Regional Variant

William J. Byrne
Cultural Facilities and Historic Resources
Alberta Community Development
Edmonton, Alberta
One Gun Phase

Terry L. Cameron
North Coast Technology
Painesville, Ohio
Serpent Mound, Great (with R. V. Fletcher)

Gayle F. Carlson
Nebraska State Historical Society
Lincoln, Nebraska
Logan Creek Complex

Roy L. Carlson
Department of Archaeology
Simon Fraser University
Burnaby, British Columbia
Bella Bella Sequence, Charles E. Borden, Lind Coulee, Microblade Tradition, Old Cordilleran Tradition, Pebble Tool Tradition, Stemmed Point Tradition

Kurt W. Carr
Pennsylvania Historical and Museum Commission
Harrisburg, Pennsylvania
Shoop Site

Jefferson Chapman
Frank H. McClung Museum
University of Tennessee
Knoxville, Tennessee
Bifurcate Tradition, Doerschuk Site, Hardaway Site, Tellico Archaic

Joseph L. Chartkoff
Department of Anthropology
Michigan State University
East Lansing, Michigan
Abalone, Acorns (California), Architecture (California), Beads (California), Borax Lake

Site, Burials (California), California
(Culture Area), California (Space-Time
Framework), Elizabeth Campbell, Central
California Prehistory, Charmstones, Comal,
Freddie Curtis, C. W. Harris Site, Emma Lou
Davis, Eastern California, Gaming Pieces
(California), Gunther Island Site, Robert
Fleming Heizer, Clement W. Meighan,
Millingstone Horizon, Milling Tools
(California), Northwestern California,
Obsidian, Olivella (California), Pismo
Clam, Pottery (California), Quartz Crystals
(California), Rock Art (California), David
Banks Rogers, Malcolm J. Rogers, Shell
Money (California), Sierra Nevada and
Cascade Ranges, Southern California Coast,
Steatite (with G. Gibbon), Stone Disks
(California), Adán Treganza, William J.
Wallace, Watercraft (California)

James C. Chatters
North American Paleoscience
Richland, Washington
Freshwater Mussels (Plateau)

Daniel Chevrier
Archeotec, Inc.
Montreal, Quebec
Quebec's Subarctic Region

Wayne T. Choquette
Ktunaxa/Kinbasket Tribal Council
Cranbrook, British Columbia
Kootenay-Pend d'Oreille Rivers Sequence

Jacques Cinq-Mars
Archaeological Survey of Canada
Canadian Museum of Civilization
Hull, Quebec
British Mountain Tradition, Engigstciak

Donald W. Clark
Archaeological Survey of Canada
Canadian Museum of Civilization
Hull, Quebec
*Koniag Culture, Northern Cordilleran
Tradition, Northwest Microblade Tradition,
Ocean Bay Tradition*

R. Berle Clay
Department of Anthropology
University of Kentucky
Lexington, Kentucky
Adena

Charles R. Cobb
Department of Anthropology
State University of New York-Binghamton
Binghamton, New York
Mill Creek Quarry

Gary Coupland
Department of Anthropology
University of Toronto
Toronto, Ontario
Kitselas Canyon Sequence

C. Wesley Cowan
Collections and Research Center
Cincinnati Museum of Natural History
Cincinnati, Ohio
*Eastern Agricultural Complex, Fort Ancient
Culture, Incinerator or Sunwatch Village*

Patricia L. Crown
Department of Anthropology
University of New Mexico
Albuquerque, New Mexico
*Ballcourt, Casa Grande, Compound, Jacal,
Rancheria, Snaketown*

I. Randolph Daniel, Jr
Department of Anthropology
East Carolina University
Greenville, North Carolina
Corner-Notched Tradition

Leslie B. Davis
Museum of the Rockies
Montana State University
Bozeman, Montana
*Antonsen Site, Barton Gulch Site, Indian Creek
Site, Lindsay Mammoth Site, Lost Terrace
Site, MacHaffie Site, Obsidian Cliff Plateau
Quarries, Pilgrim Site, Schmitt Chert Mine*

Stephen A. Davis
Department of Anthropology
St. Mary's University
Halifax, Nova Scotia
Debert/Belmont Complex

Steven L. De Vore
Intermountain Support Office
National Park Service
Denver, Colorado
*Apishapa Phase, Intermountain Tradition,
Purgatoire Phase*

Jeffrey S. Dean
Tree Ring Laboratory
University of Arizona
Tucson, Arizona
Anasazi Culture Area, Betatakin, Kayenta
Branch, Kiet Siel

D. Brian Deller
Glencoe, Ontario
Crowfield Cultural Complex (with C. Ellis)

Dena F. Dincauze
Department of Anthropology
University of Massachusetts
Amherst, Massachusetts
Boylston Street Fish Weirs, Neville Site

Clark A. Dobbs
Institute for Minnesota Archaeology
Minneapolis, Minnesota
Red Wing Locality

William H. Doelle
Desert Archaeology, Inc.
Tucson, Arizona
Hodges Ruin, University Indian Ruin

John E. Douglas
Department of Anthropology
University of Montana
Missoula, Montana
San Simon Branch of the Mogollon

Boyce N. Driskell
Moundville Archaeological Park
Moundville, Alabama
Dust Cave

Penelope B. Drooker
Center for Archaeological Investigations
Southern Illinois University
Carbondale, Illinois
Madisonville

Don E. Dumond
Department of Anthropology
University of Oregon
Eugene, Oregon
Luther Sheeleigh Cressman, Denbigh Flint
Complex, Norton Culture, Norton Tradition

James S. Dunbar
Florida Department of State
Division of Historical Resources
Bureau of Archaeological Research
Tallahassee, Florida
Aucilla River Sites

Christopher Ellis
Department of Anthropology
University of Western Ontario
London, Ontario
Crowfield Cultural Complex
(with D. B. Deller), Crowfield Site,
Thedford II

Charles H. Faulkner
Department of Anthropology
University of Tennessee
Knoxville, Tennessee
Dover Quarry

William D. Finlayson
London Museum of Archaeology
University of Western Ontario
London, Ontario
Draper Site

Paul R. Fish
Arizona State Museum
University of Arizona
Tucson, Arizona
Hohokam Culture Area

Knut R. Fladmark
Department of Archaeology
Simon Fraser University
Burnaby, British Columbia
Early Coast Microblade, Moresby Tradition,
Transitional Complex

Robert V. Fletcher
University of Pittsburgh
Pittsburgh, Pennsylvania
Serpent Mound, Great (with T. L. Cameron)

Thomas A. Foor
Department of Anthropology
University of Montana
Missoula, Montana
Pelican Lake

Richard G. Forbis
Department of Archaeology
University of Calgary
Calgary, Alberta
*Besant Phase, Cluny Earthlodge Village,
Fletcher, Old Women's Phase*

George C. Frison
Department of Anthropology
University of Wyoming
Laramie, Wyoming
*Agate Basin Complex, Agate Basin Site,
Carter/Kerr-McGee Site, Casper Hell Gap Site,
Colby Site, Finley Site, Frederick Complex
and Projectile-Point Type, Goshen Complex,
Hell Gap Complex, James (Jimmy) Allen Site
(with G. Gibbon), Lusk Complex and
Projectile-Point Type, Medicine Lodge
Creek Site, Mill Iron Site, Paleoindian*

Gayle Fritz
Department of Anthropology
Washington University
St. Louis, Missouri
Chenopodium, Corn, Sumpweed, Sunflower

Jerry R. Galm
Department of Geography and Anthropology
Eastern Washington University
Cheney, Washington
Mid-Columbia River Region Sequence

William M. Gardner
Department of Anthropology
Catholic University of America
Washington, D.C
Flint Run Complex, Thunderbird Site

Craig Gerlach
Department of Anthropology
University of Alaska-Fairbanks
Fairbanks, Alaska
Choris Culture, Ipiutak Culture

Jon L. Gibson
Department of Anthropology
University of Southwestern Louisiana
Lafayette, Louisiana
Tchefuncte Culture

Dennis Gilpin
SWCA, Inc.
Flagstaff, Arizona
Little Colorado Branch (with K. A. Hays-Gilpin)

Lynne Goldstein
Department of Anthropology
Michigan State University
East Lansing, Michigan
Aztalan

Glenn T. Goode
Highways and Public Transportation
Texas State Department
Austin, Texas
Pavo Real (with J. Henderson)

Bryan C. Gordon
Canadian Museum of Civilization
Hull, Quebec
Migod Site, Taltheilei Tradition

Richard Michael Gramly
Great Lakes Artifact Repository
Buffalo, New York
Richey Clovis Cache, Vail Site

Sheila Greaves
Athabasca University
Athabasca, Alberta
Plateau Microblade Tradition

N'omi B. Greber
Cleveland Museum of Natural History
Cleveland, Ohio
Ohio Hopewell, Seip

William Green
Office of the State Archaeologist
University of Iowa
Iowa City, Iowa
Charles Reuben Keyes, Trempealeau Locality

Joseph Greenberg
Department of Anthropology
Stanford University
Stanford, California
Language

Bjarne Grønnow
Historical-Archaeological Experimental Centre
Lejre, Denmark
Saqqaq Culture

James H. Gunnerson
University of Nebraska State Museum
Lincoln, Nebraska
Dismal River Aspect

Judith A. Habicht-Mauche
Department of Anthropology
University of California
Santa Cruz, California
Pecos Pueblo

Steven Hackenberger
Department of Anthropology
Central Washington University
Ellensburg, Washington
*Salmon River-Clearwater River Sequences
(with R. L. Sappington)*

Robert L. Hall
Department of Anthropology
University of Illinois-Chicago
Chicago, Illinois
Platform Pipe

David J. Hally
Department of Anthropology
University of Georgia
Athens, Georgia
Chauga, King Site, Ocmulgee Site

Leonard C. Ham
Archaeologist and Heritage Consultant
Delta, British Columbia
Gulf of Georgia Culture Type

Julia E. Hammett
Planning Office
Stanford University
Stanford, California
Fire

L. Adrien Hannus
Department of Anthropology
Augustana College
Sioux Falls, South Dakota
*Angostura Cultural Complex,
Lange-Ferguson Site*

Alan D. Harn
Dickson Mounds Museum
Lewistown, Illinois
Dickson Mounds

Brian Hayden
Department of Archaeology
Simon Fraser University
Burnaby, British Columbia
Classic Lillooet Culture, Pithouses (Plateau)

C. Vance Haynes
Department of Anthropology
University of Arizona
Tucson, Arizona
*San Pedro Valley Clovis Sites
(Lehner and Murray Springs)*

Kelley Ann Hays-Gilpin
Department of Anthropology
Northern Arizona University
Flagstaff, Arizona
Little Colorado Branch (with D. Gilpin)

Richard Hebda
Botany Division
Royal British Columbia Museum
Victoria, British Columbia
Western Red Cedar

Michelle Hegmon
Department of Anthropology
Arizona State University
Tempe, Arizona
Kiva, Pueblo

James W. Helmer
Department of Archaeology
University of Calgary
Calgary, Alberta
Arctic Small Tool Tradition, Pre-Dorset

Jerry Henderson
Highways and Transportation
Texas State Department
Austin, Texas
Pavo Real (with G. T. Goode)

James N. Hill
Department of Anthropology
University of California
Los Angeles, California
Broken K Pueblo

Matthew G. Hill
Department of Anthropology
University of Wisconsin-Madison
Madison, Wisconsin
Silver Mound

Philip M. Hobler
Department of Archaeology
Simon Fraser University
Burnaby, British Columbia
Bella Coola Area

John F. Hoffecker
Argonne National Laboratory
Lakewood, Colorado
Dry Creek Site, Nenana Complex,
Walker Road Site

Jack L. Hofman
Department of Anthropology
University of Kansas
Lawrence, Kansas
Domebo, Folsom Complex, Lipscomb,
Midland Complex

Vance T. Holliday
Department of Geography
University of Wisconsin-Madison
Madison, Wisconsin
Lubbock Lake (with E. Johnson)

Bruce B. Huckell
Maxwell Museum
University of New Mexico
Albuquerque, New Mexico
Southwestern Archaic, Ventana Cave

Richard E. Hughes
Geochemical Research Laboratory
Portola Valley, California
Great Basin Trade

Wilfred M. Husted
Billings, Montana
Mummy Cave, Pryor Stemmed-Lovell
Constricted

Eric Ingbar
Carson City, Nevada
Hanson Site

H. Edwin Jackson
Department of Sociology and Anthropology
University of Southern Mississippi
Hattiesburg, Mississippi
Poverty Point Culture, Poverty Point Objects,
Poverty Point Site

Joel C. Janetski
Department of Anthropology
Brigham Young University
Provo, Utah
Eastern Great Basin Lakeside Adaptations,
Parowan Valley

Ned L. Jenkins
Fort Toulouse-Jackson Park
Wetumtka, Alabama
Gulf Tradition

Alfred E. Johnson
Museum of Anthropology
University of Kansas
Lawrence, Kansas
Kansas City Hopewell, Keith Variant, Loseke
Creek Variant, Pomona Phase, Steed-Kisker
Phase, Sterns Creek Variant, Valley Variant

Ann M. Johnson
Yellowstone National Park
Mammoth Hot Springs, Wyoming
Avonlea, Big Horn Medicine Wheel, Hagen
Site, Mortlach Site, William Thomas Mulloy,
Pictograph Cave, Sonota Burial Complex

Craig M. Johnson
BRW, Inc.
Minneapolis, Minnesota
Bad River Phase, Coalescent Tradition,
Heart River Phase, Knife River Phase

Eileen Johnson
Museum of Texas Tech University
Texas Tech University
Lubbock, Texas
Lubbock Lake (with V. T. Holliday)

William Gray Johnson
Desert Research Institute
Las Vegas, Nevada
Belle Glade Culture, Fort Center Site

George T. Jones
Department of Anthropology
Hamilton College
Clinton, New York
Western Stemmed Tradition (with C. Beck)

Kevin T. Jones
Antiquities Section
Utah State Historical Society
Salt Lake City, Utah
Behavioral Ecology in the Great Basin

Scott Jones
Center for the Study of the First Americans
Oregon State University
Corvallis, Oregon
Anzick Clovis Burial (with R. Bonnichsen)

Marvin Kay
Department of Anthropology
University of Arkansas
Fayetteville, Arkansas
Goforth-Saindon and Huntsville Mounds, Kimmswick, Phillips Spring, Rodgers Shelter

Bennie C. Keel
National Park Service
Southeast Archeological Center
Tallahassee, Florida
Garden Creek Site

Alice Beck Kehoe
Department of Social and Cultural Studies
Marquette University
Milwaukee, Wisconsin
Will C. McKern, Midwestern Taxonomic System

John E. Kelly
Transportation Archaeological
Research Program
University of Illinois
Urbana, Illinois
Emergent Mississippian, Range Site

Robert L. Kelly
Department of Anthropology
University of Wyoming
Laramie, Wyoming
Stillwater Marsh, Western and Central Basin Wetland and Lakeside Adaptations

Tristram R. Kidder
Department of Anthropology
Tulane University
New Orleans, Louisiana
Coles Creek Culture

Adam King
Department of Anthropology
Pennsylvania State University
University Park, Pennsylvania
Etowah

Francis B. King
Cleveland Museum of Natural History
Cleveland, Ohio
Squash

Vernon James Knight, Jr
Department of Anthropology
University of Alabama
Tuscaloosa, Alabama
David L. DeJarnette, McKeithen Site, Moundville

Ruthann Knudson
Agate Fossil Beds National Monument
National Park Service
Harrison, Nebraska
Plainview Complex, Plainview Site

Marcel Kornfeld
George C. Frison Institute of Archaeology
and Anthropology
University of Wyoming
Laramie, Wyoming
McKean

Raymond J. Le Blanc
Department of Anthropology
University of Alberta
Edmonton, Alberta
Klo-kut and Old Chief Creek Phases, Lagoon Complex

Robert D. Leonard
Department of Anthropology
University of New Mexico
Albuquerque, New Mexico
Cibola Branch, Zuni Pueblo

Bradley T. Lepper
Ohio Historical Society
Columbus, Ohio
Fort Ancient Site, Newark Earthworks

Owen Lindauer
Intermodal Transportation Division
Arizona Department of Transportation
Phoenix, Arizona
Adobe, Platform Mounds (Southwest)

Stephanie D. Livingston
Desert Research Institute
Reno, Nevada
Humboldt Lakebed Site, Lovelock Cave

William A. Longacre
Department of Anthropology
University of Arizona
Tucson, Arizona
Carter Ranch Pueblo, Paul Sidney Martin

Julia C. Lowell
Department of Sociology and Anthropology
University of Northern Iowa
Cedar Falls, Iowa
Black River Branch, Point of Pines Ruin

Earl H. Lubensky
Columbia, Missouri
Carl Haley Chapman

John Ludwickson
Nebraska State Historical Society
Lincoln, Nebraska
Arzberger Site, Ash Hollow Cave (with J. R. Bozell), "Big Village" Site of the Omahas, Central Plains Tradition (with J. R. Bozell), Initial Coalescent, Itskari Phase (formerly "Loup River"; with J. R. Bozell), Lower Loup Phase (with J. R. Bozell), Nebraska Phase (with J. R. Bozell), Redbird Phase (with J. R. Bozell), Signal Butte (with J. R. Bozell), Smoky Hill Phase (with J. R. Bozell), St. Helena Phase, Upper Republican Phase (with J. R. Bozell), Waldo R. Wedel, White Rock/Glen Elder "Phase"

R. Lee Lyman
Department of Anthropology
University of Missouri
Columbia, Missouri
Plateau Ungulates

Margaret M. Lyneis
Department of Anthropology
University of Nevada
Las Vegas, Nevada
Southern Great Basin Late Prehistoric Period, Virgin Anasazi

David B. Madsen
Department of Natural Resources
Utah Geological Survey
Salt Lake City, Utah
Danger Cave

Martin Magne
Cultural Resource Management
Parks Canada
Calgary, Alberta
Cachepits (Plateau)

Robert C. Mainfort, Jr
Arkansas Archeological Survey
Fayetteville, Arkansas
Eva Site, Miller Culture, Pinson Mounds Site

Mary Malainey
Department of Anthropology
University of Manitoba
Winnipeg, Manitoba
Mortlach Aggregate, Wascana Ware

William H. Marquardt
Florida Museum of Natural History
University of Florida
Gainesville, Florida
Key Marco

Carol I. Mason
Department of Anthropology
University of Wisconsin-Fox Valley
Menasha, Wisconsin
Maple Sugaring

Ronald J. Mason
Department of Anthropology
Lawrence University
Appleton, Wisconsin
Lake Forest Archaic, Laurentian Archaic, Old Copper Culture, Point Peninsula Culture

R.G. Matson
Department of Anthropology and Sociology
University of British Columbia
Vancouver, British Columbia
Chilcotin Plateau (with D. L. Pokotylo)

Allen P. McCartney
Department of Anthropology
University of Arkansas
Fayetteville, Arkansas
Aleutian Tradition, Anangula, Port Moller

Karen McCullough
Arctic Institute of North America
University of Calgary
Calgary, Alberta
Ruin Island Phase

Robert J. McGhee
Archaeological Survey of Canada
Canadian Museum of Civilization
Hull, Quebec
Dorset Culture, Kittigazuit, Norse in America

Randall H. McGuire
Department of Anthropology
State University of New York-Binghamton
Binghamton, New York
Papagueria

Alan D. McMillan
Department of Archaeology
Simon Fraser University
Burnaby, British Columbia
West Coast Culture Type

James J. Miller
State Archaeologist
Florida Division of Historical Resources
Tallahassee, Florida
St. Johns Tradition

George R. Milner
Department of Anthropology
Pennsylvania State University
University Park, Pennsylvania
Cahokia, Monks Mound

Rick Minor
Heritage Research Associates, Inc.
Eugene, Oregon
Southern Northwest Coast, Willamette Valley Sequence (with K. A. Toepel)

Donald H. Mitchell
Department of Anthropology
University of Victoria
Victoria, British Columbia
Eulachon, Fraser River Canyon Sequence (with D. L. Pokotylo), Fraser River Stone Sculpture Complex, Kettle Falls Sequence, Locarno Beach Culture, Northwest Coast Culture Area, Okanagan Valley Sequence (with D. L. Pokotylo), Pacific Salmon, Queen Charlotte Strait Sequence

Charles M. Mobley
Charles M. Mobley and Associates
Anchorage, Alaska
Campus Site

Charles R. Moffat
Mississippi Valley Archaeology Center
University of Wisconsin-La Crosse
La Crosse, Wisconsin
Ridged-Field Agriculture

Elizabeth Ann Morris
Arizona State Museum
University of Arizona
Tucson, Arizona
Earl H. Morris

David Morrison
Archaeological Survey of Canada
Canadian Museum of Civilization
Hull, Quebec
Far North, Diamond Jenness, Little Ice Age (with H. E. Wright, Jr.), Therkel Mathiassen, Naujan, Pointed Mountain/Fisherman Lake, Spence River Phase, Thule Culture, Thule Tradition

Dan F. Morse
Panacea, Florida
Brand Site, Dalton, Parkin Site

Madonna Moss
Department of Anthropology
University of Oregon
Eugene, Oregon
Frederica de Laguna, Southeast Alaskan Sequence

Jon Muller
Department of Anthropology
Southern Illinois University
Carbondale, Illinois
Great Salt Spring, Salt

Cheryl Ann Munson
Department of Anthropology
Indiana University
Bloomington, Indiana
Caborn-Welborn Phase (with D. Pollack)

Ben A. Nelson
Department of Anthropology
State University of New York-Buffalo
Buffalo, New York
Mimbres Branch

Bev Nicholson
Department of Native Studies
Brandon University
Brandon, Manitoba
Killarney Focus, Vickers Focus

William C. Noble
Department of Anthropology
McMaster University
Hamilton, Ontario
Acasta Lake

George H. Odell
Department of Anthropology
University of Tulsa
Tulsa, Oklahoma

*Abrader, Anvil, Atlatl, Awl, Axe/Adze,
Bannerstone, Biface, Billet, Bipolar Percussion,
Blade/Bladelet, Bow and Arrow, Burin, Chert/
Flint, Chopper, Core, Dart/Spear Points,
Debitage/Debris, Denticulate, Disc, Discoidal/
Chunky Stone, Drill, Earspool, Flake, Flaker,
Flute, Gorget, Graver, Hammerstone, Heat
Treatment of Silicates, Hoe, Mace, Mano/
Metate, Mortar and Pestle, Needle, Notched
Piece, Panpipe, Pick, Pin, Pipe, Pitted Stone,
Plummet, Rattle, Retouch, Retouched Piece,
Scraper, Spud, Uniface*

Albert C. Oetting
Heritage Research Associates, Inc.
Eugene, Oregon

*Great Basin Archaic, Lake Abert, Northern
Great Basin Wetland and Lakeside Adaptations*

Janet D. Orcutt
National Park Service
Santa Fe, New Mexico

Rio Grande Branch

†Floyd Painter

Williamson

Robert W. Park
Department of Anthropology
University of Waterloo
Waterloo, Ontario

Dorset/Thule Transition

Christopher S. Peebles
Office of Information Services
Indiana University
Bloomington, Indiana

Angel Site and Phase

James F. Pendergast
Canadian Museum of Civilization
Hull, Quebec

Hochelaga

Peter Peregrine
Department of Anthropology
Lawrence University
Appleton, Wisconsin

World-Systems Approach

James B. Petersen
Department of Anthropology
University of Vermont
Burlington, Vermont

*Ceramics in the Far Northeast, Fiber Artifacts
and Ethnicity*

Richard M. Pettigrew
INFOTEC Research, Inc.
Eugene, Oregon

Lower Columbia River Valley Sequence

David A. Phillips, Jr
SWCA Inc., Environmental Consultants
Albuquerque, New Mexico

Southwest Culture Area

Peter J. Pilles, Jr
Coconino National Forest
Flagstaff, Arizona

Sinagua Tradition

Jean-Luc Pilon
Archaeological Survey of Canada
Canadian Museum of Civilization
Hull, Quebec

*Central Subarctic Woodland Culture, Hudson
Bay Lowlands Prehistory*

David L. Pokotylo
Department of Anthropology and Sociology
University of British Columbia
Vancouver, British Columbia

*Arrow Lakes/Slocan Valley Sequence, Charles/
St. Mungo Culture Type, Chilcotin Plateau
(with R. G. Matson), Early Period (Plateau),
Fraser River Canyon Sequence (with D. H.
Mitchell), Mazama Tephra (with J. Ryder),
Northern (Canadian) Plateau, Okanagan Valley
Sequence (with D. H. Mitchell), Plateau Culture
Area (with K. M. Ames)*

David Pollack
Kentucky Heritage Council
Frankfort, Kentucky

Caborn-Welborn Phase (with C. A. Munson)

Robert P. Powers
Intermountain Cultural Resources
   Management
National Park Service
Santa Fe, New Mexico

Bandelier National Monument

Olaf H. Prufer
Department of Anthropology
Kent State University
Kent, Ohio
McGraw

George Rapp, Jr
Archaeometry Laboratory
University of Minnesota
Duluth, Minnesota
Archaeometallurgy, Copper

John C. Ravesloot
Cultural Resource Management Program
Gila River Indian Community
Sacaton, Arizona
Casas Grandes

Robert L. Reeder
Missouri Department of Transportation
Jefferson City, Missouri
Nebo Hill Phase

J. Jefferson Reid
Department of Anthropology
University of Arizona
Tucson, Arizona
Bear Village, Bluff Village, Forestdale Branch, Grasshopper Pueblo, Mogollon Culture Area

Glen E. Rice
Office of Cultural Resource Management
Arizona State University
Tempe, Arizona
Salado Horizon

Brian S. Robinson
Quaternary Institute
University of Maine
Orono, Maine
Gulf of Maine Archaic Tradition

Thomas R. Rocek
Department of Anthropology
University of Delaware
Newark, Delaware
Pithouse

Martha Ann Rolingson
Toltec Mounds State Park
Arkansas Archeological Survey
Scott, Arkansas
Toltec Mounds Site

Tom E. Roll
Department of Sociology and Anthropology
Montana State University
Bozeman, Montana
Yonkee

Mike K. Rousseau
Antiquus Archaeological Consultants
Maple Ridge, British Columbia
Plateau Pithouse Tradition

†Guy-Marie Rousseliere
Nunguvik and Saatut Sites

Sue Rowley
Pittsburgh, Pennsylvania
Igloolik Sequence

Bret J. Ruby
Hopewell Culture National Historical Park
Chillicothe, Ohio
Mann Site

Katharine C. Ruhl
Department of Archaeology
Cleveland Museum of Natural History
Cleveland, Ohio
Hopewell Site, Turner Site

June Ryder
Terrain Analysis, Inc.
Vancouver, British Columbia
Mazama Tephra (with D. L. Pokotylo)

Jeremy A. Sabloff
Museum of Archaeology
  and Anthropology
University of Pennsylvania
Philadelphia, Pennsylvania
Gordon R. Willey

Robert J. Salzer
Department of Anthropology
Beloit College
Beloit, Wisconsin
Gottschall Site

Robert L. Sappington
Department of Sociology
  and Anthropology
University of Idaho
Moscow, Idaho
Salmon River-Clearwater River Sequences (with S. Hackenberger)

Kenneth E. Sassaman
South Carolina Institute of Archaeology
   and Anthropology
University of South Carolina
Columbia, South Carolina
Stallings Culture

Robert F. Sasso
Department of Sociology and Anthropology
University of Wisconsin-Parkside
Kenosha, Wisconsin
Sand Lake Site

Jeffrey J. Saunders
Research and Collections Center
Illinois State Museum
Springfield, Illinois
Mammoth/Mastodon

Polly Schaafsma
Museum of Indian Arts and Culture
Museum of New Mexico
Santa Fe, New Mexico
Petroglyph, Rock Art

P. Schledermann
Department of Archaeology
Arctic Institute of North America
University of Calgary
Calgary, Alberta
Inugsuk Culture

James Schoenwetter
Department of Anthropology
Arizona State University
Tempe, Arizona
*Lower Sonoran Agricultural Complex,
Upper Sonoran Agricultural Complex*

Alan R. Schroedl
P-III Associates, Inc.
Salt Lake City, Utah
Eastern Great Basin Archaic

Gerald F. Schroedl
Department of Anthropology
University of Tennessee
Knoxville, Tennessee
*Chota-Tanasee, Dallas Culture, Hiwassee
Island, Toqua*

Lynne Sebastian
Historic Preservation Division
Office of Cultural Affairs
Santa Fe, New Mexico
Casa Rinconada, Chaco Branch, Pueblo Bonito

Mark F. Seeman
Department of Anthropology
Kent State University
Kent, Ohio
Hopewell Interaction Sphere

M. Steven Shackley
Phoebe Hearst Museum of Anthropology
University of California
Berkeley, California
Patayan Culture Area

Alan H. Simmons
Department of Anthropology
University of Nevada
Las Vegas, Nevada
Oshara Tradition, Picosa

Steven R. Simms
Department of Sociology and Anthropology
Utah State University
Logan, Utah
Eastern Great Basin Late Prehistoric Period

Donald B. Simons
Grand Blanc, Michigan
Gainey Complex

Dean R. Snow
Department of Anthropology
Pennsylvania State University
University Park, Pennsylvania
*Frontenac Island Site, Iroquoian Culture,
Lamoka Lake Site, Mast Forest Archaic*

W. Geoffrey Spaulding
Dames and Moore
Las Vegas, Nevada
The Great Basin, Packrat Middens

Michael W. Spence
Department of Anthropology
University of Western Ontario
London, Ontario
Rice Lake Site

Katherine Spielmann
Department of Anthropology
Arizona State University
Tempe, Arizona
Gran Quivira

Karl T. Steinen
Department of Sociology
  and Anthropology
State University of West Georgia
Carrollton, Georgia
Kolomoki, Mandeville

James B. Stoltman
Department of Anthropology
University of Wisconsin-Madison
Madison, Wisconsin
Effigy Mounds

Peter L. Storck
Royal Ontario Museum
Toronto, Ontario
Parkhill Cultural Complex

Dee Ann Story
Department of Anthropology
University of Texas
Austin, Texas
George C. Davis Site, Alex D. Krieger

Arnoud H. Stryd
Arcas Consulting Archaeologists
Coquitlam, British Columbia
Nesikep Tradition

Alan P. Sullivan III
Department of Anthropology
University of Cincinnati
Cincinnati, Ohio
Gladwinian Classification of Cultures

Patricia D. Sutherland
Canadian Museum of Civilization
Hull, Quebec
Independence I and II

E. Leigh Syms
Manitoba Museum of Man and Nature
Winnipeg, Manitoba
Selkirk Composite, Williams Complex

Kenneth B. Tankersley
Department of Anthropology
Kent State University
Kent, Ohio
*Clovis Cultural Complex, Cumberland
Cultural Complex*

James L. Theler
Department of Sociology and Archaeology
University of Wisconsin-La Crosse
La Crosse, Wisconsin
River Snails, Shell Middens

Thomas D. Thiessen
Midwest Archeological Center
National Park Service
Lincoln, Nebraska
*Knife River Indian Villages National
Historic Site*

David Hurst Thomas
Department of Anthropology
American Museum of Natural History
New York, New York
Hidden Cave, Monitor Valley

Alston V. Thoms
Center for Ecological Archaeology
Texas A&M University
College Station, Texas
Earth Ovens, Plateau Root Foods

Lawrence C. Todd
Department of Anthropology
Colorado State University
Fort Collins, Colorado
Taphonomy

Kathryn Anne Toepel
Heritage Research Associates
Eugene, Oregon
Willamette Valley Sequence (with R. Minor)

James Tuck
Department of Anthropology
Memorial University of Newfoundland
St. John's, Newfoundland
Groswater Culture, Maritime Archaic Tradition

Donald R. Tuohy
Nevada State Museum
Carson City, Nevada
Tule Springs (with R. H. Brooks)

Susan C. Vehik
Department of Anthropology
University of Oklahoma
Norman, Oklahoma

*Antelope Creek Phase, Custer Phase, Garza
Complex, Great Bend Aspect, Henrietta Focus,
Little River Focus, Lower Walnut Focus,
Norteño Focus, Pratt Complex, Tierra Blanca
Complex, Uncas Complex, Upper Carnark
Regional Variant, Washita River Phase*

Gail E. Wagner
Department of Anthropology
University of South Carolina
Columbia, South Carolina

Tobacco

Danny N. Walker
Wyoming State Archaeologist's Office
Wyoming Department of Commerce
Laramie, Wyoming

Bison

John A. Walthall
Department of Anthropology
University of Illinois
Urbana, Illinois

Copena, Galena

H. Trawick Ward
Research Laboratories of Anthropology
University of North Carolina
Chapel Hill, North Carolina

Town Creek Site, Warren Wilson Site

Patty Jo Watson
Department of Anthropology
Washington University
St. Louis, Missouri

Indian Knoll

Fred Wendorf
Department of Anthropology
Southern Methodist University
Dallas, Texas

John Otis (Jo) Brew, Scharbauer

Kit W. Wesler
Wickliffe Mounds Research Center
Murray State University
Wickliffe, Kentucky

Wickliffe Site

Gary C. Wessen
Wessen and Associates
Seattle, Washington

Washington Ocean Coast Sequence

Frederick Hadleigh West
Peabody Museum of Salem
Salem, Massachusetts

*Beringian Tradition, Denali Complex,
Paleoarctic Tradition, Tangle Lakes District*

Nancy Marie White
Department of Anthropology
University of South Florida
Tampa, Florida

Crystal River Site, Fort Walton Site and Culture

James D. Wilde
HQ Air Force Center
San Antonio, Texas

Catlow and Roaring Springs Caves, Fremont

W.H. Wills
Department of Anthropology
University of New Mexico
Albuquerque, New Mexico

Bat Cave, Pine Lawn Branch, Tularosa Cave

Joseph C. Winter
Department of Anthropology
University of New Mexico
Albuquerque, New Mexico

Hovenweep

Regge N. Wiseman
Museum of New Mexico
Santa Fe, New Mexico

Jornada Branch of the Mogollon Culture

Thomas A. Witty, Jr
Kansas State Historical Society
Topeka, Kansas

Munkers Creek Phase, Scott County Pueblo

W. Raymond Wood
Department of Anthropology
University of Missouri
Columbia, Missouri

*Anderson Phase, Biesterfeldt Site, John
Leland Champe, Earthlodge, Fort Yates
Phase, Grand Detour Phase, Grandmother's
Lodge, Huff Phase, Hypsithermal, Donald
Jayne Lehmer, Linear Mounds (Plains),*

*Middle Missouri Tradition, Plains, Plains
Village Tradition, Ponca Fort, Thomas
Riggs Phase*

William B. Workman
Department of Anthropology
University of Alaska
Anchorage, Alaska
*Aishihik Phase, Kachemak Tradition,
Northern Archaic Tradition*

H.E. Wright, Jr
Department of Geology and Geophysics
University of Minnesota
Minneapolis, Minnesota
*Aishihik Phase, Kachemal Tradition,
Northern Archaic Tradition*

J.V. Wright
Archaeological Survey of Canada
Canadian Museum of Civilization
Hull, Quebec
*Blackduck, Laurel Culture, Northern Plano
Culture, Selkirk, Shield Culture*

Larry J. Zimmerman
Department of Anthropology
University of Iowa
Iowa City, Iowa
Crow Creek Site, Reburial Issue

About the Editor

Guy Gibbon was born in Madison, Wisconsin, in 1939 and raised in Milwaukee. After stints at Kenyon College in Ohio and in the U.S. Army he attended the University of Wisconsin-Madison, where he received B.S., M.S., and Ph.D. degrees. He has taught at the University of Illinois, the University of Wisconsin-Milwaukee, and, since 1973, at the University of Minnesota, where he is professor of anthropology and director of the Interdisciplinary Archaeological Studies (IAS) graduate program. He has received fellowships to study philosophy of science in Karl Popper's program at the London School of Economics and spent a sabbatical year at Heidelberg University in Germany, where he wrote *Explanation in Archaeology* (Blackwell, 1989). His other major publications include *Anthropological Archaeology* (Columbia University Press, 1984), edited volumes (*Oneota Studies* [1982], *Prairie Archaeology* [1983], and *The Woodland Tradition in the Western Great Lakes* [1990], all in the series *University of Minnesota Publications in Anthropology*), chapters in books, and articles in journals such as *American Antiquity*, *Plains Anthropologist*, and *Midcontinental Journal of Archaeology*. He is currently at work on an ethnography of the Sioux (Dakota/Lakota) Indians as part of Basil Blackwell's Indians of the Americas series.

Archaeology of
Prehistoric Native America

A

Abalone

Abalone (*Haliotis* spp.) is a type of marine shellfish off the Pacific Coast. Eight species occur in North American waters. The four most common in California are the red (*H. rufescens*), the black (*H. cracherodii*), the green (*H. fulgens*), and the Japanese (*H. kamtschatkana*) abalones, of which the red is the largest (30-cm [11.7-inch] diameter shell). Found in tidal zones on rocky bottoms to depths of 20 m (65.6 feet) or more, abalones were important food resources easily harvested by coastal peoples. A single red abalone shell yields up to 400 g of meat. Harvesting began at least by 6050 B.C. (8000 years B.P.). Abalone also was prized for the luminescent, mother-of-pearl quality of the shell's interior, especially in the red abalone. Abalone shell was widely traded and made into beads, pendants, and other ornaments. Whole shells were used as bowls and even to hold cremation ashes for burial. California's greatest centers for abalone shellwork were along the Santa Barbara Coast and its offshore islands, especially Santa Cruz Island. Shellworking and exchange were most prominent during the Late period (A.D. 500–1850, or 1450–100 years B.P.).

Joseph L. Chartkoff

Abbott, Charles C. (1843–1919)

A physician by training, Charles C. Abbott discovered a campsite in gravel deposits on his ancestral farm near Trenton, New Jersey, in 1873 that contained crude stone tools made of argillite that he believed were in strata dated to glacial times. His work was sponsored by Frederick Ward Putnam, who was interested in proving the great antiquity of human beings in the New World. By the late 1880s, Abbott was claiming that his materials had an age of 20,000–30,000 years and that their makers were probably not related to the American Indians but were possibly ancestors of the Inuit. In 1892, William Henry Holmes demonstrated that the tools were similar to quarry materials found at other sites in the Potomac Basin and claimed that most "paleolithic" material found in the Northeast was the work of recent Indians. Abbott's Trenton gravel "paleoliths" are an episode in early debates about the date of the first peopling of the New World.

Guy Gibbon

Further Readings

Abbott, C.C. 1876. The Stone Age of New Jersey. *Annual Report of the Smithsonian Institute for 1875*:246–380.

———. 1877. On the Discovery of Supposed Paleolithic Implements From the Glacial Drift in the Valley of the Delaware River, Near Trenton, New Jersey. *Tenth Annual Report of Trustees of the Peabody Museum* 2:33–43.

———. 1881. *Primitive Industry*. G.A. Bates, Salem.

Holmes, W.H. 1892. Modern Quarry Refuse and the Paleolithic Theory. *Science* 20:295–297.

See also HOLMES, WILLIAM HENRY; PALEOLITH; PUTNAM, FREDERICK WARD

Abrader

An abrader is a stone of coarse material, often sandstone, that is used to rub and wear away parts of another object. Throughout the

North American mid-continent, worn sandstone artifacts have been found in association with other prehistoric artifacts in the same assemblage. Although some sort of attrition has obviously occurred on them, it is difficult with contemporary techniques to determine on what sorts of tools or materials they were used. Abraders in which grooves have been worn are common in North America. This sort of wear pattern could have been caused by a variety of activities, such as the smoothing of arrow shafts, which has been documented among Plains tribes, and the manufacture of pointed bone tools, which has rarely been documented anywhere. Abrasion of cores or bifaces during flintknapping has also rarely been documented, but modern experimental replication suggests that it was probably common in prehistory.

George H. Odell

Further Readings

Flenniken, J.J., and T.L. Ozbun. 1988. Experimental Analysis of Plains Grooved Abraders. *Plains Anthropologist* 33:37–52.

Holmes, W.H. 1919. *Handbook of Aboriginal American Antiquities:1. Introductory. The Lithic Industries.* Bulletin no. 60. Bureau of American Ethnology, Smithsonian Institution, Washington, D.C.

Acasta Lake

Acasta Lake is an archaeological complex named after the type site (LiPk-1) located 137 km (85 miles) southeast of Port Radium, in the central Mackenzie District, Northwest Territories. Initially found by prospectors in 1960, the site was visited in 1967 and excavated in 1968 by William C. Noble. A quartzite erratic lodged on an east-west-trending esker in the site area provided a focus for northern Plano hunters, who were interested in utilizing the fine-grained lithic. Over a dozen sites relate to Acasta Lake, and the two consistent radiocarbon dates of 5020 B.C. ± 360 and 4900 B.C. ± 150 (6970 and 6850 years B.P.) from charcoal in hearths at LiPk-1 help fix this late period of northern Plano in the transitional forest-barrenlands region. Acasta Lake presents the earliest known human occupation of the central Mackenzie District in northern Canada.

The recovered artifact sample from LiPk-1 represents one of the largest archaeological collections from the Great Slave–Great Bear Lakes region. No fewer than 508 large bifaces, 368 scrapers, 56 projectile points, and various multigravers, spokeshaves, and transverse burins were recovered among the 968 worked items, along with 2,193 flakes. The projectile styles and their distributions indicate a contemporaneous usage of the site by peoples using late Agate Basin, Kamut-stemmed, and Acasta side-indented lanceolates. It is hypothesized that the northerly derived Kamut peoples with their stemmed points and transverse burin technology were moving southward and met the northerly moving late Agate Basin–Acasta grouping. Both shared the same lithic reduction procedures.

Settlement details at LiPk-1 are unique in that 105 pit hearths are arranged in five recognizable ring configurations. The hearth rings measure 2.1–3.6 m (7–12 feet) in diameter, which is wide enough to accommodate one or two individuals in each ring as protection from noxious insects. The hearths themselves, which are 304.8–533.4 mm (12–21 inches) in diameter, are best described as having been laid in hollowed-out pits similar to Plano hearths recorded by Millar at Fisherman's Lake, southwestern Northwest Territories. At Acasta Lake, the hearths themselves were used primarily for heat treatment of lithics in four or five steps of lithic reduction. Intense fire-reddening lined the pits and coated many of the quartzite artifact inclusions. Fauna from seven of the hearths include barren-ground caribou as the dominant species, followed by black bear, beaver, hare, and fish. In addition, a toe phalanx from a bald or golden eagle was recovered. This subsistence obviously reflects an adaptation to a forest-barrenland environment.

William C. Noble

Further Readings

Forbis, R.G. 1961. Early Point Types From Acasta Lake, Northwest Territories, Canada. *American Antiquity* 27:112–113.

Noble, W.C. 1971. Archaeological Surveys and Sequences in Central District of Mackenzie, NWT. *Arctic Anthropology* 8(1):102–135.

———. 1981. Prehistory of the Great Slave Lake and Great Bear Lake Region. In *Subarctic,* edited by J. Helm, pp. 97–106. Handbook of North American Indians, vol. 6, W.C. Sturtevant, general editor. Smithsonian Institution, Washington, D.C.

Acorns (California)

Acorns are the nutlike fruit produced by the oak tree. By the end of the Archaic period (ca. 2050 B.C., or 4000 years B.P.), acorns had become the single most significant plant food source for most prehistoric California cultures. Though acorns were used elsewhere, especially in the Eastern Woodlands, nowhere were they as important as in California. Ten species of acorn-bearing oaks grow in California, each in different habitats and elevations, making them widely available. Key species were the valley or white oak (*Quercus lobata*), blue oak (*Q. douglassii*), black oak (*Q. kelloggii*), and canyon or interior live oak (*Q. agrifolia*). Acorns possess tannic acid, which retards spoilage and insect infestation, making them easy to store but toxic to humans. By the Late Archaic period (ca. 4050–2050 B.C., or 6000–4000 years B.P.), California cultures began to develop water-leaching techniques to remove tannins. Thereafter, acorns became increasingly important to the diet. They provide all 14 amino acids humans require for protein, are rich in the B-vitamin complex, and supply large quantities of carbohydrates, fats, and calories for the energy of active hunter-gatherers. Acorns are collected when ripe in autumn. They were stored at winter villages in baskets, storage pits, or granaries. They were shelled for leaching using stone hammers and pounded into meal with mortars and pestles. Leaching was usually done by placing acorn meal in a sandy pit lined with leaves, after which baskets of boiling water were poured slowly over the meal to dilute and carry off the tannic acids. After 15–30 rinses, the meal lost its bitter taste and was safe to eat. Leached meal was added to stews and soups, prepared as a porridge, or pressed into flatbread cakes for baking. Acorn products were eaten at most meals by most California cultures.

Joseph L. Chartkoff

Further Readings

Kroeber, A.L. 1953. *Handbook of the Indians of California*. California Book, Berkeley.
Munz, P.A., and D.D. Keck. 1970. *A California Flora*. University of California Press, Berkeley.

Adena

Adena is an archaeological culture defined on the basis of a 1901 excavation at the Adena burial mound at Chillicothe, Ohio. Adena sites are concentrated in the Ohio River drainage

Adena effigy pipe. *(Prepared by R. B. Clay)*

A

from the West Virginia Panhandle to the falls at Louisville, Kentucky, an area that includes parts of the adjacent states of Ohio, West Virginia, Kentucky, and Indiana. Adena dates to ca. 500 B.C.–A.D. 200 (2450–1750 years B.P.), a range defined in part by radiocarbon dates and in part by the definition of Adena itself. Generally considered an Early Woodland culture, Adena is not the earliest Woodland culture in the region and is contemporaneous in part with the later Middle Woodland Hopewell culture. It is perhaps best considered early Middle Woodland. Often the only way to assign a late Adena burial mound to Adena rather than Hopewell is by associated artifact typology.

At the base of Adena subsistence was the same hunting-and-gathering way of life that characterized the earlier Archaic period. Deer, a major source of food, was supplemented by a variety of nut crops and by the collection of wild seeds. In addition, certain domesticated plants were used, including squash (*Cucurbita pepo*), goosefoot (*Chenopodium berlandieri*), marsh elder (*Iva annua*), and sunflower (*Helianthus annuus*). Little is known about the cultivation and harvesting of these plants; the best data on domestication come from dry rock shelters far removed from the ritual structures that have been the focus of Adena studies. There is no evidence for field agriculture and little indication that the adoption of farming caused major changes in settlement.

Adena sites are not limited to river floodplains. In many areas, such as the Central Kentucky Bluegrass, they are concentrated in uplands, although these sites are mainly burial mounds. A wide variety of camps and special-use sites must have been present, although their nature is difficult to reconstruct from burial-mound data alone. These would represent the intermittent camps of small groups on a seasonal round in the rich Eastern Mesophytic forest. As with the use of wild and domesticated plants, the settlement pattern owed much to the earlier Archaic period. While Adena camps are distinguished by hot-rock cooking ovens and specialized activity areas (where, for example, flint tools were made), evidence for substantial houses is rare and equivocal. In short, settlement data suggest low population density, mobility, and an absence of settlement nucleation.

The critical Adena addition to the earlier Archaic way of life was a greater emphasis on mortuary ritual. While it is probable that Adena burial customs grew out of simpler Archaic beginnings, neither the processes of their transformation nor their social implications are understood. It was first thought that circular post structures below mounds were houses. However, the evidence—the remains of ritual activities within distinctive buildings usually without roofs but with paired, out-leaning wall posts—indicates that they were not houses but instead were large, screened enclosures that separated ritual from secular space. Group ceremonies of ritual intensification were conducted in them, probably on a seasonal basis, that perhaps marked significant changes in the lives of individuals or in the society. Thus,

despite domestic simplicity, complex communal ceremonies were important.

Burial mounds were not planned; they were accretional structures that grew gradually as burials were added, with the final mound always the product of a series of mortuary events. Most were modest in size and covered only one or two burials. A very few, like Grave Creek mound in West Virginia, ultimately grew to considerable size. Cremation was widespread, with the ashes often deposited on the floor of the communal structure. In many other cases, the classic example being the Robbins mound in Kentucky, inhumations were added one by one. In some cases (which may be late in Adena development), log crib tombs were built to hold the body. There is evidence in these cases that the log tomb was periodically reused, as at the Wright mound in Kentucky. Artifacts often deposited with the dead included items of personal adornment, copper bracelets, mica sheets, and ornaments of cut shell and bone. Other artifacts, such as large spear points, distinctive engraved sandstone tablets, tubular pipes, and artifacts of galena and barite, were also occasionally placed in the grave. Materials used in the production of these artifacts were obtained locally and from the Great Lakes region, Georgia, and probably Alabama (copper), the Gulf Coast (shell), and the Ohio Valley (chert and galena/barite). This diversity of materials is evidence of widespread interregional trade that followed earlier patterns developed during the Archaic period.

Circular earthworks with interior ditches and exterior banks were frequently constructed. One enclosure, Mount Horeb in Kentucky, had an interior circle of paired posts like those in communal structures below mounds. Others enclosed multiple post circles (e.g., the Dominion Land Company site in Ohio). These cases suggest that the use of circular earthworks was analogous to that of screened enclosures. In certain areas with concentrations of burial mounds, large, amorphous earthwork enclosures were built (e.g., Peter Village in Kentucky). How they were used is conjectural, but they were clearly not ritual enclosures.

The location of ritual structures away from domestic sites may be critical to an understanding of Adena. It suggests that they were not "owned" by any one group but instead served to draw scattered groups together. One interpretation of the mounds and circular enclosures is that they reflect cooperation between widely dispersed social groups in a region of generally low population density. Another, which may be true for specific areas, is that a burial mound was the cemetery of a corporate social group that, presumably, lived around it.

The reconstruction of Adena society is hampered by earlier preconceptions and by a general lack of settlement information. Once thought part of a complex "Mound Builder" culture, Adena is still considered a complex society by many because of the presence of burial mounds, earthworks, and domesticated plants. However, analyses of burial populations suggest that the population was only weakly stratified, if at all. While there was widespread trade in specialized items, many of which were ultimately disposed of with the dead, there is little evidence of dramatic accumulation of personal or group wealth.

It is generally thought that the later Hopewellian culture in the Ohio Valley had its origins in the distinctive features of Adena. For instance, the large and complex Hopewell ritual sites (e.g., Mound City) seem to represent a drawing together of the scattered settlement elements of Adena: its mounds, earthworks, and habitation sites. At the same time, many Hopewellian groups retained the simplicity and diffuse settlement pattern of the earlier Adena culture. The reasons for the transformation from Adena to Hopewell or for the variability in Hopewellian complexity are not fully understood. The cultural synthesis they produced, however, was relatively brief in duration and had little direct effect on the character of Late Woodland cultures that developed by ca. A.D. 900 (1050 years B.P.) in the Ohio Valley.

R. Berle Clay

Further Readings

Clay, R.B. 1986. Adena Ritual Spaces. In *Early Woodland Archaeology,* edited by K. Farnsworth and T. Emerson, pp. 581–595. Center for American Archaeology Press, Kampsville.

Dragoo, D. 1963. *Mounds for the Dead.* Annals of the Carnegie Museum, vol. 37. Pittsburgh.

Seeman, M. 1986. Adena Houses and Their Implications for Early Woodland Settlement Models in the Ohio Valley. In *Early Woodland Archaeology,* edited by K. Farnsworth and T. Emerson, pp. 564–580. Center for American Archaeology Press, Kampsville.

See Also OHIO HOPEWELL

Adobe

Adobe is sun-dried brick made of clay and water. The term refers to the clay from which the bricks are made as well as the finished building. Adobe is made by kneading clay with vegetable fiber, such as straw, which acts as a binder and reduces shrinkage during the curing process. Water is added to give the clay a stiff plastic consistency so it can be forced by hand into a wooden mold. The brick is left outside to bake in the sun for several weeks. When not formed into bricks, adobe can be used to construct walls using an English Cob or coursed construction technique. Earth is worked into a stiff mud, into which some grass might be added. The mud is then piled in relatively thick layers to form an earth wall. In some regions, cobbles or rocks are incorporated into the layer. Additional layers are placed on top of finished sections until the desired wall height is attained. Because the mud is not fired, contact with water causes degeneration. Adobe walls thus require protection and constant repairs to ensure durability. This was the job of the *enjarradora,* the woman builder. *Enjarradora,* broadly "plasteress" in English, gave walls their final shape, color, and detail. It was also the *enjarradora* who maintained the walls by periodically replastering them. The abundance of, and ease of working, adobe made it an important construction material and technique, especially where stone raw materials were difficult to obtain. An ideal building material for areas having little rainfall, adobe is fireproof and is an excellent insulating material.

The prehistoric inhabitants of the American Southwest made extensive use of adobe to construct walls, mainly through the coursed construction technique. Adobe brick wall construction was known, though its rare use led some scholars at the turn of the twentieth century to believe that the idea of a brick was introduced by the Spanish. That was the belief of Victor Mindeleff, who studied prehistoric and historic pueblo architecture in the Tusayan and Cibola areas of Arizona and New Mexico, since the ruins and oldest buildings at pueblo villages he visited were constructed of layered stone while the Spanish church was constructed of regular and durable adobe bricks. Though absent from pueblo sites visited by Mindeleff, the use of adobe brick was rooted in the Anasazi architectural tradition. J.W. Fewkes (1910) described several adobe brick walls in a cliff dwelling in Mesa Verde. The bricks there had

A

rounded angles and hand marks, indicating wooden frames were not used. Earl Morris (1944) described two kivas near Aztec, New Mexico, that were constructed of adobe bricks. These bricks also were made without frames and coursed without bonding material. Finally, Douglas Johnson (1992) documents extensive use of adobe bricks at the Fourmile Ruin site in east-central Arizona. Unlike bricks at the sites described above, those at Fourmile Ruin were consistent in shape and size and did not show finger or hand prints, indicating that frames were used there.

Owen Lindauer

Further Readings

Feld, J. 1965. Soil Mechanics and Foundations. In *Building Construction Handbook,* edited by F.S. Merritt, pp. 40–41. 2nd ed. McGraw-Hill, New York.

Fewkes, J.W. 1910. Note on the Occurrence of Adobes in Cliff-Dwellings. *American Anthropologist* 12:434–436.

Gray, V., and A. Macrae. 1976. *Mud Space and Spirit: Handmade Adobes.* Capara Press, Santa Barbara.

Johnson, D.A. 1992. Adobe Brick Architecture and Salado Ceramics at Fourmile Ruin. In *Proceedings of the Second Salado Conference,* edited by R.C. Lange and S. Germick, pp. 131–131. Occasional Paper. Arizona Archaeological Society, Phoenix.

Mindeleff, V. 1989. *A Study of Pueblo Architecture in Tusayan and Cibola.* Reprinted, Smithsonian Institution Press, Washington, D.C. Originally published 1891, GPO, Washington, D.C.

Morris, E. 1944. Adobe Bricks in a Pre-Spanish Wall Near Aztec, New Mexico. *American Antiquity* 9:434–438.

Agate Basin Complex

In 1942, Frank H.H. Roberts, Jr., of the Smithsonian Institution and Robert E. Frison of Newcastle, Wyoming, visited what was to become the type site of the Agate Basin cultural complex. The site, which is in eastern Wyoming, had been discovered earlier by William Spencer of Edgemont, South Dakota, a nearby small town. Test excavations were carried out in 1942 by Roberts, his brother, H.B. Roberts, and Frison. World War II forced the postponement of planned large-scale investigations.

At that time, the age of what Roberts named the Agate Basin complex remained uncertain.

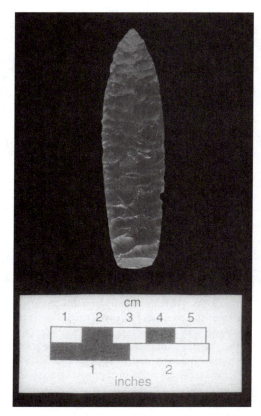

Agate Basin point, Wyoming. (Courtesy of the Wilford Archaeology Laboratory, University of Minnesota)

Although he was convinced that it was old, he was unable to place it chronologically in relationship to Folsom. The complex gained added visibility when Richard Wheeler (1954) formally proposed the Agate Basin point type. However, it was not until the early 1960s that the first unequivocal stratigraphic and chronometric evidence of the relationship of Agate Basin to other Paleoindian complexes became available in layered deposits at the Hell Gap site in southeast Wyoming. There, the Agate Basin component lay above a Midland, or Folsom, component and below a Hell Gap component. The best estimates of the age of the Agate Basin complex at the Hell Gap site are ca. 8550–8050 B.C. (10,500–10,000 years B.P.). A radiocarbon date of ca. 8450 B.C. (10,400 years B.P.) on a charcoal sample taken from the Agate Basin component at the Agate Basin site in 1979 fits well with the Hell Gap–site results.

Other Agate Basin sites include the Frazier site, a short distance south of the South Platte River in northeast Colorado; the Brewster site, which is now known to be part of the original Agate Basin site; and one component at the Carter/Kerr-McGee site in the central Powder River basin in eastern Wyoming. One radiocarbon date from the Brewster-site Agate Basin component is ca. 8050 B.C. (10,000 years B.P.) and another is ca. 7450–7350 B.C. (9400–9300 years B.P.). A Frazier-site date is ca. 7650 B.C. (9600 years B.P.). The latter three dates, and especially the last two, seem too recent.

George C. Frison

Further Readings

Frison, G.C., and D.J. Stanford (editors). 1982. *The Agate Basin Site: A Record of the Paleoindian Occupation of the Northwestern High Plains.* Academic Press, New York.

Roberts, F.H.H., Jr. 1951. The Early Americans. *Scientific American* 184(2):15–19.

———. 1961. The Agate Basin Complex. In *Homenaje a Pablo Martinez del Rio,* pp. 125–132. Instituto Nacional de Antropologia y Historia, Mexico City.

Wheeler, R.P. 1954. Selected Projectile Point Types of the United States II. *Bulletin of the Oklahoma Archaeological Society* 2:1–6.

Wormington, H.M. 1957. *Ancient Man in North America.* Popular Series no. 4. Denver Museum of Natural History, Denver.

See also AGATE BASIN SITE

Agate Basin Site

The Agate Basin site (48NO201) is located in Niobrara County in eastern Wyoming ca. 1.6 km (1 mile) from the Wyoming–South Dakota boundary. It is situated along an intermittent stream known as Agate Basin Arroyo. The site was discovered about 1916 by William Spencer of Edgemont, South Dakota. Robert E. Frison of Newcastle, Wyoming, learned about the site in a chance meeting with Spencer and informed Frank H.H. Roberts, Jr., of the Smithsonian Institution of its existence in 1941. In 1942, Roberts, his brother, and Frison conducted test excavations at the site. Several broken and complete Agate Basin–type projectile points were recovered during these excavations.

There are several exposures of the Agate Basin site along the south bank of Moss Agate Arroyo. The 1942 excavations were in a pure Agate Basin component. Between 1942 and 1961, artifact hunters dug into a bison bonebed

in another part of the site. In 1959, the University of Wyoming, under the direction of George A. Agogino, excavated in what was named the Brewster site, which is now known to be an extension of the original Agate Basin site. In 1961, Roberts returned to the site with William Bass as site foreman and excavated in an area of heaviest looting. Artifact hunters continued to dig in this area after these excavations.

A 1.5 x 3 m (5 x 10-foot) test in 1972 by the University of Wyoming revealed undisturbed deposits with large amounts of bison bone and artifacts. Beginning in 1974, University of Wyoming field crews, under the direction of George C. Frison, conducted annual short-term excavations at the site until 1978, for it did not appear that looting at the site would cease. In 1979, the National Science Foundation supported a major excavation that lasted through 1981. The Smithsonian Institution also provided some monetary assistance and several radiocarbon dates.

Agogino had exposed an Agate Basin and a Folsom component at the Brewster site in 1959. In 1961, Roberts and Bass unknowingly penetrated into a Folsom component in the heavily looted area. The Folsom component was not found by the looters, who had limited their digging to the overlying, artifact-rich Agate Basin bonebed. The University of Wyoming excavated in Folsom levels in the 1961 Roberts-Bass area and also in the Brewster site area. In addition, a large Hell Gap component was found in the Brewster site area above the Folsom component.

Geologic study of the Agate Basin site has demonstrated that a number of bison kills in the arroyo by Folsom, Agate Basin, and Hell Gap hunters probably used headcuts, artificial barriers, or both. The animal kills were made in cold weather, and caches of frozen meat were formed on the arroyo floodplain. There is evidence that the hunting groups camped in the immediate vicinity of these caches. Preservation of the site components was due to aggradation of deposits in the arroyo and subsequent downcutting episodes that in many cases departed from the course of the original arroyo. A large share of the site is still intact for future research.

George C. Frison

Further Readings

Frison, G.C., and D.J. Stanford (editors). 1982. *The Agate Basin Site: A Record of the*

Paleoindian Occupation of the North-western High Plains. Academic Press, New York.

Roberts, F.H.H., Jr. 1951. The Early Americans. *Scientific American* 184(2):15–19.

See also AGATE BASIN COMPLEX

Aishihik Phase

Aishihik is the final prehistoric phase in the southwestern Yukon Territory of Canada, stratigraphically above the eastern lobe of the White River volcanic ash (dated to ca. A.D. 700, or 1250 years B.P.) but lacking European trade goods. Characteristic traits include artifacts of native copper, abraded cobbles of uncertain function, small multibarbed bone points, small-stemmed flaked-stone arrowheads (Kavik type), and ground-stone adzes with rectangular cross sections. Items shared with the historic Bennett Lake phase include small side-notched projectile points and slate pieces with thick, flat, ground edges. Several types of notched and geometric projectile points, various end scrapers, boulder spall scrapers, stone wedges, large multibarbed bone points, flake blade cores, and blunted discoids are shared with the antecedent Taye Lake phase (ca. 2550 B.C.–A.D. 650, or 4500–1300 years B.P.). Tabular schist bifaces, flaked points with slightly concave bases, broad, thin end scrapers, and discoidal flake cores are shared among late Taye Lake, Aishihik, and Bennett Lake. Large bifaces, unifaces with thick working edges, and burins are rare to absent. Archaeological evidence for permanent structures, underground cachepits, art, and disposal of the dead is absent. Sites are typically small with meager artifact inventories, suggesting the ethnographic pattern of small mobile human groups moving seasonally over large territories. Limited faunal remains indicate exploitation of large and small game, birds, and fish. After ca. A.D. 1500 (450 years B.P.), the Aishihik phase confronted the deteriorating climatic conditions of the Little Ice Age. Available evidence suggests that Aishihik is the descendant of the antecedent Taye Lake and the immediate ancestor of the historic southern Tutchone Athapaskans.

William B. Workman

Further Readings

Clark, D.W. 1981. Prehistory of the Western Subarctic. In *Subarctic,* edited by J. Helm, pp. 107–129. Handbook of North American Indians, vol. 6, W.C. Sturtevant, general editor. Smithsonian Institution, Washington, D.C.

———. 1991. *Western Subarctic Prehistory.* Canadian Prehistory Series. Canadian Museum of Civilization, Hull.

Workman, W.B. 1917. The Prehistory of the Southern Tutchone Area. In *Problems in the Prehistory of the North American Subarctic: The Athapaskan Question,* edited by J.W. Helmer, B. Van Dyke, and F.J. Kense, pp. 46–61. Archaeological Association of the University of Calgary, Calgary.

———. 1978. *Prehistory of the Aishihik-Kluane Area, Southwest Yukon Territory.* Mercury Series Paper no. 74. Archaeological Survey of Canada, National Museum of Man, Ottawa.

Alberta Complex

Alberta is a Late Paleoindian bison-hunting cultural complex that is thought to have been present on the High Plains between the Hell Gap and the Cody complexes (Irwin-Williams et al. 1973). An estimate of its age at the Hell Gap site in southwest Wyoming is ca. 7550–7050 B.C. (9500–9000 years B.P.), and radiocarbon dates for the Hudson-Meng Alberta bison kill-site in Northwest Nebraska fall in the ca. 7850–7050 B.C. (9800–9000 years B.P.) range. However, a radiocarbon date on Alberta-associated materials at the Patten Creek site in eastern Wyoming is as recent as 6650 B.C. (8600 years B.P.), and a mixed Alberta and Cody component was found at the Carter/Kerr-McGee site in the Powder River Basin in north-central Wyoming. A "blended" Alberta-Cody component at the Horner site in northwest Wyoming is considered a possible regional variant of Alberta. In addition, a Cody knife, once considered diagnostic of the Cody complex, was found at the Hudson-Meng Alberta site. Alberta projectile points are found widely as surface finds on the High Plains and in adjacent areas.

The Alberta projectile point introduced a new concept of hafting to Paleoindian weaponry. Unlike the bases of earlier Paleoindian point types, Alberta points have a large, parallel-sided stem and abrupt shoulders (see Figure). The projectile point itself is relatively large and heavy. Since the base and shoulders of the point absorbed the shock of heavy impact, a special

Alberta projectile point. (Courtesy of the Wilford Archaeology Laboratory, University of Minnesota)

hafting technology was required to prevent the point from being driven backward into the shaft. Bruce B. Huckell (1978) has described the production, use, and reuse of Alberta points at the Hudson-Meng site.

Guy Gibbon

Further Readings

Agenbroad, L.D. (editor). 1978. *The Hudson-Meng Site: An Alberta Bison Kill in the Nebraska High Plains.* University Press of America, Washington, D.C.

Frison, G.C. 1991. *Prehistoric Hunters of the High Plains.* 2nd ed. Academic Press, San Diego.

Huckell, B.B. 1978. Hudson-Meng Chipped Stone. In *The Hudson-Meng Site: An Alberta Bison Kill in the Nebraska High Plains,* edited by L.D. Agenbroad, pp. 153–189. University Press of America, Washington, D.C.

Irwin-Williams, C., H.T. Irwin, G. Agogino, and C.V. Haynes, Jr. 1973. Hell Gap: Paleo-Indian Occupation on the High Plains. *Plains Anthropologist* 18(59):40–53.

See also CARTER/KERR-McGEE SITE; CODY; HELL GAP COMPLEX; HORNER SITE; HUDSON-MENG SITE

Albion Boardinghouse Phase

Albion Boardinghouse was originally recognized by James B. Benedict in 1975 as a complex from the high-altitude site of the same name. It was redefined in 1986 by William B. Butler as a phase within the Western Plains Early Archaic regional variant, which also includes the Mount Albion and Magic Mountain phases. Tools characteristic of the phase include the distinctive Albion Side-Notched projectile point; point preforms; crudely percussioned, bifacially flaked, thick cutting tools; steep, unifacially retouched end scrapers; manos; and unifacial slab metates (from the Front Range). Albion Side-Notched points are dated from ca. 5650 to 4050 B.C. (7600–6000 years B.P.), although they could date as late as 3050 B.C. (5000 years B.P.).While occurring in the same area as Mount Albion–phase sites, the Albion Side-Notched point style seems to predate Mount Albion–phase sites, which are associated with the Mount Albion Corner-Notched point style. Although some Albion Side-Notched points have been found in Plains and Great Basin contexts, most have been found at high altitude in the mountains. Recent research suggests that the Mount Albion phase (ca. 4050–3050 B.C., or 6000–5000 years B.P.) and Albion Boardinghouse phase (ca. 5550–4050 B.C., or 7500–6000 years B.P.) should be considered as members of the Southern Rocky Mountain Early Archaic regional variant (ca. 5550–3050 B.C., or 7500–5000 years B.P.) for mountain-oriented cultures rather than in a Plains taxa (Butler 1986).

William B. Butler

Further Readings

Benedict, J.B. 1975. The Albion Boardinghouse Site: Archaic Occupations of a

High Mountain Valley. *Southwestern Lore* 41(3):1–12.

Benedict, J.B., and B.L. Olson. 1978. *The Mount Albion Complex: A Study of Prehistoric Man and the Altithermal.* Research Report no. 1. Center for Mountain Archaeology, Ward.

Butler, W.B. 1986. *Taxonomy in Northeastern Colorado Prehistory.* Unpublished Ph.D. dissertation, Department of Anthropology, University of Missouri, Columbia.

See also MAGIC MOUNTAIN PHASE; MOUNT ALBION PHASE; SOUTHERN ROCKY MOUNTAIN EARLY ARCHAIC REGIONAL VARIANT

Alder Complex

The Alder complex is a proposed Foothill-Mountain Paleoindian cultural complex identified at the stratified Barton Gulch site (24MA171) in transmontane southwestern Montana. Found in a deeper component at the site, the Alder complex is characterized by lanceolate projectile points with parallel-oblique flaking. The 7450 B.C. (9400 years B.P.) radiocarbon date for the component extends the age of parallel-oblique flaking back into pre-Cody or earliest Cody times. But by at least 8050 B.C. (10,000 years B.P.), two separate Paleoindian subsistence adaptations apparently existed on the High Plains. The more familiar one, which is found at Hell Gap, Horner, Casper, and other bison-kill sites, was oriented toward the open plains and at least a part-time focus on bison hunting. The other, the foothill-mountain-oriented group, had adopted more diffuse "Archaic" hunting-and-gathering subsistence strategies in foothill and mountain slope areas. The Foothill-Mountain Paleoindian group is present at the deeply stratified Medicine Lodge Creek and Mummy Cave rock shelters, at Barton Gulch, and at several other sites discussed by George C. Frison (1991).

Guy Gibbon

Further Readings

Davis, L.B., S.A. Aaberg, and S.T. Greiser. 1988. Paleoindians in Transmontane Southwestern Montana: The Barton Gulch Occupations, Ruby River Drainage. *Current Research in the Pleistocene* 5:9–11.

Frison, G.C. 1991. *Prehistoric Hunters of the High Plains.* 2nd ed. Academic Press, San Diego.

See also BARTON GULCH SITE

Aleutian Tradition

Prehistoric cultural industries in the Aleutian Island chain that date to ca. 3050 B.C.–A.D. 1700 (5000–250 years B.P.) are within the Aleutian tradition. This widespread tradition is only one of two for the 1690-km (1050-mile) -long archipelago (the other being the earlier Anangula tradition). Industries of the tradition are also found at sites on the tip of the Alaska Peninsula and in the Shumagin Islands, which are located just south of the Alaska Peninsula.

Artifacts of the Aleutian-tradition are usually found in large coastal midden sites that represent the semipermanent settlements of prehistoric Aleuts. Unlike the polyhedral core and blade artifacts found at the earlier Anangula site, Aleutian tradition stone industries are primarily based on irregular cores and flakes. These include bifacially flaked projectile points, tanged and untanged knives and scrapers, and drills. Other finished tools include ground-stone adze heads and, later, ulu blades. Other typical implements are carved- and ground-stone bowls and lamps; stone net/fishline weights; scoria abraders; whetstones; bone socket pieces, harpoon heads, dart heads, wedges, and picks; birdbone awls and needles; bone fishhooks; and bone and ivory labrets. Pottery is not found in the Aleutian Islands. A rich woodworking industry was based on driftwood (trees do not grow in the Aleutians), but wooden artifacts are only rarely preserved in midden sites.

The best-dated cultural sequences for this tradition are based on large-scale excavations at eastern Aleutian midden sites, such as Chaluka midden at Nikolski, Umnak Island, and the Chulka site on Akun Island. These sites are both ca. 4 m (13 inches) deep. They contain multiple-layered but discontinuous midden stratigraphies, boulder and whale bone house structures, storage pits, and human burials. The midden matrix of these kinds of sites is usually a mix of wind-blown volcanic ash; crushed shell and urchin spines; fish, bird, and sea mammal bones; boulders; and anthropogenic soils. Russian-contact-period occupations of the mid-eighteenth century are often present in the uppermost horizons. While not necessarily continuously occupied for millennia, they do contain multiple occupations that commonly spanned many centuries. The greatest concentration of sampled midden sites is at Unalaska Bay on the northern coast of Unalaska Island. Artifacts have been collected from more than a dozen of these sites, particularly during the military occupation of World War II. Their chronology remains, however, poorly established.

The appearance of coastal midden sites corresponds to the stabilization of the sea level ca. 3050–2550 B.C. (5000–4500 years B.P.). This process created suitable reefs and other shellfish habitats for littoral collecting. Midden sites are typically found on low, protected shores, often at stream mouths and on or near spits. The Aleutian tradition ends with the introduction of Russian trade goods in the mid- to late eighteenth century A.D. Regional cultural phases of this tradition will be defined throughout the archipelago, as more archaeology takes place in this remotest part of Alaska.

Allen P. McCartney

Further Readings

Aigner, J.S. 1966. Bone Tools and Decorative Motifs From Chaluka, Umnak Island. *Arctic Anthropology* 3(2):57–85.

Denniston, G.B. 1966. Cultural Change at Chaluka, Umnak Island: Stone Artifacts and Features. *Arctic Anthropology* 3(2):84–124.

Holland, K.M. 1992. *Rethinking Aleutian Prehistory As Viewed From a Lithic Database.* Unpublished Ph.D. dissertation, Department of Anthropology, Arizona State University, Tempe.

Laughlin, W.S., and G.H. Marsh. 1951. A New View of the History of the Aleutians. *Arctic* 4(2):75–88.

McCartney, A.P. 1984. Prehistory of the Aleutian Region. In *Arctic*, edited by D. Damas, pp. 119–135. Handbook of North American Indians, vol. 5, W.C. Sturtevant, general editor. Smithsonian Institution, Washington, D.C.

Turner, C.G., II, J.S. Aigner, and L.R. Richards. 1974. Chaluka Stratigraphy, Umnak Island, Alaska. *Arctic Anthropology* 11(Supplement):125–142.

Turner, C.G., II, and J.A. Turner. 1974. Progress Report on Evolutionary Anthropological Study of Akun Strait District, Eastern Aleutians, Alaska, 1970–1971. *Anthropological Papers of the University of Alaska* 16(1):27–57.

See also ANANGULA

Anangula

Anangula (SAM-012) is the name given to the oldest known archaeological site in the Aleutian Islands, Alaska. The site is located on the small island of Ananiuliak on the northern edge of Nikolski Bay, southwestern Umnak Island. Anangula was first recognized in 1938 by William S. Laughlin and Alan G. May, while serving on a Smithsonian field expedition under the direction of Ales Hrdlicka. It was revisited and surface collected in 1952 by Laughlin, Gordon H. Marsh, and Philip Spaulding. At that time, the known site consisted of several blowout depressions above a cliff. Prismatic cores, blades, and related pieces were scattered across the depressions. In 1962, Christy G. Turner II, Laughlin, and Allen P. McCartney tested the side of one depression, where they found an in situ volcanic ash stratigraphy covering a 10–30-cm (3.9–11.7-inch) -thick cultural horizon buried approximately 2 m (6.6 feet) deep. Charcoal samples from the horizon were dated to 5710 B.C. (7660 years B.P.) and 6475 B.C. (8425 years B.P.)

Subsequent testing at Anangula, principally in 1963, 1970, and 1974, showed that the current site measures approximately 110 x 210 m (361 x 689 feet). Transverse burins of an Asian style (for example, similar to those found in Japan) and burin spalls were found, but no bifacially flaked projectile points or knives were among the thousands of pieces collected. Unlike many later microblade sites in Alaska, Anangula exhibits a continuous range of very small to large cores and blades. Other artifacts recovered from the site include core rejuvenation tablets; obsidian end scrapers; scoria abraders; hammerstones; and one carved-bowl fragment. Radiocarbon dates from tests run on charcoal samples are in the 6550–5550 B.C. (8500–7500 years B.P.) range.

Anangula is considered a settlement of early maritime hunters and gatherers who used boats for interisland travel and perhaps sea-mammal hunting and fishing. Although faunal remains have been destroyed by the acidic ashes covering the cultural horizon, the site's insular location suggests that subsistence was based on marine animals. Of the few charred bone fragments found, none has been identified as human. Several excavated depressions have been interpreted as house floors, but no structural details have been published.

The core-and-blade industry at Anangula, while duplicated in some respects at other sites found since the 1960s, remains something of a cultural enigma in the Aleutian Islands. There are few continuities between it and more recent

A

sites dating after ca. 3050 B.C. (5000 years B.P.). This distinctive industry is the defining characteristic of the Anangula tradition, a construct that presumes the existence of both earlier and later manifestations at as yet undiscovered Aleutian locales.

Allen P. McCartney

Further Readings

Aigner, J.S. 1978. *The Lithic Remains From Anangula, an 8500 Year Old Aleut Coastal Village.* Urgeschichtliche Materialhefte 3. Universität Tübingen, Institut für Urgeschichte, Tübingen.

Black, R.F. 1976. Geology of Umnak Island, Eastern Aleutian Islands As Related to the Aleuts. *Arctic and Alpine Research* 8(1):7–35.

Laughlin, W.S. 1980. *Aleuts: Survivors of the Bering Land Bridge.* Holt, Rinehart, and Winston, New York.

Laughlin, W.S., and G.H. Marsh. 1954. The Lamellar Flake Manufacturing Site on Anangula Island in the Aleutians. *American Antiquity* 20(1):27–39.

McCartney, A.P. 1984. Prehistory of the Aleutian Region. In *Arctic,* edited by D. Damas, pp. 119–135. Handbook of North American Indians, vol. 5, W.C. Sturtevant, general editor. Smithsonian Institution, Washington, D.C.

McCartney, A.P., and C.G. Turner II. 1966. Stratigraphy of the Anangula Unifacial Core and Blade Site. *Arctic Anthropology* 3(2):28–40.

See also ALEUTIAN TRADITION

Anasazi Culture Area

The major Southwestern "cultures"—Mogollon, Hohokam, Anasazi, and Patayan—are archaeological constructs based on distinguishable constellations of material traits. Their existence undoubtedly reflects the presence of important sociocultural and historical differences among subregions in this culture area. The reality behind them is obscured, however, by the near absence in their definition of the materially less visible cultural distinctions that must have existed among them. Their reality as cultures is only partial, then, and reliance on a material definition alone may obscure as much about these cultures as it reveals.

The term "Anasazi" was proposed in 1936 by A.V. Kidder as a solution to a pair of problems in Southwestern typology. First, although the Pecos classification of 1927 was designed to apply to all areas in the Southwest, subsequent research established that the Puebloan archetype embedded in the classification did not apply to the archaeological remains of the mountains and desert for which the names Mogollon and Hohokam had been proposed. Second, Kidder thought that the term "Basketmaker-Pueblo" in the classification perpetuated a false dichotomy between the Basketmaker and the Pueblo segments of the Puebloan cultural continuum. As a solution, he suggested that "Anasazi," an anglicized Navajo word for the prehistoric inhabitants of the area, be used to designate the Puebloan component of the classification. Despite some opposition, his recommendation was adopted. Today, "Anasazi" is applied to the archaeological remains of agricultural populations on the southern Colorado Plateau that differ from the remains of Mogollon, Hohokam, and Patayan populations.

"Anasazi" is defined more by cultural continuity with modern Pueblo Indians than by a homogeneous set of shared material remains. Still, despite the heterogeneous archaeological complexes subsumed under the term, broad material-culture consistencies do exist, especially in ceramics and architecture. The Anasazi ceramic tradition emphasized coil-and-scrape technology; plain and corrugated gray utility wares; and black-on-white, black-on-red, and polychrome painted wares. This tradition is continued by modern Pueblo Indian potters. Architecture is characterized by a development from pithouses to surface pueblos. Surface pueblos are made up of contiguous masonry or adobe habitation and storage rooms, and associated nondomestic structures, such as kivas, great kivas, towers, and plazas. Most of these types of structures are still used by modern Pueblo Indians.

Anasazi material culture occurs over a vast area that extends from southern Nevada east to the Pecos River in New Mexico and from the Colorado River in Utah south to the Mogollon Rim in Arizona. Anasazi-related materials are found along the western margin of the southern Great Plains on into western Kansas, at several points along the Mogollon Rim in central Arizona, and in the San Pedro Valley of southern Arizona. The remains are concentrated in three widely different physiographic provinces: the Great Basin, the Rio Grande Valley, and the southern Colorado Plateau. The flexibility of the Anasazi agriculturally based subsistence system is reflected in the adjustments that were made in adapting the system to such diverse environments.

Many geographic variants of the Anasazi tradition, called branches, developed within this diverse setting. Branches are marked by differences in ceramics, architecture, community structure, and settlement pattern. The most elaborate expressions of the general Anasazi pattern are found in the related Chaco, Cibola, and Mesa Verde branches. They were in a region that extends from the Four Corners area south along the Arizona–New Mexico border to the Mogollon Rim. To the west, the related Kayenta, Tusayan, and Virgin branches occupied the northeastern corner of Arizona, a large part of southern Utah, and the southern tip of Nevada. The Little Colorado and Winslow branches were in the middle Little Colorado River drainage in Arizona. The Rio Grande branch was a late (after A.D. 1200, or 750 years B.P.) Anasazi expression in the Rio Grande drainage of New Mexico. The Largo-Gallina branch of north-central New Mexico has many Anasazi traits, such as masonry roomblocks and towers, combined with exotic material forms, such as pointed-bottom ceramic vessels.

Superimposed on the geographical variability represented by the branch system is a larger-scale, east-west dichotomy that appears to extend many millennia back into the past. During the Paleoindian (before 6000 B.C., or 7950 years B.P.) and Archaic (6000–1000 B.C., or 7950–2950 years B.P.) periods, the dichotomy is evident in differences in artifact morphology and interregional affiliations, with eastern artifact assemblages sharing similarities with Plains cultural traditions, and western assemblages with Great Basin traditions. Subsequently, an amorphous and permeable boundary located just west of the Arizona-New Mexico border separated the eastern and western expressions of the Anasazi pattern. Before A.D. 850 (1100 years B.P.), differences in artifacts, architecture, and settlement appear to be mainly the result of different developmental histories. After this date, they appear to reflect the strength of the complex Chacoan pattern in the east and simpler patterns in the west. The dichotomy persisted into the historic period in the ethnographic distinction between eastern and western Pueblos.

The Anasazi cultural continuum has been divided in many ways, with each branch having

at least one phase or period system. Nevertheless, the original Pecos classification of 1927 remains remarkably appropriate if it is treated as a developmental rather than a chronological scheme. As a developmental scheme, stage dates are independently assigned within individual branches. This procedure shows that the west lagged significantly behind the east in achieving the level of social complexity diagnostic of each stage. Seven sequential divisions are defined in the Pecos classification: Basketmaker II to III and Pueblo I to V. Basketmaker I was a hypothetical preagricultural stage that has since been subsumed under the Archaic label.

The Basketmaker II stage originated with the addition of maize agriculture to a hunting-and-gathering Archaic economy ca. 1000 B.C. (2950 years B.P.). Although the intermittent occupation of rock shelters was succeeded by residence in hamlets composed of shallow pithouses and storage facilities, mobility remained a major means of adapting to environmental variability. For most of the span of the stage, container technology was limited to baskets and woven and hide bags. Brownware ceramics, possibly related to Mogollon prototypes, appeared among the eastern Anasazi ca. A.D. 300 (1650 years B.P.) but were rare in the west. Basketmaker II lasted until ca. A.D. 500 (1450 years B.P.) in the east and as late as 700 (1250 years B.P.) in the far west.

Basketmaker III is marked by the appearance of traits indicative of greater reliance on farming and increased sedentism. Among these are the ground-stone axe, more efficient grinding implements, the bow and arrow, the elaboration of the distinctive Anasazi ceramic tradition at the expense of less durable containers, and true pit structures. Pithouses, surface storage structures, and outdoor work areas were grouped into settlements that range from small hamlets to medium-sized villages. In the east, these settlements were integrated into larger communities through activities associated with communal ceremonial structures called great kivas. This type of community organization was virtually absent among the western Anasazi.

The transition to the Pueblo I stage occurred ca. A.D. 700 (1250 years B.P.) in the east and 850 (1100 years B.P.) in the west. Pueblo I was a period of increasing diversity as the eastern area developed greater social complexity than the western. In the eastern area, the "pithouse-to-pueblo" transition involved the construction of surface dwelling units in addition to pit structures, which now began to take on more ceremonial functions. Western settlements differed little from their Basketmaker III predecessors. In both areas, settlements ranged from hamlets to large villages. In the east, villages were integrated into larger communities by great kivas, but this structure (and, presumably, its organizational correlates) was absent in the west. The Pueblo I pattern persisted until ca. A.D. 900 (1050 years B.P.) in the east and 1000 (950 years B.P.) in the west.

The Pueblo II period is notable for the development of the Chacoan regional system, which, at its zenith, encompassed most of the San Juan Basin and surrounding areas. The Chacoan development began in the years A.D. 850–900 (100–1050 years B.P.) when several Chaco Canyon sites began to diverge from the general Pueblo I pattern. Apparently, the necessity to tap outside resources to maintain these communities was an important factor in the genesis of the regional system, which originated ca. A.D. 900 (1050 years B.P.), dominated the eastern area in the years 1000–1150 (950–800 years B.P.), and "collapsed" by 1200 (750 years B.P.). Outlying local communities, each consisting of a hierarchical grouping of settlements, were integrated by a network of roads and signaling stations into a large interaction system focused on an integrated group of "great houses" in Chaco Canyon. The canyon core apparently was a center for accumulating and perhaps distributing goods and services brought in from peripheral communities. It may have controlled the long-distance trade of turquoise south into Mesoamerica. In terms of degree of formal integration of settlements distributed over a large area, the Chacoan system was never equaled elsewhere in the Anasazi domain. It probably represents the attainment of a chiefdom level of social complexity.

The western Anasazi were impacted only minimally by the Chacoan system. The elaborate Chacoan features (great houses, great kivas, roads, elegant masonry styles, and exotic material items) were absent from this area. There is scant evidence for hierarchical settlement systems or for integration into large-scale regional networks. Rather, the large Pueblo I pithouse villages were replaced by small, scattered "homesteads," each composed of a block of living and storage rooms fronted by a subterranean kiva and a formal trash mound. During this period, western Anasazi groups reached

their maximum geographic expansion. After 1150 (800 years B.P.), however, the population began to contract toward the center. Huge areas on the periphery (including the Virgin branch) were abandoned. This population shift initiated a period of major culture change that produced the Pueblo III patterns.

Pueblo III was characterized by widespread change resulting from serious environmental deterioration and the collapse of the Chacoan system. In the east, the Mesa Verde and Cibola regional systems, each characterized by complex settlement hierarchies and interaction networks, succeeded the Chacoan system. In the Kayenta and Tusayan branches, a period of settlement flux produced, by 1250 (700 years B.P.), the strong Tsegi-phase pattern. It marked the first attainment in the west of hierarchical settlement configurations that were roughly comparable to those that had developed 150 years earlier in the east. Along the middle Little Colorado River drainage, the Winslow and Little Colorado branches developed distinctive ceramic and settlement configurations.

Pueblo III ended ca. 1300 (650 years B.P.) with the greatest population dislocations in Anasazi history. The Mesa Verde, Chaco, and Kayenta branches came to an end as the Anasazi vacated the entire San Juan drainage. People moved south and east of the drainage to join groups ancestral to the modern Pueblos. Mesa Verde emigrants augmented the extant populations in the Rio Grande Valley, the Chacoans seem to have dispersed to the south, the Cibolans concentrated in the Zuni area, and the Kayentans moved south to join their Tusayan-branch relatives in the Hopi area or continued on to Mogollon Pueblo communities in Arizona's central mountains.

Pueblo IV is the period between the abandonment of the San Juan drainage ca. 1300 (650 years B.P.) and the arrival of Spanish colonists in the Rio Grande Valley ca. 1600 (350 years B.P.). This interval was characterized by major population aggregations in the Hopi Mesas area, along the Zuni River, along western tributaries of the Rio Grande River, in the Rio Grande Valley, and on the Pecos River drainage. Although extremely large pueblos developed in these areas, regional systems comparable to those of eastern Pueblo II and III seem not to have arisen. Pueblo IV was a time of major socioreligious change. Much of this change was apparently stimulated by influences from Mesoamerica to the south and formalized trading relationships with neighboring populations, particularly those on the western Great Plains.

Pueblo V designates Puebloan groups after the arrival of Spanish and other European colonists. During this period of tumultuous relationships with the Spanish, Mexican, and U.S. governments and with other Indian tribes, modern Pueblo groups developed from the Anasazi populations of the region. From west to east, these groups are the Hopis, the Zunis, the Keresan-speaking pueblos between Zuni and the Rio Grande, and the Tiwa-, Tewa-, and Towa-speaking pueblos of the Rio Grande drainage.

Jeffrey S. Dean

Further Readings

Cordell, L.S. 1984. *Prehistory of the Southwest.* Academic Press, Orlando.

Cordell, L.S., and G.J. Gumerman (editors). 1989. *Dynamics of Southwest Prehistory.* Smithsonian Institution Press, Washington, D.C.

Crown, P.L., and W.J. Judge (editors). 1991. *Chaco and Hohokam: Prehistoric Regional Systems in the American Southwest.* School of American Research Press, Santa Fe.

Ferguson, W.M., and A.H. Rohn. 1986. *Anasazi Ruins of the Southwest in Color.* University of New Mexico Press, Albuquerque.

Gumerman, G.J. (editor). 1988. *The Anasazi in a Changing Environment.* Cambridge University Press, Cambridge, England.

Kessell, J.L. 1979. *Kiva, Cross, and Crown: The Pecos Indians and New Mexico, 1540–1850.* USDI, National Park Service, Washington, D.C.

Kidder, A.V. 1924. *An Introduction to the Study of Southwestern Archaeology, With a Preliminary Account of the Excavations at Pecos.* Papers of the Phillips Academy Southwestern Expedition no. 1. Yale University Press, New Haven.

———. 1936. *The Pottery of Pecos,* vol. 2. Yale University Press, New Haven.

Lipe, W.D. 1983. The Southwest. In *Ancient North Americans,* edited by J.D. Jennings, pp. 421–493. W.H. Freeman, San Francisco.

Powell, S., and G.J. Gumerman. 1987. *People of the Mesa: The Archaeology of Black Mesa, Arizona.* Southwest Parks and Monuments Association, Tucson; Southern Illinois University Press, Carbondale.

Vivian, R.G. 1990. *The Chacoan Prehistory of the San Juan Basin.* Academic Press, San Diego.

Anderson Phase

Sites of the Middle Missouri tradition, Initial-variant Anderson phase, are clustered near the modern town of Pierre in central South Dakota. They are situated between the mouths of the Bad and Cheyenne rivers. The best reported sites are the Breeden, Dodd, and Fay Tolton villages. Radiocarbon dates suggest an age of ca. A.D. 950 to 1250 (1000–700 years B.P.) for the phase. These semisedentary villages consist of long, rectangular houses built on high terraces overlooking the Missouri River. House entries usually faced southwest. Some sites, including Dodd and Fay Tolton, were fortified by a short ditch dug across the neck of a terrace spur. At Fay Tolton, the ditch was elaborated by the presence of four irregularly spaced bastions. The people were maize farmers, who also grew beans and squash. They augmented their diet by gathering and by hunting game, especially bison, deer, and antelope.

Well-made globular jars with cord-roughened or, rarely, simple stamped walls had either outflaring or recurved (S-shaped) rims. Vessels with recurved rims were embellished on the outer rim by incised or cord-impressed decorations. Triangular notched and unnotched arrow points, end scrapers, and bifaces are representative of the range of tools found in most sites of the Middle Missouri tradition, as are the varieties of ground-stone, bone, antler, and shell artifacts. The remains of two charred, coiled baskets contained concentrations of artifacts identified as toolkits associated with skin-working activities. Both excavated houses at Fay Tolton had been destroyed by fire. One contained the remains of five individuals who appeared to have been slain during a raid; one individual had been beheaded. Skeletal material clearly falls within the morphological range of the historic Mandan Indians, which lends strong support to the hypothesis that their ancestors were responsible for the Middle Missouri tradition as early as the Initial variant.

W. Raymond Wood

Further Readings

Brown, L. 1974. *The Archeology of the Breeden Site.* Memoir no. 10. Plains Anthropologist, Lincoln.

Lehmer, D.J. 1954. *Archeological Investigations in the Oahe Dam Area, South Dakota, 1950–51.* Bulletin no. 158. Bureau of American Ethnology, Smithsonian Institution, Washington, D.C.

Wood, W.R. (editor). 1976. *Fay Tolton and the Initial Middle Missouri Variant.* Research Series no. 13. Missouri Archaeological Society, Columbia.

See also MIDDLE MISSOURI TRADITION

Angel Site and Phase

The Angel site (12VG1) is a Middle Mississippian town ca. 40 ha (100 acres) in extent. Located on a high terrace of the Ohio River in Vanderburgh County, Indiana, opposite the mouth of the Green River, it is immune from all millennial floods. Angel contains five large truncated mounds and perhaps as many as seven smaller mounds, which surround two large plazas. The whole of the site is enclosed by a palisade set with bastions. Angel's principal occupation was in the period A.D. 1200–1450 (750–500 years B.P.), although earlier and later Mississippian components may be present. At its zenith, in the Angel 3 phase, ca. A.D. 1325–1450 (625–500 years B.P.), the resident population could have been as many as 1,000 people, although 300–500 inhabitants is a better estimate. This population clearly depended upon maize agriculture for a significant portion of its diet.

The distinctive negative painted ceramics found at Angel have been used to define the spatial and temporal extent of the Angel phase. In broad measure, these settlements are found in the Ohio River Valley in Indiana and Kentucky. They extend from the mouth of the Wabash River in extreme western Indiana to the mouth of the Anderson River in central Indiana. The earliest settlements are designated the Stephan-Steinkamp (Angel 1) phase. This phase dates to ca. A.D. 1050–1200 (900–750 years B.P.). The later settlements, which are attributed to the Angel 3 phase on the basis of ceramics, date no later than A.D. 1450. One of the enduring archaeological mysteries of this site is the cause of the demise of the Angel phase and its relations, if any, with the later Caborn-Welborn phase.

Christopher S. Peebles

Further Readings

Black, G.A. 1967. *Angel Site: An Archaeological, Historical, and Ethnological Study.* Indiana Historical Society, Indianapolis.

Hilgeman, S. 1991. *Pottery and Chronology of the Angel Site.* Ph.D. dissertation, Indiana University, Bloomington. University Microfilms, Ann Arbor.

Muller, J. 1986. *Archaeology of the Lower Ohio Valley.* Academic Press, New York.

Schurr, M. 1989. *The Relationship Between Mortuary Treatment and Diet at the Angel Site.* Ph.D. dissertation, Indiana University, Bloomington. University Microfilms, Ann Arbor.

Angostura Cultural Complex

The Ray Long site (39FA65) is located adjacent to Angostura Reservoir in the southern portion of the Black Hills in Fall River County, South Dakota. The site was initially recorded on August 6,1948, by Jack T. Hughes in the company of J.M. Shippee and Theodore E. White, who were conducting a comprehensive survey and testing of archaeological localities in the Angostura Reservoir area as part of the Missouri Basin Project of the Smithsonian Institution. Following initial testing at Locality A, additional testing was expanded in 1949 to localities identified as B and C. Richard P. Wheeler assumed direction of investigations at the site during the 1949 and 1950 seasons.

The earliest component identified within localities A and B was designated Component C by Wheeler (1957:622) and was dated from a composite sample of charcoal fragments taken from an occupation zone in Locality A. The date for Component C is reported as 7430 ± 500 B.C. (9380 years B.P.) and is associated with projectile points assigned by Wheeler to a new "type" designated as Angostura. The Angostura cultural complex identified by Wheeler is noted for its lanceolate projectile point, a point type that exhibits parallel oblique flaking.

The Angostura point, which first appeared in the literature in 1954 (Wheeler) as a specific type in the Paleoindian cultural/techno complex of the New World, has remained problematic. Several factors have contributed to the enigmatic nature of the Angostura cultural complex and its acceptance as a valid cultural typology. Consideration of the Angostura typology has long proved vexing because Wheeler's manuscript (1957) was not published, and the original specimens from which the type was identified were unavailable for further analysis, until very recently (Dennis Stanford, personal communication 1994). The Angostura debate is further complicated by the growing recognition among investigators (Frison and Bradley 1980; Frison and Stanford 1982; Hannus 1986; Frison 1991) that the current interpretation of the dynamics of the Paleoindian cultural/techno complexes on the northwestern Plains is woefully simplistic.

A number of investigators have also called attention to the lack of precision in the description of Angostura as a distinct cultural type (Thoms 1993). Wheeler (1954) noted the resemblance between Angostura points and the Agate Basin point type; however, he concluded that they must be separate morphologically and temporally. In 1982, Frison and Stanford (1982:107) noted that in naming the new type "Wheeler may have been influenced to some degree by the erroneous identification of the bison from the Agate Basin site as a modern form."

In an attempt to obtain additional data, an initial reinvestigation of the Ray Long site localities was undertaken in 1985 by the Archeology Laboratory of Augustana College, Sioux Falls, South Dakota (Hannus 1986). During the 1985 field season, localities A, B, and C were revisited. At that time, a series of deep backhoe trenches was excavated in Locality B to evaluate the geomorphology, paleoclimatic indicators, and the possibility for extant cultural deposits. This activity was undertaken under a cooperative agreement with the U.S. Bureau of Reclamation, the federal agency that manages the Angostura Reservoir lands. The work resulted in the identification of a series of ephemeral hearth features in backhoe Trench F (Hannus 1986), which produced a suite of radiocarbon dates ranging from 7000 B.C. ± 140 (8950 years B.P.) to the earliest date of 9050 B.C. ± 310 (11,000 years B.P.). These data, coupled with the extremely complex geomorphologic situation and well-preserved paleoclimatic record, encouraged the possibility of further research at the site.

Field investigations were resumed in 1992 and 1993 to further define the geomorphic circumstances at the Ray Long site. Based on an expanded understanding of the geomorphologic situation, hand excavations of limited scope were conducted at Locality B in 1994. The 1994 work identified an extant cultural horizon that produced a well-defined fire hearth with a grinding stone in direct association, as well as a living floor with lithic-reduction debitage. A radiocarbon determination with a ^{13}C value

correction of 7190 B.C. ± 230 (9140 years B.P.) was obtained from the hearth. These radiocarbon determinations demonstrate the existence of a cultural horizon directly associated with Wheeler's 1957 zone in Locality B, as well as a yet uninvestigated earlier cultural horizon at the site.

While the identification of the extant cultural horizon does not clarify the continuing debate surrounding the validity of Angostura as a distinct type in the Paleoindian toolkit of the northwestern Plains, it does provide a strong research avenue toward tightening the temporal position of the cultural/techno complex. Other encouraging developments are the fact that the Wheeler manuscript was published in 1995, and the long misplaced original specimens from the Smithsonian excavations have been located (Dennis Stanford, personal communication 1994).

L. Adrien Hannus

Further Readings

Frison, G.C. 1991. *Prehistoric Hunters of the High Plains.* 2nd ed. Academic Press, San Diego.

Frison, G.C., and B.A. Bradley. 1980. *Folsom Tools and Technology at the Hanson Site, Wyoming.* University of New Mexico Press, Albuquerque.

Frison, G.C., and D. Stanford. 1982. *The Agate Basin Site: A Record of the Paleoindian Occupation of the Northwestern High Plains.* Academic Press, New York.

Hannus, L.A. 1986. Report on 1985 Test Excavations at the Ray Long Site (39FA65), Angostura Reservoir, Fall River County, South Dakota. *South Dakota Archaeology* 10:48–104.

Thoms, A.V. 1993. Knocking Sense From Old Rocks: Typologies and the Narrow Perspective of the Angostura Point Type. *Lithic Technology* 18:16–27.

Wheeler, R.P. 1954. Selected Projectile Point Types of the United States. *Bulletin of the Oklahoma Anthropological Society* 2:1–6.

———. 1957. Archaeological Remains in the Angostura Reservoir Area, South Dakota, and in the Keyhole and Boysen Areas, Wyoming. Ms. on file, Midwest Archaeological Center, Lincoln. Reprinted, 1995, as *Archeological Investigations in Three Reservoir Areas in South Dakota and Wyoming.* J and L Reprint, Lincoln.

Antelope Creek Phase

What is presently called the Antelope Creek phase has gone by other names, most commonly Panhandle phase, Antelope Creek focus, and Optima focus. It has recently (Lintz 1986) been assigned to the Upper Canark regional variant. There are two possible subphases: early (A.D. 1200–1350, or 750–600 years B.P.) and late (A.D. 1350–1500, or 600–450 years B.P.). Occupations are concentrated along the Canadian and North Canadian rivers in the Texas and Oklahoma panhandles. The phase most likely developed in situ from earlier Woodland occupations, although it has also been proposed that the phase reflects a migration of Upper Republican–variant people from north-central Kansas. It shares a number of similarities with the Buried City complex in the northeastern Texas Panhandle.

Settlements consist of villages, campsites, and limited-purpose sites. Habitation structures vary from one-room buildings to large room-blocks. These structures often have foundations of vertically set stone slabs with more perishable superstructures. As with many members of the Plains Village tradition, altars along the back walls of structures and four center support posts are also found. Subsistence involved hunting, especially of bison but also of deer and antelope. A variety of small mammals, turtles, fish, and mussels were used, although small mammals are less varied than in the Washita River phase (A.D. 1250–1450, or 700–500 years B.P.). Nuts, grasses, and fruits were collected. Horticulture involved corn, beans, and squash/pumpkin. Bison hunting may have increased, while horticulture decreased in importance over time. Ceramics are large, globular-shaped jars that are cord marked and tempered predominantly with sand. Decoration is rare and consists of punctating, impressing, pinching, incising, or applique. Common bone tools include bison-scapula hoes and squash knives, bison-tibia digging-stick tips, split-bone awls, and pins. Stone tools include flange drills; alternately beveled, diamond-shaped knives; end scrapers; and triangular, side-notched arrow points. Shell spoons or scrapers and basketry have also been recovered.

Antelope Creek people received turquoise, Puebloan pottery, and obsidian through trade from the Southwest. Marine shell has been most commonly traced westward as well, but the Gulf and the Atlantic are also possible sources. Smoky Hill jasper (from northwest Kansas), red pipestone, and some ceramics came from the Plains. One resource traded by Antelope Creek people was Alibates agatized dolomite, the best quality of which occurred in their area. Late in time, when trade of Alibates was at its highest, settlement concentrated around the quarry sites.

The fate of Antelope Creek–phase people is uncertain. The Pawnee had an origin myth saying they once lived in stone houses, but the phase may have become the more mobile, bison-hunting Garza complex.

Susan C. Vehik

Further Readings

Hughes, D.T., and A.A. Hughes-Jones. 1987. *The Courson Archeological Projects.* Innovative, Perryton.

Lintz, C.R. 1984. The Plains Villagers: Antelope Creek. In *Prehistory of Oklahoma*, edited by R.E. Bell, pp. 325–346. Academic Press, Orlando.

———. 1986. *Architecture and Community Variability Within the Antelope Creek Phase of the Texas Panhandle.* Studies in Oklahoma's Past no. 14. Oklahoma Archeological Survey, Norman.

See also GARZA COMPLEX; PLAINS VILLAGE TRADITION; UPPER CANARK REGIONAL VARIANT

Antevs, Ernst (1888–1974)

A renowned Pleistocene geologist, Ernst Valdemar Antevs worked closely with western North American archaeologists from the mid-1930s to the mid-1950s in determining the geological associations and ages of mainly preceramic human remains and site assemblages. His collaborative work is a reflection as well of the long-term interest in arid regions of the West in the importance of the interaction between culture and environment. Antevs (1935, 1952, 1953) was particularly interested in possible associations of human remains with Pleistocene geological deposits, although he also defined, with E.B. Sayles (Sayles and Antevs 1941), the original three-stage preceramic Cochise cultural continuum. In the latter work, he and Sayles brought together stratigraphically associated geological and archaeological evidence over a broad area of southeastern Arizona and adjacent parts of New Mexico. Antevs (1955) was one of several Pleistocene geologists who established the basis of the geochronological method of dating in North American archaeology. He (1948) also labeled the cool/moist, warm/dry, and modern sequence of postglacial fluctuations in temperature and moisture in the West the Anathermal (7000–5000 B.C., or 8950–6950 years B.P.), the Altithermal (5000–2500 B.C., or 6950–4450 years B.P.), and the Medithermal (after 2500 B.C., or 4450 years B.P.). The latter sequence of paleoclimatic change is still a focus of interest among prehistorians in the West, with present-day studies concentrating on defining the complexities of local paleoclimatic changes within the broad outline established by Antevs.

Guy Gibbon

Further Readings

Antevs, E. 1935. The Occurrence of Flints and Extinct Animals in Pluvial Deposits Near Clovis, New Mexico: II. Age of Clovis Lake Beds. *Proceedings of the Academy of Natural Sciences of Philadelphia* 87:304–311.

———. 1948. Climatic Changes and Pre-White Man. In *The Great Basin, With Emphasis on Glacial and Post-Glacial Times,* edited by E. Blackwelder, pp. 168–191. Bulletin of the University of Utah, vol. 38, no. 20; Biological Series, vol. 10, no. 7. Salt Lake City.

———. 1952. Climatic History and the Antiquity of Man in California. *University of California Archaeological Survey Report* 16:23–29.

———. 1953. Artifacts With Mammoth Remains, Naco, Arizona: II. Age of the Clovis Fluted Points With the Naco Mammoth. *American Antiquity* 19:15–18.

———. 1955. Geologic-Climatic Dating in the West. *American Antiquity* 20:317–335.

Haynes, C.V., Jr. 1990. The Antevs-Bryan Years and the Legacy for Paleoindian Geochronology. In *Establishment of a Geologic Framework for Paleoanthropology,* edited by L.F. Laporte, pp. 55–68. Special Paper no. 242. Geological Society of America, Boulder.

Sayles, E.B., and E. Antevs. 1941. *The Cochise Culture.* Privately printed for the Gila Pueblo, Globe.

Smiley, T.L. 1974. Memorial to Ernest Valdemar Antevs, 1888–1974. *Geological Society of America Memorials* 1974:1–7.

See also COCHISE CULTURE; HYPSITHERMAL; HYPSITHERMAL/ALTITHERMAL

Antonsen Site

The Antonsen site (24GA660) is an open-air, multicomponent bison (*Bison bison bison*) kill and processing site located on the hillslope and

The most recent of the Late Prehistoric bison bonebeds on the north-facing hillslope at the Antonsen bison kill site on Dry Creek, Upper East Gallatin drainage. (Courtesy of Museum of the Rockies/Montana State University-Bozeman)

terrace of South Dry Creek in Gallatin County, Montana. It is north of and below a bluff along the southern extremity of the broad intermontane Gallatin Valley 8.9 km (5.5 miles) west of Bozeman. Montana State University excavated this previously disturbed site using field classes in 1972, 1974, 1976, and 1991–1993. Two spatially separate, independently formed bone middens resulting from multiple mass kills of bison were sampled, as was an extensive stratified campsite and bison-carcass-processing station situated between the two middens. The processing station contained a late Middle period (late Plains Archaic) Pelican Lake–phase component, ca. 550 B.C. (2500 years B.P.), at its base and overlying Late Prehistoric period Avonlea, ca. A.D. 950 (1000 years B.P.), and late Plains–phase, ca. A.D. 1650 (300 years B.P.), components. The westernmost middens were formed by one or more very Late Prehistoric bison-hunting events (more recent than A.D. 1770, or 180 years B.P.), while the easternmost midden resulted from Besant-phase bison procurement in the fall (tentatively) ca. A.D. 350 ± 90 (1600 years B.P.). While the Besant projectile-point assemblage included points made from Knife River flint, raw materials were dominated by Madison Plateau basalt, various local cherts, and obsidian. The obsidian, from which uncommonly numerous Besant points were made, had been imported from lithic sources some distance to the west in mountainous southeastern Idaho. The stratified late Plains projectile-point assemblages in the westernmost midden, which consisted of triangular unnotched, side-notched, and tri-notched forms, were dominated by points made from obsidian from the Idaho sources and from Obsidian Cliff in northwestern Wyoming. The Besant bison hunters were likely intrusive into the Rocky Mountains, in view of their possession of Knife River flint points, while the later Late Prehistoric bison hunters at Antonsen appear to have been locally adapted.

Leslie B. Davis

Further Readings

Davis, L.B., and C.D. Zeier. 1978. Multi-Phase Late Period Bison Procurement at the Antonsen Site, Southwestern Montana. In *Bison Procurement and Utilization: A Symposium,* edited by L.B. Davis and M. Wilson, pp. 222–235. Memoir no. 14. Plains Anthropologist, Lincoln.

Zeier, C.D. 1975. *A Morphology-Use Analysis of Besant Phase Projectile Points: Antonsen Site (24GA660), Montana.* Unpublished Master's thesis, Department of Anthropology, University of Nebraska, Lincoln.

———. 1983. Besant Projectile Points From the Antonsen Site (24GA660), Gallatin County, Montana: Within-Sample Variance. *Archaeology in Montana* 24(2):1–57.

See also AVONLEA; BESANT PHASE; PELICAN LAKE

Anvil

An anvil is both a tool and a technique. As a tool, the term refers to a large stone that is usually placed horizontally on the ground and is used as a support for percussion blows to another object resting on it. Since the stone must withstand considerable shock, it should be non-brittle and tough. Igneous and metamorphic rocks and hard sandstone effectively served this purpose in prehistory.

As a technique, anvil refers to a way of producing flakes from a core. However, usage of the term in this sense has either changed somewhat over the years or is employed differently in different parts of the world. In one use of the term, the anvil, or block-on-block, technique consists of hitting the stationary anvil with the core, from which flakes are removed (Oakley 1967:25). In another use of the term, anvil percussion refers to supporting the core on the stationary anvil in such a way that contact with the anvil is not directly in line with the force of impact (Callahan 1987:15). The resulting core exhibits basal crushing, but the flakes are usually not wedgelike, as they often are with bipolar percussion, in which contact with the anvil is directly under the point of impact.

George H. Odell

Further Readings

Callahan, E. 1987. *An Evaluation of the Lithic Technology in Middle Sweden During the Mesolithic and Neolithic.* Aun 8. Societas Archaeologica Upsaliensis, Uppsala.

Oakley, K.P. 1967. *Man the Tool-Maker.* British Museum of Natural History, London.

Anzick Clovis Burial

The Anzick site (24PA506), discovered in 1968, is the first Clovis burial locality found in North

America. The site is in an intermontane basin between the Crazy Mountains on the east and the Belt Mountains on the west in southwestern Montana. Flathead Creek, a tributary of the Shields River, is near the center of the basin. Two construction workers, Ben Hargis and Calvin Sarver, accidentally discovered the Clovis burial site with a rich array of artifacts while excavating talus from a sandstone cliff on the west side of the creek for a Wilsal School construction project. Some of the artifacts were later shared with the landowner, Dr. Melvyn Anzick. Through the efforts of L. Lahren, the collection was reunited in 1989 and is on public display at the Montana Historical Society in Helena.

The site was first reported by D.C. Taylor (1969). Later testing by L. Lahren and R. Bonnichsen (1974) exposed a lens of red ocher and a human bone fragment in the wall profile, but intact deposits had already been removed. The artifact assemblage includes three classes of data: human skeletal remains, bone foreshafts (bone rods), and flaked-stone artifacts. Several human bone fragments from the Anzick burial are from at least two juvenile individuals (Stafford 1994:49). Stafford (1994:52) has dated the human remains recovered from the Anzick cache by the radiocarbon AMS (accelerated mass spectrometry) method. The red-ocher-stained calvarium yielded seven dates that average 8730 B.C. ± 50 (10,680 years B.P.), and the bleached calvarium produced ages that averaged 6660 B.C. ± 90 (8610 years B.P.). The reliability of the calvarium dates is tenuous as there is a possibility that the collagen was degraded.

Eleven bone-tool fragments are from bone foreshafts, bone rods, or both. These specimens are probably made from mammoth bone. This total includes two complete specimens with bi-beveled ends, one specimen with a single bevel and male insertion end (Lahren and Bonnichsen 1974), four beveled ends, and five midsections. Using the end fragments as a standard, a minimum of five and a maximum of seven foreshafts are in the assemblage.

A minimum of eight fluted points are present in the Anzick assemblage. Of this total, six are complete points, one is possibly unfinished, and one is represented only by the tip end. One of the complete points was manufactured from Phosphoria chert from Wyoming. Bifaces comprise the largest class of artifacts (N = 70). Four of these can be refitted and represent two complete bifaces (MNSP = 68). Chalcedony bifaces are the largest representative class of raw materials (N = 39), while moss-agate bifaces (N = 30) and porcellanite (N = 1) account for the remainder. Four artifacts are classified as unifacial tools: two end scrapers and two side scrapers. Flake tools include a single thinning flake resembling a blade and two large spalls exhibiting possible use polish on the margins. Additionally, the assemblage includes 15 bifacial fragments and three thinning flakes. The raw-material data suggest that the flaked-stone artifacts came from at least three separate source areas in Montana and Wyoming.

The rich bounty of gravegoods associated with the Anzick burial is composed primarily of hunting and butchering implements used by mammoth hunters. It is possible that these red-ocher-covered tools indicate that Clovis peoples had a developed religion, and that the artifacts were left as offerings to children who were destined to hunt mammoths in the happy hunting ground.

Robson Bonnichsen
Scott Jones

Further Readings

Lahren, L., and R. Bonnichsen. 1974. Bone Foreshafts From a Clovis Burial in Southwestern Montana. *Science* 186:147–150.

Stafford, T.W., Jr. 1994. Accelerator C-14 Dating of Human Fossil Skeletons: Assessing Accuracy and Results on New World Specimens. In *Method and Theory in the Peopling of the Americas,* edited by R. Bonnichsen and G. Steele, pp. 45–55. Center for the Study of the First Americans, Oregon State University, Corvallis.

Taylor, D.C. 1969. The Wilsa Excavations: An Exercise in Frustration. *Proceedings of the Montana Academy of Science* 29:147–150.

See also CLOVIS CULTURAL COMPLEX

Apex Phase

The Apex phase of the Western Plains Middle Archaic regional variant was defined by William B. Butler (1986) following a reexamination of the cultural sequence at the Magic Mountain site in northeastern Colorado. The phase area extends throughout the Plains of eastern Colorado and probably dates from ca. 2550–810 B.C. (4500–2760 years B.P.), which is during the

Sub-Boreal climatic episode. Associated projectile points include McKean Lanceolate, Duncan, Hanna, and Mallory, although the McKean complex is better known from Wyoming and Montana, where it is synonymous with the Middle Archaic period. These Plains-adapted hunters and gatherers with a focus on bison left many sites in the High Plains.

William B. Butler

Further Readings

Butler, W.B. 1986. *Taxonomy in Northeastern Colorado Prehistory.* Unpublished Ph.D. dissertation, Department of Anthropology, University of Missouri, Columbia.

Irwin-Williams, C., and H.J. Irwin. 1966. *Excavations at Magic Mountain: A Diachronic Study of Plains-Southwest Relationships.* Proceedings no. 12. Denver Museum of Natural History, Denver.

See also MAGIC MOUNTAIN SITE; MCKEAN

Apishapa Phase

The Apishapa phase (A.D. 1000–1400, or 950–550 years B.P.) represents a localized manifestation of the Plains Village pattern in the Arkansas River Valley, and the Park and Chaquaqua plateaus, of southeastern Colorado and northeastern New Mexico. The term "Apishapa" was first assigned to a focus by Arnold M. Withers in 1954. The focus included several stone-circle sites along the Lower Apishapa Canyon, which were first recorded by E.B. Renaud. The artifact assemblage contained cord-marked ceramics with out-curved rims and side-notched projectile points. In the mid-1960s, Robert G. Campbell conducted extensive survey and limited excavations along the Purgatory River and its tributaries on the Chaquaqua in southeastern Colorado. According to Campbell, the Apishapa evolved out of the Graneros focus ca. A.D. 1000 (950 years B.P.), flourished for 300 years, and ended by A.D. 1400 (550 years B.P.). Based on the data available to him, he placed the focus in the Panhandle aspect. Christopher R. Lintz later questioned this placement, although he did recognize a close relationship between Apishapa and the Antelope Creek phase of the Texas Panhandle. In his 1986 revision of the Panhandle taxonomy, Lintz proposed an Upper Canark variant of the Plains Village tradition, which included Antelope Creek and Apishapa. James H. Gunnerson, like Campbell, has theorized that the Apishapa phase developed from the Graneros focus. However, he has proposed a Las Animas tradition for southeastern Colorado. This tradition would include sites, especially small ones, dating from the earlier Graneros through the end of the Apishapa phase but lacking certain diagnostic traits of the Graneros focus, such as stone enclosures, cord-marked ceramics, and small projectile points.

Three basic types of sites have been identified for the Apishapa phase: rock shelters, surface encampments, and stone/slab enclosures. The rock shelters generally occur along wide canyon portions of main streams and tributaries. Surface encampments tend to be in the upper canyons and mesas near sources of potable water. The enclosures may occur in the wide canyons but are more often in upper canyons and mesas, where they are located on isolated points encompassed by stone perimeter walls or barriers. Structures range in size from single room to multiroom enclosures. Although circular rooms are most common, various other shapes are present, including oval, semicircular, and D-shaped. Walls of structures and barriers were constructed of a combination of vertical and horizontal stone slabs incorporated into the natural boulder and outcrop exposures.

Subsistence practices reflect a diverse economy based on hunting, gathering, and limited horticulture. Material culture includes side-notched projectile points plus a variety of scrapers, gravers, choppers, knives, flanged drills, manos, metates, basketry, and cord-marked pottery. Bison-bone horticultural tools and diamond-shaped, beveled knives, common to several other Plains Village groups, are lacking. Burials are generally flexed, single-pit interments that lack associated materials. It has been suggested that the Apishapa had an extremely loose political organization and little or no apparent status differentiation.

Steven L. De Vore

Further Readings

Campbell, R.G. 1976. *The Panhandle Aspect of the Chaquaqua Plateau.* Graduate Studies no. 11. Texas Tech University, Lubbock.

Gunnerson, J.H. 1989. *Apishapa Canyon Archeology: Excavations at the Cramer, Snake Blakeslee and Nearby Sites.* Reprints in Anthropology no. 41. J and L Reprint, Lincoln.

Lintz, C.R. 1978. Panhandle Aspect and Its Early Relationship With Upper Republican. In *The Central Plains Tradition: Internal Development and External Relationships,* edited by D. Blakeslee, pp. 36–55. Report no. 11. Office of the State Archaeologist, University of Iowa, Iowa City.

———. 1986. *Architecture and Community Variability Within the Antelope Creek Phase of the Texas Panhandle.* Studies in Oklahoma's Past no. 14. Oklahoma Archeological Survey, Norman.

Lintz, C., and J.L. Anderson (editors). 1989. *Temporal Assessment of Diagnostic Materials From the Pinon Canyon Maneuver Site.* Memoirs no. 4. Colorado Archaeological Society, Denver.

Renaud, E.D. 1942. *Indian Stone Enclosures of Colorado and New Mexico.* Archaeological Series Paper no. 2. Department of Anthropology, University of Denver, Denver.

Withers, A.M. 1954. University of Denver Archeological Fieldwork. *Southwestern Lore* 19(4):1–3.

See also PLAINS VILLAGE TRADITION; UPPER CANARK REGIONAL VARIANT

Archaeoastronomy

Archaeoastronomy is an interdisciplinary study that blends aspects of archaeology and astronomy to determine the relationships between past human cultures and behavior and astronomical phenomena, such as the position at particular times of the day and year of the sun, moon, and planets. Generally ignored in North American archaeology until the 1960s, archaeoastronomical studies have proliferated as one component of a growing interest in the ideological, or symbolic, realm of precontact native societies. These studies have attempted to gauge the astronomical knowledge of precontact societies, and to determine the role it played within cosmological, religious, agricultural, and other cultural systems, by examining rock art symbols, the orientation and internal arrangement of features, and other possible "astronomical" aspects of the archaeological record. In general, astronomical observations in precontact North America seem to have focused on solar phenomena, in particular the solstices.

Astronomically related elements in the archaeological record are of various types and apparently served a variety of purposes. Some of the most striking and visible are purported astronomical observatories used to trace the seasonal movement of the sun and to mark the solstices. Examples are the stone circles called "medicine wheels" in the western Great Plains, such as Big Horn Medicine Wheel, and large circles of wooden posts called "woodhenges" at Cahokia in the American Bottom. The "henges," which are thought to date to ca. A.D. 1000 (950 years B.P.), range from 73 to 146 m (80–160 yards) in diameter. The greatest known concentration of "horizon markers" occurs, however, in the Anasazi Chaco Canyon area of New Mexico, where they are also thought to date to ca. A.D. 1000 (950 years B.P.). Among these features are apparent sunrise observation stations in pueblos, as at Pueblo Bonito, and winter solstice sunrise-related symbols on the canyon face. Horizon calendars were used by the historic Hopi Indians of Arizona to structure both ritual and agricultural practices. Still other astronomically related elements, such as the positioning of mounds at Mississippian sites like Cahokia and McKeithen in the Eastern Woodlands, may represent the cosmological configuration of a settlement or ritual center. It is likely that knowledge of astronomical regularities played a prominent role in structuring the ideological system and behavior of all precontact North American societies, but not all of these relationships are equally visible in the archaeological record.

Guy Gibbon

Further Readings
Aveni, A.F. 1981. Archaeoastronomy. In *Advances in Archaeological Method and Theory,* vol. 4, pp. 1–77. Academic Press, New York.

———. (editor). 1977. *Native American Astronomy.* University of Texas Press, Austin.

———. (editor). 1988. *World Archaeoastronomy.* Cambridge University Press, New York.

Milanich, J., A.S. Cordell, V.J. Knight, T.A. Kohler, and B.J. Sigler-Lavelle. 1984. *McKeithen Weeden Island: The Culture of Northern Florida* A.D. 200–900. Academic Press, New York.

Wedel, W.R. 1967. The Council Circle of Central Kansas: Were They Solstice Register? *American Antiquity* 32:54–63.

Williamson, R.A. 1984. *Living the Sky.* University of New Mexico Press, Albuquerque.

———. (editor). 1981. *Archaeoastronomy in the Americas.* Ballena Press, Los Altos.

Wittry, W.L. 1977. The American Woodhenge. In *Explorations in Cahokia Archaeology,* edited by M.L. Fowler, pp. 43–48. Bulletin no. 7. Illinois Archaeological Survey, University of Illinois Press, Urbana.

See also Big Horn Medicine Wheel; Medicine Wheels

Archaeological Culture

An archaeological culture can be defined as a grouping of assemblages sharing similar-appearing artifacts and features thought to represent the surviving remains of an extinct culture. A common definition of a culture is the learned behaviors, beliefs, and values generally shared by members of a particular society or group of people, although definitions of culture vary from one school of thought to another in archaeology.

Guy Gibbon

Further Readings

Willey, G.R., and J.A. Sabloff. 1993. *A History of American Archaeology.* 3rd ed. W.H. Freeman, San Francisco.

Trigger, B.G. 1989. *A History of Archaeological Thought.* Cambridge University Press, New York.

Archaeological Region

An archaeological region is a geographical area normally defined by natural geographic features, a heavy concentration of archaeological sites, or the presence of assemblages thought to represent the remains of past human communities that shared a basically similar culture-ecological adaptation. Examples are the Pine Lawn region in the Southwest and the American Bottom in the Eastern Woodlands.

Guy Gibbon

Archaeometallurgy

Archaeometallurgy is the study of the development of physical and extractive metallurgy throughout the world using the techniques of archaeology and archaeometry. Developments in metal technology took place in different ways and at different rates in various parts of the world. In the Old World, the first use of metal occurred ca. 7000 B.C. (8950 years B.P.), and a copper smelting and alloying technology was fully developed by ca. 2000 B.C. (3950 years B.P.). In North America

north of the Rio Grande, indigenous cultures did not smelt, melt, or alloy metals, relying instead on the relative abundance of native copper.

Early metal craftsmen were empiricists and traditionalists with no chemical knowledge as we understand the term. Although hampered by the random nature of archaeological discovery, archaeometallurgists have used a variety of chemical and physical analyses of artifacts, slags, and ores to trace the development of technologies for extracting, smelting, shaping, melting, alloying, casting, and hardening metals. Objects made of lead (which would require smelting) and copper slag occur in the late seventh millennium B.C. in Turkey. Casting in the Near East may go back as far as 4000 B.C. (5950 years B.P.). The problem of the sources of tin for the tin bronzes of the Bronze Age is the primary research problem for this period. The Iron Age (ca. 1000 B.C., or 2950 years B.P.) followed much later because of the much higher melting point of iron. Carbon steel has no specific point or time of origin, as it was on occasion formed as a byproduct of some smelting and forging techniques.

George Rapp, Jr.

Further Readings

Maddin, R. (editor). 1988. *The Beginning of the Use of Metals and Alloys.* MIT Press, Cambridge.

Molloy, P.M. 1986. The History of Metal Mining and Metallurgy: An Annotated Bibliography. Garland, New York.

Tylecote, R.F. 1992. *A History of Metallurgy.* rev. ed. Institute of Materials, Brookfield.

Wertime, T.A., and J.D. Muhly (editors). 1980. *The Coming of the Age of Iron.* Yale University Press, New Haven.

Archaic

A stage, period, or lifeway in North America between supposed big-game-hunting Paleoindians and peoples who had adopted some combination of pottery making, burial-mound construction, and horticulture. First proposed by William A. Ritchie in the early 1930s as an organizing concept for a portion of the Eastern Woodlands, the term was soon appropriated and applied to seemingly analogous archaeological complexes throughout the continent. The definitional basis of the concept varies both within and between culture areas.

Guy Gibbon

Further Readings

Fagan, B.M. 1991. *Ancient North America: The Archaeology of a Continent.* Thames and Hudson, New York.

Jennings, J.D. 1987. *The Prehistory of North America.* 3rd ed. Mayfield, Palo Alto.

Ritchie, W.A. 1932. The Lamoka Lake Site. *Researches and Transactions of the New York State Archaeological Association* 7(4):79–134.

Architecture (California)

A variety of architectural forms and features were produced in prehistoric California. Several forms of dwelling were used, along with several kinds of special-function structures. Subarchitectural features, such as storage pits and rock concentrations, were also common.

Semisubterranean pithouses were the most distinctive form of dwelling in California. Structures typically had round floor plans in which a dome or a cone was built over a shallow pit. Pits generally ranged in diameter from 4 to 8 m (13–26 feet), and in depth from 0.3 to 1 m (1–3.3 feet). Most had ground-level entrances, but some used tunnels, and in central California entry through a hole in the center of the roof was achieved with a ladder. Central California pithouses typically had strong interior support posts with rafters covered by sticks, wicker, and earth to create a domed structure. Elsewhere, coverings of bark, brush, or thatch were more common. Typically, the roof had a hole in its center to let out smoke from the fireplace that sat in the floor's center. Most pithouses served family-sized groups, but in a few areas, such as the northern San Joaquin Valley, long houses large enough to house a lineage were known. In late prehistory along the far northern California coast, the construction of rectangular plank houses replaced round pithouses. In the southern California deserts, brush-covered round wickiups served to house the more nomadic peoples of that region.

The sweat house was another distinctive form. Most common in central and northern California, sweat houses occurred in many medium and large villages. They generally were used for sweat baths and also served as men's gathering places and as secret-society meeting rooms. Sweat houses typically were smaller than dwellings, had round or rectangular plans, and had low roofs. Users would light a fire in the center of the structure to create heat. In many cases, stones heated in the fire were then pulled out so that cold water could be poured over them to create steam. Sweat houses generally lack female-associated artifacts and are surrounded by heaps of ashes and fire-cracked rocks.

The dance house was another distinctive form found most commonly in central and northern California. Dance houses were built like pithouses as semisubterranean structures, but they were much larger, often up to 15–20 m (49.2–65.6 feet) in diameter. Some had a shed-covered entrance that descended down from ground level to the floor in the pit. A central fireplace beneath a smoke hole in the roof also was typical. Dance houses tend to lack domestic artifacts and to possess more ideological or sociological remains. Historically, they are known to have served as gathering places for whole communities or larger groups, such as men's secret societies. In southern California, comparable public structures had a well-compacted floor surrounded by walls of brush and poles but no roof. In many areas, dance houses stood alone, sometimes in the center of the community and sometimes at the margins. In other cases, they were attached to the house of the headman, which was otherwise not significantly different from the houses of other people in the community.

Many houses had storage pits excavated into their floor. California groups also built storage silos above ground, but they are not observed archaeologically due to their perishable nature and lack of distinctive features. Village palisades, known in eastern North America from the Late Woodland period onward, are not known in California, nor are mounded earthworks. The accumulated debris of village life in California, however, frequently evolved into artificial mounds, especially along rivers and the coast, where sedentism was most pronounced. In California, such mounds are village sites rather than burial monuments, temple platforms, or effigy earthworks, as in the East.

In recent years, rock structures in highland areas have been identified in several parts of California. Three-sided mountaintop structures, called a *Tsektsel*, or prayer seat, are known in the western Klamath Mountains. Trailside rock stacks, cairns, or monuments are known from many parts of the state, but especially from the Colorado Desert to the Oregon border. In San Diego County, there are examples of curvilinear rock alignments used as windbreaks for temporary shelter, of rock enclosures containing domestic artifacts that may have been house bases, and of some possible granary bases built on flat rock outcrop surfaces. Late Prehistoric roasting pits are known in several areas. They consist of sizable flat-bottomed pits filled with thick layers of ashes and fire-affected rocks. They occur most commonly in the drier parts of the state and often have food remains, such as yucca, in their middens. Much more ubiquitous are rock features. The term is applied to any concentration of rocks caused by cultural activities. Not often studied systematically, rock features vary greatly in size, shape, density, and contents but are among the most commonly occurring structural forms in California archaeology.

Joseph L. Chartkoff

Further Readings

Carrico, R.L. 1988. Rock Rooms, Stacks and Granary Bases: The Stone Architecture of Westwood Valley. *Proceedings of the Society for California Archaeology* 1:117–124.

Chartkoff, J.L. 1983. A Rock Feature Complex From Northwestern California. *American Antiquity* 48:745–760.

Chartkoff, J.L., and K.K. Chartkoff. 1984. *The Archaeology of California.* Stanford University Press, Stanford.

Moratto, M.J. (editor). 1984. *California Archaeology.* Academic Press, New York.

Oxendine, J. 1981. Rock Enclosures in Southern California. *Journal of California and Great Basin Anthropology* 3(2):232–244.

Arctic Small Tool Tradition

The Arctic Small Tool tradition (ASTt) refers to a distinctive constellation of technological attributes dating to ca. 2550 B.C.–A.D. 950/1450 (4500–1000/500 years B.P.) that characterizes artifact assemblages found throughout the western and the eastern Arctic, from the Alaskan shores of the Bering Strait to the east coast of Greenland. This constellation of attributes commonly, though not exclusively, includes: the very small size of most, if not all, of its associated artifacts; microblades (some exhibiting further retouch) struck from an assortment of prepared microcore forms; a variety of often finely furnished, parallel-sided, stemmed (expanding or contracting), triangular, or notched bifaces (end blades and/or knives); flaked and/or ground burins; burin spalls (occasionally retouched); bifacial and/or unifacial ovate, crescentic, and/or rectangular side blades; various forms of end and side scrapers; and small, ovate, circular, or subrectangular stone lamps (commonly, though not exclusively, made of soapstone). Where the state of organic preservation permits, also present are a range of toggling and nontoggling harpoon-head forms (including tang-based, open-socketed, and closed-socketed types); lance heads; unilateral and bilateral barbed darts, bone, ivory, antler, or wood knife handles; and bone or ivory sewing needles. It is generally conceded that all cultural manifestations from across the Arctic exhibiting a majority subset of these attributes—despite the immense distances and the ca. 3500 to 4000-year time span that may separate them—share a common historical heritage.

The story of the Arctic Small Tool tradition begins with the discovery, in 1948, of the Denbigh Flint complex at the Iyatayet site in the Kotzebue Sound area of northwestern Alaska (Giddings 1951). This artifact complex was characterized by a unique combination of precision flaking and basal thinning of projectile points in association with a burin-core-blade technology. It was unlike anything hitherto known from northwestern Alaska. Between 1951 and 1958, a series of distinctive artifact assemblages was discovered at an array of prehistoric sites distributed across the length and breadth of the North American Arctic coast, from northwestern Alaska to Greenland. These assemblages included the materials from the Punyik Point site in the Brooks Range of Alaska (reported in 1951), the Saqqaq (or Sarqaq) and Sermermuit sites in western Greenland (1952), the various sites associated with the Independence I culture of northeastern Greenland (1954), the Alarnerk site in the eastern Canadian Arctic (1955), the Thyazzi site in northern Manitoba (1956), the Engigstciak site in the northwestern Yukon Territory (1956), and the Dismal II site in the central Barrens (1958). What was truly remarkable about all of these finds was the striking resemblance that each clearly bore to Gidding's Denbigh Flint complex from northwestern Alaska.

The term "Arctic Small Tool tradition" itself was introduced into the Arctic archaeological lexicon in 1957 by William N. Irving to formally acknowledge the striking typological similarities between the Denbigh Flint complex and several recently discovered artifact assemblages from the Brooks Range of north-central

Alaska. The ASTt label was used, at least initially, to differentiate the presumably related north Alaskan Denbigh Flint Brooks Range assemblages from the distinctively different western Subarctic microlithic technologies; that is, the assemblages from the Campus and Pointed Mountain sites, associated with the Boreal Forest areas of central and southern Alaska and the Yukon Territory.

This geographically constrained definition of the Arctic Small Tool tradition was subsequently expanded in 1959 by Richard S. MacNeish and again in 1962 by Irving to incorporate all those assemblages from across the North American Arctic and Greenland that contained microblades struck from conical cores; burins with extensive retouch on one or both faces; retouched burin spalls; very small, bifacially retouched inset side blades; bifacial points and knives without stems or notches; a scarcity or absence of ground or polished implements; an absence of pottery; and a unique style and technique of lithic workmanship. Subsumed under this expanded definition of the ASTt were those components associated with the Proto-Denbigh, Classic Denbigh, and Late Denbigh divisions of the western Arctic Denbigh Flint complex and the eastern Arctic Independence I, Pre-Dorset, and Saqqaq cultures (Maxwell 1984, 1985). All such local manifestations of the Arctic Small Tool tradition were assumed to be historically related and to have ultimately shared a common ancestor either in Alaska or farther to the west in northeastern Asia (Maxwell 1984, 1985).

Continued field research in both the western and the eastern Arctic quickly revealed discrepancies in the implicitly mutually exclusive list of diagnostic attributes used to define membership in the ASTt. In the western Arctic, for example, ceramics were found in possible association with some Denbigh Flint–complex components. In the eastern Arctic, ASTt assemblages lacking retouched burin spalls or, conversely, containing bifaces and/or burins with polished faces, among other inconsistencies, were encountered. Furthermore, in both the western and the eastern Arctic, assemblages containing well-preserved organic artifacts included traits, such as lance heads, harpoon heads, and needles, that were not part of the expanded list of diagnostic ASTt attributes. In each such instance, the criteria for inclusion into the Arctic Small Tool tradition was informally altered to accommodate these newly discovered exceptions and/or additions.

Developments in eastern Arctic prehistory during the late 1960s and early 1970s prompted an even more drastic shift in the definition and usage of the term. This shift was predicated on the presentation of convincing evidence that the eastern Arctic Dorset culture was a direct descendant of the ASTt Pre-Dorset culture (Taylor 1968; Maxwell 1973). It was clearly demonstrated that a majority of the diagnostic attributes of Dorset culture—including microblades struck from conical and/or polyhedral cores; burins shaped by grinding and polishing rather than spalling; small, bifacially retouched inset side blades; stemmed and notched bifacial points and knives; a unique style and technique of lithic workmanship; and a wide variety of organic tools (including lance heads, harpoon heads, and needles)—had clear typological homologues in the preceding Pre-Dorset culture. Recognition of this historical relationship ultimately led to the incorporation of the Dorset culture into the Arctic Small Tool tradition (Schledermann 1976). It soon became a common, though largely informal, practice to group the Independence I, Saqqaq, and Pre-Dorset cultures together under the heading of the early Arctic Small Tool tradition and to refer to the Dorset culture as belonging to the late Arctic Small Tool tradition (Helmer 1994). The terms "early Paleoeskimo" and "late Paleoeskimo" have also been used to distinguish between the early and late manifestations of the ASTt in the eastern Arctic (Helmer 1994).

In the western Arctic, a close analogue to the eastern Arctic Dorset culture exists in the form of the Norton tradition. There is growing uncertainty, however, over the historical relationship between this latter cultural phenomenon and the local Arctic Small Tool tradition (Dumond 1987). Although classification of the Norton tradition as the western Arctic manifestation of the late Arctic Small Tool tradition was once at least implicitly well accepted (Giddings 1967), current opinion appears to favor the position that little or no significant cultural continuity links the early Arctic Small Tool tradition with later cultural developments to the west (Dumond 1987).

The Arctic Small Tool tradition is widely believed to have emerged as a recognizable technological tradition in the Bering Strait region of the western Arctic ca. 2550–2150 B.C. (4500–4100 years B.P.). The ASTt is thought to have subsequently spread eastward to northeastern Greenland in a rapid and far-reaching movement of people. Current radiocarbon estimates for the initial appearance of the ASTt, however, are not entirely consistent with this interpretation (Maxwell 1984, 1985).

The first appearance of the Denbigh Flint complex at the Iyatayet site was initially placed at ca. A.D. 1150 (800 years B.P.) (Giddings 1951). This estimate, however, was based on the results of a single, problematic radiometric assay and is no longer considered valid (Anderson 1984; Dumond 1987). Other dates for the Denbigh Flint complex component at the Iyatayet site all postdate ca. 2000 B.C. (3950 years B.P.). The earliest date for what has been identified as a Proto-Denbigh Flint–complex component at the Onion Portage site in western Alaska is ca. 2200 B.C. (4150 years B.P.) (Anderson 1984). This date, however, was obtained on a sample recovered from a layer situated stratigraphically above a stratum at the same site that yielded a date of ca. 1750 B.C. (3700 years B.P.). Elsewhere in the western Arctic, most Denbigh Flint–complex assemblages have been radiometrically dated to ca. 1750–1050 B.C. (3700–3000 years B.P.).

Numerous ASTt sites from northeast Greenland, the Canadian High Arctic, and the eastern central Canadian Arctic in the eastern Arctic have yielded reliable dates several centuries older than the oldest currently accepted dates for the ASTt in the western Arctic. McGhee (1983) has suggested that a logical case can perhaps be made to place the initial New World appearance of the ASTt in the eastern High Arctic. From this perspective, the western Arctic Denbigh Flint complex would be considered a product of a rapid westward spread of peoples from the eastern Arctic (McGhee 1983). The current consensus, however, is that a western origin of the ASTt is more likely and that earlier ASTt occupations will ultimately be found in Alaska.

The ASTt in the western Arctic is known to span the interval from ca. 2200 to 1050 B.C. (4150 to 3000 years B.P.). Three informal temporal subdivisions of the Denbigh Flint complex are recognized. These include the Proto-Denbigh complex, the Classic Denbigh Flint complex, and the Late Denbigh Flint complex (Anderson 1984). ASTt occupation in the western Arctic ends ca. 1550 B.C. (3500 years B.P.) (in north Alaska) and 1050 B.C. (3000 years B.P.) (in southwestern Alaska) and is followed, in most parts of coastal Alaska, by an occupational hiatus of varying duration (Dumond 1987). It remains uncertain how and in what way the Arctic Small Tool tradition contributed to later cultural developments in the western Arctic.

In the eastern Arctic, the early stage of the ASTt dates to ca. 2550–1050 B.C. (4500–3000 years B.P.). Significant typological changes in the eastern Arctic variant of the ASTt begin to occur ca. 1050 B.C. (3000 years B.P.). These changes mark an in situ transition between the Pre-Dorset and Dorset stages of the Arctic Small Tool tradition. Fully recognizable Dorset culture appears in several areas of the eastern Arctic at ca. 550 B.C. (2500 years B.P.). The ASTt occupation of the eastern Arctic as a whole persists until ca. A.D. 950–1450 (1000–500 years B.P.) at which time the ASTt is displaced, replaced, or assimilated (the ultimate fate of the ASTt in the eastern Arctic remains unknown) by the bearers of the Thule culture (the immediate ancestors of the historic Inuit), who began arriving in the eastern Arctic ca. A.D. 950–1150 (1000–800 years B.P.). The latest dates in the eastern Arctic follow what appears to be a clinal distribution from north to south. In the Far North (i.e., the High Arctic Archipelago), the ASTt is thought to have ended ca. A.D. 950 (1000 years B.P.). Farther to the south, in northern Quebec and perhaps northern Labrador, elements of the ASTt may have persisted until as recently as ca. A.D. 1450 (500 years B.P.).

The ultimate origins of the Arctic Small Tool tradition remain obscure. Wherever Arctic Small Tool–tradition components are found in the western Arctic, they constitute a sharp break in the cultural continuity of occupation. In most instances, the ASTt replaces complexes belonging to the culturally and technologically unrelated Northern Archaic tradition. In most parts of the eastern Arctic, the ASTt constitutes the first human occupation of the area. The one exception to this pattern is in the central Barren Grounds of the Canadian Arctic, where the Arctic Small Tool tradition replaces the historically unrelated Shield Archaic tradition.

There has been some speculation (Dumond 1987) that the Arctic Small Tool tradition may be related to the late Pleistocene/early Holocene American Paleoarctic tradition (ca. 8050–4050 B.C., or 10,000–6000 years B.P.), which in turn has been linked by some to the northeast Asian Dyuktai culture. The ASTt and American Paleoarctic tradition do share a number of technological attributes, although the American Paleoarctic tradition is much older than the ASTt. An in situ continuity (technological or occupational) between the two complexes cannot be demonstrated anywhere in Alaska.

Other scholars (Dumond 1987) have pointed to the striking parallels that exist among the ASTt, the Siberian Neolithic Bel'Kachinsk culture, and the newly defined Kamchatka Neolithic. Dumond (1987) suggests that the Dyuktai culture, the American Paleoarctic, the Bel'Kachinsk culture, the Kamchatka Neolithic, and the Arctic Small Tool tradition may all be part of a complex and interrelated developmental sequence that occurred on both sides of the Bering Strait. Many questions clearly remain to be answered about this significant episode in the prehistory of the North American Arctic.

James W. Helmer

Further Readings

Anderson, D. 1984. Prehistory of North Alaska. In *Arctic*, edited by D. Damas, pp. 80–93. Handbook of North American Indians, vol. 5, W.C. Sturtevant, general editor. Smithsonian Institution, Washington, D.C.

Dumond, D.E. 1987. *The Eskimos and Aleuts.* 2nd ed. Thames and Hudson, New York.

Giddings, J.L. 1951. The Denbigh Flint Complex. *American Antiquity* 16:193–203.

Giddings, L.J. 1967. *Ancient Men of the Arctic.* Knopf, New York.

Helmer, J.W. 1994. Resurrecting the Spirit(s) of Taylor's Carlsberg Culture: Cultural Traditions and Cultural Horizons in Eastern Arctic Prehistory. In *Threads of Arctic Prehistory: Papers in Honour of William E. Taylor Jr.*, edited by D. Morrison and J.L. Pilon, pp. 15–34. Mercury Series Paper no. 149. Archaeological Survey of Canada, Canadian Museum of Civilization, Ottawa.

Irving, W.N. 1957. An Archaeological Survey of the Susitna Valley. *Anthropological Papers of the University of Alaska* 6(1):37–52.

———. 1962. A Provisional Comparison of Some Alaskan and Asian Stone Industries. In *Prehistoric and Cultural Relations Between the Arctic and Temperate Zones of North America*, edited by J. Campbell, pp. 55–68. Technical Paper no. 11. Arctic Institute of North America, Montreal.

MacNeish, R.S. 1959. A Speculative Framework of Northern North American Prehistory as of April, 1959. *Anthropologia* 1:1–17.

Maxwell, M.S. 1973. *Archaeology of the Lake Harbor District, Baffin Island, Canada.* Mercury Series Paper no. 6. Archaeological Survey of Canada, National Museum of Man, Ottawa.

———. 1984. Pre-Dorset and Dorset Prehistory of Canada. In *Arctic*, edited by D. Damas, pp. 359–368. Handbook of North American Indians, vol. 5, W.C. Sturtevant, general editor. Smithsonian Institution, Washington, D.C.

———. 1985. *Prehistory of the Eastern Arctic.* Academic Press, New York.

McGhee, R. 1983. Eastern Arctic Prehistory: The Reality of a Myth? *Muskox* 33:21–25.

Schledermann, P. 1976. History of Human Occupation. In *The Land That Never Melts: Auyuittyq National Park*, edited by R.Wilson, pp. 63–93. Peter Martin Associates, Ottawa.

Taylor, W.E., Jr. 1968. *The Arnapik and Tyara Sites: An Archaeological Study of Dorset Culture Origins.* Memoir no. 22. Society for American Archaeology, Washington, D.C.

Arctic Woodland Culture

Arctic Woodland culture is the name given by J.L. Giddings (1952) to a 700-year-long archaeological sequence in the Kobuk River Valley in northwestern Alaska. The sequence has four phases: Ahteut (ca. A.D. 1250, or 700 years B.P.), Ekseavik and Old Kotzebue (ca. A.D. 1400, or 550 years B.P.), Intermediate Kotzebue (ca. A.D. 1550, or 400 years B.P.), and Ambler Island (ca. A.D. 1730–1760, or 220–190 years B.P.). Since the culture was first defined in 1952, numerous Arctic Woodland sites have been found in the region. They date between ca. A.D. 1000 (950 years B.P.) and the historic period. Each phase is characterized by distinctive styles in antler and ivory weapon parts, pottery, fishing equipment, and house forms and the use of particular raw materials, like chert, jade, and ground slate.

The name of the culture refers to the peoples' adaptation to a forested region of the Arctic. Although the region is located above the Arctic Circle, dense stands of white and black spruce are present throughout the Kobuk River Valley and its major tributaries. Stands of birch and alder cover the surrounding hills. The faunal resources include both tundra species, like caribou and willow ptarmigan, and taiga species, like black bear and spruce prouse. Resident fish, like shee and whitefish, and anadromous fish, like salmon and (in the lower reaches) smelt, are also present. Sheep can be found in the nearby mountains, and seals and beluga at the mouth of the river, which empties into Kotzebue Sound. This multiple resource base is represented in most of the sites of the culture, both by faunal remains and by the implements used to harvest them. Stylistically, most of the artifacts relate to forms from coastal Eskimo cultures: toggle harpoon heads, stone and pottery lamps, pottery vessels, leister prongs, and slate knife and ulu blades. Other artifacts have links to Athapaskan culture: boulder chip scrapers known as *tci thos* and birchbark baskets.

The essential features of the culture are described in the concluding paragraph in Giddings's 1952 monograph, *The Arctic Woodland Culture of the Kobuk River:* "The Arctic Woodland Culture appears to be more than a phenomenon resulting from the meeting of two distinct forms of culture [Eskimo and Athapaskan]. It is, rather, the predictable combination of sea-river-and-forest-hunting wherever it is possible for a single ethnic group to practice these together under the special conditions of the Arctic. It is a material culture that will be practiced by whatever linguistic group happens to live in the particular environment, a culture that will outlive the physical appearance, the speech, and many of the social practices of its participants." Perhaps the most significant aspect of the Arctic Woodland construct is an approach that stresses the adaptational and regional aspects of archaeological cultures: by implication, an archaeological culture could look very different, depending on the activities carried out not only at the reference site but also at other sites in the annual round.

Douglas D. Anderson

Further Readings

Giddings, J.L. 1952. *The Arctic Woodland Culture of the Kobuk River.* University Museum, University of Pennsylvania, Philadelphia.

Arkansas Phase

The Arkansas phase of the Colorado Plains Woodland regional variant in the western Plains subarea of the Plains Woodland pattern was proposed as a provisional taxon by William B. Butler (1986, 1988). Its purpose was to reconcile the Woodland taxonomy proposed for the northeastern part of the state (i.e., the South Platte phase) with the Parker and Graneros foci of Arnold M. Withers (1954) and with three taxa proposed by Robert G. Campbell (1969) for the southeastern part. Butler found that Withers's Parker and Graneros foci were invalid constructs; Campbell's taxa were based on Withers and were thus also questioned. Campbell recognized an Archaic-Woodland transitional period (ca. A.D. 200–450, or 1750–1500 years B.P.), during which time ceramics and the bow and arrow were introduced along with cultural materials approximating those of the Parker focus. His Initial Woodland horizon (ca. A.D. 450–750, or 1500–1200 years B.P.) was seen as a local manifestation of the Graneros focus, but with above-ground architecture consisting of oval or subrectangular rooms made of rock slabs dry-laid in horizontal courses. Campbell's Terminal Woodland horizon (ca. A.D. 750–1000, or 1200–950 years B.P.) was considered similar to the preceding horizon.

The Colorado Plains Woodland peoples represented by the Arkansas phase were primarily hunters and gatherers who adopted maize horticulture between A.D. 450 and 750 (1500–1200 years B.P.). Their material culture is similar to that of the South Platte phase, in which small corner-notched arrow and dart points, small triangular side-notched and tri-notched arrow points, cord-marked ceramics with straight to slightly inverted rims and a conoidal base, and expanding-base drills are presently recognized as definitive cultural markers. However, unlike the South Platte phase, Arkansas-phase sites may include substantial above-ground, rock-walled architectural structures. The phase's closest cultural affiliation may be with the Caddoan area of the Texas and Oklahoma panhandles rather than with the greater Southwest, northern Colorado, or the central Plains. A major problem is demonstrating differences between the Woodland peoples of the Arkansas phase and the subsequent (and poorly understood) Apishapa phase (focus) of Withers and the Antelope Creek phase of the Upper Canark regional variant of Christopher R. Lintz (1986) in the Texas Panhandle. The Arkansas phase occupied the western Plains of southeastern Colorado, and probably northeastern New Mexico, and western Kansas and Oklahoma. It spanned the late third of the Sub-Boreal, the Scandic, and Neo-Atlantic times, ca. A.D. 100–1150 (1850–800 years B.P.).

William B. Butler

Further Readings

Butler, W.B. 1986. *Taxonomy in Northeastern Colorado Prehistory.* Unpublished Ph.D. dissertation, Department of Anthropology, University of Missouri, Columbia.

———. 1988. The Woodland Period in Northeastern Colorado. *Plains Anthropologist* 33(122):449–466.

Campbell, R.G. 1969. *Prehistoric Panhandle Culture on the Chaquaqua Plateau, Southeast Colorado.* Unpublished Ph.D. dissertation, Department of Anthropology, University of Colorado, Boulder.

———. 1976. *The Panhandle Aspect of the Chaquaqua Plateau.* Graduate Studies no. 11. Texas Tech University, Lubbock.

Lintz, C.R. 1986. *Architecture and Community Variability Within the Antelope Creek Phase of the Texas Panhandle.* Studies in Oklahoma's Past no. 14. Oklahoma Archeological Survey, Norman.

Withers, A.M. 1954. Reports of Archaeological Fieldwork in Colorado, Wyoming, New Mexico, Arizona and Utah in 1952 and 1953: University of Denver Archaeological Field Work. *Southwestern Lore* 19(4):1–3.

See also SOUTH PLATTE PHASE

Arrow Lakes/Slocan Valley Sequence

The Arrow Lakes/Slocan Valley area lies in the north-central portion of the Plateau culture area in a mountainous region of the west Kootenays of southeastern British Columbia. Although drained by the Columbia River, the region is distinct from the Canadian and Columbia plateaus in the higher rainfall of its heavily forested mountainous terrain. Historically, the area was occupied by the Interior Salish-speaking Lakes Indians. The first archaeological sequence for this region was developed from excavations in the late 1960s at several pithouse locations on Lower Arrow Lake and at the stratified Slocan Junction site. Later work at the Lower Slocan Valley's Vallican site led to the expanded and modified sequence presented below.

Deer Park Phase (1300–450 B.C., or 3250–2400 years B.P.). The Deer Park phase is characterized by stemmed projectile points, some medium to large corner-notched points, large side-notched eared points, cone-shaped pestles, nephrite celts, and utilized flakes. Although rare, microblades form a distinctive, additional part of the assemblage. Housepits are associated with the phase, and, from the size of these and of the settlements themselves, archaeologists have inferred that the population of the area at this time was comparatively high.

Vallican Phase (450 B.C.–A.D. 650, or 2400–1300 years B.P.). Many Deer Park–phase categories, such as the simple flake tools, continue in use in the Vallican phase. The main point forms are corner or basally notched; other distinctive stone artifacts include key-shaped or crescentic chalcedony scrapers or perforators and carefully fashioned end scrapers. Faunal remains, which are rare, include the shells of freshwater mussels and the bones of large mammals that are, most likely, ungulates. There is one housepit identified with this phase: a rimless saucer-shaped depression 7 m (23 feet) in diameter. In its characteristic scraper, perforator, and point forms, the Vallican phase closely resembles the Takumakst period of Kettle Falls in Washington, in British Columbia the South Okanagan Valley's Chiliwist phase, and the Thompson phase of the Thompson River Valley.

Slocan Phase (A.D. 650–1800, or 1300–150 years B.P.). Among the main characteristics of the Slocan phase are small side-notched points, the occasional Columbia corner-notched point, and some items of ground stone. Most lithic detritus is of Purcell siliceous siltstone (argillite), although gravers and scrapers are mainly of chalcedony. Some housepits have side entrances, while shallow rectangular depressions are likely the remains of mat lodges. Other features include distinctive hillside roasting platforms and cachepits, and hearths situated outside the dwellings. Burials are flexed and in pit graves. Faunal remains include bones of freshwater fish, salmon, and various-sized mammals. Mussel shells are common throughout, but two subphases have been suggested, with the later one (after A.D. 1450, or 500 years B.P.) distinguished by a noticeable increase in the amount of mussel shell and by the prevalence of small, thin, side-notched, flaked-stone point varieties.

The Arrow Lakes region occupies a unique and, in many respects, intermediate position between the Canadian and Columbia plateaus. The similarity of Arrow Lakes and Kettle Falls material culture suggests that Arrow Lakes formed the northern periphery of the Columbia Plateau subdivision of the Plateau culture area. Their differences may reflect seasonal variation in a settlement pattern of winter habitation in

A

the Arrow Lakes area and movement to the Columbia River in the summer and early fall for salmon fishing. An alternate model proposes that the Lakes people moved north in Late Prehistoric times from the Columbia River after separating from the linguistically related Colville people.

Donald H. Mitchell
David L. Pokotylo

Further Readings

Turnbull, C.J. 1977. *Archaeology and Ethnohistory in the Arrow Lakes, Southeastern British Columbia.* Mercury Series Paper no. 66. Archaeological Survey of Canada, National Museum of Man, Ottawa.

Arzberger Site

Arzberger (39HU6) is a famous Late Prehistoric village site located on a 40-m (130-foot) -high, isolated, east-bank Missouri River paleoterrace remnant 13 km (8 miles) southeast of Pierre, South Dakota. The village was surrounded by an elliptical ditch and stockade that were almost 1.6 km (1 mile) in circumference. The stockade, which had 24 bastions, enclosed 18 ha (44 acres) and 44 houses. Arzberger is the type site of the Initial Coalescent, a Late Prehistoric (A.D. 1200–A.D. 1350/1400, or 750–600/550 years B.P.) South Dakota manifestation possessing a majority of Central Plains–tradition traits. The fortifications reflect the fact that these invaders were under military pressure from Middle Missouri–tradition peoples during the 1200s and 1300s, which is graphically illustrated by the nearly 500 mutilated massacre victims at the Crow Creek site. Based on ceramic seriation, Arzberger is late in the sequence of Initial Coalescent sites and may have been the last bastion of the Initial Coalescent variant before final defeat and expulsion by peoples of the Extended Middle Missouri variant, Thomas Riggs phase.

Excavations under the direction of William Duncan Strong and Albert C. Spaulding of Columbia University were conducted at the site in 1939. Four houses were excavated and the fortification ditch (including one bastion) was tested. The resulting report by Spaulding, which was published in 1956, is a landmark archaeological synthesis. The site was later extensively damaged by gravel-taking operations. Both Arzberger and Crow Creek were designated National Historic Landmarks on October 15, 1966.

John Ludwickson

Further Readings

Spaulding, A.C. 1956. *The Arzberger Site, Hughes County, South Dakota.* Occasional Contributions no. 16. Museum of Anthropology, University of Michigan, Ann Arbor.
Steinacher, T.L., and D.L. Toom. 1984. Archeological Investigations at the Whistling Elk Site (39HU242), 1978–1979. *University of Nebraska Department of Anthropology Technical Report 83–04,* vol. 2, Appendix 1. U.S. Army Corps of Engineers, Omaha.

See also INITIAL COALESCENT (CAMPBELL CREEK AND/OR ARZBERGER PHASE)

Ash Hollow Cave

Ash Hollow, a well-known Oregon Trail pass through the rim of the North Platte Valley of western Nebraska, is also the location of an important archaeological site (25GD2). In 1939, local artifact collectors reported stratified archaeological deposits in a rock shelter overlooking Ash Hollow. Asa T. Hill, Nebraska State Historical Society Archaeological Survey director, recognized the importance of the site for developing a regional stratigraphic sequence and organized a major excavation. Excavations discovered sealed stratified deposits to a depth of more than 1.8 m (6 feet). Lens A contained early eighteenth-century Dismal River–phase materials; and Lens B, materials attributed to Central Plains–tradition hunters. Both Central Plains–tradition and Plains Woodland–tradition people occupied the shelter during the period of Lens C deposition, which is dated to A.D. 1250–1350 (700–600 years B.P.). The Woodland occupation is probably a component of the northeast Colorado South Platte phase, which was defined in the 1980s. A stratigraphically earlier expression of the South Platte phase was found in Lens D. Lenses E, F, and G did not contain diagnostic artifacts, but the materials are most likely associated with late Plains Archaic hunter-gatherers.

The Ash Hollow investigation and recovered materials are fully reported in a 1945 Columbia University Ph.D. dissertation by John Leland Champe. His revised manuscript, which includes dendrochronological research by Harry Weakly, was published a year later as *Ash Hollow Cave: A Study of Stratigraphic Sequence in the Central Great Plains* in the University of

Nebraska Studies series. The result was a pioneering and time-honored assessment of the stratigraphic sequence of middle and Late Prehistoric archaeological complexes in the Central Plains. The importance of Ash Hollow Cave was reaffirmed when the Nebraska Game and Parks Commission acquired the site in 1967 and developed it as a state historical park. The park features a museum and a preserved stratigraphic section of cave deposits. Ash Hollow Cave was designated a National Historic Landmark in 1966 and is one of the premier archaeological attractions of western Nebraska.

John R. Bozell
John Ludwickson

Further Readings

Champe, J.L. 1976. *Ash Hollow Cave: A Study of Stratigraphic Sequence in the Central Great Plains.* Reprints in Anthropology no. 3. J and L Reprint, Lincoln. Originally published 1946, University of Nebraska Studies, n.s., no. 1. University of Nebraska, Lincoln.

See also CENTRAL PLAINS TRADITION

Atlatl

The term "atlatl" is derived from a Nahuatl Indian word for a stick or board used for throwing spears or darts. It was employed aboriginally in almost all regions of the world and, in the Magdalenian culture of Europe, dates to at least 13,050 B.C. (15,000 B.P.). In the New World, a specimen dating to the early Holocene has been discovered at Lake Winnemucca, Nevada, and several others have been recovered, predominantly from caves and rock shelters in the Great Basin, the Southwest, Baja California, and even the Ozarks. Although the atlatl was gradually replaced by the bow and arrow, its use persisted in several locales, frequently along with the bow and arrow. For example, it was encountered by Cortez among the Aztecs, by Pizarro among the Inca, and by De Soto among southeastern North American tribes. Several accounts attest to its accuracy and effectiveness in battle.

Operationally, the spear thrower can be thought of as being composed of two parts: a handle and a mechanism for articulation with the dart. The handle may be carved or may possess one or two loops through which the hand or two fingers are inserted. Articulation with the dart occurs at the end opposite the

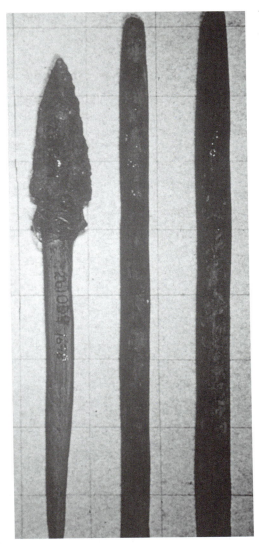

Atlatl dart foreshafts from Tularosa Cave, New Mexico. The background is ruled in one-inch squares. (Courtesy of the Wilford Archaeology Laboratory, University of Minnesota)

handle and is effected by a "male" or a "female" member or a combination of both. The "male"-type dart thrower contains a projecting part—usually a spur or a hook—that is inserted in a concavity in the nether end of the dart shaft. This projection can be attached to the throwing board or carved in whatever medium the board is made (usually wood). The "female" type possesses an indentation at its contact with the dart, while the male-female combination contains both a concavity and a small protuberance at this juncture.

The principal advantage of an atlatl is an increase in both the length of the lever arm and the amount of time the throwing board makes contact with the weapon, thus affording more thrust to the dart. Experimenters have recorded throws of more than 100 m (328 feet); more significant, they have noted substantial increases in distance over their own performances with thrusting spears. Accuracy is more difficult to quantify, but experimenters have noted considerable improvement with practice.

George H. Odell

Further Readings

Dickson, D.B. 1985. The Atlatl Assessed: A Review of Recent Anthropological Approaches to Prehistoric North American Weaponry. *Bulletin of the Texas Anthropological Society* 56:1–38.

Grant, C. 1979. The Spear-Thrower From 15,000 Years Ago to the Present. *Pacific Coast Archaeological Society Quarterly* 15:1–17.

Hester, T.R., M.P. Mildner, and L. Spencer. 1974. *Great Basin Atlatl Studies.* Ballena Press, Ramona, Calif.

Howard, C.D. 1974. The Atl-Atl: Function and Performance. *American Antiquity* 39:102–104.

Kellar, J.H. 1955. The Atlatl in North America. *Prehistory Research Series of the Indiana Historical Society* 3:281–352.

Atwater, Caleb (1778–1867)

Postmaster at Circleville, Ohio, in the early nineteenth century, Caleb Atwater studied and drew plans of many of the earthen mounds of his hometown and the surrounding region. He attributed the mounds to peoples from "Hindostan" who had migrated from India and later moved on to Mexico. Atwater worked during a period in which archaeological data and theory were rudimentary, and his conclusions were eventually proven incorrect and considered speculative. Atwater's work provided the best plans and descriptions of Ohio mounds at the time; today they serve as a useful source of information, for many of the mounds were later destroyed. One of the most important figures of this period of North American archaeology, he has been called the "first true archaeologist" by P. Mitra in his *A History of American Anthropology* (1933:99).

Guy Gibbon

Further Readings

Atwater, C. 1820. Description of the Antiquities Discovered in the State of Ohio and Other Western States. *Transactions and Collections of the American Antiquity Society* 1:105–267.

Mitra, P. 1933. *A History of American Anthropology.* Calcutta University Press, Calcutta.

Silverberg, R. 1968. *Mound Builders of Ancient America: The Archaeology of a Myth.* New York Graphic Society, Greenwich.

See also MOUND BUILDER MYTH

Aucilla River Sites

Since the mid-1980s, an underwater investigation of inundated archaeological and paleontological sites has been conducted in the Aucilla River Basin in North Florida. Statewide, the most important Paleoindian finds have occurred in karstified rivers where chert outcrops protrude from the limestone channels and spring vents connect the surface with the cavernous labyrinth that holds the subterranean Floridan Aquifer. Surface collections provide evidence of a substantial Paleoindian occupation, including sites such as a *Bison antiquus* kill in the Wacissa River. Clovis, Suwannee, and Simpson projectile points, as well as the largest collection of carved ivory foreshafts from the Americas, have been recovered from the Aucilla River. The effort to determine the scientific potential of karst river sites began with a survey in the Wacissa River and became more ambitious when the focus shifted downstream into the Aucilla River. Other surveys were also conducted offshore of the river, in Apalachee Bay. A total of 45 underwater sites range in elevation from ca. 1 m (3.3 feet) above sea level in the Wacissa River to ca. 10–12 m (32.8–39.4 feet) below sea level in sinkholes of the Aucilla River and at Ray Hole Spring, a site 32 km (20 miles) offshore. Shallow sites, particularly those in the Wacissa River, yield evidence of past subaerial exposure, while deeper sites yield evidence of damp or saturated environmental history. Charcoal, organic samples (including seeds for AMS dating), and, less frequently, bone samples from mid-river sinkholes have yielded 27 radiocarbon dates from in situ levels ranging from 32,690 ± 800 B.P. at the Simpson-Latvis site to 8905 ± 65 B.P. at the Page-Ladson site. In the search for intact Paleoindian components, three

Aucilla River sites have been the subject of small test excavations, and a fourth, the Page-Ladson site, the subject of larger, formal excavation. Two of these sites have produced artifacts and megafauna remains from in situ, contemporary levels.

The sediment sequence at the Page-Ladson site includes five zones that make up a column more than 7 m (23 feet) thick. The upper Zones A and B are middle and late Holocene fluvial deposits composed of levels of clastics interspersed with levels of organics and silt. Zone C occupies an early Holocene position in the column and represents the uppermost zone unaffected by mid- and late Holocene fluvial erosion. Zone C has Late Paleoindian to transitional and Early Archaic, Bolen (notched-point), and Kirk (notched- and stemmed-point) components. The in situ Bolen component is inundated 5 m (3.3 feet) below the river's modern low stage. The uplands adjacent to the river's modern margin also served as an occupation site during the notched-point phase. Sediment accumulation in Zone C is dominated by calcareous clays, peats, and organic soils and contrasts, with the upland sandy soils that are without organic preservation. Radiocarbon dates from Zone C range from 8330 B.C. ± 110 to 6955 B.C. ± 65 (10,280–8905 years B.P.), although the best evidence of human activity dates to Bolen times, ca. 8050–7550 B.C. (10,000–9500 years B.P.). Evidence of Paleoindian activity at the site is less substantial but occurs in Zone D.

Zone D has yielded radiocarbon dates between 11,180 B.C. ± 200 and 8570 B.C. ± 130 (13,130–10,520 years B.P.) Lithic debitage and a tusk having a set of cut marks have been recovered with the remains of extinct animal species, including *Mammut americanum*, *Equus* sp., and *Bison antiquus*, in a matrix of quartz and calcium carbonate sand containing abundant fragmentary vegetation. Samples from this matrix proved to contain proboscidean steroids and, in one sample, an epithelial cell of proboscidean (*Mammuthus* and/or *Mammut*), providing evidence that an important part of Zone D contains partially preserved digesta. A working hypothesis is that the Page-Larson site served as an occasional kill and butcher locality centered around a waterhole during Paleoindian times. This assumption is supported by the assemblage of surface-collected and in situ artifacts. There is one, and potentially a second, artifact-bearing level in Zone D. The uppermost, which produced the debitage and cut-marked tusk, dates

to ca. 10,350 B.C. (12,300 years B.P.). Compared to the notched-point phase, Zone D appears to have developed during a time when the water levels in the sinkhole were several meters (6–7 feet) lower and the bowl-shaped sinkhole bottom was accessed by large animals.

Zone E predates evidence for human involvement at the site and represents a time of swamp-forest development. Zone E has yielded a radiocarbon date of 16,480 B.C. ± 220 (18,430 years B.P.), which is about the time of the glacial maximum. Wood samples from this zone show signs of stressed growth and may indicate the driest phase of site development.

James S. Dunbar

Further Readings

Alexon, R.C. 1988. Gingery Cache (8Ta99): A Cache of Possible Paleolithic Tools Found With Mastodon Bones. *Florida Anthropologists* 41(4):483–485.

Anuskiewicz, R.J. 1988. Preliminary Archaeological Investigation at the Ray Hole Spring in the Eastern Gulf of Mexico. *Florida Anthropologists* 41(1):181–185.

Dunbar, J.S. 1991. Resource Orientation of Clovis and Suwannee Age Paleoindian Sites in Florida. In *Clovis: Origins and Adaptations*, edited by R. Bonnichsen and K.L. Turnmire, pp. 185–213. Center for the Study of the First Americans, Oregon State University, Corvallis.

Dunbar, J.S., S.D. Webb, and D. Cring. 1989. Culturally and Naturally Modified Bones From a Paleoindian Site in the Aucilla River, North Florida. In *Bone Modification*, edited by R. Bonnichsen and M.H. Sorg, pp. 473–497. Center for the Study of the First Americans, Institute for Quaternary Studies, University of Maine, Orono.

Dunbar, J.S., S.D. Webb, and M. Faught. 1991. Inundated Prehistoric Sites in Apalachee Bay, Florida, and the Search for the Clovis Shoreline. In *Paleoshorelines and Prehistory*, edited by L. Johnson and M. Stright, pp. 117–146. CRC Press, Boca Raton.

Newsom, L.A., S.D. Webb, and J.S. Dunbar. 1993. History and Geographic Distribution of *Cucurbita pepo* Gourds in Florida. *Journal of Ethnobiology* 13(1):75–97.

Richardson, S. 1988. Survey of the Aucilla River South From Ward Island on the Jefferson-Taylor County Line, Florida. *Florida Anthropologists* 41(4):471–482.

A

Serbousek, D. 1983. Exploration of a Paleoindian Site on the Aucilla River. *Florida Anthropologists* 36(1–2):88–97.

Webb, S.D. 1976. Underwater Paleontology of Florida's Rivers. *National Geographic Society Reports, 1968 Projects,* pp. 479–481. Washington, D.C.

Webb, S.D., J.S. Dunbar, and L.A. Newsom. 1992. Mastodon Digesta From North Florida. *Current Research in the Pleistocene* 9:114–116.

Webb, S.D., J.T. Milanich, R. Alexon, and J.S. Dunbar. 1984. A *Bison Antiquus* Kill Site, Wacissa River, Jefferson County, Florida. *American Antiquity* 49:384–392.

Willis, C. 1988. Controlled Surface Collection of the Little River Rapids Site (8Je603). *Florida Anthropologists* 41(4):453–470.

Avonlea

Originally defined by Thomas F. Kehoe and B.A. McCorquodale in 1961, Avonlea was the first bison-hunting culture in the northern Plains to make extensive use of the bow and arrow. The Avonlea side-notched projectile point is known for its fine workmanship and delicate form. Dates for Avonlea range from A.D. 100 to 1100 (1850–850 years B.P.). There are two hypotheses regarding its origins. The first, proposed by Kehoe in 1966, suggests that Avonlea represents Athapaskan invaders who had spread throughout the Plains from the north.

Avonlea projectile points. (Courtesy of the Wilford Archaeology Laboratory, University of Minnesota)

The second, offered by Brian O.K. Reeves in 1983, suggests that bow-and-arrow technology, which was probably borrowed from people in British Columbia during late phases of the Pelican Lake complex, transformed Pelican Lake into Avonlea.

Geographically, Avonlea is found in southern Alberta, southern Saskatchewan, southwestern Manitoba, North Dakota, Montana, South Dakota, and northern Wyoming, although the Wyoming sites, while generally accepted as having some place in Avonlea culture, do not contain materials directly comparable with the classic material culture found elsewhere. Avonlea pottery is considered Late Woodland in age and style. It has three mutually exclusive surface treatments: net impressed, parallel grooved, and smoothed. The latter treatment does not appear to have been common. As described by Ian Dyck in 1983, decoration near the rim seems absent on parallel-grooved pots, but net-impressed varieties may have one or more rows of punctates or parallel horizontal incisions near the rim. Net-impressed and parallel-grooved potteries have slightly overlapping, but primarily exclusive, geographical distributions, the meaning of which is not understood. Parallel-grooved pottery has a conoidal Middle Woodland form, while net-impressed pottery is globular in form.

Ann M. Johnson

Further Readings
Dyck, I. 1983. Prehistory of Southern Saskatchewan. In *Tracking Ancient Hunters: Prehistoric Archaeology in Saskatchewan,* edited by H.T. Epp and I. Dyck, pp. 63–139 (esp. p. 123). Saskatchewan Archaeological Society, Regina.

Frison, G.C. 1988. Avonlea and Contemporaries in Wyoming. In *Avonlea Yesterday and Today,* edited by L.B. Davis, pp. 155–170. Saskatchewan Archaeological Society, Regina.

Johnson, A.M. 1988. Parallel Grooved Ceramics: An Addition to Avonlea Material Culture. In *Avonlea Yesterday and Today,* edited by L.B. Davis, pp. 137–144. Saskatchewan Archaeological Society, Regina.

Kehoe, T.F. 1966. The Small Side-Notched Point System of the Northern Plains. *American Antiquity* 31:827–841.

Kehoe, T.F., and B.A. McCorquodale. 1961. The Avonlea Projectile Point. *Blue Jay* 19:345–353.

Morlan, R. 1988. Avonlea and Radiocarbon Dating. In *Avonlea Yesterday and Today,* edited by L.B. Davis, pp. 291–310. Saskatchewan Archaeological Society, Regina.

Reeves, B.O.K. 1983. *Culture Change in the Northern Plains: 1000 B.C.–A.D. 1000.* Occasional Paper no. 20. Archaeological Survey of Alberta, Alberta.

Awl

An awl, also called a perforator, is a pointed tool, usually of bone. The metatarsal, metacarpal, or ulna of medium- to large-sized mammals such as deer were preferred, although a splinter of long bone of any large mammal could be abraded to a point. Awls were also made from gray-fox ulna, raccoon fibula, and turkey metatarsals on sites of the Late Archaic Riverton culture of the Wabash Valley in eastern Illinois. The awl presumably was used for piercing holes in leather or other malleable substances, though little microscopic support for this contention through use-wear is available. Awls were produced from the Archaic to the Protohistoric period of North America. A nice example of a bone perforator hafted longitudinally in an antler handle was discovered in a late Caddoan deposit of the Albertson Rock Shelter in the Ozarks (Dickson 1991: Figure 127).

George H. Odell

Further Readings

Dickson, D.R. 1991. *The Albertson Site: A Deeply and Clearly Stratified Ozark Bluff Shelter.* Research Series no. 41. Arkansas Archeological Survey, Fayetteville.

Winters, H.D. 1969. *The Riverton Culture.* Reports of Investigations no. 13. Illinois State Museum, Illinois Archaeological Survey, Springfield.

Axe/Adze

A series of heavy-duty stone tool types has been distinguished by North American archaeologists. Since large morphological overlaps and few apparent functional differences exist among the types, the principal ones are described here together. The defining characteristics are morphotechnological, for abscribed functions overlap all types. Any discussion of this topic must necessarily be cautious and conditional, because the types described are not universally recognized and because consider-

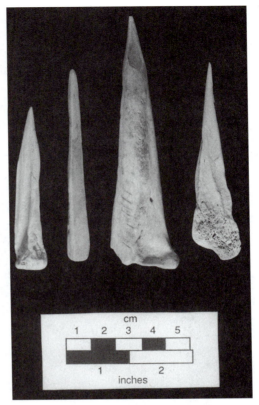

Split bone awls. (*Courtesy of the Wilford Archaeology Laboratory, University of Minnesota*)

able terminological variation exists in the naming of tools of this sort.

A fundamental distinction in the literature is whether heavy-duty stone tools were manufactured by chipping or by grinding. The distinguishing attribute of chipped types considered here is extensive bifacial flaking. The chipped-stone axe is a biface often defined as possessing a definable bit or working edge that is straight and symmetrical in cross section. By contrast, the bit of the adze, which also is definable and relatively straight, is asymmetrically beveled. The gouge is usually narrower than the axe or the adze and possesses a bit that is asymmetrical in cross section. It is distinguished from an adze in that its bit is curved, not straight, and often has a dished-out and occasionally ground underside.

Ground-stone tools are given different terminological distinctions. In traditional terminology, a ground-stone axe must possess a groove to facilitate hafting. This groove may continue around the entire periphery of the object (fully grooved) or stop at one of the narrower edges, which is flattened (three-quarter

Ground stone adze. (Courtesy of the Wilford Archaeology Laboratory, University of Minnesota)

grooved). If no hafting modification exists, the object is often termed a "celt"; a celt can therefore be considered an ungrooved axe.

Specific heavy-duty tools have served as chronological markers in North American prehistory. Among chipped-stone types, the Dalton adze was a common tool of the early Holocene Dalton culture of the Midwest and South (Morse and Goodyear 1973). Another common type is the Clear Fork gouge of the southern Plains, a later Archaic form with a straight bit and rounded or pointed butt end; it is considered to have been a woodworking tool (Hester et al. 1973; Hofman 1978). Similar small tools with a rectangular shape were associated with the Late Archaic Titterington phase of the American Midwest.

Grooved ground-stone axes were employed over a wide area: from New England through Minnesota down to the Gulf Coast, the American Southwest, and western Mexico. They occurred from the Middle/Late Archaic through the Middle Woodland and even into the Mississippian periods (Griffin 1955). In eastern North America, grooved axes are often associated with the Archaic, most notably the Late Archaic and Transitional periods (Fowler 1965). The Late Archaic Indian Knoll site, for example, yielded 159 ground-stone axes, almost all of which were fully grooved (Webb 1974).

George H. Odell

Further Readings

Fowler, W.S. 1965. The Grooved Axe: An Important Diagnostic. *Bulletin of the Massachusetts Archaeological Society* 27:5–8.

Griffin, J.B. 1955. Observations on the Grooved Axe in North America. *Pennsylvania Archaeologist* 25:32–44.

Hester, T.R., D. Gilbow, and A.D. Albee. 1973. A Functional Analysis of "Clear Fork" Artifacts From the Rio Grande Plain, Texas. *American Antiquity* 38:90–96.

Hofman, J.L. 1978. Gouge Production Strategies: Toward the Study of Archaic Local Groups on the Southern Plains. *Wyoming Contributions to Anthropology* 1:154–164.

Morse, D.F., and A.C. Goodyear III. 1973. The Significance of the Dalton Adz in Northeast

Grooved ground-stone axe. (Courtesy of the Wilford Archaeology Laboratory, University of Minnesota)

Arkansas. *Plains Anthropologist* 18:316–322. Webb, W.S. 1974. *Indian Knoll.* University of Tennessee Press, Knoxville.

Aztalan

An isolated village with no associated outlying sites, Aztalan (47JE1) is located on the Crawfish River in south-central Wisconsin. The most northerly large Middle Mississippian village, Aztalan is viewed as an outpost of Mississippian society. It was occupied primarily between A.D. 1000 and 1300 (950–650 years B.P.). Although the name "Aztalan" derives from Aztec legend, there is no Aztec relationship or link; the name postdates the occupation and results from a historical misunderstanding on the part of a chronicler in 1836.

Site areas in the village include: (1) An 8.5-ha (21-acre) palisaded precinct within which most activity occurred. Watchtowers are located at regular intervals along the palisade walls, which were plastered with clay. Several less massive inner walls further separated site activities. Within this palisaded precinct is a midden concentration where garbage was dumped, a habitation and house area, a plaza area that functioned as a public or ceremonial open space, and a pyramidal mound area. The flat-topped mounds were constructed in stages, with a ceremonial building built on top of each stage. (2) A conical mound precinct located along a ridge at the western edge of the site. Each of about 50 conical mounds in this precinct had had a large post set in its center. These posts marked the site or particular events; the mounds were generally not for burial. (3) An agricultural area to the north and south of the palisade. Only household gardens were located inside the palisade.

Both Late Woodland and Middle Mississippian people occupied the site. The first settlers—Woodland people practicing maize horticulture—came up the Rock and Crawfish rivers from northern or central Illinois, or both, ca. A.D. 800–900 (1150–1050 years B.P.). These people also settled elsewhere in southeastern Wisconsin. The more intensive Middle Mississippian presence represents the second movement of people from the south, which occurred

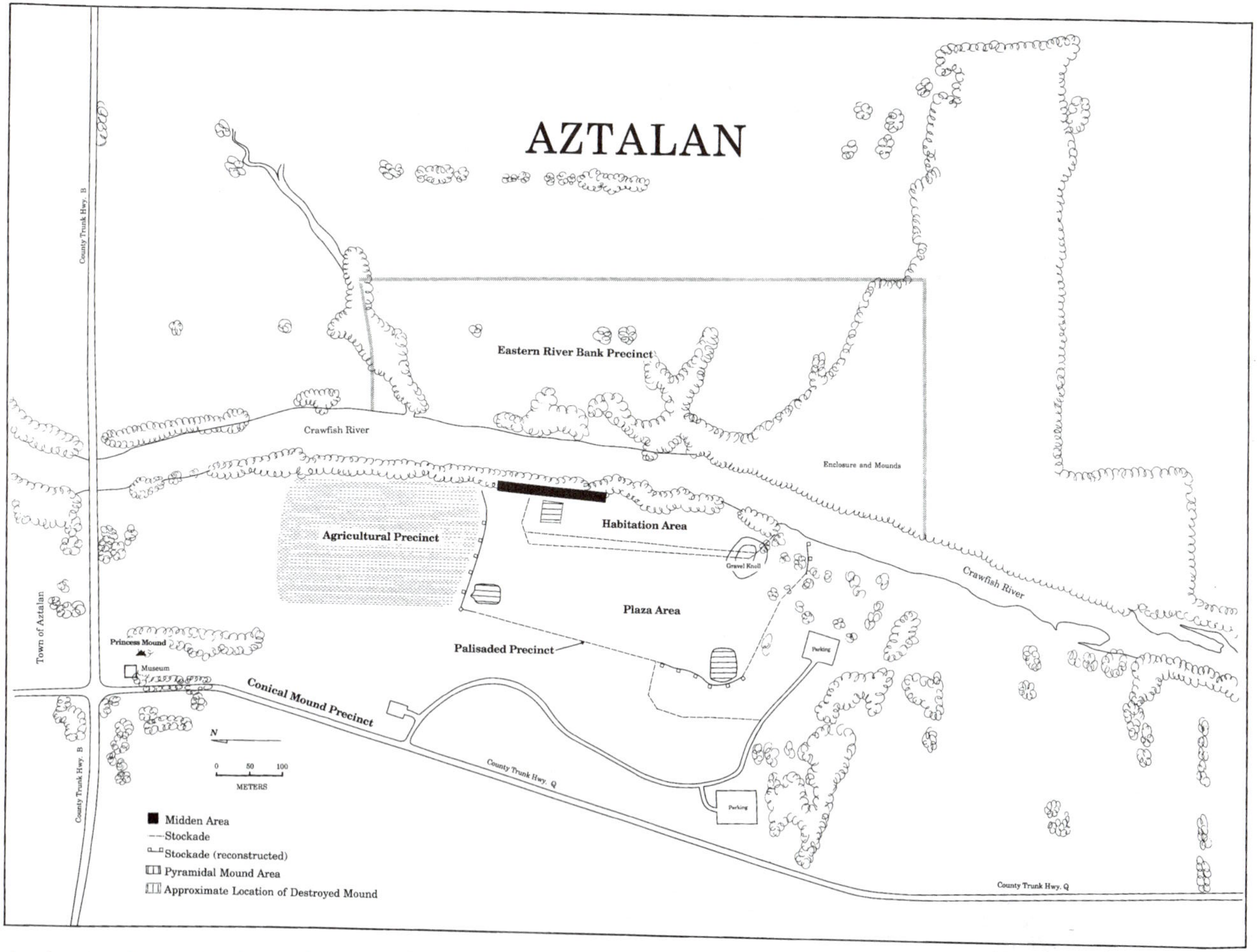

AZTALAN

Eastern River Bank Precinct

Habitation Area

Plaza Area

Palisaded Precinct

Agricultural Precinct

Conical Mound Precinct

Crawfish River

Crawfish River

Enclosure and Mounds

Great Hall

Parking

Parking

County Trunk Hwy. Q

County Trunk Hwy. Q

County Trunk Hwy. B

County Trunk Hwy. B

Town of Aztalan

Princess Mound

Museum

■ Midden Area
⊐⊐ Stockade (reconstructed)
▦ Pyramidal Mound Area
▦ Approximate Location of Destroyed Mound

N

0   50   100
METERS

Aztalan site. (Prepared by L. Goldstein)

42

100 years or so later. It reflects, perhaps, the need to find land for an expanding population. For trade, the Crawfish River would have provided transportation to locations to the south, north, and west. Aztalan's location also would have allowed easy access to all regional vegetation and resource zones. For farmers, the land is level, and its soils are well drained, easily cleared, and most suitable for maize agriculture.

On the basis of earlier reports, people invariably ask if the site's inhabitants were cannibals. Evidence for cannibalism includes some broken and split human bone in refuse pits. However, societies treat the bodies of their dead in different ways. Some parts may be curated for years, while other parts are discarded. Sometimes burial is immediate, and at other times it is not. Stages of treatment of the dead are well documented in Mississippian and Late Woodland societies. The cannibalism interpretation persists because no cemetery has been documented, few burials have been recovered, and the range of mortuary behavior is unknown. As at other Mississippian sites, the fate of Aztalan's residents is unknown; there is no evidence that they were forcibly removed or evicted, but there is also no evidence that they moved elsewhere for purely internal reasons.

Lynne Goldstein

Further Readings

Barrett, S.A. 1933. *Ancient Aztalan*. Bulletin, vol. 8. Public Museum of the City of Milwaukee, Milwaukee.

Freeman, J.E. 1986. Aztalan: A Middle Mississippian Village. In Introduction to Wisconsin Archaeology, edited by W. Green, J.B. Stoltman, and A.B. Kehoe. *Wisconsin Archeologist* 67(3–4):339–364.

Goldstein, L. 1991. The Mysteries of Aztalan. *Wisconsin Academy Review* 36(2):28–34.

A

B

Bad River Phase

The Bad River phase, a subdivision of the Post-Contact Coalescent variant, is represented by earthlodge villages along the Missouri River near Pierre, South Dakota. These communities were occupied between A.D. 1600/1675 and 1795 by ancestral Arikara and are concentrated between the Bad and Cheyenne rivers, western tributaries of the Missouri River. The villages are composed of circular, semisubterranean houses. Like all Plains Villagers, Bad River peoples relied on a dual economy of hunting and gardening. It has been suggested that the Bad River phase should be subdivided into two subphases: Bad River 1 (A.D. 1675–1740) and Bad River 2 (A.D. 1740–1795). Bad River 2 villages are characterized by circular ditches and wood palisade fortifications and by the presence of horse bones and Euro-American trade items, including gun parts. Earlier Bad River 1 sites contain smaller numbers of trade objects and lack fortifications, horse bones, and gun parts. Bad River villagers are thought to have developed directly from earlier local, Late Prehistoric Extended Coalescent groups. During the late eighteenth century, European-introduced epidemic diseases, such as smallpox, reduced Bad River and other Arikara peoples to the single consolidated village of Leavenworth along the

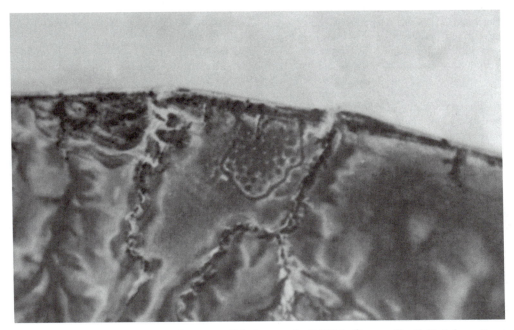

Bad River phase (Post-Contact Coalescent) Buffalo Pasture site (39ST6). (Prepared by C. M. Johnson)

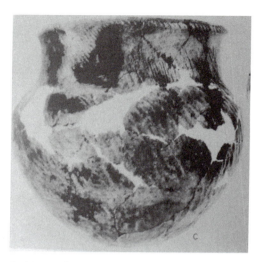

Bad River phase ceramic vessel from the Fire Creek site (32SI2). (Prepared by C. M. Johnson)

Missouri River in northern South Dakota. This village was documented in 1804 by Lewis and Clark and abandoned in 1832, when the Arikara joined the Mandan and the Hidatsa in North Dakota. Later, all three groups moved to Like-a-Fishhook Village, the abandonment of which, in 1886, ended nearly 1,000 years of village life on the northern Plains.

Bad River technology, represented by ground- and chipped-stone tools, bone tools, and ceramic vessels, suggests continuity with earlier Extended Coalescent assemblages. Tools for procuring and processing animals, such as bison, deer, elk, antelope, and fish, are present, as are horticultural implements that would have been used for growing products, like corn, beans, and squash, on the Missouri River floodplain. Euro-American trade items first appeared during the Bad River–phase contact period. The traditional date for the initial appearance of these trade items is A.D. 1675, although research since 1990 suggests a somewhat earlier date of A.D. 1650. The first trade items were obtained from nomadic native groups east or north of the Missouri River, who had received them from other aboriginal groups or directly from European trading posts in Canada or on the Great Lakes. With the passage of time, Euro-American trade goods became more abundant, and the Bad River peoples, along with other Missouri River villagers, capitalized on their middleman position in the trade system. This system included exchange of garden produce for furs and skins with Plains nomads, which were then traded for Euro-American–derived goods. Horses were added to the trade system ca. 1740, when they were acquired from the American Southwest. By then, the system also included guns coming from east of the Missouri River. This was a period of florescence and growth for Bad River–phase peoples. It was not until the period of direct American trade, which began ca. 1790 and involved the introduction of large quantities of trade goods, that the Plains Village way of life on the Missouri River began to change forever.

Craig M. Johnson

Further Readings

Ewers, J.C. 1968. *Indian Life on the Upper Missouri Before Lewis and Clark*. University of Oklahoma Press, Norman.

Johnson, C.M., S.A. Ahler, H. Hass, and G. Bonani. 1996. *A Chronology of Middle Missouri Plains Village Sites*. Smithsonian Contributions to Anthropology. Smithsonian Institution, Washington, D.C.

Krause, R.A. 1972. *The Leavenworth Site: Archeology of an Historic Arikara Community*. Publications in Anthropology no. 3. University of Kansas, Lawrence.

Lehmer, D.J. 1954. *Archeological Investigations in the Oahe Dam Area, South Dakota, 1950–1951*. Bulletin no. 158. Bureau of American Ethnology, Smithsonian Institution, Washington, D.C.

———. 1971. *Introduction to Middle Missouri Archeology*. National Park Service, Washington, D.C.

Lehmer, D.J., and D.T. Jones. 1968. *Arikara Archeology: The Bad River Phase*. Publications in Salvage Archeology no. 7. River Basin Surveys. Smithsonian Institution, Washington, D.C.

Ballcourt

Archaeologists recognize two types of ballcourts in the Southwestern United States and northern Mexico: the Hohokam and the Casas Grandes. More than 200 Hohokam ballcourts are known, all within central and southern Arizona. Hohokam ballcourts are oval in shape, with flat floors and upward-sloping side walls that form an embankment around the court. From the top of the berm, the embankments slope downward to the surrounding desert floor. The floors and side walls are often plastered to form a smooth surface. Stone or wooden markers are sometimes found on the court floors, and a few courts had pits in the floor. The Hohokam built the encircling walls of stone or dirt. Entrance into the ballcourts was often through breaks in the embankments at either end of the long axis of the oval. Some ballcourts apparently had continuous berms around the courts, and entry could be gained only through climbing the embankments. Hohokam ballcourts varied in size; the largest known, at the large site of Snaketown, was 60 m (198 feet) in length, with embankments estimated to have originally stood 5–6 m (16.5–19.8 feet) above the interior floor. Archaeologists estimate that as many as 1,240 people might have stood on the embankments to watch games or rituals enacted on the interior floor. Hohokam ballcourts were constructed between ca. A.D. 800 and 1150 (1150–800 years B.P.). David Wilcox and Charles Sternberg (1983) provide the most complete study of Hohokam ballcourts.

Beginning ca. A.D. 1300 (650 years B.P.), I-shaped ballcourts were constructed in northern Chihuahua and southwestern New Mexico. These Casas Grandes ballcourts more closely resembled traditional Mesoamerican ballcourts than do the Hohokam courts. Casas Grandes ballcourts are up to 50m (165 feet) in length, with flat floors, roughly vertical side walls, and entries on either end of the long axis of the "I." Because archaeologists have surveyed relatively little of this portion of the Greater American Southwest, no reliable estimates exist of the total number of Casas Grandes ballcourts.

Archaeologists continue to debate the function of the ballcourts. While all agree that the courts were communal structures, it is unclear whether prehistoric populations used them for actual ballgames analogous to those played in Mesoamerica or for other types of rituals, dances, or even marketplaces. The fact that ballcourts are not features of every site indicates that the sites with ballcourts (generally the larger sites) probably drew the populations from surrounding areas to whatever activity was held within the embankments. The lack of roofing and the open nature of the courts suggest that activities or rituals held within the courts were meant to be viewed by a large populace. This situation contrasts with the closed communal structures called "kivas" found in the remainder of the southwestern United States.

Patricia L. Crown

Further Readings

Gladwin, H.S., E.W. Haury, E.B. Sayles, and N. Gladwin. 1937. *Excavations at Snaketown: Material Culture.* Medallion Paper no. 25. Gila Pueblo, Globe.

Minnis, P.E. 1989. The Casas Grandes Polity in the International Four Corners. In *The Sociopolitical Structure of Prehistoric Southwestern Societies,* edited by S. Upham, K.G. Lightfoot, and R.A. Jewett, pp. 363–388. Westview Press, Boulder.

Noble, D.G. (editor). 1991. *The Hohokam: Ancient People of the Desert.* School of American Research Press, Santa Fe.

Scarborough, V.L., and D.R. Wilcox. 1991. *The Mesoamerican Ballcourt.* University of Arizona Press, Tucson.

Wilcox, D.R., and C. Sternberg. 1983. *Hohokam Ballcourts and Their Interpretation.* Archaeological Series no. 160. Arizona State Museum, University of Arizona, Tucson.

See also CASAS GRANDES; HOHOKAM CULTURE AREA; KIVA; SNAKETOWN

Bandelier, Adolph F. (1840–1914)

A Swiss-born engineer, mine administrator, and amateur anthropologist, Adolph Bandelier arrived in the Southwest in 1880 after obtaining a grant through Lewis Henry Morgan, a lawyer who was one of the most prominent American anthropologists at the time, to work in the West. During 12 years spent wandering from pueblo to pueblo on a mule with all his possessions in a saddlebag, he attempted to work out a rough chronology of prehistoric pueblo sites. He also drew the plan of the ruins of Pecos, New Mexico, and of other sites in the Rio Grande region; recorded oral traditions and local histories that stretched back into prehistory; and argued that the way to study precontact pueblo history was to work back in time in steps from the known to the unknown (Bandelier 1881). Bandelier also wrote extensively on the ancient cultures of Mexico, Peru, and Bolivia.

Guy Gibbon

Further Readings

Bandelier, A.F. 1881. Report on the Ruins of the Pueblo of Pecos. *Papers of the Archaeological Institute of America, America Series* 1:37–133.

———. 1892. Final Report of Investigations Among the Indians of the Southwestern United States. *Papers of the Archaeologi-*

cal Institute of America 4:1–591.

Hammond, G.P., and E.F. Goad (editors). 1949. *Scientist on the Trail, Travel Letters, 1880–1881.* Publications of the Quivara Society no. 10. Quivara Society, Berkeley.

Hodge, F.W. 1932. Biographical Sketch and Bibliography of Adolph Francis Alphonse Bandelier. *New Mexico Historical Revue* 7:353–370.

Lange, C.H., and C.L. Riley (editors). 1966. *Southwestern Journals, 1880–1882.* University of New Mexico Press, Albuquerque.

Schwartz, D.W. 1981. The Foundations of Northern Rio Grande Archaeology. *Archaeological Society of New Mexico, Anthropological Papers* 6:251–273.

White, L.A. (editor). 1940. *Pioneers in American Anthropology: The Bandelier-Morgan Letters, 1873–1883.* University of New Mexico Press, Albuquerque.

Bandelier National Monument

Established in 1916, by proclamation of President Woodrow Wilson, to preserve "certain prehistoric aboriginal ruins of unusual ethnologic, scientific, and educational interest," Bandelier National Monument is in the heart of the Rio Grande Anasazi province of north-central New Mexico. Known primarily for Frijoles Canyon with its hundreds of hand-hewn cave dwellings, the monument is 13,209 ha (51 square miles) in size and covers much of the southern Pajarito plateau, a high and rugged volcanic tableland incised by deep canyons and split by fingerlike mesas known as *potreros*. Nestled between the Jemez Mountain caldera and the lip of the Rio Grande gorge, Bandelier overlooks the Upper Rio Grande Valley. For reasons unclear and despite perennial streams, unlimited timber, ample game, and propitious conditions for simple agriculture, Bandelier was virtually ignored by the Anasazi until ca. A.D. 1150 (800 years B.P.), when the area was colonized by a small pioneer population. In the succeeding 150 years, these inhabitants were joined by hundreds more as the northern Southwest was depopulated due to catastrophic social, economic, and climatic upheavals that culminated in the Great Drought of 1276–1299 (674–651 years B.P.).

Initially constructing rough masonry pueblos of a dozen or so rooms, early inhabitants lived in small groups. Pueblos were built, occupied, and abandoned in quick succession as

Tyuonyi (LA82). Excavated by Edgar L. Hewett between 1908–1912, this 400-room pueblo lies at the center of a large 15th-century community of Anasazi villages in Frijoles Canyon. (Prepared by R. P. Powers)

Macaw House (LA50970). One of thirteen large cavate pueblos lining the north wall of Frijoles Canyon. Cavate pueblos were constructed by excavating rooms into the tuff cliff-face. Masonry rooms, now collapsed, were built in front of the cliff rooms as indicated here by rows of ceiling beam rests. (Prepared by R. P. Powers)

soils in nearby fields were exhausted. Around 1270 (680 years B.P.), larger, carefully constructed pueblos of 90 or more rooms appeared. One to two stories in height and built in tight blocks surrounding a plaza containing one or more kivas, these communal pueblos completely replaced the smaller pueblos in 50 years. Ongoing research suggests that population aggregation into the large pueblos was the result of a sequence of events precipitated by rapid population growth in the late 1200s (ca. 750 years B.P.). As population increased, game and wild-plant foods became scarce, forcing greater dependence on agriculture and increasing competition for arable land. As competition intensified, the time-honored option of moving to a new field location disappeared. Groups with the best agricultural land may have been the first to band together in large pueblos to reduce competition among themselves, establish permanent land-use rights, and redistribute food in the context of ritual ceremonies.

Despite these pervasive social adaptations, increasingly frequent and severe droughts in the 1400s (ca. 550 years B.P.) may have made agriculture unacceptably risky, particularly for residents of large pueblos farming on the drier *potreros*. Two of the large mesa pueblos—San Miguel and Yapashi—were abandoned by 1450 (500 years B.P.), leaving lush Frijoles Canyon, with its perennial stream and rich loamy soils, the sole enclave of year-round settlement in the park. As the Frijoles population expanded through the 1400s (550–450 years B.P.), more than 1,000 cave rooms, grouped into 13 cliff pueblos, were built along the north wall of Frijoles Canyon. The cliff pueblos, the large canyon-bottom pueblo of Tyuonyi, and a great kiva form one of the larger Late Prehistoric communities in the Southwest. Despite its size, the Frijoles Canyon community was abandoned by 1550 (400 years B.P.). As with other portions of the plateau, this departure appears to have been part of a widespread movement to lower elevations in the main river valley.

Robert P. Powers

Further Readings

Hendron, J.A. 1940. *Prehistory of El Rito de los Frijoles*. Technical Series no. 1. Southwestern Parks and Monuments Association, Coolidge.

Hubbell, L., and D. Traylor. 1982. *Bandelier: Excavations in the Flood Pool of Cochiti Lake, New Mexico*. National Park Service, Santa Fe.

Kohler, T.A. 1989. *Bandelier Archaeological Excavation Project: Research Design and Summer 1988 Sampling*. Reports of Investigations no. 61. Department of Anthropology, Washington State University, Pullman.

———. 1990. *Bandelier Archaeological Excavation Project: Summer 1989 Excavations at Burnt Mesa Pueblo*. Reports of Investigations no. 62. Department of Anthropology, Washington State University, Pullman.

———. 1992. *Bandelier Archeological Excavation Project: Summer 1990 Excavations at Burnt Mesa Pueblo and Casa del Rito*. Reports of Investigations no. 64. Department of Anthropology, Washington State University, Pullman.

Orcutt, J.D. 1991. Environmental Variability and Settlement Changes on the Pajarito Plateau, New Mexico. *American Antiquity* 56:315–332.

Preucel, R.W. 1987. Settlement Succession on the Pajarito Plateau, New Mexico. *Kiva* 53:3–33.

Bannerstones have a decidedly eastern distribution within continental North America, with the "heart area" of the Ohio Valley and Southeast their area of greatest abundance. In several areas, such as the Ohio and Illinois valleys (the Bullseye site), they have been found predominantly in mortuary mounds and cemeteries. The most extensive typology of bannerstones was produced by B.W. Knobloch in 1939. Though this evolutionary scheme was designed long before the advent of radiocarbon dating, it has not been superseded as a model of bannerstone development.

Bannerstones first appear in the early Middle Archaic period (ca. 4050–3050 B.C., or 6000–5000 years B.P.). The earliest forms were shuttles; double-edged and crescent types; and possibly double-bitted axe, knobbed lunate, and reel-shaped pieces. The next to appear were geniculate and tubular forms, and, finally, humped and triangular, hourglass, ovoid, butterfly, and bottle shapes. Bannerstones died out at the end of the Archaic period in North America and appear to have been succeeded by two-hole gorgets. This transition occurred a few centuries prior to 1000 B.C. (2950 years B.P.).

George H. Odell

Bannerstone

A "bannerstone" is usually a large pecked and ground artifact fashioned predominantly of noncherty material, such as slate, quartzite, or granite. Evidence of the possible function of the artifact appeared first at the Indian Knoll site in Kentucky, where bannerstones were discovered in proper alignment with atlatl hooks, although the more erodible intervening portions of wood and sinew or fiber had long since degraded. On the basis of this evidence, "bannerstones" were considered atlatl weights; that is, objects strapped to the body of a spear thrower to give it weight and perhaps stability. A bannerstone, called a "boatstone" in this case, was later found tied above the handle to the underside of an atlatl from early Holocene Lake Winnemucca in Nevada. Similar stones attached to spear throwers have been found in the Great Basin near Condon, Oregon, and in Hogup Cave, Utah. Although the bannerstone appears to have been functional in nature, it has never been experimentally proven that such an object improves either the accuracy or the flight distance of an atlatl dart. As a result, its ultimate function as a fetish or symbol accoutrement cannot be ruled out.

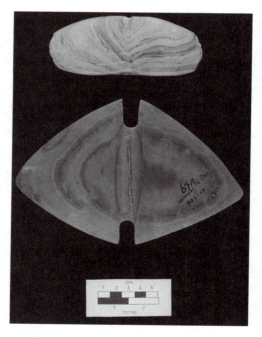

Banded-slate bannerstones from Mahoning County, Ohio. (Courtesy of the Wilford Archaeology Laboratory, University of Minnesota)

Further Readings

Hassen, H., and K.B. Farnsworth. 1987. *The Bullseye Site: A Floodplain Archaic Mortuary Site in the Lower Illinois River Valley.* Reports of Investigations no. 42. Illinois State Museum, Springfield.

Knobloch, B.W. 1939. *Banner-Stones of the North American Indian.* Privately published by the author.

Kwas, M.L. 1981. Bannerstones As Chronological Markers in the Southeastern United States. *Tennessee Anthropologist* 6:144–171.

Mildner, M.P. 1974. Descriptive and Distributional Notes on Atlatls and Atlatl Weights in the Great Basin. In *Great Basin Atlatl Studies,* edited by T.R. Hester, M.P. Mildner, and L. Spencer, pp. 7–27. Ballena Press, Ramona.

Neal, L. 1986. Preliminary Distribution of Bannerstones in Oklahoma. *Bulletin of the Oklahoma Anthropological Society* 35:51–67.

See also ATLATL

Barton, Benjamin Smith (1766–1815)

A late-eighteenth-century traveler through Ohio and adjacent areas, Benjamin Smith Barton speculated in an early book (1787) that the earthworks he had encountered were built by Danes who had later migrated to Mexico and become the Toltecs. In later publications, he suggested that ancestors of Indians had built some mounds and that Precolumbian history in the New World had considerable antiquity, perhaps even extending back before Irish Archbishop James Ussher's (1581–1656) 4004 B.C. (5954 years B.P.) date for the creation. This was one of the earliest attempts to assign a real time depth to the Indian occupation of the Americas. Barton also thought that the ancestors of the Indians had come from Asia, a view generally accepted by the end of the eighteenth century.

Guy Gibbon

Further Readings

Barton, B.S. 1787. *Observations on Some Parts of Natural History.* C. Dilly, London.

———. 1797. *New Views of the Origin of the Tribes and Nations of America.* John Bioren, Philadelphia.

———. 1799. *Fragments of the Natural History of Pennsylvania,* pt. 1. John Bioren, Philadelphia.

See also MOUND BUILDER MYTH

Barton Gulch Site

Discovered in 1972 by garnet collectors working nineteenth- and twentieth-century gold placer tailings, the Barton Gulch site (24MA171) is on a tributary of the Upper Ruby River northwest of the Greenhorn Range in Madison County, Montana. Barton Gulch, at an elevation of 1,670 m (5,480 feet), is close to Virginia City in the southwestern Montana Rockies; it was excavated by Montana State University from 1987 through 1993. This 5.85 m (19.2-foot)-deep valley fill section encloses a deeply stratified, open-air campsite that was occupied intermittently from 7450 to 2050 B.C. (9400–4000 years B.P.). Two newly recognized Paleoindian complexes sampled at the site establish Barton Gulch as the type site: the 9,400-year-old Alder complex, with its diagnostic small- to medium-sized lanceolate Ruby Valley projectile point, and the 8,700-year-old Hardinger complex, with its diagnostic large lanceolate, indented-base Metzal point.

Excavation of a 636-m^2 (6,845-square-foot) portion of the Alder-complex living floor yielded a rich and detailed bioarchaeological and cultural record. Obtained for food by hunting were mule deer (*Odocoileus hemionus*) and white-tailed deer (*O. virginianus*), jackrabbit (*Lepus* sp.), cottontail (*Sylvilagus* sp.), and porcupine (*Erithizon dorsatum*). Quantities of charred seeds recovered from earth ovens indicate that pricklypear cactus (*Opuntia polycantha*) and slimleaf goosefoot (*Chenopodium leptophyllum*), along with sunflower (*Helianthus* sp.), blazing star (*Mentzelia* sp.), limber pine (*Pinus flexilis*), and chokecherry (*Prunus virginiana*), were gathered and processed for consumption by peoples of the Alder complex at Barton Gulch. Animal remains suggest late-spring occupation, while utilized plants were gathered in late summer and early autumn. Most impressive is the fact that the 213 purposefully excavated subfloor features, exposed and recovered by recent excavations, had been arranged in 16 spatially discrete food-processing aggregates. Each of these kitchens comprised three functionally distinct features: a central charcoal-producing brazier surrounded by varying numbers of earth ovens constructed for baking or roasting meat tissue and seeds, the whole interspersed by varying numbers of postmoldlike, shallow circular depressions. Plants reduced to coals in the braziers were introduced as fuel into the earth ovens. These plants included pine (*Pinus* sp.), willow/cottonwood

Excavations of 9,400-year-old earth-oven food preparation features at the Late Paleoindian Barton Gulch site, Ruby Valley, Upper Madison River drainage. (Courtesy of Museum of the Rockies/Montana State University–Bozeman)

(Salicaceae), birch (cf. *Betula*), and sagebrush (*Artemisia* sp.). The pulverized skeletons of procured economic species were distributed irregularly across the living floor, as were large quantities of flaked-stone artifacts (points, knives, biface preforms, end and side scrapers, gravers, perforators, cores, and debitage), ground-stone (dart shaft smoothers and abrading stones), anvil stones, hammerstones, and bone artifacts (eyed needles and awls), and a carbonized dart shaft or foreshaft segment.

The material-culture inventory and associated food-processing residues at Barton Gulch, in the context of structured food-processing facilities and industrial discard, provide rare and detailed insight into the behavior of peoples associated with a specific Paleoindian complex adapted to life in the northern Rockies.

Leslie B. Davis

Further Readings

Armstrong, S.W. 1993. *Alder Complex Kitchens: Experimental Replication of Paleoindian Cooking Facilities.* Unpublished Master's thesis, Department of Sociology and Anthropology, University of Idaho, Moscow.

Davis, L.B., S.A. Aaberg, and L.S. Cummings. 1994. Northern Rocky Mountain Paleoecology in Archaeological, Paleobotanical, and Paleoethnobotanical Perspective. *Plants and Their Environments: Proceedings of the First Biennial Scientific Conference on the Greater Yellowstone Ecosystem,* edited by D.G. Despain, pp. 33–50. National Park Service, Natural Resources Publication Office, Denver.

Davis, L.B., S.A. Aaberg, and S.T. Greiser. 1988. Paleoindians in Transmontane Southwestern Montana: The Barton Gulch Occupations, Ruby River Drainage. *Current Research in the Pleistocene* 5:9–11.

Davis, L.B., S.A. Aaberg, W.P. Eckerle, J.W. Fisher, Jr., and S.T. Greiser. 1989. Montane Paleoindian Occupation of the Barton Gulch Site, Ruby Valley, Southwestern Montana. *Current Research in the Pleistocene* 6:5–7.

Bartram, William (1739–1823)
Naturalist and explorer, friend of Thomas Jefferson, and son of the famous botanist John Bartram of Philadelphia, William Bartram

traveled widely throughout the Southeast in the 1770s, describing the earthen mounds he encountered, among other features of the landscape. He observed Indians (Choctaws) constructing burial mounds and eventually concluded that some platform mounds used but not constructed by other Indians (Cherokees) had been built by earlier, unspecified Indians. Bartram provided much information on southeastern mounds to Benjamin Smith Barton, who wrote that non-Indian Mound Builders had constructed the mounds. Bartram's own extensive observations on the mounds did not become available to the general public until 1909, and some of his observations were misinterpreted, which contributed still further to the Mound Builder myth (Silverberg 1968:33–42). His *Travels* (1791) also greatly influenced English Romanticism. Bartram's observations are typical of "archaeology" in the Southeast before archaeology had appeared as a profession or even an avocation. Nonetheless, he described many mounds, and the logic of his argument is one of the earliest examples in North America of the application of the direct historical approach to the interpretation of archaeological remains.

Guy Gibbon

Further Readings

Bartram, W. 1791. *Travels Through North and South Carolina, Georgia, East and West Florida, the Cherokee Country, the Extensive Territories of the Muscogulges or Creek Confederacy and the Country of the Chactaws.* James and Johnson, Philadelphia.

———. 1853. *Observations on the Creek and Cherokee Indians (1789).* Transactions no. 31. American Ethnological Society, New York.

Earnest, E. 1940. *John and William Bartram, Botanists and Explorers, 1699–1777, 1739–1823.* University of Pennsylvania Press, Philadelphia.

Silverberg, R. 1968. *Moundbuilders of Ancient America.* New York Graphic Society, Greenwich.

See also BARTON, BENJAMIN SMITH; MOUND BUILDER MYTH

Bat Cave

In 1948, archaeologists discovered a number of small, morphologically "primitive" maize cobs in preceramic deposits at Bat Cave in the rugged highlands of western New Mexico. Radiocarbon dates associated with these maize cobs fell in the 4050–2050 B.C. (6000–4000 years B.P.) range, making Bat Cave the earliest known maize-producing site in North America at that time. The estimated age range indicated that maize had been introduced to the Southwest from Mesoamerica during the Middle Archaic cultural period (ca. 5550–2050 B.C., or 7500–4000 years B.P.). The excavations were directed by Herbert W. Dick and reported by the School of American Research in 1965. Funding for the project was provided by the Harvard Botanical Museum and Paul C. Mangelsdorf, a botanist with long-standing interests in the origin and evolution of maize.

The first description of the Bat Cave material came in botanical reports by Mangelsdorf, who considered the maize cobs to be good examples of some of the earliest domesticated maize in the New World. Mangelsdorf (1950) also argued that there was a progressive, evolutionary sequence in the maize from the lower to the upper levels of the site: The most primitive appearing cobs were found in the lowest levels, and the most modern specimens in the highest or most recent levels. By Mangelsdorf's account, the evolutionary changes in the Bat Cave maize reflected a gradual history of human cultivation without any deliberate effort at maize improvement.

Subsequent excavations at other southwestern rock shelters, particularly at Tularosa Cave in southwestern New Mexico, by other researchers discovered Archaic-period maize, but none produced reliable dates comparable in age to those from Bat Cave. In fact, there appeared to be a period of several thousand years separating the first appearance of maize at Bat Cave and the next oldest dates for maize anywhere else. Consequently, Bat Cave was an enigma.

Following the publication of the site report in 1965, several scholars suggested that the association between Middle Archaic radiocarbon dates and maize cobs might be spurious, since the stratigraphically complex deposits had been excavated in arbitrary 30.5-cm (12-inch) levels, a procedure that might have mixed materials with vastly different ages. In 1981 and 1983, the University of Michigan conducted new excavations at Bat Cave, with the objective of resolving the question of when maize had first been introduced to the area.

These new investigations provided the following results. First, sediments and rockfall have accumulated in these shelters for at least the last 14,000 years, with evidence for human use dating from ca. 8550 B.C. (10,500 years B.P.) into the modern period. Evidence for site use in the period 8550–1550 B.C. (10,500–3500 years B.P.) is limited and consists primarily of scattered hearths and chipped-stone debitage. The first indication of maize use, derived from direct dates on maize samples as well as stratigraphic context, occurred between 1550 and 1050 B.C. (3500–3000 years B.P.). The introduction of maize is associated with evidence of living floors, storage pits, dense midden deposits, and a wide range of material culture. This contrast with preceding site use suggests a shift to more intensive occupation patterns connected to local maize cultivation, processing, and storage but does not indicate year-round or sedentary adaptations. Ca. 1550 B.C.– A.D. 150 (3500–1800 years B.P.), the use of Bat Cave seems to have changed very little, and occupation does not appear to have been continuous. Following A.D. 150 (1800 years B.P.), the use of the shelter complex shifted to a specialized hunting camp, inferred from the presence of several thousand bison bones, less artifact diversity, and only sparse indications of maize. The duration of this specialized site function is not known because historic-period occupation by Apache Indians and Hispanic sheepherders effectively destroyed much of the later prehistoric deposit.

In conjunction with the new field studies at Bat Cave, the original excavation records and collections were also examined. Direct radiocarbon dates on maize specimens recovered in 1948 and 1950 from the lowest levels of the site were obtained by the Radiocarbon Laboratory at the University of Arizona. They failed to confirm the Middle Archaic dates derived from charcoal, indicating instead an oldest age of 1550–1050 B.C. (3500–3000 years B.P.). This new age range matched the dates and stratigraphic patterns produced by the University of Michigan excavations and confirmed the suspicion that the original dating was in error.

This error probably had two sources. First, the charcoal samples from the 1948–1950 excavations were among the first archaeological samples submitted for radiocarbon analysis, by Willard F. Libby at the University of Chicago. Today these early analyses are generally considered suspect due to technical problems. However, many of the original charcoal dates from Bat Cave are consistent with new radiocarbon dates and, therefore, the second source, excavation method, was likely the real problem, as many scholars had suspected. Photographs from the 1948 excavations clearly indicated that numerous pits and other features originated in upper portions of the site deposits and extended downward into earlier layers. None of these important features were noted or described in the site report of 1965. An especially large pit was recorded in the portion of the site complex where the small maize cobs were found. This feature, which was not noticed during the removal of arbitrary levels, probably is the reason that maize was recovered in association with much older charcoal (Wills 1988:117).

Richard I. Ford (1981) of the University of Michigan reexamined the maize cobs found in the 1948–1950 excavations prior to submission for new radiocarbon dates and determined that the "primitive" features described by Mangelsdorf, which had lent support to the ancient chronological estimate, were misidentified. Instead, these characteristics are attributable to stunted or tiller cobs and well within the range of later prehistoric maize varieties. Consequently, it now appears that maize cultivation at Bat Cave was much later than once thought and that the earliest forms of maize introduced to the site were highly evolved rather than primitive. According to Walton Galinat, a botanist at the University of Massachusetts, the earliest dated Bat Cave maize is fairly typical of maize specimens recovered from older Archaic southwestern sites, which indicates that the initial maize introduced to the Southwest probably belonged to a single generalized population.

However, as of 1994, the revised age range for maize at Bat Cave is still the oldest available anywhere in North America. Thus, the site remains crucial to understanding the processes underlying the diffusion of maize from Mesoamerica. Recent dates for maize and squash from sites throughout the Southwest indicate that between 1550 and 1050 B.C. (3500–3000 years B.P.) these cultigens had become a widespread component of indigenous economic systems. Some sites, such as Bat Cave, seem to reflect a fairly limited seasonal role for plant cultivation. Others, such as recently discovered open-air sites in southeastern Arizona excavated by Bruce B. Huckell of the Arizona State Museum, are associated with shelters, burials, and dense midden deposits, all features that suggest a greater degree of sedentism. Consequently, the kind of incipient food-production system associated with the occupation of Bat Cave in the Late Archaic may have been quite different from the recipient economies found in hotter, drier desert areas of the Southwest.

W.H. Wills

Further Readings

Dick, H.W. 1965. *Bat Cave.* Monograph no. 27. School of American Research Press, Santa Fe.

Ford, R.I. 1981. Gardening and Farming Before A.D. 1000: Patterns of Prehistoric Cultivation North of Mexico. *Journal of Ethnobiology* 1(1):6–27.

Mangelsdorf, P.C. 1950. The Mystery of Corn. *Scientific American* 183:20–29.

Wills, W.H. 1988. *Early Prehistoric Agriculture in the American Southwest.* School of American Research Press, Santa Fe.

Beads (California)

Beads, especially those made of shell, were a significant artifact category in most prehistoric California cultures and form an important target of archaeological analysis in this area. For most of the twentieth century, a major research goal has been the definition of distinct regional cultures based on variations. Especially valuable are artifact types with stylistic regularities. Pottery is used in many areas, but ancient Californians used little or no pottery. Analysis of bead types has met this need for California archaeologists.

Prehistoric Californians used beads for several functions, such as money, personal decoration, burial offerings, and displays of social status, and to decorate other artifacts. In most cases, the same bead form might be used for multiple functions. Among the materials used for beads were mammal and bird bone, steatite, and slate. However, seashell was the overwhelmingly common choice. Tube beads were made of bone, magnesite, steatite, and some shells. Some whole-shell beads with ends removed to allow stringing were made, especially of *Dentalium* and of *Olivella* (spire-lopped) shells. The vast majority of beads were disk shaped. Typically they were made from shells such as *Tivola* and *Saxidomus*. Shells were broken into rough squares and their centers were drilled, sometimes from one side only (uniconically) and sometimes from both

sides (biconically). Drilled pieces were strung, and strings of pieces were ground on coarse stones to create rounded shapes.

Bead use began in several Archaic cultures, but the quantity of beads increased exponentially during the last 2,000 years of prehistory (ca. 300 B.C.– A.D. 1700, or 2250–250 years B.P.). Bead making was an important craft for many coastal peoples. Both finished beads and shells for making beads were traded or exchanged inland, sometimes into the Columbia Plateau, Great Basin, and Southwest. Individual burials with up to 25,000–50,000 beads show the magnitude of social differentiation reached in many California cultures and the importance beads played in marking social distinctions. Bead preferences also mark cultural boundaries. Patterns in the choice of material, bead design, method of manufacture, and average size are as definitive as those found for pottery types or projectile-point styles.

Joseph L. Chartkoff

Further Readings

Gifford, E.W. 1940. *Californian Bone Artifacts.* University of California Anthropological Records, vol. 3, no. 2. Berkeley.

———. 1947. *Californian Shell Artifacts.* University of California Shell Artifacts, vol. 9, no. 1. Berkeley.

King, C.D. 1981. *The Evolution of Chumash Society: A Comparative Study of Artifacts Used in Social System Maintenance in the Santa Barbara Channel Region Before A.D. 1804.* Unpublished Ph.D. dissertation, Department of Anthropology, University of California, Davis.

Beans

Cultivation of the common American bean (*Phaeseolus vulgaris*) may have begun before 8050 B.C. (10,000 years B.P.) in South America. By the seventh millennium B.C., if not earlier, at least some people were growing beans, maize (corn), and squashes in Mesoamerica, from where these "Three Sisters" entered North America. Each of the three crops was adopted in the Southwest and in eastern North America at different times, with squashes, then maize, and then beans the usual sequence. Common beans probably appeared in the Southwest by 500 B.C. (2450 years B.P.) and in the Eastern Woodlands by ca. A.D. 1000 (950 years B.P.). Beans did not become a common, widespread subsistence staple in the Eastern Woodlands until after A.D. 1200 (750 years B.P.), when they appear in Late Mississippian, Upper Mississippian (e.g., Oneota, Fort Ancient), and late Late Woodland (e.g., Iroquois) agricultural contexts. In the Southwest, they have been grouped with maize and squash into an Upper Sonoran Agricultural complex (Ford 1981, 1985).

Beans were an important crop in North America, especially when grown with maize, for several reasons. A maize-based diet provides insufficient nutrition without supplementary foods, like beans or squashes, for maize lacks the vital amino acid necessary to effectively digest the protein that it provides. Because they contain a high level of this amino acid (lycene), beans greatly augment the protein content of maize-based diets. In addition, beans, like other legumes, return nitrogen to the ground, in contrast to nonleguminous terrestrial plants like maize that, because they obtain their nitrogen from the soil, deplete it. North American cultivators could maintain the fertility of their gardens longer, then, by planting maize and beans together. Isotopic analyses of the organic residues crusted to the interior of ceramic vessels also promise to help identify the presence of beans, or at least of legumes, in prehistoric diets (Renfrew and Bahn 1991). Since all legumes are terrestrial and obtain their nitrogen through the bacterial fixation of atmospheric nitrogen, they can be differentiated from marine plants and nonleguminous terrestrial plants by their nitrogen/carbon isotopic ratio.

Why beans, maize, and squashes were adopted by various peoples, the social contexts of their adoption, and the nature of their impact on these societies are topics of continued discussion in North American archaeology. Some archaeologists argue that the adoption of maize and later of bean cultivation revolutionized some North American societies by requiring a major adjustment in both settlement and subsistence patterns. In this view, large-scale gardening led to larger food surpluses, rising population densities, and more complex sociopolitical organizations. Others argue that prehistoric Indian people were aware of the existence of beans and maize long before they adopted them. In this latter view, changing social circumstances necessitated their adoption. As with other polar explanations, the truth probably lies somewhere in between. In any case, the large-scale growing of beans and maize undoubtedly helped transform the natural as well as the social environment of some areas of North America.

Guy Gibbon

Further Readings

Castetter, E.F., and W.M. Bell. 1942. *Pima and Papago Indian Agriculture.* University of New Mexico Press, Albuquerque.

Ford, R.I. 1981. Gardening and Farming Before A.D. 1000: Patterns of Prehistoric Cultivation North of Mexico. *Journal of Ethnobiology* 1(1):6–27.

———. (editor). 1985. *Prehistoric Food Production in North America.* Anthropological Paper no. 75. Museum of Anthropology, University of Michigan, Ann Arbor.

Gepts, P., K. Kmieck, P. Pereira, and F.A. Bliss. 1988. Dissemination Pathways of Common Bean (*Phaseolus vulgaris*, Fabaceae) Deduced From Phaseolin Electrophoretic Variability: 1. The Americas. *Economic Botany* 42(1):73–85.

Kaplan, L. 1965. Beans of the Wetherill Mesa. In *Contributions of the Wetherill Mesa Archaeological Project,* edited by D. Osborne, pp. 153–155. Society for American Archaeology, Washington, D.C.

Renfrew, C., and P. Bahn. 1991. *Archaeology: Theories, Methods, and Practice.* Thames and Hudson, New York, p. 241.

Wills, W.H. 1988. *Early Prehistoric Agriculture in the American Southwest.* School of American Research Press, Santa Fe.

See also UPPER SONORAN AGRICULTURAL COMPLEX

Bear Village

Bear Village (AZ P:16:1) is located on the floor of Forestdale Valley on the White Mountain Apache Reservation in east-central Arizona. It was excavated by Emil W. Haury in 1939 and 1940. The major occupation defines the Forestdale phase (A.D. 600–800, or 1350–1150 years B.P.) of the Forestdale branch of the Mogollon culture. Tree-ring dates indicate construction in the late A.D. 600s (1350–1250 years B.P.), while ceramic cross-dating suggests occupation extending into the 800s (1150–1050 years B.P.). Bear Village enlarged the geographical range of the Mogollon culture as then defined on the basis of excavations at the Mogollon and Harris villages in west-central New Mexico.

Seventeen pithouses were excavated at Bear Village, about half of the estimated total. Round pithouses predominate; three are rectangular. All exhibit a mixture of architectural features suggestive of Mogollon and Anasazi techniques. Shallow, rectangular storage structures are present. A roofed great kiva with a foot drum, four directional recesses, and a large recess to the southeast was dug deep into the alluvial terrace. Subsistence was a continuation of hunting-gathering-gardening, with increasing emphasis on maize cultivation. Mountain pottery types include Alma Plain, Alma Scored, Forestdale Plain, Forestdale Smudged, Woodruff Smudged, Woodruff Red, Forestdale Red, San Francisco Red, and Mogollon Red-on-brown. Plateau pottery types include Lino Black-on-gray, White Mound Black-on-white, Lino Gray, Adamana Brown, Woodruff Smudged, and Woodruff Red. Desert pottery types include Gila Butte Red-on-buff and Gila Plain.

Coresidence by people of different ethnic traditions is supported by architectural features and different forms of cradleboard-produced head deformation consistent with types characteristic of the Mogollon and Anasazi. The coming together of different people is compatible with population movements throughout the Southwest at this time. It may account for the relaxation of social tension seen in the movement of villages down from blufftop locations and the construction of great kivas as corporate ceremonial structures.

J. Jefferson Reid

Further Readings

Haury, E.W. 1985. *Mogollon Culture in the Forestdale Valley, East-Central Arizona.* University of Arizona Press, Tucson.

Reid, J.J. 1989. A Grasshopper Perspective on the Mogollon of the Arizona Mountains. In *Dynamics of Southwest Prehistory,* edited by L.S. Cordell and G.J. Gumerman, pp. 65–97. Smithsonian Institution Press, Washington, D.C.

See also BLUFF VILLAGE; FORESTDALE BRANCH; MOGOLLON CULTURE AREA

Behavioral Ecology in the Great Basin

Behavioral or evolutionary ecology, a theoretical perspective developed and widely applied by biologists studying animal behavior, is gaining acceptance in anthropology and has been successfully applied by a number of Great Basin archaeologists. Based on Neo-Darwinian natural-selection theory, the theories and models of behavioral ecology allow researchers to investigate prehistoric cultural behavior through the formulation and testing of explicit, theoretically informed hypotheses. The process has increased the ability to extract behavioral information from scant archaeological data.

Early applications of this perspective concentrated on optimal foraging theory, a theory that holds that foods are selected based on the ratio of benefit to cost in finding, obtaining, and processing those foods (usually calculated in terms of calories expended per hour). This approach has focused attention on the ways native peoples obtained and processed foods for consumption, with a number of researchers experimentally gathering and processing plant and animal foods, carefully tallying the time and effort involved, and measuring the caloric yield. Archaeologists have used the theory to predict the foods prehistoric peoples used and, by extension, where they lived and for how long. The results, while mixed, have produced some important insights into the human ecology of the regions where the studies have been conducted.

More recent applications of the perspective include models of central place foraging (in which foragers foray out from and return to a central place), risk management, mobility, resource transportation and storage, and migration. These approaches generally share the basic premise that organisms, including humans, will tend to make efficient use of the resources available to them, including time, energy, raw materials, manufactured goods, landscape and terrain features, food, water, and other organisms. This perspective allows researchers to make quantitative predictions about expected efficient prehistoric behavior, thus providing a baseline against which to compare archaeological data. Incorporating behavioral ecology into Great Basin archaeology has resulted in greater clarity of expectations and explanations than was previously possible.

Kevin T. Jones

Further Readings

Bettinger, R.L. 1991. *Hunter-Gatherers: Archaeological and Evolutionary Theory.* Plenum Press, New York.

Jones, K.T., and D.B. Madsen. 1991. Further Experiments in Native Food Procurement. *Utah Archaeology* 4:70–77.

B

O'Connell, J.F., K.T. Jones, and S.R. Simms. 1982. Some Thoughts on Prehistoric Archaeology in the Great Basin. In *Man and Environment in the Great Basin*, edited by D.B. Madsen and J.F. O'Connell, pp. 227–240. Society for American Archaeology, Washington, D.C.
Simms, S.R. 1987. *Behavioral Ecology and Hunter-Gatherer Foraging: An Example from the Great Basin*. British Archaeological Reports International Series no. 381. Oxford.

Bella Bella Sequence

The region occupied by those local groups who became known in the nineteenth century as the Bella Bella extended from Calvert Island in the south to Milbanke Sound in the north and from Goose Island on the far outer west coast of British Columbia eastward through the coastal islands and up the various fjords to the head of Dean Channel, ca. 180 km (112 miles) to the east. Archaeological research began in this region in the 1910–1930 period, when Harlan I. Smith looked at historic villages and rock art. Research continued with test excavations in late sites by Philip Drucker in 1938. More recently, excavations and site surveys conducted by Simon Fraser University and University of Colorado researchers from 1968 to 1983 have resulted in the present chronological picture and the recording of 592 sites. The most important excavated sites and the range of their uncorrected ^{14}C dates are: Namu, 7750 B.C.– A.D. 1450 (9700–500 years B.P.); McNaughton Island, 550 B.C. to contact (2500–200 years B.P.); Anutcix, Axeti, and Nutlitliqotlank at Kwatna River, A.D. 250 to contact (1700–200 years B.P.); Joashila at Kwatna Inlet with two components at ca. 5050 B.C.–A.D. 950 (7000–1000 years B.P.); four sites (FeSr 1, 4, 5, 7) at Kimsquit dating to the Protohistoric and historic periods (ca. 200–100 years B.P.), with a possible earlier microblade component at FeSr 4; Kisameet, 450 B.C.– A.D. 1450 (2400–500 years B.P.); Mackenzies Rock, which dates to the Protohistoric period; and Troup Passage, which dates to the nineteenth century A.D. Fort McLoughlin, established in 1830, is the only excavated Euro-Canadian site in this region. Kimsquit and Kwatna are border localities that contained both Bella Bella and Bella Coola peoples in the historic period. The other sites are all well within the boundaries of the Heiltsuk local groups, which amalgamated to become the Bella Bella in the nineteenth century.

Namu is the only site with a long continuous sequence. This sequence has been broken down into the following six chronological periods, which are based on 38 radiocarbon dates that have been tree-ring calibrated:

11,000–7000 years B.P. This period is characterized by a foliate biface, pebble tool, and flake industry to which a microblade technology was added ca. 9000 years B.P. Grooved bolas/sinkers are also present. No shell or bone has been preserved except for the enamel crowns of the molars of two people with Sinodont attributes. Obsidian was obtained through trade from the adjacent Rainbow Mountains in the interior.

7000–6000 years B.P. Lithics and trade remain the same, but there are now limited shellfish remains, preserved bone harpoons and fishhook barbs, and a full range of fish and mammal species as in later periods, with salmon the dominant class of identified vertebrates.

6000–5000 years B.P. Massive shell-midden deposits are present. While there is a decline in lithics and the microblade technology disappears, there is an increase in bone fishing and sea-hunting artifacts as well as a sharp increase in salmon remains. Atlatl spurs, needles, and labrets are also present.

5000–4000 years B.P. Period 3 industries continue with the addition of ground-stone celts, composite harpoons, and fish-form pendants. Fauna and shell-midden deposits remain the same, and the peak in salmon remains continues. Obsidian was now obtained from Oregon as well as the Rainbow Mountains.

4000–2000 years B.P. Earlier industries continue but with some stylistic changes. Fauna remains are the same except for salmon, which declines because of a rise in sea level.

2000 years B.P.–contact (ca. 200 years B.P.). There is a decline at Namu in occupation but abundant evidence at other sites of the full-blown Northwest Coast cultural pattern: winter villages of plank houses with satellite resource camps, fish traps, advanced woodworking, spindle whorls, art, and salmon-based subsistence. The waterlogged component at Axeti, which dates to the latter part of this period, yielded types of wood and basketry artifacts that probably go far back into local prehistory but which have not been preserved in earlier deposits. These items include stake-and-mat fish weirs, cedar-bark rope, wedges, twined hats,

58 BEHAVIORAL ECOLOGY IN THE GREAT BASIN

bentwood boxes and fishhooks, chisel hafts, and plaited and wicker mats and baskets. The historic-period components at Fort McLoughlin, Troup Passage, and Kimsquit provide evidence of the effect of Euro-Canadian contact on native culture.

There is strong evidence of cultural continuity throughout the sequence, particularly from Period 3 onward.

Roy L. Carlson

Further Readings

Apland, B. 1982. Chipped Stone Assemblages From the Beach Sites of the Central Coast. *Papers on Central Coast Archaeology*, edited by P.M. Hobler, pp. 13–63. Publication no. 10. Department of Archaeology, Simon Fraser University, Burnaby.

Cannon, A. 1991. *The Economic Prehistory of Namu*. Archaeology Press, Simon Fraser University, Burnaby.

Carlson, R.L. 1983. Prehistoric Art of the Central Coast of British Columbia. In *Indian Art Traditions of the Northwest Coast*, edited by R.L. Carlson, pp. 122–130. Archaeology Press, Simon Fraser University, Burnaby.

———. 1990a. Cultural and Ethnic Continuity on the Pacific Coast of British Columbia. In *Traditional Cultures of the Pacific Societies*, edited by Sang-Bok Han and Kwang-Ok Kim, pp. 79–88. Seoul National University Press, Seoul.

———. 1990b. Cultural Antecedents. In *Northwest Coast*, edited by W. Suttles, pp. 60–69. Handbook of North American Indians, vol. 7, W.C. Sturtevant, general editor. Smithsonian Institution, Washington, D.C.

———. 1991. The Northwest Coast Before A.D. 1600. In *The North Pacific to 1600*, edited by E.A.P. Crownhart-Vaughn, pp. 109–136. Oregon Historical Society Press, Portland.

Carlson, R.L., and L. Dalla Bona (editors). 1996. *Early Human Occupation in British Columbia*. University of British Columbia Press, Vancouver.

Hester, J.J., and S.M. Nelson (editors). 1978. *Studies in Bella Bella Prehistory*. Publication no. 5. Department of Archaeology, Simon Fraser University, Burnaby.

Hobler, P.M. 1990. Prehistory of the Central Coast of British Columbia. In *Northwest Coast*, edited by W. Suttles, pp. 298–305. Handbook of North American Indians, vol. 7, W.C. Sturtevant, general editor. Smithsonian Institution, Washington, D.C.

Pomeroy, J.A. 1980. *Bella Bella Settlement and Subsistence*. Unpublished Ph.D. dissertation, Department of Archaeology, Simon Fraser University, Burnaby.

Prince, P. 1992. *A People With History: Acculturation and Resistance in Kimsquit*. Unpublished Master's thesis, Department of Archaeology, Simon Fraser University, Burnaby.

Bella Coola Area

The Nuxalk (Bella Coola) archaeological area in British Columbia, Canada, is bounded by unoccupied mountainous terrain on the north and south. To the east are the Carrier people; to the west, the Heiltsuk (Bella Bella). Historically, the groups were not separated by firm boundary lines. Rather, there were intermediate zones where settlements were bilingual and intermarriage resulted in a blending of cultural traditions. The terrain consists primarily of entrenched river valleys at the heads of saltwater fjords. Nearly all Nuxalk village sites are oriented to rivers rather than to the saltwater. Food remains from excavations reflect the riverine orientation and also show extensive hunting of land mammals. The river valleys are unstable and subject to repeated flooding and channel change. Thus, although valley floors were preferred for settlement, older sites are rarely preserved in such localities. Archaeological characteristics of the area may be summarized as follows:

Midden Deposits. At Nutlitliqotlank on the Kwatna River, cultural deposits with a depth of up to 3.25 m (10.7 feet) represent ca. 1,200–1,600 years of occupation. Clam and mussel shells contribute to the volume of these deposits. The much thinner middens at village sites on other inner coast rivers reflect the near absence of shellfish and much shorter occupation of the individual villages.

Structural Remains. Archaeological work substantiates oral traditions and eighteenth-century documents that depict a surprising diversity of house types, including pile-built houses with floors up to 10 m (32.8 feet) above the ground, pithouses, surface plank houses, and possibly even skin tents. In excavations at several sites, wooden floors and posts have been found just below the surface. In two of these, remains of intact flooring are preserved from dated contexts three or more centuries prior to European contact. At Nutlitliqotlank, the surface of the glacial deposit at the base of the deep midden shows the partial outline of a house built there in the first centuries A.D. (1950–1750 years B.P.).

Burial Sites. Deposits within villages more recent than A.D. 450 (1500 years B.P.) are devoid of burial remains. At most early historic villages, burial depressions are outside of villages. The deceased were also sometimes placed in wooden boxes in trees. In the saltwater fjord areas, cedar-box burials were placed in rock shelters.

Rock Art. Red-painted pictographs are characteristic of the saltwater areas, while petroglyphs are typical of the riverine zone. Specific design elements as well as overall style crosscut the two media. Some major petroglyph panels of the Late Prehistoric and historic periods are known to have been produced by ceremonial societies at secret rehearsals.

Fish Traps. Large wooden weirs were probably once present at all Nuxalk riverine villages. Extensive remains of weirs in the Bella Coola River can still be seen during winter low-water levels. Stone-wall intertidal fish traps are not typical of Bella Coola territory.

Quarries. Two quarry sites in the Bella Coola Valley produced greenstone for rough, flaked adze blanks. Finished adzes made from these blanks are found widely on the central coast. A large andesite quarry excavated near Kwatna was in use ca. 4050–3050 B.C. (6000–5000 years B.P.) or earlier and may have been used by residents of nearby Namu.

Intertidal Refuse. Several intertidal, flaked-stone surface sites found in the fjord zone may represent settlements occupied at a time of slightly lower sea level. At Joashila, intertidal artifacts were traced directly to in situ deposits on the shore and were thus datable.

Chronology. Millennia of flooding and channel change in the Bella Coola Valley have destroyed a large segment of the prehistoric remains on the floodplain. As a result, sites older than ca. A.D. 1450 (500 years B.P.) are not preserved. In a more geologically stable area at the mouth of the Kwatna River, occupation was continuous from ca. A.D. 1 (1950 years B.P.). Prior to that time, the archaeological record is discontinuous. The presence of early flaked-stone components, whose age may be earlier than 4050 B.C. (6000 years B.P.), is evident at the intertidal lithic sites. Surface finds at two sites

on stable high terraces of the Upper Bella Coola River, as well as excavated materials from a similar rock bench at the mouth of the Dean River, hint at the possibility of a much earlier use of the adjacent floodplains. The fjord-head valleys may have been occupied since the obsidian trade began ca. 6050–5050 B.C. (8000–7000 years B.P.). The aboriginal food resources in these valleys certainly equaled those at nearby Namu near the outer coast, where the earliest archaeological deposits are close to 8050 B.C. (10,000 years B.P.).

Artifacts. Prior to ca. 50 B.C. (2000 years B.P.), flaked stone dominated Bella Coola cultural inventories. In the Bella Coola Valley, one enigmatic high-terrace site has produced quantities of pebble choppers on the surface but no other flaked stone. A nearby undated surface find of a cache of points or bifaces, also on a high terrace, resembles Paleoindian types more than those found in the early period at Namu. Intertidal sites and the related in situ materials at Joashila show a large core-flake technology in andesite-basalt in which bifaces are rare and ground and polished stone absent. Sites dating after 50 B.C. (2000 years B.P.) show a diverse technology with much stability through time. Grinding and polishing of greenstone are the principal stoneworking techniques. Bone tools are made in quantity, and many are small unipoints and bipoints that were parts of composite fishing equipment. Axeti, a prehistoric waterlogged site at Kwatna, revealed many items of perishable materials, including woven basketry, cedar-bark cordage, wooden stakes, wedges, and fishing tackle.

Philip M. Hobler

Further Readings

Hobler, P.M. 1990. Prehistory of the Central Coast of British Columbia. In *Northwest Coast,* edited by W. Suttles, pp. 298–305. Handbook of North American Indians, vol. 7, W.C. Sturtevant, general editor. Smithsonian Institution, Washington, D.C.

See also BELLA BELLA SEQUENCE

Belle Glade Culture

The Belle Glade culture refers to the prehistoric inhabitants of Florida's Lake Okeechobee Basin. Named after the type site near Belle Glade, Florida, its most distinctive features are the large, complex earthworks surrounding Lake

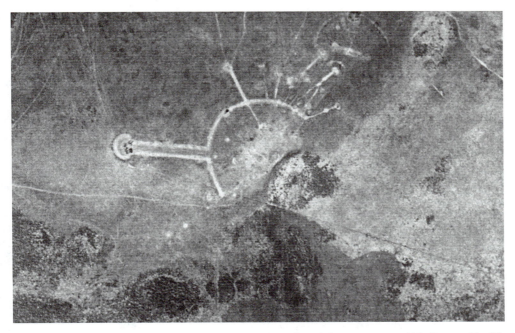

Belle Glade: The Big Circle mounds, a typical Belle Glade earthwork form at ca. A.D. 1000. (Prepared by W. G. Johnson)

Okeechobee and bordering the Kissimmee River. The earliest of these have been dated to ca. 1000 B.C. (2950 years B.P.). Changes to them through time, combined with other diagnostic artifacts, provide the basis for understanding Belle Glade chronology. Five periods have been defined that indicate continuous occupation of the region into the historic period.

The region was first inhabited during the Transitional period (ca. 1000–500 B.C., or 2950–2450 years B.P.). Evidence of earlier Archaic peoples can be found nearby in the upper reaches of the St. Johns River and along Florida's coastal margins. However, there are no sites in the Okeechobee Basin that have been assigned to the Archaic period. The earliest known occupations are at the Fort Center site, where limited numbers of semifiber-tempered ceramics are coeval with the construction of the earliest of the site's earthworks. Two semicircular ditches overlap each other inside a much larger circular ditch known as the Great Circle. The larger ditch is ca. 400 m (1,300 feet) in diameter, 10 m (33 feet) wide, and 2 m (6.6 feet) deep. A radiocarbon date indicates that it was built prior to 450 B.C. (2400 years B.P.). It is estimated that the semicircular ditches date to 1000 B.C. (2950 years B.P.).

Defined mostly by research at Fort Center, the Transitional period of occupation depicts the Belle Glade peoples as consisting of small family groups living along riverbanks on small house mounds. Fish and turtle were particularly important to their diet. Only semifiber-tempered pottery was in use at this time. Its replacement by sand-tempered plain wares signals the beginning of the Belle Glade periods.

The four Belle Glade periods (ca. 500 B.C.– A.D. 1700, or 2450–250 years B.P.) are marked by increased population sizes and social complexity. Belle Glade Ia (500 B.C.– A.D. 200, or 2450–1750 years B.P.) is defined by the presence of fully sand-tempered ceramics. The circular earthworks of the earlier periods give rise to a new form of earthwork in the Belle Glade Ib period (A.D. 200–1000, or 1750–950 years B.P.) marked by a half circle attached to a linear embankment. These sites have two mounds: one at the end of the linear feature, and the other enclosed by the half circle. The linear-feature mound has occupational debris, which indicates it served as a house mound. The other contains midden deposits that suggest it was a waste-disposal mound. Ceramics are now sand-tempered plain wares and distinctive Belle Glade plain wares. These latter artifacts, off-white to dirty light gray, can be distinguished from their sand-tempered counterparts most often by their smooth feel. Although they can be found on the coasts, they are most popular in the Belle Glade heartland around Lake Okeechobee.

Ca. A.D. 1000 (950 years B.P.), the basic half-circle, linear earthworks are modified by the attachment of additional linear embankments to the half circle, which marks the Belle Glade Iia period (A.D. 1000–1500, or 950–450 years B.P.). The largest of these are the Big Circle mounds, which cover ca. 16 ha (40 acres). As with the earlier versions, each linear embankment terminates in a house mound, and now the midden mound found within the half circle becomes larger.

During this time, approximately 20 half-circle sites are occupied in the Belle Glade area. Perhaps as many as 100 additional individual mounds and mound groups are occupied as well. Later, some of these mound groups have linear embankments leading to one of the mounds. The bulk of the material culture at these sites consists of animal bone, with turtle and fish abundantly represented. Belle Glade wares are common, along with trade wares that represent influences from other parts of Florida. Elaborate burial practices are known from Fort Center, where a large charnel platform was excavated from a small pond. Beautifully carved wooden artifacts representing a variety of animals were associated with the platform and are reminiscent of the Key Marco artifacts excavated by Frank Hamilton Cushing (1897) in the late 1800s.

Controversy concerning the subsistence base of Belle Glade peoples has led some researchers to conclude that they were a maize-based agrarian people. The evidence for this position comes from maize pollen found in a variety of archaeologically sealed deposits at Fort Center. However, there is no corroborating evidence from similar sites elsewhere in the basin. In addition, the diagnostic soil characteristics that should be present on proposed planting surfaces (i.e., the Great Circle, and later the linear embankments at Fort Center) are lacking.

Little is known about the terminus of the Belle Glade culture (Belle Glade ILb period). One ethnohistoric account of sixteenth-century South Florida native groups refers to a people who lived around a large lake known as the Mayaimi. This narrative provides scanty information on population density, subsistence, environment, and political affiliations with the coastal Calusa. Some Belle Glade sites, including Fort Center, contain European artifacts and European-derived raw materials, such as silver, iron, and gold. Thus, there exists ample evidence to indicate Belle Glade participation in a larger economy than existed solely in the Okeechobee Basin.

The demise of the Belle Glade peoples was surely linked to their participation in this larger economy. The introduction of European diseases in the sixteenth and seventeenth centuries is documented throughout the southeastern United States and is considered a major cause of death in South Florida native groups. It is thought by many researchers that by the time the Seminoles entered this part of Florida in the mid-1800s, all of the original South Florida aborigines were extinct.

William Gray Johnson

Further Readings

Cushing, F.H. 1897. Exploration of Ancient Key Dwellers' Remains on the Gulf Coast of Florida. *Proceedings of the American Philosophical Society* 35:329–448.

Johnson, W.G. 1991. *Remote Sensing and Soil Science Applications to Understanding Belle Glade Cultural Adaptations in the Okeechobee Basin.* Ph.D. dissertation, University of Florida, Gainesville. University Microfilms, Ann Arbor.

Sears, W.H. 1982. *Fort Center: An Archaeological Site in the Lake Okeechobee Basin.* University Presses of Florida, Gainesville.

Beringian Tradition

A concept intended to formally delineate a series of strongly similar late Pleistocene–early Holocene cultures that occupied eastern Siberia, Alaska, parts of the Yukon Territory, and, necessarily, the intervening land connection—the Bering Land Bridge. Botanist Eric Hultén named the former biotic province centering on this land bridge "Beringia." Its spread, distribution, and persistence show the Beringian tradition to be primarily an adjustment to the peculiar biome of Beringia. Beringian-tradition cultures are of a distinctly Upper Paleolithic character; they are marked by blade and burin technologies, with the former involving prepared cores of specific forms that produced blades ranging down to very small dimensions ("microblades").

The Beringian tradition appears in early Sartan (i.e., Wisconsinan II) times with the earliest Dyuktai culture of the Upper Lena River. It terminates in interior Alaska with the early Holocene late Denali culture. The duration of the tradition is, therefore, from ca. 28,050 to 8550 B.C. (30,000–10,500 years B.P.) for Dyuktai in Siberia to greater than 9050–6550 B.C. (11,000–8500 years B.P.) for its descendants in Alaska. The Beringian-tradition Dyuktai culture appears to represent the earliest occupation of Siberia by human hunters. While there may be other Beringian-tradition variants in late Pleistocene Alaska, Denali, which is widespread and tightly defined, is most clearly the direct Dyuktai descendent in this area. This remained an inland hunting tradition throughout its long span.

Implicit in the Beringian tradition is the assumption of a common origin, which is sustained by formal resemblances in artifact types and assemblages. The occupation of Beringia was late in human history partly because of its distance from the center of human population in Würmian times; it was surely the last corner of the contiguous Old World to be settled. Climate was another factor. As phrased in the original formulation, "one of the last major accomplishments of the genus *Homo* . . . was the adaptation to severely cold environments" (West 1981). That humans finally came to occupy these regions was a result of cultural evolution acting concurrently with pressures among burgeoning populations of hunters. The persistence of the tradition in Holocene Alaska is explained in part by the isolation of these small groups following the severing of the land-bridge connection, but also by the fact that environmental conditions approximating those of Pleistocene Beringia persisted in some—mostly mountainous—areas of Alaska well into the Holocene. The opening of the Mackenzie Corridor allowed early movement south; the Clovis culture is taken to have roots in the Beringian tradition. The first "backwash" of influences from the south was not to be until several millennia later.

Frederick Hadleigh West

Further Readings

Hoffecker, J.F., W.R. Powers, and T. Goebel. 1993. The Colonization of Beringia and the Peopling of the New World. *Science* 259:46–53.

Mochanov, Y.A. 1977. *Drevneishie Etapy Zaseleniya Chelovekom Severo-Vostochnoi Azii* (The Most Ancient Stages in the Settlement by Man of Northeast Asia). Izdatel'stsvo Nauka, Sibirskoe Otdelenie, Novosibirsk.

West, F.H. 1981. *The Archaeology of Beringia.* Columbia University Press, New York.

See also DENALI COMPLEX

Besant Phase

"Besant Phase" refers to a late middle prehistoric (late Plains Archaic) cultural entity (ca. A.D. 1–600/700, or 1950–1350/1250 years B.P.) indigenous to the Canadian Prairie Provinces and the northern Plains of the adjacent United States. First described at the Mortlach site in Saskatchewan by Boyd Wettlaufer in 1955, it was more fully defined by Brian O.K. Reeves (1983) and George C. Frison (1978).

Diagnostic, medium-sized Besant corner-to side-notched projectile points, thought to be tips for darts or thrusting spears, are sometimes accompanied by Pelican Lake points and by small points suitable for arrows. Besant points are commonly made of Knife River flint, even when found at such great distances from the North Dakota quarries as the Muhlbach pound (corral) in central Alberta. Intensive hunting by communal drives of bison is indicated particularly at numerous pounds but also at jumps. Winter campsites occupy locations on sheltered stream terraces. Associated tipi rings attest fair-weather occupation on the prairie level. Butchering and hide-working tools are common in kill and camp areas. "Bone uprights" (bison long bones or vertebrae jammed vertically into the earth) are distinctive features. A unique "ceremonial" structure of elliptical plan near the Ruby pound in Wyoming has been interpreted as evidence of shamanistic activities occurring with communal hunts (Frison 1978).

Besant points are found in the Sonota complex of the Dakotas and at other contemporaneous northern Plains Woodland sites along the eastern Plains border. Buffalo hunting was also important there, with the use of pounds inferred. Not abundant in Sonota, pottery tends to be rare or absent in Besant sites; Besant lacks burial mounds in the West. There is some question whether Sonota belongs to the Besant phase or vice versa. On the basis of exotic materials, Hopewellian connections have been proposed by Robert W. Neuman (1975) and by Reeves. At one site, High Butte in North Dakota, a "turf cut turtle effigy" is one of several features also suggesting relationships with the Eastern Woodlands. In terms of bison dependence, northern Plains Woodland seems to fall into a continuum with later sedentary farmers of the Plains Village pattern (Wood and Johnson 1973).

In the west, Besant is replaced rather abruptly by Late Prehistoric cultures in which small arrow points are dominant. The efficacious practice of driving buffalo over cliffs—the jump—tends generally to supersede the laborious construction of corrals for impoundment. Even so, Besant is sufficiently impressive in terms of bison procurement that Frison (1978:223) recognizes it as a "cultural climax" in northwestern Plains prehistory. Clearly, it did exceed previous Pelican Lake attainments in this respect, though not Old Women's.

Richard G. Forbis

Further Readings

Frison, G.C. 1978. *Prehistoric Hunters of the High Plains.* Academic Press, Orlando.

Neuman, R.W. 1975. *The Sonota Complex and Associated Sites on the Northern Great Plains.* Publications in Anthropology no. 4. Nebraska State Historical Society, Lincoln.

Reeves, B.O.K. 1983. *Culture Change in the Northern Plains: 1000 B.C.–1000 A.D.* Occasional Paper no. 20. Archaeological Survey of Alberta, Edmonton.

Wettlaufer, B. 1955. *The Mortlach Site in the Besant Valley of Central Saskatchewan.* Anthropological Series no. 1. (Saskatchewan) Department of Natural Resources, Regina.

Wood, W. R., and A.M. Johnson. 1973. High Butte, 32ME13, A Missouri Valley Woodland-Besant Site. *Archaeology in Montana* 13(3):35–83.

See also OLD WOMEN'S PHASE; PELICAN LAKE; SONOTA BURIAL COMPLEX

Betatakin

Betatakin (a Navajo word roughly translated as "ledge house") is a large cliff dwelling in the Tsegi Canyon system on the Navajo Indian Reservation in northeastern Arizona. The site was discovered in 1909 by a party led by Byron Cummings, University of Utah classics professor, and John Wetherill, trader and explorer, and was partially excavated by Cummings in that year. Subsequent archaeological work includes excavation and stabilization by Neil Merton Judd in 1917, excavation by Milton Wetherill in 1935, a tree-ring study by Jeffrey S. Dean (1969) in the 1960s, and excavation by Keith M. Anderson in the 1960s. The site has been a component of the Navajo National Monument since the latter's creation by President William Howard Taft in 1909. Excellent preservation, resulting from the dryness of the rock shelter, has made Betatakin a particularly

General view of Betatakin. (Reprinted from Bureau of American Ethnology, Bulletin 50, Plate 8, Smithsonian Institution)

Central part of Betatakin. (Reprinted from Bureau of American Ethnology, Bulletin 50, Plate 11, Smithsonian Institution)

productive locus for intensive architectural and tree-ring studies.

Betatakin consists of ca. 125 rooms and a rectangular kiva ranged in steplike fashion across the bedrock floor of an immense rock shelter in the Navajo sandstone. A second rectangular kiva is located in an adjacent shelter. Several different kinds of domestic structure can be distinguished, including living rooms, granaries, storerooms, corn-grinding rooms, and unroofed courtyards. An architectural unit called the room cluster, which typically consists of a living room and several storage chambers grouped around a courtyard, is the basic structural component of the site. At least 18 such units are present. The room cluster probably was the residence of a household that consisted of a married couple, their unmarried children, and perhaps an older adult or two. A spring at the base of the rock shelter provided water for the site's inhabitants, who farmed alluvial bottomland about a mile away in Tsegi Canyon.

Betatakin is a single-component site at which occupation was confined to the Tsegi phase (A.D. 1250–1300) of the Kayenta branch of the Anasazi cultural tradition. Tree-ring dates and architectural relationships indicate that the rock shelter was briefly occupied in the 1250s and then abandoned. A subsequent reoccupation was initiated by the construc-

tion of four isolated room clusters in 1267–1268. At least eight room clusters were added in the 1275–1278 interval and five more in the 1280s. Although the remaining clusters cannot be precisely dated, it is clear that Betatakin reached its zenith in the mid-1280s. The site was abandoned, probably in a single operation, sometime between 1286 and 1300, an event that was part of the general Anasazi exodus from Tsegi Canyon and the entire San Juan River drainage.

Betatakin is notable for its contribution to the study of prehistoric Puebloan social organization. Architectural and tree-ring analyses reveal that the community consisted of a number of relatively autonomous households that were not organized into larger residence groups within the village. Thus, the only level of social integration above the household was the village itself. The natural tendency of the village to fragment along household lines probably was offset by kiva-associated obligations that crosscut domestic units.

Jeffrey S. Dean

Further Readings

Ambler, J.R. 1985. *Navajo National Monument: An Archaeological Assessment.* Archaeological Series no. 1. Northern Arizona University, Flagstaff.

Anderson, K.M. 1971. Excavations at

Betatakin and Keet Seel. *Kiva* 37:1–29.

Dean, J.S. 1969. *Chronological Analysis of Tsegi Phase Sites in Northeastern Arizona.* Papers no. 3. Laboratory of Tree-Ring Research, University of Arizona Press, Tucson.

———. 1970. Aspects of Tsegi Phase Social Organization: A Trial Reconstruction. In *Reconstructing Prehistoric Pueblo Societies*, edited by W.A. Longacre, pp. 140–174. University of New Mexico Press, Albuquerque.

Judd, N.M. 1930. The Excavation and Repair of Betatakin. *Proceedings of the United States National Museum,* vol. 77, art. 5.

Viele, C.W. 1980. *Voices in the Canyon.* Southwestern Parks and Monuments Association, Tucson.

See also ANASAZI CULTURE AREA

Biesterfeldt Site

The Biesterfeldt site (32RMl), a fortified earth-lodge village historically documented as a Cheyenne Indian village, is sometimes called the Sheyenne-Cheyenne site because of its location on the Sheyenne River in Ransom County, southeastern North Dakota. It was excavated by Columbia University in 1938. Cartographic and historical records are consistent in identifying the village as Protohistoric Cheyenne. The village was built shortly after the Cheyenne moved east from villages on the Minnesota River in present-day Minnesota. They settled along the Sheyenne River ca. A.D. 1700 (250 years B.P.) and apparently established the site sometime later. Subsistence at the site was based on mixed hunting and horticulture. Biesterfeldt was abandoned in the closing decades of the same century, as suggested by historical records and by its inventory of European trade goods. After leaving Biesterfeldt, the Cheyenne moved farther west, where they established a number of villages and practiced horticulture on or near the Missouri River near the present North Dakota–South Dakota boundary.

The Biesterfeldt component stands alone; no earlier sites like it are known in Minnesota, and to date (1996) none of the Cheyenne village sites along the Missouri have been identified. The four-post earthlodge architecture, the ceramic inventory, and the remaining cultural assemblage at Biesterfeldt are markedly similar to those of eighteenth-century Arikara Indians.

W. Raymond Wood

Further Readings
Wood, W.R. 1971. *The Biesterfeldt Site: A*

Aerial view of the Biesterfeldt site. The view is to the southwest. (Photograph by W. R. Wood)

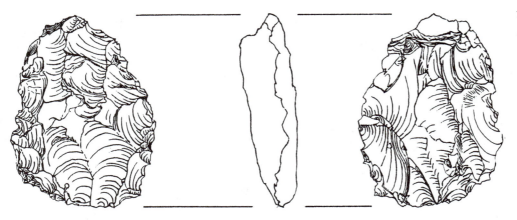

Biface. (Courtesy of the Wilford Archaeology Laboratory, University of Minnesota)

Coalescent Site on the Northeastern Plains. Contributions to Anthropology no. 15. Smithsonian Institution, Washington, D.C.

Biface

A biface is a chipped-stone implement that has been worked invasively on both surfaces (as opposed to a bifacially retouched piece whose retouch is restricted to the margins). The term was created as a purely descriptive type in an attempt to redress the functionally charged names given to other typological entities, such as "knife" and "projectile point." However, use of the term has been clouded by ambiguities of another sort: some scholars refer to a biface as any stone possessing invasive bifacial modification, a usage that would include such types as projectile points and drills, while other scholars reserve the term for an object with invasive bifacial modification that does not fit into any other category. This all-inclusive generic entity is often referred to as a "bifacial object" or a "bifacially retouched piece." Since terms are already in use for specific entities, such as projectile points and drills, and since no other readily understood term is available for bifacially worked objects that are not in these categories, the second option is favored here.

The production of bifaces entails a series of activities that can be divided into discrete stages. In creating 1,000 experimental bifaces to resolve a specific Paleoindian problem, Errett Callahan (1979) provided guidelines for interpreting these stages. This approach can be studied in still greater detail in a work by David E. Young and Robson Bonnichsen (1984), in which the products of two flint knappers are painstak-ingly compared. The abrasion of bifacial edges that occurs in the course of strengthening them for subsequent flake removal is explained in Payson D. Sheets (1973), who then interprets the accrued damage with respect to use-wear. A different approach is taken by Jay K. Johnson (1979), who employs production failures to interpret Archaic lithic trajectories in an assemblage from northeastern Mississippi.

Since the late nineteenth century, the biface has been interpreted as a core tool manufactured to serve diverse tasks and as an item conceptually distinct from a core, which possesses greater edge angles and whose primary purpose is the production of flakes. In the 1980s, concepts such as "optimal foraging" theory and the organization of hunter-gatherer mobility were increasingly instrumental in shifting the focus of studies of lithic assemblages from the creation of artifact typologies to the examination of them as adaptive technologies interdependent with human behavioral systems. In this context, Robert L. Kelly (1988) has demonstrated that bifaces could have served efficiently in many situations not only as core tools but as cores for the production of flakes for tasks less suited to bifacial edges. This interpretation blurs the easy distinctions that had been made between core and biface, but it brings us closer to understanding the roles that bifacial technologies played in human adaptation.

George H. Odell

Further Readings

Callahan, E. 1979. The Basics of Biface Knapping in the Eastern Fluted Point Tradition. *Archaeology of Eastern North America* 7:1–180.

Johnson, J.K. 1979. Archaic Biface Manufacture: A Chronicle of the Misbegotten. *Lithic Technology* 8:25–35.

Kelly, R.L. 1988. The Three Sides of a Biface. *American Antiquity* 53:717–734.

Sheets, P.D. 1973. Edge Abrasion During Biface Manufacture. *American Antiquity* 38:215–218.

Young, D.E., and R. Bonnichsen. 1984. *Understanding Stone Tools: A Cognitive Approach.* Peopling of the Americas Process Series, vol. 1. Center for the Study of Early Man, University of Maine, Orono.

Bifurcate Tradition

In 1963, erosion by the Kanawha River near Charleston, West Virginia, exposed the St. Albans site. Subsequent excavations (Broyles 1966, 1971) defined a deep stratigraphic sequence of Early Archaic–period occupations. The sequence of Kirk Corner Notched cluster projectile points was similar to that found by Joffre Lanning Coe of the University of North Carolina at Chapel Hill at the Doerschuk site in 1949 and at the Hardaway site between 1954 and 1958. Above the Kirk material was a sequence of four notched or bifurcated base projectile-point types. Bettye J. Broyles (1966) published type descriptions for three of the varieties; the fourth, the LeCroy Bifurcated Stem, had been described earlier by Madeline Kneberg (1956) but not placed chronologically. The earliest, MacCorkle Stemmed, is a large point with a notched base and basal ears that have a lobed appearance. The St. Albans Side Notched has slight side notching and deep basal bifurcation; radiocarbon dates are 6870 B.C. ± 500 and 6880 B.C. ± 700 (8820 and 8830 years B.P.). The LeCroy Bifurcated Stem has a triangular blade and a straight, deeply bifurcated stem; radiocarbon date is 6300 B.C. ± 100 (8250 years B.P.). The latest bifurcate is the Kanawha Stemmed at 6210 B.C. ± 100 (8160 years B.P.), which appears to be transitional to the later unbifurcate Stanly Stemmed type.

The discovery of a stratified Early Archaic sequence at Rose Island in the Lower Little Tennessee River Valley of east Tennessee (Chapman 1975) confirmed the St. Albans site point sequence and chronology. In 1964, James E. Fitting had suggested that bifurcate-base projectile points may provide a horizon marker. In the Rose Island site report, Chapman examined bifurcate point types from throughout eastern North America and proposed a Bifurcate tradition that commenced in the early seventh millennium B.C. and continued for 500–700 years in a geographic region that roughly coincides with the eastern deciduous forest. Additional data on bifurcate points were obtained from subsequent excavations on other Tellico Archaic sites.

Noel D. Justice (1987) has divided the bifurcate varieties in the eastern United States into two type clusters. The Rice Lobed cluster includes the MacCorkle and St. Albans Side Notched types; the LeCroy cluster includes the LeCroy and Kanawha types.

Jefferson Chapman

Further Readings

Broyles, B.J. 1966. Preliminary Report: The St. Albans Site (46KA27), Kanawha County, West Virginia. *West Virginia Archaeologist* 19:1–43.

———. 1971. *Second Preliminary Report: The St. Albans Site, Kanawha County, West Virginia, 1964–1968.* Report of Archaeological Investigations no. 3. West Virginia Geological and Economic Survey, Morgantown.

Chapman, J. 1975. *The Rose Island Site and the Bifurcate Point Tradition.* Report of Investigations no. 14. Department of Anthropology, University of Tennessee, Knoxville.

Fitting, J.E. 1964. Bifurcate-Stemmed Projectile Points in the Eastern United States. *American Antiquity* 30:92–94.

Justice, N.D. 1987. *Stone Age Spear and Arrow Points of the Midcontinental and Eastern United States.* Indiana University Press, Bloomington.

Kneberg, M. 1956. Some Important Projectile Point Types Found in the Tennessee Area. *Tennessee Archaeologist* 12:17–28.

See also DOERSCHUK SITE; HARDAWAY SITE; TELLICO ARCHAIC

Big Horn Medicine Wheel

The Big Horn Medicine Wheel (488H302) is both a contemporary Native American religious site and a prehistoric rock structure with archaeological and historical significance. Additionally, the site is a National Historic Landmark. The medicine wheel is located on the western edge of Medicine Mountain in the

Big Horn Medicine Wheel, Montana. Rock alignment in upper right marks a parking lot. (Prepared by A. M. Johnson)

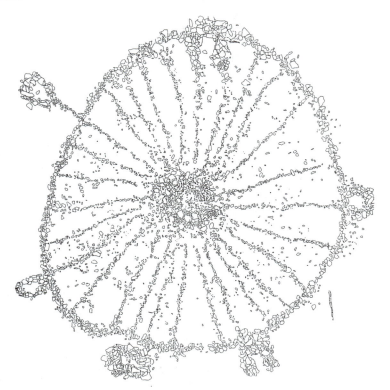

Big Horn Medicine Wheel. (Adapted by A. M. Johnson from a map drawn by Don Gray of the Wyoming Archaeological Society in August 1958)

Big Horn National Forest, Wyoming, at an elevation of 2926 m (9,600 feet), a height that provides a panoramic view of the Big Horn Basin below. The structure is an imperfect circle with a diameter of ca. 26 m (85 feet). Twenty-eight spokes radiate out from the central cairn; six other cairns or rock piles are placed unevenly just outside the rim of the circle (see Figure). It is not known who constructed the medicine wheel, but it appears to have been remodeled and modified through time. A date of origin of the site between A.D. 1400 and 1700 (550–250 years B.P.) has been proposed (Grey 1963).

The Big Horn Medicine Wheel is sacred to a number of Plains Indian tribes, who sometimes leave tobacco offerings tied to the wire fence that now protects the stone alignment. John A. Eddy (1974) believes that the rock pattern is aligned to the summer solstice. Information specific to the Big Horn Medicine Wheel has been summarized by Michael Wilson (1981).

Ann M. Johnson

Further Readings

Brumley, J.H. 1988. *Medicine Wheels on the Northern Plains: A Summary and Appraisal.* Manuscript Series no. 12. Archaeological Survey of Alberta, Edmonton.

Eddy, J.A. 1974. Astronomical Alignment of the Big Horn Medicine Wheel. *Science* 184(4141):1035–1043.

Grey, D. 1963. Big Horn Medicine Wheel Site, 488H302. *Plains Anthropologist* 8:27–40.

Grinnell, G.B. 1922. The Medicine Wheel. *American Anthropologist* 24:299–310.

Wilson, M. 1981. Sun Dances, Thirst Dances, and Medicine Wheels: A Search for Alternative Hypotheses. In *Megaliths to Medicine Wheels: Boulder Structures in Archaeology,* edited by M. Wilson, C.L. Road, and K. Hardy. Archaeological Association, Department of Archaeology, University of Calgary, Calgary.

Wyoming Archaeological Society. 1959. A Report on the Medicine Wheel Investigations. *Annals of Wyoming* 31(1):94–100.

"Big Village" Site of the Omahas

The "Big Village" (25DK5) was occupied by the Omaha tribe ca. 1775–1845, though part or all of the tribe settled on the Elkhorn River during the years 1820–1833 and 1841–1843. Sixteen km (10 miles) south of Sioux City, Iowa, the site is on a low terrace remnant on the west bank of the Missouri River where Omaha Creek emerges from the bluff line. The village site encompasses more than 518 ha (2 square miles). It once contained a hundred earthlodges and had a population of 2,500 people. Excavations were conducted in 1939–1941 by Works Progress Administration (WPA) crews under the supervision of University of Nebraska archaeologists John Leland Champe, Paul L. Cooper, and Robert Cumming. All or parts of five earthlodges were excavated, and exterior refuse areas were tested. "Big Village" typifies the "Disorganized Coalescent" period, during which native-made artifacts were being replaced with "trade goods" obtained from colonial Europeans and (later) Americans. The Omahas lived there when hit by smallpox in 1800–1801; population demography derived from two nearby, associated cemeteries (25DK2, 25DK10) suggests that the tribe also experienced the 1780–1781 epidemic. Analysis of the distribution of grave furnishings by age and sex confirms historic and ethnographic reports that Omaha society was stratified and ranked. The site has been damaged by highway and railroad construction. Though under cultivation, a thick silt mantle provides some protection to buried deposits. "Big Village" was listed on the National Register of Historic Places on August 14, 1973.

John Ludwickson

Further Readings

O'Shea, J.M. 1984. *Mortuary Variability: An Archaeological Investigation.* Academic Press, New York.

O'Shea, J.M., and J. Ludwickson. 1991. *Archaeology and Ethnohistory of the Omaha Indians: The Big Village Site.* University of Nebraska Press, Lincoln.

Billet

A billet, also called a baton or drift, is a relatively large, elongated piece of cut antler. In most cases, it possesses battering marks on at least one of its ends, a probable result of having been employed in flintknapping, either through direct percussion or with the aid of a punch. Billets have been found throughout the prehistory of the mid-continent, from Archaic sites such as Eva in Tennessee (Lewis and Lewis 1961: Plate 45) to the Caddoan occupation of the Albertson Shelter in Arkansas (Dickson 1991: Figure 108).

George H. Odell

Further Readings

Dickson, D.R. 1991. *The Albertson Site: A Deeply and Clearly Stratified Ozark Bluff Shelter.* Research Series no. 41. Arkansas Archeological Survey, Fayetteville.

Lewis, T.M.N., and M.K. Lewis. 1961. *Eva: An Archaic Site.* University of Tennessee Press, Knoxville.

Bipolar Percussion

A bipolar-percussion technique involves placing a core on an anvil and striking the core such that the direction of force directly intersects the point of contact with the anvil. Although the practical applicability of this technique, as well as its prehistoric utility, has been categorically doubted by J.B. Sollberger and L.W. Patterson (1976), their view is not the majority opinion (Hayden 1980; Shott 1989). In fact, Errett Callahan (1987) has demonstrated that this is a practical way to break up smaller nodules and cobbles that are not easy to manage with freehand percussion. Thus, bipolar percussion is often a good indicator of prehistoric economizing behavior. The technique produces cores with percussion battering on opposing surfaces and, occasionally, flakes with comparable opposed battering or even opposed ventral flake characteristics such as ripples, although it also produces flakes with a variety of other characteristics (Leaf 1979).

Although these characteristics appear superficially straightforward, other activities practiced prehistorically can cause them. For example, the hallmark of stone wedges is battering on opposed margins, and several types and degrees of wedging activities probably occurred in prehistory, such as prying out pieces of antler and splitting wood or bone. These can be shown experimentally to produce a fairly wide variety of battering traces, many of which are almost identical to the battering that accrues to bipolar cores. A less functionally charged name for these objects is *pièce esquillée,* though its use may simply beg the question of how the battering originated.

There is, then, a problem of identification. Michael J. Shott (1989) maintained that the characteristically thick objects possessing opposed battering usually illustrated in the archaeological literature were probably mostly bipolar cores. However, a number of other scholars have identified wedges in North American assemblages, particularly from Paleoindian sites

B

Bipolar percussion. (Reprinted from Smithsonian Institution, Bureau of American Ethnology, Bulletin 60, Figure 163)

like Debert in Nova Scotia and Vail in Maine, and Shott admits that the thinner varieties may well be wedges. Indeed, Raymond J. LeBlanc (1992) has argued that distinctions are best applied on a case-by-case basis. An effective way of testing hypotheses such as these is through experimental studies of manufacture and use (Callahan 1987; Sollberger and Patterson 1976) and through use-wear analyses (Ranere 1975).

George H. Odell

Further Readings

Callahan, E. 1987. *An Evaluation of the Lithic Technology in Middle Sweden During the Mesolithic and Neolithic.* Aun 8. Societas Archaeologica Upsaliensis, Uppsala.

Hayden, B. 1980. Confusion in the Bipolar World: Bashed Pebbles and Splintered Pieces. *Lithic Technology* 9:2–7.

Leaf, G.R. 1979. Variation in the Form of Bipolar Cores. *Plains Anthropologist* 23:39–50.

Le Blanc, R.J. 1992. Wedges, *Pièces Esquillées,* Bipolar Cores, and Other Things: An Alternative to Shott's View of Bipolar Industries. *North American Archaeologist* 13:1–14.

Ranere, A.J. 1975. Toolmaking and Tool Use Among the Preceramic Peoples of Panama. In *Lithic Technology: Making and Using Stone Tools,* edited by E. Swanson, pp. 173–209. Mouton, The Hague.

Shott, M.J. 1989. Bipolar Industries: Ethnographic Evidence and Archaeological Implications. *North American Archaeologist* 10:1–24.

Sollberger, J.B., and L.W. Patterson. 1976. The Myth of Bipolar Flaking Industries. *Lithic Technology* 5:40–42.

Birnirk Culture

Birnirk is the pre-Thule culture first identified by excavations in 1912 by Vilhjalmur Stefansson (1919) near Point Barrow, Alaska. The first extensive description of the culture was by J. Alden Mason (1930). It was based on collections at the University Museum of the University of Pennsylvania that were acquired in 1919 from Kugusugaruk, just south of Utkiavik (modern Barrow), by schoolteacher William B. van Valin. The first fully scientific excavations of Birnirk materials at Barrow were made by James A. Ford in 1931 and 1932, although the publication of the results was delayed until 1959. Other Birnirk sites were excavated in 1936 at Cape Prince of Wales by Henry B. Collins (1937), in 1939 at Point Hope by Helge Larsen and Froelich Rainey (1948), in 1960 and 1961 at Cape Krusenstern by J.L. Giddings (Giddings and Anderson 1986), in 1968 at Walakpa by Dennis Stanford (1976), and in 1970 and 1971 at the Kuk site near Nome by John Bockstoce (1979). Birnirk culture also appears to have existed along the northern coast of northeastern Asia as far west as the mouth of Kolyma River, where in the early 1920s H.U. Sverdrup (1978), and later A.P. Okladnikov and N.A. Beregovaia (1971), located typical Birnirk objects in middens.

The physical type of Birnirk people, described by Ales Hrdlicka (1930), is typical northern Eskimo. Birnirk settlements appear to have been rather small, with only one or two houses occupied at any one time. The houses themselves are also small and could not have been occupied by more than single families. Two forms of houses have been noted. The more common has a relatively short entrance passage and a single side bench; the other has a long entrance passage and a bench along the rear wall. Most of the houses lacked open fireplaces and were instead lighted and heated by lamps.

Birnirk culture is characterized by a wide variety of objects that closely resemble implements of historic-period northwest Alaskan Eskimo culture. This is an indication that Birnirk, along with its successor Thule culture, are in the direct line of continuity into Inupiat (Inuit) culture. The long list of artifact types includes equipment for hunting on ice, such as wound pins and seal ice scratchers for attracting seals basking on the ice in spring, and equipment for hunting seals in open water, such as bladder floats. The characteristic Birnirk-culture harpoon-head type for sealing is self-pointed and open socketed. It has a single lateral barb and an opposing chipped-stone side blade inset. The basal toggling spur is usually bifurcated or trifurcated. Another harpoon-head form is the Sicco type, a variant of the unbarbed, end-bladed Punuk-style harpoon head from St. Lawrence and Punuk islands. Birnirk is also characterized by the use of ground slate for knife and ulu blades, and thick pottery with curvilinear stamped designs.

Whether Birnirk people hunted whales or not is a subject of controversy. The settlements were too small to have permitted coordinated ice lead hunting with multiple crews, which is deemed a prerequisite to successful whaling along the northwest Alaskan coast today. Still, the presence in Birnirk of one whaling harpoon head from Barrow, a few triangular stone blades identical to those used for insetting into whaling harpoon heads from other sites, and whale effigies and baleen are difficult to explain if not related to whale hunting.

Although Birnirk culture is clearly ancestral to Thule and the historic-period Inuit culture, its own origin is still a question. The stone tools from Birnirk sites are derived stylistically from Ipiutak, an earlier northwestern Alaskan coastal and interior culture dating to the beginning of the Christian era. However, the organic implements and pottery bear no relation to Ipiutak, nor do they relate closely to other earlier coastal Beringian or Arctic cultures, such as found in Alaska, Chukchi Peninsula, St. Lawrence Island, or Canada, except in very generalized ways. The best interpretation to date (1996) is that Birnirk developed so rapidly with the introduction of specialized ice hunting practices that traces of the unique aspects of the culture of its forebearers were essentially overwhelmed by the new technology.

Douglas D. Anderson

Further Reading

Bockstoce, J. 1979. *The Archaeology of Cape Nome, Alaska.* Monographs no. 38. University Museum, University of Pennsylvania, Philadelphia.

Collins, H.B. 1937. Archeological Excavations at Bering Strait. In *Explorations and Field-Work of the Smithsonian Institution in 1936*, pp. 63–68. Washington, D.C.

Ford, J.A. 1959. *Eskimo Prehistory in the Vicinity of Point Barrow, Alaska*. Anthropological Papers, vol. 47, pt. 1. American Museum of Natural History, New York.

Giddings, J.L., and D.D. Anderson. 1986. *Beach Ridge Archeology of Cape Krusenstern*. Publications in Archaeology no. 20. National Park Service, Washington, D.C.

Hrdlicka, A. 1930. Anthropological Survey in Alaska. *Forty-Sixth Annual Report of the Bureau of American Ethnology for the Years 1928–1929:19–347.*

Larsen, H., and F. Rainey. 1948. *Ipiutak and the Arctic Whale Hunting Culture*. Anthropological Papers, vol. 42. American Museum of Natural History, New York.

Mason, J.A. 1930. Excavations of Eskimo Thule Culture Sites at Point Barrow, Alaska. *Proceedings of the Twenty-Third International Congress of Americanists, New York 1928:383–394.*

Okladnikov, A.P., and N.A. Beregovaia. 1971. *The Ancient Settlement of Cape Baranov* (in Russian). Scientific Publishing House, Siberian Department, Novosibirsk.

Stanford, D. 1976. *The Walakpa Site, Alaska: Its Place in the Birnirk and Thule Cultures*. Contributions to Anthropology no. 20. Smithsonian Institution, Washington, D.C.

Stefansson, V. 1919. *The Stefansson-Anderson Arctic Expedition of the American Museum: Preliminary Ethnological Report*. Anthropological Papers, vol. 14, pt. 1. American Museum of Natural History, New York.

Sverdrup, H.U. 1978. *Among the Tundra People* (translation of M. Sverdrup. 1938. *Hos Tundra-Folket*. Gyldendal Norsk Forlag, Oslo). Published by University of California and distributed by Scripps Institute of Oceanography, La Jolla.

See also BIRNIRK PHASE

Birnirk Phase

The Birnirk phase, which began about the sixth century A.D. and continued as late as the twelfth or thirteenth century, represents a continuation of the maritime focus of the Old Bering Sea/Okvik culture of St. Lawrence Island, the coast of northwest Alaska, and the Chukchi Peninsula of Siberia. This continuum is indicated by the persistence of a well-developed marine technology (harpoon assemblages with toggle harpoon heads, sealing darts cast by throwing boards, skin-covered boats (*kayak* and *umiak*), lances, rawhide lines, and so on) with the addition of sealskin floats, which were vital equipment in securing marine mammals. Land hunting and fishing were also important as demonstrated by the presence of bow parts, arrows, spears, bolas, and snares, and by nets, leisters (laterally barbed, multipronged fish spears) and traps. Ground-slate tools began to replace chipped-stone tools, although chipped stone tended to be retained for end and side blades on arrow points and harpoon heads. Pottery vessels were tempered with sand or grit rather than fiber; their outer surfaces were impressed with a curvilinear stamp. House structures had an entry tunnel with a cold trap, and oil lamps were used instead of a central fire pit. Major temporal changes can be noted in harpoon-head styles. Birnirk harpoon heads have an asymmetric spur, a single line hole, and a side blade and an opposing barb forward of the line hole; sockets are open. Surface decoration of objects was impoverished compared to the Old Bering Sea/Okvik culture. Harpoon heads are largely undecorated or have an occasional line or Y figure. Objects such as needle holders, combs, and items of personal adornment are decorated with spurred lines, drilled pits, and some line zonation.

The Birnirk culture is largely restricted to the Chukchi Sea, where it appears to have spread from the Bering Strait region northward. Its best expression is at Cape Krusenstern and Point Barrow on the Alaskan coast and at Cape Baranov on the East Siberian Sea (east of the Kolyma River estuary). Birnirk-type harpoon heads have been found at a number of sites along the Chukchi Peninsula, principally at Uelen as grave goods and on St. Lawrence Island as rare items at Punuk-age sites. Birnirk expansion coincided with the Early Punuk phase (A.D. 750–850, or 1200–1100 years B.P.) on St. Lawrence Island. Punuk sites are predominantly in the Bering Sea region, although several have been found along the north shore of the Chukotsk Peninsula.

Punuk sites on St. Lawrence Island and Birnirk sites near Point Barrow tend to be larger than those of the preceding Old Bering Sea and Okvik culture phases (ca. 50 B.C.– A.D. 700, or

2000–1250 years B.P.). This may represent a modest population increase triggered by growing sophistication in the hunting of sea mammals. Effective hunting of seal and walrus by Birnirk populations in the Chukchi Sea region gave them a competitive edge over earlier Norton-related peoples, who depended more on the hunting of land mammals and fishing. In the Bering Sea region, Punuk hunters not only hunted seal and walrus, but they were also active whalers. There is only slight evidence for whale hunting by Birnirk groups.

Investment in a whaling economy would have required the development of more complex social units to furnish the manpower and cooperation necessary to secure such large animals. The prestige gained from feasting and performance of whaling ceremonies would have increased rivalries among villages. The recovery of armor and special war arrows from Punuk sites on St. Lawrence Island suggests that armed conflict was the result. In the Chukchi Sea region, whaling and its consequences do not become evident until the onset of the Western Thule phase ca. A.D. 1200 (750 years B.P.).

Robert E. Ackerman

Further Readings

Ackerman, R.E. 1984. Prehistory of the Asian Eskimo Zone. In *Arctic,* edited by D. Damas, pp. 106–118. Handbook of North American Indians, vol. 5, W.C. Sturtevant, general editor. Smithsonian Institution, Washington, D.C.

Collins, H.B. 1964. The Arctic and Subarctic. In *Prehistoric Man in the New World,* edited by J.D. Jennings and E. Norbeck, pp. 85–114. University of Chicago Press, Chicago.

Ford, J.A. 1959. *Eskimo Prehistory in the Vicinity of Point Barrow, Alaska.* Anthropological Papers, vol. 47, pt. 1. American Museum of Natural History, New York.

See also Birnirk Culture; Cape Krusenstern; Old Bering Sea/Okvik Culture

Bison

The American bison (*Bison bison*) was a mainstay in the diet of the prehistoric inhabitants of North America since the first arrival of Native Americans to the continent. This is especially so in the area of the Great Plains called the "Great Bison Belt," which stretched from central Canada into Mexico and from the Rocky Mountains to the eastern Woodlands. Historically, bison were found even along parts of the eastern seacoast. The members of the genus *Bison* evolved in Asia and immigrated to North America across the Bering Strait during the late Pleistocene (pre-700,000 years B.P.). As the climate and environment changed during the latest Pleistocene (Wisconsinian, 80,000–11,000 years B.P.) and Holocene, various "species" evolved in North America as the genus adapted to those environmental changes. Paleoindians hunted *Bison antiquus* between 9050 and 7050 B.C. (11,000–9,000 years B.P.). Late Paleoindians and Early Archaic peoples used *Bison bison occidentalis* between 8050 and 3550 B.C. (10,000–5,500 years B.P.). Both taxa were distinctly larger than the two modern subspecies, *Bison bison athabascae* and *Bison bison bison,* which developed after 3050 B.C. (5000 years B.P.). This larger size is especially seen in the size of the horns. *Bison antiquus* horns may have reached 2 m (6.6 feet) from tip to tip. However, this was not the largest bison ever found in North America. During the Illinoisan (ca. 600,000–200,000 years B.P.) and Sangamonian (ca. 200,000–80,000 years B.P.) periods, *Bison latifrons* was widespread across the continent. Horn spread on this species may have approached 3–4 m (9.8–13.1 feet) from tip to tip.

Bison bison bison is the animal that most people think of when bison are mentioned. This subspecies occurred across the Great Plains in early historic times. Some estimates place the size of the herd during this time at more than 20 million animals. Some prehistoric kill sites have been recorded where it is estimated that more than 20,000 animals were killed over several years. The more common figure is 50–200 animals per kill episode. By the late A.D. 1880s, these millions of animals had been reduced to only 100–200 by Euro-Americans who were hunting them only for their hides. All bison alive today are descended from this small population, which was saved from extinction in the 1890s. Prehistoric Native Americans did not waste any part of the animals they killed. Meat and hides were the main parts of the animal used by these hunters. However, hair, hooves, tongues, brains, horns, intestines, and bones were also used in a variety of ways. Bison meat is highly nutritious and much lower in fat and cholesterol than beef. In recent years, bison meat has again become a major food source across the United States and Canada.

Danny N. Walker

Further Readings

Guthrie, R.D. 1984. Alaskan Megabucks, Megabulls, and Megarams: The Issue of Pleistocene Gigantism. *Carnegie Museum of Natural History Special Publication* 8:482–510.

———. 1990. *Frozen Fauna of the Mammoth Steppe: The Story of Blue Babe.* University of Chicago Press, Chicago.

McDonald, J.N. 1981. *North American Bison: Their Classification and Evolution.* University of California Press, Berkeley.

Meagher, M.M. 1986. *Bison bison. Mammalian Species* 266:1–8.

van Zyll de Jong, C.G. 1986. A Systematic Study of Recent Bison, With Particular Consideration of the Wood Bison (*Bison bison athabascae* Rhoads 1898). *National Museum of Canada Publications in the Natural Sciences* 6:1–69.

Black River Branch

The Mogollon people were prehistoric farmers, hunters, and gatherers who occupied the rugged mountain area of Arizona and New Mexico. Six branches of the Mogollon were defined by Joe Ben Wheat (1955): the Black River branch, along with the Mimbres, Cibola, Forestdale, San Simon, and Jornada branches. The homeland of the Black River Mogollon is the area of east-central Arizona drained by the Black River and Eagle Creek. Archaeologists today, however, often replace the designation "Black River branch" with "Point of Pines region," since this region of the San Carlos Apache Indian Reservation is the most thoroughly researched area associated with the Black River Mogollon. Extensive excavations were carried out here between 1946 and 1960 by the University of Arizona Archaeological Field School and have been described by Emil W. Haury (1989) in a unique historical account.

The Point of Pines region encompasses ca. 45,325 ha (175 square miles) of a remote and beautiful grassland plain that averages ca. 1,829 m (6,000 feet) above sea level. Its trees include ponderosa pine, juniper, and piñon. The growing season is about 165–170 days; average annual precipitation is 46 cm (18 inches) (Wendorf 1950). Although the environment is a challenge for farmers, prehistoric agricultural features are plentiful. They include terraces, linear borders, grid borders, field houses, boundary markers, wells, and reservoirs (Woodbury 1961). The region's cliff sites, where perishable materials preserve remarkably well, provide information on prehistoric domesticated plants, which included corn, squash, gourds, beans, and cotton. Wild plants included walnuts, acorns, piñon nuts, yucca, and cactus (Gifford 1980). Among the animal bones found in the region's archaeological sites are deer, antelope, bighorn sheep, rabbit, rodent, turkey, bear, bison, and domestic dog (Stein 1963).

The first Black River Mogollon phase, the Circle Prairie phase, is roughly dated from ca. A.D. 400 to 600 (1550–1350 years B.P.) (Haury 1989). Its most thoroughly excavated site is Crooked Ridge Village (Wheat 1954, 1955). Crooked Ridge was a pithouse village with more than 100 pithouses, 24 of which were excavated. Two particularly large structures were present, at least one of which was probably a great kiva, or ceremonial structure. During the Stove Canyon phase (600–900, or 1350–1050 years B.P.), people continued to live in pithouse villages. The Lunt site and the Stove Canyon site, which also had a great kiva, represent this phase. It was followed by the Nantack phase (900–1000, or 1050–950 years B.P.). At the Nantack site, 11 pithouses were excavated. They were typically semisubterranean and rectangular in shape, with lateral entries. A large rectangular great kiva also was found (Breternitz 1959).

With the onset of the Reserve phase (1000–1150, or 950–800 years B.P.), cultural changes appeared in the Mogollon homeland. These changes included the construction of aboveground masonry pueblos and the appearance of black-on-white pottery. Some archaeologists have argued that these changes reflect a cultural "swamping" of native Mogollon culture by Anasazi migrants from the north. Others emphasize the persistence of traditional Mogollon traits, which include great kivas and plain brown and red-slipped pottery, alongside the new traits. These researchers infer Anasazi influence or intermixing rather than swamping. Archaeologists variously label the post–A.D. 1000 (950 years B.P.) pueblo sites of the Mogollon cultural region as "Mogollon Pueblo," "Western Pueblo," or "Mountain Pueblo."

During the Reserve phase, people in the Point of Pines region lived in small pueblo villages with a maximum of ca. 30 rooms. Groups of these villages shared great kivas (Olson 1959). The Dry Prong site is typical of the Reserve phase (Olson 1960). It had 18 domestic rooms, a sketchily defined plaza, and a rectangular great kiva. The Stove Canyon site, in addition to its earlier pithouses, had some Reserve-phase rooms and an oval ballcourt, the only ballcourt in the region (Johnson 1961). The ballcourt suggests Hohokam influence in the Black River area, as do certain other traits, such as Hohokam pottery, stone bowls, paint palettes, artifacts of shell, and cremation as an alternative burial option to inhumation (Robinson and Spraque 1965).

The Reserve phase is followed by the Tularosa phase (1150–1275, or 800–675 years B.P.). The earliest large village of the Point of Pines region, Turkey Creek Pueblo, was constructed during this phase (Johnson 1965; Lowell 1991). This community was founded by ca. 1240 (710 years B.P.) and had 335 rooms. It was divided into two-room blocks, which may reflect a moiety or dual organizational system. The two divisions were physically united by a rectangular great kiva, and each moiety may have used one of two special sets of rooms attached to the kiva (Lowell 1991).

Aggregation into large communities like Turkey Creek Pueblo may have been a defensive maneuver, since a large settlement provides more warriors than a small one. By the thirteenth century, the Anasazi to the north and east of the Mogollon territory were on the move, and many areas of the Colorado Plateau were being abandoned as population in the mountains increased. The traditional inhabitants of the mountains may have been uneasy about this influx of newcomers.

Ca. 1275 (675 years B.P.), with the onset of the Pinedale phase (1275–1325, or 675–625 years B.P.), Turkey Creek Pueblo was abandoned, and a neighboring community, Point of Pines Pueblo, augmented by a group of Kayenta Anasazi immigrants, began to burgeon in size. Heavy occupation of Point of Pines Pueblo continued through the ensuing Canyon Creek phase (1325–1400, or 625–550 years B.P.). Cliff dwellings were intensively occupied during this time (Gifford 1980), another indication that defense continued to be of concern.

During the final phase, the Point of Pines phase (1400–1450, or 550–500 years B.P.), aggregation at Point of Pines Pueblo ceased, and people shifted back to living in small masonry villages of no more than 30 rooms, just as they had done in the Reserve phase several hundred years before (Wasley 1952; Wendorf 1950). Ca. 1450 (500 years B.P.), the Point of Pines region was abandoned completely by the Mogollon Pueblo farmers. Archaeologists have offered various explanations for why people abandoned the Black River and adjacent regions. These include threat from outsiders, environmental change, or a breakdown of the social order. However, the evidence is not compelling for any single explanation. It is not clear where the people went, although the Hopi Mesas, the Zuni area, or the Rio Grande are all possibilities. Eventually, the Black River area was settled by the Apaches, an Athapaskan group unrelated to the Mogollon.

Julia C. Lowell

Further Readings

Breternitz, D.A. 1959. *Excavations at Nantack Village, Point of Pines, Arizona.* Anthropological Papers no. 1. University of Arizona Press, Tucson.

Gifford, J.C. 1980. *Archaeological Explorations in Caves of the Point of Pines Region, Arizona.* Anthropological Papers no. 36. University of Arizona Press, Tucson.

Haury, E.W. 1989. *Point of Pines, Arizona: History of the University of Arizona Archaeological Field School.* Anthropological Papers no. 50. University of Arizona Press, Tucson.

Johnson, A.E. 1961. A Ball Court at Point of Pines, Arizona. *American Antiquity* 26:563–567.

———. 1965. *The Development of Western Pueblo Culture.* Unpublished Ph.D. dissertation, Department of Anthropology, University of Arizona, Tucson.

Lowell, J.C. 1991. *Prehistoric Households at Turkey Creek Pueblo, Arizona.* Anthropological Papers no. 54. University of Arizona Press, Tucson.

Olson, A.P. 1959. *An Evaluation of the Phase Concept in Southwestern Archaeology.* Unpublished Ph.D. dissertation, Department of Anthropology, University of Arizona, Tucson.

———. 1960. The Dry Prong Site, East Central Arizona. *American Antiquity* 26:185–204.

Robinson, W.J., and R. Spraque. 1965. Disposal of the Dead at Point of Pines, Arizona. *American Antiquity* 30:442–453.

Stein, W.T. 1963. Mammal Remains From Archaeological Sites in the Point of Pines

Region, Arizona. *American Antiquity* 29:213–220.

Wasley, W.W. 1952. *The Late Pueblo Occupation at Point of Pines, East-Central Arizona.* Unpublished Master's thesis, Department of Anthropology, University of Arizona, Tucson.

Wendorf, F. 1950. *A Report on the Excavation of a Small Ruin Near Point of Pines, East Central Arizona.* University of Arizona Bulletin, vol. 21, no. 3. Social Science Bulletin no. 19. University of Arizona Press, Tucson.

Wheat, J.B. 1954. *Crooked Ridge Village (Arizona W:10:15).* University of Arizona Bulletin, vol. 25, no. 30. Social Science Bulletin no. 24. University of Arizona Press, Tucson.

———. 1955. *Mogollon Culture Prior to* A.D. *1000.* Memoirs no. 82. American Anthropological Association, Salt Lake City.

Woodbury, R.B. 1961. *Prehistoric Agriculture at Point of Pines, Arizona,* edited by R.H. Thompson. Memoirs no. 17. Society for American Archaeology. *American Antiquity* vol. 26, no. 3, pt. 2. Salt Lake City.

See also MOGOLLON CULTURE AREA; POINT OF PINES RUIN

Blackduck

Blackduck, variously referred to as a complex, a culture, or a composite, is essentially defined by a distinctive pottery assemblage. There is thus the possibility that what is in the late twentieth century called "Blackduck" can represent both a cultural unit and, in certain instances, a ceramic style adopted by other cultures. Recognizable as early as A.D. 500 (1450 years B.P.) and extending into the period of European contact, the core area of Blackduck occupation includes the more southerly portions of northern Ontario, northern Minnesota, and most of southern Manitoba. Exclusive of the Parklands of southwestern Manitoba, this Canadian Shield region is covered by the Boreal Forest and Great Lakes–St. Lawrence vegetation provinces.

It is generally agreed that Blackduck was ancestral to historic Algonquian-speaking peoples, predominantly the Ojibwa (cf. Dawson 1987), and developed out of preceding western Laurel cultures. The approximate boundary with the eastern Ojibwa was the Michipicoten River on the north shore of Lake Superior. There are continuities with the earlier culture not only in technology, including ceramic attributes, but also in settlement patterns, subsistence, and ceremonial practices. Blackduck sites in the Parkland vegetational province, however, deviate in a number of respects from sites in the forests. Not only was bison the major prey, but certain tool categories are more typical of the Plains proper. Indeed, there appears to be some form of relationship with intrusive Middle Missouri farming populations. On the other hand, the burial mound ceremonialism found along the Ontario-Minnesota border also extends into the Parklands. Blackduck people were likely responsible for many of the vision pits and rock art sites of

Blackduck ceramics from the Smith site (21KC3) on the south bank of the Rainy River, Koochiching County, Minnesota. (Courtesy of the Wilford Archaeology Laboratory, University of Minnesota)

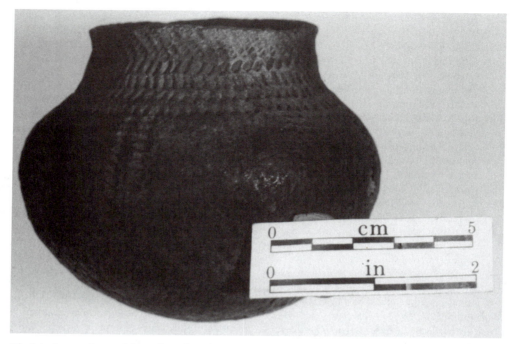

Blackduck ceramic vessel from the Lake Bronson site (21KT1), Kittson County, Minnesota. (Courtesy of the Wilford Archaeology Laboratory, University of Minnesota)

Ontario and southeastern Manitoba and, possibly, the effigy/geometric/complex petroforms of the latter region.

A noteworthy characteristic of Blackduck is its frequent and intimate association with Selkirk assemblages. Selkirk overlaps Blackduck distribution, except to the north, northwest, and south, where Selkirk is absent. Aside from for their distinctive pottery assemblages, it is extremely difficult to separate Blackduck and Selkirk on the basis of their remaining technology or by most of their other cultural systems. Since Selkirk is believed to have given rise to the historic Cree bands of the northwestern Canadian Shield, the intermingling of Blackduck and Selkirk likely reflects intermarriages between these two closely related Algonquian-speaking peoples.

J.V. Wright

Further Readings

Dawson, K.C.A. 1987. Northwestern Ontario and the Early Contact Period: The Northern Ojibwa From 1615–1715. *Canadian Journal of Archaeology* 11:143–180.

Syms, E.L. 1977. *Cultural Ecology and Economical Dynamics of the Ceramic Period of Southwestern Manitoba.* Memoir no. 12. Plains Anthropologist, Lincoln.

See also Selkirk

Blackwater Draw

The Blackwater Draw site (LA3324) in eastern New Mexico has been a famous Paleoindian site since the 1930s. It likely will be the end of the twenty-first century before its research potential is exhausted.

The initial excavators of the site were Edgar B. Howard of the Academy of Natural Sciences and John L. Cotter of the University Museum of the University of Pennsylvania. In 1932, they visited sand dune blowouts in and near the Blackwater Draw area, where they found bifaced points and fluted points, often associated with bison and mammoth remains. Actual excavations were carried out throughout 1933 and 1934. Artifacts and megafauna were found at this time, but they were not in direct association. From 1935 through 1937, Cotter, working under the direction of Howard, was the primary site supervisor. Cotter's training made him an excellent choice. He had worked with Jesse Dade Figgins, director of the then

Colorado Museum of Natural History, and with Frank H.H. Roberts, Jr., at the Lindenmeier Folsom site. Howard selected an area to excavate where gravel-quarrying operations had brought to light mammoth remains and artifacts. This area, called Locality 1, is now the Folsom type site. Excavations in this locale produced 17 artifacts in direct association with mammoth and bison remains.

E.H. Sellards, while working at Blackwater Draw in the 1950s, first defined the Clovis complex. After this time, no formal excavations were carried out until continuing quarrying operations uncovered, in 1963, four complete mammoths and the scattered remains of a possible fifth mammoth. Several hundred artifacts were also found. Three groups were initially involved with this discovery. They included Jim Warnica, an excellent amateur and the leader of the El Llano Archaeological Society; James Hester, representing the Museum of New Mexico; and Early Green, representing Texas Tech University. The situation was chaotic. The state governor finally had to decide who could excavate what. One mammoth was assigned to Texas Tech and to the El Llano group. The Museum of New Mexico retired from contention. George A. Agogino, who had recently worked at Paleoindian sites in Iowa, Wyoming, and Colorado, was hired by nearby Eastern New Mexico University to excavate the other mammoths. This arrangement worked out better than one might have expected. The chief problem was time. Sam Sanders, the quarry owner who was economically hurt by the discovery, gave the excavators only six weeks to remove the bones and artifacts. The excavators worked 12–15-hour days.

For the next decade, Agogino, as a faculty member at Eastern New Mexico University, fielded modestly funded yearly excavations along the south bank of the site. Few mammoth remains were found, since the excavations concentrated on more recent levels. The sequence of Paleoindian projectile points from oldest to most recent was Folsom, Agate Basin, Cody, Scottsbluff-Eden-Firstview, and Oblique Flaked. Archaic artifacts overlay the Paleoindian complexes. Wells dug by either Late Paleondian or Early Archaic people were found. In 1964, a possible well in the Clovis level was uncovered, although it was not publicized due to uncertainties in its interpretation; it may have simply been a holding tank for turtles, since six turtles were found roasted in a Clovis fire pit several meters (yards) away. In the early 1990s,

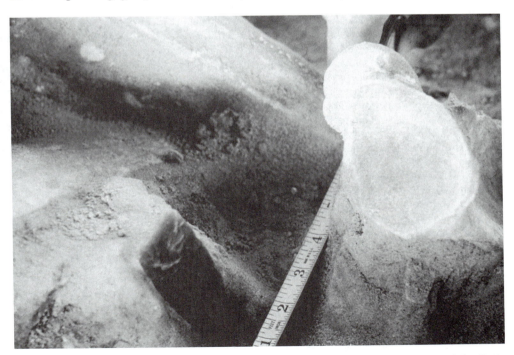

Black obsidian Clovis point in the rib cage of a mammoth at Blackwater Draw. (Photograph by G. A. Agogino)

C. Vance Haynes and Dennis Stanford joined Agogino in relocating and reexcavating this feature. To date (1996), final examination of the data is incomplete.

The site was largely unprotected for more than half a century after its discovery: Archaeologists competed with quarry operations, dune buggies, and target shooters until research was halted to preserve human life. Eastern New Mexico University sought for years to preserve the Blackwater Draw site from destruction, and it finally was designated a National Historic Landmark in 1982. It is fenced in and protected by a resident archaeologist. A small museum, located at the site, contains displays for visitors. Only 1.6 km (1 mile) away is the comprehensive Blackwater Draw Museum, developed by Agogino. Core testing indicates that productive deposits still cover much of the site area, making for a bright archaeological future at this location.

George A. Agogino

Further Readings

Agogino, G. 1964. Archaeological Excavations at Blackwater Draw, Locality No. 1, N.M., 1963–1964. *National Geographic Society Research Reports,* pp. 151–156.

Boldurian, A.T. 1981. *An Analysis of a Paleo-Indian Lithic Assembly From Blackwater Draw, Locality No. 1, in Eastern New Mexico.* Unpublished Master's thesis, Eastern New Mexico University, Portales.

Boldurian, A.T., and G. Agogino. 1982. A Reexamination of Spring Deposited Lithics From Blackwater Draw, Locality No. 1. *Plains Anthropologist* 27:211–216.

Cordell, L.S. 1984. *Prehistory of the Southwest.* Academic Press, New York.

Cotter, J.L. 1936. Clovis Field Notes. Ms. on file, University Museum, University of Pennsylvania, Philadelphia.

Haynes, C.V., and G.A. Agogino. 1966. Prehistoric Springs and Geochronology of Blackwater Draw, No. 1 Locality, New Mexico. *American Antiquity* 31:812–821.

Warnica, J.M. 1966. New Discoveries at the Clovis Site. *American Antiquity* 31:345–357.

Wormington, H.M. 1957. *Ancient Man in North America.* 4th ed. Popular Series no. 4. Denver Museum of Natural History, Denver.

See also CLOVIS CULTURAL COMPLEX

Blade/Bladelet

A blade has been operationally defined as a flake whose length is at least twice its width and whose sides are roughly parallel to each other (Crabtree 1972:42). In a study of blades from North African assemblages, Jacques Tixier (1974) made a metrical distinction between blades and bladelets, with bladelets being less than 5 cm (2 inches) long and 1.2 cm (0.5 inches) wide. This width distinction is very close to William E. Taylor Jr.'s (1962) Pre-Dorset sample from the Canadian Northwest Territories, in which a cutoff for bladelet width of 1.1 cm (0.4 inches) was established. Thus, a blade/bladelet distinction on about this order of magnitude appears to be generally valid in North America. In this discussion, blades and bladelets are considered together, for the most distinguishing factor for the production of either is the existence of a prepared-core blade technique.

Blades and bladelets were produced throughout North America, beginning with Clovis industries (Green 1963). Clovis blades, which were struck from a conical core, were large, measuring ca. 90–130 mm (3.5–5.1 inches) in length, and usually constituted a small proportion of the total assemblage. Also early were microblade industries in the Northwest Coast, which probably originated in the Paleolithic of eastern Asia and spread from there down the coast of North America. Manufactured from wedge-shaped cores, the very small individual bladelets of these industries were probably removed by pressure flaking (Kobayashi 1970).

Following the early post-Pleistocene period, blade industries in North America persisted only in specific contexts in certain regions. In the Southeast, Late Archaic Poverty Point–culture sites contain numerous bladelets manufactured from small river pebbles (Haag and Webb 1953). Some of these were fashioned into perforators for drilling shell and other hard materials. Farther north and slightly later in time, an extensive bladelet industry developed in the Middle Woodland Hopewell culture of the Midwest. Dimensions of Illinois and Ohio bladelets differ significantly (Greber et al. 1981), suggesting that each was produced locally. Use-wear on blades from mortuary contexts in the Illinois Valley is functionally specific, allowing the conclusion that blades in the Hopewell period were highly ritually charged (Odell 1994).

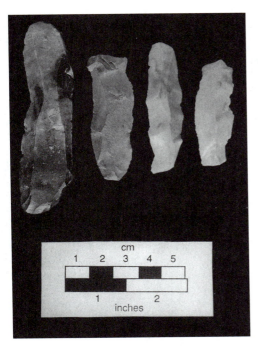

Blades. (Courtesy of the Wilford Archaeology Laboratory, University of Minnesota)

Blade production ceased in the Midwest after the Hopewell decline, but was resumed by ca. A.D. 1000 (950 years B.P.) at the Mississippian Cahokia site in Illinois (Mason and Perino 1961), where thick bladelets were employed for drilling shell (Yerkes 1983). In the west, the Channel Islands off the coast of Southern California witnessed a resurgence of bladelet production beginning near the end of the first millennium A.D. that continued for ca. 800 years. Many of the bladelets are chunky and thick and were apparently employed in drilling shell beads for coastal trade (Arnold 1985). Blade industries have also been recovered from sites in northern Minnesota and the Gulf coast of Texas. Some of the industries mentioned here may have been influenced by the vigorous Mayan blade technology in Mesoamerica, though any postulated relationship is speculative.

George H. Odell

Further Readings

Arnold, J.E. 1985. The Santa Barbara Channel Islands Bladelet Industry. *Lithic Technology* 14:71–80.

Crabtree, D.E. 1972. *An Introduction to Flintworking.* Occasional Papers no. 28.

University Museum, Idaho State University, Pocatello.

Greber, N., R.S. Davis, and A.S. DuFresne. 1981. The Micro Component of the Ohio Hopewell Lithic Technology: Bladelets. *Annals of the New York Academy of Sciences* 376:489–528.

Green, F.E. 1963. The Clovis Blades: An Important Addition to the Llano Complex. *American Antiquity* 29:145–165.

Haag, W.G., and C.H. Webb. 1953. Microblades at Poverty Point Sites. *American Antiquity* 18:245–248.

Kobayashi, T. 1970. Microblade Industries in the Japanese Archipelago. *Arctic Anthropology* 7:38–58.

Mason, R.J., and G. Perino. 1961. Microblades at Cahokia, Illinois. *American Antiquity* 26:553–557.

Odell, G.H. 1994. The Role of Stone Bladelets in Middle Woodland Society. *American Antiquity* 59:102–120.

Perry, W.J. 1994. Prismatic Blade Technologies in North America. In *The Organization of North American Prehistoric Chipped Stone Tool Technologies*, edited by P. Carr, pp. 87–98. International Monographs in Prehistory. Ann Arbor.

Taylor, W.E., Jr. 1962. A Distinction Between Blades and Microblades in the American Arctic. *American Antiquity* 27:425–426.

Tixier, J. 1974. *Glossary for the Description of Stone Tools With Special Reference to the Epipaleolithic of the Maghreb*, translated by M.H. Newcomer. Special Publication no. 1. Newsletter of Lithic Technology, Washington State University, Pullman.

Yerkes, R.W. 1983. Microwear, Microdrills, and Mississippian Craft Specialization. *American Antiquity* 48:499–518.

Bluefish Caves

Cave deposits on the Bluefish River in the Keele Range of northern Yukon Territory may contain late Pleistocene human occupations. The remains of mammoth, bison, horse, caribou, and other mammals were found in a shallow loess deposit in Bluefish Cave I spatially associated with a stone assemblage that included wedge-shaped microcores, microblades, burins, biface-trimming flakes, and other artifacts. A large pile of Ice Age mammal bones also lay outside the cave. Bone collagen radiocarbon dates are in the 23,050–10,050 B.C. (25,000–12,000 years B.P.) range. Additional arguments for a possible late Pleistocene age for the artifacts are the presence of somewhat similar microblade assemblages in the late Pleistocene Dyuktai tradition in Siberia and the "look out" position of the caves near glacial lakes that were in existence ca. 13,050 B.C. (15,000 years B.P.). Still, the relationship between the bones and the artifacts remains problematic, and the age of the artifacts has not been independently established. At present (1996), the earliest documented human occupations in central Alaska and the Yukon seem to date to ca. 10,050–9050 B.C. (12,000–11,000 years B.P.).

Guy Gibbon

Further Readings

Cinq-Mars, J. 1978. Bluefish Cave I: A Late Pleistocene Eastern Beringian Cave Deposit in the Northern Yukon. *Canadian Journal of Archaeology* 3:1–32.

Hoffecker, J.F., W.R. Powers, and T. Goebel. 1993. The Colonization of Beringia and the Peopling of the New World. *Science* 259:46–53.

Morlan, R.E. 1987. In *The Evolution of Human Hunting*, edited by M. Nitecki and D. Nitecki, pp. 267–307. Plenum Press, New York.

Bluff Village

Bluff Village (CAZP:16:20) is located on a ridge overlooking Forestdale Valley on the White Mountain Apache Reservation in east-central Arizona. It was excavated by Emil W. Haury in 1941 and 1944. The major occupation defines the Hilltop phase (A.D. 200–400, or 1750–1550 years B.P.), with three structures assigned to the Cottonwood phase (A.D. 400–600, or 1550–1350 years B.P.). Tree-ring dates verify an occupation ca. A.D. 300 (1650 years B.P.), making Bluff Village the earliest, well-dated site in the Forestdale branch of the Mogollon culture. Twenty-three pithouses were entirely or partially excavated, an estimated two-thirds of those present. During the earliest occupation, circular pithouses were dug into the fractured bedrock of the bluff. Larger pithouses (house 10 = 29 m², or 35 square yards) contain hearths, suggesting a habitation use, while smaller pithouses (mean size = 18 m², or 21.5 square yards) without hearths and with grinding equipment suggest

storage and food processing. The presence of exterior hearths indicates that cooking was not restricted to houses. The size of house 5 (83 m², or 99 square yards) suggests communal-religious functions that led Haury to postulate that it was a prototype for later great-kiva development in the valley. It is unknown how many of the circular pithouses were in use at any one time. Subsequent occupations by people who built the oval houses and later the square houses indicate a long-term selection of the locality.

The subsistence routine is unclear from the scant food remains found. Haury recovered few animal bones and, except for charred black walnut hulls, no plant remains. The presence of knives, projectile points, and grinding tools argues for a mixed strategy dominated by hunting and gathering with contributions from gardening. Pottery, though not plentiful (N = 29,000), was almost exclusively (95 percent) brown plain ware (Alma Plain, Bluff, and Forestdale varieties as well as Woodruff Smudged). Colorado Plateau types include Adamana Brown and Lino Gray; Arizona desert types include Gila Plain and late Pioneer-period red-on-buff. The Mogollon lifeway represented is little changed from that of the Late Archaic except for the addition of pottery. Although residential moves continue to be the principal means of adjusting small populations to available resources, the presence of a communal structure signals the development of focal villages in a protracted process of increasing residential stability through repeated and extended use of village localities.

J. Jefferson Reid

Further Readings

Haury, E.W. 1985. *Mogollon Culture in the Forestdale Valley, East-Central Arizona.* University of Arizona Press, Tucson.

Reid, J.J. 1989. Grasshopper Perspective on the Mogollon of the Arizona Mountains. In *Dynamics of Southwest Prehistory*, edited by L.S. Cordell and G.J. Gumerman, pp. 65–97. Smithsonian Institution Press, Washington, D.C.

See also BEAR VILLAGE; FORESTDALE BRANCH; MOGOLLON CULTURE AREA

Boas, Franz (1858–1942)

A German-born and -trained scientist whose interest in Native American cultures was aroused during a scientific expedition to Baffin Island

(1883–1884), Franz Boas became a permanent resident of the United States in 1887. In 1899, he became professor of anthropology at Columbia University, where he remained for the rest of his life. He eventually became one of the most influential of North American anthropologists and has been called the "father of American anthropology." While at Columbia, he built one of the foremost anthropology departments in the United States and largely trained the first generation of American anthropologists, including Ruth Benedict, Melville J. Herskovits, E. Adamson Hoebel, Alfred L. Kroeber, Robert Lowie, Margaret Mead, Edward Sapir, and Clark Wissler. He is notable for being one of the first anthropologists to encourage women to enter the field. Among his many other accomplishments, Boas was curator of anthropology at the American Museum of Natural History (1901–1905), directed and edited the reports of the Jesup North Pacific expedition (the first major effort in Pacific Northwest archaeology), was one of the founders of the American Anthropological Association, and was president (1931) of the American Association for the Advancement of Science.

Working within the late-nineteenth-century antievolutionary intellectual climate that had developed in reaction to the simplistic, linear schemes of an earlier generation of evolutionists, he insisted on the systematic collection of data through field investigations. Underlying Boasian anthropology was a belief in free will, psychological reductionism, and historical particularism. The result was a focus on specifically historical problems and idealist explanations, for he conceived of cultures as collections of shared concepts. Boas and his students popularized the concepts of the ethnographic culture as a basic unit of study, of cultural cores and peripheries and age/area assumptions, and of diffusion as a major cause of cultural change. He encouraged the use of the "culture area" concept as a framework for exhibiting ethnographic material, as opposed to hypothetical evolutionary sequences or continent-wide typological categories, and minimized the importance of environment as a possible explanatory factor in the development of culture.

Boasian anthropology influenced North American archaeology in numerous ways, including the view that archaeological cultures can be defined by lists of artifact types, reliance on diffusion and migration as adequate explanations of the collections of concepts formed through historical accident that form cultures, and acceptance of the concept of cultures as ways of life related to specific ethnic groups. His strong advocacy of cultural relativism and opposition to racism fostered the idea that Native Americans are capable of change and that their cultures have changed through time. He encouraged stratigraphic excavation to establish archaeological sequences and may have been instrumental in Kroeber's introduction of similarity seriation for chronological dating in the Southwest.

Neo-evolutionist writers of the 1940s and 1950s, such as Leslie White and Julian Steward, and New Archaeologists in the 1960s, in particular Lewis Binford, strongly challenged the antievolutionary and antienvironmental stance of Boasian anthropology. They argued that the search for adequate explanations of the major cultural variations that anthropologists observe is stifled by insisting that such explanations must be mentalistic and that theorizing is only possible after as much data as possible have been collected. Boas's contributions to the development of North American archaeology remain largely unappreciated, because they continue to be viewed through the distorting lens of neo-evolutionary and New Archaeology rhetoric.

Guy Gibbon

Further Readings

Anonymous. 1943. *Franz Boas, 1858–1942.* Memoir no. 61. American Anthropological Association, Menasha.

Herskovits, M.J. 1953. *Franz Boas.* Scribner, New York.

Trigger, B.G. 1989. *A History of Archaeological Thought.* Cambridge University Press, New York.

Willey, G.R., and J.A. Sabloff. 1993. *A History of American Archaeology.* 3rd ed. W.H. Freeman, San Francisco.

See also HISTORICAL PARTICULARISM

Bone Modification

From the 1970s on, taphonomy has played an increasingly important role in the study of early New World and Old World sites. Taphonomy seeks to understand the passage of animal bones from life to discovery in the fossil record. This field of study is important to paleontologists, paleoecologists, paleoanthropologists, and archaeologists who recognize that bone assemblages found in the fossil record do not always mirror living communities. In attempting to decode the processes responsible for the accumulation of bone assemblages, specialists propose that taphonomic factors influence the survivorship frequency, distribution, and bone modification patterns found in bone assemblages.

There are numerous processes that can modify bone and leave identifiable traces on the surface and in the bone microstructure. Some of the most common types of processes that affect bone-surface morphology and structure are geophysical, geochemical, biotic, biophysical, and cultural processes. At a more specific level, landslides, ice flows, expanding clay minerals, carnivore gnawing, splintering, and crunching, burning, trampling, rock-fall impact, hammering, sawing, cutting, and so on are among the many processes responsible for bone modification. These processes can be of a local nature or widespread. A thorough understanding of local environmental history is important in developing a list of taphonomic factors that could affect an assemblage.

When attempting to decode processes responsible for bone modification patterns, investigators must resort to the use of inference. This is accomplished by using modern observational and experimental analogs in which specific processes have been linked to specific patterns. Decoding occurs by comparing the modern-control analog pattern with the specimen from the fossil record in search of pattern matches. The use of modern analogs is a strong approach, yet it is not without its difficulties. Occasionally, more than one process can produce similar patterns, or "mimics." If context is considered, it is sometimes possible to determine which of two possible explanations is correct. For example, both rock fall and humans wielding hammerstones produce impact marks on a bone. If the bone is found on a floodplain, the rock-fall hypothesis can be eliminated on logical grounds.

Proposed early human sites in the Old World and the New World often contain few diagnostic artifacts. Bone modification studies are playing an important role in the interpretation of early hominid sites. Bone modification arguments now provide the basis of arguments concerning early human scavenging, marrow processing, and use of bone technology to produce bone tools.

In summary, bone modification studies since the 1970s have expanded the vision of types of information that can be retrieved from bones. Rather than simply interpreting bones as an indicator of life communities, bone modification research has contributed new knowledge about the contextual histories of individual bones and assemblages of bones. In doing so, it has increased our understanding of past environments and human adaptations.

Robson Bonnichsen

Further Readings

Bonnichsen, R., and M. Sorg (editors). 1989. *Bone Modification.* Center for the Study of the First Americans, University of Maine, Orono.

See also TAPHONOMY

Borax Lake Site

Borax Lake, part of the former extent of Pleistocene Clear Lake in California's North Coast Ranges 129 km (80 miles) north of San Francisco, is the location of an obsidian quarry site first utilized in Paleoindian times. First reported by Chester Post in the 1930s, the Borax Lake site (CALak36) was excavated in 1938, 1942, and 1945 by Mark R. Harrington of the Southwest Museum, and in 1946 by R. Sayles (see Harrington 1938a, 1938b, 1945, 1948). Harrington reported 20 fluted points and point fragments from the 250 cm (97.5 inches) of alluvial deposits. Today the points are understood to reflect variations of the Clovis pattern; they have lanceolate bodies, concave bases, and moderate channelling or fluting (70 percent are bifacially fluted, 10 percent unifacially fluted, and 20 percent too fragmentary to classify). Reexcavation by Clement W. Meighan and C. Vance Haynes (1970) provided new understandings of the site's depositional structure as a series of alluvial deposits with human activity episodes on different old surfaces dating back to a Terminal Pleistocene (equivalent to Two Creeks Interstadial) initial occupation. Obsidian hydration measurements from 77 rim cuts, including from five fluted points, ranged from 8 to 13.3 microns, which is generally consistent with an initial occupation at 10,050 B.C. (12,000 years B.P.) by a Clovis-like culture.

In his syntheses of North Coast Range prehistory (Fredrickson 1974, 1984), David A. Fredrickson recognizes three successive occupation phases at the Borax Lake site. The Clovis-like occupation is termed the "Post pattern" after site discoverer Chester Post and is dated to 10,050–9050 B.C. (12,000–11,000 years B.P.). A second occupational phase is called the "Borax Lake pattern" and is generally dated to 6050–4050 B.C. (8000–6000 years B.P.). It forms the largest component of the site and serves as the type site for the Middle Archaic mode of adaptation in the North Coast Ranges. The last component, dated to 3050–1050 B.C. (5000–3000 years B.P.), represents a later Archaic "Middle Central California complex." All three phases reflect diversified hunting-and-gathering lifeways that combined the exploitation of plant and animal resources of the lakeshore with those of the canyons and hillsides of the surrounding Coast Ranges. Not even the Clovis points, for instance, are associated with specialized big-game hunting. The early Post-pattern assemblage lacks tool types associated with specialized plant processing, but crescentic, bifacially retouched pieces may be linked with waterfowl exploitation. By Borax Lake–pattern times, millstone and manos appear, indicating the development of systematic hard-seed processing. Mortars and pestles, associated with acorn exploitation, are added by the most recent occupations. All three phases reflect systematic use of nearby obsidian sources for the production of chipped-stone tools. They also seem to reflect small-size occupations of temporary or seasonal duration by groups of minimal social complexity (Moratto 1984:82–85).

Joseph L. Chartkoff

Further Readings

Fredrickson, D.A. 1974. Cultural Diversity in Early Central California: A View From the North Coast Ranges. *Journal of California Anthropology* 1(1):41–54.

———. 1984. The North Coastal Region. In *California Archaeology,* edited by M.J. Moratto, pp. 471–527. Academic Press, New York.

Harrington, M.R. 1938a. Early Man at Borax Lake. *Carnegie Institution of Washington News Service Bulletin, School Edition* 4:259–261.

———. 1938b. Folsom Man in California. *Masterkey* 13:133–137. Southwest Museum, Los Angeles.

———. 1945. Farewell to Borax Lake. *Masterkey* 19:181–184. Southwest Museum, Los Angeles.

———. 1948. An Ancient Site at Borax Lake. *Southwest Museum Papers* 16:1–26.

Meighan, C.W., and C.V. Haynes. 1970. The Borax Lake Site Revisited. *Science* 167(3922):1213–1221.

Moratto, M.J. (editor). 1984. *California Archaeology.* Academic Press, New York.

Borden, Charles E. (1905–1978)

Carl Borden began site excavation in the Lower Fraser River region in 1945 and continued work on the prehistory of British Columbia until the day of his death. He was a professor of German at the University of British Columbia from 1939 until his retirement in 1970; in 1949, he became a lecturer in archaeology and in 1970, professor of archaeology. In 1951–1952, he secured funds for the first salvage archaeology in the province for excavation in the reservoir area behind the Kinney Dam on the Nechacko River. This project generated his "Uniform Site Designation" scheme, which has since been adopted in most of Canada. He began work at the Milliken site in the Fraser Canyon in 1959 and in the five-year excavation there established the first long chronology in British Columbia, a 9,000-year-long sequence. During this same period, he and Wilson Duff drafted and steered the 1960 Archaeological

Charles E. Borden. (Reprinted with permission from American Antiquity *45(3):472)*

and Historic Sites Protection Act through the provincial legislature. In his later years, he undertook small projects, supervised students, and continued to write articles and participate in the legal aspects of provincial archaeology. He was honored for his work by the Canadian Archaeological Association, by his university, and by both federal and provincial governments.

Roy L. Carlson

Further Readings

Borden, C.E. 1952. A Uniform Site Designation Scheme for Canada. *Anthropology in British Columbia* 3:44–48.
———. 1979. Peopling and Early Cultures of the Pacific Northwest. *Science* 203(4384): 963–971.
———. 1983. Prehistoric Art of the Lower Fraser Region. In *Indian Art Traditions of the Northwest Coast,* edited by R.L. Carlson, pp. 131–166. Archaeology Press, Simon Fraser University, Burnaby.
Carlson, R.L. 1990. History of Research in Archaeology. In *Northwest Coast,* edited by W. Suttles, pp. 107–115. Handbook of North American Indians, vol. 7, W.C. Sturtevant, general editor. Smithsonian Institution, Washington, D.C.

Bow and Arrow

When Europeans "discovered" North America, they found a Native American population whose principal weaponry was the bow and arrow. Very little ethnographic information on the manufacture and use of the bow and arrow has come down to us from the contact period. Our earliest detailed accounts date to the latter part of the nineteenth century (e.g., Mason et al. 1891). These describe how the arrowhead was manufactured through percussion and pressure flaking, how it was lashed to the shaft with sinew, the use of mastic for fastening the point and the fletching, and so on. Unfortunately, the only part of the bow-and-arrow system that usually survives archaeologically is the stone tip. Nonetheless, the tip can serve as a chronological and ethnic indicator when the myriad of available point-identification guides or attribute systems, such as the one proposed by Lewis R. Binford (1963), are employed. A comprehensive account of the development of bow technology throughout the world can be found in Gad Rausing (1967).

Despite the abundance of archaeological stone arrowheads, so many developmental and processual questions remain that, barring spectacular archaeological discoveries, resolution

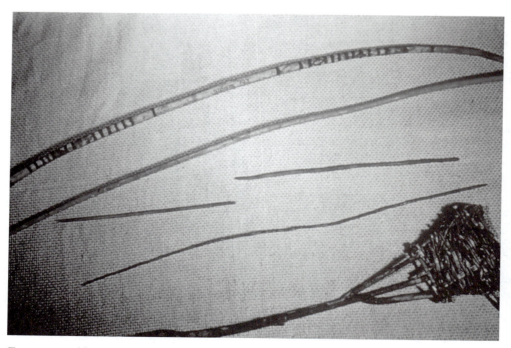

Two ceremonial bows (top), spindles (middle), and seed beater (bottom) from Tularosa Cave, New Mexico. (Courtesy of the Wilford Archaeology Laboratory, University of Minnesota)

of these questions can come only from experimentation and a more discerning observation of the archaeological record. We know something of the harvesting of bow staves from juniper trees in California, for instance, because some of the cuts and scars on these trees remain (Wilke 1988). Experimentation began in earnest in the early years of the twentieth century through the efforts of Saxton Pope. Inspired by his friendship with Ishi, the last Yahi Indian in California, Pope conducted experiments with Ishi until Ishi's death in 1916 and continued to conduct other experiments after that date. These experiments included a comparison of several aboriginal bows from various parts of the world held in museums and private collections (Pope 1923). This experimentation has been updated and rendered more consistent (cf. Bergman et al. 1988). George H. Odell and Frank Cowan (1986) have conducted experiments into the effects of bow propulsion on the stone tip and comparisons with spearheads.

The date of the inception of this projectile system in North America has been a matter of debate among prehistorians. The issue is confounded by the fact that the organic parts of the weaponry have been preserved in only some regions, such as in dry caves in the American Southwest, the Ozarks, and the Great Basin. In regions where organic portions have not been preserved, dating the origins of the system has relied on more inferential evidence, such as the size of the projectile point (Fenenga 1953; Thomas 1978). It is logical that the inception of this weaponry occurred at different times in different regions, and, indeed, the earliest dates from around the continent do differ. This is a result in part of the movement of the concept of the system across space from one or more points of origin, and in part of differing interpretations by archaeologists as to what constitutes good evidence for the presence of the system. Two schools of thought exist concerning the date of inception of the bow and arrow in the continental United States. One considers the bow and arrow no earlier than ca. A.D. 500 (1450 years B.P.) in the Midwest, but slightly earlier in the Southeast and Southwest (Heizer and Hester 1978). The second school accepts dates as early as 500 B.C. (2450 years B.P.) and, in some cases, even as early as 4000–2000 B.C. (5950–3950 years B.P.) (Odell 1988; Patterson 1992).

George H. Odell

Further Readings

Bergman, C.A., E. McEwen, and R. Miller. 1988. Experimental Archery: Projectile Velocities and Comparison of Bow Performance. *Antiquity* 62:658–670.

Binford, L.R. 1963. A Proposed Attribute List for the Description and Classification of Projectile Points. In *Miscellaneous Studies in Typology and Classification,* edited by A. White, L. Binford, and M. Papworth, pp. 193–221. Anthropological Papers no. 19. Museum of Anthropology, University of Michigan, Ann Arbor.

Fenenga, F. 1953. The Weights of Chipped Stone Points: A Clue to Their Functions. *Southwestern Journal of Anthropology* 9:309–323.

Heizer, R.F., and T.R. Hester. 1978. Great Basin. In *Chronologies in New World Archaeology,* edited by R.E. Taylor and C.W. Meighan, pp. 147–199. Academic Press, New York.

Mason, O.T., W.H. Holmes, T. Wilson, W. Hough, W. Flint, W.J. Hoffman, and J.G. Bourke. 1891. Arrows and Arrow-Makers. *American Anthropologist* 4:45–74.

Odell, G.H. 1988. Addressing Prehistoric Hunting Practices Through Stone Tool Analysis. *American Anthropologist* 90:335–356.

Odell, G.H., and F. Cowan. 1986. Experiments With Spears and Arrows on Animal Targets. *Journal of Field Archaeology* 13:195–212.

Patterson, L.W. 1992. Current Data on Early Use of the Bow and Arrow in Southern North America. *La Tierra* 19:6–15.

Pope, S. 1923. A Study of Bows and Arrows. *University of California Publications in American Archaeology and Ethnology* 13:329–414.

Rausing, G. 1967. *The Bow: Some Notes on Its Origins and Development.* Gleerups, Lund.

Thomas, D.H. 1978. Arrowheads and Atlatl Darts: How the Stones Got the Shaft. *American Antiquity* 43:461–472.

Wilke, P.J. 1988. Bow Staves Harvested From Juniper Trees by Indians of Nevada. *Journal of California and Great Basin Anthropology* 10:3–31.

B

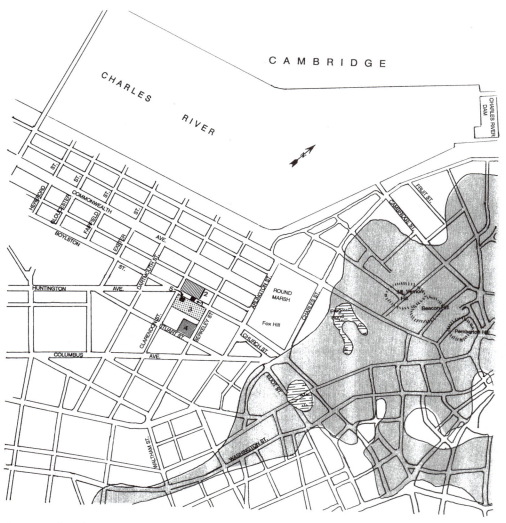

Location of Boylston Street fish weirs. (Courtesy of D. F. Dincauze)

Boylston Street Fish Weirs

The "Boylston Street Fish Weir" (19SU16) in Boston, Massachusetts, has been one of the most famous and enigmatic of New England's archaeological sites. Originally encountered beneath many feet of coastal fill during the construction of a subway in 1913, the weir was investigated during building construction in the 1930s, 1940s, and 1950s (see Maps 1, 2, 4, and 5). As a result of the initial investigations, prehistorians were left struggling to understand the function and role of an apparently huge underwater structure in the lives of people who lived in small groups and earned their living by hunting and gathering in the middle Holocene, 3050–1050 B.C. (5000–3000 years B.P.).

At that time, the regional climate was cooling from the higher summer temperatures of the early postglacial millennia. In southern New England, people were apparently living very prosperously without farming, and in Connecticut and southern Massachusetts they were building substantial houses. A rich ceremonial life complemented the adequacy of the food supplies. Smaller fish weirs of this age are known elsewhere in eastern North American rivers, but a massive fish-taking facility of the scope implied by the early investigations in the Back Bay remained a poor fit with the size of the societies archaeologists had revealed.

Investigations in 1987 and 1989 at construction sites at 500 Boylston Street and 222

Berkeley Street (see Map 3) were planned to investigate the age of the weir, the paleoenvironment, the size and function of the structure, and its role in the local economies. The investigators emphasized broad area sampling in contrast to the very localized exposures of earlier years. The investigators were spared the heroic efforts made earlier to date the weirs. Radiocarbon measurements confirmed the original age estimate made for the features at the New England Life site in the 1930s, while indicating that similar structures immediately south were older by centuries. At 500 Boylston Street, the youngest structure is dated to ca. 1750 B.C. (3700 years B.P.) and the oldest to ca. 2850 B.C. (4800 years B.P.). The stakes at the New England Life site date to ca. 1550 B.C. (3500 years B.P.), while the deepest stakes, at

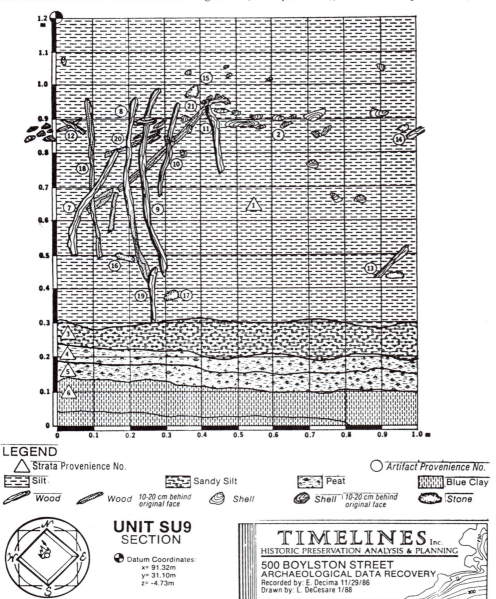

LEGEND

△ Strata Provenience No.   ○ Artifact Provenience No.

Silt   Sandy Silt   Peat   Blue Clay

Wood   Wood 10-20 cm behind original face   Shell   Shell 10-20 cm behind original face   Stone

UNIT SU9
SECTION

Datum Coordinates:
x= 91.32m
y= 31.10m
z= -4.73m

TIMELINES Inc.
HISTORIC PRESERVATION ANALYSIS & PLANNING
500 BOYLSTON STREET
ARCHAEOLOGICAL DATA RECOVERY
Recorded by: E. Decima 11/29/86
Drawn by: L. DeCesare 1/88

Profile of unit SU9. The diagram of weir elements clearly shows the relationship between the upright and slanting stakes and the layer of horizontal brushwork that they stabilized. It also shows the stratigraphy. (Courtesy of Timelines Inc., Historic Preservation Analysis & Planning)

Conjectural reconstruction of a weir feature as it might have appeared at low water, with people collecting fish. (Courtesy of Timelines Inc., Historic Preservation Analysis & Planning)

the southernmost John Hancock site, may date close to 3050 B.C. (5000 years B.P.). This broad range of time for construction and use of the features confirms irrefutably that they were many, not one.

Instead of a single huge structure built to trap large fish, the new investigations revealed that the weirs were built (1) over a long period of time, (2) on a sloping foreshore, (3) in a brackish estuary with a low tidal amplitude but rapidly rising sea level, (4) parallel to the shore near the low-tide line, (5) as small units that had a relatively short use-life, (6) in ways that required a very small, local labor force, (7) in order to produce a dependable but not dramatic supply of marine protein, and (8) in conformance to what we know elsewhere of cultural values and lifeways characteristic of the fifth and fourth millennia B.P.

Investigations of the sediments enclosing the weirs and of the included microfossils confirmed that the climate was temperate. The regional forests were dominated by hardwoods; the shores of the ancient Back Bay were rimmed by salt marshes and freshwater swamps with

alder and red maples. Analysis of diatoms (algae with siliceous cell walls) implies that the first flush of saltwater against the sloping shore in the project area occurred ca. 3650 B.C. (5600 years B.P.). For almost 2,000 years as the sea rose and the bay expanded, the bay waters remained shallow, brackish, and warm, and in a backwater location in respect to the tidal encroachment up the nearby Charles River.

Mid-Holocene people built their Back Bay weirs near shore, close to or just below low tide. During the late winter, they collected stems and branches of young wood, selecting for straightness, length (1–2 m, or ca. 3–6 feet), and diameter (less than 3 cm, or 1.2 inches). In the spring, they drove stakes into the subtidal mud in long lines and bands paralleling the shore and then forced bundles of branches down among them to create a low wall of brushwork that probably filled the water column at low tide.

The brush walls appear to have functioned as fish traps by allowing small, surface-swimming fish to move inshore with the flood tide. As the tide ebbed, the fish were held in shallow water between the brush wall and the sloping shore. People could easily scoop them out with baskets or nets. Long, shallow traps such as these would be filled twice a day with numerous small fish, offering a handy larder to the fisherfolk. By ca. 1750 B.C. (3700 years B.P.), increased tidal amplitude and energy moved more sediment in the bay. Siltation reduced the use-life of the weirs, making them less efficient and more costly in terms of labor. Construction and use of fish weirs in Back Bay ended not long after 1550 B.C. (3500 years B.P.).

Dena F. Dincauze

Further Readings

Decima-Zamecnik, E. n.d. *Mud Wrestling: Return to the Boylston Street Fish Weir.* Ph.D. dissertation in preparation, Department of Anthropology, University of Pittsburgh, Pittsburgh.

Dincauze, D.F. 1988. Sticks in the Mud. *NewsWARP* (newsletter of the Wetland Archaeology Research Project) 4:8–10.

Johnson, F. (editor). 1942. *The Boylston Street Fishweir.* Papers, vol. 2. Robert S. Peabody Foundation for Archaeology, Phillips Academy, Andover.

———. 1949. *The Boylston Street Fishweir II.* Papers, vol. 4, no. 2. Robert S. Peabody Foundation for Archaeology, Phillips Academy, Andover.

Lutins, A.H. 1992. *Prehistoric Fish Weirs in Eastern North America.* Unpublished Master's thesis, Department of Anthropology, State University of New York, Binghamton.

Brand Site

The Brand site (3PO139) is a Dalton-period (ca. 8500–8000 B.C., or 10,450–9950 years B.P.) archaeological site located in northeastern Arkansas ca. 88 km (55 miles) northwest of Memphis. The site was excavated in 1970 by the Arkansas Archeological Survey. The importance of the investigation was the recognition of a Late Paleoindian toolkit and a new interpretation of cultural behavior in Arkansas at the end of the Pleistocene.

Artifacts were clustered within the site in five 8–16-m² (9.6-square-yard) areas, each of which contained between 74 and 89 tools. Half of the tools were points or point fragments. Other tools included end scrapers and other unifaces, *pièces esquillées*, reused adze fragments, and a variety of cobble tools. Most of the Dalton-period artifacts were located stratigraphically between a lower weathered late Pleistocene clay and within the lower portion of a superimposed terminal Pleistocene wind-blown silt. The points, called Dalton points, are named after Judge S.P. Dalton of Missouri, who recognized the uniqueness of this early lanceolate and serrated fluted point style in 1948 (Chapman 1948); the presence of this style is now recognized over most of the southeastern United States. In contrast to other fluted point styles, experiments suggest that the Dalton point was primarily used as a knife that was probably used to butcher white-tailed deer. Richard Yerkes observed a pattern of microwear on selected Dalton points that indicates the cutting of meat; James Michie successfully butchered a white-tailed deer with replicated points; and Albert C. Goodyear (1974) resharpened Dalton points as if they had been used as knives, which produced a pattern of chippage that matched the observed attributes on recovered points. These experiments, along with the contents of the site, indicate that Brand was most likely a butchering camp.

The traditional settlement-pattern hypothesis for the Paleoindian period is nomadic wandering after game and stone materials. More refined hypotheses propose a seasonal round that crisscrossed environmental zones. For instance, Michael Schiffer proposed that Dalton bands crossed the three to four watersheds of the Western Lowlands in an east-to-west direction during their seasonal round. Since even the expedition of Hernando DeSoto in 1541 found this proposed route extremely difficult, an alternative settlement pattern is preferred. According to my interpretation, approximately six Dalton bands, each with ca. 25 people, were territorially restricted to watersheds that crossed one of the three major ecotones in northeast Arkansas. However, instead of wandering within the watershed, this new interpretation postulates, small work groups moved outward from a band base camp or village. Males might have moved to hunting, fishing, or quarry camps, for example, and females to food-gathering camps. The spectacular discovery in 1974 of a Dalton-period cemetery (the Sloan site) lends support to this interpretation.

Another distinctive artifact discovered at Brand and at contemporary Dalton sites is the woodworking adze. These chipped, gouge-shaped oval bifaces are the oldest true adzes known in the Americas and perhaps in the world. Paul and Hazel Delcourt have demonstrated that cypress, which was normally used to make dugouts in the area in the early historic period, did exist in the mid-South at 8500 B.C. (10,450 years B.P.), and Yerkes has observed microwear on Dalton adzes indicative of wood and charred-wood use. The presence of these adzes may indicate, then, that the tradition of making dugout canoes dates back into the Pleistocene in northeast Arkansas. Although only broken adzes reused to cut or pound were recovered at Brand, a butchering camp, complete adzes have been found at base camps and cemeteries.

The Dalton toolkit consists of fairly typical terminal Paleolithic items as well as unusual tools, such as the adzes, specialized abraders and hammers to manufacture points, long hafted unifaces with curved cutting edges, and edge-abraded cobbles to grind food. Extremely well-made artifacts include exceedingly long Dalton points probably intended only for symbolic display. Sites consist of base camps, extraction camps, and even cemeteries. Altogether the sophistication of behavior reflected by these finds is much greater than previously expected of simple hunting, gathering, and fishing folks. Brand is apparently a task-specific site within this broader settlement pattern.

Dan F. Morse

Further Readings

Goodyear, A.C. 1974. *The Brand Site: A Techno-Functional Study of a Dalton Site in Northeast Arkansas.* Research Series no. 7. Arkansas Archeological Survey, Fayetteville.

Morse, D., and P. Morse. 1987. *Archaeology of the Central Mississippi Valley.* Academic Press, New York.

See also DALTON

Brew, John Otis (Jo) (1906–1988)

Jo Brew was one of the foremost archaeologists in the American Southwest. His work on Alkali Ridge (1946) remains a landmark: it was a model for that time in the presentation of descriptive detail, but it was more important for Brew's synthesis of Mesa Verde archaeology and his analysis of classificatory systems. It was primarily for this book that he was awarded the Viking Medal in 1947. He also organized and directed two other multiyear archaeological projects for the Peabody Museum of American Archaeology and Ethnology at Harvard Univer-

sity. Probably the more important of these were the excavations on the Hopi Reservation at Franciscan Awatovi in Arizona (1936–1939), which resulted in 11 major reports, including *Franciscan Awatovi* (1949). This highly successful, multidisciplinary study included geomorphologists, artists, architects, and historians among its staff. Brew's third major archaeological research project was in the Upper Gila drainage of west-central New Mexico (1949–1954) and dealt with Mogollon-Anasazi contacts. Most of the publications resulting from the Upper Gila project were authored by his students, but Brew provided the intellectual guidance and managerial skills that made the project successful.

Although Brew's scholarship and management skills assure him a permanent place in the history of American archaeology, his most important contribution was leadership in the development of what is now known as rescue, or salvage, archaeology. Brew, together with Fred Johnson, an archaeologist at the Robert S. Peabody Foundation for Archaeology in Andover, Massachusetts, recognized the need for a national program to preserve the archaeological data being destroyed by the con-

John Otis (Jo) Brew. (Reprinted with permission from American Antiquity *55[3]:452)*

struction of dams and other economic-development projects. He organized and was chairman (1959–1974) of the Committee for the Recovery of Archaeological Remains, the group whose tireless efforts developed public awareness of the problem and led to the legislative mandate that underpins our modern program of cultural-resource management. Brew was also chairman of the International Committee for Monuments, Artistic and Historical Sites, and Archaeological Excavations for UNESCO (the United Nations Educational, Scientific, and Cultural Organization) and played the leading role in organizing and funding the International Archaeological Salvage Campaign (1961–1966) in Egyptian and Sudanese Nubia. He was primarily responsible for drafting the statement on the Preservation of Cultural Property that was adopted in November 1971 by the General Conference of UNESCO. These important precedents are the basis not only for the rescue-archaeology program in the United States, but also for many similar efforts elsewhere in the world.

Fred Wendorf

Further Readings

Brew, J.O. 1946. *The Archaeology of Alkali Ridge, Southeastern Utah, With a Review of the Prehistory of the Mesa Verde Division of the San Juan and Some Observations on Archaeological Systematics.* Papers no. 21. Peabody Museum of American Archaeology and Ethnology, Harvard University, Cambridge.

———. 1949a. The Excavation of Franciscan Awatovi. In *Franciscan Awatovi*, by R.G. Montgomery, W. Smith, and J.O. Brew, pp. 45–108. Papers no. 36. Peabody Museum of American Archaeology and Ethnology, Harvard University, Cambridge.

———. 1949b. The History of Awatovi. In *Franciscan Awatovi*, by R.G. Montgomery, W. Smith, and J.O. Brew, pp. 1–43. Papers no. 36. Peabody Museum of American Archaeology and Ethnology, Harvard University, Cambridge.

———. 1961a. Emergency Archaeology: Salvage in Advance of Technological Progress. *Proceedings of the American Philosophical Society* 105(1):1–10.

———. 1961b. Salvage in River Basins: A World View. *Archaeology* 14:232–235.

———. 1961c. The Threat to Nubia. *Archaeology* 14:268–276.

———. (editor). 1968. *One Hundred Years of Anthropology*. Harvard University Press, Cambridge.

British Mountain Tradition

But for dedicated practitioners of northwestern Boreal and Arctic archaeology, historians of the discipline, and uncritical "early man" aficionados, few archaeologists in the 1990s know what to make of a culture-historical taxonomic construct known as the British Mountain tradition (BMt). Proposed more than three decades ago (MacNeish 1959), the concept conveyed the notion that there existed, within a geographically ill-defined Mackenzie corridor, traces of those northeast Asian migrations that had led to the peopling of the New World. Derived from a small series of lithic assemblages obtained mostly from the Engigstciak site area (northern Yukon) and from northwest Alaska, and lacking chronostratigraphic integrity, the British Mountain tradition was described as characterized by large blades and flakes detached from "discoidal" cores made of siliceous sedimentary rocks and by derived "crude" unifacial and bifacial implements. These were seen as reminiscent of a then poorly understood Eurasian Levallois technology and, accordingly, indicative of great antiquity.

The British Mountain tradition did not stand the test of time or further investigations. The results of recent discoveries and analyses of BMtlike materials indicate that, as originally proposed, the tradition had subsumed at least three entirely different types of manifestations: a "crude tool" component likely associated with a number of Paleoeskimo complexes; a range of lithic-workshop detritus representative of all possible ages and reduction stages; and, ironically, an actual technocomplex whose remains, distributed along the rim of the northern Cordillera, appear to date between the end of the Pleistocene and the middle of the Holocene (Clark 1983; Greer 1991). The latter has been called the Northern Cordilleran tradition.

Jacques Cinq-Mars

Further Readings

Clark, D.W. 1983. Is There a Northern Cordilleran Tradition? *Canadian Journal of Archaeology* 7(1):23–48.

Greer, S. 1991. The Trout Lake Archaeological Locality and the British Mountain Problem. *Canadian Archaeological Asso-*

ciation *Occasional Paper* 1:15–31.

MacNeish, R.S. 1959. Men Out of Asia: As Seen From the Northwest Yukon. *Anthropological Papers of the University of Alaska* 7(2):41–70.

Broken K Pueblo

Broken K Pueblo is a single-storied, 95-room, rectangular plaza-type pueblo located in Hay Hollow Valley in east-central Arizona. It dates to A.D. 1150–1280 (800–670 years B.P.). Fifty-four rooms were excavated in 1963 by James N. Hill and John M. Fritz under the direction of Paul S. Martin of the Chicago Natural History Museum. This was one of the first attempts to demonstrate that the spatial distributions of cultural materials are patterned (nonrandom) and that activity areas can be discovered. It was one of the initial attempts by first-generation "New Archaeologists" to describe aspects of prehistoric social organization.

In an initial analysis (for it and the analyses discussed below, see Hill 1966, 1968, 1970a, 1970b; Hill and Hevly 1968), it was discovered that there were two statistically demonstrable size-based classes of rooms (large and small) in addition to ceremonial rooms (kivas). Associational analyses of artifact and ecofact distributions revealed that the large rooms (habitation rooms) had been the loci of food preparation, eating, water storage and use, and the manufacture of hunting tools; the small (storage) rooms were used for the storage of plant foods, the storage of nonplant items, and "work." The kivas exhibited evidence of ceremonial activity, weaving, and the manufacture of hunting tools.

The primary reason this research was judged important, however, was the attempt to demonstrate the presence of matrilocal (uxorilocal) residence groups at the site (as William A. Longacre [1970] claimed he had done at the Carter Ranch site in the same valley). Based on Hopi and Zuni ethnographic information, it was argued that if uxorilocal residence had existed, there should be spatially localized clusters of styles in the artifacts made by women, especially ceramics. This was so, proponents argued, because each group of related and localized women should have been learning from the others and thus sharing similar style characteristics (e.g., design elements); there should be more style sharing within each residence group than between such groups, thus leading to spatially localized style clusters.

A series of factor analyses, using both ceramic-design elements and standard pottery types, revealed five such clusters. Three of the clusters were closely related to one another and were thus judged to represent a single large residence unit (Unit I) with three subunits. The other two clusters were also closely related to each other but were quite different from the others, and were considered to have been the subunits of a second large residence unit (Unit II). Interestingly, the five subunits were differentiated from one another by nonceramic artifact styles as well; these included different styles of fire pits, numbers of storage pits, and kinds of animal bone. This hierarchy of presumed uxorilocal residence units was compared with those that Longacre had discovered at the Carter Ranch site, with interesting organizational similarities noted.

A final set of analyses dealt with temporal changes in subsistence, storage capacity, and social integration in response to a degrading environment. It is notable that while those aspects of the research dealing with uxorilocal residence units have been called into question in recent years, the study is still widely read.

James N. Hill

Further Readings
Hill, J.N. 1966. A Prehistoric Community in Eastern Arizona. *Southwestern Journal of Anthropology* 22:9–30.

———. 1968. Broken K Pueblo: Patterns of Form and Function. In *New Perspectives in Archaeology,* edited by S.R. Binford and L.R. Binford, pp. 103–142. Aldine, Chicago.

———. 1970a. *Broken K Pueblo: Prehistoric Social Organization in the American Southwest.* Anthropological Papers no. 18. University of Arizona Press, Tucson.

———. 1970b. Prehistoric Social Organization in the American Southwest: Theory and Method. In *Reconstructing Prehistoric Pueblo Societies,* edited by W.A. Longacre, pp. 11–58. University of New Mexico Press, Albuquerque.

Hill, J.N., and R.H. Hevly. 1968. Pollen at Broken K Pueblo: Some New Interpretations. *American Antiquity* 33:200–210.

Longacre, W.A. 1966. Changing Patterns of Social Integration: A Prehistoric Example From the American Southwest. *American Anthropologist* 68:94–102.

———. 1970. *Archaeology As Anthropology:*

A *Case Study*. Anthropological Papers no. 17. University of Arizona Press, Tucson.

Martin, P.S., W.A. Longacre, and J.N. Hill 1967. *Chapters in the Prehistory of Eastern Arizona, III*. Fieldiana: Anthropology, vol. 57. Field Museum of Natural History, Chicago.

Bull Brook Site

The Bull Brook site (19ES80) is a large, Early Paleoindian fluted-point site near Ipswich, Massachusetts, that dates to ca. 8600 B.C. (10,550 years B.P.). Like Debert, Vail, and some other northern Early Paleoindian sites in the Northeast, it is thought to have been a transitory hunting camp repeatedly occupied by small kin groups passing through in pursuit of herds of caribou. The buried site lacks clear vertical stratification; artifacts, animal and plant remains, and hearths seem concentrated in more than 40 circular "hot spots" arranged in a semicircle ca. 90 m (295 feet) across. The circles may be individual family activity areas that were occupied either at different times over the years or at the same time within a larger band settlement. Among the tools in the composite assemblage are fluted points, scrapers, engravers, and irregular retouched flakes. Bull Brook occupants probably engaged in gift exchanges with people to the west, for many artifacts are made of chert from Pennsylvania or the Hudson River Valley.

Guy Gibbon

Further Readings

Byers, D. 1954. Bull Brook—a Fluted Point Site in Ipswich, Massachusetts. *American Antiquity* 19:343–351.

Grimes, J.R. 1979. A New Look at Bull Brook. *Anthropology* 3(1–2):109–130.

Burials (California)

An enduring practice among North American archaeologists, and a source of continuing tension between archaeologists and Native Americans, has been the practice of excavating the burials of prehistoric Indians. California archaeology has been no exception. The practice of burial excavation in California began before the emergence of archaeology as an academic subject. Burial excavation has yielded information valuable to science in the study of nutrition, disease, growth patterns, genetic patterning, and relationships among populations, as well as the study of past culture. Many Native Americans regard such research as extremely offensive and sacreligious. Various state and federal laws now constrain burial excavation, so future contributions cannot be predicted. Constraint of study is a necessary consequence of the expansion of legal protection provided to Native American communities.

Burials have been important foci for California archaeologists for several reasons. In many prehistoric California village sites, burials were placed in and around houses, so the exposure of burials was an inevitable consequence of village excavation. In other cases, cemeteries were deliberately excavated. California burials traditionally have been accompanied by grave goods, often among the most elaborate and stylistically complex artifacts produced by a culture. Archaeologists have sought such artifacts to help identify cultural patterning and to place communities in regional sequences. Even earlier, collectors from museums sought burials to mine for display specimens. Burials have often yielded materials valuable for the reconstruction of past social and economic systems. For example, similarities and differences in the distribution of grave goods have been important in analyses of social differentiation. California researchers such as Linda B. King (1969), Thomas F. King (1970), and E.G. Stickel (1968) were among the early developers of the study of prehistoric social organization through burial analysis. They helped dispel the notion that California cultures lacked social or political complexity. Burials also have provided exotic raw materials whose identification has led to the reconstruction of past systems of exchange or trade (Hughes 1978; C. D. King 1981). Technological artifacts found with burials have been clues to patterns of subsistence and economy as well as measures of gender differentiation. Burial style and orientation have been found to reflect regional and temporal differences in culture.

Some treatments of the dead may be generalized for California as a whole for particular time periods. Prior to the Middle Archaic (6050–4050 B.C., or 8000–6000 years B.P.), evidence for burial is meager and the number of burials found in one place is small. This reflects the small size of the population and the temporary nature of settlement. In the Middle Archaic, some areas, such as coastal Santa Barbara, saw the development of larger populations and more extended seasons of village or base-camp occupation. Burials now become more common. Archaic-period burials in many parts of California are in extended or supine position. In central California, such burials tend to be aligned east-west, or toward the sunrise or sunset. Archaic burials typically are accompanied by moderate numbers of tools and relatively few artifacts that might be called ornamental, economic, or ritual in nature. An interesting variant occurs among Millingstone, or Topanga, burials along the southern California coast, where some of the deceased were covered with cairns of millingstones. In some cases, these stones had been deliberately broken, or "killed."

Pacific-period burial patterns show significant changes. In early (2050–550 B.C., or 4000–2500 years B.P.) and middle (550 B.C.–A.D. 450, or 2500–1500 years B.P.) Pacific times, the practice of extended burial gave way increasingly to flexed burial. In this practice, the deceased was placed into a shorter, rounder grave, with the body bent at the waist, knees, elbows, and neck to accommodate the smaller grave. Flexed burials show more variation in position than extended burials. Bodies may be moderately (loosely flexed) or severely (tightly flexed) constricted. They may be positioned on either side, on the back, or prone (face down). Axis or orientation of the body relative to compass directions may be more varied. The quantity of grave goods found with the deceased was greater in many cases, and more varied among individuals. This may indicate increased social complexity and differentiation within communities.

Flexed interment continued in the late (A.D. 450–1450, or 1500–500 years B.P.) and final (A.D. 1450–1769) Pacific periods, but cremation became increasingly common in several parts of the state. In areas such as San Francisco Bay, the Sacramento–San Joaquin Delta, and coastal southern California, tightly flexed burials and cremations occur in the same cemetery, sometimes in patterns that coincide with differences in the kinds and quantities of grave goods accompanying the interments. Late and final Pacific cemeteries also contain greater variation in burial styles than do previous periods. This may mean that societies experienced their greatest degrees of social complexity in these later periods. The quantity of goods with some individual burials can be impressive. A female burial at Mescalitan Island in the Goleta Slough was accompanied by more than 20,000 shell beads. A male burial in the Livermore area was found with more than 38,000 beads (Chartkoff and Chartkoff 1984:238). This degree of social differentiation is equal to that found in all but a few of the agriculturally based societies of eastern North America.

Joseph L. Chartkoff

Further Readings

Chartkoff, J.L., and K.K. Chartkoff. 1984. *The Archaeology of California.* Stanford University Press, Stanford.

Hughes, R.E. 1978. Aspects of Prehistoric Wiyot Exchange and Social Ranking. *Journal of California Anthropology* 5(1):53–66.

King, C.D. 1981. *The Evolution of Chumash Society: A Comparative Study of Artifacts Used in Social System Maintenance in the Santa Barbara Channel Region Before A.D. 1804.* Unpublished Ph.D. dissertation, Department of Anthropology, University of California, Davis.

King, L.B. 1969. The Medea Creek Cemetery (LAn-243): An Investigation of Social Organization From Mortuary Practices. *Archaeological Survey Annual Report* 11:23–68. University of California, Los Angeles.

King, T.F. 1970. *The Dead at Tiburon.* Occasional Papers no. 2. Northwestern California Archaeological Society, Petaluma.

Moratto, M.J. (editor). 1984. *California Archaeology.* Academic Press, Orlando.

Stickel, E.G. 1968. Status Differentiation at the Rincon Site. *Archaeological Survey Annual Report* 10:209–261. University of California, Los Angeles.

Burin

A burin is a chipped-stone tool characterized by a blow struck transversely to the plane of the piece or to one of its edges. The thick discard flake that results from this event, usually triangular or trapezoidal in cross section, is called a burin spall. Technically, the existence of the burin blow is the primary distinguishing feature, so a burin can be fashioned on any imaginable blank, including a flake, blade, biface, or shatter. The transverse blow creates a sturdy chisel-like tip that forms an excellent graving tool.

Burins were first recognized in European Upper Paleolithic assemblages (ca. 33,050–8050 B.C., or 35,000–10,000 years B.P.), in which they commonly constitute a prominent and diagnostic element. Since burins were often discovered in levels of French caves in which bone and antler tools and ornaments were also found, their connection with the manufacture of those items was quickly surmised. Later, associations of burins with finished antler harpoons and antler discards for roughed-out harpoon blanks at sites such as Star Carr in England indicated that they were utilized for diverse tasks and for stages in the production of complex tools. An excellent source for tracing early burin historiography and interpretation is Hallam L. Movius, Jr. (1968), and early classifications of this type have been reprinted in Jean M. Pitzer (1977a).

It is now apparent that burins exist in tool assemblages throughout the North American continent in virtually every time period, although, since they are unobtrusive, irregular in shape, and relatively difficult to recognize, they have gone largely undetected. Use-wear analysis of this type has confirmed its integrity as a graving tool in most cases, and Barbara D. Stafford (1977) has provided parameters of wear for different raw materials and modes of use. While one becomes used to regarding the burin as "the object of one's desire," it is worth noting the prehistoric utilization in Alaska of burin spalls, which are generally considered discards, as graver tips held in a handle (Giddings 1956).

George H. Odell

Further Readings

Giddings, J.L. 1956. The Burin Spall Artifact. *Arctic* 9:229–237.

Movius, H.L., Jr. 1968. Note on the History of the Discovery and Recognition of the Function of Burins As Tools. In *La Prehistoire: Problemes et Tendences*, edited by D. de Sonneville-Bordes, pp. 311–318. Centre National de la Recherche Scientifique, Paris.

Pitzer, J.M. 1977a. *Basic Sources for the Study of Burins.* Archaeological Research Facility, Department of Anthropology, University of California, Berkeley.

———. 1977b. *A Guide to the Identification of Burins in Prehistoric Chipped Stone Assemblages.* Guidebooks in Archaeology no. 1. Center for Archaeological Research, University of Texas, San Antonio.

Stafford, B.D. 1977. Burin Manufacture and Utilization: An Experimental Study. *Journal of Field Archaeology* 4:235–246.

B

Caborn-Welborn Phase

The Caborn-Welborn phase (ca. A.D. 1400–1700, or 550–250 years B.P.) is the late Mississippian occupation of southwestern Indiana, southeastern Illinois, and adjacent Kentucky. It brackets the time between the Mississippian Angel phase and the beginning of Euro-American exploration and settlement of the Lower Ohio River Valley in the eighteenth century. The Angel phase came to an end in the fifteenth century with the abandonment of Angel Mounds, the fortified central town (40 ha, or 99 acres) noted for its multiple platform mounds. About the same time, Mississippian Caborn-Welborn settlements were established to the west in a geographically restricted (55-km², or 21-square-mile) section of the Ohio Valley.

Caborn-Welborn settlements are clustered around the mouth of the Wabash River. They range from large villages (4–8 ha, or 10–20 acres) having central plazas and several clusters of rectangular houses to small villages (1–4 ha, or 2.4–10 acres) and hamlets. Villages and hamlets had associated cemeteries, but even the largest villages lacked platform mounds. The close proximity of many of these communities suggests that they were part of a larger political entity, but no single community appears to have dominated the region. Contrasts with the antecedent Angel phase in the distribution of population, mortuary patterns, and exchange of nonlocal goods point to diminished sociopolitical complexity.

Caborn-Welborn ceramics embraced the typical Mississippian array of jars, pans, bowls, bottles, and plates. The main chipped-stone tools were triangular arrow points and end scrapers, manufactured primarily of local cherts, and large hoes, made primarily of imported cherts. People lived in rectangular, single-family houses of wattle and daub construction. They relied heavily on the plants they grew, such as maize and beans, to meet their subsistence needs, but they also collected nuts, hunted, and fished.

Objects manufactured from nonlocal materials are found at many Caborn-Welborn sites. They include catlinite disk pipes, copper ornaments, bison-scapula hoes, Dover and Mill Creek chert hoes, and marine shell mask gorgets. These objects, as well as certain incised and punctated design elements on ceramic vessels, point to widespread interactions with people living to the southwest in the Lower Mississippi Valley and to the north and west in the Oneota region. While such objects as the pipes and gorgets demonstrate the acquisition of manufactured goods or raw materials from outside the home territory, some ceramic designs may reflect the presence of outsiders in Caborn-Welborn communities; these individuals could have introduced new ways of decorating vessels, which were subsequently adapted by local potters.

Historic trade goods include brass scraps and tinkling cones, glass beads, and gunflints. The low number and limited range of these materials suggest indirect contact between Caborn-Welborn peoples and Europeans, perhaps through intermediary Native American groups living closer to trading centers.

The flourishing Caborn-Welborn communities of the fifteenth century also show contrasts with settlement in adjacent regions. Regional centers in the Cahokia area were vacated, as were the large villages and towns in the central Mississippi Valley and the lowermost Ohio Valley. To the east in the central Ohio Valley,

Fort Ancient populations aggregated into large, widely separated villages. It is unclear what kinds of social and political transformations took place in the Caborn-Welborn region as a result of European presence or influence in adjacent areas. It is clear, however, that the Caborn-Welborn population abandoned—or was forced to abandon—the mouth of the Wabash prior to initial written accounts and Euro-American exploration of this locale.

Cheryl Ann Munson
David Pollack

Further Readings

Green, T.J., and C.A. Munson. 1978. Mississippian Settlement Patterns in Southwestern Indiana. In *Mississippian Settlement Patterns,* edited by B.D. Smith, pp. 293–330. Academic Press, New York.

See also ANGEL SITE AND PHASE

Cachepits (Plateau)

Cachepits are in-ground features used to store food. They are found in or next to housepit villages, or in isolated locations throughout the Northern and Columbia plateaus, during the last four millennia. They may occur as features visible from the ground surface or as subsurface features that are sometimes encountered in house excavations. Surface features usually appear as basin-shaped circular depressions, with elevated rims, that range in diameter from ca. 0.5 to 3 m (1.5–10 feet) and in depth from 0.5 to 1.5 m (1.5–5 feet). Excavation profiles reveal straight or sloping walls with thin "floors." Field distinctions between cachepits, roasting pits, and housepits may require excavation. Cachepits may differ from roasting pits by a lack of plentiful fire-cracked rock and charcoal, and from housepits by their generally smaller size, although there may be considerable overlap in size distributions among all three features. Subsurface cachepits vary considerably in form, but they appear to have higher occurrences of preserved foods, especially salmon remains and mammal bone, than do surface features, which rarely contain food remains. In-house cachepits are often located at the interior perimeters of house walls or benches.

Early ethnographers indicate that cachepits were roofed with various materials, including poles, bark, pine needles, earth, or sand. Foodstuffs (roots, berries, fish, meat) were dried, then often wrapped in birch bark, placed in baskets, or both. Pits may have been lined with bark or grass. Oral accounts exist of dried salmon remaining edible for two years in cachepits. Cachepits may have stored different kinds of food than elevated caches, which may have been used for fresh meat.

Martin Magne

Further Readings

Hayden, B. (editor). 1992. *A Complex Culture of the British Columbia Plateau: Traditional* Stl'átl'imx *Resource Use.* University of British Columbia Press, Vancouver.

Caddoan Area Mississippian

Caddoan Area Mississippian is a distinctive Late Prehistoric regional development in the prairie-forest transition zone west of the Mississippi Lowlands primarily in eastern Oklahoma, northwestern Arkansas, and southwestern Missouri. Considered the westernmost advanced Mississippian cultural system, societies in the Caddoan area shared many of the same trends toward greater complexity that characterized other "Mississippian" societies in the southeast and central Mississippi River Valley after ca. A.D. 1000 (950 years B.P.). These include increasing reliance on hoe-based maize-beans-squash agriculture, the presence of civic-ceremonial centers that often contain very large earthen mounds, population aggregation in villages or "towns," and increasingly complex social structures, at least some of which were organized at the chiefdom level.

Although considered a subtradition of the widespread Mississippian tradition, the Caddoan differs from other regional complexes, perhaps because of its location at the western margin of effective agricultural productivity using Mississippian hoe technology (Brown et al. 1978). Caddoan centers seldom display the long-term centralized planning found at "classic" Mississippian centers, such as in the American Bottom or in the Tennessee-Cumberland region, and contain a greater emphasis on burial than is typical of contemporary centers. Peculiarities in settlement patterning are thought to be related to regional environmental variables.

At least two basic site types, special-purpose extractive sites (e.g., quarries, hunting camps) and permanent-habitation sites without earthworks, and three levels of civic-ceremonial centers have been tentatively identified in the 600-year or so history of the subtradition; several developmental sequences have been proposed for this ca. A.D. 1000–1600 (950–350 years B.P.) period. Permanent habitation sites are characterized by a dense midden; permanent, roofed structures; concentration in river valley bottoms; and sizes less than 8–10 ha. Examples are the Spiro village, and the Littlefield 1, Cookson, and Horton sites. Examples of civic-ceremonial centers are Spiro, Norman, and Harlan in Oklahoma. Ritual objects and items of social display are concentrated for the most part at major civic-ceremonial centers. The largest concentration of Southeastern Ceremonial–complex material known was discovered at Spiro, the premier center. Extraordinary numbers of engraved shell artifacts, elaborately engraved polished pottery, *repoussé* (hammered design) copper items, and what appear to be retainer sacrifices, among other traits associated with elite burials, attest to the centralization of power in this social system.

In general, mound groups are located away from permanent habitation sites. The tentative three-tier hierarchy of civic-ceremonial centers is based on differing combinations of mound types. Lower-level centers usually contain low conical mounds that apparently cover the foundations of one or more buildings that may have been mortuaries that housed the dead before final interment, and simple accretional burial mounds, elongate or multilobate in plan, that probably are repositories for the burial offerings and secondary burials removed from mortuary facilities. Middle-tier centers add flat-topped pyramidal mounds, and the premier center, Spiro, a mound that combined features of both mortuary and platform mounds.

Guy Gibbon

Further Readings

Bell, R.E. 1972. *The Harlan Site, Ck-6, a Prehistoric Mound Center in Cherokee County, Eastern Oklahoma.* Oklahoma Anthropological Society, Norman.

Brown, J.A. 1975. Spiro Art and Its Mortuary Contexts. In *Death and the Afterlife in Pre-Columbian America*, edited by E.P. Benson, pp. 1–32. Dumbarton Oaks Research Library and Collections, Washington, D.C.

Brown, J.A., R.E. Bell, and D.G. Wyckoff. 1978. Caddoan Settlement Patterns in the Arkansas River Drainage. In *Mississippian Settlement Patterns*, edited by B.D. Smith, pp. 169–200. Academic Press, New York.

Davis, H.A. (editor). 1970. *Archeological and Historical Resources of the Red River Basin.* Research Series no. 1. Arkansas Archeological Survey, Fayetteville.

Hoffman, M.P. 1970. Archaeological and Historical Assessment of the Red River Basin in Arkansas. Part IV of *Archaeological and Historical Resources of the Red River Basin,* edited by H.A. Davis, pp. 135–194. Research Series no. 1. Arkansas Archeological Survey, Fayetteville.

Krieger, A.D. 1946. *Culture Complexes and Chronology in Northern Texas.* Publication no. 4640. University of Texas, Austin.

Prewitt, T.J. 1974. Regional Interaction Networks and the Caddoan Area. *Papers in Anthropology* 15(2):73–101. Department of Anthropology, University of Oklahoma, Norman.

Wyckoff, D.G. 1974. *The Caddoan Area: An Archaeological Perspective.* Garland, New York.

See also SOUTHEASTERN CEREMONIAL COMPLEX; SPIRO

Cahokia

One of the most remarkable Precolumbian sites in the United States, Cahokia (11MS2, 11S34) is located in the Mississippi River Valley near East St. Louis, Illinois. Almost a millennium ago, extensive residential areas were interspersed among more than 100 earthen mounds, other examples of monumental architecture, plazas, and borrow pits dug for the fill used to build mounds. Cahokia is the most extensive prehistoric site in the United States; it also encompasses the largest mound, known as Monks Mound. Many other nearby communities, including other mound groups, were part of a chiefdom dominated by Cahokia.

The site area was heavily occupied for hundreds of years during the Late Woodland, Emergent Mississippian, and Mississippian periods. The origins of Cahokia's rise to prominence can be traced to the Emergent Mississippian period that spanned the two centuries preceding A.D. 1000 (950 years B.P.). Its peak of development was reached in the first part of the Mississippian period, which covers the next four centuries.

Commonly accepted limits for Cahokia delineate an area of ca. 13 km^2 (5 square miles). Most mounds and habitation areas are located south of an abandoned river channel, although several mounds are situated on the north side of this swampy ground. The site limits encompass the densest concentration of mounds scattered across the valley floor. Boundary definition, however, is somewhat arbitrary. A few other mounds are located just outside the site limits, and habitation areas spread outward across the high and, hence, dry parts of the floodplain.

Mounds of various sizes and shapes were used for different purposes. High-ranking people were buried in some of them. These interments tended to be accompanied by numerous prestige-denoting artifacts, many made from exotic raw materials, and in one instance numerous human sacrifices. Flat-topped mounds supported buildings used by members of the elite social stratum. Old structure remnants often were separated by additional layers of fill that raised mounds to new heights. Many mounds were positioned so that they defined open areas, or plazas. Considerable effort was spent leveling and filling one such area delineated by mounds, the central group dominated by Monks Mound.

Mound building at Cahokia was impressive, but projects requiring much labor and organizational skill were not limited to moving great quantities of soil. Several palisades with bastions were built in succession around the central mound group. Other large constructions included circles or arcs of massive posts, called woodhenges, that were used for calendric purposes.

Local topographic relief constrained settlement choices; the site layout conformed to naturally and culturally imposed orientation axes; and the central mound cluster influenced how nearby land was used. High ground was preferred in the wet floodplain, where much of the land, including parts of the site area, was low and uninhabitable. Many mounds and intensively occupied areas were positioned along the river channel scar. Large structures perched on the crest of the south bank presumably were used by high-ranking people. This wetland-bank orientation can also be found at other major sites in the valley. The principal mound quadrangle at Cahokia, however, was oriented

at a right angle to the slough. Monks Mound overlooked swampy ground to the north, and a plaza was located to the south. The presence of several mounds north of Monks Mound in otherwise uninviting low-lying ground underscores the attraction of the site core.

Residential areas consisted of mostly rectangular houses and accompanying features, such as storage pits, hearths, and groups of posts of unknown function. House walls in the Emergent Mississippian period consisted of thatch-covered vertical poles set in individually dug holes; the wall posts in Mississippian houses typically were placed in long, narrow trenches. The sizes of rectangular dwellings for commoners increased over time, and they closely approximated the dimensions of contemporaneous houses at outlying sites. During the Mississippian period, circular sweat lodges used for ritual purposes also were located in several parts of the site. Domestic structures at Cahokia during any particular time often were similarly oriented and were organized as part of distinct communities within the site area.

Cahokia's rise to regional dominance and its subsequent slide to political obscurity were accompanied by major transformations in the internal organization of the site and the elite group's ability to command the labor needed for large construction projects. Ca. A.D. 1000 (950 years B.P.), the beginning of the Mississippian period, mound building increased dramatically, as did the influence of high-status people in this chiefdom. In addition, outlying rural communities shifted from nucleated to dispersed patterns of settlement. Alterations between the domestic and public use of space in different parts of Cahokia took place from that point forward. More or less discrete groups of mounds and residential areas were scattered across comparatively high land, all dominated by the central group including Monks Mound. Although all habitable areas were not occupied at the same time, Cahokia's population numbered in the thousands during the early Mississippian heyday. Many more people lived in outlying areas, mostly in the floodplain, not the uplands flanking the valley. The greatest capacity to organize labor for massive undertakings and to appropriate prime space for special purposes occurred early in the Mississippian period, as did the widest dissemination of Cahokia-style artifacts throughout the midcontinent.

By the twelfth century, Cahokia-dominated

society was experiencing problems. The core of Cahokia was protected by a defensive wall, and the population of the site, and that of the surrounding floodplain, was in decline. Further shifts in the site's internal configuration had taken place by the late thirteenth century, including a reversion of centrally located public space to residential use and a marked reduction in mound building. In a few more generations, the valley was all but abandoned. When Europeans first arrived in the late seventeenth century, Native Americans retained no knowledge about the mounds that so thickly dotted the valley floor.

George R. Milner

Further Readings

Bareis, C.J., and J.W. Porter (editors). 1984. *American Bottom Archaeology.* University of Illinois Press, Urbana.

Brown, J.A. (editor). 1975. *Perspectives in Cahokia Archaeology.* Bulletin no. 10. Illinois Archaeological Survey, University of Illinois Press, Urbana.

Collins, J.M. 1990. *The Archaeology of the Cahokia Mounds ICT-II: Site Structure.* Illinois Cultural Resources Study no. 10. Illinois Historic Preservation Agency, Springfield.

Emerson, T.E., and R.B. Lewis (editors). 1991. *Cahokia and the Hinterlands.* University of Illinois Press, Urbana.

Fowler, M.L. 1989. *The Cahokia Atlas: A Historical Atlas of Cahokia Archaeology.* Studies in Illinois Archaeology no. 6. Illinois Historic Preservation Agency, Springfield.

———. (editor). 1969. *Explorations into Cahokia Archaeology.* Bulletin no. 7. Illinois Archaeological Survey, University of Illinois Press, Urbana.

———. (editor). 1975. *Cahokia Archaeology: Field Reports.* Papers in Anthropology no. 3. Illinois State Museum, Springfield.

Holley, G.R., R.A. Dalan, and P.A. Smith. 1993. Investigations in the Cahokia Site Grand Plaza. *American Antiquity* 58:306–319.

Milner, G.R. 1990. The Late Prehistoric Cahokia Cultural System of the Mississippi River Valley: Foundations, Florescence, and Fragmentation. *Journal of World Prehistory* 4(1):1–43.

See also MONKS MOUND

Caldwell, Joseph R. (1916–1973)

Joseph R. Caldwell was one of a number of American archaeologists exploring ideas in the 1950s that eventually became core themes of processual archaeology. In his monograph *Trend and Tradition in the Prehistory of the Eastern United States* (1958), Caldwell ignored both the Midwestern Taxonomic Method and Gordon R. Willey's system of developmental stages, couched in terms of "traditions" and "horizons," in favor of an ecological approach in which broad, economically based patterns are crosscut by regional traditions. He argued that cultural change often results from ecological adjustments, as in the emergence at the end of the last Ice Age of a new economic pattern he called "primary forest efficiency" in response to the disappearance of big game and the spread of new resource-rich forests in the Eastern Woodlands. The name of the New Archaeology movement can be traced to his 1959 article "The New American Archeology," in which he argued that archaeologists should explain

Joseph R. Caldwell. (Reprinted with permission from American Antiquity *41[3]:303)*

change in terms of cultural processes, view artifacts as having roles within functionally integrated systems, and not regard all items of culture as equally significant in bringing about change. He also supported the assumption that a limited number of general historical processes underlay the infinite variety of the ethnographic record. Many of these ideas were extensions into archaeology of neo-evolutionary anthropology, a movement gaining popularity at the time. Caldwell also spurred interest in the study of interaction between societies with his 1964 concept of an "interaction sphere," a concept he developed to explain the spread of the Hopewellian burial cult in the Eastern Woodlands. Like many archaeologists of his generation, he received early training as a supervisor on government-funded projects in the 1930s.

Guy Gibbon

Further Readings

Caldwell, J.R. 1958. *Trend and Tradition in the Prehistory of the Eastern United States.* Memoir no. 88. American Anthropological Association, Menasha.
———. 1959. The New American Archaeology. *Science* 129:303–307.
———. 1964. Interaction Spheres in Prehistory. In *Hopewellian Studies,* edited by J.R. Caldwell and R.L. Hall, pp. 133–143. Scientific Papers, vol. 12. Illinois State Museum, Springfield.

See also WILLEY, GORDON R.

California Culture Area

The modern state of California covers 407,166 km² (157,207 square miles). It is the third-largest state in area and, with nearly 30 million inhabitants, the most populous. Its population standing was paralleled prehistorically, when its estimated 310,000–350,000 people made up nearly one-tenth of the continent's inhabitants. It is a land of immense topographic and ecological variation. Eleven major geomorphic provinces occur in the state. It possesses more than 1,931 km (1,200 miles) of Pacific coastline and has several peaks taller than 4,267 m (14,000 feet) above sea level. It also is one-third desert, and its Death Valley has the continent's lowest elevation below sea level. This great diversity is reflected in an equally complex and varied archaeological record.

This discussion of that record uses the system developed by J.L. Chartkoff and K.K. Chartkoff (1984)—see CALIFORNIA (SPACE-TIME FRAMEWORK)—that organizes California's archaeological sequences into four main divisions, called periods: Paleoindian (first human occupation to 9050 B.C., or 11,000 years B.P.), Archaic (9050–2050 B.C., or 11,000–4000 years B.P.), Pacific (2050 B.C.–A.D. 1769, or 4000–181 years B.P.), and Historic (from the first recorded European contact, ca. 1540, to the present).

Paleoindian Period. The term "Paleoindian" is used in California archaeology much as it is elsewhere, to refer to the cultures and archaeological assemblages associated with the region's first inhabitants. As elsewhere, it is assumed that California's earliest settlers had their historical, cultural, and genetic roots in northeastern Asia and crossed into the Americas during the last major (Wisconsin) glaciation, ca. 68,050–10,050 B.C. (70,000–12,000 years B.P.). California archaeologists also generally assume that the historically known Native Americans of California are descended in part from these early Paleoindian settlers, as well as from more recent migrants.

The archaeological record for Paleoindian populations in California is one of the most confusing in the hemisphere. The state has seen a host of claims for very early assemblages and human remains. In virtually every case, serious problems in evidence have caused these claims to be viewed with skepticism or to be completely dismissed by most authorities. California has also yielded better-accepted evidence for later Paleoindian materials, but because they do not closely follow patterns found elsewhere, their interpretation presents continuing problems.

California's Paleoindian archaeology may be divided into three groups. The earliest and most problematic includes materials thought to predate the development of the distinctive large-projectile-point industries found elsewhere, such as Clovis and Folsom, that date to ca. 10,050–7050 B.C. (12,000–9000 years B.P.). For convenience, these materials can be called "pre-Clovis," which indicates, among other things, that they lack a cohesive identity of their own. California also possesses examples of large projectile points. These artifacts, found both in sites and as isolated discoveries, constitute a second, "fluted-point," group of sites. A third group, slightly more recent than the fluted-point materials, has been termed the "Western Pluvial Lakes tradition" (Bedwell 1970). This tradition may represent a transition to Archaic lifeways in California at roughly the same time that large-point Plano industries are present in other areas of the continent.

Pre-Clovis materials in California include both human remains and tool assemblages claimed to be of Pleistocene age; that is, older than 10,050 B.C. (12,000 years B.P.). Both sets of materials have attracted vigorous champions, but their assumed great age has proven difficult to confirm. A series of human skeletal remains has been unearthed in California during the twentieth century for which claims of great antiquity have been made. With few exceptions these remains have been human skulls found by nonarchaeologists and removed before any systematic study could be made of the precise context from which they were taken. Examples of such finds have been made at Del Mar, La Jolla, Laguna Beach, and Sunnyvale. Claims of a Pleistocene age for these skulls rests upon such features as the great depth of the reported discovery and the absence of any cultural remains of more recent age. Aspartic-acid dates made of these crania all suggested ages between 38,050 and 13,050 B.C. (40,000–15,000 years B.P.). More recent tests of aspartic-acid results using other dating methods have produced much more recent dates for these crania. As of the mid-1990s, no human remains from California had been widely accepted by the scientific community as of Pleistocene age (cf. Fagan 1987; Jennings 1983; Moratto 1984 for reviews).

Pre-Clovis cultural remains have been reported for California even more frequently than human remains, and just as many difficulties surround them. Among the site localities claimed by some to be of Pleistocene age are Manix Lake, Calico, China Lake, Scripps, Texas Street, Farmington, Tranquillity, and Potter Creek. Their great age has been assumed primarily because of the crudeness of the tools or alleged tools found and their association with ancient land surfaces. For instance, several are associated with shorelines and beaches of Pleistocene lakes that subsequently dried up in what is now the Mohave Desert, and some are associated with buried gravel deposits from raised marine terraces or alluvial fans. The absence of more recent diagnostic artifacts and, in the case of desert finds, the occurrence of heavily patinated surfaces have also suggested to some a great age for these materials. Nonetheless, it has been shown in case after case that reasonable grounds exist to doubt their assumed Pleistocene age. Thus, while the archaeological literature for the pre-Clovis period in California is extensive, the existence of pre-Clovis cultures in the state remains unclear.

Evidence for Paleoindian occupations in California contemporary with the Clovis and Folsom traditions elsewhere is much more firmly established. These "fluted-point" traditions are less well dated in California than elsewhere but are generally understood to have occurred between 10,050 and 7050 B.C. (12,000–9000 years B.P.). Fluted-point industries have been identified in the desert lake country of southeastern California, at China Lake (Davis and Panlaqui 1978), at Borax Lake in the North Coast Ranges (Meighan and Haynes 1970), and at Tulare Lake in the southern San Joaquin Valley (Riddell and Olsen 1969). Isolated fluted points have been found as well in a variety of locations and habitats around the state. California fluted points show a wide range of variation in size, form, and material. Their channeling, or fluting, produced by the removal of one or more flakes from the base toward the tip on one or both faces, resembles the Clovis pattern. E. L. Davis (1978) recognized what she termed a proto-Clovis stage of point technology at several sites at China Lake. She thought that this proto-Clovis technology was earlier than the "classic" Clovis phase, arguing for ages of 13,050–11,050 B.C. (15,000–13,000 years B.P.) for proto-Clovis and 11,050–8850 B.C. (13,000–10,800 years B.P.) for "classic" Clovis. This relationship has not been stratigraphically established, however, and the inference of a greater age for proto-Clovis materials rests on the comparative crudeness of the points more than anything else.

There is a strong association on the Great Plains between fluted-point assemblages and the hunting of Pleistocene megafauna herds, especially mammoth and bison. In California, no direct association between fluted points and Pleistocene megafauna has been established, although the bones of megafauna have been found, especially around the shorelines of old desert lakes, and fluted-point cultural remains are found in some of the same types of settings as in the Great Plains. It is reasonable to suppose, therefore, that California's Paleoindians hunted some megafauna, such as mammoths, giant ground sloth, giant bison, and horses. Still, the lack of discovery of megafauna kill and butchering stations, despite intensive searching, suggests a much more diversified diet with less dramatic quarry. Studies since the early 1980s of Paleoindian sites in the Rockies, the Great Lakes, and New England have shown that Paleoindians in other parts of the continent also made extensive use of smaller game. The lifeways of California Paleoindians of the fluted-point traditions seem to have been more like those of the mountains and the Northeast than those of the Great Plains and the Southwest. So far, however, sites in the state with Clovis points have yielded almost no evidence of diet, and very little reliable evidence about other aspects of their life is known.

The term "Western Pluvial Lakes tradition" (WPLT) was developed by Bedwell (1970) to synthesize a series of previously defined archaeological complexes that existed during the transition ca. 9050–6050 B.C. (11,000–8000 years B.P.) from late Pleistocene to early Holocene times. The San Dieguito complex (see C.W. HARRIS SITE) is an element of this tradition, as are sites in many parts of the state, most notably at Lake Mohave, Silver Lake, and other remnant Pleistocene inland lacustrine habitats. Moratto (1984:103) holds that this tradition is an evolutionary outgrowth of the fluted-point tradition, for he believes that lacustrine environments experienced a gradual change after 10,050 B.C. (12,000 years B.P.), with woodlands and deep lakes giving way to grasslands and shallow lakes. Paleoindian cultures responded to these changes in their resource base by shifting their diet and technology. Among the characteristics of the Western Pluvial Lakes tradition are a decline in projectile-point production and an expansion of chopper-scraper production. The heavy choppers and scrapers are thought to reflect the growing importance of processing-plant resources. The Mostin site near Clear Lake in the North Coast ranges, which belongs to this tradition, seems to exhibit a greater degree of sedentism than other sites in the tradition. It also exhibits a diversified diet that utilized several kinds of resources from different microhabitats in the Clear Lake Basin: mollusks, fish, waterfowl, small and medium-sized game animals, and a number of plant foods (Kaufman 1980; King 1973; King and Berg 1973).

Although the roots and early forms of Paleoindian culture in California remain conjectural, Chartkoff and Chartkoff (1984) draw attention to some general characteristics of lifeways at that time. California's Paleoindians seem to have had somewhat more diversified and less specialized diets than did Paleoindians in most other parts of the continent. Although megafauna lived in the state at the time, there is no evidence that they were an especially significant part of the diet. Although Paleoindians lived or foraged in many parts of the state, their remains are concentrated in lakeshore environments. There is no evidence that they made use of oceanic resources, although some had access to the coast.

California Paleoindian assemblages show a less developed specialized-tool technology than do Paleoindian assemblages in other areas. Among fluted points, although some manufacturing is of excellent quality, typological consistency is very low, and the distinctive Folsom and Plano point types found to the east do not occur. Some production of distinctive chipped-stone crescents occurs in some Clovis and Western Pluvial Lakes–tradition assemblages, but many distinctive Clovis features, like prismatic and lamellar blade production from fluted cores, are absent. Also lacking are tools distinctive of later periods, such as milling tools, which suggests that procedures for processing plant foods that required a specialized technology were not yet developed. The virtual lack of bone awls and needles suggests that basketry production also remained of minor importance.

The resulting image is of a period in which societies lived by generalized foraging. They exploited a diversity of plant and animal resources but especially those that occurred widely across California and the West that did not require a very specialized technology to process. In most cases, social units seem to have been quite small, perhaps equivalent to an extended family, and the people seem to have lived a fairly nomadic life. Since small numbers of people occupied large territories, the state's population would have been quite low—perhaps no more than 1,000–2,000 people. Such societies would have been extremely egalitarian, with essentially no political structure or status differentiation.

Archaic Period. The concept of an Archaic stage to characterize forms of cultures that succeeded the Paleoindians after the close of the Pleistocene had become established in North American archaeology by the 1950s. C.W. Meighan first applied the concept to California as a whole (1959). His usage reflected a view of Archaic cultures as representing a stage in evolution toward more complex, post-Archaic forms in which the changes were defined in largely economic and technological terms, as by the adoption of pottery making and horticulture. From this perspective, California cultures remained at the Archaic level throughout prehistory. This view of California was sustained by scholars elsewhere, such as G.R. Willey (1966) and J.D. Jennings (1989) in their syntheses of continental prehistory.

This view found little acceptance among area researchers, perhaps because it failed to recognize significant changes within the California Archaic. A view more reflective of the use of the term "Archaic" in eastern North America is shown in D.A. Fredrickson's sequence of early post-Pleistocene cultures in the North Coast ranges. His regional scheme defined a Lower (6050–3050 B.C., or 8000–5000 years B.P.), Middle (3050–1050 B.C., or 5000–3000 years B.P.), and Upper (1050 B.C.–A.D. 450, or 3000–1500 years B.P.) Archaic sequence that reflected the development of seed- and acorn-based foraging strategies prior to the emergence of later florescent cultures (Fredrickson 1984:485).

California's Archaic cultures developed in ways divergent from Paleoindian patterns in several respects. The most important trends involved patterns or strategies of subsistence, settlement, technology, and social organization. These trends proceeded at somewhat different rates in different parts of the state and in varying directions. It is the occurrence of the trends, rather than the specific forms they took or the times they were manifested, that is significant. Because of differences in the timing of regional developments, the temporal boundaries of the Archaic period and its subdivisions must be regarded as useful generalizations rather than assertions of historical or evolutionary episodes.

A significant developmental trend in the California Archaic involved the gradual diversification of the food base. C.E. Cleland (1976) contrasted the focal economies of Paleoindian times with the more diffuse economies of the Archaic. By this he meant that Paleoindians utilized relatively few food species, making those they did use into primary staples. The ecology of those species exerted distinctive patterning on the lifeways of the societies that depended on them. Archaic cultures, by contrast, developed subsistence patterns in which many dozens or even hundreds of species were exploited, though none served as primary staples. This increasingly complex resource base required more complexity in seasonal movements and the scheduling of movements during the annual round.

Chartkoff and Chartkoff (1984) contrast Paleoindian and Archaic economies in terms of universality of resource base. Though Paleoindian cultures in California did not intensely concentrate on single species of megafauna, as may have occurred elsewhere, they still used relatively few of the species found in the habitats they exploited. They also concentrated on those that occurred widely and required relatively little in the way of locally developed knowledge and technology to exploit. Their resource choices were therefore generally universal throughout the environments of this culture area. Archaic cultures developed adaptations that relied increasingly on locally distinctive or unique resources. Over time, the differences among Archaic economies from one part of the state to another grew increasingly marked compared to Paleoindian strategies. Differentiation in regional technologies and settlement strategies increased correspondingly.

As Archaic cultures developed over time, they tended to create more distinctively defined territories than the Paleoindians did. Their territories tended to embrace a range of topographies and microhabitats rather than a single habitat, such as a desert lakeshore. Archaic peoples seem to have developed seasonal movement patterns that took households into greater varieties of habitats than earlier, with their movements scheduled more rigorously to give access to seasonally available resources. Archaic groups generally increased in population size and density over time and developed varied patterns of seasonal congregation and fissioning to adjust population densities to seasonal resource abundance. Over time, Archaic peoples developed increasing varieties of food-harvesting and -processing equipment, such as manos and millingstones, mortars and pestles, baskets, and seed-beaters, to allow them to make use of categories of resources that had existed in Paleoindian times but had not been used. Based on these greater intensities and efficiencies in habitat resource exploitation, Archaic cultures were able to support larger populations over time, as well as systematically occupy more parts of the state. Based on such developments, the islands of the southern California coast, the state's extensive coastal zone, most of the Central Valley, and most of its mountain ranges came to be occupied regularly for the first time. The opening of new regions for occupation as well as the development of more productive subsistence strategies helped population growth to swell compared to Paleoindian times.

Archaic cultures also developed the state's first extensive networks for the dispersal of resources across broad regions. This dispersal is often termed "exchange." Exchange is a specific pattern of social interaction and goods transfer, however, and there is uncertainty as to how much resource movement in Archaic California was due to actual exchange and how much stemmed from travel by people from their base territories to resource sources (that is, acquisition through expedition rather than through exchange or trade). Because California has a number of kinds of distinctive raw materials that can be traced to sources, it is possible to see the growth of resource movement in Archaic times even when the means of movement is not always certain. Such materials as shell from the coast, obsidian from specific quarries, and steatite (soapstone) from the few available quarry sources provide indications of this resource movement. Although a certain amount of resource movement occurred even in Paleoindian times, Archaic cultures expanded on this pattern significantly. It was much more significant by the end of the Archaic period than it had been early in the period (e.g., Chartkoff 1989). By the end of the Archaic, signs appear that social standing within communities was being displayed through the use of beads, pendants, and other ornaments. These trends are understood to have some relationship to the growth of resource movement. They suggest that California's Late Archaic cultures were developing in somewhat similar ways to the Late Archaic copper-trading cultures of the Midwest.

Archaic patterns have been defined at hundreds of sites throughout the state. Some key examples include the Windmiller site in the Delta, the Borax Lake pattern at CA-Lak-36 in the North Coast ranges (Fredrickson 1984), the Glen Annie site near Santa Barbara (Owen et al. 1964), the C.W. Harris site in San Diego County (Warren 1967), Little Lake in the Owens Valley (Bettinger and Taylor 1974), and the Menlo phase at Surprise Valley in northeastern California (O'Connell 1975). Although subsistence remains, projectile-point types, and other data vary from site to site, all areas show parallel trends toward increasing complexity of foraging economies, with increasing varieties of foodstuffs used, greater complexity of seasonal movements and scheduling, and more evolution of specialized technology to exploit productive local resources.

Pacific Period. The last few millennia in California prehistory saw the transformation of many Archaic ways of life into the cultures that were flourishing when Europeans first entered the state between A.D. 1540 and 1850. By that time, many parts of California hosted large communities with complex societies, economies, and political systems; many villages had populations of 1,000 or more people; chiefdoms existed in several areas; long-distance trade routes extended to other parts of the continent; money systems had evolved; great differences in wealth and social status were reflected in burial customs; major population movements took place; and organized warfare occurred. Populations grew until California accounted for an estimated one-tenth of all people living north of Mexico. Remarkable changes also took place elsewhere on the continent, but California is especially remarkable because, except for peoples living along the Colorado River, the growth in population occurred without aid of food production. Instead, Californians developed some of the most efficient and productive hunting and gathering strategies in world history.

The literature of California archaeology shows even less use of a standardized terminology for this remarkable era than for the Archaic period. Heizer and his colleagues (Lillard et al. 1939) developed the term "Late horizon" to refer to the last 1,500 years of prehistory in central California, but it has given way to "Late period" and, more recently, "Hotchkiss phase." For the North Coast ranges, Fredrickson (1984) uses "Gunther pattern" and "Augustine pattern." For the desert region, C.N. Warren (1984) uses "Saratoga Springs" and "Protohistoric." Rogers's (1929) "Canalino" still enjoys wide use for the southern California coast, although it is increasingly replaced by C.D. King's local use of Early, Middle, and Late periods (1981) in a way quite distinct from the central California use. The term "Bidwell" is commonly used in the Northern Sierras and northeastern California (Moratto 1984). Chartkoff and Chartkoff (1984) have used the term "Pacific period" to refer to the post-Archaic part of California prehistory as a whole.

The Pacific period is defined as the phase of California prehistory that followed the Archaic period and ended with Historic contact by Europeans and Euro-Americans (Chartkoff and Chartkoff 1984). The Chartkoffs give a starting date for the Pacific period of 2050 B.C. (4000 years B.P.) and an ending date of A.D. 1769. Contact with outside cultures occurred at different times in different parts of the state: 1539 on the Colorado River; 1849 in some parts of northern California, for example. Parts of the coast were visited by ships at different times between 1540 and 1850 when permanent European or Euro-American settlement began in different areas. The year 1769, marks the founding of California's first permanent European settlement at San Diego, and it is taken as the most appropriate single date for the onset of permanent disruption to independent native California cultures.

The Pacific period saw the transformation of California cultures from the small-scale, semi-nomadic, socially egalitarian societies of the Archaic period to the large-scale, sedentary, socially complex systems characteristic of the Protohistoric era. Several trends characterize this transformation, including the exploitation of previously underutilized ecological niches in more productive ways, the development of new kinds of focal economies, and the elaboration of sociopolitical systems.

By the end of the Archaic period, all important habitats in California had come into use, but the intensity of use was often low. The Pacific period saw the development of more effective ways to exploit resources already being used as well as the addition of previously unused resources to the diet. The result was a dramatic increase in the number of people who could be supported per unit of land. This transformation in hunter-gatherer strategies has been termed a shift from a foraging to a collecting way of life.

The collection of hard seeds and acorns had begun in Archaic times, but as the Pacific period developed, communities began to collect these resources in larger and larger surpluses above their immediate needs. Storage facilities—baskets, pits, and silos—were created to contain the surpluses. Winter camps were developed near the plant sources and were occupied for more months than previously. Houses were made more substantial to accommodate longer stays. Analogous plant resources came to be exploited in other parts of the state—pine nuts in the Sierras, mesquite beans in the deserts, and aquatic bulbs in the northeastern lake country—to provide similar surpluses.

Similar changes took place in salmon exploitation. Archaic peoples used salmon as a seasonal resource, catching enough fish for their immediate needs. In the Pacific period, salmon fishing shifted toward the harvesting of great surpluses. This change required other changes, such as the assemblage of large work forces that required organizing and the prior collection of food to support them. Preservation methods, such as smoking and drying, had to be developed to keep the meat edible for later consumption. Methods to share the catch among the many workers from different communities who participated had to be developed.

Comparable developments on the coast saw the emergence of oceangoing watercraft to improve the productivity of transportation and fishing. The use of ocean foods, such as fish, shellfish, and sea mammals, was underway in Archaic times, but Pacific-period cultures intensified their use through strategies such as net fishing and the movement of labor crews by boat.

Success with intensified food collecting sheds light on the absence of food production in California. Except for peoples along the Colorado River, who represent the margins of the Southwestern culture area, prehistoric Californians did not grow either plant or animal food. This was not because they lacked the knowledge: They were in regular trade contact with farming peoples in the Southwest, and Californians farmed tobacco for ceremonial purposes and raised domesticated dogs. Nor was it because they lacked needed natural resources: Most parts of California are more easily used for farming than the deserts of the Southwest, where prehistoric farming flourished. One possible explanation is that farming simply held no advantage for the prehistoric people in the extremely productive hunting-gathering conditions of California. Another is that simple farming might not have supported, as intensive collecting surely did, the growing population.

Intensified food collecting and the attendant population growth resulted in both larger communities and smaller territories per community. Smaller territories gave each community access to a narrower range of resources and made highly scheduled seasonal migration less productive. Instead, communities became increasingly sedentary. The use of expeditions by task groups to collect specific resources and bring them back to the community increasingly replaced community seasonal migration. At the same time, intercommunity exchange networks evolved to move more goods more effectively to consumers. An adjunct to the expansion of trade was the development of shell money systems, based mainly on strings of shell beads, to enhance trading. As C.D. King has noted, the social meaning of shell ornaments evolved over time, from the Archaic to the late Pacific period, from decorative to increasingly economic (C.D. King 1990).

These trends can be seen in many local sequences. In southern California are many coastal sequences, at such locations as Rincon Point, Dos Pueblos, and Mescalitan Island (C.D. King 1981). Inland counterparts occur at Century Ranch (C.D. King et al. 1968). One of the many Sierra Nevada examples comes from the Yosemite area, at El Portal, Crane Flat, and Hogden Ranch (Moratto 1984). In the Monterey area, G.S. Breschini and T. Haversat (1980:14–15) show these changes in their shift from the Sur to the Monterey pattern at CA-Mnt-12, 16, 170, and 298, among other sites. One of the many desert examples is offered by the Cottonwood Creek, Rose Spring, and Stahl sites (Warren 1984:373–376). In northwestern California, the change from CA-DN0-11 at Crescent City to CA-Hum-67 at Eureka shows similar trends (Fredrickson 1984:484–485).

The archaeological data from such varied cases can be quite different in detail. *Dentalium* shells on the Klamath River are replaced by clamshell discs on the San Joaquin. Plank canoes in Santa Barbara are replaced by bundled-reed canoes in the Delta. Acorn-storage silos in the Sacramento Valley are replaced by timber-lined pine-nut-storage cribs in the eastern Sierras. Obsidian exchange at Clear Lake is replaced by steatite exchange in Los Angeles. Acorn harvesting in the South Coast ranges is replaced by mesquite-bean harvesting in the deserts. Earth-covered, semisubterranean dance houses near Chico are replaced by roofless, brush-walled enclosures near San Juan Capistrano. Yet the developmental trends toward sedentism, social and political complexity, surplus-generating niche intensification, elaborate trade and exchange networks, and consequent population growth are similar across the state during the Pacific period.

Using such strategies, native Californians in late prehistory evolved some of the largest and most complex sets of cultures and societies on the continent. That they did so without food production makes their achievements all the more remarkable.

Historic Period. The fourth and last phase in the Chartkoff and Chartkoff (1984) model is the Historic period. While ostensibly beyond the limits of prehistory, Historic-period archaeology is important for the understanding of Late Prehistoric archaeology in California and elsewhere. Among other things, the Historic period covers the era when prehistoric cultures first came into contact with foreign ones. The consequences to different Native American societies varied. In addition, the entry of each culture into historical recording took place at different times. While peoples along the southern California coast began to be visited by foreigners starting in the sixteenth century, many northern Californian groups did not experience their first contacts until the nineteenth century. A particular year, such as 1750, might be within the Historic period for one culture while another was still within a prehistoric framework. Even for those groups that had come into contact with Europeans and whose existence had become historically recorded in writing, the nature of contact and its consequences could be highly variable. In some cases, individual shipwrecked Spanish sailors were rescued and cared for at Indian settlements. In others, a wrecked ship might provide access for Indians to European goods with no human contact involved. At the other extreme, Spanish military and colonial forces established permanent settlements beginning in 1769 at San Diego, with monumental impacts on all nearby Native American communities. Once European contact had commenced more systematically, the spread of introduced diseases had disastrous consequences even on some Native American communities far from direct contact.

In many parts of eastern North America, some of the most florescent prehistoric cultures had already waned before the Historic period began. In California, historical contact cut off the development of Pacific-period cultures in full flower. The first recorded contacts by Europeans took place along the Colorado River in the late 1530s. By the early 1540s, sporadic ship contacts along the California coast from Mexico had begun. They affected southern California the most. Cabrillo's expedition in 1542–1543 initiated these sea contacts. Over the next 200 years, voyages of Spanish galleons from Manila in the Philippines to Mexico brought ships to the California coast for their landfalls. The English explorer Sir Francis Drake is assumed to have stayed on the California coast for up to six weeks in 1579.

Permanent Spanish settlement began in 1769, when a fort and mission were established near modern-day San Diego. Over the following 53 years, a total of 22 missions, several forts, and four secular towns were established between San Diego and San Francisco Bay. The Spanish colonies impressed local Indians as slaves to work for their farms, ranches, and missions, at first incorporating the southern and central California coasts into their system and then raiding the Central Valley for more captives. Interior and northern California still lay beyond direct colonial impact, but the collapse of coastal cultures led to the breakdown of regional economic systems, with consequent impoverishment of the inland societies.

The Mexican Revolution of 1820–1822 ended the Spanish colonial and mission system in California. The gradual disbanding of missions left Indian survivors to cope as best they could where Europeans had taken over the great majority of the Indians' traditional resource areas. Mexican administration created a new colonial management for California; one result was the expansion of the ranch system into central California in the 1830s. In the 1840s, immigrants from Mexico began to be outnumbered by immigrants from the United States. U.S. fur traders and explorers penetrated more and more parts of previously isolated California, bringing culture contact and disease. When gold was discovered in 1848, the U.S. population rush was launched in earnest. U.S. population in California rose from less than 5,000 to more than 150,000 within 10 years. The same decade saw Indian population drop from perhaps 300,000 to less than 150,000; it kept falling, to a low of 10,000 by the year 1900.

The half-century following the 1848 California gold rush saw the breakdown of all remaining traditional cultures, as their populations were decimated by disease and privation and most of their lands were taken over by immigrants, and the end of California's independent prehistoric cultural traditions. Since then, native California populations have grown to pre-contact levels. Many traditional societies have survived to the present, though they have been radically changed due to becoming minorities, usually dispersed, in a now-dominant Euro-American population.

Joseph L. Chartkoff

Further Readings

Bedwell, S.F. 1970. *Prehistory and Environment of the Pluvial Fork Rock Lake Area of South-Central Oregon.* Unpublished Ph.D. dissertation, Department of Anthropology, University of Oregon.

Bettinger, R.L., and R.E. Taylor. 1974. *Suggested Revisions in Archaeological Sequences of the Great Basin and Interior Southern California.* Research Papers no. 5. Nevada Archaeological Survey, Reno.

Breschini, G.S., and T. Haversat. 1980. Preliminary Archaeological Report and Archaeological Management Recommendations for CA-Mnt-170, on Pescadero Point, Monterey County, California. Ms. on file, Archaeological Regional Research Center, Cabrillo College, Aptos.

Chartkoff, J.L. 1989. Exchange Systems in the Archaic of Coastal Southern California. *Proceeding of the Society for California Archaeology* 2:167–186.

Chartkoff, J.L., and K.K. Chartkoff. 1984. *The Archaeology of California.* Stanford University Press, Stanford.

Cleland, C.E. 1976. The Focal-Diffuse Model: An Evolutionary Perspective on the Prehistoric Cultural Adaptations of the Eastern United States. *Midcontinental Journal of Archaeology* 1:59–76.

Davis, E.L. (editor). 1978. *The Ancient Californians: Rancholabrean Hunters of the Mojave Lakes Country.* Science Series no. 29. Natural History Museum of Los Angeles, Los Angeles.

Davis, E.L., and C. Panlaqui. 1978. Chapters 1–5. In *The Ancient Californians: Rancholabrean Hunters of the Mojave Lakes Country,* pp. 4–152. Science Series no. 29. Natural History Museum of Los Angeles, Los Angeles.

Fagan, B.M. 1987. *The Great Journey: The Peopling of Ancient America.* Thames and Hudson, London.

Fredrickson, D.A. 1984. The North Coastal Region. In *California Archaeology,* edited by M.J. Moratto, pp. 471–528. Academic Press, Orlando.

Jennings, J.D. 1983. *Ancient North Americans.* W.H. Freeman, San Francisco.

———. 1989. *Prehistory of North America.* 3rd ed. Mayfield, Mountain View, Calif.

Kaufman, T.S. 1980. *Early Prehistory of the Clear Lake Area, Lake County, California.* Unpublished Ph.D. dissertation,

C

Department of Anthropology, University of California, Los Angeles.

King, C.D. 1981. *The Evolution of Chumash Society: A Comparative Study of Artifacts Used in Social System Maintenance in the Santa Barbara Channel Region Before A.D. 1804.* Unpublished Ph.D. dissertation, Department of Anthropology, University of California, Davis.

———. 1990. *The Evolution of Chumash Society.* Garland, New York.

King, C.D., T.C. Blackburn, and E. Chandonet. 1968. The Archaeological Investigation of Three Sites on the Century Ranch, Western Los Angeles County, California. *Archaeological Survey Annual Report* 10:12–107. University of California, Los Angeles.

King, R.F., and G. Berg. 1973. The Mostin Site: A Preliminary Report on Lake County Salvage Operations. Ms. on file, Department of Anthropology, Sonoma State University, Rohnert Park.

King, T.F. 1973. A Possible Paleoindian Cemetery and Village Site in Lake County. *Society for California Archaeology Newsletter* 6:1–2. Fullerton.

Lillard, J.B., R.F. Heizer, and F. Fenenga. 1939. *An Introduction to the Archaeology of Central California.* Bulletin no. 1. Department of Anthropology, Sacramento Junior College, Sacramento.

Meighan, C.W. 1959. California Cultures and the Concept of an Archaic Stage. *American Antiquity* 24:289–305.

Meighan, C.W., and C.V. Haynes, Jr. 1970. The Borax Lakes Site Revisited. *Science* 167(3922):1213–1221.

Moratto, M.J. (editor). 1984. *California Archaeology.* Academic Press, Orlando.

O'Connell, J.F. 1975. *The Prehistory of Surprise Valley.* Anthropological Papers no. 4. Ballena Press, Ramona, Calif.

Owen, R.C., F. Curtis, and D.S. Miller. 1964. The Glen Annie Canyon Site, SBa-142, an Early Horizon Coastal Site of Santa Barbara County. *Archaeological Survey Annual Report* 6:429–517. University of California, Los Angeles.

Ragir, S.R. 1972. *The Early Horizon in Central California Prehistory.* Contributions no. 15. University of California Archaeological Research Facility, University of California, Berkeley.

Riddell, F.A., and W.H. Olsen. 1969. An Early Man Site in the San Joaquin Valley. *American Antiquity* 34:121–130.

Rogers, D.B. 1929. *Prehistoric Man of the Santa Barbara Coast.* Santa Barbara Museum of Natural History, Santa Barbara.

Warren, C.N. 1967. The San Dieguito Complex: A Review and Hypothesis. *American Antiquity* 32:168–185.

———. 1984. The Desert Region. In *California Archaeology,* edited by M.J. Moratto, pp. 339–430. Academic Press, Orlando.

Willey, G.R. 1966. *Introduction to American Archaeology: no. 1. North and Middle America.* Prentice-Hall, Englewood Cliffs.

California (Space-Time Framework)

Regional chronologies published for California archaeology are perhaps more numerous, with smaller scales of distinction, than chronologies for anywhere else on the continent. For several parts of the state, three or more local chronological systems may be used at the same time, each with different names. In other words, unlike scholars in most parts of North America, California archaeologists have never adopted a comprehensive space-time framework within which to organize the state's archaeology. A case in point is the most detailed review of California prehistory, M.J. Moratto's *California Archaeology* (1984), which subdivides the state into several regions but lacks a comprehensive terminology and mentions few connections among the regions.

The major exception is found in J.L. Chartkoff and K.K. Chartkoff's *The Archaeology of California* (1984), in which the authors use a statewide framework they developed that follows the general structure of systems found in the eastern two-thirds of North America. The Chartkoffs' system organizes California's archaeological sequences into four major divisions, each with subdivisions. The major divisions are: the Paleoindian period (from first human occupation to 9050 B.C., or 11,000 years B.P.), the Archaic period (9050–2050 B.C., or 11,000–4000 years B.P.), the Pacific period (2050 B.C.–A.D. 1769, or 4000–181 years B.P.), and the Historic period (from the first recorded European contact, ca. A.D. 1540, to the present).

The Chartkoffs developed their system as a useful device to organize California's local sequences and to make them as compatible as possible with models and terms used elsewhere in North America. It is the only scheme in print to date (1996) that integrates the entirety of the state and all of its successive cultural stages into one unified framework. Some aspects of this model have parallels in terminology used by other California archaeologists for more restricted units of time and space (e.g., Fredrickson 1984; Meighan 1959). Although the scheme as a whole has yet to be adopted by the majority of California researchers, it is presented here (and in all California-related entries by Joseph L. Chartkoff) in the absence of any other equally comprehensive and widely used model for the state.

The use of the term "period" as an organizing device in this scheme refers to blocks of time in which definable cultural patterns prevail across a variety of regions in the state. It does not imply cultural uniformity or ethnic unity within a space-time unit, as does the term "horizon." It also does not imply a sequence of determinate cultural evolution, as does the term "stage," even though patterns of increasing complexity are recognized. It similarly does not imply a unit in which distinctive patterns of artifact or assemblage stylistic unity prevail, as does the term "phase." It recognizes local or regional variation in culture, economy, technology, and assemblage patterning across space at any moment in time, and it accommodates change over time within a unit. Its defining characteristics are meant to be at a more general level of abstraction, recognizing fundamental cultural patterns or strategies that may be manifest in varying ways by different cultural units in time and space within the division. For example, Archaic cultures are recognized as having followed settlement patterns with high degrees of seasonal movement, while Pacific-period cultures were significantly more sedentary. The "period" concept allows for trend lines to be followed by any culture within the time unit. It also allows for different cultures at different locations to display different degrees of a defining trend at the same time. The "period" scheme, therefore, is meant to be a useful organizing framework or heuristic device, not a set of classes with tightly bounded borders.

California shares some of the patterns of growth and development seen in eastern North America, although some of the most dramatic elements in the East were unimportant in the state. For instance, plant cultivation, except for tobacco, was significant in California only along the Colorado River; most California groups did not take up the practice of making pottery; and the great earthworks found in eastern North America after 2050 B.C. (4000 years B.P.) do not have any direct counterparts in California. Yet, in most aspects of cultural development—especially with respect to social and cultural complexity, economic strategies, and population levels—California parallels the eastern regions in many important ways.

Joseph L. Chartkoff

Further Readings

Chartkoff, J.L., and K.K. Chartkoff. 1984. *The Archaeology of California*. Stanford University Press, Stanford.

Fredrickson, D.A. 1984. The North Coastal Region. In *California Archaeology,* edited by M.J. Moratto, pp. 471–528. Academic Press, Orlando.

Meighan, C.W. 1959. California Cultures and the Concept of an Archaic Stage. *American Antiquity* 24:289–305.

Moratto, M.J. (editor). 1984. *California Archaeology*. Academic Press, Orlando.

See also CALIFORNIA CULTURE AREA; CENTRAL CALIFORNIA PREHISTORY; EASTERN CALIFORNIA; NORTHWESTERN CALIFORNIA; PALEOINDIAN; SOUTHERN CALIFORNIA COAST

C

Cambria

The Cambria phase is the poorest known Initial Middle Missouri phase, with almost all of the published information dealing with a single site. The Cambria site (21BE2) is on a terrace 20 m (65.6 feet) above the Minnesota River ca. 25 km (15.5 miles) northwest of Mankato, Minnesota. The river bluff and a steep ravine provide natural defenses on two sides. W.B. Nickerson excavated at the site in 1913 and 1916. The University of Minnesota excavated there in 1938 and 1941.

Cambria ceramics are grit-tempered, globular jars with constricted necks, pronounced shoulders, and smooth surfaces. Lloyd A. Wilford (1945) divided Cambria ceramics into three types based on rim form. Type A features everted rims with trailed line decoration primarily on the shoulder. Type B has S-shaped rims with trailed line or single-twisted cord decoration on the rim. Type C features rolled rims with broad trailing on the shoulder. Ruthann Knudson (1967) divided Cambria ceramics into five types based on rim form and decoration. Her types were then subdivided into

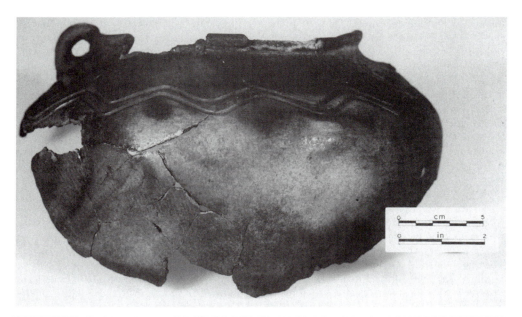

Ceramic vessels from Cambria Village (21BE2), Blue Earth County, Minnesota. (Courtesy of the Wilford Archaeology Laboratory, University of Minnesota)

varieties based on decoration. Ramey Broad Trailed and Powell Plain both feature rolled rims. Linden Everted Rim features low- to medium-height rims that are outflared. Mankato Incised features medium to high, outflaring rims with decorations on rim interiors, rim exteriors, and shoulders. Knudson's S-rim type, Judson Composite, has small lug or loop handles with trailed line and/or single-twisted cord decoration on some rims and shoulders. The Cambria site and the nearby Price site are ceramically differentiated from other Cambria habitation sites by the presence of rolled-rim sherds.

Cambria projectile points are of two basic

types: triangular/unnotched and side-notched. Scrapers make up more than half of the formal chipped-stone tools at the type site. Other stone tools include grooved stone mauls, celts, hammerstones, grinding stones, and sandstone abraders. No catlinite objects have been recovered at the Cambria or Price sites, while a western Minnesota Cambria-phase site, Gillingham, yielded a catlinite pipe and plaque. The Cambria and Gillingham sites each produced a copper awl. The Cambria site yielded a large quantity of bone tools, including scapula hoes. Worked shell is relatively scarce at Cambria sites.

Mammalian remains from the Cambria site are dominated by deer, followed by bison, *Canis* sp., beaver, and raccoon. Many of the bison remains tend to be scapula hoes and other tools. Nonmammalian remains include fish, turtle, and bird. Eleven species of freshwater mussel were recovered. Overall, Cambria subsistence features a varied assemblage of upland and wetland fauna. Nickerson collected charred maize from the Cambria site that has been identified as Eastern Eight-Row or Northern Flint. The Price site has yielded maize, cucurbits, and sunflower.

All major Cambria habitation sites are on lower or intermediate terraces of the Minnesota River. No house features have been documented, although trash/storage pits are common at the major sites. Cambria-like ceramics are typically found in small numbers in the upper levels at many of the major lacustrine habitation sites in eastern South Dakota and southwestern Minnesota. None of these sites has yielded rolled-rim ceramics or bison-scapula hoes.

Cambria burials tend to be extended primaries in mounds and are often accompanied by specialized ceramics, such as miniature vessels. Mounds identified as Cambria on Big Stone Lake in western Minnesota may have closer affiliations with other Plains Village complexes. Cambria radiocarbon dates cluster around A.D. 1200 (750 years B.P.).

It has been suggested that Cambria was linked to a Cahokia-based trade network, with the Cambria type site a dominant center in the northern extension of this network. Cambria may have been involved in the exchange of bison meat, hides, and perhaps finished clothing for cultigens and exotic materials (e.g., marine shells). Cambria exhibits a blend of Woodland, Plains Village, Middle Mississippian, and Oneota influences.

Scott F. Anfinson

Further Readings

Anfinson, S.F. 1987. *The Prehistory of the Prairie Lake Region in the Northeastern Plains.* Unpublished Ph.D. dissertation, Department of Anthropology, University of Minnesota, Minneapolis.

Johnson, E. 1961. Cambria Burial Mounds in Big Stone County. *Minnesota Archaeologist* 23:53–81.

———. 1991. Cambria and Cahokia's Northwestern Periphery. In *New Perspectives on Cahokia: Views From the Periphery,* edited by J.B. Stoltman, pp. 307–317. Monographs in World Archaeology no. 2. Prehistory Press, Madison.

Knudson, R. 1967. Cambria Village Ceramics. *Plains Anthropologist* 12:247–299.

Nickerson, W.B. 1989. Archaeological Evidences in Minnesota. *Minnesota Archaeologist* 47(2):4–40.

Ready, T. 1979. Cambria Phase. In *A Handbook of Minnesota Prehistoric Ceramics,* edited by S.F. Anfinson, pp. 51–65. Minnesota Archaeological Society, St. Paul.

Scullin, M. 1979. Price Site (21BE36): Preliminary Notes on a Previously Unidentified Site of the Cambria Focus. Ms. on file, Department of Anthropology, Mankato State University, Mankato.

Watrall, C. 1968. *An Analysis of the Bone, Stone and Shell Materials of the Cambria Focus.* Unpublished Master's thesis, Department of Anthropology, University of Minnesota, Minneapolis.

———. 1969. Analysis of the Unmodified Stone Material From the Cambria Site. *Minnesota Academy of Sciences Journal* 35:4–8.

———. 1974. Subsistence Pattern Change at the Cambria Site. In *Aspects of Upper Great Lakes Anthropology,* edited by E. Johnson, pp. 138–142. Minnesota Historical Society, St. Paul.

Wilford, L.A. 1945. Three Village Sites of the Mississippian Pattern in Minnesota. *American Antiquity* 11:32–40.

Campbell, Elizabeth (1893–1971)

Elizabeth W.C. Campbell was one of the pioneers of desert archaeology in California. Working out of the Southwest Museum in Los Angeles, Campbell and her husband, William, began a research program in the Colorado and Mojave deserts in the 1920s that helped establish the region's basic chronological sequence and culture types (Campbell 1931, 1949). Along with Malcolm J. Rogers of the San Diego Museum of Man, the Campbells created a framework for desert prehistory that is still in use. Elizabeth Campbell also is noteworthy because she was among the earliest California archaeologists to recognize the importance of climatic and environmental change and to attempt to correlate climatic patterns with culture change (Campbell 1936). She also was among the earliest California archaeologists to employ interdisciplinary research. At Lake Mojave and the Pinto Basin, she collaborated with earth scientists, such as Ernst Antevs, to help establish the geological ages of former lakeshores and to reconstruct past climatic episodes (Campbell 1936; Campbell and Campbell 1935; Campbell et al. 1937).

Joseph L. Chartkoff

Further Readings

Campbell, E.W.C. 1931. An Archaeological Survey of the Twenty-Nine Palms Region. *Southwest Museum Papers* 7:1–93.

———. 1936. Archaeological Problems in the Southern California Deserts. *American Antiquity* 1:295–300.

———. 1949. Two Ancient Archaeological Sites in the Great Basin. *Science* 109:340.

Campbell, E.W.C., and W.H. Campbell. 1935. The Pinto Basin Site: An Ancient Aboriginal Camping Ground in the California Desert. *Southwest Museum Papers* 9:1–51.

Campbell, E.W.C., W.H. Campbell, E. Antevs, C.E. Amsden, J.A. Barbieri, and F.D. Bode. 1937. The Archaeology of Pleistocene Lake Mohave. *Southwest Museum Papers* 11:1–118.

Campus Site

Stone artifacts found in 1933 at the University of Alaska campus in Fairbanks included microblades and microblade cores similar to others founds in Siberia, northern China, and Japan. Nels C. Nelson soon announced that the camp was the first evidence supporting the Bering land bridge hypothesis for human entrance into North America from Asia. Frederick Hadleigh West (1967, 1975) used the Campus site (X49FAI-001) as one of four type sites for the Denali complex, which was thought to date to 10,050–6050 B.C. (12,000–8000 years B.P.) based on typological comparisons. Restudy of collections by Charles M. Mobley (1991) identified the presence of microblade, macroblade, biface, and core/flake technologies. Except for a unique cortical cobble specimen, the 42 microblade cores have a consistent form termed "Campus-type." They are small, thin, bifacially or unifacially flaked pieces with a single platform on one edge formed by a burin scar or a deeply concave flake scar. Microblades were removed from this platform from the adjoining edge, which created a fluted face formed by microblade-removal scars. Burins include 22 Donnelly burins, which are made by notching a flake margin in one or more places to provide purchase for burin-spall removals. Bifacial tools include two notched points and several small lanceolate points with contracting stems and lateral and basal grinding. Faunal remains include bear, beaver, hare, and, probably, wolf and bison. Mobley believes that radiocarbon dates of 1550 B.C. ± 140, 910 B.C. ± 180, and 775 B.C. ± 125 (3500, 2860, and 2725 years B.P.). are associated with the microblade material, although early excavation methods and lack of stratigraphy in the shallow deposits preclude confirmation of the association.

Charles M. Mobley

Further Readings

Mobley, C.M. 1991. *The Campus Site: A Prehistoric Camp at Fairbanks, Alaska.* University of Alaska Press, Fairbanks.

Rainey, F. 1939. Archaeology in Central Alaska. *Anthropological Papers of the American Museum of Natural History* 36(4):355–405.

West, F.H. 1967. The Donnelly Ridge Site and the Definition of an Early Core and Blade Complex in Central Alaska. *American Antiquity* 32:360–382.

———. 1975. Dating the Denali Complex. *Arctic Anthropology* 12:76–81.

———. 1981. *The Archaeology of Beringia.* Columbia University Press, New York.

Cape Krusenstern

Cape Krusenstern, just north of Kotzebue Sound, Alaska, is the location of a large series of beach ridges that contain significant archaeological sites. In addition to the beach-ridge sites, Cape Krusenstern is the location of two other major archaeological localities, the Palisades and Lower Bench sites, which are situated on

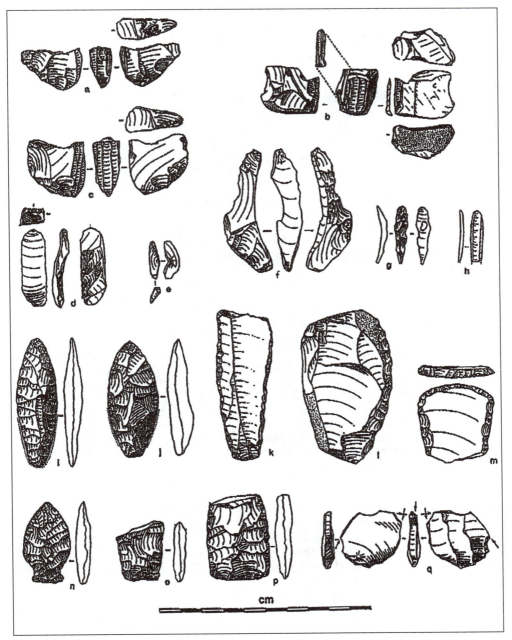

Artifacts from the Campus site: microblade cores (a–c, one with attaching microblade (b); microblade core tabley (d); gull-wing flake (e); initial microblade removals (f, g); microblade (h); lanceolate bifaces (i–j); side-notched biface (n); flat-based biface fragments (o, p); retouched macroblade (k); side- and end-retouched flakes (l, m); Donnelly burin (q). (Prepared by C. M. Mobley)

high outcrops immediately landward of the ridges. The beach-ridge sites, which were discovered in 1958 by J.L. Giddings and excavated by him between 1959 and 1962, include numerous prehistoric and historic settlements, camp-sites, grave sites, and isolated finds that span the past 4,200 years. Additional excavations were conducted there by Douglas D. Anderson in 1965. Together with the earlier Palisades and Lower Bench sites located on the hillside behind the beach ridges, Cape Krusenstern represents the most complete series of coastal and near-coastal archaeological sites in northwestern Alaska, if not in all of Alaska. Owing to the constant seaward building of the beach ridges and the tendency of coastal Eskimos to live immediately adjacent to the sea, the coastal prehistoric settlements, each quite isolated from the other, are arranged in a time series from the earliest on the inner beaches to the latest on the outermost beaches. Their isolation from each other has left them essentially undisturbed from their time of abandonment. This has provided excellent opportunities to learn about early settlement patterns in the region from unmixed contexts.

The archaeological excavations on the more than 100 Cape Krusenstern beach ridges have uncovered campsites of the Denbigh, Early Choris, Choris, Norton, and Ipiutak cultures, as well as winter villages and settlements from Old Whaling, Ipiutak, Birnirk, Western Thule, and Recent Eskimo periods. The Old Whaling Village also contains five large summer houses. Burials from the Ipiutak and Western Thule periods have been located, but they contain few grave goods and only poorly preserved skeletal remains.

The Palisades site, which overlooks the beach ridges and the Chukchi Sea from a limestone outcrop on the landward side, contained irregular-notched points of chert and obsidian and large rounded core tools that are dated by comparison to similar materials from Band 6 at the Onion Portage site on the Kobuk River to ca. 3550 B.C. (5500 years B.P.). The Lower Bench site, which also overlooks the beach ridges, though at a lower elevation than the Palisades site, contains microblades and oval platformed microblade cores once thought to represent an early form of the Denbigh Flint complex. More recently, numerous similar sites have been found all along the northwest Alaskan coast between Kotzebue Sound and Barrow. They are thought to predate Denbigh by several millennia. In the coastal plain adjacent to the beach ridges are also hundreds of other smaller, undated archaeological sites that, taken together, indicate active use of the region through time.

Cape Krusenstern is a National Monument of the U.S. National Park Service.

Douglas D. Anderson

Further Readings

Giddings, J.L. 1967. *Ancient Men of the Arctic*. Knopf, New York.

Giddings, J.L., and D.D. Anderson. 1986. *Beach Ridge Archeology of Cape Krusenstern*. GPO, Washington, D.C.

Carter Ranch Pueblo

The Carter Ranch Pueblo is located in the Hay Hollow Valley ca. 16 km (10 miles) east of the modern town of Snowflake, Arizona. It probably dates from ca. A.D. 1100 to 1250 (850–700 years B.P.). It is a fairly small site with approximately 39 pueblo rooms built around a plaza with two kivas and a detached circular great kiva with a lateral ramp entryway. The orientation of the site is to the east; that fact, and the nature of the artifacts and features, suggest that it might be an example of the late Mogollon culture. The circular great kiva, on the other hand, suggests that it may have had Anasazi ties.

The Carter Ranch site was excavated over two field seasons, 1961 and 1962, by the Southwest Expedition of the Field Museum of Natural History led by Paul S. Martin and John B. Rinaldo. As a small and not too unusual site in this area of the Southwest, the pueblo would not warrant more than a footnote in southwestern archaeology except for the innovative mode of analysis employed, for the analysis of the artifacts, especially the ceramic assemblage at the site, was one of the earliest examples of New Archaeology and experimentation with what came to be called "Ceramic Sociology." As a result, the Carter Ranch Pueblo is well known in the southwestern archaeological literature.

The analysis of pottery decoration and the distribution of design motifs at the site formed the basis for a series of inferences about postmarital residence patterns at the pueblo. This analysis was the focus of a doctoral dissertation at the University of Chicago by William A. Longacre in 1963 (Longacre 1970). In brief, he argued that the localized clustering of decoration suggested that related women were living in close proximity to one another, following matrilocal postmarital residence. If, as is likely, women were the potters and if the potting technology was passed down from mothers to daughters, such an inference seemed justified. In the analysis of the distribution of decorative motifs at the site, Longacre used a computer, one of the earliest uses of computer-assisted analysis in American archaeology. A functional study of pottery types at the site, carried out by L.G. Freeman and J.A. Brown, also used a computer.

The initial reactions to this work were quite positive. Some people saw these early examples of the New Archaeology as proof positive that archaeology could address and come to grips with issues of concern to their social-anthropological colleagues. Investigation of prehistoric social organization seemed possible. Over the years, however, the flawed nature of the excavation itself and the analyses came to be understood. The total disregard for unraveling the complex formation processes responsible for the creation of the distribution of the decoration on the sherds and whole pots was a most serious error. This plus the lack of investigation of the sources of the pottery, the places where the pots had been made, further weakened the study. No one today accepts the exciting and loud early claims made for the interpretation of prehistoric behavior and social organization at Carter Ranch Pueblo. But the work carried out there stimulated a great deal of subsequent work, both in the Southwest and elsewhere. James N. Hill's work at Broken K Pueblo in Hay Hollow Valley quickly followed, and Longacre ultimately began an ethnoarchaeological project among the Kalinga of northern Luzon, the Philippines, to investigate ceramic reflections of human behavior and organization among a living people.

William A. Longacre

Further Readings

Longacre, W.A. 1970. *Archaeology As Anthropology: A Case Study.* Anthropological Papers no. 17. University of Arizona Press, Tucson.

———. 1974. Kalinga Pottery-Making: The Evolution of a Research Design. In *Frontiers of Anthropology,* edited by M.J. Leaf, pp. 51–67. Van Nostrand, New York.

Longacre, W.A., and M.T. Stark. 1992. Ceramics, Kinship, and Space: A Kalinga Example. *Journal of Anthropological Archaeology* 2:125–136.

Martin, P.S., J.B. Rinaldo, W.A. Longacre, L.G. Freeman, J.A. Brown, R.H. Hevly, M.E. Cooley. 1964. *Chapters in the Prehistory of Eastern Arizona, II.* Fieldiana: Anthropology, vol. 55. Field Museum of Natural History, Chicago.

See also BROKEN K PUEBLO; MARTIN, PAUL SIDNEY

Carter/Kerr-McGee Site

The Carter/Kerr-McGee site (48CA12) is located in the central Powder River Basin just north of the city limits of Gillette, Wyoming. It was discovered by archaeologists in 1974 during a survey for a coal strip mine. The name is derived from its location, which straddles land to be mined by both the Carter and the Kerr-McGee mining corporations. The site had been noticed more than two decades earlier by Dan Beck of Gillette, who had found many Paleoindian projectile points eroding out of it. He realized they were different from other points he had seen in the area up to that time and even wrote a letter to the Smithsonian Institution describing the material.

A University of Wyoming field crew under the direction of George C. Frison excavated the site in 1977. It was believed at first to be only a Cody-complex bison-bone bed. However, it turned out to have not only a Cody component but also Alberta, Hell Gap, Agate Basin, Folsom, and Clovis (or possibly Goshen-Plainview) components that closely duplicated the succession of Paleoindian components at the Hell Gap site. It is a small remnant of what was once a much larger site.

It is believed to have been an arroyo bison trap. Burning of thick coal beds in late Pliocene or early Pleistocene times caused a large body of land to drop nearly 70 m (230 feet) and form a lake. Vegetation around the lake was and still is ideal for large herbivores. Subsequent drainage into the lake formed an arroyo ideal for bison trapping, and for much of Paleoindian times there was an aggradation of deposits resulting from the trapping and killing of bison. However, the cycle of erosion changed, and consequent headcutting resulted in the loss of most of the site. This kind of geologic action has probably resulted in the loss of many Paleoindian arroyo bison kills and may explain why this is the only Paleoindian bison kill found to date (1996) in the Powder River Basin.

George C. Frison

Further Readings

Frison, G.C. 1984. The Carter/Kerr-McGee Paleoindian Site: Cultural Resource Management and Archaeological Research. *American Antiquity* 49:288–314.

———. 1991. *Prehistoric Hunters of the High Plains.* 2nd ed. Academic Press, San Diego.

See also HELL GAP SITE

C

Casa Grande

Casa Grande, Spanish for Great House, is the name given to a large Hohokam Classic-period ruin located on the Gila River between Phoenix and Tucson, Arizona. The first federal reservation for a prehistoric ruin in the United States, Casa Grande Ruins National Monument encompasses not only the Great House, but also a ballcourt and numerous compounds.

The Great House is a four-story structure constructed of coursed adobe. The Hohokam made coursed adobe by piling up a wall segment of adobe by hand to a height of ca. 0.6–0.9 m (2–3 feet), allowing it to dry, and then mounding more adobe on top. The finished walls were smoothed, and sometimes polished and plastered. Roofs were constructed of juniper, pine, fir, and mesquite. Some of the wood was carried from mountains more than 80 km (50 miles) away. The lowest story was purposely filled (forming a type of platform mound), but the second and third stories had five rooms, and the uppermost story had a single towerlike room. Although ruins within the monument were occupied during the pre-Classic (before A.D. 1150, or 800 years B.P.), the Great House was apparently constructed and used ca. A.D. 1300–1450 (650–500 years B.P.). Archaeologists have proposed different functions for the Great House, including astronomical observatory and defensive stronghold.

The Great House is the most impressive portion of a larger ruin with numerous compounds. Casa Grande was one of the largest Classic-period Hohokam ruins on the Gila River. It was located at the end of an irrigation canal, and the inhabitants may have been instrumental in managing the use of water from the canal by farmers in this portion of the Gila River.

Professional excavations began at Casa Grande in the early 1900s under the direction of Jesse Walter Fewkes of the Bureau of American Ethnology. He excavated Compound A, which included the Great House, and several additional mounds nearby. Since that time, archaeologists have excavated portions of the ballcourt and several other compounds within the monument boundaries. No single report documents all of the site excavations.

No other Great Houses remain in the Hohokam area, and it is uncertain whether others existed in the past. However, on the basis of observations by early explorers in the area, many archaeologists believe that at least two other Great Houses once stood in the area between the Salt and Gila rivers of Arizona.

Patricia L. Crown

Further Readings

Andresen, J.M. 1985. Pottery and Architecture at Compound F, Casa Grande Ruins National Monument, Arizona. In *Proceedings of the 1983 Hohokam Symposium*, edited by A. Dittert and D. Dove, pp. 595–640. Occasional Paper no. 2. Arizona Archaeological Society, Phoenix.

Crown, P.L. 1987. Classic Period Hohokam Settlement and Land Use in the Casa Grande Ruins Area, Arizona. *Journal of Field Archaeology* 14:147–162.

Fewkes, J.W. 1912. Casa Grande, Arizona. *Twenty-Eighth Annual Report of the Bureau of American Ethnology*, pp. 25–180. GPO, Washington, D.C.

Wilcox, D.R., and L.O. Shenk. 1977. *The Architecture of the Casa Grande and Its Interpretation*. Archaeological Series no. 115. Arizona State Museum, University of Arizona, Tucson.

See also COMPOUND; HOHOKAM CULTURE AREA; PLATFORM MOUNDS (SOUTHWEST)

Casa Rinconada

Great kivas are one of the hallmarks of Chacoan public architecture. They are large, circular, mostly subterranean structures. Most great kivas are physically incorporated into great houses or are closely associated with them, but isolated great kivas are not uncommon. Casa Rinconada (LA841) is the largest isolated great kiva in Chaco Canyon in the San Juan Basin of northwestern New Mexico. Located on a ridge on the south side of the canyon across from Pueblo Bonito and Chetro Ketl, it is surrounded by a number of small habitation sites but not associated with any great-house structure. Casa Rinconada is 19 m (63 feet) in diameter and 3.6 m (12 feet) deep; a bench ca. 0.8 m (2 feet, 8 inches) high and wide encircles the entire chamber. The structure was apparently entered through rectangular antechambers on the north and south with stairs descending to the bench. The southern antechamber is a single room; the northern antechamber was one of a complex of at least three and possibly six rooms. Date of construction is uncertain, but based on ceramics from a layer of construction debris below the floors and some tentatively dated tree-ring specimens from a wall niche, original construction probably occurred in the A.D. 1070s.

Features on the original floor include a raised, square firebox; a low, curving fire screen between the firebox and the south antechamber; four circular seating pits for socketing the large, upright timbers that supported the roof; and two rectangular raised "floor vaults." The latter are enclosures ca. 1.8 m (6 feet) by 2.6 m (8.5 feet) by 0.6 m (2 feet) in depth, approximately half of the depth being subfloor. The function of the floor vaults is not certain, but many researchers believe they were covered with planks and used as foot drums or sounding platforms for dancers. This earlier floor contains two unique features: a subfloor passageway 0.9 m (3 feet) deep and wide and 11.9 m (39 feet) long, and a circular trench ca. 0.3 m (1 foot) in depth by 15–23 cm (6–9 inches) wide and 4.9 m (16 feet) in diameter. The passageway extends from the northern antechamber to the circular feature, which surrounds one of the upright roof supports and may have been the base of a screened enclosure. The combination of the subfloor passage and such an enclosure would have permitted performers in kiva ceremonies to enter the structure unseen to appear suddenly and dramatically at the appropriate moment in the proceedings.

The later floor in Casa Rinconada lies ca. 10 cm (4 inches) above the first floor. This remodeling included minor changes to the firebox, floor vaults, and seating pits; application of a new veneer to the front and top of the encircling bench; and filling in of the subfloor passageway and the circular trench associated with the first floor. The major wall features in the great kiva are 28 evenly spaced wall niches, ca. 0.3 m (1 foot) in each dimension and less than 0.9 m (3 feet) above the bench top; six other niches were placed lower on the wall. These latter niches are more variable in size and less regular in spacing.

Most researchers view the great kivas as having been the venue for public ceremonies, religious or otherwise. Some have also suggested that Casa Rinconada in particular served as an astronomical or calendrical observatory, but the evidence is limited and arguable.

Lynne Sebastian

Further Readings

Marshall, M.P., J.R. Stein, R.W. Loose, and J.E. Novotny. 1979. *Anasazi Communities of the San Juan Basin*. Public Service Company of New Mexico, Albuquerque; New Mexico State Planning Division, Santa Fe.

Vivian, G., and P. Reiter. 1965. *The Great Kivas of Chaco Canyon and Their Relationships*. University of New Mexico Press, Albuquerque.

Williamson, R.A. 1987. Light and Shadow, Ritual, and Astronomy in Anasazi Structures. In *Astronomy and Ceremony in the Prehistoric Southwest*, edited by J.B. Carlson and W.J. Judge, pp. 99–119. Papers no. 2. Maxwell Museum of Anthropology, Albuquerque.

Zeilik, M. 1984. Archaeoastronomy at Chaco Canyon. In *New Light on Chaco Canyon*, edited by D.G. Noble, pp. 65–72. School of American Research Press, Santa Fe.

Casas Grandes

Casas Grandes, or *Paquimé* as it is commonly called, is situated on the first terrace of the Rio Casas Grandes River in northwestern Chihuahua, Mexico. *Paquimé*, a Nahuatl word, has the same meaning as the Spanish *casas grandes* ("great houses"). The massive ruin of Casas Grandes has been a subject of intense curiosity and speculation since it was first described by early sixteenth-century Spanish and later American explorers. However, the first large-scale scientific excavations were not conducted at this impressive site until the late 1950s.

Much of what we know about Casas Grandes is the result of excavations conducted in the years 1958–1961 by the Joint Casas Grandes Expedition. Directed by Charles C. Di Peso of the Amerind Foundation, the excavations focused on the western portion of the ruin. Evidence of ballcourts, a walk-in well, an extensive water and sewer system, an elaborate mortuary complex that socially differentiated members of the society, human sacrifice, and single and multistoried domestic, public, and ceremonial architecture was uncovered. At its height, Casas Grandes is estimated to have covered 35.7 ha (88 acres) and to have contained more than 2,000 people.

The discovery of large quantities of worked and unworked marine shell, copper and turquoise artifacts, and the remains of more than 500 macaws led Di Peso (1974) to conclude that Casas Grandes was a trading outpost or center in a large-scale Mesoamerican-Southwest exchange system. Mesoamerican merchants, or *puchteca,* constructed the site, in this view, to establish and monopolize trade in rare and exotic raw materials, such as turquoise. Turquoise was a highly valued commodity of the elite classes of Toltec society, whom these merchants were presumed to have served.

On the basis of the excavations at Casas Grandes and several other sites in the general vicinity, the Joint Casas Grandes Expedition established a provisional chronological sequence for the region, which is called the Gran Chichimeca. The six major occupational periods defined are Preceramic (pre-A.D. 1, or 1950 years B.P.), Plainware (A.D. 1–700, or 1950–1250 years B.P.), Viejo (A.D. 700–1060, or 1250–890 years B.P.), Medio (A.D. 1060–1340, or 890–610 years B.P.), Tardio (A.D. 1340–1660, or 610–290 years B.P.), and Espanoles (A.D. 1660–1821, or 290–129 years B.P.). Casas Grandes was occupied primarily during the Medio period, which contains three phases: Buena Fe (1060–1205), Paquimé (1205–1261), and Diablo (1261–1340).

Many of Di Peso's ideas about Casas Grandes have been questioned since they were originally published in 1974. Until the early 1980s (LeBlanc 1980; Lekson 1984; Dean and Ravesloot 1993), criticism focused on his chronological reconstructions, particularly the beginning and ending dates for the Medio period. Archaeologists working in the American Southwest had assumed, on the basis of tree-ring-dated pottery types, such as Gila Polychrome, that the florescence of Casas Grandes occurred after A.D. 1300 (650 years B.P.). The temporal sequence proposed by the Joint Casas Grandes Expedition implied that its zenith was several hundred years earlier than thought. According to this interpretation, the site was occupied at the same time as Chacoan towns, such as Pueblo Bonito.

A reevaluation of tree-ring specimens collected by the Joint Casas Grandes Expedition from Casas Grandes indicates that major episodes of building occurred in the 1200s and 1300s. Construction and repair activities may have lasted into the late 1400s. On the basis of this reanalysis, a revised chronology for Casas Grandes has been proposed that places the Medio period between A.D. 1200 and 1450 (750–500 years B.P.). Consequently, Casas Grandes was not occupied at the same time as Pueblo Bonito. It was contemporaneous instead with other major prehistoric southwestern groups, such as the Classic Hohokam and Salado of southern and central Arizona.

John C. Ravesloot

Further Readings

Bradley, R.J. 1993. Marine Shell Exchange in Northwest Mexico and the Southwest. In *The American Southwest and Mesoamerica: Systems of Prehistoric Exchange,* edited by J.E. Ericson and T.G. Baugh, pp. 123–151. Plenum Press, New York.

Carey, H.A. 1931. An Analysis of the Northwestern Chihuahua Culture. *American Anthropologist* 33:325–374.

Dean, J.S., and J.C. Ravesloot. 1993. The Chronology of Cultural Interaction in the Gran Chichimeca. In *Culture and Contact: Charles C. Di Peso's Gran Chichimeca,* edited by A.I. Woosley and J.C. Ravesloot, pp. 83–103. University of New Mexico Press, Albuquerque.

Di Peso, C.C. 1974. *Casas Grandes: A Fallen Trading Center of the Gran Chichimeca,* vols. 1–3. Northland Press, Flagstaff.

Di Peso, C.C., J.B. Rinaldo, and G.J. Fenner. 1974. *Casas Grandes: A Fallen Trading Center of the Gran Chichimeca,* vols. 4–8. Northland Press, Flagstaff.

LeBlanc, S.A. 1980. The Dating of Casas Grandes. *American Antiquity* 45:799–806.

Lekson, S.H. 1984. Dating Casas Grandes. *Kiva* 50(1):55–60.

Minnis, P.E. 1984. Peeking Under the Tortilla Curtain: Regional Interaction and Integration on the Northern Periphery of Casas Grandes. *American Archeology* 4:181–193.

———. 1989. The Casas Grandes Polity in the International Four Corners. In *The Sociopolitical Structures of Prehistoric Southwestern Societies,* edited by S. Upham, K. Lightfoot, and R. Jewett, pp. 269–305. Westview Press, Boulder.

Minnis, P.E., M.E. Whalen, J.H. Kelley, and J.D. Stewart. 1993. Prehistoric Macaw Breeding in the North American Southwest. *American Antiquity* 58:270–276.

Ravesloot, J.C. 1988. *Mortuary Practices and Social Differentiation at Casas Grandes, Chihuahua, Mexico.* Anthropological Papers no. 49. University of Arizona Press, Tucson.

Casper Hell Gap Site

The Casper Hell Gap site (48NA304) is located on the uppermost terrace on the north side of the North Platte River within the city limits of Casper, Wyoming. It was discovered by two avocational archaeologists, Roderick Laird and Dave Egolf, who were exploring an area of sand dunes disturbed by industrial development. Part of the site was excavated by the University of Wyoming in 1971; the remainder, also by the University of Wyoming, in 1975 when the decision was made to continue industrial expansion. A segment of the site had been unknowingly destroyed several years earlier by pipeline construction.

This unique site was a Hell Gap cultural complex bison kill. It contained the partial remains of about 80 bison of an extinct subspecies that has many characteristics of *Bison antiquus* and some of *Bison occidentalis*. Along with the bison were nearly the same number of broken and complete Hell Gap–type projectile points and butchering tools. The site represents a single kill or perhaps more than one kill that occurred in late fall or early winter. The animals were driven into the windward end of a long, narrow parabolic sand dune with steep sides and leeward end, which served as an impediment to the animals. No evidence of an associated processing area or camp was located. Radiocarbon dates on both charcoal and bone are 8050 B.C. (10,000 years B.P.), which fits well with dates on Hell Gap from the Hell Gap site in southwest Wyoming. Remains of a single *Camelops* were recovered with the bison bones, suggesting this species may have survived nearly 1,000 years longer on the northern Plains than formerly believed.

George C. Frison

Further Readings

Frison, G.C. 1974. *The Casper Site: A Hell Gap Bison Kill on the High Plains*. Academic Press, New York.

———. 1991. *Prehistoric Hunters of the High Plains*. 2nd ed. Academic Press, San Diego.

Wilson, M. 1978. Archaeological Kill Site Populations and the Holocene Evolution of the Genus *Bison*. In *Bison Procurement and Utilization: A Symposium*, edited by L.B. Davis and M. Wilson, pp. 9–22. Memoir no. 14. Plains Anthropologist, Lincoln.

See also HELL GAP COMPLEX

Catlinite

Catlinite is an easily carved, reddish brown argillite stone that was formed mainly into pipes but also into tablets and ornaments. Catlinite artifacts were widely distributed in the Plains and Upper Midwest during the Historic and Late Prehistoric periods, having been obtained in trade or directly from the quarry named after painter, writer, and explorer George Catlin, who visited and described it in 1836. The Native American quarry at Pipestone National Monument in southwestern Minnesota is the type locality for catlinite. Although the term "catlinite" has been used for any red argillite that was used to make aboriginal pipes, it should be reserved for stone of the same mineralogical and chemical makeup as that derived from Pipestone National Monument. Stone of similar appearance can be obtained from primary and secondary deposits in Minnesota, South Dakota, Wisconsin, Nebraska, Kansas, Iowa, Ohio, Arkansas, and Arizona. Red argillite from these sources and from other as yet unidentified sources is also referred to as "pipestone." Source identification of catlinite and pipestone by neutron activation has not been very successful, but a limited application of X-ray diffraction has produced promising results. Pipestone artifacts are rare in the Plains and Midwest until after A.D. 1100 (850 years B.P.),

Indian miner breaking up the exposed margin of a pipestone layer in a quarry. (Reprinted from Smithsonian Institution, Bureau of American Ethnology, Bulletin 60, Figure 128)

Section of a pipestone quarry showing the layer of pipestone (B), quartzite strata (C), and dump (E). (Reprinted from Smithsonian Institution, Bureau of American Ethnology, Bulletin 60, Figure 129)

when they begin to occur in higher frequencies, especially in the form of pipes. Historically, pipes made of this material are common and are sometimes referred to as calumet pipes. X-ray-diffraction analysis of a few Late Prehistoric, Protohistoric, and Historic Plains samples reveal that early samples were derived primarily from local pipestone sources, while historic samples were primarily catlinite. It is not known when use of the catlinite quarry at Pipestone National Monument began, but its primary use appears to be Historic. Quarrying has exposed a gradually sloping, thin layer of catlinite that was revealed after removal of several feet of quartzite. Quarry operations continue at Pipestone National Monument but are limited to Native Americans using traditional techniques.

William T. Billeck

Further Readings

Gundersen, J.N., and J.A. Tiffany. 1986. Nature and Provenance of Red Pipestone From the Wittrock Site (13OB4), Northwest Iowa. *North American Archaeologist* 7:45–67.

Sigstad, J.S. 1973. *The Age and Distribution of Catlinite Red Pipestone.* Unpublished Ph.D. dissertation, Department of Anthropology, University of Missouri, Columbia.

Woolworth, A.R. (compiler). 1983. The Red Pipestone Quarry of Minnesota: Archaeological and Historical Reports. *Minnesota Archaeologist* 42:1–137.

Catlow and Roaring Springs Caves

Catlow and Roaring Springs caves, in southeastern Oregon, were carved into the basalt cliffs of eastern Catlow Valley by ancient Lake Catlow. The lake dropped below the level of the caves ca. 11,050 B.C. (13,000 years B.P.). It was reduced to a string of marshes in the center of the valley ca. 8050 B.C. (10,000 years B.P.). Small bands of foragers began using Roaring Springs Cave (38HA433) around this time, but Catlow Cave does not seem to have been used until 5050 B.C. (7,000 years B.P.). Thereafter, both caves were used sporadically by Native American groups until early in the Historic period. The most intensive use of both caves occurred between 850 B.C. and A.D. 1150 (2800–800 years B.P.).

Catlow Cave was studied in 1935, 1937, and 1938 by University of Oregon crews led by Luther S. Cressman. It was the scene of one of the first stratigraphically and horizontally controlled excavations in the western United States. Roaring Springs Cave was excavated in 1938 and differed in excavation from Catlow Cave in that meters rather than feet were used for all measurements. Cressman's University of Oregon crews at Catlow and Roaring Springs caves included Alex Krieger, Fred Voget, Robert L. Stephenson, and others who forged successful careers in archaeology and anthropology.

Both caves contained large numbers and varieties of perishable artifacts, including twined and coiled basketry, woven sandals, bison-hide moccasins, mats, nets, ropes, feathers, rawhide, and wooden dart and arrow shafts, atlatls, and bow parts. They also contained abundant stone tools, such as projectile points, grinding stones, and scrapers. A few pieces of Late Prehistoric pottery were found on the surface, and human remains were reported from the basal levels of Catlow Cave. Cressman claimed that these were in association with

Pleistocene horse remains, but others argued that the horse bones were modern and had fallen into an excavation pit during a bout of heavy and dusty shoveling. The remains of at least four humans were found in the upper levels of Roaring Springs Cave.

Extensive vandalism and rodent disturbance stopped an attempt to excavate a portion of Catlow Cave during the Steens Mountain Prehistory Project in 1979. The 1930s collections from Catlow and Roaring Springs caves were reanalyzed during the Steens Project (Wilde 1985). Results showed that occupations of the caves generally corresponded with periods of decreasing or low precipitation, when valley marshes were shrinking. Occupational intensity was reduced during periods of increased effective moisture, possibly because people moved out into the valleys to exploit the expanding marshlands.

James D. Wilde

Further Readings

Cressman, L.S. 1942. *Archaeological Researches in the Northern Great Basin.* Publications no. 538. Carnegie Institute of Washington.

Wilde, J.D. 1985. *Prehistoric Settlements in the Northern Great Basin: Excavations and Collections Analysis in the Steens Mountain Area, Southeastern Oregon.* Unpublished Ph.D. dissertation, Department of Anthropology, University of Oregon, Eugene.

Central California Prehistory

Central California refers here to the state's Central Valley and regions west to the coast, excluding the North Coast ranges, which are discussed elsewhere. This region was the birthplace of modern archaeology in California and has remained at the center of academic debate among California archaeologists. M.J. Moratto (1984) has summarized that intellectual history.

The region's geography consists of five major units. The Central Valley, running for more than 600 km (372 miles) west of the Sierra Nevada, forms the drainages of two great river systems: the Sacramento on the north and the San Joaquin on the south. Each river constitutes a separate ecological entity even though together they form one great valley. These streams join east of San Francisco to create a vast delta. Though technically part of the Cen-

tral Valley, the Delta is unique enough to stand as a third unit on its own. The Delta was a vast waterland of freshwater marshes and islands covering more than 10,000 km² (3,860 square miles). It extends up the two major river channels, which used to maintain floodplains up to 30 km (19 miles) wide. Rimming the floodplain both east and west of the rivers were broad grasslands. Only in the southwest corner was the Central Valley dry enough to support semi-desert vegetation. Otherwise, prior to the arrival of Europeans, it was a zone of almost unbelievable ecological wealth. The Delta and floodplains teemed with fish, tule elk, migratory waterfowl, and hundreds of species of water plants. The grasslands were rich in hard seeds and supported herds of antelope. At their margins, the adjacent foothills were blanketed with chaparral and punctuated with oak-filled canyons. Deer, rabbits, hard seeds, and acorns occurred in vast supply.

The merged rivers drain west through the Delta into San Francisco Bay, which is a separate ecological zone with climate affected by the Pacific Ocean and waters made salty by the sea. It supported great numbers of fish, shellfish, waterfowl, and shore plants, while surrounding hills were dense with chaparral, oaks, and deer. Beyond the Bay lies the Pacific coastline, and for central California the coast extends for more than 200 km (124 miles) from below the Big Sur region to above Bodega Bay. As elsewhere along the coast, the shoreline is ecologically complex—a succession of sandy beaches, rocky points, marshy estuaries, and freshwater-stream mouths. After San Francisco Bay, Monterey Bay is the next largest feature on this coast.

The last unit is the South Coast ranges, lying between the San Joaquin Valley and the coast. Neither as tall nor as broad as the North Coast ranges, the South Coast ranges have not emerged as a separate ecological or cultural unit archaeologically, but instead seem to have served as resource areas that formed a back country for peoples living in the Central Valley or along the coast.

Central California at the time of European contact was occupied by native California peoples speaking several languages, each with many dialects and numbering up to 30,000–50,000 people per language. People with languages of the Penutian stock occupied the Central Valley and Bay area: Wintun-speakers west of the Sacramento River and Maidu-speakers east; Yokuts-speakers in the San Joaquin Valley;

Miwoks in and around the Delta; Coast Miwoks north of San Francisco Bay; and Ohlones (Costanoans) from the south side of the Bay to below Big Sur. Smaller communities of Hokan-speakers lived south of the Ohlones: Esselen- and Salinan-speakers (cf. Heizer 1978).

Central California was the first part of the state in which a sequence of prehistoric cultures was recognized. N.C. Nelson (1907, 1909) did pioneering work at Ellis Landing and other Bay-area sites, where he defined an earlier and a later pattern of cultures. The most influential work was done in the Delta, however, when J.B. Lillard et al. (1939) developed their central-California sequence of Early, Middle, and Late horizons based on results from mound excavations in which they were able to recognize changes over time in mode of burial and styles of accompanying artifacts. This taxonomic approach to organizing the past culminated in R.K. Beardsley's (1954) development of the Central California Taxonomic system, applying ideas from W.C. McKern's Midwestern Taxonomic method (1939) that had earlier influenced archaeologists in eastern North America.

Further research began to show the limits of a taxonomic approach to identifying past cultures. B.A. Gerow (1954, 1974a, 1974b; Gerow and Force 1968), S.R. Ragir (1972), and others, aided by the development of dating methods such as radiocarbon, were able to show that separate archaeological patterns, like the Early horizon and Middle horizon, actually overlapped each other to a great extent, even in the same area. In addition, sites showing these patterns were found to be quite variable as to which diagnostic traits they would or would not possess. As a result, some writers began to re-define local sequences to try to establish units that might reflect actual cultures that could be variable from one site to another. Ragir (1972), for example, developed the models of the Windmiller, Cosumnes, and Hotchkiss cultures to replace the Early, Middle, and Late horizons, respectively, and her terminology is still widely used. D.A. Fredrickson (1974) offered the Berkeley and Augustine patterns as broad units to express change throughout central California, and his terminology also is still widely used.

As elsewhere in the state, no one set of terms is used universally, so the model developed by J.L. Chartkoff and K.K. Chartkoff (1984) is used in this discussion to help create a more comparative framework. At the same time, the archaeology for the earlier half of the record (10,050–4050 B.C., or 12,000–6000 years B.P.) is sporadically defined for central California (as in several other parts of the state), so the Chartkoff and Chartkoff model may be applied to gaps in present knowledge as well as to the better-defined parts.

The archaeological record for central California begins in Paleoindian times (10,050–8050 B.C., or 12,000–10,000 years B.P.), not surprising since the Clovis-period site at Borax Lake is just to the north of the Bay area (Moratto 1984). Fluted-point finds have been made elsewhere in the region, however (e.g., Simons et al. 1985). More importantly, early occupations in the southern San Joaquin Valley at Tulare and Buena Vista lakes may have beginnings in Late Paleoindian times and are believed to reflect a local variant of the Western Pluvial Lakes tradition (Warren and McKusick 1959). These early materials, though falling mostly into the Early Archaic, reflect a lifeway found elsewhere in California by Late Paleoindian times: tiny groups of people, living for at least a good part of the year in lakeshore habitats, following a generalized foraging way of life that exploited varieties of large and small animals, waterfowl, and plant foods. They did not have the fluted-point technology of the Clovis pattern; they lacked the ground-stone tools of later times associated with the milling of hard seeds; and they did not fish even though they lived around lakes.

Data in central California are sporadic for sites of the Early Archaic (8050–6050 B.C., or 10,000–8000 years B.P.) and Middle Archaic (6050–4050 B.C., or 8000–6000 years B.P.) periods. Not until the Late Archaic (4050–2050 B.C., or 6000–4000 years B.P.) do most of the local, continuous cultural sequences become identifiable. Nevertheless, several sites have been identified in the region that show people present during the Early and Middle Archaic. In the Lower Sacramento Valley, for example, materials apparently contemporary with Buena Vista Lake were found by A.E. Treganza (1952) at Farmington Reservoir. A site (CA-SCr-177) in Scotts Valley in the Santa Cruz area yielded radiocarbon dates and a collection of chert and obsidian tools dating to this period (Cartier 1982), while in the Bay area south of San Jose, site CA-SCl-178, near Coyote Creek, is equally old (Stickel, personal communication, 1980). Moratto (1984:110) notes some interesting finds at SCl-178, including a mano, an *Olivella* shell bead, and a notched stone that could be a net weight. These may be the earliest such artifacts in all central California, and they suggest something of regional differences in adaptive behavior at an early date.

For the Middle Archaic period (6050–4050 B.C., or 8000–6000 years B.P.), there are no defined cultural patterns for the Sacramento and San Joaquin valleys or the Delta. Only the Bay area yields sites from that period. Near Santa Clara, site CA-SCl-64 was found to have been first occupied during the Middle Archaic, and nearby CA-SCl-106 also belonged to that period. From them, R.R. Cartier (1979) has defined a "Santa Theresa complex." This complex is like Middle Archaic sites elsewhere in the state in that it shows a diversified foraging economy by small groups that moved camp seasonally and exploited a wide range of plants and animals. The presence of some millingstones and manos shows the start of hard-seed exploitation. Absent are any associations with shoreline adaptations, such as shellfish, fish bones, or waterfowl remains. The Santa Theresa complex is not so much a distinctive regional form of Middle Archaic culture as it is a contrast with later cultures of the same area that became much more aquatically oriented.

During the Late Archaic period (4050–2050 B.C., or 6000–4000 years B.P.), continuous culture sequences were established in most parts of central California. The foundations of the Lillard-Heizer-Fenenga Early horizon (1939) emerged in the Delta, the Bay area, and the Lower Sacramento and San Joaquin rivers ca. 3050 B.C. (5000 years B.P.) The type site for this pattern, Windmiller, served primarily as a burial mound at that time. Burial styles and their accompanying artifacts became, and still largely remain, the defining elements of this period: a propensity for extended burials, mostly oriented east-west, most accompanied by grave goods, but with relatively little indication of status distinction among individuals. Hunting was suggested by the presence of large projectile points, usually stemmed and made more of chert or slate than obsidian. Fishing was suggested by baked-clay net weights. A variety of well-crafted ground-stone charmstones were found, along with round *Olivella* and square *Haliotis* shell beads and ornaments. Ground-stone pipes were common, but bone tools, such as needles and awls, were less so. Milling tools, both mano-millingstone and mortar-pestle sets, occurred, but infrequently, suggesting the modest scale of hard-seed and acorn use at that time.

In the San Joaquin Valley, the Positas complex is the Early Archaic equivalent of the Windmiller material. It is present at several sites at the western edge of the valley, such as the Grayson site (Olsen and Payen 1969). As dry-area sites, they understandably do not reflect fishing but show more emphasis on milling and pounding tools. Ornaments, however, reflect trends similar to those at Windmiller. In the Bay area, a continuous-occupation sequence did not emerge during the Late Archaic, but isolated artifacts continued to be found, reflecting some level of occupation. The Stanford II site, the Sunnyvale site, the BART skeleton, and SCl-106 have been dated between 3050 and 2550 B.C. (5000–4500 years B.P.) (Moratto 1984). A sequence does emerge in the Monterey area, however, where the Sur pattern, as defined by G.S. Breschini and T. Haversat (1979, 1980), began by 3050 B.C. (5000 years B.P.) and continued into the Pacific period. At sites such as CA-Mnt-16, CA-Mnt-116, CA-SCr-93, and CA-SCr-7, Monterey-pattern sites showed occupations along shorelines that made modest use of local shellfish and other maritime resources while relying on a wide variety of plant and animal land resources from the nearby hills, valleys, and terraces. In appropriate Archaic fashion, these communities subsisted through diversification, seasonal movement, and backup strategies rather than intensive, focal concentration on any one resource.

By early Pacific times (2050–550 B.C., or 4000–2500 years B.P.), continuous sequences were underway throughout central California. Some archaeologists think that in many cases these sequences reflect the ancestry of the ethnic peoples living there when the Historic era began ca. A.D. 1769. Other analysts believe that a good deal of population movement took place after the start of this era.

The early Pacific-period pattern for the Delta and lower river valleys is the Windmiller culture (Ragir 1972), discussed on the previous page in terms of the Early horizon. It continued to ca. 550 B.C. (2500 years B.P.). In the Bay area, the contemporary cultural pattern has been termed the "Berkeley pattern." It emerged as early as 1850 B.C. (3800 years B.P.) at the West Berkeley site (Elsasser 1978). The stylistic characteristics of the Berkeley pattern are shared to some degree with the Windmiller culture of the Delta, and to some extent with the Cosumnes culture (or Middle horizon) that succeeded the Windmiller after 550 B.C. (2500 years B.P.). In the Berkeley pattern, as in the Cosumnes culture, a greater emphasis is put on the use of acorns as a food staple, and the mortar and pestle become more common. In Berkeley cemeteries, the flexed burial was more common than the extended, Windmiller burial. Fewer grave goods occur than with Windmiller burials, and there is a modest tendency for rich grave lots, which may indicate greater status differentiation. Stylistic differences in projectile points and beads also occur. Some writers see these changes as reflecting the movements of stylistic preferences across established populations, while others see the changes as indicating actual population movements (Moratto 1984:204–209). Whichever may have been the case, the data from the Early Pacific period show marked growth in populations, increasing conflict among communities in the burial traumas, increasing importance of exchange and ornamentation, and a developing focal emphasis on acorns as a food staple.

The early Pacific-period archaeology for the San Joaquin Valley features the Pacheco complex in the Merced County area, as well as a sequence at the southern end of the valley called Buena Vista Lake (after the lake of the same name where the archaeology occurred). The early Buena Vista Lake phase (ca. 2550–1550 B.C., or 4500–3500 years B.P.) starts somewhat earlier than the Windmiller materials in the Delta but shows some stylistic similarities, such as the preference for extended burials, although its burials are accompanied by no grave goods (Warren and McKusick 1959).

Analysis of skeletons from early Pacific burials reveals the recurrence of stresses. Injuries from blows show up in numbers of skeletons. In addition, burial orientation may indicate season of death. P.D. Schulz (1970) found that 80 percent of all Windmiller burials he analyzed have orientations that coincide with the position of the setting sun on the horizon during winter. Dietary studies suggest early Pacific populations emphasized hunting more than the gathering of storable seeds, indicating that winter starvation may have been a common problem. This idea is supported by X-ray studies done by H. McHenry (1968). Longbone X rays show high incidences of childhood growth interruptions, generally stemming from starvation or serious disease. There is evidence of both childhood dietary stress and burial orientation associated with winter decrease in the subsequent middle and late Pacific periods,

when area populations put more emphasis on collecting hard-seed and acorn surpluses and storing them for the winter.

At the same time, the early Pacific period gives evidence for regionwide contacts not found in older eras. Artifacts from Delta sites include obsidian from at least two North Coast Range sources and three Great Basin sources, as well as several varieties of coastal shells, quartz crystals, and alabaster from the Sierras, and imported asphaltum (Ragir 1972). Regional exchange networks were in active operation by the early Pacific period and were already moving exotic and ornamental materials over distances of 200 km (124 miles) or more.

The middle Pacific period (550 B.C.–A.D. 450, or 2500–1500 years B.P.) saw trends rather than revolutionary changes in the archaeology of central California. In the Delta area, it is reflected in the Middle horizon, or Cosumnes culture (Ragir 1972). In the Bay area, it is reflected in the last millennium of the Berkeley pattern as exemplified by the Ellis Landing facies (Fredrickson 1974) In the San Joaquin Valley, the Pacheco complex changes to the Gonzaga complex (Olsen and Payen 1969), and the early Buena Vista Lake phase is replaced by the middle Buena Vista phase (Warren and McKusick 1959). In the Monterey area, the middle Pacific period saw the start of the Monterey pattern at sites such as CA-Mnt-12 (Breschini and Haversat 1979, 1980).

In each area, the styles of projectile points, beads, and other crafted artifacts vary, but more general trends are parallel. Food economies move during the middle Pacific toward greater reliance on resources that can be harvested in surplus and stored for later use during times of scarcity. Acorns are the single most important such food in most areas. Mortars and pestles become increasingly common, while millingstones and manos become rare in most sites. Greater reliance on stored foods appears to have led middle Pacific people to become more sedentary, at least during the winter half of the year. Cemeteries accumulate at winter basecamp villages, and a preference for flexed burials largely replaces the earlier preference for extended burials, especially in the Delta. Interestingly, the use of grave goods to accompany burials becomes less common in middle Pacific times than earlier. The grave donations that do occur tend to suggest shaman's kits by the use of such artifacts as quartz crystals, and there is some tendency toward marking social differences by giving lavish burial accompaniments to a few individuals. These well-endowed burials often are the few cremations in a cemetery.

While these patterns predominate in the middle Pacific of the Delta and the Bay area, in the San Joaquin Valley south of Stockton the styles characteristic of the early Pacific persisted. This variance has suggested ethnic differences to some writers. Excavations in this area at French Camp slough show that middle Pacific villagers were relying mainly on water-related resources: perch, squawfish, freshwater clams, ducks, geese, and tules, in addition to deer, elk, and acorns from the foothills (Johnson 1971). Whether these regional differences stem from cultural differences or differences in adaptive strategies by allied populations in different microhabitats is not clear.

The middle Pacific period developed into the final Pacific period (A.D. 450–1450, or 1500–500 years B.P.) across central California ca. A.D. 500 (1450 years B.P.) and represents a new florescent phase in regional prehistory. Lillard et al. (1939) originally defined the era after A.D. 500 (1450 years B.P.) as the "Late horizon" and cited characteristics mostly related to burial practices: A new preference for cremations, a new concentration on contributed grave goods with much greater differences between grave lots than ever before, new styles of beads and projectile points, adoption of the bow and arrow, the preeminence of the mortar and pestle over the millingstone and mano, and the abundance of clamshell disc beads are only some features.

Ragir (1972) attempted to shift this trait-oriented, burial-focused definition to a more culturally oriented concept when she substituted "Hotchkiss culture" for Late horizon. Fredrickson (1973) had similar goals in his concept of the "Augustine pattern" but also sought to show broader relationships over a larger part of California than Ragir's model indicated. In both cases, archaeologists developed understandings of central California cultures in the late Pacific period as having larger populations, with greater degrees of social differentiation and wealth, with greater degrees of ceremonialism, and more complex political systems. Late Pacific economies were understood to be more reliant on exchange and trade than ever before, and to have begun to develop money systems based on shell beads. Late Pacific-period subsistence was more focused on the collection and storage of seasonal surpluses of acorns, salmon, and other locally available wild resources.

Craftwork in fashioning baskets, mortars and pestles, arrow tips and knives, pipes, tubes, pendants, and other creations reached new levels of artistry. Distinctive artifact forms, such as flanged tubular pipes, carved bone tubes, Gunther barbed and Desert Side-notched projectile points, and barbed bone harpoon tips, characterized styles of the era. Architecture reached new levels of elaboration with the spread of semisubterranean pithouses, dance houses, and sweathouses over much of central California. Degrees of village sedentism increased compared to earlier times, and much seasonal village migration was replaced by specialized task-group expeditions from permanent settlements. Definition of territories became more formal, and conflict among communities seems to have increased.

These trends have been revealed at a great many excavations throughout central California, from the Finch site (Chartkoff and Chartkoff 1984) near Chico to the Gonzaga phase at the Grayson site (Olsen and Payen 1969) near Los Banos and from the Bakersfield area (Warren and McKusick 1959) to Emeryville (cf. Moratto 1984:227–230) in the Bay area as well as Monterey-pattern sites around Monterey Bay (e.g., CA-Mnt-112, CA-Mnt-116, and Mnt-170; Dietz and Jackson 1981). Archaeologists are generally convinced that the Late-period archaeology of the region reflects the ancestors of the ethnographically known peoples found there in historic times. When those ancestors arrived, which other peoples they displaced, and why the changes took place as they did are still being debated (e.g., Moratto 1984:276–283).

The last prehistoric phase, the final Pacific period (A.D. 1450–1769, or 500–181 years B.P.), clearly reflects the archaeology of central California's ethnic groups as found by European and Euro-American contacts. The established sequences recognize that in these last few centuries some distinctive elements appear archaeologically. Some elements result from early contact with outsiders, such as the appearance of Chinese porcelains on the Marin County coast (e.g., Treganza and King 1968). Other elements reflect indigenous changes in technology, economy, and style, such as Fredrickson's (1973) distinction of the (final Pacific) Fernandez facies of the Augustine pattern at A.D. 1450 (500 years B.P.) from the preceding Emeryville facies (3050 B.C.–A.D. 450, or 5000–1500 years B.P.).

C

The differences between periods reflect more evolution than dramatic change: Fernandez-facies beads, for example, include magnesite and steatite cylinders, punched and lipped *Olivella* shell beads, and great numbers of small clamshell disc beads, while there are far fewer clamshell disc beads among Emeryville facies beads, *Olivella* beads that are thin rectangles with center perforations, and few or no steatite or magnesite tube beads. Such obscure-sounding differences are understood to reflect changes of greater importance. The development of the bead-money systems used by native Californians began in the late Pacific period but grew dramatically in the final Pacific period. The increase in sheer numbers of beads reflects a growing shift of bead function from ornamentation to wealth and a growing difference in social and economic standing of families within communities. New forms of wealth, such as magnesite and steatite cylinders, appear to have served the same sort of purpose that a $1000 bill does to replace a thousand $1 bills today.

The final Pacific period, then, saw the last series of innovations arise to perfect the efficiencies of hunter-gatherer economies on the Pacific coast. At the same time, it was the era in which outsiders first appeared from other parts of the planet. From sporadic visits in the 1500s to wholesale migrations in the eighteenth and nineteenth centuries, these newcomers eventually overwhelmed the indigenous cultures and brought their traditional ways of life to a close.

Joseph L. Chartkoff

Further Readings

Beardsley, R.K. 1954. *Temporal and Areal Relationships in Central California Archaeology.* Reports nos. 24–25. University of California Archaeological Survey, University of California, Berkeley.

Breschini, G.S., and T. Haversat. 1979. Archaeological Overview of the Central Coast Counties. Ms. on file, Department of Human Sciences, Cabrillo College, Aptos.

———. 1980. Preliminary Archaeological Report and Archaeological Management Recommendations for CA-Mnt-170, on Pescadero Point, Monterey County, California. Ms. on file, Archaeological Regional Research Center, Cabrillo College, Aptos.

———. 1981. *Archaeological Test Excavations at CA-SCR-93, With a Discussion of Models of Central California Prehis-*

tory. Coyote Press, Salinas.

Cartier, R.R. 1979. Lower Archaic Culture in Santa Clara County. *Society for California Archaeology Newsletter* 13(5–6):5

———. 1982. Current Research. *American Antiquity* 47(1):229.

Chartkoff, J.L., and K.K. Chartkoff. 1984. *The Archaeology of California.* Stanford University Press, Stanford.

Dietz, S.A., and T.L. Jackson. 1981. Report of Archaeological Excavations at Nineteen Archaeological Sites for the Stage I Pacific Grove-Monterey Consolidation Project of the Regional Sewerage System. Ms. on file, Archaeological Consulting and Research Services, Santa Cruz.

Elsasser, A.B. 1978. Development of Regional Prehistoric Cultures. In *California,* edited by R.F. Heizer, pp. 37–58. Handbook of North American Indians, vol. 8, W.C. Sturtevant, general editor. Smithsonian Institution, Washington, D.C.

Fredrickson, D.A. 1973. *Early Cultures of the North Coast Ranges, California.* Unpublished Ph.D. dissertation, Department of Anthropology, University of California, Davis.

———. 1974. Cultural Diversity in Early Central California: A View from the North Coast Ranges. *Journal of California Anthropology* 1(1):41–54.

Gerow, B.A. 1954. The Problem of Culture Sequences in Central California. Paper presented at the annual meetings of the American Association for the Advancement of Science, Berkeley.

———. 1974a. Comments on Fredrickson's "Cultural Diversity." *Journal of California Anthropology* 1(2):239–246.

———. 1974b. *Co-Traditions and Convergent Trends in Prehistoric California.* Occasional Papers no. 8. San Luis Obispo County Archaeological Society, San Luis Obispo.

Gerow, B.A., and R. Force. 1968. *An Analysis of the University Village Complex With a Reappraisal of Central California Archaeology.* Stanford University Press, Stanford.

Heizer, R.F. (editor). 1978. *California.* Handbook of North American Indians, vol. 8, W.C. Sturtevant, general editor. Smithsonian Institution, Washington, D.C.

Johnson, J.J. 1971. Preliminary Report on the French Camp Slough Site, Sjo-91. Ms.

on file, Department of Anthropology, California State University, Sacramento.

Lillard, J.B., R.F. Heizer, and F. Fenenga. 1939. *An Introduction to the Archaeology of Central California.* Bulletins no. 2. Department of Anthropology, Sacramento Junior College, Sacramento.

McHenry, H. 1968. Transverse Lines in Long Bones of Prehistoric California Indians. *American Journal of Physical Anthropology* 29(1):1–18.

McKern, T.W. 1939. The Midwestern Taxonomic Method As an Aid to Archaeological Culture Study. *American Antiquity* 4(40):301–313.

Moratto, M.J. (editor). 1984. *California Archaeology.* Academic Press, Orlando.

Nelson, N.C. 1907. San Francisco Bay Shellmounds. Ms. no. 349 on file, University of California Archaeological Survey, Berkeley.

———. 1909. Shellmounds of the San Francisco Bay Region. *University of California Publications in American Archaeology and Ethnology* 7(4):309–356.

Olsen, W.H., and L.A. Payen. 1969. *Archaeology of the Grayson Site, Merced County, California.* Archaeology Reports no. 12. California Department of Parks and Recreation, Sacramento.

Pritchard, W.E. 1967. *The Archaeology of Lower Los Banos Creek.* Unpublished Master's thesis, Department of Anthropology, California State University, Sacramento.

———. 1970. *Archaeology of the Menjoulet Site, Merced County, California.* Archaeology Reports no. 13. California Department of Parks and Recreation, Sacramento.

Ragir, S.R. 1972. *The Early Horizon in Central California Prehistory.* Contributions no. 15. Archaeology Research Facility, University of California, Berkeley.

Riddell, F.A. 1951. *The Archaeology of Site Ker-74.* Reports no. 10. University of California Archaeological Survey, University of California, Berkeley.

Schulz, P.D. 1970. Solar Burial Orientation and Paleodemography in the Central California Windmiller Tradition. *Center for Archaeological Research at Davis Publications* 2:185–198. University of California, Davis.

Treganza, A.E. 1952. *Archaeological Investigations in the Farmington Reservoir Area, Stanislaus County, California.* Reports no. 14. University of California Archaeological Survey, University of California, Berkeley.

Treganza, A.E., and M.H. Heicksen. 1969. *Salvage Archaeology in the Black Butte Area, Glenn County, California.* Occasional Papers no. 2. Anthropology Museum, San Francisco State College, San Francisco.

Treganza, A.E., and T.F. King. 1968. Archaeological Studies in Point Reyes National Seashore, 1959–1968. Ms. on file, National Park Service, San Francisco and Tucson.

Warren, C.N., and M.B. McKusick. 1959. A Burial Complex From the Southern San Joaquin Valley. *Archaeological Survey Annual Report* 1:17–26. University of California, Los Angeles.

C

Central Plains Tradition

The Late Prehistoric Central Plains tradition (ca. A.D. 1000–1400, or 950–550 years B.P.) consists of five recognized "phases" that occur along the Missouri River and its western tributaries in the Kansas and Platte River basins in Nebraska, Kansas, and western Iowa. Sites in the western High Plains may deserve separate phase-level recognition. The phases are Upper Republican, Smoky Hill, Nebraska, Itskari (formerly Loup River), and St. Helena. The Initial Coalescent variant of central South Dakota is also similar enough to be included within the tradition.

The Upper Republican phase may have emerged earliest (ca. A.D. 1000, or 950 years B.P.), but the Smoky Hill and Nebraska phases appear by or soon after A.D. 1000 (950 years B.P.), and Itskari and St. Helena by A.D. 1100 (850 years B.P.). The phases are nearly contemporaneous, and each is a regional adaptation to available resources of the Central Plains–tradition pattern. Rather than having formed historical sequences, the phases interacted and influenced one another through time. The Central Plains tradition was influenced by and influenced other traditions, especially the Middle Missouri and Mississippian.

Houses are square to rectangular, sometimes slightly rounded, wattle-and-daub structures with an extended entry passage and four central roof-support posts arranged around a central fire basin. Several cylindrical-to-"bell-shaped" subfloor storage/refuse chambers occur. Sites consist of solitary houses, hamlets of two to five houses, and perhaps small "villages" of up to 12 houses, which are scattered along terraces or upon bluffs overlooking streams. Pottery is cord roughened with decorated or plain, unthickened, and "collared" rims. Pottery pipes and "spindle whorls" are present. Chipped-stone tools include triangular side-notched projectile points, unnotched points or preforms, drills, bifacial knives and choppers, end scrapers, side scrapers, modified flakes, and core tools. Other tools include sandstone abraders, cobble hammerstones, stone pipes, ground and polished celts, bison-scapula hoes and knives, awls of split deer/pronghorn metapodials, other bone and antler tools and ornaments, and shell beads and scrapers. Subsistence included hunting of a broad spectrum of vertebrates, fishing, gathering wild plant food, and gardening. Large-scale exploitation of bison is not evident. The dead were buried in ossuaries with few (often no) grave furnishings.

The Central Plains–tradition adaptation evolved in the southern portion of its range and spread from there rapidly, a movement that most likely benefited from the favorable environmental conditions of the Neo-Atlantic climatic episode. The subsequent Pacific episode apparently stressed this adaptation and contributed to the demise and disappearance of the tradition. In the 1100s, some peoples of the Central Plains tradition migrated to South Dakota, warred with peoples of the Middle Missouri tradition, and were killed or expelled. Warfare between later Nebraska-phase and Mill Creek peoples also occurred. The Central Plains tradition ceased to exist by A.D. 1350–1400 (600–550 years B.P.).

John R. Bozell
John Ludwickson

Further Readings

Blakeslee, D.J. (editor). 1978. *The Central Plains Tradition: Internal Dynamics and External Relationships.* Report no. 11. Office of the Iowa State Archaeologist, University of Iowa, Iowa City.

Bozell, J.R. 1991. Fauna From the Hulme Site and Comments on Central Plains Tradition Subsistence Variability. *Plains Anthropologist* 36(136):229–253.

Roper, D.C. 1990. Artifact Assemblage Composition and the Hunting Camp Interpretation of High Plains Upper Republican

Sites. *Southwestern Lore* 56(4):1–19.

Wedel, W.R. 1986. *Central Plains Prehistory: Holocene Environment and Culture Change in the Republican River Basin.* University of Nebraska Press, Lincoln.

Willey, P. 1990. *Prehistoric Warfare on the Great Plains: Skeletal Analysis of the Crow Creek Massacre Victims.* Garland, New York.

Wood, W.R. (editor). 1969. Two House Sites on the Central Plains. Memoir no. 6. *Plains Anthropologist,* 14(44), pt. 2.

Central Riverine Archaic

The expression "Central Riverine Archaic" refers to a cluster of largely contemporaneous Late Archaic (ca. 4050–1050 B.C., or 6000–3000 years B.P.) cultures centered on resource-rich river valleys in the Midwest and the Southeast, in particular the Cumberland, Mississippi, Ohio, and Tennessee valleys and some of their major tributaries. Their highly successful riverine adaptations were the product of thousands of years of cultural and biotic adjustment to stabilizing mid-continent drainage systems in the earlier middle Holocene. Although widely scattered in spatially restricted environmental zones and possessing stylistically different material cultures, Central Riverine Archaic cultures are generally considered components of the same adaptive tradition because they shared a pattern of exploitation of interior river valley floodplains and bordering deciduous forests that made them, as a group, the most elaborate and socially complex Late Archaic societies in the mid-continent. Among their often cited shared characteristics are relatively high population densities, semisedentary lifeways, a diverse and rich array of tools (especially of bone and antler), exotic grave goods, extensive trade or exchange contacts, and restricted mobility within well-demarcated territories, as exemplified by the limited distribution of their diagnostic artifact and site types.

Particularly well-known examples of Central Riverine Archaic cultures occur along and adjacent to the middle portion of the Green River Valley in west-central Kentucky, the Lower Illinois Valley in Illinois, the central Wabash Valley along the divide between Indiana and Illinois, and the middle and western Tennessee River and its tributaries in Tennessee and portions of adjacent states. The Green River culture is best known for its 45 or more large shell-midden sites, a site type that led at one time to the designation "Shell Midden" Archaic for this and many other Central Riverine Archaic cultures. Of these sites, the most famous is Indian Knoll, where excavations by C.B. Moore in 1916 and W.S. Webb in the 1930s uncovered more than 1,000 burials. Accumulated over hundreds of years, the meat in the freshwater shells that form the middens was most likely only a seasonal supplement to a diet resulting from the capture of deer, many small mammals, fish, and waterfowl, and the harvesting of a range of wild-vegetable foods, such as hickory nut. The presence of small-scale horticulture is documented by the remains of squash and other domesticates at Green River–culture sites. Although the society was apparently egalitarian, the distribution among burials of grave goods, which include conch shells, shell beads, cups, gorgets, and small items made of Lake Superior copper, suggests the presence of the initial stages of social differentiation. In the Lower Illinois Valley, 100 to 150 Helton-phase people lived year-round at the Koster site in a 2-ha (5-acre) village from which they also harvested a broad spectrum of vegetable, animal, and aquatic foods. A small cemetery at the edge of the village contained eight burials. H. Winters (1968) has documented still another Central Riverine Archaic lifeway, called the Riverton culture, along a 64 km (40-mile) stretch of the central Wabash River. Included in their settlement round were seasonal stays at large, 0.4–1.2 ha (1–3-acre), shell-midden base camps in the valley from mid-May to late September, temporary fall foraging camps, and cold-weather settlements on promontories overlooking the floodplain. The approximate 16 km (10-mile) distance between major warm-weather base camps suggests the presence of subgroup exploitation territories.

Among the processes suggested to explain some Central Riverine Archaic characteristics are stress induced by population growth and restricted territorial mobility within circumscribed resource-exploitation zones, and increasing conflict with people in neighboring regions with less diverse and abundant food resources.

Guy Gibbon

Further Readings

Chapman, J. 1985. *Tellico Archaeology.* University of Tennessee Press, Knoxville.

Fagan, B.M. 1991. *Ancient North America.* Thames and Hudson, New York.

Marquardt, W.H., and P.J. Watson. 1983. The Shell Mound Archaic in Western Kentucky. In *Archaic Hunters and Gatherers in the American Midwest,* edited by J. Phillips and J. Brown, pp. 323–339. Academic Press, New York.

Smith, B.D. 1986. The Archaeology of the Southeastern United States: From Dalton to de Soto, 10,500 to 5000 BP. *World Archaeology* 5:1–92.

Struever, S., and F. Holton. 1979. *Koster: Americans in Search of the Prehistoric Past.* Anchor Press, New York.

Webb, W.S. 1974. *Indian Knoll. Site Oh 2, Ohio County, Kentucky.* Reprinted (with an introduction by H. Winters), University of Tennessee Press, Knoxville. Originally published 1946. Reports in Anthropology, vol. 4, no. 3, pt. 1. Department of Anthropology, University of Kentucky, Lexington.

Winters, H. 1968. *The Riverton Culture.* Illinois State Museum, Springfield.

See also INDIAN KNOLL; KOSTER; MOORE, CLARENCE B.; TELLICO ARCHAIC; WEBB, WILLIAM SNYDER

Central Subarctic Woodland Culture

As in many parts of North America, the beginning of the Woodland pattern in the central Subarctic is defined by the appearance of ceramics. While a coincidence with an intensification of gathering or incipient plant domestication may be suggested in areas farther south, the more rigorous climate of the central Subarctic did not allow the expansion of these new food resources into northern Ontario and Manitoba. Of possible significance, however, is the documentation of wild-rice gathering in the Boundary Waters area beginning in the first few centuries following the introduction of ceramics. A hunting-and-fishing subsistence pattern, established during the earliest occupations by Paleoindian and later Archaic peoples, continued with little real change until contact with Europeans initiated a departure from this economic orientation.

In Subarctic Ontario and Manitoba, ceramic sherds, which are elsewhere attributed to the Early Woodland period, can literally be counted on the fingers of one hand. Good evidence for the local manufacture of pottery is not found until the second century B.C., when Laurel ceramics (a Middle Woodland–period cultural expression first defined in the 1940s) are found on sites in the Rainey River/Boundary Waters region immediately west of Lake Superior. These ceramics seem to have been grafted onto an existing, local Archaic culture. As a result of the lateness of the arrival of a ceramic technology in the central Subarctic, some researchers are more comfortable describing the first pottery-making cultures of this region as Initial Woodland rather than Middle Woodland.

Variously described as a focus, a tradition, and a culture, Laurel has recently (Reid and Rajnovich 1991) been organized into a series of regional composites on the basis of local stylistic and chronological patterning in Laurel ceramics. In general, these ceramics are characterized by conoidal-shaped pots, which were made by a coiling technique, that have little or no neck constriction. Temper is coarse, and vessel walls relatively thick. Decoration usually covers less than half the outer surface. It was executed with a variety of tools that usually have a toothed or sinuous edge. Their impression resulted in a wide range of stamped or incised decorative motifs variously described as dentate stamped, pseudo-scallop-shell impressed, drag-stamped, and push-pull, among other terms. Punctations with or without bosses also occur, as do plain surfaces and interior brushing. Laurel ceramics spread rapidly over a broad area. They reached their maximum geographical extent sometime around the eighth century A.D., at which time they were being manufactured in east-central Saskatchewan, most of Manitoba, and in a wide band across northern Ontario from the Manitoba border to the western fringes of central Quebec.

But Laurel is not only a ceramic complex. Burial mounds have been associated with Laurel in the Boundary Waters area, and their presence farther south in Minnesota during the same period suggests that Laurel burial ceremonialism resulted from the sharing of ideas with groups from that direction and ultimately the Hopewell tradition. In fact, items clearly imported from the Hopewell heartland have been found in some Laurel burials. Laurel may thus be described as part of a vast mid-continent interaction sphere. Others think there is an economic/ecological basis for a group of cultures termed "Northern Tier" or "Lake Forest" Middle Woodland. Additional elements of Laurel material culture include bone and antler implements, such as fishing harpoons, the use of native copper in the manufacture of a wide range of decorative and utilitarian items, side- and corner-notched as well as stemmed projectile points, a variety of scrapers, and the use of bipolar cores. The systematics of these artifact classes have yet to be fully developed. Laurel houses have been identified that resemble the dome-shaped lodges noted in historic times in the central Subarctic.

The origins of Laurel are a mystery. A working hypothesis proposed by J.V. Wright in 1967 connected Laurel through linked cultures to cultures in Siberia. The explosion of research since then has failed to find any hint of the postulated Asian connection. The distinctiveness of Laurel ceramics is shared with the Saugeen and Point Peninsula cultures of southern Ontario and the Malmo focus of Minnesota. The temporal cline between Laurel and the closely related ceramic complexes of southern Ontario suggests that the main source of this new technology was from that region. Although the influence of Hopewellian mortuary ceremonials is evident in the burial mounds of the Rainy River/Boundary Waters region, the distinctive use of denticulated instruments in the decoration of Hopewell ceramic vessels is virtually unknown.

The Late Woodland of northern Ontario and Manitoba is also often designated by a more pragmatic term, the Terminal Woodland period. Two main expressions of this period have been recognized, Blackduck and Selkirk. The Blackduck focus or culture is primarily located along the southern reaches of the central Subarctic from the north shore of Lake Superior west into southern Manitoba. Blackduck ceramics have been found as far east as western Quebec and as far north as the Hudson Bay Lowlands. The ceramics are characterized by rounded or globular thin-walled pots with constricted openings. Rims and necks are most often decorated with cord-wrapped stick impressions and punctates, and bodies marked with cord-wrapped paddle or fabric impressions. Again, as with earlier Laurel, Blackduck appears to have been influenced by ideas found to the south, both in terms of certain elements of its ceramics and in the use of burial mounds in its western range. Although an intense effort has not been made to determine the nature of Blackduck origins, a small number of late Laurel collections, which date ca. A.D. 600–800 (1350–1150 years B.P.), seem to possess decorative elements evocative of the following Blackduck tradition, but the relationship is far from well documented. Contact-period collections strongly suggest the makers of Blackduck ceramics were the ancestors of the related Algonkian speakers loosely referred to as Ojibwa.

A Laurel group appears to have persisted until the twelfth century A.D. northwest of the area occupied by Blackduck potters. At that time, the boreal forest of east-central Saskatchewan and adjacent Manitoba witnessed the emergence of Selkirk ceramics, which have the more globular shape of the Blackduck vessel body but maintain the earlier near-vertical rim. Punctates are prominent decorative elements and usually appear in combination with textile or net impressions over most surfaces. In northern Manitoba, distinctive platters were manufactured, too. One cannot help wonder if proximity to Neoeskimo groups along the edge of Hudson Bay served as an inspiration for their manufacture. A number of regional expressions (complexes) of Selkirk have been identified that seem to correspond well with historically documented ethnic groups collectively known as Cree.

Lithic assemblages in both major Terminal Woodland cultures appear to shift to smaller and less complex implements. Projectiles have become simple triangular forms, some of which are notched. Other components of the lithic inventory are relatively nondescript with the exception of a prevalence of *pièces esquillées,* or wedges, in many assemblages. Since the actual function of these implements is far from certain, we cannot begin to gauge their significance.

Although the brief picture of the Woodland cultures of the central Subarctic presented above suggests clear and straightforward categories, such is not the reality when the cultures are examined in detail. To the ethnic mix of the contact period can be added the presence of Assiniboin groups in the region who some have suggested were the authors of Blackduck pottery in Manitoba and northwestern Ontario. Along the shores of eastern Lake Superior, Late Prehistoric sites have very few sherds of local ceramics but instead pottery types known from Michigan. Many of the sites of the interior of the central Subarctic contain few if any ceramic sherds, which has resulted in the curious site designation "aceramic Woodland." If nothing else, this term is indicative of the work still required to address some of the fundamental archaeological questions of the central Subarctic.

Jean-Luc Pilon

Further Readings

Dawson, K.C.A. 1983. Prehistory of the Interior Forest of Northern Ontario. In *Boreal Forest Adaptations,* edited by A.T. Steegman, Jr., pp. 55–84. Plenum Press, New York.

Meyer, D., and D. Russell. 1987. The Selkirk Composite of Central Canada: A Reconsideration. *Arctic Anthropology* 24(2): 1–31.

Reid, C.S., and G. Rajnovich. 1991. Laurel: A Re-Evaluation of the Spatial, Social, and Temporal Paradigms. *Canadian Journal of Archaeology* 15:193–234.

Stoltman, J.B. 1973. *The Laurel Culture in Minnesota.* Minnesota Prehistoric Archaeology Series no. 8. Minnesota Historical Society, St. Paul.

Wright, J.V. 1967. *The Laurel Tradition and the Middle Woodland Period.* Bulletin no. 217. National Museum of Canada, Ottawa.

See also BLACKDUCK; LAUREL CULTURE; SELKIRK; SELKIRK COMPOSITE

Ceramics in the Far Northeast

A nearly 3,000-year sequence of ceramic manufacture has been defined for the full span of the Woodland and early contact period (ca. 1100 B.C.–A.D. 1750, or 3050–200 years B.P.) in far northeastern North America. This sequence documents a combination of broad-scale technological and stylistic changes. The close study of this data base is important, for Native American ceramic industries usually record prehistoric social interaction and ethnicity more clearly than do other artifact forms. Although it is still difficult to define precise relationships between ceramics and particular cultural groups, and to identify specific patterns of social interaction, in the Far Northeast, some aspects of these endeavors are being addressed in ongoing research and are summarized here (Petersen and Sanger 1991).

Ceramic technology first appeared in far northeastern North America ca. 1100 B.C. (3050 years B.P.) in the context of Terminal Archaic– or Early Woodland–period native hunter-gatherer groups. Older in the Mid-Atlantic region and older still in the Southeast, native ceramic production almost certainly developed in the Far Northeast (here defined as New England and the Maritime provinces) as the result of exogenous forces. The source was most likely the Mid-Atlantic on the basis of correspondences with evidence that is dated there before 1100 B.C. (3050 years B.P.) (Custer 1989; Stewart 1982).

The earliest easily recognizable ceramic form in the Far Northeast, the "Vinette I" type (Ritchie and MacNeish 1949), was widespread across the region and present as well farther to the west and south (Petersen and Hamilton 1984). No clear source area has yet been defined. Available radiocarbon dates seem to suggest a near uniform and very rapid adoption of this ceramic form in most of the Far Northeast by ca. 1050–850 B.C. (3000–2800 years B.P.). Ceramic production in the northernmost portion of the region, specifically the Canadian Maritimes, may have begun slightly later (Petersen and Sanger 1991).

These early ceramics were tempered with crushed-up rocks, or "grit," and characteristically preserve evidence of coil construction and related fabric-paddled surface finish on both interior and exterior surfaces. Only rare examples of punctate and incised decoration are known thus far. Even earlier ceramic forms may be present, including some with steatite temper, an attribute present in some early Mid-Atlantic forms. However, these latter ceramics are rare and may fall within the temporal range of the early fabric-paddled forms (Petersen and Hamilton 1984; Petersen and Sanger 1991). Thus, one or perhaps more forms are attributable to Ceramic period (CP) 1, the oldest of a seven-part regional sequence. CP 1 is generally dated to ca. 1100–200 B.C. (3050–2150 years B.P.).

On the basis of preserved evidence, these small conoidal vessels apparently served primarily as containers for cooking. They are present in small numbers at habitation sites and are known from a few contemporaneous cemeteries (Heckenberger et al. 1990). Although little evidence of intraregional variation has been recognized among CP 1 ceramics in the Far Northeast, such evidence is apparently present when their full distribution to the west is considered. Still, some subdivisions in the Far Northeast can be demonstrated, using attributes of fabrics and other textiles used in vessel construction. For example, different technological traditions (and presumably cultural groups) were apparently present in the Gulf of Maine area. Fabrics with S-wefts predominate in the noncoastal ceramics of CP 1, while coastal ceramics exhibit fabrics with predominant Z-wefts, in spite of the

fact that both areas shared a standardized form of ceramic.

By the time CP 2 ceramics appear in the early Middle Woodland period (ca. 200 B.C.–A.D. 300, or 2150–1650 years B.P.), ceramic production had increased, and ceramics are relatively common across the region. In addition, they now more clearly reflect intraregional variation through a combination of widespread forms, decoration, and other attributes. Like generally comparable ceramics far to the west in the Great Lakes region, nearly all of these vessels were elaborately decorated on smoothed exterior surfaces using stamping tools, such as dentate and pseudo-scallop-shell forms; fabric-paddled surfaces temporarily disappeared (Petersen and Power 1985). Techniques of tool application, including simple, drag (push-pull), and rocker stamping, varied spatially within the region and extraregionally as well. Across the region (and far to the west), CP 2 vessels represent an early mastery of ceramic production. Most vessels were still small and apparently used for cooking; mortuary finds are unknown at this time in the Far Northeast.

During the middle and later portions of the Middle Woodland period, ceramic production diversified still further in the Far Northeast. However, despite the greater range in vessel shapes and sizes present, the general conoidal form of earlier ceramics persisted. Ceramics of CP 3 (ca. A.D. 300–600, or 1650–1350 years B.P.) and CP 4 (ca. A.D. 600–1000, or 1350–950 years B.P.) have various forms of surface finish, including fabric and other textile impressions, with impressions occurring only on exterior vessel surfaces. Channeling was sometimes used on the interior surface, but these surfaces were predominantly smooth. A new temper type, marine shell, appeared in coastal and near coastal areas near the end of CP 4 times, while grit temper persisted in noncoastal areas.

Ceramic decoration also diversified during CP 3 and CP 4. While dentate (but not pseudo-scallop-shell) stamping continued, new tools for applying decoration are inferred, including cylindrical and other punctate tools and cord-wrapped "stick" tools. Cord-wrapped sticks completely replaced dentate tools over time, although design motifs show continuity. Some techniques of application, such as drag stamping and rocker stamping, disappeared, but simple stamping and impression persisted.

Fabric (and other textile) impressions that resulted from surface finishing *and* the cordage used in decorative tools reflect technological and cultural differences between coastal and non-coastal locales during CP 4, at least within the Gulf of Maine area, as during CP 1. A similar distinction is apparently present to the north in the Maritimes, although the distribution pattern there may be the opposite of that in the Gulf of Maine area, with an S-orientation in coastal settings and a Z-orientation in the interior.

Sometime in the early portion of the Late Woodland period during the subsequent CP 5 (ca. A.D. 1000–1300, or 950–650 years B.P.), horticulture became well established in the region, at least in southern and western New England (Heckenberger et al. 1992). This shift in subsistence was accompanied by further changes in regional ceramics. While shell temper was dominant in all coastal areas before or by the time of the first local horticulture, cord-wrapped-stick and cylindrical-punctate decoration proliferated, and fabric-paddled surface finishing re-emerged, at least in the southern and western areas. New, small vessel forms, likely bowls and cups, were now present, along with large jar forms; ceramic pipes also became more common or appeared for the first time in many regions.

Wherever shell temper was used, whether in coastal or noncoastal settings, cordage, fabrics, and other textiles show the coastal Z-orientation. Marine-shell temper has been identified at far interior settings in the Connecticut, Androscoggin, and Kennebec River drainages; its presence in these drainages was most likely the result of the long-distance transport of ceramics or, less likely, the result of the adoption of shell temper (Heckenberger et al. 1992). This same situation apparently occurred in later times, too.

A resurgence of grit temper occurred in Late Prehistoric CP 6 ceramics (ca. A.D. 1300–1550, or 650–400 years B.P.) near the end of the Late Woodland period in all settings. CP 6 ceramics presage later ceramics in terms of their remarkable thinness. Vessel forms became more globular at this time, too, a trend present in many other regions of eastern North America. While the frequency of cord-wrapped-stick decoration did not change, incised decoration, which was often added to the vessel surface by various noncylindrical punctate tools, became more common over the region, as did undecorated vessels.

These ceramics were similar to, but distinct from, Iroquoian and proto-Iroquoian ceramics to the north and west in Quebec, Ontario, and New York State, although Iroquoian and proto-Iroquoian ceramics are present in small numbers in some assemblages, perhaps because of trade, visitation, or some other mechanism (Petersen 1990). It has been difficult to identify distinctive CP 6 ceramics in the Far North in the Maritimes, and it may be that CP 5 forms persisted late there. Ceramics completely different from actual Iroquoian or Iroquoian homologies developed during CP 6 in more southerly areas, too. They were probably made by local cultural groups, such as the Western Abenaki and the Wampanoag.

Native ceramics in the Far Northeast were transformed by early European contact after ca. A.D. 1550 (400 years B.P.), and disappeared by A.D. 1700–1750 (250–200 years B.P.), at the latest. Fine-quality ceramics of CP 6 persisted into CP 7, the final period, but new forms appeared in some places, at least some of which copied European forms. In the Maritimes and perhaps in coastal settings to the south, native ceramics disappeared early, for ethnohistoric accounts fail to mention them. It seems clear, however, that native ceramics were manufactured as late as ca. A.D. 1700 (250 years B.P.) or later in several areas of New England well after other traditional technologies (e.g., stone working) had been abandoned (Petersen and Sanger 1991).

In sum, the long history of native ceramic manufacture in the Far Northeast chronicles an emergent pattern of aboriginal ethnicity, with long-term distinctions between coastal and noncoastal settings, and between particular areas within this broad region. At the same time, local ceramic production shared certain general developments with other native cultures and culture provinces in the Eastern Woodlands of North America because of broad-scale contacts. These contrasting levels of interaction are reflected in the various combinations of attributes of ceramic manufacture and decoration that occur at the local and regional level in the Far Northeast.

James B. Petersen

Further Readings

Custer, J.F. 1989. *Prehistoric Cultures of the Delmarva Peninsula: An Archaeological Study.* University of Delaware Press, Newark.

Heckenberger, M.J., J.B. Petersen, and N.A. Sidell. 1992. Early Evidence of Maize Agriculture in the Connecticut River Valley of Vermont. *Archaeology of Eastern North America* 20:125–149.

Heckenberger, M.J., J.B. Petersen, L.A. Basa, E.R. Cowie, A.E. Spiess, and R.E. Stuckenrath. 1990. Early Woodland Period Mortuary Ceremonialism in the Far Northeast: A View from the Boucher Cemetery. *Archaeology of Eastern North America* 18:109–144.

Petersen, J.B. 1990. Evidence of the Saint Lawrence Iroquoians in Northern New England: Population Movement, Trade, or Stylistic Borrowing? *Man in the Northeast* 40:31–39.

Petersen, J.B., and N.D. Hamilton. 1984. Early Woodland Ceramic and Perishable Fiber Industries From the Northeast: A Summary and Interpretation. *Annals of Carnegie Museum* 53:413–445.

Petersen, J.B., and M.W. Power. 1985. Three Middle Woodland Ceramic Assemblages From the Winooski Site. In *Ceramic Analysis in the Northeast: Contributions to Methodology and Culture History*, edited by J.B. Petersen, pp. 109–159. Occasional Publications in Northeastern Anthropology, vol. 9, no. 20. Department of Anthropology, Franklin Pierce College, Rindge.

Petersen, J.B., and D. Sanger. 1991. An Aboriginal Ceramic Sequence for Maine and the Maritime Provinces. In *Prehistoric Archaeology in the Maritimes*, edited by M. Deal and S. Blair, pp. 121–178. Council of Maritime Premiers, Fredericton.

Ritchie, W.A., and R.S. MacNeish. 1949. The Pre-Iroquoian Pottery of New York State. *American Antiquity* 15(2):97–124.

Stewart, R.M. 1982. Prehistoric Ceramics of the Great Valley of Maryland. *Archaeology of Eastern North America* 10:69–94.

See also FIBER ARTIFACTS AND ETHNICITY

Chaco Branch

The term "Chaco branch" is used to describe a division of the Anasazi culture area, although the term was originally intended as a label for a spatial division that encompassed most of the San Juan Basin of northwestern New Mexico. Chacoan affiliation is defined largely on the basis of architecture and settlement pattern plus some ceramic markers.

The term "Chaco" comes from the name of a canyon in the central San Juan Basin where the earliest and most impressive manifestations of Chacoan architecture and settlement are found. Beginning in the A.D. 900s (1050–950 years B.P.), a series of large pueblo structures referred to in Chacoan archaeology as "great houses" was constructed in the canyon. Initially similar in design to the numerous small "village" sites in the canyon but larger in scale, these great houses were expanded over the next 200 years through the construction of multiple, often large, and carefully planned and constructed additions. Ultimately, the larger great houses contained hundreds of rooms and dozens of kivas. These structures were associated with large, apparently ceremonial structures called great kivas, with mounds and other earthworks, and with roads and stairways leading from site to site and out of the canyon.

Through time, this pattern of large-scale, planned, well-built great houses associated with great kivas, earthworks, roads, and surrounding communities of small sites, spread outward from the canyon, first to the south and west, then to the north. The outliers, as these isolated great houses are called, often were built in existing communities of small sites. Occasionally, a new community and associated great house were built or a great house without an associated community was established. Most often, the outliers were connected to one another and to the canyon great houses by a network of perfectly straight, well-engineered roads, some of them 9 m (29.5 feet) wide. The road network within the San Juan Basin is dendritic, with the major roads converging on Chaco Canyon. By A.D. 1100 (850 years B.P.), very large outliers on the San Juan and Animas rivers in far northwestern New Mexico may have rivaled the canyon great houses in power and importance.

What has become clear only recently is that by the early 1100s (850–800 years B.P.) this pattern of great houses with associated communities had spread well beyond the San Juan Basin into southwestern Colorado and eastern Arizona. These far-flung great houses also have associated road segments, but it is not clear yet whether these local roads were connected to the road system leading to Chaco Canyon.

The material culture of the Chaco branch shows considerable variability across space. Despite an overlay of Chacoan traits, most outliers and their communities have a very local assemblage of artifacts; most materials that can be sourced drop off in frequency with distance to the source as would be expected in a direct procurement and simple exchange economy. The distribution of material culture does not support the idea of a redistributive or otherwise managed economy centered in Chaco Canyon. In contrast, Chacoan sites show evidence of a widespread procurement and exchange system. Copper bells and tropical birds from Mesoamerica, shells from the Gulf and Pacific coasts, and cotton from the Hohokam region all appear in sites in Chaco Canyon. Ceramic imports into Chaco from the Cibola region to the southwest, from the San Juan region to the north, and especially from the Chuska Valley to the west reached remarkable proportions. For instance, by 1100 (850 years B.P.), at least 50 percent of the ceramics at Pueblo Alto, one of the canyon great houses, were imports. Another major item being moved through the basin and into Chaco Canyon was wood. An estimated 200,000 large beams were required just for the roofs and upper-story floors of the great houses; all had to be carried from upland regions around the basin edges 70 km (43 miles) or more away.

There is considerable disagreement about the organization and degree of integration of the Chacoan cultural system—and, indeed, about whether there was a system in any unified sense. Opinions among Chacoan scholars range from the statement that what we have called "Chaco" is just a description of the basic late Pueblo II–period eastern Anasazi settlement pattern to the argument that there was a unified Chacoan cultural system administered from Chaco Canyon and marked by colonization efforts based in the Chaco-style great houses at the outliers. There are those who view Chaco as socially and politically egalitarian, and those who see evidence of political and social differentiation; those who describe a Chacoan polity dominated by elite individuals or lineages, and those who envision a theocracy.

Chaco has been studied at varying levels of intensity since the late nineteenth century. Sometimes it seems that the list of what we do not know about this archaeological phenomenon is longer than the list of what we do know. For example, we do not know how to estimate population (or the related phenomena of carrying capacity or organizational requirements) for Chaco Canyon or for the outlier communities because we do not really understand the function(s) of the great houses. We do not know much about the function(s) of the Chacoan roads, about how the outliers operated, or about how they related to the sites in the can-

yon. Until the late 1980s, we did not even know that the archaeological manifestations that we call outliers were to be found far beyond the borders of the San Juan Basin, the original boundaries of the Chaco branch (Fowler and Stein 1992).

The prehistoric pueblo people of the Chacoan world built remarkable public and private architecture, practiced sophisticated water control to support their agricultural systems, maintained widespread trade and social relations, and enjoyed a rich material culture and an elaborate ceremonial life. Beginning in the 900s (1050–950 years B.P.), the cultural pattern that began in Chaco Canyon expanded areally and grew in power and magnificence. Then, after a prolonged drought in the mid-1100s, Chaco Canyon and, indeed, the whole center of the San Juan Basin was largely abandoned.

The northern and western portions of the Chaco Anasazi region continued to be occupied, experiencing increasing population and aggregation of that population. The organization of the cultural system seems to have changed, however, with the abandonment of Chaco Canyon. The branch ended as an entity when the architectural and settlement traits that defined it changed or were lost over the next 100 years.

Lynne Sebastian

Further Readings

Crown, P.L., and W.J. Judge (editors). 1991. *Chaco and Hohokam: Prehistoric Regional Systems in the American Southwest.* School of American Research Press, Santa Fe.

Fowler, A.P., and J.R. Stein. 1992. The Anasazi Great House in Space, Time, and Paradigm. In *Anasazi Regional Organization and the Chaco System*, edited by D.E. Dovel, pp. 101–122. Maxwell Museum of Anthropology Papers no. 5. Maxwell Museum of Anthropology, Albuquerque.

Judge, W J., and J.D. Schelberg (editors). 1984. *Recent Research on Chaco Prehistory.* Reports no. 8. Chaco Center, National Park Service Southwest Region, Santa Fe.

Lister, R.H., and F.C. Lister. 1981. *Chaco Canyon: Archaeology and Archaeologists.* University of New Mexico Press, Albuquerque.

Sebastian, L. 1992. *The Chaco Anasazi: Sociopolitical Evolution in the Prehistoric Southwest.* Cambridge University Press, Cambridge.

Champe, John Leland (1895–1978)

Following a successful business career in Lincoln, Nebraska, John L. Champe was entranced by exposure to archaeology through his friend William Duncan Strong. He began spending time in the field with Strong and pioneer archaeologist A.T. Hill and published his first paper (1936) on the Sweetwater site even before obtaining formal anthropology training. When he was 43 years old, he retired from business and returned to school at Columbia University, where Strong was then teaching. Completing his doctoral course work, he returned to Lincoln and was appointed instructor in anthropology and director of the Laboratory of Anthropology at the University of Nebraska. Champe's dissertation on Ash Hollow Cave (1946) established the stratigraphic relations of many Late Prehistoric cultures of the central Plains.

Champe's fieldwork and demanding teaching established many standards observed by Central-Plains archaeologists, and his Laboratory of Anthropology provided a home for the first few years of the Smithsonian Institution's River Basin Surveys. His first excavations were at Big Village, a historic Omaha Indian village in northeastern Nebraska. Among the many sites he dug for the Interagency Archaeological Program was White Cat village, an Apache community in south-central Nebraska that provided an outlet for his deep interest and competence in ethnohistory, particularly in historical cartography (1949). For 13 years following World War II, Champe and the Laboratory of Anthropology hosted the annual Plains Conference. Following his retirement in 1963, he became involved in research as a consultant and expert witness in three Indian land-claims cases (Yankton, Three Affiliated Tribes, and Hoopa).

W. Raymond Wood

Further Readings

Champe, J.L. 1936. The Sweetwater Culture Complex. In *Chapters in Nebraska Archaeology,* edited by E.H. Bell, pt. 3. University of Nebraska Press, Lincoln.

———. 1946. *Ash Hollow Cave: A Study in Stratigraphic Sequence in the Central Great Plains.* University of Nebraska Studies, n.s., no. 1. University of Nebraska Press, Lincoln.

———. 1949. White Cat Village. *American Antiquity* 14:285–292.

John L. Champe. (Reprinted with permission from American Antiquity *45[2]:268)*

Chapman, Carl Haley (1915–1987)

Known for years as "Mr. Missouri Archaeology," Carl H. Chapman became interested in archaeology when as a youth he visited the prehistoric mounds at Cahokia, Illinois. In 1934, at the age of 19, he worked on an archaeological survey in Crawford County, Missouri, directed by Professor Jesse Wrench of the University of Missouri. Wrench encouraged Chapman to study archaeology and lent him his first year's tuition in 1935. In 1939, Chapman received his B.A. degree in sociology. In 1941, he began work at the University of New Mexico on an M.A. degree, which he received in 1946 after serving in World War II. He was a prisoner of war in Germany after parachuting from his stricken plane. Chapman completed his Ph.D. at the University of Michigan in 1959.

Chapman was, with Wrench, a guiding force over the years of the Missouri Archaeological Society and of the Archaeological Survey

Carl H. Chapman and wife Eleanor. (Reprinted with permission from American Antiquity *55[2]:222)*

of Missouri; he was also well known for his encouragement of amateur archaeologists. He conducted excavations and research at many sites in the Table Rock and Pomme de Terre reservoirs, at Graham Cave, the Vernon County Osage Indian sites, and at the Utz, Libourn, Campbell, and Towosahgy sites. He was a professor and director of the American Archaeology Division in the Anthropology Department at the University of Missouri until his retirement in 1985.

Chapman was active on a national level with the Society for American Archaeology and was instrumental in bringing about the passage of the Archaeological and Historical Preservation Act (the Moss-Bennett bill) by the U.S. Congress. He was awarded the Distinguished Service Award by the Society for American Archaeology, the Conservation Award of the Society for Conservation Archaeology, and the Thomas Jefferson Award by the University of Missouri.

Chapman is known for his two-volume *Archaeology of Missouri* (1975, 1980). These volumes and the popular *Indians and Archaeology of Missouri* (1983) were illustrated by his wife, Eleanor, who illustrated many of his writings and other publications by the Missouri Archaeological Society. Both he and Eleanor died in an automobile accident in Florida in 1987.

Earl H. Lubensky

Further Readings

Bray, R.T., and D.R. Henning. 1990. Carl Haley Chapman (1915–1987) and Eleanor Finley Chapman (1917–1987). *American Antiquity* 55:222–228.

Chapman, C.H. 1975. *The Archaeology of Missouri,* vol. 1. University of Missouri Press, Columbia.

———. 1980. *The Archaeology of Missouri,* vol. 2. University of Missouri Press, Columbia.

Chapman, C.H., and E.F. Chapman. 1983. *Indians and Archaeology of Missouri.* University of Missouri Press, Columbia.

Charles/St. Mungo Culture Type

The Charles/St. Mungo culture existed from ca. 3550 to 1350 B.C. (5500–3300 years B.P.) in the Strait of Georgia region of southwestern British Columbia. The term "Charles" was originally used by C.E. Borden in 1975 to define a regional phase that included three local phases: St. Mungo in the Fraser River Delta, Mayne in the Gulf Islands, and Esilao in the Lower Fraser River canyon. These three phases share a sufficient number of archaeological characteristics to be considered collectively the Charles regional culture type. At least 18 components from sites along the Lower Fraser River Valley from the canyon downriver to the delta and the Strait of Georgia are assigned to the Charles culture type. As it is best known from excavations at the St. Mungo and Glenrose Cannery sites in the Fraser River Delta, many Charles-culture attributes are based on St. Mungo–phase materials from these two sites. The Charles culture existed from 2500 to 1500 B.C. (4450–3450 years B.P.) in the Fraser Delta area, although it may have started as early as 3500 B.C. (5450 years B.P.) at the Esilao site in the Lower Fraser River Canyon and 3000 B.C. (4950 years B.P.) at the Helen Point site in the Gulf Islands.

The Charles culture is generally acknowledged to be a development toward the historic Northwest Coast cultural pattern. A number of significant Northwest Coast characteristics first appear in Charles components: shell middens; bone, antler, and ground-stone industries; art and sculpture; substantial dwellings; a riverine and maritime subsistence pattern that emphasized fish (particularly salmon) and shellfish; significant woodworking capability; and evidence of social complexity. The origins of the culture type are in the preceding Old Cordilleran culture, as evidenced by the continuity of many artifact types, albeit in different proportions.

Flaked-stone industries predominate Charles-culture assemblages. Leaf-shaped points, pebble tools, and expedient flake tools continue from earlier times. New artifact types include points with parallel or contracting stems and some with shoulders, drills, formed unifaces (scrapers), and small quartz-crystal flakes produced by bipolar flaking. Although ground-stone artifacts constitute a relatively small proportion of any Charles-culture assemblage, they indicate the use of new manufacturing techniques on an expanded range of lithic materials. In general, slate points and knives in coastal sites are partially flaked and ground, whereas the upriver Esilao site in the Fraser Canyon contains well-made ground- and polished-slate knives. Other ground-stone artifacts present are abrasive stones, disk beads, and decorated objects. The most distinctive decorated items are thin fragments of soft stone (slate, schist, steatite, siltstone) with notched edges and simple incised geometric patterns along the margins, and small, segmented spindlelike artifacts that resemble grubs or insect larvae that are possibly gaming pieces. Small pin-shaped labrets, adzes, and totally ground-slate knives have been reported at coastal locations but are rare and may occur only at the end of the culture.

A wide range of bone, antler, and shell artifacts are preserved in many Charles-culture shell-midden sites. The most characteristic artifact type in the Charles-culture bone-and-antler industry is the decorated bone pendant. Spindlelike objects, identical to those carved from stone, were also fashioned from bone. A wide variety of awls, unilaterally and bilaterally barbed fixed points, bilaterally barbed harpoons, and wedges are present. The fixed points and harpoons provide the first direct evidence of fishing and sea-mammal-hunting technology in the region. Disk beads and adze and knife blades were made from mussel shell. The shell adzes and antler wedges provide a basic woodworking toolkit, but it does not approach the level of proficiency found in later archaeological cultures. A small, finely carved antler anthropomorphic figure from the Glenrose Cannery site shows little stylistic similarity to historic Northwest Coast artistic tradition but indicates that the roots of these traditions extend back at least 4,000 years.

Architectural remains at the Hatzic and Maurer sites in the Lower Fraser River Valley, midway between the delta and the canyon, suggest that a shift in settlement patterns toward semisedentism was under way in the area by the beginning of the Charles culture. The Maurer site has two semisubterranean dwellings dated at 2830 B.C. (4780 years B.P.) and 2290–2270 B.C. (4240–4220 years B.P.), respectively. The more recent structure has been completely excavated. It has a 7.5 x 5.5 m (24.6 x 8 foot) central pit area that is 1.5–2.0 m (4.9–6.6 foot) deep and contains a large hearth offset from the center. A 1-m (3.3-foot) -wide bench surrounds the depression and an entranceway cut through the bench at one end. The arrangement of postmolds suggests an earth-covered superstructure with gabled walls and a flat roof. The Hatzic site has evidence of multiple structures. Two houses have been dated to 2580 B.C. (4530 years B.P.) and 2980–2470 B.C. (4930–4420 years B.P.), respectively The second, possibly older structure has ca. 75 percent of its floor area excavated. An 8 x 11 m (26.2 x 36.1-foot) dwelling, it was set into the side of the riverbank. It has a bench along the north margin of the depression and a substantial hearth in the center. More than 75 postmolds suggest a dwelling with vertical walls, possibly covered with planks, that was rebuilt during the lifespan of the structure. It is difficult to determine from the limited evidence whether the Maurer and Hatzic structures are typical of Charles-culture habitations throughout the region. Less substantial structures, represented by small postmolds, hearths, and thin cultural layers thought to be occupation floors, may be present at coastal sites such as St. Mungo.

Faunal assemblages from the Glenrose, St. Mungo, and Crescent Beach sites provide detailed information on Charles-culture subsistence. The subsistence pattern at these delta locations stressed coastal and riverine resources, particularly fish and shellfish, but evidence of intensive harvesting and storage of key resources is absent. Salmon were the most important fish species utilized, and shellfish either equaled or exceeded both land and sea mammals in economic importance.

The appearance of art objects (some of which may have been status symbols), substantial architecture, and ground-stone and bone-antler industries all indicate that considerable material-culture change was under way during the Charles-culture period. One would expect that some degree of social change was associated with these developments, but direct archaeological evidence for social ranking is limited. Relatively few burials are reported, but they include extended and cairn burials. Some human skeletal remains exhibit labret wear and artificial cranial deformation. These mortuary data suggest some degree of emerging social complexity during the Charles culture, but its specific nature is not yet determined.

David L. Pokotylo

Further Readings

Borden, C.E. 1975. *Origins and Development of Early Northwest Coast Culture, to About 3000 B.C.* Mercury Series Paper no. 45. Archaeological Survey of Canada, National Museum of Man, Ottawa.

Matson, R.G. (editor). 1976. *The Glenrose Cannery Site.* Mercury Series Paper no. 52. Archaeological Survey of Canada, National Museum of Man, Ottawa.

Charmstones

Charmstones are ground-stone artifacts dating to after 2050 B.C. (4000 years B.P.) that are found in several parts of central California. They are elongated, usually have round cross sections, and have finely finished surfaces. Length commonly is 60–120 mm (2.3–4.7 inches) and diameter 25–40 mm (1–1.6 inches). Forms vary. Examples are cylindrical, bionically tapered, teardrop (fishtail), and phallic shapes. They are usually made from fine-grained stones that are readily polished, such as schist, alabaster, marble, and amphibolite. Some specimens have a hole drilled near one end (perforate), while others do not (imperforate). Charmstones have been found archaeologically in association with human burials and, therefore, are thought to be ritually important artifacts; some writers associate them with shaman's kits or shamanistic practices. They have been found most frequently around San Francisco Bay and in the Delta of the San Joaquin and Sacramento rivers, but more widely in the Central Valley, the Monterey region, the southern half of the North Coast region, and the Sierra Nevada foothills. Excavators have found perforated charmstones in early Pacific-period burials, while imperforate charmstones occurred in middle Pacific-period graves. It was initially thought that charmstones did not occur in late and final Pacific-period burials, but more recent excavations have found imperforate charmstones in sites that date as recently as the nineteenth century.

Joseph L. Chartkoff

Further Readings

Chartkoff, J.L., and K.K. Chartkoff. 1984. *The Archaeology of California.* Stanford University Press, Stanford.

Fredrickson, D.A. 1974. Cultural Diversity in Early Central California: A View From the North Coast Ranges. *Journal of California Anthropology* 1(1):41–54.

———. 1984. The North Coastal Region. In *California Archaeology,* edited by M.J. Moratto, pp. 471–528. Academic Press, Orlando.

Moratto, M.J. (editor). 1984. *California Archaeology.* Academic Press, Orlando.

Chauga

The Chauga site (38OC47) is located in the floodplain of the Tugalo River near the mouth of the Chauga River in Oconee County, South Carolina. Chauga was excavated by A.R. Kelly and R.S. Neitzel in 1958 prior to its inundation by Lake Hartwell. The site consisted of a single rectangular platform mound and a habitation area of undetermined size. Site utilization occurred at various times during the Middle Archaic, Middle Woodland, and Mississippian periods. The major components, those responsible for mound construction and presumably most of the features exposed in the limited village excavation, belong to the Jarrett and Tugalo phases. Jarrett is a local manifestation of the widespread Etowah culture and dates to ca. A.D. 1100–1200 (850–750 years B.P.). Tugalo is a local manifestation of the widespread Lamar culture and dates to ca. 1500–1600 (450–350 years B.P.). A final, Estatoe-phase occupation, dating to the early eighteenth century, is identifiable as historic Cherokee.

The Chauga mound measured ca. 4 m (13 feet) in height and 35 m (115 feet) across at the base. In typical Mississippian fashion, the mound was constructed in a number of stages, each consisting of a mantle of earth placed over the preceding mound. The summit of each construction stage probably supported one or more buildings, but a large looter's pit in the center of the mound destroyed almost all evidence of such structures. The first six mound stages were constructed during the Jarrett occupation, while the last four date to the Tugalo occupation. The presence of Estatoe-phase pottery in outwash deposits at the base of the mound suggests that it may have been used by the historic Cherokee occupants of the site as well.

With its platform mound, the Chauga site can be identified as the administrative and ceremonial center for Jarrett- and Tugalo-phase chiefdoms located on the headwaters of the Savannah River. The eighteenth-century occupation has been identified with the historic Cherokee town of Chauga, but, in the absence of contemporary maps depicting that town's exact geographic location, this identification must be considered as tentative.

David J. Hally

Further Readings

Anderson, D.G., D.J. Hally, and J.L. Rudolph. 1986. The Mississippian Occupation of the Savannah River Valley. *Southeastern Archaeology* 5:323–351.

Hally, D.J. 1986. The Cherokee Archaeology of Georgia. In *The Conference on Cherokee Prehistory,* assembled by D.G. Moore, pp. 95–121. Warren Wilson College, Swannanoa.

Kelley, A.R., and R.S. Neitzel. 1961. *Chauga Mound and Village Site (38OC1) in Oconee County, South Carolina.* Laboratory of Archaeology Series Report no. 3. University of Georgia, Athens.

Chenopodium

Plants in the genus *Chenopodium* were used by indigenous North Americans for medicines, foods, and flavorings. Seeds of *C. ambrosiodes* (known as "wormseed") are effective for killing some intestinal parasites, and at least four other native species were observed to have medicinal uses. Chenopod leaves were, and still are, gathered as edible greens. They are delicious both raw and cooked, either alone or combined with other foods in stews. Individual chenopod plants can produce tens—or even hundreds—of thousands of seeds, and these can be harvested, parched, and ground to form a meal or flour, then cooked alone or in combination with other seeds to make porridge or bread.

One species, *C. berlandieri,* was domesticated in eastern North America and used as a native seed crop for at least 3,000 years. Modern researchers did not realize until recently that many of the millions of chenopod seeds found in archaeological sites did not come from wild

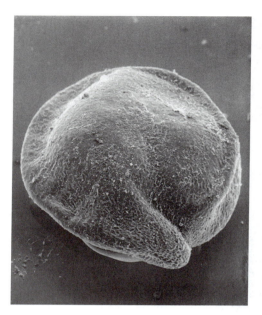

Cultigen Chenopodium berlandieri *(ssp* jonesianum) *from the Cow Ford site, Benton County, Arkansas. Note the truncate margin on the right and the smooth seed coat visible on the top of the seed where the net-like pericarp is eroded. (Photograph by G. Fritz)*

populations, but instead represent a domesticated food source. Unlike seeds of other native crops, including sunflower (*Helianthus annuus* var. *macrocarpus*) and sumpweed (*Iva annua* var. *macrocarpa*), chenopod seeds in this region did not increase appreciably in size with domestication. Instead, selection was for thinner seed coats, simultaneous ripening, more densely packed seed heads, and plants with indehiscent seeds that did not shatter and fall away before or during harvesting.

The history of domestication of eastern North American *Chenopodium berlandieri* spp. *jonesianum,* as the prehistoric cultigen is classified, can be summarized as follows. Between 3000 and 2000 B.C. (4950–3950 years B.P.), harvesting of chenopod increased, but the seeds appear wild in form with thick, rounded, pitted seed coats. By 1500 B.C. (3450 years B.P.), chenopod seeds from rock-shelter sites in Kentucky had the dramatically thinner and smoother seed coats with truncate margins that mark them as domesticated. The thin-testa cultigen form appears in numerous archaeological sites across the Midwest between 1200 and 300 B.C. (3150–2250 years B.P.). Chenopod flourished as an important seed crop between 300 B.C. and A.D.

1300 (2250–650 years B.P.), becoming even more important in places such as Cahokia in Illinois and the surrounding American Bottom area after corn was introduced and intensified.

Chenopod seeds are rich in the amino acids lysine and tryptophan, which corn has little of, making them a good source of both protein and carbohydrates. By A.D. 500 (1450 years B.P.), at least one variety of chenopod had been developed with seed coats so thin as to make them pale yellow or creamy in color rather than black, similar to the related and independently domesticated pale-colored South American grain known as quinoa (*Chenopodium quinoa*). In spite of its many virtues, the North American cultigen chenopod declined to the point of extinction after 1300 (650 years B.P.). Casual sowing and harvesting by the Natchez in Mississippi of an enigmatic plant called *choupichoul*, noted by the French in the early 1700s, might be the latest record of native North American chenopod cultivation.

The archaeological record for chenopod domestication attests to the skills of ancient North American farmers. Both botanists and anthropologists suspect that some of the germ plasm of the native crop persists in weedy *C. berlandieri* growing today in the Midwest, and some speculate that this resource might one day be tapped for breeding an improved, high-protein grain.

Gayle Fritz

Further Readings

Fritz, G.J., and B.D. Smith. 1988. Old Collections and New Technology: Documenting the Domestication of *Chenopodium* in Eastern North America. *Midcontinental Journal of Archaeology* 13:3–27.

Reinhard, K.J., J.R. Ambler, and M. McGuffie. 1985. Diet and Parasitism at Dust Devil Cave. *American Antiquity* 50:819–824.

Smith, B.D. 1992. *Rivers of Change: Essays on Early Agriculture in Eastern North America.* Smithsonian Institution Press, Washington, D.C.

C

Cherokee Sewer Site

The Cherokee Sewer site (13CK405) is a deeply stratified, multicomponent site incorporated into an alluvial fan in the Little Sioux River

Cherokee Sewer Site: Bison processing camps stratified in an alluvial fan on the Little Sioux River, northwestern Iowa, 1976. Level 1 (above) occurred 9 feet below the ground surface (Middle Archaic, 6500 years B.P.); Level 2 (Middle Archaic, 7400 years B.P.); Level 3 (Late Paleoindian, 8500 years B.P.). Dark bands in the profile represent buried soil horizons. (Photograph by D. Anderson)

Valley near Cherokee, Iowa. It was excavated by Duane C. Anderson, Holmes A. Semken, and Richard Shutler, Jr., in 1973 and 1976. The earliest components, representing two separate Late Paleoindian bison-processing camps dating to ca. 6500 B.C. (8450 years B.P.), contained projectile points reminiscent of the Agate Basin and Hell Gap types. Two Middle Archaic occupations, dating to 5300 and 4450 B.C. (7250–6400 years B.P.), respectively, were also present. Each contained choppers, scrapers, bifaces, and flake tools. At each camp, bison were disarticulated and stripped of meat, then fractured to obtain marrow and render for grease. All levels at the site bearing cultural materials also yielded micromammals, gastropods, plant macrofossils, and charred wood. The upper level contained the butchered remains of a domestic dog, and a fragmentary bird-bone flute. The second level produced one of the earliest millingstones in the Midwest. Extensive use of heat-treated cherts was in evidence on all levels.

Duane Anderson

Further Readings

Anderson, D.C., and H.A. Semken (editors). 1980. *The Cherokee Excavations: Holocene Ecology and Human Adaptation in Northwestern Iowa*. Academic Press, New York.

Chert/Flint

"Chert" and "flint" are words used to describe a wide variety of cryptocrystalline sedimentary rocks that also include jasper, chalcedony, novaculite, agate, and hornstone. They are composed primarily of quartz and are members of the silicate rock group with basic elemental composition of SiO_2. Chert and flint, which form through processes of chemical precipitation, are considered the more general and common of these rock types. They have frequently been distinguished from each other in the geological and archaeological literature on the basis of texture, color, or place of origin; however, since their composition is identical, most of these attempts appear arbitrary or contain massive overlaps. As a result, there are no universally accepted criteria for their differentiation.

Because of its special characteristics, chert/flint has been preferred by human beings throughout history as a source of stone for tool manufacture. These characteristics include its fine-grained internal structure, brittleness, and

isotropic qualities, which assure that its physical properties are the same in all directions. This quality is essential for making stone tools, or flintknapping, because the direction and force of the blow, rather than internal properties of the stone itself, such as planes or platy structure, determine the characteristics of fracture. Thus, breakage can be controlled by the flintknapper and can be comprehended through principles of fractural mechanics.

George H. Odell

Further Readings

Luedtke, B.E. 1992. *An Archaeologist's Guide to Chert and Flint*. Archaeological Research Tools no. 7. Institute of Archaeology, University of California, Los Angeles.
Shepherd, W. 1972. *Flint: Its Origin, Properties and Uses*. Faber and Faber, London.

Chilcotin Plateau

The Chilcotin Plateau of south-central interior British Columbia covers the area west of the Fraser River that is drained by the Chilcotin River; it extends to the eastern slopes of the Coast ranges. Although the region lies at the interface between the Plateau and the Subarctic culture areas, the Chilcotin River has abundant salmon resources. The plateau also marks the northern limit of the lodgepole pine/aspen plant community, which is replaced by spruce forests immediately to the north. At historic contact, Athapaskan-speaking Chilcotin Indians occupied all but the eastern edge of the region. They replaced the Salish-speaking Shuswap Indians even in that area after smallpox epidemics in the 1850s.

Ethnographic and limited archaeological evidence indicates that the Chilcotin Indians are relatively recent inhabitants over most of the region, but the timing and nature of their migration remains an outstanding issue. Three additional major issues in Chilcotin Plateau–culture history are the nature of pre-pithouse occupations, the origins of very large "Lillooet phase" pithouse villages, and the character and extent of the more typically Plateau "Kamloops phase." The latter two issues are extensions of cultural developments along the mid-Fraser and the Thompson rivers, for these two phases show close similarities to that region. However, it is not certain that either the pre-pithouse or the later Athapaskan development parallels events occurring elsewhere in the Plateau culture area.

Pre-pithouse cultural remains are found at a number of sites, but they are not well dated. At the junction of the Fraser and Chilcotin rivers, undated "Chert Debitage" sites with atlatl projectile points are found in areas of high overlook. The Poplar Grove site on the Chilanko River, a tributary of the Chilcotin, has a nonmicroblade assemblage of probable pre-pithouse age that includes atlatl projectile points, but it shows no clear affinities with any well-dated cultures elsewhere.

Microblade assemblages are found at a number of locations, including Alexis Creek, Eagle Lake, Horn Lake Southwest, and the extreme northwest portion of the Chilcotin region at Anahim Lake. If these assemblages date to greater than 2050 B.C. (4000 years B.P.), as to the north along the Skeena River, the north coast of British Columbia, and in most other interior locations, they would be pre-pithouse in age. An argument has been made, however, that microblade use extended much later in time at Anahim Lake.

Although the earliest pithouse sites elsewhere in the Plateau area precede the large Lillooet-phase sites, this pattern has yet to be

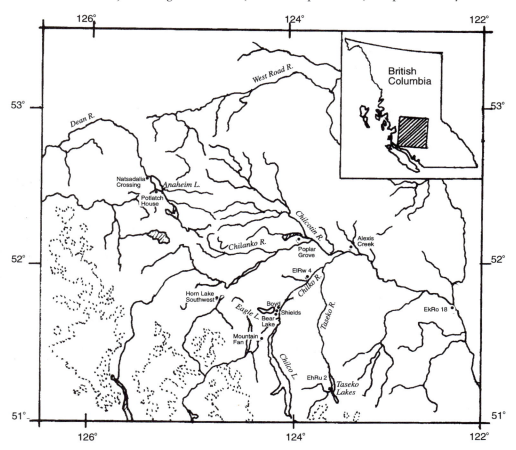

CHILCOTIN PLATEAU

SCALE 1:2,000,000

Locations of archaeological sites in the Chilcotin Plateau. (Map by R. G. Matson and D. L. Pokotylo)

identified in the Chilcotin. Instead, the oldest dated pithouse sites in the region are aggregations of very large (up to 15 m, or 49 feet) and very deep housepits adjacent to the Chilcotin River and two of its tributaries. At the mouth of the Chilcotin River, site EkRo 18, which exhibits Lillooet-phase characteristics, dates to this 150 B.C.–A.D. 950 (2100–1000 years B.P.) period, and sites EkSa 5 and ElRw 4 on the Chilko River fit this pattern. Site EhRv 2 at the head of the Taseko River also has Lillooet-phase attributes and three radiocarbon dates all within the expected time period. Given the tight fit between these cultural phenomena and salmon abundance, including the possibility that the Lillooet culture collapsed ca. A.D. 950 (1000 years B.P.) after a large slide on the middle Fraser River, it is significant that few salmon resources are available near EhRv 2 today.

The Kamloops phase, the archaeological representative of ethnographic Plateau culture, is found along the Chilcotin River and its salmon-bearing tributaries. Not only are there a number of such sites (including two dated ones) at the mouth of the Chilcotin, they also extend up to Chilko Lake at the head of the Chilko River. Excavations at the Boyd and Shields sites, two tightly clustered housepit sites near Eagle Lake and the Chilko River, have produced dates of A.D. 1200 and 1450 (750–500 years B.P.) and typical Kamloops-phase assemblages. The similarity of these Kamloops-phase features and assemblages, and the settlement patterns found at the mouth of the Chilcotin and at Eagle Lake, allow the fairly secure inference that this culture was ethnically Salish. It is not presently found west of the Chilko River, the western limit of abundant salmon resources, but it was well within Chilcotin territory at contact.

The arrival of the Athapaskan-speaking Chilcotin is evident at Eagle Lake and Anahim Lake. At Eagle Lake, the Kamloops-phase occupation is truncated by a culture using rectangular lodges and stemmed Kavik or Klo-Kut projectile points. This culture is found at the Bear Lake site with a "Lulua phase" historic component dendrochronologically dated to 1877 and a prehistoric "Eagle Lake phase" component occurring prior to that but no earlier than A.D. 1450 (500 years B.P.). An occupation similar to the Lulua phase is found at the Potlatch House site at Anahim Lake. Slightly earlier prehistoric assemblages found in relatively isolated pithouses near Anahim Lake (Component Cluster IV) and at Natsadalia Crossing are also probable Chilcotin occupations. Earlier assemblages from isolated housepits at Anahim Lake (Component Clusters I–III) have an uncertain association in this area, which lacks salmon resources and a clear Kamloops-phase occupation.

Investigations at Potato Mountain adjacent to Eagle Lake show an intensive occupation of the subalpine parkland zone. In accord with Chilcotin ethnographic accounts, this occupation was undoubtedly associated with the summer exploitation of spring beauty or mountain potato (*Claytonia lanceolata*) roots. Small roasting pits are abundant and date to A.D. 50 (1900 years B.P.), indicating this use also occurred in pre-Athapaskan occupations. A component dated to 350 B.C. (2300 years B.P.) at the Mountain Fan site shows even earlier use of this zone, although it is not associated with roasting pits.

The Chilcotin Plateau is a large region with significant internal cultural and environmental variability. The actual amount of archaeological work carried out is minimal, making the framework given above tentative and subject to substantial change.

R.G. Matson
David L. Pokotylo

Further Readings

Ham, L. 1975. *Shuswap Settlement Patterns.* Unpublished Master's thesis, Department of Archaeology, Simon Fraser University, Burnaby.

Magne, M. 1985. *Lithics and Livelihood: Stone Tool Technologies of Central and Southern Interior British Columbia.* Mercury Series Paper no. 133. Archaeological Survey of Canada, National Museum of Man, Ottawa.

Magne, M., and R.G. Matson. 1982. Identification of "Salish" and "Athapaskan" Side-Notched Points From the Interior Plateau of British Columbia. In *Approaches to Algonquian Archaeology,* edited by M.G. Hanna and B. Kooyman, pp. 57–80. Archaeological Association, University of Calgary, Calgary.

———. 1987. Projectile Point and Lithic Assemblage Ethnicity in Interior British Columbia. In *Ethnicity and Culture,* edited by R. Auger, M.F. Glass, S. MacEachern, and P.H. McCartney, pp. 227–242. Archaeological Association,

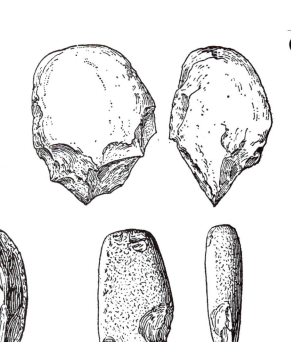

Choppers. (Reprinted from Smithsonian Institution, Bureau of American Ethnology, Bulletin 60, Figure 198)

University of Calgary, Calgary.

Mitchell, D.H. 1970. Archaeological Investigations on the Chilcotin Plateau, 1968. *Syesis* 3:45–65.

Wilmeth, R. 1978. *Anahim Lake Archaeology and the Early Historic Chilcotin Indians.* Mercury Series Paper no. 77. Archaeological Survey of Canada, National Museum of Man, Ottawa.

Chopper

A chopper is a stone tool whose periphery was modified to a limited extent to form a relatively sharp edge. The unmodified portions often consist of cortexual surfaces. The chopper was largely unshaped and, therefore, crude in appearance. Still, it was undoubtedly a very utilitarian implement. Although technological criteria are used in their definition, most choppers possess robust wear patterns, including fracturing and striating, that confirm their predominant use in a chopping mode. In North America, no chopper/chopping tool distinctions have been made on the basis of unifacial or bifacial retouch, as has been the practice for the Far Eastern Paleolithic.

George H. Odell

Further Readings

Winters, H.D. 1969. *The Riverton Culture.* Reports of Investigations no. 13. Illinois State Museum, and Illinois Archaeological Survey, Springfield.

Choris Culture

Choris culture is named after a site on the Choris Peninsula in Alaska, which itself was named for Adelbert von Choris, a naturalist on the von Kotzebue voyage of 1815–1818. The first indications of the existence of the Choris culture were end blades and points discovered by Helge Larsen in 1948 at Trail Creek Caves. J.L. Giddings formally defined the culture following the recovery in 1956 of similar lithic artifacts and a sizable organic toolkit on Choris Peninsula. Extravagant claims are made for the Choris culture, ranging from Aleut affinities to reindeer domestication. Despite the presence of whalebone on Choris ridges at Cape Krusenstern, few archaeologists claim Choris peoples hunted bowhead or beluga whales. Instead, faunal data suggest a subsistence specialization centered on the hunting of ringed seal from breathing holes, as in the ethnographic present.

Labrets and oil lamps are found only at the

Choris Peninsula locality, where preservation is exceptional. Other evidence found there includes postmolds; double-barbed, single-line-hole harpoon heads; bone needles and awls; and the faunal remains of beluga, caribou, and seal. More widespread lithics and linear-stamp ceramics are distinguishing characteristics of Choris, especially the diagonally flaked biface. Diagonally flaked bifaces are often of substantial length (5–7 cm, or 2–2.7 inches) and often have a shouldered midsection for hafting. Lanceolate spear points with concave bases are common in some sites. Burinization of bifaces was presumably linked with bone insets and perhaps with the production of microblades. Microblades (or bladelike flakes) occur most prominently within Band 3, level 2, and "Old Hearth" at Onion Portage; microblades are not widely accepted as part of the Choris assemblage. The range and size of biface forms, especially in hafting characteristics, are diverse. The presence of some of these forms in the Kayuk complex at Anaktuvuk Pass could mean that the complex is related to the Choris culture. House remains are comparatively rare. Only two are documented: a 15-m (49-foot) -long oval activity area at Choris and a square 8 x 5 m (26 x 16.4-foot) "winter house" at Onion Portage.

The distribution of Choris sites has an abrupt boundary through the Seward Peninsula, where it extends north, possibly, to the problematic Walakpa site near Barrow. Scattered Choris sites or artifacts (labrets, pottery, harpoon heads) also occur across the Brooks Range to the Atigun River and to the coast of northern Yukon Territory. The greatest concentration of Choris materials, over 180 site localities, is from two areas: Cape Krusenstern and Cape Espenberg. Most of these sites are diffuse surface scatters of lithic tools on top of prominent lookout stations; presumably these were used to sight game. Choris bifaces are reported at Lake Minchumina and Chugwater in the Tanana Valley; otherwise the sites are limited to tundra regions. The notable decline in Choris traits inland implies that the most characteristic Choris sites are along the coast. The sudden appearance of well-fired, decorated pottery dates to 1050 B.C. (3000 years B.P.). Its presence implies increased sedentism and possibly trade in perishable commodities.

Choris seems to be a horizon; that is, a comparatively brief period of time during which a distinctive people or ideas spread throughout a region; Choris peoples apparently had unequal impacts on their various neighbors. Age control over Choris sites is, however, limited. The four best-dated sites (Choris, Espenberg, Onion Portage, Trail Creek) are radiocarbon dated to 950–250 B.C. (2900–2200 years B.P.). There are substantial occupational hiatuses over and below Choris layers at the stratified Onion Portage site, which is often considered a type site of the culture. A single date of 1450–1250 B.C. (3400–3200 years B.P.) at this site has been used to argue for an older age for Choris. Sites in the Brooks Range are often palimpsests of many occupations and have proven unreliable for chronometric estimates.

The cultural affinities of Choris trouble archaeological taxonomists in northern Alaska. Some see clear links between the Arctic Small Tool tradition (ASTt) and Choris, and even with the presumably older bifacial-tool complexes, Northern Archaic and Old Whaling. Some researchers believe that there is a clear break between ASTt and Choris. A few even derive Choris from an interior substratum. Nonetheless, few would argue that there are definite links between Choris and the younger Norton tradition. Some archaeologists even refer colloquially to a hybrid culture termed "Chorton." Much of the confusion stems from the use of Onion Portage and Cape Krusenstern as informal type localities for the Choris culture. Most claims for continuity between the earlier Denbigh complex, which is part of the Arctic Small Tool tradition, and Choris rest on the common occurrence of isolated traits, such as burinization or microblades. This type of inference is subject to personal taste and is offered instead of stratigraphic succession or near contemporaneity in radiocarbon ages. Lengthy occupational hiatuses within Krusenstern beach ridges and at Onion Portage have confused the issue too.

Craig Gerlach

Further Readings
Giddings, J.L. 1967. *Ancient Men of the Arctic.* Knopf, New York.
Giddings, J.L., and D.D. Anderson. 1986. *Beach Ridge Archeology of Cape Krusenstern.* GPO, Washington, D.C.

See also CAPE KRUSENSTERN

Chota-Tanasee
Chota-Tanasee (40MR2 and 40MR62) refers to the two separate eighteenth-century A.D. Chero-

kee villages that were located adjacent to each other on the Lower Little Tennessee River in Monroe County, Tennessee. Chota or Itsa'sa is also spelled Echota and Chote, while Tanasee, from which the state of Tennessee derives its name, also appears as Tanasi. The original meanings of both names, according to James Mooney (1900), have been lost. Chota and Tanasee were part of the Cherokee Overhill settlements found in east Tennessee. The village names are hyphenated because the towns cannot be distinguished from each other by archaeological studies of artifacts or by their distributions. Historic records suggest that initially the Cherokee recognized only a single town, Tanasee, at this location. English traders began visiting Tanasee in the late seventeenth century, and formal diplomatic missions and sustained contact were firmly established by the early eighteenth century. Between 1740 and 1750, the town of Chota formally emerged and superseded its neighbor in economic, political, and military power. At this time, the town probably had a population of 300–500 individuals living in ca. 60 houses. Chota quickly assumed regional importance. It was regarded as the principal town of the Overhills and eventually as the

capital of the Cherokee people. After the American Revolutionary War, the town dwindled in size and importance. It was abandoned by the early nineteenth century.

Archaeological investigations were made at Chota-Tanasee by a University of Tennessee Work Projects Administration (WPA) crew in 1939. Further investigations were carried out at the site from 1969 through 1974 by the university's Tellico Archaeological Project. Excavations totaling ca. 2 ha (5 acres), or about 10 percent of the site area, were conducted. These investigations recorded the remains of 37 Cherokee structures and more than 1,000 features, including 736 pit features and 117 Cherokee burials. These contexts and their associated artifacts are a primary source for describing eighteenth-century Overhill Cherokee material culture and for inferring patterns of culture change. Two superimposed council houses are present at the site. The earliest building measures ca. 15 m (49 feet) in diameter and contains a central hearth, four major roof-support posts, and bench-support posts surrounding the central floor area. The second building is slightly larger (18 m, or 59 feet, in diameter) and duplicates the smaller building's plan except that

Artist reconstruction of Chota-Tanasee ca. A.D. 1760. (Drawing by Tom Whyte, courtesy of the Frank H. McClung Museum, University of Tennessee)

there are eight major roof-support posts. Next to these buildings was a rectangular summer townhouse or pavilion facing a plaza; it measured ca. 7 x 15 m (23 x 49 feet). Near this building were the skeletal remains of the Cherokee leader Chief Oconastota, who was buried at the site in 1783. Most domestic structures consist of a circular winter house ca. 7 m (23 feet) in diameter with four roof-support posts and a central hearth. A rectangular summer house ca. 5 x 9 m (16.4 x 29.5 feet) was built adjacent to these buildings. Several other forms of rectangular buildings also represent houses at the site. Prior to completion of the Tellico Reservoir in 1979, the central portion of the site in the vicinity of the townhouses was covered with fill by the Tennessee Valley Authority (TVA). In cooperation with the Eastern Band of the Cherokee, the TVA dedicated a monument at the site in the 1980s.

Gerald F. Schroedl

Further Readings

Mooney, J.M. 1900. Myths of the Cherokees. *Nineteenth Annual Report of the Bureau of American Ethnology*, pp. 3–576. Smithsonian Institution, Washington, D.C.

Schroedl, G.F. (editor). 1986. *Overhill Cherokee Archaeology at Chota-Tanasee*. Report of Investigations no. 38. Department of Anthropology, University of Tennessee, Knoxville.

Chucalissa

Chucalissa (40SY1) is located on the crest of the loess bluffs overlooking the Mississippi River floodplain in southwestern Memphis, Tennessee. Covering an area of ca. 5 ha (12.4 acres), this late Mississippian town includes a moderately large rectangular substructural mound (4.5 m, or 14.8 feet, tall), one smaller mound, an artificially raised habitation ring surrounding an open plaza, and outlying residential areas. The largest mound evidently supported two structures on its uppermost preserved summit. One of these structures, presumably representing the residence of a political or religious (or political and religious) leader, was roughly 15 m² (17.9 square yards), with a slightly sunken floor and a roof supported by cypress posts. Several large storage pits were located within the structure. Preliminary testing indicates that the adjacent second structure was smaller. Radiocarbon evidence suggests that the excavated structure was built ca. A.D. 1430 (520 years B.P.) (calibrated). At least one subsequent (i.e., overlying) mound summit was probably destroyed by plowing and erosion.

Houses flanking the plaza, suspected to represent the dwellings of high-ranking families, were constructed on small mounds and averaged 6 m² (7.2 square yards) in size. A number of burials also occur throughout the house-mound ring. Several radiocarbon determinations indicate that occupation of the circumplaza residential ring continued until ca. 1500 (450 years B.P.), if not somewhat beyond. This raises the possibility that Chucalissa may have been occupied at the time of the Hernando de Soto expedition, which crossed the Mississippi River somewhere south of Memphis in A.D. 1541. Excavations in selected off-mound residential areas have disclosed midden accumulations of as much as 1 m (3.3 feet) or more, suggesting intensive, long-term occupation of the site, perhaps spanning as many as 200 years. Portions of numerous roughly square houses, including examples of both wall-trench and simple post construction, are present in some of these residential areas.

As is common for Mississippian-period sites, corn (primarily 10- and 12-row) and deer meat were the foundation of subsistence at Chucalissa. Other reported plant remains include beans, sunflower seeds, hickory nuts, and acorns. Fish and migratory waterfowl are not well represented, presumably a reflection of the site's upland location. The ceramics and lithics from Chucalissa are typical of the Late Mississippian period in the central Mississippi Valley. Many examples of willow-leaf (Nodena) arrow points have been found, as well as small triangular (Madison) points. Deer antler tines were also fashioned into points. Other characteristic lithic artifacts include ground-stone discoidals ("chunky stones"), flaked and polished celts, and drills. The distinctive Late Mississippian ceramic complex is much in evidence at Chucalissa. Numerous finely crafted examples of decorated types, such as Walls Engraved, Nodena Red and White, Rhodes Incised, and Parkin Punctated, are present, as are various effigy forms that are usually manufactured from a fine shell-tempered (Bell Plain) paste. These ceramic types are typically associated with burials, while undecorated wares were used for domestic purposes.

The site is owned by Memphis State University and is managed as an archaeological park, with an on-site museum and several reconstructed Mississippian structures.

Robert C. Mainfort, Jr.

Further Readings

Lumb, L.C., and C.H. McNutt. 1988. *Chucalissa: Excavations in Units 2 and 6, 1959–67*. Occasional Paper no. 15. Anthropological Research Center, Memphis State University, Memphis.

Smith, G.P. 1990. The Walls Phase and Its Neighbors. In *Towns and Temples Along the Mississippi,* edited by D. Dye and C. Cox, pp. 135–169. University of Alabama Press, Tuscaloosa.

Cibola Branch

In 1934, Winifred and Harold S. Gladwin formalized a new conception of southwestern prehistory. Dissatisfied with some aspects of the developmental classification developed at Pecos, New Mexico, in 1929 by southwestern archaeologists, the Gladwins created a conceptual scheme that they thought better described the variation they saw in the archaeological record and more accurately reflected the chronological complexities of the region's cultural development. Their ideas resulted in the creation of an evolutionary tree with roots, stems, and branches that historically connected the deepest past of prehistory in the region to the contemporary pueblos of today over the broad geographic area of the American Southwest. Each root, stem, and branch was considered associated with a particular linguistic stock and was crosscut chronologically by periods that were subdivided by phases. Each phase had associated pottery types, architecture, dates, and type sites.

At the time, the Cibola branch referred to prehistoric development in west-central New Mexico and eastern Arizona. The linguistic stock was considered as possibly Keresan; the root, Basketmaker and Caddoan; and the stem, the Little Colorado. This scheme was considered a conceptual framework that outlined the prehistory of the modern Zuni people who reside in Zuni Pueblo in west-central New Mexico. If present-day archaeologists were to rewrite this scheme, they would call the southern influence Mogollon rather than Caddoan and would know that the linguistic evidence is much more complex than the Gladwins could possibly have known. As recent linguistic research suggests, the Zuni language may be related to the Penutian language used by many Native Americans in California.

While few archaeologists still use the Gladwins' system, many refer to the Cibola area, or to the Cibola branch, in discussing the same area the Gladwins did and archaeological remains considered to be ancestral Zuni. This likely has more to do with the romance associated with the word "Cibola" and Spanish explorer Francisco Coronado's sixteenth-century search for the mysterious Seven Cities of Cibola than with the archaeological utility of the Gladwins' concept.

The Cibola area is very complex archaeologically, and Zuni Pueblo itself as well as ancestral sites in the area lie at or near the boundary between what are often referred to as the Anasazi culture area to the north and the Mogollon culture area to the south. The constellation of features found at Zuni that reflect aspects of both the Anasazi and the Mogollon traditions reinforces the point that concepts such as Anasazi and Mogollon are of dubious utility. But irrespective of the utility of the concepts, many have noted that there are changes through time that do reflect a more northern or a more southern influence, depending on the time period.

Paleoindian and Archaic remains are found throughout the Cibola area, but generally the Cibola concept is intended to refer to the agricultural peoples of the area who used ceramics and lived in pithouse villages. The earliest ceramics are brown wares that date to ca. A.D. 300 (1650 years B.P.). Their presence reflects a more southern Mogollon influence to many researchers, although Andrew Fowler has presented evidence that indicates that they were made locally. Shortly after, La Plata and White Mound Black-on-white ceramics appear, suggesting a shift to a more northern influence. By A.D. 800–900 (1150–1050 years B.P.), the shift of influence to the north is complete. Archaeological materials are now largely indistinguishable from the rest of the northern Anasazi world. The shift from the almost exclusive use of pit structures to above-ground jacal structures occurs as well at this time. Ca. 900 (1050 years B.P.), the shift to above-ground structures called pueblos had begun. In general, this time period is little known and remains problematic.

Between 1000 and 1130/1150 (950–820/800 years B.P.), the archaeology of the area was clearly influenced by Chaco. Gallup-style ceramics in the tradition of Chaco Black-on-white are common, as are other Chacoan types.

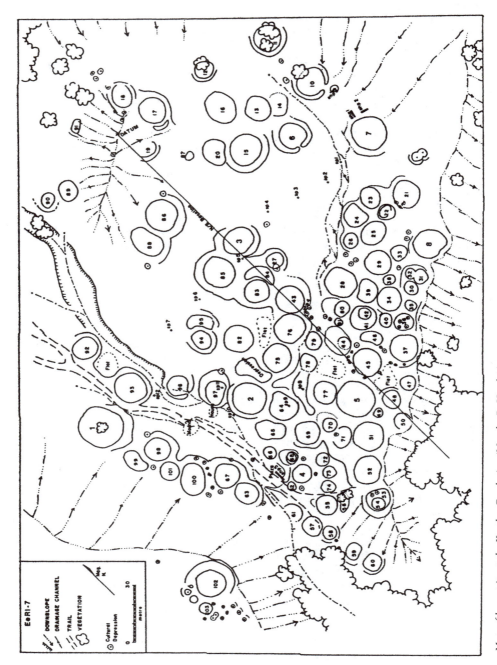

Map of housepits at the Keatley Creek site. (Map by B. Hayden)

Chaco-style architecture is common as well, and structures known as great kivas and great houses appear in the Cibola area. While the great houses were not constructed on the same scale as the great houses in Chaco Canyon, they are nonetheless large formidable structures of perhaps 20–60 rooms. Many are associated with great kivas and Chacoan road segments that connect them with nearby sites. One of the most famous is Village of the Great Kivas in the Nutria Valley on the Zuni Reservation. Excavated by Frank H.H. Roberts, Jr., in the 1930s, the Village of the Great Kivas is perhaps the best known Chacoan outlier in the area. Exactly how the Village of the Great Kivas and other large Cibolan-area settlements functioned in the Chacoan system is unclear. Some researchers see Chaco as a panregional belief system focused on great houses, great kivas, and roads, while others see it as a regional economic system in which outlying areas, such as Cibola, participated in an exchange network centered in Chaco Canyon. Still other researchers believe that outlying areas were largely economically independent of the canyon, yet were influenced to varying degrees by architectural and ceramic traditions centered in the canyon.

With the Chacoan collapse in the mid-1100s (ca. 800 years B.P.), ceramic evidence again indicates increasing ties to the south, as evident in an increase in abundance of Reserve and Tularosa ceramics. White Mountain red wares, centered probably to the south and west, also became common. By the mid-1200s (ca. 700 years B.P.), there is an increase in larger settlements located in higher-elevation settings, such as the El Morro Valley, although settlement continues in other settings. A major shift also occurs at this time from residence in small dispersed settlements, many of which were centered around great houses, to large aggregated pueblos with hundreds of rooms. Researchers have suggested a variety of processes to explain this shift, such as climatic change, population growth, warfare, the structure of labor, and changes in social organization. This trend continued until historic times. It is these large aggregated sites that drew researchers' attentions for many years.

By Coronado's arrival in 1540, settlement in the Zuni area was centered around six or seven villages along the Zuni River: Hawikku, Kwa'kin'a, Halona:wa (Zuni Pueblo), Mats'a:kya, Kyaki:ma, Kechiba:wa, and possibly Chalo:wa. These villages are the legendary Seven Cities of Cibola that were sought by Coronado in 1540. During the Pueblo revolt of 1680, their residents took refuge on the top of Dowa Yallane, a 305 m (1,000-foot) -high mesa near Halona:wa, or Zuni Pueblo. After the revolt, the Zuni people coalesced at Halona:wa, where, as of the mid-1900s, about 8,500 tribal members lived. This is the same region their ancestors occupied for hundreds, if not thousands, of years.

Robert D. Leonard

Further Readings

Ferguson, T.J., and E.R. Hart. 1985. *A Zuni Atlas.* University of Oklahoma Press, Norman.

Gladwin, W., and H.S. Gladwin. 1934. *A Method for the Designation of Cultures and Their Variations.* Medallion Paper no. 15. Gila Pueblo, Globe.

Kintigh, K. 1985. *Settlement, Subsistence, and Society in Late Zuni Prehistory.* Anthropological Papers no. 44. University of Arizona Press, Tucson.

LeBlanc, S.A. 1989. Cibola: Shifting Cultural Boundaries. In *Dynamics of Southwest Prehistory,* edited by L.S. Cordell and G.J. Gumerman. Smithsonian Institution Press, Washington, D.C.

See also ZUNI PUEBLO

Classic Lillooet Culture

The Classic Lillooet culture is a regional manifestation of the Plateau Pithouse tradition of south-central British Columbia. It is distinguished from other contemporaneous Plateau cultures by the exceptionally large size of its villages/towns and by its unusually large residential structures and their distinctive socioeconomic characteristics. The basic elements of this cultural florescence were apparently established sometime during the Shuswap horizon (1550–450 B.C., or 3500–2400 years B.P.), when most of the large (15–22 m, or 49–72-foot, diameter) and medium (10–14 m, or 33–46-foot, diameter) housepits were first occupied. The greatest numbers of housepits and the greatest size diversity apparently occurred during the Plateau horizon (450 B.C.–A.D. 750, or 2400–1200 years B.P.). A major cultural collapse may have occurred in the region ca. A.D. 850 (1100 years B.P.), for large Classic Lillooet settlements seem to have been abruptly abandoned at that time.

The major villages of this culture have from 20 to well over 100 housepits. As many as 8–10 such villages may have been present along the middle Fraser River near Lillooet. Some have been destroyed and only two sites have been systematically excavated, the Bell site with 23 housepits and the Keatley Creek site with 118 housepit-size depressions. Some tests have also been conducted at the Bridge River site.

The special characteristics of the Classic Lillooet culture are almost certainly related to the unusually productive fisheries—the richest in the Canadian Plateau—that occur along this stretch of the Fraser River. Salmon transiting through this region had optimal fat content and, once dried, were highly valued in trade. The hot, dry, and windy climate was ideal for drying them. The principal trade corridor from the coast also emerged at the present townsite of Lillooet. All of these factors made the Lillooet region an unusually rich salmon-exporting and -trading center. Most of the wealth resulting from trade was ultimately deposited with burials. However, since very few burials have been excavated in the Lillooet region, it is difficult to compare wealth and prestige objects with other regions for which there is abundant data, such as The Dalles on the Columbia River.

Excavation of large, medium, and small housepits at the Keatley Creek site (see Figure) has demonstrated that large houses constituted corporate groups that controlled the best fishing locations as well as separate hunting-and-gathering grounds in the mountains. Hearth areas inside large houses were clearly ranked, with one domestic area apparently reserved for a chief administrator. About half of the families consisted of members of the owning lineage or clan, while the other half consisted of commoners or slaves. On the basis of raw-material differences between houses, some corporate groups were associated almost from the beginning of the Classic Lillooet culture until its end with the same houses. People living in small houses generally lived in a much more communal, nonranked fashion and were poorer, although a few of the small houses were probably occupied by relatively rich specialists.

The demise of the Classic Lillooet culture is best explained by a massive landslide that dammed the Fraser River some time prior to A.D. 750 (1200 years B.P.) and blocked the salmon runs that were critical for survival. For unknown reasons, most of the major Classic Lillooet village sites were never reoccupied to any significant degree even after the salmon runs had been reestablished in the centuries following the regional collapse.

Brian Hayden

Further Readings
Hayden, B., and J. Ryder. 1991. Prehistoric Cultural Collapse in the Lillooet Area. *American Antiquity* 56:50–65.
Hayden, B., and J. Spafford. 1993. The Keatley Creek Site and Corporate Group Archaeology. *B.C. Studies* 99:106–139.
Richards, T., and M. Rousseau. 1987. *Late Prehistoric Cultural Horizons on the Canadian Plateau.* Publication no. 16. Department of Archaeology, Simon Fraser University, Burnaby.
Schulting, R. 1995. *Mortuary Variability and Status Differentiation on the Columbia-Fraser Plateau.* Archaeology Press, Simon Fraser University, Burnaby.
Stryd, A. 1973. *The Later Prehistory of the Lillooet Area, British Columbia.* Unpublished Ph.D. dissertation, Department of Archaeology, University of Calgary, Calgary.

Cliff Palace

Nestled in a sheltered alcove near the head of Cliff Canyon in southwestern Colorado, Cliff Palace (5MV625) is the largest cliff dwelling in Mesa Verde National Park and one of the most frequently visited Anasazi (ancestral Pueblo) ruins in the Southwest. The discovery of Cliff Palace is attributed to Richard Wetherill and Charley Mason in December 1888, though local ranchers claimed to have visited the site as early as 1881. The ruin gained international fame largely through the activities of the Wetherill family, who guided tourists and artifact hunters into the ruins of Mesa Verde during the late nineteenth century. One of the most important early visitors was Gustav von Nordenskiöld, a Swedish baron who excavated at Cliff Palace and other Mesa Verde ruins. His classic monograph, *Cliff Dwellers of the Mesa Verde* (1893), was one of the first publications of systematic archaeological work undertaken on an Anasazi site. Jesse Walter Fewkes directed an extensive excavation and reconstruction of Cliff Palace in 1909. Fewkes (1911) noted that by 1909 the site had been almost completely stripped of significant artifacts, a result of

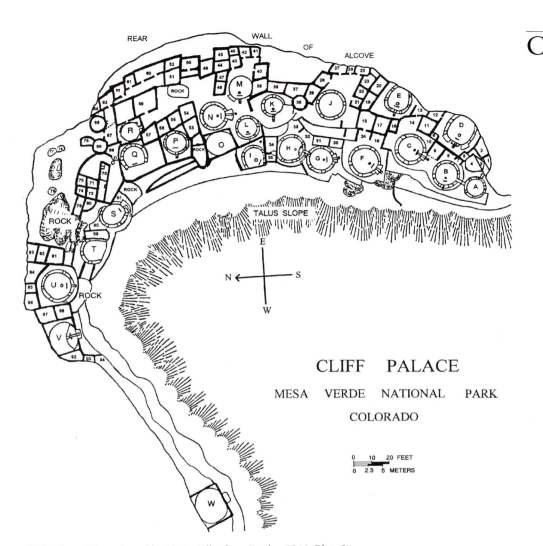

Cliff Palace. (Map adapted by M. A. Adler from Fewkes 1911, Plate 8)

nearly 20 years of looting by local ranchers and visitors.

Of the 36 wooden beams in Cliff Palace that have been tree-ring dated, some date as early as A.D. 1050. However, most of the timbers used in site construction were felled between 1190 and 1279. A similar pattern of site occupation is found across the Mesa Verde region, with the Anasazi moving off the mesas and into cliff-alcove sites during the late twelfth and early thirteenth centuries.

Cliff Palace contains 220 rooms and 23 kivas, numbers consistent with the room-to-kiva ratio of 10:1 found in many contemporary Anasazi settlements. Population at the height of occupation in the mid-thirteenth century prob-

ably reached 200–300 people. Buildings in Cliff Palace are constructed of large blocks of sandstone masonry, many of which have been pecked or ground to shape and bonded with a silty mortar. While most of the structures stand one to two stories in height, some reached as high as four stories, as evidenced by the square tower on the south end of the settlement. Many of the residential rooms at Cliff Palace were plastered on both internal and external walls, and several have painted decorations. Red-and-white wall paintings depicting mountains and an abstract textile design can still be seen inside the square tower. Fewkes divided the site into four "quarters," a reflection of his perception that breaks in the site's architecture represent construction sequences and the functional differentiation of space. Later research into the structure of Cliff Palace indicates that multi-household social groups were present. Arthur H. Rohn (1977) has suggested that groups of related households clustered their individual domiciles around a common courtyard or small plaza. Kivas, constructed within these plazas, served as integrative spaces for the courtyard-based groups.

Cliff Palace is one of 33 cliff dwellings that make up a portion of what Rohn calls the Cliff–Fewkes Canyon settlement, a cluster of contemporaneously occupied sites whose occupants shared common water sources, agricultural fields, and nearby ceremonial sites, such as Sun Temple and Hew Fire House. Occupation ended at Cliff Palace and in the rest of the Cliff-Fewkes settlement sometime between 1280 and 1300 (670–650 years B.P.), a period that coincides with the Anasazi's complete abandonment of the Four Corners region of the Southwest.

Michael A. Adler

Further Readings

Fewkes, J.W. 1911. *Antiquities of the Mesa Verde National Park: Cliff Palace.* Bulletin no. 51. Bureau of American Ethnology, Smithsonian Institution, Washington, D.C.

Nordenskiöld, G. von. 1893. *Cliff Dwellers of the Mesa Verde.* Norstedt and Söner, Stockholm.

Rohn, A.H. 1977. *Cultural Change and Continuity on Chapin Mesa.* Regents Press of Kansas, Lawrence.

See also Kiva; Pueblo; Sand Canyon Pueblo

Climatic Episodes (Holocene)

D.A. Baerreis and R.A. Bryson (1965) and W.M. Wendland and Bryson (1974) have shown that there are globally preferred times of climatic change. The intervals between these changes are called climatic episodes. These climatic shifts, at various places and regionally, appear to be as abrupt as the thermal mass of the ocean and land will allow. Judging by pollen proxies, for example, the change from the late Pleistocene climate to the Holocene climate (ca. 8850 B.C., or 10,800 years B.P., to the present), the largest climatic change for which we have detailed information, took place within a couple of centuries—or less if the growth times of the biota are taken into account, as T. Webb and Bryson (1972) have suggested. Indeed, adjusting for the lag of plant communities behind the climate suggests about one century for the duration of the largest climatic change of the past 20 millennia.

The existence of globally synchronous, identifiable times of climatic change indicates that climatic history can be described as a series of episodes. Synchroneity is to be expected because the entire global atmosphere is dynamically interlinked, so there can be no local change without that change having some global effect. However, it is clear that climate does not change uniformly around the globe or even within a single hemisphere. Anomalous patterns, whether for months, years, or decades (and apparently for centuries), show regions of greater or less difference as well as regions of opposite sign. Thus, the expression of the climate during an episode will vary from region to region. As a consequence, it is not to be expected that all cultures would be exposed to the same kind of climatic impact, of equal importance, or, for that matter, to any change of climate at all.

The fact that climatic change varies in magnitude and sign from region to region indicates that if the episodes are named, the names should not define the nature of the climate during the episode. This was recognized in the early part of the twentieth century by palynologists working in Europe, such as R. Sernander. Since the episodes they identify for Europe are now seen to define global episodes, as pointed out by Wendland and Bryson in 1974, it is reasonable to adopt the terminology known as the Blytt-Sernander sequence (see Table). At the time of development of this terminology, it was believed that what is called here the "Post Sub-Atlantic" could not be separated from the Sub-Atlantic and that the entire period to the present represented, in the pollen profiles, the effects and subsequent consequences of the Neolithic farming revolution. Since then, exploration of climatic history in areas other than Europe has shown that the Sub-Atlantic and later times could indeed be subdivided on the basis of climatic change not related to human activities. The term "Post Sub-Atlantic" is thus used provisionally pending general acceptance of an identifier of nondescript nature. The subepisodes within the Post Sub-Atlantic have been identified and named, however. Perhaps the geological tradition of naming intervals for type localities where they are particularly well defined should be used. The main climatic episodes of the Holocene appear to have been one to three millennia in length, and the subepisodes several centuries. The subepisodes are best defined in more recent times. Of particular inter-

TABLE 1

Tentative Division of the Holocene into Climatic Episodes, Based on Globally Preferred Dates of Climatic Change

CLIMATIC EPISODE	SUB-EPISODE	PROVISIONAL TERMINI	POSSIBLE SUB-DIVISION TERMINI	CHARACTER
		Present		
	Modern			Maximum warmth ca. 1945 (NH)
		**************1915-1920 AD	1915 AD	Cool n. hemisphere
	Neo-Boreal		1885	Mild n. hemisphere
	("Little Ice Age")		1820	Generally cold n. hemisphere
			1765	Mild n hemisphere
Post Sub-Atlantic			1720	Coldest 1600-1630, 1670-1720 (NH)
			1600	Rapid drop of temperature, esp N Atlantic area
		**************1550 AD		Warm N Atlantic
	Pacific		1400	Cooler N America-N Atlantic
		**************1150-1200 AD		
	Neo-Atlantic		1000	"Medieval warm period"
		**************700-750 AD		
	Scandic			Character largely unknown
		**************************300-400 AD		
Sub-Atlantic	S-A III			
		**************50-100 BC		Beginning of 2000-yr general decline of N. Amer. summer temperature.
	S-A II			
		**************ca 500 BC		Highly unstable, weak monsoon NW India, freq. drought in China
	S-A I			
		**************************ca 950 BC		
Sub-Boreal	S-B II			Monsoon failure NW India, expanded tundra, glacial advances
		**************2100 BC		
	S-B I			

(continued on page 160)

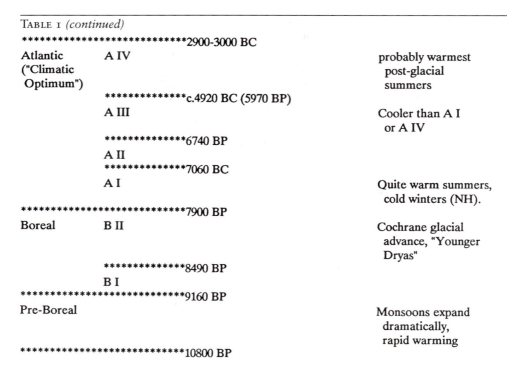

TABLE I *(continued)*

****************************2900-3000 BC			
Atlantic ("Climatic Optimum")	A IV		probably warmest post-glacial summers
	*************c.4920 BC (5970 BP)		
	A III		Cooler than A I or A IV
	*************6740 BP		
	A II		
	*************7060 BC		
	A I		Quite warm summers, cold winters (NH).
****************************7900 BP			
Boreal	B II		Cochrane glacial advance, "Younger Dryas"
	*************8490 BP		
	B I		
****************************9160 BP			
Pre-Boreal			Monsoons expand dramatically, rapid warming
****************************10800 BP			

Note: BC = calendar date, BP = radiocarbon date. Calendar dates are used as far back as reliable conversion of radiocarbon date to calendar date is available. The transition times between episodes were identified using radiocarbon data however, in all cases except those in the past two centuries.

(After Bryson and Padoch, 1981).

est is the fact that the Neo-Boreal episode ended during the time of instrumental observation. This provides an opportunity to establish a probable mode of change, especially if paired with times of opposite change to avoid spurious correlations with parameters that happened to change in the same direction.

While synchronous over the globe, the climatic expression of the episode must vary with location. A pattern of changes with increases in some regions, decreases in others, and with some regions of no change is normal to the behavior of the atmosphere and is indeed required by the dynamics of flow on a rotating sphere. For example, it was moist enough ca. A.D. 1000 (950 years B.P.) in the northern Plains of the United States for nonirrigated corn cultivation, but the rainfall rapidly declined ca. 1150 (800 years B.P.) to a long drought, while the southern Plains became wetter in summer. In the Far North, the boreal forest extended to 55 km north of its present position, then rapidly re-treated southward at the end of the episode. In the desert of northwestern India, the same period appears to have been wetter than at the present, as indicated by transfer function analysis of pollen records and by the expansion of the Osian Republic northwest of Jodhpur. This region appears to have become even wetter during the first phase of the following couple of centuries. When this wet phase ended, the Oswali left the region and dispersed.

R.A. Bryson

Further Readings

Baerreis, D.A., and R.A. Bryson. 1965. Climatic Episodes and the Dating of the Mississippian Cultures. *Wisconsin Archeologist* 46(4):203–220.

Bryson, R.A. n.d. Some Regional Aspects of the Neo-Atlantic Climatic Episode (submitted to *Climate Change*).

Bryson, R.A., and C. Padoch. 1980. On the Climates of History. *Journal of Interdis-*

ciplinary History 10(4):583–597.

Webb, T., III, and R.A. Bryson. 1972. The Late- and Post-Glacial Sequence of Climatic Events in Wisconsin and East-Central Minnesota: Quantitative Estimates Derived From Fossil Pollen Spectra by Multivariate Statistical Analysis. *Quaternary Research* 2(1):70–115.

Wendland, W.M., and R.A. Bryson. 1974. Dating Climatic Episodes of the Holocene. *Quaternary Research* 4(1):9–24.

Clovis Cultural Complex

Clovis is one of the oldest unambiguous archaeological complexes in the New World. It dates to the terminal Pleistocene (ca. 9550–9250 B.C., or 11,500–11,200 years B.P.). Most archaeologists believe that its origins can be traced to Upper Paleolithic Malta-Afontova sites in eastern Siberia, central Asia, and eastern Europe. The Clovis complex shares more than 10 traits with Old World Upper Paleolithic sites: shaft wrenches, cylindrical objects of ivory and bone with single-beveled ends and cross-hachured incised surface, ivory semifabricates, ivory billets and/or burnishers, large prismatic blades, polyhedral blade cores, bifaces, end scrapers, side scrapers, burins, portable art, red

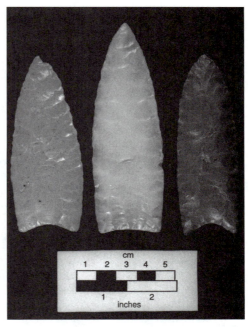

Clovis projectile points. (Courtesy of the Wilford Archaeology Laboratory, University of Minnesota)

ocher, and amber. The single most diagnostic artifact of the Clovis complex is a biface referred to as the Clovis point. While Clovis

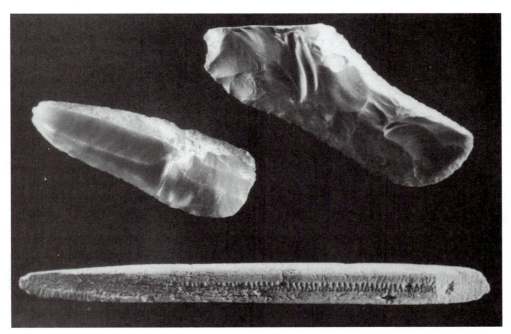

Flaked stone and ground bone Clovis tools from the East Wenatchee site. (Photograph by Pete Bostrom, courtesy of K. B. Tankersley)

A variety of Clovis blades and cores from across North America (Photograph by Pete Bostrom, courtesy of K. B. Tankersley)

points vary in overall shape and size, they display a remarkable degree of homogeneity in their method of manufacture. Clovis points were made from large pieces of high-quality, exquisitely colored stone. Initially, large percussion-produced thinning flakes, struck from carefully prepared platforms, were removed from one edge of the biface to the next in an alternating manner from one side to the other of the biface. Basal thinning flakes (flutes) were subsequently removed to the maximum width of the biface. The bifaces were then refined with percussion and/or pressure flaking. Early-stage thinning flakes were recycled into a variety of cutting and scraping tools. Numerous Clovis points have been recovered from sites located hundreds, sometimes even thousands, of kilometers from the sources of the stone from which they were manufactured.

Archaeological sites associated with the Clovis cultural complex have a pan-North American distribution. Clovis site types include kills, habitations, workshops, caches, and burials. Kill sites are located near water, especially along small tributary streams, ponds, and springs. Clovis weaponry and butchering tools have been found at these sites in direct association with the partially disarticulated or culturally

modified remains of mammoth, mastodon, bison, musk-ox, camel, horse, ground sloth, bear, pronghorn, mountain sheep, peccary, tapir, deer, rabbit, and a wide spectrum of amphibians, reptiles, and birds. Habitation sites are situated on elevated areas that overlook a kill site, stream confluence, shallow crossing, or wetland. Very little information is known about Clovis dwellings. At one site, a circular pattern of postmolds has been interpreted as the remains of a structure. At other sites, shallow bathtub-shaped depressions may represent semisubterranean shelters. Hearths appear as small, shallow, circular features. Artifacts at habitation sites occur adjacent to hearth features. They include broken or exhausted weaponry and tools, raw materials, and lithic debris from tool-maintenance activities. Workshop sites are found near sources of abundant, high-quality stone that occurs in large masses. Lithic debris includes bifaces discarded at all stages of manufacture, debitage that weighs by the ton, and broken or exhausted finished points and tools. Caches occur in a variety of settings and include finished weaponry, preforms, food and raw material-processing tools, portable art, and red ocher. At least one cache, located in a shallow rock shelter in Montana, is associated with a grave. Meat caches, represented by stacked bone, are also known.

Chronometrically, the Clovis cultural complex correlates with the end of the Pleistocene, the last gasp of the last ice age, which was a period of rapid and widespread drying. The drought conditions of this time subjected many of the large gregarious herbivores, such as mammoths, to extreme environmental stress at the same time they were being hunted by Clovis peoples. While the archaeological record demonstrates that smaller animals and plant foods were also procured, these animals likely provided Clovis groups with a source of backup or second-choice foods. Big-game hunting seems to have been the driving force in the Clovis economy.

Kenneth B. Tankersley

Further Readings

Bonnichsen, R., and K.L. Turnmire (editors). 1991. *Clovis Origins and Adaptations.* Center for the Study of the First Americans, Oregon State University, Corvallis.

Frison, G.C. (editor). 1991. *Prehistoric Hunters of the High Plains.* 2nd ed. Academic Press, New York.

Haynes, C.V. 1991. Geoarchaeological and Paleohydrological Evidence for a Clovis-Age Drought in North America and Its Bearing on Extinction. *Quaternary Research* 35:438–450.

Sofer, O., and N.D. Praslov (editors). 1993. *From Kostenki to Clovis: Upper Paleolithic-Paleoindian Adaptations.* Plenum Press, New York.

C

Cluny Earthlodge Village

Cluny Earthlodge Village (EePf-1) is a short-lived occupation site located on the north bank of the Bow River, south of the town of Cluny on the Blackfoot Reserve ca. 97 km (60 miles) east of Calgary, Alberta. It dates to ca. A.D. 1740. The site is marked by 11 circular to oval depressions that may represent former house-pits; it is enclosed by a semicircular fortification trench abutting the river bank. A palisade wall runs inside and parallel to the ditch, with the pits between them. Thus, the palisade was not designed to protect the pits. So few features and artifacts were recovered in the pits that their identification as residential quarters, much less earthlodges, can be questioned. However, this identification relies on a Blackfoot (Siksika) tra-

Cluny Earthlodge Village, Alberta (Courtesy of the Department of Archaeology, University of Calgary)

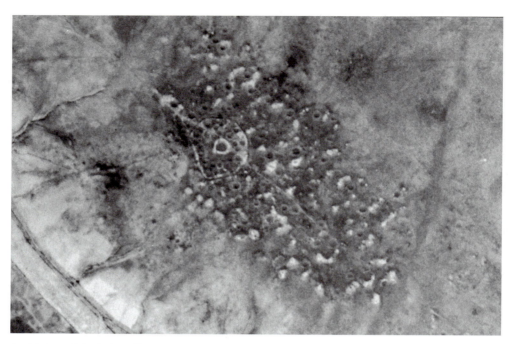

Aerial view of the Oahe Village (39HU2), a Post-Contact Coalescent, Le Beau phase, earthlodge village. (Photograph by C. M. Johnson)

dition referring to the ancient occupants of the site as *Tsawkoyee*, or "Earth Lodge People." A thin layer of cultural debris, suggesting brief habitation, is concentrated on the flats inside the palisade, where impermanent structures (tipis?) evidently were erected. Butchered bones of bison and other animals indicate an economy based on hunting. Horse bones are present. There is no evidence of horticulture; scapula hoes and squash knives are absent.

Architecturally, Cluny has its closest counterparts in Post-Contact Coalescent earthlodge settlements of the Plains Village pattern on the Missouri River in North and South Dakota. Artifact comparisons support this contention even though Cluny has no exact counterpart in the Dakotas. The distinctive pottery complex constitutes the foundation for the One Gun phase, which is intrusive into southern Alberta. It stands in contrast to the indigenous Saskatchewan Basin complex of southern Alberta, which William J. Byrne (1973) ascribes to the Old Women's phase. The route by which these people arrived from the Dakotas is uncertain in the absence of prehistoric fortified sites in Montana and Saskatchewan. From ceramic studies, Byrne (1973:503–504) believes that they moved up the South Saskatchewan rather than the Missouri River drainage.

Identifying Cluny with known historic tribes remains highly speculative. Probably the Protohistoric group living at the site was either of the Siouan linguistic stock (a splinter group of Hidatsa?) or was strongly influenced by Siouans of the Middle Missouri region. An Algonquian affiliation cannot be entirely dismissed.

Richard G. Forbis

Further Readings

Byrne, W.J. 1973. *The Archaeology and Prehistory of Southern Alberta As Reflected by Ceramics.* Mercury Series Paper no. 14. Archaeological Survey of Canada, National Museum of Man, Ottawa.

Forbis, R.G. 1977. *Cluny, an Ancient Fortified Village in Alberta.* Occasional Paper no. 4. Department of Archaeology, University of Calgary, Calgary.

Coalescent Tradition

The Coalescent tradition represents the late prehistoric and early historic remains of the Mandan, Hidatsa, Arikara, and Pawnee who once lived along the major river valleys in North Dakota, South Dakota, and Nebraska. They lived in circular, semisubterranean earthlodges and subsisted on a dual economy of horticulture and hunting. Their villages are organized into a number of variants: Initial (A.D. 1300–1500), Extended (1450–1600/1650) and Post-Contact (1600/1650–1862). The Post-Contact variant is traditionally subdivided into six phases: Knife River (Mandan and Hidatsa), Heart River (Mandan and Hidatsa), Bad River (Arikara), Le Beau (Arikara), Talking Crow (Arikara), and Lower Loup (Pawnee).

Most Coalescent villages are located along the terraces of the Missouri River in North and South Dakota, a segment of the river termed the "Middle Missouri subarea." The North Dakota sites represent the ancestral villages of the Mandan near Bismarck and of the Hidatsa who lived near the mouth of the Knife River. Coalescent villages along the Missouri River in South Dakota are thought to have been occupied by ancestral Arikara. Most of the nineteenth-century Mandan, Hidatsa, and Arikara lived in a few communities near the Knife River, some of which were documented by explorers such as Lewis and Clark, George Catlin, and Prince Maximilian. The last village, Like-a-Fishhook, is upstream from these villages and was the home for the few surviving members of all three tribes. It was abandoned in 1886. A smaller group of villages at or near the confluence of the Loup and Platte rivers in Nebraska in the Central Plains represents the remnants of Pawnee

Initial Coalescent ceramic vessel from the Partizan site. (39LM218). (Prepared by C. M. Johnson)

settlements. The last Pawnee earthlodge settlement, Genoa Village, was abandoned in 1876.

Initial-variant villages have a plan characterized by houses surrounded by a fortification ditch and an interior post palisade marked by bastions at regular intervals. Extended Coalescent sites, while retaining this fortification system, are more commonly unfortified communities of loosely arranged houses scattered over large areas. During the Post-Contact period, there is an increase in village size; about a third of these villages are fortified by ditches and

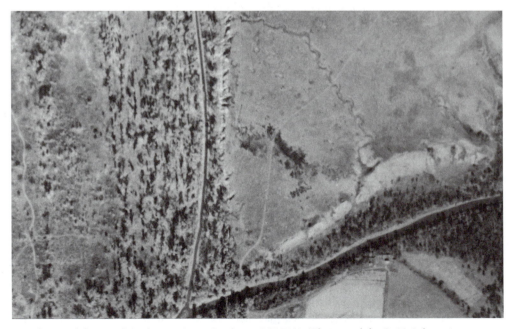

Aerial view of the Initial Coalescent Crow Creek site (39BF11). (Photograph by C. M. Johnson)

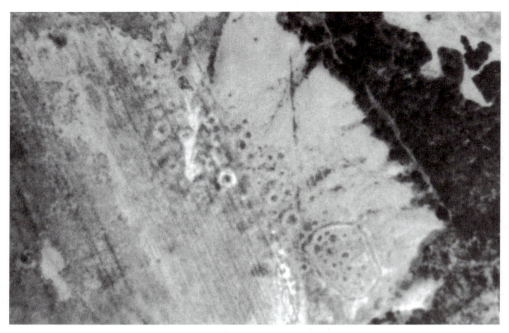

Aerial view of the Potts Village site (39CO19), an extended Coalescent earthlodge village. (Photograph by C. M. Johnson)

palisade systems lacking bastions. Circular houses are characteristic of the Coalescent tradition and are made of a wood frame covered by grass, sticks, and earth. They typically have a central hearth and a number of storage/refuse pits in their floors. Human burials are in cemeteries near the villages, particularly during the Post-Contact Coalescent.

Native technology consisted of ground- and chipped-stone tools, ceramic vessels, and bone implements used to procure and process animals, such as bison, deer, elk, antelope, birds, and fish, and horticultural products, like corn, beans, and squash. Ground-stone tools include manos, metates, grooved mauls and abraders, and smoking pipes and ornaments; chipped-stone tools, which are found in large quantities, include arrow points, scrapers, knives, and drills. Bone tools, fashioned primarily from bison, include scapula hoes, awls, knives, shaft wrenches, and fishhooks. Ceramic vessels are globular jars having a wide variety of rim and shoulder decorations consisting of trailing or incising and cord or tool impressions. Shell, sometimes imported from the Pacific, Atlantic, or Gulf coasts via a Native American trading network, was also used for ornaments. Euro-American trade items appear during the Post-Contact variant. This was a time of flores-

cence and growth of Plains Village populations, who took advantage of their "middleman" trade status between Plains nomadic groups and Euro-Americans to exchange garden produce, animal furs, and skins for guns, horses, and other Euro-American–derived products.

There continues to be disagreement over the origins of Coalescent peoples and the relations of the various variants and phases. It is believed that Initial Coalescent villagers came from a Central Plains–tradition stock in Nebraska and/or Kansas ca. A.D. 1300 (650 years B.P.) in response to widespread drought. Upon arrival at the Missouri River southeast of Pierre, South Dakota, they came into hostile contact with resident Initial Middle Missouri–village groups, hence the need for fortifications. The Coalescent villagers appear to have prevailed and are thought to have evolved in time into the Extended Coalescent, although there is a temporal overlap between the two and discontinuities in material culture that suggest multiple origins. Initial and Extended Coalescent villages are located in South Dakota and are believed to represent ancestral Arikara. The Extended Coalescent, in turn, was transformed into the Post-Contact variant with the addition of artifacts of Euro-American derivation. A number of late Extended-variant villages at the southern limits of the Middle Missouri subarea may represent ancestral Pawnee communities, although this view is not shared by all archaeologists.

Craig M. Johnson

Further Readings

Ahler, S.A., T.D. Thiessen, and M.K. Trimble. 1991. *People of the Willows*. University of North Dakota Press, Grand Forks.

Lehmer, D.J. 1971. *Introduction to Middle Missouri Archeology*. National Park Service, Washington, D.C.

Smith, C.S., and R.T. Grange, Jr. 1958. *The Spain Site (39LM301)*. Bulletin no. 169. Bureau of American Ethnology, Smithsonian Institution, Washington, D.C.

Spaulding, A.C. 1956. *The Arzberger Site, Hughes County, South Dakota*. Occasional Contributions no. 16. Museum of Anthropology, University of Michigan, Ann Arbor.

Wedel, W.R. 1936. *An Introduction to Pawnee Archeology*. Bulletin no. 112. Bureau of American Ethnology, Smithsonian Institution, Washington, D.C.

Wood, W.R. 1974. Northern Plains Village Cultures: Internal Stability and External Relationships. *Journal of Anthropological Research* 30:1–18.

Cochise Culture

In 1941, E.B. Sayles and Ernst Antevs published a seminal monograph, *The Cochise Culture*, in which they proposed a three-stage, preceramic cultural sequence for southeastern Arizona and adjacent portions of New Mexico. This influential publication marshaled stratigraphically associated geological and archaeological evidence over a broad region to outline a developmental continuum of hunter-gatherers (or foragers) from the late Pleistocene to horticultural village communities dating to ca. 50 B.C. (2000 years B.P.). The Cochise culture was originally divided into three stages that together were thought to represent a distinct and uninterrupted sequence of regional cultural evolution. The earliest of these, the Sulphur Spring stage, was dated to 10,050 B.C. (12,000 years B.P.) on the basis of a direct geologic association with extinct mammals, such as mammoth, horse, bison, and dire wolf. Paradoxically, the economy of this stage was inferred to be heavily dependent on plant food collecting and processing due to the preponderance of grinding implements and the general paucity of chipped-stone tools. The subsequent Chiricahua stage was dated to 4050 B.C. (6000 years B.P.). It was composed of hearths, middens, and artifacts overlying deposits containing Sulphur Spring material. Artifacts typically associated with this stage included not only ground stone but considerable quantities of chipped stone and some projectile points. The San Pedro stage was thought to date between 3050 and 550 B.C. (5000–2500 years B.P.) and to contain a distinctive artifactual assemblage with basin-shaped metates, large handstones, and long-stemmed triangular projectile points with pressure flaking. Notably, San Pedro–stage sites possessed shallow depressions indicative of house structures, bell-shaped pits, and trash deposits. The perceived advancements in the chipped-stone industry suggested an increase in the importance of hunting. Following additional fieldwork at the Double Adobe site in the 1950s, Sayles added the Cazador stage to the Cochise-culture sequence. It existed between the Sulphur Spring and Chiricahua stages at ca. 7050–6050 B.C. (9000–8000 years B.P.).

The concept of the Cochise culture as an evolutionary continuum in the Southwest and its chronostratigraphic foundations have been discussed and challenged in the decades since it was originally proposed by Sayles and Antevs. Two substantive issues that have received attention and some clarification involve the temporal association of Sulphur Spring material culture with extinct fauna and the alluvial geomorphology of the region. Some scholars found it anomalous that the association of a ground-stone industry and extinct Pleistocene animals occurs in no other area but southeastern Arizona. It was suggested that the Pleistocene fossils were redeposited with later Archaic-period ground stone. It was also proposed that Sulphur Spring sites were merely specialized plant-processing localities of the Clovis tradition. Michael Waters (1986) has explored these and other questions related to the geochronology of the Cochise culture along Whitewater Draw in southeastern Arizona. He concluded that Pleistocene faunal remains are probably not in primary association with Sulphur Spring–stage artifacts, which date to between 8050 and 6050 B.C. (10,000–8000 years B.P.). Further, he found little support for a distinctive Cazador stage, concluding instead that the material culture of the purported stage appeared to be an amalgam of Sulphur Spring and later Archaic material.

Chronometric reassessment of the other Cochise stages by numerous other researchers throughout the region have, in similar fashion, resulted in changes to the alluvial-based chronology proposed by Sayles. More refined estimates for the Chiricahua stage place it between 3550 and 1550 B.C. (5500–3500 years B.P.), and the San Pedro stage is now generally dated to 1550–50 B.C. (3500–2000 years B.P.).

While some of the substantive interpretations of Sayles and Antevs have been questioned, the character and tenor of much of the discussions have been directly influenced by paradigmatic changes and methodological advancements in archaeology since 1941. Fred Plog, for example, seriously doubted the value of the "stage" concept and its cultural historical links as a valid means of understanding evolutionary change and human adaptation. Implicit in the normative, developmental scheme proposed by Sayles and Antevs is that cultures evolve and change along some progressive trajectory. This perspective has little support among those who research hunter-gatherer cultures (cf. Bettinger 1991), for it cannot readily account for observed archaeological variability. The analytical value of Sayles and Antevs's developmental continuum, the "Cochise culture," is of less importance today than the significant influence it had on the character of Archaic-period research in the Southwest.

Frank E. Bayham

Further Readings

Bettinger, R.L. 1991. *Hunter-Gatherers: Archaeological and Evolutionary Theory.* Plenum Press, New York.

Irwin-Williams, C. 1979. Post-Pleistocene Archaeology: 7000–2000 B.C. In *Southwest,* edited by A. Ortiz, pp. 31–42. Handbook of North American Indians, vol. 9, W.C. Sturtevant, general editor. Smithsonian Institution, Washington D.C.

Martin, P.S., and F. Plog. 1973. *The Archaeology of Arizona.* Doubleday/Natural History Press, New York.

Sayles, E.B. 1983. *The Cochise Cultural Sequence in Southeastern Arizona.* Anthropological Papers no. 42. University of Arizona Press, Tucson.

Sayles, E.B., and E. Antevs. 1941. *The Cochise Culture.* Medallion Paper no. 29. Gila Pueblo, Globe.

Waters, M.R. 1986. *The Geochronology of Whitewater Draw, Arizona.* Anthropological Papers no. 45. University of Arizona Press, Tucson.

Cody

"Cody" is a term applied by archaeologists to a prehistoric time period and assemblage of artifact types primarily known from the North American High Plains. Usually called the Cody complex, this material falls within what is known as the Paleoindian stage (ca.10,050–5050 B.C., or 12,000–7,000 years B.P.). Most known Cody-complex sites are locations where large numbers of now extinct bison were killed and butchered. However, several hunting camps have also been investigated. Dating of a number of Cody-complex sites ranges from 7250 to 6850 B.C. (9200–8800 years B.P.).

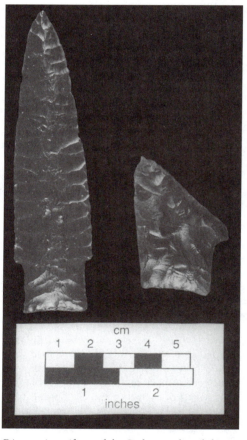

Diagnostic artifacts of the Cody complex: (left) Scottsbluff point from Saskatchewan; (right) Cody knife from the Mathieson site, New Mexico. (Illustration by B. A. Bradley)

After the discovery in the 1920s and 1930s that human cultures in North America coexisted with now extinct forms of large mammals, many more such discoveries were made. Initially, only a couple of differences in stone-tool and projectile-point styles were distinguished (Folsom and Yuma), but as new discoveries were made, it became clear that there were a number of distinguishable forms. By the late 1950s, several additional types were defined and the Yuma type was discredited. Several distinct styles of projectile points were found together at the Horner site near Cody, Wyoming, and the different styles were subsumed under the term "Cody complex." This work was carried out by expeditions from Princeton University and the Smithsonian Institution between 1949 and 1952. Two main projectile-point styles (Eden and Scottsbluff) and a distinctive shouldered-knife form (Cody knife) were all found together in this site. Scottsbluff points have wide triangular- to parallel-sided blades, distinctly indented parallel-sided stems, straight bases, and moderately controlled pressure flaking that tends to be perpendicular to the edges and overlaps near the middle. Eden points are relatively narrow and parallel-sided with slightly indented parallel-sided stems (occasionally produced only by grinding), straight bases, and highly controlled serial pressure flaking that is perpendicular to the edges and meets evenly in the middle, producing a distinct diamond cross section. Two types of Cody knives have been described. The most distinctive has a triangular blade that is set at an oblique angle to a straight-sided, straight-based stem, produced by indenting only one side. These are sometimes referred to as shouldered Cody knives. The second form has a symmetrical, triangular blade with a centered square stem (originally identified as a Scottsbluff-point variant). Both types are very thin, exhibit evidence of knife use and resharpening, and are technologically distinct from Cody projectile points.

Originally, the projectile point forms had been recovered and described separately in southwestern Wyoming (Eden) and western Nebraska (Scottsbluff). Additional investigations and analyses showed that these forms most often occur together. Over the years, there have been several theories as to why two distinct projectile-point types sometimes occur separately and sometimes together. A common explanation is that each represents a distinct cultural group and that sites that yield both

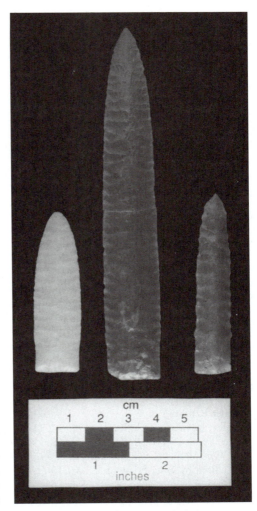

Cody complex Eden points: (left and center) the Claypool site; (right) Saskatchewan. (Illustration by B. A. Bradley)

types represent combined hunts and activities of the two groups. Another idea has been that there may have been different functions for the different styles and that the various sites represent these separate or combined functions. Although Eden and Scottsbluff points are usually considered distinct enough to recognize, when large collections are studied there are enough intermediate forms to indicate a continuity of style rather than a clear distinction. At least one study (Bradley and Stanford 1987) has made a case that the different forms simply represent different manufacture stages within a technological continuum. As more sites are investigated, even the distinctions between Cody points and the earlier Alberta-point style are becoming less obvious.

Relevant questions are, When does Cody begin? and Does it really represent a distinct cultural development? As with most Paleoindian materials, Cody sites with good archaeological contexts are rare, and what looks like distinct differences from earlier sites may be primarily a result of sample size. This was demonstrated as a likely possibility in the late 1970s when the University of Wyoming reopened the Horner site and found a previously unknown deposit that contained projectile points that, in technology and style, fell between Eden/ Scottsbluff- and the earlier Alberta-point style (Frison and Todd 1987). It is likely that this situation will continue to occur as more sites are discovered and studied. Cody-complex projectile points are considered to be some of the best-made projectile points in the High Plains from any time period. The skill and care that were used to produce them went well beyond what was necessary to make functional projectile points. Several interpretations have been presented, ranging from simple functional need to ritual/spiritual enhancement of the forms.

Bruce A. Bradley

Further Readings

Bradley, B.A., and D.J. Stanford. 1987. The Claypool Study. In *The Horner Site: The Type Site of the Cody Cultural Complex,* edited by G.C. Frison and L.C. Todd, pp. 405–434. Academic Press, New York.
Frison, G.C., and L.C. Todd. 1987. *The Horner Site: The Type Site of the Cody Cultural Complex.* Academic Press, New York.
Wheat, J.B. 1972. *The Olsen-Chubbuck Site: A Paleo-Indian Bison Kill.* Memoir no. 26. Society for American Archaeology, Washington, D.C.

Colby Site

The Colby mammoth-kill site (48WA322) is located in the central Bighorn Basin in northern Wyoming east of the Bighorn River. Don Colby, a heavy equipment operator, discovered the site in 1962 when he uncovered a fluted Clovis point during reservoir construction. More than a decade later, in 1973, after a heavy thunderstorm, a pair of extremely deteriorated mammoth mandibles appeared at the surface in the same location. Excavations in 1973, 1975, and 1978 by University of Wyoming field crews under the direction of George C. Frison recovered parts of at least eight mammoths and three fluted Clovis points. Although the lithic technology of the points is unquestioningly Clovis, two have rounded corners unlike other known Clovis points.

Two piles of mammoth bones at the Colby site are believed to have been cold-weather meat caches. One consisted of a front quarter of a mammoth underneath long bones of at least three other animals. The skull of a young male mammoth had been placed on top of the pile, which was intact and had not been opened. The other pile had apparently been opened and utilized, for the bones were more widely dispersed. These features are reminiscent of frozen meat caches in the Arctic.

The mammoth remains were in the bottom and floodplain of an old arroyo whose topography has changed dramatically since Clovis times. What was then a wide, deep, steep-sided arroyo is now a more mature dendritic type of topography. The old arroyo had filled entirely, but, fortunately, subsequent cycles of erosion paralleled the old arroyo, leaving parts of it with the mammoth remains intact. The site may have been an arroyo-kill situation in which wounded individual animals were separated from the herd and trapped. Small numbers of other bones in the site include camel, horse, pronghorn, and jackrabbit. No evidence of a processing area or camp was found.

George C. Frison

Further Readings

Frison, G.C. 1976. Cultural Activity Associated With Prehistoric Mammoth Butchering and Processing. *Science* 194:728–730.
Frison, G.C., and L.C. Todd. 1986. *The Colby Mammoth Site: Taphonomy and Archaeology of a Clovis Kill in Northern Wyoming.* University of New Mexico Press, Albuquerque.

See also CLOVIS CULTURAL COMPLEX

Cole, Fay-Cooper (1881–1961)

Fay-Cooper Cole was an important guiding figure in the development of anthropology in North America between 1930 and 1950, though his participation in American archaeology was subsidiary to his many other, largely administrative endeavors. He began his career in 1906 as an ethnologist for the Field Museum of Natural History in Chicago, where he was known for his work in the Philippines and Malaysia. By 1924, he was a lecturer in anthropology at the University of Chicago, and in 1929 he became head of the newly formed Department of Anthropology. He devoted his considerable energy and managerial skill to building that department in the 1930s. Always intensely interested in science, excellence, and rigorous field training, Cole helped initiate, support, and direct archaeological field training in Illinois for scores of University of Chicago students from 1925 into the mid-1930s. His two tangible contributions to the field, *Rediscovering Illinois* (1937), coauthored with Thorne Deuel, and *Kincaid: A Prehistoric Illinois Metropolis* (1951), were syntheses of information gathered during these field-school exercises. *Rediscovering Illinois* provided one of the first descriptions of the sequence of prehistoric cultures in the Midwest and was an important precursor to early functionalist approaches to archaeological materials in the United States. In their descriptions, Cole and Deuel grouped all artifact types from a component at a site into functional categories, such as "agriculture and food-getting," "architecture and house life,"

and "costume and dress." Although their functional approach was rudimentary—they did not, for example, use their categories to infer seasonal activities at different sites—it did help spur a shift in focus in archaeological investigations from individual objects to sets of activities. Cole influenced North American archaeology in many other, less tangible ways, too. He participated in the formulation and adoption of the Midwestern Taxonomic system, helped initiate dendrochronological studies in the Midwest, and hosted the organizational meeting for the Society for American Archaeology in his Chicago office. Cole also served as president of the American Anthropological Association and was a founder of the Social Science Research Council.

Guy Gibbon

Further Readings

Cole, F.-C. 1951. *Kincaid: A Prehistoric Illinois Metropolis*. University of Chicago Press, Chicago.

Cole, F.-C., and T. Deuel. 1937. *Rediscovering Illinois*. University of Chicago Press, Chicago.

Jennings, J.D. 1962. Fay-Cooper Cole: 1881–1961. *American Antiquity* 27:573–575.

C

Fay-Cooper Cole. (Reprinted with permission from American Antiquity 27[4]:573)

Coles Creek Culture

The Coles Creek culture was first identified by James A. Ford in 1936. It has since come to occupy an important place in the prehistory of the Lower Mississippi Valley and adjacent parts of the Southeast for the period ca. A.D. 700–1200 (1250–750 years B.P.). Coles Creek culture is notable for its distinctive ceramics and for building flat-topped mounds around an open plaza.

Coles Creek groups are found in the Lower Mississippi Valley and adjacent tributaries and along the Gulf Coast from the Sabine River eastward to the Pearl River. The northern limit of distribution is along an east-west line drawn just below the mouth of the Arkansas River. Sites extend up the major tributaries on the east and west banks of the Mississippi, where they are largely confined to the wider floodplains. Major Coles Creek culture groupings are found in the Yazoo, Tensas, Boeuf, Ouachita, and Red River basins of southeastern Arkansas, northeastern Louisiana, and west-central Mississippi; along the Natchez Bluffs; in the Atchafalaya-Teche waterways; along the Chenier Plain of west Louisiana; and eastward to the Mississippi Delta.

Coles Creek is dated from ca. A.D. 700 to

1200 (1250–750 years B.P.), although there are few radiocarbon dates to securely place its beginning and ending points. This culture is subdivided into a series of regionally distinct archaeological phases with internally consistent stratigraphic sequences. The phases are thought to correlate, to some degree, with the distribution of different subgroups ("tribes"?) throughout Coles Creek territory. In each region, there are usually early, middle, late, and often transitional phases that mark the evolution of ceramic assemblages and of other aspects of material culture.

The settlement pattern appears to be hierarchically organized and can be divided into at least three major classes. In the river basins and adjacent tributaries, there are a limited number of large mound sites. These sites have between five and nine flat-topped mounds, with one mound usually considerably larger than the rest. Mounds supported perishable structures for civic and religious leaders, although some earlier mounds were also used as mortuaries. These edifices were built around a central plaza and were generally associated with large village occupations. Some sites may have been "vacant" ceremonial centers with small resident populations. Smaller mound sites, usually with three mounds facing a plaza, are distributed throughout Coles Creek territory. Numerous small hamlets or villages, and isolated artifact scatters, are found dispersed along relic levees and on higher ground adjacent to rivers or streams.

The assumption that Coles Creek peoples were sedentary farmers, growing corn and other tropical domesticates, has been challenged by new data recovered from sites in northeast Louisiana since 1989 (Kidder 1992; Fritz and Kidder 1993; Kidder and Fritz 1993). Corn was apparently not part of the Coles Creek diet until after A.D. 1000 (950 years B.P.). It may not have been dietarily significant until ca. 1200 (750 years B.P.). Coles Creek populations apparently subsisted on a diet of wild-plant foods, especially acorns and other nuts, persimmon, palmetto, and maygrass. Squash and, possibly, tobacco were cultivated. There is no evidence for other domesticated foods until the introduction of corn. Fish, turtle, deer, squirrel, raccoon, opossum, and rabbit were important to most Coles Creek populations.

Coles Creek ceramics were tempered with grit, sand, and grog (crushed fired clay). The most common design consisted of parallel lines incised around the mouths of bowls, jars, and beakers. Temporal and spatial distinctions are identified by variations in the numbers of lines and their placement on the vessel surface. Minor but important ceramic variants are found, some of which seem to relate to broader trends along the Gulf Coast and westward into the Red River Valley. These are critical in distinguishing regional interaction. Coles Creek groups do not appear to have spent much time making or using stone tools. The most common finished tool on sites is the small barbed arrow point. Chipped-stone bifaces are occasionally recovered, but they are rare. Almost all chipped-stone tools and debris are made from locally available chert gravel. An exception seems to be the manufacture or importation of small- to medium-sized green or black stone celts found on some Coles Creek sites. Along the Gulf Coast, bone tools are important and take the place of stone, which is scarce. The only piece of Coles Creek art, found in southwestern Louisiana, is a human effigy figure carved from antler.

Most archaeologists believe that Coles Creek culture was socially and politically complex. They generally characterize it as a chiefdom (or group of chiefdoms). The most important evidence comes from settlement data, which indicate a hierarchical, and possibly ranked, sociopolitical organization. There is not much other evidence for social, economic, or political differentiation, however, and the precise nature of Coles Creek society is unknown. Economically, Coles Creek people were relatively conservative; nonlocal, rare, or exotic commodities are not often found at Coles Creek sites. Coles Creek–style ceramics are found in many parts of the Southeast, especially to the north at sites in the American Bottom near St. Louis. Cultures that are related to Coles Creek, and that probably interacted with it on a regular basis, include the Plum Bayou in the Arkansas River Valley, early Caddo cultures along the Red River, later Weeden Island on the eastern Gulf Coast, and Miller III in eastern Mississippi and western Alabama.

In the period ca. 1100–1200 (850–750 years B.P.), Coles Creek cultures underwent a series of changes that culminated in the emergence of the Mississippi-period Plaquemine culture. One of the factors involved may have been the shift in subsistence from largely wild foods to mostly domesticated crops. Political centralization intensified. A few large sites grew bigger and dominated the political and social landscape. In the Yazoo Basin on the northern fringe of Coles Creek culture, contact with Cahokia or Cahokian-related groups may have stimulated social change, although this was not the sole cause of, or reason for, the appearance of the later Plaquemine culture. Material traits also changed. Characteristic Coles Creek pottery slowly gave way to newer ceramic innovations. Although Coles Creek culture eventually disappeared, it provided not only the material, but also the genetic and generic background, for the Indians who were alive in the area at European contact in the sixteenth and seventeenth centuries A.D.

Tristram R. Kidder

Further Readings

Ford, J.A. 1936. *Analysis of Indian Village Site Collections From Louisiana and Mississippi.* Anthropological Study no. 2. Louisiana Department of Conservation, New Orleans.

———. 1951. *Greenhouse: A Troyville-Coles Creek Period Site in Avoyelles Parish, Louisiana.* Anthropological Papers, vol. 44, pt. 1. American Museum of Natural History, New York.

Fritz, G.J., and T.R. Kidder. 1993. Recent Investigations Into Prehistoric Agriculture in the Lower Mississippi Valley. *Southeastern Archaeology* 12:1–14.

Kidder, T.R. 1992. Coles Creek Period Social Organization and Evolution in Northeast Louisiana. In *Lords of the Southeast: Social Inequality and the Native Elites of Southeastern North America,* edited by A. Barker and T. Pauketat, pp. 145–162. Archaeological Papers no. 3. American Anthropological Association, Washington, D.C.

Kidder, T.R., and G.J. Fritz. 1993. Subsistence and Social Change in the Lower Mississippi Valley: The Reno Brake and Osceola Sites, Louisiana. *Journal of Field Archeology* 20:281–297.

Phillips, P. 1970. *Archaeological Survey in the Lower Yazoo Basin, Mississippi, 1949–1955.* Papers no. 60. Peabody Museum of American Archaeology and Ethnography, Harvard University, Cambridge.

Williams, S., and J.P. Brain. 1983. *Excavations at the Lake George Site, Yazoo County, Mississippi, 1958–1960.* Papers no. 74. Peabody Museum of American Archaeology and Ethnography, Harvard University, Cambridge.

Collins, Henry B. (1899–1987)

A pioneer synthesizer of Arctic prehistory. In his 1929 and 1930 excavations on St. Lawrence Island, Alaska, Henry B. Collins was the first to use beach ridge sequences and stratigraphy to order archaeological cultures chronologically; his report, *The Archeology of St. Lawrence Island, Alaska* (1937), was awarded a gold medal by the Royal Academy of Sciences and Letters in Denmark and is an important landmark in Arctic archaeology. After 1948, he conducted an extensive series of excavations in the Canadian Arctic islands that provided much of the early substantive data on Thule and Dorset occupations in the Canadian Arctic, and in 1954 he was the first to use the term "Pre-Dorset." His excavations of village sites in Mississippi in the late 1920s are among the first village (as opposed to mound) site excavations in the southeastern United States.

Guy Gibbon

Further Readings

Collins, H.B. 1937. *The Archeology of St. Lawrence Island, Alaska.* Miscellaneous Collections, vol. 96, no. 1. Smithsonian Institution, Washington, D.C.

———. 1954. *Arctic Area.* Pan American Institute of Geography and History no. 160a. Mexico.

———. 1964. The Arctic and Subarctic. In *Prehistoric Man in the New World,* edited by J.D. Jennings and E. Norbeck, pp. 85–114. University of Chicago Press, Chicago.

Dekin, A.A., Jr. 1973. The Arctic. In *The Development of North American Archaeology,* edited by J.E. Fitting, pp. 14–48. Anchor Books, Garden City.

Colorado Plains Woodland Regional Variant

Defined by William B. Butler as a taxon that includes the South Platte and Arkansas phases, the Colorado Plains Woodland regional variant dates between ca. 100 and 1150 (1850–800 years B.P.) and includes the Woodland occupations in the Plains of eastern Colorado and adjacent states.

William B. Butler

Further Readings

Butler, W.B. 1986. *Taxonomy in Northeastern Colorado Prehistory.* Unpublished Ph.D. dissertation, Department of Anthropol-

ogy, University of Missouri, Columbia.
———. 1988. The Woodland Period in Northeastern Colorado. *Plains Anthropologist* 3(122):449–466.

See also ARKANSAS PHASE; SOUTH PLATTE PHASE

Comal

A Spanish term for griddle, "comal" is used by California archaeologists for flat sheets of steatite that served as frying surfaces for various foods among a number of prehistoric southern California cultures. Comals average 20–40 cm (7.8–15.6 inches) in length, are usually oval in shape, and sometimes have a hole drilled near one end. A comal was placed over an open fire and was used for frying. Flat cakes made from leached acorn meal or milled hard seeds were frequently cooked on comals. Most often made of steatite from Santa Catalina Island, comals were developed as early as 4000 B.C. (5950 years B.P.) but became most common after ca. 250 B.C. (2200 years B.P.).

Joseph L. Chartkoff

Further Readings

King, C.D. 1981. *The Evolution of Chumash Society: A Comparative Study of Artifacts Used in Social System Maintenance in the Santa Barbara Channel Region Before A.D. 1804.* Unpublished Ph.D. dissertation, Department of Anthropology, University of California, Davis.

Complex

"Complex" is a concept in culture-historical analysis that refers to arbitrary chronological subdivisions of artifact and feature forms, such as stone tool, pottery, house, and grave types, that can be used to define regional time-space sequences and to correlate sequences between regions. Stylistically sensitive complexes like pottery and projectile points are most often used in these analyses. In culture-historical interpretations, complexes are used to chronicle aspects of technological and cultural change and regional interrelationships.

Guy Gibbon

Component

Associated artifacts, debris, and features thought to represent one occupation unit at a site, with occupation unit variously interpreted as, among other things, phases of a settlement, a settlement no matter its duration or developmental history, or all parts of the archaeological record associated with a single archaeological culture. Sites with one occupation unit are single-component sites, those with more than one are multicomponent sites. Regional chronologies, settlement-subsistence systems, and other integrative frameworks are constructed by synthesizing components from different sites. Component is the smallest unit in the Midwestern Taxonomic system.

Guy Gibbon

Compound

Compounds are architectural forms that consist of clusters of rooms surrounded by enclosing walls. The rooms typically share contiguous walls, and the compound wall encloses both the rooms and an open area used as a "plaza" for extramural activities. The back walls of rooms frequently form one or more sides of the enclosing rectangle, with the remaining sides formed by freestanding walls. The compound differs from typical architectural forms in two major respects. First, plazas within pueblos are generally open areas surrounded by blocks of rooms, whereas plazas within compounds rarely have rooms on all sides. Second, pueblos lack enclosing walls, while compounds are completely surrounded by walls. Constructed of adobe, jacal, or masonry, compounds appear in the southwestern United States and northern Mexico after A.D. 900 (1050 years B.P.) and increase in frequency through time. They are particularly common in central and southern Arizona.

Patricia L. Crown

Further Readings

Haury, E. 1945. *The Excavation of Los Muertos and Neighboring Ruins in the Salt River Valley, Southern Arizona.* Papers, vol. 24, no. 1. Peabody Museum of American Archaeology and Ethnology, Harvard University, Cambridge.

Nabokov, P., and R. Easton. 1989. *Native American Architecture.* Oxford University Press, New York.

Nelson, B.A., and S.A. LeBlanc. 1986. *Short-Term Sedentism in the American Southwest: The Mimbres Valley Salado.* Maxwell Museum of Anthropology, Albuquerque.

See also ADOBE; HOHOKAM CULTURE AREA; JACAL; PITHOUSE; SALADO HORIZON

Copena

The term "Copena," derived from the first three letters of copper and the last three letters of galena, was coined in the 1930s as the name for a distinctive Middle Woodland burial complex. Found in the highland middle Tennessee Valley region of northern Alabama, the Copena complex displays a number of characteristics that link it with the Hopewell trade network centered in the Ohio Valley area between 100 B.C. and A.D. 400 (2050–1550 years B.P.). Most characteristic of the Copena complex are low, conical mounds that contain subfloor burial pits and secondary extended burials in the mound fill. Burials in natural-cave tombs are known, and at least one Copena ceremonial encampment, the Walling site, included a small, flat-top nonmortuary mound. The most typical offerings accompanying Copena burials are copper ornaments and celts, galena nodules up to 40 pounds in weight, marine-shell cups, steatite elbow pipes, and greenstone hoes and celts. A distinctive, recurvate, triangular stone biface, called the Copena point, has also been found at several of the more than 50 known mounds in the region.

John A. Walthall

Further Readings

Cole, G.G. 1981. *The Murphy Hill Site (1Ms300): The Structural Study of a Copena Mound and Comparative Review of the Copena Mortuary Complex.* Reports of Investigations no. 3. Office of Archaeological Research, University of Alabama, Tuscaloosa.

Walthall, J.A. 1979. Hopewell and the Southern Heartland. In *Hopewell Archaeology*, edited by D.S. Brose and N.M.B. Greber, pp. 200–208. Kent State University Press, Kent.

———. 1985. Early Hopewellian Ceremonial Encampments in the Southern Appalachian Highlands. In *Method and Process in Southeastern Archaeology*, edited by R.S. Dickens and H.T. Ward, pp. 243–262. University of Alabama Press, Tuscaloosa.

Copper

Archaeological interest in the sources of North American artifact copper centers on trade relations and network systems. If exchange networks are to be accurately modeled, positive identification of source areas is vital. North American copper technology began in preceramic times, most likely in the Upper Great Lakes region. In the middle 1800s, copper prospectors in the Lake Superior district observed mined pits in which stone hammers and vein copper were found. Indigenous cultures north of the Rio Grande did not melt or smelt copper or copper ores, nor did they cast copper. There is no evidence that they were able to fuse separate particles except by hammering and annealing to the desired shape.

Much of the copper was literally there for the taking. In some Alaskan and Lake Superior localities, copper nuggets covered large surface areas. Native copper is found in lode deposits, as rounded nuggets in river or lag deposits, and as nuggets in glacial till. Subject only to some surface alteration, native copper is nearly indestructible in the surface geologic environment. Although native copper forms in a diversity of geologic environments, most sources are mafic lavas—including extensive deposits in the Lake Superior region, along the Copper and White rivers in Alaska, on the Coppermine River in the Northwest Territories, and in Cap d'Or, Nova Scotia. The second most common source is the oxidized zone of copper-sulfide deposits in the west and southwest sections of the United States. Most native copper available at or near the surface in prehistoric North America came from mafic igneous rock.

Since 1975, the Archaeometry Laboratory at the University of Minnesota at Duluth has been involved in locating and trace-element "fingerprinting" North American native copper deposits. As of 1996, approximately 1,000 samples from these deposits had been analyzed by neutron-activation techniques to provide discrete chemical signatures for many of these deposits. The trace elements found to be useful discriminators are antimony, arsenic, cadmium, chromium, cobalt, europium, gold, indium, iridium, iron, mercury, molybdenum, nickel, scandium, selenium, silver, and zinc. Using multivariate discriminate procedures, analyzed copper artifacts often can be assigned to a source deposit.

George Rapp, Jr.

Further Readings

Drier, R.W., and O.J. Du Temple (editors). 1961. *Prehistoric Copper Mining in the*

Lake Superior Region: A Collection of Reference Articles. Privately printed. Calumet, Michigan; Hinsdale, Illinois.

Griffin, J.B. 1961. *Lake Superior Copper and the Indians.* Anthropological Papers no. 17. Museum of Anthropology, University of Michigan, Ann Arbor.

Rapp, G., Jr., J. Allert, and G. Peters. 1990. The Origins of Copper in Three Northern Minnesota Sites: Pauly, River Point, and Big Rice. In *The Woodland Tradition in the Western Great Lakes: Papers Presented to Elden Johnson,* edited by G. Gibbon, pp. 233–238. Publications in Anthropology no. 4. University of Minnesota, Minneapolis.

Rapp, G., Jr., E. Hendrickson, and J. Allert. 1990. Native Copper Sources of Artifact Copper in Pre-Colombian North America. In *Archaeological Geology of North America,* edited by N. Lasca and J. Donahue, pp. 479–498. Centennial Special Volume no. 4. Geological Society of America, Boulder. (This paper has an extensive bibliography.)

Cordilleran Ice Sheet

During the many cold periods of the Pleistocene (the last 2 million years or more) and especially in the Late Wisconsin, culminating ca. 18,000 B.C. (19,950 years B.P.), glaciers expanded or developed in the Canadian Rockies and coastal ranges until they filled the intermontane valleys, thereby producing the Cordilleran ice sheet. Lobes extended southward onto the Columbia Plateau and the lowlands of Washington. The expansion of the ice westward was inhibited by the deep waters of the Pacific coastal region. Expansion eastward beyond the base of the Rocky Mountains was limited by the precipitation shadow caused by the mountains and by the mass of the ice sheet itself. At the eastern piedmont of the Rocky Mountains, the ice was confluent with the western margin of the Laurentide ice sheet. When the two ice sheets retreated ca. 10,000 B.C. (11,950 years B.P.), the Alberta corridor was open to the immigration of plants, animals, and humans. The chronology of ice advance and retreat was probably roughly similar to that of the Laurentide ice sheet, although it differed somewhat from the pattern for the alpine glaciers of the Cascade Mountains of Washington, which were smaller and apparently reacted more quickly to climatic changes, retreating ca. 12,000 B.C. (13,950 years B.P.).

H.E. Wright, Jr.

Further Readings

Ruddiman, W.F., and H.E. Wright, Jr. (editors). 1987. *North America and Adjacent Oceans During the Last Deglaciation.* Geology of North America, vol. K-3. Geological Society of America, Boulder.

Core

The initial act in the manufacture of stone tools is the procurement of the stone from which the tool is to be made. This natural piece of rock is called a nodule or a cobble, depending on its origin and context. When the toolmaker removes a flake from that piece, the piece becomes a core. In a general sense, then, any piece of stone from which a flake has been removed is technically a core. However, this is not the sense in which most archaeologists use the term, and it is at this point that confusion clouds the picture.

Normal archaeological usage takes account of the fact that prehistoric people needed sharp tools for tasks such as cutting and scraping. The sharpest natural entity available for these purposes was siliceous stone, which could be knapped into flake tools. Prehistoric people, therefore, had great need for flakes, which they would produce from cores. This, then, is the sense in which most archaeologists employ the term—as a specific material entity created for the production of flakes. The act of specifically chipping tools for the purposes of shaping, blunting, or sharpening, but not for producing usable flakes, is called "retouch."

Potential for confusion also occurs with the "core tool," an implement fashioned by adroitly removing flakes from the periphery of the parent blank. In this case, the purpose of the activity was to shape the tool, not to create usable flakes. Core tools, which include Abbevillian choppers and Acheulean hand axes, are ancient, and they continue throughout human history up to the bifaces manufactured by Native Americans immediately before such implements were replaced by metal ones. Regarding the situation from an emic perspective, it is logical that stone-tool-using hunter-gatherers would find it advantageous, under certain conditions, to carry a biface for use as both a tool and a core from which flakes could be removed. That is, biface-thinning flakes are sharp and usable,

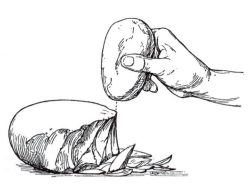

Core. (Reprinted from Smithsonian Institution, Bureau of American Ethnology, Bulletin 60, Figure 161)

and there is no reason that hunters on forays should not have sharpened their bifaces with the intention of also employing the resulting flakes for appropriate tasks (Kelly 1988). This situation, of course, blurs the functional distinctions between a core and a biface. From an archaeological perspective, the most reasonable solution to this dilemma is to define these entities using mechanical criteria; that is, the degree and kind of marginal shaping and edge angles (cores typically possess edges with angles more than 70°; bifaces, less than that).

Research involving cores has not played a major role in American archaeology, because prehistoric core technologies have been neither distinctive nor consistent in shape and size. Recently, however, core technologies have contributed to a reinterpretation of the development of sedentary lifestyles on the North American continent (Johnson and Morrow 1987, esp. the article by Parry and Kelly).

George H. Odell

Further Readings

Johnson, J.K., and C.A. Morrow (editors). 1987. *The Organization of Core Technology*. Westview Press, Boulder.

Kelly, R.L. 1988. The Three Sides of a Biface. *American Antiquity* 53:717–731.

Parry, W.J., and R.L. Kelly. 1987. Expedient Core Technology and Sedentism. In *The Organization of Core Technology*, edited by J.K. Johnson and C.A. Morrow, pp. 285–304. Westview Press, Boulder.

Corn

Corn (*Zea mays* ssp. *mays*) was the most important crop for most Late Prehistoric Native American farming societies in the Southwest, the Great Plains, the Great Lakes region, the Midwest, the Southeast, and the Northeast, and it was the single most important food for many of these groups. Because of its economic primacy then and now, a great deal of research has focused on the evolution of corn and corn-based agricultural systems. Although much is known, big questions remain unanswered. Major debates surround issues such as how domesticated corn evolved from teosinte (probably the subspecies *Zea mays* ssp. *parviglumis*), when and how gradually this process occurred, how and when corn spread from Mexico into various regions of North America, what the routes of dispersal were, and how rapidly corn was accepted and integrated into local economies.

Firm dates on Archaic-period corn and squash (*Cucurbita pepo* ssp. *pepo*) from sites in the U.S. Southwest indicate diffusion from western Mexico no later than 1200 B.C. (3150 years B.P.). Some experts argue for a northward expansion or migration of farming groups. Others believe seeds were passed from farmers to indigenous hunter-gatherers. Disagreement also exists between those who see little evidence for a radical initial impact of crops and those who think their arrival triggered a rapid transformation from foraging to farming. Settled farming communities did not exist earlier than A.D. 100 (1850 years B.P.) in either the Sonoran Desert (Hohokam region) or the Colorado Plateau (Anasazi region), but the tradition of Southwestern agriculture was under way from then on. Many other crops were valued, especially in the Hohokam region, but corn attained such a central role in religion and the economy that, for Pueblo societies, it is symbolized as Mother and Life itself. Ritual requirements associated with corn flour and perfect ears of corn with kernels of particular colors have aided the survival of traditional agriculture on the Colorado Plateau and in the Rio Grande Valley.

People in different subregions in the East accepted and intensified corn according to different schedules. Around the great ceremonial center of Cahokia in Illinois, corn was virtually absent (or below the level of archaeological visibility) before A.D. 750 (1200 years B.P.). It was intensified along with native crops between 800 and 1000, and it became the dominant product of a multicropping system that persisted until the demise of the American Bottom–area chiefdoms after 1250 (700 years B.P.). Corn did not become a major item in the Lower Mississippi Valley until after 1100 (850 years B.P.). It appears to have been the first cultigen there, possibly excluding gourds, that made a difference to already complex fisher-gatherer-hunter societies.

At Moundville in Alabama, corn agriculture rapidly intensified between 900 and 1050 (1050–900 years B.P.), just before the consolidation of chiefly power. A close temporal connection between agricultural intensification and the emergence of Mississippian chiefdoms has inspired scenarios pointing to either the plant or the elites as stimulating the rise of the other. Leaders' needs for surplus food served at feasts and other social exchanges may have been an important factor in the adoption and intensification of corn-based agriculture in the Southeast.

The transition from foraging to farming in much of the Northeast appears to have occurred swiftly ca. A.D. 1000 (950 years B.P.). The eight-row race of corn later known as Northern Flint dominated the Northeastern harvest and probably evolved in this region. The success of Iroquois agriculture as documented by early European observers and early ethnographers is a testament to the skills of the Indian women who farmed the fields and whose ancestors or neighbors bred the eight-row variety later used as one parent in commercial hybrids that made many non-Indian Americans prosperous.

Gayle Fritz

Further Readings

Doebley, J. 1990. Molecular Evidence and the Evolution of Maize. *Economic Botany* 44(3):6–27.

Johannessen, S., and C.A. Hastorf (editors). 1993. *Corn and Culture in the Prehistoric New World.* Westview Press, Boulder.

Scarry, C.M. (editor). 1993. *Foraging and Farming in the Eastern Woodlands.* University Press of Florida, Gainesville.

Wills, W.H. 1992. Plant Cultivation and the Evolution of Risk-Prone Economies in the Prehistoric American Southwest. In *Transitions to Agriculture in Prehistory,* edited by A.B. Gebauer and T.D. Price, pp. 153–176. Monographs in World Prehistory no. 4. Prehistory Press, Madison.

Corner-Notched Tradition

During the summer of 1948, test pits along the Yadkin River demonstrated for the first time that stratified alluvial sites of some antiquity existed in the Carolina Piedmont. The stratig-raphy at two of these sites, Lowder's Ferry and Doerschuk, allowed Joffre L. Coe to distinguish a sequence of Archaic complexes that was virtually unknown elsewhere in the Southeast and to make temporal sense of a "hodgepodge of projectile point types" previously known in the Piedmont from surface collections and shallow plow-zone deposits. Although both sites were deeply stratified, the earliest identified component dated only to the Middle Archaic period (ca. 6050–3050 B.C., or 8000–5000 years B.P.). A relatively undisturbed Early Archaic (ca. 7050–6050 B.C., or 9000–8000 years B.P.) sequence was found at yet another site first tested that summer, the Hardaway site located just upstream on the Yadkin River from Doerschuk and Lowder's Ferry. Somewhat paradoxically, it was neither deeply stratified nor located in the floodplain of the Yadkin, but on a hilltop high above the river. Nevertheless, the early sequence at Hardaway was eventually linked to Doerschuk and Lowder's Ferry. In 1964, Coe published *The Formative Cultures of the Carolina Piedmont,* which defined the Archaic sequence of the region on the basis of the stratigraphic sequences at these sites.

The recognition of a Corner-Notched tradition in the Southeast essentially began with the identification of two Early Archaic corner-notched-point types at Hardaway: Palmer and Kirk Corner-Notched. Subsequent work in the late 1960s by Betty J. Broyles (1971) at the St. Albans site in West Virginia and by Jefferson Chapman (1976, 1977) in Tennessee during the late 1970s confirmed the Early Archaic placement for the Corner-Notched tradition in the Southeast. Variously referred to as the "Kirk complex," "Kirk horizon," or "Kirk Corner-Notched cluster," the Corner-Notched tradition in the Southeast is stratigraphically preceded by side-notched points and followed by bifurcate points. Typically, the Corner-Notched tradition is marked by a small- to medium-sized point exhibiting small but deep U-shaped corner notches. Point bases are straight and sometimes ground. Blade shapes are roughly triangular, with straight to slightly excurvate blade margins that are commonly serrated and sometimes alternately beveled. While Kirk points are widely recognized as a cultural-historical type in the Southeast, local variants also exist, such as Palmer Corner-Notched in North Carolina, Charleston Corner-Notched in West Virginia, Lost Lake in Alabama, and Pine Tree in Mississippi.

The majority of radiocarbon dates for the Corner-Notched tradition come from the Little Tennessee River Valley and cluster between 7550 and 7050 B.C. (9500–9000 years B.P.). The Little Tennessee River sites also provide the best contexts for defining Corner-Notched–tradition assemblages. In addition to projectile points, a distinctive end-scraper form demonstrates continuity with earlier Dalton and fluted-point assemblages. Unifacially flaked and often highly formalized in shape, these small and probably hafted tools were used in hide working. Other less formalized tools that were used in a variety of scraping and cutting tasks include side scrapers, blade-like flakes, drills, *pièces esquilées*, and a variety of bifaces. Bifacially flaked and partially ground celts, apparently used as heavy-duty woodworking tools, are also present. The processing of plant foods has been inferred from the presence of cobble and other large stone tools used as grinding stones. Similar assemblages are represented in other Early Archaic contexts elsewhere in the Southeast. Although stone tools continue to be the focus of many assemblage studies, the remains of basketry and netting preserved as impressions in prepared clay hearths at several Little Tennessee River sites provide a tantalizing glimpse of a broader material assemblage.

Following the identification of tool use and the functional grouping of tool types, research since the 1970s has focused on the identification of Early Archaic site function and settlement patterns. In the Little Tennessee River Valley, for example, probable residential base camps were situated in bottom lands near food and stone sources. These base camps were occupied seasonally, as were smaller habitation or special-use sites elsewhere on the floodplain and in the uplands. For the South Atlantic Slope, David G. Anderson and Glen T. Hanson (1988) have proposed a regional model of Early Archaic settlement based on analyses of local and regional resource structure, theoretical arguments about the biocultural needs of hunter-gatherer populations, and evidence from the archaeological record along the Savannah River. They suggest that individual bands, which foraged within the large drainage systems along the south Atlantic, were part of a larger macroband unit that maintained viable mating networks. The regional (macroband) territory included watersheds that extended from the Ocmulgee drainage in Georgia to the Neuse drainage in North Carolina. Seasonal movement occurred along drainages between the Piedmont and the Coastal Plain. Residential base camps were located in the Coastal Plain during the winter, and short-term base camps were scattered across both regions during the remaining part of the year. The focus of settlement along river valleys is believed to be a result of the presumed distribution of food resources along the South Atlantic Slope. Furthermore, some cross-drainage movement occasionally took place when groups from adjacent watersheds would aggregate at lower Piedmont or upper Coastal Plain locations for social and economic reasons.

An alternative model proposed by I. Randolph Daniel, Jr. (1994), views Early Archaic settlement as conditioned less by the availability of food resources than by the limited occurrence of high-quality knappable stone. According to this model, Early Archaic settlement was tethered to two major stone resources along the South Atlantic Slope: extensive rhyolite outcrops in the Uwharrie Mountains along the eastern Piedmont of North Carolina, and Coastal Plain Allendale chert exposures along the Savannah River of South Carolina. As a result, prehistoric settlement mobility included regular cross-drainage movement. Evidence for this model is the high frequency of Early Archaic points made from both stone types and the great distances of these points from their sources. The archaeological pattern is a commonality in raw stone material both along and across drainages.

I. Randolph Daniel, Jr.

Further Readings

Anderson, D.G., and G.T. Hanson. 1988. Early Archaic Settlement in the Southeastern United States: A Case Study From the Savannah River. *American Antiquity* 53:262–286.

Broyles, B.J. 1971. *Second Preliminary Report: The St. Albans Site, Kanawha Valley.* Report of Archaeological Investigations no. 3. West Virginia Geological and Economic Survey, Morgantown.

Chapman, J. 1976. The Archaic Period in the Lower Little Tennessee River Valley: The Radiocarbon Dates. *Tennessee Anthropologist* 1:1–12.

———. 1977. *Archaic Period Research in the Lower Little Tennessee River Valley-1975, Icehouse Bottom, Thirty Acre Island, Calloway Island.* Report of Investigations no. 18. Department of Anthropology, University of Tennessee, Knoxville.

Coe, J.L. 1964. *The Formative Cultures of the Carolina Piedmont.* Transactions of the American Philosophical Society, vol. 54, no. 5. Philadelphia.

Daniel, I.R., Jr. 1994. *Hardaway Revisited: Early Archaic Settlement in the Southeast.* Unpublished Ph.D. dissertation, Department of Anthropology, University of North Carolina, Chapel Hill.

Crab Orchard

The term "Crab Orchard" refers to a regional Woodland-period ceramic tradition and/or to one or more archaeological cultures centered in extreme southern Illinois and adjacent portions of southwestern Indiana, western Kentucky, and southeastern Missouri. Crab Orchard was originally defined by M.S. Maxwell as a focus in the Midwestern Taxonomic system, based on his 1939–1941 work in the Big Muddy River drainage of southern Illinois. The type site, Sugar Camp Hill, was on Crab Orchard Creek. More recently, the term has been used as a regional expression for closely related cultures along the Lower Ohio (Baumer) and Lower Wabash and Little Wabash rivers. Crab Orchard is best known from work in the Big Muddy and Saline river valleys in interior southern Illinois. Crab Orchard groups existed in areas dominated by oak-hickory forests; they made little penetration into prairie-dominated landscapes to the north occupied by Havana-tradition peoples.

As a ceramic tradition, Crab Orchard extends from ca. 600 B.C. to A.D. 400 (2550–1550 years B.P.); it is the regional ceramic tradition in both the Early and Middle Woodland periods. As a relatively distinct regional expression, it is primarily Middle Woodland (100 B.C.–A.D. 400, or 2050–1550 years B.P.). Crab Orchard represents the northernmost extension of J.R. Caldwell's Middle Eastern ceramic tradition and, as such, exhibits general affinities to ceramic complexes to the south and east. Crab Orchard ceramics are easily distinguished from the Havana tradition. They are less readily distinguished from similar ceramic expressions in southeast Missouri (Tchula period) and western Kentucky (Long Branch/Birmingham). The early portion of the Crab Orchard sequence is not well known. Ceramics first appear in the southern Illinois area 700–600 B.C. (2650–2550 years B.P.), but they are not common on sites until ca. 300 B.C. (2250 years B.P.). The relationship between early Crab Orchard and neighboring Early Woodland complexes both north and south is not yet clear. Future work may define a separate Early Woodland unit in the region that is contemporaneous with expressions in the American Bottom and Lower Illinois Valley.

Crab Orchard ceramic vessels are typically deep conoidal to subconoidal forms with flat, flowerpotlike bases, grit or grit-clay temper mixtures, and cord- and fabric-marked (generally cord-wrapped, dowel-impressed) surfaces. Decoration, other than punched nodes, is rare. It usually consists of dowel lip notches and, occasionally, stamped or incised decorative elements derived from ceramics of the late Havana tradition. As a ceramic tradition, Crab Orchard is conservative; change is gradual, individual ceramic lots are highly variable, and reliable temporal markers are few. Individual occupations are often difficult to seriate on the basis of ceramics alone. The Crab Orchard sequence will eventually be divided into temporal phases; until then, most researchers separate components into gross early, middle, and late divisions. Recent attempts at finer divisions based on type-variety ceramic analysis (Moffat 1992) are of uncertain utility.

Chipped-stone-tool technology is biface dominated, with a variety of stemmed and notched projectile-point forms. Corner-notched/expanding-stem types are typical of the Middle Woodland portion of the sequence. Heavy woodworking tools (adzes, chisels, and heavy scrapers) are common, and small chert hoes are present. The lamellar or prismatic blade technology of the Havana tradition is poorly represented except at a small number of sites. Crab Orchard sites in the Mississippi drainage exhibit a distinctive biface-core technology based on the high-quality Cobden chert that occurs within the area. Cobden disk cores were widely traded northward; they are sometimes found on Havana-tradition sites.

The long temporal span of Crab Orchard complicates descriptions of subsistence and settlement patterns. Short-term camps and rock-shelter sites are abundant, but large base camps, intensively occupied settlements with midden accumulation and numerous pits, are fairly common along major streams or near large areas of riverine or aquatic resources. By Middle Woodland times, a significant proportion of the components seem to represent year-round occupations. Still, the overall impression is that the settlement system, at any one time, exhibited great variability in the size and duration of individual settlements. Storage pits are common on most sites. Identifiable architecture is rare. Lightly built wigwamlike structures were probably the norm, although a few more heavily built single-post structures, in a variety of shapes and sizes, have been found. Subsistence data indicate that Middle Woodland Crab Orchard groups practiced limited horticulture involving, primarily, chenopodium and maygrass with some knotweed, squash, and little barley, along with a variety of uncultivated seeds, nuts, and fruits. Nut resources appear to have remained important in the subsistence economy. Although the importance of cultivated plant foods increased through time, Crab Orchard groups apparently were always less dependent on cultivated foods than neighboring Havana-tradition peoples. Faunal remains indicate a pattern of faunal exploitation typical of most other groups in the southern Midwest and middle South.

Mortuary patterns are not well known. Other than a few enclaves along major rivers, such as Twenhafel on the Mississippi River and the Wilson Mounds on the Little Wabash, burial-mound construction and elaborate Middle Woodland burial ceremonialism with exotic trade goods are not characteristic of Crab Orchard. Most burials are simple inhumations within the settlement.

This picture of Crab Orchard as a conservative and rather unsophisticated Middle Woodland culture is based heavily on data from interior riverine drainages in southern Illinois (Hargrave and Stephens 1993). Large Crab Orchard sites exist in the Mississippi and Ohio River floodplains, but they are poorly known. Their study may greatly alter impressions of Crab Orchard subsistence, settlement, and mortuary patterns.

Brian M. Butler

Further Readings

Butler, B.M., and R.W. Jefferies. 1986. Crab Orchard and Early Woodland Cultures in the Middle South. In *Early Woodland Archaeology*, edited by K.B. Farnsworth and T.E. Emerson, pp. 523–534. Kampsville Seminars in Archaeology no. 2. Center for American Archaeology Press, Kampsville.

Caldwell, J.R. 1958. *Trend and Tradition in the Prehistory of the Eastern United States.* Memoir no. 88. American Anthropological Association, Washington, D.C.

Hargrave, M.L., and B.M. Butler. 1993. Crab Orchard Settlement Patterns and Residential Mobility. In *Highways to the Past, Essays on Illinois Archaeology in Honor of Charles J. Bareis*, edited by T. Emerson, A. Fortier, and D. McElrath. *Illinois Archaeology* 5:181–192.

Hargrave, M.L., and J.E. Stephens. 1993. Hopewell and Crab Orchard: The Middle Woodland Period in Southern Illinois. Paper presented at the Annual Midwestern Archaeological Conference, Milwaukee.

Maxwell, M.S. 1951. *The Woodland Cultures of Southern Illinois: Archaeological Investigations in the Carbondale Area.* Publications in Anthropology, Bulletin no. 7. Logan Museum, Beloit College, Beloit.

Moffat, C.R. 1992. Ceramic Analysis. In *The Little Muddy Rockshelter: A Deeply Stratified Prehistoric Site in the Southern Till Plains of Illinois*, edited by C.R. Moffat, pp. 139–278. Cultural Resources Management Report no. 186. American Resources Group, Carbondale.

Cressman, Luther Sheeleigh (1897–1994)

L.S. Cressman received his Ph.D. from Columbia University (1925) in sociology, with some anthropology classes from Franz Boas. In 1929, he was invited to the University of Oregon to develop courses in cultural anthropology, the first university anthropologist in the Northwest. Untrained in archaeology, he nevertheless responded and excavated when a burial ground was reported in southeastern Oregon in 1930. He next studied Oregon petroglyphs and then excavated caves in the northern Great Basin with the encouragement of John C. Merriam of the Carnegie Institution and the support of specialists in climate and geology. The latter work (Cressman et al. 1942) revised downward the cultural chronology of the Great Basin, which had previously been treated as a derivative of the Southwest, although general acceptance of this revision came only when the new radiocarbon method dated sandals from Fort Rock Cave in south-central Oregon at ca. 7050 B.C. (9000 years B.P.) (Cressman 1951). Moving to the edge of the Basin to study Klamath Indian prehistory (Cressman 1956), he became interested in coastal and river adaptations and shifted to the Columbia River. At Five Mile Rapids, he and his students produced a sequence suggesting occupation before 8050 B.C. (10,000 years B.P.) and a developed riverine adaptation almost as early (Cressman et al. 1960). His last field project was again in the Great Basin, where he and a student interpreted the evidence as indicating occupation in 11,050 B.C. (13,000 years B.P.). His final synthesis was published in 1977; an autobiography, in 1988. He was head of the Department of Anthropology at the University of Oregon from its founding in 1935 until his retirement in 1963. Cressman received honors from the University of Oregon, Pennsylvania State University (his undergraduate institution), and the Society for American Archaeology.

Don E. Dumond

Further Readings

Cressman, L.S. 1951. Western Prehistory in the Light of Carbon-14 Dating. *Southwestern Journal of Anthropology* 7:289–313.
———. 1956. *Klamath Prehistory: The Prehistory of the Culture of the Klamath Lake Area.* Transactions, n.s., vol. 46, no. 4. American Philosophical Society, Philadelphia.
———. 1977. *Prehistory of the Far West: Homes of Vanished Peoples.* University of Utah Press, Salt Lake City.
———. 1988. *A Golden Journey.* University of Utah Press, Salt Lake City.
Cressman, L.S., F.C. Baker, H.P. Hansen, P. Conger, and R.F. Heizer. 1942. *Archaeological Researches in the Northern Great Basin.* Publication no. 538. Carnegie Institution of Washington, Washington, D.C.
Cressman, L.S., D.L. Cole, W.A. Davis, T.M. Newman, and D.J. Scheans. 1960. *Cultural Sequences at The Dalles, Oregon: A Contribution to Northwest Prehistory.* Transactions, n.s., vol. 50, no. 10. American Philosophical Society, Philadelphia.

Crow Creek Site

Located along the Missouri River in central South Dakota, the Crow Creek village (39BF11) is a National Historical Landmark site with two prehistoric components. The earlier, labeled Crow Creek, is an Initial Middle Missouri variant–occupation dating to ca. A.D. 1100 (850 years B.P.); the later, Wolf Creek, is an Initial Coalescent variant–component dating to ca. A.D. 1325 (625 years B.P.). A bastioned, deep fortification ditch nearly 400 m (1,312 feet) long is visible on the surface. It protected the more than 50 earthlodges that constituted the Initial Coalescent village. In 1954–1955, the Nebraska State Historical Society excavated lodges of both components and tested the fortification ditch. Excavations in 1978 by the University of South Dakota unearthed the remains of nearly 500 people who had been killed in a massacre. Many had been scalped and mutilated. Their partly decomposed bodies were thrown into a mass grave near one end of the fortification ditch and covered with a thin layer of soil. Radiocarbon dates and pottery firmly link the massacre to the Initial Coalescent component. Causes and perpetrators of the massacre are unknown. Possible explanations of the massacre include competition from upstream Middle Missouri peoples, unknown nomadic groups, and internecine warfare between Initial Coalescent villages. Evidences of nutritional stress in the skeletons suggest that malnutrition was a contributory factor, with competition between

Crow Creek bone bed. (Photograph by L. J. Zimmerman)

Initial Coalescent villages over garden space a feasible cause of warfare. The site is the largest prehistoric massacre known in the Americas and has challenged archaeological understandings of prehistoric Plains Indian warfare.

Larry J. Zimmerman

Further Readings

Kivett, M.F., and R. Jensen. 1976. *Archeological Investigations at the Crow Creek Site (39BF11)*. Publications in Anthropology no. 7. Nebraska State Historical Society, Lincoln.

Willey, P.J. 1990. *Prehistoric Warfare on the Great Plains: Skeletal Analysis of the Crow Creek Massacre Victims*. Garland, New York.

Zimmerman, L.J., and R.G. Whitten. 1980. Mass Grave at Crow Creek in South Dakota Reveals How Indians Massacred Indians in 14th Century Attack. *Smithsonian* 11(6):100–109.

Zimmerman, L.J. (editor). 1981. *The Crow Creek Site Massacre: A Preliminary Report*. U.S. Army Corps of Engineers, Omaha District, Omaha.

Crowfield Cultural Complex

The Crowfield complex or, as some prefer, phase is named after the type site located in southwestern Ontario. The Crowfield site is a small campsite or way station, which, besides a small amount of unheated normal occupation debris, included a large cache of heat-fractured artifacts interpreted as grave goods associated with a decayed cremation burial. Crowfield-complex material has been reported within an area that extends from eastern Michigan, southern Ontario, and northern Ohio eastward to western and southern New England. Besides the Crowfield site itself, and several isolated finds of diagnostic fluted stone projectile tips, other known sites with Crowfield-complex components include the Bolton, Zander, and Hussey sites in Ontario, the Reagan site in Vermont, and the Plenge site in New Jersey. All of these components seem to represent relatively small campsites; the spatially extensive, multilocus sites characteristic of other suggested northeastern Early Paleoindian complexes, such as the Gainey and Parkhill complexes or phases, have yet to be reported. Moreover, in the Great Lakes region, Crowfield-complex sites do not seem to be as strongly associated with the strandlines of

pro-glacial lakes as are other Early Paleoindian materials. A reliance on more local stone materials has been used to suggest a relatively reduced settlement mobility versus some other, and presumably earlier, Paleoindian complexes.

Although the type-site materials are predominantly from a probable grave cache, the evidences of resharpening and recycling of tools in the cache, combined with the fact that subsequently reported sites seem to be strictly occupation or resource-exploitation sites, demonstrate that the diagnostic Crowfield artifacts do not represent specially made grave goods or items intended solely for ceremonial use. The most characteristic Crowfield-complex artifacts are fluted stone projectile points (see Figure). Distinctive aspects of these points include: a very thin cross section (less than 5 mm, or 0.2 inches, thick); shallow basal concavities (ca. 2–3 mm, or 0.08–0.1 inches); narrow bases (less than 20 mm, or 0.8 inches); lateral edges that markedly expand from the base toward a point of maximum width at or above midpoint; often multiple, but still well-executed, fluting, especially considering the thinness of the points; a lack of fishtails; and an overall pentagonal or "pumpkinseed" outline. A characteristic of a small percentage of Crowfield points, and one that makes them unique among reported varieties of fluted points, is the presence of a shoulder and more extensive edge resharpening on one lateral edge than is normally found on fluted points. These latter items resemble Cody knives of the Late Paleoindian Cody complex of western North America. Like them, the shouldered Crowfield items seem to represent a specialized form of hafted knife rather than a projectile head. The remainder of the Crowfield-complex toolkit is comparable to that seen on other Paleoindian sites. Included are such pan-Paleoindian items as trianguloid end scrapers, concave side scrapers, beaks, and gravers or micropiercers. However, other items often considered typical of northeastern Paleoindian assemblages, such as *pièces esquillées*, seem to be lacking from the Crowfield complex. The Crowfield site itself has also yielded a distinctive form of small ovoid biface with one thickened and somewhat narrowed end ("leaf-shaped bifaces") that to date (1996) has not been reported from other suggested northeastern fluted-point-complex sites.

There are no radiocarbon dates available for Crowfield-complex sites. However, of all of the varieties of fluted points reported from the Northeast, Crowfield points most closely resemble subsequent Late Paleoindian unfluted points, in particular points reported from such sites as Holcombe in Michigan. On this basis, the Crowfield complex is believed to represent the most recent, or terminal, Early Paleoindian manifestation in the eastern Great Lakes/western New England area; it is guess dated to ca. 8550–8350 B.C. (10,500–10,300 years B.P.).

Christopher Ellis
D. Brian Deller

Diagnostic Crowfield complex/phase fluted bifaces from sites in Ontario (a, c, d: fluted points, Crowfield site; b: single shouldered fluted point, Crowfield site; e: single shouldered fluted preform, Bolton site; f: fluted point, Rice site. Arrows show locations of shoulders. (Illustration by C. Ellis)

Further Readings

Deller, D.B., and C.J. Ellis. 1984. Crowfield: A Preliminary Report on a Probable Paleo-Indian Cremation in Southwestern Ontario. *Archaeology of Eastern North America* 12:41–71.

———. 1988. Early Paleo-Indian Complexes in Southwestern Ontario. In *Late Pleistocene and Early Holocene Paleoecology and Archaeology of the Eastern Great Lakes Region*, edited by R.S. Laub, N.G. Miller, and D.W. Steadman, pp. 251–263. Bulletin, vol. 33. Buffalo Society of Natural Sciences, Buffalo.

———. 1992. Excavation at the Bolton Site: An Early Paleo-Indian Crowfield Phase Site in Southwestern Ontario. *Current Research in the Pleistocene* 9:4–7.

Ritchie, W.A. 1953. A Probable Paleo-Indian Site in Vermont. *American Antiquity* 18:249–258.

Stewart, A.L. 1984. The Zander Site: Paleo-Indian Occupation of the Southern Holland Marsh Region of Ontario. *Ontario Archaeology* 42:45–79.

Storck, P.L. 1979. *A Report on the Banting and Hussey Sites: Two Paleo-Indian Campsites in Simcoe County, Southern Ontario*. Mercury Series Paper no. 93. Archaeological Survey of Canada, National Museum of Man, Ottawa.

See also CROWFIELD SITE

Crowfield Site

The Crowfield Early Paleoindian site (AfHj-31) is located in the Sydenham River drainage, just southwest of the city of London, Ontario. It is the type site of what has come to be called the Crowfield complex or phase in the eastern Great Lakes region. The site, which is estimated to date to ca. 8350 B.C. (10,300 years B.P.) on typological grounds, is in a cultivated field and covers ca. 250 m² (299 square yards) of which ca. 208 m² (249 square yards) were excavated in 1981 and 1982. The site yielded a small amount of unheated stone-flaking debris, fluted and unfluted preforms broken in manufacture, and exhausted, discarded tools typical of several other known small Paleoindian campsites or way stations in the Great Lakes area. However, and atypically, the excavations also uncovered the remains of at least one plow-truncated circular feature ca. 150 cm (58.5 inches) in diameter that extended ca. 20 cm (7.8 inches) into the subsoil below the plow zone. Excavation of the subsoil feature remnant, as well as plottings of the density of items in the plow zone and refitting of recovered artifact fragments, revealed that the feature contained more than 175 heat-shattered Paleoindian stone artifacts, including more than 29 fluted points and preforms characterized by multiple fluting, shallow basal concavities, very thin cross sections, and, in a few cases, a distinct shoulder on one edge (see CROWFIELD CULTURAL COMPLEX entry illustration). Also included were a minimum 40 unfluted preforms; 14 stone biface "knives" with a flat backing for hafting or holding the tools along one side edge; 35 unifaces dominated by side scrapers with concave edges but also including beaked tools and a single graver or micropiercer; 40 large flakes that presumably are blanks for unifacial tools; and several miscellaneous items, including two or more "drills," two large biface "knives" resharpened by the alternate edge-beveling of their foresection edges, and at least two tools, possibly hammerstones or abraders, on nonsiliceous materials. Notable by their absence are such common Paleoindian tool forms as trianguloid end scrapers. The heat-shattered tools, preforms, and blanks on siliceous materials are largely of Onondaga chert from bedrock outcrops ca. 100 km (60 miles) southeast of the site. A small number of items are made from Fossil Hill chert, whose source is 200 km (120 miles) northeast of Crowfield.

Analyses of the feature artifacts indicate that few, if any, were discarded because of breakage in manufacture or use. Unlike the situation on the vast majority of campsites where fluted-point basal sections predominate, the feature contained only complete points. The lack of definitive chert wastage in the feature, the large amount of material recovered from a single feature, which is unheard of on sites of this age, and the fact the material seems to have been deliberately burned led the investigators to suggest that the pit is a ceremonial feature—most likely a Paleoindian cremation, the osteological remains of which decayed during 10,000 years of exposure to the site's acidic soils. Given that the artifacts in the feature were not specially made grave goods, as indicated by the resharpening of tool edges dulled by use and by the recycling of some items, it is even possible that the assemblage represents an individual's functioning toolkit.

Christopher Ellis

Further Readings

Deller, D.B. 1988. *The Paleo-Indian Occupation of Southwestern Ontario: Distribution, Technology and Social Organization.* Unpublished Ph.D. dissertation, Department of Anthropology, McGill University, Montreal.

Deller, D.B., and C.J. Ellis. 1984. Crowfield: A Preliminary Report on a Probable Paleo-Indian Cremation in Southwestern Ontario. *Archaeology of Eastern North America* 12:41–71.

Ellis, C.J. 1984. *Paleo-Indian Lithic Technological Structure and Organization in the Lower Great Lakes Area: A First Approximation.* Unpublished Ph.D. dissertation, Department of Archaeology, Simon Fraser University, Burnaby.

Ellis, C.J., and D.B. Deller. 1990. Paleo-Indians. In *The Archaeology of Southern Ontario to A.D. 1650,* edited by C.J. Ellis and N. Ferris, pp. 37–63. Occasional Publications no. 5. London [Ontario] Chapter, Ontario Archaeological Society, London.

See also CROWFIELD CULTURAL COMPLEX

Crystal River Site

Crystal River (8CII) is a famous mound-and-midden complex on the bank of a spring-fed river more than 7 km (4 miles) from the Gulf of Mexico in west Citrus County, Florida. It covers an estimated 5.7 ha (14 acres) and includes at least two temple mounds; two shell mounds that are part of a long, irregularly shaped shell-midden ridge; two burial mounds, the larger one of which has a surrounding platform enclosed by a circular embankment; and a large habitation area that includes other shell middens. Inhabited from at least Middle Woodland through Mississippian times (ca. A.D. 200–1400, or 1750–550 years B.P.), the site has produced spectacular evidence of burial-mound ceremonialism and interaction with similar mortuary systems in the Midwest and in other parts of the Southeast. Famous early southeastern investigator C.B. Moore dug in the large burial mound three times between 1903 and 1918. Florida archaeologist Ripley Bullen and others continued investigations from 1951 onward. Bullen interpreted two large limestones with crude incised lines (with one set resembling a face and upper body) as "stelae" with astronomical alignments.

The major occupation of the site is charac-

Stele I at the Crystal River site, Citrus County, Florida. The stele is in a metal cage for protection. (Photograph by N. M. White)

Midden Mound "K," Crystal River site, Citrus County, Florida, view facing the southwest. (Photograph by N. M. White)

terized by Swift Creek–early Weeden Island ceremonial ceramics and other exotic artifacts associated with ca. 600 burials that consist of primary, bundle, and single skull interments. Stone artifacts include chert points (some of which are ceremonially broken), knives, and hammers; ground-stone hammers, celts, cigar-shaped stones, and bar amulets; and imitation animal teeth, sheet mica, beads, pendants, and plummets. Among the stone raw materials are quartz crystal, banded slate, catlinite, and limestone. Shell artifacts include chisels, gouges, basally perforated cups, hammers, discs, beads, and gorgets of various shapes, including a rosette (scalloped circle). Other unusual specimens of animal origin are turtle shells, stingray-spine points, canine teeth, cut panther and other jaws, modern and fossil shark teeth, bone points, and a bone fishhook. Abundant copper artifacts include panpipes, plummets, ear spools sometimes plated with silver or meteoric iron (with one inset with pearls), embossed sheets or tablets, and beads. Also present is a lump of bitumen; bitumen coats some shell and stone plummets, probably as an adhesive.

Pipes of clay, limestone, and soapstone are of the elbow, tube, and monitor, or platform, type. Platform pipes are clear evidence of con-nections with contemporaneous Hopewellian burial mounds in Ohio and other areas to the North. Pottery of unusual shapes and with zoned red and negative painting, tetrapodal supports, complicated stamps, incising, and elaborately modeled decoration further mark Crystal River's important position as the most southerly node within the Hopewellian and, more broadly, the Middle Woodland interaction system. However, this evidence is not thought to indicate population movements or the acceptance of a foreign burial cult. Rather, the local, economically diffuse hunter-gatherer and probably incipient horticulturalist population may have been intensifying and expanding their external contacts as their densities grew and their egalitarian pattern of organization gave way to a more elaborately ranked one.

It is unknown whether occupation of the site persisted through the Late Woodland. There is somewhat better evidence of use during Late Prehistoric times by Safety Harbor people, who had a peninsular Gulf Coastal variant of Mississippian culture. Though some of the site has been destroyed, Crystal River is a state park with a small museum and recreation area, located 97 km (60 miles) north of Tampa.

Nancy Marie White

Further Readings

Brose, D.S. 1979. An Interpretation of the Hopewellian Traits in Florida. In *Hopewell Archaeology: The Chillicothe Conference*, edited by D. Brose and N. Greber, pp. 141–149. Kent State University Press, Kent.

Milanich, J.T. 1994. *Archaeology of Precolumbian Florida*. University Press of Florida, Gainesville.

Weisman, B.R. 1995. *Crystal River: A Ceremonial Mound Center on the Florida Gulf Coast*. Florida Archaeology no. 8. Florida Bureau of Archaeological Research, Tallahassee.

Cultural Resource Management

Cultural Resource Management (CRM) involves the identification, protection, and interpretation of archaeological sites, historic structures, and other elements of cultural heritage through survey, evaluation, and treatment strategies. CRM is often used synonymously with "historical preservation," although CRM refers to a more systematic approach incorporating long-range planning. In the United States, archaeological-site management began in the Southwest in the late nineteenth century with attempts to protect pueblo ruins. The first florescence of CRM was associated with Depression-era employment programs in the 1930s. A second expansion occurred in the post–World War II period associated with the "salvage" of archaeological sites during reservoir construction.

A more comprehensive CRM approach appeared in the early 1970s following the passage of a series of federal laws. These laws were adopted as a result of public recognition that cultural resources are important elements of the environment and that the significance of such resources should be judged at the local as well as the federal level. The most important law was the Historic Preservation Act of 1966, which established the National Register of Historic Places (NRHP), gave states a key role in CRM with the appointment of State Historic Preservation Officers (SHPOs), and required all federal agencies not only to consider the effects of their undertakings on cultural resources but to survey federal lands to identify such resources. The National Park Service (NPS) has gradually become the leading federal agency in CRM, providing interagency services, coordinating SHPO activity, and directing the NRHP. State and local governments have also taken some CRM responsibilities, but their level of participation varies greatly.

Since the widespread establishment of CRM in the 1970s, the practice of archaeology in the United States has been greatly altered. Prior to 1970, most archaeologists were affiliated with universities or museums, and most archaeological activities focused on education and research. Nearly 30 years later, most archaeologists are employed by government agencies or private contracting firms where emphasis is on fulfilling agency responsibilities or contract obligations. The massive influx of funding since the 1970s has greatly increased employment, expanded site inventories, promoted a large number of excavations, and provided for the widespread availability of scientific procedures, such as radiocarbon dating. Many sites have been saved from destruction.

The effects of CRM archaeology have not all been positive. The scope of research has been somewhat narrowed by a necessary focus on particular land parcels and management needs rather than broad research questions. Emphasis on preservation rather than data recovery (salvage) has saved some sites from publicly sponsored destruction only to see them destroyed by associated private development. Strict interpretation of preservation has even encouraged a "hands off" mentality in some land managers about site excavation, although data gathering is a critical archaeological function. Most of all, little CRM archaeology has been adequately published, leading to accusations of mismanagement and unscholarly conduct.

Issues in CRM archaeology in the mid-1990s include significance evaluation (how to establish which sites are worth saving), incorporating Native American perspectives, refining methods of site protection to reduce the damage done by erosion and vandalism, and providing better training for CRM professionals. A broader definition of archaeological resources is also being recognized, leading to expanded attention to urban, industrial, and shipwreck archaeology.

Scott F. Anfinson

Further Readings

Fowler, D. 1982. Cultural Resource Management. In *Advances in Archaeological Method and Theory* 5:1–50. Academic Press, New York.

King, T. 1987. Prehistory and Beyond: The Place of Archaeology. In *The American*

Mosaic: Preserving a Nation's Heritage, edited by R. Stipe and A. Lee, pp. 236–264. United States Committee/International Council on Monuments and Sites, Washington, D.C.

Knudson, R. 1986. Contemporary Cultural Resource Management. In *American Archaeology Past and Future,* edited by D. Meltzer, D. Fowler, and J. Sabloff, pp. 395–413. Smithsonian Institution Press, Washington, D.C.

McGimsey, C., and H. Davis (editors). 1977. *The Management of Archaeological Resources: The Airlie House Report.* Special Publication. Society for American Archaeology, Washington, D.C.

Schiffer, M., and G. Gumerman (editors). 1977. *Conservation Archaeology: A Guide for Cultural Resource Management Studies.* Academic Press, New York.

Culture Areas

Culture areas are large-scale spatial units defined in principle by a commonality of cultural and environmental attributes. In archaeology, culture areas generally coincide with natural physiographic zones and with the broad ethnographic culture areas identified by early anthropologists. The traditional culture areas of North America are the Arctic, the Subarctic, the Great Plains, the Northeast, the Southeast, California, the Great Basin, the Southwest, the Northwest Coast, and the Plateau. The concept was pioneered in North America late in the nineteenth century by ethnologists who were attempting to organize cultural similarities and differences in terms other than hypothetical evolutionary sequences. The first detailed ethnographic treatment of the culture areas of North America was published by Otis Mason in 1896, and, soon after, Clark Wissler (1914) used the concept as an aid in organizing North American ethnographic collections for display at the American Museum of Natural History in New York City. The concept eventually became a conceptual unit of synthesis within the cultural-historical approach, although broad "culture characterization areas" had been used earlier by William Henry Holmes. Archaeological culture areas are much larger spatial units than archaeological regions and have less integrity than ethnographic culture areas because of the changing boundaries of archaeological cultures through time. Archaeologists working within a culture

area usually share common terminology, concepts, and research concerns, and many regional syntheses and annual conferences occur for this level of organization.

Guy Gibbon

Further Readings

Fagan, B.M. 1991. *Ancient North America.* Thames and Hudson, New York.

Holmes, W.H. 1914. Areas of American Culture Characterization Tentatively Outlined As an Aid in the Study of the Classic Maya Collapse. *American Anthropologist* 16(3):413–446.

Mason, O.T. 1896. Influence of Environment Upon Human Industries and Arts. *Annual Report of the Smithsonian Institution for 1895,* pp. 639–665. Washington, D.C.

Wissler, C. 1914. Material Cultures of the North American Indians. *American Anthropologist* 16:447–505.

Cumberland Cultural Complex

The Cumberland cultural complex is restricted to the midwestern and midsouthern United States. Although there are no unequivocal chronometric dates for the Cumberland complex, it is thought to postdate the Clovis complex (ca. 9550–9250 B.C., or 11,500–11,200 years B.P.), a period of rapid environmental change. The Cumberland complex shares several traits with pan-North American Clovis sites, including fluted bifaces, flake tools, end scrapers, side scrapers, and gravers. The Cumberland cultural complex is thought to derive from the Clovis complex because of these shared traits. The only artifact that is unique to the Cumberland complex is a biface known as the Cumberland point. Stylistically and technologically, Cumberland points resemble Folsom points from the Plains and Southwest as well as Barnes points from the Great Lakes and Northeast. Like Folsom and Barnes, Cumberland points display a single basal-thinning flake, or flute, that extends to the tip of the biface. Morphologically, Cumberland points are long, narrow, recurvate lanceolates with a pronounced constriction in the haft element just above the base that creates a fish-tailed appearance. The basal and lateral edges of the haft element are heavily ground. Cumberland points have been recovered almost exclusively from open habitations and rock shelters on terraces and in upland settings. The

Cumberland cultural complex is thought to be associated with foragers that began to settle in the landscape during the Pleistocene-Holocene transition (ca. 8550–7550 B.C., or 10,500–9500 years B.P.). Additional temporal, ecological, and economic aspects of the Cumberland complex are yet to be discovered.

Kenneth B. Tankersley

Further Readings

Lewis, T.N. 1954. The Cumberland Point. *Bulletin of the Oklahoma Archaeological Society* 11:7–8.

Tankersley, K.B., and B.L. Isaac (editors). 1990. *Early Paleo-Indian Economies of Eastern North America*. Research in Economic Anthropology Supplement no. 5. JAI Press, Greenwich.

Curtis, Freddie (1913–1996)

Freddie Curtis was an important early excavator of prehistoric sites in coastal southern California. She was a leading member of one of California's most significant amateur, or avocational, archaeological societies, the Archaeological Survey Association (ASA) of Los Angeles. Although the ASA included some academic and professional members, such as William J. Wallace, most members were, like Curtis, devotees who conducted research at professional levels of competence and contributed to the growth of archaeological knowledge through publication. Curtis is particularly notable for two projects. In the 1950s, she directed excavations at the Arroyo Sequit site, a Late Prehistoric occupation site on the Los Angeles County coast near the Ventura County border. This project joined the ASA with the Los Angeles Museum of Natural History, the Southwest Museum in Los Angeles, and the UCLA Archaeological Survey. Curtis's monograph on Arroyo Sequit (Curtis 1959) has become a standard reference for southern California archaeology. During the 1960s, along with Roger C. Owen and Donald S. Miller (Owen et al. 1964), she undertook excavations at a much older site in the Santa Barbara area, the Glen Annie site. Curtis subsequently undertook an analysis of evidence in that region for sedentary village life during the Middle Archaic period (Curtis 1965). Although later analyses have not fully supported her, she directed scholars to reconsider their entire basis for interpreting early cultural patterns and paved the way for substantial rethinking of the nature of Archaic society and culture (e.g., Erlandson and Colton 1991).

Joseph L. Chartkoff

Further Readings

Curtis, F. 1959. *Arroyo Sequit: Archaeological Investigations of a Late Coastal Site in Los Angeles County, California*. Papers no. 4. Archaeological Survey Association, Los Angeles.

———. 1965. The Glen Annie Site (SBa-142): A Case for Sedentary Village Life. *Archaeological Survey Annual Report* 7:1–18. University of California, Los Angeles.

Erlandson, J.M., and R.H. Colton. 1991. *Hunter-Gatherers of Early Holocene Coastal California*. Perspectives in California Archaeology no. 1. Institute of Archaeology, University of California, Los Angeles.

Owen, R.C., F. Curtis, and D.S. Miller. 1964. The Glen Annie Canyon Site, SBa-142, an Early Horizon Coastal Site of Santa Barbara County. *Archaeological Survey Annual Report* 6:431–520. University of California, Los Angeles.

Cushing, Frank H. (1857–1900)

A Smithsonian Institution anthropologist and leader of the privately sponsored Hemenway Expedition, Frank H. Cushing arrived at Zuni pueblo in west-central New Mexico in 1879 on a brief excursion and stayed for four and a half years. Primarily an ethnographer, he learned to speak the Zuni dialect fluently and was a pioneer of participant observation in anthropology, becoming famous for his descriptions of Zuni life. Cushing was also a pioneer of the direct historical approach to the interpretation of archaeological data, arguing that how prehistoric artifacts had been made and used could best be determined by comparing them with items of similar appearance made by their presumed makers' descendents among living Indians; that is, by working back from the present to the past. The argument was predicated on the assumption current in the late nineteenth century that there was no significant difference between life in historic and prehistoric pueblos. Although the assumption was false, it did have the effect of bringing archaeologists into close contact with ethnographers and native peoples. In 1896, Cushing dug into the muck of Key Marco in southwestern Florida, recovering a spectacular collection of preserved wooden artifacts.

Guy Gibbon

Further Readings

Cushing, F.H. 1886. A Study of Pueblo Pottery As Illustrative of Zuni Culture Growth. *Fourth Annual Report of the Bureau of American Ethnology*, pp. 467–521. Smithsonian Institution, Washington, D.C.

Mark, J. 1980. *Four Anthropologists: An American Science in Its Early Years.* Science History, New York.

Custer Phase

Originally defined as a focus, the Custer phase dates from A.D. 800 to 1250 (1150–700 years B.P.). Located in west-central Oklahoma, sites occur along portions of the North Fork of the Red River, as well as portions of the Canadian and the Washita rivers. The Custer phase likely developed in situ from Woodland-period societies, especially the Pruitt complex, and was ancestral to the Washita River phase.

Settlements consist of hamlets, camps, and shelters. Hamlets seem to involve only a few houses, but excavations have been few and limited. Houses are rectangular in outline, constructed of wattle and daub, with a grass roof. Subsistence was based on hunting, gathering, and horticulture. Corn was grown and possibly beans and squash, although neither has been identified. The role of horticulture may have been limited, especially in western sites. A variety of wild plants and nuts were collected. While both deer and bison were hunted, deer seems to have been the more important resource. A variety of small mammals, turtles, birds, and fish were also eaten. Ceramics are globular shaped and most commonly cord marked, although some vessels have plain surfaces. Decoration, which is rare, includes applique and punctates as well as notching on lips. Temper is primarily coarse grit. Bone artifacts include tips of bison-tibia digging sticks, split-bone awls, arrow-shaft straighteners, and beads. Stone tools include small corner-notched points, triangular side-notched points, end scrapers, and expanding-base and plain-shafted drills. Evidence for trade is limited. There are small amounts of Florence-A chert from north-central Oklahoma, marine shell probably from the Gulf, and Arkansas River Valley Caddo pottery, although the latter could be a local imitation.

Susan C. Vehik

Further Readings

Drass, R.R., and P. Flynn. 1990. Temporal and Geographic Variations in Subsistence Practices for Plains Villagers in the Southern Plains. *Plains Anthropologist* 35:175–190.

Drass, R.R., and M.C. Moore. 1987. The Linville II Site (34RM492) and Plains Village Manifestations in the Mixed Grass Prairie. *Plains Anthropologist* 32:404–418.

Hofman, J.L. 1984. The Plains Villagers: The Custer Phase. In *Prehistory of Oklahoma*, edited by R.E. Bell, pp. 287–305. Academic Press, Orlando.

C.W. Harris Site

The C.W. Harris site (CASDi149), located on the banks of the San Dieguito River ca. 32 km (20 miles) north of San Diego and 24 km (15 miles) inland, is the type site for the Early Archaic San Dieguito tradition of southern California. Malcolm J. Rogers of the San Diego Museum of Man recorded the site in 1928 and excavated there 10 years later (Rogers 1938, 1966). The UCLA Archaeological Survey conducted additional investigations in the early 1960s (Warren and True 1961; Warren 1967).

The Harris site yielded three phases of occupation in an environment that gave inhabitants access to a variety of riverine, grassland, and chaparral habitats. The earliest phase, which Rogers termed "San Dieguito" after the river, has been dated to 8050–6050 B.C. (10,000–8,000 years B.P.) with ^{14}C assays of 6450 B.C. ± 400, 6540 B.C. ± 400, and 7080 B.C. ± 350 (8400, 8490, and 9030 years B.P.) (Warren 1967). Its distinctive assemblage has relatively few tool types. Among them are a series of elongated, bifacially retouched points or knives; a variety of heavy scrapers rendered on thick primary flakes and cores; and some choppers and cleavers. The bifaces include some that are termed points, blanks, or crescentics (Warren and True 1961:252). The assemblage resembles those of the Lake Mohave complex of the same age, but the latter assemblages are found along the shorelines of former inland Pleistocene lakes. Though found near the ocean, the San Dieguito material at the Harris site lacks evidence that either aquatic or hard-seed resources were utilized.

The subsequent occupation at the Harris site reflects the next stage of cultural development in coastal southwestern California, termed "La Jolla" by Rogers. La Jolla represents the local equivalent of Middle to Late Archaic adaptations. Cumulative dates place La Jolla between ca. 6050 and 1050 B.C. (8000–3000 years B.P.) A ^{14}C determination of 4350 B.C. ± 240 (6300 years B.P.) from the Harris site places it in the early part of this sequence (Warren 1967, 1968). Numbers of manos and millstones are found in the La Jolla assemblage, reflecting the systematic exploitation of hard-seed resources. Retouched cobble-core tools also are abundant. La Jolla sites closer to the coast also reflect the exploitation of shellfish, while two La Jolla sites in Orange County have yielded a remarkable early ceramic tradition of fired-clay vessels and effigies. La Jolla sites, though not the Harris site, also often yield remarkable ground-stone disks and cogged disks, or cogstones.

La Jolla sites as a whole indicate a direct evolution into the precursors of the historically or ethnographically known peoples of the region, Ipai and Tipai speakers belonging to the Hokan language family. This suggests that Hokan-speaking peoples had occupied the region for millennia. At the Harris site, a stratigraphic break separates the La Jolla materials, which might represent early Hokan settlers, from the Protohistoric component, called "Yuman" by Claude N. Warren and Delbert L. True (1961). The Yuman component continues the production of millstones and adds the mortar and pestle. Its small projectile points are generally thought to reflect the introduction of the bow and arrow. A ceramic industry, the undecorated Tizon Brown ware, is represented, as are varieties of ornaments of shell and steatite (soapstone). This Yuman pattern is more fully described as the San Luis Rey tradition of northern inland San Diego County (True et al. 1974; cf. Moratto 1984:153–155).

Joseph L. Chartkoff

Further Readings

Moratto, M.J. (editor). 1984. *California Archaeology.* Academic Press, New York.

Rogers, M.J. 1938. Archaeological and Geological Investigations in an Old Channel of the San Dieguito Valley. *Yearbook of the Carnegie Institution of Washington* 37:344–345.

———. 1966. *Ancient Hunters of the Far West.* Union-Tribune, San Diego.

True, D.L., C.W. Meighan, and H. Crew. 1974. *Archaeological Investigations at Molpa, San Diego County, California.* Publications in Anthropology no. 11. University of California Press, Berkeley.

Warren, C.N. 1967. The San Dieguito Complex: A Review and Hypothesis. *American Antiquity* 32:168–185.

———. 1968. Cultural Traditions and Ecological Adaptation on the Southern California Coast. In *Archaic Prehistory in the Western United States,* edited by C. Irwin-Williams, pp. 1–14. Contributions in Anthropology, vol. 1, no. 3. Eastern New Mexico University, Portales.

Warren, C.N., and D.L. True. 1961. The San Dieguito Complex and Its Place in California Prehistory. *Archaeological Survey Annual Report 1960–61:*246–338. University of California, Los Angeles.

D

Dallas Culture

The Dallas culture or phase refers to the Late Prehistoric Mississippian period (ca. A.D. 1300–1600, or 650–350 years B.P.) culture of East Tennessee. Based on ceramics or artistic styles, especially on carved-shell gorgets, some researchers have attempted to divide Dallas into early, middle, and late periods. Others have suggested that a more appropriate terminal date is A.D. 1700 (250 years B.P.). Sites attributed to the phase are well represented along the main channel of the Tennessee River and its tributaries from ca. 50 km (31 miles) north of Knoxville to Chattanooga, Tennessee. M.R. Harrington, C.B. Moore, and William S. Webb recognized many of the major characteristics of the Dallas culture from their explorations of sites in the early twentieth century. Thomas M.N. Lewis and Madeline Kneberg, through their extensive work in the late 1930s, especially in the Chickamauga Reservoir Basin at the Davis, Dallas, Hixon, Hiwassee Island, and Sale Creek sites, named and defined the culture in detail. Their published descriptions of Dallas community plans, mortuary patterning, architecture, and ceramic, stone, bone, and shell artifacts are found in their 1946 book *Hiwassee Island: An Archaeological Account of Four Tennessee Indian Peoples.* Excavations at the Toqua site on the Little Tennessee River in the 1970s (Polhemus 1987), new theoretical perspectives on the social and religious organization of chiefdoms, modern analyses of faunal and botanical remains, and alternative interpretations of sixteenth-century European contact have added greatly to the picture of the Dallas culture.

Dallas-culture ceramics are predominantly shell tempered and are believed to have developed out of the ceramic tradition of the earlier Hiwassee Island culture (A.D. 1000–1300, or 950–650 years B.P.). Dallas vessel forms include a variety of globular jars, plain and carinated bowls, hooded and open-mouth bottles, and large shallow "salt" pans. Plain and cord-marked surface treatments occur most frequently on vessels; the greater occurrence of cord marking on Dallas vessels is especially important in distinguishing them from Hiwassee Island ceramics. Incising and burnishing tend to occur most often on bowls, while pans are most often fabric impressed. Negative-painted, red-on-buff, and red-filmed bottles and bowls also are found in Dallas ceramic assemblages. Lug-and-strap handles commonly occur on jars, and modeled human, bird, and animal effigies are present, especially on the rims of bowls. Most vessel rims are plain, filleted, or notched.

Primary Dallas settlements consisted of large, palisaded towns ca. 2 ha (4.9 acres) in area. They contained a village plaza and a platform or substructure mound on which community buildings were erected. In most cases, there was a single structure with an accompanying arbor or pavilion built on the mound summit. In other instances, pairs of structures were erected on the mound summit. A small number of towns have a second mound at the opposite side of the plaza area that served primarily for mortuary activities. Villages contained 30–50 houses and had populations of 100–500 individuals. Domestic structures, constructed of wattle and daub, were 7–10 m (23–33 feet) on a side with a central, prepared clay hearth, four major roof-support posts, and benches along the interior wall. Adjacent to these dwellings were sheds or arbors, elevated corn-storage cribs, and open areas for outdoor activities. Groups of these structures may represent kin-related household aggregates. Communal fields where corn, squash, and beans were grown were located around the town. Additional areas, some far beyond the village periphery, were exploited for arboreal seeds, especially hickory nuts, acorns, walnuts, and chestnuts, and for animal resources, especially deer, turkey, and raccoons, and many small mammals, fish, and turtles.

Dallas towns contain numerous human burials. These are generally single primary inhumations placed in a rectangular pit. Burial location, grave goods, and age and sex of the individuals strongly suggest status differences and indicate a hierarchy of social positions. Burials of all ages and both sexes occur in village areas in and around domestic structures; individuals with grave goods have simple utilitarian items, such as pottery vessels, or ornaments, such as shell beads. Burials in mound contexts, in contrast, are more frequently adult males who were interred with a variety of grave goods, including shell masks, gorgets, and cups; monolithic stone axes; copper ornaments, such as earspools, headdresses, and collars; and chipped-stone artifacts made from nonlocal raw materials.

Based on the complexity of community and mortuary patterns, researchers believe that Dallas society possessed a hierarchy of status positions conforming to a chieftain level of sociopolitical organization. Differences in the size, complexity, and location of Dallas towns, hamlets, isolated farmsteads, and special-purpose sites suggest that, at any one time, several economically autonomous polities may have existed that were spaced 50–75 km (31–46 miles) apart. These polities, to varying degrees, formed political alliances, established kinship ties among elites, engaged in economic tribute or trade, participated in reciprocal ritual exchange and religious ceremonies, and carried out military action against one another. Some historians and archaeologists believe that certain Dallas sites correspond to villages associated with the Chiefdom of Coosa, which was visited by sixteenth-century A.D. Spanish explorers. The Spanish introduced epidemic diseases, such as smallpox and measles. The deaths caused by them contributed to the collapse of Dallas culture in the sixteenth and seventeenth centuries.

Gerald F. Schroedl

Further Readings

Hatch, J.W., and P.S. Willey. 1974. Stature and Status in Dallas Society. *Tennessee Archaeologist* 30:107–131.

Lewis, T.M.N., and M. Kneberg. 1946. *Hiwassee Island: An Archaeological Account of Four Tennessee Indian Peoples.* University of Tennessee Press, Knoxville.

Lewis, T.M.N., and M.D. Kneberg Lewis. 1995. *The Prehistory of the Chickamauga Basin in Tennessee.* 2 vols. Compiled and edited by L.P. Sullivan. University of Tennessee Press, Knoxville.

Polhemus, R. 1987. *The Toqua Site: A Late Mississippian Dallas Phase Town.* 2 vols. Report of Investigations no. 41. Department of Anthropology, University of Tennessee, Knoxville.

———. 1990a. Dallas Phase Architecture and Sociopolitical Structure. In *Lamar Archaeology: Mississippian Chiefdoms in the Deep South,* edited by M. Williams and G. Shapiro, pp. 125–138. University of Alabama Press, Tuscaloosa.

———. 1990b. Phase Characteristics, East Tennessee River. In *Lamar Archaeology: Mississippian Chiefdoms in the Deep South,* edited by M. Williams and G. Shapiro, pp. 39–41. University of Alabama Press, Tuscaloosa.

Dalton

About 1948, S.P. Dalton of Jefferson City, Missouri, later chief justice of the Missouri Supreme Court, showed Carl Chapman, state archaeologist of Missouri, some distinctive lanceolate points and end scrapers. Some had been recovered at depths of 1.5–2.4 m (5–8 feet) in a highway borrow pit now known as the Dalton site. They were not characteristic of known later Archaic sites. Chapman speculated that they were very early in date and named them Dalton points in honor of Judge Dalton, who was the first to recognize them as significant. In 1949 and 1950, excavations at Graham Cave in Missouri confirmed the early stratigraphic position of Dalton points.

Until ca. 1960, Dalton points were thought to be concentrated mostly within Missouri, although Marie Wormington (1957) had recognized by 1957 that they were also widespread outside the state. By 1960, Cambron and Hulse (1960) had discovered in a survey of points in Alabama that 1.25 percent of all points and point fragments found at 21 archaeological sites in the Lower Tennessee Valley were Dalton (for perspective, Mississippian Triangular points constituted only 2.25 percent of the total, while the largest category [29.41 percent] was "distal ends and mid sections"). In 1960–1961 excavations at the Stanfield–Worley Bluff Shelter in Alabama, Dalton and side-notched points were the only point forms in the basal level; it was learned later that Dalton was restricted to the lowest stratigraphic level. In 1961–1962, the Ford-Redfield survey (Redfield 1971) for Dalton points searched collections in an area that stretched from southeast Missouri through eastern Arkansas and into northeast Louisiana. Rodgers Shelter in Missouri was excavated between 1963 and 1968, the Arkansas Brand site in 1970, and the Arkansas Sloan site in 1974. By 1980, archaeologists recognized that Dalton points were extremely widespread. Daltonlike points are found throughout the eastern United States; they occur in significant numbers in Florida, Georgia, Alabama, Mississippi, Louisiana, Arkansas, South Carolina, Tennessee, Illinois, Missouri, and Kentucky. The closely related Merserve point is found bordering this distribution in the Plains.

Dalton is thought to date between ca. 8750 and 8250 B.C. (10,700–10,200 years B.P.). While the fluting technology developed from Clovis, Dalton remains have never been associated with extinct megafauna, such as mastodon. Therefore, Dalton must postdate ca. 9000 B.C. (10,950 years B.P.). At the Brand and Sloan sites, no side-notched points were associated with the large, excavated samples. Side-notched points are associated with the Holocene, which began ca. 8000 B.C. (9950 years B.P.). Two radiocarbon dates from Rodgers Shelter in Missouri are 8580 B.C. ± 650 and 8250 B.C. ± 330 (10,530 and 10,200 years B.P.).

The Dalton point is a fluted point with lateral retouch usually obscuring all or most of the flutes that removed the central ridge on each face. The point is often serrated, a major clue to its main function as a cutting tool. Resharpened points are alternately beveled and usually serrated. Impact fractures are rare and normally restricted to unsharpened specimens. Replicated points have functioned well to butcher white-tailed deer, and microwear analyses indicate that Dalton points were used to cut meat. Small chert hammers and notched abraders to grind lateral and basal edges of Dalton points also occur.

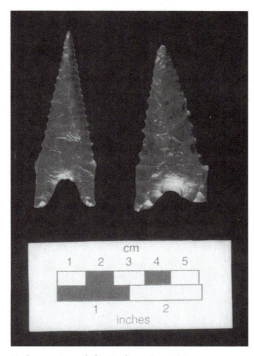

Dalton points: (left) Graham Cave, Montgomery, Missouri; (right) Sloan site, Greene County, Arkansas. (Illustration by D. F. Morse)

End scrapers made on flakes had the bulb of percussion thinned for hafting. According to microwear analyses, they functioned to scrape skins. Based on bulbular thinning and lateral retouch, other unifaces, some made on blades, were often also hafted. They range from nicely made stemmed and backed spokeshaves to expedient flake tools, including graver forms. A strong woodworking tradition is reflected by the presence of formal true adzes. They were made on cobbles and often retain cortex on the butt end. Lateral and surface grinding for hafting is present, and microwear analyses indicate the haft involved leather. The gougelike bits exhibit straight striations on one face only. Microwear analyses indicate that wood and charred wood were both worked. They probably functioned to manufacture cypress dugout canoes, as well as a variety of wooden items, possibly even masks. Larger grooved abraders may have been used to grind lateral edges. Edge-abraded cobbles probably functioned to grind vegetable foods. To date (1996), these tools have been reported only in northeast Arkansas, but they probably exist elsewhere. Other cobble tools appear to be more expedient and include a variety of hammers and anvil functions. Other Dalton artifacts include small-pointed bifaces, microblades, red ocher, and *pièces esquillées*. Bone artifacts include an eyed needle found at Graham Cave.

Sites range from bluff shelters to open sites. Rodgers Shelter contained hearths. No structures have been identified at these sites, but the expertise in woodworking as exemplified by the Dalton adze would indicate that houses, outbuildings, drying racks, and storage facilities may have been constructed. Most known Dalton sites appear to have been expedient or specialized extraction sites. Many are rock shelters. The Brand site in northeast Arkansas may have been the location of several successive deer-butchering camps, based on five areas of artifact concentration discovered there. They may be tent or house sites, but the tools recovered seem appropriate for butchering and skin processing. At the nearby Lace site, which was destroyed by farming activities in the 1970s, a much greater variety of tools were recovered from the surface. Lace has been interpreted as a base camp or village.

The Sloan site, also located in northeast Arkansas, has been interpreted as a cemetery. Pristine artifacts were recovered from the upper 50 cm (19.5 inches) of a stabilized and partially eroded sand dune. The tools were clustered into several dozen grave-sized areas within the 12 x 12 m (39.4 x 39.4-foot) excavation. Due to the high activity of the dune, only very small and rare human bone fragments were associated with approximately half the clusters. Dalton points made up one-third of the recovered 450 artifacts. Some appeared to have been hafted on foreshafts as knives. Adzes, abraders, hammers, end scrapers, a variety of bifaces and unifaces, and an edge-abraded cobble were also recovered. Points ranged up to 20 cm (7.8 inches) in length and have pristine working edges.

The distribution of ca. 800 Dalton sites in northeast Arkansas indicates the presence of single clusters within separate watersheds. Each watershed crosses one of the three major ecotones (transition areas) in northeast Arkansas, allowing access to upland gravel deposits and lowland lakes with significant food sources. Sites cluster together within each of the watersheds within the Delta. Each cluster is thought to include one or more cemeteries and base camps/villages plus other camps. There seem to be six clusters, which may indicate the presence of six bands. The total population must have

been ca. 150–300. Bands would have been organized into a network that involved trade in better local cherts and exotic cherts from farther north in the Missouri Ozarks. Waste in chert, an indication of the importance of trade, is inferred from the large number of discarded adzes and longer points.

Dan F. Morse

Further Readings

Cambron, J.W., and D.C. Hulse. 1960. The Transitional Paleo-Indian in North Alabama and South Tennessee. *Journal of Alabama Archaeology* 6(1):7–33.

Morse, D.F., and P.A. Morse. 1987. *Archeology of the Central Mississippi Valley.* Academic Press, New York.

Redfield, A. 1971. *Dalton Project Notes.* Museum of Anthropology, University of Missouri, Columbia.

Wormington, H.M. 1957. *Ancient Man in North America.* Popular Series no. 4. Denver Museum of Natural History, Denver.

See also BRAND SITE; RODGERS SHELTER

Danger Cave

Danger Cave (42TO13) is a dry cave site on the western edge of the Great Salt Lake desert near the border town of Wendover. The site has been the focus of repeated excavation work over more than 50 years due to the presence of highly stratified deposits spanning more than the last 10,000 years. The cave was first excavated by Elmer Smith in the late 1930s, when it was known as Hands-and-Knees Cave. It is best known from the work of Jesse D. Jennings in the early 1950s (cf. Jennings 1957). Jennings first established the long chronology of Danger Cave and used it as the basis for his definition of the "Desert Archaic," a long-lived pattern defined as a mobile hunting-and-gathering lifestyle dependent on the wide array of plants and animals found in the varied desert and mountain environments of western North America. Later work conducted by Gary Fry in 1968 and David Madsen in 1986 further refined the chronology and food-collecting practices at the site. The dominance of seeds, pine nuts, and small game in the subsistence economy is evident from the earliest occupations, dating to ca. 8550–8050 B.C. (10,500–10,000 years B.P.), to historic occupations dating to ca. A.D. 1800–1950. The cave area was seasonally occupied, probably during the winter months, with the cave interior serving primarily as a seed-processing and storage area and possibly secondarily as a sleeping area. Most daily activities probably took place at the cave mouth or exterior.

David B. Madsen

Further Readings

Fry, G.F. 1978. *Prehistoric Diet at Danger Cave, Utah, As Determined by the Analysis of Coprolites.* University of Utah Press, Salt Lake City.

Grayson, D.K. 1988. *Danger Cave, Last Supper Cave, and Hanging Rock Shelter: The Faunas.* American Museum of Natural History, New York.

Jennings, J.D. 1957. *Danger Cave.* Memoir no. 14. Society for American Archaeology, Washington, D.C.

Madsen, D.B., and D. Rhode. 1990. Early Holocene Pinyon *(Pinus monphylla)* in the Northeastern Great Basin. *Quarterly Research* 33:94–101.

Dart/Spear Points

Dart and spear points are pointed, usually bifacially flaked, stone objects suitable for hafting on the end of a shaft. A dart is hafted to a relatively short shaft that can be thrown or, more frequently, launched with the aid of an atlatl or spear thrower. A spear is attached to a longer shaft and is designed to be a thrusting weapon. Because of the rarity in prehistoric contexts of preserved organic shafts with intact stone tips, it is usually impossible to determine whether a prehistoric "point" tipped a dart or a spear shaft or was used as some other kind of implement.

A dart or spear point has a rear "haft element" for attachment to a shaft and an anterior "blade element" for penetration. Attrition of the blade element through use usually resulted in its periodic resharpening or reshaping, processes that altered its size and shape. Since the haft element was less likely to incur attrition or damage, it was usually not modified after its initial manufacture. This latter element of a dart or a spear is also usually its most distinctive part, for hafting was facilitated through a variety of basal shapes, which included side, corner, and basal notches, and the creation of stems, lobes, and tangs (projecting ears).

These distinctive features have been employed in the development of elaborate typological systems for classifying these objects, as it has been found that dart/spear points were often manufactured to specific shapes by separate cultural groups in particular periods. They therefore serve as useful markers of prehistoric chronological placement or cultural affiliation. Projectile-point typologies have been created for every region of North America. These systems are regionally specific and are meant to remain so, as the meaning of classifications derives from the association of similar objects with a common history of development; that is, two projectile points existing thousands of miles apart may look alike, but it makes little sense to associate them in any way if they originated in different traditions and developed separately.

Because of their usefulness as cultural and temporal indicators, dart/spear points have received more attention by archaeologists than have other classes of stone tool. It is important to note, however, that an item's classification as a projectile point is a totally arbitrary and artificial decision based solely on the shape and size of the object. "Points" also possess sharp edges that could have been used for cutting, scraping, shaving, and a variety of other tasks, and a tip that could have served as a drill or a graver spur. Use-wear analysis of the edges and surfaces of some of these objects suggests that they were employed in a variety of tasks and that many probably never actually functioned as projectile points. This issue and the frequent use of bifacially flaked projectile points as multifunctional knives have been recognized in the United States since the early twentieth century.

Experimental studies have explored the problems of recognizing dart and spear points and of evaluating their effectiveness. Examples include the thrusting of stone-tipped spears into the carcass of an elephant by Bruce B. Huckell (1982) to investigate efficiency and breakage patterns; the thrusting of 39 replicated Elko Corner-Notched points into a variety of materials by Gene L. Titmus and James C. Woods (1986) to inspect breakage patterns within this Great Basin typological series; and a comparison by George H. Odell and Frank Cowan (1986) of the efficiency of penetration, breakage patterns, and use-wear indicators of spear points and arrowheads and of retouched and unretouched points.

George H. Odell

D

Further Readings

Huckell, B.B. 1982. The Denver Elephant Project: A Report on Experimentation With Thrusting Spears. *Plains Anthropologist* 27:217–224.

Justice, N.D. 1987. *Stone Age Spear and Arrow Points of the Midcontinental and Eastern United States.* Indiana University Press, Bloomington.

Odell, G.H., and F. Cowan. 1986. Experiments With Spears and Arrows on Animal Targets. *Journal of Field Archaeology* 13:195–212.

Perino, G. 1985. *Selected Preforms, Points and Knives of the North American Indians,* vols. 1–2. Points and Barbs Press, Idabel.

Titmus, G.L., and J.C. Woods. 1986. An Experimental Study of Projectile Point Fracture Patterns. *Journal of California and Great Basin Anthropology* 8:37–49.

Davis, Edwin H. (1811–1888)

A physician from Chillicothe, Ohio, Edwin H. Davis surveyed and excavated large numbers of earthworks in Ohio and adjacent regions in the mid-1840s with E.G. Squier, who was junior author to Davis of the early exemplar of the descriptive phase of North American archaeology, *Ancient Monuments of the Mississippi Valley* (1848).

Guy Gibbon

See also SQUIER, EPHRAIM G.

Davis, Emma Lou (1905–1988)

Emma Lou Davis was among the most significant scholars in the scientific study of Paleoindian archaeology in the California deserts. Davis came to archaeology late in her career, after first earning a fine-arts degree from Vassar College in 1927 and following a career in commercial art for 30 years. Deciding to retrain in archaeology, she completed a Ph.D. at UCLA in 1965, focusing on the early archaeology of the Panamint Valley for her dissertation. She subsequently worked for the San Diego Museum of Man, where she continued her desert studies, with a particular emphasis on the China Lake region in southern California, and expanded them into other areas of California and into Nevada. Before retiring from the museum, she established the Great Basin Foundation, through which she continued her studies after retirement. The Great Basin Foundation became especially prominent in focusing paleoenvironmental research on Paleoindian questions and in publishing the results of that research. Davis was one of the most important figures in bringing scientific rigor and credibility to Paleoindian archaeology in California.

Joseph L. Chartkoff

Further Readings

Blackburn, T.C. (editor). 1985. *Woman, Poet, Scientist: Essays in New World Anthropology Honoring Dr. Emma Lou Davis.* Anthropological Papers no. 29. Ballena Press, Los Altos.

Davis, E.L. 1961. The Mono Craters Petroglyphs, California. *American Antiquity* 27:236–239.

———. 1963. The Desert Culture of the Western Great Basin: A Lifeway of Seasonal Transhumance. *American Antiquity* 29:202–212.

———. 1964. An Archaeological Survey of the Mono Lake Basin and Excavation of Two Rockshelters, Mono County, California. *Archaeological Survey Annual Report* 6:251–392. University of California, Los Angeles.

———. 1967. Man and Water at Pleistocene Lake Mojave. *American Antiquity* 32:345–353.

———. 1968a. Early Man in the Mojave Desert. In *Contributions in Anthropology,* vol. 1, no. 4. Edited by C. Irwin-Williams, pp. 42–47. Eastern New Mexico University, Portales.

———. 1968b. A Rare Find: A Fluted Point in Process. *San Diego Museum of Man News Bulletin* April-May 1968.

———. 1970. Archaeology of the North Basin of Panamint Valley, Inyo County, California. *Nevada State Museum Anthropological Papers* 15:83–141.

———. 1973. The Hord Site: A Paleo-Indian Camp. *Pacific Coast Archaeological Society Quarterly* 9(2):1–26.

———. 1974. Paleo-Indian Land Use Patterns at China Lake, California. *Pacific Coast Archaeological Society Quarterly* 10(2):1–16.

———. 1975. The "Exposed Archaeology" of China Lake, California. *American Antiquity* 40(1):39–53.

———. (editor). 1978. *The Ancient Califor-*

nians: *Rancholabrean Hunters of the Mojave Lakes Country*. Science Series, vol. 29. Natural History Museum, Los Angeles.

Davis, E.L., and R. Shutler, Jr. 1969. Recent Discoveries of Fluted Points in California and Nevada. *Nevada State Museum Anthropological Papers* 14:154–169.

Davis, E.L., C.W. Brott, and D.L. Weide. 1969. *The Western Lithic Co-Tradition*. Papers, vol. 6. San Diego Museum of Man, San Diego.

Dawson, John W. (1820–1899)

Eminent professor of geology and principal of McGill University, Montreal (1855–1893), John W. Dawson was an early pioneer of the direct historical approach and has been credited with the birth of Canadian archaeology. He attempted to link artifacts from a site in western Montreal with the Iroquoian village of Hochelaga visited by French explorer Jacques Cartier in 1535. Contrary to other commentators of the period, Dawson tried to use what was known of the archaeological record in North America to flesh out prehistoric life in western Europe, arguing that the European archaeological record was too little known to support many widely accepted claims. He proposed that cultures at different levels of complexity coexisted throughout human history, that the presence of human remains with extinct animals (discovered by French prehistorian Jacques Boucher de Perthes in geological deposits of the the Somme River Valley) confirmed only the recent date of the Pleistocene gravels in which they were found rather than great age (Dawson 1901), and that the developmental sequence favored by European archaeologists could represent only idiosyncratic local trends. Dawson thought that archaeologists should view artifacts from the perspective of their makers rather than concentrate solely on their form. Many of his conclusions are summarized in his widely read 1880 work *Fossil Men and Their Modern Representatives*. Dawson was elected fellow of the Royal Society in 1862 and was knighted in 1884.

Guy Gibbon

Further Readings

Dawson, J.W. 1880. *Fossil Men and Their Modern Representatives*. Dawson Brothers, Montreal.

———. 1901. *Fifty Years of Work in Canada, Scientific and Educational*. Ballantyne and Hanson, London.

Trigger, B.G. 1966. Sir John Dawson: A Faithful Anthropologist. *Anthropologia* 8:351–359.

Debert/Belmont Complex

The Debert/Belmont Paleoindian complex is the oldest evidence for human habitation in the Maritime Provinces of eastern Canada. It is associated with the Clovis period in the Far Northeast. The artifactual material represents a continuum of a broad, continent-wide adaptation to the hunting of late Pleistocene fauna. The people involved in this adaptive strategy were the descendants of the immigrants who crossed Beringia and settled in the heart of North America. From this core area, they spread west to California, east to New England, and northeast into the Maritimes. The carbon dates from the 1963–1964 excavations at Debert gave an average of 8650 B.C. ± 47 (10,600 years B.P.) for the occupation of this site. The five new sites at Belmont have received only limited testing and surface collection. Therefore, this summary of the data presently known from Nova Scotia relies heavily on George F. MacDonald's 1968 publication *Debert: A Paleo-Indian Site in Central Nova Scotia.*

MacDonald identified two aspects of the subsurface deposits at Debert that he deemed of archaeological significance: structural horizons and soil-weathering horizons. Their determination is complicated in that they are derived from a single parent matrix, the underlying site bedrock, which is composed of red Wolfville sandstone. The stratigraphy was poorly defined, for interfaces based upon changes in color or texture were difficult to determine. Further, over the past 10 millennia, factors such as ice, water, wind, organic agents, and insects have reworked each of the strata. These same agents have also contributed to the vertical displacement of the artifactual materials. A detailed discussion of these horizons can be found in MacDonald's report.

Although various natural agents caused vertical displacement of artifacts, their horizontal positioning was not significantly altered. The excavations recovered 4,471 lithic specimens associated with 25 distinct features. These were used by MacDonald to define 11 discrete activity areas, eight of which were concentrated across a ridge in the central portion of the site. This same area produced the major percentage (92 percent) of artifactual material.

Most of the lithics collected from Debert are fashioned from two varieties of chalcedony. The most common (40.4 percent) is an opaque, brecciated variety, and the second is a translucent chalcedony (34.2 percent). Since few cortex flakes of either variety were found, the initial manufacturing of tools probably occurred elsewhere than on the site. An attempt to locate the source of these chalcedonies has not, however, been successful; a best-guess location is offshore near the present community of Parrsboro, Nova Scotia. The remaining lithics are represented by silicified siltstone of unknown origin and porphyritic rhyolite, which is locally available in the underlying till.

MacDonald recognized 11 different types of tools manufactured from the various stone materials, with the most diagnostic being a fluted projectile point that closely resembles the Clovis type. End scrapers were the type most common (34.7 percent), followed by retouched flakes (19.8 percent). The percentage of scrapers suggests that animal-hide processing was a dominant activity at the site. The high humic acid content of the Debert/Belmont soils has negated any opportunity to recover faunal remains. To date (1996), one projectile point has been subjected to blood-residue analysis, which produced evidence that the residue was that of caribou.

It is anticipated, on the basis of the preliminary investigations, that the new sites will duplicate the results achieved by MacDonald. However, it is clear that a much more complex culture history exists within the Debert/Belmont area than originally thought. With additional archaeological, palynological, geological, and soils analyses, we will be in a position to better understand the events surrounding the oldest occupation of Nova Scotia.

Stephen A. Davis

Further Readings

Davis, S.A. 1991. Two Concentrations of Paleo-Indian Occupation in the Far Northeast. *Revista de Arqueologia Americana* 3:31–56.

MacDonald, G.F. 1968. *Debert: A Paleo-Indian Site in Central Nova Scotia.* Anthropology Papers no. 16. National Museum of Canada, Ottawa.

Debitage/Debris

The terms "debitage" and "debris" are considered by most North American lithic analysts to be synonymous. Debitage (or debris) is the result of lithic fracturing, and most perceive it as a byproduct of a bifacial or core trajectory; that is, the removals from a biface, or the flakes or blades struck from a core. Debris is thus distinguished from objects manufactured by abrasive techniques (e.g., ground axes) and from objects exhibiting use-pecking or grinding (e.g., hammerstones, manos) by having been the result of fracturing. It is distinguished from morpho-technologically derived tool types by its lack of retouch, or secondary modification of the margins of the stone subsequent to procurement (if a nodule) or initial removal from the core (if a flake).

Although flakes from lithic reduction constitute the largest share of most collections of lithic debitage from a site, archaeologists generally also include shatter from flake production that does not possess flake characteristics, fire-crazed chunks, and natural blocky fragments, if they are present in an obvious cultural horizon or assemblage. The issue of the cultural or noncultural origin of flakes, hotly debated during the first half of the twentieth century, was finally put to rest by Alfred S. Barnes (1939) and others.

Debitage used to be considered devoid of cultural information and was, therefore, thrown away, but modern archaeologists have begun to grasp its manifold advantages. First, unlike retouched tools or ground-stone implements, debitage is not usually picked up by modern collectors—nor, presumably, by more ancient ones. Second, it was not likely to be curated by its makers and thereby removed to another location as a tool; therefore, most flakes have probably remained where they were knapped or discarded. And third, since one core or biface was potentially the origin of several flakes, debris is almost always considerably more abundant than modified tools, even discounting the effects of collecting and curation. This means that debris sample sizes are almost always larger than those of typed lithic artifacts, and more sophisticated statistical techniques can be applied to them.

A suitable analysis of debitage can render several kinds of information, among which are: (1) the type of reduction trajectory in use, such as flake, blade, bipolar, or biface; (2) the kind of percussor used, such as hard or soft hammer, pressure flaker, or punch; (3) for a biface-producing people, the position of an assemblage with respect to the sequence of lithic reduction (early or late); (4) the sources of raw material, which in turn often engender hypotheses concerning the origin of the material, the means of procuring it, and the position of the site with respect to prehistoric trade networks; (5) the intensity of activity in any given area of a site; (6) functional and technological parameters of specific areas; and (7) human behavioral issues, such as the curation rate of formal tools (which would be expected to have been high if the amount of debris greatly exceeds the amount of formal tools left on the site).

Several types of analyses have been marshaled to elicit the kinds of information listed above. Although relevant studies have assumed different forms, most of them rely on experimental data for comparison with archaeological material, and most are concerned with the size and/or shapes of the flakes. Alan P. Sullivan III and Kenneth C. Rozen (1985), for example, produced a simple and immediately popular flake-categorization system based on the extent of flake breakage. Other research has emphasized the tiniest flakes, or "microdebitage," under the assumption that these are the most likely to still be in primary context (Fladmark 1982). Several studies have taken individual flake attributes as their elemental units of analysis (e.g., Dibble and Whittaker 1981; several studies in Amick and Maulden 1989). Other studies, however, have employed graded screens to produce aggregate samples of specific size classes, usually relating that information to experimentally derived comparative collections (Stahle and Dunn 1984; Ahler 1989).

George H. Odell

Further Readings

Ahler, S.A. 1989. Mass Analysis of Flaking Debris: Studying the Forest Rather Than the Trees. In *Alternative Approaches to Lithic Analysis*, edited by D. Henry and G. Odell, pp. 85–118. Archaeology Papers no. 1. American Anthropological Association, Menasha.

Amick, D.S., and R.P. Mauldin (editors). 1989. *Experiments in Lithic Technology.* International Series no. 528. British Archaeological Report, Oxford.

Barnes, A.S. 1939. The Difference Between Natural and Human Flaking on Prehistoric Flint Implements. *American Anthropologist* 41:99–112.

Dibble, H.L., and J. Whittaker. 1981. New Experimental Evidence on the Relation Between Percussion Flaking and Flake Variation. *Journal of Archaeological Science* 6:283–296.

Fladmark, K.R. 1982. Microdebitage Analysis: Initial Considerations. *Journal of Archaeological Science* 9:205–220.

Magne, M., and D. Pokotylo. 1981. A Pilot Study in Bifacial Lithic Reduction Sequences. *Lithic Technology* 10:34–47.

Shott, M.J. 1994. Size and Form in the Analysis of Flake Debris: Review and Recent Approaches. *Journal of Archaeological Method and Theory* 1:69–110.

Stahle, D.W., and J.E. Dunn. 1984. *An Experimental Analysis of the Size Distribution of Waste Flakes From Biface Reduction.* Technical Paper no. 2. Arkansas Archeological Survey, Fayetteville.

Sullivan, A.P., III, and K.C. Rozen. 1985. Debitage Analysis and Archaeological Interpretation. *American Antiquity* 50:755–779.

DeJarnette, David L. (1907–1991)

The state of Alabama's foremost archaeologist from the 1930s to the 1970s, David Lloyd DeJarnette was born in Bessemer, Alabama, on

David L. Dejarnette. (Reprinted with permission from American Antiquity *58[4]:622)*

June 2, 1907. His archaeological career began in 1930 with employment as curator of the Alabama Museum of Natural History in Tuscaloosa. Formal training in archaeology was acquired at Fay-Cooper Cole and Thorne Deuel's University of Chicago field school in 1932. During the Depression years, DeJarnette, using relief labor, played a leading role in Alabama-area archaeological projects of unprecedented scale. He oversaw salvage excavations in the Pickwick, Wheeler, and Guntersville basins in the Tennessee River Valley and coauthored fundamental publications with William S. Webb that defined such entities as the Shell Mound Archaic, the Copena mortuary-mound complex, and Koger's Island Mississippian culture (Webb and DeJarnette 1942). At Moundville, Alabama, he laid the archaeological groundwork for the restoration of this Mississippian ceremonial complex by the Civilian Conservation Corps (CCC) and the National Park Service. Also during the 1930s, he orchestrated the Works Progress Administration (WPA) archaeological program in Alabama and the operation of the Central Archaeological Laboratory in Birmingham. After World War II, DeJarnette left the Alabama Museum of Natural History to become the first curator of the Museum of Atomic Energy in Oak Ridge, Tennessee, a post he held for five years. Lured back to archaeology and Alabama, he returned to Moundville as its curator and accepted a faculty position at the University of Alabama, from which he directed a long succession of annual field schools between 1958 and 1975. DeJarnette ended his professional career having authored the first synthesis of Alabama archaeology (DeJarnette 1952) and having worked out much of the framework of its culture history. His last major project was the excavation of the Stanfield–Worley Bluff Shelter, which resulted in the definition of a Transitional Paleoindian cultural horizon in the Tennessee Valley (DeJarnette et al. 1962). He died at Foley, Alabama, on January 16, 1991.

Vernon James Knight, Jr.

Further Readings

Cambron, J.W., and D.C. Hulse. 1964. *Handbook of Alabama Archaeology,* edited by D.L. DeJarnette. Archaeological Research Association of Alabama, Moundville.

DeJarnette, D.L. 1952. Alabama Archeology: A Summary. In *Archeology of Eastern United States*, edited by J.B. Griffin, pp. 272–284. University of Chicago Press, Chicago.

———. 1975. *Archaeological Salvage in the Walter F. George Basin of the Chattahoochee River in Alabama.* University of Alabama Press, Tuscaloosa.

DeJarnette, D.L., and S.B. Wimberly. 1941. *The Bessemer Site.* Museum Paper no. 17. Geological Survey of Alabama, University of Alabama, Tuscaloosa.

DeJarnette, D.L., E. Kurjack, and J. Cambron. 1962. Stanfield-Worley Bluff Shelter Excavations. *Journal of Alabama Archaeology* 8(1–2).

Webb, W.S., and D.L. DeJarnette. 1942. *An Archaeological Survey of Pickwick Basin in the Adjacent Portions of the States of Alabama, Mississippi, and Tennessee.* Bulletin no. 129. Bureau of American Ethnology, Smithsonian Institution, Washington, D.C.

Demography

Demography is the study of the physical characteristics, or "vital statistics," of human populations, such as group size, density, distribution, age-sex structure, age-group life expectancies, and health. When determined through the analysis of archaeological data or sketchy early contact reports, the study is called paleodemography. Notable examples of paleodemographic studies in North America include Jane Buikstra's (1976, 1977, 1981) investigations of ancient populations in the Eastern Woodlands and examinations of the more than 2,000 human burials recovered by A.V. Kidder at Pecos Pueblo in New Mexico. Paleodemographic studies are essential in the reconstruction of lifeways and culture histories. They help explain, among many other critical aspects of past lifeways, the nature of social systems and the transition from one kind to another, offer a measure of the adaptational success of a lifeway or of the impact of a technological innovation, expose periods of population stability or instability, allow the investigation of fluctuations in the lifespan of both sexes under different circumstances, and measure the strain on the carrying capacity of the resources of a region.

Paleodemographic studies derive their information from a variety of sources, including human skeletal samples; the size, number, and content of archaeological sites; models based on modern demographic studies; and early written observations at first European contact. Studies of human bone can determine the age, sex, health status, and diet of individuals (Ubelaker 1989). The sex of an individual can be assessed by the structure of the pelvis, and age by degree of fusion of sutures between bones of the skull or by the eruption sequence and degree of wear of teeth. Estimates of population size have been based on settlement and mortuary data and on the assumed carrying capacity, or food potential, of a particular environment. Among the settlement data used are site size, numbers of dwellings thought to have been occupied at the same time, amount of floor area, and number of sites of an archaeological culture in a region. Most of these estimates are based on models derived from modern demographic studies. An example is Raoul Naroll's (1962) suggestion that the population of a prehistoric site is equal to one-tenth the total floor area in square meters. Others have refined his estimate for particular groups or types of houses, offering such suggestions as: Population sizes equal one-third of the total floor area in square meters in pueblos in the American Southwest and one-sixth of the floor area in square meters in New World multifamily houses. Still others have used ethnographic cross-cultural studies to suggest that average band size among hunter-gatherers is 25 people and that average tribe size is 500 people.

Paleodemographic estimates like these are usually no more than guesses or rough guides, for a variety of reasons. For example, since band size varies considerably with the seasons and through time, a 25-person estimate is at best a statistical average. Likewise, population aggregation is difficult to differentiate from population growth; a cemetery population may not be representative of the behavioral population from which it was derived; available sample sizes may be too small; estimates of sex and age at death may be wrong; and assignments of archaeological complex and time period may be in error. Even where early historic records are available, determinations of parameters such as the population size of a community or region vary considerably (Verano and Ubelaker 1992).

Like other aspects of the study of prehistoric Native American peoples, paleodemography is based on assumptions, and the fundamentals of sampling and reliable chronology. Because it rests, perhaps uncomfortably, between archaeology and physical anthropology, paleodemography has not experienced the concerted effort to clarify basic issues and evaluate methods that has characterized other areas of the study of ancient peoples in North America—in spite of its obvious and fundamental importance in this endeavor.

Guy Gibbon

Further Readings
Bocquet-Appel, J., and C. Masset. 1982. Farewell to Paleodemography. *Journal of Human Evolution* 11:321–333.

Buikstra, J.E. 1976. *Hopewell in the Lower Illinois Valley: A Regional Study of Human Biological Variability and Prehistoric Mortuary Behavior.* Scientific Papers no. 2. Northwestern University Archeological Program, Evanston.

———. 1977. Biocultural Dimensions of Archeological Study: A Regional Perspective. In *Biocultural Adaptation in Prehistoric America,* edited by R.L. Blakely, pp. 67–84. Proceedings of the Southern Anthropological Society no. 11. University of Georgia Press, Athens.

———. 1981. Mortuary Practices, Palaeodemography, and Palaeopathology: A Case Study From the Koster Site (Illinois). In *The Archaeology of Death,* edited by R. Chapman, I. Kinnes, and K. Randsborg, pp. 123–132. Cambridge University Press, Cambridge.

Buikstra, J.E., and L. Konigsberg. 1985. Paleodemography: Critiques and Controversies. *American Anthropologist* 87:316–333.

Hassan, F.A. 1981. *Demographic Archaeology.* Academic Press, New York.

Mobley, C.M. 1980. Demographic Structure of Pecos Indians: A Model Based on Life Tables. *American Antiquity* 45:518–530.

Naroll, R. 1962. Floor Area and Settlement Population. *American Antiquity* 27(4):319–348.

Ubelaker, D.H. 1989. *Human Skeletal Remains: Excavation, Analysis, Interpretation.* 2nd ed. Taraxacum, Washington, D.C.

Verano, J.W., and D.H. Ubelaker (editors). 1992. *Disease and Demography in the Americas.* Smithsonian Institution Press, Washington, D.C.

See also HEALTH AND DISEASE

D

Denali Complex

The Denali complex is a distinctive late Pleistocene–early Holocene cultural grouping that has a wide geographical distribution, although the majority of known sites are in noncoastal Alaska and western Yukon Territory. Denalicomplex assemblages are typically Upper Paleolithic in general form, with their distinctive core-and-blade technology, burins, and simple bifaces. They resemble, with a high degree of specificity, Dyuktai culture assemblages from the greater Aldan drainage of Yakutia (Sakha Republic).

The complex was first proposed and defined in 1967 (West 1967) on the basis of the content of four sites. Of these, three were discoveries made in the early 1960s (Teklanika West, Teklanika East, and Donnelly Ridge). The fourth, the Campus site, was recorded and compared by N.C. Nelson (1937) with the site of

Early excavations at the Dry Creek site, the main component of which belongs to the Denali complex. (Photograph by F. H. West)

Shabarakh Usu in the Gobi Desert. For the Americanist, the Campus site remained unique and essentially uninterpretable until the Teklanika and Donnelly Ridge sites were discovered. Like the Campus site, which is near Fairbanks, these sites are also in the interior: The Teklanika sites are within the Denali National Park, and the Donnelly Ridge site is on the north flank of the Alaska Range south of Fairbanks. The Teklanika sites were extensively tested in 1961; Donnelly Ridge was excavated in its entirety in 1964. Donnelly Ridge produced a very small but critically important assemblage with a relatively wide array of artifact forms. Unlike most shallow interior sites, the assemblage was also not mixed with assemblages from other periods. It thus seemed that Donnelly Ridge would be exceptionally useful in the delineation of the new complex. Dating of these sites was necessarily inferential and based on typological comparisons with Siberian sites with accessible descriptions. These included the Trans-Baikalian sites of Afontova Gora II, Verkholenskaya Gora, and Krasnyi Yar, which have an accepted age range of ca. 13,050–8050 B.C. (15,000–10,000 years B.P.). It was suggested at the time that this bracket was also applicable to the Denali complex.

More sites assignable to the complex were soon recognized following the appearance of the 1967 West publication. Among them were a series in the Tangle Lakes district on the south flank of the Alaska Range (including the Phipps site–Mt. Hayes 111); the earliest horizons at the deeply stratified Onion Portage site on the Kobuk River (Kobuk and Akmak assemblages); further finds in the Brooks Range; sites in the Nenana River Valley south of Fairbanks (especially Dry Creek); others in southwestern and south-central Alaska, one directly on Cook Inlet (Beluga Point); and still others on the Kenai Peninsula and in southeast Alaska. With these, fortunately, came the possibility of attaining credible radiocarbon dates for the complex. In the Tangle Lakes district, the Phipps site is radiocarbon dated at 8200 B.C. ± 265 (10,150 years B.P.) and Mt. Hayes 149 at 7110 B.C. ± 425 (9060 years B.P.). An assay of 6205 B.C. ± 265 (8155 years B.P.) was obtained on humic acid from the A horizon overlying the paleosol containing the Denali assemblage at the Phipps site. Akmak, which is Denali related, has yielded a date of 7907 B.C. ± 155 (9857 years B.P.), and Kobuk, which is also Denali related, a date of 6261 B.C. ± 84 (8211 years B.P.). The Denali

The Alaska range seen from the Donnally Ridge site, one of the original constituents of the Denali complex. (Photograph by F. H. West)

component at Dry Creek II has been dated at 8740 B.C. ± 250 (10,690 years B.P.). Bluefish Cave in northwest Yukon Territory has produced several assays in the vicinity of 10,950 ± 100 (12,900 years B.P.), but the exact relationship of the small Denali-related assemblage to these dates, which are associated with extinct fauna, remains problematic. Finally, two Denali-related sites in southeast Alaska have also produced dates of interest: Ground Hog Bay has a date of 7200 B.C. ± 130 (9150 years B.P.), and Hidden Falls has four assays averaging 7887 B.C. (9837 years B.P.), with the oldest 8125 B.C. ± 75 (10,075 years B.P.).

From the outset, dating problems caused some uncertainty in the interpretation of the complex, for most of these sites are in relatively shallow, mixed soil. That, combined with the effects of natural burning, which is ubiquitous in the interior, produced a number of clearly spurious assays that were, nonetheless, accepted at face value by some scholars. In the main, these problems have been overcome by firm evidence of stratigraphy, bolstered by radiocarbon dates that confirm the estimations based upon comparative typologies. Nevertheless, for a time, a few researchers proposed that there were *two* Denali complexes, one early, the other late. Seldom discussed were questions about how great the time separating them was and *where* the Denali people might have been in a hypothetical intervening time of thousands of years (during which new and different cultures appeared). The dual-Denali position has been generally discarded. Its vestige seems to be the conviction that microblades and possibly some other elements of the late Pleistocene–early Holocene Denali lithic tradition may have filtered down to relatively recent times. Once more, the evidence is equivocal.

The position that Denali represents the first incursion into the Americas from Northeast Asia has been challenged by a few archaeologists, who propose instead that a "Nenana complex" preceded Denali. Evidence for the possible existence of this complex comes from a small series of sites in the Nenana River Valley, of which Dry Creek is the best known. The evidence comes primarily from Component I at Dry Creek and from the Walker Road site, which is also in the Nenana Valley. In both instances, clear-cut Denali materials are underlain by small assemblages that have been interpreted as pre-Denali or Nenana complex. That interpretation is supported by a radiocarbon date of 9170 B.C. ± 85 (11,120 years B.P.) for Component I at Dry Creek and by four assays in excess of 9050 B.C. (11,000 years B.P.) from Walker Road. In the opinion of some, these collections are sufficiently small and equivocal that the possibility of their being part of the Denali complex cannot, on present evidence, be ruled out.

The time placement of the Denali complex or culture seems secure, with radiocarbon assays placing it between 9050 and 7050 B.C. (11,000–9000 years B.P.). It will likely be shown eventually to date somewhat earlier. Its relationship to Siberian sites became infinitely clearer with the publication by the Mochanovs of their research

in the Aldan. Where comparability with Afontova Gora II, Verkholenskaya Gora, and other sites was previously limited by an absence of extensive detailed descriptions of materials, typological correspondences can now be clearly demonstrated. The antecedents of Denali clearly lie in northeast Siberia (Dyuktai) in sites firmly dated as early as 16,050 B.C. (18,000 years B.P.). Examples are Upper Troitskaya (16,350 B.C. ± 180, or 18,300 years B.P.), Dyuktai Cave (12,150 B.C. ± 100, or 14,100 years B.P.), and Berelekh (10,980 ± 80, or 12,930 years B.P.), which display a span of dates that approach the beginning of Denali. Some assays, as for Ust-Mil and Ikhine, which are as early as 28,050 B.C. (30,000 years B.P.), are perhaps questionable. However, no dates are more recent than ca. 9550 B.C. (11,500 years B.P.). The virtual identity between Dyuktai and Denali assemblages also supports the conclusion that the two complexes were close together in time.

All early complexes with a distinctive Siberian Upper Paleolithic cast have been grouped into a Beringian tradition in the conviction that the recognition of this entity has both analytical and heuristic value. These peoples appear to have been the first successful colonists of America, with only one other significant migration apparently following theirs, that of the ancestral Eskimos. Prior to 10,050 B.C. (12,000 years B.P.), sub-Laurentian ice sheet America appears to have been without human occupants. Beginning ca. 9550 B.C. (11,500 years B.P.), Clovis hunters appeared and spread explosively throughout the empty continents. It seems clear that the Upper Paleolithic Beringian tradition—with Denali-Dyuktai as its most clearly delineated member—is the matrix from which Clovis developed. The place of these early northern hunters in American prehistory is, therefore, of fundamental importance.

Frederick Hadleigh West

Further Readings

Mobley, C.M. 1991. *The Campus Site: A Prehistoric Camp at Fairbanks, Alaska.* University of Alaska Press, Fairbanks.

Nelson, N.C. 1937. Notes on Cultural Relations Between Asia and America. *American Antiquity* 2:267–272.

West, F.H. 1967. The Donnelly Ridge Site and the Definition of an Early Core and Blade Tradition in Central Alaska. *American Antiquity* 32:360–382.

———. 1981. *The Archaeology of Beringia.* Columbia University Press, New York.

———. 1983. The Antiquity of Man in America. In *The Late Pleistocene,* edited by S.C. Porter, pp. 364–382. Late-Quaternary Environments of the United States, vol. 1, H.E. Wright, general editor. University of Minnesota Press, Minneapolis.

See also CAMPUS SITE; DRY CREEK SITE; NENANA COMPLEX; WALKER ROAD SITE

Denbigh Flint Complex

The original Denbigh Flint complex of Alaska was discovered in 1948 by J.L. Giddings as he was exploring the base of the Iyatayet site on Cape Denbigh in Norton Bay, Norton Sound. Only stone artifacts were preserved in the thin and convoluted deposit underlying the occupation of what Giddings named the Norton culture. These tools were of especially small size and delicate workmanship. They consisted of small bipointed projectile blades apparently designed for both end- and side-hafting in arrow or small dart shafts; some triangular projectile points presumably for use in harpoon heads; numerous microblades; many chipped grooving implements repeatedly resharpened to create what Giddings called "mitten-shaped burins"; spalls from the burin resharpening, often retouched as graving tools; some polished groovers apparently used like burins; and a few small chipped adze blades with polished bits that Giddings at first mistakenly assigned to the overlying Norton deposit.

Almost immediately after the Cape Denbigh find, sites with similar materials were discovered by Giddings on Seward Peninsula and around Kotzebue Sound and by others in the Brooks Range of north Alaska and in the eastern Arctic, where they predated the known Dorset culture. These widespread similarities led William Irving (1962) to encompass all of them in his Arctic Small Tool tradition, in which the term "Denbigh Flint complex" was at first reserved for the collection from Iyatayet. Giddings, however, continued to apply the same term to all comparable finds he made between Cape Denbigh on Norton Sound and Cape Krusenstern on the Chukchi Sea. Because his students and others have followed suit, the term "Denbigh Flint complex" has come to embrace all such assemblages in northern Alaska.

Struck by the "microlithic" nature of the Cape Denbigh materials, Giddings compared them to the European Mesolithic and to the early Siberian Neolithic, despite the absence of pottery, and was inclined to assign them comparable dates. Although the radiocarbon evidence was ambiguous, the date for materials in the original collection by Giddings and the geologist David M. Hopkins was finally put between 3000 and 2500 B.C. (4950–4450 years B.P.) (Giddings 1964). Continued work in northwestern Alaska suggests that even this might be too early for the Cape Denbigh assemblage. Similar materials have been dated to 2000 and 1600 B.C. (ca. 3950–3550 years B.P.), and, until the 1990s, only a single deposit at the site of Onion Portage, referred to as "proto-Denbigh," had provided an earlier date of 2100 B.C. (4050 years B.P.) (Anderson 1984). For the eastern Brooks Range, radiocarbon determinations suggest that comparable assemblages date after 1050 B.C. (3000 years B.P.). Nevertheless, the earliest elements of the Denbigh Flint complex in western Alaska are generally thought to represent the first stage of the widespread Arctic Small Tool tradition and to be ancestral to the Pre-Dorset and Independence I cultures of the eastern Arctic.

At Cape Denbigh and other coastal sites, the occupation remains of the Denbigh complexes are interpreted as the temporary sealing camps of seasonal visitors who primarily hunted caribou on the interior tundra. When evidence of semisubterranean houses is encountered, it is at interior, tundra-edge locations known as caribou crossings or migration paths. In the Brooks Range, Denbigh Flint–complex occupations have also been found at interior lakes that must have provided fish.

South of Norton Bay, related complexes are less plentiful except along the interior river drainages of the northern Alaska Peninsula. These complexes have been given local names in preference to "Denbigh Flint complex" and are dated to the period 2000–1100 B.C. (3950–3050 years B.P.) (Dumond 1984). Semisubterranean houses suggest recurrent winter use, presumably in connection with the hunting of the large peninsula caribou herd, although the small amount of organic trash surviving on house floors points to summer salmon fishing.

The origin of the Denbigh Flint complex is not clear. Some investigators suggest a local derivation from much earlier microblade-making peoples of interior Alaska. Others argue for a migration from Siberia in the early third millennium B.C. In apparent support of this latter position, recent research by the U.S. National

D

Park Service on Seward Peninsula appears to date Denbigh Flint–related occupations as early as ca. 2700 B.C. (4650 years B.P.) (Harritt 1994). The end is similarly uncertain, with evidence for a hiatus following the Denbigh Flint occupation in some areas. Nonetheless, many tool classes show evidence of technological continuity between the Denbigh complex and the succeeding Norton and Ipiutak cultures.

Don E. Dumond

Further Readings

Anderson, D.D. 1984. Prehistory of North Alaska. In *Arctic,* edited by D. Damas, pp. 80–93. Handbook of North American Indians, vol. 5, W.C. Sturtevant, general editor. Smithsonian Institution, Washington, D.C.

Dumond, D.E. 1984. Prehistory of the Bering Sea Region. In *Arctic,* edited by D. Damas, pp. 94–105. Handbook of North American Indians, vol. 5, W.C. Sturtevant, general editor. Smithsonian Institution, Washington, D.C.

Giddings, J.L. 1964. *The Archeology of Cape Denbigh.* Brown University Press, Providence.

Harritt, R.K. 1994. Eskimo Prehistory on the Seward Peninsula, Alaska. *Resources Report* NPS/ARORCR/CRR-93/21. National Park Service, Alaska Regional Office, Anchorage.

Irving, W.N. 1962. A Provisional Comparison of Some Alaskan and Asian Stone Industries. In *Prehistoric Cultural Resources Between the Arctic and Temperate Zones of North America,* edited by J.M. Campbell, pp. 55–68. Technical Paper no. 11. Arctic Institute of North America, Montreal.

See also ARCTIC SMALL TOOL TRADITION

Denticulate

The denticulate is a chipped-stone tool that possesses a regular row of teeth on at least one portion of its periphery. It differs from a notched piece in that the retouched indentations that produced the denticulate teeth are smaller than those of a notched piece; they also do not serve to isolate the notch itself. In its simplest form, the tool can be made on a flake, a blade, or a blocky fragment blank; it can vary in size; and the retouch can be on either the dorsal or the ventral surface. Occasionally, denticulated edges occur on bifacial implements. In these instances, the choice of calling the implement a denticulate or retaining the piece within its principal technological or formal category is a matter of personal preference. In the Normandy Reservoir Project in Tennessee, for instance, a distinction was made between a "denticulate" and a "denticulate flake," with the former being bifacial and the latter unifacial. The denticulate was most likely useful for sawing, shredding, and starting grooves in hard substances, such as antler. This type of tool has existed in most of North America since at least the early Holocene period.

George H. Odell

Further Readings

Faulkner, C.H., and Major C.R. McCollough. 1973. *Introductory Report of the Normandy Reservoir Salvage Project: Environmental Setting, Typology, and Survey.* Normandy Archaeological Project, vol. 1. Report of Investigations no. 11. Department of Anthropology, University of Tennessee, Knoxville.

Deptford Culture

The Deptford culture existed during the Early Woodland period (500 B.C.–A.D. 300, or 2450–1650 years B.P.) on the Coastal Plain in the southeast corner of the United States. Its culture area included southeastern Alabama, all of northern and west-central Florida, eastern Georgia, and southeastern South Carolina. Two internal Deptford areas have been identified, the Atlantic and the Gulf. Only a few of the many different societies within these two areas have been defined by archaeologists.

There were two ways of life in the Deptford culture, coastal and riverine, with most of the population within 75–100 miles of the coast living directly on the coastal strip. The population in the interior lived in the large river valleys. The coastal way of life was one of the first adaptations by Southeast Indians to the modern marine environment. Sea level had stabilized just prior to the Deptford period, and the ecology of the lagoons and bays along the South Atlantic and the northern Gulf of Mexico had developed large sea-grass beds that supported large populations of fish and shellfish that could be easily harvested by people. In addition to the new marine food resources, the coast line was dotted with groves of oak and hickory trees that provided nutritious nuts and also drew deer herds and turkey flocks. Nuts, deer, and turkey had been primary food resources for Southeast Indians for many millennia prior to the Deptford culture. Archaeologists think that it was the addition of easily captured marine food (fish and shellfish) to the traditional nut-deer-turkey dietary mainstays that "pulled" the previous Late Archaic and early Deptford populations to the coastal strip. Deptford settlements were usually located in oak-hickory hammocks adjacent to extensive salt marshes near the mouths of creeks. Many archaeologists think that the coastal villages were permanent, with at least part of the population living there year-round.

Deptford coastal archaeological sites are characterized by general refuse, called a shell midden, that is composed of food waste, such as bones, shells, and charred plants; charcoal from firewood; broken pottery; and other lost and discarded items. Larger sites often contain subterranean pits and postmolds. A few Deptford houses have been found on Cumberland Island off the Georgia coast. They indicate that, by the first century A.D., different houses were used during cool and warm seasons. The cool-season house was a solid, walled, oval structure ca. 10.7 x 9.1 m (35 x 30 feet) in size with a cooking and sleeping room. The warm-season structure had open walls of widely spaced posts and a bell-shaped storage pit in the center. Most Deptford settlements were linear and paralleled the marsh edge, but one site on Cumberland Island was organized in a donutlike circle ca. 67 m (220 feet) in diameter. The Deptford coastal population appears to have expanded throughout its existence, as many new settlements were established and grew in size. By the end of the period, the typical Deptford settlement had 15–25 house structures. At least along the Atlantic Coast, villages were spaced about every 12.9–16 km (8–10 miles).

Deptford culture reached the interior river valleys by at least 100 B.C. Two large settlements have been documented in the interior: the Mandeville site on the edge of the Chatahoochee Valley in southwest Georgia, and the Durant Bend site on the Alabama River in central Alabama. At both of these settlements, a low, large, rectangular platform mound was constructed and covered with a thick layer of food remains and many pits and postmolds, which indicate that the mounds were used for eating or feasting, or both.

The best-known aspect of the material culture of Deptford is its ceramics, which were made from a sandy clay that was coiled to make deep and cylindrical containers with conical bases. Supports were occasionally attached to vessel bases. The most frequent surface treatment is a check pattern made with a wooden or clay stamp inscribed with parallel or perpendicular grooves. Impressing pottery surfaces with fabric is a technique that was occasionally used during the early portion of the period. During the later half of the period, some ceramics were decorated with cord impressions, brushing, and a combination of check and curvilinear (complicated) stamping.

The stone tools made and used by the Deptford people included a small, stemmed, chipped-stone point with a triangular blade. A wide range of stone tools was made of flint, sandstone, quartzite, and limestone for cutting, scraping, abrading, pounding, and chopping activities. Ground-stone tools included celts, axes, and bannerstones. In coastal areas, shell was used to make ladles, dippers, scrapers, chisels, hoes, fishhooks, and harpoons. Both shell and stone were used to make personal adornments such as beads, gorgets, and pendants. Bone was used for needles, awls, pins, harpoons, and basket-weaving "fids." Textiles are poorly preserved, but impressions in pottery reveal that the Deptford people made good mesh nets and woven cloth.

The primary source of information about Deptford social organization is how the people treated their dead. Mounds were built to cover the graves of select individuals in some Deptford societies. The oldest known mounds are on St. Catherines Island off the coast of Georgia. The mounds were constructed on a cleared, burned surface into which a rectangular pit or tomb had been excavated. One or more bodies were placed into the tomb with a few artifacts (usually projectile points). The pit was filled, covered with shells and pottery fragments, and then covered with a low mound of sand ca. 0.9 m (3 feet) high. Human remains in the tombs included individuals who had recently died and bundles of bones prepared from earlier deaths. Some mounds were reused by adding a second layer of fill on top of the old mound into which burials were interred. Only one Deptford burial mound has been found in the Gulf culture area: the Oakland Mound near Tallahassee, Florida. It was a large mound 29 x 23 x 2.4 m (95 x 75 x 8 feet) in size.

D

Study of Deptford burial practices and skeletal remains has revealed that nearly twice as many females were selected for mound burial than males. However, no individual in the mounds was buried with a disproportionate share of grave goods, suggesting that their social organization was egalitarian. In egalitarian societies, people are born relatively equal, and status and wealth are based on individual accomplishments in life.

The Deptford culture was dominant among the southern southeastern Indians during the Early Woodland period (500 B.C.–A.D. 300, or 2450–1650 years B.P.). They were the first people to adapt to the modern coastal environment and to construct platform and burial mounds. The Deptford coastal way of life remained essentially unchanged in much of the area for 2,000 years.

Judith A. Bense

Further Readings

Bense, J.A. 1985. *Hawkshaw: Prehistory and History in an Urban Neighborhood in Pensacola, Florida.* Reports of Investigations no. 7. Archaeology Institute, University of West Florida, Pensacola.

Milanich, J.T. 1994. *Archaeology of Precolumbian Florida.* University of Florida Presses, Gainesville.

Smith, B.A. 1975. *A Re-Analysis of the Mandeville Site, 9Cla1, Focusing on Its Internal History and External Relations.* Unpublished Ph.D. dissertation, Department of Anthropology, University of Georgia, Athens.

Thomas, D.H. 1979. *The Anthropology of St. Catherines Island: 2. The Refuge-Deptford Mortuary Complex.* Anthropological Papers, vol. 56, no. 1. American Museum of Natural History, New York.

See also MANDEVILLE

Dickson Mounds

The Dickson Mounds site (11F34) is a large, Late Prehistoric burial complex located in the central Illinois River Valley near the confluence of the Illinois and Spoon rivers. This complex contains at least two unmounded cemeteries, 10 burial mounds, and a truncated pyramidal mound. Its estimated burial population is 3,000 individuals.

Burial began at the site before A.D. 800 (1150 years B.P.) during the early Late Woodland Myer-Dickson phase. It continued through the later Maples Mills and Sepo Late Woodland phases. By 1000 (950 years B.P.), Mississippian Eveland-phase burials began to appear. Mississippian burials ended after 1250 (700 years B.P.) in the Larson phase. Contacts with Plains cultures are also mirrored in burials at the Dickson site. These contacts are evident in stylistic influences and trade items among the burial furniture. A portion of the site containing 248 burials was excavated and left in situ by the Dickson family in the late 1920s. These burials became the central exhibit in museum complexes operated initially by the Dicksons and later by the state of Illinois. Heightened sensitivity to the display of human skeletal remains resulted in the closing of the exhibit in 1992.

The Dicksons' excavations and excavations in the 1960s by the Illinois State Museum at the mounds site have produced one of the largest and best-documented collections of human skeletal remains from one complex in the Midwest. This collection is of particular importance to studies that measure changes through time in the interaction between physiology and culture. Scholars from diverse fields have undertaken lengthy, unparalleled investigations of the impact of nutritional, sociopolitical, and other forms of stress on the population at the site though time (cf. Buikstra and Milner 1989). These investigations have provided unique temporal perspectives for assessing indigenous Late Woodland and intrusive Early Mississippian dynamics along the northern frontier of Cahokia (Harn 1975, 1980).

Alan D. Harn

Further Readings

Blakely, R.L. 1973. *Biological Variation Among and Between Two Prehistoric Indian Populations at Dickson Mounds.* Unpublished Ph.D. dissertation, Department of Anthropology, Indiana University, Bloomington.

Buikstra, J.E., and G.R. Milner. 1989. *The Dickson Mounds Sites: An Annotated Bibliography.* Reports of Investigations no. 44. Dickson Mounds Museum Anthropological Studies, Illinois State Museum, Springfield.

Goodman, A.H., and G.J. Armelagos. 1985. Disease and Death at Dr. Dickson's Mounds. *Natural History* 94(9):12–18.

Harn, A.D. 1975. Cahokia and the Mississippian Emergence in the Spoon River Area of Illinois. *Transactions of the Illinois State Academy of Science* 68:414–434.

———. 1980. *The Prehistory of Dickson Mounds: The Dickson Excavation.* 2nd ed. Reports of Investigations no. 35. Illinois State Museum, Springfield.

Lallo, J.W. 1972. *The Skeletal Biology of Three Prehistoric American Indian Populations From Dickson Mounds.* Unpublished Ph.D. dissertation, Department of Anthropology, University of Massachusetts, Amherst.

Disc

A disc is a flattened, round object made of stone. At least two separate manifestations of this type of stone object have occurred in North American prehistory. The first type of disc was made of chert and has been discovered in Middle Woodland contexts in burial mounds or as caches. A reanalysis of the Baehr Mounds in the Illinois Valley, excavated in the late nineteenth century, has established that flint objects of this type can be reclassified into crude bifaces, bifacial disc cores, and flat discs (Morrow 1991). Interpretations of these items vary, from talismen, or votive offerings, to preforms for more intensively reduced projectile points or knives. The second type of disc is different in several respects. Although it is also round and flat, it is made of slate or shale and is frequently decorated and drilled. Slate discs have been discovered in Ohio in Middle and Late Woodland contexts. These were chipped into circular flat slabs and then often ground and polished on their periphery. They are crudely manufactured, and their function remains enigmatic. Shale discs from Michigan's Thunder Bay region bordering Lake Huron, on the other hand, were quite carefully manufactured and frequently decorated with objects, such as Thunderbirds and the Great Medicine Tree, that are associated with Ojibwa water symbolism. Holes were drilled in some of these discs, suggesting that they were hung as pendants; others possess no drilled holes but exhibit extensive wear, as though they had been carried around in a bag. They have been interpreted as amulets related to personal safety and appear to have originated in the Late Woodland period in this region.

George H. Odell

Further Readings
Cleland, C.E., R.D. Clute, and R.E. Haltiner. 1984. Naub-Cow-Zo-Win Discs From Northern Michigan. *Midcontinental Journal of Archaeology* 9:235–249.

Converse, R.N. 1973. *Ohio Stone Tools.* Special Publication. Archaeological Society of Ohio, Columbus.

Morrow, C.A. 1991. Observations on the Baehr Mounds Chert "Disks": The American Museum of Natural History Collections. *Illinois Archaeology* 3:77–92.

Discoidal/Chunky Stone

"Discoidal" is an archaeological term for a disclike, flattened stone that is round in plain view, usually bifacially concave, and variable in size. Objects of this nature have been recovered more frequently in midden deposits then in burials. They occurred late in North American prehistory, beginning in Late Woodland times (ca. A.D. 700, or 1250 years B.P.) and continuing through the Mississippian and into the historic period. Several styles of chunky stones, including the Bradley, Cahokia, Jersey Bluff, Prairie du Pont, and Salt River types, have been recognized in prehistoric contexts. Because of their occurrence among historically documented Indian tribes, we know that stones of this nature were employed in the game of "chunkey." This sport was derived from hoop-and-pole gambling games and was a characteristically male activity. In a common version, two players would run side by side. One would toss the chunky and both would hurl or shoot a pole, spear, or arrow at the chunky. The hurled object whose business end fell nearest the chunky was the winning toss. Warren R. DeBoer (1993) has proposed that increased standardization of archaeologically recovered chunky stones in the later Mississippian periods indicates control of the game by the resident elite class. If so, that would provide an interesting parallel to the control of modern sports by the media and certain moneyed "elites."

George H. Odell

Further Readings
DeBoer, W.R. 1993. Like a Rolling Stone: The Chunkey Game and Political Organization in Eastern North America. *Southeastern Archaeology* 12:83–92.

Link, A.W. 1980. Discoidals and Problematical Stones From Mississippian Sites in

Minnesota. *Plains Anthropologist* 25:343–352.

Perino, G.H. 1971. The Mississippian Component at the Schild Site (No. 4), Greene County, Illinois. In *Mississippian Site Archaeology in Illinois I*, pp. 1–148. Bulletin no. 8. Illinois Archaeological Survey, University of Illinois Press, Urbana.

Dismal River Aspect

A.T. Hill, W.D. Strong, and W.R. Wedel first recognized Dismal River sites in the mid-1930s along the Dismal River in western Nebraska—hence the name. The designation Dismal River "aspect" or complex followed excavations in 1939 at the Lovitt site, a large village in Chase County in southwestern Nebraska. Additional data came from excavations in west-central Kansas, especially in Scott County, and at White Cat Village in Harlan County, in south-central Nebraska. To date (1996), Dismal River sites have been reported from the ninety-ninth meridian west in Kansas and Nebraska to the foothills of the Rockies and from southwestern South Dakota to southeastern Colorado. Large villages are found along the east-central border of this area, where horticulture was an important addition to a basically hunting economy. The complex was soon attributed to the Apaches, an identification that has continued to be strengthened, with the Quartelejo and Paloma Apaches of the 1600s and early 1700s considered the most likely groups.

The more thoroughly investigated Dismal River sites are large villages, located on small permanent streams near garden plots, of up to 15–20 semipermanent structures. The structures are apparently not arranged in any particular pattern. A typical house is represented by a circle of five center posts surrounding an unprepared hearth at a radius of ca. 2 m (6.6 feet). There are often two entrance posts opposite the east or southeast side of the pentagon ca. 4 m (13 feet) from the hearth. The entrance posts were apparently placed against a circle of poles that leaned against the framework of the center posts. The houses, which are ca. 8 m (26.2 feet) in diameter, were covered with brush and perhaps dirt. Bell-shaped, heavily burned baking pits, some of which contain human burials, are characteristic features. Trash-filled pits, which may once have been borrow pits, are also common. Artifacts resemble those of other Protohistoric Plains complexes, with chipped-stone tools dominated by heavy, crude, hide-working choppers and scrapers. Projectile points are small, well-made, unnotched or side-notched, triangular forms. Bone and antler points are rare, but stone drills are common. A

Artist's reconstruction of the framework for a Dismal River house. (Prepared by J. H. Gunnerson)

diagnostic trait is an artifact that resembles a double-pointed drill with one or more projections at the midpoint.

Pottery consists of smooth bowls and smooth or simple stamped ollas (jars). Decoration is restricted to ollas and consists of incised lines or punctations on the lips. Simple stamping and lip decoration decreases as one goes from north to south. Trade pottery, from the Southwest, consists of Tewa polychrome and Ocate micaceous, a type of micaceous pottery made by the Jicarilla Apache in New Mexico betwen ca. A.D. 1600 and 1750 (350–200 years B.P.). Some turquoise has also been found. A few portable, well-made, Jicarilla-type metates have been found in western Kansas sites and are common in related Jicarilla sites in northeastern New Mexico. Tree rings date Dismal River sites to the last quarter of the 1600s and the first quarter of the 1700s, with ethnohistory pushing the complex back to the mid-1600s. To date (1996), presedentary Plains Apache sites, starting with the arrival on the Plains of Apaches from western Canada in ca. A.D. 1500 (450 years B.P.), have not been identified. The Dismal River people (the Paloma and Quartelejo Apaches of Spanish documents) were friends of the Spanish, but they were pushed off the central Plains in the third decade of the 1700s by the French and by Pawnees from the east and Comanches from the west. Dismal River survivors eventually joined the Jicarilla and Lipan Apaches. Others had earlier joined the Kiowa in the Black Hills area and, with them, later migrated south, where they became known as the Kiowa Apache.

James H. Gunnerson

Further Readings

Champe, J.L. 1949. White Cat Village. *American Antiquity* 14(4):285–292.

Gunnerson, D.A. 1956. The Southern Athabascans: Their Arrival in the Southwest. *El Palacio* 63(11–12):346–365.

———. 1974. *The Jicarilla Apaches: A Study in Survival.* Northern Illinois University Press, De Kalb.

Gunnerson, J.H. 1960. An Introduction to Plains Apache Archeology—the Dismal River Aspect. Anthropological Paper no. 58. *Bulletin of the Bureau of American Ethnology* 173:129–260.

———. 1968. Plains Apache Archaeology: A Review. *Plains Anthropologist* 13(41):167–189.

———. 1979. Southern Athapaskan Archeology. In *Southwest,* edited by A. Ortiz, pp. 162–169. Handbook of North American Indians, vol. 9, W.C. Sturtevant, general editor. Smithsonian Institution, Washington, D.C.

Gunnerson, J.H., and D.A. Gunnerson. 1971. Apachean Culture: A Study in Unity and Diversity. In *Apachean Culture History and Ethnology,* edited by K.H. Basso and M.E. Opler, pp. 7–27. Anthropological Papers no. 21. University of Arizona, Tucson.

Hill, A.T., and G. Metcalf. 1942. A Site of the Dismal River Aspect in Chase County, Nebraska. *Nebraska History* 22(2): 158–226.

D

Doerschuk Site

Doerschuk (31MG22) is a deeply stratified, multicomponent site on the Yadkin River in Montgomery County, North Carolina. Excavations under the direction of Joffre L. Coe in 1948–1949 recovered more than 6,800 artifacts and enormous quantities of debitage representing eight cultural complexes spanning more than 8,000 years. Coe's research at Doerschuk and later at the Hardaway site was seminal in Archaic-period research for defining the typological chronology of Archaic-period projectile points based on stratigraphy. The deep cultural stratigraphy of the Doerschuk site was an important impetus for later archaeological work by Betty Broyles at the St. Albans site in West Virginia and by Jefferson Chapman in the Tellico Reservoir in eastern Tennessee.

Although scattered Early Archaic material was recovered at Doerschuk, the first in situ occupation was that of the Middle Archaic Stanly complex. Ascending stratigraphy defined by Coe included the Archaic Morrow Mountain, Guilford, and Savannah River complexes overlain by the Woodland Badin and Yadkin, the Mississippian Pee Dee, and the historic Caraway components.

Jefferson Chapman

Further Readings

Broyles, B.J. 1966. Preliminary Report: The St. Albans Site (40KA27), Kanawha County, West Virginia. *West Virginia Archaeologist* 19:1–43.

Chapman, J. 1985. *Tellico Archaeology:*

12,000 Years of Native American History. University of Tennessee Press, Knoxville.

Coe, J.L. 1964. *The Formative Cultures of the Carolina Piedmont.* Transactions, n.s., vol. 54, pt. 5. American Philosophical Society, Philadelphia.

Oliver, B.L. 1985. Tradition and Typology: Basic Elements of the Carolina Projectile Point Sequence. In *Structure and Process in Southeastern Archaeology,* edited by R.S. Dickens, Jr., and H.T. Ward, pp. 195–211. University of Alabama Press, Tuscaloosa.

See also TELLICO ARCHAIC

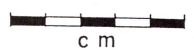

c m

Clovis points from the Domebo site (34CD50) made from Edwards chert. (Drawn by Frederic Sellet; courtesy of J. L. Hofman)

Domebo

The Domebo site (34CD50) in Oklahoma is a Clovis age (9250–9050 B.C., or 11,200–11,000 years B.P.) mammoth bonebed with associated artifacts that was excavated in 1962. Since 1966, when a detailed interdisciplinary report on the site (Leonhardy 1966) was published, it has remained a key reference for the Clovis cultural complex, for studies of Paleoindian mammoth hunting, for paleoecology of the Pleistocene-to-Holocene transition in the southern Plains, and for the cultural history of the Plains region. The research at Domebo helped establish the geographic distribution of the Llano complex, which had been defined based on the repeated association of Clovis fluted projectile points and mammoth remains in the Plains region. At Domebo, the remains of a single mammoth were recovered from gray sandy clay deposits at the base of a small canyon. Associated with the mammoth bones were three small flakes and three Clovis projectile points, one represented by a midsection only. Two butchering tools and another Clovis projectile point were found in the vicinity of the bones but had eroded out of the mammoth and gray sandy clay unit. The source of the stone material used in making the Clovis points, flakes, and tools from Domebo is the Edwards formation in central Texas ca. 250 km (155 miles) to the south. Whether the Clovis points were actually used to kill the Domebo mammoth has remained a point of discussion, although the association between the points and the mammoth bones is well documented. It is possible that the points represent spears used to finish off a sick or disabled animal or that they were used as knives to aid in the butchering of an animal that had died by other means.

The Domebo site's significance is due in part to the variety of paleoecological studies that were conducted in conjunction with the archaeological research. Evidence from pollen,

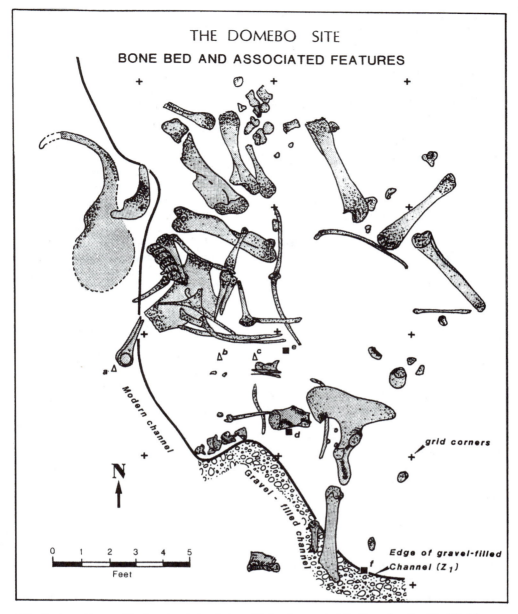

THE DOMEBO SITE
BONE BED AND ASSOCIATED FEATURES

grid corners

N

0 1 2 3 4 5
Feet

Modern channel

Gravel - filled channel

Edge of gravel-filled
Channel (Z₁)

Distribution of bones, Clovis points (triangles), and flakes (squares) at the Domebo site. (Modified from Leonhardy 1966; drawn by J. L. Hofman)

snails, vertebrate faunal remains, stratigraphy, and radiocarbon dating has made the site a key reference locality for studies of southern-Plains paleoenvironments at the end of the Pleistocene. The climate of the region at the time apparently was more moderate, with less severe winters and cooler summers, as indicated by the variety of species in the deposit. More recently, developments in accurate radiocarbon dating of fossil bone using accelerator mass spectrometry have relied upon the Domebo mammoth assemblage as a key sample. The site is one of the better dated Clovis-age deposits in the New World.

Jack L. Hofman

Further Readings

Ferring, C.R., and S.A. Hall. 1987. Domebo Canyon. In *Late Quaternary Stratigra-*

phy, *Neotectonics and Geoarchaeology of Southwestern Oklahoma*, pp. 56–66. Guidebook for the Fifth Annual Field Trip of the South Central Cell. Friends of the Pleistocene, Lawton.

Hofman, J.L. 1988. Dating the Lower Domebo Formation in Western Oklahoma. *Current Research in the Pleistocene* 5:86–88.

Leonhardy, F.C. (editor). 1966. *Domebo: A Paleo-Indian Mammoth Kill in the Prairie-Plains*. Contributions no. 1. Museum of the Great Plains, Lawton.

Stafford, T.W., Jr., P.E. Hare, L. Currie, A.J.T. Juil, and D.J. Donahue. 1991. Accelerator Radiocarbon Dating at the Molecular Level. *Journal of Archaeological Science* 18:35–72.

See also CLOVIS CULTURAL COMPLEX

Dorset Culture

The term "Dorset culture" refers to the later phases of the Paleoeskimo (Arctic Small Tool) tradition in the eastern North American Arctic. Dorset culture appears to have developed from earlier Pre-Dorset complexes as a result of technological and economic changes that occurred between ca. 1050 and 550 B.C. (3000–2500 years B.P.). A series of new artifacts and stylistic innovations appear at this time in various regional subtraditions of the Pre-Dorset complex: polished burinlike tools, small soapstone lamps, needles with flattened ovate cross sections, new forms of chipped-stone points with notched hafts, a new technique of sharpening bifaces by removing large thin flakes from the tip (tip-fluting), and new styles of bone or ivory harpoon and lance heads. A few of these elements had appeared at low incidences in some local Pre-Dorset complexes prior to 1050 B.C. (3000 years B.P.), and some did not occur in other local traditions until after 550 B.C. (2500 years B.P.). During the centuries between these dates, however, there appears to have been increased communication and transmission of technological innovations throughout the eastern Arctic. Local complexes that participated in this process are known as Independence II in the High Arctic and the Groswater phase in Labrador and Newfoundland; the term "transitional" has generally been applied elsewhere.

By ca. 550 B.C. (2500 years B.P.), a more uniform complex—apparently centered on the general area of Baffin Island, Foxe Basin, northern Hudson Bay, Hudson Strait, and northern Labrador—had emerged in the eastern Canadian Arctic. Throughout this area, sites assigned to the Early Dorset phase are characterized by a uniform set of artifact styles, including harpoon heads with closed sockets, small rectangular soapstone lamps with sloping sides, flat needles with gouged elongate eyes, nephrite burinlike tools, flat multinotched ground-slate knives, numerous microblades, triangular end blades in chipped stone, notched bifaces with a relatively high incidence of tip-fluting, and occasional small carvings representing animals and humans or humanlike beings. Two items of technology important to Pre-Dorset people, the drill and the bow and arrow, appear to have gone out of use. These technological changes appear coincidentally with a marked increase in the size and duration of occupations represented by Early Dorset archaeological sites.

Many Early Dorset sites also produce evidence of greater reliance on, and probably more efficient exploitation of, sea-mammal resources than is apparent in most Pre-Dorset complexes. This change in economic adaptation may have been related to environmental changes during the final millennium B.C. Evidence from throughout the eastern Arctic indicates that this millennium saw generally cooling climatic conditions, and that in some areas this process accelerated after ca. 500 B.C. (2450 years B.P.). Although such a climatic change was probably not conducive to increased sea-mammal populations, an increase in the seasonal duration and extent of sea ice may have increased the effectiveness of Dorset ice-hunting techniques. Although a few fragments of wooden frames from kayaklike watercraft have been recovered from Dorset sites, techniques for open-water hunting do not appear to have been highly developed. Most Dorset weapons could be effectively used for hunting seals at breathing holes and other sea mammals from the ice edge; the importance of ice hunting and traveling is also indicated by the use of ivory crampons to walk on ice and shoes for small sled runners. A dependable supply of sea-mammal meat and oil may have allowed the adoption of a more sedentary way of life, a change suggested by the first appearance at some eastern Arctic sites of large semisubterranean winter houses built from boulders and turf. These houses must have been heated and lit by oil-burning lamps.

Victoria Island, in the central Arctic, was

occupied by an Early Dorset variant that shared much of the technology of eastern Arctic Dorset culture but based its economy on the hunting of caribou and musk-ox. This development appears to have been based in a local Pre-Dorset tradition that had been influenced by contact with both Early Dorset peoples to the east and Alaskanlike peoples to the west, now known from sites on Banks Island and Cape Bathurst on the adjacent mainland coast. Although there is very slight evidence for the transmission of technological elements between Dorset culture and the developing maritime hunting traditions of Alaska, such diffusion may have played a small part in the development of Early Dorset culture.

The florescence of Early Dorset culture appears to have lasted for only a few centuries. A poorly defined middle Dorset period is usually considered to have begun by at least 50 B.C. (2000 years B.P.) and to have lasted until ca. A.D. 450 (1500 years B.P.). The period is defined by relatively minor technological changes. More significant, however, Dorset occupations throughout the central and eastern Arctic appear to have been smaller and more scattered, and a widespread population decline is postulated. The major exception to this pattern is on the coast of Labrador and around the coasts of the island of Newfoundland, which saw a major Dorset occupation throughout this period. The largest Dorset sites in Newfoundland are associated with areas where Harp seals can be hunted on the spring ice, but the Newfoundland Dorset people also occupied ice-free coasts and were obviously adapted to such Subarctic conditions. The only human burials that can be definitely ascribed to the Dorset population are found in Newfoundland caves, and the few skeletons that have been recovered are indistinguishable in physical type from Inuit.

While the Dorset people withdrew from Newfoundland and southern Labrador at some time after A.D. 450 (1500 years B.P.), the following 500 years saw a major expansion of Dorset occupation across the central and eastern Arctic and northward to the High Arctic islands and Greenland. This Late Dorset complex is characterized by widespread uniformity in artifact styles, which suggests the establishment of effective communication networks. The Late Dorset period also saw a major florescence in artistic activities, and most specimens of Dorset carving derive from sites of this time. Many of the carvings appear to have been related to shamanic or other ritual activities, which are also evidenced by the manufacture of items like masks and drums. Another feature of Late Dorset sites is long enclosures up to 45 m (148 feet) long and 6 m (20 feet) wide that are built of boulders. These structures show little evidence of occupation. They are often associated with rows of hearths, which may be the remains of linear tent encampments in an area external to the enclosure. The purpose of such structures is not known, but it has been suggested that they may have been related to the ritual activities evidenced by the frequent carvings and ritual artifacts found in Late Dorset sites.

Late Dorset sites throughout most of the Arctic are not known after ca. A.D. 1000 (950 years B.P.), except in the northern Quebec/Labrador peninsula, where Dorset occupation may have continued until as recently as A.D. 1500 (450 years B.P.). Elsewhere, the Dorset disappearance appears to coincide with the immigration of Thule-culture Inuit from Alaska. It seems likely that the newcomers, who brought a maritime hunting technology significantly more efficient than that of the Dorset people, quickly replaced the last of the Paleoeskimo occupants from most Arctic regions.

Robert J. McGhee

Further Readings

Dumond, D. 1987. *Eskimos and Aleuts*. 2nd ed. Thames and Hudson, New York.

Maxwell, M. 1985. *The Prehistory of the Eastern Arctic*. Academic Press, New York.

Dorset/Thule Transition

Did the people of the Thule culture find the Canadian Arctic and Greenland uninhabited when they ventured eastward from Alaska or did they meet people of the Dorset culture? Most archaeologists believe that such a meeting took place and that the Dorset either joined Thule communities and quickly adopted their way of life or retreated to ecologically marginal areas where they were unable to survive for long. However, these conclusions are based on circumstantial types of evidence, for sites have not been found that provide even reasonably unambiguous proof of their face-to-face contact.

Perhaps the most persuasive evidence for contact comes from Inuit legends concerning a people known as Tunit who inhabited the land before the Inuit. Many archaeologists believe that the Tunit were the Dorset. However, we also know that the Thule used abandoned Dorset sites and thus need never have come into contact with Dorset people to be aware that someone had lived there before them. Hence the Thule might just have made up stories about their unknown predecessors without ever having actually met them.

Overlapping radiocarbon dates support the possibility of contact between these two groups. The earliest reliable Thule radiocarbon estimations from the Canadian Arctic and Greenland date to the late tenth century A.D. While there are almost no reliable Dorset dates later than the ninth century from most of that vast region, dates as late as the sixteenth century have been attributed to Dorset in the Labrador-Ungava Peninsula. However, the cultural affiliation of these very late dates has been challenged (Park 1993).

The final line of evidence supporting contact comes from an apparent transfer of technology from Dorset to Thule, especially harpoon-head styles. Dorset-influenced Thule harpoon heads are found only at very late Thule sites, however, and not in sites dating to the period when the two groups are presumed to have been in contact. It may be that late Thule people simply copied Dorset harpoon heads found at abandoned Dorset sites. Many researchers also suggest that the Dorset taught the Thule how to build snowhouses and to make pots and lamps out of soapstone. However, the Thule may have made snowhouses before meeting the Dorset, and soapstone vessels would have been a logical invention for the Thule to make in the clay-poor Canadian Arctic as substitutes for ceramic pots and lamps. Thus, the available evidence supporting Thule-Dorset contact can be explained almost equally well by Thule salvage and reuse of abandoned Dorset sites and artifacts. Further research will be required to finally determine whether contact took place or whether the Dorset had already disappeared for reasons unrelated to the Thule migration.

Robert W. Park

Further Readings

Dumond, D. 1987. *Eskimos and Aleuts.* 2nd ed. Thames and Hudson, New York.
Maxwell, M. 1985. *The Prehistory of the Eastern Arctic.* Academic Press, New York.
Park, R.W. 1993. The Dorset-Thule Succession in Arctic North America: Assessing Claims for Culture Contact. *American Antiquity* 58:203–234.

See also DORSET CULTURE; THULE CULTURE

Douglass, Andrew Ellicott (1867–1962)

An astronomer interested in tree rings as a means of relating cyclic climatic episodes on Earth to periods of sunspot activity, A.E. Douglass invented dendrochronology (tree-ring dating) in the first decades of the twentieth century. Beginning in 1901 with living trees in the arid U.S. Southwest, he eventually searched prehistoric pueblos for progressively older wood specimens. By 1929, he had connected long tree-ring sequences with the historic period; by the mid-1930s, he had constructed an accurate chronology of late prehistory in regions of the northern Southwest. Douglass founded the Laboratory of Tree-Ring Research at the University of Arizona in Tucson in 1938. Since then, archaeologists in the Southwest and elsewhere have increasingly followed his lead in using tree rings in paleoecological studies.

Guy Gibbon

Further Readings

Douglass, A.E. 1935. *Dating Pueblo Bonito and Other Ruins of the Southwest.* National Geographic Society Contributions, Technical Paper no. 1. National Geographic Society, Washington, D.C.

Andrew E. Douglass. *(Reprinted with permission from* American Antiquity *28[1]:87)*

Judd, N.M. 1962. Andrew Ellicott Douglass: 1867–1962. *American Antiquity* 28:87–89.

Webb, G.E. 1983. *Tree Rings and Telescopes: The Scientific Career of A.E. Douglass.* University of Arizona Press, Tucson.

Dover Quarry

Prehistoric Native Americans in eastern North America made most of their stone-cutting and piercing tools out of flint or chert, a tractable silica rock that can be flaked in predictable ways. Flint, a popular generic term, or chert as it is usually called by geologists and archaeologists, occurs in limestone bedrock in thick tabular layers or in spherical masses called nodules. Tabular pieces and nodules were directly mined out of the bedrock in quarries, or nodules were collected in streams into which they had eroded. The most famous prehistoric chert quarry in eastern North America is the Dover quarry southeast of the town of Dover in Stewart County, Tennessee. The quarry pits cover ca. 2 ha (5 acres); debris from the making of stone tools extends over at least 20 ha (50 acres). Geological opinion is divided as to whether the gray-to-dun-colored chert nodules and tabular pieces mined there are from the lower St. Louis or the Warsaw geological formations. A neutron activation study of Dover chert has compared it to other lower St. Louis chert, but the results have been inconclusive (Nance 1979).

Dover chert may have been picked up for thousands of years in the quarry area by aboriginal toolmakers. However, extensive digging in the quarry apparently occurred only during the Mississippian period (ca. A.D. 800–1600, or 1150–350 years B.P.). While high-quality chert was abundant throughout this region of western Tennessee and Kentucky for the manufacture of projectile points and various other smaller, utilitarian objects, large nodules and tabular pieces were available only at Dover quarry. These large chunks of chert were used to make utilitarian hoes and adzes and, especially, the ceremonial objects coveted by Mississippian peoples, such as bipointed swords, batons, discs, and maces. The latter are superb examples of the chertknapper's art, with some of the swords reaching a length of 69 cm (27 inches).

Archaeological survey and excavation at the quarry have revealed numerous pits from which the nodules and tabular pieces were dug. The pits are ringed by piles of waste flakes and discarded broken pieces from flaking blanks or rough preforms of intended finished artifacts. Two kinds of pits have been identified: shallow excavations where nodular chert may have been dug and worked, and deep pits where the tabular chert was derived. Nodules were probably dug out with digging sticks and stone hoes or spades. Tabular chunks may have been dislodged with heat, water, and levers. Near the pits are extensive workshops where Mississippian craftspersons produced finished utilitarian and ritual objects. Domestic structures and burials around the quarry indicate that full-time artisans probably lived and died at the site. The artifacts they produced were traded in a regional exchange system that extended throughout the southeastern United States, particularly during the late Mississippian period (A.D. 1350–1500, or 600–450 years B.P.). Artifacts tentatively identified as made from Dover chert have been found in Mississippian villages and mounds in eastern Tennessee, southern Illinois, Georgia, Alabama, Florida, and Oklahoma.

Charles H. Faulkner

Further Readings

Gramly, R.M. 1992. *Prehistoric Lithic Industry at Dover, Tennessee.* Persimmon Press, Buffalo.

Nance, J.D. 1979. A Preliminary Report on Neutro-Activation Analysis of the Dover Flint Quarry, Stewart County, Tennessee. Paper presented at the Thirty-Eighth Annual Meeting, Southeastern Archaeological Conference, Atlanta.

———. 1984. Lithic Exploitation Studies in the Lower Tennessee-Cumberland Valleys, Western Kentucky. In *Prehistoric Chert Exploitation: Studies from the Midcontinent*, edited by B.M. Butler and E.E. May, pp. 101–127. Occasional Paper no. 2. Center for Archaeological Investigations, Southern Illinois University Press, Carbondale.

Draper Site

The Draper site, northeast of Toronto, was a late-fifteenth-century A.D. prehistoric village and town occupied by the Huron Indians. Iroquoian-speaking slash-and-burn horticulturalists, the Huron occupied south-central Ontario, Canada, between A.D. 1400 and 1650 (550–300 years B.P.). The proposed destruction of the site by the new Toronto International Airport

D

project resulted in small-scale salvage excavations in 1972 and 1973. These excavations were funded by the Canadian Museum of Civilization (CMC). By 1974, less than 4 percent of the site had been investigated. Major rescue excavations, funded by the Ministry of Transport, CMC, and Employment and Immigration Canada, were directed by the author in 1975 and 1978. More than 42,869 m² (51,271 square yards) of the site were excavated, including 1,747 1 x 1 m (3.3 x 3.3 foot) units in undisturbed middens and 3,283 1 x 1 m (3.3 x 3.3 foot) units in undisturbed longhouses.

Excavations revealed that Draper began as a 1.2 ha (3-acre) village containing at least seven longhouses surrounded by four rows of palisades. Its population at the time is estimated at 396. During its relatively short occupation (50 years or less), the village expanded five times to become a town of 3.4 ha (8.4 acres) with at least 35 longhouses and an estimated population of 1,944. As the village expanded, the longest houses—interpreted as those occupied by civil and war chiefs—were placed on the outer edges of the village. This placement assisted in the defense of the village by creating long, narrow, easily defended corridors and central "plazas." Two groups of houses of similar orientation with estimated populations of at least 216 individuals were in separate segments of the village. Their presence suggests that clan segments, which are documented for the historic period,

were also present among the Huron before European contact. An unpalisaded satellite or hamlet containing seven widely spaced longhouses was adjacent to the village. It is uncertain whether this was a year-round satellite, a seasonally occupied hamlet associated with an earlier or later village, or a settlement occupied by an immigrant population prior to its incorporation into the village.

The Draper excavations allowed experimentation with bulldozers and road graders in stripping large areas of subsoil to expose house and palisade patterns. Mechanical screens and high-pressure water from firefighting pumps were used to screen midden and undisturbed living-floor deposits. Data on more than 43,966 postmolds and 2,134 features were processed, illustrated, and analyzed by computer, as were data for all other major classes of artifact. The excavation of several complete middens made it possible to evaluate random-sampling strategies. These evaluations indicated that, at Draper, small middens (less than 100 1 x 1 m units) had to be totally excavated to attain a reliable profile of their content. At least 60 percent of medium-sized middens (100–250 1 x 1 m units) and 40–45 percent of large middens (more than 300 1 x 1 m units) had to be excavated using a systematic transverse sampling method to attain similarly secure results.

An archaeological survey of 5,463 of the 7,487 ha (13,500 of 18,500 acres) expropriated

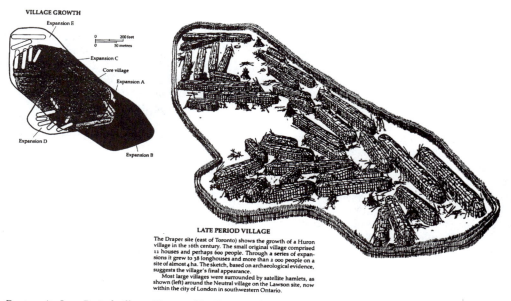

VILLAGE GROWTH
Expansion E
0   200 feet
0   50 metres
Expansion C
Core village
Expansion A
Expansion D
Expansion B

LATE PERIOD VILLAGE

The Draper site (east of Toronto) shows the growth of a Huron village in the 16th century. The small original village comprised 11 houses and perhaps 600 people. Through a series of expansions it grew to 38 longhouses and more than 2 000 people on a site of almost 4 ha. The sketch, based on archaeological evidence, suggests the village's final appearance.
Most large villages were surrounded by satellite hamlets, as shown (left) around the Neutral village on the Lawson site, now within the city of London in southwestern Ontario.

Draper site Late Period village. (Prepared by W. D. Finlayson)

Core Village   Expansion 1

D

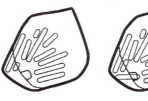

Expansion 2

Expansion 3

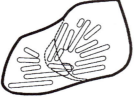

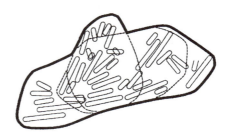

Expansion 4

Expansion 5

Draper site village growth. (Prepared by W. D. Finlayson)

for airport construction discovered 14 new Iroquoian sites. The survey demonstrated that Draper was only one of more than 26 sites on Duffin Creek and that the Iroquoian occupation of this area dated to at least the ninth century A.D. A 30-minute movie and a multimedia kit for public schools, both entitled *To Know the Hurons,* were made by the National Film Board of Canada.

William D. Finlayson

Further Readings

Bellhouse, D.R., and W.D. Finlayson. 1979. An Empirical Study of Probability Sampling Designs. *Canadian Journal of Archaeology* 3:105–123.

Finlayson, W.D. 1985. *The 1975 and 1978 Rescue Excavations at the Draper Site: Introduction and Settlement Patterns.* Mercury Series Paper no. 130. Archaeological Survey of Canada, National Museum of Man, Ottawa.

Hayden, B. (editor). 1979. *Settlement Patterns of the Draper and White Sites.* Publication no. 6. Department of Archaeology, Simon Fraser University, Burnaby.

Trigger, B.G. 1985. Introduction. In *The 1975 and 1978 Rescue Excavations at the Draper Site: Introduction and Settlement Patterns,* pp. 5–18. Mercury Series Paper no. 130. Archaeological Survey of Canada, National Museum of Man, Ottawa.

Drill

The drill is employed for making circular holes in things. The hole is necessarily circular, because the drill bit is rotated in the material in which the hole is desired. Projected uses for these tools in prehistory run the gamut from stitching in hide clothing, to the attachment of a bone harpoon, to the repairing of pots. Drilling experiments in stone (Rau 1868) indicate that this is an intensive activity requiring a long time to complete. Several types of drills have been recognized, with the key differences between them defined by the energizing component. The earliest was undoubtedly the manually held rotary drill. This was replaced by more complex kinetic apparatus, such as the bow drill and the pump drill. The drill is so basic to human needs that it has been an integral constituent of human tool assemblages since at least the Upper Paleolithic period. In North America, drills have been dated as far back as Paleoindian times and are found in all subsequent periods. In the Late Prehistoric Mississippian period, they have been associated with an interesting cottage industry involving considerable craft specialization. Flint microdrills at Cahokia and nearby settlements were employed to bore holes in shells for a vibrant bead industry.

George H. Odell

Drills. (Reprinted from Smithsonian Institution, Bureau of American Ethnology, Bulletin 60, Figure 210)

Further Readings

Meyer, D., and H. Liboiron. 1990. A Paleoindian Drill From the Niska Site in Southern Saskatchewan. *Plains Anthropologist* 35:299–302.

Rau, C. 1868. Drilling in Stone Without Metal. *Annual Report of the Smithsonian Institution,* pp. 392–400. Washington, D.C.

Wylie, H.G. 1975. Pot Scrapers and Drills From Southern Utah. *Kiva* 40:121–130.

Yerkes, R.W. 1983. Microwear, Microdrills, and Mississippian Craft Specialization. *American Antiquity* 48:499–518.

Dry Creek Site

Dry Creek (HEW-005) is a stratified early prehistoric site in central Alaska that contains remains assigned to several major cultural traditions, including Palaeoindian (Nenana complex) and American Palaeoarctic (Denali complex). The site is located in the northern foothills of the Alaska Range near the town of Healy and occupies a southeast-facing bluff on the north side of Dry Creek in the Nenana Valley. The site was discovered and initially investigated by C.E. Holmes in 1973 and subsequently excavated by W.R. Powers in 1974 and 1976–1977; a total of 347 m² (415 square yards) has been exposed (Powers et al. 1983).

The artifacts and other remains are buried

in loess and aeolian sand deposits that cap a glaciofluvial outwash terrace of possible late middle Pleistocene age (ca. 250,000–130,000 years B.P.). These deposits, which vary between 1 and 2 m (3.3–6.6 feet) in depth, unconformably overlie the outwash and span the last 12,000 years. The lowermost unit (Loess 1) is devoid of archaeological remains. It is overlain by a sandy silt (Loess 2) that contains the lowermost archaeological component (Component I) and is radiocarbon dated to 9170 B.C. ± 85 (11,120 years B.P.). A sand lens separates Loess 2 from overlying Loess 3, which is another sandy silt unit containing archaeological Component II (8740 B.C. ± 250, or 10,690 years B.P.). Loess 3 also contains a series of thin organic lenses distributed throughout the unit (Palaeosol 1), and is capped with two more strongly developed and continuous organic bands (Palaeosol 2) that date to the earliest Holocene (8050–6050 B.C., or 10,000–8000 years B.P.). The upper portion of the aeolian sequence at Dry Creek comprises a series of alternating loess and aeolian sand units that span the remainder of the Holocene. It contains a soil complex (Palaeosol 3) composed of a series of organic bands and lenses that dates to ca. 6650–4300 B.C. (8600–6250 years B.P.) and may be correlated with the Altithermal; it contains scattered artifacts. The uppermost part of the sequence contains a buried-forest soil complex (Palaeosol 4a and 4b) dated to the middle and late Holocene (2650 B.C., or 4600 years B.P., to the present). The lower part of the complex (Palaeosol 4a) yielded an assemblage of several thousand artifacts (Component IV) (Thorson and Hamilton 1977).

A small quantity of poorly preserved mammalian faunal remains was recovered from the site; identifiable specimens are confined to isolated tooth fragments. Remains excavated from Component I (Loess 2) were identified as Dall sheep (*Ovis dalli*) and wapiti (*Cervus canadensis*), and fragments from Component II (Loess 3/Palaeosol 1) were assigned to steppe bison (*Bison priscus*) and Dall sheep (Guthrie 1983).

Three large artifact concentrations were mapped on the Component I occupation floor. They ranged in size from 2 to 5 m² (2.4–6.0 square yards) and contained between 110 and 1,160 items; isolated faunal remains and charcoal fragments were found in association with the concentrations. Smaller accumulations of debris, including a concentration of faunal remains, are scattered across the occupation area. More than 4,500 artifacts, including four cores and 56 tools (1.2 percent), were recovered from this level; raw materials include brown chert, gray chert, rhyolite, and quartzite. Among the tools are a small bifacial projectile point, two projectile-point bases, small bifaces, side scrapers, end scrapers, planes, wedges, and cobble tools. The projectile point is triangular in form, and the point bases appear to be derived from similar points. Component I has been assigned to the Nenana complex on the basis of the presence of small triangular/teardrop-shaped points (or Chindadn points), end scrapers, planes, and wedges, and the absence of wedge-shaped microblade cores, microblades, and polyfaceted burins (Powers and Hoffecker 1989; Goebel et al. 1991).

Fourteen large debris concentrations were uncovered in Component II. They range from 4 to 13 m² (4.8–15.5 square yards) in size and contain 350–3,500 items; most of the concentrations are associated with isolated faunal remains and charcoal fragments. The concentrations vary significantly in terms of content: Some contain microblade cores, microblades, and burins, while others contain bifacial points or other tool types. The Component II assemblage contains more than 28,000 artifacts, including more than 120 cores and core fragments and more than 300 tools (1.2 percent); raw materials include quartzite, rhyolite, various cherts (gray, brown, black, and green), chalcedony, obsidian, quartzite, argillite, diabase, pumice, and sandstone. The cores and core fragments include more than 20 wedge-shaped microblade cores and numerous microblade core parts; more than 1,700 microblades were recovered from this level. Among the tools in this assemblage are burins (including polyfaceted types), small and large bifaces, and various types of scrapers. The bifaces include a small lanceolate projectile point and projectile-point tips and bases; the point bases are apparently derived from lanceolate or stemmed forms. Component II is assigned to the Denali complex (West 1967), primarily on the basis of the presence of wedge-shaped microblade cores, microblades, and polyfaceted burins (Powers et al. 1983; Powers and Hoffecker 1989).

The uppermost assemblage yielded more than 2,300 artifacts, which include 241 rocks and bone fragments and 16 tools (0.8 percent); raw materials comprise rhyolite, quartzite, obsidian, chert, and siltstone. The tools include several stemmed/side-notched points, end scrapers, and retouched flakes. The assemblage is assigned to the Northern Archaic tradition on the basis of the point typology.

John F. Hoffecker

Further Readings

Goebel, F.E., W.R. Powers, and N.H. Bigelow. 1991. The Nenana Complex of Alaska and Clovis Origins. In *Clovis Origins and Adaptations,* edited by R. Bonnichsen and K. Turnmire, pp. 49–79. Center for the Study of the First Americans, Oregon State University, Corvallis.

Guthrie, R.D. 1983. Paleoecology of the Dry Creek Site and Its Implications for Early Hunters. In *Dry Creek: Archeology and Paleoecology of a Late Pleistocene Alaskan Hunting Camp,* edited by W.R. Powers, R.D. Guthrie, and J.F. Hoffecker, pp. 209–287. Report on file, National Park Service, Washington, D.C.

Powers, W.R., and J.F. Hoffecker. 1989. Late Pleistocene Settlement in the Nenana Valley, Central Alaska. *American Antiquity* 54:263–287.

Powers, W.R., R.D. Guthrie, and J.F. Hoffecker (editors). 1983. *Dry Creek: Archeology and Paleoecology of a Late Pleistocene Alaskan Hunting Camp.* Report on file, National Park Service, Washington, D.C.

Thorson, R.M., and T.D. Hamilton. 1977. Geology of the Dry Creek Site: A Stratified Early Man Site in Interior Alaska. *Quaternary Research* 7:149–176.

West, F.H. 1967. The Donnelly Ridge Site and the Definition of an Early Core and Blade Complex in Central Alaska. *American Antiquity* 32:360–382.

See also DENALI COMPLEX; NENANA COMPLEX; NORTHERN ARCHAIC TRADITION

Dust Cave

Located in the limestone bluffs bordering the Tennessee River in northwestern Alabama, Dust Cave (1Lu496) was a locus of prehistoric occupation by Late Paleoindian times (8550 B.C., or 10,500 years B.P.). Use of the cave continued until ca. 3250 B.C. (5200 years B.P.), when deposits filled the entrance to an extent that made continued use unattractive (Driskell 1992). Subsequent roof breakdown and colluvium from the entrance sealed and protected the cave's archaeological deposits. Archaeological deposits, up to 5 m (16.5 feet) in thickness, occur mostly in the small entrance chamber ca. 100 m² (119.5 square yards) and steeply sloping talus in front of the cave mouth. Two known passageways lead to inner chambers; neither was used much in prehistoric times. Unlike most sites in the area, there has been little vandalism; bioturbation (natural churning of sediments by worms, roots, small animals, etc.) has been the biggest disturbance factor. The cave was first explored, mapped, and named by Dr. Richard Cobb (Cobb 1987), a local educator and amateur archaeologist/

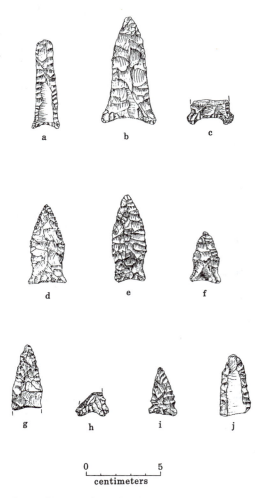

Projectile Points from the Late Paleoindian component at Dust Cave (a. Cumberland reworked to a drill-like artifact; b–c. Quad; d–f. Beaver Lake; g–h. Dalton-like; i. Hardaway Side Notched; j. fluted distal fragment). (Courtesy of the Journal of Alabama Archaeology)

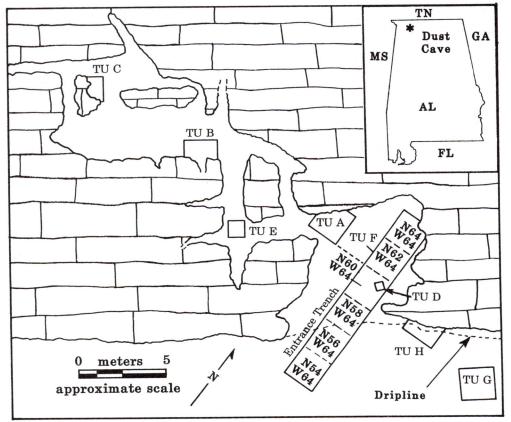

Plan view of Dust Cave and the placement of excavation units, 1989 to 1994. (Courtesy of the Journal of Alabama Archaeology)

speleologist, who reported the site to the Alabama Archaeological Site File in 1987.

Excavations at the site (1989–1996) by the University of Alabama Summer Field School reveal five superimposed, isolable, and well-preserved archaeological components within the deposits in the entrance chamber and adjacent talus (Driskell 1994). To date (1996), 40 radiocarbon dates support estimated date ranges for each component. A Late Paleoindian component dominated by Beaver Lake, Quad, and similar projectile points resides in the basal deposits dated to ca. 8550–8050 B.C. (10,500–10,000 years B.P.). This is overlain by an Early Archaic component containing side-notched projectile points similar to Big Sandy or Bolen points dated to ca. 8050–7050 B.C. (10,000–9000 years B.P.). This deposit is in turn overlain by a younger Early Archaic component dominated by Kirk Stemmed and Kirk Serrated projectile points dated to ca. 6550–5050 B.C. (8500–7000 years B.P.). An Eva/Morrow Moun-

tain component overlies the earlier ones and is dated to ca. 5050–4050 B.C. (7000–6000 years B.P.). The uppermost component is of the late Middle Archaic Seven Mile Island phase dominated by Benton and similar projectile points. The age of this youngest component is ca. 4050–3250 B.C. (6000–5200 years B.P.).

Because of complex natural and cultural factors not yet fully understood, thin or even microscopic layers, organic-laden lenses, and cultural features are remarkably well preserved and reminiscent of cave and shelter deposits in much dryer climates. While radiometric determinations suggest a rather straightforward depositional history, morphology is complex and demands a field methodology that emphasizes small-size excavation units and tight provenance control. Thus, routine field collaboration of micromorphologists (Goldberg and Sherwood 1994) has been pivotal in continuing investigation of stratigraphy and morphology, and resultant refinement of excavation strategy

Entrance trench to Dust Cave at the close of the 1993 excavations. (Courtesy of B. N. Driskell)

and technique. Initial attempts to reconstruct depositional history within and around the cave and to describe the local geomorphology have also been made (Collins et al. 1994).

Although analysis of various categories of artifacts and organic remains from the 1989–1994 excavations is only in its infancy, it is already clear that Dust Cave is an almost unprecedented resource for new data, particularly for the Late Paleoindian and Early Archaic periods. These excavations have provided considerable new information on stone-tool assemblages and tool function (Meeks 1994). No doubt, the quality and quantity of faunal (Parmalee 1994; Grover 1994; Goldman-Finn and Walker 1994; Morey 1994) and floral (Gardner 1994) remains will lead to an enhanced understanding of early prehistoric diet, subsistence, and economy in the mid-South. Collection of large samples for flotation (water separation of light materials with recovery of heavier materials larger than 1 mm) and fine screening has become an important part of the field strategy.

Research at Dust Cave has been supported through grants from the Tennessee Valley Authority, the National Geographic Society, the Alabama Historical Commission, and the Alabama Archaeological Society, and through ef-

forts of numerous volunteers and students of the University of Alabama Summer Field School. Additional excavation is anticipated, with active research extending well into the twenty-first century.

Boyce N. Driskell

Further Readings

Cobb, R.M. 1987. A Speleoarchaeological Reconnaissance of the Pickwick Basin in Colbert and Lauderdale Counties in Alabama. Ms. on file, Office of Archaeological Research, University of Alabama, Tuscaloosa.

Collins, M.B., W.A. Gose, and S. Shaw. 1994. Preliminary Geomorphological Findings at Dust and Nearby Caves. *Journal of Alabama Archaeology* 40(1–2): 35–56.

Driskell, B.N. 1992. Stratified Early Holocene Remains at Dust Cave, Northwest Alabama. In *Paleoindian and Early Archaic Period Research in the Lower Southeast: A South Carolina Perspective*, edited by D.G. Anderson, K.E. Sassaman, and C. Judge, pp. 273–278. Council of South Carolina Professional Archaeologists, Columbia.

———. 1994. Stratigraphy and Chronology at Dust Cave. *Journal of Alabama Archaeology* 40(1–2):17–34.

Gardner, P.S. 1994. Preliminary Analysis of Carbonized Plant Remains From Dust Cave. *Journal of Alabama Archaeology* 40(1–2):192–211.

Goldberg, P., and S.C. Sherwood. 1994. Micromorphology of Dust Cave Sediments: Some Preliminary Results. *Journal of Alabama Archaeology* 40(1–2):57–65.

Goldman-Finn, N.S., and R.B. Walker. 1994. The Dust Cave Bone Tool Assemblage. *Journal of Alabama Archaeology* 40(1–2):107–115.

Grover, J. 1994. Fauna Remains From Dust Cave. *Journal of Alabama Archaeology* 40(1–2):116–134.

Meeks, S. 1994. Lithic Artifacts From Dust Cave. *Journal of Alabama Archaeology* 40(1–2):79–106.

Morey, D.F. 1994. *Canis* Remains From Dust Cave. *Journal of Alabama Archaeology* 40(1–2):163–172.

Parmalee, P.W. 1994. Freshwater Molluscs From Dust and Smith Bottom Caves. *Journal of Alabama Archaeology* 40(1–2):135–162.

E

Early Coast Microblade

The "Early Coast Microblade complex" represents all coastal Late Lithic-substage occurrences on the northern Northwest Coast, including northern British Columbia and southeastern Alaska. It dates to ca. 8050–3050 B.C. (10,000–5000 years B.P.). The complex occurs as far south as the site of Namu on the central mainland coast of British Columbia, although microblades are no longer thought to occur in the oldest occupation at that site. Other Early Coast Microblade components include the Moresby-tradition sites of the Queen Charlotte Islands, and Groundhog Bay and Hidden Falls on the coast of southeastern Alaska. Because of the lack of organic preservation in most sites, little is known about the overall lifeways of Early Coastal Microblade people other than some details of their lithic technology. Some degree of maritime or littoral-intertidal adaptation is implied by the beachfront site locations.

Knut R. Fladmark

Further Readings

Carlson, R.L. 1996. Early Namu. In *Early Human Occupation in British Columbia*, edited by R.L. Carlson and L. Dalla Bona, pp. 83–102. University of British Columbia Press, Vancouver.

Fedge, D.W., J.B. McSporran, and A.R. Mason. 1996. Early Holocene Archaeology and Paleoecology at the Arrow Creek Sites in Gwaii Haanas. *Arctic Anthropology* 33(1):116–142.

Fedge, D.W., A.P. Mackie, J.B. McSporran, and B. Wilson. 1996. Early Period Archaeology in Gwaii Haanas: Results of the 1993 Field Program. In *Early Human Occupation in British Columbia*, edited by R.L. Carlson and L. Dalla Bona, pp. 133–150. University of British Columbia Press, Vancouver.

Fladmark, K.R. 1982. An Introduction to the Prehistory of British Columbia. *Canadian Journal of Archaeology* 6:95–156.

———. 1986. Lawn Point and Kasta: Microblade Sites on the Queen Charlotte Islands. *Canadian Journal of Archaeology* 10:39–58.

———. 1989. The Native Culture History of the Queen Charlotte Islands. In *The Outer Shores,* edited by G.G.E. Scudder and N. Gessler, pp. 199–221. Queen Charlotte Islands Museum, Skidegate.

See also MORESBY TRADITION

Early Period (Plateau)

The Early period of human occupation in south-central interior British Columbia extends from deglaciation (ca. 10,050/9050 B.C., or 12,000/11,000 years B.P.) to 5050 B.C. (7000 years B.P.). Most of the Canadian Plateau was suitable for human occupation by 10,050 B.C. (12,000 years B.P.), but securely dated archaeological evidence is not available until 6550 B.C. (8500 years B.P.). Information for the initial part of the Early period is limited to surface finds of fluted, stemmed, leaf-shaped, and Planolike points and knives. These artifacts may reflect contemporary but independent regional variants of several widespread early cultural-technological traditions defined for the Pacific Northwest—Plano, Early Stemmed Point, Old Cordilleran, and possibly Western Fluted Point. However, there is no consensus on the proper interpretation of the present data. After 6550

B.C. (8500 years B.P.), the sequence has a firmer chronological footing. Three sites located in the Thompson River/South Thompson-Shuswap Lakes regions are radiocarbon dated to 6550–5050 B.C. (8500–7000 years B.P.).

Evidence of a Western Fluted Point tradition, which dates as early as 8550 B.C. (10,500 years B.P.) in adjacent areas to the north and south, is equivocal for the Canadian Plateau. Three specimens from the Thompson River region might be attributed to the tradition. Evidence for the Early Stemmed Point tradition in British Columbia is also minimal. Stemmed points from the mid-Fraser-Thompson River and Kootenay regions may have been introduced ca. 8550–8050 B.C. (10,500–10,000 years B.P.) by peoples affiliated with the Lind Coulee tradition and/or Windust phase on the Columbia Plateau. Finely made lanceolate, stemmed, and foliate points from the Fraser-Thompson and Okanagan regions are highly similar to Plano-tradition types from the northwestern Plains. Such point forms may represent a northward extension of early Columbia Plateau populations influenced by Plains cultures and Plano technology shortly after deglaciation. Leaf-shaped points and pebble choppers in surface collections throughout the Canadian Plateau may be derived from the Old Cordilleran tradition on the Columbia Plateau and the south and central coasts of British Columbia. Although they may be early, these artifact types persist throughout the Canadian Plateau archaeological sequence.

The Landels site in Upper Oregon Jack Creek Valley has the earliest conclusive evidence for human occupation in the Canadian Plateau. A "pre-Mazama" component with two short occupations dated at 6450 B.C. ± 90 and 5720 B.C. ± 80 (8400 and 7670 years B.P.) contains a small assemblage of microblades, a microblade-core-rejuvenation flake, retouched and utilized flakes, and a bipolar core fragment. Associated faunal remains indicate a subsistence focus on deer. The cultural affiliation of the component is unknown, but it may relate to the Early Coast Microblade complex of the northern Northwest Coast that dates as early as 8050–7050 B.C. (10,000–9000 years B.P.).

The Gore Creek "burial" site in the South Thompson River Valley contained the postcranial remains of a young adult male accidentally killed and buried by a mudflow. The skeletal remains lay immediately beneath a layer of Mazama tephra and yielded a radiocarbon date of 6300 B.C. ± 115 (8250 years B.P.). No cultural material was associated with the human remains, but stable-carbon-isotope analysis indicates that the individual's diet included 8 ± 10 percent marine-origin protein, most likely salmon. If the Gore Creek individual's diet is representative, human subsistence at this time focused on terrestrial rather than riverine resources: perhaps on land mammals rather than salmon.

The Drynoch Slide site in the Thompson River Valley is the third reliably dated Early-period occupation. Although the site has not been systematically studied, charcoal from a small, exposed cultural deposit buried beneath 20 m (65.5 feet) of earth-flow deposits and Mazama tephra is dated at 5580 B.C. ± 270 (7530 years B.P.). Reported recoveries include a stemmed point, three microblades, and unifacial and unretouched flake tools. Faunal remains recovered include deer, elk, and fish (possibly salmon). To date (1996), the cultural relationships of this material are unknown, but they may be similar to those suggested for the Landels site.

The lack of Early-period data more likely reflects past research emphases on river valley bottoms and site survey methods, rather than the nature of the archaeological record. A speculative model for Early-period adaptations proposes Sub-Periods I-III that span 10,050–8050 B.C. (12,000–10,000 years B.P.), 8550–7050 B.C. (10,500–9000 years B.P.), and 7050–5050 B.C. (9000–7000 years B.P.), respectively. Initial occupants during Sub-Period I may have been big-game hunters associated with the Western Fluted Point tradition, while Sub-Periods II and III may reflect a shift away from big-game hunting to a more diversified subsistence economy as groups of other cultural traditions entered the Canadian Plateau from adjacent regions.

David L. Pokotylo

Further Readings

Chisholm, B.S., and D.E. Nelson. 1983. An Early Human Skeleton From South-Central British Columbia: Dietary Inference From Carbon Isotopic Evidence. *Canadian Journal of Archaeology* 7:85–86.

Cybulski, J.S., D.E. Howes, J.C. Haggarty, and M. Eldridge. 1981. An Early Human Skeleton From South-Central British Columbia: Dating and Bioarchaeological Inference. *Canadian Journal of Archaeology* 5:49–59.

Rousseau, M.K. 1993. Early Prehistoric Occupation of South-Central British Columbia: A Review of the Evidence and Recommendations for Future Research. *BC Studies* 99:140–183.

Stryd, A.H., and M. Rousseau. 1996. The Early Prehistory of the Mid Fraser-Thompson River Area of British Columbia. In *Early Human Occupation of British Columbia,* edited by R.L. Carlson and L. Dalla Bona, pp. 177–204. University of British Columbia Press, Vancouver.

Early Woodland

Early Woodland is the first period or stage of the Woodland tradition in the Eastern Woodlands. Its beginning was thought at one time to be marked by the contemporaneous appearance of pottery vessels, earthen burial mounds, and horticulture. Subsequent investigations demonstrated, however, that these traits are present in some areas in earlier Archaic complexes. Today, the period's inception in any region is more commonly defined by the first appearance of Woodland pottery and, to a lesser extent, by the presence of burial mounds.

Early Woodland pottery consists mainly of heavy, thick jars that have a wide mouth and a flat-to-rounded base. Unlike earlier Late Archaic "fiber-tempered" vessels in some more southern regions, these coil-built and poorly fired vessels are grit tempered. Resembling flower pots in shape, they were paddled on the inner and outer surfaces with a cord-wrapped instrument to consolidate the paste and thin the walls. Vessels gradually became thinner and more skillfully made in some areas, perhaps because manufacturing skills improved or vessel function changed. Woodland pottery appears throughout the Eastern Woodlands between ca. 1000 and 400 B.C. (2950–2350 years B.P.). The end of the period is generally marked by the first appearance of Middle Woodland pottery between ca. 400 B.C. and A.D. 1 (2350–1950 years B.P.).

Archaeologists find the pieces of ceramic vessels that survive in sites very useful taxonomic tools. Their comparison allows them to identify regional "cultural" complexes on the basis of variation in style or technology. The origin and significance of Woodland pottery remain speculative. Similar-appearing vessels entered the Seward Peninsula of Alaska from Asia by 1000 B.C. (2950 years B.P.), and a stimulus from northwestern Europe remains a remote possibility. Many archaeologists believe it has indigenous origins from steatite prototypes. Decisive evidence confirming one of these or some other origin is lacking. In some areas, the adoption or invention of ceramic vessels may have been a response to the growing need for a durable, easy to make waterproof container within which large numbers of hickory nuts or other seeds could be efficiently processed. However, the spread of Woodland pottery into areas where these plant resources were absent indicates that the vessels served a variety of purposes.

Distinguishing characteristics of the Early Woodland period are, in general, the product of interrelated processes whose origins extend back into the Middle Archaic period, if not earlier. Among these are: gradually increasing population densities; the "packing" of regions by larger numbers of bands through fissioning of larger groups and migration; a trend toward smaller, better defined, and more circumscribed group territories; more sedentary lifeways; the increasingly specialized and intensive exploitation of diverse food resources in more highly localized environments; an increasing emphasis on the gathering and gardening of seed-bearing plants; a growing sense of corporate identity; the emergence of more complex societies; the development of mechanisms to assure increasing social and economic stability; intensification of local and often interregional exchange and of formal exchange mechanisms; increasing numbers of boundary markers (such as mounds and projectile-point differences); and elaboration of burial rites. These processes are visible archaeologically in the presence of greater numbers of substantial habitation sites with extensive middens in resource-rich areas; more diverse food-procurement and -processing toolkits that now include ceramic vessels; denser remains of diverse food resources, such as deer, raccoon, turkey, fish, turtle, waterfowl, shellfish, acorns, hickory nuts, and some cultigens; earthen burial mounds; and variations in artifact style that are confined to more limited environmental zones. Together, these traits make Early Woodland sites more visible archaeologically than most earlier Archaic sites.

The Early Woodland landscape was occupied by a mosaic of highly localized complexes that include the Adena culture in the central Ohio Valley, the Morton complex in Illinois, the Tchefuncte culture in the Lower Mississippi Valley, the Deptford complex in Georgia, the

Meadowood in the eastern Great Lakes region, and Middlesex in parts of New England and adjacent areas. This diversity is most likely a result of the playing out of the processes listed above in a very large and environmentally heterogeneous area. Some archaeologists have identified significant organizational differences between northern and southern Early Woodland groups. According to their argument, these differences were based on the degree of severity of seasonal weather contrasts, the impact of these contrasts on the year-round availability of food energy, and the degree to which food resources were localized or evenly dispersed. In more northern portions of the Eastern Woodlands, where seasonal contrasts were more marked and food resources more highly localized, local territories tended to be better defined, and exchange relationships more formally structured. Similar elaborations are not found in more southern portions of the Eastern Woodlands, where seasonal contrasts are less marked, and food abundance less restricted in time and space. It is not surprising within this context, then, that the most spectacular evidence of elaborate mortuary ceremonialism occurs in the northern tier and is associated with the Adena culture in resource-rich sections of Ohio, Indiana, Kentucky, West Virginia, and Pennsylvania. Copper, mica, ocean shell, and other exotic materials flowed into central Ohio at this time.

In broad perspective, the Early Woodland is a continuation and gradual intensification of earlier Archaic trends. Life was not dramatically different from that in the earlier Late Archaic in most areas. People still lived by gathering and hunting wild foods. While the domestication process continued within the Eastern Agricultural complex, cultigens and semicultigens remained a dietary supplement. For the most part, groups of less than 50 people continued to aggregate and disperse throughout the year and to live in small communities of less than a half-dozen loosely clustered houses. The most visible change from an archaeological perspective was the appearance of Woodland pottery and of simple, conical burial mounds in most regions of the Eastern Woodlands.

Guy Gibbon

Further Readings

Braun, D.P. 1983. Pots As Tools. In *Archaeological Hammers and Theories*, edited by J. Moore and A. Keene, pp. 107–134. Academic Press, New York.

Farnsworth, K.B., and T.E. Emerson (editors). 1986. *Early Woodland Archeology.* Kampsville Seminars in Archeology, vol. 2. Center for American Archeology Press, Kampsville.

Keegan, W.F. (editor). 1987. *Emergent Horticultural Economies of the Eastern Woodlands.* Center for Archaeological Investigations, Southern Illinois University Press, Carbondale.

Smith, B.D. 1986. The Archaeology of the Southeastern United States. *Advances in World Archaeology* 5:1–92.

———. 1992. *Rivers of Change: Essays on Early Agriculture in Eastern North America.* Smithsonian Institution Press, Washington, D.C.

Steponaitis, V. 1986. Prehistoric Archaeology in the Southeastern United States 1970–1985. *Annual Review of Anthropology* 15:363–404.

Taladay, L., D.R. Keller, and P.J. Munson. 1984. Hickory Nuts, Walnuts, Butternuts, and Hazelnuts: Observations and Experiments Relevant to Their Aboriginal Exploitation in Eastern North America. In *Experiments and Observations on Aboriginal Wild Plant Foods in Eastern North America,* edited by P.J. Munson, pp. 338–359. Prehistoric Research Series, vol. 6, no. 2. Indiana Historical Society, Indianapolis.

See also ADENA; DEPTFORD CULTURE; EASTERN AGRICULTURAL COMPLEX; TCHEFUNCTE CULTURE

Earspool

An earspool, or "earplug," is a relatively flat, rounded object inserted in a hole in one's earlobe like an earring. It is worn for purposes of decoration, social symbolism, or status. The earliest extensive use of earspools occurred more than 2,000 years ago in the Hopewell culture, where they have been found almost exclusively in burial context. Their distribution centered in Ohio, though they have also been discovered in Illinois, southern Wisconsin, northern Georgia, and several other regions. Hopewell earspools usually consisted of a copper stem and plates wrapped together in a discoidal, or bicymbal, shape. Occasionally, the manufacturer added clay filling between the plates, an overlay of metal other than copper (usually silver or iron), or both. K.C. Ruhl's (1992; Greber and Ruhl 1989) stylistic analyses of Hopewell earspools in Ohio suggest chronological development within regions, as well as differences among regions and even among individual sites. Earspool manufacture was arrested ca. A.D. 500 (1450 years B.P.) with the demise of the Hopewell manifestation and its attendant symbolic trappings.

After several centuries of absence, earspools again became popular among Mississippian cultural groups of the mid-continent beginning ca. A.D. 900 (1050 years B.P.). An early locus of this revival was the Harlan site in eastern Oklahoma, which yielded several open-centered pulley-shaped and a few ring-shaped earspools. Most of these were made of sandstone; several had traces of copper sheathing covering the outside of the object. Popularity of the pulley-shaped earspool continued in the region; more than 400 such earspools, made of shale and cedar and covered with embossed copper, were discovered at the Spiro site. The specificity of earspool styles renders them useful as markers of cultural affiliation and contact. For example, the presence of locally manufactured tufa earspools of Illinois style in a north-central Ohio Late Woodland inhumation allowed D.S. Brose (1993) to postulate an uneven exchange of ideas or techniques with the Mississippian cultures of the central Mississippi and/or Illinois valleys, an exchange associated perhaps with the southerly movement of Northern Flint corn.

George H. Odell

Earspools from the Kampsville site. (Courtesy of the Wilford Archaeology Laboratory, University of Minnesota)

Further Readings

Bell, R.E. 1972. *The Harlan Site, Ck-6, a Prehistoric Mound Center in Cherokee County, Eastern Oklahoma.* Memoir no. 2. Oklahoma Anthropological Society, Oklahoma City.

Brose, D.S. 1993. Early Mississippian Con-

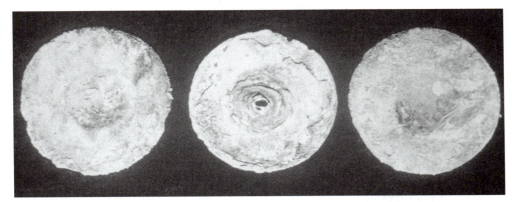

Hopewellian copper earspools, 2¹/₁₆" in diameter. (Courtesy of the Wilford Archaeology Laboratory, University of Minnesota)

nections at the Late Woodland Mill Hollow Site in Lorain County, Ohio. *Midcontinental Journal of Archaeology* 18:97–130.

Greber, N.B., and K.C. Ruhl. 1989. *The Hopewell Site*. Westview Press, Boulder.

Ruhl, K.C. 1992. Copper Earspools From Ohio Hopewell Sites. *Midcontinental Journal of Archaeology* 17:46–79.

Willoughby, C.C. 1916. The Art of the Great Earthwork Builders of Ohio. *Annual Report of the Smithsonian Institution for 1916*, pp. 489–500.

Earth Ovens

Ethnographic, ethnohistoric, and archaeological data indicate that earth ovens (also called pit ovens, steaming/baking pits, or oven mounds) were used throughout the Plateau (the interior parts of southwest Canada and the northwest United States) to cook meat, fish, shellfish, nuts, fruits, seeds, and especially root foods. Earth ovens are found from the subalpine zone and hilly flanks in forested, montane regions to the river valley bottoms and grasslands in dry regions. Most ovens have one basic construction/use pattern (see Figure 1), with morphological variations attributable, in part, to differences in sediments and terrain. Oven mounds functioned well where sediments were too wet or hard; oven pits worked best in well-drained sediments; and oven platforms cut into hillsides were used on sloping terrain (see Figure 2).

The oldest known ovens in the Plateau date from ca. 3550 B.C. to A.D. 1850 (5500–100 years B.P.) at camas- (*Camassia quamash*) processing sites in northeastern Washington's Calispell Valley. Remains of wood charcoal, camas bulbs, skunk cabbage (*Lysichitum americanum*), and other plants likely used as packing materials were recovered from large (1.5–3.0 m, or 6–10-foot, diameter) earth ovens with up to 1,000 kg (2,200 lbs) of fire-cracked rock. These feature dimensions match nineteenth-century descriptions of ovens used to cook 1,000 kg (2,200 lbs) of camas. In the Calispell Valley, where salmon were not readily available, large earth ovens were common by 1550 B.C. (3500 years B.P.). Large ovens were not prevalent until 550 B.C. (2500 years B.P.) in the Plateau's salmon-rich river valleys, well after the onset of the winter-pithouse-village pattern.

Archaeological sites primarily consisting of large earth-oven features probably functioned as bulk processing loci where the year's supply of root foods was prepared, including sites in the Calispell Valley, the Potomac Valley of western Montana, Upper Hat Creek Valley and Scheidam Flats of southern interior British Columbia, the Yakima and Columbia valleys of central Washington, and Grand Ronde Valley in Oregon. Repeatedly used earth-oven sites tend to be found where fuel, rocks, and foodstuffs were readily accessible. These sites contain an abundance of fire-cracked rock and carbon-stained sediments and a dearth of chipped-stone artifacts.

Sites primarily consisting of small (1-m, or 3.3-foot, diameter) rock-filled earth ovens dating to the last 2,500 years have also been recorded. Ovens at Potato Mountain in south-central interior British Columbia yielded charred Indian potato tubers (*Claytonia* sp.). Camas bulbs were reported from small ovens at a site along the Columbia River near Colville in north-central Washington. An Oregon grape seed (*Mahonia* sp.) was recovered from an oven at the Parker site in southern interior British Columbia, and an earth oven along the Spokane River in eastern Washington yielded charred onion bulbs (*Allium* sp.).

Small meat-processing earth ovens containing calcined bone and numerous bone flakes are known from sites in the Kootenai Valley of northwest Montana, the Upper Clearwater Basin in Idaho, and the Upper Snake River Valley in Wyoming. Rock shelters dated to 2550 B.C.–A.D. 450 (4500–1500 years B.P.) in the Lemhi Valley and other parts of central Idaho have rock-filled earth ovens up to 1.5 m (5 feet) in diameter containing burned canid bones. Smaller (50 cm, or 19.5-inch, diameter) earth ovens probably used to cook river mussels were excavated at sites dated to 4050–2050 B.C. (6,000–4,000 years B.P.) near the confluence of the Okanogan and Columbia rivers in central Washington.

Alston V. Thoms

Further Readings

Pokotylo, D.L., and P. Froese. 1983. Archaeological Evidence for Prehistoric Root Gathering on the Southern Interior Plateau of British Columbia: A Case Study From Upper Hat Creek Valley. *Canadian Journal of Archaeology* 7(2):127–157.

Smith, A.H. 1984. *Kutenai Indian Subsistence and Settlement Patterns, North-*

A pit of the appropriate size is dug, filled with firewood and rocks, then burned; the result is a layer of red hot rocks on the bottom and sides of the pit.

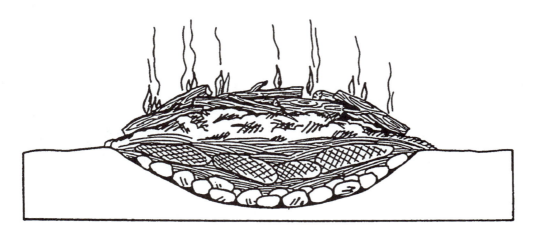

Moist, green plants are placed over the hot rocks, then fresh camas and perhaps other foods are put into sacks of woven vegetal fibers, stacked on top of the layer of green plants, and covered with another layer of plants; sometimes there are several layers of camas separated by green packing material; sometimes a fire is built on top of the mound.

After the camas has cooked for a day or more, the layers of hot coals, earth, and packing materials are pulled back, and the sacks of steam-cooked camas are removed, leaving a shallow, rock-lined depression which eventually fills in with the surrounding sediments.

Fig. 1. Schematic illustration of the construction and use of a camas oven that is typical of earth ovens found in the Plateau area. (Illustration by A. V. Thoms)

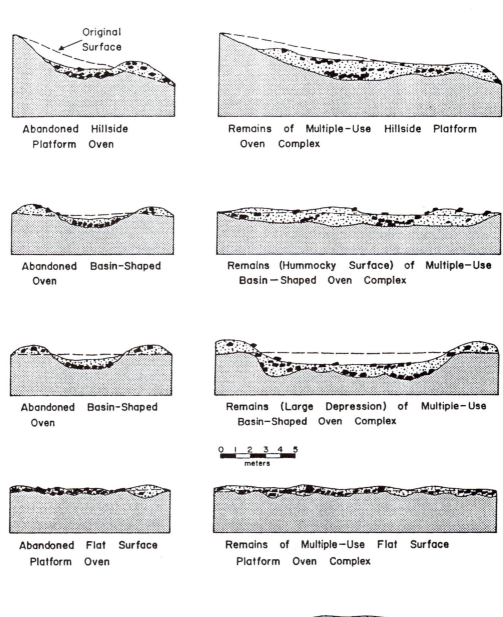

Fig. 2. *Schematic illustrations of various types of camas ovens typical of types of earth ovens found in the Plateau area. (Illustrations by A. V. Thoms)*

west Montana. Cultural Resources Investigations for Libby Reservoir, Lincoln County, Northwest Montana, vol. 2. Project Report no. 2. Center for Northwest Anthropology, Washington State University, Pullman.

Thoms, A.V. 1989. *The Northern Roots of Hunter-Gatherer Intensification: Camas and the Pacific Northwest.* Unpublished Ph.D. dissertation, Department of Anthropology, Washington State University, Pullman.

See also NORTHERN (CANADIAN) PLATEAU; SOUTHERN (COLUMBIA) PLATEAU

Earthlodge

An earthlodge is an earth-covered structure, best known in North America as a late-prehistoric-to-historic Plains Indian dwelling. Historically, the lodge was circular, with a dome-shaped roof supported by vertical wall posts and by four, six, or eight posts set around a central hearth. Rafters radiating from the stringers between the center posts provided support for successive layers of grass, willow branches, and earth and sod. A short, covered passage on one side of the lodge provided entry, and a hole in the roof center provided an exit for smoke. The earth cover provided extra warmth in the winter and coolness in the summer. These structures were built, with minor variation, by Plains Village tribes (Arikara, Hidatsa, Mandan, Omaha, Oto, and Pawnee), by some of their prehistoric ancestors, and by the eastern Dakota (Yankton, Yanktonai). The structure typically was a dwelling, but some were used as sites for ceremonials. Prehistorically, the lodge is best known in the Central Plains tradition, where it is a subrectangular structure with four or more center posts.

W. Raymond Wood

Further Readings

Wilson, G.L. 1934. *The Hidatsa Earth Lodge.* Anthropological Papers, vol. 33, pt. 5. American Museum of Natural History, New York.

Earthworks (Eastern Woodlands)

Earthworks are artificial, above-ground constructions made chiefly of earth, such as burial mounds, fortifications, and ridges that demarcate special spaces. Some archaeologists restrict the term to nonburial-mound constructions.

The earliest known earthwork in North America is an earth-and-stone burial mound dated to 5600 B.C. (7550 years B.P.) that covers the grave of a child at the L'Anse Amour site in Labrador (McGhee and Tuck 1977). In the Eastern Woodlands, the earliest earthworks are small bluff-top conical burial mounds that may date as early as 4000 B.C. (5950 years B.P.) (the late Middle Archaic period) in some resource-rich areas in the central Mississippi drainage (Charles and Buikstra 1983). Earthen burial mounds and other earthworks are clearly present in this culture

Photograph taken in 1871 by W. H. Jackson of a Pawnee earthlodge village. (Reprinted from Smithsonian Institution, Bureau of American Ethnology, Bulletin 77, Plate 50)

area in the Late Archaic period (ca. 4000–700 B.C., or 5950–2650 years B.P.). The most spectacular examples are associated with the Poverty Point culture in the Lower Mississippi Valley and adjacent Gulf Coast. At the unique Poverty Point site in Louisiana, six concentric semicircular earth ridges were constructed during the period 1000–700 B.C. (2950–2650 B.P.) using ca. 35,000 m³ of basket-loaded soil. A nearby mound is more than 20 m (66 feet) high and 200 m (660 feet) long. To the northeast in Labrador, Late Archaic Maritime Archaic burial mounds date as early as 3500 B.C. (5450 years B.P.).

Various explanations have been offered for the construction of early earthworks. Those at Poverty Point, for example, are thought by some archaeologists to have cosmological and perhaps political significance, for they seem connected with astronomical observations. According to some interpretations, burial mounds marked group boundaries, enhanced the visibility of markers, commemorated kin affiliations, and legitimized the right of kin groups to local food resources by signifying that this was "the land of the ancestors" (e.g., Charles and Buikstra 1983). They may also be

material representations of aspects of a widespread Eastern Woodlands cosmology.

A florescence of earthwork construction is a characteristic of many later cultures in the Midwest and the Southeast. Earthen burial mounds and associated circular enclosures, thought to have been meeting places for kin groups using the mounds, were important components of Early Woodland Adena people after 500 B.C. (2450 years B.P.). And later Middle Woodland Hopewell communities constructed large clusters of burial mounds and enclosures at sites like Mound City, Hopewell, Newark, and Seip. Some of the most distinctive Late Woodland burial mounds were effigies constructed in the shape of animals and birds in southern Wisconsin and in the bordering areas of adjacent states. Conical and oval burial mounds remained a distinctive feature of Woodland cultures in many regions of the Eastern Woodlands until the widespread adoption of maize horticulture and a Mississippian way of life at the end of the first millennium A.D. After this date, earthen burial mounds continued to be built to the historic period in some peripheral areas, such as the wild-rice-harvesting region of northern Minnesota, where they were

Curly-tailed panther mound from the Mendota State Hospital Mound group near Madison, Wisconsin. (Courtesy of James B. Stoltman)

Grand Mound (21KC3) (also known as Smith or Laurel Mound) is the largest earthwork in Minnesota. It is located on the southern bank of the Rainy River in Koochiching County. (Courtesy of the Wilford Archaeology Laboratory, University of Minnesota)

still being constructed in the A.D. 1600s.

A different kind of earthwork, the square-to-rectangular, layered platform mound, was first constructed in many areas of the Southeast in the first millennium A.D. An early example is a low, large rectangular platform at the Deptford culture Mandeville site in Georgia. Other early examples are associated with the Weeden Island culture and somewhat later with the Coles Creek culture. The number and size of platform mounds increased dramatically throughout areas of the Southeast and the Midwest with the florescence of Mississippian cultures after ca. A.D. 1000 (950 years B.P.). The largest Precolumbian earthwork in North America is Monks Mound, a platform mound at the Cahokia site in Illinois that covers 7 ha (17.3 acres) and is ca. 30 m (98 feet) high. Earthworks of various sizes and shapes served a variety of functions at many Mississippian centers. While many were imposing platforms for temples, some contained burials, were markers in the astronomical arrangement of a center, or served some combination of these and other functions. Platform mounds were still being used to support temples in some southeastern communities when Spanish explorers first traveled through the region in 1539–1541.

Guy Gibbon

Further Readings

Charles, D.K., and J.E. Buikstra. 1983. Archaic Mortuary Sites in the Central Mississippi Drainage: Distribution, Structure, and Implications. In *Archaic Hunters and Gatherers in the Midwest*, edited by J. Phillips and J. Brown, pp. 117–145. Academic Press, New York.

Fagan, B.M. 1991. *Ancient North America*. Thames and Hudson, New York.

McGhee, R., and J.A. Tuck. 1977. An Archaic Indian Burial Mound in Labrador. *Scientific American* 235(5):122–129.

See also CAHOKIA; EFFIGY MOUNDS; HOPEWELL SITE; MANDEVILLE; MONKS MOUND; NEWARK EARTHWORKS; POVERTY POINT SITE; SEIP; WEEDEN ISLAND CULTURE

Eastern Agricultural Complex

The term "Eastern Agricultural complex" refers to a group of annual plants that were either domesticated or cultivated by American Indians throughout a broad area of the Midwest, the mid-South, and the eastern prairies. These plants include squash (*Cucurbita pepo*), sumpweed (*Iva annua* var. *macrocarpa*), goosefoot (*Chenopodium berlandieri* ssp. *jonesianum*), sunflower (*Helianthus annuus*), maygrass (*Phalaris caroliniana*), erect knotweed (*Polygonum erectum*), little barley (*Hordeum pusillum*), and probably ragweed (*Ambrosia trifida*).

"Eastern Agricultural complex" is a term first given credence by Ralph Linton (1944) when he noted the differences in maize agriculture in Mexico, the Southwest, and the eastern United States. Without mentioning any specific plants, Linton suggested that it was at least possible that peoples in the Eastern Woodlands grafted maize agriculture onto a preexisting pattern based upon the cultivation of grain crops that were indigenous to eastern North America. Linton's ideas were expanded by the pioneering ethnobotanists Melvin R. Gilmore and Volney H. Jones through their examination of desiccated plant remains recovered from dry-cave and rock-shelter sites in the Arkansas Ozarks and the mountains of eastern Kentucky. In the 1940s, George Quimby began utilizing the term "Eastern complex" in his lectures in anthropology at the University of Chicago. In the 1960s, Stuart Streuver and his colleagues stimulated renewed interest in the idea of the Eastern Woodlands as an independent center for the development of plant husbandry. As flotation became a standard recovery technique in the 1970s and 1980s, and the technological means to examine morphological details of ancient seeds through scanning electron microscopy became widely available, archaeobotanists eventually confirmed the existence of ancient premaize plant husbandry in eastern North America. Since then, the name "Eastern Agricultural complex" has been consistently applied to the plants that were either domesticated or cultivated by American Indians in the Eastern Woodlands before the advent of maize.

While "Eastern Agricultural complex" is the moniker for these plants, the term should probably be dropped and replaced with the general term "indigenous seed crops." "Complex" implies an invariant group of crop plants as well as a related technology. In reality, there is considerable variability in the kinds and amounts of indigenous seed crops grown from one area to the next in the Midwest and the mid-South; there is no standard group of plants. "Agriculture" conjures up a vision of field cropping that emphatically did not characterize the premaize farming systems in use before maize emerged as the dominant crop plant. Finally, good evidence exists for the cultivation of several of the members of the "complex" as far

west as the eastern Plains; the indigenous seed crops were not restricted to eastern North America.

Until recently, most archaeologists and archaeobotanists thought that the initial "kick" that ultimately led to domestication of indigenous eastern North American plants came from Mexico (Smith 1992). Squash (*Cucurbita pepo*) was one of the first plants domesticated in Mesoamerica (ca. 7050 B.C., or 9000 years B.P.). On the basis of this evidence, it was generally assumed that the plant was introduced into eastern North America. Carbonized and desiccated cucurbit rinds have been found in several archaeological sites in the Eastern Woodlands dated to ca. 4050–2050 B.C. (6000–4000 years B.P.). Originally, these finds were accepted as positive evidence of the diffusion of horticulture from Mexico. This "event" was seen as a prime mover that propelled eastern populations down a road that led to the domestication of native plants ca. 1550 B.C. (3500 years B.P.).

Within the past few years, evidence has accumulated from paleontology and modern botanical fieldwork that leaves this scenario in serious doubt. Genetic analysis of contemporary *Cucurbita pepo* populations has revealed that there are two lineages of squash, one rooted in Mexico and one in eastern North America. Botanical fieldwork has revealed the existence of an apparently wild, indigenous gourd (*Cucurbita pepo* var. *ovifera* ssp. *ozarkana*) that could easily be the progenitor of the eastern lineage. Finally, paleontologists have discovered hundreds of small *Cucurbita* seeds in late Pleistocene sediments along the Aucilla River in Florida in the absence of human activity. On the basis of these findings, it is now apparent that a wild gourd, indigenous to eastern North America, was likely domesticated by American Indians by ca. 2050 B.C. (4500 years B.P.) in the absence of any Mesoamerican contacts.

By 1550 B.C. (3500 years B.P.), American Indians in the Eastern Woodlands had domesticated at least three species of plants (squash, sunflower, and sumpweed) and were cultivating several others. Each of these plants shares a number of common characteristics. First, they are all annuals; that is, they are dependent upon the seeds produced during one growing season to provide the stock for next year's population. They all produce seed in prolific quantities, and each produces its grain in neat packages. In this sense, the seeds are relatively easy to harvest, making them "preadapted" for human use. Finally, each of the plants thrives in open disturbed habitats, such as the annually reworked levees of rivers and streams.

In general, the seeds of the plants can be classified as either possessing oily (sumpweed, sunflower) or starchy (goosefoot, maygrass, erect knotweed, little barley) edible portions. With the exception of sumpweed, sunflower, and goosefoot, the evidence for intensive cultivation of indigenous seed crops comes from either large seed masses found in storage pits, their consistent presence in flotation samples, or their archaeological presence in areas far outside their contemporary natural range. In this sense, only squash, sumpweed, sunflower, and goosefoot are known as actual domesticates; that is, genetically altered plants whose morphology is drastically different from their wild ancestors.

Evidence for the domestication of sumpweed and sunflower is primarily morphological. The seeds (technically, achenes) of both underwent radical changes in size, with both ultimately reaching lengths nearly three to four times the size of their wild ancestors. Goosefoot seeds underwent a dramatic change in the thickness of the seed coat (testa), which changed the natural pattern of seed dormancy and enhanced the ability of the seed to imbibe water during cooking. Unlike the sunflower, the domesticated forms of both goosefoot and sumpweed are extinct and known only through archaeological finds.

The importance of indigenous seed crops in premaize subsistence economies seems to have dramatically increased between 1050 B.C. and A.D. 250 (3000–1700 years B.P.). By A.D. 1050–1150 (900–800 years B.P.), sizable quantities of various combinations of the indigenous crops were produced in many areas of the Midwest and mid-South, including the central Mississippi Valley, the central and Lower Ohio valleys, and the Tennessee-Cumberland drainages of Tennessee and Alabama. There is little evidence for the use of indigenous crops in the Lower Mississippi Valley, the Gulf Coastal Plain of the Southeast, or along the Atlantic or Gulf coasts. With the rise of maize as a crop plant after ca. A.D. 1150 (800 years B.P.), indigenous crop plants became less important and, gradually, were almost totally supplanted by this Mesoamerican grass.

C. Wesley Cowan

Further Readings

Linton, R. 1944. North American Cooking Pots. *American Antiquity* 9:369–380.
Smith, B.D. 1992. *Rivers of Change: Essays on Early Agriculture in Eastern North America.* Smithsonian Institution Press, Washington, D.C.

Eastern California

Eastern California includes the arid lands east of the Cascade, Sierra Nevada, Transverse, and Penninsular ranges. It extends more than 1,100 km (682 miles) north-south from Baja California to Oregon. Because California's arbitrary eastern boundary has no bearing on geography, the boundary intrudes into the Sierra Nevada at Lake Tahoe, dividing eastern California into two unequal parts: the state's northeastern region, and the Mojave and Colorado deserts in the southeast. The northeastern boundary is formed by a high margin of the northern Great Basin and retains some of the broad, shallow lakes that dotted the Great Basin during the Pleistocene. The Mojave Desert, at a somewhat lower elevation, is part of the much drier, hotter basin-and-range country that characterizes most of the Great Basin. The Colorado Desert, which is partly drained by the Colorado River, is an even lower basin-and-range complex (although Death Valley in the Mojave Desert possesses the lowest elevation in North America). Eastern California makes up one-third of the state's area. Though all parts of eastern California are arid, generally receiving less than 250 mm (9.8 inches) of precipitation annually, the region has so much topographic and ecological variability that its prehistoric cultural patterns are comparably varied.

No generally accepted model exists for the cultural sequences of both northeastern and southeastern California. Though the amount of fieldwork in this part of the state was modest until recently, a profusion of local sequences and several more general ones have now been proposed. Perhaps the most widely used regional model in the late twentieth century is C.N. Warren's (1984) for southeastern California. C. Raven's review (1984) of northeastern California prehistory probably has been the most influential discussion of that region's archaeology, but it does not offer a synthetic model comparable to Warren's. This discussion merges the above two models and places them within the more general framework developed by J.L. Chartkoff and K.K. Chartkoff (1984).

Southeastern California is home to some of the state's claimed pre-fluted-point Paleoindian sites (China Lake, Calico Hills, Manix Lake, Yuha Burial, Yuha Pinto Wash) as well as to the majority of fluted-point sites known for California (Davis 1978). M.J. Moratto (1984) recognizes two demonstrated Paleoindian patterns: the Fluted-Point tradition, whose diagnostic element is the Clovislike point; and the Western Pluvial Lakes tradition, which overlaps the first tradition in time. In the west, the Fluted-Point tradition begins by at least 10,050 B.C. (12,000 years B.P.) and continues to 7050 B.C. (9000 years B.P.). The Western Pluvial Lakes tradition lasts from 9050 to 6050 B.C. (11,000–8000 years B.P.). The western Fluted-Point tradition represents the local variant of the Paleoindian period in the Chartkoff and Chartkoff model, while the Western Pluvial Lakes tradition represents their Early Archaic period. The fact that the two patterns overlap in time in the same area may indicate that their assemblages are associated with particular adaptive behaviors rather than with historically separate cultural traditions—some may have been produced by the same families. So far, neither Paleoindian nor Western Pluvial Lake–tradition sites have been reported for northeastern California. However, archaeologists believe that these materials will turn up in that area with further searching.

Fluted-point finds in the southeastern California deserts are best known from the shorelines of former Pleistocene China Lake. The richest assemblage is from a locality there called Basalt Ridge. As elsewhere in California, China Lake lacks buried deposits in which unarguably human artifacts can be shown to be in direct association with Pleistocene megafauna and deposits of Pleistocene age. The demonstration in other parts of the continent that fluted Clovis points date to the terminal Pleistocene period, however, lends support to the idea that fluted points at China Lake also are that old. Basalt Ridge alone has yielded more than 500 artifacts, including some fluted points, on surfaces formed between 12,050 and 10,050 B.C. (14,000–12,000 years B.P.). Some surface tools are in close association with exposed bones of mammoth, camelid, and horse, some of which are charred. Artifacts reflect selection of good-quality cherts and obsidian, some heat treatment of stone before flaking, and careful pressure flaking. In addition to fluted points, tools include crescentics, bifaces or preforms (some possibly used as knives), varied scrapers with serrated beaked, notched, and straight edges, and some pounding or possibly milling tools. The mode of living suggested by these discoveries implies small groups exploiting varied plant and animal resources within lacustrine habitats, with Pleistocene-period large mammals the most dramatic forms. The lack of houses and midden deposits suggests frequent moves and little repetition of camping on the same spot. Although some technological aspects of this western Fluted-Point tradition resemble those of Great Plains Llano or Clovis assemblages, differences also occur, and the subsistence patterns of the two areas are quite different.

The Western Pluvial Lakes tradition (WPLT) is better represented in eastern California than is the western Fluted-Point tradition. Proposed by S.F. Bedwell (1970), the WPLT incorporates the desert San Dieguito complex defined by M.J. Rogers (1958) and C.N. Warren (1967), along with the Lake Mojave culture defined by E.W.C. Campbell and W.H. Campbell (1935) and W.J. Wallace (1962). WPLT sites tend to be found along or near the shorelines of the former Pleistocene shallow lakes and marshes that once filled the bottoms of almost every valley in eastern California's basin-and-range topography, and along stream courses that drained into those lakes. WPLT sites often have buried deposits, so organic remains may be preserved, and undisturbed associations between artifacts and other remains can be discovered. Faunal remains show the use of a variety of large, medium, and small mammals and birds but no use of Pleistocene megafauna. Plant remains show diversified foraging practices, but the lack of milling tools indicates that hard seeds, acorns, mesquite beans, and screwbean pods were not exploited to any degree. Lake Mojave and San Dieguito assemblages share the presence of heavy core and flake scrapers, cleavers, choppers, knives, and crescentics. Lake Mojave sites also contain a series of projectile points in addition to the elongated bifacial knives or foliate points found in both groups. Lake Mojave points are diamond shaped with longer stems than bodies. Silver Lake points are triangular with wide stems or stems expanding below side notches. San Dieguito assemblages generally lack projectile points, though in eastern California they often are found in similar settings of the same time period as Lake Mojave sites.

Warren (1984) recognizes a Pinto period (5050–2050 B.C., or 7000–4000 years B.P.) as successor to the Western Pluvial Lakes tradition. The preceding three millennia saw increasing aridity in the desert West. Many lakes and marshes dried up, and grasslands gave way to deserts. The wetlands adaptations found during the Paleoindian and Early Archaic periods shifted to desert adaptations. While some writers argue for a severe dry-hot phase between 5050 and 3050 B.C. (7000–5000 years B.P.) that virtually depopulated eastern California (Wallace 1962; Kowta 1969), others see no hiatus between WPLT and subsequent Pinto occupations (Tuohy 1974). Whichever was true, Pinto occupations were fewer than those in the earlier Western Pluvial Lakes tradition; the best examples include Pinto Basin (Campbell and Campbell 1935), Salt Springs (Rogers 1939), the Stahl site (Harrington 1957), and Death Valley (Wallace 1977). These occupations would generally fit in the Middle and Late Archaic periods in the Chartkoff and Chartkoff (1984) model.

Pinto assemblages are distinguished by Pinto points, a type of large, generally triangular, and often coarsely flaked point with a straight or expanding stem and a strongly concave or bifurcated base. Heavy keeled scrapers and mano-millingstone tools were found by the Campbells at Pinto Basin. Farther to the east, Rogers (1939) found fewer scrapers and no milling tools. Later finds show that tools associated with plant processing are more common in western Pinto sites than in eastern ones. This difference may reflect local environmental variation. In almost all cases, though, Pinto sites suggest the presence of tiny desert populations in very small groups that were exploiting the resources of arid lands for brief periods of time. This contrasts with the earlier lake-and-marsh focus of the Western Pluvial Lakes tradition.

Materials contemporary with Pinto have been found in northeastern California. The Karlo site in eastern Lassen County was the first significant open-air site excavated in the Great Basin (Riddell 1960). Its first phase of occupation, Madeline Dunes, occurred between 5050 and 2550 B.C. (7000–4500 years B.P.). The Nightfire Island site, in the southern Klamath Lake Basin of northeastern Siskiyou County, had its initial occupation, Phase I, between 4550 and 3250 B.C. (6500–5200 years B.P.), while Phase II occurred between 3250 and 2250 B.C. (5200–4200 years B.P.) (Johnson 1968;

Grayson 1976). J.F. O'Connell (1975) established a sequence in Surprise Valley, eastern Modoc County, at the King's Dog site and elsewhere, beginning with the Menlo phase (4750–2650 B.C., or 6700–4600 years B.P.). These occupations, though contemporary with Pinto and often containing Pinto points (as well as other, more regionally distinctive types, such as Elko Eared, Rose Spring Corner-Notched, and Northern Side-Notched), show more in common adaptively with WPLT occupations. Pinto-era sites in northeastern California typically occur along lakeshores. They reflect diversified hunting-and-gathering adaptations, including the use of deer, elk, antelope, mountain sheep, small mammals, and waterfowl. The Menlo-phase occupation at King's Dog Site even includes pithouse architecture and other evidence of semisedentism. The severe dryness felt in southeastern California during Pinto times does not seem to have characterized the northeastern area.

The subsequent Gypsum period (2050 B.C.–A.D. 450, or 4000–1500 years B.P.) occurred during a wetter climatic phase in southern California's deserts. Most writers consider Gypsum an outgrowth of Pinto-era cultures, but with larger populations with more connections to other regions. Newberry Cave (C. Davis 1981), Rose Spring (Clewlow et al. 1970), Gypsum Cave (Heizer and Berger 1970), Ash Meadows (Muto et al. 1976), and Atlatl Rock Shelter (Warren 1982) all contain important Gypsum occupations. There are split-twig animal effigies at Newberry Cave, an apparent link with the Grand Canyon area. The occurrence of Elko Eared and Elko Corner-Notched points indicates connections with the Great Basin at several Gypsum sites, and the presence of abalone (*Haliotis*) and *Olivella* shell artifacts at some sites indicates contacts with the Pacific Coast. The occurrence of bead and pendant styles characteristic of the Delta area's "Middle horizon" indicates links with central California. This degree of regional interaction is much greater than in earlier periods (cf. Warren 1984:415–418).

Characteristic Gypsum assemblages include a series of distinctive projectile-point types, including the Gypsum point. Millingstones and manos become more common over time, and mortars and pestles appear, indicating the systematic use of hard seed, nut, and legume resources. Heavy and light scrapers, as well as choppers, T-drills, planoconvex scrap-

E

ers, and hammerstones are common. Ornamental artifacts, such as shell beads and rings, pendants, tubes, pipes, and incised tablets, also occur, along with shaft straighteners and atlatl parts.

In northeastern California, materials contemporary with Gypsum are well documented. At Surprise Valley, the Bare Creek (2550–1050 B.C., or 4500–3000 years B.P.) and Emerson (1050 B.C.–A.D. 450, or 3000–1500 years B.P.) phases form the local equivalent of the early and middle Pacific periods in the Chartkoff and Chartkoff (1984) model. This period saw some gradual changes in lifeways. Perhaps due to climatic change, the importance of large mammals to the diet declined, while small mammals and waterfowl became more important. This contrasts with Nightfire Island, where waterfowl already had been important. Bison had been hunted in Surprise Valley but disappear at this time. Houses are less substantial than in the Menlo phase, suggesting shorter stays in base camps. Milling tools remain important.

While Gypsum cultures and their contemporaries constitute their regions' variants of the Chartkoffs' early and middle Pacific periods, Warren's Saratoga Springs period (Warren and Crabtree 1972) is generally equivalent to the Chartkoffs' late Pacific period. The Saratoga Springs period (A.D. 500–1200, or 1450–750 years B.P.) reflects significant involvement with Southwestern cultures as well as continuation of cultural and technological patterns from the previous Gypsum period. Warren (1984) recognizes four regional southeastern California cultures during Saratoga Springs times. The two closest to the Southwest understandably show the strongest Southwestern elements and the most radical changes. At the same time, the region as a whole shares traits in common.

Saratoga Springs–period cultures reflect the replacement of the spear and atlatl by the bow and arrow. Atlatl parts disappear from the archaeological record, and distinctive small projectile points appear. Types such as Rose Spring, Eastgate, Cottonwood Triangular, and Desert Side-Notched are typical. Rock art reflects this weapon change as well. Manos and millingstones as well as mortars and pestles are widely distributed, attesting to the importance of plant food staples in a hunting-and-gathering economy. Along the Colorado River, the peripheral Southwestern culture called Hakataya occurs at this time. Hakataya farming is limited to the Colorado River Valley, but pottery of this

culture is found widely in the eastern Colorado desert in Saratoga Springs sites. In southern Nevada, a western variant of Southwestern Anasazi culture has been documented. Anasazi pottery is distributed well into the eastern Mojave Desert from Death Valley southward. South of Death Valley, Malcolm J. Rogers noted the occurrence of turquoise mines near Halloran Springs (Rogers 1929), where Anasazi pottery is widely distributed among hundreds of small turquoise mines. Whether this pattern reflects Anasazi occupation or local mining for purposes of trading with the Anasazi is not clear. In the western deserts, there is little evidence of Southwestern contact, but there is a good deal of material from other parts of California, including the coast and the Central Valley. Shell beads and steatite are much more abundant in western village sites than in the eastern deserts.

Comparable to the Saratoga Springs period in northeastern California is the Alkali phase in Surprise Valley (O'Connell 1975) and at Tommy Tucker Cave (Riddell 1960). The bow and arrow appear during the Alkali phase (A.D. 500–1500, or 1450–450 years B.P.). Included are several projectile-point types that also occur in southeastern California, such as Rose Spring and Eastgate. Foliate bifaces or knives, ground-stone spheroids, and tubular pipes are found in these assemblages. Subsistence continues to rely upon smaller mammals and waterfowl, with waterfowl more important than in the previous Emerson phase. Houses continue in the pattern developed in the Emerson phase, which involves smaller, less substantial houses with shallower pit floors than in Menlo times (Hester and Heizer 1973).

Warren defines the last phase in southeastern California prehistory as the Protohistoric period (A.D. 1200–1750, or 750–200 years B.P.). On linguistic as well as archaeological grounds, it is assumed that the historically known peoples of the region, speakers of Shoshonean languages, migrated into this region at or not long before the start of the period. Differences between eastern and western desert communities also are found in this era, although specific artifact categories change. The most distinctive Protohistoric artifact type is the Desert Side-Notched projectile point, though it first appears during Saratoga Springs times. Anasazi pottery stops appearing in California ca. A.D. 1150 (800 years B.P.), just before the end of Saratoga Springs, but Hakataya pottery types continue to occur in eastern desert village sites well into the Protohistoric period. In addition, an undecorated brown ceramic type, made by the paddle-and-anvil technique, called Tizon Brown Ware, becomes widely used in the Colorado and eastern Mojave deserts. Extensive trade routes were maintained across the deserts from the coast to the Southwest during Protohistoric times. Quantities and varieties of coastal artifacts, such as shell beads and steatite shaft straighteners, were more abundant in western desert sites than they had been during Saratoga Springs times. The maintenance of larger villages in the eastern deserts along key trade routes, such as the Mojave River, occurred in the Protohistoric period.

Just as Warren's Protohistoric period reflects the emergence of historically known cultures in the southeastern deserts, the Late Prehistoric sequence of northeastern California is tied to ethnographically known cultures (Warren 1984; Raven 1984). O'Connell's last period, the Bidwell phase (A.D. 1500–1769, or 450–181 years B.P.) (O'Connell 1975) is equivalent to Chartkoff and Chartkoff's final Pacific period (1984). The Surprise Valley area, studied by O'Connell, was home to Shoshonean-speaking peoples, as was the southeastern desert area. The broader Surprise Valley region, by contrast, was held by Penutian speakers at that time, while the area from Eagle Lake to Trinity Reservoir was occupied by speakers of Hokan languages (Moratto 1984:560–574). The greater linguistic diversity in this area may help explain its greater diversity in assemblages compared to southeastern California. Also relevant are differences in the influences of neighboring cultures. Southeastern desert peoples interacted with Southwest farming peoples and coastal maritime cultures, while northeastern California societies interacted with northern Great Basin, southern Columbia Plateau, and inland groups from northern California and southern Oregon. In both cases, the interactions were most intensive in the last phases of prehistory and helped promote greater cultural complexity than in earlier phases (the Menlo phase excepted). The patterns of material culture in the two areas showed greater differences than earlier, however, because the sources of interaction were so different.

At the same time, certain fundamental similarities link the two regions. Both areas lie on parts of the western periphery of the Great Basin and the eastern periphery of the California culture area. Both areas have long been characterized by arid environments with diversified local topography and lacustrine habitats. The greater aridity in the south promoted the greater loss of lakes prehistorically, so strategies concerning resource choice and use that continued in northeastern California, such as the exploitation of waterfowl and aquatic-plant tubers, were increasingly abandoned in the south as prehistory wore on. Yet the two areas shared many similarities in settlement, social organization, technology, and modes of economic behavior, even by the end of prehistoric times.

Joseph L. Chartkoff

Further Readings

Arkush, B.S. 1990. The Protohistoric Period in the Western Great Basin. *Journal of California and Great Basin Anthropology* 12(1):28–36.

Bedwell, S.F. 1970. *Prehistory and Environment of the Pluvial Fort Rock Lake Area of South-Central Oregon.* Unpublished Ph.D. dissertation, Department of Anthropology, University of Oregon, Eugene.

Campbell, E.W.C., and W.H. Campbell. 1935. *The Pinto Basin Site: An Ancient Aboriginal Camping Ground in the California Desert.* Papers no. 9. Southwest Museum, Los Angeles.

Campbell, E.W.C., W.H. Campbell, E. Antevs, C.E. Amsden, J.A. Barbieri, and F.D. Bode. 1937. *The Archaeology of Pleistocene Lake Mohave.* Papers no. 11. Southwest Museum, Los Angeles.

Chartkoff, J.L., and K.K. Chartkoff. 1984. *The Archaeology of California.* Stanford University Press, Stanford.

Clewlow, C.W., Jr., R.F. Heizer, and R. Berger. 1970. An Assessment of Radiocarbon Dates for the Rose Spring Site (CA-Iny-372), Inyo County, California. *Contributions of the University of California Archaeological Research Facility* 7:19–25.

Davis, C.A. 1981. Newberry Cave: An Elko Religious Site in San Bernardino County, California. Unpublished Master's thesis, Department of Anthropology, University of California, Riverside.

Davis, E.L. (editor). 1978. *The Ancient Californians: Rancholabrean Hunters of the Mojave Lakes Country.* Science Series no. 29. Los Angeles County Museum of Natural History, Los Angeles.

Grayson, D.K. 1976. The Nightfire Island Avifauna and the Altithermal. In *Holocene Environmental Change in the Great Basin,* edited by R. Elston, pp. 73–103. Research Papers no. 6. Nevada Archaeological Survey, Reno.

Harrington, M.R. 1957. *A Pinto Site at Little Lake, California.* Papers no. 17. Southwest Museum, Los Angeles.

Heizer, R.F., and R. Berger. 1970. Radiocarbon Age of the Gypsum Cave Culture. *Contributions of the University of California Archaeological Research Facility* 7:13–18.

Hester, T.R., and R.F. Heizer. 1973. *Review and Discussion of Great Basin Projectile Points: Forms and Chronology.* Archaeological Research Facility, Department of Anthropology, University of California, Berkeley.

Johnson, L. 1968. Obsidian Hydration Rate for the Klamath Basin of California and Oregon. *Science* 165:1354–1355.

Kowta, M. 1969. *The Sayles Complex: A Late Milling Stone Assemblage From Cajon Pass and the Ecological Implications of Its Scraper Planes.* Publications in Anthropology no. 6. University of California Press, Berkeley.

Lindstrom, S.G. 1992. Submerged Tree Stumps As Indicators of Mid-Holocene Drying Trends Within the Lake Tahoe Region. *Proceedings of the Society for California Archaeology* 5:315–321.

Moratto, M.J., (editor). 1984. *California Archaeology.* Academic Press, Orlando.

Muto, G.R., P.J. Mehringer, Jr., and C.N. Warren. 1976. A Technological Analysis of Projectile Points From a Burial, Amargosa Desert, Nevada. *Kiva* 41:267–276.

O'Connell, J.F. 1975. *The Prehistory of Surprise Valley.* Anthropological Papers no. 4. Ballena Press, Ramona, Calif.

Pinto, D.G. 1989. *The Archaeology of Mitchell Caverns.* Archaeological Reports no. 25. California Department of Parks and Recreation, Sacramento.

Raven, C. 1984. Northeastern California. In *California Archaeolgy,* edited by M.J. Moratto, pp. 431–469. Academic Press, Orlando.

Riddell, F.A. 1960. *The Archaeology of the Karlo Site (Las-7), California.* Reports no. 53. University of California Archaeo-

logical Survey, University of California, Berkeley.

Rogers, M.J. 1929. *Report on an Archaeological Reconnaissance in the Mojave Sink Region.* Papers no. 1. San Diego Museum of Man, San Diego.

———. 1939. *Early Lithic Industries of the Lower Basin of the Colorado River and Adjacent Desert Areas.* Papers no. 3. San Diego Museum of Man, San Diego.

———. 1958. San Dieguito Implements From the Terraces of the Rincon-Patano and Rillito Drainage System. *Kiva* 24(1):1–23.

Schneider, J.S. 1989. *The Archaeology of the Afton Canyon Site.* San Bernardino County Museum Association Quarterly, vol. 36, no. 1.

Sutton, M.Q. 1980. Some Aspects of Kitanemuk Prehistory. *Journal of California and Great Basin Anthropology* 2(2):214–225.

Tuohy, D.R. 1974. A Comparative Study of Late Paleo-Indian Manifestations in the Western Great Basin. *Nevada Archaeological Survey Research Papers* 5:91–116.

Wallace, W.J. 1962. Prehistoric Cultural Development in the Southern California Deserts. *American Antiquity* 28:172–180.

———. 1977. A Half-Century of Death Valley Archaeology. *Journal of California Anthropology* 4(2):249–258.

Warren, C.N. 1967. The San Dieguito Complex: A Review and Hypothesis. *American Antiquity* 32:168–185.

———. 1982. Prehistoric Developments at Atlatl Rock. Ms. on file, Nevada Division of State Parks, Carson City.

———. 1984. The Desert Region. In *California Archaeology,* edited by M.J. Moratto, pp. 343–430. Academic Press, Orlando.

Warren, C.N., and R.H. Crabtree. 1972. The Prehistory of the Southwestern Great Basin. In *Great Basin,* edited by W.L. D'Azevedo. Handbook of North American Indians, vol. 11, W.C. Sturtevant, general editor. Smithsonian Institution, Washington, D.C.

Eastern Great Basin Archaic

The term "Eastern Great Basin Archaic" is used to refer to a specific time period in the prehistory of the eastern Great Basin and to the lifeways of the people who inhabited the region during this period. The Eastern Great Basin Archaic spans ca. 7,000 years: 6000 B.C.–A.D. 700 (7950–1250 years B.P.). During this time span, the population of this area was composed of small, nomadic hunting-and-gathering groups, usually the size of one or more extended families. These small kinship groups subsisted primarily by harvesting and processing a wide variety of plants. While hunting was probably of secondary importance, small mammals, such as jackrabbit and cottontail, were their main protein source.

Attire for these Eastern Great Basin Archaic people included loincloths, rabbit-skin robes, sandals, and leather moccasins. Subsistence-related tools included a variety of projectile points, knives, scrapers, and other stone and bone tools, as well as millingstones and hand stones for processing plant remains. Wood and plant fiber were used to construct an array of useful items, such as dart shafts, digging sticks, rope, cordage, nets, and an assortment of winnowing, storage, and burden baskets. Among the nonutilitarian items that have been recovered are shell and bone beads, pendants, and incised and painted stone. Generally, Eastern Great Basin Archaic assemblages are notable for their variety of notched and stemmed projectile points and hand stones and millingstones. These classes of artifact distinguish Archaic occupations from those of the earlier Paleoindians.

Most archaeological data pertaining to the Eastern Great Basin Archaic have been derived through the excavation of large, stratified rock shelters, including Danger Cave, Hogup Cave, Black Rock Cave, and Swallow Shelter. A result of the excavation at Danger Cave was the formulation by Jesse D. Jennings (1978) of the concept of a Desert culture. According to this concept, Archaic people throughout the Great Basin had a meager lifeway that was, nonetheless, exquisitely adapted to the desert environment. Jennings believed that this lifeway remained relatively static and unchanged for thousands of years. Other archaeologists have challenged this concept. Recent research (Madsen 1982) has shown that during the last 10,000 years environmental conditions, such as rainfall and temperature, fluctuated in the region. It is now thought that these shifting environmental conditions forced adjustments in local hunting-and-gathering patterns. Madsen (1982) has also proposed that a pattern of regional transience existed, with local groups moving back and forth between valley bottoms and nearby mountain slopes to take advantage of the shifting availability of plant and animal resources. To test these hypotheses, archaeologists are focusing their efforts on determining the role that small, open Archaic campsites played in the overall seasonal pattern of movement in the area.

By ca. A.D. 700 (1250 years B.P.), changes in the artifact assemblage represent the end of the Archaic period and the beginning of the Late Prehistoric period (A.D. 700–1850, or 1250–100 B.P.). In the southeastern part of the Great Basin, this transition was marked by the appearance of sedentary populations that lived in primitive permanent structures, relied heavily on maize horticulture, and made pottery. In the northeastern part, the environment was not conducive to maize horticulture. Local groups there maintained their Archaic subsistence pattern of hunting and gathering throughout the Late Prehistoric period until European contact in the 1800s. Still, archaeologists generally end the Eastern Great Basin Archaic period at ca. 700. The end of this period is conveniently marked by the introduction of Rose Spring projectile points.

Alan R. Schroedl

Further Readings

Aikens, C.M., and D.B. Madsen. 1986. Prehistory of the Eastern Area. In *Great Basin*, edited by W.L. D'Azevedo, pp. 149–160. Handbook of North American Indians, vol. 11, W.C. Sturtevant, general editor. Smithsonian Institution, Washington, D.C.

Condie, C.J, and D.D. Fowler (editors). 1986. *Anthropology of the Desert West: Essays in Honor of Jesse D. Jennings.* Anthropological Papers no. 110. University of Utah Press, Salt Lake City.

Jennings, J.D. 1978. *Prehistory of Utah and the Eastern Great Basin.* Anthropological Papers no. 98. University of Utah Press, Salt Lake City.

Madsen, D.B. 1982. Get It Where the Gettin's Good: A Variable Model of Great Basin Subsistence and Settlement Based on Data From the Eastern Great Basin. In *Man and Environment in the Great Basin*, edited by D.B. Madsen and J.F. O'Connell, pp. 207–226. Papers no. 2. Society for American Archaeology, Washington, D.C.

E

Eastern Great Basin Lakeside Adaptations

The Great Basin of western North America drains internally. Water from snowmelt and precipitation accumulates along the western and eastern rims forming large, shallow, often saline lakes. On the eastern periphery, the primary bodies of water are, or were, the Great Salt Lake, Utah Lake, and Sevier Lake (now usually dry). The resources available to aboriginal peoples in or along the edges of these large lacustral systems varied depending on the presence of fresh water. Both Great Salt Lake and Sevier Lake are highly saline, although fresh or brackish waters in the vicinity of inflowing rivers and streams formed extensive marshlands (Simms et al. 1991). This is especially the case along the eastern shore of the Great Salt Lake, which was fed by the Bear, Weber, and Jordan rivers. Sevier Lake was filled by the waters of the Sevier River only, and marshes there were restricted to the immediate vicinity of the river mouth (Janetski 1991).

The productive wetlands adjacent to the river mouths in the saline lakes consist of relatively flat, wet meadows of bulrush, salt grass, pickleweed, and other water-loving, salt-tolerant species whose distribution was determined by the microtopography of the marshes. In the case of the Great Salt Lake, those marshes extend for miles along the southeast, east, and northeast shores. Waterfowl are abundant throughout the warm, as well as much of the colder, periods of the year, and wetland mammals (muskrat especially) were once common. Native fishes, especially Utah chubs, were present in the feeder streams but not in these saline lakes.

Utah Lake, drained by the Jordan River, is the only freshwater, lowland lake in the eastern Basin. Fringing marshes with resources similar to those described for the Great Salt Lake are present everywhere except for the western shore, and extensive wetlands are found in Provo and Goshen Bay. In the past, the lake supported a highly productive fishery of trout, suckers, and chubs (Janetski 1991).

The importance of the lake-edge environment for hunter-fisher-gatherers during the Archaic period (8050 B.C.–A.D. 450, or 10,000–1500 years B.P.) has been documented through archaeological research. Both Danger Cave (Jennings 1957) and Hogup Cave (Aikens 1970) on the west side of the Great Salt Lake contained evidence of the extensive use of lacustral resources, including the salt-loving pickleweed (*Allenrolfea occidentialis*), bulrush (*Scirpus* spp.), cattail (*Typha latifolia*), and waterfowl. Deadman Cave (also Archaic in age) at the south end of the Great Salt Lake likewise contained numerous marsh birds (Parmalee 1980) and what appear to be net weights or sinkers (E. Smith 1952:21–22) that suggest fishing activities.

Fishing was a significant activity around Utah Lake. Archaic sites, such as Spotten Cave (Mock 1971) in the foothills south of Utah Lake and Goshen Island (ca. A.D. 100–300, or 1850–1650 years B.P.) on the south shore of Goshen Bay, contained abundant fish, waterfowl, and muskrat bones, and quantities of eggshell (Janetski and Nauta 1994). Artifactual evidence of Archaic fishing includes sinkers, harpoons, and probable composite fishhooks. Uplands adjacent to the marshes were also important

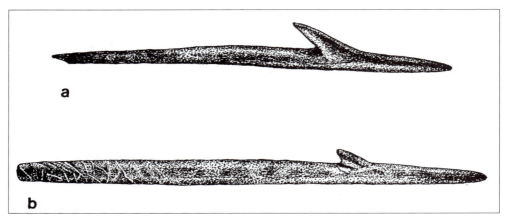

Bone harpoons from Woodard Mound, a late Fremont site in Utah Valley, Utah. (Modified by J. C. Janetski from Richens 1983)

during the Archaic, especially for the procurement of large game, primarily deer and mountain sheep.

Despite the introduction of farming after ca. A.D. 500 (1450 years B.P.), marsh resources continued to be important to eastern Basin peoples. At Backhoe Village, a Fremont site on the middle Sevier River south of the Wasatch Front wetlands, David B. Madsen and LaMar W. Lindsay (1977) found abundant cattail pollen on house floors. With these data as a basis, they argued that marsh plants were at least as important as domesticated crops for Fremont farmers on the eastern Basin rim and spurred scholarly interest in wetland adaptations generally. Better support for the importance of lacustral resources during the Fremont period (A.D. 400–1300, or 1550–650 years B.P.) comes from the east shore of the Great Salt Lake, where numerous Fremont burials exposed by the high water of the 1980s provide evidence of the heavy use of the marshes during this period (Simms et al. 1991). At Fremont sites along the Wasatch Front from the Bear River sites on the north to Woodard Mound in Utah Valley, waterfowl, fish, muskrat, bulrush, and knotweed are important dietary items. Fishing gear is scarce but includes harpoons from Woodard Mound and the Bear River 2 site (Aikens 1967). The majority of Fremont residential settlements cluster along streams somewhat back from the lake in order, apparently, to better access drained soil for farming; however, Fremont peoples, like their Archaic predecessors, continued the exploitation of the uplands for deer and mountain sheep.

Farming declined after ca. A.D. 1350 (600 years B.P.), and aboriginal peoples appear to have intensified their use of marsh resources during the early Late Prehistoric (Promontory) period. In this time, settlement shifts downward in Utah Valley and apparently along the Great Salt Lake as well. Sites (probably winter camps) with extensive middens and storage pits are located at the mouths of streams (Janetski 1990b). Fish bones swamp all other faunal remains, and pits for storage are common in Utah Valley and at the Orbit Inn site just north and east of the Bear River marshes (Simms and Heath 1990). Superpositioning of pits suggests redundant use of these sites. Muskrats and waterfowl bones, bulrush and grass seeds, and more limited remains of small and large mammals are present in most sites. Fishing gear is almost nonexistent, although stone sinkers are common in surface scatters along the Utah Lake shore; fishhooks were likely used, although none have been dated (Hunter 1991). Interestingly, Late Prehistoric sites are rare in the uplands during the Promontory period, and the use of the uplands appears more transitory than in the earlier Archaic and Fremont periods. After ca. A.D. 1600 (350 years B.P.), site location appears to shift away from the marshes, perhaps due to the Little Ice Age, which raised lake levels and probably flooded marshes as it had 3,000 years earlier during the Medithermal (cf. Murchison 1989).

Ethnographic research (Steward 1970 [1938]; Stewart 1942; A. Smith 1974; Janetski 1991) has demonstrated the importance in the region of lacustral plants and animals for food, houses, bags, mats, clothing, and other essential needs. Aboriginal populations clustered in the lake valleys, with settlement patterns reflecting the importance of stores of dried fish and bulrush, for winters were spent in the valleys rather than near the pine-nut groves as was the case in the central Great Basin. Early Spanish explorers laud the riches of Utah Valley and, in their journals, describe the Lagunas (people of the lake, or Timpanogos Ute) and the abundance and importance of fish, waterfowl, and other resources in the valley (see Janetski 1991 for a synthesis).

From as early as 10,000 years ago, eastern Great Basin lakes and their accompanying marshes were critical in the lives of early aboriginal peoples. Today, as they were in the past, the lake valleys are centers of population.

Joel C. Janetski

Further Readings

Aikens, C.M. 1967. *Excavations at Snake Rock Village and the Bear River No. 2 Site.* Anthropological Papers no. 87. University of Utah Press, Salt Lake City.

———. 1970. *Hogup Cave.* Anthropological Papers no. 93. University of Utah Press, Salt Lake City.

Hunter, R.J. 1991. Archaeological Evidence of Prehistoric Fishing at Utah Lake. *Utah Archaeology* 4:46–57.

Janetski, J.C. 1990a. Utah Lake: Its Role in the Prehistory of Utah Valley. *Utah Historical Quarterly* 58(1):4–31.

———. 1990b. Wetlands in Utah Valley Prehistory. In *Wetland Adaptations in the Great Basin,* edited by J.C. Janetski and D.B. Madsen, pp. 233–258. Occasional

E

Papers no. 1. Museum of Peoples and Cultures, Brigham Young University, Provo.

———. 1991. *The Ute of Utah Lake.* Anthropological Papers no. 116. University of Utah Press, Salt Lake City.

Janetski, J.C., and L.T. Nauta. 1994. Fishing and Fowling: Late Archaic Subsistence in the Eastern Great Basin. Paper presented at the Twenty-Fourth Great Basin Anthropological Conference, Elko.

Jennings, J.D. 1957. *Danger Cave.* Anthropological Papers no. 57. University of Utah Press, Salt Lake City.

Madsen, D.B., and L.W. Lindsay. 1977. *Backhoe Village.* Antiquities Section Selected Papers, vol. 4, no. 12. Utah State Historical Society, Salt Lake City.

Mock, J. 1971. *Archaeology of Spotten Cave, Utah County, Central Utah.* Unpublished Master's thesis, Department of Anthropology and Archaeology, Brigham Young University, Provo.

Murchison, S.B. 1989. *Fluctuation History of Great Salt Lake, Utah, During the Last 13,000 Years.* NASA contract NAAS5-28753. Limneotectonics Laboratory Technical Report no. 89–2. Department of Geography, University of Utah, Salt Lake City.

Parmalee, P.W. 1980. Utilization of Birds by the Archaic and Fremont Cultural Groups of Utah. In *Papers in Avian Paleontology Honoring Hildegarde Howard,* edited by K.E. Campbell, Jr., pp. 237–250. Contributions in Science no. 330. Los Angeles County Museum of Natural History, Los Angeles.

Richens, L.D. 1983. *Woodard Mound: Excavations at a Fremont Site in Goshen Valley, Utah County, Utah 1980–1981.* Unpublished Master's thesis, Department of Anthropology, Brigham Young University, Provo.

Simms, S.R., and K.M. Heath. 1990. Site Structure of the Orbit Inn: An Application of Ethnoarchaeology. *American Antiquity* 55:797–813.

Simms, S.R., C.J. Loveland, and M.E. Stuart. 1991. *Prehistoric Human Skeletal Remains and the Prehistory of the Great Salt Lake Wetlands.* Ms. on file, Utah Department of Natural Resources. Department of Sociology, Social Work, and Anthropology, Utah State University, Logan.

Smith, A.M. 1974. *Ethnography of the Northern Utes.* Papers in Anthropology no. 17. Museum of New Mexico Press, Albuquerque.

Smith, E.R. 1952. *The Archaeology of Deadman Cave, Utah, A Revision.* Anthropological Papers no. 10. University of Utah Press, Salt Lake City.

Steward, J.H. 1970. *Basin-Plateau Aboriginal Sociopolitical Groups.* Reprinted. University of Utah Press, Salt Lake City. Originally published in 1938, Bulletin no. 120. Bureau of American Ethnology, Smithsonian Institution, Washington, D.C.

Stewart, O.C. 1942. Cultural Element Distributions: XVIII, Ute-Southern Paiute. *Anthropological Records* 6(4):231–356. University of California Press, Berkeley.

Eastern Great Basin Late Prehistoric Period

The Late Prehistoric period is a chronological category for the eastern Great Basin. It began with the demise of Fremont farming in the late fourteenth century A.D. and ended at the beginning of the Protohistoric period, which is defined by the introduction of the horse in the eighteenth or, perhaps, the seventeenth century.

The Fremont "demise" was fragmented. It varied in expression across space and in the timing of the abandonment of farming. As a result, it included lifeways ranging from full-time hunting and gathering to settled agriculture; farmer/forager systems possibly existed simultaneously. Rather than a monolithic and sudden shift from sedentary to nomadic peoples, the Late Prehistoric period may represent a more gradual deletion of farming from the economic repertoire. This process would have involved a narrowing of adaptive diversity over time and an accompanying shift in the way many people organized their lifespace. It is also possible that the demographic fluidity of this period contributed to the historic distributions of some Native American languages.

Diversity in Late Prehistoric lifeways in the eastern Great Basin falls into two broad categories: desert valley/mountain exploitation and wetland exploitation. In both cases, housing consisted of brush windbreaks and of wickiups of brush, woven mats, or logs covered with earth. Ceramic vessels were used at certain sites. Stone-tool manufacture and use varied from one kind of site to another and in relation to the distance to stone sources. Obsidian was a common raw material, and the most frequently made type of projectile point was a small side-notched form. Some specialized technologies were used in the exploitation of the wetlands.

Desert valley/mountain lifeways in the Late Prehistoric period remain largely unsynthesized and are known primarily from surface collections. However, they probably fall within the range of lifeways that one would expect to find in an Archaic-stage existence. Rather than being fully nomadic, these foragers probably moved intermittently in response to the distribution and abundance of food resources. Subsistence was based on large and small mammals, birds, reptiles, insects, and a wide variety of roots and seeds. Camps that were occupied for a few days to more than a month are found in all ecosystems except in the highest altitudes. Winter residential camps, which required a wood supply and depended on stored food, were often located in the warmer inversion belt along the lower edge of the piñon-juniper vegetation community. They were occupied from a few weeks to several months.

In the large wetlands associated with Utah Lake and the Great Salt Lake, Late Prehistoric lifeways were characterized by high population densities and tethering to wetland habitats. The presence of recurrently occupied residential camps indicates that there was a greater degree of settlement stability in this area compared to desert areas. Grinding stones, which included specialized stone balls and V-shaped cobbles, were common, as were subsurface pits for storage and roasting. Subsistence resources included waterfowl, fish, large and small mammals, roots, and seeds. A decrease in the exploitation of bison and an increase in the capture of deer, antelope, bighorn sheep, muskrat, and beaver may have occurred in the period. The long-held notion that the Great Basin wetlands were a settlement focus still holds to some degree, but it is unrealistic to maintain that they were a focus of sedentary settlement systems.

Artifact use shows both continuity and discontinuity during the Fremont–Late Prehistoric transition. These shifts are related to the elimination of residential farming bases from the subsistence-settlement system with the abandonment of farming, and to the resulting trend toward a less logistic organization of seasonal activities. For instance, the quality of ceramics and the range of vessel forms decrease in the Late Prehistoric period. These ceramics are variously referred to as Promontory, Shoshone,

or simply Late Prehistoric wares. Most were manufactured by coiling, as were the preceding Fremont wares. Studies of temper size and homogeneity, wall thickness, and surface preparation show variability in both periods. There has been some success in matching the degree of investment in ceramic quality with differences in mobility both within and between Fremont and Late Prehistoric collections. Late Prehistoric side-notched projectile points (e.g., Bear River, Uinta, and Desert Side-Notched types), rather than falling within clusters of discrete traits, are highly diverse. Basketry in the two periods contrasts sharply.

The Promontory culture is limited to the northeastern Great Basin. It exhibits connections with Plains cultures in ceramics and in a very small sample of other traits, such as moccasins and shields. Based largely on ceramics, the term "Promontory" may be a taxonomic excess. However, the term does stress that the Late Prehistoric was a varied, dynamic period rather than a homogeneous one as might be inferred by the ethnographic record.

There is continuity with the Fremont in the northeastern Great Basin until ca. A.D. 1600 (350 years B.P.). The Great Salt Lake expanded and flooded many wetlands ecosystems between 1550 and 1700 (400–250 years B.P.). Ceramic use decreased. The wares that did remain in use are similar to those in use in the Protohistoric and historic periods. The settlement pattern changed at this time, and the human presence in the area seems to have decreased, too. While the transgression of the Great Salt Lake was certainly an important influence in these trends, the wetlands would have been available for later recolonization. Perhaps the change in settlement pattern was a result of the introduction of the horse. If so, the Protohistoric period began earlier in this region than the mid-eighteenth-century date indicated by the ethnohistoric records. Another possibility is depopulation resulting from diseases introduced by Europeans in the early 1500s, as documented in the southeastern and northwestern United States. The necessary population densities were present for the transmittal of diseases, although arid environments act as disease filters. However, the actual causes of these changes remain undocumented for this region.

The Numic-language groups that were present in this region in the historic period may have entered the area in the Late Prehistoric period. These language groups are the Shoshoni,

E

Ute, and Southern Paiute. Linguistic studies indicate that they differentiated into their historic ranges less than 1,000 years ago. The timing of this spread is debated among archaeologists and, to a lesser extent, among linguists. If the Numic spread is associated with the transition from Fremont to Late Prehistoric, migrants would have encountered foragers either living among or descendant from the Fremont. This would explain why there is little evidence of a Late Prehistoric presence at Fremont farming sites. Alternatively, Numic migrants may have arrived well before the Late Prehistoric began or well after the transition from Fremont to Late Prehistoric, perhaps during the settlement shift in the sixteenth or seventeenth century. The most frequent form of migration in history is the movement of individuals and small groups, not mass movements. Furthermore, demographic fluidity is a hallmark of foraging societies. Thus, the Numic spread is likely the terminus of a continuous process.

Steven R. Simms

Further Readings

D'Azevedo, W. (editor). 1986. *Great Basin.* Handbook of North American Indians, vol. 11, W.C. Sturtevant, general editor. Smithsonian Institution, Washington, D.C.

Grayson, D.K. 1993. *The Desert's Past: A Natural Prehistory of the Great Basin.* Smithsonian Institution Press, Washington, D.C.

Janetski, J.C. 1991. *The Ute of Utah Lake.* Anthropological Papers no. 116. University of Utah Press, Salt Lake City.

Janetski, J.C., and D.B. Madsen (editors). 1990. *Wetland Adaptations in the Great Basin.* Occasional Papers no. 1. Museum of Peoples and Cultures, Brigham Young University, Provo.

Madsen, D.B., and J.F. O'Connell (editors). 1982. *Man and Environment in the Great Basin.* Publications no. 2. Society for American Archaeology, Washington, D.C.

Madsen, D.B., and D. Rhode (editors). 1994. *Across the West: Human Population Movement and the Expansion of the Numa.* University of Utah Press, Salt Lake City.

Simms, S.R., and M.E. Stuart. 1993. Prehistory and Past Environments of the Great Salt Lake Wetlands. In *Archaeological Test Excavations in the Great Salt Lake Wetlands and Associated Analyses,* pp. 5–31. Contributions to Anthropology no. 14. Utah State University, Logan.

See also FREMONT; NUMIC EXPANSION

Eastern Woodlands Archaic

In the Eastern Woodlands, the term "Archaic" has been used to designate a period, stage, tradition, type of artifact assemblage, taxonomic unit, or some combination of these and other uses. In the late twentieth century, the term has been generally defined by constellations of artifact and site types or by trends in subsistence and settlement patterning. According to trait-based definitions, the Archaic is separated from later Woodland assemblages by the absence of Woodland ceramics, and from earlier Paleoindian sites by the presence in the Archaic of new traits, including projectile-point forms with notches or stems; reliance on a wider range of more localized, less flakable lithic raw materials; ground- and polished-stone tools like manos, axes, celts, and bannerstones; more varied and numerous bone tools; a proportionately large number of only lightly flaked stone tools; and greater regional variability in types of sites and their content (Ellis et al. 1990). Subsistence-settlement definitions have often contrasted a generalized Archaic hunter-gatherer lifeway that gradually became ever more efficient in the exploitation of the varied resources of the eastern forests with that of free-wandering Paleoindian big-game hunters and Woodland horticulturalists. According to initial formulations of this latter perspective, this long, adaptive shift prepared Archaic "broad-spectrum" hunter-gatherers for emerging new lifeways that required ever more complex social organizations and the harvesting of domesticated "tropical" plant foods like maize (corn) and beans.

There are problems with both of these general approaches. Trait-based approaches, for example, perpetuate the limited taxonomic and chronological goals of culture history. Although essential goals of the archaeological enterprise, they are by themselves sterile for they cannot explain either the archaeological record or past cultural activities. Subsistence–settlement pattern approaches, while couched in an explanatory format, have often made what have proven to be false assumptions. For instance, nearly all initial reconstructions of Archaic lifeways were based on the idea that Woodland peoples were "tribal" horticulturalists, while their Archaic ancestors were simpler, band-level hunter-gatherers. Visible features of the new Woodland lifeway were thought to be ceramic vessels to store surplus crops and earthen burial mounds, which the surplus gave them the leisure time to construct. Among the discoveries in recent years that have undermined this picture are Late Archaic ceramics in the Southeast that date from 2500 B.C. (4450 years B.P.) onward, Middle and Late Archaic earthen mounds, and the remains of cultivated weedy plants, gourds, and squash in Late Archaic contexts south of the Great Lakes (Neusius 1986; Smith 1986; Steponaitis 1986).

In retrospect, a problem with some more recent lifeway approaches is the simplistic assumption that trends throughout the Archaic can be explained by a single process, an ever increasing "efficiency" in the exploitation of an ever broader spectrum of natural food resources until a "primary forest efficiency" was achieved (Phillips and Brown 1983; Jeffries 1995). Evidence for this "settling in" is the appearance in the Archaic of specialized resource-procurement and -processing equipment, such as plant-food grinders, heavy woodworking tools, and fishing paraphernalia; a focus on less mobile resources than big game within smaller exploitation territories; larger and more permanent sites; less portable toolkits; and an increase in human population sizes that "filled in" space so that earlier "free" wandering lifeways became a decreasing option. But the processes involved were certainly more complex. Among other likely possibilities are the impact of postglacial climatic trends that reached a peak between 7000 and 3000 B.C. (8950–4950 years B.P.) in the warm-dry Hypsithermal interval; rapid melting of northern glaciers, which led to a continued rise in sea levels and a flattening of the gradient of interior streams; and lake and drainage maturation. In combination, these processes may have led to an increasing aggregation of denser populations within rich but circumscribed resource zones, restricted mobility, semisedentism, increased conflict over resources, new tools to exploit a wider range of the resource base, and so on. Regional variations on these themes add to the complexity of this emerging picture. It is most likely the combined effects of these natural processes and of less visible cultural processes like the logic of culture histories that account for observed changes in the Archaic archaeological record.

Still other problems exist with the lifeway approach. In contrast to Paleoindian big-game hunters on the Plains, earlier Paleoindian economies south of the late glacial environments of the Great Lakes were apparently already diverse, with deer, smaller mammals, fish, and plants integral components of the diet. And later, as broad-spectrum economies continued to develop in the deciduous forests of the Eastern Woodlands, more focal economies continued to exist for thousands of years in some regions of the Upper Great Lakes and the Northeast. Broad generalizations about the Eastern Woodland Archaic are, then, often difficult to draw.

Since the 1950s, the Archaic in the Eastern Woodlands has been subdivided into Early, Middle, and Late segments. However, the beginning and end dates of the Archaic, and the timing of the divisions between the Early-to-Middle and the Middle-to-Late Archaic, may differ widely depending on whether the Archaic is investigated through lists of traits or as a perceived adaptive shift. Some archaeologists begin the Late Archaic, for example, at 4000 B.C. (5950 years B.P.); others, at 2500 B.C. (4450 years B.P.). In areas of the Upper Great Lakes, Paleoindian complexes persisted until the middle of the Middle Archaic (ca. 5000 B.C., or 6950 years B.P.), and Woodland ceramics appeared hundreds of years earlier in some coastal and southern areas than they did in the Upper Mississippi Valley. Even when Woodland ceramics were adopted, many peoples seemed to have continued living what is traditionally considered an Archaic lifeway. These shifting boundaries affect what archaeological complexes are included in one division or another, as well as the primary processes that are thought to be at work, among many other aspects of the Archaic.

Guy Gibbon

Further Readings

Bense, J. 1994. *Southeastern Archaeology.* Academic Press, New York.

Custer, J.F. 1984. *Delaware Prehistoric Archaeology: An Ecological Approach.* University of Delaware Press, Newark; Associated University Presses, London and Toronto.

Ellis, C.J., I.T. Kenyon, and M. Spence. 1990. The Archaic. In *The Archaeology of Southern Ontario to A.D. 1650,* edited by

E

C. Ellis and N. Ferris, pp. 65–124. Occasional Publications no. 5. London [Ontario] Chapter, Ontario Archaeological Society, London.

Fagan, B. 1991. *Ancient North America.* Thames and Hudson, New York.

Jeffries, R.W. 1995. The Status of Archaic Period Research in the Midwestern United States. *Archaeology of Eastern North America* 23:199–244.

Mason, R. 1981. *Great Lakes Archaeology.* Academic Press, New York.

Morse, D., and P. Morse. 1983. *Archaeology of the Central Mississippi Valley.* Academic Press, New York.

Neusius, S.W. (editor). 1986. *Foraging, Collecting, and Harvesting: Archaic Period Subsistence and Settlement in the Eastern Woodlands.* Center for Archaeological Investigations, Southern Illinois University, Carbondale.

Phillips, J.L., and J.A. Brown. (editors). 1983. *Archaic Hunters and Gatherers in the American Midwest.* Academic Press, New York.

Smith, B.D. 1986. The Archaeology of the Southeastern United States: From Dalton to de Soto, 10,500 to 500 Years B.P. *Advances in World Archaeology* 5:1–92.

Snow, D. 1980. *The Archaeology of New England.* Academic Press, New York.

Steponaitis, V. 1986. Prehistoric Archaeology in the Southeastern United States 1970–1985. *Annual Review of Anthropology* 15:363–404.

See also ARCHAIC; EASTERN WOODLANDS EARLY ARCHAIC; EASTERN WOODLANDS LATE ARCHAIC; EASTERN WOODLANDS MIDDLE ARCHAIC

Eastern Woodlands Culture Area

The Eastern Woodlands culture area is, in a very general sense, that portion of North America east of the western Plains and prairies and south of the boreal forest. This general definition is neither accurate nor particularly useful, however, for the locations of the borders of these plant communities were dramatically different at times in the past. Southward-creeping glacial ice pushed bands of tundra and boreal forest into the southern Great Lakes region and New England, and grasslands thrust a wedge deep into the heart of the Midwest during the later warm-dry Hypsithermal climatic episode (7000–3000 B.C., or 8950–4950 years B.P.). An important component of early Eastern Woodlands prehistory, then, is the adaptation of ancient Americans to these shifting late Pleistocene and mid-Holocene conditions. For these reasons, the boundaries of the culture area are more often defined in terms of map coordinates or political divisions. In a still useful definition, G.R. Willey (1966) separates the Eastern Woodlands from the Plains "by a line drawn through the western portions of Minnesota, Iowa, and Missouri and the eastern edges of Oklahoma and Texas" and includes southern Manitoba, Ontario, and Quebec, and New Brunswick and Nova Scotia within the northern boundary. This cultural division of North America should not be confused with eastern North America, a geographic division that extends eastward from the Rocky Mountains to the Atlantic and southward from southern Canada to the Gulf of Mexico and northeastern Mexico.

North-south-trending temperature and plant-community gradients and physiographic contrasts created diverse landscapes in the Precolumbian Eastern Woodlands. The continental climate ranged from humid and cold in the north to humid and subtropical in the south. Forests shifted from deciduous hardwoods mixed with conifers in the north (the "Lake Forest" ecotone), to deciduous oak-hickory woodlands in midlatitudes, to mixed hardwood forests with numerous swamplands, such as the Florida Everglades, in the south. Prairie grasslands with wooded river valleys stretched westward from Illinois. Major physiographic divisions are the Coastal Plain, the Appalachian Mountains, the Central Lowlands in the interior north, and the Ozark-Ouachita hills in Missouri and Arkansas. Numerous rivers and streams with broad floodplains and rich alluvial soils course throughout the area, and the Great Lakes and thousands of smaller lakes stretch across the northern section. The primary natural food resources were white-tailed deer, small game, fish, shellfish, nuts, and wild seed and root foods. Because this enormous region is so diverse, it is often subdivided into smaller, more environmentally homogenous units, such as Southeast and Northeast, or Southeast, Northeast, and Midwest. In a more extensive scheme, Willey (1966) divided the region into nine subareas: Upper Mississippi, Ozark, Lower Mississippi Valley, Southeast, Ohio Valley, Great Lakes, Northeast, Middle Atlantic, and Glades.

Prehistoric archaeological complexes in the Eastern Woodlands have been grouped by archaeologists into a series of sequential traditions, stages, or periods. From earliest to latest (with approximate time spans), these are the Paleoindian (9500–8000 B.C., or 11,450–9950 years B.P.), the Archaic (8000–1000 B.C., or 9950–2950 years B.P.), the Woodland (1000 B.C.–A.D. 700/1700, or 2950–1250/250 years B.P.), and the Mississippian (A.D. 700–1700, or 1250–250 years B.P.). The major language groups represented in the culture area in the early historic period were Muskogean, Iroquoian, Algonquian, Siouan, and Caddoan.

Guy Gibbon

Further Readings

Bense, J. 1994. *Southeastern Archaeology.* Academic Press, New York.

Fagan, B.M. 1991. *Ancient North America.* Thames and Hudson, New York.

Griffin, J.B. 1967. Eastern North American Archaeology: A Summary. *Science* 156:175–191.

Jennings, J.D. 1987. *The Prehistory of North America.* 3rd ed. Mayfield, Palo Alto.

———. (editor). 1983. *Ancient North Americans.* W.H. Freeman, San Francisco.

Mason, R. 1981. *Great Lakes Archaeology.* Academic Press, New York.

Morse, D., and P. Morse. 1983. *Archaeology of the Central Mississippi Valley.* Academic Press, New York.

Muller, J. 1986. *Archaeology of the Lower Ohio River Valley.* Academic Press, New York.

Smith, B.D. 1986. The Archaeology of the Southeastern United States: From Dalton to de Soto, 10,500 to 500 Years B.P. *Advances in World Archaeology* 5:1–92.

Snow, D. 1980. *The Archaeology of New England.* Academic Press, New York.

Steponaitis, V. 1986. Prehistoric Archaeology in the Southeastern United States 1970–1985. *Annual Review of Anthropology* 15:363–404.

Willey, G.R. 1966. *An Introduction to American Archaeology: 1. North and Middle America.* Prentice-Hall, Englewood Cliffs.

Eastern Woodlands Early Archaic

In areas to the west in the Upper Great Lakes, Late Paleoindian lanceolate projectile point forms persisted to ca. 5000 B.C. (6950 years B.P.).

Elsewhere in the Eastern Woodlands, these forms had been replaced by apparent areawide sequences of notched and stemmed point forms by 8000 B.C. (9950 years B.P.). The basis of these sequences was established in the 1950s by Joffre Coe's excavations at deeply stratified alluvial floodplain sites, such as Doerschuk, Lowder's Ferry, and Gaston, and at Hardaway on a promontory above the Yadkin River in the North Carolina Piedmont (Coe 1964), and later by Bettye Broyles's work at the St. Albans site in West Virginia (Broyles 1971). Because of the layered nature of these deep sites, it was possible to develop a secure ordering of point styles. Still later, James A. Tuck (1974) proposed, on the basis of radiocarbon determinations, that the Early Archaic period in the Eastern Woodlands was characterized by three point horizons—Dalton (Hardaway), Big Sandy, and Kirk—and a uniformity of hunter-gatherer lifeways that stretched from the Southeast into the Far Northeast. More recent work by Jefferson Chapman (1985) in the Little Tennessee Valley in eastern Tennessee at floodplain sites like Icehouse Bottom and Rose Island resulted in the addition of a fourth, "Bifurcate," horizon to this Early Archaic sequence. Chapman also proposed that the style horizons or traditions were widespread throughout the Eastern Woodlands and that style differences within phases of the Bifurcate horizon could be used as chronological markers over much of this area.

The sequence of projectile-point forms begins with a Dalton horizon (ca. 8500–8000 B.C., or 10,450–9950 years B.P.) characterized by Dalton or Daltonlike points, such as Hardaway Side-Notched and Hi-Lo, that are thought to have been directly derived from Clovislike fluted points in many regions of the Eastern Woodlands, for some Dalton points have thinning flakes that resemble flutes. Dalton or Daltonlike points have been found at Brand and other sites in northeastern Arkansas, over much of the Southeast, and in New England and westward across the southern Great Lakes in smaller numbers. Each of the subsequent horizons—the Side-Notched (ca. 8000–7700 B.C., or 9950–9650 years B.P.), Corner-Notched (ca. 7700–6900 B.C., or 9650–8850 years B.P.), and Bifurcate (ca. 6900–6000 B.C., or 8850–7950 years B.P.)—contains point forms with names like Big Sandy, Kessel Side-Notched, Eva, LeCroy, and Morrow Mountain or some cluster designation like Kirk Corner-Notched. Many archaeologists regard the Dalton horizon as a transitional phase and start the Early Archaic with the first appearance of notched points. In this scheme, the Early Archaic extends from ca. 8000 to 6000 B.C. (9950–7950 years B.P.); if the Dalton horizon is included, the period begins at ca. 8500 B.C. (10,450 years B.P.). Other stone tools in Early Archaic toolkits were generally similar throughout much of the Eastern Woodlands. These include large triangular bifaces, expanding-base "drills," celts with ground bits, grinding slabs, mullers, pitted cobbles, and polished-slate celts (Ellis et al. 1990). Settlements were apparently relatively small and used seasonally for only short periods of time. The light structures that served as shelters reflect this mobile lifeway.

Many basic questions about Early Archaic projectile-point forms remain unanswered, such as: Why were the forms uniform over such vast areas? What do the changes in form mean in cultural terms? How were the points used? (For more on the proposals, studies, and hypothesis discussed here, see Coe 1964; Broyles 1971; Chapman 1985; Anderson and Hanson 1988.) One proposed reason for the uniformity of point styles is based on the need for scattered, small groups of people to maintain contact to exchange information, mates, and material, among other transactions. According to this argument, as the small family bands of the Early Archaic became increasingly anchored to circumscribed territories, they began to establish networks in which points were one of a number of gifts that groups gave to one another in a pattern of reciprocal exchange. It has been proposed, too, that this process was facilitated by the presence throughout the Eastern Woodlands at the time of related Algonquian-Gulf languages. Reasons for the change from lanceolate to notched and stemmed forms remain elusive, but they may reflect shifts in how hunting weapons were used. The shift from side-notch to corner-notch is thought, for example, to accompany a change from thrusting spears to lighter shafts propelled by an atlatl (throwing stick), and bifurcate forms are considered possible adaptations for hunting particular species of forest game. Other studies of these points have concentrated on their patterns of wear. They show that, among other uses, many "projectile points" functioned as knives and saws, or some combination of these.

The gradual adaptive shift of ancient Americans in the Eastern Woodlands from a free-wandering Paleoindian lifeway focused on the capture of megafauna like mastodon and caribou to one based on a broader spectrum of forest foods like white-tailed deer, nuts, and plants as big game vanished and oak-dominated deciduous forests spread northward is a hypothesis that has been used to structure research. Regardless of the economy of earlier people in the area, these trends in the Early Archaic seem to have been accompanied by the development within more restricted territories of regular seasonal movements from one base camp to another in pursuit of a broadening spectrum of rich animal, plant, and aquatic food resources that included deer, opossum, raccoon, rabbit, turkey, fish, hickory nuts, roots, and berries. This general picture is supported by food and artifact remains in stratified deposits, especially in the Southeast. To the north, in the mixed hardwood forests of the Upper Great Lakes, some Late Paleoindian projectile-point styles persisted throughout this period, but their makers, too, may have been exploiting a broadening spectrum of resources within their more limited environment. A variety of models of Early Archaic lifeways have been proposed by Jefferson Chapman, David G. Anderson, and Dan F. and Phyllis A. Morse, among others.

Guy Gibbon

Further Readings

Anderson, D.G., and G.T. Hanson. 1988. Early Archaic Settlement in the Southeastern United States: A Case Study From the Savannah River Valley. *American Antiquity* 53:262–286.

Broyles, B. 1971. *Second Preliminary Report: The St. Albans Site, Kanawka County.* West Virginia Geological and Economic Survey, Morgantown.

Chapman, J. 1985. *Tellico Archaeology.* University of Tennessee Press, Knoxville.

Coe, J. 1964. *The Formative Cultures of the Carolina Piedmont.* Transactions, vol. 54, no. 5. American Philosophical Society, Philadelphia.

Ellis, C.J., I.T. Kenyon, and M.W. Spence. 1990. The Archaic. In *The Archaeology of Southern Ontario to A.D. 1650,* edited by C. Ellis and N. Ferris, pp. 65–124. Occasional Publications no. 5. London [Ontario] Chapter, Ontario Archaeological Society, London.

Morse, D.F., and P.A. Morse. 1983. *Archaeology of the Central Mississippi Valley.* Academic Press, New York.

Tuck, J.A. 1974. Early Archaic Horizons in Eastern North America. *Archaeology of Eastern North America* 2(1):72–80.

See also BIFURCATE TRADITION; BRAND SITE; CORNER-NOTCHED TRADITION; DALTON; EASTERN WOODLANDS ARCHAIC; HARDAWAY SITE; TELLICO ARCHAIC

Eastern Woodlands Late Archaic

The time range of the Late Archaic period in the Eastern Woodlands varies from one region to another for several reasons. Archaeologists disagree, for instance, on what traits mark its beginning, and the Woodland pottery whose appearance is conventionally taken to mark its end did not appear in all regions at the same time but gradually spread inward and northwestward from the coasts. Some archaeologists even group "Late Archaic" and nonagricultural Woodland societies together, for they believe that their lifeways had more in common with each other than either did with lifeways of earlier Early and Middle Archaic societies. As a result, the beginning of the Late Archaic period is generally placed somewhere between 4000 and 2500 B.C. (5950–4450 years B.P.), and its termination between 1000 and 400 B.C. (2950–2350 years B.P.). If "Late Archaic" and nonagricultural Woodland societies are lumped together, the Archaic ends by ca. 3000–2500 B.C. (4950–4450 years B.P.). The somewhat arbitrary bracket of 4000–700 B.C. (5950–2650 years B.P.) adopted here for the Late Archaic is for convenience, for a longer time frame has the advantage of simplicity in a review of a plethora of somewhat similar processes and events that occurred at different times in different regions. The basic problem is a familiar one in subdividing cultural continuums into smaller but still meaningful taxonomic units for analysis and discussion: Concentration on the defining criteria of units tends to mask internal variability, promote discussions of difference, and detract from investigations of the nature of the continuum as a whole.

Most regions of the Eastern Woodlands attained their modern climate and biome (plant and animal community) distribution by ca. 3000 B.C. (4950 years B.P.) as the warm-dry Hypsithermal climatic episode came to an end. With the final wastage of the northern glaciers, the Atlantic Ocean became warmer and attained its modern level. Together these and other natural processes changed still further the character and distribution of the eastern forests. Because of the cooler, moister climate, deciduous trees spread northward and out onto the prairies to the west and northwest, and the carrying capacity of many uplands in the interior improved once again. Higher sea levels raised water levels in the Great Lakes and flooded river estuaries. As stream gradients were reduced and water flow became more sluggish, more swampy backwaters, resource-rich floodplains, oxbows, and other riverine habitats formed, expanding the aquatic-exploitation niche of Archaic hunter-gatherers. These conditions also led to a northward expansion along the Atlantic Coast of fish and shellfish habitats, and the warmer water improved fishing conditions in the Great Lakes.

The Late Archaic is traditionally regarded as the period in which the seeds of "primary forest efficiency" sown in the Early Archaic or Late Paleoindian periods reached their fruition. The results were far-reaching changes that culminated in a florescence and climax of the Archaic way of life. Among the distinguishing features of this period are a trend toward greater social complexity and sophistication, with the emergence of social ranking and increasingly elaborate mortuary customs; a sharp rise in human population size (as reflected in much higher site densities); intensification of long-distance exchanges to obtain a wider range of materials, including copper, galena, seashells, and foreign cherts; more sedentary lifeways and the appearance of sites with large, dense middens and evidence of substantial dwellings; more restricted food-procurement territories; a probable increase in the intensity of hunting and foraging (possibly to meet demands for trade goods); increasing numbers of subterranean storage pits and advances in the technology of storage, with the first use of heavy containers of stone and pottery; the deliberate cultivation in small gardens of indigenous wild plants, such as sunflowers, marsh elder, and knotweed, as an ancillary food and plant product resource; the appearance of "tropical" cultigens (squashes and gourds); construction of earthen burial mounds and other earthworks in some areas of the Midwest and the Southeast; and greater regional variation in artifact and stylistic traditions, especially after 2000 B.C. (3950 years B.P.). Archaeologists usually consider these characteristics to have been causally intertwined, linked in part to higher population densities, and temporal expressions of long-term processual trends in the Eastern Woodlands.

Not all of these Late Archaic characteristics were present in all regions of the Eastern Woodlands or reached their Archaic peak at the same time. Squashes and gourds, for example, were present in some localities of the Midwest and the Southeast in the third millennium B.C., while cultivated indigenous plants like sunflower appear in the second millennium B.C. Fiber-tempered clay containers, which were possibly used for cooking and storage, are present along the coastal plain of Georgia and South Carolina by 2500 B.C. (4450 years B.P.), in the Lower Mississippi Valley by ca. 1300 B.C. (3250 years B.P.), and in northern Alabama by 1000 B.C. (2950 years B.P.). Steatite and sandstone vessels were present even earlier in some areas of the Southeast, with pottery containers possibly a heavy-container adaptation in areas farther from the sources of these stone materials.

Since the 1960s, the geographic variability of Late Archaic complexes has been organized into a series of regional variants based on contrasting adaptations to different kinds of environmental zones. These include the Shield culture on the northern border of the Eastern Woodlands; the Maritime, Lake Forest, and Mast Forest traditions in the Upper Midwest and the Northeast; the Central Riverine Archaic in the major river valleys of the southern Midwest and the Southeast; and the Poverty Point culture in the Lower Mississippi Valley and along the adjacent Gulf Coast.

Guy Gibbon

See also CENTRAL RIVERINE ARCHAIC; EASTERN AGRICULTURAL COMPLEX; EASTERN WOODLANDS ARCHAIC; LAKE FOREST ARCHAIC; MARITIME ARCHAIC TRADITION; MAST FOREST ARCHAIC; POVERTY POINT CULTURE; SHIELD CULTURE

Eastern Woodlands Middle Archaic

The temporal bracketing of the Middle Archaic period in the Eastern Woodlands by archaeologists varies widely because the nature and timing of natural and cultural processes during the mid-Holocene (ca. 6500–2000 B.C., or 8450–3950 years B.P.) were not uniform throughout this vast culture area. While most dating schemes begin the period at ca. 6000 B.C. (7950 years B.P.), its termination is placed anywhere from 4000 to 2500 B.C. (5950–4450 years B.P.).

Some archaeologists even terminate the Archaic period itself at 3000–2500 B.C. (4950–4450 years B.P.), because they believe that cultural adaptations after that date resemble Woodland adaptations more closely than they do those of Early and Middle Archaic cultures. The 6000–4000 B.C. (7950–5950 years B.P.) bracket adopted here is rather arbitrary, then, but it does allow a contrast between earlier (ca. 6000–4500 B.C., or 7950–6450 years B.P.) Middle Archaic adaptations and later (ca. 4500–4000 B.C., or 6450–5950 years B.P.) trends that eventually culminated in the florescence of the Archaic in the Late Archaic period.

Early Middle Archaic (ca. 6000–4500 B.C., or 7950–6450 years B.P.) lifeways continued the trend toward an ever more "efficient" exploitation of a broadening range of food resources within increasingly restricted and circumscribed territories that began in the Early Archaic, if not still earlier in the Late Paleoindian period. Small, scattered populations with a generalized hunter-gatherer economy apparently briefly occupied a series of warm-weather base camps along floodplain levees and terraces, where they hunted white-tailed deer and smaller mammals, fished, and harvested seasonal plant foods, such as roots and hickory nuts. During cold-weather months, they may have exploited deer from smaller transitory camps in the uplands and along stream tributaries. The greatest occupational densities at this time seem to have been in river valleys and perhaps along the Atlantic and Gulf coasts, where rich animal or plant resources, or both, were concentrated. The exploitation of coastal sea mammals and fisheries remains hypothetical, for the water level of the Atlantic Ocean, which did not stabilize until ca. 3000–2500 B.C. (4950–4450 years B.P.), gradually inundated this region of the coastal strip as northern ice masses continued to waste during the mid-Holocene. However, the existence of a rich coastal lifeway is supported by the discovery of evidence of sea-mammal hunting and an earthen and stone burial mound dated to ca. 5600 B.C. (7550 years B.P.) at the site of L'Anse Amour far to the north in Labrador. The site was preserved when land rose as the weight of nearby ice sheets diminished. Shell mounds dating to ca. 5000 B.C. (6950 years B.P.) have been found as well on high bluffs bordering the Lower Hudson River Valley in New England. Apparently, at the time, a fairly uniform hunter-gatherer culture stretched from the Piedmont in the Southeast far into the northern sector of the Eastern Woodlands. Only minor variations in projectile-point styles seem to distinguish one culture from another in the archaeological record.

Although human population in the Eastern Woodlands was still low, these accelerating early Middle Archaic trends seem to have resulted in more permanent settlement as people became increasingly concentrated in areas with a greater diversity of food resources. Among the processes possibly responsible for these more circumscribed lifeways were gradual population growth, which may have stressed the carrying capacity of less favored environments, and a warmer, drier climate, which may have reduced the carrying capacity of bordering river valley uplands. Often cited evidence of reduced territoriality is a more exclusive use of local raw materials, with the implication that these and other processes had restricted the range within which people were able to move in their annual settlement-subsistence round so that they now had to gather food and raw materials from within a smaller area.

The last centuries (ca. 4500–4000 B.C., or 6450–5950 years B.P.) of the Middle Archaic period were marked by the onset of dramatic changes that heralded the florescence of Late Archaic lifeways. Among these are the appearance of more substantial and increasingly permanent floodplain midden sites formed by habitation debris that are located near shellfish beds, fish spawning grounds, and backwaters; a dramatic increase in the use of riverine aquatic resources; increased numbers of shell midden sites; even more restricted mobility within increasingly fixed territories; more careful seasonal scheduling to maximize the procurement of a narrower range of readily exploitable "first-line" food resources (the attainment of "primary forest efficiency"); evidence of increased competition for resources and territories; fewer numbers of sites in some areas; the first appearance of bluff-top mounds; and increasing regional variability in projectile-point styles.

The reasons for these changes remain a focus of Middle Archaic research. However, they may have included climatic change (the peak of the Hypsithermal at ca. 4000 B.C., or 5950 years B.P.), rising sea levels, continued population growth, and the incursion of people associated with new language families. The warm-dry Hypsithermal climatic episode resulted in the encroachment of prairie along the western border of the Eastern Woodlands; low-ered water levels in lakes, streams, and rivers in much of the Midwest and the Southeast; and a further reduction of the carrying capacity of the upland forests. Rising sea levels after 4500 B.C. (6450 years B.P.) changed the gradients of interior streams and rivers, which stabilized drainage systems, increased the number of oxbows and backwaters, and resulted in the accumulation of silt in floodplains. These latter processes enhanced aquatic habitats for mussels and bottom fish and led in general to an increase in the level of aquatic biomass. Together, these and other processes apparently "pushed" people from areas with dwindling resources and "drew" them to the enriched resources of favored river valleys. Aquatic food resources now became increasingly important components of the Middle Archaic diet in these areas. According to this hypothetical scenario, as these still-egalitarian societies became "fixed" in circumscribed river-valley localities, some kin groups began to symbolically legitimize their right to local food resources by burying more people in their settlements and in nearby cemeteries and by constructing low earthen mounds in highly visible locations, such as bluff tops.

As in the Early Archaic, early Middle Archaic projectile-point forms, such as Kirk Stemmed, Stanly/Neville Stemmed, and Morrow Mountain Stemmed, were regional expressions of a Stemmed horizon that extended throughout much of the Eastern Woodlands. By the late Middle Archaic, an apparent increasing regional variability in point form seems to parallel the increased restriction of people to a smaller number of scattered, river-valley or lake-edge locations. Other characteristics of the Middle Archaic toolkit include the appearance of fully ground and polished stone tools, like the grooved axe and the bannerstone, and of notched pebbles, which were probably used as net sinkers; an increasing and extensive use of a wide range of lower-grade stone materials for the manufacture of flaked tools; and an increase in numbers of plant-processing artifacts, such as grinding stones and manos (Ellis et al. 1990).

Changes in Middle Archaic lifeways have been traced at least in part at many archaeological sites in the Eastern Woodlands, including Icehouse Bottom and Rose Island in the Little Tennessee Valley; Koster, Carrier Mills, and Modoc Rock Shelter in Illinois; Rodgers Shelter and Graham Cave in central Missouri; and Neville in New Hampshire.

Guy Gibbon

Further Readings

Chapman, J. 1985. *Tellico Archaeology.* University of Tennessee Press, Knoxville.

Dincauze, D. 1976. *The Neville Site: 8000 Years at Amoskeag.* Peabody Museum of American Archaeology and Ethnology, Harvard University, Cambridge.

Ellis, C.J., I.T. Kenyon, and M.W. Spence. 1990. The Archaic. In *The Archaeology of Southern Ontario to A.D. 1650,* edited by C. Ellis and N. Ferris, pp. 65–124. Occasional Publications no. 5. London [Ontario] Chapter, Ontario Archaeological Society, London.

McGhee, R., and J.A. Tuck. 1977. An Archaic Indian Burial Mound in Labrador. *Scientific American* 235(5):122–129.

Morse, D., and P. Morse. 1983. *Archaeology of the Central Mississippi Valley.* Academic Press, New York.

Snow, D. 1980. *The Archaeology of New England.* Academic Press, New York.

See also EASTERN WOODLANDS ARCHAIC; KOSTER; MODOC ROCK SHELTER; NEVILLE SITE; RODGERS SHELTER; TELLICO ARCHAIC

Effigy Mounds

Effigy mounds are prehistoric earthworks with outlines resembling life forms, the most common appearing like mammals in profile and variously referred to as panthers, canines, bears, or deer, depending upon such features as tails, ears, or antlers. There are two instances of human effigy mounds. In addition, birds with outstretched wings are common, and turtle and lizard forms also occur. Despite their distinctiveness, effigy forms are normally minority types within groups composed predominantly of conical and linear mounds.

The majority of effigy-mound groups are in southern Wisconsin, with lesser numbers in contiguous portions of Minnesota, Iowa, and Illinois. Within this region, effigy mounds typically are situated on elevations near rivers and lakes. While most groups have fewer than 50 mounds, the Harpers Ferry group in northeast Iowa reportedly had 895 mounds, 174 of which were effigies. The largest reported effigy mound, near Madison, Wisconsin, is of a bird with a wingspan of 190 m (624 feet). While the sheer numbers and linear dimensions of these mounds are impressive, their low stature—

Bird effigy mounds, Effigy Mounds National Monument. (Photograph by Allan Zarling. Courtesy of the Effigy Mounds National Monument, National Park Service, Harpers Ferry, Iowa)

Great Bear mound group, found in the North Unit, Effigy Mounds National Monument. This mound group is located along the main trail of the North Unit and is about one mile walking distance from the visitor center. It includes the only bear lying on its left side and facing up river. (Courtesy of the Effigy Mounds National Monument, National Park Service, Harpers Ferry, Iowa)

rarely do they exceed 2 m (6.6 feet) in height—has made them easy prey to destruction by plowing and urban expansion. Fortunately, numerous effigy mounds still survive within community parks throughout the region; the most informative and accessible to the general public is Effigy Mounds National Monument near McGregor in northeast Iowa. The meaning of the effigy forms remains unknown, but their primary purpose was for burial of the dead, who were usually interred either in the flesh in a flexed position or as secondary reburials of bones not in anatomical order. Burials were placed in subfloor pits, upon the mound floor, or in the mound fill, depending upon the episode of mound construction. Graves contained one or multiple individuals, with at least two known instances of mass graves, containing the remains of 35 and 45 individuals, respectively. Grave goods are generally sparse or absent. Peoples of Effigy Mound culture apparently practiced a mobile lifestyle, for evidence of sedentary villages is rare. Their subsistence seems to have been primarily based upon hunting and gathering, although there are indications that maize was present, but not yet important, in their diet. Their inventory of material goods was modest. Thin-walled pottery jars with corded surfaces and cord-impressed decoration were probably used to cook gruels and stews. Small stemmed and notched projectile points suggest the presence of the bow and arrow (which they sometimes used on one another, as evidenced by at least one burial with

The Marching Bear group is the largest group of effigy mounds in the Effigy Mounds National Monument. This group follows a ridgetop above the Mississippi River. (Photograph by Allan Zarling. Courtesy of the Effigy Mounds National Monument, National Park Service, Harpers Ferry, Iowa)

a point embedded in bone). Elbow pipes of clay indicate the practice of smoking, while a few items of native copper suggest exchange with neighbors to the north. Taxonomically, archaeologists assign Effigy Mound culture to the Late Woodland stage. The primary period of its existence was A.D. 750–1050 (1200–900 years B.P.). Unfortunately, no successor culture has been reliably identified in the Upper Mississippi Valley region, so that it has been impossible to identify any present-day native peoples as the descendants of this culture.

James B. Stoltman

Further Readings

Barrett, S.A., and E.W. Hawkes. 1919. *The Kratz Creek Mound Group*. Bulletin no. 13. Public Museum of the City of Milwaukee, Milwaukee.

Hurley, W.M. 1975. *An Analysis of Effigy Mound Complexes in Wisconsin*. Anthropological Papers no. 59. Museum of Anthropology, University of Michigan, Ann Arbor.

Mallam, R.C. 1976. *The Iowa Effigy Mound Manifestation: An Interpretive Model*. Report no. 9. Office of the State Archaeologist, Iowa City.

McKern, W.C. 1928. *The Neale and McClaughry Mound Groups*. Bulletin, vol. 3, no. 3. Public Museum of the City of Milwaukee, Milwaukee.

———. 1930. *The Kletzien and Nitschke Mound Groups*. Bulletin, vol. 3, no. 4. Public Museum of the City of Milwaukee, Milwaukee.

Rowe, C.W. 1956. *The Effigy Mound Culture of Wisconsin*. Publications in Anthropology no. 3. Public Museum of the City of Milwaukee, Milwaukee.

Emergent Mississippian

In the Eastern Woodlands, Mississippian culture represents the climax of Native American societies. Distributed unevenly throughout much of the Southeast in the Late Prehistoric period, Mississippian societies have been characterized as ranked agriculturalists and as politically unstable chiefdoms. At the time of European contact in the sixteenth century, Mississippian chiefdoms had been in existence for 500 years. The shift to Mississippian chiefdoms from earlier Late Woodland societies involved a complex set of processes that varied in many respects from one area of the Southeast to another. The concept of an "Emergent Mississippian" culture was formally introduced into the literature of the American Bottom in 1984 to highlight the presence of this set of processes in that region, a 100-km (62-mile) long segment of the central Mississippi River Valley between the mouths of the Missouri and Kaskaskia rivers (Kelly et al. 1984). The unusually large Early Mississippian mound center, Cahokia, is located at its northern end, near present-day East St. Louis, Illinois. A dispersed series of smaller mound centers, including five with multiple mounds, is located within a 30-km (18.6-mile) radius of the Cahokia mound complex.

By A.D. 1000 (950 years B.P.), Cahokia and a number of the other mound centers in the American Bottom had emerged as dominant political entities on the local landscape. Their emergence is rooted in the preceding 250-year Emergent Mississippian period, for which two spatially distinct traditions, Late Bluff and Pulcher, have been delineated. Each of these traditions has been divided into a series of phases. In the northern third of the American Bottom, the Late Bluff tradition consists of the Collinsville, Loyd, Merrell, and Edelhardt phases, while the Pulcher tradition in the central third of the region consists of the Dohack, Range, George Reeves, and Lindeman phases.

Elements of the Pulcher-tradition Lindhorst phase persist into the Early Mississippian period (A.D. 1000–1100, or 950–850 years B.P.). Although changes between phases can be identified, there was considerable continuity within both traditions and a noticeable cross-fertilization between them. In addition, their spatial limits were subject to varying degrees of fluidity through time.

Ceramics have been used as the primary means of differentiating between these spatial and temporal divisions. However, the shift to an Emergent Mississippian culture involved, more importantly, significant settlement and subsistence changes. It was noted in initial studies (Kelly et al. 1984) that the shift was marked by a sudden and widespread presence of maize in archaeological features. Paleoethnobotanical analyses (Kelly et al. 1990) indicated, too, that maize, while now more important in the diet, augmented an already existing substantial suite of native starchy seed food resources. By 1991, it had been determined that maize is present in 30 percent of the features associated with the terminal Late Woodland Sponemann phase (A.D. 750–800, or 1200–1150 years B.P.). While some archaeologists regard this phase as the first segment of the Emergent Mississippian

E

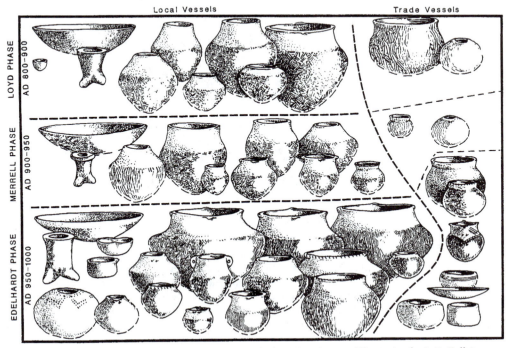

Emergent Mississippian ceramic assemblages from Cahokia–Merrel tract. (Illustration by J. E. Kelly)

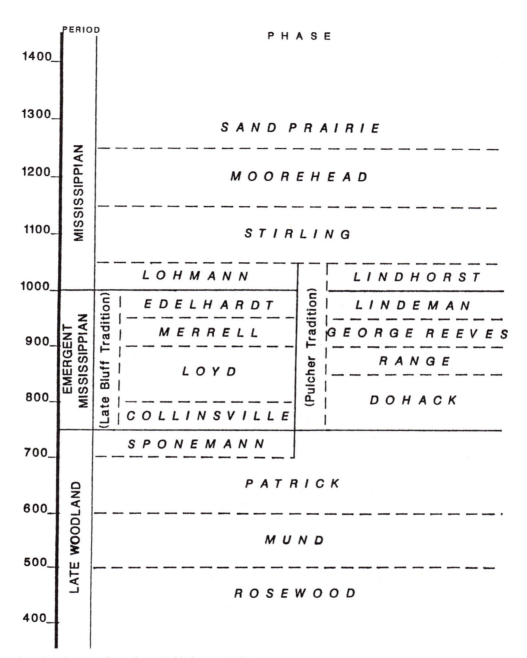

PERIOD			PHASE	

American Bottom chronology. (Table by J. E. Kelly)

culture, it is considered a Late Woodland manifestation here on the basis of ceramics and other criteria.

The complexes assigned to the initial half (A.D. 750–900, or 1200–1050 years B.P.) of the Emergent Mississippian sequence exhibit some degree of continuity and thus affinity with their Late Woodland antecedents. An example of a shared trait is the presence of small aggregated villages. However, while they are of this general settlement pattern, Emergent Mississippian villages are more complex, with groups of structures sometimes distributed around community squares. The community squares of the Emergent Mississippian villages at the Range and Westpark sites are dominated by a set of central features consisting of one of three patterns: a quadrapartite arrangement of four pits about a central post; a large rectangular post structure; or an isolated central post. These central facilities were not only imbued with certain symbols, but also served as mechanisms to integrate the communities. By contrast, Late Woodland societies were apparently based on a segmentary kinship system in which competition for leadership roles led to the fusion and fissioning of communities. Conflict appears to have been minimized during the initial part of the Emergent Mississippian when leadership roles became established along kinship lines and subject to principles of primogeniture. Distribution of resources, particularly agricultural land, probably became integrated into rituals of agricultural renewal and may have played an important role in this shift in social organization. Control of these rituals and their associated symbols ultimately became an important part of the role of these incipient elites.

During the latter half (A.D. 900–1000, or 1050–950 years B.P.) of the Emergent Mississippian, the ceramic assemblage became more diversified, and interaction with coeval societies to the south increased. Mill Creek chert hoes were being imported from sources in southern Illinois at this time, if not earlier. While there is little change in botanical assemblages, changes in settlement patterns included a proliferation of large nucleated villages and the possible emergence of mound centers at Pulcher and Cahokia. Although an extensive area containing Emergent Mississippian materials has been identified at both sites, mound construction has not been documented to date (1996).

The basic elements that underlie Cahokia's overall configuration are apparent in the layout of the large George Reeves–phase Emergent Mississippian village at the Range site. These elements consist of a large central plaza flanked by a series of courtyards, with the set of central features that dominated initial Emergent Mississippian villages carefully and symmetrically arranged within the various courtyards and plaza. Presumably, these elements and their arrangements embody certain symbolic meanings and were associated with particular segments of the society, such as clans or phratries (groupings of clans). The layout of the Range village also provides the first clear evidence of societal ranking in the American Bottom.

The Emergent Mississippian concept has been used primarily in the American Bottom. Its applicability to other areas of the Southeast depends upon the nature of local Late Woodland-Mississippian transformations.

John E. Kelly

Further Readings

Kelly, J.E. 1987. Emergent Mississippian and the Transition From Late Woodland to Mississippian: The American Bottom Case for a New Concept. In *The Emergent Mississippian*, edited by R.A. Marshall, pp. 87–101. Proceedings of the Sixth Mid-South Archaeological Conference, June 6–9, 1985, Starkville. Occasional Papers. Cobb Institute of Archaeology, Mississippi State University, Starkville.

———. 1990. The Emergence of Mississippian Culture in the American Bottom Region. In *The Mississippian Emergence*, edited by B.D. Smith, pp. 113–152. Smithsonian Institution Press, Washington, D.C.

Kelly, J.E., S.J. Ozuk, D.K. Jackson, D.L. McElrath, F.A. Finney, and D. Esarey. 1984. Emergent Mississippian Period. In *American Bottom Archaeology: A Summary of the FAI–270 Project Contribution to the Culture History of the Mississippi River Valley*, edited by C.J. Bareis and J.W. Porter, pp. 128–157. University of Illinois Press, Urbana.

Marshall, R.A. (editor). 1987. *The Emergent Mississippian.* Proceedings of the Sixth Mid-South Archaeological Conference, June 6–9, 1985, Starkville. Occasional Papers. Cobb Institute of Archaeology, Mississippi State University, Starkville.

Nassaney, M.S., and C.R. Cobb (editors). 1991. *Stability, Transformation, and Variation: The Late Woodland Southeast.* Plenum Press, New York.

Smith, B.D. (editor). 1990. *The Mississippian Emergence.* Smithsonian Institution Press, Washington, D.C.

See also CAHOKIA; MISSISSIPPIAN CULTURE; RANGE SITE

Engigstciak

Engigstciak is a large, stratified, multicomponent archaeological deposit located a few kilometers (a mile or two) from the Arctic Ocean on the Firth River at the western end of the Yukon Coastal Plain in Canada. It became known for

E

a while in the 1960s as a locality of some significance, primarily because of its purported potential to help elucidate issues pertaining to the peopling of the New World, the later initial colonization of the Arctic, and the development of regional Neo-Eskimo culture history. Unfortunately, a combination of factors, including the realization that much of the deposit had been heavily disturbed by gelifluction, the lack of integrity of the proposed very ancient British Mountain tradition, the absence of dates, and what might be euphemistically called a series of paradigmatic shifts in northern archaeology, caused this initial interest to subside. Engigstciak soon became just another pioneering episode in the history of regional research.

Recently, however, the results of continued investigations and a better understanding of site-formation processes have led to a resurgence of scientific attention in the site (Cinq-Mars et al. 1991). For example, the recent dating of butchered bison bones indicates that in one important locus of the site, where chronostratigraphic integrity has been retained, there is in situ evidence of human exploitation of local resources dating back to ca. 8000 B.C. (9950 years B.P.). Together with new information on an early Paleoeskimo presence and a better appreciation of the site's strategic location, these data show that Engigstciak may well have retained a good deal of its originally hypothesized interpretive potential.

Jacques Cinq-Mars

Further Readings

Cinq-Mars, J., C.R. Harington, D.E. Nelson, and R.S. MacNeish. 1991. Engigstciak Revisited: A Note on Early Holocene AMS Dates From the "Buffalo Pit." *Canadian Archaeological Association Occasional Paper* 1:33–44.

MacNeish, R.S. 1959. Men Out of Asia: As Seen From the Northwest Yukon. *Anthropological Papers of the University of Alaska* 7(2):41–70.

Etowah

Etowah (9BR1) is a large Mississippian-period mound center located in the northwestern corner of Georgia. It is situated on an expanse of alluvial bottomland that lies just below the point where the Etowah River flows out of the Piedmont and into the Great Valley of the Ridge and Valley province. These floodplain soils are some of the most productive in the area, and this productivity undoubtedly was an important factor in Etowah's rise to prominence.

The site is physically impressive, dominated by six mounds, several large borrow pits, and a defensive ditch that encloses 21 ha (52 acres). The largest mound, Mound A, measures 19 m (62 feet) in height, while the other mounds range from 3 to 7 m (10–23 feet) high. Originally, the ditch had a palisade with bastions on its inner edge and ran to the Etowah River on each side. Despite its size, Etowah is best known for the spectacular collection of finely crafted items excavated from the site's mortuary mound. From burials in Mound C, excavators recovered items associated with the Southeastern Ceremonial complex, such as flint swords, embossed copper plates, carved shell gorgets, and the famous Etowah marble statues. Similar items have been found at other major Mississippian centers, such as Spiro in Oklahoma and Moundville in Alabama.

The earliest Mississippian occupation of the site began ca. A.D. 950 (1000 years B.P.). By A.D. 1050 (900 years B.P.), Mounds A and B were both in existence and Etowah emerged as an important political center in the region. Between A.D. 1150 and 1200 (800–750 years B.P.), the site experienced a brief period of abandonment but it was reoccupied and reached its peak by A.D. 1350 (650 years B.P.). During this period, Mounds A, B, and C were substantially enlarged, the ditch and palisade were completed, and a large plaza paved with red clay and lined with a low rock wall was constructed to the east of Mound A. Also at this time, the Southeastern Ceremonial–complex items were buried with Etowah's elites in Mound C. By A.D. 1300 (650 years B.P.), Etowah had become the capital of a complex chiefdom, with between two and four subsidiary centers, and was clearly one of the most important polities in northern Georgia. However, by A.D. 1350 (600 years B.P.), Etowah's importance had waned, and the site again was abandoned. In the summer of 1540, Hernando de Soto and his army spent six days visiting the town of Itaba, now known to be the Etowah site. At that time, the summit of Mound B was in use and at least one (Mound D) of the three smallest mounds was constructed. According to de Soto, Itaba was part of the paramount chiefdom of Coosa, whose capital lay 54 km to the north at the Little Egypt site. Within 50 years of de Soto's visit, Etowah, along with much of the valley, was again abandoned and remained so until the Cherokee moved into the area in the eighteenth century.

Since the first investigations in the late nineteenth century, a great deal of archaeological research has been conducted at the site. Most has involved intensive excavations in limited areas related to mound contexts. Consequently, more is known about the structure and chronology of the mounds than about overall site structure and how it changed through time.

Adam King

Further Readings

Kelly, A.R., and L.H. Larson. 1957. Explorations at the Etowah Indian Mounds Near Cartersville, Georgia: Seasons 1954, 1955, and 1956. *Archaeology* 10(1):39–48.

Larson, L.H. 1971. Archaeological Implications of Social Stratification at the Etowah Site. In *Approaches to the Social Dimensions of Mortuary Practices,* edited by J.A. Brown, pp. 58–67. Memoir no. 25. Society for American Archaeology, Washington, D.C.

———. 1972. Functional Considerations of Warfare in the Southeast During the Mississippi Period. *American Antiquity* 37:383–392.

Moorehead, W.K. (editor). 1932. *The Etowah Papers.* Yale University Press, New Haven.

Thomas, C. 1894. *Report on the Mound Explorations of the Bureau of Ethnology.* Twelfth Annual Report. Bureau of Ethnology, Smithsonian Institution, Washington, D.C.

Eulachon

Eulachon *(Thaleichthys pacificus)* is an anadromous smelt that was an important source of food oil for populations of the Northwest Coast. Early each spring, vast numbers of eulachon leave the sea to spawn in the larger rivers between northern California and Alaska's Bristol Bay. Most then die, but some drift back to saltwater and return the next spring. Spawning takes place after the fish reach three years of age. The maximum lifespan appears to be five years. Eulachon are of such exceptionally high oil content that when dried they can be lit and burned as a small torch, a property that has earned them the popular name of "candlefish." To the aboriginal people, however, it was their

food value that was of importance. Freshly caught smelt, available just as winter supplies of dried salmon and halibut reached their lowest levels, were welcome fare. In addition, many were air dried or smoked for later consumption, and huge quantities were processed by boiling to extract their soft, buttery oil.

Although widely distributed, eulachon run in a limited number of streams. The exploitation of these fisheries brought together some of the largest seasonal aggregations of Northwest Coast populations. The Nass River fishery, for example, drew people from virtually all Coast Tsimshian and Nishga local groups as well as a contingent of southern Tlingit. Those groups without direct access often traded for the product. The resulting trade network extended well inland, with the oil brought to settlements east of the coastal mountains along the so-called "grease trails."

Donald H. Mitchell

Further Readings

Macnair, P.L. 1971. Descriptive Notes on the Kwakiutl Manufacture of Eulachon Oil. *Syesis* 4:169–177.

Scott, W.B., and E.J. Crossman. 1973. *Freshwater Fishes of Canada.* Bulletin no. 184. Fisheries Research Board of Canada, Ottawa.

Eva Site

The Eva site (40BN12) is on a small knoll within the Tennessee River floodplain in Benton County, Tennessee. It was one of many sites excavated with WPA (Works Progress Administration) labor prior to the construction of dams by the Tennessee Valley Authority. The Eva site is now submerged beneath Kentucky Lake, which was created in 1944. Although the site apparently was intermittently occupied over a period of ca. 8,000 years or more, its primary importance lies in its intensive Middle and Late Archaic occupations.

The Middle Archaic "Eva component" has been radiocarbon dated to ca. 5000 B.C. (6950 years B.P.). These occupations are represented stratigraphically by a ca. 2 m (6.6-foot) -thick deposit containing shell middens. With the exception of burials, very few identifiable features were encountered during the excavations. A large number of chert projectile points were recovered from the site. They provide data that continue to be central to studies of regional projectile-point typologies and their temporal relationships. Eva is the type site for the large, basally notched projectile point/knife of the same name. Eva points are heavily concentrated in the Middle Archaic component, and the point form itself occurs primarily within the Lower Tennessee River Valley. A variety of stemmed points of various types characterize the later Archaic occupations.

Besides shellfish (the importance of which is only cursorily mentioned in the site report), deer were the major source of protein during all periods of the site's occupation (Lewis and Lewis 1961). Bear, raccoon, opossum, turkey, turtle, and various species of fish are also present. Shellfish and fish may have assumed greater importance during the post–Eva component occupations. However, there appear to be problems with the arbitrary stratigraphic divisions proposed for the site. These problems make an assessment of changing subsistence strategies difficult. There are no paleobotanical data from the site, for Eva was excavated long before the advent of modern water-screening and flotation techniques. The presence of "nutting stones" and of various grinding stones may reflect the importance of nuts in the diet.

Eva has produced an important body of mortuary data. Within the relatively small excavation area, 180 human and 18 dog burials, dating primarily to the Late Archaic period, were recovered. Virtually all of the human skeletons were flexed and placed in pits scattered throughout the midden deposits. Grave goods were associated with approximately one-third of the interred individuals. The most frequent inclusions were various forms of projectile points (although several may have been responsible for the death of the individual), followed by red ocher, bone-splinter awls, and bone beads; copper beads were present in a single grave. A study of Eva mortuary practices found little evidence of social differentiation, suggesting that the Middle and Late Archaic people who occupied the site had basically egalitarian social systems (Magennis 1977).

Robert C. Mainfort, Jr.

Further Readings

Lewis, T.M.N., and M.K. Lewis. 1961. *Eva: An Archaic Site*. University of Tennessee Press, Knoxville.

Magennis, A.L. 1977. *Middle and Late Archaic Mortuary Patterning: An Example From the Western Tennessee Valley*. Unpublished Master's thesis, Department of Anthropology, University of Tennessee, Knoxville.

F

Far North

The Far North includes two distinct culture areas: the Arctic and the Subarctic. Roughly divided by the tree line, they cover most of Canada and nearly all of Alaska. Their culture histories can be discussed separately, for neither seems to have exerted a profound influence on the other.

The Subarctic is a land of long, cold winters; short, warm summers; and seemingly impenetrable spruce forests. At the time of European contact between A.D. 1600 and 1800 (350–150 years B.P.), it was the home of two great Indian-language families: the Algonquian, spoken in the Canadian Shield area; and the Athapaskan, spoken north and west of northern Saskatchewan. Despite different origins, the speakers of these two language families shared a cultural configuration that was based primarily upon hunting and fishing. With population densities among the lowest in the world, their social groups were everywhere comparatively small. These groups were also fluid in composition; social units of varying sizes moved throughout the seasons from one food resource to another. This pattern of nearly constant movement is reflected in their toolkits, which were light and multipurpose. Among the important food animals exploited throughout the Subarctic were caribou, moose, waterfowl, small game, and freshwater fish. Only in the Pacific drainage of the Far West were there salmon streams rich enough to support a slightly more secure and settled way of life.

Archaeological research in the Subarctic is particularly challenging, for the acid soils of the boreal forest destroy most organic materials, such as wood, antler, and animal bone, and the nomadic way of life and very difficult landscape mean that sites are scattered, small, and difficult to locate. One difference between the archaeology of the eastern and western Subarctic is the presence of pottery in some areas of the eastern Subarctic. This pottery was a result of trade and other connections with cultures to the south. The various periods that make up the eastern Subarctic cultural sequence have been defined in part by whether they occur before or after the first appearance of pottery. Periods in the sequence, from oldest to most recent, are the Plano Paleoindian (a designation primarily based on the presence of lanceolate points, which dates from 5500 B.C., or 7450 years B.P., or earlier to ca. 3000 B.C., or 4950 years B.P., depending on locale); the Archaic (Shield Archaic, which dates to ca. 4500–500 B.C., or 6450–2450 years B.P.; and Maritime Archaic, which dates to ca. 5500–1000 B.C., or 7450–2950 years B.P.—both preceramic complexes with notched points); and, finally, a succession of Woodland periods (defined on the basis of the presence of various kinds of Woodland ceramics). There is no clear evidence throughout of cultural discontinuity. It has been suggested that local Paleoindian groups were the direct cultural and, presumably, biological ancestors of the Cree, the Montagnais, and the Naskapi (Innu) who still occupy most of this vast territory.

The archaeology of the western Subarctic appears to be more complex. The earliest clear signs of a human presence in Alaska and the Yukon (Nenana complex) date to the end of the last glacial period (ca. 9500 B.C., or 11,450 years B.P.). These groups are considered ancestral Paleoindian. They were immediately followed by a range of "cultures" or "complexes" that contained microblades, wedge-shaped microblade cores, and a variety of burins. These groups, which are represented by an abundant amount of evidence, have generally been grouped into an all-embracing American Paleoarctic tradition. The characteristic microblades and burins suggest an origin in northeastern Asia.

Beginning ca. 4500 B.C. (6450 years B.P.), the American Paleoarctic tradition was influenced by, or in some places replaced by, the spread of Archaic technologies and peoples from the south. Characteristic notched projectile points appear widely, sometimes in association with microblade technology, and sometimes not. The resultant "Northern Archaic" or "Northwest Microblade" tradition has been seen by some as directly ancestral to the culture of historic Athapaskan-speakers, but the matter remains problematic. Whatever the exact cultural connection, microblades and other early traits gradually drop out of local cultural assemblages and, at least by the late precontact period,which began ca. A.D. 450 (1500 years B.P.), we are almost certainly dealing with Athapaskan-speakers everywhere in the western Subarctic. Examples of some of these late-precontact cultural entities include the Klo-kut phase in the northern Yukon, the Spence River phase in the Mackenzie River Valley, and the Taltheilei tradition in the barren-ground/transitional forest zone west of Hudson Bay.

The Arctic is most easily defined as the area north of the tree line. It is characterized by even longer winters than the Subarctic, cool summers, and the absence of trees. Although a useful approximation, the tree line has not always correlated perfectly with cultural boundaries. Shield Archaic "Indians," for instance, once occupied the tundra zone west of Hudson Bay, as did historic Athapaskan speakers during the eighteenth century. Conversely, Dorset "Eskimos" at one time lived as far south as the island of Newfoundland.

As well as the presence or absence of trees, another way of defining the geocultural distinction between the Arctic and the Subarctic is to contrast the continental interior with its northern coastline. Few Arctic areas are far from the sea, and, with few exceptions, Arctic cultures both past and present have depended on sea-mammal hunting for a large portion of their subsistence needs.

Archaeology in the Arctic enjoys a number of practical advantages. In nonacidic, permanently frozen soils, organic preservation tends to be good, even spectacular. Since the Arctic toolkit has always tended toward the complex, arctic archaeologists usually have a great deal more data to work with than their colleagues working in the forests to the south.

In the Arctic, archaeologists appear to be dealing with the prehistory of a single people: speakers of Eskaleut, a language family that comprises Aleuts, the Yupik-speaking Eskimos (Yuit) of southwestern Alaska and eastern Siberia, and the Inuktitut/Inupiaq-speaking Eskimos (Inuit) of northern Alaska, Canada, and Greenland. It must be remembered, however, that not all cultures represented in the archaeological record are necessarily the direct ancestors of any living group.

Aleut prehistory may be traceable back to the occupation, ca. 6000 B.C. (7950 years B.P.), of the Anangula site on the Aleutian Islands. More confidently, it dates to Sandy Beach Bay, which is dated to ca. 2500 B.C. (4450 years B.P.), from which stems the Aleutian tradition.

Within the Eskimo area to the north and east, the Alaska Peninsula seems to have functioned as an important cultural boundary throughout much of the past. As a result, two distinct cultural sequences can be defined on either side of it. To the south is a sequence going back at least 6,500 years from the culture of the historic Koniag (Yuit) through Kachemak III, II, and I and allied phases to Ocean Bay. To the north is the "classic" Arctic cultural sequence beginning with the Arctic Small Tool tradition. Joining these threads into a common strand, as a linguistic model suggests should be possible, has proved elusive. It may be, however, that each of the three areal sequences—Aleutian, north Pacific, and Bering Sea—has a common origin in the microblade-using cultures of early and middle Holocene Alaska and Siberia.

The Arctic Small Tool tradition (ASTt) is the first really widespread Arctic cultural phenomenon. It appeared in western Alaska ca. 2500 B.C. (4450 years B.P.) and spread rapidly into Arctic Canada and Greenland. Important regional variants include the Denbigh Flint complex (Alaska), Pre-Dorset (Arctic Canada), Independence I (High Arctic), and Saqqaq (Greenland). East of Amundsen Gulf, ASTt seems to have developed fairly directly into the Dorset culture, while, farther west in the Canadian Arctic, the Lagoon complex seems to represent a related local development. In Alaska, ASTt is succeeded by a group of cultures sometimes classified together as elements of a "Norton tradition." These include Choris,

Ipiutak, and Norton proper. There is no consensus on the precise nature of the relationship among these cultures, and between them and the Arctic Small Tool tradition. It seems likely, however, that there is some kind of relationship. Both Choris and Norton have a ceramic component that also testifies to cross-ties with northeastern Siberia at this time (ca. 3500–3000 years B.P.).

The next major development in Arctic prehistory took place on the easternmost tip of Siberia and on the islands in Bering Strait. This was the appearance ca. 50 B.C. (2000 years B.P.) of the Old Bering Sea culture (OBS). While the origins of OBS are poorly understood, it appears to be on a line of cultural development that led directly to the culture of more recent Eskimo, both Inuit and Yuit. In its Bering Strait homeland, it leads directly to the Punuk culture, while, on the Alaskan mainland to the east, it appears partially ancestral to Birnirk and thus ultimately to the Thule culture.

Thule culture (ca. A.D. 900–1400, or 1050–550 years B.P.) represents the second great adaptive explosion in Arctic prehistory. Beginning ca. A.D. 950 (1000 years B.P.), Thule Inuit began a series of rapid migrations to the east, where they successfully displaced earlier Dorset occupants and colonized all of the Canadian Arctic and Greenland. Thule underlies all subsequent cultural developments from the Bering Strait to eastern Greenland and provides the common linguistic and cultural heritage of all native Inuktitut speakers.

Thule culture also spread south from the Bering Strait as far as the north Pacific area. However, in this most densely populated part of the Arctic, its mechanism of spread seems to have been influence and diffusion more than migration and population replacement. For instance, the Yupik-speaking Eskimos of southwestern Alaska retain a firm cultural footing in Kachemak and the late Norton culture, while, at the same time, they share in the Thule-culture heritage of their northern kinsmen.

David Morrison

Further Readings

Clark, D. 1991. *Western Subarctic Prehistory.* Canadian Prehistory Series, Canadian Museum of Civilization, Hull.

Damas, D. (editor). 1984. *Arctic.* Handbook of North American Indians, vol. 5, W.C. Sturtevant, general editor. Smithsonian Institution, Washington, D.C.

Dumond, D. 1987. *The Eskimos and Aleuts.* 2nd ed. Thames and Hudson, New York.

Helm, J. (editor). 1981. *Subarctic.* Handbook of North American Indians, vol. 6, W.C. Sturtevant, general editor. Smithsonian Institution, Washington, D.C.

Maxwell, M. 1985. *Prehistory of the Eastern Arctic.* Academic Press, New York.

McGhee, R. 1978. *Canadian Arctic Prehistory.* Canadian Prehistory Series, National Museum of Man, Ottawa.

Tuck, J. 1976. *Newfoundland and Labrador Prehistory.* Canadian Prehistory Series, National Museum of Man, Ottawa.

Wright, J. 1972. *Ontario Prehistory.* Canadian Prehistory Series, National Museum of Man, Ottawa.

———. 1979. *Quebec Prehistory.* Canadian Prehistory Series, National Museum of Man, Ottawa.

F

Fatherland Site

The Fatherland site (22AJ501) was the Grand Village of the historic Natchez Indians that figured so prominently in French descriptions of early life in Louisiana. It is located on the west bank of St. Catherine Creek within Natchez, Mississippi. There are three linearly arranged platform mounds at Fatherland, but only two of them (Mounds B and C) were occupied between 1680 and 1730 when the French explorers and settlers wrote about the region. Mound A is totally prehistoric and has had only minor excavations. Mound B served as the Great Sun's (principal chief) house, while Mound C was the temple. Excavations at Fatherland by James A. Ford (1936) and Moreau B. Chambers in the early twentieth century focused on the burials associated with the temple. Robert S. Neitzel's investigations in the 1960s and 1970s were to retrieve settlement data (Neitzel 1965, 1983).

As with earlier Plaquemine-culture mound centers in the Natchez Bluffs region, Fatherland was a chiefly compound. Although it was the ceremonial center for the surrounding population, probably only the Great Sun, his immediate family, various retainers, and some priestly personages occupied the site year-round. Despite its low population density, the remains of a considerable number of buildings were discovered. Twenty-two structures have been detected both within the mounds and around the plaza between the mounds. Nine were associated with Mound B, and three with Mound C.

Ten buildings were found in nonmound contexts. All of the Mound B structures were rectangular, wall-trench buildings arranged according to cardinal directions. The premound surface and Building Level 1 supported two structures simultaneously, but the upper three building levels held only one structure at any one time. Two structures had been built on Level 3, but the second one was not erected until the earlier one had been demolished. The door for all Mound B structures was in the southeast corner. These buildings typically had a hearth located just inside the door, presumably to allow smoke from the fire to dissipate through the door. The premound structures date to either the Anna (A.D. 1200–1350, or 750–600 years B.P.) or the Foster (1350–1500, or 600–450 years B.P.) phase of the Plaquemine culture. The Building Level 1 structures date to the Foster phase, the Level 2 structure to the Foster or the Emerald phase (1500–1680, or 450–270 years B.P.), and Level 3 structures to the Emerald phase. The Building Level 4 structure is historic Natchez (1680–1730).

The three buildings that were discovered in Mound C are unusual in that they are compound structures consisting of a back room and a portico. This structural arrangement certainly exists for the prehistoric buildings, but an analysis by James A. Brown (1990) has suggested that the historic temple probably did not have this attachment. The lower stages of Mound C lacked buildings altogether. Perhaps the temple and the chief's house were positioned adjacent to each other on the Phase I mantle of Mound B at this time (Foster phase). The first Mound C building was erected on top of the third mantle during the Emerald phase. The other two, nearly identical, compound structures were built sequentially in this location. They were not, however, aligned along the cardinal directions, as the longest dimensions of the structures were oriented north-northeast by south-southwest. Located on Building Level 1, the two structures had porticos that were narrower than the rear rooms. Two hearths were used in the rear rooms during each building stage. The entryway in each of the three temples was located in the north wall of the back room.

The Fatherland site is now the Grand Village of the Natchez Indians Museum and is owned by the State of Mississippi. Mounds B and C have been totally rebuilt for interpretive purposes, while Mound A is being conserved as

it was at the beginning of this project. There are reconstructions of a wattle-and-daub house and other features that would have been associated with a Natchez Indian household.

Ian W. Brown

Further Readings

Brown, I.W. 1985. Plaquemine Architectural Patterns in the Natchez Bluffs and Surrounding Regions of the Lower Mississippi Valley. *Midcontinental Journal of Archaeology* 10(2):251–305.

Brown, J.A. 1990. Archaeology Confronts History at the Natchez Temple. *Southeastern Archaeology* 9(1):1–10.

Ford, J.A. 1936. *Analysis of Indian Village Site Collections From Louisiana and Mississippi.* Anthropological Study no. 2. State of Louisiana, Department of Conservation, Louisiana Geological Survey, New Orleans.

Neitzel, R.S. 1965. *Archeology of the Fatherland Site: The Grand Village of the Natchez.* Anthropological Papers, vol. 51, pt. 1. American Museum of Natural History, New York.

———. 1983. *The Grand Village of the Natchez Revisited: Excavations at the Fatherland Site, Adams County, Mississippi, 1972.* Archaeological Report no. 12. Mississippi Department of Archives and History, Jackson.

See also PLAQUEMINE CULTURE

Federally Funded Archaeology

Federal support has at times dramatically affected the nature of archaeological investigations in North America. Some of the more striking examples in the United States are the Smithsonian Institution's impact on archaeological thought and practice in the second half of the nineteenth century, federal relief programs between 1933 and 1942, river-basin surveys between 1945 and 1969, National Science Foundation funding for scholarly research since the 1950s, and federal legislation in the 1960s and more recently that mandates the management and conservation of archaeological and other cultural resources. Founded in 1846, the Smithsonian Institution in Washington, D.C., laid the foundations of prehistoric archaeology in the United States in both an empirical and a theoretical sense in the second half of the nine-

Lloyd Wilford and federal work relief crew at La Moille Cave (21HU1), Houston County, Minnesota. (Courtesy of the Wilford Archaeology Laboratory, University of Minnesota)

teenth century. Many of the most influential archaeologists of the period, such as Cyrus Thomas, John Wesley Powell, and William Henry Holmes, were employed by the Smithsonian or in two of its divisions, the Bureau of Ethnology (founded in 1879; renamed the Bureau of American Ethnology [BAE] in 1894) and the National Museum (founded in 1879). Among their many accomplishments were the disproof of the Mound Builder myth, the systematic cataloging of mound and other prominent sites in the Eastern Woodlands in large-scale surveys, and the establishment of scientific principles of field procedure and analysis. The impact of federal relief programs, like the Civil Works Administration (CWA) and the Works Progress Administration (WPA), between 1933 and 1942 was also revolutionary in many areas of the country, but particularly in the Southeast. A federal response to reduce unemployment during the Great Depression, the programs hired large numbers of unskilled workmen and put them to work in large-scale excavations under the supervision of a few professional archaeologists. Under the scientific direction of the Smithsonian Institution, CWA and WPA crews excavated many important sites, as along

the Tennessee Valley for the Tennessee Valley Authority (TVA). In the process, they amassed a huge corpus of artifacts and site information that served as a stimulus to the development of organizational formats in the late 1930s, such as the Midwestern Taxonomic system, and the emergence of professional, anthropological archaeology in the Southeast. These projects, which served as a training ground for many young archaeologists at the time, were under the overall direction of Mathew Stirling (BAE chief from 1928 to 1957) and, in the Southeast, William Snyder Webb, who was the most prolific publisher of relief-program excavations in that area.

Planned, large-scale reservoir projects after World War II also resulted in massive excavation programs in many parts of the country between 1945 and 1969. The largest of these were managed by the Smithsonian Institution. A prime example is the Missouri River project, which was administratively directed by Frank H.H. Roberts, Jr., the national director of river-basin surveys, and organized by Waldo R. Wedel, both Smithsonian Institution archaeologists. Like the earlier federal relief projects, river-basin archaeology produced massive amounts of information and numerous publications. A different kind of federal support for archaeology was initiated in the 1950s when funds for research became available through the Social Sciences Division of the National Science Foundation. The millions of dollars provided by this program spurred research investigations not necessarily tied to conservation issues. As large as the sums of money were for all previous federal initiatives, they pale compared to the huge sums of money made available to archaeology since the 1960s through federal legislation for the protection of archaeological and historical sites. Among the most important pieces of legislation are the National Historic Preservation Act of 1966 (amended 1976 and 1980), which created a national program for site protection and a National Register of Historic Places that lists significant sites; the National Environmental Policy Act of 1969, which requires an assessment of the impact of development programs on cultural resources; and the Federal Abandoned Shipwreck Act of 1988, which provides protection for sunken ships of archaeological interest. Cultural resource management rapidly transformed North American archaeology, with more archaeologists (and funds) now employed in this area of archaeology than all other areas combined.

Guy Gibbon

Further Readings

Fowler, D. 1982. Cultural Resources Management. *Advances in Archaeological Method and Theory* 5:1–50.

Goldschmidt, W. (editor). 1979. *The Uses of Anthropology.* Special Publication no. 11. American Anthropological Association, Washington, D.C.

Haag, W.G. 1985. Federal Aid to Archaeology in the Southeast, 1933–1942. *American Antiquity* 50:272–280.

Hinsley, C.M. 1981. *Savages and Scientists: The Smithsonian Institution and the Development of American Anthropology, 1846–1910.* Smithsonian Institution Press, Washington, D.C.

Jennings, J.D. 1985. River Basin Surveys: Origins, Operations, and Results, 1945–1969. *American Antiquity* 50:281–296.

Lyon, E.A. 1996. *A New Deal for Southeastern Archaeology.* University of Alabama Press, Tuscaloosa.

Meltzer, D.J., D.D. Fowler, and J. Sabloff (editors). 1986. *American Archaeology Past and Future.* Smithsonian Institution Press, Washington, D.C.

Petsche, J.E. 1968. *Bibliography of Salvage Archaeology in the United States.* River Basin Surveys Publications in Salvage Archaeology no. 10.

Quimby, G.I. 1979. A Brief History of WPA Archaeology. In *The Uses of Anthropology,* edited by W. Goldschmidt, pp. 1101–123. Special Publication no. 11. American Anthropological Association, Washington, D.C.

Yellen, J.E. 1983. Archaeology and the National Science Foundation. In *The Socio-Politics of Archaeology,* edited by J.M. Gero, D.M. Lacy, and M.L. Blakey, pp. 59–65. Research Report no. 23. Department of Anthropology, University of Massachusetts, Amherst.

See also CULTURAL RESOURCE MANAGEMENT; HOLMES, WILLIAM HENRY; POWELL, JOHN WESLEY; PUTNAM, FREDERICK WARD; ROBERTS, FRANK H.H., JR.; THOMAS, CYRUS; WEBB, WILLIAM SYNDER; WEDEL, WALDO R.

Fiber Artifacts and Ethnicity

The study of Native American fiber artifacts has had a long tenure in archaeological research in North America, although some scholars have abandoned material culture analyses in favor of processual issues and other concerns. Nonetheless, fiber artifacts continue to provide intriguing glimpses of culturally sensitive attributes that can be used to reconstruct these technologies and their economic, social, ceremonial, and perhaps even symbolic functions in the past. Various researchers maintain, too, that it is possible to study "ethnicity" in the archaeological record using native fiber artifacts (e.g., Maslowski 1984; Adovasio 1986; Petersen 1996).

Native fiber artifacts, fiber "perishables," or "textiles," as they are variably called, include a potentially diverse (but often little known) range of industries in the archaeological record, such as basketry, sandals, other fabrics, cordage, and netting. All of these artifacts have an established utility in reconstructing human behavior, whether preserved as fragmentary (or, much more rarely, complete) specimens due to unusual conditions (e.g., aridity, water saturation, carbonization, replacement by metallic salts; Weltfish 1932; Andrews and Adovasio

1980), or as preserved in negative impressions on ceramics (Petersen and Hamilton 1984; Drooker 1992).

Basketry, other fabrics, cordage, and other fiber artifacts are some of the most culturally sensitive forms of material culture in general, with many of their attributes reflecting remarkably stable, culturally determined choices. Leading North American textile researchers, such as Mary Elizabeth King and J.M. Adovasio, have long noted this fact. King (1975:11) reports: "I have come to regard [textiles] as perhaps the most culturally revealing of all categories of artifacts." Adovasio (1977:4) is even more explicit in speaking of basketry: "no class of artifacts available to the archeologist possesses a greater number of culturally bound and still visible attributes. No two populations appear to have ever manufactured basketry in precisely the same fashion, whether their products were coiled, twined or plaited, flexible, semi-rigid or rigid. This situation is demonstrable ethnographically and seems to be valid archeologically as well."

Numerous cases can be mustered to support this view, but several attribute categories are cited here as an example: weft slant for twined basketry or initial spin and final twist for cordage. All are readily derivable from fragmentary archaeological specimens, no matter how small, and often can be derived from negative impressions on ceramics. Many archaeological examples and essentially all ethnographic samples provide documentation of the distinctive patterning that characterizes technological-learning networks, with the preferred twist or weft slant ranging from 70 to 80 percent and often exceeding 90 percent in large samples of fiber artifacts. Whether derived from the archaeological or ethnographic record, one or the other of the binary attribute states (S or Z) typically dominates a site-specific or regionally derived sample. The important point is that once a population adopts a particular cordage twist or twined weft, they rarely, if ever, change it. When used in conjunction with other attributes, where possible, these attributes can contribute to definitions of prehistoric and ethnographic ethnicity.

Using this perspective, given adequate temporal control, archaeologists can analyze available samples of native fiber artifacts to build local and regional inventories of attribute variability, thereby providing a means to establish patterning and boundaries in the archaeological record (e.g., Andrews and Adovasio 1980). Although interpretation of such data is subject to debate, their empirical, readily testable nature is important. Several brief examples suggest how important this research (and debate) may be.

Drawing from the archaeological record of eastern North America, the native fiber artifacts of the Adena culture in the Midwest and the related Middlesex complex (or phase) in the Northeast share notable commonalties in spite of space and time. They include a broad, but predictable, range of complicated constructions, including basketry, other fabrics, and cordage, from a substantial number of Adena and Middlesex sites (ca. 850–150 B.C., or 2800–2100 years B.P.) attributable to some or all of the Early Woodland period (Petersen and Hamilton 1984). Remarkably, all such specimens reflect a preference for S-weft slant and S-twist constructions where these pertain, which suggests a broad-scale series of manufacture imperatives over an immense region and a long period. We cannot say that these and other attributes define Adena and Middlesex native fiber artifacts, but they clearly allow us to exclude unrelated attributes that have been identified in other contemporaneous samples from the region.

Hinds Cave in the Lower Trans-Pecos region of Texas has produced a substantial and important sample of fiber artifacts. This sample documents a site-specific (and broader regional) sequence that demonstrates notable continuity for more than 9,000 years; that is, between ca. 7500 B.C. and A.D. 1600 (9550–350 years B.P.) (Andrews and Adovasio 1980). In this case, although the configurations of weft slant among the twining and cordage final twist were different between the two industries, both were consistent within these industries over time. Of the twined basketry specimens (N = 19), 84 percent exhibit S-wefts and the balance Z-wefts. Of the numerous cordage specimens (N = 717), 87 percent have a final Z-twist, 12 percent have a final S-twist, and less than 1 percent have a combination of both twists (Andrews and Adovasio 1980). This and other evidence has led to recognition of a long-lasting, distinctive Archaic tradition in the Lower Trans-Pecos region and adjacent portions of Mexico.

Another example may be even more instructive. Detailed analysis of a large sample of ethnographic material culture from the Yanomama of Roraima, Brazil, establishes a striking preference for particular weft-slant and cordage-twist configurations (Couture-Brunette

F

1985, 1986; Petersen 1996). Of 45 twined "bowl" baskets, *all* have an S-weft slant, while among 44 cotton and other fiber "aprons," three separate components share this pattern as well as strongly dominant S-twist cordage. The three components are "belt," "fringe," and "cord," of which 83 percent of those with belts (N = 23) have S-wefts, 83 percent of those with fringe (N = 42) have S-wefts, and 91 percent of those with cords (N = 44) have an S-twist as their final configuration. These and other constructions establish strong cultural preferences among Yanomama fiber artifacts and thereby contribute to definition of their ethnicity.

The implications of these three examples should be a powerful inducement for further analyses of native fiber artifacts, wherever such artifacts occur and wherever they can be reconstructed. Attributes of native fiber artifacts may be variably correlated with particular cultural or "ethnic" groups on local and/or regional scales, as known from both archaeological and ethnographic examples. However, this cannot be presumed a priori; it remains to be tested in each and every case, within the limits of archaeological preservation.

Although extant archaeological fiber artifacts are never likely to be common in most parts of North America, the potential information derivable from such native fiber industries is well worth further study. Likewise, the potentially equal wealth of information preserved on ceramics has yet to be fully realized in many areas. Both avenues of study should be pursued rigorously as a means of potentially delimiting cultural patterning and ethnicity in the archaeological record.

James B. Petersen

Further Readings

Adovasio, J.M. 1977. *Basketry Technology: A Guide to Identification and Analysis.* Aldine, Chicago.

————. 1986. Artifacts and Ethnicity: Basketry As an Indicator of Territoriality and Population Movements in the Prehistoric Great Basin. In *Anthropology of the Desert West, Essays in Honor of Jesse D. Jennings,* edited by C.J. Condie and D.D. Fowler, pp. 44–88. Anthropological Papers no. 110. University of Utah Press, Salt Lake City.

Andrews, R.L., and J.M. Adovasio. 1980. *Perishable Industries From Hinds Cave, Val Verde County, Texas.* Ethnology Monographs no. 5. Department of Anthropology, University of Pittsburgh, Pittsburgh.

Couture-Brunette, L. 1985. Yanomama Material Culture in the Carnegie Museum of Natural History. Part I: Food Procurement and Household Articles. *Annals of Carnegie Museum* 54(15):487–532.

————. 1986. Yanomama Material Culture in the Carnegie Museum of Natural History. Part II: Wearing Apparel and Festival Artifacts. *Annals of Carnegie Museum* 55(4):63–93.

Drooker, P.B. 1992. *Mississippian Village Textiles at Wickliffe.* University of Alabama Press, Tuscaloosa.

King, M.E. 1975. Archaeological Textiles. In *Archaeological Textiles,* edited by P.L. Fiske, pp. 9–16. Textile Museum, Washington, D.C.

Maslowski, R.F. 1984. The Significance of Cordage Attributes in the Analysis of Woodland Pottery. *Pennsylvania Archaeologist* 54(1–2):51–60.

Petersen, J.B. (editor). 1996. *A Most Indispensable Art: Native Fiber Industries From Eastern North America.* University of Tennessee Press, Knoxville.

Petersen, J.B., and N.D. Hamilton. 1984. Early Woodland Ceramic and Perishable Fiber Industries From the Northeast: A Summary and Interpretation. *Annals of Carnegie Museum* 53:413–445.

Weltfish, G. 1932. Problems in the Study of Ancient and Modern Basket Makers. *American Anthropologist* 34(2):108–117.

Finley Site

The Finley site (48SW5) is located near the small town of Eden in north-central Wyoming, in the northwest part of the Killpecker sand dunes, one of the largest active sand dune areas in North America. Orion Finley found several projectile points on the surface of the site in 1940. Harold Cook, a geologist, tested the subsurface and found several more points later the same year. Cook notified Edgar B. Howard at the University of Pennsylvania Museum, who sent Linton Satterthwaite, Jr., and Charles Bache to excavate the site that same year. In 1941, both the University of Pennsylvania Museum and the Nebraska State Museum sponsored excavations at the site under the direction of Howard and C. Bertrand Schultz, respectively. The site produced both Eden and Scottsbluff projectile points and tools, along with a large quantity of foot bones of extinct bison but few long bones. The first geological work at the site was by John T. Hack; later work was by John H. Moss (Moss et al. 1951).

In 1971, bison bone was exposed ca. 200 m (219 yards) north of the original Finley-site excavations. The bones were too large for modern bison, and the possibility that the kill area for the Finley site had been found was raised. It was believed at first to be an in situ occurrence. However, the bones appeared to have been moved earlier, probably by artifact hunters, and covered again with sand. When the bones were salvaged, however, a small number of them were found to be still in situ. Several broken Eden and Scottsbluff points were recovered, too, a further indication that this may have been the kill area of the Finley site. The bones are a valuable collection of osteological research materials. They consist of the partial remains of at least 59 animals that were killed in late fall—about the same time of year as the bison at the Horner site in northwest Wyoming. The original Finley site may have been a special bison-processing area, while the kill itself may have been in a sand dune similar to the one at the Casper Hell Gap site in central Wyoming.

George C. Frison

Further Readings

Howard, E.B. 1943. Discovery of Yuma Points, In Situ, Near Eden, Wyoming. *American Antiquity* 8:224–234.

Howard, E.B., L. Satterthwaite, Jr., and C. Bache. 1941. Preliminary Report on a Buried Yuma Site in Wyoming. *American Antiquity* 7:70–74.

Moss, J.H., K. Bryan, G.W. Holmes, L. Satterthwaite, Jr., H.P. Hansen, C.B. Schultlz, and W.D. Frankforter. 1951. *Early Man in the Eden Valley*. Monographs no. 6. University Museum, University of Pennsylvania, Philadelphia.

Wormington, H.M. 1957. *Ancient Man in North America*. Popular Series no. 4. Denver Museum of Natural History, Denver.

Fire

Fire was the primary source of fuel for cooking and heating in prehistoric North America. It was also used as a source of lighting, in the manufacture of ceramics and stone and bone tools, and in many ceremonies. One widely overlooked use was its role in resource management. Prescribed burning was an important management tool throughout native North America. The historical use of fire for wildlife harvesting has been well documented for the Southeast by J.E. Hammett (1992), the Northeast by E. Russell (1983), the Subarctic by H.T. Lewis and T.A. Ferguson (1988), the Great Basin by C. Fowler (1986), and California by Lewis (1973), and J. Timbrook et al. (1982). In the Southeast, prescribed burning apparently often occurred in conjunction with communal hunts when large groups of people gathered together. Native Californians used prescribed burning in coastal grassland areas to rejuvenate fields of seed crops. In the Subarctic, edge areas of fire-managed corridors and patches provided resource managers with a greater abundance of plant and animal resources and a higher measure of hunting predictability.

The prehistoric evidence for prescribed burning is less conclusive than the historic evidence because of inherent problems related to interpreting archaeological stratigraphy. In particular, problems stem from deposition and perturbation factors and the difficulty of distinguishing between cultural and nonhuman sources of fire. Because prehistoric humans used fire as their main source of fuel for heating and cooking, it is difficult to isolate evidence of its use as a management tool from other uses. However, archaeological evidence in concert with modern ecological data and historical analogues can provide indirect evidence for prehistoric resource management. Modern demographic studies of plant and animal species have identified organisms that are considered "fire tolerant" and "fire loving"; that is, that benefit in numbers and health from periodic burning. Prehistoric zooarchaeological evidence from the Southeast presented by G.A. Waselkov (1978) and archaeological evidence from California studied by Hammett (1991) document the long-term exploitation of species and sets of organisms that benefit from controlled burning programs. This circumstantial evidence indicates that burning was almost certainly a significant factor in prehistoric subsistence and management strategies. The ethnohistorical record indicates a perpetuation of this management practice into early historic times. These kinds of observations, without concomitant evidence of nonfire causes, are probably the best evidence

F

for the use of fire as a management tool in the prehistoric period. To date (1996), evidence for the use of fire as a management tool in North America extends back 1,000 years.

Julia E. Hammett

Further Readings

Fowler, C.S. 1986. Subsistence. In *Great Basin*, edited by W.L. D'Azevedo, pp. 64–97. Handbook of North American Indians, vol. 11, W.C. Sturtevant, general editor. Smithsonian Institution, Washington, D.C.

Hammett, J.E. 1991. *The Ecology of Sedentary Societies Without Agriculture: Paleoethnobotanical Indicators From Native California.* Unpublished Ph.D. dissertation, Department of Anthropology, University of North Carolina, Chapel Hill.

———. 1992. Ethnohistory of Aboriginal Landscapes and Land Use in the Southeastern United States. *Southern Indian Studies* 41:1–50.

Lewis, H.T. 1973. *Patterns of Indian Burning in California: Ecology and Ethnohistory.* Anthropological Papers no. 1. Ballena Press, Ramona.

Lewis, H.T., and T.A. Ferguson. 1988. Yards, Corridors and Mosaics: How to Burn a Boreal Forest. *Human Ecology* 16(1):57–77.

Russell, E. 1983. Indian-Set Fires in the Forests of the Northeastern United States. *Ecology* 64(1):78–88.

Timbrook, J., J.R. Johnson, and D.D. Earle. 1982. Vegetation Burning by the Chumash. *Journal of California and Great Basin Anthropology* 4(2):162–186.

Waselkov, G.A. 1978. Evolution of Deer Hunting in the Eastern Woodlands. *Midcontinental Journal of Archaeology* 3(1):15–34.

Fish Weirs and Traps (Eastern Woodlands)

A fish weir is a fence or wattle of stakes, brushwood, or similar material set in a stream, river estuary, or tideway to catch or retain fish. The loosely knit framework allows water to flow through but stops the passage of larger fish. Traps are usually baskets or cages of cane or sticks. Fish are often driven into them through stone-wall funnels. While fishhooks, spears, leisters, and gorges are more visible in the archaeological record, weirs, traps, and nets were probably as widely used, for they are more efficient in capturing larger numbers of fish. If the early historic record is a measure, weirs and traps were familiar sights in the waterways of prehistoric North America.

There are many ethnographic accounts of Native Americans employing weirs and traps to capture large numbers of fish, which they often dried for use in leaner months. Anadromous species—that is, fish that migrate upstream to spawn—such as Arctic char and salmon, were favorite quarry. Because of their fragile nature, weirs disintegrate over time if they are not maintained, and nearly all that did exist at historic contact have been destroyed by modern waterway use. Still, remnants of ancient weirs or rock funnels do provide direct evidence that they were used before contact. A well-known and until recently puzzling example is the Boylston Street fish weirs in Boston. The weirs, which are now covered by about 5 m (16 feet) of seawater, were once thought to be a single huge Late Archaic structure. Radiocarbon dating on material collected in the late 1980s has demonstrated that the structure is instead a composite of many small weirs built between 3000 and 1000 B.C. (4950–2950 years B.P.). Perhaps the oldest dated fish weir in North America is at Sebasticool Lake in Maine, with multiple radiocarbon dates of ca. 3850–3150 B.C. (5800–5100 years B.P.) (Petersen et al. 1994). Other, less direct evidence for the presence of weirs or traps includes the numbers and kinds of fish in archaeological deposits; artifacts possibly used in their construction or use, such as notched pebbles; and the location of settlements near fish-rich river estuaries or along the banks of major salmon streams. While weirs and traps were probably in use in the Eastern Woodlands at least as early as the Middle Archaic period, evidence for their presence is much more common in the Late Archaic and more recent periods.

Guy Gibbon

Further Readings

Chapman, J. 1985. *Tellico Archaeology.* University of Tennessee Press, Knoxville.

Johnson, F. (editor). 1949. *The Boylston Street Fishweir II.* Papers, vol. 4, no. 1. Robert S. Peabody Foundation for Archaeology, Phillips Academy, Andover.

Lutins, A.H. 1992. *Prehistoric Fish Weirs in Eastern North America.* Unpublished

Master's thesis, State University of New York, Binghamton.

Petersen, J.B., B.S. Robinson, D.F. Belknap, J. Stark, and L.K. Kaplan. 1994. An Archaic and Woodland Period Fish Weir Complex in Central Maine. *Archaeology of Eastern North America* 22:197–222.

See also Boylston Street Fish Weirs

Flake

A flake is a removal from a solid material. In archaeology, the flake is usually associated with the manufacture of stone tools, though some bone implements were also flaked in prehistory. Flaking occurs through exertion of a force greater than the tensile strength of the materials, resulting in fracture. The fracture is initiated through impaction; it propagates and then terminates on the outside of the core or nodule on which the force was applied. Depending on the amount of impact, the nature of the impactor, and the raw material, the interior (ventral) surface of the resulting flake may exhibit several attributes characteristic of its removal. Such traits include bulb of percussion, "lipping" of striking platform over ventral surface, concentric ripples, lateral fissures or hackle marks, "gull wings," and "eraillure," or bulbar scar.

Different technological contexts necessitate manipulation of material in a manner specific to the task at hand. Archaeologists have often attempted to identify the context in which a flake was produced from the attributes of the flakes themselves. Context may apply to all possible manufacture trajectories or may be diagnostic of a particular trajectory. In the general case, many, if not most, flint and obsidian—North America's principal tool materials—are found naturally encased in a coating or rind called "cortex." For most tool applications, the cortex is worthless and must be removed. A flake whose outer, or dorsal, surface contains cortex signifies, therefore, an early stage in the reduction of the initial cobble or nodule from which it was removed and is called a "decortication flake." Flakes that lack cortex and any other special distinguishing features are termed "interior flakes." Occasionally, from use-wear or other characteristic marks on the piece's dorsal surface, one can determine that a flake was removed from a tool in the process of rejuvenating the margin and prolonging the tool's use-life; such an object is known as a "sharpening flake."

Specific trajectories often produce certain kinds of flakes that are diagnostic of that trajectory. For example, removals in a core trajectory that bear evidence of having been instrumental in altering the angle between striking platform and exterior surface, thereby facilitating subsequent removals, are "core rejuvenation flakes." The results of a core-splitting technology in which the bottom of the core is rested on a hard surface are known as "bipolar flakes." Byproducts of bifacial technologies can be particularly distinctive, and pieces that bear such evidence are termed "bifacial reduction flakes." Mistakes in bifacial reduction in which force incorrectly applied carries to the opposite face of the core, causing the flake termination to include the core's bottom surface, are called "outrepasse," or "overshot," flakes. The readings listed below concentrate on the manner in which flakes are formed; that is, the transmission of force through a brittle solid.

George H. Odell

F

Further Readings

Bonnichsen, R. 1977. *Models for Deriving Cultural Information From Stone Tools.* Mercury Series Paper no. 60. Archaeological Survey of Canada, National Museum of Man, Ottawa.

Cotterell, B., and J. Kamminga. 1987. The Formation of Flakes. *American Antiquity* 52:675–708.

Lawn, B., and D. Marshall. 1979. Mechanisms of Microcontact Fracture in Brittle Solids. In *Lithic Use-Wear Analysis*, edited by B. Hayden, pp. 63–82. Academic Press, New York.

Speth, J.D. 1972. Mechanical Basis of Percussion Flaking. *American Antiquity* 37:34–60.

See also Blade/Bladelet; Burin

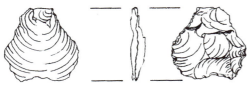

Drawing of a flake showing flake scars and retouch on the dorsal surface, and striking platform, bulb of percussion, and concentric ripples. (Courtesy of the Wilford Archaeology Laboratory, University of Minnesota)

Flaker

A flaker is an elongated, snub-nosed, pointed object that is easily held and manipulated in the hand. The preferred blank was antler tine of a large ungulate, such as deer, elk, or moose. A splinter of animal bone occasionally served as a flaker, as in the Late Archaic Riverton culture of the Wabash Valley, which forms the border between the states of Illinois and Indiana (Winters 1969:47). Many implements with these characteristics possess pitting on the more pointed end, a pattern reproduced by flint-knapping experiments. It is apparent that a large proportion of prehistoric flakers were pressure flakers used in the manufacture of chipped-stone implements. Their importance in tool production suggests that they have existed in North America as long as hominids have.

George H. Odell

Further Readings

Lewis, T.M.N., and M.K. Lewis. 1961. *Eva: An Archaic Site.* University of Tennessee Press, Knoxville.

Winters, H.D. 1969. *The Riverton Culture.* Reports of Investigations no. 13. Illinois State Museum, Springfield; Illinois Archaeological Survey, Urbana.

Fletcher

Fletcher is a Late Paleoindian site (DjOw-1 in the Uniform Site Designation scheme for Canada) located at a water hole on the level plains of southern Alberta just north of the Sweetgrass Hills of Montana and ca. 257 km (160 miles) southeast of Calgary. The artifact assemblage contains Plano projectile points (Alberta and Scottsbluff types). A side-notched projectile point as well as chipped-stone knives, scrapers, gravers and spokeshaves, hammerstones, and a grooved-stone maul were also found in a concentration of bison bone. The artifact assemblage suggests that Fletcher was a campsite and butchering station, situated near a spring where large numbers of bison were killed and processed. There is no evidence to suggest that either natural features or deliberate human constructions such as corrals were employed to assist in the communal driving or impounding of bison. The exact method of hunting, though clearly productive, remains enigmatic. Attempts at radiocarbon dating have proved unsuccessful; however, geological estimates of pre-Altithermal to late glacial age are compatible with typological dates for the Fletcher artifacts of ca. 8050–6050 B.C. (10,000–8000 years B.P.). A comparable pre-Altithermal component at the MacHaffie site, ca. 241 km (150 miles) south near Helena, Montana, is radiocarbon dated to ca. 6250 B.C. (8200 years B.P.). In contrast to rare but still earlier Folsom and Clovis Paleoindian points, Plano variants are relatively common surface finds on the Canadian short-grass plains (e.g., the Little Glen complex of Alberta and the Mortlach region of Saskatchewan).

Richard G. Forbis

Further Readings

Forbis, R.G. 1968. A Paleo-Indian Site in Alberta. *American Antiquity* 33:1–10.

Flint Run Complex

The Flint Run complex consists of four interrelated but functionally different types of sites centered around a jasper quarry in Warren County, Virginia. Included in the complex are the jasper quarry, which is located on Flint Run; reduction stations, of which the Lockhart site is the prototype; a large base camp, the Thunderbird site; and maintenance stations, of which the Fifty site is the most well studied. Thunderbird and Fifty are both stratified Paleoindian-through-Early Archaic sites. They provide the bulk of the information on change and continuity during the period of occupation, which begins ca. 9500–9200 B.C. (11,450–11,150 years B.P.) with an Eastern Clovis horizon at each site and extends to ca. 6800 B.C. (8750 years B.P.), the beginning of the Bifurcate horizon.

The environmental structure of the local setting probably accounts for the spatial separation of what really is a single interdependent operation of quarrying, toolkit replenishment, day-to-day living, and necessary subsistence activities, for the South Fork of the Shenandoah River cuts through the center of the site complex. The south side of the river, where the jasper outcrop is located, receives minimal sunlight and maximal wind during much of the year. It is hilly and dissected, and water is not immediately available at the outcrops. In contrast, the north side of the river, where the Thunderbird site is located, has a southern aspect, is sheltered from the wind, and at one time was well watered with springs. The reduction stations are close to the quarry but adjacent to the nearest available water. All of these sites are underlain by limestone, except the maintenance stations, which are on alluvial fans overlooking poorly drained localities in the contiguous shale bedrock areas. The distance from Thunderbird to Fifty is 0.8 km (0.5 mile), from Thunderbird to Lockhart ca. 152 m (500 feet), and from Lockhart to the jasper outcrops ca. 30.5 m (100 feet). The total area for all known sites is no more than 0.4 x 3.2 km (0.25 x 2 miles), or ca. 129.5 ha (0.5 square mile).

The basic elements of the quarry locations are large blocky pieces of jasper, some of which have been shaped into crude bifaces, and debitage characterized by significant quantities of weathered cortex and botryoidal-crusted surfaces. The reduction stations, as at Lockhart and Gooney Run, contain for the most part further reduced and shaped bifaces that are still, however, mainly in the early stages of reduction, as is evident in the common occurrence of primary decortication flakes. Tools are rare at both of these types of site. The lithic material at the base camp, Thunderbird, ranges from preliminarily shaped and transported bifaces and cores to nearly finished and finished late-stage bifaces, preforms and broken unused points, and discarded, extensively curated points of nonlocal materials. The overwhelming impression is that the Thunderbird stone assemblage is composed primarily of bifaces and an abundant amount of debitage. The bifaces were discarded at varying stages because they were broken, mistakes had been made in the reduction strategy, or flaws existed in the material.

Thunderbird is more than just a workshop site, however, for it contains artifact concentrations that integrate two major sets of spatially separate activities into a functioning whole. These are toolmaking, primarily of projectile points and transportable bifaces, and generalized maintenance activities. The most well-studied location of this type is Area 1B, which is 15.2–21.3 m x 76.2 m (50–70 feet x 250 feet) in extent. The maintenance activities are located the farthest from the old river edge and are associated with a postmold pattern that measures ca. 6 x 12 m (20 x 40 feet). The toolmaking area consists of a series of knapping clusters that contain evidence of production stages that range from the reduction of single cores to final-stage reduction and projectile-point finishing. The high frequency of extensively curated points, which were discarded, indicates that a major activity was replenishment of weaponry.

In contrast to the base camp, the mainte-nance camps, of which Fifty is the prototype, have a much higher proportion of processing tools of varying sizes and shapes, and their projectile points were broken and discarded during use rather than during manufacture. Intrasite variation is evident at Fifty, with the area closest to the swamp containing mostly large crushing, smashing, and cutting tools, and the upslope location containing small (ca. 1.2 x 1.5 m [4 x 5-foot] to 1.2 x 2.4 m [4 x 8-foot]) activity areas with more refined, smaller, and more diverse processing tools as well as the discarded and broken projectile points.

One of the keys to understanding the complex is that each site is a constituent element in an integrated whole; no one of the sites can be fully understood without reference to the whole. The sites as a complex show a number of differences from other Paleoindian sites in the Middle Atlantic region. For instance, the characteristic Paleoindian toolkit is present, but it is only a minor element in the total assemblage and is not present in total at any one of the sites. Scrapers, except for the curated and discarded ones of nonlocal raw material, do not have accessories, such as graver spurs. The sites being close to the quarry, conspicuous consumption of lithics was the norm, and no attempt was made at curation. Expedient, minimally used tools are the rule.

The projectile-point phases at Thunderbird are, from earliest to latest levels, Clovis, Mid-Paleo, Dalton, Corner-Notched (Palmer Corner-Notched, which is radiocarbon assayed at 7990 B.C., or 9940 years B.P., and Kirk Corner-Notched), Side Notched (Big Sandy II/Warren), and Kirk Stemmed (radiocarbon assayed at 7200 B.C., or 9150 years B.P.). At Fifty, Mid-Paleo and Dalton are absent. While change is evident throughout this sequence, continuity is equally evident. One of the major changes is in the form of the points, with the most striking formal shift, at a macro level, from a lanceolate to a notched form. It has been suggested that this reflects the change from the use of a hand-thrown spear to one propelled by a spear thrower. In terms of raw material used, except for exhausted artifacts brought into Thunderbird everything is made of jasper at the earliest levels. By the first part of the Early Archaic (ca. 8000–7500 B.C., or 9950–9450 years B.P.), a more diverse range of lithics was being selected, including nonmicrocrystalline materials, such as rhyolite and quartzite. By the end of the complex (ca. 6800 B.C., or 8750 years B.P.) in the last half of the Early Archaic, jasper was no longer being selected and Thunderbird was abandoned, as were the reduction stations and the quarry. Fifty continued to be occupied, but more sporadically now, and jasper was not being selected there either. Nonetheless, a biface core-flake reduction projectile point manufacturing strategy continued throughout the Paleoindian and the Early Archaic periods.

During the Early Archaic, the areal extent of living floors and the number of sites increased, reflecting population growth, stays of longer duration, or both. Viewed overall, the pace of change in all aspects accelerated so that, by the end of the Early Archaic, little resemblance with the ancestral Clovis occupation can be seen. While these cultural and technological changes were occurring, changes in climate, vegetation, and drainage were transforming the region as well.

William M. Gardner

Further Readings

Carr, K.W. 1991. *A Distributional Analysis From the Fifty Site.* Unpublished Ph.D. dissertation, Catholic University of America, Washington, D.C.

Gardner, W.M. 1989. An Examination of Cultural Change in the Late Pleistocene and Early Holocene (ca. 9200–6800 B.C.). In *Paleoindian Research in Virginia, a Synthesis,* edited by M. Wittkofski and T.R. Reinhart. Special Publication no. 19. Archeological Society of Virginia, Diets Press, Richmond.

See also THUNDERBIRD SITE

Flute

A flute is the negative of a relatively large elongated flake taken off specific Paleoindian projectile points, of which the most well known are Clovis and Folsom. The blow emanated from the base and removed a piece part way (Clovis) or most of the way (Folsom) to the tip. The flake that resulted from such a blow is called a "channel flake." In most instances, flakes of this sort were removed from both surfaces of the object. The existence of flutes on a projectile point is usually diagnostic of its Paleoindian affiliation. Although no Clovis or Folsom point has ever been found in its haft, the probable reason for the flute was to facilitate a specific kind of hafting mechanism.

An extensive literature has grown up around the techniques of manufacturing a Paleoindian point and of providing the tell-tale flutes, particularly in replicating the kind of classic Folsom point discovered at the Lindenmeier site. D.E. Crabtree's (1966) successes in removing a channel flake using a pressure technique involving a chest crutch with a clamp and an anvil rest stimulated further experimentation. J.J. Flenniken (1978) established that fluting was not the last stage in the production process and that vises or clamps were probably not used prehistorically. Subsequent experiments have indicated that hand-held fluting was definitely possible, if not preferred (Gryba 1988), but that certain types of vises may, in fact, have resulted in a higher fluting-success rate overall than other methods of removal (Sollberger 1985).

George H. Odell

Further Readings

Boldurian, A.T., P.T. Fitzgibbons, and P.H. Shelley. 1985. Fluting Devices in the Folsom Tradition: Patterning in Debitage Formation and Projectile Point Basal Configuration. *Plains Anthropologist* 30:293–303.

Crabtree, D.E. 1966. A Stoneworker's Approach to Analyzing and Replicating the Lindenmeier Folsom. *Tebiwa* 9:3–39.

Flenniken, J.J. 1978. Reevaluation of the Lindenmeier Folsom: A Replication Experiment in Lithic Technology. *American Antiquity* 43:473–480.

Gryba, E.M. 1988. A Stone Age Pressure Method of Folsom Fluting. *Plains Anthropologist* 33:53–66.

Sollberger, J.B. 1985. A Technique for Folsom Fluting. *Lithic Technology* 14:41–50.

Folsom Complex

The Folsom technological complex represents one of the more famous, distinctive, and widespread early prehistoric cultures in the Plains, Rocky Mountain, and Southwest areas of the United States. Folsom technology is well known through detailed studies of collections from sites such as Lindenmeier in Colorado and Agate Basin and Hanson in Wyoming. Isolated finds of artifacts, bison-kill sites, campsites with ephemeral surface hearths, small-tool sets from hunting overlooks, and lithic workshops or stone-tool-production sites are documented from Montana and North Dakota to Texas and

New Mexico. Campsites often occur in close association with kills or lithic sources, such as at Hanson and Agate Basin, Lake Ilo in North Dakota, Cattle Guard in Colorado, and Adair-Steadman in Texas. Characteristic artifacts include delicately made, thin, fluted projectile points; distinctive projectile-point preforms and channel flakes from fluting; bifacial cores used to make flakes for tool production; end scrapers with spurred corners; pointed gravers and other distinctive tools made on flakes; eyed needles of bone; decorated bone pieces; and a recurrent association with red ocher.

The complex was first recognized and acquired historical significance when discoveries between 1926 and 1928 at the Folsom type site in Colfax County, northeastern New Mexico, established beyond doubt that human groups had lived in the New World during the late Pleistocene, before 8000 B.C. (9950 years B.P.). The age of the site was initially determined through detailed stratigraphic correlations and the presence of an extinct form of bison. The Folsom site is ca. 19.3 km (12 miles) west of the town of Folsom, from which the cultural complex derives its name. The site was first excavated in 1926 by paleontologists from the Denver Museum of Natural History who were searching for a bison skeleton for a museum exhibit; the site itself had been discovered in 1908 by a local ranch foreman, George McJunkin. Work continued in 1927, when a number of archaeologists were invited to view finds of artifacts in place among the bison skeletons. In 1928, paleontologists working for Barnum Brown of the American Museum of Natural History in New York conducted more extensive excavations at the site and recovered additional bison skeletons and Folsom projectile points. Little else was done at the site until the early 1970s when Adrienne Anderson, C. Vance Haynes, and associates conducted detailed studies of the stratigraphy and collected samples of bone and charcoal, which have provided radiocarbon dates for the site. These dates indicate that Folsom bison hunters were at the Folsom site ca. 8800 B.C. (10,750 years B.P.). Available radiocarbon dates from numerous sites have established the age range of the Folsom complex between 8800 and 8200 B.C. (10,750–10,150 years B.P.). One of the more significant Folsom sites is Lindenmeier, which is located in north-central Colorado near the Wyoming border. Excavations between 1934 and 1940 by Frank H.H. Roberts, Jr., of the

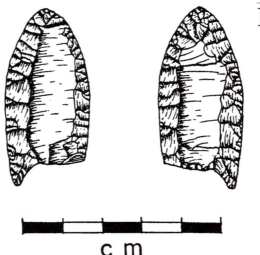

F

A Folsom point from the type site. This point is on display at the Denver Museum of Natural History. (Drawing by J. L. Hofman)

Smithsonian Institution yielded what remains the premiere assemblage of Folsom materials from the bison bonebed and multiple camp areas at this site.

Distribution of the Folsom complex has been found, based on site excavations and the study of surface occurrences, to extend from the plains of Canada to southern Texas and northern Mexico and from Idaho, eastern Arizona, and Utah to the prairie peninsula region of Missouri and Illinois. The greatest density of sites and finds appears to be in the High Plains region and is strongly correlated with the distribution of the large Pleistocene bison (Bison bison antiquus). The economy of these early hunters is assumed to have been diverse, as demonstrated in part by the presence of rabbits, deer, antelope, and lesser mammals in assemblages at several Folsom sites. Without question, however, bison were the primary staple of the Folsom economy, as remains of this animal are dominant at most sites from which bones have been recovered. Seasonal or situational variation in the use of bison and other species is expected to have occurred, but such variation, like the significance of plant foods in the diet, remains largely undetermined.

Folsom bison-kill sites include cases with very few animals, such as at Lubbock, Texas, and some with large numbers of kills: At least 56 bison are represented in the apparently single-kill-event bonebed at Lipscomb, Texas.

Reuse of the same site by Folsom people for multiple bison kills is evident at the Cooper site in Oklahoma, where at least three distinct kill events are represented in a small gully tributary of the North Canadian River.

Folsom groups were highly mobile and are believed to have moved over regions of considerable size during the course of their hunting activity. Studies of stone-tool sources suggest fairly common movement up to 200–400 km (124–248 miles) from locations where lithics were acquired for tool manufacture. Because of the presumed low population density and the rarity of recurrently occupied sites, archaeologists believe that direct acquisition of lithic material for tool manufacture, rather than trade, was the primary means for obtaining the critically important stone.

Little evidence exists to resolve questions about stature, longevity, physical condition, or pathologies of the Folsom people. Such concerns must await discovery and study of skeletal remains.

Red ocher was mined by Folsom and other Paleoindian people at the Powers II site in eastern Wyoming. This red pigment was found on the surface of the floor in a small circular lodge at Agate Basin; it was also used to paint a zigzag line on a bison skull at the Cooper site. A specialized feature at the Lake Theo Folsom site in the Texas Panhandle consisted of a bison skull placed on a support formed of leg bones and mandibles. Although its purpose is unknown, this feature could represent an offering, a hunting ritual, or a marker for a storage cache of meat, hides, or other material. Potential ritual activity, perhaps indicated by the projectile-point fluting process, has also been suggested by the occurrence of fluted but unfinished projectile points at sites such as Agate Basin and Lindenmeier. While the archaeological record left by these early hunting people has revealed a successful and relatively long-lived cultural tradition, much remains to be learned about Folsom lifeways.

Jack L. Hofman

Further Readings

Frison, G.C. 1991. *Prehistoric Hunters of the High Plains*. 2nd ed. Academic Press, San Diego.

Frison, G.C., and B. Bradley. 1980. *Folsom Tools and Technology at the Hanson Site, Wyoming*. University of New Mexico Press, Albuquerque.

Judge, W.J. 1973. *Paleoindian Occupation of the Central Rio Grande Valley in New Mexico*. University of New Mexico Press, Albuquerque.

Meltzer, D.J. 1993. *Search for the First Americans*. Smithsonian Books. St. Remy Press, Montreal.

Stanford, D.J., and J.S. Day (editors). 1992. *Ice Age Hunters of the Rockies*. University Press of Colorado, Niwot.

Wilmsen, E.N., and F.H.H. Roberts, Jr. 1978. *Lindenmeier, 1934–1974: Concluding Report of Investigations*. Contributions to Anthropology no. 24. Smithsonian Institution Press, Washington, D.C.

Folsom Site

The Folsom site (LA8121), which lies 19.3 km (12 miles) west of the town of Folsom, New Mexico, is the type site for the Folsom culture. Although it is in the Great Plains, the Rocky Mountains are just 40.2 km (25 miles) to the west. The site represents the location where a herd of longhorn bison (*Bison bison antiquus*) was driven up an arroyo, killed, and partially butchered. Folsom became the first widely accepted evidence for a Pleistocene human occupation of the New World, when stone projectile points with distinctive flutes were found embedded among the rib cages of the skeletons of this extinct species of bison in 1927 (Cook 1927; Figgins 1927). Acceptance of this site legitimized subsequent research in Paleoindian studies and greatly expanded the time scale of Native American occupation in the New World (Brown 1929; Bryan 1937).

It is generally believed that George McJunkin, a local ranch foreman of African-American heritage, identified the site. On the afternoon of August 27, 1908, 33 cm (13 inches) of rain fell on Johnson Mesa in the Dry Cimmaron Valley. A massive flood resulted that devastated the town of Folsom and deepened many local stream channels. Following the torrential rainstorm, McJunkin noticed the erosion of some very large bison bones in the bottom of Wild Horse Arroyo ca. 2.4–3.7 m (8–12 feet) below the surface. McJunkin's role in bringing professional attention to the site is poorly understood (Agogino 1971; Jackson and Thacker 1992). Jesse D. Figgins (1927:232) states that Fred Howarth and Carl Schwachheim of Raton, New Mexico, reported the site to the Colorado Museum in the summer of 1925.

Figgins, of the Colorado Museum, sent crews to dig the site in 1926 and 1927. Many scientists remained skeptical of the first reports from Folsom, and verification by respected professionals was needed. The field season of 1927 exposed fluted points in place among the bison skeletons. Work ceased, and Alfred V. Kidder, Frank H.H. Roberts, Jr., and Barnum Brown were summoned to view the excavations. They concluded that the association of human artifacts with extinct bison was secure. Brown, a paleontologist with the American Museum of Natural History in New York, joined the crew during the third season of digging in 1928. Based on a review of original field notes, Lawrence C. Todd and Jack L. Hofman (1994) estimate that 268.4 m² of sediment were uncovered at the site between 1926 and 1928. The materials from these excavations are curated at the Denver Museum of Natural History and the American Museum of Natural History.

Recent research on the assemblage and its depositional context has greatly increased our understanding of the Folsom site. C. Vance Haynes et al. (1992) provide a generalized geologic cross section of Wild Horse Gulch at the Folsom site and reliable radiocarbon ages for the distinct depositional units. The Folsom bones and artifacts are contained within a 10–30-cm (4–12-inch) zone that appears to have been subjected to some slope washing during burial. Six accelerator radiocarbon dates are determined on wood charcoal from the Folsom level. These dates average 8940 B.C. ± 50 (10,890 years B.P.), which establishes the Folsom site as one of the earliest and best-dated Folsom occupations. Haynes (Haynes et al. 1992) advocates that this average charcoal date should replace the earlier unreliable radiocarbon dates on bone from the site.

Original reports state that 23 bison were present. Reanalysis by Todd and Hofman (1994) suggests a minimum of 28. Dentition wear patterns on the lower mandibles indicate there were three calves, four yearlings, two juveniles, and 19 adults. The patterns of tooth eruption and wear are consistent with an early fall death for all individuals. It is probable that Folsom represents a single kill-and-butchery event. Evidence of sexual dimorphism based on limb bone measurements indicate that 45–55 percent of the group are cows. Some complete or nearly complete bison skeletons are present at the site, which suggests it represents the actual location of death. The remaining carcasses show limited and selective processing. This butchery pattern contrasts with the intensive processing of bison seen at Late Prehistoric sites.

Bison may not have been the only animals exploited at Folsom. O.P. Hay and H.J. Cook (1930) also report mule deer (*Odocoileus hemionus*), prairie dog (*Cynomys ludovicianus*), ground squirrel (*Citellus* sp.), and jackrabbit (*Lepus californicus*). An unpublished list by Gordon Tucker, Jr., of the University of Colorado identifies 13 additional genera in the Folsom collection at the Denver Museum. They are: cottontail (*Sylvilagus* sp.); yellow-bellied marmot (*Marmota flaviventris*); squirrel (*Scurius* sp. and *Otospermophilus* sp.); canids (*Canis* sp.); fox (*Vulpes* sp.); horse (*Equidae* sp.); pronghorn (*Antilocapra* sp.); pika (*Ochotona* sp.); pocket gopher (*Thomomys* sp.); woodrat (*Neotoma* sp.); mouse (*Peromyscus* sp.); and vole (*Microtus* sp.). However, the association of these bones with the Folsom deposit is uncertain.

A total of 19 stone projectile points and two tools made on stone flakes were originally reported. The Ele Baker collection, which is housed in Denver, also contains a quartzite scraping tool (*dejeté*) that is known to have come from the site. E.B. Renaud (1931) provides measurements for 16 of the points, and Jack L. Hofman (1991) reports stone-source information on them (six Alibates, four Tecovas, three Edwards, and three other). Sources of Alibates are 230 km (144 miles) southeast of the Folsom site, while Tecovas sources lie 360 km (225 miles) and Edwards sources 575 km (360 miles) to the southeast. These distances support the notion that Folsom people were highly mobile. They may also imply a directional pattern of movement. Gradual stone replacement might have occurred while these people were traveling north and west from the southern Plains of central Texas to the foothills of the Rockies.

Daniel S. Amick

Further Readings

Agogino, G. 1971. The McJunkin Controversy. *New Mexico Magazine* 49(3):41–44.

Brown, B. 1929. Folsom Culture and Its Age, With Discussion by Kirk Bryan. *Geological Society of America Bulletin* 40:128–129.

Bryan, K. 1937. Geology of the Folsom Deposits in New Mexico and Colorado. In *Early Man*, edited by G.G. MacCurdy, pp. 139–152. Lippincott, Philadelphia.

Cook, H.J. 1927. New Geological and Pale-ontological Evidence Bearing on the Antiquity of Mankind in America. *Natural History* 27:240–247.

Figgins, J.D. 1927. The Antiquity of Man in America. *Natural History* 27:229–239.

Hay, O.P., and H.J. Cook. 1930. *Fossil Vertebrates Collected Near, or in Association With, Human Artifacts at Localities Near Colorado, Texas; Frederick, Oklahoma; and Folsom, New Mexico.* Proceedings, vol. 9, no. 2. Colorado Museum of Natural History, Denver.

Haynes, C.V., Jr., R.P. Beukens, A.J.T. Jull, and O.K. Davis. 1992. New Radiocarbon Dates for Some Old Folsom Sites: Accelerator Technology. In *Ice Age Hunters of the Rockies,* edited by D.J. Stanford and J.S. Day, pp. 83–100. University Press of Colorado, Niwot.

Hofman, J.L. 1991. Folsom Land Use: Projectile Point Variability As a Key to Mobility. In *Raw Material Economies Among Prehistoric Hunter-Gatherers,* edited by A. Montet-White and S. Holen, pp. 335–355. Publications in Anthropology no. 19. Department of Anthropology, University of Kansas, Lawrence.

Jackson, L.J., and P.T. Thacker. 1992. Harold J. Cook and Jesse D. Figgins: A New Perspective on the Folsom Discovery. In *Rediscovering Our Past,* edited by J.E. Reyman, pp. 217–240. Avebury Press, Hamshire.

Renaud, E.B. 1931. *Prehistoric Flaked Points From Colorado and Adjacent Districts.* Proceedings, vol. 10, no. 2. Colorado Museum of Natural History, Denver.

Todd, L.C., and J.L. Hofman. 1994. Variation in Folsom Age Bison Assemblages: Implications for the Interpretation of Human Action. In *Folsom Archaeology: An Overview of Early Holocene Environments and Human Adaptation,* edited by D.J. Stanford and M.A. Jodry. Smithsonian Institution Press, Washington, D.C.

See also FOLSOM COMPLEX

James A. Ford. (Reprinted with permission from American Antiquity 34[1]:63)

Ford, James Alfred (1911–1968)

In the late 1920s, shortly after graduating from high school, James A. Ford was excavating burial mounds for the Mississippi Department of Archives and History and met Henry B. Collins. At the time, Collins, another Mississippian, was employed by the Bureau of American Ethnology at the Smithsonian Institution; he became Ford's early mentor. Ford assisted Collins in local village excavations and accompanied him to the Point Barrow area of Alaska in the early 1930s. In Alaska, Ford learned the fundamental principles of stratigraphy, seriation, and artifact typology. In 1933, he received a National Research Council grant to search for and excavate sites in Mississippi and Louisiana, which resulted in his first major publication, *Analysis of Indian Village Site Collections From Louisiana and Mississippi* (1936). In this project as in subsequent projects with WPA (Works Progress Administration) labor at Crooks, Greenhouse, and Tchefuncte, also in Mississippi and Louisiana, and at sites in the Lower Mississippi River Valley, he was concerned with applying stratigraphic, typological, and seriational techniques to define regional cultural sequences. His "An Interpretation of the Prehistory of the Eastern United States" (1941) with Gordon R. Willey introduced a stage (Archaic, Burial Mound I and II, Temple Mound I and II) alternative to W.C. McKern's

(1939) system of arbitrary taxonomic units and provided one of the first culture-history syntheses for the region, although a short chronology of less than 1,200 years was adopted.

Ford was as concerned with methodological issues as he was with insightful field procedures. He (1954) regarded types as tools constructed by archaeologists for historical analysis and engaged in a debate with A.C. Spaulding, a theoretician at the University of Michigan, over their reality. He also argued that archaeology should become a "science of culture" whose primary goal was the discovery of general principles of long-range culture change. However, he believed that change occurred only gradually, and then mainly through diffusion, which, in the southeastern United States, meant ultimately from Mesoamerica. His approach lacked a sense of process and remained best suited to chronological ordering, as evident in his diffusionist *A Comparison of Formative Cultures in the Americas: Diffusion or the Psychic Unity of Man?* (1969), in which he attempted to trace southeastern traits to northwestern South America and, in part, back across the Pacific Ocean. Nonetheless, Ford remains a seminal, creative figure in the development of modern archaeology of the southeastern United States.

Guy Gibbon

Further Readings

Brown, I.W. 1978. *James Alfred Ford, the Man and His Works*. Special Publications no. 4. Southeastern Archaeological Conference, Morgantown.

Ford, J.A. 1936. *Analysis of Indian Village Site Collections From Louisiana and Mississippi*. Anthropological Study no. 1. State of Louisiana, Department of Conservation, Louisiana State Geological Survey, New Orleans.

———. 1954. On the Concept of Types. *American Anthropologist* 56:42–53.

———. 1959. *Eskimo Prehistory in the Vicinity of Point Barrow, Alaska*. Anthropological Papers, vol. 47, pt. 1. American Museum of Natural History, New York.

———. 1962. A *Quantitative Method of Deriving Cultural Chronology*. Technical Manual no. 1. Pan American Union, Department of Social Affairs, Washington, D.C.

———. 1969. *A Comparison of Formative Cultures in the Americas: Diffusion or the Psychic Unity of Man?* Contributions to Anthropology no. 2. Smithsonian Institution, Washington, D.C.

Ford, J.A., and G.R. Willey. 1941. An Interpretation of the Prehistory of the Eastern United States. *American Anthropologist* 43:325–363.

McKern, W.C. 1939. The Midwestern Taxonomic Method As an Aid to Archaeological Study. *American Antiquity* 4:301–313.

Willey, G.R. 1988. *Portraits in American Archaeology*. University of New Mexico Press, Albuquerque.

Forestdale Branch

The Forestdale branch of the Mogollon culture was defined by Emil W. Haury based on excavations in Forestdale Valley by the University of Arizona archaeological field school (1939–1941). The valley lies on the White Mountain Apache Reservation at 1,981 m (6,500 feet) above sea level. It is in the mountain transition zone of east-central Arizona, 6.4 km (4 miles) south of the Mogollon Rim, the southern boundary of the Colorado Plateau, and 13 km (8 miles) south of the modern town of Show Low. Haury's culture-phase sequence, the core of the Forestdale branch construct, is predicated on four major assumptions: (1) continuity of valley occupation and occupants; (2) limited inmigration throughout the sequence; (3) gradual assimilation of Anasazi traits by resident Mogollon, which resulted in a loss of Mogollon identity; and (4) gaps between tree-ring-dated phases, which were filled by assigning transitional remains to postulated, intermediate phases. Haury's original formulation is presented here, except where recent chronological evidence has altered time spans.

Hilltop Phase (A.D. 200–400, or 1750–1550 years B.P., one cutting and six noncutting tree-ring dates; 238–322). Pithouses, which are generally circular with a side entrance, are on ridges or hills. These large pit structures served communal-religious functions and as prototypes for great kivas. Diet was based on corn (inferred from metates), supplemented by hunting and gathering. Pottery types are Alma Plain and Woodruff Smudged (from the mountain area), Adamana Brown (plateau), and Gila Plain and, possibly, late Pioneer-period Hohokam Red-on-Buff (desert). Definition of this phase was based on the excavation of Bluff Village.

Cottonwood Phase (A.D. 400–600, or 1550–1350 years B.P., no tree-ring dates). Pithouses, which are generally subrectangular and slab-lined with a side entrance, are on ridges. The economy was the same as in the Hilltop phase. Pottery types are Alma Plain, Forestdale Smudged, and Woodruff Red (mountain), Adamana Brown and, possibly, Lino Gray (plateau), and Gila Plain (desert). Definition of this phase was based on three pithouses at Bluff Village.

Forestdale Phase (A.D. 600–800, or 1350–1150 years B.P., 10 noncutting tree-ring dates: 563–702). Although generally round, pithouses exhibit a variety of forms and architectural features. For example, a bench, a defector-ventilator complex, a roof entrance, or a side entrance may be present or not. Great kivas are present. Subsistence was balanced between hunting and agriculture. Pottery types are Mogollon Red-on-brown, Alma Plain, Scored, Incised, and Neck Banded, Forestdale Plain, Red, and Smudged, San Francisco Red, and Woodruff Smudged and Red (mountain); Lino Black-on-gray, White Mound Black-on-white, Adamana Brown, and Lino Gray (plateau); Gila Butte Red-on-buff and Gila Plain (desert). Burials are semiflexed and usually have offerings. Definition of this phase was based on excavations at Bear Village.

Corduroy Phase (A.D. 800–900, or 1150–1050 years B.P., no tree-ring dates). Assignment of only three pithouses to this phase precludes determination of architectural changes other than the use of stone to encircle one house. No great kiva has been identified. Corduroy Black-on-white pottery is presumed to have been locally made. Plateau pottery types include Kana'a Black-on-white, Kiatuthlanna Black-on-white, and Red Mesa Black-on-white. Definition of this phase was based on three pithouses at Tla Kii Pueblo.

Dry Valley Phase (A.D. 900–1000, or 1050–950 years B.P., no tree-ring dates). A single, shallow, square pit structure had edges circled with stone to increase wall height. It is viewed as transitional between pithouse and pueblo construction. Pottery includes the first examples of all-over corrugation. Definition of this phase was based on one architectural feature, several burials, and ceramics from Tla Kii Pueblo.

Carrizo Phase (A.D. 1000–1150, or 950–800 years B.P., three cutting and 49 noncutting tree-ring dates; 1008–1115). Architecture is masonry pueblo with detached kiva and a cir-cular, semisubterranean, masonry great kiva. Mountain pottery includes McDonald Painted Corrugated, Alma Plain, Forestdale Smudged, Reserve Smudged, and Linden Corrugated. Black-on-white pottery was locally made and decorated in plateau styles. Plateau pottery includes a variety of black-on-white types, Wingate Black-on-red, and Puerco Black-on-red. Desert types include Gila Plain. Definition of the phase was based on excavations at Tla Kii Pueblo.

Linden Phase (A.D. 1150–1250, or 800–700 years B.P., no tree-ring dates). Evidence for this phase in Forestdale Valley is equivocal. True to the assumptions of the original branch construct, it fills the gap between the end of the Carrizo phase and the beginning of the Pinedale phase. The site (AZ P:16:9) tested by Haury to define the Linden phase is now recognized as belonging to the subsequent Pinedale phase.

Pinedale Phase (A.D. 1250–1300, or 700–650 years B.P., a considerable number of tree-ring dates from areas outside Forestdale Valley). A low-wall, masonry pueblo of ca. 40 rooms, an enclosed plaza, and an attached circular great kiva are present. Mountain pottery continues traditions of brown plain, corrugated, and red-slipped ceramics, with a decrease in finely patterned and painted corrugated. Plateau pottery includes black-on-white types painted in Puerco, Snowflake, Reserve, Tularosa, and Pinedale styles, White Mountain Red Ware types (St. Johns, Springerville, Pinedale), and Roosevelt Red Ware (Pinto Black-on-red and Polychrome). This phase is represented in Forestdale Valley by AZ P:16:9, a site tested by Haury and assigned by him to the Linden phase. Chodistaas and Grasshopper Spring are contemporaneous, excavated pueblo ruins in the Grasshopper region; Turkey Creek is in the Point of Pines region.

Canyon Creek Phase (A.D. 1300–1400, or 650–550 years B.P., a considerable number of tree-ring dates from areas outside Forestdale Valley). This phase is characterized by population aggregation into masonry pueblos of up to 800–1,000 rooms. The pueblos are often several stories high and have an enclosed plaza, rectangular small kivas, and, at the largest pueblos, a great kiva incorporated into the roomblock. The 200-room Tundastusa pueblo in Forestdale Valley has not been excavated. Utility pottery is dominated by brown obliterated corrugated. Decorated pottery includes White Mountain Red Ware (Pinedale, Cedar

Creek, Four Mile), Roosevelt Red Ware (Pinto, Gila, Tonto), and an increase in the number of locally manufactured decorated ceramics. Definition of the phase was based on excavations at Canyon Creek cliff dwellings, and at Show Low and Kinishba pueblos. Point of Pines and Grasshopper are contemporaneous, excavated pueblos.

J. Jefferson Reid

Further Readings

Haury, E.W. 1985. *Mogollon Culture in the Forestdale Valley, East-Central Arizona.* University of Arizona Press, Tucson.

Reid, J.J. 1989. A Grasshopper Perspective on the Mogollon of the Arizona Mountains. In *Dynamics of Southwest Prehistory,* edited by L.S. Cordell and G.J. Gumerman, pp. 65–97. Smithsonian Institution Press, Washington, D.C.

See also BEAR VILLAGE; BLUFF VILLAGE; GRASSHOPPER PUEBLO; MOGOLLON CULTURE AREA; POINT OF PINES RUIN

Fort Ancient Culture

"Fort Ancient culture" is a term applied to agricultural societies occupying the central Ohio Valley ca. A.D. 1000–1650 (950–300 years B.P.). The Fort Ancient heartland covers ca. 50,000 km² (31,000 square miles). It is roughly bounded by Parkersburg, West Virginia, on the east, by a line just downstream from Cincinnati, Ohio, on the west, by Richmond, Kentucky, on the south, and by Columbus, Ohio, on the north. The name "Fort Ancient" was first applied to materials recovered from an ancient village on the floodplain of the Little Miami River in Warren County, Ohio. The village was below the famous Hopewell-culture (100 B.C.–A.D. 400, or 2050–1550 years B.P.) hilltop enclosure of the same name. William C. Mills (1906, 1907), an archaeologist at the Ohio Historical Society, theorized that the hilltop enclosure was a defensive fortification that the floodplain villagers retreated to in time of war. With the advance of radiocarbon dating in the 1950s, it quickly became apparent that neither was related. Still, the name for the floodplain culture stuck, and today "Fort Ancient" culture is the accepted moniker for Late Prehistoric and Protohistoric agricultural societies in the central Ohio Valley. This name was given further credence by James B. Griffin (1943) of the University of Michigan, who made a massive study of related museum collections in the 1940s.

Traditionally, archaeologists speak of *a* Fort Ancient culture. Such a term masks the considerable variability that existed both temporally and spatially in the late prehistory and protohistory of the central Ohio River Valley. As more research is conducted, it is becoming apparent that, while they are unified by various material traits, the best way to view Fort Ancient societies is to take into account regional adaptations to local conditions. In Ohio, each of the main rivers that drains south into the Ohio River produces evidence of unique historical developments. These were noted long ago by Griffin and continue to have utility. In Kentucky, there are apparent differences in the Fort Ancient societies that occupied the Inner versus the Outer Bluegrass. For each of these areas of Fort Ancient development, it is possible to trace a similar evolutionary trajectory that encompasses three broad stages: (1) the development of small, seemingly unplanned pithouse communities in the eleventh and twelfth centuries A.D.; (2) the emergence of large villages with evidence of a true community plan by the thirteenth century; and (3) the disintegration of planned villages, followed by the virtual abandonment of the central Ohio Valley in the second half of the seventeenth century.

Fort Ancient cultures are assumed to have developed in situ from Late Woodland cultural stock that was strongly influenced by cultural developments elsewhere in the Southeast and the Midwest. These developments are associated with the rise of Mississippian societies. Postulated influences include the adoption of crushed freshwater mussel shell as a ceramic-tempering agent, the adoption of a bow-and-arrow hunting technology, and the use of maize as a dietary mainstay. On the basis of available radiometric evidence (current to 1996), these traits diffused into the central Ohio Valley ca. A.D. 900–1000 (1050–950 years B.P.). Early Fort Ancient communities were composed of a series of households arranged in a linear fashion along a river terrace or in an amorphous scatter over a broad ridge top overlooking a nearby stream or river. Houses discovered at the Muir site in Jessamine County, Kentucky, are probably typical of Early Fort Ancient structures. They were extremely small, rectangular in shape, and semisubterranean. Large, shallow storage pits were associated with the exterior of each household. Evidence for the use of maize is abundant at Muir, which was occupied during the eleventh century. Early Fort Ancient mortuary practices are poorly known, but they seem to follow an earlier Late Woodland tradition of interment away from habitation sites. Some burials were placed in stone platforms or cairns, although it seems likely that most individuals were buried in less elaborate circumstances.

In the period A.D. 1000–1200 (950–750 years B.P.), scattered pithouse villages became large, perhaps through consolidation of isolated villages or through slow internal growth. By A.D. 1200–1250 (750–700 years B.P.), seemingly unplanned Early Fort Ancient communities were replaced by carefully planned towns or villages that were home to several hundred individuals. Each of these Middle-period towns consisted of a roughly circular settlement, with houses surrounding an open public space or plaza. While the earliest of these towns were unprotected, by the late fourteenth century many were encircled by a wooden stockade with carefully restricted points of entry. Whether these stockades were defensive in nature, or simply used to demarcate village space from the surrounding environment, is unknown. Some early towns have earthen mounds associated with the village plan. The mounds were invariably used for burial. In most areas, the mounds were relatively low and amorphous in shape, but in the central Scioto Valley of central Ohio, most mounds were truncated and pyramidal in shape. At least one contained evidence of some sort of structure.

The basic economic unit of Fort Ancient societies was probably the nuclear family, although each family was undoubtedly part of some larger social unit, such as a clan. While each family was probably responsible for producing the food needed to feed the household, preparing fields and planting the crop may have involved the corporate labor of the clan. The Fort Ancient subsistence economy was based upon a mix of agricultural produce and food derived from wild animals and plants. Corn was the principal crop, but squash, beans, sunflower, and tobacco were also grown. Surplus crops, along with dried meat and fish, were stored in underground silos. Lined with poles and mold-resistant bluestem grass, the pits were capable of holding 25–35 bushels of corn. The corn could have been kept without significant spoilage for as much as a year. Pits were dug around houses and, at some villages, were located in a broad band that encircled the village

plaza. The village plaza was the focus of important public ceremonies and social gatherings. At the Sunwatch village, the plaza was dominated by a 0.6 m (2-feet)-in-diameter post of eastern red cedar surrounded by a series of smaller poles. This post-and-pole complex is thought to have been utilized to track seasonal movements of the sun. It formed the basis for scheduling important ritual observances of the village residents. Regional distinctions among Middle-period Fort Ancient populations are most marked in distinct ceramic styles. Incising of the vessel neck, and the presence or absence of vessel handles, serves to establish these differences. Most are associated with individual river drainages, which suggests that natural barriers served to channel local cultural developments. These river valley–to–river valley distinctions imply that social interaction was most intense among villages occupying the same river drainage.

After A.D. 1450 (500 years B.P.), regional distinctions among Fort Ancient cultures seem to have softened. Ceramic diversity lessens, and, while minor distinctions continue to exist, neck decoration of ceramic jars virtually disappears. Ceramic forms are now more or less uniform throughout the Fort Ancient heartland. A "Madisonville horizon" (A.D. 1450–1690, or 500–260 years B.P.) has been proposed by archaeologists to denote this collapse of regional diversity. Many archaeologists think that the "Madisonville horizon" reflects increasing interaction of formerly disparate cultural groups and heralds the emergence of some pantribal organization (Henderson 1992). There is some suggestion that over the course of the Madisonville horizon—at least in parts of the central Ohio Valley—the overall number of Fort Ancient towns decreases and portions of formerly occupied river drainages in the state of Ohio appear to have been abandoned.

After A.D. 1500 (450 years B.P.), European objects were available to Fort Ancient communities. Copper and brass beads made from scraps of kettles, and occasionally glass beads and iron celts and axes, mark the first evidence of contact between central Ohio Valley populations and other Native Americans who had access to European commodities. Most of the objects on central Ohio Valley sites cannot be specifically dated, but iron kettle lugs and bails recovered from the Madisonville site near Cincinnati, Ohio, are of a type traded into the Gulf of St. Lawrence by Basque fishermen ca. A.D. 1580–1600 (370–350 years B.P.). In addition to this obvious northeastern entryway, at least some European commodities found their way into the Ohio Valley through a southeastern connection. A "Clarksdale" bell manufactured of copper was recovered from the Madisonville site and is of the type made available almost exclusively by sixteenth- and seventeenth-century Spanish sources. The southeastern connection is also apparent in the appearance, after A.D. 1550 (400 years B.P.), of both "Citico"-style shell gorgets and shell masks that were most likely manufactured in eastern Tennessee by late Dallas-phase Mississippian craftsmen.

By the late sixteenth century, the highly structured community plan evident in earlier Fort Ancient villages seems to have given way to unorganized amalgams of houses and associated features. House styles in these unplanned villages also changed. At the Hardin village in Greenup County, Kentucky, for example, structures are multiple-family residences as long as 21.3 m (70 feet). Some archaeologists think that the latest Fort Ancient sites may have been occupied by the historically recorded Shawnee Indians. The absolute connection between late Madisonville-horizon sites and the Shawnee is difficult to prove with absolute certainty. By the middle of the seventeenth century, the Iroquois Confederacy began raiding the Ohio Valley. According to Jesuit records, the Iroquois claimed to have driven the Shawnee from what is now the state of Ohio. These accounts largely agree with the archaeological record; no Fort Ancient villages are documented later than the mid-seventeenth century.

C. Wesley Cowan

Further Readings

Cowan, C.W. 1987. *First Farmers of the Ohio Valley.* Cincinnati Museum of Natural History, Cincinnati.

Griffin, J.B. 1966. *The Fort Ancient Aspect.* Anthropological Papers no. 28. Museum of Anthropology, University of Michigan, Ann Arbor. Originally published 1943, as *The Fort Ancient Aspect: Its Cultural and Chronological Position in Mississippi Valley Archaeology.* University of Michigan Press, Ann Arbor.

Henderson, G. (editor). 1992. *Fort Ancient Cultural Dynamics in the Central Ohio Valley.* Prehistory Press, Madison.

Mills, W.C. 1906. Baum Prehistoric Village. *Ohio State Archaeological and Historical Quarterly* 16(2):113–193.

———. 1907. Explorations of the Edwin Harness Mound. *Ohio State Archaeological and Historical Quarterly* 25(3):262–398.

See also FORT ANCIENT SITE; INCINERATOR, OR SUNWATCH VILLAGE; MADISONVILLE

Fort Ancient Site

The Fort Ancient earthworks (33WA2) are the foremost example of that class of monumental earthworks termed "Works of Defense" by E. Squier and E. Davis in their seminal 1848 work *Ancient Monuments of the Mississippi Valley.* Although denominated a "fort" by nineteenth-century archaeologists largely on the basis of its formidable strategic location, it is doubtful the site ever served as a work of defense. The 5.7 km (3.5 miles) of winding earthen embankments enclose 51 ha (126 acres) of a high, flat bluff top 80 m (262.5 feet) above the east bank of the Little Miami River in southern Ohio. In some areas, ditches or moats are located inside the walls. These excavations may have originated as borrow pits that provided the earth for the walls, but some, lined with stone and clay, served as reservoirs for water.

This great hilltop enclosure includes "two grand divisions" (Squier and Davis 1848:20): the North and South Forts, which are connected by a long, narrow neck of embankments called the Middle Fort. Although the walls of Fort Ancient were constructed by the Hopewell culture (ca. 100 B.C.–A.D. 400, or 2050–1550 years B.P.), the site has given its name to the Fort Ancient culture (ca. A.D. 1000–1550, or 950–400 years B.P.). A group of Late Prehistoric farmers had thoughtlessly built their village within the already antique earthwork enclosure, which confused early archaeologists, who concluded that the villagers also built the surrounding walls.

The earth and stone walls of the enclosure are 1–7 m (3–23 feet) in height. The embankments, which generally follow the contours of the bluff, are broken by more than 60 gateways. These openings are sometimes associated with more elaborate "gateway" constructions, such as mounds or especially high walls. A few open onto paved roadways or terraced hill slopes, facilitating access from the surrounding valleys and ravines. The most prominent of the gateways is the northeastern, where large twin mounds frame the entrance, and a set of paral-

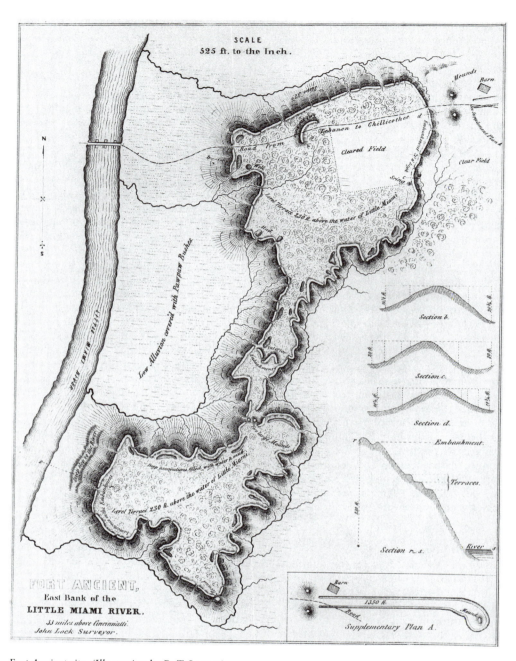

Fort Ancient site. (Illustration by B. T. Lepper)

lel embankments extends 840 m (920 yards) to the northeast. These embankments end in a cul de sac that encloses yet another large mound. Patricia Essenpreis and David Duszynski (1989) have suggested that significant astronomical alignments are encoded into the structure of the site. Caches of copper, mica, and obsidian arti-

facts have been discovered in the vicinity of the parallel walls. These discoveries support the interpretation of this earthwork as a place of ceremony and ritual rather than of protracted warfare.

Essenpreis, who worked at the Fort Ancient site between 1982 and 1990, and Robert

Connolly (1992), who joined her in 1987 and has continued to work at the site, excavated the remains of an extensive habitation area just outside the northeastern gateway. Substantial houses, fire pits, and other features that relate to the Hopewell occupation of the site were identified. This discovery indicates that, although the interiors of Hopewellian enclosures are frequently vacant, habitation sites can be directly associated with these great ceremonial centers.

Bradley T. Lepper

Further Readings

Connolly, R. 1992. The Evidence for Habitation at the Fort Ancient Earthworks, Warren County, Ohio. In *Ohio Hopewell Community Organization,* edited by W.S. Dancey and P.J. Pacheco. Kent State University Press, Kent.

———. 1993. Prehistoric Land Modification at the Fort Ancient Hilltop Enclosure—A Model of Formal and Accretive Development. In *Hopewell Archaeology: A View From the Core,* edited by P. Pacheco. Ohio Archaeological Council, Columbus.

———. 1996. *Middle Woodland Hilltop Enclosures: The Built Environment, Construction and Function.* Unpublished Ph.D. dissertation, Department of Anthropology, University of Illinois, Urbana.

Essenpreis, P.S., and D.J. Duszynski. 1989. Possible Astronomical Alignments at the Fort Ancient Monument. Paper presented at the Fifty-Fourth Annual Meeting of the Society for American Archaeology, April 9, 1989.

Essenpreis, P.S., and M.E. Moseley. 1984. Fort Ancient: Citadel or Coliseum? Past and Present Field Museum Explorations of a Major American Monument. *Field Museum of Natural History Bulletin,* June 1984, pp. 5–26.

Moorehead, W.K. 1890. *Fort Ancient: The Great Prehistoric Earthwork of Warren County, Ohio, Compiled From a Careful Survey, With an Account of Its Mounds and Graves.* Cincinnati.

Morgan, R.G. 1950. *Fort Ancient.* Ohio Archaeological and Historical Society, Columbus.

Squier, E., and E. Davis. 1848. *Ancient Monuments of the Mississippi Valley.* Contributions to Knowledge no. 1. Smithsonian Institution, Washington, D.C.

Thomas, C. 1886. Fort Ancient, Warren County, Ohio. *Science* 8:538–540.

See also HOPEWELL INTERACTION SPHERE

Fort Center Site

Named for the fort that was established at the site during the second Seminole War, Fort Center (8GL13) is known mostly for its prehistoric inhabitants. Beautifully carved wooden figures were excavated from a charnel pond, along with hundreds of burials and evidence of prehistoric maize. William H. Sears's excavations at the site in the 1960s transformed it from a little-known archaeological deposit to the most widely recognized example of the Belle Glade culture (Sears 1982). At the time, Sears employed all of the most innovative archaeological methods, including floral and faunal analyses. The results of his research led him to believe that maize-based agricultural practices allowed the Fort Center inhabitants to develop a sustainable economic base that supported their society for thousands of years.

Subsequent research at the site and in the area questions the maize-based-agriculture hypothesis (Johnson and Collins 1993), but no one refutes the presence of maize pollen grains that Sears documented at the site (Milanich 1994:287). Thus, the maize question remains open to debate and likely will remain unanswered until similar Belle Glade sites are examined for maize.

Fort Center is one of 20-plus sites in the Lake Okeechobee Basin that boast Belle Glade earthworks. Circular trenches and borrows join with linear embankments and numerous mounds to form the peculiar shapes that are the hallmark of the Belle Glade culture. Dating from as early as 1000 B.C. (2950 years B.P.), the Belle Glade earthworks have been compared to Hopewellian constructions in Ohio. The largest of these at Fort Center, known as the Great Circle, is ca. 400 m (1,312 feet) in diameter, 10 m (33 feet) wide, and 2 m (6.6 feet) deep. A radiocarbon date indicates construction took place prior to 450 B.C.

Sears documented continuous occupation of the site until it was abandoned some time during the historic period. European artifacts and European-derived raw materials, such as silver, iron, and gold, were recovered from the site, indicating participation in a larger economy than existed solely in the Okeechobee

F

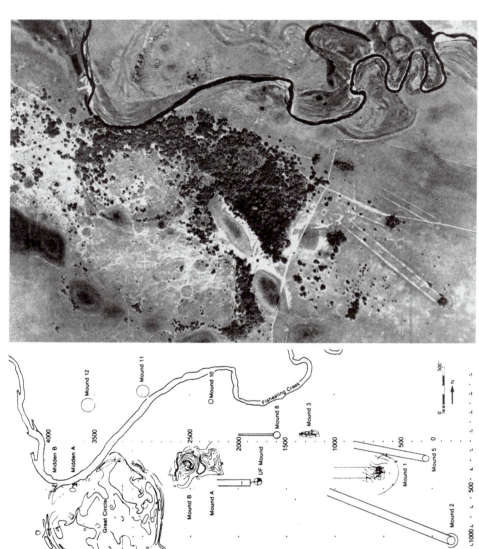

Plan view and aerial photograph of the Fort Center site. (Adapted by W. G. Johnson from Sears 1982)

Basin. Abandonment of the site by Belle Glade peoples was surely linked to their participation in this larger economy. The introduction of European diseases is documented throughout the southeastern United States and is considered a major cause in the abandonment of many of the South Florida contact-period sites. Many researchers believe that by the time the Seminoles entered into this part of Florida, South Florida's native populations were extinct.

William Gray Johnson

Further Readings

Johnson, W.G., and M.E. Collins. 1993. Can Soil Evidence Prove that Prehistoric Maize Was not the Basis for Complex Cultural Developments in the Lake Okeechobee Basin? *Proceedings of the First International Pedo-Archaeology Conference, February 16–20, 1992.* Special Publication 93–04, pp. 157–160. Agricultural Experiment Station, University of Tennessee, Knoxville.

Milanich, J.T. 1994. *Archaeology of Precolumbian Florida.* University Press of Florida, Gainesville.

Sears, W.H. 1982. *Fort Center: An Archaeological Site in the Lake Okeechobee Basin.* University Press of Florida, Gainesville.

See also BELLE GLADE CULTURE

Fort Walton Site and Culture

A Late Prehistoric ceremonial and habitation site, Fort Walton (8OK6) is located near the entrance to Choctawhatchee Bay on Santa Rosa Sound in northwest Florida not far from the Gulf of Mexico. The temple mound at the site was estimated to be 8 m (26 feet) high and to have a summit measuring 80 x 45 m (87.5 x 49 yards) at the time it was first recorded in 1885. It was also thought at the time to be associated with nearby sand and shell mounds. Later investigations by C.B. Moore, Gordon Willey, and others uncovered deeper midden strata that contained Early through Late Woodland ceramics. The mound produced 61 primary, bundle, and single-skull burials accompanied by typical Mississippian goods, such as pottery, points, discoidal stones, shell ear pins, and stone, bone, and shell beads. Since all of the burials are shallow and close to the surface, the mound is thought to have been used primarily for structural (temple) support. Today, the habitation

F

Fragment of small Fort Walton Incised bowl from the Corbin-Tucker site (8CA142), Calhoun County, northwest Florida. (Photograph by N. M. White)

areas are covered or destroyed by modern development. The mound itself was saved by William and Yulee Lazarus, notable amateur archaeologists, who scientifically explored the mound and persuaded the city of Fort Walton Beach to build an excellent museum adjacent to it and even to construct a temple on its summit. The Fort Walton site was originally named the type site of the Fort Walton culture, the northwest Florida variant of the Late Prehistoric Mississippian-stage adaptation in the Southeast. It is now considered more representative, however, of another Mississippian variant, the Pensacola culture, which extended from the westernmost portion of the Florida Panhandle westward through Alabama. Both of these variants are defined mostly on the basis of ceramics.

The Fort Walton culture itself is unusual among Mississippian variants in that it is the only one with predominantly grit- or sand-tempered pottery; other Mississippian variants, including the Pensacola, have shell-tempered wares. In much of northwest Florida, Fort Walton sites also have a paucity of chipped-stone tools. Fort Walton groups are thought to have been organized at the level of stratified chiefdoms, with the centralized polities supported by intensive maize agriculture in the riverine interior. The presence of large numbers of village sites with temple mounds supports this characterization. There is less agreement about the organization of adjacent coastal and estuarine groups, whose shell-midden sites, which have yet to produce much evidence for the use of cultivated crops, suggest seasonal gathering. Fort Walton culture is generally regarded as an in situ development out of a late Weeden Island (Late Woodland) indigenous adaptation ca. A.D. 1000 (950 years B.P.). The development is thought to have involved a shift of growing populations away from a settlement pattern of widely scattered villages that took advantage of wild resources in a diverse array of environments to a new pattern focused on alluvial lands better suited for agriculture and interaction along major waterways. Participation of Fort Walton chiefdoms in the Southeastern Ceremonial complex is evident at several sites, notably the Lake Jackson mounds in Tallahassee, which produced elaborate elite burials with exotic grave goods that include embossed copper plates and engraved shell with typical iconography. Fort Walton peoples now identified with the Apalachee Indians in the Tallahassee area were the first Native Americans in northwest Florida to encounter the Spanish. In other areas,

Large portion of Fort Walton Incised 5-pointed open bowl, from the Corbin-Tucker site (8Ca142), Calhoun County, northwest Florida. (Photograph by N. M. White)

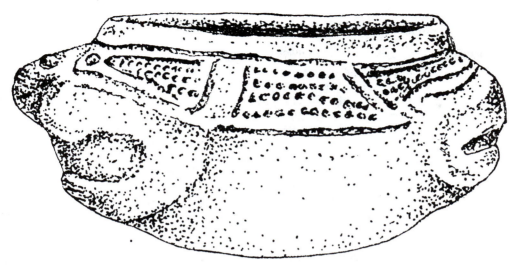

Fort Walton Incised frog effigy bowl from the Curlee site (8Ja7), Jackson County, northwest Florida. (Drawing by C. Maggiora; courtesy of N. M. White)

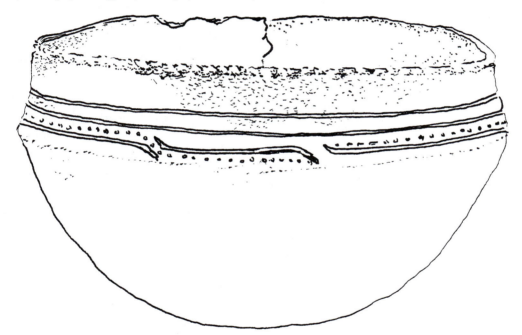

Fort Walton Incised Casuela bowl from the Bartow's Landing site (9Se106), Seminole County, southwest Georgia. (Drawing by M. Council; courtesy of N. M. White)

Fort Walton peoples disappeared without historic record, leaving only a few European artifacts in their graves.

Nancy Marie White

Further Readings

Lazarus, Y., and C.B. Hawkins. 1976. *Pottery of the Fort Walton Period.* Temple Mound Museum, Fort Walton Beach.

Milanich, J.T. 1994. *Archaeology of Precolumbian Florida.* University Press of Florida, Gainesville.

Willey, G.R. 1949. *Archaeology of the Florida Gulf Coast.* Miscellaneous Collections no. 113. Smithsonian Institution, Washington, D.C.

Fort Yates Phase

Villages of this Middle Missouri Extended variant Late Prehistoric phase were built on high terraces along the banks of the Missouri River from about the North Dakota–South Dakota border to the mouth of the Heart River in south-central North Dakota. Radiocarbon dates suggest the phase dates from ca. A.D. 1100 to ca. 1500 (850–450 years B.P.). The Thomas Riggs phase is a closely related and contemporaneous phase that occupied the Missouri Valley downriver in present-day central South Dakota. Most communities are relatively small and unfortified, although at least one of them (Havens) had 56 houses. A few villages near the North Dakota–South Dakota border, like the Helb site, are enclosed by shallow ditches. The long rectangular houses that typify the phase have vertical side walls and a central ridge pole. A covered entry faces southwest. The houses were usually not placed in any particular order, though some are roughly arranged in rows.

The pottery consists of well-made, moderately sized jars and small bowls. Rims are either straight or collared (an angular "S" rim), with most of the decoration on rims of the latter variety. Other items of baked clay include animal effigies, beads, and pipes. Small, triangular chipped-stone arrow points, drills, end scrapers, and a variety of bifaces are common. Ground-stone tools include grooved mauls, axes, celts, and a variety of grinding stones. Worked bone is dominated by bison-scapula hoes, but many tools are of this material. Lesser numbers of objects are made of antler or shell. The villages of the phase are believed to have coalesced into much larger, fortified communities that were the antecedents of the Huff phase, beginning sometime before ca. A.D. 1500 (450 years B.P.). The latter phase is believed to have provided the ancestral base of the Mandan Indians.

W. Raymond Wood

Further Readings

Falk, C.R., and F.A. Calabrese. 1973. Helb: A Preliminary Statement. *Plains Anthropologist* 18(62):336–343.

Lehmer, D.J. 1966. *The Fire Heart Creek Site.* Publications in Salvage Archeology no. 1. River Basin Surveys, Smithsonian Institution, Lincoln.

Wood, W.R., and A.R. Woolworth. 1964. The Paul Brave Site (32SI4), Oahe Reservoir, North Dakota. *Bureau of American Ethnology Bulletin* 189:1–66.

See also MIDDLE MISSOURI TRADITION; THOMAS RIGGS PHASE

Fraser River Canyon Sequence

The area to which British Columbia's Fraser River Canyon sequence applies includes the lower portion of the Fraser River Canyon and the eastern part of the Lower Fraser River Valley. Home to several Coast Salish local groups at contact, the region's plentiful salmon resources and superior fish-drying conditions attracted many seasonal Salish visitors from Strait of Georgia villages. Excavations at 14 sites provide the basis for the following sequence of culture types. All are represented at one or the other of the adjoining Milliken and Esilao sites, excavated by Charles E. Borden (1968a, 1968b, 1975), within the canyon. Because preservation of most organic material is poor, stone artifacts are almost the only category recovered. Thus, archaeological units are distinguished mainly by the technological characteristics of stone tools. Although faunal remains are virtually absent, stable carbon isotope analysis of human bone from burials at four sites provides information on Late Prehistoric diet.

Old Cordilleran (7000–4500 B.C., or 8950–6450 years B.P.). This early culture type includes both the Milliken and the Mazama phases of the Milliken site and probably at least part of the Pasika complex of the South Yale site. Artifacts, almost all of which are flaked stone, include large leaf-shaped points, pebble tools, flake unifaces, utilized flakes, hammerstones, a microblade, and some fragments of ground-stone artifacts. At first presented as a late Pleistocene or early postglacial occupation of the area, the large Pasika assemblage of crude unifacial pebble tools and utilized or retouched primary flakes is now viewed as a specialized woodworking complex associated with both the Old Cordilleran and the Charles culture types. Available radiocarbon age estimates, however, fall only within the Charles period.

Charles (4500–1700 B.C., or 6450–3650 years B.P.). The canyon manifestation of this culture type is also known as Eayem. Chief among its characteristic artifacts are stemmed points and drills of flaked stone; partially ground, partially flaked slate points; and ground-slate knives. At the western periphery of the region, the Hatzic and Maurer sites in the Lower Fraser River Valley contain semisubterranean houses dating to 2980–2270 B.C. (4930–4220 years B.P.). The two dwellings at Maurer date to 2830–2270 B.C. (4780–4220 years B.P.). Dates for two of the three houses at Hatzic range from 2980 to 2470 B.C. (4930–4420 years B.P.). One house depression at each site has been extensively excavated to provide architectural information. Both feature rectangular depressions (ranging in size from 5.5 x 7.5 m, or 18 x 24.6 feet, at Maurer to 8 x 11 m, or 26.2 x 36 feet, at Hatzic), large hearths, earthen benches, and large- and small-sized postmolds that suggest substantial superstructures. However, their rather different construction styles distinguish each from the other as well as from later prehistoric and historic interior and coastal dwellings. The Maurer pithouse was 1.5–2 m (4.9–6.6 feet) deep and had gabled walls and a flat roof that were earth covered. The Hatzic dwelling was excavated into the side of a riverbank, and the size and alignment of postmolds suggest vertical walls possibly covered with planks. These dwellings indicate that a semisedentary settlement pattern was developing in the region as early as 3000 B.C. (4950 years B.P.). However, the Maurer and Hatzic sites have no direct evidence of subsistence resource specialization, and storage features are absent within the structures or settlements.

Baldwin (1700–500 B.C., or 3650–2450 years B.P.). The distinctive assemblages of this form feature a prominent soft-stone-carving industry producing small carved figures, earspools, labrets, disk beads, and rings. There are variously sized and shaped stemmed and unstemmed flaked-stone points, pebble-core and cortex-spall tools, microblades and microcores, quartz microflakes, and quantities of both retouched and utilized flakes. Celts, ground-slate knives, and hammerstones are also present. Baldwin assemblages resemble those of the Strait of Georgia's contemporaneous Locarno Beach–culture type.

Skamel (500 B.C.–A.D. 500, or 2450–1450 years B.P.). In contrast with its predecessor, there is little evidence of microblade technology or of the soft-stone industry in this culture type. Flaked-stone artifacts include such point varieties as leaf shaped, contracting stemmed, corner notched, and basal notched; pebble-core tools; drills; formed unifaces; and retouched and utilized flakes. There are also celts, ground-slate knives, disk beads, saws, and irregular abrasive stones. Both house and cache pits are present.

Mortuary data from the Scowlitz site, a large village-and-burial-mound site located in the Lower Fraser River Valley, provide direct evidence of complex social organization at the end of the Skamel culture through the early stages of the subsequent Canyon-culture type. The site contains more than 30 earthen burial mounds and boulder cairns. These features have three distinct size groupings that may indicate a three-level social hierarchy. Excavations of two mounds disclose that this type of burial was practiced from at least A.D. 350 to 850 (1600–1100 years B.P.). The largest mound was constructed between A.D. 350 and 550 (1600–1400 years B.P.) and is ca. 3 m (10 feet) high and 12 m (39 feet) across at the base. It contained the remains of an adult male with artificial cranial deformation interred in an elaborate stone-covered burial pit. The burial contained abundant grave goods, including abalone-shell pendants, copper disks, and thousands of *Dentalium* shell beads. This individual may have had exceptionally high social rank in the region.

Canyon (A.D. 500–1800, or 1450–150 years B.P.). This type incorporates the Eayem and Esilao phases that have been distinguished by some. Working in soft stone returns to prominence with the production of figurines, beads, and straight pipes. Flaked-stone points are generally small and many are side notched. Other characteristic artifacts include drills, cortex-spall tools, retouched flakes, utilized flakes, celts, ground-slate knives, saws, hand mauls, and abraders. The use of house and cache pits continues. One excavated pithouse at Esilao, dating from the early postcontact period (A.D. 1800–1830), evidently had four upright columns supporting sloped rafters, much as described by ethnographers of the canyon's Thompson and Upper Stalo Salish. Stable carbon isotope analysis of eight individuals from four sites indicates that an average of 68 percent of the protein in their diet was from marine species, most likely salmon. Individual values range from 41 to 95 percent.

The Fraser River Canyon sequence shows some degree of technological change over the last 9,000 years. However, the general pattern is one of cultural continuity over time from which one may infer an in situ development of the Fraser River Canyon variety of Coast Salish culture.

Donald H. Mitchell
David L. Pokotylo

Further Readings

Borden, C.E. 1968a. A Late Pleistocene Pebble Tool Industry of Southwestern British Columbia. In *Early Man in Western North America,* edited by C. Irwin-Williams, pp. 55–69. Contributions in Anthropology, vol. 1, no. 4. Eastern New Mexico University, Portales.

————. 1968b. Prehistory of the Lower Mainland. In *Lower Fraser Valley: Evolution of a Landscape,* edited by A.H. Seimens, pp. 9–12. Geographical Series. University of British Columbia Press, Vancouver.

————. 1975. *Origins and Development of Early Northwest Coast Culture, to About 3000 B.C.* Mercury Series Paper no. 45. Archaeological Survey of Canada, National Museum of Man, Ottawa.

Mitchell, D. 1990. Prehistory of the Coasts of Southern British Columbia and Northern Washington. In *Northwest Coast,* edited by W. Suttles, pp. 340–358. Handbook of North American Indians, vol. 7, W.C. Sturtevant, general editor. Smithsonian Institution, Washington, D.C.

Von Krogh, G.H. 1980a. The 1974 Katz Salvage Project. In *Current Research Reports,* edited by R. Carlson, pp. 68–82. Publications no. 3. Department of Archaeology, Simon Fraser University, Burnaby.

————. 1980b. *Archaeological Investigations at the Flood and Pipeline Sites, Near Hope, British Columbia.* Occasional Papers no. 4. British Columbia Heritage Conservation Branch.

Fraser River Stone Sculpture Complex

Items considered members of the Fraser River Stone Sculpture complex have been found primarily along the middle and lower reaches of the Fraser River and in the Strait of Georgia area in southwest British Columbia and northwest Washington. Subjects are varied, but several general categories are evident:

Seated-Human-Figure Bowls. A sitting human with an emaciated or even skeletal body but with a fully fleshed face embraces a bowl with its arms and legs. The face often tilts upward, and the mouth is usually wide open or the lips shaped to form an O. Topknots are common and may have served as suspension knobs. Another figure—often an amphibian or reptile—or a face is sometimes on the front of the bowl. In some, the body of a snake trails down the back, perhaps representing the spinal column. Bowls range in height from ca. 9 to 40 cm (3.5–15.6 inches).

Human-Head Bowls. Bowl set into the top of a head or situated behind a masklike face. Heights range from 9 to ca. 30 cm (3.5–11.7 inches).

Zoomorphic Bowls. Bowl set into the back or belly of animals or supernatural beings with animal characteristics. One common form is a tortoise that often has a fan-shaped tail; another is a reclining owl-like bird. Lengths range from 12 to 30 cm (4.7–11.7 inches).

Many kinds of locally available rock were selected for these sculptures, but the finest bowls are of steatite (soapstone), a common material in the Fraser River Canyon. Cruder specimens are frequently made from sandstone. The age of the complex is uncertain, as the vast majority of specimens have been accidental discoveries and isolated finds. The very few recovered during site excavations have come from Marpole-culture assemblages, which date to 400 B.C.–A.D. 400 (2350–1550 years B.P.). Some pieces, perhaps themselves relics from an earlier past, are known to have been used in late-nineteenth-century rituals.

Two ethnographic accounts (Boas 1890; Hill-Tout 1899) suggest that some seated-human-figure bowls represent women giving birth and tie the bowls specifically to puberty ceremonies. In one of them, Franz Boas (1890) described how a Shuswap shaman led a girl back from her place of seclusion, while carrying a dish carved of steatite in one hand: "The dish represents a woman giving birth to a child, along whose back a snake crawls. The child's back is hollowed out and serves as a receptacle for water. In the other hand, the shaman carries certain herbs. When they returned to the village the herbs were put into the dish, and the girl was sprinkled with water."

In selected details, most notably the treatment of eyes, a few of the more carefully carved pieces show similarity to the well-known northern Northwest Coast wood-sculpture style. Generally, however, the resemblances lie with later south-central Northwest Coast or Salish wood art. A reasonable interpretation is that the distinctive Fraser River Stone Sculpture complex is an early form of the Salishan variant of northwest North American aboriginal art.

Donald H. Mitchell

Further Readings

Boas, F. 1890. *The Shuswap*. Sixth Report on the Northwestern Tribes of Canada. British Association for the Advancement of Science, London.

Duff, W. 1956. *Prehistoric Stone Sculpture of the Fraser River and Gulf of Georgia*. Anthropology in British Columbia no. 5. British Columbia Provincial Museum, Victoria.

———. 1975. *Images Stone B.C., Thirty Centuries of Northwest Coast Indian Sculpture*. Hancock House, Saanichton.

Hill-Tout, C. 1899. *Notes on the Prehistoric Races of British Columbia and Their Monuments*. British Columbia Mining Record, Vancouver.

Wingert, P. 1952. *Prehistoric Stone Sculpture of the Pacific Northwest*. Portland Art Museum, Portland.

Frederick Complex and Projectile-Point Type

The Frederick projectile-point type was named during the examination of materials recovered from the excavation of the Hell Gap site in southeast Wyoming from 1962 to 1966. Frederick represents the next to the youngest component at the site and was named after the landowner, Ruth Frederick. Henry T. Irwin, in notes recovered after his death, stated that instead of Frederick, the point type should have been called James (Jimmy) Allen.

George C. Frison

Further Readings

Irwin-Williams, C., H.T. Irwin, G. Agogino, and C.V. Haynes, Jr. 1973. Hell Gap: Paleo-Indian Occupation on the High Plains. *Plains Anthropologist* 18(59):40–53.

See also HELL GAP SITE

Fremont

The prehistoric Fremont culture was centered along the eastern edge of the Great Basin and the western part of the northern Colorado Plateau, in what we know as Utah. It reached at various times into Colorado, Wyoming, Idaho, and Nevada. This is a region of highly variable geography, with fir, aspen, and spruce forests within a few hours walk of dry salt flats and sage- or greasewood-covered valleys. It is hot in the summer and cold in the winter and subject to periodic droughts in an already dry climate. Water is scarce. Streams and rivers run clear and cold down high mountains before becoming lost in the dry valleys below. It is along these streams and rivers that Fremont people thrived in their villages and houses for almost 1,000 years, between A.D. 500 and 1350 (1450–600 years B.P.). Fremont is the name of an archaeological culture that may be the product of several different ethnic cultures. Although these various groups might not have shared common languages, beliefs, or customs, they did share basic environmental adaptations and strategies in growing and gathering food.

The climate seems to have been somewhat wetter, with longer growing seasons, ca. 50 B.C. (2,000 years B.P.), when maize agriculture came into the region from the south. In a sense, nature selected for this new system of growing food, for it was more efficient and productive than was gathering wild foods in relatively moist and warm conditions. Even so, agriculture did not spread quickly, nor did it become the primary source of food until many centuries after its arrival in the region. The earliest maize in the Fremont region comes from Glen Canyon on the Colorado River in southern Utah. This sample has been dated to ca. 400–200 B.C. (2350–2150 years B.P.). Slightly more recent maize, from near Elsinore in central Utah, dates to ca. 200 B.C. (2150 years B.P.). The people growing and storing these maize crops did not live in villages, although some seem to have lived in sturdy semisubterranean houses. This suggests that they had begun to settle down, at least for part of the year. These structures, called pithouses, distinguish early farmers from other peoples in the region, who continued to move from place to place, following hunting-and-gathering patterns established ca. 8000 B.C. (9950 years B.P.).

Farmers need to store food and seeds to be effective food producers. Evidence for such storage in deep bell-shaped pits comes from sites near Elsinore, Vernal, and Emery, Utah. They range in age from 200 B.C. to A.D. 300 (2150–1650 years B.P.). Only the latest site, on the Muddy River near Emery, has evidence of houses associated with the storage pits. Archaeologists assume that pithouses must have been located near the earlier storage sites. Sites near Kanab and Sevier, Utah, contain semisubterranean houses dated before A.D. 300 (1650 years B.P.), and a site in Richfield, Utah, has a pithouse dated to ca. 400 B.C. (2350 years B.P.). Neither bell-shaped nor other kinds of long-term storage features were found in these sites, probably because only the houses were excavated. No searches for exterior features were made.

A bow-and-arrow hunting technology came from the south ca. A.D. 200 (1750 years B.P.) and replaced or was added to the existing spear-thrower (atlatl) and dart technology. Ceramic technology also came up from the south. It seems to have become established with the appearance of Fremont gray wares ca. A.D. 500 (1450 years B.P.). Small communities appeared at about this time, too, which suggests that ceramic vessels were necessary to store enough produced food to support growing populations and aggregating groups of people. "Fremont" is said to exist when all of these traits came together ca. A.D. 500 (1450 years B.P.). Some archaeologists, however, believe Fremont started with the advent of maize farming in the region at ca. 200 B.C. (2150 years B.P.). Still others argue that the culture did not come into existence until after A.D. 900 (1050 years B.P.), when larger communities became widespread (Berry 1980; Anderson 1983; Madsen 1989).

Fremont culture is characterized by geographical variety and temporal homogeneity; that is, Fremont groups in various places have distinct sets of traits, but they show relatively little change in their basic patterns of material culture through time. The importance of geographical varieties has been debated for more than 60 years. The debate began as archaeologists tried to show that prehistoric farmers in southern Utah were either closely related to, or were distinct from, ancestors of the Pueblo peoples of the American Southwest. Most early archaeologists called these remains the "Puebloan" and "puebloid" cultures on the "northern periphery" of the Southwest. Noel Morss first defined the Fremont as distinct from Anasazi farmers to the south in *The Ancient Culture of the Fremont River in Utah* (1931). He focused on the presence of traits not found in the Southwest, such as moccasins, clay figurines, and distinctive rock art. The Fremont became defined by these traits, as well as by gray ceramics, storage bins and structures, round or square pithouses, stone balls, a variety of small arrow points, and a style of trough-grinding stones called "Utah" metates.

Not all of these traits were spread through-out the Fremont area, however, and many that were showed considerable variety from place to place. These factors fueled the debate, and archaeologists argued for some time about whether the Fremont should be considered a distinct cultural entity (Jennings 1978; Hogan and Sebastian 1980). Many focused on geographical variability to define two, three, or five distinct groups (Marwitt 1986). The natures of these groups have also been debated, with some claiming that they are "variants" of the overall Fremont archaeological culture (Marwitt 1986). These debates reached their peak in the late 1970s and early 1980s. They subsided when archaeologists realized that such arguments did not help them understand how these ancient peoples lived their lives (Simms 1986; Madsen 1989).

How did they live their lives? Discussions continue to focus on variability, but attention has shifted from trait varieties between areas to variation in food-gathering techniques and other cultural strategies. A growing number of archaeologists agree that the Fremont are defined by variability. Their strategies for living changed from place to place, and from time to time in the same places, in such things as growing and gathering food, building houses, moving about the landscape, and the employment of basic technologies. As David B. Madsen says in *Exploring the Fremont* (1989), Fremont groups lived in large and sedentary villages where and when local resources would support such human density, and in highly mobile family groups in other places and times when resources were scarce or dispersed over the landscape. They seem to have been most consistent in farming and maintaining communities in a "core area" along the zone where the eastern Great Basin meets the western Colorado Plateau (Talbot and Wilde 1989). Sedentary communities were occupied in this core for the whole of the Fremont period. Communities came into existence and were abandoned one or more times in favor of more mobile strategies in other areas of the Fremont region. Major expansions of sedentary communities away from the core occurred in the periods A.D. 900–1050 (1050–900 years B.P.), A.D. 1050–1200 (900–750 years B.P.), and A.D. 1250–1350 (700–600 years B.P.). Few or no sedentary communities were occupied outside the core in the years A.D. 1200–1250 (750–700 years B.P.). Only the Texas Creek Overlook area of northwestern Colorado is known to have small Fremont-like sedentary villages occupied after A.D. 1350 (600 years B.P.) (Creasman and Scott 1987). The Fremont culture disappeared after this time.

What happened to the Fremont? Many different theories have been proposed (Anderson 1983; Marwitt 1986). One suggests that northern Fremont groups moved out into the Great Plains to join farmers already there. Groups in the eastern area became hunter-gatherers similar to other Plains peoples. The southern Fremont moved southward with the Anasazi to eventually become the Pueblos. Other theories suggest that Fremont farmers were pushed out of the area by large groups of Numic-speaking ancestral Utes, Shoshones, and Paiutes, who had moved into the eastern Great Basin and Colorado Plateau from southern California. This would explain why the last Fremont habitation site is in northwestern Colorado, the most distant area from the postulated migration route of the invaders. Research by workers in northern Utah (Janetski 1995; Simms 1995) suggests that Fremont peoples stayed where they were, but they responded to climatic conditions that no longer favored farming by becoming full-time foragers. This seems to have been the case near the Great Salt Lake in Utah and possibly near Utah Lake. Fremont in other areas may have selected the same response, even if ancestral Numic groups invaded the region. Others may have joined the Anasazi migrations, and still others may have been displaced or exterminated. In any case, the last half-century of Fremont existence seems to have been one of fragmentation in community structures, food-gathering strategies, technologies, and belief systems (Lindsay 1986).

Important research has been undertaken in central Utah by the University of Utah in Gooseberry Valley, by the National Park Service and Metcalf Archaeological Consultants at Hogan Pass, by the Utah Department of Transportation, the University of Pittsburgh, and Alpine Archaeologists in the San Rafael Swell, and by Brigham Young University in Sevier Valley and Clear Creek Canyon. Most of these projects have not yet produced final reports. Northern Utah Fremont research has been advanced by the work of Utah State University along the the eastern margins of the Great Salt Lake (Fawcett and Simms 1993) and by Brigham Young University near Utah Lake (Janetski 1995). An important project at Baker, Nevada, between 1990 and 1994 was the result of a cooperative effort between the Bureau of Land Management

and Brigham Young University (Wilde and Soper 1994). Much of the notable work done in the 1960s and 1970s was led by Jesse D. Jennings from the University of Utah (cf. Jennings 1978).

Most of the important studied Fremont sites are large habitations. Examples are Paragonah, Beaver, Median Village, and Evans Mound in southwestern Utah; Pharo Village, Nawthis Village, Backhoe Village, Icicle Bench, Five Finger Ridge, Radford Roost, Poplar Knob, Snake Rock, Old Woman, Round Spring, Point Pithouse, and Pahvant Park in central Utah; Woodard Mound, Hinckley Mounds, Nephi Mounds, Willard Mound, the Bear River sites, Orbit Inn, Hogup Cave, and Grantsville in northwestern Utah; Whiterocks and Caldwell Village in northeastern Utah; Turner-Look in western Colorado; and the Bull Creek sites and Coombs Village in southern Utah.

One of the most important Fremont sites is Baker Village in eastern Nevada (Wilde 1992; Wilde and Soper 1994). This site is a large concentration of pithouses and surface structures built to a plan around a large mud-walled surface house. Buildings occupied A.D. 1200–1300 (750–650 years B.P.) were carefully placed to lie along diagonal axes of the large surface house, or along sight lines to solstice and equinox sunrise locations on the eastern horizon. Some structures seem to align the center of the large house to sunrise and sunset locations over prominent peaks and notches on the western and eastern horizons. Sunrises over these eastern landmarks and along building alignments appear to make up a horizon calendar that marks off six, four, three, and two lunar months before the winter solstice. The alignments of long axes of small buildings east of the large house coincide exactly with sunrise two months before and two months after the winter solstice. A clue to what this might mean comes from Hopi villages that begin their new year with a major ceremony about two lunar months before the winter solstice; they conduct a major early spring ceremony two months after the winter solstice. Hopi horizon calendars mark these and other important times with sunrises and sunsets over specific peaks and notches.

Fremont studies are beneficiaries of new and exciting ideas, techniques, and questions. Future research will undoubtedly focus on defining variability within regional catchments of large and small sites. Studies of Fremont trade are beginning to benefit from new material-sourcing techniques and the growing understanding of long-distance trade in obsidian, shells, and turquoise throughout western North America and Mexico. Fremont diets, agriculture, hunting and transportation techniques, material uses, ceramic production and centers of production, and social structure will all be more explicitly addressed in the coming years, helping us better understand Fremont life and times.

James D. Wilde

Further Readings

Anderson, D.C. 1983. Models of Fremont Culture History: An Evaluation. *Journal of Intermountain Archaeology* 2:1–27.

Berry, M.S. 1980. Fremont Origins: A Critique. In *Fremont Perspectives,* edited by D.B. Madsen, pp. 17–25. Antiquities Section Selected Papers, vol. 7, no. 16. Utah State Historical Society, Salt Lake City.

Creasman, S.D., and L.J. Scott. 1987. Texas Creek Overlook: Evidence for Late Fremont (Post A.D. 1200) Occupation in Northwestern Colorado. *Southwestern Lore* 53(4).

Fawcett, W.B., and S.R. Simms (editors). 1993. *Archaeological Test Excavations in the Great Salt Lake Wetlands and Associated Sites.* Contributions to Anthropology no. 14. Utah State University, Logan.

Gunnerson, J.H. 1969. *The Fremont Culture: A Study in Cultural Dynamics on the Northern Anasazi Frontier.* Papers no. 59. Peabody Museum of American Archaeology and Ethnology, Harvard University, Cambridge.

Hogan, P., and L. Sebastian. 1980. The Variants of the Fremont: A Methodological Evaluation. In *Fremont Perspectives*, edited by D.B. Madsen, pp. 13–17. Antiquities Section Selected Papers, vol. 17, no. 16. Utah State Historical Society, Salt Lake City.

Janetski, J.C. 1995. Recent Transitions in Eastern Great Basin Prehistory: The Archaeological Record. In *Across the West: Human Population Movement and the Expansion of the Numa,* edited by D.B. Madsen and D. Rhode, pp. 157–178. University of Utah Press, Salt Lake City.

Jennings, J.D. 1978. *Prehistory of Utah and the Eastern Great Basin.* Anthropological Papers no. 98. University of Utah Press, Salt Lake City.

Lindsay, L.W. 1986. Fremont Fragmentation. In *Anthropology of the Desert West: Essays in Honor of Jesse D. Jennings,* edited by C.J. Condie and D.D. Fowler, pp. 229–252. University of Utah Press, Salt Lake City.

Madsen, D.B. 1979. The Fremont and the Sevier: Defining Prehistoric Agriculturalists North of the Anasazi. *American Antiquity* 44:711–722.

Marwitt, J.P. 1986. Fremont Cultures. In *Great Basin,* edited by W.L. D'Azevedo, pp. 161–182. Handbook of North American Indians, vol. 11, W.C. Sturtevant, general editor. Smithsonian Institution, Washington, D.C.

Simms, S.R. 1986. New Evidence for Fremont Adaptive Diversity. *Journal of California and Great Basin Anthropology* 8(2):204–216.

———. 1995. Unpacking the Numic Spread. In *Across the West: Human Population Movement and the Expansion of the Numa,* edited by D.B. Madsen and D. Rhode, pp. 76–83. University of Utah Press, Salt Lake City.

Talbot, R.K., and J.D. Wilde. 1989. Giving Form to the Formative: Shifting Settlement Patterns in the Eastern Great Basin and Northern Colorado Plateau. *Utah Archaeology* 2:3–18.

Wilde, J.D. 1992. Finding a Date: Some Thoughts on Radiocarbon Dating and the Baker Fremont Site in Eastern Nevada. *Utah Archaeology* 5:39–54.

Wilde, J.D., and R. Soper. 1994. *Baker Village: A Preliminary Report on the 1991, 1992, and 1993 Archaeological Field Seasons at 26WP63, White Pine County, Nevada.* Museum of Peoples and Cultures, Technical Series 93–10. Brigham Young University, Provo.

Freshwater Mussels (Plateau)

The large freshwater mussels of the Plateau belong to seven species in three genera: *Margaritifera falcata* (freshwater pearl); *Gonidea angulata* (Rocky Mountain ridged); *Anodonta kennerlyi, A. nuttalliana, A. oregonensis,* and *A. californiensis* (western, winged, Oregon, and California floaters). As resources, mussels share three characteristics: They can be transported live for several hours before consumption; portions of their flesh can be easily dried and preserved for long periods; and each individual provides only a small amount of protein and fat to the consumer. Unless they can be mass harvested, they are inefficient sources of nutrition.

M. falcata prefers clear, cold, sand-to-gravel-bottomed lakes and streams. In suitable habitats, it can be found in concentrations that obscure the streambed. It is slow growing and long-lived, with recorded ages of more than 130 years. As they age, the shells conform to their substrate, making them essentially sessile. Sessile habits and dense populations made *Margaritifera* a reliable resource; their slow growth rate left them vulnerable to overexploitation.

G. angulata occupies streams with more turbid, warmer waters and sand-to-mud bottoms. Faster growing, it reaches maximum ages of 60–70 years. It, too, can form dense colonies on the streambed, but it remains mobile throughout its life in adaptation to its more mutable sandy habitat. It is, therefore, less spatially predictable as a resource.

All species of *Anodonta* occupy mud-bottomed lakes and streams. All are fast growing and rarely live beyond 15 years. Unlike *Margaritifera* and *Gonidea,* they tend to be dispersed throughout their habitat, making mass harvest difficult and acquisition unpredictable.

Ethnohistorical accounts from throughout the Plateau indicate that native peoples utilized freshwater mussels but did not consider them an important resource. Archaeological evidence, however, has shown that, for some times of year and during some periods of the Holocene (8000 B.C., or 9950 years B.P., to the present), mussels assumed a greater significance.

Margaritifera, Gonidea, and, occasionally, *Anodonta* have been found in sites spanning the Holocene, although they first appear in strata dating to ca. 8000 B.C. (9950 years B.P.) at Marmes Rock Shelter. Middle Holocene (6500–2000 B.C., or 8450–3950 years B.P.) sites along the Snake, Columbia, Fraser, and Thompson rivers often contain large middens that typically hold higher ratios of *Gonidea* to *Margaritifera* than occur in sites postdating 2050 B.C. (4000 years B.P.). Collection occurred at any time of year the mussels were accessible. Middens are also found along the Columbia and Snake rivers after 2050 B.C. (4000 years B.P.) but largely disappear from the Thompson and Fraser after

3050 B.C. (5000 years B.P.). Ca. 150–50 B.C., or 3500–2000 years B.P., mussel collection was primarily confined to the late summer and held a significant place in the seasonal round. Mass harvesting and processing are evident in sites such as Game Farm on the Upper Columbia River. In later prehistory, mussels declined in importance and became an emergency resource at springtime foraging camps and at camps established for harvesting less predictable resources.

James C. Chatters

Further Readings

Clarke, A.H. 1981. *The Freshwater Molluscs of Canada.* National Museum of Natural Sciences/National Museums of Canada, Ottawa.

Ingram, W.M. 1948. The Larger Freshwater Clams of California, Oregon and Washington. *Journal of Entomology and Zoology* 40:72–92.

Front Range Phase

The Front Range phase of the Western Plains Late Archaic regional variant was defined by William B. Butler (1986) following a reexamination of the Magic Mountain site in northeastern Colorado. Although a series of dates are available from components said to be in the Late Archaic period (ca. 810 B.C.–A.D. 100, or 2760–1850 years B.P.), few unmixed single components have been described in the literature. Projectile points found from this interval do not include any of the Middle Archaic McKean series, and the large-to-medium corner-notched types present also range well into Woodland times. The recognition of point types that would serve as good Late Archaic–period markers has yet to be accomplished, but possible candidates are large corner-notched or basally notched points/knives with straight bases.

Little is known about the Late Archaic period in Colorado except that it occurs during the cool and wet Sub-Atlantic episode, follows the Middle Archaic, and precedes the introduction of ceramics and the bow and arrow, which marks the beginning of the Plains Woodland period.

William B. Butler

Further Readings

Butler, W.B. 1986. *Taxonomy in Northeastern Colorado Prehistory.* Unpublished Ph.D.

dissertation, Department of Anthropology, University of Missouri, Columbia.

Irwin-Williams, C., and H.J. Irwin. 1966. *Excavations at Magic Mountain: A Diachronic Study of Plains-Southwest Relationships.* Proceedings no. 12. Denver Museum of Natural History, Denver.

See also MAGIC MOUNTAIN SITE

Frontenac Island Site

Frontenac (2089) is an island ca. 0.4 ha (1 acre) in size that lies in the reedy northern part of Cayuga Lake in the state of New York. It is the only substantial island in the Finger Lakes and, for millennia, has been ideally situated as a campsite for people seeking to exploit the fish and waterfowl resources of the area. During excavations there in 1939, 1940, and 1953, William A. Ritchie (1945) turned up 163 burials and a thick layer of habitation refuse that covered the entire island.

The mantle of refuse varied in thickness from 25 to 75 cm (10–29 inches) across the island, but Ritchie observed no clear stratification despite the long occupation. Graves had been dug into and through the refuse at various times during its accumulation, creating additional stratigraphic confusion that could not be interpreted easily.

Deer, bear, and elk, in that order, dominated the faunal remains. While turkey bones were more numerous than other bird bones, the bones of both bird and fish species were remarkably rare considering the location of the site. It is likely that this resulted from the relative size of large mammals and the rudimentary recovery techniques used by archaeologists at the time of the excavations.

Most of the occupation of Frontenac Island occurred within the Late Archaic period (4000–1700 B.C., or 6800–3900 cal years B.P.). Four radiocarbon age determinations, when calibrated, strongly suggest that the site was occupied sometime between 2570 and 2150 B.C. (4400–4000 cal years B.P.). Overall, the adaptation of the Frontenac Island inhabitants was typical of the Mast Forest Archaic, stressing a combination of plant and animal resources that were abundant in the oak-deer-maple biome that gradually emerged in central New York after the close of the Ice Age. Projectile points of the Lamoka, Genesee, and Brewerton types were recovered. Fishing equipment included stone net sinkers and plummets as well as gorges, fishhooks, and barbed harpoon points of bone. Slate points, a slate semilunar knife (ulu), and spear-thrower weights were also found.

Preservation of organic materials was good, but the rarity of carbonized acorns and other nuts and the low frequency of stone mortars, mullers, and pestles suggest that this camp was more for hunting and fishing than for the gathering of vegetable foods. Chert drills and scrapers, together with scrapers, needles, and awls made of bone (and in one case copper), indicate domestic tasks. Hides were doubtless processed and turned into garments on the site. Necklaces, bracelets, combs, and pendants of stone, bone, claw, antler, tooth, and marine shell, most of them found in burials, indicate a broad range of personal ornamentation. At least some of these were imported from distant sources. Marine-shell objects were typically associated with the graves of children. Turtle-shell rattles and bone flutes and whistles were typically found with adult male burials. Several adult males also showed evidence of wounds received in combat, some of which were probable causes of death.

Caches of small round pebbles were found, often associated with hearths. These have been inferred to have been used for stone boiling. House remains were not located. Shelter was probably found in temporary structures in the warm months, which is when the site was apparently used.

The remains of dogs were found in two sizes. All but one were buried with adult male humans, along with hunting equipment and other personal belongings. Various chipped-stone tools typical of Archaic sites were also found on the site, as were masses of limonite, which is a yellow mineral. The latter were the decayed remains of iron pyrites that had apparently been used with chert as fire-making kits.

The sample of 163 individuals is one of the largest known for the Northeast. Using analytical procedures that were current at the time, Ritchie hypothesized that there were two distinct populations present and that these later merged. This conclusion, which was based on now discredited cranial measurements, is no longer generally accepted. Forensic techniques were used to re-create faces for some of the individuals. The faces can be seen on the human figures in the life-size Lamoka Lake diorama at the New York State Museum in Albany.

Dean R. Snow

Further Readings

Ritchie, W.A. 1945. *An Early Site in Cayuga County, New York*. Research Records no. 7. Rochester Museum of Arts and Sciences, Rochester.

————. 1980. *The Archaeology of New York State*. Harbor Hill Books, Harrison, New York.

Ritchie, W.A., and R.E. Funk. 1973. *Aboriginal Settlement Patterns in the Northeast*. Memoir no. 20. New York State Museum and Science Service, Albany.

F

G

Gainey Complex

The Gainey complex or phase is named after the type site in southern Genesee County in east-central Lower Michigan (Simons 1980, 1997; Simons et al. 1984). It is further defined here as an early fluted-point industry distinguished by the use of cherts from the Great Lakes region. Gainey (20 GS49) is positioned near the end of a morainic lobe north of a 200-ha (494-acre) lake/marsh complex. Clusters of diagnostic artifacts are distributed with features over an area of ca. 2.5 ha (6 acres). With work ongoing late in the sixteenth season, excavations at Gainey total 5482 m² (6,556 square yards). The count for whole and fragmentary tools exceeds 4,000, and a preliminary count of debitage exceeds 29,000 pieces.

Well more than half the tools and the vast majority of the debitage are of Upper Mercer chert most likely from east-central Ohio. A large portion of the tool assemblage is also made of Ten Mile Creek chert from northwestern Ohio. Minor chert types include Bayport and Flint Ridge. Bayport chert, with a sample size of eight fluted bifaces and five unifaces, is probably from exposures northwest of Saginaw Bay ca. 145 km (90 miles) north of the site. The Flint Ridge chert, the material of two small fluted points, a point ear, biface fragments, one graver, three end scrapers, and a small amount of debitage may be from sources just west in Coshocton County in eastern Ohio. Finally, a single end scraper is made of Onondaga chert probably from an exposure along the northeast shore of Lake Erie in Ontario. Chert exhibiting the appearance of exposure to high temperatures is widespread at Gainey. Pot-lidding, crazing (fine angular cracks), crenated edges, luster, and color changes are evident on tools and debitage in a pattern suggesting a bias by material, with heated chert declining in order of occurrence from Flint Ridge, Upper Mercer, and Bayport to Ten Mile Creek.

Exotic chert materials are key elements in the assemblage at the Gainey type site because they provide clues to group movements and exchange relations. The character and distribution of clusters of stone artifacts and pit features at Gainey indicate repeated visits over an indeterminable length of time. The chert types are strong directional indicators for southern populations expanding into Michigan, perhaps during a period of colonization (Deller 1983; Deller and Ellis 1988; Anderson 1990; Simons 1997).

Fluted projectile points are the most diagnostic artifacts at the Gainey site (see Figure). The total number recorded as of September 1996 was 116 whole and fragmentary bifaces with fluting. Unbroken points have a parallel-sided to slightly expanded form, a relatively deep-to-shallow basal concavity, and flutes, struck from prepared beveled platforms, often extending more than half the distance from the base toward the tip. Multiple flutes are common. Points occur in two sizes and (rarely) may be fluted from both ends. Similar point forms are found from the Midwest to the East Coast, although they were often made from different materials. Examples of Gainey-like points are found at Bull Brook in Massachusetts (Byers 1955), Vail in Maine (Gramly 1982), Lamb in New York (Gramly 1988), Udora in Ontario (Storck 1988), miscellaneous sites in western Pennsylvania (Lantz 1984), and Nobles Pond (Gramly and Summers 1986), Sandy Springs (Seeman and Prufer 1982), and Welling (Prufer and Wright 1970) in Ohio.

Gainey Complex Fluted Bifaces. (Photograph by D. B. Simons)

Additional elements of the Gainey complex are very large bifacial cores, ovoid bifaces, late-stage bifaces with heavily ground tips, relatively large triangular end scrapers almost always without notches, side scrapers, gravers, and small quartzite core tools or wedges. Rare items include small multigrooved sandstone abraders; burins; heavy scrapers with convergent lateral edges; edged choppers made from split quartzite boulders; and beaked gravers. In Michigan, other sites besides Gainey with similar stone-tool assemblages include Butler (Simons et al. 1987; Simons and Wright 1992; Simons 1994), Leavitt (Shott 1993), and Grey (Daniel Wymer, personal communication, ca. 1987). Notable examples of small sites or single point find spots include Plank (Wright 1981), Wiles (Beld 1986), Varner (Topping 1992), and Reaume (Tom LaDuke, personal communication, ca. 1989).

Preliminary thermoluminescence dates on burned flint from pit features and typological evidence suggest that the Gainey complex dates to ca. 9050 B.C. (11,000 years B.P.) on the radiocarbon calendar. D. Brian Deller and Christopher Ellis have discussed the typological evolution of fluted points in the Great Lakes. They (1988:255) have "been able to demonstrate in detail the presence of at least three point types in southern Ontario: Gainey, Barnes and Crowfield. . . . These types are used as diagnostic indicators of three fluted point complexes or industries. Point specimens are assigned to a particular type based on the consistent co-occurrence of certain technological, morphological, and metrical characteristics. . . ." The Gainey site data support this hypothesis and typological sequence.

The Gainey complex is part of a widespread cultural expression. Defining this complex helps expand our understanding of colonizing populations in the Lower Great Lakes region.

Donald B. Simons

Further Readings

Anderson, D.G. 1990. The Paleoindian Colonization of Eastern North America: A View From the Southeastern United States. In *Early Paleoindian Economics of Eastern North America,* edited by K.B. Tankersley and B.L. Isaac, pp. 163–216. Research in Economic Anthropology Supplement no. 5. JAI Press, Greenwich.

Beld, S.G. 1986. A Fluted Point Find, 20GR162, From Gratiot County, Michigan. *Michigan Archaeologist* 32(4):156–163.

Byers, D.S. 1955. Additional Information on the Bull Brook Site, Massachusetts. *American Antiquity* 20:274–276.

Deller, D.B. 1983. Paleo-Indian Utilization of Exotic Lithic Raw Materials: Data Suggesting Seasonal Resource Scheduling and Social Interaction in the Great Lakes Region. Paper presented at the Ninth Annual McMasters University Archaeology Symposium: Early Man in the Northeast, Hamilton, Ontario.

Deller, D.B., and C.J. Ellis. 1988. Early Paleo-Indian Complexes in Southern Ontario. *Bulletin of the Buffalo Society of Natural Sciences* 33:251–263.

Gramly, R.M. 1982. *The Vail Site: A Paleo-Indian Encampment in Maine.* Bulletin, vol. 30. Buffalo Society of Natural Sciences, Buffalo.

———. 1988. Discoveries at the Lamb Site, Genesee County, New York, 1986–87. *Ohio Archaeologist* 38(1):4–10, edited by R.N. Converse. Archaeological Society of Ohio, Richardson.

Gramly, R.M., and G.L. Summers. 1986. Nobles Pond: A Fluted Point Site in Northeastern Ohio. *Midcontinental Journal of Archaeology* 11(1):97–124.

Lantz, S.W. 1984. Distribution of Paleo-Indian Projectile Points and Tools From Western Pennsylvania: Implications for Regional Differences. *Archaeology of Eastern North America* 12:210–230.

Prufer, O., and N. Wright. 1970. The Welling Site (33CO-2): A Fluted Point Workshop in Coshocton County, Ohio. *Ohio Archaeologist* 20(4):259–268.

Seeman, M.F., and O.H. Prufer. 1982. An Undated Distribution of Ohio Fluted Points. *Midcontinental Journal of Archaeology* 7(2):155–169.

Shott, M.J. 1993. *The Leavitt Site: A Parkhill Phase Paleo-Indian Occupation in Central Michigan.* Memoirs no. 25. Museum of Anthropology, University of Michigan, Ann Arbor.

Simons, D.B. 1980. The Gainey Site in Genesee County. *Archaeology of Eastern North America* 8:16.

———. 1997. The Gainey and Butler Sites As Focal Points of the Northern Hemisphere. In *Caribou and Reindeer Hunters of the Northern Hemisphere,* edited by L.J. Jackson and P. Thacker. Worldwide Archaeology Series. Avebury Press, Aldershot.

Simons, D.B., and H.T. Wright. 1992. Butler 1991: Excavations at a Fluted Point Site in the Central Great Lakes (20GS104). *Current Research in the Pleistocene* 9:35–37.

Simons, D.B., M.J. Shott, and H.T. Wright. 1984. The Gainey Site: Variability in a Great Lakes Paleo-Indian Assemblage. *Archaeology of Eastern North America* 12:266–279.

———. 1987. Paleoindian Research in Michigan: Current Status of the Gainey and Leavitt Projects. *Current Research in the Pleistocene* 4:27–30.

Storck, P.L. 1988. Recent Excavations at the Udora Site: A Gainey/Clovis Occupation Site in Southern Ontario. *Current Research in the Pleistocene* 5:23–24.

Topping, W. 1992. A Gainey Point From Varner. Ms. in file, Baldwin, Mich.

Wright, H.T. 1981. A Fluted Point From the Muskegon Valley. *Michigan Archaeologist* 27(3–4):87–89.

Galena

Galena (PbS), or lead ore, is a heavy, gray-colored mineral that, when crushed or ground, produces a bright silver, sparkling glitter. When this powdered form of the mineral is allowed to oxidize, it turns pure white and can be used as a source of paint. Although prehistoric peoples occasionally made ornaments, such as beads, from galena or carried pieces of the mineral as magical charms, there is overwhelming evidence that its major use prior to European contact was as glitter or paint. Galena was used by North American prehistoric peoples for more than 8,000 years. Two periods, the Middle Woodland (A.D. 100–300, or 1850–1650 years B.P.) and the Mississippian (A.D. 900–1400, or 1350–550 years B.P.), were times of peak galena trade and use. Trace element analysis of galena specimens from source areas and from archaeological contexts indicates that, during the Middle Woodland period, the major source of this mineral was the Upper Mississippi Valley region near the present borders of Illinois, Iowa, and Wisconsin. Mississippian trade included a large quantity of galena from the upland deposits of southeast Missouri (with the nearby Cahokia chiefdom as a major consumer and exporter of galena). After European contact in the late seventeenth century A.D. (post 1673) and the introduction of firearms, galena was mined by the Illinois, Winnebago, and other Mississippi Valley tribes and smelted into lead for molding into shot.

John A. Walthall

Further Readings

Walthall, J.A. 1981. *Galena and Aboriginal Trade in Eastern North America.* Scientific Papers no. 17. Illinois State Museum, Springfield.

Walthall, J.A., S.H. Stow, and M.J. Karson. 1980. Copena Galena: Source Identification and Analysis. *American Antiquity* 45:21–42.

Gaming Pieces (California)

California Indians practiced a wide range of guessing and gambling games. Some were played predominantly by women, others by men. Some have left no archaeological traces, but others involved artifacts that turn up in excavations. The gaming piece is an example.

Gaming pieces were made of bone, often from the leg bones of deer. A typical piece was rectangular with rounded corners or ends. A typical size was ca. 5–6 cm (2–2.3 inches) long x 2 cm (0.8 inches) wide x 35 mm (1.4 inches) thick. Gaming pieces were often polished on their outer, convex surfaces. Some were marked with incised cuts or pits, while others were left blank. In the "hand game," usually played by teams of men, a player from one team held two gaming pieces behind his back. One piece was marked, and the other was blank. Players from the other team had to guess which hand held the marked or the blank piece. Often, gambling on the outcome was involved. When teams represented whole villages or kin groups, the amount of wealth risked could be very great. Women usually played dice games with similar pieces. In a dice game, each piece had a different number of spots carved on its surface. In some versions, betting was done on how many spots would turn up when the pieces were thrown as cast die. In other versions, the guessing involved how many pieces would fall face up or face down.

Gaming pieces, being made of bone, often are preserved archaeologically. Many have been found in houses or burials. They were especially distinctive of Pacific-period (2050 B.C.–A.D. 1769, or 4000–181 years B.P.) sites.

Joseph L. Chartkoff

Further Readings

Heizer, R.F. (editor). 1978. *California*. Handbook of North American Indians, vol. 8, W.C. Sturtevant, general editor. Smithsonian Institution, Washington, D.C.

Garden Creek Site

The Garden Creek site is composed of three mounds (31HW1 to 3) and a village site (31HW7). It is situated on the south bank of the Pigeon River 4.8 km (3 miles) west of Canton, North Carolina. In the period 1965–1967, the three prehistoric mounds that mark this locality were extensively investigated by the University of North Carolina. The mounds, which had suffered considerable deterioration from extensive farming, previous excavations, and residential-subdivision development, were substantially smaller at the time of these investigations than when they were initially described in the 1880s (Valentine et al. 1880).

In 1919, George Heye (1919) described Mound 1 as 5.5 m (18 feet) high and 24.4 m (80 feet) in diameter. By 1965, the mound had been reduced to less than half its former height. Built during the Pisgah phase (A.D. 1000–1500, or 950–450 years B.P.) in two separate but apparently brief intervals, Mound 1 was constructed over two earthlodges joined by a narrow passageway; the floor of each lodge was 2.6 m² (28 feet square). Each of the successive platforms supported rectangular ceremonial structures (temples); the most complete floor plan indicated a structure measuring 15.2 x 21.3 m (50 x 70 feet). A number of burials recovered from the mound suggest that the people interred in it had ascribed high social status. Village domestic architecture featured squarish single-set post walls with wall-trench entrances. Subsistence remains indicate that maize agriculture was important but that hunting and gathering continued to provide substantial nourishment. A small Qualla phase (A.D. 1500–1838, or 450–112 years B.P.) component marked the final Indian occupation of this area.

In 1880, Mound 2 stood 2.1–2.4 m (7–8 feet) high. By 1965, intensive farming had reduced its height to ca. 0.9 m (3 feet). Built during the Connestee phase (200 B.C.–A.D. 400, or 2150–1550 years B.P.), it was constructed in two separate building episodes on the surface of a thin midden that dated from the Late Archaic (2000–1000 B.C., or 3950–2950 years B.P.) through the initial part of the Connestee phase. The superposition of artifacts in the premound midden and sequential mound stages allowed the chronological ordering of the Swannanoa (1000–600 B.C., or 2950–2550 years B.P.), Pigeon (600–200 B.C., or 2550–2150 years B.P.), and Connestee phases and the delineation of some of their cultural content. Prismatic blades of Flint Ridge chalcedony and limestone-tempered rocker-stamped pottery demonstrated contact with Scioto Hopewell cultures ca. 100 B.C. (2050 years B.P.).

Mound 3 was 0.6–0.9 m (2–3 feet) high when excavated by Heye in 1915. It was incompletely reported, and little can be said other than that it may have been constructed on top of a midden similar to the one present at Mound 2 during the Pisgah phase. A 15.2-cm (6-inch) elevation in the vegetable garden of a recently constructed residence was all that remained of the mound in 1965.

Developed from these excavations at the site were the Appalachian Summit Area cultural sequence ca. 1000 B.C.–A.D. 1500 (2950–450 years B.P.), as well as much of the cultural content of the local Woodland (Swannanoa, Pigeon, and Connestee) and Mississippian (Pisgah and Qualla) phases and their external relations.

Between 1966 and 1971, investigations at the Warren Wilson, Gashes Creek, Tuckasegee, Townson, and Coweeta Creek sites confirmed this sequence and added details to the defined phases. The Early Woodland Swannanoa phase is characterized by thick grit-tempered, fabric-impressed and cord-marked ceramics that suggest an affiliation with Northern-tradition cultures of the Midwest. This influence lessened but did not completely disappear during the Pigeon phase, when carved, paddle-stamped ceramics made their appearance from the south. Northern influence was reasserted in ceramics in the Connestee phase with a marked increase in cord-marked vessels and trade relations with the Ohio Hopewell. The Mississippian Pisgah phase seems to have grown out of evolving Mississippian cultures in the central Ohio River Valley. It shares a number of characteristics with the Dallas and Mouse Creek phases of eastern Tennessee.

Bennie C. Keel

G

Further Readings

Dickens, R.S., Jr. 1976. *Cherokee Prehistory: The Pisgah Phase in the Appalachian Summit Area.* University of Tennessee Press, Knoxville.

Heye, G.G. 1919. Certain Mounds in Haywood County, North Carolina. *Contributions From the Museum of the American Indian-Heye Foundation* 5:35–43. New York.

Keel, B.C. 1976. *Cherokee Archaeology: A Study of the Appalachian Summit.* University of Tennessee Press, Knoxville.

Valentine, M.S. et al. 1880. *Notes Taken in North Carolina, 1880s.* Valentine Museum, Richmond.

Garza Complex

Garza-complex sites are known from the southern Texas Panhandle/northwestern Texas and adjacent eastern New Mexico areas. The origins of the Garza complex, which dates to A.D. 1450–1700 (500–250 years B.P.), are uncertain. Garza has a number of cultural similarities to the Wheeler phase in western Oklahoma, with which it is contemporaneous; it may simply be a western extension of that phase.

Known site types include bison kills, short-term campsites, and more permanent villages. House types have not been defined. Some settlements appear to have been fortified. Subsistence strategies, especially strategies used to obtain plant foods, are uncertain. Horticultural tools are rare. Bison hunting was a major activity. Ceramics are very similar to Wheeler-phase ceramics. There is a plain-surfaced, flat-bottomed, sand-tempered ware. There is also a small globular vessel with striated surfaces that resembles Southwestern utility wares. Bone tools include a few bison-scapula hoes and bison-tibia digging-stick tips. Bone-fleshing tools and split bone awls (commonly associated with hide working) are more frequent. Stone tools include small triangular unnotched, side-notched, and basal-notched projectile points; expanding-base drills; alternately beveled, diamond-shaped knives; two-edged, alternately beveled knives; flake knives; end scrapers; and manos and metates. Trade materials include puebloan ceramics; turquoise; *Olivella*, conus, or oliva shells; possibly Edwards chert from central Texas and Alibates agatized dolomite from the Texas Panhandle; and New Mexico obsidian. Caddoan ceramics are also present.

The Garza complex is considered an archaeological reflection of the Teya encountered by Spanish explorer Francisco Vásques de Coronado in 1541. While some have thought the Teya were Apache, it seems more likely that they were Plains Caddoans.

Susan C. Vehik

Further Readings

Baugh, T.G. 1986. Culture History and Protohistoric Societies in the Southern Plains. *Plains Anthropologist Memoir* 21:167–187.

Habicht-Mauche, J.A. 1992. Coronado's Querechos and Teyas in the Archaeological Record of the Texas Panhandle. *Plains Anthropologist* 37:247–259.

George C. Davis Site

The George C. Davis site (41CE19) is a major habitation and mound center on the middle reaches of the Neches River in the pine-hardwood forest of East Texas. It is listed on the National Register of Historic Places and is a designated Texas Archeological Landmark. Extensive and well-controlled excavations carried out intermittently between 1939 and 1983 have revealed a long record of occupation that includes Paleoindian, Archaic, Woodland (or early Ceramic), Caddoan, and Anglo-American components. Of these, the Caddoan is the most extensive and important.

The most prominent of the Caddoan remains are three earthen mounds. One is a burial mound, and the other two are capping and substructural mounds. Occupational debris is reasonably abundant and extends continuously but unevenly over ca. 112 ha (276.8 acres). Probably founded by a Caddoan-speaking group from northwestern Louisiana, this ceremonial center and associated village established and dominated the southwestern frontier of the Caddoan area for at least four centuries. Numerous radiocarbon assays place the initial Davis-site settlement in the late ninth or early tenth century A.D. and its abandonment at ca. A.D. 1300 (650 years B.P.).

Several circumstances make the Davis site of special archaeological interest. First, it is one of the comparatively few major mound centers in Texas. Second, it evidently marks the initial expansion of Caddoan-speaking peoples into the middle Neches River Basin. Third, it is the type site for the Alto focus. Lastly, as one of the

George C. Davis, Cherokee County, Texas. Two excavated houses (one partially) in a large village area surrounding the three mounds. Structures were circular in plan, pole and thatch construction, and conical or traditional beehive shaped. All that remains today are stains where the poles once stood (cleaned in this photo). Typical village structures were 6–9 m in diameter. (Illustration by D. A. Story)

more intensively investigated Caddoan sites, it has revealed certain patterns more clearly than have other Caddoan centers. Foremost among them are, first, the architectural details and spatial arrangements that distinguish special-purpose buildings (such as temples and elite residences) from ordinary domiciles; and, second, the elaborate mortuary behavior of these people, gleaned from the tight associations and excellent stratigraphy in the burial mound. This mortuary behavior was likely associated with the interment of only certain members, presumably the elites, of the Caddoan community.

Dee Ann Story

Further Readings

Creel, D. 1979. *Archeological Investigations at the George C. Davis Site, Cherokee County, Texas, Summer 1978.* Texas Antiquities Committee Permit Series Report no. 1. Texas A&M University and Texas Antiquities Committee, Austin.

Newell, H.P., and A.D. Krieger. 1949. *The George C. Davis Site, Cherokee County, Texas.* Memoir no. 5. Society for American Archaeology, Washington, D.C.

Story, D.A. (editor). 1981. *Archeological Investigations at the George C. Davis Site, Cherokee County, Texas: Summers of 1979 and 1980.* Occasional Papers no. 1. Texas Archeological Research Laboratory, University of Texas, Austin.

Story, D.A., and S. Valastro, Jr. 1977. Radiocarbon Dating and the George C. Davis Site, Texas. *Journal of Field Archaeology* 4(1):63–89.

Giddings, James Louis (1909–1964)

Henry B. Collins, a pioneer synthesizer of Arctic prehistory, described J.L. Giddings as one of the ablest, most brillant, and most productive of the Arctic archaeologists. His important archaeological discoveries include three of the major sites that have defined northwestern Alaskan prehistory: Iyatayet at Cape Denbigh;

Cape Krusenstern, located immediately north of Kotzebue Sound; and Onion Portage on the Kobuk River. These three sites, and several others around Kotzebue Sound, such as on Choris Peninsula, are the type sites from which Giddings named and described the Denbigh Flint complex, the Old Whaling culture, and the Palisades, Choris, and Norton complexes.

Among Giddings's important intellectual contributions were his recognition that the Bering Strait region was a center of, not a barrier to, cultural developments between northeast Asia and northwest North America, and his still debated suggestion that the initial peopling of North America from Asia occurred by gradual population spread rather than by successive waves of migrations.

Prior to his major archaeological discoveries, Giddings conducted extensive ethnographic and archaeological research in the Kobuk River Valley, where he described the Arctic Woodland culture, an Eskimo culture that combined elements of both coastal and interior forest adaptations. His focus on adaptation as well as culture history was a departure from earlier Arctic research orientations, and it remains a fundamental theoretical perspective for many Arctic archaeologists. His perspective is best summed up by the concluding paragraph in his monograph *The Arctic Woodland Culture of the Kobuk River*: "The Arctic Woodland Culture appears to be more than a phenomenon resulting from the meeting of two distinct forms of culture [Eskimo and Athapaskan]. It is, rather, the predictable combination of sea-river-and-forest-hunting wherever it is possible for a single ethnic group to practice these together under the special conditions of the Arctic. It is a material culture that will be practiced by whatever linguistic group happens to live in the particular environment, a culture that will outlive the physical appearance, the speech, and many of the social practices of its participants."

Giddings is also credited with developing and applying tree-ring dating in the Arctic. His Arctic Woodland–culture sequence, which spanned 700 years (ca. A.D. 1100–1800, or 850–150 years B.P.) of riverine Eskimo prehistory, was based on his own dendrochronological research in the Kobuk River Valley (Giddings 1952). He also developed several tree-ring chronologies for portions of central Alaska, but these were never able to be put to archaeological use there because there were no associated archaeological materials. In addition to his research in

northwest Alaska, Giddings conducted an archaeological survey in the Keewatin district, which produced some of the earliest archaeological materials then known from interior Arctic Canada. His ethnographic studies among northwestern Alaskan Eskimos resulted in several publications on the oral history, social organization, and folklore of the Kobuk River Eskimos. Among his findings is that the "Eskimo type" kinship system was rare, if present at all, in any of the Alaskan Eskimo groups.

Douglas D. Anderson

Further Readings

Giddings, J.L. 1952. *The Arctic Woodland Culture of the Kobuk River.* University Museum, University of Pennsylvania, Philadelphia.

———. 1964. *The Archaeology of Cape Denbigh.* Brown University Press, Providence.

———. 1967. *Ancient Men of the Arctic.* Knopf, New York.

Gladwinian Classification of Cultures

Among his many accomplishments, Harold S. Gladwin developed a system for classifying Southwestern archaeological data. Prior to Gladwin's initial work in the late 1920s, archaeologists had concluded that some type of systematization was required to achieve data comparability. A major step in this direction was taken in 1927 when Alfred V. Kidder (1927) published nomenclatural accords reached by participants of the first Southwestern Archaeological Conference (now known as the Pecos Conference). These accords, provisionally developed by Earl H. Morris (1921) six years earlier, represented the first consensually based pan-regional classification scheme for prehistoric Southwestern ceramics and puebloan architecture. But as archaeologists began to apply the "Pecos Classification," its limitations became evident in classifying, for example, nonpuebloan architectural remains and buffware ceramics found in Arizona's Sonoran Desert.

To rectify this problem, Gladwin and his associates at Gila Pueblo (a private archaeological research foundation located in Globe, Arizona, between 1928 and 1950; see Haury 1988) developed methods to record data consistently "with the primary purpose of merely defining the boundaries of various culture areas of the Southwest" (Gladwin and Gladwin 1934:2). The first volume in Gila Pueblo's Medallion Papers publication series issued rules for numerically recording sites on U.S. Geological Survey (USGS) topographic sheets to discourage the assigning of names to ruins and to avoid institutional hegemony (Gladwin and Gladwin 1928a). The second volume of Medallion Papers outlined procedures for securing information about surface ceramic assemblages (Gladwin and Gladwin 1928b). These procedures included random sherd collections, sherd classification by decoration category (e.g., black-on-white, black-on-red, brown-on-yellow, red-on-buff, polychrome, corrugated, indented, slipped plainware, and unslipped plainware), and selection of voucher specimens to facilitate rapid and accurate comparisons of ceramic variability (Gladwin and Gladwin 1930).

With these empirical protocols, Gladwin and his associates were now positioned to reconstruct Southwestern culture history (Gladwin 1957) by means of a hierarchical taxonomy (Gladwin and Gladwin 1934). At the most fundamental level were *roots*, such as Basketmaker or Hohokam, that represented the archaeological counterparts of linguistically distinctive "later peoples" (e.g., Keresan speakers or Piman speakers, respectively). Roots were divided into *stems*,

which corresponded to prominent geographical areas, such as the San Juan or Little Colorado basins. Within stems, various *branches* identified important culture areas, such as the Cibola, Chaco, Salado, and Mimbres branches of the Little Colorado stem. Branches were subdivided further into *phases*, which were temporal/spatial units defined by homogeneous types of architecture and ceramics. Interestingly, a temporal taxon called the *period*, albeit never mentioned as a taxonomic level, was positioned hierarchically between the branch and the phase (see Figure). Although Gladwin (1936:258) indicated that a subdivision of the phase, called a *component*, would be added to the classification system, it evidently never was. To illustrate how the system actually worked, in the figure below Tusayan Ruin (a single-story, 16-room pueblo located on the south rim of the Grand Canyon) and Wupatki Pueblo (a three-story, 102-room pueblo located 56.3 km [35 miles] northeast of Flagstaff, Arizona) are classified according to Gladwinian procedures.

Gladwinian methods for organizing survey data continue to be used for the Southwest (Wasley 1980). Although modified by Harold S. Colton (1939) to accommodate archaeological phenomena of northern Arizona, the basic

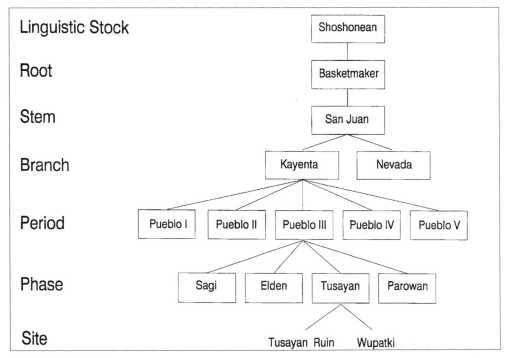

Example of a Gladwinian classification. (Drawn by A. P. Sullivan III)

structure of the (Gladwinian) system has changed little and represents a lasting conceptual contribution to Southwestern archaeology.

Alan P. Sullivan III

Further Readings

Colton, H.S. 1939. *Prehistoric Culture Units and Their Relationships in Northern Arizona.* Bulletin no. 17. Museum of Northern Arizona, Flagstaff.

Gladwin, H.S. 1936. Methodology in the Southwest. *American Antiquity* 4:256–259.

———. 1957. *A History of the Ancient Southwest.* Bond Wheelwright, Portland.

Gladwin, W., and H.S. Gladwin. 1928a. *A Method for Designation of Ruins in the Southwest.* Medallion Paper no. 1. Privately printed, Pasadena.

———. 1928b. *The Use of Potsherds in an Archaeological Survey of the Southwest.* Medallion Paper no. 2. Privately printed, Pasadena.

———. 1930. *A Method for the Designation of Southwestern Pottery Types.* Medallion Paper no. 7. Gila Pueblo, Globe.

———. 1934. *A Method for Designation of Cultures and Their Variations.* Medallion Paper no. 15. Gila Pueblo, Globe.

Haury, E.W. 1988. Gila Pueblo Archaeological Foundation: A History and Some Personal Notes. *Kiva* 54:1–77.

Kidder, A.V. 1927. Southwestern Archaeological Conference. *Science* 66:489–491.

Morris, E.H. 1921. Chronology of the San Juan Area. *Proceedings of the National Academy of Science* 7:18–22.

Wasley, W.W. 1980. Method of Site Number Designation. In *The Arizona State Museum Archaeological Site Survey System,* compiled by L.E. Vogler, pp. 9–12. Archaeological Series no. 128. Arizona State Museum, University of Arizona, Tucson.

Goforth-Saindon and Huntsville Mounds

Goforth-Saindon (3BE245) and Huntsville Mounds (3MA22), two Late Prehistoric Caddoan civic-ceremonial centers in the southwestern Ozark highland of Arkansas, have been the subject of systematic archaeological investigations since 1980. Goforth-Saindon is in the Illinois River Valley in western Benton County near the state line with Oklahoma; Huntsville is within War Eagle Creek Valley in Madison County. A third, related Arkansas site, the Collins Mound group in Washington County, has been mapped but not excavated. All three sites have superficially similar landscape associations: Each is in the center of a large alluvial valley and is positioned on an essentially flood-free terrace set off from the remainder of the valley by an active stream channel and one or more high-water channels. The overall impression is being in the bowl of an amphitheater with a commanding panorama of the uplands up and down the valley. The sites, however, differ in overall size and number and placement of mounds. Solstice alignments are apparent for mound pairs at Collins and Huntsville but not at Goforth-Saindon. At both Goforth-Saindon and Huntsville, the partial excavations of mortuary structures, or charnel houses, demonstrate a preferred orientation of their extended entryways to the winter-solstice sunset. The same orientation of similar mortuary structure entryways in eastern Oklahoma indicates a more widespread patterning to these mortuary rituals within the Caddoan area.

Calibrated radiocarbon assays for the initial charnel houses at Goforth-Saindon and Huntsville most likely date to within the 2σ cal A.D. intervals of 1152–1279 (798–671 years B.P.) for Goforth-Saindon and 1256–1304 (694–646 years B.P.) for Huntsville. These intervals are statistically different from each other and imply that initial mound construction at Goforth-Saindon was older, if only slightly. Final mound construction at either site, however, dates roughly to the fourteenth century A.D., or perhaps slightly later.

Flat-topped mound construction at the two sites was similar to that of other Caddoan mounds in the Arkansas River Basin of eastern Oklahoma. Deliberately prepared and often carefully fired mound surfaces were used as platforms. Occasionally, buildings were erected directly on these platforms. More commonly, however, a structural basin was dug into the mound, and a charnel house used to store the dead was assembled in the basin. After removal of the dead, the charnel house was carefully cleaned, its floor replastered, and its entryway blocked. It was then destroyed by fire, after which another charnel house would be built above the ruins of the first. This process would be repeated until the structural basin was nearly filled, then another basin would be dug that often intersected, or truncated, a previous structural basin. Periodically, the vertical height of a mound would be increased by the addition of another prepared mound surface. This would initiate another cycle of ritual construction and mortuary ceremonialism by these agrarian people, who were dependent on maize agriculture. The mound centers themselves do not appear to have been the primary place of residence for the supporting population. The description of similar eastern Oklahoma sites by Robert E. Bell (1984) as empty or vacant centers would seem to be especially apt when applied to Goforth-Saindon and Huntsville.

Although we are confident these sites and related ones in the Arkansas River Basin of eastern Oklahoma were built and used by Caddoan speakers, we do not know which Caddoan group was responsible, or even if the group, or groups, survived into the historic period. It does seem likely, however, that they were not the Caddo identifiable in the Red River Basin of southwestern Arkansas, northwest Louisiana, and East Texas.

Marvin Kay

Further Readings

Bell, R.E. (editor). 1984. *Prehistory of Oklahoma*. Academic Press, New York.

Kay, M., G. Sabo III, and R. Merletti. 1989. Late Prehistoric Settlement Patterning: A View From Three Caddoan Civic-Ceremonial Centers in Northwest Arkansas. In *Contributions to Spiro Archaeology: Mound Excavations and Regional Perspectives*, edited by J.D. Rogers, D.G. Wyckoff, and D.A. Peterson, pp. 129–157. Studies in Oklahoma's Past no. 16. Oklahoma Archeological Survey, Norman.

Sabo, G., III (editor). 1986. *Contributions to Ozark Prehistory*. Research Series no. 27. Arkansas Archeological Survey, Fayetteville.

Gorget

The gorget is a piece of stone, frequently made of slate, through which (usually) two holes, symmetrically oriented on the long axis, have been drilled. Although supporting evidence is weak, they are traditionally considered to have been pendants, probably for body ornamentation. Gorgets come in a wide variety of shapes, including rectangular, ovoid, semiconcave, quadriconcave, constricted center, expanded center, humped, reel shaped, and boat shaped. Although usually thin and flat, spineback, semikeeled, and some other types are relatively thick. Although gorgets occur in low quantities elsewhere, a preponderance of them has been discovered in Ohio. These have been dated to Early and Middle Woodland contexts, and, more specifically, to the Glacial Kame and Adena cultures of this region. Hopewell examples have been found in the Hopewell, Harness, and Tremper mounds. Late Prehistoric gorgets were recovered from the Spiro Mound in eastern Oklahoma. Made of shell, these gorgets typically possess two or three holes placed close together and feature intricately engraved geometric and anthropomorphic designs.

George H. Odell

Further Readings

Converse, R.N. 1978. *Ohio Slate Types*. Special Publication. Archaeological Society of Ohio, Columbus.

Hamilton, H.W. 1952. The Spiro Mound. *Missouri Archaeologist*, vol. 14.

Webb, W.S., and C.E. Snow. 1945. *The Adena People*. Publications of the Department of Anthropology and Archaeology, vol. 6. University of Kentucky, Lexington.

Goshen Complex

During the terminal phase of the Hell Gap–site excavations in 1966, the deepest cultural level encountered in Locality 1 was first thought to be Folsom and then Clovis. It was finally decided that it was neither, and it was given the name the Goshen complex after the county in Wyoming where the Hell Gap site is located. Goshen was not given further serious consideration until the discovery and investigation of the Mill Iron site in southeast Montana in the 1980s. AMS radiocarbon dates on charcoal from the Goshen complex are close to 9050 B.C. (11,000 years B.P.). Its relationship to Clovis and Folsom is unresolved. Goshen projectile points are difficult to separate typologically from Plainview on the southern Plains, which is believed to be post-Folsom in age. It has been proposed (Frison 1996) that the name Goshen be dropped in favor of Plainview. However, since these complexes do not date to the same period, it is further proposed that Goshen-Plainview be used when referring to Goshen to avoid confusion.

George C. Frison

G

Further Readings

Frison, G.C. 1991. The Goshen Paleoindian Complex: New Data for Paleoindian Research. In *Clovis Origins and Adaptations,* edited by R. Bonnichsen and K.L. Turnmire, pp. 131–151. Center for the Study of the First Americans, Oregon State University, Corvallis.

———. (editor). 1996. *The Mill Iron Site.* University of New Mexico Press, Albuquerque.

Irwin-Williams, C., H.T. Irwin, G. Agogino, and C.V. Haynes, Jr. 1973. Hell Gap: Paleo-Indian Occupation on the High Plains. *Plains Anthropologist* 18(59): 40–53.

See also HELL GAP SITE; MILL IRON SITE; PLAINVIEW COMPLEX

Gottschall Site

The Gottschall site (47IA80) is a sandstone rock shelter in the unglaciated area of southwestern Wisconsin. It contains more than 6 m (20 feet) of clearly stratified floor deposits that incorporate exceptionally well-preserved debris left by the peoples who periodically made use of the shelter in the period 1500 B.C.–A.D. 1850 (3450–100 years B.P.). The walls of the overhang are adorned with more than 40 prehistoric and historic paintings of animal and human figures in an art style that, until the paintings were discovered in 1974, was completely unknown. Specialized photography and computers were used to enhance one group of five figures that illustrates the main characters, and a portion of the plot, in the Hochungara (Winnebago) Indian legend of Red Horn. This story, which was written down by tribal elders ca. 1910, describes the exploits of a famous hero. These rock paintings (pictographs) illustrate Mississippian motifs found on engraved marine-shell cups at the Spiro site in Oklahoma. Radiocarbon analysis indicates that they date to A.D. 900–1000 (1050–950 years B.P.), a time when both Mississippian and Oneota cultures were beginning to develop. The artwork indicates, then, a widespread sharing of prehistoric ideologies. These dates also prove the persistence of at least some kinds of oral literature over a span of ca. 1,000 years.

Stratigraphic information indicates that the Red Horn group was painted during the latter stages of the manufacture and deposition of an unconsolidated special dirt made of a mixture of wood and grass ashes, burned and powdered exotic limestone, and ground clam shells. Available data indicate that these dirts began to be made and laid down after ca. A.D. 350 (1600 years B.P.) and are associated with pottery of the late Middle Woodland (Millville phase: ca A.D. 350–600, or 1600–1350 years B.P.), early Late Woodland (Effigy Mound tradition: A.D. 700–1300, or 1250–650 years B.P.), and early Oneota (McKern phase: A.D. 1000–1100, or 950–850 years B.P.) peoples. Since the Hochungara believe that their ancestors built the effigy mounds in Wisconsin, it is significant that Effigy Mound styles of pottery are present at the site. However, archaeologists have long believed that the Hochungara's predecessors were part of the Oneota culture. Since occupations by both groups are present, this debate remains unresolved. A carefully sculpted and painted sandstone head that dates to ca. A.D. 1000–1100 (950–850 years B.P.) and is stylistically similar to the Red Horn composition was also found at the site.

The Gottschall site is interpreted as a shrine, possibly an ancestral shrine, that was periodically used over a span of at least 600 years to commemorate former leaders of the prehistoric Hochungara people. The head may be a likeness of a particular ancestor. This site also documents the time when the most complex prehistoric development known for North America, the Mississippian culture, was emerging. The data imply that the Effigy Mound and/or the emerging Oneota culture, at least for a while, shared the ideology of those more southern groups.

Robert J. Salzer

Further Readings

Gartner, W.G. 1993. *The Geoarchaeology of Sediment Renewal Ceremonies at the Gottschall Rockshelter, Wisconsin.* Unpublished Master's thesis, Department of Geography, University of Wisconsin, Madison.

Radin, P. 1948. *Winnebago Hero Cycles: A Study in Aboriginal Literature.* Indiana University Publications in Anthropology and Linguistics. Waverly Press, Baltimore.

Salzer, R.J. 1987. Preliminary Report on the Gottschall Site (47Ia80). *Wisconsin Archeologist* 68(4):419–473.

Gouge

A gouge is an asymmetrically beveled ground- or chipped-stone tool that looks much like an adze. It is not always distinguished from adzes, but, when it is, the distinction is based primarily on the width of the bit. A gouge has a narrow bit that usually curves toward the flatter, beveled side; an adze has a wider, straighter bit whose beveled surface is more planar.

George H. Odell

Further Readings

Converse, R.N. 1973. *Ohio Stone Tools*. Special Publication. Archaeological Society of Ohio, Columbus.

Graham Cave

Graham Cave (23MT2) is a well-known site that is thought to document the transition from Late Paleoindian to Archaic artifact assemblages along the Plains-Eastern Woodlands interface in the 8050–5050 B.C. (10,000–7000 years B.P.) period. It is located near the top of a side ravine of the Loutre River Valley 3–4 km (several miles) north of its confluence with the Missouri River in central Missouri; the cave's more than 2.1 m (7 feet) of fill was composed of dirt, living debris, and ash lenses. Although extensive mixing had obviously occurred, the artifact assemblage retains some stratigraphic integrity, for fluted projectile points/knives were concentrated in the lower levels, Archaic materials in the middle levels, and a small sample of late Middle Woodland ceramics in the top levels. In the early historic period, the landscape was rolling prairie with scattered stands of trees concentrated along waterways.

Excavated in 0.3-m (1-foot) arbitrary levels, the lowest artifact-bearing levels (6 and 5) were associated with radiocarbon dates of 7750–6050 B.C. (9700–8000 years B.P.) and fluted Paleoindian projectile points/knives (Logan 1952). Included were one Dalton point and at least nine points with concave bases and basal grinding that W.L. Logan, the excavator, considered similar to Clovis points. In the second 0.3-m (1-foot) cut, Level 5, Late Paleoindian parallel-flaked, lanceolate (Meserve) projectile points were also present, as were Archaic stemmed and deeply corner-notched forms and other typical "eastern" Archaic artifacts. Archaic artifacts, which first appear in number in Level 5, dominate the content of more recent levels. Among these artifacts are flaked-stone drills, thumbnail and ovoid scrapers, and flake scrapers; ground-stone manos and millingstones, hammerstones, grooved axes, and nutting stones; a shell pendant; bone needles, tubes, spatulas, and ulna and split-bone awls; antler wrenches and flakers; and a perforated wolf canine tooth. A single sherd of fiber-tempered pottery was in Level 4, a clay impression of a coiled basket in Level 6, and clay impressions of twined weaving in Levels 2, 4, and 5. Large quantities of animal bones were found throughout the deposit. The species, in order of decreasing frequency, are deer, squirrel, turkey and raccoon, elk, and fox; smaller numbers of other species were present, too. Some fish bones were recovered, as were one walnut and two charred acorns.

Logan interpreted the change in content from one level to the next as evidence of a transition from a Paleoindian big-game-hunting lifeway to a more diffuse Archaic one. Other interpretations have been offered, including interaction between small bands of Archaic and Paleoindian people in a transitional ecotone between the Eastern Woodlands and Plains heartland of each tradition.

Guy Gibbon

Further Readings

Logan, W.L. 1952. *Graham Cave: An Archaic Site in Montgomery County, Missouri*. Memoir no. 2. Missouri Archaeological Society, Columbia.

Graham Tradition

The term "Graham tradition" refers to a cultural epoch on the Queen Charlotte Islands that lasted from ca. 3000 B.C. (4950 years B.P.) to historical contact in A.D. 1774. It is the most recent of the three sequential cultural "complexes" defined for the islands and spans the period when Haida culture assumed much of its complex social organization, ceremonialism, and elaborate material inventory. By definition, the tradition includes all area shell-midden sites that contain pecked- and ground-stone or bone artifacts, among other items. It coincides with the period of declining sea levels on the Queen Charlotte Islands. While a degree of continuity with earlier lithic technologies is maintained in the form of cobble and cortical-spall tools, unifacial tools, and *pièces-esquillées* (small wedge-shaped lithic tools made by bipolar battering and flaking presumably used in making pronged salmon spears), a number of attributes are credited to a mainland origin or influence. These include bifacially flaked as well as pecked- and ground-stone technologies. Noticeably absent from the assemblage is the older microblade industry of the preceding Moresby tradition.

Common to the period are small flaked adze or chisel blades, finished by pecking and grinding, that are unique to the islands. Bifacial tools, some of which are made from mainland obsidian, were thought to date relatively late in the Graham tradition, but recent evidence (Ham 1990; Fedje et al. 1996) suggests a much earlier presence of this tool type. Bone and antler tools include barbed harpoons, harpoon valves, fishhook shanks, a variety of awls and punches, needles, leister barbs (small, narrow, double-pointed barbs used in making pronged salmon spears), and rare single-piece fishhooks. Items of personal adornment complete the assemblage; these include bone combs, pendants, and beads of bone, tooth, ivory, and shell as well as labrets made of stone. The prevalence of bone and antler tools during this period must be viewed in the context of site characteristics, however. Given the buffering effect a shell midden has on the normally deleterious acidic conditions of forest soils, preservation as much as cultural practice likely accounts for tool numbers. Abraders, a tool type commonly used in the manufacturing of bone implements, do occur in earlier nonshell sites.

A number of Graham burials from Blue Jackets Creek, dating to 2900–2000 B.C. (4850–3950 years B.P.), are found to differ noticeably in cranial form and stature from historic Haida. While the prehistoric population shows a tendency to long-headedness reminiscent of the Tsimshian on the adjacent mainland, modern-day Haida show a tendency to be brachycephalic, or round-headed. The sample population, however, is neither large enough nor covers sufficient time depth to permit firm conclusions on whether we are dealing with a biological evolutionary process within a single cultural group or different populations on the islands that could, in turn, be linked to the introduction of various mainland lithic traits.

Emphasis on flaked-stone technologies, the unique form of woodworking tools, and the higher relative frequency of stone tools to bone and antler found at Prince Rupert Harbor sites tend to differentiate the Graham tradition from mainland developments. These differences appear to diminish after 1000 B.C. (2950 years B.P.)

with the appearance of artifact assemblages dominated by ground bone in late sites on the southern Queen Charlottes; these assemblages contain little or no pecked and ground stone. Parallels in bone-artifact types can also be drawn with Middle and Late period assemblages dating to ca. 3050 B.C. (5000 years B.P.) from the Central Coast region. A greatly expanded maritime subsistence base is indicated for this period, with marine resources, including a variety of pelagic species, composing the majority of the faunal assemblage. Evidence of a settlement pattern more permanent than that of the preceding period is inferred from a modest assemblage of structural features identified at Blue Jackets Creek, as well as in the appearance of shell-midden accumulations throughout the islands at this time. Massive midden deposits indicative of large settlements, however, appear relatively late. Small, sedentary village aggregates may, in fact, have typified the settlement pattern prior to historical contact.

The Graham tradition owes its origins as a concept to work conducted at four Graham Island sites, the most important being Blue Jackets Creek on Masset Inlet. Uncertainty concerning the representativeness of components from these few sites for the islands was one early acknowledged weakness of the concept. One manifestation of this problem is the ongoing debate in the literature since the late 1980s on the nature of the relationship between this tradition and that known as the Transitional complex (Fladmark 1989; Fladmark 1990). In addition to sharing a number of lithic traits, the two concepts overlap chronologically. The Transitional complex, with its emphasis on a bipolar-core-reduction industry, was first conceived as the immediate predecessor of the Graham tradition. Since the 1980s, the complex has been treated as either a contemporaneous cultural form distinct from the Graham tradition or, alternatively, as evidence of special-use sites or activities associated with the Graham tradition.

The Graham tradition remains a broad concept. Causal explanations for the appearance of shell middens, along with accelerated growth in the number of sites and material inventory, have been fundamentally ecological and stress the greater resource availability and/or extraction capabilities on the part of the island's inhabitants during this period. The basis for these developments remains vague, however, because of the general lack of detailed data needed to decipher Graham-tradition settlement and subsistence behavior.

Steven Acheson

Further Readings

Fedje, D.W., A.P. Mackie, J.B. McSporran, and B. Wilson. 1996. Early Period Archaeology in Gwaii Haanas: Results of the 1993 Field Program. In *Early Human Occupation in British Columbia*, edited by R.L. Carlson and L. Dalla Bona, pp. 133–150. University of British Columbia Press, Vancouver.

Fladmark, K. 1989. The Nature Culture History of the Queen Charlotte Islands. In *The Outer Shores, Proceedings of the Queen Charlotte Islands First International Scientific Symposium, University of British Columbia*, edited by G.G.E. Scudder and N. Gessler, pp. 199–221. Queen Charlotte Islands Museum, Skidegate.

Fladmark, K.R., K.M. Ames, and P.D. Sutherlands. 1990. Prehistory of the Northern Coast of British Columbia. In *Northwest Coast*, edited by W. Suttles, pp. 229–239. Handbook of North American Indians, vol. 7, W.C. Sturtevant, general editor. Smithsonian Institution, Washington, D.C.

Ham, L.C. 1990. The Cohoe Creek Site: A Late Moresby Tradition Shell Midden. *Canadian Journal of Archaeology* 14:199–221.

Severs, P. 1974a. Archaeological Investigations at Blue Jackets Creek FlUa 4, Queen Charlotte Islands, British Columbia, 1974. *Canadian Archaeological Association Bulletin* 6:163–205.

———. 1974b. A View of Island Prehistory: Archaeological Investigations at Blue Jackets Creek, 1972–73. *The Charlottes: A Journal of the Queen Charlotte Islands* 3:2–12.

See also TRANSITIONAL COMPLEX

Gran Quivira

Gran Quivira (LA 120) is a large pueblo site in central New Mexico whose occupation spanned the prehistoric through early historic periods. It sits on an arm of Chupadero Mesa, east of the Rio Grande and the Manzanos Mountains, on the western border of the Plains. Gran Quivira is one of the large pueblos in the Salinas province. The Salinas pueblos are named for the saline lakes in the Estancia Basin, which provided salt used in exchange both historically and, no doubt, prehistorically.

The earliest occupation at the site dates to the fourteenth century A.D. and is represented by a large circular pueblo (Hayes 1981b). Circular-pueblo construction is rare in the Rio Grande area, the best-known example being Tyuonyi at Bandelier National Monument well north of the Salinas province. After a hiatus of unknown duration in the fifteenth century (Spielmann 1993), the site was reoccupied and grew to at least 20 roomblocks in size.

In the sixteenth century, early Spanish explorers rarely visited the site, given its distance from the Rio Grande, the heart of the eastern pueblo world in the 1500s. Gran Quivira is mentioned in some early documents, however, as a Tompiro-speaking pueblo, whose language was very similar to Piro, the language of pueblos on the Rio Grande in the Socorro area of New Mexico. Mention is also made of trade with Plains bison hunters. In fact, the pueblo is often referred to in these documents as the pueblo of the "Xumanos." The Jumanos were nomadic bison hunters who occupied the Texas Plains in the Protohistoric period (ca. A.D. 1450–1600, or 500–350 years B.P.). Two explanations have been proposed for the "Xumanos" designation for Gran Quivira: Either a portion of the population at Gran Quivira was composed of Jumanos people (Scholes and Mera 1940; Vivian 1964), or the designation reflects their importance as trade partners (Hayes 1981b). Prehistoric Plains artifacts found at Gran Quivira, such as bison bone and beveled knives made of Alibates dolomite, attest to the prehistoric antecedents of the historically documented Plains trade (Hayes 1981b; Spielmann 1993).

Gran Quivira was missionized in 1629 by Fray Francisco Letrado, who oversaw the construction of the small church of San Isidro. Letrado left shortly thereafter, and Gran Quivira was not assigned another friar until the late 1650s, when Fray Diego de Santander arrived and began the construction of a large church, San Buenaventura, and monastery complex. The pueblo was abandoned in 1672, as a result of a devastating combination of drought, epidemic disease, and Apache raids that caused Gran Quivirans to flee to the pueblos of Abo and Quarai farther to the west. The entire Salinas province was abandoned by the late 1670s, and the population moved west to the Rio Grande.

The site became a National Monument in 1909. Excavations at Gran Quivira began in the 1920s under the direction of Edgar Hewett, who focused primarily on the San Buenaventura mission. Hewett also tested a number of roomblocks. No report on these excavations is available. Little further work was conducted at the site until the National Park Service undertook excavations in 1951 under the direction of Gordon Vivian. A portion of the rectangular roomblocks (Mound 10), a kiva, and San Isidro were excavated (Vivian 1964). This work was followed in the late 1960s by a three-year excavation of the largest roomblock at the site, Mound 7 (Hayes 1981a and 1981b). In the mid-1980s, Katherine A. Spielmann directed three seasons of excavation in the middens on the south side of the pueblo (Spielmann 1993). Her work focuses on Plains trade, diet, and economic change at the pueblo.

In 1980, Gran Quivira was incorporated into Salinas Pueblo Missions National Monument, which includes the three Salinas pueblos that contain large, well-preserved, seventeenth-century Spanish missions: Quarai, Abo, and Gran Quivira (Ivey 1988).

Katherine Spielmann

Further Readings

Hayes, A.C. 1981a. *Contributions to Gran Quivira Archeology*. Publications in Archaeology no. 17. National Park Service, Washington, D.C.

———. 1981b. *Excavation of Mound 7*. Publications in Archaeology no. 16. National Park Service, Washington, D.C.

Ivey, J.E. 1988. *In the Midst of Loneliness: The Architectural History of the Salinas Missions*. Professional Papers no. 15. Southwestern Cultural Resources Center, Santa Fe.

Scholes, F.V., and H.P. Mera. 1940. *Some Aspects of the Jumano Problem*. Contributions to American Anthropology and History, vol. 6, no. 34. Carnegie Institution of Washington, Washington, D.C.

Spielmann, K.A. 1993. *Subsistence and Exchange at Gran Quivira Pueblo, New Mexico*. Ms. on file, National Park Service, Southwestern Regional Office, Santa Fe.

Vivian, G. 1964. *Excavations in a Seventeenth Century Jumano Pueblo, Gran Quivira*. Publications in Archaeology no. 8. National Park Service, Washington, D.C.

Grand Detour Phase

The Grand Detour phase, a rather loosely defined Middle Missouri–tradition, Initial variant phase, is based on three village sites on the Missouri River in central South Dakota in what is popularly known as the "Big Bend" or "Grand Detour" area. The Pretty Head, Jiggs Thompson, and Langdeau sites date ca. A.D. 1100–1200 (850–750 years B.P.). The latter site was not fortified, but the others were defended by a shallow ditch that isolated a spur of the terrace on which they were built. There is some variation in the long rectangular pithouses of the phases, and there was no consistent placement of the houses. Each dwelling had a central ridgepole and an entry that faced southwest. Maize, beans, and squash were the major crops. They were supplemented by gathering and by the hunting of bison and other game. Globular jars with outflaring or recurved (S-shaped) rims had cord-roughened bodies and limited, if sometimes complex, embellishments on the vessel lip. Triangular arrow points, end scrapers, drills, and a wide variety of bifaces constitute the chipped-stone industry, and grooved mauls and celts dominate the ground-stone tools. Scapula hoes and a wide variety of other bone tools were augmented by a number of esoteric items of conch and other shell derived from the Gulf Coast. These southern Extended Middle Missouri–tradition sites are most closely related to sites of the Anderson phase that are farther north and west along the Missouri River.

W. Raymond Wood

Further Readings

Caldwell, W.W., and R.E. Jensen. 1969. *The Grand Detour Phase*. Publications in Salvage Archaeology no. 13. River Basin Surveys. Smithsonian Institution, Washington, D.C.

See also ANDERSON PHASE; MIDDLE MISSOURI TRADITION

Grandmother's Lodge

Grandmother's Lodge (32ME59) is a small Middle Missouri Extended-variant site in Mercer County, North Dakota. It is represented by a single, excavated, long rectangular house near the mouth of the Little Missouri River. The locale was revered by the Mandan, Hidatsa, and Crow Indians, because it was said to be the home of "Grandmother," or the "Old Woman who never dies," a supernatural being in the mythology of these tribes that ensured the fertility of crops. The artifacts found at Grandmother's Lodge, though of typical Extended-variant forms, were not sufficiently distinctive to assign the site to a named subunit of the variant. Grandmother's Lodge is further enigmatic in being ca. 112.6 km (70 river miles) upstream from any other Extended-variant site or village. It has not been dated.

W. Raymond Wood

Further Readings
Woolworth, A.R. 1956. Archeological Investigations at Site 32ME59 (Grandmother's Lodge). *North Dakota History* 23(2): 79–102.

Grasshopper Pueblo

Grasshopper is a 500-room, Mogollon pueblo ruin on the White Mountain Apache Reservation in the mountains of east-central Arizona. It was the location of the University of Arizona archaeological field school between 1963 and 1992. Grasshopper may be assigned to the Canyon Creek phase of the Forestdale branch of the Mogollon culture.

A small population during the Great Drought (A.D. 1276–1299, or 674–651 years B.P.) grew exponentially from A.D. 1300 to 1330 (650–620 years B.P.), a time of high rainfall, through the aggregation of local inhabitants and immigration from as far as the Colorado Plateau. The Grasshopper locality was well suited for habitation because of a spring, abundant wood for fuel and construction, ample building stone, and proximity to the largest expanse of agricultural land in the region. Diet was initially a continuation of the long-term hunting (mule deer, turkey, rabbit, squirrel), gathering (piñon, acorn, walnut, agave, cactus), and gardening (maize, beans, squash) strategy characteristic of the mountain Mogollon. Because of population increase, it shifted rapidly in the early 1300s to a total reliance on maize agriculture. Domesticated animals included dogs and, perhaps, turkeys.

Community organization began with households that varied in the occupation and use of domestic space. Groups of related households shared ceremonial rooms and kivas; a roofed, rectangular great kiva incorporated into a roomblock served the entire community. Four male societies are identified by stylized ornaments—shell pendants, conus shell tinklers, bone hairpins, and arrows—worn as part of ceremonial attire. A Mogollon man, 40–45 years old, was head of the arrow and bone-hairpin societies, from which post he provided community leadership. At least two ethnic groups, Mogollon and Anasazi, lived together in apparent harmony.

Ceramic assemblages are marked by variability. Decorated pottery includes five distinct wares: White Mountain Red Ware (St. Johns, Pinedale, Cedar Creek, Four Mile), Roosevelt Red Ware (Pinto, Pinto-Gila, Gila, Tonto), Grasshopper Ware, Cibola White Ware (Pinedale), and painted corrugated ware (Cibicue). Decorated ceramics occurring in trace frequencies include Kinishba Polychrome, Jeddito Black-on-yellow, and Zuni-area ceramics. Undecorated pottery is dominated by brown obliterated corrugated with red-slipped (Salado Red) and brown plain in lesser quantities. White Mountain Red Ware predominated in public-use contexts, Roosevelt Red Ware and painted corrugated in mortuary contexts, and Grasshopper Ware in domestic contexts.

The Grasshopper-pueblo database includes several thousand whole vessels, several million sherd and lithic artifacts, 696 individuals (before removal of human remains ceased in 1979), 167 dated tree-ring specimens, and 106 excavated pueblo rooms. Plaza 1 (15 percent), Plaza 2 (45 percent), and the Plaza 3 great kiva (100 percent) were excavated, and numerous trenches in extramural areas were mechanically excavated.

Abandonment of the pueblo was gradual and may have begun as early as A.D. 1325 (625 years B.P.) with movement to satellite communities during a time of reduced rainfall that lasted until A.D. 1355 (595 years B.P.). The large population of the fourteenth century was unable to adjust to the marginal, unstable environmental conditions the Grasshopper region posed for people newly dependent on maize agriculture. A final, noncutting, tree-ring date of A.D. 1373 (577 years B.P.) accords with an estimated abandonment of the pueblo and region by A.D. 1400 (550 years B.P.)

J. Jefferson Reid

Further Readings
Longacre, W.A., S.J. Holbrook, and M.W. Graves. 1982. *Multidisciplinary Research at Grasshopper Pueblo, Arizona.* Anthropological Papers no. 40. Univer-

sity of Arizona Press, Tucson.

Reid, J.J. 1989. A Grasshopper Perspective on the Mogollon of the Arizona Mountains. In *Dynamics of Southwest Prehistory,* edited by L.S. Cordell and G.J. Gumerman, pp. 65–97. Smithsonian Institution Press, Washington, D.C.

See also FORESTDALE BRANCH; MOGOLLON CULTURE AREA

Graver

With minor exceptions, the graver was a more prominent constituent of Paleoindian toolkits than of the toolkits of later periods. Paleoindian assemblages throughout the continent normally contain some gravers, though they never dominate the collections. In the Southwest (Judge 1973:116) and Great Plains (Irwin and Wormington 1970), the apogee of this type occurred in the Folsom complex, approaching 10 percent or more of total modified tools. In most cases, the graver consists of a simple flake, the side or end of which has been chipped to a fine point. Often, the graver spur was combined with other typological attributes, such as a notch or a scraper bit. As a result, its characteristic projection is frequently masked by these traits, and the graver is subsumed within other tool types. Considered together, these attributes can be very distinctive. For example, the occurrence of "spurred end scrapers" on Pleistocene terraces but not on Holocene ones in Kansas provides strong evidence that this typological combination constitutes a diagnostic Paleoindian tool type. Graver function has engendered considerable debate, as the projection itself is often delicate and cannot withstand much pressure. Experiments by R.W. Nero (1957) and M.J. Lynott (1975) suggest that a graver is easily destroyed when employed for heavy incising of bone, shell, or wood, although it could be used for precision work and when beginning a groove on these materials. It could also have been used for piercing, tattooing, and other lighter tasks.

George H. Odell

Further Readings

Irwin, H.T., and H.M. Wormington. 1970. Paleo-Indian Tool Types in the Great Plains. *American Antiquity* 35:24–34.

Judge, W.J. 1973. *Paleoindian Occupation of the Central Rio Grande Valley in New Mexico.* University of New Mexico Press, Albuquerque.

Lynott, M.J. 1975. Explanation of Microwear Patterns on Gravers. *Plains Anthropologist* 20:121–128.

Nero, R.W. 1957. A "Graver" Site in Wisconsin. *American Antiquity* 22:300–304.

Rogers, R.A. 1986. Spurred End Scrapers As Diagnostic Paleoindian Artifacts: A Distributional Analysis on Stream Terraces. *American Antiquity* 51:338–341.

Great Basin, The

The Great Basin is a region encompassing more than 300,000 km^2 (115,800 square miles) between the Sierra Nevada of California and the Wasatch Range of Utah. It was named by John C. Frémont after his 1843–1844 U.S. government survey expedition. Frémont recognized that drainages there do not flow to the ocean but end in closed valleys. This hydrographic Great Basin occupies much of Nevada and western Utah and portions of southeastern Oregon, northeastern California, and southern Idaho. It should be distinguished from two other common usages of the term that rely on floristic and cultural criteria. The Great Basin Desert excludes the Mojave Desert of the southwestern hydrographic Great Basin. It incorporates regions where sagebrush steppe or saltbush scrub are dominant, such as the Snake River plains of Idaho and parts of the Colorado Plateau. The Great Basin culture area encompasses the ethnohistoric range of Numic-speaking peoples. It includes even more of the Colorado Plateau, parts of Wyoming, much of southern Idaho, and part of the Lower Colorado River Valley. Unfortunately, many references do not specify whether the "Great Basin" under consideration is hydrographically, floristically, or culturally defined. Readers need to exercise caution in this regard. This discussion focuses on the hydrographic Great Basin.

The lowest elevation in North America is in the southwestern Great Basin, where Death Valley lies below sea level. The Lahontan and Bonneville sinks, on the western and eastern margins of the Great Basin, respectively, also represent relatively low terrain with valley bottoms that seldom exceed 1,200 m (3,937 feet) in elevation. In the central Great Basin, however, regional uplift has resulted in valleys that are 1,600–1,800 m (5,249–5,905 feet) high, and surrounding mountains that exceed 3,000 m

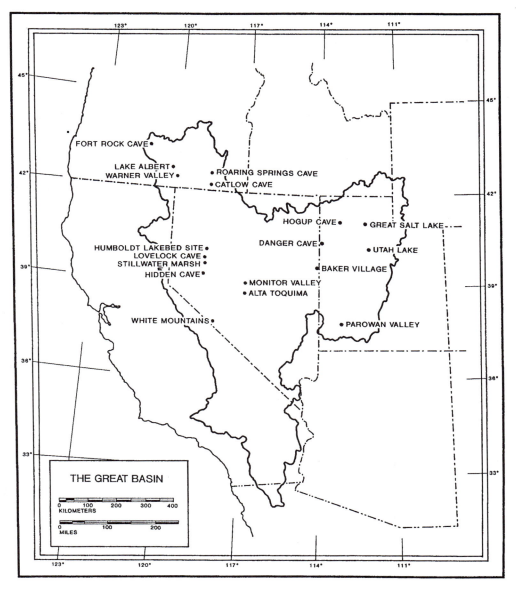

Great Basin sites. (Drawn by W. G. Spaulding)

(9,840 feet). More than 100 isolated mountain ranges lie within the Great Basin. Most are oriented north-south. Many support woodland or forest vegetation. These are separated by broad, arid-to-semiarid valleys supporting sagebrush steppe, saltbush scrub, or, in the far southwest of the region in the Mojave Desert, creosotebush scrub.

Since the late nineteenth century, geologists have recognized that many closed valleys in the Great Basin supported freshwater or "pluvial"

lakes during the last Ice Age. The largest were truly vast: Pluvial Lake Lahontan of western Nevada and adjacent California covered more than 22,000 km² (8,490 square miles). The Great Salt Lake in Utah is but a small, postglacial remnant of Lake Bonneville. In the Mojave Desert to the southwest, greatly enhanced runoff from the central Sierra Nevada and the San Bernadino Mountains formed a chain of lakes connected by the now dry Owens and Mojave rivers that, ultimately, flowed into Death Valley's pluvial Lake

Manly. Ancient shorelines carved by wave action high on valley flanks can still be seen in many areas. Barren salt pans attest to the dissolved mineral load that these water bodies once contained. However, many valleys in the southern Great Basin were either dry or supported only marshes. The flanks of these valleys lack the ancient shorelines commonly found in the central and northern parts of the region.

The chronology and nature of the climate changes responsible for the development and desiccation of pluvial lakes have long been subjects of study. The interrelationship of high shorelines of Lake Bonneville and glacial outwash debris from the Wasatch Range led the pioneering nineteenth-century geologist G.K. Gilbert to conclude that pluvial climates were largely synchronous with glacial ages. In the early twentieth century, Ernest Antevs suggested that the movement of massive continental ice sheets in the north caused a southward shift in the winter storm track; this shift enhanced precipitation in the Great Basin. Unfortunately, the equation of pluvial climates with glaciations has been uncritically extended to other deserts in more southerly latitudes, where past episodes of

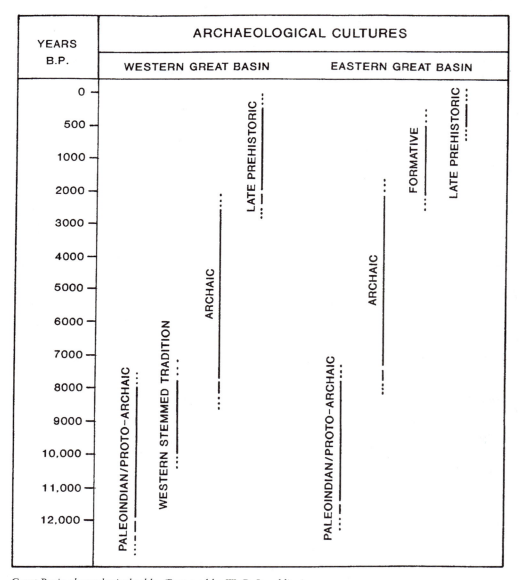

Great Basin chronological table. (Prepared by W. G. Spaulding)

increased rainfall were associated with *warmer* climates and enhanced monsoons. Subsequent research in the Great Basin identified the importance of cloudy weather and low temperatures in reducing evaporation rates during pluvial climatic episodes. However, debate still exists regarding the nature of the Ice Age climate in the Great Basin. Two different models best summarize this debate. The "equable glaciopluvial" model holds that winters were not much cooler but summers considerably colder than present, and that mean annual precipitation was nearly double today's amounts. The "cold, dry" model holds that winter temperatures were severe, and that precipitation was not more than 50 percent above the modern mean. In the latter model, low temperatures are a key to reducing evaporation, which allowed the pluvial lakes to fill.

In the central Great Basin, pluvial Lakes Lahontan and Bonneville reached their maximum high stands ca. 13,050–12,050 B.C. (15,000–14,000 years B.P.). By 10,050 B.C. (12,000 years B.P.), pluvial lakes throughout the Great Basin had shrunk to small remnants, although they still represented extensive lake systems. Episodic high stands occurred during the Paleoindian period at most lakes, but most were dry by 5550 B.C. (7500 years B.P.). Paleoecological data indicate that this period was typified by increasing aridity, albeit with some reversals and, perhaps, with enhanced summer rainfall in the southeastern Great Basin. The next 2,000 years were typified by temperatures exceeding current annual averages and by enhanced aridity in the valleys. Relaxation of aridity began ca. 3550–2550 B.C. (5500–4500 years B.P.). Evidence for the subsequent filling of dry basins is found throughout the Great Basin. The dates of these events, which cluster in the period ca. 1650–50 B.C. (3600–2000 years B.P.), correlate with the neoglaciation of the Sierra Nevada and Rocky Mountains. A return to aridity was followed by a final period of enhanced precipitation and higher lake levels, which occurred during the Little Ice Age (ca. A.D. 1350–1850, or 600–100 years B.P.). Although colder temperatures and increased rainfall typified these late postglacial "minipluvials," the consequent lakes were quite small relative to their glacial-age antecedents.

W. Geoffrey Spaulding

Further Readings

Benson, L.V., D.R. Curry, R.I. Dorn, K.R. Lajoie, C.G. Oviatt, S.W. Robinson, G.I. Smith, and S. Stine. 1990. Chronology of Expansion and Contraction of Four Great Basin Lake Systems During the Past 35,000 Years. *Palaeogeography, Palaeoclimatology, Palaeoecology* 78:241–286.

COHMAP Project Members. 1988. Climatic Changes of the Last 18,000 Years: Observations and Model Simulations. *Science* 241:1043–1052.

Cronquist, A., A.H. Holmgren, N.H. Holmgren, and J.L. Reveal. 1972. *Intermountain Flora: Vascular Plants of the Intermountain West, U.S.A.,* vol. 1. Hafner, New York.

D'Azevedo, W.L. (editor). 1986. *Great Basin.* Handbook of North American Indians, vol. 11, W.C. Sturtevant, general editor. Smithsonian Institution, Washington, D.C.

Mifflin, M.D., and M.M. Wheat. 1979. *Pluvial Lakes and Estimated Pluvial Climates of Nevada.* Bulletin no. 94. Nevada Bureau of Mines and Geology, Carson City.

Morrison, R.B. 1965. Quaternary Geology of the Great Basin. In *The Quaternary of the United States,* edited by H.E. Wright, Jr., and D.G. Frey, pp. 265–286. Princeton University Press, Princeton.

Shreve, F. 1942. The Desert Vegetation of North America. *Botanical Review* 8:195–246.

Smith, G.I., and F.A. Street-Perrott. 1983. Pluvial Lakes of the Western United States. In *The Late Pleistocene,* edited by S.C. Porter, pp. 190–214. University of Minnesota Press, Minneapolis.

Spaulding, W.G. 1990. Vegetational and Climatic Development of the Mojave Desert: The Last Glacial Maximum to the Present. In *Packrat Middens: The Last 40,000 Years of Biotic Change,* edited by J.L. Betancourt, P.S. Martin, and T.R. Van Devender, pp. 166–199. University of Arizona Press, Tucson.

Thompson, R.S. 1990. Late Quaternary Vegetation and Climate in the Great Basin. In *Packrat Middens: The Last 40,000 Years of Biotic Change,* edited by J.L. Betancourt, P.S. Martin, and T.R. Van Devender, pp. 200–239. University of Arizona Press, Tucson.

Van Devender, T.R., R.S. Thompson, and J.L. Betancourt. 1987. Vegetation History of the Deserts of Southwestern

North America: The Nature and Timing of the Late Wisconsin-Holocene Transition. In *North America and Adjacent Oceans During the Last Deglaciation,* edited by W.F. Ruddiman and H.E. Wright, Jr., pp. 323–352. Geological Society of America, Boulder.

Great Basin Archaic

The term "Archaic" denotes the general hunter-gatherer lifeway in North America; "Western Archaic" encompasses the settlement and subsistence strategies employed by hunter-gatherer groups in the Great Basin (Aikens 1983; Jennings 1989). The Archaic is best conceptualized as a flexible and resilient socioeconomic adaptive strategy in which a broad spectrum of wild plant and animal resources available in a regional mosaic of microenvironments is efficiently extracted and used by people who are knowledgeable in the distribution and seasonality of these resources. This adaptive strategy was flexible, since the particular environments and resources exploited varied regionally and the technologies, extractive techniques, and residential patterns used by the people likewise varied as needed (Jennings 1986, 1989). It continued to be an effective adaptation, too, as climate changed through time and populations changed in size. The "Archaic period" is the time period when this strategy was employed.

In the demanding environment of the Great Basin, resources are often dispersed, their occurrence is usually seasonal, and their abundance is not reliably predictable (Aikens 1983; Grayson 1993). To utilize the available resource base effectively, people exploited a wide variety of potential foods, made the best use of available resources, and took advantage of occasional abundances. Distinctive regional expressions of this general strategy developed and evolved through the Archaic period (Lyneis 1982; Thomas 1982; Aikens and Madsen 1986; Elston 1986). Groups developed locally specific socioeconomic adaptations and cultural traditions to exploit the spectrum of available resources. In general, people employed a tethered settlement/subsistence system in which they wintered together in lowland villages and then dispersed into family groups to procure seasonal resources as they became available. Where resources were sparse and scattered, residential groups tended to be small and fluctuated in composition, residential mobility was high,

reoccupation of residential sites was irregular, and, while a set pattern of seasonal movement to exploit particular resources was followed, the routes varied from year to year. Where resources were more plentiful or predictable, groups were larger in size, residential sites were occupied longer and reused annually, and seasonal patterns of movement were more regular (Elston 1982; Oetting 1994).

Archaic strategies were being employed in parts of the Great Basin by 7050 B.C. (9000 years B.P.). They continued to be used in much of the region by the Shoshone, Paiute, and other Great Basin peoples into the nineteenth century. This long time frame is usually divided into three or four periods, the Paleo-Archaic, Early Archaic, Middle Archaic, and Late Archaic (Jennings 1986; Oetting 1994). Each roughly corresponds to general Holocene climatic episodes. The timing and duration of these periods varied somewhat from one region to another in the Great Basin.

The Initial or Paleo-Archaic (ca. 9050–5050 B.C., or 11,000–7000 years B.P.) represents early cultural adaptations to the changing early Holocene environment and its cool moist Anathermal climate. Some researchers view this period as pre-Archaic, a period when specialized hunting or lake-marsh economies dominated, and few other resources were exploited (Jennings 1986). Others view it as a time when groups were beginning to diversify and use new resources (Willig and Aikens 1988). Although many sites are located in lakeside settings, they are also found in many other lowland and upland environments. Plant-processing implements are present but infrequent. Hunting remained the primary economic focus, and many types of animals were procured. Population sizes were low, and groups were probably mobile.

The Early Archaic (ca. 5050–2050 B.C., or 7000–4000 years B.P.) witnessed the warmest and driest climatic conditions of the Holocene. This climatic episode is referred to as the Altithermal. Population densities were low. Since preferred foods were less plentiful, an increasing range of foods had to be exploited. Long-term winter camps were located in lowland, watered areas; smaller sites occurred in a wide array of microenvironments. Large numbers of ground-stone tools indicate that plant processing was much more common, though hunting was still a major economic pursuit.

The Middle Archaic (ca. 2050–50 B.C., or 4000–2000 years B.P.) reflects human responses to the ameliorating Medithermal climate of the later Holocene. This climatic episode began with a distinctly moister climatic interval (the neoglacial) and then shifted toward the current climatic regime. The tempo of human activity increased markedly throughout the Great Basin as population densities rose and resource use increased. More types of resources were used, and plant processing became increasingly important. However, in some areas, fewer microenvironments were being used, for a greater abundance and variety of resources were now available in particular ecozones because of the improved climate. Distinct regional socioeconomic adaptations developed as local groups focused on using the resource base available in their immediate areas, especially those in riverine and lake-marsh areas. While groups in arid, resource-poor areas continued to be relatively small and mobile, those in better subsistence settings became larger in size, resided longer in regularly reoccupied villages, and made shorter, more predictable seasonal moves. These people resided in substantial semisubterranean houses. Their artifact forms were more elaborate and diverse, and trade was more evident.

In the Late Archaic (ca. 50 B.C.–historic period, or 2000–150 years B.P.), the modern climate developed through a mild drying trend punctuated by short, moister intervals. The beginning of this period was marked by the introduction of small narrow-necked projectile points that indicate the presence of a bow-and-arrow technology. Pottery appeared during this period. Although the general environment and available resources stayed about the same as in Middle Archaic times, the diversity of resources used increased, the use of particular resources intensified, and more ecozones were exploited. These trends suggest higher population densities and increasing population stress. Exploitation of key resources, such as piñon pine nuts, grass/Chenopod seeds, and wetlands plants and animals, intensified. In some riverine and lake-marsh areas, this intensification enabled stable village settlements to continue. Elsewhere, settlements became more dispersed, and residential occupations were shorter. Mobility increased as groups sought resources from more ecozones, and high-altitude environments were used much more. In the eastern Great Basin, Late Archaic broad-spectrum subsistence was replaced or supplemented ca. A.D. 350–1300 (1600–650 years B.P.) by the Formative maize horticulture of the Fremont cultures (Aikens and Madsen 1986). The Late Archaic is also thought to be marked by the appearance of Numic-speaking groups ancestral to the modern native groups in the region (Elston 1986). Linguistic evidence suggests that they spread rapidly, but this has not been verified in the archaeological record.

Albert C. Oetting

Further Readings

Aikens, C.M. 1983. The Far West. In *Ancient North Americans,* edited by J.D. Jennings, pp. 149–201. W.H. Freeman, San Francisco.

Aikens, C.M., and D.B. Madsen. 1986. Prehistory of the Eastern Area. In *Great Basin,* edited by W.L. D'Azevedo, pp. 149–160. Handbook of North American Indians, vol. 11, W.C. Sturtevant, general editor. Smithsonian Institution, Washington, D.C.

Elston, R.G. 1982. Good Times, Hard Times: Prehistoric Culture Change in the Western Great Basin. In *Man and Environment in the Great Basin,* edited by D.B. Madsen and J.F. O'Connell, pp. 186–206. SAA Papers no. 2. Society for American Archaeology, Washington, D.C.

———. 1986. Prehistory of the Western Area. In *Great Basin,* edited by W.L. D'Azevedo, pp. 135–148. Handbook of North American Indians, vol. 11, W.C. Sturtevant, general editor. Smithsonian Institution, Washington, D.C.

Grayson, D.K. 1993. *The Desert's Past: A Natural Prehistory of the Great Basin.* Smithsonian Institution Press, Washington, D.C.

Jennings, J.D. 1986. Prehistory: Introduction. In *Great Basin,* edited by W.L. D'Azevedo, pp. 113–119. Handbook of North American Indians, vol. 11, W.C. Sturtevant, general editor. Smithsonian Institution, Washington, D.C.

———. 1989. *Prehistory of North America.* Mayfield, Mountain View.

Lyneis, M.M. 1982. Prehistory in the Southern Great Basin. In *Man and Environment in the Great Basin,* edited by D.B. Madsen and J.F. O'Connell, pp. 172–185. SAA Papers no. 2. Society for American Archaeology, Washington, D.C.

Oetting, A.C. 1994. Chronology and Time Markers in the Northwestern Great Basin: The Chewaucan Basin Cultural

G

Chronology. In *Archaeological Researches in the Northern Great Basin: Fort Rock Archaeology Since Cressman,* edited by C.M. Aikens and D.L. Jenkins, pp. 41–62. Anthropological Papers no. 50. Department of Anthropology and State Museum of Anthropology, University of Oregon, Eugene.

Thomas, D.H. 1982. An Overview of Central Great Basin Prehistory. In *Man and Environment in the Great Basin,* edited by D.B. Madsen and J.F. O'Connell, pp. 156–171. SAA Papers no. 2. Society for American Archaeology, Washington, D.C.

Willig, J.A., and C.M. Aikens. 1988. The Clovis-Archaic Interface in Far Western North America. In *Early Human Occupation in Far Western North America: The Clovis-Archaic Interface,* edited by J.A. Willig, C.M.Aikens, and J.L. Fagan, pp. 1–40. Anthropological Papers no. 21. Nevada State Museum, Carson City.

Great Basin High-Altitude Adaptations

Research in high-altitude adaptations in the Great Basin is concerned with lifeways in Alpine Tundra communities above the upper limit of tree growth (the tree line), which occurs at ca. 3,048–3,352 m (10,000–11,000 feet). Adaptations in such areas are intrinsically interesting because high-altitude environments provide very limited kinds of resources, are difficult of access, and are physically challenging to live and work in. Relative to those at lower elevations, alpine environments are more seasonal and more productive of game than plant resources. Because these attributes are heavily influenced by temperature and rainfall, which vary with geographical location, the definition of "high altitude" varies somewhat within the Great Basin. Some "high-altitude" research in the eastern Great Basin deals with localities below 3,048 m (10,000 feet).

The ethnographic record consistently portrays Great Basin peoples using the Alpine Tundra sparingly and for relatively short periods. Mountain sheep (*Ovis canadensis* spp.) migrating there for summer rangeland were the principal attraction. Hunters working singly or in small parties traveled into the highlands for daily forays or longer bouts involving two- or three-day camps. Sheep were ambushed near watering spots or driven to hunters waiting in blinds built in the rocky talus slopes their prey favored as escape terrain. Larger communal hunts, occasionally in conjunction with pole-and-brush corrals or V-shaped wing traps, are also reported. Secondary alpine resources included roots, berries, fish, and eagles (for feathers and other valued body parts), the first three being especially important in the eastern and northern Great Basin.

Alpine archaeology has been seriously pursued only in the 1990s, prior to which attention was concentrated on the excavation of rich, lowland-cave and open sites. Limited early work suggested a pattern of short-term occupation centered on hunting similar to that indicated in ethnographic accounts. A small number of probabilistic regional surveys conducted in the 1970s encompassed limited alpine tracts that also produced sparse remains consistent with the picture of limited use indicated in ethnographic accounts. Interpretations of prehistoric alpine adaptation changed dramatically between 1978 and 1983, as the result of archaeological surveys in the Toquima Range of central Nevada and the White Mountains of eastern California, which located a series of villages at elevations between 3,050 and 3,850 m (3,335–4,210 yards), far higher than had previously been reported anywhere in North America.

The White Mountain and Toquima Range alpine villages vary in size and quantity of cultural materials represented. Nonetheless, they invariably contain the remains of at least one family-sized dwelling and display a diverse array of chipped- and ground-stone tools that document village use as seasonal base camps for plant and animal procurement. Alta Toquima, one of the two villages located on Mount Jefferson in the Toquima Range, is the largest-known example of its kind and contains at least 31 rock structures, most of which are houses. The 12 White Mountain villages that have been excavated are all smaller than Alta Toquima, most likely because the White Mountain Alpine Tundra is much larger and contains many more suitable camp locations than the Toquima Range Alpine Tundra.

The cultural deposits contained within alpine village houses are frequently rich: A single house at Alta Toquima produced 135 typeable projectile points, and one from the White Mountains produced in excess of 600. Faunal assemblages recovered are dominated by highly fragmented skeletal elements of mountain sheep

(*Ovis canadensis*) and marmots (*Marmota flaviventris*), indicating that these animals were the favored targets of hunters. Charred plant remains, abundant milling equipment, and crude cobble pulping tools indicate that roots, seeds, and two kinds of pine nuts (*Pinus flexilis* and *P. monophylla*) were important. The piñon pine (*P. monophylla*) is not an alpine tree, and the abundance of macrofossils attributed to that species in the White Mountain alpine villages indicates partial reliance on resources obtained and cached previously at lower elevations. The other resources indicate village occupation in the months between June and September. Tools and waste related to activities other than food procurement, including tool manufacture and repair, suggest fairly lengthy occupations within this interval, anywhere from six weeks to three months.

The interpretation that has emerged from extensive study of the White Mountain and Toquima Range villages has individual nuclear or extended families or groups of families moving from lower elevations in nearby valleys to gather and hunt alpine plants and animals during the warmest three months of the year. Such use is remarkable because the alpine settings in which these sites are located are so obviously marginal for hunters and gatherers. It is unlikely that any substantial surplus of alpine game, roots, or seeds could have been laid away for winter use by groups summering in alpine villages. Groups must have relied on fall piñon crops in the winter, using what was left over the following summer to offset the food shortages that were periodically experienced in alpine villages.

Villages constitute a small fraction of the high-elevation archaeological record in the White Mountains and the Toquima Range, where most sites are simple rock hunting-blinds and sparse tool and waste-flake scatters thought to represent the activities of individual hunters or hunting parties pursuing large game, most probably mountain sheep. A variety of dating methods, including radiocarbon, time-sensitive projectile points, tephrochronology (stratigraphic dating with reference to volcanic ash [tephra] layers linked to eruptions of known age), and lichenometry (dating of rock constructions by measurement of lichen growth), indicate that the first alpine villages appeared sometime in the period A.D.1–1000 (1950–950 years B.P.), much later in time than the bulk of these hunting blinds and lithic scatters, which began

to appear by 2500 B.C. (4450 years B.P.). This indicates that the alpine zones of the White Mountains and the Toquima Range have been in use for a minimum of 4,500 years, during the first 2,500 of which there is little evidence of plant procurement or extended seasonal occupation. In this early period, aboriginal activity revolved around the hunting of mountain sheep. A major change in alpine land use occurred when alpine villages appeared, marking the replacement of an existing pattern of limited and specialized alpine use by a more intensive and generalized one in which both plant and animal procurement was important. In the White Mountains, this intensification is believed to mark the point at which regional populations had grown larger than traditional lowland resources could sustain, and additional resources in more marginal settings were required. The same is probably true in the case of Alta Toquima. There is good reason to believe that the high-altitude villages that have been found in the White Mountains, which flank Owens Valley to the east, are associated with the development of an intensive exploitative strategy that Robert L. Bettinger and Martin A. Baumhoff (1982; Bettinger 1991) believe can explain the Late Prehistoric spread of Numic-speaking peoples into the Great Basin. This spread is thought to have begun ca. A.D. 1000 (950 years B.P.) from a homeland in the general vicinity of Owens Valley. Termination of the alpine village pattern probably occurred in very early historic times as a result of Euro-American contact, which would explain why there is no record of alpine village peoples in ethnographic accounts.

The White Mountain and the Toquima Range alpine villages have understandably rekindled interest in high-altitude adaptations throughout the Great Basin. Preliminary surveys aimed at locating alpine villages have been conducted in most Nevada ranges and many Utah ranges that reach elevations in excess of 3,000 m (9,842.5 feet). However, these surveys have resulted in the location of only one possible additional village, in the Toiyabe Range, which lies between the Toquima Range and the White Mountains. The absence of villages east of the Toquima Range is likely due in part to the impoverishment of the Alpine Tundra communities of nearly all of those ranges, which do not appear to contain the quantity of resources needed to sustain intensive village occupation. The research, however, raises the possibility that

G

there are fundamental differences in prehistoric alpine land use in the eastern and the western Great Basin. In eastern Nevada and Utah, alpine sites are small but routinely contain plant-processing tools; such tools are rare in western Great Basin alpine sites other than villages. This implies that eastern Great Basin alpine land use characteristically involved short-term residential occupation for a mixture of hunting and gathering. In the western Great Basin, alpine land use was almost universally logistical and focused on hunting. This latter focus was replaced in a few localities by long-term residential use as witnessed by the presence of alpine villages. The eastern alpine pattern is relatively stable over time and suggests a more foragerlike hunter-gatherer strategy than the western alpine pattern, which varies in intensity through time and is more collectorlike.

Robert L. Bettinger

Further Readings

Bettinger, R.L. 1991. Aboriginal Occupation at High Altitude: Alpine Villages in the White Mountains of Eastern California. *American Anthropologist* 93:656–679.

Bettinger, R.L., and M.A. Baumhoff. 1982. The Numic Spread: Great Basin Cultures in Competition. *American Antiquity* 47(3):485–503.

Grayson, D.K. 1991. Alpine Faunas From the White Mountains, California: Adaptive Change in the Late Prehistoric Great Basin? *Journal of Archaeological Science* 18:483–506.

Thomas, D.H. 1982. *The 1981 Alta Toquima Project: A Preliminary Report.* Technical Report Series no. 27. Desert Research Institute Social Sciences Center, Reno.

Great Basin Trade

When native peoples of the Great Basin were encountered by Euro-Americans in the early nineteenth century A.D., and when they were later studied by anthropologists in the early twentieth century, a wide variety of perishable and nonperishable materials were observed circulating among families and social groups. Food (animal meats, fish, crickets, roots, acorns, seeds, and salt), animals (horses and dogs), clothing (skins and hides, furs, blankets, dresses, and moccasins), and artifacts (baskets, nets, knives and knife handles, shell beads and ornaments, obsidian projectile points, pottery, turquoise, bullets, horse bridles, and steel fishhooks) were all items of historic trade among native Great Basin peoples. Exchange of such materials commonly took place on an informal basis at all times of the year whenever people got together. The best-known social event fostering the widespread dispersal of both perishable and nonperishable materials was the festival (sometimes called the "fandango"). Festivals were held during the fall for periods ranging from a few days to a week, usually in areas of abundant local resources. They attracted people of all ages from neighboring areas who congregated to dance, gamble, socialize, and trade.

Prior to the introduction of the horse into the Great Basin, perhaps as early as the late 1600s, trade and acquisition of materials for trade were constrained largely by pedestrian considerations. The horse accelerated the speed at which people could move and dramatically expanded the territory and distances over which trade took place. Examples are stone smoking pipes introduced to Great Basin peoples from eastern North America, and obsidian from south-central Idaho that was conveyed as far south as Kansas, Oklahoma, and southern Texas.

Although much research has been devoted to the study of prehistoric trade in the region, less is known about it than historic-period trade largely because written records documenting the social contexts in which prehistoric trade took place and the commodities involved are lacking. In addition, less of the material likely to have been traded prehistorically (perishable foodstuffs, clothing, and certain types of artifacts) is preserved in most archaeological sites (except under special circumstances in caves and rock shelters). Because studies of prehistoric trade must rely largely on nonperishable materials like stone and bone, we know little about the role of perishables in prehistoric trade, although we assume that they were important.

Studies of two nonperishable commodities, shell and obsidian, provide an indication of the timing and areal extent of prehistoric trade networks. Shell beads manufactured from Pacific Coast species were conveyed across the Sierra Nevada into western Nevada and at least as far east as northwestern Utah ca. 5050 B.C. (7000 years B.P.). The peak of trade in shell beads and ornaments between California and the Great Basin appears to have occurred ca. 2050–50 B.C. (4000–2000 years B.P.). Over the last 2,000 years, trade in shell appears to have declined throughout the Great Basin. It reached its lowest point in the prehistoric period just prior to the arrival of Euro-Americans.

Chemical analyses of obsidian (a naturally occurring volcanic glass used by native peoples to manufacture projectile points, knives, and other implements) show that use of, and trade in, this material began during the earliest known period of human occupation. For instance, an analysis of a Clovis spear point from Blackwater Draw, New Mexico, indicated that it was derived from a geologic obsidian deposit in west-central Utah. Obsidian studies have revealed variability in the use-life histories of particular geologic sources, in addition to showing that trade in obsidian varied through time, and by artifact class, in the Great Basin. Formal tools, such as projectile points, recovered from archaeological sites are frequently made from distant, nonlocal obsidian sources, whereas casual tools and flakes were most often made from obsidian closest at hand. This suggests that much obsidian trade was confined to finished products rather than unfinished raw material.

The differences already discovered between trade in the historic period and trade in the prehistoric period suggest that future work will provide exciting new insights into the variability and complexity of movement of materials throughout the Great Basin and between this region and adjacent areas.

Richard E. Hughes

Further Readings

Bennyhoff, J.A., and R.E. Hughes. 1987. *Shell Bead and Ornament Exchange Networks Between California and the Western Great Basin.* Anthropological Papers, vol. 64, pt. 2. American Museum of Natural History, New York.

Hughes, R.E. 1994. Mosaic Patterning in Prehistoric California–Great Basin Exchange. In *Prehistoric Exchange Systems in North America,* edited by T.G. Baugh and J.E. Ericson, pp. 363–383. Plenum Press, New York.

Hughes, R.E., and J.A. Bennyhoff. 1986. Early Trade. In *Great Basin,* edited by W.L. D'Azevedo, pp. 238–255. Handbook of North American Indians, vol. 11, W.C. Sturtevant, general editor. Smithsonian Institution, Washington, D.C.

Great Bend Aspect

A more accurate name for the Great Bend aspect would probably be the Great Bend regional variant, given the trend in other parts of Plains archaeology to replace the term "aspect" with "variant." Regardless, as originally defined, the Great Bend aspect occupied two relatively discrete areas in central and south-central Kansas. More research has identified a larger spatial distribution covering the area from north-central Oklahoma to central Kansas and from the Great Bend, Kansas, area to the Verdigris and Neosho River valleys in eastern Kansas. There are two named foci: the Little River focus in central Kansas, and the Lower Walnut focus in south-central Kansas and adjacent parts of Oklahoma. A third grouping may be represented by occupations in east-central Kansas.

Great Bend sites include large villages and small, special-purpose camps. Low, mounded accumulations of refuse occur at village sites. Some sites are characterized by "council circles" that may be associated with solstice observances. Houses have proven hard to locate, but they were apparently the straw, beehive-shaped forms documented historically. The cultural assemblages of Great Bend–aspect members share many similarities with other members of the Plains Village tradition, particularly the Central Plains Village tradition and the Southern Plains Village tradition. Pottery is plain surfaced, ovate in shape, with round or flat bases. Stone tools include end scrapers; hafted knives; triangular, unnotched projectile points; a variety of drills; and ground-stone manos and metates. Bone tools include bison-scapula hoes. Subsistence has not been systematically assessed. Horticulture and hunting of bison and deer are indicated. Trade was conducted with societies to the north, east, west, and south; however, each of the three spatial groupings had slightly different sets of external relations.

Susan C. Vehik

Further Readings

Rohn, A.H., and A.M. Emerson. 1984. *Great Bend Sites at Marion, Kansas.* Wichita State Publications in Anthropology no. 1. Department of Anthropology, Wichita State University, Wichita.

Wedel, W.R. 1961. *Prehistoric Man on the Great Plains.* University of Oklahoma Press, Norman.

Great Oasis

Great Oasis is one of the earliest and most widespread Plains Village phases. It was first defined in 1945 by Lloyd Wilford following excavations at the Great Oasis type site (21MU2) in southwestern Minnesota. Great Oasis was J.N. Nicollet's name for a large wooded area in the southwestern Minnesota prairie that was protected from fires by several large adjoining lakes; the type site is on a peninsula in this area. Great Oasis ceramics are found in eastern and central South Dakota, northern Iowa, southwestern Minnesota, and northeastern Nebraska. These ceramics have also been reported in western Illinois and southern Manitoba. The densest concentration of Great Oasis sites is in northwestern Iowa, although several Middle Missouri sites in South Dakota (e.g., Oldham, Mitchell) have significant amounts of Great Oasis ceramics.

Great Oasis ceramics have been divided into two wares, High Rim and Wedge Lip. Both feature well-made globular vessels that are grit tempered with smooth rims and smooth or cord-marked-smoothed exterior bodies. High Rim vessels have straight, outflaring rims 2–5 cm (0.8–2 inches) in height with flat lips and sharp rim-shoulder junctions. Most rim exteriors are decorated with fine trailing in bands of horizontal and oblique parallel lines. Wedge Lip

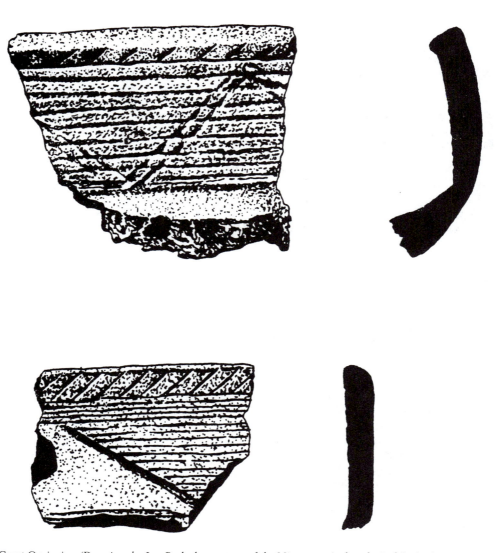

Great Oasis rims (Drawings by Lee Radzak, courtesy of the Minnesota Archaeological Society)

vessels have low, outcurving rims with broad, flat, outwardly beveled lips; the rims thicken toward the lip, resembling a wedge. The rim-neck junction is also thickened, giving this area of the vessel more strength than the High Rim ware. Wedge Lip vessels are occasionally decorated on the lip, rim, and shoulder with trailed line cross-hatching and/or tool impressions. The High Rim ware is closely related to Chamberlain Ware found at Mill Creek sites and the Anderson High Rim type from Over-phase sites. Great Oasis High Rim may be ancestral to other Initial Middle Missouri high-rim types. Great Oasis Wedge Lip closely resembles Mill Creek Sanford ware and some Over-phase Anderson-ware types.

Great Oasis projectile points are usually small, side-notched or unnotched, triangular varieties. Ground-stone tools are celts, arrow-shaft abraders, and hammerstones; a few manos and metates have been recovered. Bone tools include awls, chisels, quill flatteners, shaft wrenches, and antler-tine flaking tools; bison-scapula hoes are rare. Shell objects include dippers, clamshell crosses, and beads.

Great Oasis subsistence patterns closely resemble local Woodland patterns that used a wide range of upland and aquatic species. Bison usage increases moving west. Maize kernels, as well as some sunflowers and squash, have been found at most Great Oasis sites. Great Oasis sites in the Prairie Lake region of the northeastern Plains occupy traditional Woodland locations on the islands, peninsulas, and isthmuses of the larger shallow lakes. Typical site locations outside of the Prairie Lake region are on first terraces above stream or river floodplains. Only a few large sites, such as Broken Kettle West in northwestern Iowa, appear to have house structures; houses were rectangular in shape, 6.5–12 m (21–39 feet) long, 5–7.5 m (16.4–24.6 feet) wide, and semisubterranean with entryways.

At least three Great Oasis burial sites are known. The Gypsum Quarry site in central Iowa featured two mounds on a low terrace above the Des Moines River. Two High Rim vessels were recovered from one mound, but only fragmentary human remains were noted. At the nearby West Des Moines site, at least 18 individuals were unearthed in single flexed and multiple burials associated with two High Rim vessels, eight shell crosses, and *Anculosa* sp. beads. At the Ryan site in northeastern Nebraska, Great Oasis and Woodland burials were found together; the Great Oasis burials appeared to be secondary bundles.

Radiocarbon dates from charcoal recovered at sites in Minnesota, South Dakota, and Iowa indicate that Great Oasis may have been as early as A.D. 800 (1150 years B.P.) and may have persisted as late as A.D. 1250 (700 years B.P.), although the usually accepted chronological range is A.D. 900–1200 (1050–750 years B.P.). There is some disagreement as to whether Great Oasis should be considered part of the Middle Missouri tradition, since it has stronger Woodland influences than other Initial-variant phases and lacks certain Middle Missouri traits, such as fortified villages and S-rim ceramics. There does seem to be general agreement, however, that Great Oasis is ancestral to Initial Middle Missouri.

Scott F. Anfinson

Further Readings
Anfinson, S.F. 1979. Great Oasis Phase. In *A Handbook of Minnesota Prehistoric Ceramics,* edited by S.F. Anfinson, pp. 87–94. Minnesota Archaeological Society, St. Paul.
———. 1987. *The Prehistory of the Prairie Lake Region in the Northeastern Plains.* Unpublished Ph.D. dissertation, Department of Anthropology, University of Minnesota, Minneapolis.
Henning, D.R. 1971. Great Oasis Culture Distributions. In *Prehistoric Investigations,* edited by M. McKusick, pp. 125–133. Report no. 3. Office of the State Archaeologist, Iowa City.
Henning, D.R., and E.P. Henning. 1978. Great Oasis Ceramics. In *Some Studies of Minnesota Prehistoric Ceramics,* edited by A.R. Woolworth and M.A. Hall, pp. 12–26. Minnesota Archaeological Society, St. Paul.
Johnson, C.M. 1973. House Four at Broken Kettle West. Ms. on file, Department of Anthropology, University of Nebraska, Lincoln.
Johnson, E. 1969. Decorative Motifs on Great Oasis Pottery. *Plains Anthropologist* 14:272–276.
Johnson, R.B. 1967. *The Hitchell Site.* Publications in Salvage Archaeology no. 3. River Basin Surveys. Smithsonian Institution, Lincoln.
Knauth, O. 1963. Mystery of the Crosses. *Annals of Iowa* 37:81–91.

Tiffany, J.A. 1983. An Overview of the Middle Missouri Tradition. In *Prairie Archaeology,* edited by G.E. Gibbon, pp. 87–108. Publications in Anthropology no. 3. University of Minnesota Press, Minneapolis.

Wilford, L.A. 1945. Three Village Sites of the Mississippian Pattern in Minnesota. *American Antiquity* 11:32–40.

Williams, P. 1975. The Williams Site (13PM50): A Great Oasis Component in Northwest Iowa. *Journal of the Iowa Archaeological Society* 22:1–33.

Great Salt Spring

The Great Salt Spring is perhaps the best known of a series of Mississippian salt-production localities in the upper Southeast (see Keslin 1964; Brown 1980 for other salt-production sites). The Great Salt Spring site is located in southern Illinois near present-day Shawneetown. The site was reported as an archaeological site in the early nineteenth century (Cramer 1966 [1814]), although it was known as a historical and aboriginal salt-production area for nearly a century before that. Archaeological excavations date from the 1870s to the present (Sellers 1877; Peithman 1953; Blasingham 1972; Muller 1984). The entire Great Salt Spring site consists of both bottomland and adjacent blufftop areas. Site areas were largely devoted to salt production and auxiliary activities from A.D. 800 to historic times (1150–300 years B.P.). The floodplain salt-production zone extends for more than 500 m (1,640 feet) with as much as 3 m (10 feet) of debris from salt production in the areas closest to the main saline springs. The extensive remains gave rise to the common interpretation that the site was the focus of full-time specialization in salt production (Driver 1969:172). However, more recent work has shown that production at the site was carried out by small groups of producers whose use of the site was transient (Muller 1984, 1986a, 1986b, 1987). These data are in accord with the predominantly "household" character of production known to exist elsewhere in Lower Ohio Valley Mississippian societies (Muller 1986a, 1987). The Great Salt Spring site stands as an example cautioning us that production in many chiefdomlike societies does not correspond to models postulating the growth of specialized production systems (Muller 1987).

Jon Muller

Further Readings

Blasingham, E. 1972. The Prehistoric and Historic Uses of the Saline Springs, Gallatin County, Illinois. Ms. on file, Center for Archaeological Investigations, Southern Illinois University, Carbondale.

Brown, I. 1980. *Salt and the Eastern North American Indian: An Archaeological Study.* Lower Mississippi Survey Bulletin no. 6. Peabody Museum of American Archaeology and Ethnology, Harvard University, Cambridge.

Cramer, Z. 1966 [1814]. *The Navigator; Containing Directions for Navigating the Ohio and Mississippi Rivers.* 8th ed. Cramer, Spear and Eichbaum. 1966. facsimile reprint. University Microfilms, Ann Arbor.

Driver, H.E. 1969. *Indians of North America.* 2nd ed. University of Chicago Press, Chicago.

Keslin, R.O. 1964. Archaeological Implications on the Role of Salt and an Element of Cultural Diffusion. *Missouri Archaeologist* 26:1–181.

Muller, J. 1984. Mississippian Specialization and Salt. *American Antiquity* 49(3):489–507.

———. 1986a. *Archaeology of the Lower Ohio River Valley.* Academic Press, New York.

———. 1986b. Pans and a Grain of Salt: Mississippian Specialization Revisited. *American Antiquity* 51(2):405–409.

———. 1987. Salt, Chert, and Shell: Mississippian Exchange and Economy. In *Specialization, Exchange, and Complex Societies,* edited by E. Brumfield and T. Earle, pp. 10–21. Cambridge University Press, Cambridge.

———. (editor). 1992. The Great Salt Spring: Mississippian Production and Specialization. Ms. on file, U.S. Forest Service, Shawnee National Forest, Harrisburg.

Peithman, I. 1953. A Preliminary Report on Salt-Making and Pottery Manufacture at a Prehistoric Site in Gallatin County, Illinois. *Illinois State Archaeological Society Journal* 3(1):67–74.

Sellers, G.E. 1877. Aboriginal Pottery of the Salt-Springs, Illinois. *Popular Science Monthly* 40:573–585.

Griffin, James B. (1905–1997)

James Griffin was, since the 1940s, the major synthesizer of Eastern Woodlands archaeology.

Of equal importance, as an enlightened practitioner of the cultural-historical approach, Griffin was often the first to systematically apply innovations in other fields to regional archaeological problems. On a more familiar level, "Jimmy" was a constant presence at local and national meetings, where his wit, sharp tongue, and enormous knowledge enlightened generations of colleagues.

As a student of Fay-Cooper Cole at the University of Chicago, the first major archaeological training center in the Midwest, Griffin participated in Cole and Thorne Deuel's field training program in Illinois. While still a graduate student at the University of Chicago, in 1933 he accepted a fellowship in the Ceramic Repository at the University of Michigan to help bring order to midwestern prehistoric ceramics. The creation of the repository was one step in a plan initiated in the 1920s by Alfred V. Kidder, the chairman of the National Research Council's Committee on State Archaeological Surveys, to improve archaeology in the Midwest. As an assistant in the repository, Griffin traveled widely to examine collections and talk with archaeologists. After receiving his Ph.D. in 1936 from the University of Michigan (the first Ph.D. granted by the Department of Anthropology), he became a research associate in the Museum of Anthropology there and eventually director of the museum (1946) and chairman of the Department of Anthropology. During this period, he was intimately involved in bringing the museum and the department to national prominence. Although he retired from his positions as director of the museum, curator of archaeology, chairman of the Department of Anthropology, and professor of anthropology in the summer of 1975, he remained active in Eastern Woodlands archaeology.

Among his synthetic works are his edited "Green Bible," *Archeology of Eastern United States* (1952), and influential articles (1946, 1961b, and 1967). He was the first or one of the first to systematically apply the Midwestern Taxonomic system (1935, 1943), radiocarbon dating (1952), and neutron activation analysis (Griffin et al. 1969) to archaeological problems in the Eastern Woodlands, and to actively explore ethnohistoric relationships (1943), the sources of archaeological copper (1961a), and the influences of climatic change (1960b, 1965) and of other regions of the Americas (1960b, 1966) on that culture area. Griffin received numerous awards in recognition of his accom-

James B. Griffin (Reprinted with permission from American Antiquity *45[4]:661)*

plishments, including the Viking Fund Award and Medal and election to the National Academy of Sciences. Needless to say, this brief review presents only a glimpse of an extraordinary career and personality.

Guy Gibbon

Further Readings

Cleland, C.E. (editor). 1976. *Cultural Change and Continuity: Essays in Honor of James Bennett Griffin.* Academic Press, New York.

Ford, R.I., and V.H. Jones (compilers). 1977. Published Works of James Bennett Griffin. In *For the Director: Research Essays in Honor of James B. Griffin,* edited by C.E. Cleland, pp. 343–362. Anthropological Papers no. 61. Museum of Anthropology, University of Michigan, Ann Arbor.

Griffin, J.B. 1935. *An Analysis of the Fort Ancient Culture.* Notes no. 1. Ceramic Repository for the Eastern United States, Ann Arbor.

———. 1943. *The Fort Ancient Aspect: Its*

Cultural and Chronological Position in Mississippi Valley Archaeology. University of Michigan Press, Ann Arbor.

———. 1946. Cultural Change and Continuity in Eastern United States Archaeology. In *Man in Northeastern North America,* edited by F. Johnson, pp. 37–95. Papers, vol. 35. Robert S. Peabody Foundation for Archaeology, Phillips Academy, Andover.

———. 1960a. Climatic Change: A Contributory Cause of the Growth and Decline of Northern Hopewellian Culture. *Wisconsin Archeologist* 41(1):21–33.

———. 1960b. Some Prehistoric Connections Between Siberia and America. *Science* 131(3403):801–812.

———. 1961b. North America: Prehistory and Archaeology. *Encyclopaedia Britannica,* vol. 16, pp. 506–513. Encyclopaedia Britannica, Chicago.

———. 1961c. Some Correlations of Climatic and Cultural Change in Eastern North American Prehistory. *New York Academy of Science Annals* 95(1):710–717.

———. 1965. Late Quaternary Prehistory in the Northeastern Woodlands. In *The Quaternary of the United States,* edited by H.E. Wright and D.G. Frey. Princeton University Press, Princeton.

———. 1966. Mesoamerica and the Eastern United States in Prehistoric Times. In *Archaeological Frontiers and External Connections*, edited by G.F. Ekholm and G.R. Willey, pp. 111–131. Handbook of Middle American Indians, vol. 4, R. Wauchope, general editor. University of Texas Press, Austin.

———. 1967. Eastern North American Archaeology: A Summary. *Science* 156(3772):175–191.

———. (editor). 1952. *Archeology of Eastern United States.* University of Chicago Press, Chicago.

———. (editor). 1961a. *Lake Superior Copper and the Indians: Miscellaneous Studies of Great Lakes Prehistory.* Anthropological Papers no. 17. Museum of Anthropology, University of Michigan, Ann Arbor.

Griffin, J.B., A.A. Gordus, and G.A. Wright. 1969. Identification of Sources of Hopewellian Obsidian in the Middle West. *American Antiquity* 34:1–14.

Jones, V.H. 1976. James Bennett Griffin, Archaeologist. In *Cultural Change and Continuity: Essays in Honor of James Bennett Griffin,* edited by C.E. Cleland, pp. xxxix–xxvii. Academic Press, New York.

Groswater Culture

The term "Groswater culture" is applied to a Paleoeskimo culture found along the coasts of Labrador and the island of Newfoundland. It was first defined by William Fitzhugh on the basis of an unusual collection of finely fashioned, chipped-stone tools and weapons found along the shores of Groswater Bay of the central Labrador coast. The culture was first called "Groswater Dorset" because of its presumed historical relationship to the somewhat more recent Dorset Eskimo culture of the eastern Arctic. Although some researchers continue to regard the Groswater culture as the progenitor of the Dorset cultures of Newfoundland and Labrador, comparisons of tool and weapon styles, as well as radiocarbon dates, do not indicate a strong historical relationship between the two peoples.

The chipped-stone tool-and-weapon complex of the Groswater people is distinctive by virtue of being manufactured largely from cherts obtainable only along the west coast of Newfoundland; these cherts are even found in Groswater sites as far north as the central Labrador coast. The side-notched harpoon end blades (and a few organic harpoons from Phillips Garden in western Newfoundland into which the end blades fit perfectly), expanding-corner end scrapers, chipped-stone knives of a variety of forms, microblades, and small polished stone adzes are among the hallmarks of the Groswater tool-and-weapon complex. In every case, it is difficult to see specific resemblances between these specimens and those manufactured by the succeeding Dorset Eskimo people.

Radiocarbon dates clearly place the Groswater culture in the first millennium B.C., ca. 950–150 B.C. (2900–2100 years B.P.). Most researchers consider Groswater culture the final expression of an "Early Paleoeskimo tradition" in Newfoundland and Labrador. This tradition began with the arrival of the first Paleoeskimos from the north ca. 2050 B.C. (4000 years B.P.) and ended with what appears to be a disappearance (at least from the archaeological record) of the Groswater people ca. 50 B.C. (2000 years B.P.). In northern Labrador, there is a chronological overlap between the latest Groswater radiocarbon dates and those of the Early Dorset culture, which first appears ca. 550 B.C. (2500 years B.P.). Early Dorset artifacts are distinctive from those of the Groswater culture, and some researchers think that their presence signals the arrival of a new people. Groswater culture disappears from both the island of Newfoundland and the coast of Labrador slightly prior to 50 B.C. (2000 years B.P.). Present evidence indicates that there was little, if any, survival into later Dorset times. If there was a Groswater-to-Dorset transition, it does not seem to have taken place either along the Labrador coast or on the island of Newfoundland.

James Tuck

Gulf of Georgia Culture Type

The Gulf of Georgia culture type is the most recent (ca. A.D. 450–1750, or 1500–200 years B.P.) archaeological culture of the Coast Salish Indians of the Strait of Georgia and Puget Sound region in British Columbia and Washington State. It is synonymous with Developed Coast Salish culture at the time of contact with European cultures in the late 1700s. The distribution of Gulf of Georgia–culture type sites indicates a more extensive Coast Salish nation than in the historic period (at ca. A.D. 1800). This recent period of the Coast Salish sequence was first identified at Musqueam (South Vancouver) in the late 1940s. Several regional variants have been postulated, including the Stselax, San Juan, Esilao, and Whalen II phases. These variants appear to derive from different Coast Salish linguistic groups. Like preceding archaeological cultures (Marpole, Locarno Beach, and Charles culture types), it developed among Central Coast Salish who controlled access to Fraser River salmon. The Fraser was one of the most productive salmon rivers in the world, exceeded only by the Yukon and the Columbia.

A range of settlement types has been identified. Included are permanent house site clusters, late winter camps for herring and shellfish harvesting, spring camps for eulachon and sturgeon fishing, summer camps for salmon fishing and berrying, and autumn fish-weir sites and camps. Other types of sites include trails; rock art (petroglyphs and pictographs); women's menstrual seclusion features; shallow, rectangular bathing pools; burial mounds; culturally modified trees; fortified or defensive sites; and fish weirs and traps. Most sites excavated have proven to be seasonally occupied. Faunal assemblages are dominated by fish, land mammals, and waterfowl. Most significant are Pacific salmon. Other important species include sturgeon, flatfish, herring, eulachon, and rock cod. Deer and wapiti are the most important land mammals, followed by beaver and bear. Sea-mammal remains are not common and consist largely of seal, with some sea lion. Bird remains are primarily waterfowl, with ducks the most important, then geese. Shellfish remains are present at most sites and are especially plentiful at shellfish-harvesting sites. Plant foods, such as berries and roots, were probably at least as important as intertidal resources.

More than 100 different artifact classes can be assigned to the Gulf of Georgia culture type. Many are similar to those from earlier archaeological cultures, but there is an overall increase in the quantity of bone, antler, and ground-slate artifacts. Flaked-stone artifacts are very rare at some sites. Distinctive artifacts include small flaked-stone arrow points (plain triangular, side-notched, corner-notched, and stemmed varieties); slotted, channeled, and tapered composite toggling harpoon valves of antler; thin, triangular ground-slate points with thinned bases; triangular points made of ground sea mussel; slender cylindrical bone and antler points; small wedge-based bone points (for arming toggling harpoons); large bone points with unilateral, multiple enclosed barbs; fishhook shanks; small bone unipoints (for arming composite fishhooks and herring rakes) and small bone bipoints used as gorge hooks; small, thin ground-slate knives; large, well-made ground-nephrite celts; flat-topped stone hand mauls; decorated antler combs; plain and decorated bone and antler blanket pins; decorated and plain bone (and possible stone) spindle whorls; steatite pipes; and small stone slabs with incised lines. Other artifacts include biface knives, bipolar cores, pebble cores, flake tools (scrapers, knives), flaked-slate knives, numerous split and sectioned bone awls, nipple-top mauls, antler wedges, bone chisels, net gauges, and antler hafts. Water-logged deposits have yielded a range of sizes of twisted-withe cordage; checker-weave, open-plain-twining, open-wrapped-twining and plain-twined basketry; mats; wooden wedges; bentwood fishhooks; and canoe bailers made from cedar bark. Com-

G

mon at all sites are fractured pebbles from heating water and cooking with hot rocks.

Within the type, there are noticeable differences among assemblages. Flaked stone, while rare at some sites, is common at others. Ground-slate artifacts, in particular knives, are most common in the area occupied by Halkomelem Salish, who controlled access to the Fraser River salmon, but are rare in the northern Strait of Georgia and in Puget Sound south of Whidbey Island. Although this distribution seems to suggest there is some relationship between the ground-slate knife and the Fraser River salmon runs, no evidence has been presented that such a knife is any more efficient for butchering salmon than a hafted flake or a unifacial or bifacial flaked-stone knife.

Trade was extensive. Raw materials, such as slate, sandstone, nephrite, obsidian, and whalebone, as well as many types of finished artifacts, such as arrow points, slate artifacts, and basketry, were probably traded throughout the region. Examples of art are rare in Gulf of Georgia–culture type sites, largely due to the sparsity of excavated permanent house sites. In addition, the primary medium for Coast Salish art was wood. Examples recovered indicate distinct regional styles that may be traced back to the early part of the Gulf of Georgia culture type.

Burial practices were varied, as might be expected in a society with marked social differentiation. They include loosely flexed midden burials, sitting position, and cairn midden burials. In addition, scattered human remains indicate the use of tree and other surface burials. Grave goods are rare, suggesting most midden burials are low-class or poor people. At contact, people of high status were interred in small plank mortuary houses, raised canoes, or box burials in trees in designated cemeteries. This form of burial does not preserve well. Fronto-lambdoidal, also known as the Cowichan type of, cranial deformation, which appeared during the earlier Marpole culture, is the dominant form. Labret use is noted in early Gulf of Georgia–culture sites but disappears by A.D. 950 (1000 years B.P.).

Considerable distortion may exist in the database for the Gulf of Georgia culture type. The original number of Gulf of Georgia–culture type sites is not known; thus, the statistical significance of recovered assemblages cannot be estimated. The majority of assemblages are from seasonal settlements, and sampling is not adequate to segregate those site areas occupied by wealthy and by low-class people. Site constituents could vary significantly. However, differences in wealth, and the shifting fortunes, influences, and alliances of the large extended Coast Salish families who controlled access to the Fraser River salmon runs probably account for at least some of the temporal and areal differences in the archaeological record.

Leonard C. Ham

Further Readings

Bernick, K. 1983. *A Site Catchment Analysis of the Little Qualicum River Site, DiSc 1: A Wet Site on the East Coast of Vancouver Island, B.C.* Mercury Series Paper no. 118. Archaeological Survey of Canada, National Museum of Man, Ottawa.

Burley, D.V. 1989. *Senewélets: Culture History of the Nanaimo Coast Salish and the False Narrows Midden.* Memoir no. 2. Royal British Columbia Museum, Victoria.

Haggarty, J.C., and J.H.W. Sendey. 1976. *Test Excavations at Georgeson Bay, British Columbia.* Occasional Papers no. 19. British Columbia Provincial Museum, Victoria.

Ham, L.C. 1982. *Seasonality, Shell Midden Layers, and Coast Salish Subsistence Activities at the Crescent Beach Site, DgRr 1.* Unpublished Ph.D. dissertation, Department of Anthropology and Sociology, University of British Columbia, Vancouver.

Mitchell, D. 1971. Archaeology of the Gulf of Georgia Area, a Natural Region and Its Culture Types. *Syesis* 4 (Supplement no. 1).

———. 1990. Prehistory of the Coasts of Southern British Columbia and Northern Washington. In *Northwest Coast*, edited by W. Suttles, pp. 340–358. Handbook of North American Indians, vol. 7, W.C. Sturtevant, general editor. Smithsonian Institution, Washington, D.C.

Gulf of Maine Archaic Tradition

"Gulf of Maine" is an Archaic tradition in the Northeast lacking bifacial stone projectile points. The Gulf of Maine Archaic tradition has been defined as a technological pattern that spans the period ca. 7750–4050 B.C. (9500–6000 years B.P.) in the coastal region from the

Merrimack River in Massachusetts, north to central Maine and probably to the Canadian Maritimes. The tradition is dominated by core-and-flake industries and the development (by 6050 B.C., or 8000 years B.P.) of a variety of ground-stone tools, including full-channeled gouges, adzes, celts, and rods. No single artifact type is considered unique to the tradition or region. Rather, identification is based on whole assemblages and frequencies of characteristic artifacts. The technological tradition generally lacks bifacial projectile points, which may largely account for both its late recognition and the former models of low population density in the region. In contrast, other Early and Middle Archaic units of culture history, especially to the south and west, have been identified primarily by diagnostic projectile points (e.g., bifurcate-base tradition, Neville and Stark complexes) (Dincauze 1976).

Because the tradition lacks diagnostic artifacts that are exclusive to it, definition of the tradition requires well-isolated components. The most thorough discussion of the tradition occurs in *Early Holocene Occupation in Northern New England* (Robinson et al. 1992), which includes reports on three deeply stratified sites from central Maine (Brigham, Sharrow, and Blackman Stream) and three comparable sites from New Hampshire (Weirs Beach, Wadleigh Falls, and the Eddy site); Middle Archaic (6050–4050 B.C., or 8000–6000 years B.P.) mortuary sites are also discussed. The Gulf of Maine Archaic tradition includes both regional and temporal variation that has not been reconciled with evidence of other culture subsystems. As a result, it is not defined as a "whole culture" unit. For example, the Morrill Point burial complex, dating to ca. 6050–5050 B.C. (8000–7000 years B.P.), includes artifacts characteristic of the Gulf of Maine Archaic tradition, but it is not yet known if the burial complex coincides with, or only partially overlaps, the technological pattern. Hence, the limited definition of the tradition.

Regional and temporal variation within this tradition is recognized but little understood to date (1996). In the Merrimack River Valley of New Hampshire, Early Archaic (ca. 7050–6050 B.C., or 9000–8000 years B.P.) assemblages are characterized almost exclusively by a quartz-core-and-uniface technology with ground-schist rods and crude tabular "choppers" or "knives." This pattern, with its emphasis on quartz technology, persists into the Middle Archaic period in this area with the addition of ground-stone

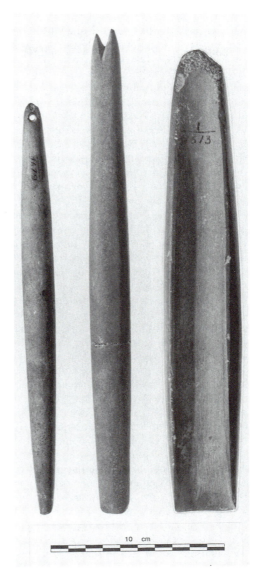

G

Ground stone tools characteristic of the Gulf of Maine Archaic tradition, as found in the Morrill Point burial complex (ca. 8000–7000 years B.P.). Perforated rods (left and center) and full-channeled gouge (right) from the Haffenreffer Museum of Anthropology and the James P. Whittal collection (center).

woodworking tools. It was apparently replaced by the biface-dominated Neville complex within a few hundred years before or after 5550 B.C. (7500 years B.P.) (Dincauze 1976).

While this Early Archaic quartz-core technology is prevalent at some sites (e.g., Brigham) in the Penobscot River drainage of central

Maine, larger felsite cores occur more frequently (e.g., at the Sharrow and Blackman Stream sites), in contrast to Merrimack River sites. In Penobscot River sites, crude tabular choppers apparently occur throughout the duration of the tradition. Other tool forms were added to the assemblage over time without abrupt changes in the remaining assemblage (e.g., ground-slate points are well represented by 4450 B.C., or 6400 years B.P., at the Sharrow site). Specialized-production sites also occur, such as at the Gilman Falls site (Sanger 1996). Hundreds of phyllite stone rod fragments occur (ca. 5350–4350 B.C., or 7300–6300 years B.P.) at this latter site, along with full-channeled gouges, celts, and phyllite choppers, all in various stages of production. While Gulf of Maine Archaic–tradition technology was replaced in the Merrimack River Valley by that of the Neville complex during the Middle Archaic period, the proposed end of the tradition in the Penobscot River drainage is more arbitrarily defined at ca. 4050 B.C. (6000 years B.P.). At that time, large side-notched bifaces characteristic of the Late Archaic Laurentian tradition, as well as short-channeled gouges and plummets, were introduced (Petersen 1991). However, much of the technology of the Laurentian tradition in Maine (Cox 1991) occurs in the preceding Middle Archaic period without apparent discontinuity in technologies.

Boundary definition of the Gulf of Maine Archaic tradition is complicated by the different criteria used to define archaeological units of culture history. Although few archaeologists would suggest that projectile-point types are equivalent to cultures, the practical use of such artifacts for site identification and distributional studies often dominates interpretation. Less distinctive artifact assemblages may be appended to more visible (but unrelated) diagnostic artifacts or written off as minor specialized activities, if they are recognized at all, as happened in this region. Former assumptions about the relationship of projectile points to people in some areas of the Northeast resulted in a proposed population hiatus, at what now appears to be the center of a thriving culture area. The Gulf of Maine Archaic tradition facilitates interpretation of some of the less distinctive artifact assemblages in the area, providing a new focus for the study of cultural origins, culture interaction, environmental change, and adaptation.

Brian S. Robinson

Further Readings

Cox, S.L. 1991. Site 95.20 and the Vergennes Phase in Maine. *Archaeology of Eastern North America* 19:135–161.

Dincauze, D.F. 1976. *The Neville Site: 8000 Years at Amoskeag.* Monographs no. 4. Peabody Museum of American Archaeology and Ethnology, Harvard University, Cambridge.

Petersen, J.B. 1991. *Archaeological Testing at the Sharrow Site: A Deeply Stratified Early to Late Holocene Cultural Sequence in Central Maine.* Occasional Publications in Maine Archaeology no. 8. Maine Historic Preservation Commission and Maine Archaeological Society, Augusta.

Robinson, B.S., J.B. Petersen, and A.K. Robinson (editors). 1992. *Early Holocene Occupation in Northern New England.* Occasional Publications in Maine Archaeology no. 9. Maine Historic Preservation Commission, Augusta.

Sanger, D. 1996. Gilman Falls Site: Implications for the Early and Middle Archaic of the Maritime Peninsula. *Canadian Journal of Archaeology* 20:7–28.

Gulf Tradition

The Gulf tradition refers to the consistent recurrence of specific ceramic decorative treatments that developed south of the Fall Line hills in the Southeast. For ca. 2,000 years (2000–100 B.C., or 3950–2050 years B.P.), they occurred almost exclusively within the Gulf Coastal Plain. These decorative treatments include incising, punctating, fingernail pinching, stamping (both rocker and straight-dentate stamping techniques), and the production of rim bosses punched through from the interior to form a band below the exterior vessel lip. The Gulf tradition initially appeared on the southern Atlantic Coast in the form of the Stallings Island and Orange ceramic complexes. In the period 1500–500 B.C. (3450–2450 years B.P.), many attributes of these complexes diffused westward as a result of trade centered on the Poverty Point site. The Bayou la Batre complex appeared in the Mobile Bay region ca. 1000–500 B.C. (2950–2450 years B.P.). It should be noted that almost all of the attributes that identify early Gulf ceramics have antecedents in northern South America (Ford 1969).

As these ceramic ideas spread throughout

the Coastal Plain, they occurred in different combinations both spatially and temporally. By the Middle Woodland period, the evolving arrangements of ceramic ideas comprised such ceramic complexes as Marksville, Porter, and Havana. In the midwestern United States after 100 B.C. (2050 years B.P.), the decorative elements of the Gulf tradition were combined with cord- or fabric-marked complexes, while, in the southern Coastal Plain and the Mississippi Valley, plain ceramics predominated. Even by A.D. 600–700 (1350–1250 years B.P.), ceramic series like Weeden Island in the eastern Gulf Coastal Plain and Troyville in the western Coastal Plain continued to be characterized by complexes dominated by plain-surfaced ceramics. (Weeden Island and Weeden Island-related complexes were restricted geographically to the area south of the Fall Line and had a Coastal Plain adaptation.)

After A.D. 1000 (950 years B.P.), most Mississippian ceramic series east of the Chattahoochee River were characterized by complexes marked by 85–90 percent plain pottery and incised decorations. Although new motifs had certainly been added, many old motifs, such as the chevron, line-filled triangles, zone punctation, and fingernail punctation, were still present.

Ned L. Jenkins

Further Readings

Ford, J.A. 1969. *A Comparison of the Formative Cultures in the Americas.* Contributions to Anthropology no. 2. Smithsonian Institution, Washington, D.C.

Jenkins, N.J. 1975. The Wheeler Series and Southeastern Prehistory. *Florida Anthropologist* 18:17–26.

Jenkins, N.J., D.H. Dye, and J.A. Walthall. 1986. Early Ceramic Development in the Gulf Coastal Plain. In *Early Woodland Archaeology,* edited by K. Farnsworth and T. Emerson. Kampsville Seminars in Archaeology, vol. 2. Center for American Archaeology, Kampsville.

Walthall, J.A., and N.J. Jenkins. 1976. The Gulf Formational Stage in Southeastern Prehistory. Southeastern Archaeological Conference, *Bulletin* 19:43–49.

Gunther Island Site

The Gunther Island site (CAHum67), located on an island in Humboldt Bay at Eureka, was the first site to be systematically excavated in northwestern California and has served as the type site for the Late Prehistoric period of that area's coast. The historic Wiyot village of Tolowot was located on the island until 1860, when a night raid by local American settlers led to the massacre of many of its inhabitants and the flight of survivors. Archaeological research began in 1918, when L.L. Loud of the University of California, Berkeley, first excavated the mounded midden. The rich variety of artifacts from his and later studies has defined what D.A. Fredrickson (1984:485) describes as the "Gunther pattern," typical of the region's coast after A.D. 450 (1500 years B.P.). However, a more recently obtained ^{14}C assay from the midden's base (Elsasser and Heizer 1966:2) dated to A.D. 900 ± 200 (1050 years B.P.) suggested to Fredrickson that the founding of the site might have been more recent than the suggested date of A.D. 450 (1500 years B.P.) for the beginning of the Gunther pattern.

The Gunther Island assemblage reflects a variety of technologies and subsistence strategies at this southern periphery of the Northwest Coast–culture area (e.g., Driver 1961:Map 2). The distinctive Gunther Island Barbed projectile point, often made of imported obsidian or local chert, serves as a regional time marker for the A.D. 950–1750 (1000–200 years B.P.) period. Ground-stone and chipped-pebble net weights are associated with intensive fishing, as are bone harpoon toggles and toggle-harpoon spurs. Barbed bone-harpoon points reflect sea-mammal hunting, while widespread use of bone and antler from deer and elk indicates the systematic hunting of land mammals. Beads and ornaments of abalone, clamshell, *Olivella*, and *Dentalium* reflect extensive maritime exploitation and, in several cases, extensive exchange relations. *Dentalium* in the area, for example, derives from Puget Sound. These artifacts also reflect the region's shell-money system and ranked societies. Antler wedges and stone adze handles and blades indicate evolved woodworking crafts. Mortars and pestles are associated with the processing of several kinds of plant and animal foods. Imported steatite, or soapstone, was widely used for making bowls, smoking pipes, and some of the region's distinctive zoomorphic effigies. While zoomorphs are not characteristic of central and southern California, they are known from many sites in northwestern California and Oregon. Identification of sources of the obsidian found at Gunther Island and nearby sites indicates that it was imported differentially in considerable quantity. Utilitarian artifacts are made almost exclusively of obsidian from eastern Siskiyou County, ca. 225 km (140 miles) distant. Distinctive obsidian ceremonial bifaces, some up to 89 cm (35 inches) in length, come from different sources in northwest Nevada and southern Oregon more than 402 km (250 miles) from the coast (Hughes 1982).

This evidence, combined with the lack of local archaeological indications for the gradual evolution of the Gunther pattern, has suggested to some that its inception reflects the migration of Algic-speaking (Algonquian) and Athapaskan-speaking peoples from the north and east into northwestern California between A.D. 450 and 950 (1500–1000 years B.P.) (Moratto 1984:564–566). If so, the Gunther Island site may represent the first wave of such migrants, who are presumed to be the ancestors of the historically established Wiyot people whose descendants still live in the area (Elsasser and Heizer 1964).

Joseph L. Chartkoff

Further Readings

Driver, H.E. 1961. *Indians of North America.* University of Chicago Press, Chicago.

Elsasser, A.B., and R.F. Heizer. 1964. Archaeology of Hum-67, the Gunther Island Site in Humboldt Bay, California. *University of California Archaeological Survey Reports* 62:5–122.

———. 1966. Excavation of Two Northwestern California Coastal Sites. *University of California Archaeological Survey Reports* 67:1–149.

Fredrickson, D.A. 1984. The North Coast Region. In *California Archaeology,* edited by M.J. Moratto, pp. 471–547. Academic Press, Orlando.

Hughes, R.E. 1982. Age and Exploitation of Obsidian From the Medicine Lake Highland. *California Journal of Archaeological Science* 9(2):173–185.

Loud, L.L. 1918. Ethnogeography and Archaeology of the Wiyot Territory. *University of California Publications in American Archaeology and Ethnology* 17(6):355–372.

Moratto, M.J. (editor). 1984. *California Archaeology.* Academic Press, Orlando.

H

Hagen Site

The Hagen site (24DW2) is a Plains village near Glendive, Montana, that was excavated by the Montana Works Progress Administration (WPA) in 1939. William T. Mulloy (1942) suggested that it might represent one stage in the western migration of the Crow after their split from the Hidatsa. This hypothesis was based on site content, which included a large number of scapula hoes and ceramics (20,000 sherds), and the site's location on the northwestern Plains 322 km (200 miles) from other known Plains villages. The hypothesis has never been seriously evaluated, although some archaeologists have accepted it as fact. The cultural affiliation of the Hagen site appears to be generalized Middle Missouri tradition, but more precise relationships have not been identified. The site may contain two or more ceramic components, with the earlier possibly related to the Middle Missouri Extended variant. Hagen has not been adequately dated, but it probably dates to ca. A.D. 1400–1650 (550–300 years B.P.).

Ann M. Johnson

Further Readings

Davis, L.B. (editor). 1979. *Symposium on the Crow-Hidatsa Separations.* Archaeology in Montana, vol. 20, no. 3. Montana Archaeological Society, Billings.

Mulloy, W.T. 1942. *The Hagen Site, A Prehistoric Village on the Lower Yellowstone.* Publications in the Social Sciences no. 1. University of Montana, Missoula.

Hammerstone

Hammerstones are stones that are used to batter other objects or materials. Because of the traumatic nature of the activity, they were usually made from durable, relatively nonbrittle substances, such as igneous or metamorphic rock. Although a variety of objects, from tent pegs to tubers, might have been pounded by prehistoric peoples, a common use of hammerstones must have been to break other rocks. Indeed,

Hammerstones, a. b. c. show battering from use, d. are hammers that have been chipped into shape. (Reprinted from Smithsonian Institution, Bureau of American Ethnology, Bulletin 60, Figure 142)

experimental flintknapping invariably produces wear on hammers that is identical to wear on similar stones discovered in archaeological contexts throughout North America. The wear pattern is a pecked, pulverized attrition of the surface produced by the loss of individual grains of igneous or sedimentary stone, or by a jagged breakage contour of microcrystalline ones. Hammers are common on archaeological sites. Many of the so-called "spheroids" found on sites in North America were probably not intentionally shaped as such but became rounded as a result of their use as hammerstones.

George H. Odell

Further Readings

McGuire, J.D. 1891. The Stone Hammer and Its Various Uses. *American Anthropologist* 4:301–312.

Witthoft, J. 1967. Stone Spheres and Hammers. *Maryland Archaeologist* 2:4–10.

Hanson Site

The Hanson site (48BH329) is a buried Paleoindian locality on the western slope of the Bighorn Mountains in northwestern Wyoming. Abundant artifacts, mostly chipped stone, lie buried within the T3 sediments of a third-order foothill drainage. Diagnostic artifacts recovered from the site indicate an extensive Folsom-period use of the paleosurface buried there. Radiocarbon dates from this Folsom occupation range from 8750 B.C. ± 670 to 8130 B.C. ± 330 (10,700–10,080 years B.P.). The site appears to have served as a lithic workshop and camp during the Folsom period, perhaps for 500 or more years. Investigations at the site have revealed a younger Paleoindian level above the Folsom surface. No typological indicators have been recovered from this younger stratum, but a single radiocarbon age determination of 7335 B.C. ± 90 (9285 years B.P.) has been made from it. The primary excavations at the site, conducted by George C. Frison of the University of Wyoming, exposed 225 m² (269 square yards) of an estimated 3,000 m² (3,588 square yards) of buried Paleoindian material.

Eric Ingbar

Further Readings

Frison, G.C. 1991. *Prehistoric Hunters of the High Plains*. 2nd ed. Academic Press, San Diego.

Frison, G.C., and B.A. Bradley. 1980. *Folsom*

Tools and Technology at the Hanson Site, Wyoming. University of New Mexico Press, Albuquerque.

Ingbar, E.E. 1992. The Hanson Site and Folsom on the Northwestern Plains. In *Ice Age Hunters of the Rockies*, edited by D.J. Stanford and J.S. Day, pp. 169–192. Denver Museum of Natural History, Denver.

Hardaway Site

The Hardaway site is situated on a promontory more than 76 m (250 feet) above the Yadkin River in Stanly County, North Carolina, and 6.4 km (4 miles) upstream from the Doerschuk site. Excavations in 1948 and 1955–1958 under the direction of Joffre L. Coe, and the intermittent investigations to date (1996), have recorded more than 7 metric tons of material, including more than 5,000 projectile points. The site has ca. 71 cm (28 inches) of midden deposit resting on a thin humus of the original land surface. Coe observed that debitage and lithic implements, primarily argillite and novaculite, were so dense in the midden that they accounted for 40 percent of the volume.

The site is important for data pertaining to the transition from Paleoindian to Early Archaic on the Carolina Piedmont. The first occupation is represented by the Hardaway complex; the Hardaway point is thought to be a regionalized variant of Paleoindian projectile points, and the Hardaway Side-Notched point a variant of the widespread Dalton type. Subsequent Early Archaic occupants were defined by Coe as Palmer and Kirk; Kirk points were divided typologically into Kirk Corner-Notched, Kirk Serrated, and Kirk Stemmed. Plow-zone deposits contained cultural material from Stanly, Guilford, Morrow Mountain, and Savannah River complexes, which had been stratigraphically defined at the nearby Doerschuk site; Woodland complexes were also represented in the plow zone.

Jefferson Chapman

Further Readings

Coe, J.L. 1964. *The Formative Cultures of the Carolina Piedmont*. Transactions, n.s., vol. 54, pt. 5. American Philosophical Society, Philadelphia.

Daniels, I.R., Jr. 1986 *An Analysis of Unifacial Stone Tools From the Hardaway Site,*

North Carolina. Southern Indian Studies no. 35. Research Laboratories of Anthropology, University of North Carolina, Chapel Hill.

Oliver, B.L. 1985. Tradition and Typology: Basic Elements of the Carolina Projectile Point Sequence. In *Structure and Process in Southeastern Archaeology,* edited by R.S. Dickens, Jr., and H.T. Ward, pp. 195–211. University of Alabama Press, Tuscaloosa.

Ward, H.T. 1983. A Review of Archaeology in the North Carolina Piedmont: A Study of Change. In *Prehistory of North Carolina: An Archaeological Symposium,* edited by M.A. Mathis and J.J. Crow, pp. 53–81. North Carolina Division of Archives and History, Department of Cultural Resources, Raleigh.

See also DOERSCHUK SITE

Havana Hopewell

The Havana Hopewell culture was an important center of Middle Woodland Hopewell development in the Lower Illinois River Valley and the adjacent Mississippi River Valley in west-central Illinois ca. 200 B.C.–A.D. 400 (2150–1550 years B.P.). Havana Hopewell pottery jar types, in par-

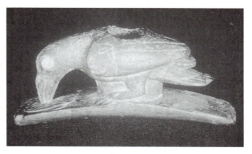

Hopewell bird effigy platform pipe from the Kampsville site, Illinois (4¹/₂" in length, 2" in height). (Courtesy of the Wilford Archaeology Laboratory, University of Minnesota)

ticular Havana Zoned Stamped and associated types, are present in site assemblages by ca. 200 B.C. (2150 years B.P.); classic Hopewell Zoned pottery, by ca. 100 B.C. (2050 years B.P.). Although the early relationship of Havana Hopewell and Ohio Hopewell remains obscure, both regions were centers in a large, interregional exchange network called the Hopewell Interaction Sphere; it is possible that the "Hopewell" phenomenon originated in this region of Illinois and spread to Ohio, where it attained its greatest elaboration. Familiar Hopewell Interaction Sphere items found in Havana Hopewell graves and settlements include cups, beads, and pendants made from *Busycon* and *Cassis* shells;

Baked clay human figurines from the Knight site, Illinois (left figure is 3¹/₈" in height). (Courtesy of the Wilford Archaeology Laboratory, University of Minnesota)

Hopewell Zoned ceramic vessel from the Meppen site, Calhoun County, Illinois (5 3/4" in height, 4 1/2" in diameter at the shoulder). (Courtesy of the Wilford Archaeology Laboratory, University of Minnesota)

copper pendants, gorgets, earspools, and plates with *repoussé* designs; platform pipes; and baked-clay human figurines.

Havana Hopewell subsistence was based on hunting, fishing, fowling, gathering, and the likely cultivation of starchy seeds, such as maygrass, knotweed, and goosefoot. Village–burial mound complexes ranging in size from ca. 2 ha to 15 ha (5–37 acres) were "packed" along the floodplain of the Lower Illinois and adjacent Mississippi valleys, with each apparently having access to an exploitation zone that stretched ca. 20 km (12.4 miles) along the river. Burial mounds are also present on the bluffs overlooking the valleys.

Guy Gibbon

Further Readings

Asch, D.L., K.B. Farnsworth, and N.B. Asch. 1979. Woodland Subsistence and Settlement in West Central Illinois. In *Hopewell Archaeology,* edited by D.S. Brose and N. Greber, pp. 80–85. Kent State University Press, Kent.

Braun, D.P. 1979. Illinois Hopewell Burial Practices and Social Organization: A Reexamination of the Klunk-Gibson Mound Group. In *Hopewell Archaeology,* edited by D.S. Brose and N. Greber, pp. 66–79. Kent State University Press, Kent.

———. 1985. Ceramic Decorative Diversity and Illinois Woodland Regional Integration. In *Decoding Prehistoric Ceramics,* edited by B.A. Nelson, pp. 128–153. Southern Illinois University Press, Carbondale.

———. 1986. Midwestern Hopewellian Exchange and Supralocal Interaction. In *Peer Polity Interaction and Sociopolitical Change,* edited by C. Renfrew, pp. 117–126. Cambridge University Press, Cambridge.

Brown, J.A. 1979. Charnel Houses and Mortuary Crypts: Disposal of the Dead in the Middle Woodland Period. In *Hopewell Archaeology,* edited by D.S. Brose and N. Greber, pp. 211–219. Kent State University Press, Kent.

Buikstra, J. 1979. *Hopewell in the Lower Illinois Valley: A Regional Approach to the Study of Human Biological Variability and Prehistoric Behavior.* Scientific Papers no. 2. Archaeology Program, Northwestern University, Evanston.

Caldwell, J.R., and R. Hall (editors). 1964. *Hopewellian Studies.* Illinois State Museum, Springfield.

Charles, D.K., S.R. Leigh, and J.E. Buikstra (editors). 1988. *The Archaic and Woodland Cemeteries at the Elizabeth Site in the Lower Illinois Valley.* Published for the Illinois Department of Transportation by the Center for American Archeology, Kampsville Archeological Center, Research Series, vol. 7. Kampsville.

Cole, F.-C., and T. Deuel. 1937. *Rediscovering Illinois.* University of Chicago Press, Chicago.

Farnsworth, K.B., and A.L. Koski. 1985. *Masey and Archie: A Study of Two Hopewellian Homesteads in the Western Illinois Uplands.* Published for the Illinois Department of Transportation by the Center for American Archeology, Kampsville Archeological Center, Research Series, vol. 3. Kampsville.

Griffin, J.B., R.E. Flanders, and P.F. Titterington. 1970. *The Burial Complexes of the Knight and Norton Mounds in Illinois and Michigan.* Memoir no. 2. Museum of Anthropology, University of Michigan, Ann Arbor.

See also HOPEWELL INTERACTION SPHERE; MIDDLE WOODLAND; OHIO HOPEWELL

Haven, Samuel F. (1806–1881)

Influential scientist and librarian of the American Antiquarian Society, Samuel F. Haven was commissioned by Joseph Henry, first secretary of the Smithsonian Institution, to prepare a historical review of the archaeology of the United States, which was published in 1856 as *Archaeology of the United States*. In the review, Haven surveyed existing knowledge and current speculation about North American prehistory and, intent on stopping "where evidence ceases," cautiously concluded that the Mound Builder theory was untenable, that Indians had been in North America for a considerable period, and that their closest affinities were with "Asiatic races." Haven's reasoned and dispassionate review, written at a time when speculative works dominated the literature, typified the new, descriptive mode of scholarly inquiry being promoted at the time by government scientists, a mode of inquiry that came to dominate late-nineteenth- and early-twentieth-century North American archaeology.

Guy Gibbon

Further Readings

Haven, S.F. 1856. *Archaeology of the United States*. Smithsonian Institution, Washington, D.C.

See also MOUND BUILDER MYTH

Hawkshaw

Hawkshaw (8ES01287) was an Early Woodland Deptford settlement on Pensacola Bay, Florida. In 1985, the well-preserved remains of this 2,000-year-old settlement were discovered near downtown Pensacola. It is situated on the edge of a bluff overlooking Pensacola Bay, at the mouth of a small, spring-fed stream in a grove of oaks and hickories. Several factors make Hawkshaw an unusual Deptford site. First, the deposits, which were less than 0.6 m (2 feet) deep, were covered only by a deposit of sand. Most Deptford sites are located at the bottom of dense shell middens several feet thick. Second, the site had been occupied only by Deptford people. Other known Deptford sites had been used repeatedly over the millennia, an occupation history that has usually resulted in the mixture of old and young materials. Third, the site contained almost 200 small pits (ca. 0.9–1.5 m, or 3–5 feet, wide x 0.6–1.2 m, or 2–4 feet, deep) full of household refuse. Few other Deptford sites have sealed pits. Instead, they are composed of built-up surface debris (midden), a matrix that is susceptible to disturbance by the activities of people, animals, and generations of large trees. To an archaeologist, the presence of these three factors means that Hawkshaw contains "pure" information about a Deptford occupation. In addition, the site's sealed small pits contained materials that had been used and discarded at the same time, which means that information about the material culture of a people at a point in time can be obtained.

More than 165 Deptford refuse pits were excavated at Hawkshaw. The carefully removed contents included pieces of pottery, charred wood, nuts and seeds, stone and shell tools, and animal bones. These contents were studied by specialists such as stone-tool technologists, paleobotanists, and archaeozoologists. Charcoal bits from 10 pits were also radiocarbon dated. From the contents and organization of the sealed trash pits, and these dates, archaeologists have been able to deduce much information about the Deptford group that lived at Hawkshaw. For example, the radiocarbon dates from all but one pit were the same (averaging A.D. 212, or 1738 years B.P.). From this information, it can be inferred that most of the material recovered from the site was from a single occupation. The trash pits were organized into clusters of 5–15 pits, and there were many more pieces of pottery that fit together within these clusters than between them. From this information, archaeologists have suggested that the clusters were related to separate households or perhaps even extended families. The bones of small pinfish and mullet were recovered in great numbers. From this information, it is reasonable to conclude that the Deptford people used small-mesh seine nets in shallow near-shore waters to capture schools of fish. Other information indicates that they fished for bass in the freshwater stream and hunted deer in the nearby woods. The presence of acorns, hickory, and deer skulls with antlers attached indicates that Deptford people lived at this site during the summer and fall seasons. From the size of their pots, we know that everyone used large, deep pots that are good for simmering stews and gruels. Each cluster also had fragments of small bowls and beakers that were well made and decorated with different designs than the cooking pots. Archaeologists infer from this information that these were personal eating and drinking containers most likely traded in from the Lower Mississippi Valley.

Information continues to be gleaned from the pristine time capsules found at the Early Woodland Deptford Hawkshaw site. It is sites like Hawkshaw that enable archaeologists to develop more detailed and comprehensive information about the lifeways of early Native Americans.

Judith A. Bense

Further Readings

Bense, J.A. 1985. *Hawkshaw: Prehistory and History in an Urban Neighborhood in Pensacola, FL.* Reports of Investigations no. 7. Archaeology Institute, University of West Florida, Pensacola.

Head-Smashed-In Buffalo Jump

Located in southwestern Alberta, Canada, Head-Smashed-In Buffalo Jump (DkPj-1) is one of the premier examples of the great communal-bison-kill sites used by the native peoples of the northern Plains. The components of this complex site, called HSI for short, include a collecting area ca. 40 km² (25 square miles) in size where the bison were gathered in preparation for the drive to the cliff. This natural landform is an enormous bowl-shaped topographic basin that helped contain the bison, enhancing the likelihood of a suc-

cessful and productive kill. Found throughout the basin are a network of lines of small rock piles known as drive lanes. Thousands of rock piles form lanes that converge in a funnel-shaped manner. They served to direct the movement of the stampeding bison toward the cliff. The cliff, or jump off, consists of a 10-m (33-foot) -high wall of bedrock, at the base of which are found the archaeological materials that have been deposited over thousands of years. The final component of HSI is an immense camp and butchering area situated on the prairie below the jump. Here, the laborious task of cutting up and processing the spoils of the kill transpired.

It is estimated that several hundred thousand bison met their death by being stampeded over the cliffs of HSI. Archaeological materials at the bottom of the cliff have been recorded from near the existing ground surface to a depth of 11 m (36 feet). This massive deposit of bison bone and stone tools spans nearly 6,000 years of time, with the earliest use of the jump occurring ca. 3850 B.C. (5800 years B.P.). This makes HSI one of the earliest—perhaps the earliest—example of the use of the jump as a means of killing large numbers of bison at a single time. The jump was used almost continuously afterward. Although a few historic-period artifacts, such as metal trade points, have been found at the site, the introduction of the gun and especially the horse brought an

Head-Smashed-In buffalo jump showing the main cliff and kill site. (Photograph by J. Brink)

end to the use of the jump by ca. A.D. 1850.

Archaeological investigations at HSI began in 1938 with a visit by Junius Bird of the American Museum of Natural History in New York. More significant excavations were conducted in 1949 by Boyd Wettlaufer, and the 1960s saw excavations organized by Richard G. Forbis and directed by Brian Reeves. It was Reeves's work (1978, 1983) that established the cultural and chronological framework for HSI, leading to the recognition of the significance of this site in chronicling the prehistory of the northern Plains. Head-Smashed-In has been designated a Provincial Historic Site, a National Historic Site, and, in 1981, a UNESCO World Heritage Site. An interpretive center at the site is open to the public year-round.

Jack Brink

Further Readings

Reeves, B.O.K. 1978. Head-Smashed-In: 5500 Years of Bison Jumping in the Alberta Plains. In *Bison Procurement and Utilization: A Symposium,* edited by L.B. Davis and M. Wilson, pp. 151–174. Memoir no. 14. Plains Anthropologist, Lincoln.
———. 1983. Six Millenniums of Buffalo Kills. *Scientific American* 249(4):120–135.

Health and Disease

While reconstruction of the state of health of Precolumbian Native American populations is a problem of formidable complexity, ethnographic accounts, historical records of postcontact epidemics, and observations of identifiable disease in archaeological human remains can be employed to fashion a useful perspective.

The behavior of postcontact epidemics established clearly that certain diseases common among Europeans were foreign to New World natives. Smallpox, for example, accompanied Hernán Cortés and his forces into Tenochtitlan in the early sixteenth century, allowing this handful of Spaniards to enter what is now Mexico City to find half of its Aztec population dead or dying of that disease; a century later, the disease had spread throughout the central valley of Mexico and slashed its population to one-tenth of its precontact level (Crosby 1972). Such experiences were repeated again and again as this highly infectious disease spread northward as far as the Arctic areas and southward to decimate the Andean populations as well. Other illnesses with similar consequences include measles and later malaria and yellow fever (introduced through the slave trade). Such a response is characteristic of "virgin soil" epidemics in which a new infectious agent is introduced into a nonimmune population.

However disastrous these epidemics were, the absence in the Americas of these typically European infectious agents does not validate an image of a disease-free New World. Tuberculous skeletal and soft-tissue lesions are numerous in ancient skeletons, in both North and South America. Though uncommon prior to A.D. 1000 (950 years B.P.) in North America (Buikstra 1981), many examples are contemporary with the evolution of a maize agricultural subsistence pattern (Cook 1984). The various forms of spirochetal infections grouped under the term "treponematosis" are clearly defined in many early American populations as early ca. 2000 B.C. (3950 years B.P.). However, until methods are developed that are more specific than those currently available, it will not be possible to determine whether these infections are related to the European syphilis epidemic that began ca. A.D. 1502 (Crosby 1969). Coccidioidomycosis, a major fungus infection in the southwestern United States in the twentieth century, has been demonstrated in Precolumbian skeletal lesions (Merbs 1992).

Parasites, too, have been found in many studies of coprolites (desiccated ancient intestinal content). Fish tapeworm (*Diphyllobothrium pacificum*) was incurred by ancient fishermen earlier than 2000 B.C. (3950 years B.P.) on the coast of Chile by eating unheated, infected marine fish (Verano and Ubelaker 1992). Calcified liver or lung cysts suggestive of dog tapeworm (*Echinococcus granulosus*) have also been reported. The lesions of American trypanosomiasis (Chagas' disease), endemic in the late twentieth century in certain parts of South America, are evident in Precolumbian mummies from those same areas (Fornaciari et al. 1992). Numerous other organisms with lesser health effects, such as pinworm (*Enterobius*) and roundworm (*Ascaris*), are represented within ancient bodies. More puzzling are reports of hookworm (*Ancylostoma*) infestation in mummies dating as far back as 5000 B.C. (6950 years B.P.). Since this infection is transmitted to humans via the skin of bare feet by larvae hatched from ova discharged in the soil, one would not expect this disease to survive a trans-Beringian trek.

Noninfectious diseases were also abundant in ancient Americans. Degenerative joint disease was common, particularly among those living physically strenuous lives like the residents of the Mesa Verde site in southwestern Colorado ca. A.D. 750 (1200 years B.P.). Congenital deformities, such as spina bifida, parallel the frequency in many modern and older European populations. Traumatic lesions, indicative of both interpersonal violence and group warfare, are numerous in many peoples of both North and South America. Even metabolic aberrations like osteoporosis can be found in groups ranging from the Arctic to northern Chile.

In addition to these specific diseases, it is possible to assess the general health of a population on the basis of lesions caused by life-threatening conditions producing sufficient metabolic demands ("stress") to arrest or retard growth temporarily. These lesions include radiologically evident transverse lines representing, among other things, arrest in long-bone growth, foci of enamel growth impairment ("dental hypoplasia"), thickness of long-bone cortex, length of life span, and adult stature. Such lesions are called "nonspecific stress indicators" because they reflect a serious health problem without identifying its specific etiology. Many ancient American populations reveal high frequencies of such indicators. These indicators are often correlated with archaeological evidence of famine or other stressful situations, such as adaptations to new environments following forced translocation.

It is clear that Precolumbian New World populations were subject to many disease agents. Patterns of diseases were shaped then, as now, by interactions of the biology of the disease agent, the environment, and human behavior. Stable circumstances often were accompanied by excellent human adaptations. Substantial variations in disease frequency among native populations reflect instability of disease-affecting conditions. The complete absence of several European disease agents, including smallpox, typhoid fever, and measles, in their environments left Precolumbian Americans uniquely susceptible to their devastating epidemic impact following European contact.

Arthur C. Aufderheide

Further Readings

Buikstra, J.E. 1981. *Prehistoric Tuberculosis in the Americas.* Scientific Paper no. 5. Archaeology Program, Northwestern University, Evanston.

Cook, D.C. 1984. Subsistence and Health in the Lower Illinois Valley: Osteological Evidence. In *Paleopathology at the Origins of Agriculture,* edited by M.N. Cohen and G.J. Armelagos, pp. 235–269. Academic Press, New York.

Crosby, A.M., Jr. 1969. The Early History of Syphilis: A Reappraisal. *American Anthropologist* 71:218–227.

———. 1972. *The Columbian Exchange: Biological and Cultural Consequences of 1492.* Contributions in American Studies no. 2. Greenwood Press, Westport.

Fornaciari, G., M. Castagna, P. Viacava, A. Tognetti, and G. Bevilacqua. 1992. Chagas' Disease in Peruvian Incan Mummy. *Lancet* 339:128–129.

Merbs, C.F. 1992. A New World of Infectious Disease. *Yearbook of Physical Anthropology Series* 35:3–42.

Verano, J.W., and D.H. Ubelaker, Jr. (editors). 1992. *Disease and Demography in the Americas.* Smithsonian Institution Press, Washington, D.C.

Heart River Phase

The Heart River phase is a subdivision of the Coalescent tradition. It consists of 24 circular earthlodge villages along the Missouri River in North Dakota between the Heart and the Knife rivers that were occupied in the period A.D. 1450/1500–1780 by the ancestors of the Mandan and the Hidatsa. Many of the sites have deep middens, up to 2.7 m (9 feet) thick, suggesting long and intensive occupations. There is disagreement over divisions within the phase. The traditionally accepted, but tentative, view, which is based on geographic location, suggests Heart River 1 and 2 subphases. Heart River 1 villages near the Heart River were occupied by the Mandan, while Heart River 2 communities near the Knife River are ancestral Hidatsa. This taxonomic system also suggests A.D. 1675–1780 for the time span of the Heart River phase. Later cultural-historical summaries date the Heart River phase at A.D. 1450/1500–1780 and do not propose further divisions, although the geographic separation between villages occupied by the Mandan and the Hidatsa continues to be recognized.

Ten of the villages are fortified with curvilinear ditches. Mandan villagers are believed to be direct descendants of the Late Middle Missouri–tradition peoples who lived along the Missouri near Bismarck, North Dakota; the

Aerial view of the Double Ditch site, Heart River phase. (Photograph by C. M. Johnson)

Hidatsa have multiple, but unclear, origins. The few Mandan and Hidatsa to survive the devastating epidemic diseases introduced by Europeans and Americans lived in the last earthlodge village, Like-a-Fishhook, until 1886.

Excavated Heart River sites contain diverse chipped- and ground-stone, pottery, and bone-tool assemblages used in the procurement and processing of animals, such as bison, and horticultural products, like corn, beans, and squash, grown on the Missouri River floodplain. As early as A.D. 1600 and certainly by 1675, Euro-American trade goods began to be used by the Heart River and other Protohistoric villagers along the Missouri River in North and South Dakota. The period that includes trading in these and other items has been divided into four units, based on the type of trade contact: indirect (A.D. 1600–1740), intermittent (A.D. 1740–1790), frequent (A.D. 1790–1822), and local (A.D. 1822–1860). During the first period, all Missouri River villagers acted as "middlemen" in the trading system that included their own garden produce, skins, and furs, as well as Euro-American items. The second period began with the introduction of the horse from the American Southwest via Plains nomadic groups and guns brought in by other nomadic groups from Canadian and Great Lakes trading posts. It was not until the period of di-

rect Euro-American trade that glass bead and metal knives, scrapers, and containers began to replace native pottery vessels and stone and bone tools. The early part of the trade period resulted in great material wealth and a florescence in Heart River–phase culture.

There is historical documentation relating to several Heart River–phase communities during the trade period. The earliest of these is by La Vérendrye, a French trader and explorer who visited several Mandan villages in the vicinity of the Heart River in 1738–1739. During their expedition in 1804–1806, Lewis and Clark recorded a number of abandoned communities near the Heart River, identified as Mandan with the help of native informants. Some of these can be associated with modern-day archaeological sites. After Lewis and Clark, the number of contacts by European and American traders, trappers, explorers, and adventurers grew significantly—leading eventually to the demise of much of the traditional lifeways of the Mandan and the Hidatsa.

Craig M. Johnson

Further Readings

Lehmer, D.J. 1971. *Introduction to Middle Missouri Archeology.* National Park Service, Washington, D.C.

Thiessen, T.D. 1993. *The Phase I Archeological Research Program for the Knife River Indian Villages National Historic Site: 2. Ethnohistorical Studies*. Midwest Archeological Center, National Park Service, Lincoln.

Will, G.F., and H.J. Spinden. 1906. *The Mandans: A Study of Their Culture, Archeology and Language*. Papers, vol. 3, no. 4. Peabody Museum of American Archaeology and Ethnology, Harvard University, Cambridge.

Wood, W.R. (editor). 1986. *Papers in Northern Plains Prehistory and Ethnohistory*. Special Publication no. 10. South Dakota Archaeological Society, Sioux Falls.

Heat Treatment of Silicates

The heating of chert or flint above certain temperatures causes internal changes in the stone that are favorable for tool production. This concept, first introduced to American archaeology by D.E. Crabtree and B.R. Butler (1964), has been confirmed ethnographically as an aboriginal practice (Hester 1972). Heat changes cause an increase in compressive strength, reduction in point tensile strength, more effective control of flaking and fracture, and a decrease in the occurrence of hinge and step fractures while flaking (Purdy 1974).

Controlled heating of cherts appears to cause fusion and/or recrystallization on a molecular level, perhaps facilitated by impurities in the silicate material that act as fluxes. The result is greater internal vitreousness and homogeneity but also a reduction in fracture toughness or resistance to fracture (Purdy and Brooks 1971; Domanski and Webb 1992). This produces sharper edges but also increased brittleness, an undesirable property when contemplating percussive activities that require durability. Heating also affects the use of tools: heat-treated implements wear more quickly than unheated ones and yield more step- and hinge-fracture terminations from use (Olausson 1983). Proper length of firing time and optimal temperatures vary with the material; for the Florida cherts tested by B.A. Purdy, critical temperatures were in the 350°–400°C range.

Visual properties of the silicates can also be altered with firing. Silicates usually, but not always, become more lustrous with firing. Silicates that contain iron are oxidized and turn pink or red, while cherts that lack iron either do not change color or intensify their original color. The white Burlington chert tested by J.W. Rick (1978) occasionally became whiter. From an archaeologist's point of view, visual assessments of the existence of prehistoric heat alteration are quick and easy—but frequently inaccurate. More accurate results for any particular stone may be obtained through thermoluminescence (Melcher and Zimmerman 1977), investigation of isothermal remanent magnetism (Borradaile et al. 1993), or inspection through a scanning electron microscope (Olausson and Larsson 1982).

George H. Odell

Further Readings

Borradaile, G.J., S.A. Kissin, J.D. Stewart, W.A. Ross, and T. Werner. 1993. Magnetic and Optical Methods for Detecting the Heat Treatment of Chert. *Journal of Archaeological Science* 20:57–66.

Crabtree, D.E., and B.R. Butler. 1964. Notes on Experiments in Flint Knapping: I. Heat Treatment of Silica Minerals. *Tebiwa* 7:1–6.

Domanski, M., and J.A. Webb. 1992. Effect of Heat Treatment on Siliceous Rocks Used in Prehistoric Lithic Technology. *Journal of Archaeological Science* 19:601–614.

Hester, T.R. 1972. Ethnographic Evidence for the Thermal Alteration of Siliceous Stone. *Tebiwa* 15:63–65.

Melcher, C.L., and D.W. Zimmerman. 1977. Thermoluminescent Determination of Prehistoric Heat Treatment of Chert Artifacts. *Science* 197:1359–1362.

Olausson, D.S. 1983. Experiments to Investigate the Effects of Heat Treatment on Use-Wear on Flint Tools. *Proceedings of the Prehistoric Society* 49:1–13.

Olausson, D.S., and L. Larsson. 1982. Testing for the Presence of Thermal Pretreatment of Flint in the Mesolithic and Neolithic of Sweden. *Journal of Archaeological Science* 9:275–285.

Purdy, B.A. 1974. Investigations Concerning the Thermal Alteration of Silica Minerals: An Archaeological Approach. *Tebiwa* 17:37–66.

Purdy, B.A., and H.K. Brooks. 1971. Thermal Alteration of Silica Minerals: An Archaeological Approach. *Science* 173:322–325.

Rick, J.W. 1978. *Heat-Altered Cherts of the*

Lower Illinois Valley: An Experimental Study in Prehistoric Technology. Prehistoric Records no. 2. Archaeology Program, Northwestern University, Evanston.

Heizer, Robert Fleming (1915–1979)

Robert F. Heizer was the first California archaeologist to hold a tenured faculty appointment in the University of California system. Trained under the guidance of A.L. Kroeber, Heizer was brought into Kroeber's Department of Anthropology in 1946 after completing his Ph.D., in order to make the study of California archaeology a regular part of the department's research and scholarship mission. A prolific author and field researcher, Heizer directed the doctoral programs of most California archaeologists trained between the late 1930s and the late 1950s, including Clement W. Meighan, Adán Treganza, William J. Wallace, James Bennyhoff, Martin Baumhoff, Franklin Fenenga, Albert Elsasser, William Clewlow, Jr., Lewis K. Napton, and Francis W. Riddell.

Heizer's first and arguably most enduring contribution to California archaeology was his development, with Jeremiah B. Lillard and Franklin Fenenga, of the first model of a culture sequence for central California. During the 1930s, they excavated a series of sites around

Robert F. Heizer. (Reprinted with permission from American Antiquity *47[1]:99)*

the Delta country, a vast network of marshes and islands formed by the confluence of the Sacramento and San Joaquin rivers east of San Francisco. Many of these sites proved to be burial deposits. Prehistoric burials in California were often accompanied by finely crafted artifacts, which Heizer and his colleagues sought in order to study the artifact styles characteristic of different eras in the region's past. The results, presented in numerous papers from 1937 onward, defined the "Central California sequence." In this model, Heizer and his colleagues recognized three successive cultural episodes or stylistic horizons: the Early horizon, the Middle horizon, and the Late horizon. Time spans attributed to each horizon were later refined as absolute dating methods became available.

The Central California sequence quickly became the basic chronological ordering device for much of the archaeology of northern California. Over time, it began to evolve as new discoveries were made and ideas changed. Heizer and others took part in this reconfiguration. By the 1950s, the term "horizon" was giving way to "period," reflecting a shift in emphasis from time units as episodes in the stylistic history of artifacts to a concern for the histories of past cultures as analytic units. As archaeological research became more extensive in other parts of northern California, local sequences with different terms and dates emerged, and the Central California sequence became more fully confined to the Delta area. By the 1970s, the time units of "Early," "Middle," and "Late" had been replaced by periods with local site or region names: the Early period became Windmiller; the Middle period, Cosumnes; and the Late period, Hotchkiss. This shift reflected a trend away from the evolutionary progression of the Early-Middle-Late series. Nonetheless, these terms, especially "Late period," came into greater use elsewhere in the state to refer to general stages of California prehistory. "Late period" now serves the sort of function in much of California archaeology that is served by such terms as "Late Woodland" or "Mississippian" in eastern North America.

Heizer and his students made contributions regarding other parts of the state as well. In the late 1940s, they did pioneering excavations in Topanga Canyon in western Los Angeles County, helping define the Millingstone horizon. In the 1950s, his students helped him define the first regional sequence for the High Sierras and surrounding region with the Martis and Kings Beach cultures. In the 1960s, Heizer led research along the northwestern California coast, where his *Four Ages of Tsurai* (1952), written with John Mills, served as a guide and helped define the emergence of the region's complex coastal cultures. Heizer devoted most of the last two decades of his research career, though, to the archaeology of the Great Basin in western Nevada at such sites as Humboldt and Lovelock caves. He nevertheless remained a profound factor in California archaeology, continuing to publish and to direct students doing research in the field.

Joseph L. Chartkoff

Further Readings

Baumhoff, M.A. 1980. Robert Fleming Heizer, 1915–1979. *American Anthropologist* 82:843–847.

Clark, J.D. 1980. Memorial to Robert Fleming Heizer (1915–1979). *Journal of California and Great Basin Anthropology* 1:241–245.

Heizer, R.F. 1937. Baked Clay Objects of the Lower Sacramento Valley, California. *American Antiquity* 3:34–50.

———. 1949. The Archaeology of Central California: 1. The Early Horizon. *University of California Anthropological Records* 12(1):1–84.

———. 1953. The Archaeology of the Napa Region. *University of California Anthropological Records* 12(6):225–338.

———. 1974. *The Destruction of California Indians: A Collection of Documents From the Period 1847 to 1865 in Which Are Described Some of the Things That Happened to Some of the Indians of California.* Peregrine Smith, Santa Barbara.

———. (editor). 1978. *California.* Handbook of North American Indians, vol. 8, W.C. Sturtevant, general editor. Smithsonian Institution, Washington, D.C.

Heizer, R.F., and A.F. Almquist. 1971. *The Other Californians: Prejudice and Discrimination Under Spain, Mexico and the United States to 1920.* University of California Press, Berkeley.

Heizer, R.F., and M.A. Baumhoff. 1962. *Prehistoric Rock Art of Nevada and Eastern California.* University of California Press, Berkeley.

Heizer, R.F., and W. Clewlow, Jr. 1973. *Prehistoric Rock Art of California.* Ballena Press, Ramona, Calif.

Heizer, R.F., and A.B. Elsasser. 1953. *Some Archaeological Sites and Cultures of the Central Sierra Nevada.* Reports no. 21. University of California Archaeological Survey, University of California, Berkeley.

———. 1964. Archaeology of Hum-67, the Gunther Island Site in Humboldt Bay, California. *University of California Archaeological Survey Reports* 62:5–122.

Heizer, R.F., and J. Mills. 1952. *The Four Ages of Tsurai.* University of California Press, Berkeley.

Heizer, R.F., and M.A. Whipple (editors). 1971. *The California Indians: A Source Book.* 2nd ed. University of California Press, Berkeley.

Hester, T.R. 1982. Robert Fleming Heizer, 1915–1979. *American Antiquity* 47:99–107.

Lillard, J.B., R.F. Heizer, and F. Fenenga. 1939. *An Introduction to the Archaeology of Central California.* Bulletins no. 2. Department of Anthropology, Sacramento Junior College, Sacramento.

Hell Gap Complex

The Hell Gap complex is named after the Hell Gap site in southeast Wyoming. Two Paleoindian points were found eroding out of a cut bank of an arroyo at this site in the late 1950s. Since they were different from other point types recognized at that time, they were named Hell Gap from the site location, which is at the south end of the Hartville Uplift a short distance north of Guernsey, Wyoming.

First investigations at the location led the investigator, George A. Agogino, who at that time was teaching at the University of Wyoming, to believe that the Hell Gap projectile point might be one of the older Paleoindian point types. However, after careful stratigraphic work this proved not to be the case, for the Hell Gap complex followed the Agate Basin complex in time.

The results of the Hell Gap site excavations placed the Hell Gap complex at ca. 8050–7550 B.C. (10,000–9000 years B.P.). Further confirmation of this age range was provided by both bone and charcoal radiocarbon dates at the Casper Hell Gap bison kill in Wyoming of ca. 8050 B.C. (10,000 years B.P.). Another Hell Gap bison-kill site, the Jones-Miller site in eastern Colorado, also has a radiocarbon date of ca. 8050 B.C. (10,000 years

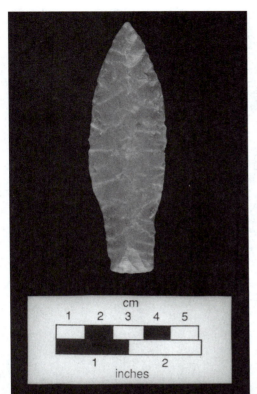

Hell Gap point from the Hell Gap site, Wyoming. (Courtesy of the Wilford Archaeology Laboratory, University of Minnesota)

B.P.). A radiocarbon date on a Hell Gap component at the Agate Basin site is ca. 8450 B.C. (10,400 years B.P.). A mixed and undated Agate Basin–Hell Gap level was present at the Carter/Kerr-McGee site in eastern Wyoming stratigraphically between a Cody-Alberta level and a Folsom level.

George C. Frison

Further Readings

Frison, G.C. 1974. *The Casper Site: A Hell Gap Bison Kill on the High Plains.* Academic Press, New York.

Irwin-Williams, C., H.T. Irwin, G. Agogino, and C.V. Haynes, Jr. 1973. Hell Gap: Paleo-Indian Occupation on the High Plains. *Plains Anthropologist* 18(59):40–53.

Stanford, D.J. 1978. The Jones-Miller Site: An Example of Hell Gap Bison Procurement Strategy. In *Bison Procurement and Utilization: A Symposium,* edited by L.B. Davis and M. Wilson, pp. 90–97. Memoir no. 14. Plains Anthropologist, Lincoln.

See also HELL GAP SITE

Hell Gap Site

James Duguid and Malcom McKnight, then students at the University of Wyoming, found the Hell Gap site (48GO305) in the Haystack Range, 13 km (8 miles) north of Guernsey, Wyoming, in 1959. Realizing the potential value of the site, the students showed its location to George A. Agogino, then teaching at the University of Wyoming. He began work using a student crew in the summer of that year. The first two years' excavation developed the basic sequence, from earliest to most recent, of Folsom, Midland, Agate Basin, Hell Gap, Alberta, Scottsbluff, Eden, and Oblique Flake cultures. The Hell Gap point was identified as a new Paleoindian point type in these excavations by Agogino, who obtained a radiocarbon date indicating its age at ca. 8050 B.C. (10,000 years B.P.).

In 1960, Agogino was joined by Harvard University students Cynthia and Henry Irwin. They worked together for the next six years (1961–1966) under the directorship of Jo Brew, chairman of the Department of Anthropology at Harvard. An unofficial staff member was Kay Irwin, mother of Henry and Cynthia. Agogino's initial research had already developed a sequence of cultures and first identified and dated the Hell Gap level. Under Brew's leadership, more areas in the canyon were tested, and living floors were found at three separate locations. The Goshen point, which resembles an unfluted Clovis point and is dated at ca. 9050 B.C. (11,000 years B.P.), was associated with the base cultural horizon. A possible house structure, identified by post holes, was found in the Agate Basin level.

Following the seventh season of their joint excavation (1960–1966), the excavators decided to close the project and write a final publication. To help prepare the report, Kay and Cynthia Irwin took partial collections to Harvard, while Henry Irwin took artifacts to Washington State University. Lingering illness caused both Henry and Cynthia to delay writing reports. In succession, Henry, Kay, and Cynthia Irwin died. The artifacts seemed hopelessly scattered in various institutions. Agogino, then working at Blackwater Draw, had little time to collect the scattered notes and artifacts.

Top: Hell Gap site, Agate Basin level bone and chip floor. (Photograph by G. A. Agogino) Bottom: View of the valley in which the Hell Gap site is located and the Harvard University–University of Wyoming base camp. (Photograph by G. A. Agogino)

However, even before Cynthia Irwin's death, George C. Frison at the University of Wyoming had, with the permission of the excavators, begun reassembling Hell Gap artifacts. Frison is currently (1996) studying the artifacts, and he plans additional work at Hell Gap; he has also secured legal protection for the site. A final report of all research at the site will be completed under his leadership.

George A. Agogino

Further Readings

Agogino, G. 1961. A New Point Type From Hell Gap Valley, Eastern Wyoming. *American Antiquity* 26:558–560.

———. 1965. The Hell Gap Site, Wyoming: An Archaeological Sketch. *Wyoming Archaeologist* 3:35–39.

———. 1966. Resume of Cultural Complexes at the Hell Gap Site. *Wyoming Archaeologist* 9:11–13.

———. 1983. The Hell Gap Point: A Twenty-Year Evaluation. *Masterkey* 14(4):155–157.

Irwin, C., H. Irwin, and G. Agogino. 1968. Archaeological Investigations at the Hell Gap Site Near Guernsey, Wyoming, 1964. *National Geographic Society Research Reports, 1963 Projects,* pp. 151–156.

———. 1969. Archaeological Investigations at the Hell Gap Site, Guernsey, Wyoming, 1964. *National Geographic Society Research Reports, 1964 Projects,* pp. 113–115.

Henrietta Focus

Henrietta was initially designated a focus. Generally, foci have become phases in more recent classification schemes. Henrietta, however, now is more often considered a complex because it is poorly defined spatially and temporally. Material-culture associations are also poorly known, although the complex does belong to the Southern Plains Village tradition. Henrietta is guess-dated to after A.D. 1450 (500 years B.P.). The main area of occupation is north-central Texas, especially the Red River Valley, its tributaries, and the Trinity and Brazos headwaters. Henrietta origins are uncertain, but it may have developed out of an indigenous Woodland-period occupation. Similarities have also been seen to the Washita River phase. It is uncertain what happened to Henrietta-focus people; they may be ancestral to the Norteño focus.

Very little research has been done on Henrietta sites since the 1940s, when they were first studied. Small villages or hamlets with thick midden deposits exist. There is very little information on subsistence. Bison, deer, fish bones, and mussel shells were used for tools. Bone tools commonly used in horticultural activities are also present. Ceramics are shell tempered, plain surfaced, and ovate in shape with flat-to-round bases. Decoration is rare but includes appliqué, punctation, and incising. Bone tools include bison-scapula and horn-core hoes, awls of several types, and fishhooks. Stone tools include small, triangular, side-notched or unnotched points; expanding-base drills; end scrapers; alternately beveled, diamond-shaped knives; and two-edged, alternately beveled knives. Ground stone includes several types of manos and metates, and shaft smoothers and pipes. Trade material includes Southwestern pottery, obsidian, *Olivella* shell, Alibates agatized dolomite (Texas Panhandle), and probably Caddoan pottery.

Susan C. Vehik

Further Readings

Krieger, A.D. 1947. *Culture Complexes and Chronology in Northern Texas.* Publication no. 4640. University of Texas, Austin.

Hidden Cave

Hidden Cave was formed ca. 19,000 B.C. (20,950 years B.P.), when the waves of rising Lake Lahontan gouged out a huge cavity beneath the tufa-cemented gravels in the Stillwater Range, which overlooks central Nevada's now-arid Carson Desert. The floor of this cavern was alternately flooded and exposed until shortly after 8000 B.C. (9950 years B.P.). Ca. 4950 B.C. (6900 years B.P.), the Mazama volcanic ash washed into Hidden Cave. During brief intervals in the Holocene (the geologic period from 8000 B.C., or 9950 years B.P., to the present), Native American groups visited Hidden Cave, leaving behind a well-stratified, well-preserved archaeological record. Natural and cultural deposits continued to accumulate inside until the cave entrance gradually became choked with a debris cone. Hidden Cave was rediscovered in the 1920s, and teams of archaeologists excavated there in the 1940s, 1950s, and late 1970s.

Even today, the entrance to Hidden Cave remains difficult to find; hence, the name. But once inside, the visitor realizes that the cavern is huge. It is ca. 45.7 m (150 feet) long and 29 m

Hidden Cave excavation taken from the rear of the cave. (Courtesy of the American Museum of Natural History. Photograph by D. H. Thomas)

(95 feet) wide; in places, the roof rises 6 m (20 feet) above the cave floor. But, now as then, the interior of Hidden Cave is pitch-black, and walking across the surface raises suffocating clouds of dust. No matter how well sheltered, Hidden Cave was never a good place to live.

The various excavations have shown that the archaeological deposits of Hidden Cave are riddled with dozens of ancient storage pits, most of them emptied of their contents millennia before archaeologists got there. During precontact times, the site was used mostly to temporarily store personal gear and, to a lesser extent, food supplies. Only occasionally did people camp inside; once in a great while, deceased were buried inside.

Most of the cultural materials inside Hidden Cave were left there ca. 3050–1250 B.C. (5000–3200 B.P.). Analysis of plant and animal remains shows that Native American people used Hidden Cave from spring through fall, but most intensively during the summer, when the cave's cool interior provided a temporary respite from the searing desert heat outside.

David Hurst Thomas

Further Readings

Ambro, R.D. 1966. Two Fish Nets From Hidden Cave. *University of California Archaeological Survey Reports* 66:101–135.

Roust, N.L., and C.W. Clewlow. 1968. Projectile Points From Hidden Cave (NV-Ch-16), Churchill County, Nevada. *University of California Archaeological Survey Reports* 71:103–116.

Thomas, D.H. 1985. The Archaeology of Hidden Cave, Nevada. *Anthropological Papers of the American Museum of Natural History* 61(1):1–430.

Historical Particularism

Historical particularism is an approach to cultural analysis championed by Franz Boas in the early twentieth century that viewed each culture as a collection of individual traits that had largely come together through the chance operation of diffusion. Research involved, then, identification and description of the myriad attributes of specific cultures, as well as a search for the unique combinations of diffusional events that had shaped their development. Historical particularism was, in part, a reaction against the excesses of the grand schemes of late-nineteenth-century unilineal cultural evolutionism that had concentrated on cross-cultural regularities. Although Boas did not deny that such regularities might exist, he believed that cultures were so complex that detailed historical studies of particulars were essential before general trends could be rigorously examined. The approach influenced how archaeologists approached and organized the archaeological record, resulting, for instance, in an emphasis on identifying archaeological cultures by lists of traits, as in the Midwestern Taxonomic method. While under attack by New Archaeologists in the 1960s and 1970s, some elements of historical particularism, especially the emphasis on the complexity of culture, the necessity of a historical approach, and rejection of the view of cultures as integrated systems, reemerged as viable viewpoints in the 1980s.

Guy Gibbon

Further Readings

Boas, F. 1940. *Race, Language, and Culture.* Macmillan, New York.

Trigger, B.G. 1989. *A History of Archaeological Thought.* Cambridge University Press, New York.

See also BOAS, FRANZ

Hiwassee Island

Hiwassee Island (40MG31) is located at the confluence of the Hiwassee and Tennessee rivers in Meigs County, Tennessee. The island is triangular in plan, measures 2 x 3 km (1.2 x 1.9 miles), and covers ca. 316 ha (781 acres). Beginning in the nineteenth century, various archaeologists showed interest in the rich archaeological record of the island. Intensive archaeological studies were conducted on Hiwassee Island in conjunction with the construction of the Chickamauga Reservoir from April 1937 through March 1939 by Works Progress Administration (WPA) investigators under the supervision of Thomas M.N. Lewis and Madeline Kneberg. From these studies, and comparative data gathered at other sites in the reservoir, Lewis and Kneberg defined the Late Prehistoric culture sequence that, with few modifications, continues to be used in the region. Their characterization of the Late Woodland Hamilton culture, the Early Mississippian Hiwassee Island culture, and the Late Mississippian Dallas culture remains largely the standard against which modern culture-history studies are measured. Lewis and Knebert hypothesized that this sequence represented the replacement of Woodland people by Muskogean or Creek-speaking peoples, who in turn were replaced by the historic Cherokee. The Hiwassee Island report (Lewis and Kneberg 1946) is considered a classic study in southeastern archaeology; Hiwassee Island itself is among the best-known archaeological sites in the United States.

On Hiwassee Island, numerous small scatters of river-mussel shells, mostly attributed to Late Woodland–period habitation, were recorded. Five Late Woodland burial mounds containing 173 interments were completely excavated. The primary focus of investigations, however, were the large platform mound and associated Mississippian-period palisaded village that covered ca. 1.6 ha (4 acres). The mound was 7 m (23 feet) high and 45 m (148 feet) in diameter at its base. Including the premound surface, there were eight major construction phases with associated community buildings. The initial four phases (G, F, E1, E2) represented Hiwassee Island culture, with the remaining four (D, C, B, A) attributed to the Dallas culture. Two structures with accompanying porch or arbor were built on each mound summit. Ca. 1500 m² (1,794 square yards) of the village were excavated, and the palisade was traced for 260 m (853 feet). Thirty Hiwassee Island–culture and five Dallas-culture domestic structures were excavated. The former were rectangular buildings mostly of small-pole single-post or wall-trench construction, while the latter were square houses mostly of log single-post wall construction, with four roof supports and wall-trench entrances. Attributed to the Dallas occupation were 188 burials, most of which were interred in rectangular pits in the vicinity of domestic structures. Burial goods included a rich array of ceramic vessels, stone tools, bone tools and ornaments, marine and freshwater shell beads, and marine-shell cups and gorgets. The gorgets exhibited engraved anthropomorphic, zoomorphic, and geometric designs. Pottery from the site was used to define Late Woodland Hamilton Cord-Marked and Plain types; Early Mississippian Hiwassee Island Red Filmed and Red-on-Buff types; and Late Mississippian Dallas Decorated and Modeled types. Dallas culture was distinguished from Hiwassee Island culture by the greater incidence of shell-tempered, cord-marked pottery and the more frequent occurrence of strap and lug handles on jars.

Gerald F. Schroedl

Further Readings

Lewis, T.M.N., and M. Kneberg. 1946. *Hiwassee Island: An Archaeological Account of Four Tennessee Indian Peoples.* University of Tennessee Press, Knoxville.

H

Hochelaga

On Sunday, October 3, 1535, a delegation of headmen from Hochelaga met French explorer Jacques Cartier when he landed at St. Mary's Current on the St. Lawrence River to lead him through the forest and cornfields to their palisaded village near the mountain where Montreal now stands. As a result, Hochelaga holds the mixed distinction of being the first Iroquoian village to be visited by Europeans. More than 70 years would elapse before John Smith encountered the Susquehannock on Chesapeake Bay in 1608, and ca. 80 years before Kleyntijen would visit the Mohawks in 1614 and Champlain the Hurons in 1615.

Cartier described Hochelaga as a village having some 50 houses that were "about 50 or more paces in length and 12 to 15 in width," which would make them ca. 38 m (125 feet) long and 9–12 m (30–40 feet) wide. Archaeological investigations of contemporary longhouses in this region indicate that their length could vary considerably, but that they were consistently 6.4 m (21 feet) wide. The round-ended houses, which were as high as they were wide, were framed with poles set vertically in the ground. They were roofed over with saplings to form an arch, which led Europeans to describe them as arbors. This pole frame was sheeted with large pieces of bark as broad as a table. Inside the longhouse along each wall were many compartments facing onto a central corridor in which were located several fires more or less evenly spaced to enable two families, one on each side of the corridor, to share a single hearth. As was characteristic of Iroquoian villages of this period, the Hochelaga longhouses were surrounded by a roughly circular palisade. Cartier estimated this palisade to be two lances high, a typical European lance at that time being ca. 6 m (20 feet) long. Iroquoian palisade construction varied. Cartier's description of the Hochelaga palisade indicates it was constructed of closely spaced posts set vertically in the ground to form a wall that was braced with parallel rows of smaller posts set on either side of the vertical posts so as to cross at the top. He described this structure as a pyramid. Often the palisade was stabilized by heaping soil at the foot of the vertical posts and by weaving saplings into the spaces between the posts. At Hochelaga, ladders were placed inside the palisade to provide access to galleries at the top where rocks were stored to cast down upon attackers. The Hochelaga palisade had but one gate, which

could be barred, to provide access to the village. Undoubtedly, Hochelaga was a fortress built to defend a community of Iroquoian farmers from attack, principally by other Iroquoians, for war was endemic at that time throughout Iroquoia.

Estimates regarding the size of the Hochelaga population on the basis of Cartier's statement that there were some 50 houses in the village would be speculative without knowing the length of each house. The number of persons living in a longhouse varied greatly, depending on the length of the house, and archaeological evidence indicates that house length varied greatly at this time. Suffice it to note Cartier's estimate that more than 1,000 men, women, and children came to meet him, which suggests that Hochelaga was a sizable village. After two days visiting Hochelaga, Cartier departed to return to his ships, which were moored downstream at Stadacona, present-day Quebec City. During his stay, he had been regaled with several of the ritualistic ceremonies Iroquoians traditionally accorded visitors, and he responded by giving gifts of European material. He also had been taken to the top of Mount Royal, where he was shown the surrounding countryside as if to impress upon him the extent of the territory claimed by the Hochelagans.

Cartier's account of his third voyage to the Canada region in 1541 makes no mention of Hochelaga. He relates briefly how he visited the town of Tutonaguy, which he locates two leagues from the first rapid at St. Mary's Current. Tutonaguy may have been another name for Hochelaga or an altogether different village. Alternatively, it may have been a distinct Iroquoian fishing station near the Lachine Rapids. In any event, his having been met by only some 400 people in 1541 contrasts sharply with the 1,000 and more Hochelagans who greeted him in 1535. There is the possibility, too, that the local population had been depleted by European disease introduced by Cartier. In two accounts of subsequent European visits to Montreal Island, neither Jacques Noel's account of his having scaled Mount Royal before 1587 nor Champlain's account of his visit to the Lachine Rapids in 1603 mentions Hochelaga. The presumption is that Hochelaga had ceased to exist sometime between 1541 and 1603, probably ca. A.D. 1580.

Some nineteenth-century scholars drew upon early French records to suggest that Hochelaga was a Huron village occupied by a Huron-Iroquois people. Others drew upon different French documentation to identify the Hochelagans as Mohawks. Subsequently, both these hypotheses gave way to the suggestion that undifferentiated Iroquoians had migrated into the St. Lawrence Valley from the west on a route north of Lakes Erie and Ontario. In this model, the Hurons had settled Hochelaga only to be driven out sometime after Cartier's visit by Mohawks, who made Hochelaga their capital. Later, it was alleged that some Mohawks moved from the St. Lawrence Valley to the Mohawk Valley in New York State, where they were encountered by Europeans. The Mohawk who remained in the St. Lawrence Valley were named Laurentian Iroquois. A variant of this eastward-migration hypothesis would have some of these undifferentiated Iroquoians driven from the St. Lawrence Valley by the Adirondacks (Algonquians) into New York State, where they became the Mohawks, Onondaga, and Oneidas. For a time, most Iroquoianists supported these hypotheses largely because of perceived similarities between the pottery excavated on the Dawson site in downtown Montreal, which may be Hochelaga, and the ceramics excavated on contemporary Mohawk, Onondaga, and Oneida archaeological sites in New York State. These hypotheses have been eclipsed by a greatly expanded archaeological database, which indicates that Cartier's Hochelaga was a village, probably the terminal village, of a distinct indigenous people. This conclusion has been borne out by recent linguistic research, which demonstrates that portions of the Cartier vocabularies are also distinct. It is now thought the Hochelagans were Iroquoians descended from a people who, having entered the St. Lawrence Valley after glaciation and the emergence of the land from the Champlain Sea, had long lived in several regions of the valley. These Iroquoians have been named the St. Lawrence Iroquoians.

The disappearance of the St. Lawrence Iroquoians from their ancient homeland has been attributed to their neighbors to the west, the Huron. Both amicable and hostile scenarios have been proposed. Archaeological evidence suggests that hostility originated ca. A.D. 1450 and continued with varying intensity until the St. Lawrence Iroquoians were destroyed ca. A.D. 1580. After the appearance of Europeans on the St. Lawrence River in the sixteenth century, the demise of the St. Lawrence Iroquoians was accelerated, principally as a result of European disease against which they had no immunity.

There is good archaeological evidence to demonstrate that some took refuge with the Mohawk, Onondaga, and Oneida Iroquois in New York State. Some fled eastward to the Abenaki Algonquians in New England. Most were assimilated by the Hurons and Petuns, as is demonstrated by the presence of distinctive St. Lawrence Iroquoian pottery on their archaeological sites.

James F. Pendergast

Further Readings

Biggar, H.P. 1924. *Voyages of Jacques Cartier.* Publication no. 11. Public Archives of Canada, Ottawa.

Jamieson, J.B. 1990. The Archaeology of the St. Lawrence Iroquoians. In *The Archaeology of Southern Ontario to A.D. 1650,* edited by C.J. Ellis and N. Ferris, pp. 385–404. Occasional Publications no. 5. London [Ontario] Chapter, Ontario Archaeological Society, London.

Pendergast, J.F. 1991. St. Lawrence Iroquoians: Their Past, Present and Immediate Future. *New York State Archaeological Association Bulletin* 102:47–74.

———. 1993. *More on When and Why the St. Lawrence Iroquoians Disappeared.* Occasional Papers in Northeastern Archaeology no. 8. Copetown Press, Dundas.

Pendergast, J.F., and B.G. Trigger. 1972. *Cartier's Hochelaga and the Dawson Site.* McGill-Queens University Press, Montreal.

Trigger, B.G., and J.F. Pendergast. 1978. Saint Lawrence Iroquoians. In *Northeast,* edited by B.G. Trigger, pp. 357–362. Handbook of North American Indians, vol. 15, W.C. Sturtevant, general editor. Smithsonian Institution, Washington, D.C.

Hodges Ruin

During the 1930s, Gila Pueblo, the private research foundation established in 1929 by Harold S. Gladwin, actively pursued its goal of defining the "Red-on-buff," or "Hohokam," culture of the southern Arizona desert area. Broad regional surveys were followed by excavations in the Tonto Basin at Roosevelt 9:6 by Emil Haury in 1932, at the site of Snaketown in 1935–1936, and at the Hodges Ruin (AZ AA:12:18) in Tucson in 1936–1938. The results of the first two excavations were published rapidly (Haury 1932; Gladwin et al. 1937) and provided an outline of Hohokam development along the Salt and Gila rivers (the Phoenix Basin). Isabel Kelly's manuscript on the Hodges excavations, however, had a much more limited impact, for it remained in an unfinished and unpublished state for 40 years after the completion of fieldwork. Its publication in 1978 served, however, to accelerate an awareness of, and interest in, the Hohokam archaeology of the Tucson Basin.

The Hodges site is located on the second terrace overlooking the floodplains of the Santa Cruz and Rillito rivers. The portion of the site gridded for the 1930s excavations was just less than 12 ha (30 acres) of a much larger area covered with the surface remains of a dense occupation. Excavations at the site in 1936 were directed by Carl Miller, who was hired by property owner Wetmore Hodge. Isabel Kelly was hired by Gladwin in 1937, and she supervised the excavation and analysis of material until the end of the project in 1938. Kelly's largely completed manuscript was organized in the same manner as the Snaketown report in that it traced material-culture change through time, with an emphasis on ceramics and pithouse architecture. Kelly saw sufficient differences in the ceramics to merit a separate phase sequence for the Tucson area. Of major importance was the documentation of a large ballcourt at Hodges, which was excavated in 1937 by Haury, who had found a court almost the exact length and orientation during his excavations at Snaketown. In addition, excavation of several cremation areas showed that certain burial practices, including the use of stone palettes and censers, were shared by the Tucson and the Phoenix Basin Hohokam.

Recent research (Layhe 1986; Doelle and Fish 1988; Doelle and Wallace 1991) has placed the Hodges site within broader, regional perspectives. For example, ballcourts are now known to be present at nearly all Tucson Basin Hohokam villages that date to the Cañada del Oro (A.D. 750–850, or 1200–1100 years B.P.), Rillito (A.D. 850–925, or 1100–1025 years B.P.), or Early Rincon (A.D. 925–1000, or 1025–950 years B.P.) phases; more than 20 ballcourts have been identified in the region. Similarly, the abundance of Phoenix Basin decorated buffware ceramics at the Hodges site is seen to be part of a broader Tucson Basin pattern, although buff wares are relatively scarce in the southern Tucson Basin, where the local produc-

tion of Red-on-brown ceramics is believed to have been much greater. The Arizona State Museum's 1985 excavations at Hodges (Layhe 1986) have also provided basic information about past regional environments and subsistence practices, for this kind of information had not been gathered during the earlier excavations. The presence of cultigens, such as corn, beans, and cotton, and evidence of a wide range of wild plants establish that the occupants of Hodges followed a rather typical Hohokam subsistence pattern. Recent research (Layhe 1986; Doelle and Fish 1988; Doelle and Wallace 1991) at Hodges and at other contemporary regional sites has documented, too, a major shift in settlement pattern during the Rincon phase. Among the settlement changes were the apparent abandonment of the ballcourt system and a greater dispersal of large villages. While initial research at the Hodges Ruin established the basic outline of Hohokam development in the Tucson Basin, ongoing research is adding to our understanding of this development.

William H. Doelle

Further Readings

Doelle, W.H., and P.R. Fish (editors). 1988. *Recent Research on Tucson Basin Prehistory: Proceedings of the Second Tucson Basin Conference.* Anthropological Papers no. 10. Institute for American Research, Tucson.

Doelle, W.H., and H.D. Wallace. 1991. The Changing Role of the Tucson Basin in the Hohokam Regional System. In *Exploring the Hohokam: Prehistoric Desert Peoples of the American Southwest,* edited by G.H. Gumerman, pp. 279–346. University of New Mexico Press, Albuquerque.

Kelly, I.T. 1978. *The Hodges Ruin: A Hohokam Community in the Tucson Basin.* Anthropological Papers no. 30. University of Arizona Press, Tucson.

Layhe, R.W. 1986. *The 1985 Excavations at the Hodges Site, Pima County, Arizona.* Archaeological Series no. 170. Arizona State Museum, University of Arizona, Tucson.

Hoe

The hoe is a large, bifacially manufactured implement employed for digging in the soil. The principal distinguishing feature of a hoe is the

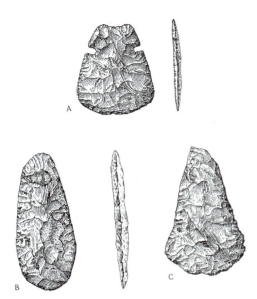

Chipped stone hoe blades: a. with specialized hafting element; b. c. ovate-lanceolate and triangular blades ready for hafting. (Reprinted from Smithsonian Institution, Bureau of American Ethnology, Bulletin 60, Fig 70 & 71)

presence of very bright surface polish ("use sheen") extending far from the edge and covering interior ridges and scar negatives alike. This is termed "phytolith polish" to suggest its genesis in the chemical interaction of a flint surface, in the presence of water, with opal contained in plant stems, leaves, and roots (Kamminga 1979). Occasionally, the prehistoric presence of hoes on a site can be deduced by recovery of sharpening flakes, known as "hoe chips," that contain phytolith polish on their dorsal surfaces. The similarity of use sheen on hoes to that on sickles employed for cutting grasses has been recognized for years (Witthoft 1967), and it is probable that at least some of the same processes are involved in the formation of each. Little experimentation on the effectiveness of, or the wear on, hoes had been conducted before that of J. Sonnenfeld (1962). He produced not only the characteristic polish, but also beveling and "scour grooving" of the surface near the bit.

Because of its close association with agriculture, the hoe did not come into common use in North America until relatively intensive agriculture was practiced during Middle Woodland times. Middle Woodland hoes of the midcontinent were bifacially flaked and contained edges that expanded toward the bit (Montet-White 1968:84–85). As agriculture intensified

in later prehistory, the quantity of hoes increased. Mississippian hoes were considerably more variable in shape than earlier hoes. Commonly ovate, they were also occasionally manufactured in triangular, trapezoidal, or rectangular forms. Some of the more diagnostic ones possess side notches or a stem to facilitate hafting or a slightly denticulate bit. In later prehistory, hoes became a major trade item. Hoes of Mill Creek chert from southern Illinois were perhaps the principal import into Cahokia, just east of St. Louis, Missouri, from where they were distributed to smaller polities in the region (Kelly 1991:83).

George H. Odell

Further Readings

Kamminga, J. 1979. The Nature of Use-Polish and Abrasive Smoothing on Stone Tools. In *Lithic Use-Wear Analysis*, edited by B. Hayden, pp. 143–157. Academic Press, New York.

Kelly, J.E. 1991. The Evidence for Prehistoric Exchange and Its Implications for the Development of Cahokia. In *New Perspectives on Cahokia: Views From the Periphery*, edited by J. Stoltman, pp. 65–92. Prehistory Press, Madison.

Montet-White, A. 1968. *The Lithic Industries of the Illinois Valley in the Early and Middle Woodland Period*. Anthropological Papers no. 35. Museum of Anthropology, University of Michigan, Ann Arbor.

Sonnenfeld, J. 1962. Interpreting the Function of Primitive Implements. *American Antiquity* 28:56–65.

Witthoft, J. 1967. Glazed Polish on Flint Tools. *American Antiquity* 32:383–388.

Hogup Cave

Hogup Cave overlooks the now-dry bed of Pleistocene Lake Bonneville from a point near the terminus of the Hogup Range, ca. 120 km (75 miles) northwest of Salt Lake City, Utah. A suite of 23 radiocarbon dates from 16 culture-bearing strata shows that human occupation there extended ca. 6850 B.C.–A.D. 1450 (8800–500 years B.P.). Dry deposits of 3.4–4.3 m (11–14 feet) in thickness yielded a rich record of biotic remains and organic as well as lithic artifacts. The stratigraphic profile of these deposits showed many very thin lenses, or layers, of campfire ash, antelope hair, chaff of seeds milled in the cave, and other such traces of short-term activities, presenting a graphic record of innumerable human visits to Hogup Cave over a span of more than 8,000 years (Aikens 1970).

Yielding a premier archaeological record of the Great Basin Desert Archaic culture, Hogup Cave is important in supporting and extending the evidence from Danger Cave (ca. 97 km [60 miles] away on the western edge of the Bonneville Salt Flats), on the basis of which the Desert-culture concept was originally formulated (Jennings 1957). Hogup Cave also preserved a clear biotic record of change over time in the regional environment, as the early Holocene remnant of Lake Bonneville shrank to form present-day Great Salt Lake, and it yielded a concomitant cultural sequence leading from the Desert Archaic through Fremont culture to Late Prehistoric evidence of the region's ethnographically known Numic-speaking peoples.

C. Melvin Aikens

Further Readings

Aikens, C.M. 1970. *Hogup Cave*. Anthropological Papers no. 93. University of Utah Press, Salt Lake City.

Jennings, J.D. 1957. *Danger Cave*. Anthropological Papers no. 27. University of Utah Press, Salt Lake City. Also released as Memoir no. 14. Society for American Archaeology, Washington, D.C.

Hohokam Culture Area

The Hohokam were prehistoric farmers in the northeast sector of the Sonoran Desert in southern Arizona. Although members of the Hohokam tradition inhabited a territory spanning nearly 120,000 km² (45,000 square miles), archaeological interpretations have emphasized spatial uniformity in cultural and stylistic expression. Models characterizing this homogeneity have attributed cultural cohesiveness to the existence of a single or closely related set of ethnic groups; an underlying economic adaptation or peasant tradition; and an interaction sphere, horizon style, or regional system grounded in religious ideology. Changes in material culture and society through time have been explained as the result of intrusions from Mexico or the northern Southwest and as religious transformations connected with ideological upheavals in Mesoamerica.

The name "Hohokam" is usually reserved for pottery-making peoples who lived between A.D. 200 and 1450 (1750–500 years B.P.), for their Late Archaic predecessors were already farming in some locations by 700 B.C. (2650 years B.P.). One of the major archaeological traditions in the southwestern United States, Hohokam assemblages are distinguished by the presence, during all but the initial and the final segments of the ceramic sequence, of repetitious designs of numerous small elements in red paint on buff, brown, or gray pottery. Discovery of the geographic extent of these diagnostic ceramics was a major research thrust of the Gila Pueblo Archaeological Foundation which, in the 1920s, began the first sustained study of Hohokam.

Since the 1920s, a variety of other traits have come to characterize the Hohokam. Villages consist of dispersed houses and house clusters, with larger settlements more formally organized around plazas, ballcourts, and platform mounds. Cremation was the primary method for disposal of the dead until ca. A.D. 1300 (650 years B.P.), when inhumation also became common. Canal networks tapped desert rivers, with the longest lines, which linked multiple settlements or communities, carrying water up to 30 km (15 miles). A variety of floodwater and run-off techniques completed a versatile agricultural repertoire. Widespread trade networks involved large amounts of marine shell; exotic stone such as argillite, steatite, and obsidian; and highly stylized craft products. A set of carved-stone ritual objects that included palettes and effigy censers and bowls, as well as an iconography that emphasized desert fauna and human forms, further distinguished the Hohokam.

The Hohokam had strong cultural ties with northwestern Mexico. In both artistic style and settlement pattern, the Hohokam resembled historic riverine cultures in southern Sonora and Sinaloa more than Puebloans in the uplands to the north and east. A Tepiman linguistic corridor stretches from central Arizona along the western coast of Mexico as far south as Nayarit. This broad band of mutually comprehensible languages would have provided an avenue for the exchange of personnel, goods, and information. Ceramic traits with Mesoamerican associations include incising, grooving, repetitious small design elements, and specialized vessel forms such as chile grinders, tripods, and censers. In the earlier part of the sequence, figurines, censers, and palettes form a set of ritual items that are rare in the Southwest beyond the northern extent of Hohokam occupation. Likewise, mounds and ballcourts are classes of public architecture with distributional continuity to the south. More than other aspects of material culture, such ceremonial, ideological, and iconographic expressions have been the criteria used by contemporary researchers to delimit the boundaries of the Hohokam tradition.

Hohokam in all reaches of the tradition shared the challenges of a relatively low and hot desert environment. Its geographic extent to the north and east coincided closely with the vegetational attributes demarcating the Sonoran Desert. Bimodal rainfall promotes a greater diversity among plant communities and a more arborescent vegetation than under winter-dominant precipitation to the west and summer-dominant precipitation to the east. Even in the vicinity of the larger mountain ranges in the basin and range country of southern Arizona, settlements were concentrated in basin interiors, seldom exceeding elevations of 1,100 m (3,300 feet). Although annual precipitation throughout is less than 380 mm (15 inches), the highest average amounts exceed the lowest by a factor of two. The broad, flat Phoenix Basin experiences the lower range of precipitation, at 180 mm (7.5 inches), and the hottest temperatures, with more than 90 days above 56°C (100°F). An arc of somewhat higher elevation, lower temperatures, and increased rainfall surrounds the Phoenix Basin to the north, east, and south.

The Sonoran Desert offered a rich and varied set of food resources to the Hohokam. Desert plants tend to store starchy reserves, fruiting quickly and profusely in response to sporadic moisture. Many of these, such as mesquite beans and cholla buds, are seasonally predictable, easy to harvest, found in large quantities, and readily processed into storable states. These were combined with a suite of cultigens that are both drought tolerant and varied, including "60-day" corn, tepary beans, grain amaranth, agave, little barley, and other typical southwestern crops. Arable land in Hohokam territory is both abundant and widely distributed. The major drainages flow through numerous basins with considerable elevational diversity. Some of these rivers, particularly the Salt and the Gila, are perennial or have perennial segments with terraces suitable for large-scale irrigation agriculture. Elevational ranges result in a variety of native-plant resources and different kinds of agricultural land spread over short horizontal distances. This pattern is so common

that individual Hohokam groups would usually have had comparable access to most important resources within a day's walk.

While food for large populations could be supplied by the Sonoran Desert, important restrictions to settlement were present. The spotty availability of potable water was one of the most significant. Many areas containing much potential plant food or cultivable land were never exploited or were used only during periods of highest population density because of the absence of sustained surface water. Furthermore, direct-rainfall agriculture is impossible in all Sonoran Desert basins. Supplemental water must be provided to crops through technologies requiring considerable cooperative investment in fields and water-delivery systems.

The initial interval of Hohokam ceramic manufacture is now known from numerous locations throughout the region during the first few centuries of the Christian era. Compared to the tree-ring–dated chronologies of the northern Southwest, several parallel Hohokam sequences are not refined or well synchronized among subregions of the tradition. However, large numbers of newly reported radiocarbon and archaeomagnetic dates are the basis for a growing consensus regarding general temporal parameters for most phases.

Throughout the sequence, the Hohokam lived in pithouses with wattle-and-daub superstructures. Adobe rooms were added near the beginning of the Classic period ca. A.D. 1150 (800 years B.P.) and were often grouped within the walls of a compound. Earthen-banked ballcourts were the common form of public architecture before the Classic period, when they were superseded by platform mounds supporting adobe structures. Public architecture was constructed at large, focal sites in differentiated settlement patterns. The community, defined as a central site and an integrated set of surrounding settlements, was the basic Hohokam territorial and sociopolitical unit.

Even the largest and most nucleated Hohokam sites appear to have had limited populations, typically numbering in the hundreds rather than the thousands. Appreciable segments of the Hohokam population lived in dispersed rancherias or farmsteads and hamlets. Communities embody the institutions that integrated multiple settlements into bounded territorial units. Such units are thought to have provided a framework for allocating water among sites in the Phoenix vicinity sharing irrigation networks and for mobilizing and coordinating labor in the construction and maintenance of canals. In regions without perennial rivers, communities linked sites in diverse basin segments, thus encompassing a variety of productive potentials and risks. The flexible community structure appears to have been the basis for cooperation, specialization, and risk management throughout the Hohokam tradition.

Recently, much progress has been made in delineating the archaeological components of communities and interpreting their social correlates. A set of two to six structures forming a courtyard group has been identified with a household in an economic sense and with the basic residential unit in kinship structure. Multiples of courtyard groups frequently shared facilities such as pit ovens, cemeteries, and trash mounds. These groups are often equated with lineages, but since ethnographic groups in southern deserts were almost universally bilateral, other types of social arrangements seem equally plausible. Courtyard households are the building blocks of both smaller and larger sites.

A watershed in Hohokam development occurred with the transition to the Classic period in the twelfth century. Canal systems reached their greatest extent, and acreage cultivated by other water-harvesting and irrigation strategies was expanded in many areas. Maximum population densities at the largest settlements and highest overall densities for most subregions were achieved after this transition. Greater investment in integrative organization can be seen in the construction of the most massive examples of public architecture, with which socially differentiated personnel appear to have been associated.

Appropriate characterization of social and organizational complexity for the Hohokam is a subject of extended discourse and controversy. In the Southwest, the Hohokam, Chaco Canyon, and Casas Grandes are usually considered to have attained the greatest complexity and hierarchy. Attributes of complexity for the Hohokam include construction of the largest prehistoric canal system north of Peru, dense and permanent populations, and the erection of relatively massive public architecture. The necessity for cooperation and coordination in the construction and use of canals greater than 30 km (15 miles) in length is apparent. However, conclusions concerning levels of effort, the need for centralized control and social hierarchy, and the relationship of canal networks to political entities are not matters of consensus.

The study of Hohokam archaeology has followed a significantly different historical trajectory from that of neighboring southwestern traditions. Until recently, investigations have focused on the examination of a few large sites, and major publications have been sporadic. More than other regional cultures, areas of greatest prehistoric population density and cultural elaboration have coincided with modern cities and agriculture, limiting many types of archaeological study. Furthermore, the basic Hohokam sequence and evolutionary scheme were constructed on the basis of intensive excavations at only one site, the long-inhabited and elaborate site of Snaketown in the Phoenix Basin, rather than through the integration of research from multiple locations. This emphasis promoted a model of Hohokam culture as emanating from a strong central source, surrounded by less well developed, imitative, and colonial spheres. This core/periphery dichotomy has also been cast as a distinction between riverine and nonriverine or outlying desert regions, based on the implications of differential opportunities for large-scale irrigation and the development of an associated religious and integrative ideology in the Phoenix Basin. However, the strength of this contrast is being modified by the increasing documentation of unanticipated levels of population and of centers with public architecture outside the core.

There has been an explosion in primary data for the Hohokam since the mid-1980s, resulting from development-related funding required by environmental legislation. With hundreds of large and small excavations and survey projects throughout southern Arizona, the pace of recent Hohokam research is unparalleled in North America. As the resulting information is assimilated and synthesized, existing perceptions of "facts" for Hohokam prehistory are bound to be changed significantly. Already, this mass of new data is allowing Hohokam archaeologists to challenge regional and holistic models formulated from only a few well-studied sites.

Paul R. Fish

Further Readings

Crown, P.L. 1987. Classic Period Hohokam Settlement and Land Use in the Casa Grande Ruin Area, Arizona. *Journal of Field Archaeology* 14(2):147–162.

———. 1990. The Hohokam of the American Southwest. *Journal of World Prehistory* 4:223–255.

Crown, P.L., and W.J. Judge (editors). 1991. *Chaco and Hohokam: Prehistoric Regional Systems in the American Southwest.* School of American Research Press, Santa Fe.

Doyel, D.E. (editor). 1987. *The Hohokam Village: Site Structure and Organization.* Southwestern and Rocky Mountain Division of the American Association for the Advancement of Science, Glenwood Springs.

Fish, P.R. 1989. The Hohokam: 1,000 Years of Prehistory in the Sonoran Desert. In *Dynamics of Southwest Prehistory,* edited by L. Cordell and G. Gumerman, pp. 19–63. Smithsonian Institution Press, Washington, D.C.

Fish, S.K., P.R. Fish, and J.H. Madsen. 1992. *The Marana Community in the Hohokam World.* Anthropological Papers no. 56. University of Arizona Press, Tucson.

Gumerman, G.P. (editor). 1991. *Exploring the Hohokam: Prehistoric Desert Peoples of the American Southwest.* University of New Mexico Press, Albuquerque.

Haury, E.W. 1976. *The Hohokam: Desert Farmers and Craftsmen.* University of Arizona Press, Tucson.

Masse, R.B. 1981. Prehistoric Irrigation Systems in the Salt River Valley, Arizona. *Science* 214:408–415.

Noble, D.G. 1991. *The Hohokam: Ancient People of the Desert.* School of American Research Press, Santa Fe.

Wilcox, D.R. 1991. The Mesoamerican Ballgame in the American Southwest. In *The Mesoamerican Ballgame,* edited by V.L. Scarborough and D.R. Wilcox, pp. 101–128. University of Arizona Press, Tucson.

Holmes, William Henry (1846–1933)

An important figure in the professionalization of North American archaeology, William Henry Holmes began his career in 1872 as an artist with F.V. Hayden's U.S. geological survey of the Rocky Mountain area. He became interested in geology and, eventually, archaeology through his geological explorations of cliff dwellings in Utah. Appointed curator of aboriginal ceramics in the U.S. National Museum in Washington, D.C., in 1882, Holmes launched a study of the

William Henry Holmes. (Courtesy of the National Anthropological Archives, Smithsonian Institution, Photograph No. 45–A)

pottery of the Mississippi Valley and of Clarence B. Moore's extensive Florida collections, believing that pottery was a valuable medium through which to explore chronological and historical problems. In 1889, Holmes joined the Bureau of American Ethnology, which had published his early studies of Native American art, and began the analysis of ceramics collected by Cyrus Thomas's mound survey and of ceramics in other collections. The result was his classic "Aboriginal Pottery of the Eastern United States" (Holmes 1903), the first systematic, comparative attempt to classify prehistoric pottery in the Eastern Woodlands and an early exemplar of the culture-historical approach in North American archaeology. In a later work (Holmes 1914), he defined ceramic "provinces" and divided the whole of North America into 26 "cultural characterization areas" in conjunction with a geographic model without time depth that was replacing the

Mound Builder Myth that had been discredited by the early 1890s.

Holmes served as chief of the U.S. Bureau of American Ethnology (1902–1909) and as curator of anthropology at Chicago's Field Museum of Natural History (1894–1897) and the U.S. National Museum (1897–1902, 1910–1920), where, with Ales Hrdlicka, a physical anthropologist at the museum, he challenged and critically appraised claims for great antiquity in the New World. He demonstrated that most "Paleolithic" material found in the Northeast was the work of recent Native Americans (Holmes 1897) and that claims of great age for the Calavaras skull in California did not meet scientific standards (Holmes 1901). Although often overbearing and strong-willed in promoting the view of the past held by scientists in the federal government, Holmes was a pioneer with others in transforming archaeology into a "scientific" discipline. He also made important contributions to Mesoamerican archaeology in the late 1890s by describing pottery and other antiquities and noting the presence of stratigraphic deposits.

Guy Gibbon

Further Readings

Anonymous. 1933. *American Anthropologist* 35:755–764.

Holmes, W.H. 1897. Stone Implements of the Potomac-Chesapeake Tidewater Province. *Fifteenth Annual Report of the Bureau of American Ethnology,* pp. 3–152.

———. 1901. Review of the Evidence Relating to Auriferous Gravel Man in California. *Annual Report of the Smithsonian Institution for 1899,* pp. 419–472.

———. 1903. Aboriginal Pottery of the Eastern United States. *Twentieth Annual Report of the Bureau of American Ethnology,* pp. 1–201.

———. 1914. Areas of American Culture Characterization Tentatively Outlined As an Aid in the Study of Antiquities. *American Anthropologist* 16:413–446.

———. 1992. *The Archaeology of William Henry Holmes,* edited with an introduction by D.J. Meltzer and R.C. Dunnell. Smithsonian Institution Press, Washington, D.C.

Mark, J. 1980. William Henry Holmes. In *Four Anthropologists: An American Science in Its Early Years,* by J. Mark, pp. 131–171. Science History, New York.

Meltzer, D. 1983. The Antiquity of Man and the Development of American Archaeology. *Advances in Archaeological Method and Theory* 6:1–51.

See also HRDLICKA, ALES; MOORE, CLARENCE B.; THOMAS, CYRUS

Holocene

The Quaternary Era of geologic time is divided into the Pleistocene (roughly encompassing the ice ages) and the Holocene. The beginning of the Holocene is arbitrarily placed at 8050 B.C. (10,000 years B.P.), because that is about the time of the pronounced climatic change that transformed the Ice Age climate into conditions similar to those of today. This temporal boundary is rarely applied exactly, however, because so many environmental changes accompanied the transition that the strict designation of a particular year has little practical value. Even the identification of the time is difficult, because the radiocarbon time scale, on which most chronology is based, experienced strong perturbations about this time. It is, therefore, difficult to establish exact ages in absolute terms.

The rapidity of the environmental changes at the beginning of the Holocene decreased over time in most areas, as environmental conditions similar to the present prevailed. Once-glaciated landscapes became covered with vegetation, the succession of plants and animals was characterized by differential rates of dispersal from Ice Age refuges, by competition, by progressive development of soils and geomorphic surfaces, and by the ever-changing pattern of minor climatic changes. The last factor is particularly well illustrated by the early Holocene expansion of lakes and vegetation cover in the now-desert basins of northern and eastern Africa, which was the result of enhanced monsoonal climates related to shifts in Earth/Sun orbital patterns. The same factor may have been involved in the temporary shift eastward of the border between prairie and forest in the American Midwest in the middle Holocene, although this shift was delayed in comparison with the African sequence because of the persisting climatic influence of the still existing ice sheet in Canada.

The Holocene was a time when human populations first had a significant effect on the natural scene. In North America, hunters migrated from Alaska to the Great Plains ca. 10,000 B.C. (11,950 years B.P.) as the retreat of the Laurentide and Cordilleran ice sheets opened the Alberta corridor. Extinction of large mammals in both North and South America at this time is believed by many to have been the result of overkill by Paleoindians, although the contemporaneous changes in climate and vegetation may have been a contributing or a major factor. Subsequently in North America, the changes in the vegetation and other elements of the landscape during the Holocene may be attributed almost entirely to natural causes, at least until the last two centuries of the second millennium A.D., when extensive agricultural development altered vegetation throughout much of the area. In Europe and other areas where agriculture formed the economic base for Neolithic and subsequent cultures, the impact on vegetation in particular was significant through much of the Holocene, leading to widespread deforestation, soil erosion, and other local environmental modifications.

Holocene history can be reconstructed from the stratigraphic analysis of lake sediments, peat, cave sediments, stream deposits, archaeological sites, or any other accumulations in which fossils or artifacts are preserved or in which the geological materials themselves provide clues to environmental history. Pollen grains are perhaps the most widely used fossils for reconstruction of vegetation history, but plant macrofossils, insects, vertebrate bones and teeth, and aquatic organisms such as diatoms and mollusks are also useful. Chemical components of lake sediments, including stable isotopes of oxygen and carbon, are also used to infer changes in lake and landscape history.

H.E. Wright, Jr.

Further Readings

Roberts, N. 1989. *The Holocene: An Environmental History.* Basil Blackwell, New York.

Wright, H.E., Jr. (editor). 1984. *The Late Quaternary of the United States: 2. The Holocene.* University of Minnesota Press, Minneapolis.

Hopewell Interaction Sphere

The Hopewell Interaction Sphere defines those cultural systems that fostered multidimensional, comparatively intense, interregional communication across a substantial portion of eastern North America during the Middle Woodland period. It operated ca. A.D. 1–400 (1950–1550

years B.P.), and was one of several long-distance exchange and information networks that periodically developed, flourished, and disassembled in the Eastern Woodlands. First defined by Joseph R. Caldwell in 1964, the Interaction Sphere represented an alternative explanation to migration, colonization, or diffusion as a way of accounting for the long-recognized similarities of "Hopewell" style, material culture, and ritual practice across numerous regions during a relatively brief time period. As originally formulated, the Interaction Sphere emphasized the importance of interregional ideological or religious interchange as a basis for increased innovation and cultural evolution. The broad acceptance of certain ideological constructs, drawn from a diversity of sources, was responsible for breaking tradition-bound, regional patterns. The particular mechanisms and social contexts involved, however, were left largely unspecified.

Subsequent to Caldwell's definition, the "Interaction Sphere" concept was revised substantially. Emphasis shifted from the potential effects of an Interaction Sphere on subsequent complexity toward its importance as a structured response, or as a set of structured responses, to immediate, and essentially local, societal needs. The increased manipulation and trade of Hopewell-style valuables are more understandable in this context; they provided a mechanism for validating competing claims among potential leaders or groups. However, the

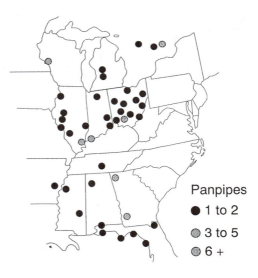

Distributions of Panpipes in the Eastern Woodlands. (Map by M. F. Seeman)

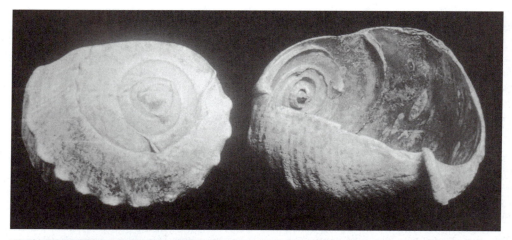

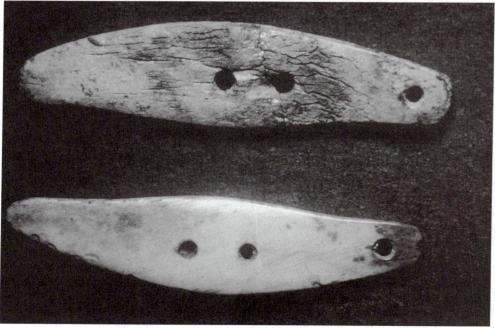

Top: *Hopewell marine shell containers (Courtesy of the Wilford Archaeology Laboratory, University of Minnesota) Bottom: Imitation bear canines (Courtesy of the Wilford Archaeology Laboratory, University of Minnesota)*

high degree of stylistic copying present in Hopewell-style artifacts across regions, the diversity of employed symbols, and the panregional distribution of certain ritual details assure that the Hopewell Interaction Sphere involved more than just an exchange of valuables among potential leaders; it was really the conjunction of both social and symbolic systems, and their relative expressions were complexly textured, varying in particular local, regional, and interregional situations.

Certain materials, artifact classes, design motifs, and their contexts provide the basis for tracing the operation of the Hopewell Interaction Sphere. Many of the raw materials—for example, meteoric iron, silver, copper, obsidian, grizzly bear canines, galena, rock crystal, conch shell, freshwater pearls, sharks' teeth, mica, chlorite, and certain flint types—were no doubt quite costly as a function of distance-to-source or rarity. Specific source areas include the Rocky Mountains, the Florida Gulf Coast, the Canadian Shield, and the southern Appalachian Mountains. Most of these exotic materials were used to carefully craft even more exotic classes of highly conventionalized artifacts, such as ear ornaments, breastplates, oversized spears, head-dresses, smoking pipes, panpipes, mirrors, containers, necklaces, costumes, and celts. The majority were ultimately destined for use in public mortuary rituals, which at the same time served to assure a continued demand. Although not as intensive as once thought, the actual exchange, direct procurement, or both of Hopewell Interaction Sphere raw materials and finished artifacts remain impressive in scope (see Figure).

Evidence for direct participation in the Hopewell Interaction Sphere can be found in archaeological sites from Florida to southern Ontario and from North Carolina to Kansas. More than 300 sites in eastern North America have produced Interaction Sphere goods. The cross-cultural connections responsible for these patterns progressed unevenly, changed considerably over time, and were more complex in the Midwest than in the Southeast. The most notable pattern of all is the out-of-scale demand for Interaction Sphere products in southern Ohio.

The Hopewell Interaction Sphere does not easily fit any known ethnographic template. At the same time, the social conditions that fostered it—for example, the development of "tribal" organizations with low population densities, nonnucleated residence patterns, and centuries of preceding, intermittent interregional relationships—are difficult to duplicate in ethnographic contexts.

Mark F. Seeman

Further Readings

Binford, L.R. 1965. Archaeological Systematics and the Study of Cultural Process. *American Antiquity* 31:203–210.

Braun, D.P. 1986. Peer Polity Interaction and Socio-Polical Change. In *Peer Polity Interaction and Socio-Political Change,* edited by C. Renfrew and J. Cherry, pp. 117–172. Cambridge University Press, Cambridge.

Caldwell, J.R. 1964. Interaction Spheres in Prehistory. In *Hopewellian Studies,* edited by J. Caldwell and R. Hall, pp. 133–143. Scientific Papers no. 12. Illinois State Museum, Springfield.

Schortman, E.M. 1989. Interregional Interaction in Prehistory: The Need for a New Perspective. *American Antiquity* 54:52–55.

Seeman, M.F. 1979. *The Hopewell Interaction Sphere: The Evidence for Interregional Trade and Structural Complexity.* Prehistory Research Series, vol. 5, no. 2. Indiana Historical Society, Indianapolis.

Hopewell Site

The Hopewell site (33RO27) is located in Ross County, Ohio, on the North Fork of Paint Creek. Ephraim G. Squier and E.H. Davis's plan of the earthworks appears as Plate X in *Ancient Monuments of the Mississippi Valley* (1848). Warren K. Moorehead excavated extensive sections of the site in 1891–1892 for the Columbian Exhibition of 1893. Further excavations were carried out in the period 1922–1925 by the Ohio Historical Society under the direction of Henry Clyde Shetrone. A major portion of the site is now protected by the Ar-

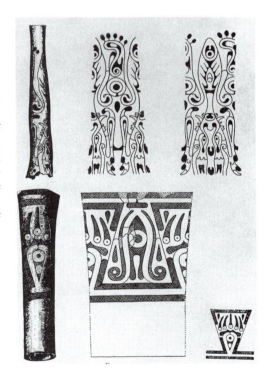

Designs engraved on human bone. The lower is a portion of a human femur with engraved bear foot and claw motif, from the Hopewell site. The upper specimen is a portion of a human arm bone engraved with a conventionalized carnivorous animal, from the Hopewell site. (Reprinted from Smithsonian Institution, Bureau of American Ethnology, Annual Report, 1916, Plate 6)

chaeological Conservancy. The most prominent feature at the Hopewell site was the Great Enclosure, a roughly rectangular earthwork more than 40 ha (99 acres) in area that followed the contours of the second and third terraces of the North Fork and a small stream. A large geometric square conjoined the enclosure's eastern side. Within the Great Enclosure were a circle and a "D-shaped" earthwork that surrounded the largest mound at the site. The exact number and location of other mounds at the site are unknown, but it is thought that there were 38; those known ranged in size from very small to one that was more than 150 m (492 feet) long and 9 m (29.5 feet) high. Their structure and contents varied as much as their size. Mound 25, the largest, consisted of three segments that covered a central building complex flanked by plaza areas. The central buildings, which contained burials and deposits of artifacts, were destroyed before the final construction of the mound. Evidence for intermediate stages and ceremonies in this mound implies some time depth. Although much variation is noticeable, some of the smaller mounds exhibited similar evidence but on a reduced scale. Others, such as Mound 2, which contained a deposit of more than 7,000 exotic flint discs, appear to represent single activities or construction episodes. Because of extensive excavation and cultivation across most of the site, very little of these walled enclosures and mounds is still visible.

Excavators discovered the gamut of burial and artifact types associated with the Hopewell complex within the mounds. The artifacts themselves were the primary focus of early excavators. The variety of raw materials and the high level of craftsmanship make this understandable, although more contextual information, which was not well recorded, would add greatly today to their use as sources of cultural information. Exotic materials from distant locations, such as mica, copper, obsidian, and marine shell, were evidently prized for their rarity, beauty, and possible symbolic significance. Artifacts depict birds and animals as well as more abstract symbols that can be quite complex. When combined with the now long decayed organic components, these objects would have formed an elaborate display that is today largely incomprehensible. It is thought that the nature and quantity of grave goods associated with burials may have reflected an individual's status or role in the regional cultural system. Cremation and inhumation were both prac-

ticed. Besides burial, there is evidence for other ritual activities that involved fire and the deposition of quantities of artifacts in specially prepared basins; the remains of other ritual activities capped small preliminary mounds. Because of the variety of practices present, the Hopewell site probably served as a ritual center for a number of different groups in the region.

Although the Hopewell site encompasses most of the characteristics seen in the Hopewell complex, it is certainly not a typical type site. Its extraordinary complexity, variety of content, and size make it unique among Hopewell sites.

Katharine C. Ruhl

Further Readings

Greber, N.B., and K.C. Ruhl. 1989. *The Hopewell Site*. Westview Press, Boulder.

Moorehead, W.K. 1922. The Hopewell Mound Group of Ohio. *Anthropological Series* 6:73–184. Field Museum of Natural History, Chicago.

Shetrone, H.C. 1926. Exploration of the Hopewell Group of Prehistoric Earthworks. *Ohio Archaeological and Historical Quarterly* 35:154–168.

Squier, E.G., and W.H. Davis. 1848. *Ancient Monuments of the Mississippi Valley.* Contributions to Knowledge no. 1. Smithsonian Institution, Washington, D.C.

See also HOPEWELL INTERACTION SPHERE; OHIO HOPEWELL

Horizon

A horizon is a unit of time bracketing the rapid spread, often over an enormous area, of a technical procedure, set of artifacts, art style, religious cult, or other archaeological phenomenon that endures for only a short time. Since these traits transcend cultural boundaries, the concept allows cross-dating of many local sequences in phases often hundreds of miles apart. A major integrative principle in Gordon R. Willey and Philip Phillips's (1958) New World cultural historical synthesis, the concept has been infrequently used in North American archaeology.

Guy Gibbon

Further Readings

Willey, G.R., and P. Phillips. 1958. *Method and Theory in American Archaeology.* University of Chicago Press, Chicago.

Horner Site

The Horner site (48PA29) is an archaeological site on the western edge of the Big Horn Basin near Cody, Wyoming. It is located on Sage Creek ca. 0.5 km (0.3 miles) south of the Shoshone River. The site is on a Pleistocene gravel terrace where a poorly drained, shallow depression probably held water during wet years. The location is considered the type site of the Cody complex. It was discovered in 1939 by an amateur archaeologist; scientific excavations were undertaken by Princeton University in the years 1949–1952, and jointly with the Smithsonian Institution in 1952. Additional excavations were done by the University of Wyoming in 1977–1978. The site has been divided into two locations based on the spatial separation between the early and late excavations. Horner I is the area that was investigated by Princeton and the Smithsonian. Animal remains, stone tools, and hearth areas were discovered. The majority of the animals were an extinct form of large bison (*Bison bison antiquus*), with ca. 100–200 individuals represented. The other animal species were represented by only a small number of individuals and included deer, antelope, dog/coyote, and various small mammals, reptiles, and amphibians. Horner I was characterized by scattered remains with two areas of concentration, one on the north and one to the south. These concentrations seemed to represent hearth-centered activity areas. Activities included killing and butchering of bison, hide preparation, and possibly short-term occupations. Originally, it was thought that the two areas might have represented different occupations, but the evidence was equivocal. Reinvestigations and reanalyses of these areas by the University of Wyoming supported this contention. Artifacts included projectile points, bifacial knives, butchering tools, and end scrapers. A wide range of projectile-point forms were described, but most were Eden and Scottsbluff types. Cody knives were also a common form. Reevaluation of this assemblage during the University of Wyoming research indicated that there are two different, but related, artifact assemblages present. Cody-complex materials from Horner I date to ca. 6950–6550 B.C. (8900–8500 years B.P.).

The second area is known as Horner II. This location was slightly separated from the first and yielded the remains of a bison-kill area. Evidently, a small herd of bison was killed in late fall or winter and, minimally, butchered. Activity and postdepositional reconstructions led to the conclusion that only a low proportion of the available food products was exploited. This pattern seems to be a common trait of Paleoindian procurement strategies and quite unlike Late Prehistoric kill sites where bison kills were maximally exploited. It looks like Horner II was a short-term kill, processing, and possibly frozen meat cache. The artifact assemblage consisted of projectile points, butchering tools, and a single shouldered knife. The projectile points were different enough in form and manufacture technology to be classified as other than Scottsbluff and Eden. They fall between Cody points and the earlier Alberta points and have been called Alberta/Cody points. They are the same as some of the points from Horner I and help to corroborate that two different occupations are represented there. Dates for Horner II fall between 8110 and 7925 B.C. (10,060–9875 years B.P.).

Bruce A. Bradley

Further Readings

Frison, G.C., and L.C. Todd (editors). 1987. *The Horner Site: The Type Site of the Cody Cultural Complex*. Academic Press, New York.

Jepsen, G.L. 1953. Ancient Hunters of Northwestern Wyoming. *Southwestern Lore* 19:19–25.

Wormington, H.M. 1957. *Ancient Man in North America*. Popular Series no. 4. Denver Museum of Natural History, Denver.

See also CODY

Hovenweep

Hovenweep, on the southern Utah-Colorado border, is an Anasazi region famous for its one-, two-, and three-story masonry towers. The heart of Hovenweep (which means "deserted valley" in the local Ute language) is five noncontiguous National Monument units administered by Mesa Verde National Park. The pottery and masonry at Hovenweep reflect its location within the general Mesa Verde Anasazi culture, but, in contrast to the cliff dwellings at Mesa Verde, many of the Hovenweep ruins are residential pueblos with towers perched on boulders at the heads of canyons, often overlooking springs.

Top: *Rim Dam at Hovenweep Castle. (Prepared by J. C. Winter) Bottom: South side of Hovenweep Castle at the head of Square Tower Canyon. (Reprinted from Smithsonian Institution, Bureau of American Ethnology, Bulletin 70, Plate 8)*

Research carried out in and around Hovenweep National Monument suggests that the towers represent a multipurpose architectural style rather than a special-purpose, single-function one. Test excavations at various towers have revealed a variety of features, including kivas, habitation rooms, storage units, grinding areas, and toolmaking locations. Astronomical observations during the summer and winter solstices and at other times of the year raise the possibility that certain portholes and other tower features may have served as agricultural and ceremonial calendars. Defense, lookouts, signaling, and community centers are other possible uses for various towers.

Earlier Basketmaker, Archaic, and even Paleoindian sites can be found on mesas around the canyons. The tower-building sequence began ca. A.D. 1000 (950 years B.P.) with the construction of small, single-story towers attached to L- and U-shaped Pueblo II ridge-top-unit pueblos. Beginning ca. A.D. 1160 (790 years B.P.), massive canyonhead residential complexes of roomblocks, kivas, modified springs, rim dams, arroyo-check dams, and spring-fed talus gardens were built in association with graceful towers. Most canyonhead towers were built after A.D. 1230 (720 years B.P.) and abandoned by A.D. 1277 (673 years B.P.) as the Anasazi left the Four Corners region.

Research at Hovenweep began with the explorations of W.H. Jackson (1878) and W.H. Holmes (1878) in the late nineteenth century and continued with the surveys and excavations of T.M. Prudden (1903), S.G. Morley (1908), and J.W. Fewkes (1919, 1925) in the early twentieth century. Aside from work by C.L. Riley (1950) and A.H. Schroeder (1967–1968), there were few projects in the 1950s and 1960s. In the 1970s, J.C. Winter began a National Science Foundation investigation of the Anasazi agricultural economy at Hovenweep, and J.E. Reyman (1975) and R. Williamson investigated the astronomical features of the towers (Williamson et al. 1977; Williamson 1978). Although there have been a few cultural-resource-management projects in the general area, there have been no full-scale excavations at Hovenweep. The National Monument is still relatively undeveloped and rarely visited (at least in comparison with Mesa Verde, Aztec, and Chaco Canyon). Hovenweep will probably remain an intriguing, yet poorly understood, deserted valley for years to come.

Joseph C. Winter

Stronghold House, Square Tower Canyon, Hovenweep. (Reprinted from Smithsonian Institution, Bureau of American Ethnology, Bulletin 70, *Plate 17)*

H

Further Readings

Fewkes, J.W. 1919. *Prehistoric Villages, Castles, and Towers*. Bulletin no. 70. Bureau of American Ethnology, Smithsonian Institution, Washington, D.C.

———. 1925. The Hovenweep National Monument. *Annual Report of the Smithsonian Institution for 1923*, pp. 465–480.

Holmes, W.H. 1878. Report on the Ancient Ruins of Southwestern Colorado, Examined During the Summers of 1875 and 1876. *Tenth Annual Report, United States Geological and Geographical Survey of the Territories for 1876*, pp. 383–408.

Jackson, W.H. 1878. Report on the Ancient Ruins Examined in 1875 and 1877. *Tenth Annual Report, United States Geological and Geographical Survey of the Territories for 1876*, pp. 411–450.

Morley, S.G. 1908. *The Excavation of the Cannonball Ruins in Southwestern Colorado*. Papers no. 2. School of American Archaeology, Archaeological Institute of America, Santa Fe.

Prudden, T.M. 1903. The Prehistoric Ruins of the San Juan Watershed in Utah, Arizona, Colorado, and New Mexico. *American Anthropologist* 5:224–258.

Reyman, J.E. 1975. The Nature and Nurture of Archeoastronomical Studies. In *Archaeoastronomy in Pre-Columbian America,* edited by A.F. Aveni, pp. 205–215. University of Texas Press, Austin.

Riley, C.L. 1950. "Defensive" Structures in the Hovenweep Monument. *El Palacio* 57(11):339–344.

Schroeder, A.H. 1967–1968. An Archaeological Survey Adjacent to Hovenweep National Monument. *Southwestern Lore* 33(3–4):61–94.

Williamson, R. 1978. Native Americans Were Continent's First Astronomers. *Smithsonian Magazine* 9(7):78–84.

Williamson, R., H.J. Fisher, and D. O'Flynn. 1977. Anasazi Solar Observatories. In *Essays in Native American Astronomy,* edited by A.F. Aveni, pp. 203–217. University of Texas Press, Austin.

Winter, J.C. 1975. *Hovenweep 1974.* Archeological Report no. 1. Anthropology Department, San Jose State University, San Jose.

———. 1976. *Hovenweep 1975.* Archeological Report no. 2. Anthropology Department, San Jose State University, San Jose.

———. 1977. *Hovenweep 1976.* Archeological Report no. 3. Anthropology Department, San Jose State University, San Jose.

———. 1981. Anasazi Agriculture at Hovenweep: 2. The Development and Use of Towers. *Contract Abstracts and CRM Archeology* 2(2):28–36.

———. 1991. Hovenweep Through Time. In *Understanding the Anasazi of Mesa Verde and Hovenweep,* edited by D.C. Noble. School of American Research Press, Santa Fe.

See also ANASAZI CULTURE AREA

Hrdlicka, Ales (1869–1943)

Founder (1918) and editor of the *American Journal of Physical Anthropology* and founder (1929) and first president of the American Association of Physical Anthropologists, Ales Hrdlicka was hired in 1903 as an assistant curator to organize the division of physical anthropology at the U.S. National Museum in Washington, D.C., where he became curator in 1910. He was an early exponent of an Asian origin for Native Americans and rigorously examined all human skeletal remains claimed to date to the Glacial Age. Although he believed that people were in the New World by at least 8000 B.C. (9950 years B.P.), he demonstrated that none of the remains then known were that old. He also conducted excavations in southwestern Alaska and elsewhere as part of his continued interest in the physical anthropology of Native Americans. Although correct in his general ideas about the peopling of the Americas, Hrdlicka (with William Henry Holmes, an associate at the Smithsonian Institution) is usually regarded today as an overbearing government scientist who used his power and prestige—and scathing attacks on younger scholars—to impose his view of the past on his contemporaries, thereby impeding the study of the peopling of the New World.

Guy Gibbon

Further Readings

Hrdlicka, A. 1918. *Recent Discoveries Attributed to Early Man in America.* Bulletin no. 66. Bureau of American Ethnology, Smithsonian Institution, Washington, D.C.

———. 1925. The Origin and Antiquity of the American Indian. *Annual Report of the Smithsonian Institution for 1923,* pp. 481–494.

———. 1930. *The Skeletal Remains of Early Man.* Smithsonian Institution, Washington, D.C.

Meltzer, D.J. 1983. The Antiquity of Man and the Development of American Archaeology. *Advances in Archaeological Method and Theory* 6:1–51.

See also HOLMES, WILLIAM HENRY

Hudson Bay Lowlands Prehistory

Known archaeological sites in the Hudson Bay Lowlands of Ontario are few, and their contents are sparse. To date (1996), systematic investigations have taken place only along the lower courses of the Severn and Albany rivers. However, it is possible to describe a distinctive adaptive pattern in this unique environmental zone that began as early as 5050 B.C. (7000 years B.P.).

Human remains dating to that time on Big Trout Lake are associated with a ground-stone gouge of possibly late Plano or Early Archaic affiliation. Although the site is outside the lowlands proper, its proximity to the then-active shores of the receding Tyrrell Sea provides the earliest actors for this emerging stage. The earliest evidence of a sustained presence in the lowlands is at present the archaeological remains of later Archaic groups who may have occupied the region in 1050–50 B.C. (3000–2000 years B.P.). Their toolkit included corner-notched projectile points, a variety of bifaces and scrapers, and notched implements that were probably used as spokeshaves. While these materials share general relationships with Shield Archaic assemblages, they are most similar to Pelican Lake–related assemblages in northern Manitoba.

The transition in the lowlands from clearly Archaic to Woodland-period occupations is not well known. However, a distinctive and well-documented human adaptive pattern had emerged in the lowlands by ca. A.D. 950 (1000 years B.P.). It was a pattern still followed by the *omaške·ko·w,* or West Main Cree, who were the first in the region to encounter European explorers. This adaptive pattern was based on the exploitation of a wide range of scattered subsistence species, of which caribou was a focal resource. The material culture of this period reflects the significant distances that had to be traveled to successfully exploit the lowlands on a year-long basis.

Ceramics were only occasionally acquired, and then most likely through trade. Pottery typical of the Initial Woodland period (Laurel) was recovered in small quantities stratigraphically below a component containing Late Woodland Blackduck ceramics. The strata containing Laurel sherds have been radiocarbon dated to A.D. 1080 ± 100 (870 years B.P.). Fabric-impressed body sherds reminiscent of Late Woodland Selkirk ceramics were recovered from an assemblage left behind by people who had traveled to the Hudson Bay Company fort at the mouth of the Severn River between 1685 and 1690. Bone and antler were probably more important raw materials for the manufacture of tools than was stone, which, in contrast to the earlier Archaic assemblages, was now used in a very expedient fashion. The Severn River Late Prehistoric assemblages stand in marked contrast to those of neighboring areas to the east, south, and west. Contacts with these distant regions are, however, demonstrated by the occurrence of triangular and notched projectile points. The most frequently used items in the lithic inventory remained, nonetheless, a variety of used and minimally retouched flakes and *pièces esquillées.*

From an archaeological perspective, contact with Europeans, although obvious in certain categories of material items, such as hunting weapons, had little effect on the general lifestyle of these people until the mid- to late nineteenth century. The subsistence-settlement pattern underwent important changes at that time that coincided with declining caribou populations.

Jean-Luc Pilon

Further Readings
Pilon, J.-L. 1987. *Washahoe Inninou Dahtsuounoaou: Ecological and Cultural Adaptation Along the Severn River in the Hudson Bay Lowlands of Ontario.* Report no. 10. Conservation Archaeology Report, Northwest Region, Ministry of Citizenship and Culture, Toronto.
———. 1988. Culture History and Ethnicity in the Hudson Bay Lowlands. In *Boreal Forest and Sub-Arctic Archaeology,* edited by C.S. Reid, pp. 100–120. Occasional Publications no. 6. London [Ontario] Chapter, Ontario Archaeological Society, London.
———. 1990. Historic Native Archaeology Along the Lower Severn River, Ontario. *Canadian Journal of Archaeology* 14:123–142.

See also BLACKDUCK; LAUREL CULTURE; PELICAN LAKE; SELKIRK; SHIELD CULTURE

Hudson-Meng Site

Hudson-Meng (25SX115) is an Alberta-complex bison-kill site in the High Plains of northwest Nebraska. Three radiocarbon determinations date the separate kill episodes at the site to 7850–7050 B.C. (9800–9000 years B.P.). Alberta projectile points and a Cody knife were recovered, along with the remains of several hundred bison. Bruce B. Huckell has described the production, use, and reuse of these points (Huckell 1978). The small, stemmed, shouldered biface from the site was produced using the same basic technological processes as those used to make the points. Larry D. Agenbroad, the investigator, has suggested that the procurement strategy at the site was a bison jump (Agenbroad 1978). George C. Frison notes that landform changes in the site area since its use as a bison-procurement station obscure what the terrain was like at the time; a natural or artificial trap of some sort is an alternative possibility (Frison 1991).

Guy Gibbon

Further Readings

Agenbroad, L.D. 1978. *The Hudson-Meng Site: An Alberta Bison Kill in the Nebraska High Plains.* University Press of America, Washington, D.C.

Frison, G.C. 1991. *Prehistoric Hunters of the High Plains.* 2nd ed. Academic Press, San Diego.

Huckell, B.B. 1978. Hudson-Meng Chipped Stone. In *The Hudson-Meng Site: An Alberta Bison Kill in the Nebraska High Plains,* edited by L.D. Agenbroad, pp. 153–189. University Press of America, Washington, D.C.

See also ALBERTA COMPLEX

Huff Phase

The Huff phase, a Late Prehistoric expression of the Terminal variant of the Middle Missouri tradition, is centered in Morton County, south-central North Dakota. The several semipermanent villages of the phase are set on high terraces along the Missouri River between the mouths of the Heart and the Cannonball rivers. The type site is the Huff village; a second excavated site is Shermer on the opposing bank of the Missouri River. Radiocarbon dates suggest that the Huff phase dates between ca. A.D. 1550 and 1675 (400–275 years B.P.). It predates the arrival of Euro-American trade goods.

The Huff site is a 3.4-ha (8.5-acre) fortified village on the west bank of the Missouri River near the present-day hamlet of the same name. The village, which is rectangular in plan, was surrounded by a prominent ditch within which was a palisade line reinforced at regular intervals by bastions. The defenses enclose 103 long rectangular houses set in irregular rows around an open, central "plaza." These dwellings were supported by a central ridge pole and had a covered entry that faced southwest. They were not earthlodges, although they may have been banked with, or partly covered by, earth. The people depended on maize, beans, and squash, food gathering, and the hunting of bison and other game.

The complex pottery industry was devoted to making globular jars, often with elaborate decorations on the rim and shoulder. The inventory of chipped and ground stone, shell, and bone objects is representative of Middle Missouri–tradition sites, but trade pottery from Extended Coalescent sites was also present at the Huff site. These sherds, and the presence of a subrectangular four-post earthlodge, reveal the beginnings of the downriver contact that was to lead to changes in the content of the phase. These changes were in the direction of historic Mandan Indian material culture. The Mandans, who lived to the north along the Missouri River in historic times, are probably the direct descendants of the people of this phase.

W. Raymond Wood

Further Readings

Sperry, J.E. 1968. *The Shermer Site (32EM10).* Memoir no. 2. Plains Anthropologist, Lincoln.

Wood, W.R. 1982. *An Interpretation of Mandan Prehistory.* Reprinted. J and L Reprint, Lincoln. Originally published 1967, Bulletin no. 198. Bureau of American Ethnology, Smithsonian Institution, Washington, D.C.

See also MIDDLE MISSOURI TRADITION

Humboldt Lakebed Site

The Humboldt Lakebed site (26CH15) includes three of the 19 artifact concentrations that L.L. Loud mapped on the southeast shore of Humboldt Lake while working at Lovelock Cave in 1912. It is a large, Late Prehistoric village located on a low dune on one of the main channels draining the Humboldt River into Humboldt Lake. It is sometimes flooded by Humboldt Lake or lying on a dry lakebed, depending on the year.

The site is ca. 855 m (2,800 feet) east-west and 365 m (1,200 feet) north-south. It includes 719 features classified as houses, burial pits, storage pits, hearths, smudge pits, and seep wells. Artifacts have been collected from this area over the last eight decades by both professionals and amateurs. To date (1996), there are 1,801 reported projectile points, including Desert, Rosegate, Elko, and Gatecliff series, as well as a number of specimens that cannot be placed in any of the recognized Great Basin series. The remainder of the artifact assemblage comprises ground stone, debitage, shell, and bone, with a few fragments of basketry associated with burials. There are eight radiocarbon dates for the site: six on charcoal or sediments from house floors that date to A.D. 580–990 (1370–960 years B.P.), one of 740 B.C. (2690 years B.P.) on organic material from a burial, and one of A.D. 1400 (550 years B.P.) on organic material from a storage pit.

Stephanie D. Livingston

Further Readings

Harrington, M.R. 1927. Some Lake-Bed Camp-Sites in Nevada. *Indian Notes* 4(1):40–47. Museum of the American Indian-Heye Foundation, New York.

Heizer, R.F., and C.W. Clewlow, Jr. 1968. Projectile Points From Site NV-CH-15, Churchill County, Nevada. *University of California Archaeological Survey Report* 71:59–88.

Livingston, S.D. 1986. The Archaeology of the Humboldt Lakebed Site. *Journal of California and Great Basin Anthropology* 8(1):99–115.

———. 1991. Aboriginal Utilization of Birds in the Western Great Basin. In *Beamers, Bobwhites, and Blue-Points: Tributes to the Career of Paul W. Parmalee*, edited by J.R. Purdue, W.E. Klippel, and B.W. Styles, pp. 341–357. Scientific Papers no. 23. Illinois State Museum, Springfield.

See also LOVELOCK CAVE

Hypsithermal

"Hypsithermal" is the name of the middle stage in a three-step Holocene climatic scheme comprising the Boreal, Hypsithermal, and Neoglacial. It was the period of maximum warmth and dryness that affected much of North America and Europe in postglacial times. It is a time-transgressive period formally defined as the time represented by four pollen zones, V–VIII, in the Danish system (Boreal, Atlantic, Subboreal), or the period ca. 7050–550 B.C. (9000–2500 years B.P.) (Deevey and Flint 1957). Temperatures were as much as 2–3°C warmer then than now, although warm/dry periods alternated with cooler/moister periods. The stage is known by a variety of older terms, including Altithermal, Climatic Optimum, Megathermal, Wärmezeit, and Xerothermic interval. When the Hypsithermal ended, the last glacial ice in Canada was gone, and alpine glaciers had receded as far as they were to do so. The stage was followed by a cooler period, the Neoglacial, in which glaciers were reborn in alpine settings worldwide.

An earlier term, the Altithermal, is widely used by archaeologists in the western United States due to its introduction and use in two influential reconstructions by Ernst Antevs (1948, 1955). The Altithermal was one of three geologic-climate units (Anathermal, Altithermal, and Medithermal) he defined for the postglacial (Neothermal) period.

W. Raymond Wood

Further Readings

Antevs, E. 1948. Climatic Changes and Pre-White Man. In *The Great Basin, With Emphasis on Glacial and Post-Glacial Times*, edited by E. Blackwelder, pp. 168–191. Bulletin of the University of Utah, vol. 38, no. 20. Biological Series, vol. 10, no. 7. Salt Lake City.

———. 1955. Geologic-Climate Dating in the West. *American Antiquity* 20(4):317–335.

Deevey, E.S., Jr., and R.F. Flint. 1957. Postglacial Hypsithermal Interval. *Science* 125:182–184.

Hypsithermal/Altithermal

Evidence is strong, especially in midwestern North America, that a warm/dry climate reached a maximum during the middle Holocene. The border between the prairie and the forest in the Minnesota area was displaced eastward ca. 6050–3050 B.C. (8000–5000 years B.P.), and lake levels were lower. The term "Hypsithermal" has been applied to this interval, with dating originally based on correlation with the "postglacial Climatic Optimum" of Europe. The interval was followed by the Neoglacial period, when glaciers in the Rocky Mountains expanded after a long interval of recession. Although the original correlation with the European sequence is no longer relevant, the term "Hypsithermal" still expresses significant climatic trends in much of North America. The basic cause is believed to be the gradual shift in the distribution of summer solar radiation related to Earth/Sun orbital cycles. Maximum insolation in the continental interior was reached ca. 8050 B.C. (10,000 years B.P.), but the climatic manifestations were delayed in the Midwest by the lingering effects of the retreating Laurentide ice sheet. The inception of the Hypsithermal in the Great Plains came as early as 7550 B.C. (9500 years B.P.) because this region was farther from the influence of the ice sheet. The climatic expression of the insolation maximum is strongest in the continental interior and is less marked east of the Midwest. Here the hydrological budget is less subject to the incidence of drought and other climatic causes for vegetational and lake-level change.

"Altithermal" is a term used largely in the American Southwest for a comparable interval of warm/dry climate. It is probably also related to insolational changes, but the timing may be different because the climate of the western mountains and plateaus is largely controlled by the nature of the Pacific air masses that dominate.

H.E. Wright, Jr.

Further Readings

Wright, H.E., Jr., J.E. Kutsbach, T. Webb III, W.F. Ruddiman, F.A. Street-Perrot, and P.J. Bartlein (editors). 1993. *Global Climates Since the Last Glacial Maximum.* University of Minnesota Press, Minneapolis.

I

Ice-Free Corridor

During the last glacial maximum (ca. 18,050 B.C., or 20,000 years B.P.), the Laurentide and Cordilleran ice sheets merged along the piedmont of the Canadian Rocky Mountains in Alberta to form a continuous barrier to migration of plants, animals, and humans between the Alaska/Yukon area and the northern Great Plains. As the two ice sheets wasted after the maximum, a continuous corridor of ice-free land became available for colonization and travel. The time of opening of the corridor and the occupation of numerous sites of the Clovis culture throughout the United States, especially in the West, are more or less contemporaneous, leading to the hypothesis that the peopling of the New World south of Alaska awaited the climatic change that effectively opened the corridor. It is also a main element of the hypothesis that the abrupt migration of human hunters through the corridor resulted in the contemporaneous decimation of American megafauna, which was not accustomed to human predators. Both of these hypotheses have opponents. Difficulties with the first come from the finding of archaeological sites south of the ice sheet that predate the opening of the corridor (e.g., Meadowcroft in Pennsylvania, with a date at least as old as 12,050 B.C. [14,000 years B.P.], and Monte Verde in Chile, with a date of ca. 11,050 B.C. [13,000 years B.P.]). Opposition to the second comes from the leading alternative explanation for megafaunal extinction, namely the effects of the climatic change itself, which may have caused such rapid changes in the vegetation that the megafauna could not adapt. The critical point in the problem is the chronology of deglaciation in the Alberta area and the nature of the landscape during deglaciation,

although some reviewers avoid the problem by postulating a migration route along the coast or off the coast rather than through the corridor.

The ice-sheet confluence that was the future site of the corridor was several tens of kilometers long. The general inaccessibility of this heavily forested area and the paucity of geologic studies have resulted in inadequate information about the course of deglaciation and the nature of the landscape as the corridor developed. It is possible that as the ice thinned it became stagnant, and, as a result, a great mass of buried ice persisted for a long time. This would have produced a very rugged terrain, but one in which vegetation could develop on the debris covering the dead ice and through which animals and humans could have passed at an early time. But such speculation is irrelevant in the absence of geologic reconstruction of the course of deglaciation in the region. A distinct standstill of the retreating Laurentide ice sheet is recorded by the Cree Lake moraine near the western end of huge Lake Athabaska, which is well dated to ca. 8050 B.C. (10,000 years B.P.). Prior to this time, events are poorly recorded. A drained proglacial lake to the west has a radiocarbon date of 10,050 B.C. (12,000 years B.P.), which is about the best control for a minimum date for the opening of the corridor, at least in that area. A radiocarbon date for the basal sediments of a lake in southern Alberta, Goldwater Lake, of ca. 16,050 B.C. (18,000 years B.P.) was first thought to indicate that this area near the base of the mountains was already open by this time. But study of moss remains and other macrofossils in a nearby lake indicate that aquatic mosses utilize carbon derived in part from groundwater deficient in radiocarbon and thus yield dates that are too old. It may be some time before a reliable date for the opening of the corridor emerges.

A more direct approach to the archaeological implications of the Alberta corridor might be further search for archaeological sites in the south to refine the chronology of migration, which is already fairly well constrained. Inasmuch as Meadowcroft and Monte Verde are not Clovis sites and are substantially older than the best dates for the opening of the corridor, migration to those sites may have been earlier and thus may not have involved the corridor.

H.E. Wright, Jr.

Further Readings

Dillehay, T.D., and D.J. Meltzer. 1991. *The First Americans: Search and Research.* CRC Press, Boca Raton.

Igloolik Sequence

The Igloolik sequence of Paleoeskimo cultures was established by Jorgen Meldgaard following fieldwork in the vicinity of Igloolik Island, northern Foxe Basin, Northwest Territories in 1954, 1957, and 1962. It represents the earliest attempt to establish such a sequence. Northern Foxe Basin is ideally suited to studies of culture change through time for three reasons: (1) since it has always been an area rich in marine mammal resources, the record of human occupation is a continuous one; (2) much of the region is limestone, which has resulted in the excellent preservation of antler, bone, and ivory despite the shallow depth of most archaeological sites; and (3) during the Wisconsin glaciation, this region was heavily glaciated. Following the retreat of the glacier, the land began to rebound, and this process continues. Generally, hunters exploiting large marine mammals choose to live close to the coast. As the land rose, people would establish new camps at lower elevations rather than return to camp sites at higher elevations. Therefore, sites in this region are rarely superimposed on one another. In most cases, depending on the local topography, the higher the elevation the older the site.

At Igloolik, the earliest Paleoeskimo sites are associated with the Pre-Dorset culture (termed the Sarqaq by Meldgaard). The earliest radiocarbon dates for the Pre-Dorset occupation of this region are 1750 B.C. ± 300 (3700 years B.P.). Meldgaard divided this period into three phases, Early, Middle, and Late, based on the elevation of sites. The later Paleoeskimo

sites are associated with the Dorset culture. They are located on beach ridges that are ca. 8–22 m (26–72 feet) above sea level and date to ca. 700 B.C.–A.D. 1300 (2650–650 years B.P.). The transition from Pre-Dorset to Dorset is abrupt and includes changes in house styles, material culture, and even use of raw materials. This abrupt change led Meldgaard to hypothesize that a possible diffusion from southerly boreal-forest cultures or even a migration of new peoples into the eastern Arctic had taken place. These ideas have not found favor with other Arctic specialists, who see a more gradual in situ transition taking place mostly as a result of climate change and concomitant changes in resource availability.

Meldgaard's (1960) Dorset sequence, which is based on his work at the Alarnerk site on Melville Peninsula, consists of five periods. The sequence has been corroborated by work at four other large sites in the region. Period I marks the transition from Pre-Dorset to Dorset. Period II is a stable period with little variability in material culture, whereas during Period III there are many changes. Periods IV and V mark the end of the Dorset period. Period V houses are found at the same elevations as the earliest Neoeskimo houses. These periods are defined by elevations at the site, by changes in type fossils, most importantly harpoon heads, and by the presence and absence of certain artifacts.

Sue Rowley

Further Readings

Meldgaard, J. 1960. Prehistoric Culture Sequences in the Eastern Arctic As Elucidated by Stratified Sites at Iglulik. In *Men and Cultures,* edited by A.F.C. Wallace, pp. 588–595. Selected Papers of the Fifth International Congress of Anthropological and Ethnological Sciences, 1956. University of Pennsylvania Press, Philadelphia.

Incinerator, or Sunwatch Village

Incinerator, or Sunwatch Village, is a reconstructed thirteenth-century A.D. Fort Ancient village, situated on the west bank of the Great Miami River on the outskirts of Dayton, Ohio. Designated a National Historic Landmark in 1990, the site is maintained by the Dayton Museum of Natural History, which operates a visitors center at the village. Staff and volunteers from the museum have reconstructed several houses and offer village tours and special programs related to Native Americans throughout the year. Sunwatch village is the most completely excavated site of its type in the Ohio Valley.

The plan of Sunwatch village is probably typical of thirteenth- and fourteenth-century Fort Ancient communities. Covering ca. 1.2 ha (3 acres), it was a permanently occupied village that was home to ca. 150–300 individuals, who lived in 25–30 wattle-and-daub houses regularly arranged around an open plaza. A stockade of irregularly spaced wooden poles surrounded the core area of the village, with the wall overlapping in two areas to form narrow openings into the village interior. The overall layout of the village was circular to slightly oval in shape.

A group of large wooden posts, some made of Eastern red cedar (*Juniperus virginiana*), occupied the center of the village plaza. One structure on the west side of the plaza is considerably larger and seems to have played a part in the astronomical alignments associated with the post complex in the plaza. Dayton Museum archaeologists and astronomers believe that this pole-and-post compound was used to track the movement of the sun in order to regulate community-wide agricultural rituals. While most of the houses at Sunwatch are fairly regular in size, one house on the west side of the plaza was slightly larger than most and was built in a shallow pit. The house also incorporated a number of cedar poles in its walls. Based on the abundance of flint tools and the byproducts from their manufacture on the floor of the house, Sunwatch archaeologists theorize that this structure was not a true residence but a special "men's house" in which village men conducted special activities. A number of pits containing quantities of charred maize as well as stone tobacco pipes were also associated with the house.

The fitting together of broken pottery jars and stone tools recovered from abandoned, trash-filled storage pits has revealed a series of patterns within the village. The Dayton Museum staff suggests that these patterns indicate the presence of at least four distinct residential zones in the village that are probably related to kinship groupings, such as clans. These groupings may have been the social units that made up the village.

The dietary mainstay of the Sunwatch residents was maize, and dried agricultural products were stored in underground pits, or silos,

that ringed the space between the houses and the plaza. Village residents were buried in front of the ring of pits at the edge of the plaza. In addition to maize, beans, squashes, and sunflowers were grown. Wild plants of all sorts were collected to provide both sustenance and variety to an otherwise carbohydrate-dominated diet. Animal foods, particularly white-tailed deer and turkey, were intensively hunted, and the nearby Great Miami River was a source of important aquatic resources.

C. Wesley Cowan

Further Readings

Heilman, J.A., M.C. Lileas, and C.A. Turnbow. 1988. *A History of 17 Years of Excavation and Reconstruction—A Chronicle of 12th Century Human Values and the Built Environment.* Dayton Museum of Natural History, Dayton.

Robertson, J.A. 1984. Chipped Stone and Functional Interpretations: A Fort Ancient Example. *Midcontinental Journal of Archaeology* 9:251–267.

See also FORT ANCIENT CULTURE

Independence I and II

The Independence culture takes its name from Independence Fjord in the Pearyland region of northern Greenland, where remains of the culture were first recognized by Eigil Knuth in 1949. Knuth named and described two temporal phases: Independence I, considered to be the earliest evidence of occupation in the High Arctic, and Independence II, thought to be coeval with late Pre-Dorset variants of the central and eastern Arctic.

Independence I is now seen as an early and distinctive variant of the Arctic Small Tool tradition, with occupation centered in the polar desert regions of northern Greenland and the northern Queen Elizabeth Islands of Arctic Canada. Radiocarbon dates suggest that Independence people may have reached the area as early as 2550 B.C. (4500 years B.P.); most sites appear to date to ca. 2050–1650 B.C. (4000–3600 years B.P.). The Independence I adaptation was based primarily on the hunting of musk-oxen. Waterfowl, arctic char, and caribou were secondary resources; relatively little dependence was placed on sea mammals. The most notable characteristics that distinguish Independence I assemblages from other early Paleoeskimo variants include contracting-stem end blades and small bipoints; thin triangular end blades; a wide variety of struck burins, including large forms with multiple notches for hafting; and fine flaking of stone tools with deep edge serration. Structural remains are limited to tent foundations, frequently with central box hearths and midpassage features.

Independence II, a poorly defined complex, is known from a limited number of sites in northern Greenland and the Queen Elizabeth Islands of Arctic Canada. It is generally thought to date to ca. 1050–550 B.C. (3000–2500 years B.P.). As the term implies, this complex shares a number of characteristics with Independence I, including the midpassage or axial style of dwelling, which continues with slight variations, and an adaptation based largely on the interior resources of the High Arctic. However, Independence II hunters appear to have made greater use of sea mammals than did their predecessors. Most Independence II artifacts resemble those of late Pre-Dorset and early Dorset complexes of more southerly Arctic regions. Such similarities include toggling harpoon heads, lance heads with "cloven-hoof" bases, end blades with wide side notches, large round side blades, small soapstone vessels, burinlike tools, needles with oval-to-flat cross section, and adze blades of the Dorset type. Independence II is one of several distinctive complexes that developed across Arctic Canada at the time of the Pre-Dorset–Dorset transition.

Patricia D. Sutherland

Further Readings

Knuth, E. 1967. *Archaeology of the Musk-Ox Way.* Contributions du Centre d'Etudes Arctiques et Finnoscandinaves no. 5. Ecole Pratique des Hautes Etudes, Sorbonne, Paris.

Maxwell, M.S. 1985. *Prehistory of the Eastern Arctic.* Academic Press, New York.

See also ARCTIC SMALL TOOL TRADITION; DORSET CULTURE

Indian Creek Site

The Indian Creek Site (24BW626) is a deeply stratified, multicomponent campsite located within the south valley floodplain of extensively placered Indian Creek. It is at an elevation of 1,640 m (5,380 feet) inside the southeast flank of the Elkhorn Mountains in the Upper Missouri River drainage, west of Townsend in

Excavation unit 3 at the Downstream Locality of the Indian Creek site, west-central Montana, Upper Missouri River drainage. Folsom peoples occupied the excavated surface nearly 11,000 years ago. (Courtesy of Museum of the Rockies/Montana State University–Bozeman)

Broadwater County, west-central Montana. The Indian Creek site was discovered in 1979 and excavated in the years 1982–1985 by Montana State University. Twenty-eight different occupations within 7.3 m (24 feet) of valley fill were sampled. The initial Paleoindian Folsom or Folsom-related occupation in the Downstream Locality was radiocarbon dated at 9030 B.C. ± 110 (10,980 years B.P.). It was preceded by a Glacier Peak Layer G ashfall, which was dated at 9175 B.C. ± 130 (11,125 years B.P.). The lithic artifact assemblage associated with the initial Paleoindian occupation consisted predominantly of butchering (marginally retouched flakes), bone or woodworking (multibitted gravers), and hide-working (spurred end scrapers and side scrapers) tools, a bifacial core, debitage, and a few projectile-point fragments. Successive Paleoindian occupations dated at 8210 B.C. ± 90 (10,160 years B.P.), 7920 B.C. ± 130 (9870 years B.P.), 7340 B.C. ± 120 (9290 years B.P.), and 6390 B.C. ± 100 (8340 years B.P.) lacked diagnostic artifacts in the Downstream Locality. Upstream, a Folsom debris-discard feature radiocarbon dated at 8680 B.C. ± 280 (10,630 years B.P.) was stratigraphically overlain by Agate Basin and Hell Gap–complex components, with ages of 8060 B.C. ± 110 (10,010 years B.P.) and 7910 B.C. ± 70 (9860 years B.P.) for the Hell Gap occupation. The Folsom discard feature yielded eight tools (end and side scrapers and projectile points) and ca. 2,400 waste flakes, including channel flakes, and skeletal remains of utilized bison (*Bison* sp.), deer or pronghorn antelope (*Odocoileus* sp; *Antilocapra americana*), yellow-bellied marmot (*Marmota flaviventris*), large hare (*Lepus* sp.), black-tailed prairie dog (*Cynomys ludovicianus*), and vole (*Microtus* sp.). The other occupations in the Downstream Locality are associated with early Middle Prehistoric (Middle Plains Archaic) and Bitterroot occupations, ca. 5250–4950 B.C. (7200–6900 years B.P.). Bison and, to a lesser extent, marmot continued to be of local economic importance into the late Middle period. Mountain sheep (*Ovis canadensis*) were an important food species during the Middle period at Indian Creek, as elsewhere in the Northern Rockies. Overall, the Indian Creek site was occupied on different occasions from late spring through early autumn over an 8,000-year span by hunter-gatherers in transit between the Townsend Basin and mountainous areas to the south, west, and north, and vice versa.

Leslie B. Davis

Further Readings

Davis, L.B. 1984. Late Pleistocene to Mid-Holocene Adaptations at Indian Creek, West-Central Montana Rockies. *Current Research in the Pleistocene* 1:9–10.

———. 1986. Age and Source Analysis for Obsidian Hell Gap Complex Artifacts in the Montana Rockies. *Current Research in the Pleistocene* 3:27–28.

Davis, L.B., and S.T. Greiser. 1992. Indian Creek Paleoindians: Early Occupation of the Elkhorn Mountains' Southeast Flank, West-Central Montana. In *Ice Age Hunters of the Rockies*, edited by D.J. Stanford and J.S. Day, pp. 225–283. Denver Museum of Natural History, Denver; University Press of Colorado, Niwot.

Davis, L.B., S.T. Greiser, and T.W. Greiser. 1987. Spring Cleanup at a Folsom Campsite in the Montana Rockies. *Current Research in the Pleistocene* 4:5–6.

Davis, L.B., S.T. Greiser, and N. Toth. 1985. Use-Wear Analyses of Paleoindian Unifaces From the Initial Occupation at the Indian Creek Site. *Current Research in the Pleistocene* 2:45–46.

Davis, L.B., S.T. Greiser, J.P. Albanese, R.J. Ottersberg, G.E. Fredlund, and L.S. Cummings. 1997. Indian Creek and MacHaffie: Folsom Campsites in the Elkhorn Range, North Rocky Mountains. In *Folsom Archaeology and Late Pleistocene Paleoecology*, edited by M.A. Jodry and D.J. Stanford. In preparation for the Smithsonian Inquiry in Archaeology Series.

Indian Knoll

The mound known as Indian Knoll (15OH2) was first excavated by C.B. Moore in 1915 (Moore 1916). It lies on the right bank of Green River in Ohio County, west-central Kentucky, and now, although still under cultivation, is a National Historic Landmark. Moore's work and that of Works Progress Administration (WPA) archaeologists in 1939, 1940, and 1941 have made Indian Knoll the most famous of the 45 or so prehistoric shell mounds along and adjacent to the middle portion of the Green River.

W.S. Webb (1946:119) described the site as an elliptical mound ca. 137 x 67 m (450 x 220 feet) whose long axis paralleled the river. The archaeological deposits were 1.5–2.4 m

(5–8 feet) deep at the mound center and contained thousands of artifacts and artifact fragments, hundreds of human burials, and 21 dog burials. Skeletal remains of human burials were removed from Indian Knoll by Moore (who reports a total of 298) and by the WPA archaeologists (who report 880). Human osteological materials excavated by the WPA are at the Museum of Anthropology at the University of Kentucky in Lexington, but apparently only 66 of the 298 dug up by Moore were sent on to the U.S. National Museum in Washington, D.C. The University of Kentucky series has been analyzed or described by several different researchers. The function of these shell mounds as cemeteries continues to be debated (Claassen 1991).

Webb (1951) obtained four radiocarbon determinations on antler from Indian Knoll in the early period of Willard F. Libby's work on the technique: 2013 B.C. ± 350, or 3963 years B.P. (from the 1.4-m [4.5-foot] level); 2332 B.C. ± 250, or 4282 years B.P. (from the 0.3-m [1-foot] level); 2944 B.C. ± 560, or 4894 years B.P., and 3759 B.C. ± 350, or 5709 years B.P. (from the 0.3-m [1-foot] level; the sample was run twice). Traditional and accelerator mass spectrometry (AMS) dates from other Green River shell mounds obtained more recently are in the range 5224 B.C.–A.D. 130 (7174–1820 years B.P.) (Marquardt and Watson 1983).

For some 50 years, Green River shell mounds have been assumed to exemplify a well-developed Late Archaic tradition in the west-central Kentucky portion of the Ohio drainage. This attribution is generally correct, but evidence from artifact finds, projectile-point typology, and some radiocarbon dates suggests that there are also Middle Archaic and Woodland to Mississippian components at some sites. Indian Knoll yielded 792 potsherds to WPA archaeologists; 21 were shell tempered, and the other 171 grit tempered. Most were from the upper part of the deposit. Webb and William Haag thought that these sherds postdated occupancy of the shell mound by "the Shell Heap People" (Haag 1946:362).

The best-known artifacts from Indian Knoll are grave goods, such as conch shells, shell beads (probably made from conchs), atlatl hooks and weights, tortoise-shell rattles, and a few small copper items. Fishhooks and abundant antler and bone tools of various sorts are also characteristic of Indian Knoll and other Green River shell mounds.

Interpretation of overall site function for Indian Knoll and the other Green River shell mounds is under debate, with much stronger emphasis than previously on their role as mortuary sites. Detailed understanding of shell-mound subsistence is also accumulating for a few sites. Besides forest species (deer, turkey, small mammals, nuts, berries) and riverine species (fish, crustaceans, and shellfish), there are fragments of charred *Cucurbita pepo* rind at the Carlston Annis mound and the Bowles site, both part of the Green River shell mounds. The *Cucurbita* is presumably *C. pepo ovifera,* an indigenous wild plant, or a cultivated or semi-cultivated variety derived from the indigenous wild population. In the 1990s, research in the Indian Knoll/Green River shell-mound region has focused on relations between shell mounds and contemporaneous midden mounds (burnt-rock middens, dirt mounds) and on the details of seasonal indicators at the shell mounds.

Patty Jo Watson

Further Readings

Claassen, C. 1991. Gender, Shellfishing, and the Shell Mound Archaic. In *Engendering Archaeology,* edited by J. Gero and M. Conkey, pp. 276–300. Basil Blackwell, New York.

Crawford, G.W. 1982. Late Archaic Plant Remains From West-Central Kentucky: A Summary. *Midcontinental Journal of Archaeology* 7:205–224.

Haag, W. 1946. Pottery From Indian Knoll. In *Indian Knoll,* by W. Webb, pp. 356–365. Reports in Anthropology and Archaeology, vol. 4, no. 3, pt. 1. University of Kentucky, Lexington.

Hensley, C.K. 1991. The Middle Green River Shell Mounds: Challenging Traditional Interpretations Using Internal Site Structure Analysis. In *The Human Landscape in Kentucky's Past: Site Structure and Settlement Patterns,* edited by C. Stout and C.K. Hensley, pp. 78–97. Kentucky Heritage Council, Frankfort.

Marquardt, W.H., and P.J. Watson. 1983. The Shell Mound Archaic of Western Kentucky. In *Archaic Hunters and Gatherers in the American Midwest,* edited by J. Phillips and J. Brown, pp. 323–339. Academic Press, New York.

Moore, C.B. 1916. Some Aboriginal Sites on Green River, Kentucky. *Journal of the Academy of Natural Sciences of Philadelphia,* ser. 2, 16(3).

Perzigian, A.J. 1976. The Dentition of the Indian Knoll Skeletal Population: Odontometrics and Cusp Number. *American Journal of Physical Anthropology* 44:113–122.

Rolingson, M.A. 1967. Temporal Perspectives on the Archaic Cultures of the Middle Green River Region. Unpublished Ph.D. dissertation, Department of Anthropology, University of Michigan, Ann Arbor.

Snow, C.E. 1948. *Indian Knoll Skeletons of Site Oh2, Ohio County, Kentucky.* Reports in Anthropology and Archaeology, vol. 4, no. 3, pt. 2. University of Kentucky, Lexington.

Stewart, T.D. 1962. Comments on the Reassessments of the Indian Knoll Skeletons. *American Journal of Physical Anthropology* 20:143–148.

Webb, W.S. 1946. *Indian Knoll. Site Oh2, Ohio County, Kentucky.* Reports in Anthropology and Archaeology, vol. 4, no. 3, pt. 1. University of Kentucky, Lexington.

———. 1951. Radiocarbon Dating of Samples From the Southeast. In *Radiocarbon Dating,* edited by F. Johnson. Memoir 8:30. Society for American Archaeology, Washington, D.C.

Winters, H. 1974. Introduction to the New Edition. In *Indian Knoll. Site Oh2, Ohio County, Kentucky.* Reports in Anthropology and Archaeology, vol. 4, no. 3, pt. 1, pp. v–xxvii. University of Kentucky, Lexington. Reprinted. University of Tennessee Press, Knoxville.

Initial Coalescent (Campbell Creek and/or Arzberger Phase)

The "Initial Coalescent" is a Late Prehistoric archaeological manifestation in South Dakota and northeast Nebraska. Initial Coalescent sites were organized as a variant of the Coalescent tradition on the assumption they were the first stage of a later Coalescent tradition. Newer investigations (Steinacher and Toom 1984) make this interpretation untenable. Possessing a majority of traits of the Central Plains tradition, "Initial Coalescent" is a one-phase (Arzberger, Campbell Creek, or Anoka phase) phenomenon of about a dozen village sites dating to ca. A.D. 1150–1350 (800–550 years B.P.).

Initial Coalescent houses range from nearly square to round wattle-and-daub structures erected over shallow, excavated housepits, with an entry passage extending from the middle of one wall and four central roof-support posts around a central fire basin. One house, however, has a double row of three postholes, which suggests a gabled roof, possibly borrowed from Middle Missouri–tradition architecture. Villages of up to 50 houses were grouped into ditched and palisaded, bastioned sites on the Missouri River terraces (e.g., Whistling Elk, Crow Creek, Talking Crow, Black Partizan) or on isolated, high paleoterrace remnants (Arzberger, Lynch). Villages may have contained 200–800 people.

Pottery consists of globular jars with unthickened, collared, or (rarely) beveled-lip rims. Rim exteriors of all forms may bear incised or trailed decoration; lips of all forms often have tool-impressed or finger-pinched decoration. Jar bodies were formed using a cord-wrapped paddle or a grooved or thong-wrapped paddle; many vessels were subsequently thoroughly smoothed. A small number of jar shoulders were decorated, and some jars have elliptical mouths, traits likely borrowed from Oneota sources; several actual Oneota shell-tempered jars were found at the Lynch site.

Stone tools include small, triangular, side-notched and unnotched arrow points; drills; ovate and four-edge-beveled knives; plate chalcedony knives; end scrapers; graving tools; and retouched or utilized flake and core tools. Raw materials are often from western Nebraska and South Dakota sources, a pattern similar to the Itskari phase of central Nebraska. Groundstone tools include a variety of sandstone and "clinker" abraders, red pipestone (catlinite?) pipes, pecked-and-polished celts and grooved axes, grooved mauls, and hammerstones. Bone, antler, and shell tools include bison-scapula digging tools, scapula cleavers, and polygonal knives, split proximal deer/antelope metapodial awls, rarer distal deer/antelope metapodial awls, rib face awls, "quill flatteners," cancellous tissue abraders, bone fishhooks, antler-tine flakers, and shell disc beads. Subsistence focused on bison hunting and gardening.

Simple-stamped surface treatment of Initial Coalescent pottery, some architecture, and the fortifications were borrowed from Extended Middle Missouri–variant sources, which were most likely invaders under military pressures, as indicated by the construction of Initial Coalescent fortifications. This interpretation is also graphically illustrated by the nearly 500 mutilated skeletons in the Crow Creek–site fortification ditch. The Initial Coalescent was terminated as a result of war with peoples of the Middle Missouri tradition in the thirteenth and fourteenth centuries. At the end of this period, not only was Initial Coalescent gone, but also Initial Middle Missouri (including Mill Creek sites). The inheritors of the Dakotas were Extended Middle Missouri, Thomas Riggs–phase peoples.

John Ludwickson

Further Readings

Caldwell, W.W. 1966. *The Black Partizan Site.* Publications in Salvage Archeology no. 2. River Basin Surveys. Smithsonian Institution, Lincoln.

Freed, M.L. 1954. *The Lynch Site, 258D1.* Unpublished Master's thesis. Department of Anthropology, University of Nebraska, Lincoln.

Kivett, M.F., and R.E. Jensen. 1976. *The Crow Creek Site (39BF11).* Publications in Anthropology no. 7. Nebraska State Historical Society, Lincoln.

Smith, C.S. 1977. *The Talking Crow Site: A Multi-Component Earthlodge Village in the Big Bend Region, South Dakota.* Publications in Anthropology no. 9. Department of Anthropology, University of Kansas, Lawrence.

Spaulding, A.C. 1956. *The Arzberger Site, Hughes County, South Dakota.* Occasional Contributions no. 16. Museum of Anthropology, University of Michigan, Ann Arbor.

Steinacher, T.L., and D.L. Toom. 1984. *Archeological Investigations at the Whistling Elk Site (39HU242), 1978–1979.* University of Nebraska Department of Anthropology Technical Report 83–104, vol. 2, Appendix 1. U.S. Army Corps of Engineers, Omaha.

Willey, P. 1990. *Prehistoric Warfare on the Great Plains: Skeletal Analysis of the Crow Creek Massacre Victims.* Garland, New York.

See also ARZBERGER SITE; CROW CREEK SITE

Intermountain Tradition

Intermountain was originally defined by William Mulloy in the early 1950s as a Late Prehistoric ceramic tradition in the intermountain regions of Montana and Wyoming. The ceramics are flat-bottomed vessels with a slight constriction above the base and a body that flares outward from the constriction to a maximum diameter at the shoulder. The upper portion of the vessels curves slightly inward to the mouth. Vessel shape resembles a flower pot. Jack R. Rudy defined a similar kind of pottery as Shoshone Ware in his survey of western Utah (Rudy 1953). Intermountain, or Shoshonean, ceramics have been accepted as an indicator of Shoshonean occupation of the northeastern Great Basin and surrounding intermountain areas of eastern Idaho, northern Utah, southwestern Montana, and western Wyoming during the Late Prehistoric period. While there is an apparent ethnographic association of this pottery with Shoshonean (Numic) groups of the Great Basin culture area, an archaeological association of Intermountain ceramics with a proposed Shoshonean (Numic) migration or expansion into the area is less clear. This migration hypothesis is based upon four primary assumptions: (1) the homeland for all Numic groups is probably the southwestern corner of the Great Basin culture area; (2) all Numic languages show dialect differences by A.D. 1000 (950 years B.P.); (3) dialect differences are directly associated with a rapid expansion of Numic groups northward and eastward across the Great Basin and into the intermountain areas of Idaho, Montana, Wyoming, and possibly Colorado; and (4) the temporal and geographic distribution of Intermountain ceramics reflects this migration (Miller 1966; Madsen 1975). An opposing hypothesis suggests an in situ development of ancestral Shoshonean speakers in the intermountain areas beginning at least 5050–3050 B.C. (7000–5000 years B.P.) (Swanson 1972; Wright 1978). Archaeological investigations of the Upper Snake and Salmon river country (Butler 1979) indicate a more complex cultural developmental scheme than implied by either the migration or the in situ hypothesis.

Steven L. DeVore

Further Readings

Butler, B.R. 1979. The Native Pottery of the Upper Snake and Salmon River Country. *Idaho Archaeologist* 3(1):1–10.

———. 1981. *When Did the Shoshoni Begin to Occupy Southern Idaho? Essays on the Late Prehistoric Cultural Remains From the Upper Snake and Salmon River Country.* Occasional Papers no. 32. Idaho Museum of Natural History, Pocatello.

Coale, G.L. 1963. A Study of Shoshonean Pottery. *Tebiwa* 6(2):1–11.

Madsen, D.B. 1975. Dating Paiute-Shoshoni Expansion in the Great Basin. *American Antiquity* 40:82–85.

Mulloy, W. 1958. *A Preliminary Historic Outline for the Northwest Plains.* University of Wyoming Publications, vol. 2, no. 1. Laramie.

Rudy, J.R. 1953. *Archeological Survey of Western Utah.* Anthropological Papers no. 12. University of Utah Press, Salt Lake City.

Swanson, E.H., Jr. 1972. *Birch Creek: Human Ecology in the Cool Desert of the Northern Rocky Mountains, 9000 B.C.– A.D. 1850.* Idaho State University Press, Pocatello.

Tuohy, D.R. 1956. Shoshoni Ware From Idaho. *Davidson Journal of Anthropology* 2(1):55–72.

Wright G.A. 1978. The Shoshonean Migration Problem. *Plains Anthropologist* 23(80):113–137.

Inugsuk Culture

The first Thule-culture Inuit crossed the icy waters separating northern Greenland from Ellesmere Island late in the twelfth century A.D. At the time, Norse farmers had occupied southern Greenland for nearly two centuries and hunted on a regular basis in the Disko Bay region and occasionally farther north. In the 1930s, Danish archaeologist Therkel Mathiassen excavated Thule-culture houses and middens at the Inugsuk site on an island in the Upernavik district. Based on an analysis of the data, he defined the Inugsuk culture as a later phase of the Thule culture that showed evidence of Inuit/ Norse interaction. Subsequent excavations at the Sermermiut Thule-culture midden in Disko Bay yielded additional Norse finds, providing further evidence, as far as Mathiassen was concerned, of a strong cultural influence by the medieval Norse on Inuit culture.

As the Thule-culture Inuit penetrated farther south along the west coast of Greenland, Inuit/Norse contact undoubtedly intensified until the last of the Norse settlements was abandoned ca. A.D. 1500 (450 years B.P.). The degree to which the Inuit presence determined the fate of the Norse settlers remains a point of debate, as does the amount of influence the Norse asserted on Thule culture. Most present-day Arctic prehistorians view the Norse influence on the west Greenland Thule culture as fairly insignificant. More recent discoveries of large numbers of Norse artifacts in the earliest Thule-culture sites on Ellesmere Island further erode the importance of Mathiassen's original definition of the Inugsuk culture.

The Thule Inuit arrived in west Greenland with an extremely well-developed maritime subsistence culture. Apart from securing iron and perhaps wood, they had comparatively little to gain from their Norse neighbors. Most of the Norse items found on Inuit sites, such as pieces of woven fabric, chess and draught gaming pieces, chain-mail rings, spindle whorls, loom weights, and fragments of church bells, were novelty items that had no practical application. The Inuit artisans did occasionally imitate Norse objects like spoons, casks, and the occasional carved small wooden figures representing Norsemen. These objects and images indicate some degree of interaction. However, in general, the two peoples seem to have learned little from each other—their association was characterized more by quarrels and fights than mutual cooperation.

In the late twentieth century, the Inugsuk culture is thought of principally as a developed form of Thule culture that existed in west and east Greenland from the middle of the thirteenth century to the period of renewed European contact in the early seventeenth century. Some historians prefer a more restricted time frame that encompasses only the period during which the Inuit were influenced directly by the Norsemen. Regardless of the definition, it is clear that there was no significant change in Inuit culture during the nearly three centuries of contact with the Norse. Nor do most finds prove direct contact. For instance, iron items and other interesting finds may have been obtained by the Inuit by digging in collapsed buildings and extensive middens after the abandonment of the Norse Vesterbygd settlement ca. A.D. 1350 (600 years B.P.). Not until the arrival of European whalers in the early seventeenth century was there a marked European influence on Inuit culture.

The Thule culture of west and east Greenland did not evolve in response to the Norse but to changing environmental and ecological conditions, for these immigrant hunters moved southward from the Smith Sound area to warmer regions with more open and different ecological parameters. As a result, there was greater emphasis on kayak hunting and snow-houses, and ice hunting became less important except during colder climatic episodes such as the Little Ice Age (A.D. 1650–1850, or 300–100 years B.P.).

P. Schledermann

Further Readings

Jordan, R.H. 1979. Inugsuk Revisited: An Alternative View of Neo-Eskimo Chronology and Culture Change in Greenland. In *Thule Eskimo Culture: An Anthropological Retrospective,* edited by A.P. McCartney. Mercury Series Paper no. 88. Archaeological Survey of Canada, National Museum of Man, Ottawa.

Mathiassen, T. 1931. Inugsuk: A Mediaeval Eskimo Settlement in the Upernavik District, West Greenland. *Meddelelser om Grønland* 77(4):147–340.

McCullough, K. 1989 *The Ruin Islanders: Thule Culture Pioneers in the Eastern High Arctic.* Mercury Series Paper no. 74. Archaeological Survey of Canada, National Museum of Man, Ottawa.

See also NORSE IN AMERICA; THULE CULTURE

Ipiutak Culture

In 1939, J.L. Giddings observed the shallow depressions of Ipiutak houses on beaches near Point Hope in the Bering Strait region of Alaska. The remains of a mystifying culture of astonishing aesthetic and mortuary sophistication emerged at Point Hope in the next two years through excavations by Giddings, Froelich Rainey, and Helge Larson. Their collection of organic artifacts and grave goods remains the largest body of data for the Ipiutak culture; its size has also considerably biased interpretations of the culture. The 1939–1941 research project uncovered more than 135 burials and 72 houses out of the total of 575 houses mapped on the Point Hope spit. Linear-dot and abstract-animal Ipiutak design elements were thought to have stylistic similarities to the culture's near contemporary, Old Bering Sea, and to Scythian and Siberian motifs. The latter similarities provided the first age estimates for Ipiutak of ca. 200 B.C.–A.D. 200 (2150–1750 years B.P.); limited radiocarbon estimates now indicate that the culture's occupation layers at the site date to the more recent period of ca. A.D. 400–800 (1550–1150 years B.P.). The high num-ber of house remains, many now eroded by storms, was thought to represent the remains of a large village or the presence of an annual trade fair. Too few of these remains are dated, however, to determine whether they were contemporary.

Ipiutak is distinct in its lack of ceramics, in contrast to other late Holocene north Alaskan cultures, a circumstance that has generated considerable controversy. Slate is also lacking in Ipiutak, as are burinization and microblades. Organic artifacts are comparatively more common than in earlier cultures. The distinguishing characteristics of Ipiutak, however, are its widespread lithics, especially the discoidal flaked biface and end blades with straight or concave bases. The character of Ipiutak outside Point Hope is often difficult to determine because of numerous resemblances between Ipiutak lithic artifacts and those of the Norton culture. Despite this difficulty, many sites in the Brooks Range, a mountain range in Alaska north of the Arctic Circle, contain lithic types identical to those at Point Hope. Because the Norton culture used pottery, aceramic sites are often considered Ipiutak by default. The bow and arrow appears to have been the preeminent Ipiutak weapon. House remains are comparatively well documented, especially at Point Hope. Ipiutak houses were ca. 4 m (13 feet) square and were placed within shallow basins ca. 50 cm (19.5 inches) deep; the basins were apparently covered by skin superstructures. Art is well represented at some sites, with etched pebbles being especially widespread across the Brooks Range. Faunal data suggest a subsistence specialization focused, as in the ethnographic present, on ringed seal hunted through breathing holes and caribou. Lakes were used as drive sites. Evidence for fishing is comparatively rare. Site densities on the coast imply seasonal transhumance between spring/summer sealing on the coast and interior wintering sites.

The distribution of Ipiutak sites shows an abrupt boundary through the Seward Peninsula that excludes Wales and extends north to the Point Lay vicinity. Sites occur at Cape Krusenstern (Ridges 29 to 35), Kotzebue, Deering, and Cape Espenberg. They are particularly common along the foothill lakes of the north slope of the Brooks Range: Feniak Lake, Tukuto Lake, and Itkillik Lake. The notable decline in Norton traits inland implies that coastal sites are "true" Ipiutak. The absence of pottery may also imply increased mobility. The increased number and the internal complexity of sites have led some archaeologists to argue for a dramatic population increase.

Age control over any one Ipiutak site is limited, although many are reasonably well dated. As mentioned above, the Ipiutak component at Point Hope dates to A.D. 400–800 (1550–1150 years B.P.); this large component is used informally as the type site of the culture. Sites in the Brooks Range are often palimpsests of many occupations and prove unreliable for chronometric estimates; perhaps significantly, the oldest Ipiutak dated lithics and designs are from Feniak Lake and fall at ca. 50 B.C.–A.D. 150 (2000–1800 years B.P.). On the younger end of the time range, sites in the central and eastern Brooks Range indicate a persistence there until the Thule expansion (ca. A.D. 1150, or 800 years B.P.).

Most researchers postulate an in situ development for the Ipiutak culture, and most northern Alaska researchers see clear cultural links between it and the Arctic Small Tool tradition (ASTt), which includes Choris and Norton cultures. Still, the cultural affinities of Ipiutak continue to be disputed by archaeological taxonomists in Alaska for several reasons. Taxonomic confusion exists because of the use of the possibly anomalous Point Hope locality as a type site, and because Ipiutak and Norton lithics are very similar. Some archaeologists also claim cultural continuity between the earlier Denbigh complex (= ASTt) and Ipiutak, because they share some isolated traits, such as collateral flaking styles. This type of inference is subject, however, to personal taste and is offered in lieu of stratigraphic succession or near contemporaneity in radiocarbon years.

Craig Gerlach

Further Readings

Dumond, D. 1987. *Eskimos and Aleuts*. 2nd ed. Thames and Hudson, New York.

Giddings, J.L. 1964. *The Archaeology of Cape Denbigh*. Brown University Press, Providence.

———. 1967. *Ancient Men of the Arctic*. Knopf, New York.

Larsen, H., and F. Rainey. 1948. *Ipiutak and the Arctic Whale Hunting Culture*. Anthropological Papers, vol. 42. American Museum of Natural History, New York.

Shaw, R.D., and C.E. Holmes (editors). 1982. The Norton Interaction Sphere. *Arctic Anthropology* 19(2):1–149.

Iroquoian Culture

Northern Iroquoian speakers once lived primarily in the Lower Great Lakes portions of what are now southern Ontario and the state of New York. Some nations extended into the St. Lawrence lowlands of Quebec, the Mohawk Valley of eastern New York, and the Upper Susquehanna Valley of Pennsylvania. Related Northern Iroquoians that were living in the middle Atlantic region at the time of first contact with Europeans moved northward to join the Iroquois Confederacy in the eighteenth century. The Cherokees are the only survivors of the Southern Iroquoian branch and are excluded from this summary of Iroquoian culture.

The St. Lawrence Iroquoians, who were visited by French explorer Jacques Cartier early in the sixteenth century, disappeared within a few decades. They were apparently absorbed by the Hurons and other Northern Iroquoian nations. This process also explains the disappearance of other Iroquoian groups in the region that are known only through archaeology.

All Northern Iroquoians depended upon swidden (shifting) horticulture that focused on maize, beans, and squash as staples. All lived in compact and usually palisaded villages of multifamily longhouses. Villages relocated every decade or two as fields lost their fertility and structures decayed. The lack of large domesticated animals meant that horticulture had to be carried on without bulk transportation, the plow, or fertilizer to renew fields.

Longhouses were consistently ca. 7 m (23 feet) in width and height but varied in length depending upon the sizes of the matrilineal clan segments they were built to house. Pairs of nuclear families shared hearths sunk into the center aisle of a longhouse. Each hearth thus served two families, each family on average having about five members. The female head of each nuclear family was typically a sister, daughter, or granddaughter of the head of the clan segment that lived in the longhouse. Adult men in the longhouse were husbands drawn from other clans. They were thus in some sense visitors in the homes of their wives. Although this status often prompts men in other matrilineal societies to build central men's houses, the Northern Iroquoians achieved the same result by spending much of their time away from the village on diplomatic or military missions.

The importance of women in Iroquois society is frequently cited, and their role is reflected in the origin myth that is shared by all of the Northern Iroquoian nations. Sky Woman is the principal character in this myth, which, in turn, is the first of the three main pieces of Iroquois cosmology.

The Iroquois structured the annual round in terms of a sequence of seasonal ceremonies, the most important of which was the midwinter ceremony. Most ceremonies focused on one or another of the traditional staples, whether wild or domesticated. In all cases, the Iroquois stressed the giving of thanks for things received rather than supplication for things desired.

People were born to one of three to nine clans, depending upon the nation. Each clan was known by its animal totem, and clans within a nation were grouped into two moieties. Members of the same clan felt a special kinship with one another and behaved accordingly. In certain ceremonies, for planning group games, and on other occasions, opposite moieties served as predetermined sides. On the death of an individual, members of the opposite moiety provided condolence services to the grieving clan. Death was rarely considered natural, witchcraft was often suspected, and vengeance was a strong impulse. Consequently, the condolence ceremony was an important means by which feuding was averted and harmony was restored to a grieving community.

The clan system and the condolence ceremony were raised to the level of international politics by the League of the Iroquois. The league comprised the Mohawk, Oneida, Onondaga, Cayuga, and Seneca nations. Migrating Tuscaroras were later incorporated, as were several dependent nations. It was probably founded in the fifteenth or early sixteenth century, and the legend of its founding is the second of the three main pieces of Iroquois cosmology. Major roles are played in the legend by a man known as the peacemaker, whose name, Deganawidah, is sacred to many modern Iroquois. Almost as important was Hiawatha, usually said to have been initially Onondaga but later adopted by the Mohawks, whose name was still later appropriated for other purposes by the poet Henry Wadsworth Longfellow. Together, Deganawidah and Hiawatha contrived the structure of the league, convinced the five nations to join, and symbolically converted the wicked Onondaga shaman Thadodaho along the way.

Fifty league chiefs (sachems) were appointed by the matrons of an equal number of clan segments from the five nations to govern the organization. Among these, the reformed Thadodaho was made first among equals. The nations were divided into two moieties for reciprocal purposes. Upon the death of a league chief, chiefs from the opposite side consoled the grieving nation, and a new man was appointed to assume the name of the deceased chief. The dead chief was raised up again in the form of a younger man who assumed the name and identity of the office. The structure of the league was thus built upon a preexisting clan system and funerary ritual. The principal ceremonies of the league came to focus on recitation of its history and operating principles, the condolence rite, and the requickening ceremony in which new chiefs were raised up.

The League of the Iroquois required unanimity in all decisions, so much time was spent in debate and consensus building. The history and charter of the organization were maintained as oral tradition. These features produced a system in which oratorical skill and lengthy formulaic addresses predominated. The League of the Iroquois came to be linked first to Dutch and later to English interests. Although the French competed with the English for Iroquois allies, by the eighteenth century the league was linked most strongly with the English through the metaphorical union known as the Covenant Chain.

Members of the league systematically destroyed other Northern Iroquoian nations and confederacies, in many instances absorbing the survivors. The Erie, Huron, Petun, Neutral, Wenro, and Susquehannock nations were all destroyed by the middle of the seventeenth century. Some of them fled westward, where they reconstituted themselves as Wyandots. Absorption of many others by the Iroquois nations enabled the latter to survive the severe population decline brought about by epidemics of smallpox and other diseases as well as warfare during the colonial period.

By the end of the eighteenth century, the Iroquois had lost their economic base in the fur trade and their political base between competing political powers. The longhouse disappeared both as a standard dwelling and as a metaphor for the disintegrating League of the Iroquois. A Seneca visionary known as Handsome Lake led a religious revival that eventually spread to most Iroquois reservations. The code he established forms the third main piece of Iroquoian cosmology.

Iroquois culture was popularized by early

anthropologists Lewis Henry Morgan, William Beauchamp, and others beginning in the middle nineteenth century. Iroquois medicine societies with their distinctive False Face and Bushy Head masks, Iroquois folklore, the game of lacrosse, and other features of Iroquois culture have since become widely appreciated. Today, the Iroquois live largely on reservations scattered around New York, southern Ontario, and Quebec.

Dean R. Snow

Further Readings

Snow, D.R. 1980. *The Archaeology of New England*. Academic Press, New York.
Trigger, B. 1985. *Natives and Newcomers*. McGill-Queen's University Press, Montreal.

Itskari (formerly "Loup River") Phase

One of five recognized taxa of the Late Prehistoric Central Plains tradition (A.D. 1000–1400, or 950–550 years B.P.), the Itskari (Pawnee for "many potatoes river") phase was renamed from "Loup (French for "wolf") River phase" to avoid persistent confusion with the Protohistoric "Lower Loup phase." Itskari-phase sites occur in the Lower Loup River Basin, along Wood River, on Shell Creek, and along the Big Blue River in east-central Nebraska. Formerly classified within the Upper Republican phase or regional variant, the Itskari phase is distinct.

Itskari-phase peoples, who become culturally recognizable by ca. A.D. 1100 (850 years B.P.), colonized the Loup River Basin during the favorable Neo-Atlantic climatic episode, ca. A.D. 1000–1250 (950–700 years B.P.). They adjusted their lifeway during the early part of the succeeding, drier Pacific episode, whose effects were perhaps buffered by Sand Hills groundwater reservoirs tapped by the Loup River system. The Itskari phase is similar to the Initial Coalescent and the St. Helena phases, but its relations with phases of the Central Plains tradition are more collateral than developmental. Once thought to be transitional between the Central Plains tradition and the Lower Loup phase (Protohistoric Pawnee, A.D. 1600–1750, or 350–200 years B.P.), the end of the Itskari phase is now well dated to ca. A.D. 1350–1400 (600–550 years B.P.).

Houses are nearly square-to-oval, wattle-and-daub structures built in pits excavated 0.3–0.6 m (1–2 feet) deep, with four central roof supports around a central fire basin. An extended entry passage emerges from the middle of one wall. Several subfloor, cylindrical or bell-shaped storage/refuse pits are usually present. Itskari-phase houses are far smaller than other Central Plains–tradition houses, with 80 percent of excavated houses only 56–93 m² (100–600 square feet) in area. Settlements include solitary houses, small hamlets, and small villages of up to a dozen houses. External work/storage areas are present. The dead were buried in communal ossuaries with a few modest grave goods.

The Itskari phase existed in a region with few or no lithic resources. Raw materials present in sites reflect an eclectic pattern of acquisition but with a preference for materials from western Nebraska, South Dakota, and eastern Wyoming. Chipped-stone tools include triangular side-notched and multiple side-and-base notched arrow points; unnotched triangular points; point preforms or knives; bifacial drills; narrow and broad ovate and alternately beveled lozenge-shaped knives; end scrapers; gravers; and side scrapers. Ground-stone tools include Oglala and Dakota sandstone abraders, pebble hammerstones, ground and polished celts, stemmed and nonstemmed pipes of red pipestone and limestone, calcite beads, one grooved cobble maul, and other miscellaneous items. Bone tools include bison-scapula digging/hoeing tools, cleavers, and other knives. Awls are of split (quartered) deer/pronghorn metapodial proximal ends, proximal ulnas, rib edges, and bone splinters. Eyed needles, shaft wrenches of deer tibias and bison ribs, bone fishhooks, halved elk metapodial gouges or fleshers, deer-mandible corn shellers, and other bone tools and ornaments (e.g., tubular beads) also occur. Antler tools include cylinders, flaking tools, shaft wrenches, bracelets and bowguards, and other implements. Mussel-shell disc beads and some marine-shell objects have been found. Itskari-phase people fished, hunted a wide range of mammals, gathered wild plants, and tended gardens.

Itskari-phase pottery consists of sand-tempered, globular jars with cord-roughened surfaces. They have either unthickened or collared rims that are plain or decorated with a variety of incised (less commonly cord-impressed) motifs. Handles and all kinds of appendages are moderately abundant. Other vessels have narrow broad-beveled lips that resemble unthickened rims but are decorated like collared rims. Bowls occur in small numbers. Spindle whorls, or clay beads, have been found. Pottery pipe forms also occur. They sometimes have human or animal effigy forms resembling Nebraska-phase types.

John R. Bozell
John Ludwickson

Further Readings

Ludwickson, J., D.J. Blakeslee, and J.M. O'Shea. 1987. *Missouri National Recreational River, Native American Cultural Resources*. Publications in Anthropology no. 3. Wichita State University Press, Wichita.

Ludwickson, J., J.R. Bozell, and A. Koch. 1993. Highway Archaeological Investigations at the Olsen Site, 25CU23, an Itskari Phase Settlement in the Upper Mud Creek Basin, Custer County, Nebraska. Report prepared for the Nebraska Department of Roads by the Nebraska State Historical Society, Lincoln.

———. 1993. Highway Archaeological Investigations at the Palmer Johnson Site, 258U37, an Itskari Phase Settlement in the Upper Big Blue River Basin, Butler County, Nebraska. Report prepared for the Nebraska Department of Roads by the Nebraska State Historical Society, Lincoln.

Iyatayet

Iyatayet (49NOB002) is a stratified archaeological site located along the northern shores of Norton Sound, Alaska, on the northwest side of Cape Denbigh. It is the type site for the Denbigh Flint complex and Norton cultures and contains materials of the Nukleet culture, which is a regional variant of Western Thule culture. The Denbigh Flint complex is also the type complex for the Arctic Small Tool tradition, which is distributed throughout the entire Inuit world. Discovered by J.L. Giddings in 1949, Iyatayet produced the first stratigraphic demonstration of the considerable antiquity of microblade assemblages in Alaska. Prior to the discovery of the Denbigh Flint complex, microblade assemblages had been located at the shallow Campus site at the University of Alaska, Fairbanks, and at other isolated localities throughout Alaska. Still, there was considerable debate as to whether microblades were as old in Alaska as they were in Europe and Asia, where they were associated with Mesolithic and early Neolithic cultures. It was possible that they had "survived" in the Arctic until recent prehistoric times. The Iyatayet excavations clearly indicated that microblades were old, although just how old remained a subject of controversy for many years. Denbigh at Iyatayet was one of the first archaeological complexes in Alaska to be radiocarbon dated, but the dates of 4050–3050 B.C. (6000–5000 B.P.) were initially considered too recent, for geological evidence suggested a date of 6050–4050 B.C. (8000–6000 years B.P.). It was not until the 1970s that additional radiocarbon dates of Denbigh materials from excavations at Onion Portage and elsewhere in northwestern Alaska confirmed a date of ca. 2450–1650 B.C. (4400–3600 years B.P.).

Norton culture at Iyatayet was represented by thick cultural deposits from an abandoned winter village, now dated to ca. 850–350 B.C. (2800–2300 years B.P.). These deposits, which overlay the Denbigh layer, indicate the presence of a people who were primarily engaged in seal, beluga, and walrus hunting; fish and caribou, which are also represented in the midden, appear to have been less important. Some archaeologists regard Norton as the last general Eskimo cultural stage in Alaska before the divergence of the Yupik and Inupik Eskimo languages.

Nukleet-culture remains, first identified at a nearby winter village site on the southeast side of Cape Denbigh, were present in the uppermost 0.6 m (2 feet) of deposits at Iyatayet. The culture extends from the twelfth to the eighteenth century. During this period, the people subsisted on a diet equally balanced between seals, beluga, fish, and caribou. Especially noteworthy in these excavations was Giddings's conclusion that Nukleet is directly ancestral to modern Norton Bay Eskimo culture.

Douglas D. Anderson

Further Readings

Dumond, D.E. 1987. *The Eskimos and Aleuts*. rev. ed. Thames and Hudson, New York.

Giddings, J.L. 1964. *The Archaeology of Cape Denbigh*. Brown University Press, Providence.

See also DENBIGH FLINT COMPLEX; NORTON CULTURE; NORTON TRADITION

J

Jacal

Derived from the Spanish for "shack" or "hut," the term "jacal" is used by archaeologists to refer to a particular form of architectural construction. Jacal construction consists of a superstructure of upright poles set in the ground that have thatch or branches, or sometimes simply pole crosspieces, interwoven between them. The framework is then covered with mud or puddled adobe. This form of wattle-and-daub architecture was common prehistorically and historically throughout the American Southwest. It was particularly suited to areas that lacked tabular stone that could be used in masonry construction, although it was also often used in constructing partitions within masonry structures.

Patricia L. Crown

Further Readings

Nabokov, P., and R. Easton. 1989. *Native American Architecture.* Oxford University Press, New York.

Roberts, F.H.H., Jr. 1931. *The Ruins at Kiatuthlanna, Eastern Arizona.* Bulletin no. 100. Bureau of American Ethnology, Smithsonian Institution, Washington, D.C.

Sayles, E.B. 1937. Houses. In *Excavations at Snaketown,* by H.S. Gladwin, E.W. Haury, E.B. Sayles, and N. Gladwin, pp. 59–90. Medallion Paper no. 25. Gila Pueblo, Globe.

See also HOHOKAM CULTURE AREA; PITHOUSE

James (Jimmy) Allen Site

James (Jimmy) Allen (48AB4) is a Paleoindian bison-procurement site ca. 14 miles south of Laramie, Wyoming, in the southern Laramie Basin with a radiocarbon date of ca. 6050 B.C. (8000 years B.P.). Discovered in 1949 by James Allen, it was excavated by the University of Wyoming under the direction of William T. Mulloy in 1951, 1953, and 1954. James (Jimmy) Allen is an important archaeological site, for it is one of the few bison kills known on the northwestern Plains that dates between Cody complex and middle Early Archaic times. Ca. 15 animals (*Bison bison occidentalis* or *antiquus*) were killed in what was probably a single hunt. Measurements of bison metapodials indicated

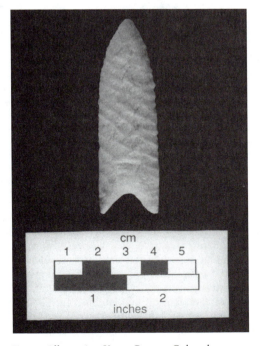

Jimmy Allen point, Yuma County, Colorado. (Courtesy of the Wilford Archaeology Laboratory, University of Minnesota)

the animals were larger than the present-day subspecies. A few scrapers, 30 nearly complete to framentary projectile point/knives, and 60 unretouched flakes and cores were found in association with the bonebed. The relatively long, roughly parallel-sided lanceolate points are characterized by concave bases and excellent oblique, parallel flaking. Called Allen points by Mulloy, varieties of the same general style have been called Yuma, Oblique Yuma, and Browns Valley, among other names, in other contexts. Since the site is in open country with almost no topographic relief, it is assumed that some kind of surround or, possibly, artificial corral structure, perhaps a buck-type fence, was used to trap the animals. No population or seasonality studies of the bison bone, apparently the only kind of procured animal bone in the bed, were made before the bone was discarded.

George C. Frison
Guy Gibbon

Further Readings

Berman, J.E. 1959. Bison Bones From the Allen Site, Wyoming. *American Antiquity* 25:116–117.

Frison, G.C. 1991. *Prehistoric Hunters of the High Plains.* 2nd ed. Academic Press, San Diego.

Mulloy, W.T. 1959. The James Allen Site Near Laramie, Wyoming. *American Antiquity* 25:112–116.

Wormington, H.M. 1957. *Ancient Man in North America.* Popular Series no. 4. Denver Museum of Natural History, Denver.

Jefferson, Thomas (1743–1826)

An extraordinarily learned man and third president of the United States (1801–1809), Thomas Jefferson has often been referred to as the "father of American archaeology" for his precocious excavation of a small prehistoric Indian burial mound by the Rivanna River on his Virginia estate prior to 1782. He was also an ardent student of the natural sciences, scientific farming, the Bible, and philosophy, among numerous other interests. An active and influential intellectual in Philadelphia's coffeehouse society, he speculated with others about American Indian life and the origin of the earthworks scattered across the Eastern Woodlands. In deciding to test these conflicting speculations, Jefferson initiated what Sir Mortimer Wheeler

(1954:6) has labeled "the first scientific excavation in the history of archaeology." Jefferson's attempt to resolve the Mound Builder problem was unique at the time in that he formulated a problem and excavated carefully to resolve it, although his contribution was constrained by the near absence at the time of knowledge of New World prehistory. He concluded that more information was necessary to resolve the Mound Builder problem. The excavation probably was the first stratigraphic excavation anywhere. Unfortunately, it fell, as Wheeler (1954:43) noted, "upon infertile soil" and was not emulated for generations afterward. In 1799, while president of the American Philosophical Society, Jefferson distributed a circular soliciting information about Indian artifacts, earthworks, and tumuli as part of the society's active investigation of the Mound Builder problem.

Guy Gibbon

Further Readings

Jefferson, T. 1787. *Notes on the State of Virginia.* J.W. Randolph, Richmond.

Martin, E.T. 1952. *Thomas Jefferson: Scientist.* Schuman, New York.

Schachner, N. 1951. *Thomas Jefferson.* 2 vols. Appleton-Century-Crofts, New York.

Wheeler, M. 1954. *Archaeology From the Earth.* Oxford University Press, Oxford.

Willey, G.R., and J.A. Sabloff. 1993. *A History of American Archaeology.* 3rd ed. W.H. Freeman, San Francisco.

See also MOUND BUILDER MYTH

Jenness, Diamond (1886–1969)

Canada's most distinguished pioneer anthropologist, Diamond Jenness was born at Wellington, New Zealand, in 1886 and educated in New Zealand and at Oxford in England. In 1926, he became Edward Sapir's replacement as chief anthropologist at the National Museum of Canada, a position Jenness held on and off until his retirement in the late 1940s. Primarily a social anthropologist and Eskimologist, he laid the groundwork for the scientific study of archaeology in the North American Arctic. In 1914, he undertook what was arguably the earliest controlled archaeological excavation in the Arctic at Barter Island near the Canada-Alaska border. In 1925, he brilliantly identified the extinct Dorset culture of the eastern Arctic on the basis of a culturally mixed archaeologi-

Diamond Jenness. *(Reprinted with permission from American Antiquity 37[1]:86)*

became immersed in Fay-Cooper Cole's excavation program at Kincaid and other Illinois sites and, during the Works Progress Administration (WPA) and Tennessee Valley Authority (TVA) days of the 1930s, dug at various places in the Midwest and Southeast. This period also saw stints of excavation in New Mexico and in Guatemala, where he and his wife, Jane Chase Jennings, worked with A.V. Kidder at Kaminaljuyu. It was this later work that formed the basis of Jennings's doctoral dissertation, which he wrote before he went off to service in World War II and defended during a leave; he was awarded the degree in absentia in 1943 while serving as a U.S. Navy lieutenant in Iceland.

After the work at Kaminaljuyu, Jennings entered the National Park Service in 1937. First serving as a park ranger at Montezuma Castle in Arizona, he subsequently became acting superintendent at Ocmulgee National Monument in Georgia, then archaeologist on the Natchez Trace Parkway in Mississippi. Following the war, Jennings resumed his work on the Natchez Trace, staying until 1947, when he became Region II (Plains) archaeologist, based in Omaha, Nebraska. Faced with a promotion and transfer to Washington, D.C., in

cal collection donated to the museum. And in 1926, Jenness's excavations at Bering Strait established the basic cultural sequence in Arctic Alaska, from Old Bering Sea culture (which he first identified) to the nineteenth century.

David Morrison

Further Readings

Jenness, D. 1922. *The Life of the Copper Eskimos.* Report of the Canadian Arctic Expedition, 1913–18, vol. 12. F.A. Acland, Ottawa.

———. 1928. *The People of the Twilight.* Macmillan, New York.

———. 1933. The Problem of the Eskimo. In *The American Aborigines: Their Origin and Antiquity,* edited by D. Jenness, pp. 373–396. University of Toronto Press, Toronto.

———. 1957. *Dawn in Arctic Alaska.* University of Minnesota Press, Minneapolis.

Morrison, D. 1992. *Arctic Hunters: The Inuit and Diamond Jenness.* Canadian Museum of Civilization, Hull.

Jennings, Jesse D. (1909–1997)

Jesse David Jennings began his anthropological career in 1929, when he entered the graduate program at the University of Chicago. He soon

Jesse D. Jennings. *(Reprinted with permission from American Antiquity 47[3]:483)*

1948, he resigned from the National Park Service and took a position as professor of anthropology at the University of Utah. After more than 30 years at Utah, Jennings left his position as Distinguished Professor there and moved to Oregon in 1980. As late as 1996, Jennings taught and did research as adjunct professor at the University of Oregon.

At Utah, Jennings established a statewide archaeological survey and the University of Utah Anthropological Papers, which have, over the years, generated an enormous amount of research and well over 100 volumes of published scholarship. Jennings's work at Danger Cave, begun soon after his arrival at Utah, was a tour de force of what is now called "environmental archaeology" and led to the seminal concept of a Great Basin Desert culture, which has centered and influenced all subsequent research in the region (Jennings 1957). The Glen Canyon Archaeological Salvage project (1957–1965), and work over a period of years thereafter in Utah and Polynesia, saw research crews annually in the field under his direction, with voluminous published results.

In addition to his research, Jennings's teaching—in both field and classroom—has strongly influenced North American archaeology in the twentieth century, and many professionals active in the field today learned the discipline of archaeological field research and publication from him. His pioneering *Prehistory of North America* (1st ed., 1968), now in its third edition, has also introduced thousands of undergraduate students to the continent's human past. Yet another avenue of influence has come through Jennings's establishment of the Utah Museum of Natural History, beginning with only a concept in 1963 and culminating in 1971 with accreditation of the fully launched institution by the American Association of Museums.

Jennings's professional service and honors have been extensive. He was editor of *American Antiquity* (1950–1954); a member of the executive board of the American Anthropological Association (1953–1956); a member of the National Research Council division of anthropology and psychology (1954–1956); recipient of the Viking Medal in Archaeology (1958); president of the Society for American Archaeology (1959–1960); vice president and Section H chairman, American Association for the Advancement of Science (1961, 1971); and a founding member of the Society of Professional Archaeologists. Jennings was elected to the National Academy of Sciences in 1977 and received the Distinguished Service Award of the Society for American Archaeology in 1982. In 1995, he received the prestigious A.V. Kidder Award of the American Anthropological Association in recognition of his outstanding achievements in American archaeology.

C. Melvin Aikens

Further Readings

Jennings, J.D. 1957. *Danger Cave.* Memoirs no. 14. Society for American Archaeology, Washington, D.C.; also released as Anthropological Papers no. 27. University of Utah Press, Salt Lake City.

———. 1964. The Desert West. In *Prehistoric Man in the New World,* edited by J.D. Jennings and E. Norbeck, pp. 149–174. University of Chicago Press, Chicago.

———. 1966. *Glen Canyon: A Summary.* Glen Canyon Series no. 31. Anthropological Papers no. 81. University of Utah Press, Salt Lake City.

———. 1968. *Prehistory of North America.* 1st ed. McGraw-Hill, New York.

———. 1978. *Prehistory of Utah and the Eastern Great Basin.* Anthropological Papers no. 98. University of Utah Press, Salt Lake City.

———. 1986. American Archaeology 1930–1985: One Person's View. In *American Archaeology, 1935–1985,* edited by D.J. Meltzer, D.D. Fowler, and J.A. Sabloff. Smithsonian Institution Press, Washington, D.C.

———. 1994. *Jesse D. Jennings, Accidental Anthropologist.* University of Utah Press, Salt Lake City.

———. (editor and contributor). 1979. *Prehistory of Polynesia.* Harvard University Press, Cambridge.

Stout, C., J. Condie, and D.D. Fowler (editors). 1986. *Anthropology of the Desert West: Essays in Honor of Jesse D. Jennings.* University of Utah Press, Salt Lake City.

Jones-Miller Site

The Jones-Miller site (5YM8) is a large and unusually well-preserved Hell Gap Paleoindian bison kill near the town of Wray in northeastern Colorado that has possible ritual features. In a grassland setting more than 240 km (150 miles) east of the mountain front, the site is at the head of a shallow draw ca. 45 cm (18 inches) deep that drains into a tributary of the Arickaree River. A bonebed ca. 30 m (98 feet) long x 20 m (66 feet) wide along the bottom and sides of the draw has been radiocarbon dated to ca. 8050 B.C. (10,000 years B.P.). The remains of some 300 almost totally disarticulated *Bison bison antiquus* were stacked in piles in a number of separate butchering units. A homogeneous lithic technology of Hell Gap projectile points/knives, scrapers, flakes, and bone implements was associated with the piles. The butchering units were most likely the remains of a number of nearby kills of nursery herds—mainly of cows, calves, and yearlings— in what may have been one winter. Dennis J. Stanford, the excavator, believes that herds may have been stampeded down an adjacent snow-packed slope into a simple corral, where they were killed using spears and spear throwers (Stanford 1974, 1978). Possible shamanistic activity associated with the kill is represented by traces of a stout wooden "shaman" pole, a miniature projectile point, and an apparent antler flute that were clustered together near the corral. Similar associations between bison kills and shamanistic activity have been described in early historic ethnographic reports and are not that unusual in Archaic bison kills (Frison 1971).

Guy Gibbon

Further Readings

Davis, L., and M. Wilson (editors). 1978. *Bison Procurement and Utilization: A Symposium.* Memoir no. 14. Plains Anthropologist, Lincoln.

Frison, G.C. 1971. The Buffalo Pound in Northwestern Plains Prehistory: Site 48CA302. *American Antiquity* 36:77–91.

———. 1991. *Prehistoric Hunters of the High Plains.* 2nd ed. Academic Press, San Diego.

Stanford, D.J. 1974. Preliminary Report on the Excavation of the Jones-Miller Hell Gap Site, Yuma County, Colorado. *Southwestern Lore* 40(3–4):29–36.

———. 1978. The Jones-Miller Site: An Example of Hell Gap Bison Procurement Strategy. In *Bison Procurement and Utilization: A Symposium,* edited by L. Davis and M. Wilson, pp. 90–97. Memoir no. 14. Plains Anthropologist, Lincoln.

Jornada Branch of the Mogollon Culture

The Jornada branch refers to a group of heterogeneous, prehistoric cultural manifestations involving semisedentary and sedentary lifestyles, architecture, hunting-gathering-horticultural subsistence strategies, pottery, and, in the last phases, a wide-reaching exchange network. The earliest documented Jornada manifestation appeared in the El Paso, Texas, region ca. A.D. 200 (1750 years B.P.) and disappeared sometime in the fifteenth century A.D.

D.J. Lehmer (1948) first defined the Jornada branch for south-central New Mexico, far west Texas, and northern Chihuahua, Mexico. The concept has since been expanded to include virtually all of southeastern New Mexico. Recognized subareas include the Sierra Blanca/Roswell, the Middle Pecos River, the Guadalupe Mountains (and adjacent portion of the Pecos River Valley), and the area between the Pecos River and the Texas state line. Sequences of named phases have been developed for each subarea. Not all scholars agree that this vast area should be characterized as a single branch, and some even question whether Jornada is properly considered to be Mogollon.

Jornada culture developed from an Archaic base, but no single tradition underpinned the entire Jornada area. Rather, each subarea of the Jornada reflects the nearest Archaic tradition: Cochise on the west, Chihuahua on the south, Trans-Pecos on the southeast, and Central Texas on the east. To date (1996), the effects of the Oshara (northwestern New Mexico) and the Plains Archaic have not been evaluated. Throughout prehistory, Jornada traits continued, in part, to reflect contemporary developments in the adjacent Mimbres-Mogollon (west), Rio Grande Anasazi (northwest), southern Plains (east), and Trans-Pecos Texas (southeast) areas.

Pottery is the one trait that marks the transition of the Jornada branch from the Archaic. In the El Paso and perhaps the Sierra Blanca subareas, Archaic hunting-and-gathering pattern(s) included pithouses and horticulture, but east of the Pecos River and in the Guadalupe Mountains, the Archaic apparently lacked both of these characteristics.

Initially, settlements were small, consisting of one or a few loosely clustered pit structures and associated extramural storage pits and hearths. Sites are located in a variety of topographic situations, probably reflecting a generalized subsistence strategy. In most areas, the earlier occupations were probably also seasonal. Later settlements were larger and more restricted in their geographic distribution. Contiguous-room pueblos of adobe, rock, or more flimsy construction were the primary domicile except in the southern Sierra Blanca, where pit structures prevailed throughout the Jornada period. However, the abandonment of pit structures was never complete in the other subareas, for underground ceremonial chambers and even small pit domiciles continued until abandonment.

Subsistence practices throughout the Jornada varied fairly consistently through time and space. Wild-plant and -animal foods were important in all subareas at all times. Hunting evidently was very important in the Sierra Blanca and in the vicinity of Roswell until abandonment. Corn, later supplemented by beans and squash, was more important in the west, less so in the Sierra Blanca subarea, and evidently never grown in the Guadalupe subarea or east of the Pecos River. Where practiced, horticulture probably involved a variety of dry-farming and simple water-diversion techniques, though ditch irrigation was also employed in the El Paso subarea.

If numbers of items per site or subarea are an indication, contacts with peoples residing outside the Jornada area evidently were not numerous or of importance. During pithouse times, contacts were primarily with the Mimbres peoples, who traded their distinctive painted potteries eastward. Smaller amounts of Anasazi Black-on-White and Red-on-Brown pottery from northern Mexico also found their way into Jornada-branch sites. Sherds of these vessels are found throughout the Jornada Branch, though the actual numbers are very small.

In later phases, the volume and scope of contacts increased, though overall numbers of nonlocal items still represent only a small percentage of the artifacts recovered from any site. Contacts included northern Mexico, the Salado, the Zuni-Acoma regions, the Middle Rio Grande, the southern Plains, and the Trans-Pecos. Pottery, lithic materials, copper bells, turquoise, macaws, and beveled knives are some of the more notable items received by the Jornadans.

Relations between Jornadans and outside peoples, or among the Jornadans themselves, were not always peaceful. Several sites have produced evidence of violence in the form of disarticulated and burned skeletons (Rosewell

area), unburied skeletons in defensive postures (Sierra Blanca), arrow points imbedded in human bones (Sierra Blanca and east of the Pecos River), and mass cremation of many individuals (Sierra Blanca and Roswell).

Although some archaeologists question the data and the interpretations, most subareas of the Jornada branch appear to have been abandoned ca. A.D. 1350–1450 (600–500 years B.P.). Documented exceptions include the historic Mansos on the Rio Grande in the vicinity of El Paso and the abandoned villages of unidentified hunter-gatherers observed by Spanish explorers along the Pecos River in the Guadalupe subarea. Though not yet systematically and thoroughly investigated, the prehistoric Jornadans are believed to have joined several different historic groups, including the Mansos and other groups in far west Texas and northern Mexico, the Piro, Tompiro, and Jumano pueblos of central New Mexico, the Plains-dwelling Kiowa-Apaches, and perhaps other southern Plains peoples.

Regge N. Wiseman

Further Readings

Jelinek, A.J. 1967. *A Prehistoric Sequence in the Middle Pecos Valley, New Mexico.* Anthropological Papers no. 31. Museum of Anthropology, University of Michigan, Ann Arbor.

Katz, S.R., and P. Katz. 1984. *The Prehistory of the Carlsbad Basin, Southeastern New Mexico: Technical Report of Prehistoric Archaeological Investigations in the Brantley Project Locality.* Incarnate Word College, San Antonio.

Kelley, J.H. 1984. *The Archaeology of the Sierra Blanca Region of Southeastern New Mexico.* Anthropological Papers no. 74. Museum of Anthropology, University of Michigan, Ann Arbor.

Lehmer, D.J. 1948. *The Jornada Branch of the Mogollon.* Social Science Bulletin no. 17. University of Arizona Press, Tucson.

Leslie, R.H. 1979. The Eastern Jornada Mogollon, Extreme Southeastern New Mexico (A Summary). In *Jornada Mogollon Archaeology: Proceedings of the First Jornada Conference,* edited by P.H. Beckett and R.N. Wiseman, pp. 179–199. Cultural Resources Management Division, New Mexico State University, Las Cruces; Historic Preservation Bureau, Department of Finance and Administration, Santa Fe.

Sebastian, L.S., and S. Larralde. 1989. *Living on the Land: 11,000 Years of Human Adaptation in Southeastern New Mexico*. Cultural Resources Series no. 6. New Mexico State Office, Bureau of Land Management, Santa Fe.

Judd, Neil Merton (1887–1976)

A pioneer in the systematic study of Southwestern archaeology, Neil Judd had a distinguished curatorial career at the Smithsonian Institution in Washington, D.C., where he worked from 1911 until his retirement in 1949. While at the Smithsonian, he was assistant curator in the Department of Anthropology (1918), curator of American archaeology in the Division of Archeology (1919–1930), and curator of the Division of Archeology (1930–1949). As a prelude to his professional career, Judd served as a student assistant on archaeological reconnaissance trips (1907, 1909) to the Four Corners area of the Southwest with an uncle, Byron Cummings, and on an Archaeological Institute of America expedition (1910) to El Rito de los Frijoles, New Mexico, led by E.L. Hewett.

In spite of his demanding curatorial responsibilities, Judd was actively involved in field investigations in the Southwest into the early 1930s. From 1915 through 1923, he conducted surveys and excavations from the Great Salt Lake to the Grand Canyon for the Bureau of American Ethnology; this was the first systematic archaeological work in the Intermontane West. In 1917, he also partially excavated and restored the large cliff ruin of Betatakin, in Navajo National Monument, for the U.S. Department of the Interior. From 1920 through 1927, he directed intensive surveys and excavations, with the assistance of the National Geographic Society, in Chaco Canyon. His work during this period at Pueblo Bonito, the largest-known pueblo ruin, is considered by many to be his major contribution to American archaeology (Judd 1954, 1964).

Judd was also directly involved in establishing tree-ring dating and detailed aerial survey as essential sources of information in Southwest archaeology. With the support of the National Geographic Society, he led the First Beam Expedition in 1923 to search for datable wood and charcoal specimens at sites in Arizona, Colorado, and New Mexico; he was also the leader of the Third Beam Expedition in

Neil M. Judd. (Reprinted with permission from American Antiquity *43[3]:399)*

1929 to sites in Arizona. After carrying out a ground reconnaissance of prehistoric canals in the Gila and Salt River valleys in 1929, he served as science director of a joint U.S. War Department and Bureau of American Ethnology aerial survey of the area in 1930 (Judd 1931).

Among the awards Judd received were the Alfred Vincent Kidder Award from the American Anthropological Association (1965) and the Franklin L. Burr Award from the National Geographic Society (1953, 1962). He was president of the Anthropological Society of Washington (1925–1927), the American Anthropological Association (1945), and the Society of American Archaeology (1939). He also served as vice president of the American Association for the Advancement of Science (1939). Judd was a member of many societies and councils and a delegate to a number of national congresses. His reminiscences were published in 1968 in *Men Met Along the Trail*.

Guy Gibbon

Further Readings

Judd, N. 1931. Arizona's Prehistoric Canals From the Air. In *Explorations and Fieldwork of the Smithsonian Institution in 1930*, pp. 157–166. Smithsonian Institution, Washington, D.C.

———. 1954. *The Material Culture of Pueblo Bonito*. Miscellaneous Collections, vol. 124. Smithsonian Institution, Washington, D.C.

———. 1964. *The Architecture of Pueblo Bonito*. Miscellaneous Collections, vol. 147, no. 1. Smithsonian Institution, Washington, D.C.

———. 1967. *The Bureau of American Ethnology*. University of Oklahoma Press, Norman.

———. 1968. *Men Met Along the Trail*. University of Oklahoma Press, Norman.

Wedel, W.R. 1978. Neil Merton Judd, 1887–1976. *American Antiquity* 43:399–404.

Jurgens Site

Jurgens (5WL53) is a Late Paleoindian Cody-complex site on a South Platte River terrace ca. 14.5 km (9 miles) east of Greeley in northeastern Colorado. Like the Frasca site in northeastern Colorado, and the Horner, Finley, and Carter\Kerr-McGee sites in Wyoming, Jurgens was the scene of extensive bison-procurement operations at a time when bison herds were diminishing with the progression of the warm/dry Altithermal climatic episode. Radiocarbon dated to ca. 7150 B.C. (9100 years B.P.), the site is important within this context, for it apparently contained the remains of three functionally distinct activity areas: a long-term habitation, a short-term camp, and a butchering station. Among the 2,635 stone and bone artifacts recovered were 63 long lanceolate projectile points (called Kersey points), 32 knives, 84 end scrapers, 271 utilized flakes, 2,023 debitage flakes, 30 ground-stone tools, 55 stone or mineral specimens, and nine bone artifacts. Many fractured and fragmented bones were apparently also used as "expedient" tools. The ground stone included abrading stones, anvil/hammerstones, handstones, grooved shaft-abraders, and a tube that may have been a pipe. The bone items were atlatl hooks, an antler flaking-hammer, and an ulna with engraved designs on both faces.

Joe Ben Wheat, the excavator, skillfully compared the distribution of categories of artifact and bone in the three functional areas (Wheat 1979). Area 1, the habitation, contained a wide range of artifacts and evidence of tool production, skin preparation, and general everyday activities. Area 2, the short-term camp, contained a wide, but reduced, assemblage compared to Area 1. Parts of dismembered bison were taken for processing to Area 3, as is apparent from the parts present. These were, for the most part, easily transported units, such as hindlimbs, forelimbs, and segments of vertebrate columns. Less productive animal sections like whole or nearly whole skulls and pelvic units were absent or rare. Most of the bone was disarticulated, and the tools present were mainly for killing and butchering. Bison remains in Areas 1 and 2 were what one would expect in a living, as compared to a butchering, zone. At least 35 animals were represented in the Area 3 bonebed. Although the kills must have occurred nearby, the means of procurement are uncertain, for no natural traps are in the immediate area. The age group structure of the herd and the season of the kills were not determined.

Guy Gibbon

Further Readings

Frison, G.C. 1991. *Prehistoric Hunters of the High Plains*. 2nd ed. Academic Press, San Diego.

Wheat, J.B. 1979. *The Jurgens Site*. Memoir no. 15. Plains Anthropologist, Lincoln.

K

Kachemak Tradition

Named in honor of pioneer work in Kachemak Bay, the Kachemak tradition persisted for more than 2,000 years on the Kodiak Archipelago. Although its early stages are poorly documented, Kachemak appears to be present on Kodiak from the middle of the second millennium B.C. (Old Kiavak phase). The oldest manifestation on the outer Kenai Peninsula (Kachemak I) is not reliably dated. On Kodiak, the tradition endured until after A.D. 1000 (950 years B.P.). Kachemak Bay may have been abandoned four to five centuries earlier. Contemporary cultures on the Alaska Peninsula and in Prince William Sound show some similarities. They might be grouped with the Kachemak tradition within a cotradition framework.

The origins of the Kachemak tradition have yet to be demonstrated convincingly. An antecedent tradition, Ocean Bay, occupied this territory ca. 4050–1850 B.C. (6000–3800 years B.P.). While late Ocean Bay and Kachemak share a few technological elements, the few centuries that separate them would appear inadequate to derive Kachemak from Ocean Bay without postulating revolutionary culture change. However, in the absence of other candidates, the Kachemak tradition will probably prove to be rooted in a variant of late Ocean Bay. Traits that characterize the Kachemak tradition include a developed maritime economy centered on the procurement of smaller sea mammals, deep-sea fishes, salmon, birds, and intertidal invertebrates, and villages of solid semisubterranean houses. Burial was typically in the villages rather than in separate cemeteries. Kachemak technology features both flaked cryptocrystalline stone and ground slate (although the percentages may vary geographically and temporally), as well as cobbles made into heavy implements, such as lamps, net and line weights, and cortex-flake tools.

Kachemak hunters favored barbed darts over toggling harpoons. They used compound fishhooks with straight bone barbs and wooden or animal-rib shanks to catch halibut and cod. Bird bone was used for awls and needles. Backed (single-edged) ground-slate knives (ulus) occur throughout, as do ground-slate knives and points. The latter are often stemmed and sometimes stem notched (stem serration). Small flaked and ground adzes were used. Large adzes are rare. Flaked-stone implements include points, a few end scrapers, unifaces, and retouched flakes. Biface knives are relatively rare. Small projectile points persisted longer than other flaked implements as ground-slate tools grew in popularity. Shaping and finishing were accomplished with coarse- and fine-grained abraders; those of scoria (unfragmented ash) and pumice are especially prominent. Stone saws were used more often on bone than slate. Distinctive lip ornaments (labrets) were worn from earliest times. A high-quality representational art epitomized by small sculpted figures, many of probable supernatural significance, is also characteristic. Representational art is seldom found on utilitarian implements. These may be exquisitely made, incised with fine lines, or endowed with ownership marks, but the impression is one of exacting craftsmanship rather than integration of implement function and magical power.

Although finer subdivisions have been proposed, the Kachemak tradition may be most profitably divided into an Early (Old Kiavak on Kodiak, Kachemak I and II in Cook Inlet) and a Late stage (Three Saints Bay on Kodiak,

Kachemak Sub-III and III in Cook Inlet). The Early stage is known only from a few small site collections. A distinctive plummet-shaped stone weight is characteristic. Flaked-stone artifacts are more common relative to ground slate than they are later. Archaic-looking, self-armed toggle harpoon heads and primitive, expanding-base barbed darts are known, but they co-occur with more advanced types. Much of the definition of the earlier Kachemak tradition hinges on what is lacking in relation to later Kachemak. Early in the first millennium B.C., abundant end-notched pebbles for weighting fishing and/or fowling nets appear. Fairly large at first, they become smaller later. Ground-slate implements increase in popularity, and new styles were innovated. There was significant interaction with the Norton culture of the Bering Sea after 500 B.C. (2450 years B.P.). By ca. 100 B.C. (2050 years B.P.), cultural elaboration had reached a point where the Late Kachemak stage can be recognized to have emerged. Late Kachemak is the regional cultural climax in craftsmanship, art, and, especially, mortuary ceremonialism. An almost compulsive emphasis on symmetry and surface finish, which even extended to utilitarian tools like adzes and bone wedges, pervades the material culture. Artifacts diversify. An increasing emphasis on ornaments such as labrets, beads, pendants, and other jewelry of exotic materials perhaps indicates a growing societal emphasis on status. Spectacularly decorated stone lamps appear, probably indicating an increasingly rich ceremonial life. Perhaps most distinctive is the unusual mortuary complex, which features multiple burials; dismembered burials; curated skulls; cut, drilled, and mutilated human bones; ritual(?) cannibalism(?); occasional skulls with artificial eyes inserted in the orbits; and death masks. Routine interment with grave goods is poorly documented.

Settlement and subsistence patterns do not appear to have changed significantly, although populations may well have become larger. Trade and probably warfare were thriving. The Late Kachemak tradition had significant influence on adjacent cultures. A high degree of artifactual similarity and participation in common long-term trends indicate that the Kachemak peoples of Kodiak and Cook Inlet shared a common origin and sustained intimate contacts for more than 1,000 years.

The peoples of the Late Kachemak tradition withdrew from Kachemak Bay by A.D. 500–600 (1450–1350 years B.P.), leaving a partial cultural vacuum. The tradition lasted into the early second millennium A.D. on Kodiak. While the scenarios of investigators differ considerably, all seem to agree that the Kachemak tradition contributed significantly to the formation of the second millennium A.D. Koniag phase, which is directly ancestral to the modern native inhabitants. Rapid cultural change early in the second millennium A.D. resulted in the loss of many elements of the Kachemak tradition. The addition of new elements suggests to most workers that there must have been significant extralocal, as well as Kachemak-tradition, inputs into the formation of the Koniag phase. It seems highly unlikely that the Kachemak folk spoke an ancestral form of the Yupik (Bering Sea) Eskimo spoken on Kodiak in the late A.D. 1700s.

William B. Workman

Further Readings

Clark, D.W. 1970. The Late Kachemak Tradition at Three Saints and Crag Point, Kodiak Island, Alaska. *Arctic Anthropology* 6(2):73–111.

———. 1984. Prehistory of the Pacific Eskimo Region. In *Arctic*, edited by D. Damas, pp. 136–148. Handbook of North American Indians, vol. 5, W.C. Sturtevant, general editor. Smithsonian Institution, Washington, D.C.

Dumond, D.E. 1987. *The Eskimos and Aleuts.* rev. ed. Thames and Hudson, New York.

Laguna, F. de. 1975. *The Archaeology of Cook Inlet, Alaska.* Reprinted. Alaska Historical Society, Anchorage. Originally published 1935, University Museum, University of Pennsylvania, Philadelphia.

Workman, W.B. 1980. Continuity and Change in the Prehistoric Record From Southern Alaska. *Senri Ethnological Studies* 4:49–101. National Museum of Ethnology, Osaka.

———. 1992. Life and Death in a First Millennium A.D. Gulf of Alaska Culture: The Kachemak Tradition Ceremonial Complex. In *Ancient Images, Ancient Thought: The Archaeology of Ideology,* edited by S. Goldsmith, S. Garvie, D. Selin, and J. Smith, pp. 19–25. Proceedings of the Twenty-Third Annual Chacmool Conference, Archaeological Association, Calgary.

Kansas City Hopewell

Kansas City Hopewell is a western variant of the Middle Woodland Hopewellian Interaction Sphere, a sociopolitical/economic/religious system involving differential participation on the part of widely spread local populations in the eastern United States during the period ca. 500 B.C.–A.D. 750 (2450–1200 years B.P.). Long thought to represent a migration up the Missouri River to the Kansas City vicinity from a homeland in eastern Missouri or Illinois, recent demonstration (Johnson 1992:129–136) of a well-developed pre-Hopewell Early Woodland presence in eastern Kansas and western Missouri presents an alternative possibility of local development stimulated by ongoing interaction with the east. Kansas City Hopewell settlements are centered about the junction of the Kansas and Missouri rivers, with an extension to the north along the east side of the Missouri nearly to St. Joseph, Missouri. Other sites are known on the west bank of the Missouri and along the Kansas River in eastern Kansas. Large (ca. 2 ha [5 acres]) and long-occupied villages are recognized, as are small, probably seasonally occupied, camps. Earthen burial mounds covering dry-laid stone masonry tombs are present on bluff tops above the stream-terrace village and camp locations. Throughout the history of Kansas City Hopewell, subsistence was based on a wide range of local plants and animals. Especially important were white-tailed deer, turkeys,

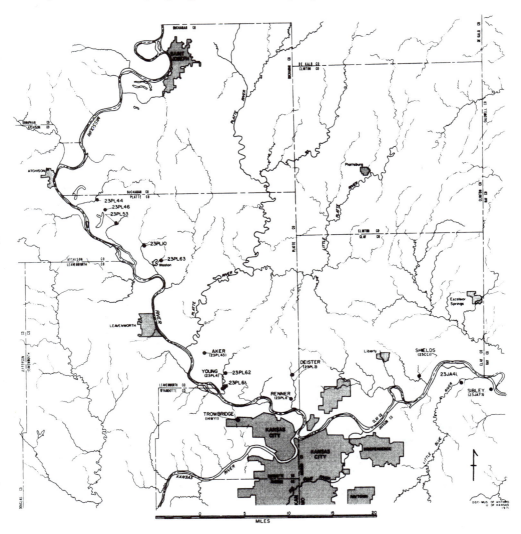

Locations of Kansas City Hopewell sites. (Map by A. E. Johnson)

fish, nuts, and chenopod and amaranth seeds. Horticulture is present as a supplement at least after A.D. 250 (1700 years B.P.). Domesticates identified to date (1996) include maize, squash, marsh elder, and sunflower.

The Kansas City Hopewell sequence, which is a continuum of gradual change, includes three phases based primarily on variations in ceramic form and design (Kansas City, A.D. 1–250, or 1950–1700 years B.P.; Trowbridge, A.D. 250–500, or 1700–1450 years B.P.; Edwardsville, A.D. 500–750, or 1450–1200 years B.P.). The Edwardsville phase is equivalent to early Late Woodland development in the Illinois River Valley. The dissolution of Kansas City Hopewell after 750 years of successful adaptation is not well understood, but it may be related to increasing population, limitations in the availability of natural resources, and the necessity of a switch to a heavier dependence on agriculture. The subsequent late Late Woodland period in the Kansas City locality is marked by dispersed hamlets, which were probably reliant on agriculture for their basic subsistence needs.

Alfred E. Johnson

Further Readings

Johnson, A.E. 1979. Kansas City Hopewell. In *Hopewell Archaeology: The Chillicothe Conference,* edited by D.S. Brose and N. Greber, pp. 86–93. Kent State University Press, Kent.

———. 1992. Early Woodland in the Trans-Missouri West. *Plains Anthropologist* 37(139):129–136.

———. (editor). 1976. *Hopewellian Archaeology in the Lower Missouri Valley.* Publications in Anthropology no. 8. Department of Anthropology, University of Kansas, Lawrence.

Wedel, W.R. 1940. Cultural Sequence in the Central Great Plains. *Miscellaneous Collections,* vol. 100, pp. 291–352. Smithsonian Institution, Washington, D.C.

———. 1943. *Archaeological Investigations in Platte and Clay Counties, Missouri.* Bulletin no. 183. U.S. National Museum, Washington, D.C.

Kayenta Branch

Four distinct Southwestern sociocultural "traditions" (Anasazi, Hohokam, Mogollon, and Patayan) are recognized on the basis of systematic differences in archaeological content.

Anasazi refers to the pattern on the southern Colorado Plateau; it represents a continuum of development into the modern Puebloan groups of the region. The Kayenta branch is one of several localized variants of the Anasazi, the others being the Virgin, Tusayan, Winslow, Little Colorado, Cibola, Chaco, Mesa Verde, Largo-Gallina, and Rio Grande branches. While these units are defined on the basis of archaeological evidence, it is assumed that these similarities and differences reflect important behavioral and cultural phenomena in the past.

Archaeological remains of Kayenta affiliation occur over a large area of northern Arizona and southern Utah that extends from west of the Grand Canyon to the Chuska Mountains and from the Colorado River to the Little Colorado River. The distribution of Kayenta material culture, which varied through time, reached its maximum area in the twelfth century. Kayenta groups on the periphery of this distribution were in regular contact with adjacent populations: Mesa Verde Anasazi on the northeast and north; Fremont on the northwest; Virgin Anasazi on the west; Cohonina and Sinagua on the southwest; Little Colorado, Tusayan, and Winslow Anasazi on the south; Cibola Anasazi on the southeast; and Chaco Anasazi on the east. The Kayenta manifestation is in general less culturally complex than the Chaco and Mesa Verde branches, roughly equivalent to the Tusayan, Winslow, and Little Colorado branches, and more complex than the Virgin branch. Kayenta populations never achieved the level of social complexity and hierarchy evident in the Chacoan regional interaction system, which developed in the San Juan Basin in the years A.D. 900–1200 (1050–750 years B.P.), or in the post-A.D. 1150 (800 years B.P.) Mesa Verde Pueblo III system. Furthermore, developments in the Kayenta branch lagged behind similar achievements in the Chaco and Mesa Verde areas.

The Kayenta branch is distinguished archaeologically from other branches by differences in ceramics, architecture, site configuration, and settlement pattern. In addition to diagnostic versions of the plain and textured gray wares and black-on-white painted wares that characterize all Anasazi divisions, the Kayenta branch is unique in possessing an orange ware with distinctive two-, three-, and four-color designs. Kayenta architecture is characterized by simple coursed masonry, adobe, and jacal walls; several typical room features; the late

Kayenta dipper, left, 4¹/₂ inches tall. Kayenta food bowl, right, 6 inches in diameter. (Reprinted from Smithsonian Institution, Bureau of American Ethnology, Bulletin 50, Plate 15)

occurrence of pithouses; grouping of dwellings and storage chambers into a domestic unit called a room cluster; a wide range of kiva forms and features; and an absence of great kivas and biwall and triwall structures. Kayenta sites are smaller and less functionally differentiated than their eastern Anasazi counterparts. Central and satellite sites do not occur until long after their appearance in the Chacoan area. Finally, the Kayenta area lacks road networks like those that connected the components of the Chacoan system.

The Kayenta expression passed through a typically Anasazi developmental sequence. Paleoindian and Archaic materials testify to a sparse occupation of the area by hunting-and-gathering groups before 1000 B.C. (2950 years B.P.). Although these early remains differ from those in the eastern Anasazi area, the Kayenta branch cannot properly be said to have begun until the Basketmaker II period (ca. 1000 B.C.–A.D. 550/600, or 2950–1400/1350 years B.P.), which saw the beginnings of farming, permanent residences (pithouses), and the grouping of dwellings into small hamlets. The succeeding Basketmaker III period (A.D. 550/600–850, or 1400/1350–1100 years B.P.) was marked by a number of technological innovations (the bow and arrow, the ground-stone axe, more efficient maize-grinding tools, and ceramics), an increased commitment to agriculture, more substantial pithouses and storage facilities, the agglomeration of dwellings into fairly large villages, and the construction of the only known Kayenta great kiva, at the Juniper Cove site. The Pueblo I period (A.D. 850–1000, or 1100–

950 years B.P.) differed little from Basketmaker III. People still lived in pithouse-storage structure units grouped into large villages located near the fields that produced the bulk of their food. The great kiva had disappeared from the Kayenta architectural inventory. During Pueblo II (A.D. 1000–1150, or 950–800 years B.P.), residence shifted from pithouses to "unit pueblos," which consisted of small blocks of contiguous masonry and jacal living and storage rooms fronted by semisubterranean structures that can be recognized as true kivas. The large Pueblo I villages situated near arable land were succeeded by a dispersed settlement pattern in which small unit-pueblo homesteads were scattered widely across the landscape. Kayenta populations achieved their maximum geographic spread during this period.

Pueblo II was followed by a century-long Transition period (A.D. 1150–1250, or 800–700 years B.P.), which saw major demographic and settlement changes. The peripheries of the area and upland localities within the area were abandoned as the population converged on favorable locations in the core area. Agricultural intensification in the form of terracing and ditch irrigation was practiced in these special areas. The unit pueblo was augmented by other habitation-site configurations, including plaza-oriented pueblos and pithouse villages. The changes wrought during the Transition period crystallized into the distinctive Tsegi phase (A.D. 1250–1300, or 700–650 years B.P.) pattern. Population was concentrated in three discontinuous areas: the Marsh Pass, Rainbow Plateau, and Klethla Valley. Habitation sites of several different kinds

A large Kayenta black-on-white vase, height, 17 inches. (Reprinted from Smithsonian Institution, Bureau of American Ethnology, Bulletin 50, Plate 18)

(unit pueblo, courtyard, plaza, and pithouse) were clustered around central pueblos that served as the organizational focus of these communities. Line-of-sight relationships between central pueblos linked these communities into visually connected larger groups. Thus, Kayenta populations finally achieved a settlement hierarchy more than two to three centuries after the Chaco Anasazi to the east.

This social achievement came to an end with the abandonment of the Kayenta area ca. 1300 (650 years B.P.), an event that was part of the general Anasazi abandonment of the San Juan drainage. Most Kayenta people probably moved south, the majority joining closely related Tusayan groups in the Little Colorado drainage. Others, however, continued farther south to the large Mogollon pueblo at Point of Pines, to the Safford Valley, and even to the San Pedro Valley in extreme southern Arizona. There, the Kayenta spoor is lost, although these people undoubtedly formed an important part of the population that evolved into the modern-day Hopis.

Jeffrey S. Dean

Further Readings

Dean, J.S. 1970. Aspects of Tsegi Phase Social Organization: A Trial Reconstruction. In *Reconstructing Prehistoric Pueblo Societies,* edited by W.A. Longacre, pp. 140–174. University of New Mexico Press, Albuquerque.

Gumerman, G.J. 1984. *A View From Black Mesa: The Changing Face of Archaeology.* University of Arizona Press, Tucson.

Gumerman, G.J., and J.S. Dean. 1989. Prehistoric Cooperation and Competition in the Western Anasazi Area. In *Dynamics of Southwest Prehistory,* edited by L.S. Cordell and G.J. Gumerman, pp. 99–148. Smithsonian Institution Press, Washington, D.C.

Haury, E.W. 1958. Evidence at Point of Pines for a Prehistoric Migration From Northern Arizona. In *Migrations in New World Culture History,* edited by R.H. Thompson, pp. 1–6. University of Arizona Bulletin, vol. 29, no. 2. Social Science Bulletin no. 27. University of Arizona Press, Tucson.

Kidder, A.V. 1924. *An Introduction to the Study of Southwestern Archaeology, With a Preliminary Account of the Excavations at Pecos.* Papers of the Phillips Academy Southwestern Expedition no. 1. Yale University Press, New Haven.

Lindsay, A., Jr. 1969. *The Tsegi Phase of the Kayenta Cultural Tradition in Northeastern Arizona.* Ph.D. dissertation, University of Arizona, Tucson. University Microfilms, Ann Arbor.

Lipe, W.D. 1983. The Southwest. In *Ancient North Americans,* edited by J.D. Jennings, pp. 421–493. W.H. Freeman, San Francisco.

Plog, F. 1979. Prehistory: Western Anasazi. In *Southwest,* edited by A. Ortiz, pp. 108–130. *Handbook of North American Indians,* vol. 9, W.C. Sturtevant, general editor. Smithsonian Institution, Washington, D.C.

Keith Variant

Keith-variant components extend westward from central Kansas and south-central Nebraska to the western portions of these states and have a north-south distribution from the Platte to the Arkansas River. A majority of the radiocarbon determinations available for the variant suggest a Late Woodland placement (A.D. 600–900, or 1350–1050 years B.P.).

Open sites and rock shelters were both occupied. Judging from their small size and limited quantity of cultural debris, which includes animal-bone refuse, hunting tools, and grinding implements, many served as temporary hunting-gathering stations. Villages of larger size with greater accumulations of refuse are also present, as indicated by excavations at sites 25FT70 and 25FT18 in the Medicine Creek Reservoir of southwestern Nebraska. Domestic structures in the villages include circular-to-oval basins excavated from 30.5–45.7 cm (12–18 inches) into sterile soil. These are probably house floors, for they have poorly defined fireplaces. Keith-variant burials include primary or secondary inhumations within occupation sites, burial mounds, and ossuaries, and offerings frequently occur. They include utilitarian artifacts, such as pottery vessels, projectile points, knives, scrapers, and grinding stones, and personal ornaments, such as tubular bone beads, shell disk beads, and shell pendants.

The subsistence base of the Keith variant centered on hunting and gathering. Large mammals of importance were deer, bison, and antelope. Small mammals and rodents were hunted, too, and aquatic resources utilized included freshwater mussels and fish. The exploitation of wild-vegetable products is indicated by grinding slabs and handstones, but cultigens have not been recognized from Keith-variant sites. The single pottery type that has been defined for the Keith variant is Harlan Cord Roughened (Kivett 1953:131–134). Vessels are elongated jars with conoidal bottoms and straight to slightly outflaring rims. Decoration is rare and limited to the rim. Exterior surfaces are vertically cord marked; interior rim surfaces occasionally bear horizontal or diagonal cord marking. Temper is usually ground calcite, although other types of stone tempering occur.

Alfred E. Johnson

Further Readings

Kivett, M.F. 1949. Archaeological Investigations in Medicine Creek Reservoir, Nebraska. *American Antiquity* 14:278–284.

———. 1952. *Woodland Sites in Nebraska.* Publications in Anthropology no. 1. Nebraska State Historical Society, Lincoln.

———. 1953. *The Woodruff Ossuary: A Prehistoric Burial Site in Phillips County, Kansas.* Bulletin no. 154. Bureau of American Ethnology, Smithsonian Institution, Washington, D.C.

Kettle Falls Sequence

Situated on the middle portion of the Columbia River in Washington State, Kettle Falls was one of the great salmon fisheries of the Pacific Northwest. Investigation of its lengthy history of use has resulted in the long, although in places sketchy, sequence outlined below. The sequence is built on work at several sites in the Kettle Falls vicinity.

Shonitkwu Period (7600–6800 B.C., or 9550–8750 years B.P.). The earliest components are characterized by side- and corner-notched points; small- and medium-sized leaf-shaped points; thick quartzite-slab tools, such as choppers and notched-pebble sinkers; utilized flakes, including some that are large; and, most distinctively, microblades and keeled cores. A crude pestle or hand maul, some manos, and a possible fragment of a tubular pipe were also found. Faunal remains include bones of grizzly bear, waterfowl, and an extinct species of large tortoise. The assemblages are thought to represent the presence of relatively small groups of people at the falls to catch salmon. In line with this interpretation, it is suggested that the plentiful crude chopping tools may have been used to construct weirs and fishing platforms. Alliances with the Windust and Cascade phases to the south are suggested by similarities in projectile-point styles. Microblades, on the other hand, provide evidence of ties to the north.

Slawntehus Period (6800–5300 B.C., or 8750–7250 years B.P.). A notable decline in local population and in use of the fishery is thought to result from reduction in the number of salmon available, perhaps because a warming climate had increased the amount of sediment in the glacier-fed headwaters of the Columbia River. Assemblages include leaf-shaped points with faintly visible shoulders, side- and corner-notched points, and pebble tools. Ca. 30 km (19 miles) upriver from the falls is a site containing sinkers, many grinding stones, and the floors of small shelters.

Ksunku Period (2800–1600 B.C., or 4750–3550 years B.P.). Artifacts include medium-sized points with shallow side notches; contracting and square-stemmed points; medium-sized hawk-tail side-notched points; leaf-shaped points; formed unifaces and bifaces, including both convex and concave scrapers; and flaked-stone perforators. Fire-cracked rocks, the inferred remains of boiling stones, are abundant. Although there are no sinkers to provide evidence of net use, bones of salmon are plentiful. Clearly, the falls was once more an important fishery. Ksunku origins seem to lie in those rare, small assemblages found during the little known period of ca. 5300–2800 B.C. (7250–4750 years B.P.).

Skitak Period (1600–800 B.C., or 3550–2750 years B.P.). During the last few centuries of the Ksunku period and the first few at the beginning of the Skitak, human occupation is not much in evidence. What eventually appear are assemblages that, except in point forms, are not much different from those in the preceding period. Characteristic artifacts (many of which are made from cryptocrystalline materials) include moderate-to-small-sized leaf-shaped points, points with either square or contracting stems, formed unifaces and bifaces, flaked-stone perforators, and a few pebble-based cutting tools.

Takumakst Period (800 B.C.–A.D. 300, or 2750–1650 years B.P.). The period is said to exhibit the lowest level of skill in stone technology of any component at Kettle Falls. This may have been the result of the prevailing choice of quartzite as a flaking material. Other characteristics of the assemblages include such artifacts as small-to-medium contracting-stem and side- and corner-notched (including barbed) points, formed unifaces and bifaces, flaked-stone perforators and drills, some of them key-shaped in form; carved and polished tubular pipes with thin, flaring bowls; and small choppers. There are also 1–2-m (3.3–6.6-foot) -deep pithouses and storage pits, at least some of which have a quartzite slab—henceforward, the sequence may be identified with the Plateau Salish. In contrast to the succeeding Sinaikst period, the Takumakst period appears to be a time of stylistic uniformity. Such uniformity may be an indication of ethnic homogeneity.

Sinaikst Period (A.D. 300–1400, or 1650–550 years B.P.). Deep pithouses similar to those of the Takumakst period continue in use. In contrast to their common interpretation on the Plateau as winter dwellings, these seem to have been occupied in summer. The most common Sinaikst projectile point is a small side-notched variety, but a wide range of other forms are also represented. As this diversity is attended by a notable increase in exotic raw materials, one might see this as evidence of greater contact with neighboring groups through an expanded trade network or, alternatively, as the seasonal assembly at the fishery of an ethnically diverse population. Whatever the interpretation, the presence of substantial pithouses, and both the size and the number of contemporaneously occupied settlements, suggest lengthy residence of a considerable population.

Shwayip Period (A.D. 1400–1800, or 550–150 years B.P.). Although still present, signs of ethnic diversity are much less evident. Estimates of the number of people assembling at the fishery are also considerably reduced. Pithouses are no longer built at the falls, having been replaced as the dominant dwelling by the stilt house form described at early contact (ca. A.D. 1810, or 140 years B.P.). The period is characterized by abundant small, ovate, quartzite knives that presumably were used to prepare salmon for drying, and by the almost exclusive presence among projectile points of a small, thin, side-notched triangular form.

Donald H. Mitchell

Further Readings

Chance, D.H. 1986. *People of the Falls.* Kettle Falls Historical Society, Colville.

Chance, D.H., and J.V. Chance. 1977. *Kettle Falls 1976: Salvage Archaeology in Lake Roosevelt.* Anthropological Research Manuscript Series no. 39. University of Idaho, Moscow.

———. 1982. *Kettle Falls 1971 and 1974: Salvage Archaeology in Lake Roosevelt.* Anthropological Research Manuscript Series no. 69. University of Idaho, Moscow.

———. 1985. *Kettle Falls 1978: Further Archaeological Excavations in Lake Roosevelt.* Anthropological Research Manuscript Series no. 84. University of Idaho, Moscow.

Chance, D.H., J.V.Chance, and J.L. Fagan. 1977. *Kettle Falls: 1972 Salvage Excavation in Lake Roosevelt.* Anthropological Research Manuscript Series no. 31. University of Idaho, Moscow.

Key Marco

Key Marco (8CR49) is an archaeological site located on Marco Island, Collier County, Florida. Discovered in 1895 by property owner W.D. Collier, the site was tested by C.D. Durnford (1895) and extensively excavated under the direction of F.H. Cushing in 1896 (Cushing 1897). Its material culture is thoroughly documented by M.S. Gilliland (1975), who also provides an authoritative account of Cushing's expedition (Gilliland 1989).

Cushing's investigations were systematic. He constructed a site map, employed a grid, took detailed notes, and interpreted his finds anthropologically. Working without the benefit of modern equipment, Cushing excavated with difficulty in wet, mucky sediments. Although a number of Florida wet sites have been excavated in the intervening century (Purdy 1991), Key Marco is still unparalleled in terms of diversity of items and quality of organic preservation. Among the wooden items recovered were carved masks, figurines, figureheads, plaques, stools, containers, pestles, arrows, weapons, canoe paddles, and tool handles. Netting made of palm fiber was found with wooden float pegs and shell weights still attached. Marine shells were used for line sinkers, net gauges, knives, woodworking tools, and hammers. Points, pins, and fishing gear were made from deer bones. Sharks' teeth served as cutting and engraving tools, antler as knife handles and adze sockets, and turtle carapace as net gauges (Gilliland 1975; Walker 1992).

The dating of the site and its cultural affiliation are controversial. John Goggin believed that the site dated to the fifteenth century. However, five of six radiocarbon assays fall in the A.D. 600–900 (1350–1050 years B.P.) period, and a sixth is dated at A.D. 100 (1850 years B.P.) (corrected dates). J.T. Milanich (1978) thinks that the dates may be spurious due to contamination by pesticides while in storage. B.J. Widmer (1988:91–93) believes that the site was occupied over a several-hundred-year period and that a society capable of producing the artifacts was in place in southwest Florida by A.D. 800 (1150 years B.P.).

Was Key Marco a Calusa site? J. Griffin (1988:135–137) argues on the basis of pottery traditions that the Ten Thousand Islands area, of which Marco Island represents the northern extremity, was not related to the heartland of the historic Calusa (i.e., to Charlotte Harbor) until very late precontact times, ca. A.D. 1400 (550 years B.P.). Thus, however remarkable the artifacts of Key Marco, they must not automatically be considered Calusa.

William H. Marquardt

Further Readings

Cushing, F.H. 1897. Exploration of Ancient Key Dweller Remains on the Gulf Coast of Florida. *Proceedings of the American Philosophical Society* 35:329–448.

Durnford, C.D. 1895. The Discovery of Aboriginal Netting Rope and Wood Implements in a Mud Deposit in Western Florida. *American Naturalist* 29:1032–1039.

Gilliland, M.S. 1975. *The Material Culture of Key Marco, Florida.* University Presses of Florida, Gainesville.

———. 1989. *Key Marco's Buried Treasure: Archaeology and Adventure in the Nineteenth Century.* University Presses of Florida, Gainesville.

Goggin, J. n.d. The Archaeology of the Glades Area, Southern Florida. Ms. on file, Florida Museum of Natural History, Gainesville.

Griffin, J. 1988. *The Archaeology of Everglades National Park: A Synthesis.* Southeastern Archeological Center, National Park Service, Tallahassee.

Feline figurine, wood 15 cm high, National Museum of Natural History catalogue no. 24915. (Photograph courtesy NMNH, Smithsonian Institution)

K

Milanich, J.T. 1978. The Temporal Placement of Cushing's Key Marco Site, Florida. *American Anthropologist* 80:682.

Purdy, B. 1991. *The Art and Archaeology of Florida's Wetlands.* CRC Press, Boca Raton.

Walker, K.J. 1992. The Zooarchaeology of Charlotte Harbor's Prehistoric Maritime Adaptation: Spatial and Temporal Perspectives. In *Culture and Environment in the Domain of the Calusa,* edited by W.H. Marquardt, pp. 265–366. Monograph no. 1. Institute of Archaeology and Paleoenvironmental Studies, University of Florida, Gainesville.

Widmer, R.J. 1988. *The Evolution of the Calusa: A Non-Agricultural Chiefdom on the Southwest Florida Coast.* University of Alabama Press, Tuscaloosa.

Keyes, Charles Reuben (1871–1951)

Charles Reuben Keyes was for most of his adult life a professor of German at Cornell College in Mount Vernon, Iowa. His recognition as an eminent midwestern archaeologist derives from work he did, largely in his spare time, from 1922 through 1950, when he directed the Iowa Archaeological Survey (IAS). The IAS was a systematic, statewide program of investigations that collected baseline data and put Iowa on the nation's archaeological map. A project of the State Historical Society of Iowa, the IAS recorded more than 400 sites and obtained more than 108,000 specimens. During the 1930s and 1940s, it was funded and jointly administered by the University of Iowa in Iowa City. Following his retirement from Cornell in 1941, Keyes was able to devote himself full-time to archaeology as visiting research professor of anthropology at the University of Iowa. Despite his advanced age, he vigorously pursued survey work and writing, and he initiated excavations as well. His final summary of Iowa archaeology was published a month after his death (Keyes 1951).

Keyes's close contacts with the principal eastern U.S. archaeologists of his era ensured Iowa's involvement in the development of survey methods and the establishment of regional taxonomic and classification systems. Keyes was instrumental in establishing the Plains Conference for Archaeology. He hosted the Third Plains Conference in Iowa in 1936, bringing Plains and Midwest archaeologists together to discuss the newly developed Midwest Taxonomic system. In the 1930s, Keyes and his colleague Ellison Orr directed WPA (Works Progress Administration) excavations at Nebraska-phase and Mill Creek sites in western Iowa. Keyes's concise 1949 summary of Plains-affiliated Iowa complexes helped solidify western Iowa's identification with the Plains and structured research directions for the following decades.

Although the time and resources Keyes had for detailed analyses and writing were extremely limited, he published nearly three dozen papers on Iowa archaeology, most of which were culture-history summaries and field reports. The Charles R. Keyes Collection at the State Historical Society of Iowa in Iowa City remains a principal repository of Plains-Midwest material.

William Green

Further Readings

Anderson, D.C. 1975. The Development of Archaeology in Iowa: An Overview. *Proceedings of the Iowa Academy of Science* 82:71–86.

Green, W. 1992. Charles Reuben Keyes and the History of Iowa Archaeology. *Journal of the Iowa Academy of Science* 99:80–85.

Keyes, C.R. 1949. Four Iowa Archeologies With Plains Affiliations. In *Proceedings of the Fifth Plains Conference,* pp. 96–97. Notebook Series no. 1. Laboratory of Anthropology, University of Nebraska, Lincoln.

———. 1951. Prehistoric Indians of Iowa. *Palimpsest* 32:285–344.

Tiffany, J.A. 1986. Curating the Charles R. Keyes Archaeological Collection. *Council for Museum Anthropology Newsletter* 10(2):15–22.

Tiffany, J.A., S.J. Schermer, and D.Z. Baker. 1990. Documenting Archaeological Sites in the Charles R. Keyes Collection. *Journal of the Iowa Archeological Society* 37:87–91.

Kidder, Alfred V. (1885–1963)

Alfred V. Kidder was an early-twentieth-century innovator in Southwestern archaeology who also strongly influenced many other North American archaeologists at the time. Among his innovative perspectives and activities were the

Alfred V. Kidder. (Reprinted with permission from American Antiquity 7[4]:269)

he also took a course in field methods with George Reisner, an Egyptologist and leading excavator of the period. He surveyed and excavated in the Four Corners area with Samuel Guernsey from 1914 through 1917, but began to focus his attention on Pecos Pueblo in 1915, where he carried out 10 seasons of work through 1929. Many students and professionals learned the stratigraphic method of excavation from Kidder at Pecos and then applied the concepts to other areas of North America. On the basis of his years of excavation and survey, Kidder structured the archaeological materials from nine river drainages into four developmental periods, stages, or cultures—Basket Maker, Post-Basket Maker, Pre-Pueblo, and Pueblo—in his 1924 synthesis. The classificatory scheme adopted at the First Pecos Conference in 1927 had strong roots in his early work. Kidder's research at Pecos and in the Four Corners area was supported by the Peabody Museum of American Archaeology and Ethnology at Harvard and the Robert S. Peabody Foundation for Archaeology of Phillips Academy in Andover, Massachusetts. He also worked in the Mayan area of Mesoamerica later in his career. Two biographies have been written about Kidder's life and career (Woodbury 1973; Givens 1992), and he set down his own reminiscences in 1958.

Guy Gibbon

first large-scale application in the Southwest of the stratigraphic method; the development of a five-step regional strategy of cultural-chronological research; the first attempted culture-historical synthesis of any part of North America (his 1924 *An Introduction to the Study of Southwestern Archaeology*); an early use of the concept of an archaeological culture; an insistence on an in situ rather than a diffusionist origin of Southwest cultures; the idea that the ultimate goal of archaeological research should be the establishment of generalizations about human behavior rather than the reconstruction of prehistory; excavation by natural and arbitrary layers where appropriate; the development of seriations of changing ceramic, stone, and bone artifact styles; and recognition of the importance of major site operations, which he conducted at Pecos in the Upper Pecos Valley of New Mexico.

Alfred Vincent Kidder was trained under Alfred M. Tozzer at Harvard University, where

Further Readings

Givens, D.R. 1992. *Alfred Vincent Kidder and the Development of American Archaeology.* University of New Mexico Press, Albuquerque.

Guernsey, S.J., and A.V. Kidder. 1921. *Basket-Maker Caves of Northeastern Arizona.* Papers, vol. 8, no. 2. Peabody Museum of American Archaeology and Ethnology, Harvard University, Cambridge.

Kidder, A.V. 1924. *An Introduction to the Study of Southwestern Archaeology, With a Preliminary Account of the Excavations at Pecos.* Papers of the Phillips Academy Southwestern Expedition no. 1. Yale University Press, New Haven.

———. 1927. Southwestern Archaeological Conference. *Science* 66:486–491.

———. 1932. *The Artifacts of Pecos.* Papers of the Phillips Academy Southwestern Expedition no. 6. Yale University Press, New Haven.

———. 1958. *Pecos, New Mexico: Archaeological Notes.* Papers no. 5. Robert S.

Peabody Foundation for Archaeology, Phillips Academy, Andover.

———. 1962. *An Introduction to the Study of Southwestern Archaeology, With an Introduction, "Southwestern Archaeology Today," by Irving Rouse.* Yale University Press, New Haven.

Kidder, A.V., and Charles Avery Amsden. 1931. *The Pottery of Pecos,* vol. 1. Papers of the Phillips Academy Southwestern Expedition no. 5. Yale University Press, New Haven.

Kidder, A.V., and Samuel J. Guernsey. 1919. *Archaeological Explorations in Northeastern Arizona.* Bulletin no. 65. Bureau of American Ethnology, Smithsonian Institution, Washington, D.C.

Kidder, A.V., and A.O. Shepard. 1936. *The Pottery of Pecos,* vol. 2. Papers of the Phillips Academy Southwestern Expedition no. 7. Yale University Press, New Haven.

Woodbury, R.B. 1973. *Alfred V. Kidder.* Columbia University Press, New York.

Kiet Siel

Kiet Siel (from a Navajo term meaning "broken pottery") is a large "cliff dwelling" on the Navajo Indian Reservation in northeastern Arizona. It is located near the head of Kiet Siel Canyon, a tributary of Tsegi Canyon. The site was discovered in January 1895 by a party led by Richard Wetherill, who returned in 1897 with the Bowles-Whitmore Expedition to excavate the site. Subsequent research included excavation by Byron Cummings in 1909, excavation and stabilization by a Civil Works Administration crew directed by Irwin Hayden and John Wetherill in the winter of 1933–1934, tree-ring collection by the Rainbow Bridge–Monument Valley Expedition in the 1930s, an intensive tree-ring study by Jeffrey S. Dean in the 1960s (Dean 1969), and excavation by Keith M. Anderson in the 1960s (Anderson 1971). Like Betatakin, Kiet Siel is one of the original components of Navajo National Monument.

Kiet Siel consists of 155 rooms with one rectangular and four circular kivas built on a bedrock shelf in a large rock shelter in the Navajo sandstone. A lower level contains several poorly preserved rooms and a possible circular tower. Two circular kivas in nearby Turkey Cave probably were used by the people of Kiet Siel. The same types of domestic feature identified at Betatakin are evident at Kiet Siel: living rooms, granaries, storerooms, corn grinding rooms, and courtyards organized into 25 room clusters. Two other "public" structures are the tower and at least two ceremonial annexes (D-shaped rooms that adjoin kivas). Artificial fill behind a retaining wall 4 m (13 feet) high and 60 m (197 feet) long forms a level building surface in the eastern half of the site.

While Kiet Siel is a Tsegi-phase (A.D. 1250–1300, or 700–650 years B.P.) site, the rock shelter was also inhabited in Basketmaker III (A.D. 600–850, or 1350–1100 years B.P.), Pueblo I (A.D. 850–1000, or 1100–950 years B.P.), and

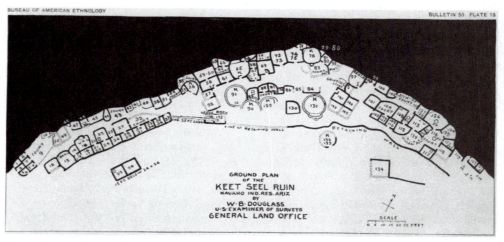

Ground plan of Kiet Siel. (Reprinted from Smithsonian Institution, Bureau of American Ethnology, Bulletin 50, Plate 13)

Pueblo II (A.D. 1000–1250, or 950–700 years B.P.) times. Tree-ring dates and architectural data provide an unusually complete picture of the complex developmental history of this site. Kiet Siel was begun ca. 1245 and by 1271 consisted of a rectangular kiva with 12 clusters of rooms distributed along the back wall of the shelter. Construction of the retaining wall ca. 1272 allowed considerable expansion, and by 1275 the site included at least 16 room clusters, one rectangular kiva, and three circular kivas. A decade of room construction, remodeling, and abandonment produced the final configuration in 1286 of 23 room clusters, three circular kivas, and the two kivas in Turkey Cave. Abandonment followed between 1286 and 1300.

Kiet Siel seems to have been less tightly organized than Betatakin. Relatively autonomous households were integrated into the village structure through crosscutting participation in kiva groups and ceremonies. Kiet Siel households, however, exhibit a greater degree of independence than their Betatakin counterparts. These groups seem to have been fairly mobile, moving into Kiet Siel, taking their place in the village structure for a time, and then moving on to be replaced by like units. As a result of this process, Kiet Siel probably was founded and abandoned through the uncoordinated movement of individual households rather than through the concerted action of a single community, as probably was the case at Betatakin.

Jeffrey S. Dean

Further Readings

Ambler, J.R. 1985. *Navajo National Monument: An Archaeological Assessment.* Archaeological Series no. 1. Northern Arizona University, Flagstaff.

Anderson, K.M. 1971. Excavations at Betatakin and Keet Seel. *Kiva* 37:1–29.

Dean, J.S. 1969. *Chronological Analysis of Tsegi Phase Sites in Northeastern Arizona.* Papers of the Laboratory of Tree Ring Research no. 3. University of Arizona Press, Tucson.

———. 1970. Aspects of Tsegi Phase Social Organization: A Trial Reconstruction. In *Reconstructing Prehistoric Pueblo Societies,* edited by W.A. Longacre, pp. 140–174. University of New Mexico Press, Albuquerque.

Fewkes, J.W. 1911. *Preliminary Report on a Visit to the Navaho National Monument, Arizona.* Bulletin no. 50. Bureau of American Ethnology, Smithsonian Institution, Washington, D.C.

Viele, C.W. 1980. *Voices in the Canyon.* Southwestern Parks and Monuments Association, Tucson.

See also BETATAKIN

Killarney Focus

The Killarney focus is known only from surface collections from four sites in the lightly forested stretch of rolling terrain between Killarney Lake to the south and the Pembina River to the north in Manitoba. The nature of the ceramic variability in this donated collection clearly indicates a multicomponent assemblage. Since the materials were lumped together from all four sites, which are in close proximity, it is not possible to determine whether the sites are multicomponent or represent discrete occupations. The lithics are undistinguished but include Knife River flint as well as local Swan River chert and agate.

Unusual ceramics form the basis for definition of the Killarney focus. A wide range of manufacturing techniques are evident from the body sherds, but use of a cord-wrapped paddle seems to predominate. The paste is hard and well worked. Grit temper is usual. Many vessels display a sharply inward-turned neck angle with a vertical section above. This configuration is consistent with a collared vessel. Castellations are absent. All of the vessels displaying this neck/rim morphology have cord-wrapped-object (CWO) -impressed decoration in oblique, horizontal, or chevron configurations. The lips may be CWO decorated or smoothed. While the CWO decorative patterning and method of application are consistent with Blackduck practices, the vessel shape is not. Antecedents for these vessels have not been identified elsewhere.

Many of the vessels in this collection are consistent, however, with Vickers-focus wares, and the presence of these vessels is sufficiently great to postulate a Vickers occupation in the area. Nonetheless, there is an abundance of other material that clearly falls outside the Vickers-focus range of variability. A few of these materials are consistent with a Wascana or Mortlach occupation, but others are clearly unique to the region. The presence of Vickers-

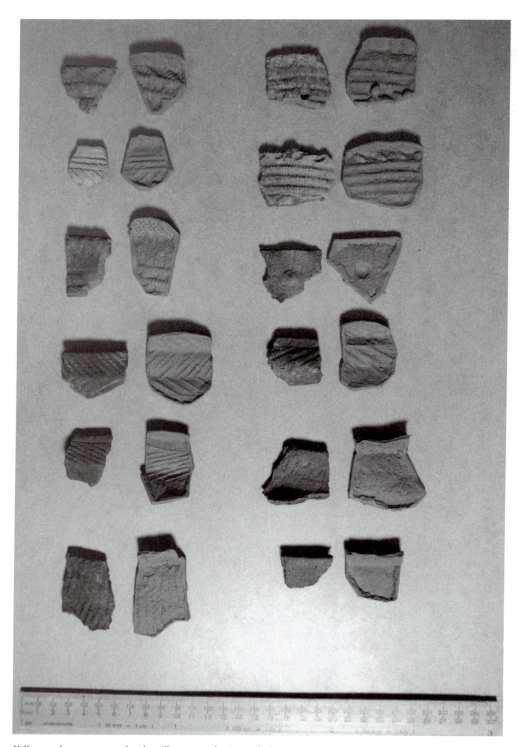

Killarney focus pottery sherds. (Illustration by B. Nicholson)

focus materials suggests a probable date of A.D. 1450 (500 years B.P.).

Bev Nicholson

Further Readings

Nicholson, B.A. 1990. Ceramic Affiliations and the Case for Incipient Horticulture in Southwestern Manitoba. *Canadian Journal of Archaeology* 14:33–60.

———. 1991. Modeling a Horticultural Focus in South-Central Manitoba During the Late Prehistoric Period—The Vickers Focus. *Midcontinental Journal of Archaeology* 16(2):163–188.

Kimmswick

The Kimmswick site (23JE2, 23JE334), Jefferson County, Missouri, is south of St. Louis on the west side of the Mississippi River Valley. It is at the base of a south-facing limestone bluff near a mineral spring. Kimmswick has long been a subject of archaeological and paleontological investigations. In 1839, Albert C. Koch collected late Pleistocene fossils from the locality and claimed an association of extinct animals and artifacts. Other investigations continued sporadically during the nineteenth and mid-twentieth centuries, at which time the site was developed as a limestone quarry and severely damaged. Most notable were the discovery of a Clovis point near the turn of the twentieth century and later excavations of the bonebed by R.M. Adams. However, it was not until renewed excavations in 1979 and 1980 that the relationship of the uppermost bonebed with Clovis was established; it was the first unequivocal association of the American mastodont (*Mammut americanum*) and Clovis culture (ca. 9350–9050 B.C., or 11,300–11,000 years B.P.).

The upper bonebed actually consists of at least two stratified ponded deposits, or shallow basins, both of which contain Clovis diagnostics. These are sealed from each other by coarse colluvium from the bluff and are overlain by ca. 2 m (6.5 feet) of additional bluff-derived colluvium. The latter sediment contains early Holocene (ca. 7050 B.C., or 9000 years B.P.) artifacts unambiguously separated from the Clovis-material remains. In addition to mastodont, the two Clovis units contain a diverse vertebrate fauna assemblage, dominated by rodents, deer, and turtle, that is also related to transitional late glacial conditions. The Clovis component is noteworthy for the associated remains of two other extinct taxa, *Mylohyus nasutus* (a cursorial peckary) and *Glossotherium harlani* (a giant ground slouth), and for the condition of the mastodont teeth, which are from animals undergoing extreme physiological stress. The *G. harlani* elements are all dermal ossicles, which attach to the skin rather than the appendicular skeleton. Their occurrence without other skeletal elements suggests that *G. harlani* skins were brought to the site.

Clovis tools and de facto refuse of chipped-stone-tool manufacture are equally conspicuous in the two ponded deposits. The most important of the tools are fluted points fashioned from nearby chert sources. These are unambiguous and follow the conventions of Clovis-point typology. The three complete specimens (including the one found at the turn of the twentieth century) have impact-fractured tips and consistent microwear evidence of use as projectile points, or weapon heads. A Clovis-point preform from the lower unit was broken in an attempt to flute the base and is clear evidence of tool fabrication at the site. Most artifacts are microdebitage produced in tool manufacture, use, or maintenance. While, the artifact inventory is meager, it is highly specific in terms of function and meaning: It is clearly an artifact assemblage normally associated with a big-game kill.

The Kimmswick site is preserved as Mastodon State Park.

Marvin Kay

Further Readings

Graham, R., and M. Kay. 1988. Taphonomic Comparisons of Cultural and Noncultural Faunal Deposits at the Kimmswick and Barnhart Sites, Jefferson County, Missouri. In *Late Pleistocene and Early Holocene Paleoecology and Archeology of the Eastern Great Lakes Region*, edited by R.S. Laub, G. Miller, and D.W. Steadman, pp. 227–240. Bulletin, vol. 33. Buffalo Society of Natural Sciences, Buffalo.

Graham, R.W., C.V. Haynes, D.L. Johnson, and M. Kay. 1981. Kimmswick: A Clovis-Mastodon Association in Eastern Missouri. *Science* 213:1115–1117.

King, J.E., and J.J. Saunders. 1984. Environmental Insularity and the Extinction of the American Mastodont. In *Quaternary Extinctions: A Prehistoric Revolution*, edited by P.S. Martin and R.G. Klein, pp. 315–339. University of Arizona Press, Tucson.

King Site

The King site (9FL5) is a mid-sixteenth-century A.D. aboriginal town located on the Coosa River in northwestern Georgia. Pottery from the site is identifiable as Barnett, a phase belonging to the Lamar culture that extended over most of Georgia and adjacent portions of Alabama, North and South Carolina, and Tennessee during the fifteenth and sixteenth centuries.

King is the westernmost of five known contemporary towns located along a 20-km (12.4-mile) stretch of the Coosa River west of the present-day city of Rome. These towns probably constituted a politically centralized society or chiefdom. A sixth site, with an earthen platform mound, may have been the adminis-trative and ceremonial center for this polity. Located in downtown Rome at the junction of the Oostanaula and Etowah rivers, this site was destroyed by urban development in the late nineteenth century.

Iron tools of Spanish origin have been recovered from several burials at the King site. Research by Charles Hudson and others indicates that the expeditions of Spanish explorers Hernando de Soto and Tristán de Luna y Arellano passed through the Rome area in A.D. 1540 and 1560, respectively. According to Hudson's reconstruction of the Spanish expedition routes, the King-site chiefdom may have been de Soto's province of Ulibihali (Hudson et al. 1985).

In addition to its status as a probable Spanish contact site, King is important for the insight it provides into the nature of late Mississippian towns in the region. Sixty percent of the site area has been excavated and mapped, resulting

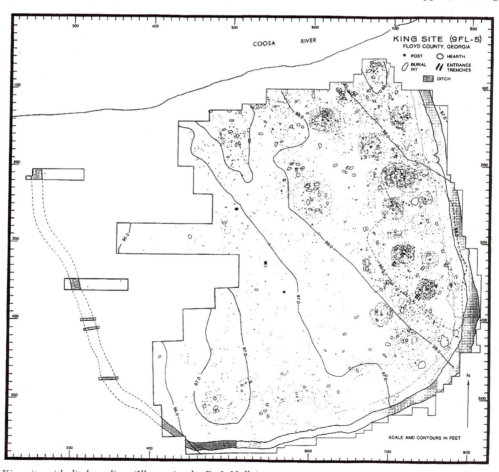

King site with ditch outline. (Illustration by D. J. Hally)

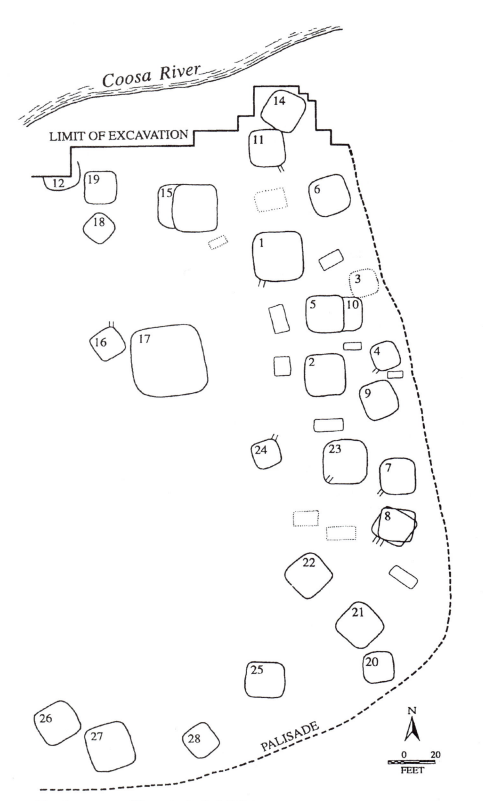

K

King site structures. (Illustration by D. J. Hally)

in a detailed picture of the town's layout and architecture. King covers 2.3 ha (5.7 acres) and is bounded by a ditch-and-palisade system on three sides and by the Coosa River on the north (see Figure). A large open plaza occupied the center of the town and was surrounded by a domestic habitation zone. A single large post, ca. 1 m (3.3 feet) in diameter, marked the geographic center of the plaza and town. Two buildings occupied the northern portion of the plaza. One resembles domestic structures in the habitation zone and may have been the residence of the village chief. The second, the largest structure on the site, probably had public and ceremonial functions.

The habitation zone contained approximately 40 domestic structures. Measuring between 5.5 and 9.5 m² (6.6–11.4 square yards), these were erected in shallow basins, with earth banked against their exterior walls and a pitched roof. Inside was an open central floor space containing a hearth. Low wattle-and-daub walls divided the outer floor area into a number of cubicles that served as work, storage, and sleeping areas. Foodstuffs were stored in smaller rectangular structures erected adjacent to the domestic structures.

Large extended-family households may be represented by groups of two to four domestic structures arranged around small open "courtyards." The largest structures in these groupings were occupied longer than the smallest and tend to be located adjacent to the town plaza. The founders of such households may have resided in the former, while their grown and married daughters may have resided in the latter.

The King site was occupied for less than 50 years (A.D. 1520–1560). Its peak population probably never exceeded 250 people. The Spanish may have introduced diseases, such as smallpox and measles, to the region, leading to the death of large numbers of native inhabitants. Whether for this or other unidentified reasons, the King site and the Upper Coosa River Valley as a whole were abandoned within a few decades of Spanish contact.

David J. Hally

Further Readings

Blakely, R.L. (editor). 1988. *The King Site: Continuity and Contact in Sixteenth-Century Georgia.* University of Georgia Press, Athens.

Hally, D.J. 1993. The 1992 and 1993 Excavations at the King Site (9FL5).

Early Georgia 23(2):30–44.

Hally, D.J., M.T. Smith, and J.B. Langford, Jr. 1990. The Archaeological Reality of de Soto's Coosa. In *Columbian Consequences: 2. Archaeological and Historical Perspectives on the Spanish Borderlands East,* edited by D.H. Thomas, pp. 121–138. Smithsonian Institution Press, Washington, D.C.

Hudson, C., M. Smith, D. Hally, R. Polhemus, and C. DePratter. 1985. Coosa, A Chiefdom in the Sixteenth Century Southeastern United States. *American Antiquity* 50:723–737.

Smith, M.T. 1987. *Archaeology of Aboriginal Culture Change in the Interior Southeast.* University of Florida Press, Gainesville.

Kitselas Canyon Sequence

Kitselas Canyon is a narrow, 2-km (1.2-mile) long gorge on the Lower Skeena River in northwestern British Columbia ca. 150 km (93 miles) inland from the Pacific coast. Ethnographically, the canyon was occupied by the Kitselas people, a Tsimshian-speaking group sometimes called the "Canyon Tsimshian," whose territory separated the Coast Tsimshian tribes from their inland neighbors, the Gitksan. The age range for the prehistoric cultural sequence at Kitselas Canyon is ca. 3050–50 B.C. (5000–2000 years B.P.) or later. It includes five named phases represented at two excavated sites in the canyon: Gitaus and the Paul Mason site. Gitaus has a deeply stratified archaeological deposit, with radiocarbon estimates in the 2350–450 B.C. (4300–2400 years B.P.) range, although the latter is probably not a terminal date. The Paul Mason site, also deep and stratified, has radiocarbon dates in the 3050–750 B.C. (5000–2700 years B.P.) range.

Bornite Phase (3050–2350 B.C., or 5000–4300 years B.P.). The Bornite phase, identified so far only at the Paul Mason site, is characterized by pebble, flake, and microblade tools. The microblades are manufactured mainly from obsidian, which comes from the Anahim Peak area of central British Columbia and perhaps from Mount Edziza in northern British Columbia. The presence of microblades is unique among mainland components on the northern coast of British Columbia; the Bornite-phase dates are relatively late compared with dates from other microblade components on the central coast of British Columbia, the Queen Charlotte Islands, and southeastern Alaska. Bornite appears to be a late manifestation of the North Coast Microblade tradition. This component at Kitselas Canyon is interpreted as a limited-activity camp, probably associated with salmon fishing, although faunal evidence to support this inference is lacking.

Gitaus Phase (2350–1650 B.C., or 4300–3600 years B.P.). The Gitaus phase, represented at Gitaus and the Paul Mason site, is interpreted as a purely coastal manifestation, probably representing seasonal movement to inland riverine locations for summer salmon fishing. Similarities with early coastal material from the Prince Rupert Harbor area include high proportions of pebbles and flake tools, ground-stone implements, such as abraders and slate points, and rare flaked-stone points. Microblades are absent. Evidence for the importance of summer fishing includes an abundance of cortex spalls, which may have replaced microblades as fish-processing implements; remains of birchbark rolls, which may have been used as torches for night fishing; and a carved fish effigy.

Skeena Phase (1650–1250 B.C., or 3600–3200 years B.P.). The Skeena phase, represented at Gitaus, includes a greater occurrence of implements typically associated with land-mammal hunting. Formed unifacial and bifacial flaked-stone tools, including a distinctive lanceolate, Planolike point form, predominate in this phase. The technological changes from the preceding phase are substantial and may represent a population replacement in the canyon, perhaps a downriver incursion of inland groups. Alternatively, these changes may be associated with in situ developments in the existing lower Skeena settlement-subsistence system. As in the previous phases, there is no evidence for winter habitation. The Skeena phase at Gitaus appears to represent a base camp with summer-fall occupation.

Paul Mason Phase (1250–750 B.C., or 3200–2700 years B.P.). Important changes in technology, subsistence, and settlement occur at Kitselas Canyon during this phase, which is represented at the Paul Mason site. Flaked stone declines sharply from the preceding Skeena phase, while use of pebble, flake, and ground stone and inferred use of bone tools all increase. Hexagonal ground-slate points and blunt, rod-like implements commonly called "pencils" appear for the first time. Both types also appear in the coastal middens at Prince Rupert Harbor at about this time. Faunal evidence and the re-duced proportion of flaked-stone hunting tools indicate a decline in the importance of land mammals and a concomitant increase in the importance of fishing during the phase. The presence of a single, 4-m (13-foot) -long hearth feature, widespread scatters of fire-cracked rock, and cachepits reflect the importance of intensive food processing and storage. The most important new element in the phase is a series of 10 rectangular-house-floor features that reflect permanent house construction and village organization. The house-floor features were arranged side by side in two rows facing the river. Internal patterns were similar in two excavated floors. Each had two hearths and, along either side, lateral raised benches perhaps for sleeping and storage. House floors were consistent in size, averaging ca. 62 m^2 (74 square yards).

Kleanza Phase (550 B.C., or 2500 years B.P., to ?). The poorest known of the five phases at Kitselas Canyon, the Kleanza phase, represented at Gitaus, has a radiocarbon date of 450 B.C. (2400 years B.P.), which is probably associated with the beginning of the phase rather than with its end. The artifact assemblage is generally similar to that of the Paul Mason phase, except for the addition of a few items that may be related to changes in social status differentiation. Labrets, slate mirrors, and a ground-slate dagger, which all appear for the first time, may have been status markers. Slate mirrors, for example, were worn historically only by Tsimshian women of high status. Widespread scatters of fire-cracked rock reflect continued intensive processing of food resources during the Kleanza phase, but there is no direct evidence for storage or permanent winter habitation at Gitaus.

The Kitselas Canyon sequence begins with the Bornite phase, a late manifestation of the North Coast Microblade tradition, during the early period of occupation of the northern Northwest Coast. Subsequent phases reflect developments in the lower Skeena settlement-subsistence system, which culminates with the emergence of permanent village life and storage in the Paul Mason phase. The ensuing Kleanza phase provides evidence of social inequality, perhaps the quintessential feature of the developed Northwest Coast cultural pattern.

Gary Coupland

Further Readings

Allaire, L. 1978. *L'Archeologie des Kitselas d'apres le Site Stratifie de Gitaus (GdTc*

2) sur la Riviere Skeena en Colombie Britannique. Mercury Series Paper no. 72. Archaeological Survey of Canada, National Museum of Man, Ottawa.

———. 1979. The Cultural Sequence at Gitaus: A Case of Prehistoric Acculturation. In *Skeena River Prehistory,* edited by R. Inglis and G. MacDonald, pp. 18–52. Mercury Series Paper no. 87. Archaeological Survey of Canada, National Museum of Man, Ottawa.

Coupland, G. 1985. Household Variability and Status Differentiation at Kitselas Canyon. *Canadian Journal of Archaeology* 9:39–56.

———. 1988a. *Prehistoric Cultural Change at Kitselas Canyon.* Mercury Series Paper no. 138. Archaeological Survey of Canada, National Museum of Man, Ottawa.

———. 1988b. Prehistoric Economic and Social Change in the Tsimshian Area. In *Prehistoric Economies of the Pacific Northwest Coast,* edited by B. Isaac, pp. 211–243. Research in Economic Anthropology Supplement no. 3. JAI Press, Greenwich.

Kittigazuit

Kittigazuit (NiTr-2) is the site of the central village of the traditional Kittegaryumiut, the largest subgroup of the Inuvialuit who occupy the Mackenzie delta region of the western Canadian Arctic. The village was located at the mouth of East Channel, where the dominant channel of the Mackenzie River delta flows into shallow Kugmallit Bay on the Beaufort Sea coast. This location was adjacent to a wide expanse of shoal water that was heavily utilized during the summer months by herds of feeding beluga. The Kittegaryumiut took advantage of this situation with a highly organized and extremely efficient communal beluga hunt. Up to 200 kayak-hunters are reported to have proceeded in line across the 8-km (5-mile) width of Kugmallit Bay before turning upstream to drive the beluga among the shoals, where they could be easily harpooned and lanced. Several hundred whales are reported to have been killed in some of these hunts. Up to 1,000 people may have occupied the beaches around Kittigazuit during the summer hunts, and a smaller number lived at the site during the winter.

During the late nineteenth century, the wintering population occupied six large semisubterranean houses built of driftwood logs and turf in a distinctive cruciform pattern. Archaeological excavations at the site found more than 1 m (3.3 feet) of accumulated deposits rich in beluga bones, which indicates a time depth of ca. 500 years for the village and associated whale hunt. The village was abandoned in 1902 after two disastrous measles epidemics had decimated the Kittegaryumiut.

Robert J. McGhee

Further Readings

McGhee, R. 1974. *Beluga Hunters*. Institute of Social and Economic Research, Memorial University of Newfoundland, St. John's.

Kiva

Kiva is a Hopi word for the underground ceremonial chambers of Pueblo Indians. Since the late nineteenth century, archaeologists have applied the term "kiva" to prehistoric structures in the Southwest, particularly in the Anasazi and parts of the Mogollon region. Many prehistoric kivas are round, semisubterranean structures, a form that developed from early pithouses more than 2,000 years ago. Thus, a consideration of kivas links the modern Pueblo people to their ancient roots in the Southwest.

Kivas have been identified and defined in a number of ways. Very commonly, prehistoric structures that are round (or rectangular in the Mogollon area), subterranean, and masonry-lined and that have features including an encircling bench, a fire pit and ventilator, wall niches, and a sipapu (a hole or vault feature that symbolizes where the ancestors emerged from the underworld) are called kivas (see Figures). Most kivas are fairly small (10–25 m², or 12–30 square yards). Great kivas were built as early as A.D. 500 (1450 years B.P.), though regular kivas first become common in the tenth century A.D.

Kivas have also been defined in terms of their presumed function. Archaeologists in the first Pecos Conference, held in 1927 at Pecos Pueblo in New Mexico argued that a kiva is a chamber constructed especially for ceremonial purposes. Unfortunately, this definition has been problematic because it does not provide guidelines for identifying kivas archaeologically. Furthermore, it appears that both modern kivas and rooms identified as prehistoric kivas were used for domestic activities (e.g., grinding corn and cooking) as well as for ceremonies.

Top photo: Features inside a kiva. Plaza D, Spruce-Tree House cliff dwelling, Mesa Verde, Colorado. (Reprinted from Smithsonian Institution, Bureau of American Ethnology, Bulletin 41, Plate 12). Bottom photo: Reconstructed kiva roof/plaza and kiva entrance. Plaza D, Spruce-Tree House cliff dwelling, Mesa Verde, Colorado. (Reprinted from Smithsonian Institution, Bureau of American Ethnology, Bulletin 41, Plate 12)

Prior to A.D. 1300 (650 years B.P.), many small kivas were associated with a small suite of surface rooms, an arrangement known as a unit pueblo. Presumably, the two or three households that lived in the surface rooms shared the kiva. Early (before A.D. 1000, or 950 years B.P.) unit pueblos included subterranean pit structures that often had a sipapu, a ventilator, and a fire pit but lacked masonry lining, were subrectangular, and had frequent evidence of domestic activities. These early pit structures are sometimes called protokivas.

The organization of pueblo architecture changed dramatically when the northern Southwest was abandoned ca. A.D. 1300 (650 years B.P.), and many people moved into large villages along the Rio Grande and the Little Colorado River. These large pueblos lack unit-style architecture. Instead, they have one or a few larger kivas. The newly organized architecture suggests that before and after A.D. 1300 (650 years B.P.) kivas played very different roles: Most early ones were shared by only a few households, while the later ones could be used by many members of a community.

Michelle Hegmon

Further Readings

Brew, J.O. 1946. *The Archaeology of Alkali Ridge, Southeastern Utah.* Papers no. 21. Peabody Museum of American Archaeology and Ethnology, Harvard University, Cambridge.

Hawley, F. 1950. Big Kivas, Little Kivas, and Moiety Houses in Historical Reconstruction. *Southwestern Journal of Anthropology* 6:286–302.

Judd, N.M. 1922. Archaeological Investigations at Pueblo Bonito, New Mexico. *Smithsonian Miscellaneous Collections* 72(15):106–117.

Lekson, S. 1988. The Idea of the Kiva in Anasazi Archaeology. *Kiva* 53:213–234.

Lipe, W.D., and M. Hegmon (editors). 1989. *The Architecture of Social Integration in Prehistoric Pueblos.* Occasional Papers no. 1. Crow Canyon Archaeological Center, Cortez.

Smith, W. 1952. *When Is a Kiva? and Other Questions About Southwestern Archaeology,* edited by R.H. Thompson. University of Arizona Press, Tucson.

Klo-kut and Old Chief Creek Phases

The Late Prehistoric period (1050 B.C.–A.D. 1850, or 3000–100 years B.P.) in the northern Yukon is divided into two sequential phases, a division based primarily on the excavation of two large, deeply stratified sites, Klo-kut (MjV1-1) and Rat Indian Creek (MjVg-1), along the middle Porcupine River and of two smaller sites, Old Chief Creek (MjVk-7) and Lazarus (MjVk-4), in the same region. These sites are located 10–100 km (6–62 miles) up-stream from the modern *Vuntut Gwichin* village of Old Crow. The stratified sites represent hunting camps intended for the seasonal interception of migrating caribou.

The earlier of the two phases, Old Chief Creek (1050/550 B.C.–A.D. 700, or 3000/2500–1250 years B.P.), is represented by the lowest two levels (6 and 6A) at Rat Indian Creek and by components at Old Chief Creek and Lazarus. It is characterized by the use of fine-quality cherts for the production of a wide range of bifacial tools and large, unfacially retouched flakes. The later and much better known Klo-kut phase (A.D. 110–1850, or 1840–100 years B.P.) includes all of the prehistoric levels at Klo-kut, the major prehistoric cultural level (5) at Rat Indian Creek, and the last prehistoric component at Old Chief Creek. It is characterized by a rich and elaborate bone and antler industry that was produced using a limited range of simple flake tools, such as retouched flakes and scrapers, that were themselves produced through the reduction of small chert cores made from locally collected waterworn pebbles. There is also evidence for the use of unmodified quartzite cobble spalls for a range of functions such as hide working and butchering, the ubiquitous Athapaskan hide scraper known as the *chi-tho*, and artifacts made of native copper and obsidian. These are exotic raw materials that may have come from sources several hundred kilometers away in Alaska (copper and obsidian), the southern Yukon (obsidian), and the Northwest Territories (copper).

Among the notable changes between the two phases is the dramatic decrease in chert bifacial technology after A.D. 700 (1250 years B.P.). Indeed, after this date there are remarkably few bifaces made of this material, perhaps because many of their functions (e.g., projectile points and knives) could be fulfilled equally well by bone or antler implements. Other changes between the two phases include distinct morphological and size differences in scrapers and a shift in raw-material usage. Larger, higher quality stone was exploited in the Old Chief Creek phase; smaller pebble cherts, in the Klo-kut. The latter change may have contributed to the much more expedient nature of the lithic component of Klo-kut-phase technology.

Raymond J. Le Blanc

Further Readings

Le Blanc, R.J. 1984. *The Rat Indian Creek Site and the Late Prehistoric Period in the Interior Northern Yukon.* Mercury

Series Paper no. 120. Archaeological Survey of Canada, National Museum of Man, Ottawa.

Morlan, R.E. 1973. *The Later Prehistory of the Middle Porcupine Drainage, Northern Yukon Territory.* Mercury Series Paper no. 11. Archaeological Survey of Canada, National Museum of Man, Ottawa.

Klunk-Gibson Mound Group

The Klunk-Gibson Mound Group (11C4,5,43), is a large Middle Woodland Hopewellian burial site in the Lower Illinois River Valley that has been a focus of studies that attempt to discern social organization, such as the presence or absence of hereditary elites, from burial data. Covering a probable 100–200-year time span in the period ca. A.D. 100–300 (1850–1650 years B.P.), Klunk-Gibson is a seemingly ideal choice for such studies in the Midwest, for the site is one of the few mound groups in the area that has had most of its mounds completely and systematically excavated. It is also one of the few in which the human remains—more than 500 individuals recovered from 13 earthen mounds and one natural knoll—have been extensively analyzed for a range of data, including age, sex, stature, epigenetic trait distributions, and postmortem manipulation of body parts; and in which a range of artifact forms, burial features, and local and nonlocal raw materials exists that can be correlated with individual interments. In addition, osteological analyses indicate that all ages of both sexes, except for the very young, are represented without apparent bias. Among the burial features are log-walled and log-and-slab-roofed features; among the artifacts, shell objects, earspools, copper adzes, and bear-teeth and animal-jaw pendants. As at most other Havana Hopewell mound centers, the mounds were "tombs" associated with charnel facilities within which a range of postmortem treatments of individual corpses occurred.

Guy Gibbon

Further Readings

Braun, D.P. 1979. Illinois Hopewell Burial Practices and Social Organization: A Reexamination of the Klunk-Gibson Mound Group. In *Hopewell Archaeology,* edited by D.S. Brose and N. Greber, pp. 66–79. Kent State University Press, Kent.

Buikstra, J.E. 1976. *Hopewell in the Lower Illinois Valley: A Regional Approach to the Study of Human Biological Variability and Prehistoric Behavior.* Scientific Papers no. 2. Archaeology Program, Northwestern University, Evanston.

Perino, G.H. 1969. The Pete Klunk Mound Group, Calhoun County, Illinois: The Archaic and Hopewell Occupations (With an Appendix on the Gibson Mound Group). In *Hopewell and Woodland Site Archaeology in Illinois,* edited by J.A. Brown, pp. 9–124. Bulletin no. 6. Illinois Archaeological Survey, University of Illinois Press, Urbana.

Tainter, J.A. 1975. The Archaeological Study of Social Change: Woodland Systems in West Central Illinois. Unpublished Ph.D. dissertation, Department of Anthropology, Northwestern University, Evanston.

———. 1977. Woodland Social Change in West Central Illinois. *Midcontinental Journal of Archaeology* 2:67–98.

See also HAVANA HOPEWELL

Knife River Flint

Knife River flint is a dark brown, fine-grained, translucent flint that was used extensively for chipped-stone tools. The excellent flaking qualities of the flint account, at least in part, for its widespread distribution in the Plains and the Midwest. Under certain weathering conditions, the flint obtains a white patina with age. The degree of patination has been used with some success as a relative dating technique. The primary source is a 2,000-km² (750-square-mile) area in western North Dakota that contains one of the most extensive series of quarries and associated workshops in North America. Quarry sites vary from 0.5 to 32 ha (1–80 acres) and contain as many as 2,400 surface depressions of quarry pits. Quarry pits were dug into sandy unconsolidated alluvial and colluvial Pleistocene and Holocene deposits to obtain secondary deposits of flint in the form of weathered pebbles, cobbles, and boulders. Knife River flint has a cellular microstructure, indicating it formed from silicified plant fragments. The flint appears to have originally derived from an Eocene Age formation destroyed by erosion. A large amount of Knife River flint was obtained from the quarries, but it is also available in lesser quantities in secondary deposits adjacent to the primary source area. In addition, small pieces of Knife River flint occasionally can be found in terrace gravel along the Missouri River and in till deposits up to several miles from the quarry.

The flint is found in archaeological sites from western Montana to western Pennsylvania and from northern New Mexico to central Saskatchewan, but it is most common in the northern Plains. Its use spans the entire Native American occupation of North America from Paleoindian to historic contact. The most widespread use occurred during the Paleoindian (ca. 10,000–7000 B.C., or 11,950–8950 years B.P.) and Middle Woodland (ca. 300 B.C.–A.D. 400, or 2250–1550 years B.P.) periods. Paleoindian artifacts of Knife River flint are found as far away as Pennsylvania and New Mexico. Knife River flint artifacts dating to the Middle Woodland are found in Hopewell Interaction Sphere sites. Large broad-bladed bifacial tools are found as far away as Wisconsin, Illinois, and Ohio in Hopewell mortuary contexts.

William T. Billeck

Further Readings

Ahler, S. 1986. *The Knife River Flint Quarries: Excavations at Site 32DU508.* State Historical Society of North Dakota, Bismarck.

Braun, D.P., J.B. Griffin, and P.F. Titterington. 1982. *The Snyders Mounds and Five Other Mound Groups in Calhoun County, Illinois.* Technical Reports no. 13. Museum of Anthropology, University of Michigan, Ann Arbor.

Clark, F. 1984. Knife River Flint and Interregional Exchange. *Midcontinental Journal of Archaeology* 9:173–198.

Clayton, L., W.B. Bickley, Jr., and W.J. Stone. 1970. Knife River Flint. *Plains Anthropologist* 15:282–290.

Knife River Indian Villages National Historic Site

Administered by the U.S. National Park Service, the Knife River Indian Villages National Historic Site preserves several village sites occupied in Late Prehistoric and early historic times by the Hidatsa Indians, a Siouan-language-speaking tribe linguistically related to their close neighbors, the Mandan. In the late eighteenth and nineteenth centuries A.D., the locale about the confluence of the Knife and Missouri rivers in central North Dakota was home to three Hidatsa villages and two Mandan villages. The villages are collectively referred to as the "five traditional villages" of the Mandan and the Hidatsa and were an important center of trade with many other northern Plains tribes in prehistoric times. The Hidatsa and the Mandan also attracted Euro-American fur traders: first, French and British traders from Canada; later, Spanish and Americans from St. Louis, Missouri. The villagers lived by growing corn, beans, and squash on the Missouri River floodplain and by hunting bison in the valley and uplands.

The Hidatsa were organized into three subgroups called the Awatixa, the Awaxawi, and the Hidatsa-proper. Each lived in separate villages and possessed separate origin and migration myths, language dialects, and customs. The Awatixa believed that they always lived in the Missouri Valley in North Dakota, and archeological evidence of their presence is believed to date as early as A.D. 1100 (850 years B.P.). The Awaxawi and the Hidatsa-proper reached the Missouri Valley several hundred years later and settled near their Awatixa relatives. In the park, the Big Hidatsa Village was first settled by the Awatixa ca. A.D. 1400–1450 (550–500 years B.P.) and later by Hidatsa-proper, who lived there ca. A.D. 1600–1845 (350–105 years B.P.). The other two Hidatsa settlements, Sakakawea Village and Amahami Village, were established by Awatixa and Awaxawi, respectively, shortly before A.D. 1800 and were destroyed by the Sioux in 1834. Weakened by successive epidemics of smallpox, which swept through the villages in the eighteenth and early nineteenth centuries, the Hidatsa and neighboring Mandan were stationary targets for the militarily stronger, nomadic Sioux, who increasingly raided and harassed the villagers. As a consequence, the Hidatsa left the Knife River region in 1845 and founded a new settlement, Like-a-Fishhook Village, ca. 80.5 km (50 miles) up the Missouri, where they were eventually joined by the Mandan and the Arikara, a Caddoan-speaking people who practiced a similar economy based an horticulture and bison hunting. Living together for mutual defense, these three peoples blended into a single society. They abandoned Like-a-Fishhook Village in 1886. Their descendants today live on the Fort Berthold Reservation in west-central North Dakota and are called the Three Affiliated Tribes.

Thomas D. Thiessen

Further Readings

Ahler, S.A., T.D. Thiessen, and M.K. Trimble. 1991. *People of the Willows: The Prehistory and Early History of the Hidatsa Indians.* University of North Dakota Press, Grand Forks.

Bowers, A.W. 1965. *Hidatsa Social and Ceremonial Organization.* Bulletin no. 194. Bureau of American Ethnology, Smithsonian Institution, Washington, D.C.

Meyer, R.W. 1977. *The Village Indians of the Upper Missouri: The Mandans, Hidatsas, and Arikaras.* University of Nebraska Press, Lincoln.

Wood, W.R., and T.D. Thiessen (editors). 1985. *Early Fur Trade on the Northern Plains: Canadian Traders Among the Mandan and Hidatsa Indians, 1738–1818.* University of Oklahoma Press, Norman.

Knife River Phase

The Knife River phase or complex of the Coalescent tradition consists of about two dozen circular earthlodge villages near the confluence of the Knife and Missouri rivers in central North Dakota. Two additional communities are farther upstream on the Missouri River. These villages were occupied by the Mandan and the Hidatsa A.D. 1780–1845. Both groups had a dual economy based on hunting bison and other native species in addition to growing corn, beans, squash, and other cultigens on the Missouri River floodplain. The phase has been divided, based on whether the villages were occupied by the Mandan (subphase I) or the Hidatsa (subphase II). This traditional view of the phase has been modified by more recent investigations in 1991 and 1993 that propose a Knife River complex (A.D. 1600–1886) consisting mostly of Hidatsa communities but that also includes a few late Mandan and Arikara villages. Four phases within this revised scheme have been defined: Willows (A.D. 1600–1700), Minnetaree (A.D. 1700–1785), Roadmaker (A.D. 1785–1830), and Four Bears (A.D. 1830–1886). Origin traditions of the Hidatsa have one band, the Hidatsa-proper, arriving at the Missouri River from the east from the Devils Lake, North Dakota, or southern Wisconsin areas, while the Awatixa Hidatsa claim to have always lived along the Missouri. The last village to have been occupied by Mandan, Hidatsa, and Arikara survivors of various introduced epidemic diseases, such as smallpox, is Like-a-Fishhook Village. Nearly 1,000 years of traditional village life on the Missouri River ended when it was abandoned in 1886.

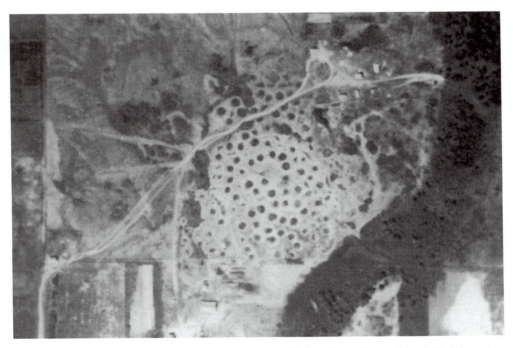

Aerial view of the Big Hidatsa site, a Knife River phase earthlodge village. (Prepared by C. M. Johnson)

During the course of the Knife River phase or complex, there was increasing trade between the plains villagers and French, British, Spanish, American, and native nomadic neighbors west and east of the Missouri River. Furs and skins, items of Euro-American manufacture, and garden produce were exchanged. During the Willows and Minnetaree phases, this trade in Euro-American items derived from French and British trading posts in Canada and along the Great Lakes. It was indirect and intermittent, with few of these items found in village archaeological sites. Most of these goods were passed on in trade, prompting researchers to call the villagers "middlemen" in the trade system. This role intensified as guns from the east and horses from the American Southwest were added to the system in about 1740. More frequent and direct contacts with Euro-American traders during the Roadmaker and Four Bears phases resulted in the gradual replacement and disappearance of native technologies, along with much of traditional culture. Many of the most experienced craftsmen and artisans as well as other individuals were lost in the first historically documented smallpox epidemic, which spread throughout the Plains in 1780–1781. The construction of American Fur Company and other posts on the Upper Missouri, which began in 1830, eliminated the plains village "middlemen" as a key component in the native–Euro-American trading system. These posts were an outgrowth of the 1804–1806 Lewis and Clark expedition that stimulated American interest in the newly acquired lands of the Louisiana Purchase. Lewis and Clark, in addition to a number of later American traders, trappers, and explorers departing from St. Louis and other locations, documented native village life at many of the Knife River–complex communities.

Craig M. Johnson

Further Readings

Ahler, S.A., T.D. Thiessen, and M.K. Trimble. 1991. *People of the Willows: The Prehistory and Early History of the Hidatsa Indians*. University of North Dakota Press, Grand Forks.

Lehmer, D.J. 1971. *Introduction to Middle Missouri Archeology*. National Park Service, Washington, D.C.

Meyer, R.W. 1977. *The Village Indians of the Upper Missouri: The Mandans, Hidatsas, and Arikaras*. University of Nebraska Press, Lincoln.

Smith, G.H. 1972. *Like-a-Fishhook Village and Fort Berthold, Garrison Reservoir, North Dakota*. National Park Service, Washington, D.C.

Wilson, G.L. 1934. *The Hidatsa Earthlodge*. Anthropological Papers, vol. 33, pt. 5, American Museum of Natural History, New York.

———. 1987. *Buffalo Bird Woman's Garden*. Minnesota Historical Society, St. Paul.

Wood, W.R. (editor). 1986. *Papers in Northern Plains Prehistory and Ethnohistory*. Special Publication no. 10. South Dakota Archaeological Society, Sioux Falls.

Wood, W.R., and T.D. Thiessen (editors). 1985. *Early Fur Trade on the Northern Plains: Canadian Traders Among the Mandan and Hidatsa Indians, 1738–1818*. University of Oklahoma Press, Norman.

Kolomoki

Kolomoki (9ER1), located ca. 9.7 km (6 miles) east of the Chattahoochee River in Early County, Georgia, has provided important information about the Woodland period (A.D. 300–700, or 1650–1250 years B.P.) of the Gulf Coastal Plain. Kolomoki is a large, multimound site that has all the appearances of a Mississippian-period (A.D. 900–1500, or 1050–450 years B.P.) civic center—elaborate burial mounds (Mounds D and E), a large pyramid-shaped mound (Mound A), and a crescent-shaped village area—but it clearly dates to the Woodland period.

The ceramics in the village area indicate a late Swift Creek and Weeden Island I occupation. The late Swift Creek (called Kolomoki by W.H. Sears) materials are found in a crescent-shaped midden surrounding three sides of an open plaza in front of Mound A. The later Weeden Island I materials are found only on the southern side of the plaza. The two burial mounds that were excavated contained numerous elaborate mortuary vessels, central burials, indications of retainer sacrifice, and curated skeletons. Mound E dates to the late Swift Creek occupation, while Mound D dates to the later Weeden Island I occupation. The radiocarbon dates for the site argue for an overall occupation period of ca. A.D. 250–600 (1700–1350 years B.P.). Sears (1951a, 1951b, 1953, 1956) originally argued that for the Kolomoki site, and for an undefined geographic area surrounding it, complicated stamping (what he defined as Kolomoki Complicated Stamped, a type that is a regional development of Late Swift Creek Complicated Stamped) postdated early Weeden Island and that complicated stamping was never replaced by check stamping. This interpretation differs from the widely accepted chronology defined by Willey (1949); in a 1992 article, Sears withdrew his controversial interpretation of the Kolomoki site and of ceramic sequences in South Georgia.

Kolomoki is significant because it represents an elaborate development of sociopolitical organization on the eastern Gulf Coastal Plain before the evolution of Mississippian society. The size of the site, the lack of low-status burials, and the presence of high-status burials accompanied by elaborate burial goods in large mounds indicate that Kolomoki was the focus of a sociopolitical system developing toward chiefdom status. However, Kolomoki appears to have remained a protochiefdom that failed to develop into a Mississippian system. Reasons for this failure have not been determined.

Karl T. Steinen

Further Readings

Sears, W.H. 1951a. *Excavations at Kolomoki, Season I—1948.* Series in Anthropology no. 2. University of Georgia Press, Athens.

———. 1951b. *Excavations at Kolomoki, Season II: Mound E.* Series in Anthropology no. 3. University of Georgia Press, Athens.

———. 1953. *Excavations at Kolomoki, Seasons III and IV: Mound D.* Series in Anthropology no. 4. University of Georgia Press, Athens.

———. 1956. *Excavations at Kolomoki: Final Report.* Series in Anthropology no. 5. University of Georgia Press, Athens.

———. 1964. The Southeastern United States. In *Prehistoric Man in the New World,* edited by J. Jennings and E. Norbeck, pp. 259–290. University of Chicago Press, Chicago.

———. 1992. Mea Culpa. *Southeastern Archaeology* 11(1):66–711.

Willey, G.R. 1949. *Archaeology of the Florida Gulf Coast.* Miscellaneous Collections, vol. 113. Smithsonian Institution, Washington, D.C.

Koniag Culture

"Koniag" refers to the archaeological aspect of the Koniags (or Kaniagmiut), the historic Eskimo inhabitants of Kodiak Island and the adjacent coast of the Alaska Peninsula and ancestors of today's Alutiiqs. It is not simply a precontact phase, inasmuch as the excellence of its maritime adaptations, which were well suited to the needs of the Europeans who subjugated the Koniags but had inferior hunting technology, continued to be followed into the nineteenth century A.D. and are documented in the excavation of historic components. The Koniags, or Alutiiqs as they call themselves in their historic Russianized aspect, are well known from several historical ethnographies and were featured in the Smithsonian Institution's 1988 Crossroads of Continents exhibition (Fitzhugh and Crowell 1988).

"Koniag" appears to be derived from the Aleut name for the Eskimo inhabitants of Kodiak. The name was eventually passed on to the Russians as they explored eastward along the Aleutian chain. It was first applied archaeologically by Ales Hrdlicka (1945) to the upper levels collections and skeletal populations from the Uyak, or Our Point, site. His work on Kodiak Island remains the largest single archaeological excavation ever undertaken in Alaska, though also one of the most infamous because of the technique of "mining" used to excavate it. Considered in retrospect, occupation of the Uyak site appears to have ceased before historic contact, but the gap of a few centuries has been filled through later excavation of Late Prehistoric and contact-period Koniag sites. Stylistic and technological development of the archaeological culture can be traced to the end of the Kachemak tradition, ca. A.D. 1100–1200 (850–750 years B.P.).

Koniag prehistory has received considerable attention from anthropologists because the Koniags appear to be an intrusive Yupik-speaking Eskimo community whose presence is explained to some extent by linguistic change and migration to the Gulf of Alaska. Nevertheless, the evidence indicates that Koniag's basic roots are in the antecedent Kachemak population, with stylistic and technological updating to Neo-Eskimo modes and changes in social organization (as reflected in house size and complexity) (Knecht 1996). Not all change and population movement were coincident with the beginning of the archaeological phase, for some of these processes were probably still in

K

progress at the time of Russian conquest in 1784. Other changes date to the end of the Kachemak tradition. In effect, the Koniag culture was a small-scale tradition that encompassed local variants or phases and an ongoing sequential development due in part to stimulus and increments of new peoples at various times from the Bering Sea (Western Eskimo region) and the Northwest Coast culture area. Some Koniag culture elements are clearly derived from the Bering Sea region by way of the Alaska Peninsula. Pottery is an example. The origins of many other cultural elements have yet to be determined. It is possible that much of what is known as Western Eskimo and as Northwest Coast culture (e.g., Eyak, Tlingit) originated in the Koniag culture of Kodiak Island and its closely related conjoiners of the outer Kenai Peninsula and Prince William Sound.

Temporal and local Kodiak variants are poorly formalized, though work in the 1980s (Knecht 1996) points to transitional (Kachemak-Koniag), early, developed, and late aspects. There were also ceramic and aceramic areas that roughly divided the island in half. These areas persisted for several centuries to the time of historic contact in the 1760s. Other differences tend to correlate with these two areas. Several closely related, temporally and spatially discrete local phases have been defined for the Alaska Peninsula, but none have been termed "Koniag" by their investigators.

Koniag archaeological culture is defined by contrast with the antecedent Kachemak tradition, by its technological composition, and by reference to the populous early historic Koniags. The majority of implements show at least minor stylistic change when compared with earlier tools. Though only a few Kachemak traits dropped out during or at the beginning of the Koniag phase, many innovations appeared. Among these were pottery, the large grooved splitting adze, a marked increase in planing adzes, profuse sweat-bath rubble (fire-cracked rock), an incised figurine ritual, petroglyph making (dating not certain), absence of effigy representations in stone lamps, and a change from numerous small notched pebble weights (probably for nets) to fewer, heavier notched cobbles (mainly for fishing in the sea). The technology of cutting tools, including weapon end blades or tips, was based almost exclusively on ground slate and again exhibited changing stylistic modes. Most of these trait changes have strong implications: changes in fishing technol-

ogy (the weights), a tremendous increase in woodworking (why? what was being built?), and changes in ritual and ceremony (the lamps, figurine cult, petroglyphs, the sweat bath). And, especially later during the phase, house forms changed to large dwellings with a common room and appended family apartments. The historic Koniags were masters of sewing, with waterproof rain parkas among their productions. But, strangely and in contrast with the locally antecedent Ocean Bay and Kachemak traditions, fine needles are unknown in their prehistoric refuse deposits. Confronted with these contrasts and profound temporal changes, and by the Eskimo presence on the Pacific Coast, archaeologists and ethnologists find an intellectual challenge in working with the Koniag culture.

Donald W. Clark

Further Readings

Clark, D.W. 1974a. *Contributions to the Later Prehistory of Kodiak Island, Alaska.* Mercury Series Paper no. 20. Archaeological Survey of Canada, National Museum of Man, Ottawa.

———. 1974b. *Koniag Prehistory.* Tubinger Monographien Sur Urgeschichte, vol. 1. Verlag W. Kohlhammer, Stuttgart.

———. 1992. "Only a Skin Boat Load or Two": The Role of Migration in Kodiak Prehistory. *Arctic Anthropology* 29(1): 2–17.

Dumond, D.E. 1981. *Archaeology on the Alaska Peninsula: The Naknek Region, 1960–1975.* Anthropological Papers no. 21. Department of Anthropology, University of Oregon, Eugene.

Dumond, D.E., and G.R. Scott. 1991. *The Uyak Site on Kodiak Island: Its Place in Alaskan Prehistory.* Anthropological Papers no. 44. Department of Anthropology, University of Oregon, Eugene.

Fitzhugh, W.W., and A. Crowell (editors). 1988. *Crossroads of Continents: Cultures of Siberia and Alaska.* Smithsonian Institution Press, Washington, D.C.

Harritt, R.K. 1988. *The Late Prehistory of Brooks River, Alaska.* Anthropological Papers no. 38. Department of Anthropology, University of Oregon, Eugene.

Heizer, R.F. 1956. *Archaeology of the Uyak Site Kodiak Island, Alaska.* Anthropological Records, vol. 17, no. 1. University of California, Berkeley.

Hrdlicka, A. 1945. *The Anthropology of Kodiak Island.* Wistar Institute of Anatomy and Biology, Philadelphia.

Jordan, R.H., and R.A. Knecht. 1988. Archaeological Research on Western Kodiak Island, Alaska: The Development of Koniag Culture. In *Late Prehistoric Development of Alaska's Native People,* edited by R.D. Shaw, R.K. Harritt, and D.E. Dumond, pp. 225–306. Monograph Series, Aurora IV. Alaska Anthropological Association.

Knecht, R.A. 1985. Nunakakhnak: A Historic Koniag Village in Karluk, Kodiak Island, Alaska. *Arctic Anthropology* 22(2):17–35.

———. 1996. The Late Prehistory of the Alutiiq People: Culture Change on the Kodiak Archipelago From 1200–1750 A.D. Unpublished Ph.D. dissertation, Department of Anthropology, Bryn Mawr College, Bryn Mawr.

Kootenay-Pend d'Oreille Rivers Sequence

The Kootenay and Clark Fork/Pend d'Oreille watersheds of southeastern British Columbia, northeastern Washington, and northern Idaho form the Columbia River headwaters. This mountainous area between the Plains and the Plateau has exceptionally high biological diversity. West of the Purcell-Cabinet-Bitterroot mountains, aquatic and vegetal resources, including anadromous salmon and camas, thrived under maritime influence. The parklands and grasslands leeward of this divide were range for white-tailed and mule deer, elk, mountain sheep, moose and, in late precontact time, bison and antelope.

Over the past 12,000 years, alpine, boreal, steppe, semidesert, and maritime biomes changed in response to cool-wet through hot-dry climatic cycles. In immediate postglacial times, steppe tundra above the shores of proglacial lakes supported megafauna. Subsequent warming and drying conditions supported coniferous forests and grasslands after 8550 B.C. (10,500 years B.P.). More diverse vegetational mosaics developed during moister and increasingly colder cycles after 5050 B.C. (7000 years B.P.). Aquatic and riparian resources attained their greatest abundance in the 3050–550 B.C. (5000–2500 years B.P.) period. The last 2,000-year cycle facilitated the expansion of bison and antelope in the intermontane basins

until A.D. 1450 (500 years B.P.), after which time they were extirpated during the Little Ice Age.

At European contact at the beginning of the nineteenth century A.D., the Ktunaxa, speakers of a unique language, inhabited the core area along the Kootenay River. They were surrounded in the Columbia drainage by the Salishan-speaking Shuswap, Flathead, Pend d'Oreille, Kalispel, and Sinixt Indians.

The region's culture history is presented here as a series of strategies for land and resource use representing adaptive responses to changing climate and geological and biotic-resource distributions. The Ktunaxa, who were apparently the first inhabitants, at ca. 8050 B.C. (10,000 years B.P.), maintained a diversified economy in the core Kootenay River area, a region of great biodiversity, and encroached as well on peripheral regions, where more specialized cultures focused on the rich salmon, root-crop, and bison resources of those regions. The rise and fall of these superabundant resources, and the populations of specialists, is manifest in discontinuous cultural sequences at sites south and east of the core area. There are no correlative breaks in the record of the Kootenay River area for the 10,000-plus years of human occupation. This is not surprising given the Ktunaxa's status as a linguistic isolate and the presence of many unique traits in their culture.

Fluted spear points have been found in the region, but large stemmed points are the most widespread projectiles in immediate postglacial settings. They typify the Goatfell complex, which appears to reflect a northward movement of people from the Great Basin as pluvial lakes dried up. Other characteristics of the Goatfell complex include a preference for quartzite and tourmalinite lithic material, bifacial cores with platform abrasion for the production of large knives and side-struck flake tools, and a settlement pattern focused on well-drained landforms associated with proglacial lakes in the southern Purcell and Selkirk mountains.

Cultural deposits of the slightly later "Shonitkwu" cultural period (7600–6800 B.C., or (9550–8750 years B.P.) (see KETTLE FALLS SEQUENCE) are also found in riverine settings to the north. Use of argillite and rhyolite for microblades differentiates Shonitkwu from Goatfell assemblages and suggests the presence of a separate, northwestward-oriented cultural group.

Above timberline in the Purcell and Rocky mountains, stemmed and side-notched projectile points and high-elevation quarries suggest increased ungulate carrying capacity due to an early mid-Holocene drought. However, no formal archaeological units have yet been defined because most archaeological work has been done in valley bottoms. With the increased influence of the westerlies ca. 5050 B.C. (7000 years B.P.), forest cover west of the region increased, but the rain shadow effect expanded the grasslands to the east. At the western entrance to Crowsnest Pass, extensive bison hunting took place in the montane grasslands. Significant continuities with the Goatfell complex during this time include the high-terrace orientation of the settlement pattern and an identical lithic technology based on tourmalinite and quartzite. Stemmed and shouldered projectile points are still present, but notching also occurs now.

As the climate became cooler and moister during the last 5,000 years, the upland orientation gave way to a more intensive focus on valley-bottom resources. Evidence of fishing, plant gathering, and hunting of waterfowl becomes more important. Fire-broken rock is much more common than previously and often occurs as concentrations, indicating adoption of stone boiling as a new cooking method. A number of discrete cultural units can be defined, all characterized by a focus on local lithic materials. Microcrystalline stone was still preferred, from both quarries and gravel sources. The lithic technology remained similar to that of earlier times, along with the common occurrence of stemmed points. In the eastern part of the region, the localized distribution of lithic material, the large number, but small size, of sites, and relatively sparse deposits suggest a more spatially confined food quest and distinct subsistence territories. To the west, however, a very significant population focus, supported by fish and root crops, is evident.

The Inissimi complex (3050–550 B.C., or 5000–2500 years B.P.) encompasses a distinctive set of assemblages on the Kootenay River and its major tributaries from the big bend in northwestern Montana to the north arm of Kootenay Lake. Sites are located by river confluences, outlets, large eddies, and rapids. The complex is also characterized by an expanding-stem projectile-point form with a ground, convex base and acute-to-right-angled shoulders, and a predominance of Kootenay Argillite, a distinctive stone quarried only beside the north arm of Kootenay Lake. Its distribution well up the Kootenay River system strongly suggests canoe

travel and a subsistence quest that included salmon fishing near the Kootenay River mouth. The lithic industry is essentially the same as that of the Goatfell and succeeding complexes.

The Deer Park phase (1300–450 B.C., or 3250–2400 years B.P.) of the Arrow Lakes and the falls on the Lower Kootenay River was contemporary with a period of high fluvial discharge and high salmon carrying capacity. It ended during an interval of instability correlated with the Neoglacial advance that began ca. 850 B.C. (2800 years B.P.). The phase is characterized by pithouse settlements; parallel and expanding-stem, corner-notched, and lanceolate projectile points; phyllite knives; conical pestles; and nephrite adzes. It represents an upriver focus on the salmon fisheries and coincides with an occupational hiatus at Kettle Falls.

Evidence of occupation within the last 2,000 years, a period of reduced fluvial discharge, is less common along the Arrow Lakes and Lower Kootenay River. Occupations of the Vallican (450 B.C.–A.D. 650, or 2400–1300 years B.P.) and Slocan (A.D. 650–1800, or 1300–150 years B.P.) phases are found on lower terraces and at major river confluences. A distinctive cultural development occurred in the southern Purcell Trench, where a different seasonal-flow pattern after 550 B.C. (2500 years B.P.) affected the timing of flooding on the Kootenay River delta that made an economic focus on freshwater fish and waterfowl possible. The distinctive social institutions of the ethnographic Lower Ktunaxa were developed to better organize the taking and distribution of these resources.

On the Lower Pend d'Oreille River, intensive camas processing may have begun as early as 2550 B.C. (4500 years B.P.). It led to increasingly permanent residential sites, most of which date to 1050–50 B.C. (3000–2000 years B.P.). In sites farther up the Pend d'Oreille during this time period, Kootenay Argillite was replaced by stone from the Montana Rockies, indicating an eastward shift in geographic orientation that probably correlated with the divergence of the Flathead and the Pend d'Oreille ethnolinguistic groups.

A similar eastward shift is also manifest in the southern Rocky Mountain Trench, where significant changes in subsistence-settlement pattern and lithic technology occurred during the last two millennia. The Akanohonek complex (ca. A.D. 450–1800, or 1500–150 years B.P.) is typified by large, intensively inhabited sites on alluvial terraces, and smaller encampments on high terraces and along tributaries. Other characteristics include adoption of the bow and arrow, a significant reduction in tool size, and cryptocrystalline stone as the preferred tool stock. Top of the World Chert from the Rocky Mountains reaches its highest proportions in lithic assemblages. Hunting of herd ungulates increases significantly and includes the taking of bison west of the Continental Divide. In contrast to small, relatively isolated bands of previous times, Akanohonek social organization was apparently more complex—a large population wintered on the Tobacco Plains and dispersed as summer arrived into smaller task groups to procure a wide range of subsistence resources. There is also emerging evidence of a contemporary, but as yet undefined, occupation associated with the ungulate winter range farther north at the Columbia River headwaters.

Wayne T. Choquette

Further Readings

Choquette, W.T. 1987. A Palaeoclimatic Model for the Upper Columbia River Drainage Basin. In *Man and the Mid-Holocene Climatic Optimum,* edited by N. McKinnon and G. Stuart, pp. 311–344. Students' Press, Calgary.

———. 1996. Early Post-Glacial Habitation of the Upper Columbia Region. In *Early Human Occupation of British Columbia,* edited by R. Carlson and L. Dalla Bona, pp. 45–50. University of British Columbia Press, Vancouver.

Thoms, A., and G. Burtchard (editors). 1984. Prehistoric Land Use in the Northern Rocky Mountains: A Perspective From the Middle Kootenay Valley. *Project Report* 4:57–119. Center for Northwest Anthropology, Washington State University, Pullman.

Koster

The Koster site (11GE4) is a large open-air site containing a stratified sequence of occupations that details important changes in subsistence and settlement that have taken place among hunter-gatherers over the last 9,000 years. The site is located in west-central Illinois at the edge of the Lower Illinois River Valley where the river drives a broad palustrian system of enhanced primary productivity. The thick colluvial fan in which the site is embedded has preserved in its calcareous sediments a continuous record of artifacts and dietary remains. Starting from an unusual record of Early Archaic bone and antler tools, a long record of punctuated sedentary occupations is documented within a changing environment.

The site is best known for its well-preserved archaeological record of 23 distinct occupations in 10 m (32.8 feet) of deposit. These extend from the Early Archaic at 7050 B.C. (9000 years B.P.) to the early Late Archaic at 1050 B.C. (3000 years B.P.). Over this span of time, the site records the effect of an increasingly stable wetland-resource base upon subsistence and settlement practices that leads to the establishment of sedentary communities ca. 3550–3050 B.C. (5500–5000 years B.P.). For most of its history, the site was occupied by small residential camps. At three times, this use pattern was punctuated by relatively dense occupations, in 6550 B.C. (8500 years B.P.), 5050 B.C. (7000 years B.P.), and 3250–3050 B.C. (5200–5000 years B.P.). These occupations, labeled Horizon 11, 8C, and 6A, respectively, record the progressive experimentation of hunter-foragers with increasing degrees of sedentism. Large rectangular houses of post-and-beam interior-support construction appear in Horizons 8C and 6A. Burial plots are associated with Horizons 11 and 6A/B. Primitive squash seeds appear in Horizon 8C. But only in the meter-thick deposit of Horizon 6A/B, when sedentism becomes permanent, does the heretofore conservative chipped-and-ground-stone technology begin to change. During this period, oily seeds are systematically collected, and evidence can be found for long-distance exchange in native copper and other items.

James A. Brown

Further Readings

Brown, J.A. 1985. Long-Term Trends to Sedentism and the Emergence of Complexity in the American Midwest. In *Prehistoric Hunter-Gatherers: The Emergence of Cultural Complexity,* edited by T.D. Price and J.A. Brown, pp. 201–231. Academic Press, New York.

Brown, J.A., and R. Vierra. 1983. What Happened in the Middle Archaic? An Introduction to an Ecological Approach to Koster Site Archaeology. In *Archaic Hunters and Gatherers in the American Midwest,* edited by J.L. Phillips and J.A. Brown, pp. 165–195.

K

Academic Press, New York.

Cook, T.G. 1976. *Koster: An Artifact Analysis of Two Archaic Phases in West-Central Illinois*. Prehistoric Records no. 1. Archaeology Program, Northwestern University, Evanston.

Hajic, E.R. 1990. *Koster Site Archeology I: Stratigraphy and Landscape Evolution*. Research Series, vol. 8. Center for American Archeology, Kampsville.

Krieger, Alex D. (1911–1991)

Alex Krieger was a graduate of the University of California at Berkeley (B.A., 1936), the University of Oregon (M.A., 1938), and the Universidad Nacional Autónoma de México (D. Sc., 1955). His most important archaeological work concerned artifact typologies, southern Caddoan culture history and its broader relationships, southeastern United States–Mesoamerican connections, and the early peopling of the New World. While at Berkeley, he and other students, including Robert Heizer and Richard K. Beardsley, dug Humboldt Cave, a major occupation and cache site in the western part of the Great Basin. Between 1937 and 1939, he continued work in the Great Basin as a University of Oregon field archaeologist. In the following 17 years, he worked in various research capacities with the Anthropology Department at the University of Texas at Austin. This was the most productive period in his long professional career. Working closely with Clarence H. Webb, a major figure in Louisiana archaeology, he developed a ceramic typology and an encompassing culture-historical framework for the interpretation of southern Caddoan prehistory. Although much modified over the years, this framework is one of the better examples of the application of the Midwestern Taxonomic system.

In 1946, Krieger published *Cultural Complexes and Chronology in Northern Texas,* one of the most significant monographs to come out of Texas archaeology. It demonstrated contact between the Anasazi and Caddoan areas, chronologically related complexes in the Southwest and the eastern United States, respectively, and synthesized much previously unpublished information. For this and other distinguished contributions, he was awarded the Viking Medal in Archaeology in 1948. The next year another important work, *The George C. Davis Site, Cherokee County, Texas,* appeared. Coau-

Alex D. Krieger. (Reprinted with permission from American Antiquity 58[4]:614)

thored with H. Perry Newell, who excavated the site but died before the analysis was completed, this volume remains a classic site report. Between 1954 and 1956, Krieger coauthored three other major monographs, one on Texas archaeology, another on the purportedly early Midland skeleton, and the third on Humboldt Cave. While all of these works are notable contributions, *An Introductory Handbook of Texas Archeology* (Krieger et al. 1954) stands out as one of the then few statewide archaeological summaries. It was also a pioneer in its use of cultural stages and definitions of named projectile-point types (some new, some not). In addition to these volumes, Krieger wrote many landmark articles on issues that ranged from method and theory in artifact classification to New World culture history, and he was a frequent contributor to the book-review sections of major journals. In the years 1950–1958, he was an assistant editor of *American Antiquity,* compiling the Early Man section of "Notes and News." Rich in detail, these vignettes provide useful tidbits of information as well as a valuable perspective on the history of the study of the early peopling of the Americas.

In 1956, Krieger left the University of Texas to become director of a municipal museum in Riverside, California. In 1960, he moved to Seattle, Washington, where he became involved in an archaeological highway salvage program and later (1964–1979) taught in the Department of Anthropology at the University of Washington. Although he continued to publish incisive book reviews, the latter part of his career focused more on teaching than on original research.

Dee Ann Story

Further Readings

Krieger, A.D. 1944. The Typological Concept. *American Antiquity* 9:271–288.
———. 1945. An Inquiry Into Supposed Mexican Influences on a Prehistoric "Cult" in the Southern United States. *American Anthropologist* 47:483–515.
———. 1946. *Culture Complex and Chronology in Northern Texas, With Extension of Puebloan Datings to the Mississippi Valley.* Publication no. 4640. University of Texas, Austin.
Krieger, A.D., and H.P. Newell. 1949. *The George C. Davis Site, Cherokee County, Texas.* Memoirs no. 5. Society for American Archaeology, Washington, D.C.
Story, D.A. 1993. Obituary for Alex D. Krieger 1911–1991. *American Antiquity* 58:614–621.
Story, D.A., A.D. Krieger, and E.B. Jelks. 1954. *An Introductory Handbook of Texas Archeology.* Bulletin no. 25. Texas Archeological Society, San Antonio.

K

L

Lagoon Complex

The Lagoon complex is a regional Paleoeskimo manifestation in the eastern Mackenzie Delta–Banks Island area of the western Canadian Arctic. Elements of the complex were first recognized at the Lagoon site on the southwestern coast of Banks Island and subsequently at the Crane site on Cape Bathurst Peninsula on the mainland opposite Banks Island. A small assemblage from Melville Island north of Banks Island may also be related. The complex represents an amalgam of Pre-Dorset and Dorset traits, with the possibility of minor Norton-culture influences from western Alaska. The Pre-Dorset relationship can be seen clearly in the bone and antler implements, particularly in bilaterally barbed, open-socketed harpoons and in bird-bone needles with drilled eyes; the harpoons also show similarities with Norton varieties. The lithic artifacts, on the other hand, show strong parallels with Dorset-culture assemblages, particularly in such things as transverse-oblique scrapers. Ten radiocarbon dates from the two sites, all on terrestrial mammal bone, are in the 830–200 B.C. (2780–2150 years B.P.) range, which overlaps with the transitional period of Pre-Dorset-to-Dorset cultural development in eastern and High Arctic Canada.

Raymond J. Le Blanc

Further Readings

Arnold, C.D. 1981. *The Lagoon Site (OjRl-3): Implications for Paleoeskimo Interactions.* Mercury Series Paper no. 107. Archaeological Survey of Canada, Canadian Museum of Civilization, Hull.

Le Blanc, R.J. 1994. *The Crane Site (ObRv-1) and the Palaeoeskimo Period in the Western Canadian Arctic.* Mercury Series Paper no. 148. Archaeological Survey of Canada, Canadian Museum of Civilization, Hull.

Laguna, Frederica de (1906–)

Using archaeology to reconstruct prehistoric ethnography, Frederica de Laguna integrated ethnohistory, oral history, and linguistics into her study of northern North American cultures—in the best Boasian tradition. Although she has excavated in the American Southwest and Europe, her pioneering research in Greenland, Alaska, and Canada is best known. In 1929, she worked with Arctic archaeologist Therkel Mathiassen in Greenland; a year later she began study of Pacific Eskimos. She initiated scientific archaeology in several parts of Alaska, and, in addition to her excavations, her reports typically describe archaeological survey and native place-names. In *The Archaeology of Cook Inlet, Alaska* (1975 [1934]), she defined the distinctive Kachemak series from excavations on Yukon Island and Cottonwood Creek. *Chugach Prehistory: The Archaeology of Prince William Sound, Alaska* (1966 [1956]) established a cultural sequence from excavations at Palugvik and Palutat rock shelters. Work with Athapaskan Indian cultures of the Yukon inspired her ambitious *Prehistory of Northern North America As Seen From the Yukon* (1947), which included detailed distributional analyses of cultural traits found across northern North America and North Asia. *The Story of a Tlingit Community* (1960) and *Under Mount St. Elias* (1972) are original contributions to Northwest Coast Indian prehistory and ethnography that are unmatched in scope and depth. Many of her insights into prehistory derive from her expert use of the direct historical method and intensive work with Native Americans who are experts. Laguna was the first vice president of the Society for American Archaeology and received that organization's fiftieth-anniversary award in 1986. That same year she was presented with the Distinguished Service Award of the American Anthropological Association.

Madonna Moss

Further Readings

Laguna, F. de. 1947. *The Prehistory of Northern North America As Seen From the Yukon.* Memoir no. 3. Society for American Archaeology, Washington, D.C.

———. 1960. *The Story of a Tlingit Community: A Problem in the Relationship Between Archeological, Ethnological and Historical Methods.* Bulletin no. 172. Bureau of American Ethnology, Smithsonian Institution, Washington, D.C.

———. 1966 [1956]. *Chugach Prehistory: The Archaeology of Prince William Sound, Alaska.* Publications in Anthropology no. 13. University of Washington Press, Seattle.

———. 1972. *Under Mount St. Elias: The History and Culture of the Yakutat Tlingit.* Contributions to Anthropology no. 7. Smithsonian Institution, Washington, D.C.

———. 1975 [1934]. *The Archaeology of Cook Inlet.* University of Pennsylvania Press, Philadelphia.

———. 1977. *Voyage to Greenland: A Personal Initiation into Anthropology.* Norton, New York.

Laguna, F. de., F.A. Riddell, D.F. McGeein, K.S. Lane, and J.A. Freed. 1964. *Archeology of the Yakutat Bay Area, Alaska.* Bulletin no. 192. Bureau of American Ethnology, Smithsonian Institution, Washington, D.C.

McClellan, C. 1990. Frederica de Laguna and the Pleasures of Anthropology. *American Ethnologist* 16(4):766–785.

Lake Abert

Lake Abert is a closed-basin lake in the northern Great Basin in south-central Oregon fed by the Chewaucan River that passes through the Chewaucan Marshes in the same basin. More than 300 archaeological sites are found around the lake, river, and marshes, including 76 with house features (Pettigrew 1985; Oetting 1988, 1989, 1990). In the years 2050–50 B.C. (4000–2000 years B.P.), sites were located in diverse settings across the basin, but, after 50 B.C. (2000 years B.P.), they were primarily located near wetlands (Oetting 1989). Pithouse villages were first occupied ca. 2050 B.C. (4000 years B.P.), but most were inhabited after 50 B.C. (2000 years B.P.). All are located adjacent to wetlands. These settlement patterns suggest the development of an increasingly sedentary lifestyle focused on the use of wetlands resources (Oetting 1989).

Albert C. Oetting

Further Readings

Oetting, A.C. 1988. *Archaeological Investigations on the East Shore of Lake Abert, Lake County Oregon,* vol. 2. OSMA Report 88–6. Oregon State Museum of Anthropology, Eugene.

———. 1989. *Villages and Wetlands Adaptations in the Northern Great Basin: Chronology and Land Use in the Lake Abert-Chewaucan Marsh Basin, Lake County, Oregon.* Anthropological Papers no. 41. Department of Anthropology, University of Oregon, Eugene.

———. 1990. Testing Housepits at the ZX Ranch Site, Lake County, Oregon: A Report on the 1939 Investigations. *Journal of California and Great Basin Anthropology* 12(1):101–111.

Pettigrew, R.M. 1985. *Archaeological Investigations on the East Shore of Lake Abert, Lake County, Oregon,* vol. 1. Anthropological Papers no. 32. Department of Anthropology, University of Oregon, Eugene.

Lake Forest Archaic

Lake Forest Archaic is a useful, if flawed, heuristic concept that draws attention to the cultural traits that are shared by the diverse Middle to Late Archaic (ca. 4050–1050 B.C., or 6000–3000 years B.P.) cultures of the region that includes the western Great Lakes, the St. Lawrence Valley, and northern New England. These cultures constitute the Lake Forest Archaic Culture Area. Lake Forest is also the name of a biological region, as described below. The flaw is the temptation to assume that the distribution of the culture area exactly coincides with the boundaries of a biotic area. Cultures are rarely so rigidly bounded. Nevertheless, sufficient general correlation has been demonstrated in this instance to persuade archaeologists of its utility for purposes of generalization. Indeed, in certain parts of the Lake Forest Archaic cultural area, the correspondence with the distribution of the Lake Forest biotic area itself is exact and statistically impressive. In southern Ontario, for example, all known sites of the Laurentian culture, the best-defined eastern expression of the Lake Forest Archaic, are confined to the easternmost section of the boundaries of that forest type. Numerous specimens of Laurentian and Laurentianlike artifacts—particularly projectile points—occur well west of this boundary in southernmost Ontario and on into the lower peninsula of Michigan. But they do not recur in regular and repeated association with the suite of artifacts that collectively defines the culture.

The name "Lake Forest Archaic" derives from the Lake Forest, or Canadian, biome of mixed conifers (mainly hemlock and pine) and northern hardwoods (principally beech, sugar maple, yellow birch, white ash, and basswood). This biological zone is transitional between the coniferous Boreal Forest to the north, the Hudsonian biome across central and northern Canada south of the tree line, and the broadleaf, deciduous, Carolinian forest to the south and southeast. Like the Hudsonian zone with its Shield Archaic culture, and the Carolinian with its "Narrow Point" Archaic cultures, the Lake Forest biome roughly coincides with the distribution of Lake Forest Archaic cultures, which are thought to exhibit adaptations appropriate to the biome's particular mix of resources.

The most conspicuous exemplars of the Lake Forest Archaic are the so-called Old Copper culture of Wisconsin and Michigan, and the Vergennes, Brewerton, and other "Laurentian Archaic" cultures of upstate New York, southern Ontario and Quebec, and northern (especially northwestern) New England. These and related manifestations are believed to date to ca. 3500–1000 B.C. (5450–2950 years B.P.). Broad-bladed, side-notched projectile points, called Otter Creek, Raddatz, and other regional names, are often associated with gouges, adzes, plummets, stemmed points and/or knives, ulus (half-moon-shaped knives), simple forms of bannerstones, and tanged and barbed bone and antler points and harpoons. Many remarkably similar examples of these forms made of ground slate in the eastern part of the Lake Forest region were made of native copper in the west.

Through the former, clear connections may be seen with the Maritime Archaic cultures of coastal New England, the Maritimes, and Newfoundland-Labrador. Although important, heavy ground and polished stone tools are not as numerous in the Lake Forest Archaic as in contemporary cultures to the south.

Fishing was of great importance to Lake Forest people, although the techniques of capture used differed somewhat from those used by people to the south. While fishhooks and gorges of bone and copper were used by both, leisters and harpoons, as well as nets, were much more important in the Lake Forest region. Hunting was regionally and seasonally imperative, especially the taking of white-tailed deer, black bear, and beaver, in addition to gray squirrels, raccoon, and cottontail rabbits. Wild-vegetable foods were not as prominent in the diet as they were in the Carolinian forest, perhaps because they were not as varied or as abundant. Accordingly, stone mortars, pestles, and milling implements are uncommon in Lake Forest Archaic tool assemblages.

As attested by the location of sites, the heaviest human occupation in the Lake Forest region occurred along lake shores and at river mouths, where fishing was best, and in those districts that supported the best hardwood stands, where game animals were consistently present. The presence of sites on many islands, and of adzes and gouges, strongly hints at the making of dugout canoes. Canoes would have had a significance for more than subsistence practices. Such watercraft, which could have included bark canoes, would have facilitated the level of communication—of social interaction—implied by the sharing of so many artifact types and styles throughout the vastness of the Lake Forest biome. The Lake Forest Archaic, in short, may have been a cultural tradition as well as an adaptation.

Ronald J. Mason

Further Readings

Ellis, C.J., I.T. Kenyon, and M.W. Spence. 1990. The Archaic. In *The Archaeology of Southern Ontario to A.D. 1650,* edited by C.J. Ellis and N. Ferris, pp. 65–124. Occasional Publications no. 5. London [Ontario] Chapter, Ontario Archaeological Society, London.

Fitting, J.E. 1975. *The Archaeology of Michigan.* rev. ed. Cranbrook Institute, Bloomfield.

L

Ritchie, W.A. 1965. *The Archaeology of New York State*. Natural History Press, Garden City.

Snow, D.R. 1980. *The Archaeology of New England*. Academic Press, New York.

Tuck, J.A. 1978. Regional Cultural Developments, 3000 to 300 B.C. In *Northeast,* edited by B.G. Trigger. Handbook of North American Indians, vol. 15, W.C. Sturtevant, general editor. Smithsonian Institution, Washington, D.C.

Lamoka Lake Site

William Ritchie excavated on the Lamoka Lake site (2173) in Schuyler County, New York, in 1925, 1958, and 1962. At other times, the site has been compromised by amateur digging. The site is the type site for Lamoka culture, which is regarded as a local variant within a more widespread Mast Forest Archaic adaptation that flourished during the Late Archaic period (4000–1700 B.C., or 5950–3650 cal years B.P.). The site lies on a knoll overlooking the head of the lake from which it takes its name. Diagnostic artifacts include the narrow, stemmed Lamoka point and the beveled adze. A portion of the Lamoka Lake site has been re-created as a life-size diorama with human figures in the New York State Museum in Albany. Calibration of eight radiocarbon age determinations from the Lamoka Lake site strongly suggests that it was occupied sometime in the 3350–3100 B.C. (5300–5050 cal years B.P.) period. This makes it several centuries older than the Frontenac Island site, with which it shares many traits.

White-tailed deer dominated the faunal assemblage, although there were more than 20 other mammalian species present. Remains of passenger pigeons were more frequent than all other bird species combined. Turtles were abundant in the refuse, and bullheads were the most common fish. Good preservation conditions also produced a wide range of bone tools and even coprolites (fossil excrement). Awls, needles, gorges, and shuttles of bone that were used for sewing and net making were numerous. Excavators also recovered bone scrapers, punches, daggers, points, and shaft straighteners. Personal objects included bird-bone tubes, flutes, and whistles, and pendants of antler, tooth, and bone. Barbed points, or harpoon heads, were not present. Neither the chert and pyrite fire-making kits nor the pebbles used for stone boiling that were found at the later Frontenac Island site were recovered at Lamoka Lake.

The chipped-stone-tool inventory was dominated by the narrow-stemmed Lamoka point type. This was probably used on spear-thrower darts, as the bow and arrow had not yet been introduced to the region. Ground-stone tools included mortars, pestles, mullers, beveled adzes, celts, and hammerstones; stone plummets were absent. Heavy woodworking tools imply the manufacture of dugout canoes. The remains of acorns and hickory nuts in pits and around hearths combine with food-grinding implements to indicate that the gathering of mast was an important subsistence activity. The tool inventory also suggests that the site was used as a base for both fishing and hunting. Floral and faunal data suggest that seasonal occupation extended through the warm months and into the fall.

Ritchie also found 14 complete flexed burials and portions of 34 others. The initial analysis of these remains suggested that there were two populations present at Lamoka Lake, one long headed and the other broad headed. This distinction and the speculations about intrusion, miscegenation, and assimilation that it inspired have all since been discredited. Dog remains were recovered from refuse layers, but dog burials were not found. Some human remains were also found mixed with other refuse. Fractures of human long bones identical to those found on deer and other game suggest occasional cannibalism. Two burials were of headless, mutilated young men. These and at least one other burial on the site had embedded spear points as evidence of violent death.

Many hearths, pits, and postmolds were found during Ritchie's excavations. Ritchie inferred that these represented the remains of at least 10 full or partial outlines of roughly rectangular houses averaging ca. 4 m (13 feet) on their longer axes. It is likely that no more than two structures ever existed at the same time and that the archaeological pattern has been confused by repeated occupations and rebuilding episodes.

Dean R. Snow

Further Readings

Ritchie, W.A. 1932. The Lamoka Lake Site. *Researches and Transactions of the New York State Archeological Association* 7:4.

———. 1980. *The Archaeology of New York State.* Harbor Hill Books, Harrison.

Ritchie, W.A., and R.E. Funk. 1973. *Aboriginal Settlement Patterns in the Northeast.* Memoir no. 20. New York State Museum and Science Service, Albany.

See also FRONTENAC ISLAND SITE; MAST FOREST ARCHAIC

Lange-Ferguson Site

The Lange-Ferguson site (39SH33) is a mammoth kill-butchering locality preserved in sediments of a late Pleistocene/early Holocene pond or bog in the White River Badlands of South Dakota. Excavations conducted at the site by L. Adrien Hannus of Augustana College, Sioux Falls, South Dakota, in 1980–1984 established the presence of a Clovis technocultural complex.

Cultural deposits are preserved in at least two butte remnants situated between intermittent drainages that transport runoff into the White River, located to the north. The primary activity area of the site consists of the butchered remains of an adult and a juvenile mammoth killed or scavenged by Clovis hunters. Both animals were systematically butchered using culturally modified elements of mammoth bone. A second activity area at the site, in a context stratigraphically related to the first area, contained three Clovis points.

The recovery of bone expediency tools provides insights into butchering systematics associated with the Clovis culture. Reconstruction of the butchering sequence is supported by the secure stratigraphic context of the site and excellent taphonomic data. Clovis hunters used heavy cleaving tools and bone flakes shaped on mammoth flat-bone and long-bone units. This bone technology appears to mimic that of Euro-Asiatic sites of the Upper Paleolithic.

A suite of radiocarbon age determinations has been obtained for Lange-Ferguson. One date, obtained from a sample of adult mammoth bone (collagen carbon), puts the butchering event at 8780 B.C. ± 530 (10,730 years B.P.). The age of a second sample, derived from organic material sealing the sediments encasing the bonebed, is 8720 B.C. ± 300 (10,670 years B.P.). Both ages are based on the ^{14}C half-life of 5,568 years. Reconstruction of the local environment at Lange-Ferguson is based on corroborating evidence from invertebrate (mollusks) and vertebrate fauna, geomorphological and sedimentary analyses, and fossil pollen and phytoliths.

L. Adrien Hannus

Further Readings
Frison, G.C. 1991. *Prehistoric Hunters of the High Plains.* 2nd ed. Academic Press, San Diego.

Hannus, L.A. 1989. Flaked Mammoth Bone From the Lange-Ferguson Site, White River Badlands Area, South Dakota. In *Bone Modification,* edited by R. Bonnichsen and M. Sorg, pp. 395–412. Center for the Study of the First Americans, University of Maine, Orono.

———. 1990a. The Lange-Ferguson Site: A Case for Mammoth Bone Butchering Tools. In *Megafauna and Man: Discoveries of America's Heartland,* edited by L. Agenbroad, J. Mead, and L. Nelson, pp. 86–99. Mammoth Site of Hot Springs, South Dakota; Northern Arizona University, Flagstaff.

———. 1990b. Mammoth Hunting in the New World. In *Hunters of the Recent Past,* edited by L.B. Davis and B.O.K. Reeves, pp. 47–67. Unwin Hyman, London.

Language

The number of indigenous languages of North America, those still spoken and extinct ones that have left some record, is estimated at ca. 400. Given the indeterminacy of the language-dialect distinction, an exact figure is not possible. The large number of languages is matched by their grammatical and phonological diversity. However, such differences of structure do not exclude common origin, as shown by the structural difference between, for example, English and Armenian—both Indo-European. To derive hypotheses of interest to archaeologists and historians requires a classification into families of languages with correct hierarchic subdivisions, each reflecting common origin from a single earlier language with subsequent differentiation. A large number of such groupings of a lower level—on the order of the Romance languages, for example—are discernible even on a superficial inspection. Of such groupings, some consist of single isolated languages, whereas others, like Algonkian, are widespread and contain numerous languages. The most influential of classifications of this type was that of John Wesley Powell (1891), which assigned the languages north of Mexico to 58 separate stocks. Beginning shortly after 1900, a number of investigators like Alfred E. Kroeber and Roland B. Dixon, who worked in California, which contained 22 of Powell's stocks, consolidated many of these stocks into larger groupings like Na-Dene, Penutian, Hokan, and Uto-Aztecan. Particularly striking was Edward Sapir's (1913) linking of Algonkian to two small stocks in California, Wiyot and Yurok, now accepted after long controversy. Beginning ca. 1950, a conservative trend developed whose results are summarized in a work edited by Lyle Campbell and Marianne Mithun (1979) in which 63 independent stocks—more than Powell's—are distinguished for North America, excluding Mexican outliers. In 1987, Joseph Greenberg, reversing this trend, presented a drastically different picture with three stocks for all the Americas. The first is Eskimo-Aleut, with affiliations in northern Asia; the second is Na-Dene, centered in the Canadian northwest; and the third is Amerind, which embraces all of the remaining languages. As noted in Greenberg et al. (1986), this classification shows close agreement with the dental and genetic evidence. From these results, there derives a theory of the peopling of the Americas by three migrations. The oldest must be Amerind because of its extensive territory, most southerly location, and great internal differentiation. It has been identified with the Clovis culture that first appeared ca. 9550 B.C. (11,500 years B.P.) and rapidly spread to Central and South America. The Na-Dene was probably the second, and the Eskimo-Aleut would be the most recent. This certainly holds for the linguistic expansion of the Inuit Eskimo from central Alaska to Greenland with hardly more than dialectal divergence, but the split with Yuit Eskimo and particularly the earlier one with Aleut might predate the Na-Dene. Glottochronological dates suggest ca. 7050 B.C. (9000 years B.P.) for the Na-Dene and 2050 B.C. (4000 years B.P.) for Eskimo-Aleut.

Joseph Greenberg

Further Readings

Campbell, L., and M. Mithun (editors). 1979. *The Languages of Native America: Historical and Comparative Assessment.* University of Texas Press, Austin.

Greenberg, J. 1987. *Language in the Americas.* Stanford University Press, Palo Alto.

Greenberg, J., C. Turner, and P. Zegura. 1986. The Settlement of the Americas: A Comparison of the Linguistic, Dental, and Genetic Evidence. *Current Anthropology* 27:477–497.

Powell, J.W. 1891. *Indian Linguistic Families North of Mexico.* Annual Report of the Bureau of American Ethnology, vol. 7. Smithsonian Institution, Washington, D.C.

Sapir, E. 1913. Wiyot and Yurok, Algonkin Languages of California. *American Anthropology* 17:188–194.

Largo-Gallina Branch

The Largo-Gallina branch is situated east of the San Juan Basin and northwest of the Rio Grande region of north-central New Mexico. The area is contained within the southern Colorado Plateau physiographic province. The rugged landscape in the core of the Largo-Gallina habitat, with elevations of 2,250–2,500 m (2,460–2,734 yards), is characterized by alternating high mesas, steep ridges, narrow valleys, and badlands. Tree-ring dates reveal that the Largo-Gallina locale was colonized by Anasazi farmers soon after A.D. 1050 (900 years B.P.). The lack of reported remains dating to the eleventh and twelfth centuries, however, reflects investigative biases inherent in the body of available survey data rather than an actual paucity of early occupation. The density of cultural properties is particularly high in the Llaves Valley after A.D. 1250 (700 years B.P.), and numerous, clustered tree-ring dates indicate that the settlement of the locale by large, permanent populations persisted until the end of the thirteenth century. Following this time, the Largo-Gallina branch—like the central San Juan Basin and the Four Corners region—was abandoned by prehistoric Pueblo farmers.

The archaeological reconstruction of the culture history of the Largo-Gallina Anasazi is based primarily on the study of late Gallina phase (A.D. 1200–1275, or 750–675 years B.P.) villages, which are typically composed of two to eight circular pithouses and rectangular, surface masonry structures, or "unit houses," composed of one to four rooms. Pithouses, which possess hearths, ventilators, air-flow deflectors, storage bins, and benches, are associated with habitation. Unit houses, in contrast, appear to have been used for a variety of other purposes, such as drying agricultural produce, storing food, and keeping turkeys.

Even though the settlement pattern is dominated by mixed pithouse and unit-house communities that are often tightly packed on the crests of high ridges, the Largo-Gallina branch is best known in the archaeological literature for spectacular, even if uncommon, cliff houses and towers. Cliff houses resemble ridge-top unit houses architecturally, but these picturesque sites are situated in remote rock shelters. The circular, masonry towers occur in some of the larger mixed pithouse and unit-house communities. Although some investigators suggest that towers may have been constructed as part of an intercommunity network of signal stations, not all of these features are found in settings that provide good overlooks of the enclosing landscape. Excavation data, furthermore, indicate that most of these structures were used for storage of foodstuffs.

Prevailing interpretations of Largo-Gallina settlement patterns are subject to question because of the focus of most research on the large, more easily visible villages of the late Gallina phase. Residential settlements of the early Gallina phase (A.D. 1000–1200, or 950–750 years B.P.) are small, with only one to three pit structures. Even though there are hundreds of shallow pithouse depressions dating to this early phase throughout the Largo-Gallina area, the scattered distribution of the settlements across mesa tops, slopes of low hills, gently rising valley sides, and drainage bottomlands contributes to their oversight in many archaeological accounts.

One consequence of the prevailing research emphasis on late Gallina-phase manifestations is the depiction by archaeologists of Largo-Gallina Anasazi as geographically isolated, culturally conservative, and prone to endemic warfare. Interpretations of cultural isolation are based upon the poverty of material traces that would suggest contact between the Largo-Gallina Anasazi and other Puebloan peoples in the northern Rio Grande Valley, the San Juan Basin, and the Mesa Verde district. The high degree of homogeneity in the manufacture and design of Gallina pottery through time and across geographic space is interpreted as evidence of the prevailing conservatism of Largo-Gallina Anasazi. The fact that most excavated late pithouse villages possess defensive locations and are protected by wooden palisades and other fortifications, and the evidence of burning are considered indicators of widespread conflict.

Characterizations of Largo-Gallina peoples as "aberrant and war-like provincials" are problematic because of significant limitations in the research designs with which archaeologists have studied Largo-Gallina cultural phenomena (after Seaman 1976:122). The supposition that the isolation, conservatism, and violence of these Puebloan peoples were an inevitable consequence of competition for basic economic resources underlies traditional archaeological interpretations of the culture history of this locale. Investigators, however, have neglected to consider the dynamic ecological and cultural contexts of regional Anasazi populations. These may be the processes responsible for archaeologically observed changes in local subsistence and settlement patterns over time.

J. Mackey and S.J. Holbrook (1978) provided the first significant attempt to address the problem of Largo-Gallina culture history from a systemic perspective. These researchers suggest that decreased frequencies of tree pollen, the appearance of stunted maize cobs and kernels, a reduction in the numbers of moisture-adapted rodents, and evidence of streambed downcutting demonstrate that the Largo-Gallina area became increasingly arid in the years A.D. 1250–1300 (700–650 years B.P.). They conclude that environmental deterioration was the primary causal factor behind the outbreak of open hostilities and the abandonment of this locale by Anasazi populations at the end of the thirteenth century.

Although Mackey and Holbrook's explanatory framework is an important contribution to understanding processes of change over time, it discounts the possible role that Anasazi peoples themselves may have played in actively changing their own conditions for living. In a review of diverse paleoclimatological and archaeological evidence, K.F. Anschuetz (1991) suggests that despite their intensification of agricultural practices, Largo-Gallina farmers were unable to produce sufficient harvests to support themselves in the face of significantly drier climatic conditions in the late thirteenth century. Because of a regional framework of open competition among neighboring populations for the control of local territories, the Largo-Gallina population could not easily immigrate to new areas. Instead, they chose to intensify their hunting of mule deer and elk to make up for shortfalls in their farming economy. The subsequent rapid depletion of large-bodied game animals evidenced in the

L

archaeological record, however, appears to have heightened food shortages in the long term. The persistence of stressful conditions resulted in the need for the Largo-Gallina Anasazi to develop new, more costly cultural mechanisms that permitted their removal to other locales, possibly the Jemez Canyon area to the south. An interesting question is why a segment of the Largo-Gallina population did not remain in permanent residence in their traditional homeland after A.D. 1300 (650 years B.P.), for it apparently continued to offer sufficient plant, animal, and arable land resources to support a smaller community of Anasazi peoples.

Kurt F. Anschuetz

Further Readings

Anschuetz, K.F. 1991. Natural Periodicity and Human Agency: Reevaluating the Anasazi Abandonment of the Gallina District, New Mexico. Paper presented at the Fourteenth Annual Conference of the Society of Ethnobiology, St. Louis.

Dick, H.W. 1976. *Archeological Excavations in the Llaves Area, Santa Fe National Forest, New Mexico, 1972–1974: 1. Architecture.* Archaeology Report no. 13. U.S. Forest Service, Southwest Region, Albuquerque.

Eddy, F.W. 1966. *Prehistory in the Navajo Reservoir District, Northwestern New Mexico.* Papers in Anthropology no. 15, pts. 1–2. Museum of New Mexico Press, Santa Fe.

Ellis, F.H. 1988. *Canjilon Mountain: Hunting and Gathering Sites. From Drought to Drought: An Archaeological Record of Life Patterns As Developed by the Gallina Indians of North-Central New Mexico (A.D. 1050–1300),* vol. 1. Sunstone Press, Santa Fe; Florence Hawley Ellis Museum of Anthropology at Ghost Ranch, Abiquiu.

Fiero, K. 1978. Archaeological Investigations at LA 11850: A Gallina Phase Village on the Continental Divide, Rio Arriba County, New Mexico (review draft). Laboratory of New Mexico Note no. 111f. Research Section, Museum of New Mexico, Santa Fe.

Ford, R.I., A.H. Schroeder, and S.L. Peckham. 1972. Three Perspectives on Puebloan Prehistory. In *New Perspectives on the Pueblos,* edited by A. Ortiz, pp. 19–39. University of New Mexico Press, Albuquerque.

Hall, E.T., Jr. 1944. *Early Stockaded Settlements in the Governador, New Mexico.* Studies in Archaeology and Ethnology, vol. 2, pt. 1. Columbia University Press, New York.

Hibben, F.C. 1937. *Excavation of Riana Ruin and Chama Valley Survey.* Anthropology Series Bulletin no. 300, vol. 2, no. 1. University of New Mexico Press, Albuquerque.

———. 1938. The Gallina Phase. *American Antiquity* 4:131–136.

———. 1948. The Gallina Architectural Forms. *American Antiquity* 14:32–36.

———. 1949. The Pottery of the Gallina Complex. *American Antiquity* 14:194–202.

Holbrook, S.J., and J.C. Mackey. 1976. Prehistoric Environmental Change in Northern New Mexico: Evidence From a Gallina Phase Archaeological Site. *Kiva* 41:309–317.

Mackey, J., and S.J. Holbrook. 1978. Environmental Reconstruction and the Abandonment of the Largo-Gallina Area. *Journal of Field Archaeology* 5(1):29–49.

Mera, H.P. 1938. Some Aspects of the Largo Cultural Phase, Northern New Mexico. *American Antiquity* 3:236–242.

Pattison, N.B. 1968. *Nogales Cliff House: A Largo-Gallina Site.* Master's thesis, Department of Anthropology, University of New Mexico, Albuquerque.

Robinson, W.J., B.G. Harrill, and R.L. Warren. 1974. *Tree-Ring Dates From New Mexico B, Chaco-Gobernador Area.* Laboratory of Tree-Ring Research, University of Arizona, Tucson.

Robinson, W.J., and R.L. Warren. 1971. *Tree-Ring Dates From New Mexico C-D, Northern Rio Grande Area.* Laboratory of Tree-Ring Research, University of Arizona, Tucson.

Seaman, T.J. 1976. Excavation of LA 11843: An Early Stockaded Settlement of the Gallina Phase. Archeological Investigations on the San Juan-to-Ojo 345 kV Transmission Line for the Public Service Company of New Mexico. Laboratory of New Mexico Note no. 111g. Research Section, Museum of New Mexico, Santa Fe.

Whiteaker, R.J. 1976. Excavation of LA 11841. Laboratory of New Mexico Note no. 111d. Research Section, Museum of New Mexico, Santa Fe.

Late Wisconsin

The Quaternary era of geologic time was characterized by many intervals of continental glaciation, as shown by the oxygen-isotope stratigraphy of deep-sea sediment cores. This stratigraphy records the volume of water extracted from world oceans and stored in ice sheets. Major continental glaciations occurred about every 100,000 years, with the last one in North America called the Wisconsin. The maximum of the last interglaciation was ca. 125,000 years ago. Thereafter, ice sheets grew and fluctuated in size several times during the Early and Middle Wisconsin and came to a climax in the Late Wisconsin. This last phase of the Wisconsin glaciation is generally dated on a global basis at ca. 18,050–16,050 B.C. (20,000–18,000 years B.P.), although the terminal moraines of some of the lobes of the Laurentide ice sheet in the Midwest may be as old as 22,050 B.C. (24,000 years B.P.) (e.g., in Ohio) and as young as 12,050 B.C. (14,000 years B.P.) (e.g., in Iowa). These fluctuations in ice-sheet size are largely a direct response to global climatic change as controlled by cyclical shifts in the Earth/Sun orbital relations, which determine the seasonal distribution of solar radiation at different latitudes. The buildup of Late Wisconsin ice sheets was thus a result of the decrease in solar radiation received in the Northern Hemisphere in summer—a cycle that reached its maximum ca. 18,050 B.C. (20,000 years B.P.). The wastage of the ice sheets resulted from an increase in summer temperature in the Northern Hemisphere, which reached a maximum ca. 8050 B.C. (10,000 years B.P.). Because of the vast mass of the ice sheets, a certain lag in response to both growth and wastage was involved, and the Laurentide ice sheet was not completely wasted from Canada until ca. 4050 B.C. (6000 years B.P.), at which time sea level, which had been lowered when the ocean water was stored in the ice sheets, rose to its modern position.

Minor fluctuations in the margins of the several ice lobes in the Great Lakes region, resulting in the formation of recessional moraines, may have been caused by minor climatic fluctuations, but some of them may reflect certain instabilities in the flow patterns of the ice itself, as controlled by the thickness, temperature, and water content of the ice and the nature of the glacial bed. As a result, the advances of adjacent ice lobes are not in all cases concurrent.

Because of the gradual nature of climatic changes during the Quaternary, the assignment of particular years for the beginning and end of the subdivisions is somewhat arbitrary. The Quaternary consists of the Pleistocene and the Holocene. The boundary between them should reasonably be placed at the time of maximum rate of climatic change as recorded by various proxy records, providing the records can be dated. Because glacier margins, vegetation, or other landscape features respond to climatic change with lags, and because the climatic changes themselves are gradual and cross various thresholds for different indicators, assigning a date to the end of the Late Wisconsin has been controversial. Resolution of the problem was reached by designating the figure of 8050 B.C. (10,000 years B.P.) for the Pleistocene/Holocene boundary. This does not solve the problem completely, however, because radiocarbon years, on which the ages of most features are determined, are not the same as calendar years, which are better established on the basis of tree-ring chronologies. In fact, radiocarbon years are as much as 1,000 years younger than dendroyears from 8050 B.C. (10,000 years B.P.). Furthermore, the calibration of radiocarbon years with dendroyears indicates that the radiocarbon content of the atmosphere has varied substantially over time and that during an interval lasting ca. 400 dendroyears, all of the radiocarbon dates indicate about the same age, ca. 7550 B.C. (9500 years B.P.). Thus, the end of the Late Wisconsin, although designated as 8050 B.C. (10,000 years B.P.) in radiocarbon years as a matter of convenience, still has its problems in definition. As long as no independent, more accurate chronologies are available for particular events, such as written documents of historic time, the radiocarbon chronology is still the most practical means of reconstructing past events. And that certainly applies to the Late Wisconsin.

The Wisconsin was named for the extensive glacial landforms in the state of that name. These landforms include moraines, drumlins, eskers, tunnel valleys, lake plains, lake-outlet valleys, and many other features. They are now all assigned to the Late Wisconsin, for the glacial record of the Early and Middle Wisconsin has been buried or eroded and has been identified in only a few localities in Canada. Similar features are found in other states of the Great Lakes region, as well as farther east into New England and the Canadian maritime provinces and farther west in the northern Great Plains and the Canadian prairie provinces. In fact, the term "Late Wisconsin" is appropriately applied over the western, northern, and eastern perimeters of the Laurentide ice sheet. The term was introduced to differentiate a time term from a materials term, but it has not been widely used.

Contemporaneous with the Late Wisconsin glaciation of the Laurentide ice sheet was the development of the Cordilleran ice sheet in the mountains of western Canada, extending in ice lobes into northern Washington, Idaho, and Montana. At the same time, mountain glaciers and ice caps developed in the western United States, especially on the Yellowstone Plateau, the Sierra Nevada, and the northern and middle Rocky Mountains. The term "Late Pinedale," taken from the Wind River Mountains and applied to other ranges in the Rocky Mountains, is correlative with the Late Wisconsin. The Laurentide ice sheet was joined with the Cordilleran along the Rocky Mountain front in Canada, and their separation during wastage of the two ice sheets near the end of the Late Wisconsin formed the Alberta Corridor for the immigration of plants and animals, including Paleoindians.

Besides expansion of the Laurentide ice sheet and fluctuations of its various ice lobes in the Great Lakes region, the Late Wisconsin was characterized by vegetation that was distinctly different from today's, not only in distribution but also in composition. The Late Wisconsin forest of the Midwest, characterized by spruce and minor amounts of north-temperate hardwoods, has no modern analogue today, for the Boreal Forest of Canada has no such hardwoods and has abundant jack pine. Vertebrate microfaunas recovered from caves and other Late Wisconsin deposits include species that today have disparate distributions; for example, western types mixed with eastern. These "disharmonious" assemblages must be attributed to climatic regimes that today are found nowhere in North America, perhaps because of different seasonality patterns related to Earth/Sun orbital changes. The change in climatic and vegetational patterns at the end of the Late Wisconsin is considered by some to be the ultimate cause for the extinction of the Pleistocene megafauna.

In the American Southwest, the most distinctive feature of the Late Wisconsin was the expansion of lakes in the now-desert basins. Although the colder summer climates were effective in lowering the vegetation zones in the mountains and reducing evaporation in the lowland areas, a more important factor in controlling lake levels was the greater precipitation—the result of the southward displacement of the mid-latitude jet stream, which controls the location of storm tracks in the west. This displacement resulted from the existence of the massive Laurentide-Cordilleran ice sheet in Canada, which formed a major barrier to the entry of the jet stream into the continent. The relations are demonstrated by the results of numerical paleoclimatic models of the general circulation of the atmosphere. Another result of the model simulation for the time of the Late Wisconsin maximum was the identification of a branch of the jet stream that passed along the northern margin of the ice sheet near the Arctic Coast, bringing cold air southeastward into the North Atlantic and causing the expansion of sea ice far to the south. This, in turn, affected the climate of Europe, which at that time was characterized by permafrost and tundra vegetation all the way to the Alps; treeless vegetation prevailed even in the Mediterranean lowlands.

Elsewhere in the world, the climate of the time equivalent to the Late Wisconsin was greatly different from that of today, with details depending on location. Even in the Southern Hemisphere, the climatic patterns were similar, according to records contained in cores of the Antarctic ice sheet and the ocean sediments and in the glacial and paleoecological sequences in the Andes, Australia, and other southern regions. The massive extent of the North American ice sheets in the Late Wisconsin apparently directly or indirectly affected the climate of much of the globe.

H.E. Wright, Jr.

Further Readings

Porter, S.C. (editor). 1983. *The Late Quaternary Environments of the United States: 1. The Late Pleistocene.* University of Minnesota Press, Minneapolis.

Ruddiman, W.F., and H.E. Wright, Jr. 1987. *North America and Adjacent Oceans During the Last Deglaciation.* Geology of North America, vol. K-3. Geological Society of America, Boulder.

Wright, H.E., Jr., J.E. Kutzbach, T. Webb III, W.F. Ruddiman, F.A. Street-Perrot, and P.J. Bartlein (editors). 1993. *Global Climates Since the Last Glacial Maximum.* University of Minnesota Press, Minneapolis.

Late Woodland

The Late Woodland is the third and last period or stage of the Woodland tradition in eastern North America. Like the initial Early Woodland period, the Late Woodland time span varies widely from one region to another. In the Southeast and the southern Midwest, Late Woodland societies are thought to be present by A.D. 200–450 (1750–1500 years B.P.), and to have transformed to local Mississippian cultures in the A.D. 750–1000 (1200–950 years B.P.) period. By contrast, in the Upper Midwest, the Late Woodland period extends from ca. A.D. 400 (1550 years B.P.) to the historic period (the A.D. 1600s); in the Northeast, from ca. A.D. 1000 (950 years B.P.) to the historic period (the A.D. 1500s). There are three main reasons for these dating differences. First, the transition from the Middle to the Late Woodland and the transformation of Late Woodland societies to Mississippian were processes rather than discrete events. As a result, archaeologists place the dividing lines between these units at different times, include 200–300-year transition periods (that may have special names, such as Emergent Mississippian), or both. In addition, the processes may have occurred at different times in different regions. Second, different criteria are often used to define the start and end of the Late Woodland period in different regions and even in the same region by different archaeologists. For example, in the Upper Mississippi drainage, the beginning of the period is set at the transition from Havana-Hopewell ceramics to something else (ca. A.D. 250–400, or 1700–1550 years B.P.), while, in the Northeast, it is generally set at the introduction of maize agriculture and large, nucleated settlements (ca. A.D. 1000, or 950 years B.P.). Third, while the emergence of maize-based Mississippian agricultural societies to the south by ca. A.D. 1000 (950 years B.P.) is used to mark the end of the Woodland tradition in that area, an equally dramatic and abrupt, if less spectacular, transition of maize-based agricultural societies in the Northeast is considered to have occurred within the Woodland tradition, mainly because these societies continued to use "Woodland" pottery. The latter is a vestige of the taxonomic period in Eastern Woodlands archaeology, during which archaeological units were defined using lists of traits rather than adaptive settlement-subsistence strategies. It is probably fair to conclude that the "Late Woodland" concept is fairly well defined in specific regions but lacks integrity at broader geographic levels of integration.

Interpretations of the Late Woodland in cultural terms are closely tied to ideas about its relationship with the preceding Hopewell phenomenon (Yerkes 1988). Middle Woodland "Hopewell" societies were archaeologically spectacular compared to their Late Woodland descendants. The emergence of Late Woodland societies is marked by a striking decline in burial ceremonialism and amounts of exotic trade goods and by a disappearance of the ceremonial-art materials for which Hopewell is famous. At one time, archaeologists generally agreed that the disappearance of these traits heralded a decline in the Woodland tradition. Among the reasons given for this seemingly drastic decline were the onset of colder climatic conditions ca. A.D. 400 (1550 years B.P.), a shift from the spear and atlatl to the bow and arrow at about the same time, and population growth. According to these interpretations, these changes led to a decrease in natural-food resources (climatic deterioration); greater hunting success, a decimation of game herds, population growth, and a rise in warfare (bow and arrow); and a new, more dispersed settlement pattern and a more diffuse range of subsistence practices (population growth).

In contrast, more recent interpretations generally consider the Late Woodland a dynamic, fascinating period that was a logical consequence of long-term social processes that extend back into the Archaic period (ca. 8050–1050 B.C., or 10,000–3000 years B.P.). According to one interpretation, an increasing reliance on horticultural produce (the Eastern Agricultural complex) led to a leavening of subsistence differences between regions, which decreased the incentive for the long-distance exchange relationships that in this reading were the glue that held the Hopewell Interaction Sphere together. In another, not incompatible, interpretation, the same growing reliance on horticultural produce increased the chances of serious subsistence risk through catastrophic fluctuations in rainfall or temperature, or both, by removing the buffer provided by a more diffuse resource base. Countering strategies developed to minimize this risk included the development of food-storage systems, diversification of the crops planted, scattering gardens in more diverse locations, and the development of reciprocal ties with more distant kin to ensure an alternative settlement location in case of local subsistence failure. In both views, distinctive Late Woodland subsistence-settlement systems were the product of an increasing domestic orientation after A.D. 200 (1750 years B.P.) that was a result of the increasing success and importance of cultivation as a resource base. From this perspective, the dramatic decrease in the importance of personal prestige, long-distance trade, ceremonial-center construction, and manufacture of Hopewell Interaction Sphere items is an anticipated outcome of these processes.

Whatever the processes that produced Late Woodland societies, they did transform after A.D. 800 (1150 years B.P.) in the Southeast and the southern Midwest into the riverine cultures associated with the Mississippian tradition. In the Southeast in particular, this transformation is preceded by gradual increases in population densities, more complex settlements, increasing reliance on cultivated plants by sedentary communities, continued intercommunity exchange, and more elaborate forms of social organization. Notable examples are the Weeden Island culture along the Gulf Coastal Plain between Florida, Alabama, and Georgia, and the Troyville-Issaquenna culture in the Lower Mississippi Valley in Louisiana and Mississippi. Both exhibit a strong emphasis on ceremonialism centered on the burial of a "chief." Low platform mounds associated with charnel houses appear in Florida, Georgia, Tennessee, Alabama, and Mississippi ca. A.D. 150–400 (1800–1550 years B.P.). Other southeastern Late Woodland cultures are Coles Creek along the Louisiana coast and St. Johns in Florida. McKeithen in northern Florida and Kolomoki in Georgia are among the many important sites of the period. In the years A.D. 700–1000 (1250–950 years B.P.), most but not all of these Late Woodland societies became Mississippian societies dependent on maize agriculture. This transformation was accompanied by dramatic and seemingly abrupt changes in settlement pattern, technology, sociopolitical integration, and subsistence orientation.

To the north in the Mississippi River drainage, Late Woodland peoples adopted at the same time or slightly later a variety of less complex "Upper Mississippian" lifeways that were also based on maize-centered horticulture, settlement aggregation, and changes in technology and sociopolitical organization. Examples are the Fort Ancient and the Oneota cultures in the Midwest. Still farther north where a shorter growing season limited maize production and in the Northeast, local societies continued within the Woodland tradition in the historic period in the A.D. 1500s. Some peoples, such as those who became the Iroquois in New York and southern Ontario, experienced changes in lifeways after A.D. 800–1000 (1150–950 years B.P.) that also included a growing dependence on maize and other cultigens; aggregation into large, often fortified villages; and changes in sociopolitical integration. By A.D. 1400 (550 years B.P.), some of the largest Iroquois settlements contained as many as 1,500 people. Maxon-Derby and Draper represent different types of village sites within this tradition. Comparable changes were even made along the northern periphery of the Eastern Woodlands, where the growing season is also short, by some people who harvested wild rice as a substitute for maize. An example is those people in northern Minnesota who made Sandy Lake pottery. Other "Woodland" peoples along the northern periphery of the eastern Woodlands and in the southern part of the adjacent Subarctic culture area continued an "Archaic" lifeway to the historic period in the A.D. 1600s

Guy Gibbon

Further Readings

Bentz, C. (editor). 1988. *Late Woodland Sites in the American Bottom Uplands.* American Bottom Archaeology, vol. 18. Published for the Illinois Department of Transportation by the University of Illinois Press, Urbana.

Custer, J.F. 1986. *Late Woodland Cultures of the Middle Atlantic Region.* University of Delaware Press, Newark; Associated University Presses, Cranbury.

Fagan, B.M. 1991. *Ancient North America: The Archaeology of a Continent.* Thames and Hudson, New York.

Mason, R. 1981. *Great Lakes Archaeology.* Academic Press, New York.

McPherron, A. 1967. *The Juntunen Site and the Late Woodland Prehistory of the Upper Great Lakes Area.* Anthropological Papers no. 30. Museum of Anthropology, University of Michigan, Ann Arbor.

Moeller, R.W. 1992. *Analyzing and Interpreting Late Woodland Features.* Archaeological Services, Bethlehem.

Nassaney, M.S., and C.R. Cobb (editors). 1991. *Stability, Transformation, and Variation: The Late Woodland Southeast.* Plenum Press, New York.

Reinhart, T.R., and M.E.N. Hodges (editors). 1992. *Middle and Late Woodland Research in Virginia: A Synthesis.* Special Publication no. 29. Archeological Society of Virginia, Richmond.

Snow, D. 1980. *The Archaeology of New England.* Academic Press, New York.

Yerkes, R.W. (editor). 1988. *Interpretations of Culture Change in the Eastern Woodlands During the Late Woodland Period.* Occasional Papers in Anthropology no. 3. Department of Anthropology, Ohio State University, Columbus.

Laurel Incised vessel from the Smith site (21KC3), Koochiching County, Minnesota. (Courtesy of the Wilford Archaeology Laboratory, University of Minnesota)

Laurel Culture

Laurel culture is the descendant of Shield culture in the western half of the Canadian Shield. It occupied an area extending from eastern Quebec across northern Ontario and central and southeastern Manitoba into east-central Saskatchewan and northern Minnesota and Michigan. Resource variety and availability were extremely variable across this region, with food-energy potential increasing as one moved from the Lichen Woodland in the north to the Boreal Forest and then the Great Lakes–St. Lawrence vegetation provinces. Regional expressions of the Laurel culture have been recognized. The descendants of Laurel culture were the Blackduck and Selkirk cultures, which have been equated with the historic Ojibwa and Cree, respectively, although this dichotomy is, in part, simplistic. Laurel culture occupied a region interconnected by major east-west-trending rivers and lakes with numerous other drainage connections, particularly from the north. Thus, exploitation of the often limited food resources of extensive areas could be achieved through an exceptional degree of mobility, which was accomplished by water transport.

It was the diffusion of a northern horizon of pottery technology from eastern Canada, which possibly began as early as 700 B.C. (2650 years B.P.) and eventually extended from the Atlantic Coast to the edge of the Plains, that transformed western Shield-culture bands into the Laurel culture. The Shield-culture occupants of most of northern Quebec did not accept pottery or participate in certain other developments and thus are excluded from the Laurel classification. In addition to the distinctive pottery vessels, bow-and-arrow technology largely replaced earlier spear-thrower and lance weapon systems. The remainder of the toolkit, however, remained basically unchanged, including a wide range of tools and ornaments manufactured from locally available native copper. Fortunately, a few Laurel-culture sites have produced bone tools and debris. Items include socketed toggling harpoons, barbed harpoons, beaver-incisor knives, awls, and snowshoe netting needles. These same sites, all in the southern area of the Laurel-culture distribution, contained mainly moose, beaver, and fish remains, although a wide range of species were exploited. Wild rice has also been recovered from a site in northern Minnesota in what appear to be specialized pits for the preparation of the grain. Base camps were occupied seasonally during the warm months and tended to occur along major river and lake systems, particularly at river mouths or adjacent to fishing pools at the foot of rapids. It is assumed that during the colder portion of the year, small groups of related families moved to winter hunting territories with their fall food reserves.

In the southwestern portion of the Laurel-culture distribution, particularly along the Rainy River between Ontario and Minnesota, large burial-mound clusters are frequently associated with large seasonal base camps. These mounds likely represent a form of territorial marker. While burial-mound ceremonialism undoubtedly diffused to the region from the south, many mound features are distinctly local. Included among these are the construction of accretionary mounds that covered multiple secondary burials, often with clear evidence of the removal of the brain and long-bone marrow. Other than red ocher, grave offerings are rare but do occur within the mound fill, presumably as part of ceremonies related to the mound itself rather than directly to the bodies per se. Such offerings range from a platform pipe likely obtained from the Ohio Valley to projectile points manufactured from North Dakota chalcedony. To the east, in Michigan, an ossuary containing articulated bodies with grave offerings has been recorded. Also, some of the features found in boulder beaches in southeastern Manitoba and along the north shore of Lake Superior, inferred to represent pits used by individuals in search of visions, very likely pertain to Laurel culture.

The distributions of distinctive pottery styles and exotic cherts and native copper indicate that major contacts existed with neighboring cultures in the lower Great Lakes to the east and in the Plains to the west and south. The exotic pottery styles have been interpreted as a product of female intracultural marriages arranged to establish social rights and obligations necessary for trade and other relationships between otherwise unrelated peoples.

Throughout most of its territory, Laurel society was probably unchanged from that of its Shield-culture predecessors. An exception existed in the boundary area between Ontario and Minnesota, where exceptionally rich wild rice and other plant foods, game, and fish resources permitted large population aggregations. This included clustered multifamily dwellings. Certainly, the maintenance of burial-mound ceremonialism over a considerable period of time at specific site locales suggests a level of social organization unlikely to have existed elsewhere in Laurel culture.

The inclination of some scholars to place greater interpretive weight upon radiocarbon dates and ceramic seriation as opposed to stratigraphy, component isolation by isostatic rebound, or the analysis of the totality of cultural systems and the extent of Laurel culture; the characteristically thin deposits at multicomponent sites; and other factors have resulted in conflicting views of Laurel-culture chronology and development. Isostatic rebound refers to the tendency of the Earth's crust to maintain a state

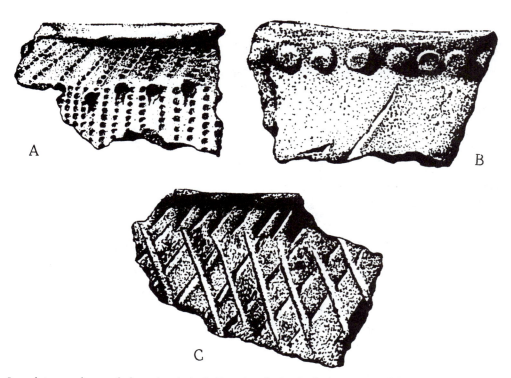

Laurel rims: a, dentate; b, bossed; c, incised. (Drawings by Lee Radzak; courtesy of the Minnesota Archaeological Society)

of equilibrium, with the result that when the crust is depressed by the weight of glacial ice it will recover, or "rebound," when the weight is lessened or removed. In areas such as the north shore of Lake Superior, this leads to archaeological sites of different time periods being isolated on beaches of different elevations above the lake. For an alternate view from what has been presented here, see C.S. Reid and G. Rajnovich (1991).

J.V. Wright

Further Readings

Reid, C.S. "Paddy," and G. Rajnovich. 1991. Laurel: A Re-evaluation of the Spatial, Social and Temporal Paradigms. *Canadian Journal of Archaeology* 15:193–234.

Stoltman, J.B. 1973. *The Laurel Culture in Minnesota*. Minnesota Prehistoric Archaeology Series, Minnesota Historical Society, St. Paul.

Wright, J.V. 1967. *The Laurel Tradition and the Middle Woodland Period*. Bulletin no. 217. National Museum of Canada, Ottawa.

Laurentian Archaic

Laurentian Archaic is one of the principal components of the Lake Forest Archaic. The Laurentian is a Late Archaic cultural continuum of New York, Vermont, and southern Ontario. Its diagnostic attributes, as first described by William A. Ritchie in the 1930 and 1940s, are mainly broad-bladed, side- or corner-notched, chipped projectile points; barbed bone projectile points; ground-slate stemmed projectile points and knives that are often equipped with multinotched tangs, barbs, and ridged blade backs or beveled edges; chipped- or ground-slate ulus, or crescent-bladed knives; winged bannerstones, or atlatl weights; plummets; and ground-stone adzes and gouges. Skeletal remains found with this complex are often those of brachycephalic, or broad-headed, people. Individual artifact traits of what has come to be called the Laurentian tradition have a much wider occurrence than their collective association. As those discrete traits have been traced in their wider distributions, they have been linked to more and more diverse assemblages across a broader area of northeastern North America; the result is a more attenuated Laurentian "culture."

The most tightly defined manifestations of the Laurentian Archaic include the "core" regional cultures: Brewerton, Vosburg, and Vergennes. They appear to span a good two millennia, from 3500–1500 B.C. (5450–3450 years B.P.). Together, they reflect a high degree of interaction with other Archaic cultures from the western Great Lakes to the Gulf of St. Lawrence and southward to the Ohio Valley and even beyond. In their settlement and subsistence practices, Laurentian Archaic people, while exhibiting some local specializations, participated in the successful adaptational pattern common to all members of the Lake Forest Archaic cultural family. Some archaeologists believe that some or all of the Iroquoian-speaking tribes of the Northeast are the remote descendants of the ancient people responsible for the Laurentian Archaic culture.

Ronald J. Mason

Further Readings

Ritchie, W.A. 1944. *The Pre-Iroquoian Occupations of New York State*. Memoir no. 1. Rochester Museum of Arts and Sciences, Rochester.

———. 1969. *The Archaeology of New York State*. rev. 2nd ed. Natural History Press, Garden City.

Tuck, J.A. 1977. A Look at Laurentian. In *Current Perspectives in Northeastern Archeology, Essays in Honor of William A. Ritchie*, edited by R.E. Funk and C.F. Hayes III. Researches and Transactions of the New York State Archaeological Association no. 1. Rochester.

See also LAKE FOREST ARCHAIC

Laurentide Ice Sheet

At many times during the Pleistocene, cooler summers resulted in snow accumulation across Canada until an ice sheet built up and covered the country from the Labrador coast to the base of the Rocky Mountains. It extended north to cover most of the Arctic islands and south to fill the Great Lakes basins, covering the area roughly north of the Missouri and Ohio rivers, which were formed in their present courses as a result of diversion of preglacial streams and sand. Ice lobes protruding from the ice sheet, especially in the Great Lakes region, formed complex patterns of moraines and outwash plains as the ice margins fluctuated in response to climatic changes and to instabilities in the mechanism of ice flow. Because of cyclical climatic changes, the Laurentide ice sheet was built up and destroyed many times during the Pleistocene. As a result, most is known about the last (Wisconsin) glaciation, particularly about the Late Wisconsin ca. 18,000 B.C. (20,050 years B.P.) when the ice sheet extended into the Great Lakes area. The ice sheet's fluctuating retreat brought its terminus north of the Great Lakes by ca. 8050 B.C. (10,000 years B.P.), and its remnants disappeared from the Quebec/Labrador Plateau ca. 4050 B.C. (6,000 years B.P.). At its maximum, the load of ice depressed the Earth's crust, with the greatest effect in the Hudson Bay area, which indicates that the ice was thickest there (perhaps 2,500 m, or 2,734 yards). With ice wastage, the crust has been slowly uplifting; the process is so slow that Hudson Bay may ultimately be drained.

H.E. Wright, Jr.

Donald J. Lehmer. (Reprinted with permission from American Antiquity 41[2]:178)

Further Readings

Porter, S.C. (editor). 1983. *Late Quaternary Environments in the United States: 1. The Late Pleistocene.* University of Minnesota Press, Minneapolis.

Ruddiman, W.F., and H.E. Wright, Jr. (editors). 1987. *North America and Adjacent Oceans During the Last Deglaciation.* Geology of North America, vol. K-3. Geological Society of America, Boulder.

Lehmer, Donald Jayne (1918–1975)

The most enduring archaeological contributions by Donald J. Lehmer have been in the area of the Great Plains, but he was also influential in early studies of the Mogollon in southern Arizona (Lehmer 1948) and worked in northern Mexico and Texas. He built on his early work in the Southwest in developing a synthesis of Late Prehistoric Great Plains prehistory that remains a standard for Plains horticultural village tribes (Lehmer 1954, 1971), although since the mid-1970s its overall validity has faced increasing criticism.

Between 1950 and 1952, Lehmer was an archaeologist for the Smithsonian Institution's Missouri Basin Project in Lincoln, Nebraska; during his employment there, he excavated the Phillips Ranch and Dodd sites on the Missouri River in South Dakota. This work provided the background for his doctoral dissertation at Harvard University (Lehmer 1954), a tour de force that demonstrated his anthropological insight and brought order to the Plains Village tradition. He later taught at the University of Washington (1953) and at Dana College in Blair, Nebraska (1961–1975). The latter institution provided a base for him until his death; it is where he continued his studies of northern Plains Village cultures and their environmental settings (Lehmer 1970). His 1971 monograph, *Introduction to Middle Missouri Archeology*, was his last major work, for his untimely death cut short his contributions to understanding the culture history and ecology of the Hidatsa and their neighbors in the area between the Oahe and Garrison reservoirs, North Dakota.

W. Raymond Wood

Further Readings

Lehmer, D.J. 1948. *The Jornada Branch of the Mogollon.* Bulletin, vol. 19, no. 2. University of Arizona Press, Tucson.

———. 1954. *Archeological Investigations in the Oahe Dam Area, South Dakota, 1950–51.* River Basin Surveys Papers no. 7. Bulletin no. 158. Bureau of American Ethnology, Smithsonian Institution, Washington, D.C.

———. 1970. Climate and Culture History in the Middle Missouri Valley. In *Pleistocene and Recent Environments of the Central Great Plains*, edited by W. Dort, Jr., and K. Jones, Jr., pp. 117–129. University of Kansas Press, Lawrence.

——. 1971. *Introduction to Middle Missouri Archeology*. Anthropological Papers no. 1. National Park Service, Washington, D.C.

Leonhardy, Frank Clinton (1935–1991)

Frank C. Leonhardy, with David Rice, developed the synthesis of Lower Snake River prehistory that remains the longest cultural chronology on the Plateau and, in some ways, the master sequence for the Plateau (Leonhardy and Rice 1970). Leonhardy's work built on earlier research by Richard Daugherty (1956) at Lind Coulee and Marmes Rock Shelter and by Roderick Sprague, Harvey Rice, and others. His approach was based on rigorous field techniques relying on large exposures and the application of geomorphic and soil-science methods at a time when the term "site formation processes" had yet to be invented. His doctoral dissertation was a monographic description of the Granite Point site (Leonhardy 1970). All of his other Snake River excavation reports are in the M.A. and Ph.D. theses of his students, first at Washington State University and then at the University of Idaho. His work was deeply influenced by his interest in, and relationship with, the Nez Perce of central Idaho. He also excavated the Domebo PaleoIndian site in Oklahoma and the Late Prehistoric Iron Gate site in southern Oregon. The development of his career was profoundly affected by serious heart problems. Leonhardy died of heart failure in the field, after completing the excavation of a pithouse in Hell's Canyon, in eastern Oregon. He was, in many ways, the embodiment of the North American "dirt archaeologist."

Kenneth M. Ames

Further Readings

Daugherty, R.D. 1956. Archaeology of the Lind Coulee Site, Washington. *Proceedings of the American Philosophical Society* 100(3):223–278.

Leonhardy, F.C. 1970. *Artifact Assemblages and Archaeological Units at Granite Point Locality 1 (45WT41), Southeastern Washington*. Unpublished Ph.D. dissertation, Department of Anthropology, Washington State University, Pullman.

Leonhardy, F.C., and D.G. Rice. 1970. A Proposed Culture Typology for the Lower Snake River Region, Southeastern Washington. *Northwest Anthropological Research Notes* 4(1):1–29.

Libby, Willard F. (1908–1980)

Willard F. Libby is the University of Chicago chemist who revolutionized prehistoric archaeology with the discovery in the late 1940s of the radiocarbon dating method. Libby won the 1960 Nobel Prize for chemistry for his discovery.

Guy Gibbon

Further Readings

Libby, W. 1955. *Radiocarbon Dating*. 2nd ed. University of Chicago Press, Chicago.

Lime Creek

The Lime Creek site (25FT41) is a deeply buried Paleoindian site near the confluence of Medicine and Lime creeks in Frontier County, southwestern Nebraska. Excavations at the site in 1947 by University of Nebraska paleontologists, and in 1949–1950 by archaeologists under the direction of E. Mott Davis, revealed three archaeological levels associated with buried soils. As yet (1996) unpublished radiocarbon analyses of soil organics date these between 8140 B.C. ± 450 and 6030 B.C. ± 1000 (10,090 and 7980 years B.P.). These levels produced three antler and 197 retouched stone artifacts, as well as several thousand flakes. In contrast to the nearby Allen site, which was occupied at the same time as Lime Creek and produced a wide range of domestic debris, including eyed needles and other bone tools, grinding stones, and a variety of stone tools, the Lime Creek flaked-stone assemblage is dominated by debris from the manufacture of stone tools, particularly unfinished bifaces (termed "Lime Creek knives" by Davis but now recognized as production rejects). These implements are made from Smoky Hills jasper, which outcrops extensively in the vicinity of the site. The collection from the site thus appears to represent primarily workshop rather than general-habitation material. The two diagnostic projectile points from the lowest cultural level, which produced the majority of the collection, fall into the Scottsbluff type; two diagnostic points from the uppermost level resemble Plainview points; and one other point shows an oblique flaking pattern typical of the Late Paleoindian period on the Plains. In contrast to most Paleoindian sites on the Plains, only the most recent (ca. 6050 B.C., or 8000 years B.P.) fauna from Lime Creek are dominated by bison; beaver and antelope are more common in the lower (Scottsbluff) level.

Douglas B. Bamforth

Further Readings

Bamforth, D.B. 1991. Population Dispersion and Paleoindian Technology at the Allen Site. In *Raw Material Economies Among Prehistoric Hunter-Gatherers,* edited by A. Montet-White and S. Holen, pp. 357–374. Publications in Anthropology no. 19. University of Kansas Press, Lawrence.

Davis, E.M. 1953. Recent Data From Two Paleoindian Sites on Medicine Creek, Nebraska. *American Antiquity* 18:380–386.

———. 1962. *The Archaeology of the Lime Creek Site in Southwestern Nebraska.* Special Publication no. 3. University of Nebraska State Museum, Lincoln.

Wedel, W. 1986. *Central Plains Prehistory.* University of Nebraska Press, Lincoln.

Lind Coulee

The Lind Coulee (45GR97) site is located near the town of Warden in eastern Washington State. It was first excavated under the direction of Richard D. Daugherty (1956) of Washington State University in 1951–1952, and again between 1968 and 1972 by a team that included at various times Ann Irwin, Roald Fryxell, Benny Keel, Henry Irwin, and Carl Gustafson. Daugherty's initial investigations demonstrated the first definite association of artifacts with extinct bison remains in the Columbia Basin. Radiocarbon dates on burned bone from this initial work are 7450 B.C. ± 980 and 6568 B.C. ± 460 (9400 and 8518 years B.P.), and on bone from the later excavation, 6770 B.C. ± 299 (8720 years B.P.). Upper St. Helens J tephra, dated elsewhere at 6950 B.C. ± 300 (8900 years B.P.), is found in the lower site sediments. Detailed stratigraphic analysis by Ula L. Moody (1978) discerned a minimum of 65 microstratigraphic levels and seven occupational levels within an estimated time interval of 50–200 years, of which the earliest is associated with the upper St. Helens J tephra. Abundant remains of full-term fetal elk and bison indicate an early spring occupation. Projectile points, bone needles, and gravers occurred consistently with the bones of large herbivores. Muskrat and beaver and other mammalian and bird remains were also recovered. Artifacts consist primarily of stemmed projectile points, numerous scrapers, flaked-stone crescents, flake knives, ocher grinding implements, bone needles, and barbed-bone harpoon heads and fixed points.

Overall, the types and distributions of artifactual and faunal remains indicate that the site was an early spring hunting camp utilized as part of a seasonal round of subsistence activities. Sites such as Marmes Rock Shelter were probably used by the same peoples during other seasons of the year. Taxonomically, the Lind Coulee–site assemblage belongs to the Stemmed Point tradition, which is found throughout the Columbia drainage and south into the Great Basin. The Stemmed Point tradition (ca. 6050 B.C., or 8000 years B.P.) dates between the earlier Fluted Point tradition and later cultural traditions in which salmon fishing had replaced hunting as the primary subsistence activity.

Roy L. Carlson

Further Readings

Daugherty, R.D. 1956. Archaeology of the Lind Coulee Site, Washington. *Proceedings of the American Philosophical Society* 100:223–278.

Moody, U.L. 1978. *Microstratigraphy, Paleoecology, and Tephrochronology of the Lind Coulee Site, Central Washington.* Unpublished Ph.D. dissertation, Department of Anthropology, Washington State University, Pullman.

See also STEMMED POINT TRADITION

Lindenmeier Site

Lindenmeier is an undisturbed, stratified, multicomponent archaeological site (5LR13) on the Plains in northern Colorado that is best known for its extensive Folsom base camps. Located ca. 74 km (46 miles) north of Fort Collins, the site was excavated by Frank H.H. Roberts, Jr., in the mid-1930s (Roberts 1935) but not adequately reported until the 1970s (Wilmsen 1973; Wilmsen and Roberts 1978). Dated at 8850 B.C. (10,800 years B.P.), the Folsom occupation was a series of localized concentrations of artifacts, debitage, food remains, and fire hearths. Once on the banks of a late Pleistocene lake in a small valley near the grasslands, the village debris gradually became covered by sediments eroding from surrounding hills. The toolkit included fluted and "unfluted" Folsom projectile points, spokeshaves, flake knives, scrapers, drills, and small pieces of delicately incised bone. Generations of Folsom bison hunters apparently camped on a regular basis at the site, where they seem to have trapped and butchered many bison.

Since most known Folsom sites are kills, large campsites like Lindenmeier and Hanson in the Bighorn Basin of north-central Wyoming expand our understanding of Folsom culture. Edwin N. Wilmsen, who examined the site materials in the 1970s, thought the site was visited by two or more related family groups who interacted socially and participated in communal bison hunts, perhaps seasonally. The site was also used in ca. 9050 B.C. (11,000 years B.P.) by earlier Clovis hunters, who captured an occasional mammoth, and by more recent Early Plains Archaic people at 3050 B.C. (5000 years B.P.).

Guy Gibbon

Further Readings

Roberts, F.H.H., Jr. 1935. A Folsom Complex: A Preliminary Report on Investigations at the Lindenmeier Site in Northern Colorado. *Smithsonian Miscellaneous Collections* 94:1–35.

———. 1936. Additional Information on the Folsom Complex. *Smithsonian Miscellaneous Collections* 95:1–38.

Wilmsen, E.N. 1973. *Lindenmeier: A Pleistocene Hunting Society.* Harper and Row, New York.

Wilmsen, E.N., and F.H.H. Roberts, Jr. 1978. *Lindenmeier: 1934–1974.* Contributions to Anthropology no. 24. Smithsonian Institution Press, Washington, D.C.

See also FOLSOM COMPLEX

Lindsay Mammoth Site

The nearly complete skeleton of a mature bull imperial mammoth (*Mammuthus* cf. *imperator*) (24DW501) that expired while in its prime more than 11,000 years ago was excavated in 1967 by Montana State University. The skeleton was exposed by county roadbuilding and the later erosion of the borrow pit. It was found near the townsite of Lindsay, Dawson County, Montana, 12.4 km (20 miles) northwest of Glendive in rolling plains uplands north of the Lower Yellowstone River. This largely disarticulated skeleton of a 4.3-m (14-foot) -tall bull with 2.7-m (8.8-foot) -long tusks was incorporated within the lower part of a 1.2-m (3.9-foot)

1967 excavation of the Late Pleistocene Lindsay mammoth beneath and adjacent to a county road in east-central Montana, Lower Yellowstone River drainage. (Courtesy of Museum of the Rockies/Montana State University–Bozeman)

thick late Pleistocene loess cap deposited atop a truncated Fort Union Formation section. Taphonomic and related facts suggest that the carcass might have been scavenged by humans, although no artifacts were found. Both of the femora were found stacked atop one another, overlying several thoracic ribs. Intrusive, amorphous blocks of sandstone (combined weight, 4.5 kg, or 10 lbs) were found beneath and adjacent to the scattered humeri, both of which had sustained battering. Certain bone fractures indicative of patterned early postmortem breakage by humans suggested the intentional accessing of marrow cavities. While cause of death is unknown, a blow or blows to the front of the animal's mandible had dislodged several front molar plates, which were found beneath a segment of spinal column several meters from the mandible. The Lindsay Mammoth may have died as a result of injuries inflicted by another mammoth. The carcass was found and scavenged by Paleoindians who, by 9550 B.C. (11,500 B.P.) were occupying eastern Montana.

Leslie B. Davis

Further Readings

Davis, L.B. 1986. In Search of Early Elephants. *Montana Outdoors* 17(6):27–31.

Davis, L.B., and M.C. Wilson. 1985. The Late Pleistocene Lindsay Mammoth (24DW501): A Possible Man-Mammoth Association. *Current Research in the Pleistocene* 2:97–98.

Linear Mounds (Plains)

Linear mounds are best known in the Upper Mississippi drainage area, but they are also common features in the northeastern Plains, especially along the Missouri River in west-cen-

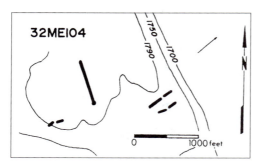

Map of Stanton mound group, 32ME104, Mercer County, North Dakota. (Adapted by W. R. Wood from Chomko and Wood 1973: Figure 3)

tral North Dakota near the present town of Stanton. They once existed by the hundreds, but farming has leveled the bulk of them. Most of these low, elongated earthen features are probably of Woodland origin, although no firm evidence exists to so identify them or to date them. Some mounds also may be products of Late Prehistoric Assiniboine Indians. Mounds may occur singly, in pairs, or in groups of six or seven structures. The size of those along the Missouri River varies considerably, from 26 m to more than 457 m (85 to more than 1,500 feet) in length. Many of them have a low, dome-shaped tumulus attached to one or both ends. One dome-shaped mound at the Washburn mound group in Oliver County, North Dakota, was attached to a linear mound outlined by a shallow trench cut in the sod. One of the terminal dome-shaped mounds at the Levis mound group in McLean County, North Dakota, yielded the remains of an adult, a child, and an infant in a shallow submound pit, but there were no diagnostic artifacts to permit an estimate of their age or cultural affiliation.

W. Raymond Wood

Further Readings

Chomko, S.A., and W.R. Wood. 1973. Linear Mounds in the Northeastern Plains. *Archaeology in Montana* 14:1–19.

Lipscomb

The Lipscomb site (41LP1) is a Folsom-age (8850–8250 B.C., or 10,800–10,200 year B.P.) Paleoindian bison-kill and -processing site located in the northeastern corner of the Texas Panhandle. At present (1995), Lipscomb is the largest Folsom bison bonebed known. The bonebed is situated on the eastern margin of the southern High Plains on a tributary of Wolf Creek, which drains into the North Canadian River. The site was first investigated by paleontologists from the University of Nebraska State Museum in 1939 and 1946. Stone artifacts found in the bonebed included Folsom points, some butchering tools, and flakes from the shaping and resharpening of tools. The site has commonly served as an example of a typical Folsom bison-kill site. Interpretations by archaeologists of how the bison were killed have varied dramatically, but detailed information about the site was not generally available until reinvestigation of the site and museum collections began in the 1980s. This is one of many

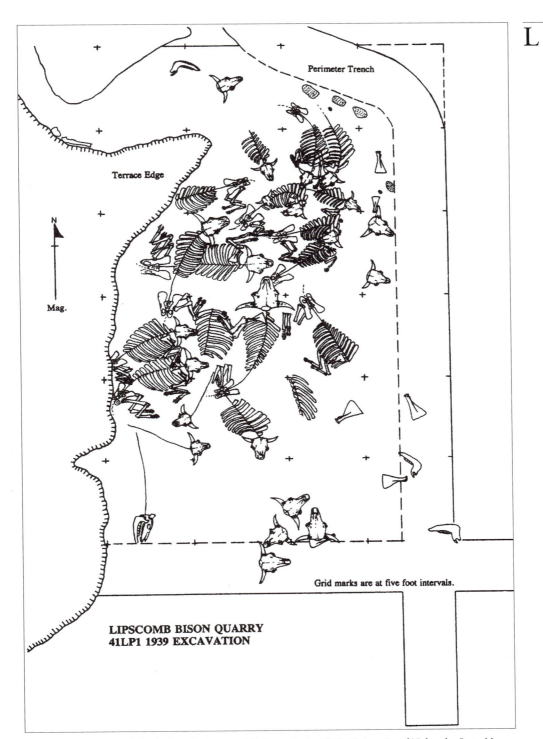

L

Perimeter Trench

Terrace Edge

N

Mag.

Grid marks are at five foot intervals.

LIPSCOMB BISON QUARRY
41LP1 1939 EXCAVATION

Plan map of the bison bone bed at the Lipscomb Folsom site in 1939. University of Nebraska State Museum excavation. (Drawing by J. L. Hofman) examples in which the restudy of long-known sites using new methods has enhanced our understanding of the archaeologial record. At least 56 large bison of the late Pleistocene subspecies *Bison bison antiquus* were killed within a small area at this site. Based on the study of bison bones, it appears that most of the herd was composed of cows while a quarter were bulls. Based on tooth eruption and wear patterns, all appear to have died within a short period during late summer or early fall, perhaps late September or early October.

The stone tools found at the site were manufactured primarily from two distinctive types of stone derived from known sources. Most of the projectile points and a few tools were manufactured from Edwards chert from the central Texas region. The nearest sources are located ca. 350 km (217 miles) south or southeast of the site. Many of these Edwards-chert Folsom points exhibit evidence of having been used, broken, and resharpened, suggesting that they had been used in one or more previous bison-kill and -processing events or similar activities. Other projectile points and a number of butchering tools are made from Alibates agate derived from sources on the Canadian River ca. 125 km (77.5 miles) southwest of the site. Unlike the Edwards-chert projectile points, those made from Alibates show no evidence of having been broken and reworked prior to their use at Lipscomb. This evidence suggests that the Edwards-chert lithic-source area, located far to the south, was visited first and that this group of Folsom hunting-and-gathering people moved northward on the southern High Plains, perhaps while hunting bison. After a series of tool-using events, they replenished their tool supply from the Alibates lithic-source area and subsequently killed and butchered the bison at Lipscomb at the end of summer or early fall. This suggests a sequence of movement from south to north during the summer and the use of an extensive hunting region by such groups.

Several skeletons remained largely articulated. There is little evidence for use of bone marrow or for the intensive butchering common at Late Prehistoric bison-kill sites on the Plains. The people at Lipscomb utilized only a portion of the bison resources they had captured. Perhaps this was a small group and could take only a portion of the resources with them when they left. If the weather was warm, some of the carcasses may have spoiled before they could be used, or the people may have been more interested in hides than meat. There are many unanswered questions about the Lipscomb deposit. Ongoing study of the geologic setting of the site, the available samples, and excavation of areas away from the bonebed should help us learn much more about this Folsom bison-kill and -processing site.

Jack L. Hofman

Further Readings

Hofman, J.L., L.C. Todd, and C.B. Schultz. 1989. Further Investigations of the Folsom Bison Kill at Lipscomb, Texas. *Current Research in the Pleistocene* 6:16–18.

Hofman, J.L., L.C. Todd, C.B. Schultz, and W.J. Hendy. 1989. The Lipscomb Bison Quarry: Continuing Investigations of a Folsom Site on the Southern Plains. *Bulletin of the Texas Archaeological Society* 60:149–189 (published in 1991).

Schultz, C.B. 1943. Some Artifact Sites of Early Man in the Great Plains and Adjacent Areas. *American Antiquity* 8:242–249.

Todd, L.C., J.L. Hofman, and C.B. Schultz. 1990. Seasonality of the Scottsbluff and Lipscomb Bison Bonebeds: Implications for Modeling Paleoindian Subsistence. *American Antiquity* 55:813–827.

———. 1992. Faunal Analysis and Paleoindian Studies: A Reexamination of the Lipscomb Bison Bonebed. *Plains Anthropologist* 37(139):137–165.

Lithic Technology (Paleoindian)

The processes by which stone was intentionally modified to produce tools, weapons, and other objects are collectively referred to as lithic technology. During Paleoindian times (ca. 10,050–5050 B.C., or 12,000–7000 years B.P.), the main method of the production of stone tools was flaking: Stones that had conchoidal (glasslike) fractures were selected and modified by the application of force that removed pieces, usually called flakes. Force applied by direct percussion, indirect percussion, and pressure were used to varying degrees. Although flakes were made from single and multiplatform cores, the most common process used was the manufacture of bifacial cores. Often, these cores were the initial stages of the manufacture of complex knives and projectile points, but the flakes were also being produced to be used as, or modified into, implements. What distinguishes Paleoindian bifacial technologies from many later ones is the complexity of some of the projectile-point manufacturing sequences. The earliest point types often exhibit a distinctive trait known as a flute. This occurred when relatively large thinning flakes were removed from the straight or indented bases of the points near the end of the manufacturing sequence. There are a number of fluted-point types, but probably the best known are Clovis, Folsom, and Cumberland. Other Paleoindian point types also exhibit complex flaking sequences, especially those from the North American High Plains. Many of these were finished with highly controlled pressure-flaking sequences that produced distinctive flake scar patterns. Probably the best known and described are Eden points. This style was made by several sequential pressure-flaking series, in which the flakes terminated at the midline, eventually producing a diamond cross section. Another distinctive flaking process is exhibited by Clovis-biface manufacture. In this case, the process is not well represented on finished projectile points, but several caches of unfinished bifaces, in various stages of completion, exhibit a distinctive process. Very large thinning flakes were struck from the bifaces in such a way as to extend across the entire surface and remove a portion of the opposite edge. Wide spacing of these flake removals allowed even very large bifaces to be substantially thinned and flattened by the removal of only a few flakes. The various technological processes, combined with variations in final forms, have allowed specific types to be defined and named. A complete study of flaked-stone technology cannot be done through the examination of the finished points and tools alone; the majority of information concerning the manufacturing processes is obtained by studying the byproducts, or debitage. It is also rare to have an entire technological process represented in the assemblage of a single site. Different manufacturing activities occurred in different locations, depending on many factors. Since Paleoindian groups were not sedentary, complete processes seldom occur in the same localities. There has been much research done on Paleoindian flaked-stone technology, resulting in a large and growing literature.

Bruce A. Bradley

Further Readings

Bradley, B.A. 1991. Lithic Technology. In *Prehistoric Hunters of the High Plains,* by G.C. Frison, pp. 369–395. 2nd ed. Academic Press, San Diego.

Bradley, B.A., and D.J. Stanford. 1987. The Claypool Study. In *The Horner Site: The Type Site of the Cody Complex,* edited by G.C. Frison and L.C. Todd, pp. 405–434. Academic Press, New York.

Callahan, E. 1979. The Basics of Biface Knapping in the Eastern Fluted Point Tradition: A Manual for Flintknappers and Lithic Analysts. *Archaeology of Eastern North America* 7(1):1–56.

Collins, M.B. 1975. Lithic Technology As a Mean of Processual Inference. In *Lithic Technology,* edited by E. Swanson, pp. 3–39. Mouton, The Hague.

L

Little Colorado Branch

Regional environments in the Little Colorado River Basin in Arizona include alpine meadows at the Little Colorado headwaters, ponderosa pine forests and piñon-juniper woodland in the highlands, desert grasslands over most of the central basin, and the Painted Desert along the lower reaches of the river. Most archaeologists do not believe that archaeological sites in this diverse environment represent the remains of a distinct cultural entity that persisted through time. For example, the phrase "Little Colorado branch" is not present in any general text on Southwestern archaeology. Fred Plog's 1981 archaeological overview of the basin for the U.S. Forest Service and the Bureau of Land Management, which focused on its upper and central portions, divided the basin into six "cultural provinces" (Zuni, Upper Little Colorado, Chevelon-Chavez, Flagstaff, Hopi Buttes, and Black Mesa), and demonstrated that all major cultural historical periods recognized in the Southwest (Paleoindian, Archaic, Formative, and Historic) are represented in this area, too. Beginning with the Formative period (ca. A.D. 200–1600, or 1750–350 years B.P.), occupants of the basin drew upon diverse sources to develop rapidly shifting cultural adaptations; while boundaries and affiliations were highly changeable over time, the Hopi Buttes and the Chevelon areas, which straddle the middle Little Colorado, remained the core of the Little Colorado branch of the Anasazi culture area.

Archaeological sites in the basin were first reported in the mid-nineteenth century by explorers, such as Edward Fitzgerald Beale, Lorenzo Sitgreaves, and Amiel Weeks Whipple, who were seeking transportation corridors

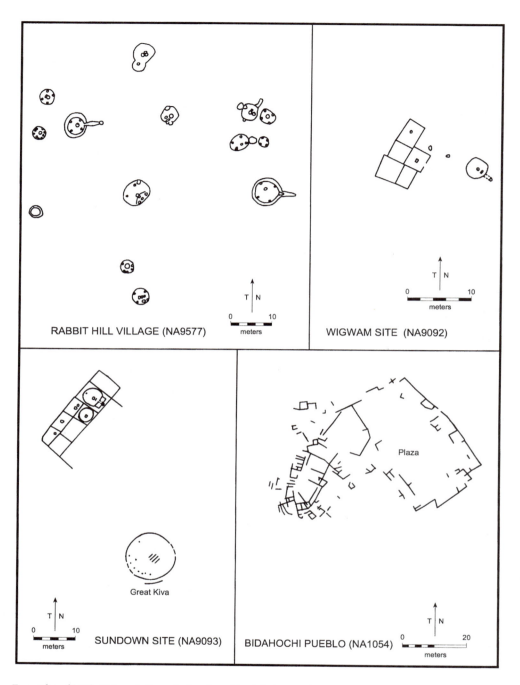

RABBIT HILL VILLAGE (NA9577)

WIGWAM SITE (NA9092)

Great Kiva

SUNDOWN SITE (NA9093)

BIDAHOCHI PUEBLO (NA1054)

Plaza

Examples of Little Colorado Branch site plans. Top left: late Basketmaker III (ca. A.D. 700s. Top right: late Pueblo II (A.D. 1000–1100). Bottom left: middle Pueblo III (A.D. 1100–1250). Bottom right: early Pueblo IV (A.D. 1300s). (Courtesy of K. A. Hays-Gilpin and D. Gilpin)

across the region. Pioneering archaeologists Jesse Walter Fewkes (1898, 1904), Walter Hough (1903), and Harry Percival Mera conducted the first archaeological surveys and ex-

cavations in the area in the late nineteenth and early twentieth centuries. In the 1920s and 1930s, archaeologists began to classify the archaeological remains in the basin into different chronological and regional typologies. For instance, sites on Black Mesa and in the portion of the Little Colorado River below Grand Falls were assigned to the Kayenta branch of the Anasazi, while sites west of Grand Falls were classified as Sinagua and Cohonina. Sites of the Upper Little Colorado Basin (south of Holbrook, Arizona) were recognized as more closely related to those in the Zuni (Cibola) area in west-central New Mexico and to the Mogollon culture. The central Little Colorado Valley, from Grand Falls to Holbrook and north to Indian Wells, which encompasses the Hopi Buttes and Winslow areas, was termed the Winslow branch of the Anasazi by Harold S. Colton in his 1939 cultural classification. Colton defined the Winslow branch on the basis of ceramics. Salvage archaeology, begun in the 1950s, added new information that helped refine temporal and spatial classifications. In the 1960s, George Gumerman recorded more than 200 sites in the southwestern Hopi Buttes as part of a multidisciplinary geological research project. Paul Martin's (1962) field school for the Field Museum of Natural History, Chicago, investigated sites in the Upper Little Colorado Basin between 1958 and 1971. Subsequent research has focused on the Homolovi Ruins State Park near Winslow (Adams 1989, Adams and Hays 1992), the Petrified Forest National Park (Stewart 1980), and lands east of the Petrified Forest acquired for Navajo relocated from Hopi land.

L

Painted ceramic sequence for the Little Colorado Branch. Top left: Holbrook Black-on-white, A.D. 1050–1150 (Museum of Northern Arizona (MNA) NA2098A.42). Top right: Walnut A Black-on-white, A.D. 1100–1250 (MNA NA1139.34). Bottom left: Walnut B Black-on-white, A.D. 1200–1250 (MNA NA9096.R.4.2). Bottom right: Homolovi Polychrome, A.D. 1280–1350 (Chicago Field Museum 72443). (Courtesy of K. A. Hays-Gilpin and D. Gilpin)

Little Colorado Branch. Hopi oral traditions place the home of the Mother of Game Animals in the Little Colorado River valley. These Pueblo III period (A.D. 1100–1300) petroglyphs from Petrified Forest (top) and Wupatki (bottom) National Monuments depict this deity. (Courtesy of Patricia McCreery)

Paleoindian Clovis and Folsom projectile points and Archaic Pinto projectile points regularly appear as surface finds in the Little Colorado drainage, but no diligent search for early sites has been made, and evidence for early occupations remains rare. Some 70 scatters of crude flaked-stone artifacts, known as Tolchaco sites, along the Little Colorado River between Holbrook and Cameron, Arizona, were described in the 1940s (Bartlett 1943) as stone quarries and workshops that may predate the

Anasazi occupation of the area. Subsequently, these sites have been interpreted as Anasazi lithic-procurement areas, where initial reduction of raw material took place (Keller and Wilson 1976). Similar sites appear in the Hopi Buttes, where lag gravels are exposed.

By ca. A.D. 200 (1750 years B.P.) (Basketmaker II period, A.D. 1–500, or 1950–1450 years B.P.), pottery, slab-lined storage facilities, and permanent habitation structures were present at the Flattop site and Sivu'ovi in the

Petrified Forest. The Flattop site has at least 25 small, slab-lined pithouses associated with a brown pottery (Adamana Brown) shaped by paddle and anvil, a technique that was most commonly used to the south and the west.

Basketmaker III (A.D. 500–700, or 1450–1250 years B.P.) and Pueblo I (A.D. 700–900, or 1250–1050 years B.P.) sites in the central Little Colorado Basin include the Finger Rock and Kol sites in the southwestern Hopi Buttes. These sites have Tusayan White Ware and Tusayan Gray Ware pottery associated with pithouse architecture similar to the Lino and Marsh Pass phases of the Kayenta Anasazi. Architecture and pottery at the Basketmaker III Twin Butte site in the Petrified Forest suggest affinity closer to the Chacoan or Cibolan branches of the Anasazi than to the Kayenta branch. The Pueblo I NA6583 site excavated by David Breternitz east of Winslow had a mixture of Kayentalike and Mogollonlike architecture and pottery, together with shell artifacts and a cremation that suggested Hohokam contacts. White Mound Village, a Basketmaker III–Pueblo I site east of the Petrified Forest, consists of pithouses in front of arcs of semisubterranean jacal storage rooms.

Pueblo II (A.D. 900–1100, or 1050–850 years B.P.) sites in the Little Colorado Basin are mostly small, scattered, unit pueblos and pithouse clusters that are distinctive enough to warrant a separate phase designation: the Holbrook phase. Chacoan-style great houses with great kivas and roads extend as far west as central Black Mesa and the Petrified Forest. Ca. A.D. 1070 (880 years B.P.), the southwestern Hopi Buttes experienced a major population increase. The use of pithouses continued, but pottery technology diverged from the Kayenta Anasazi norm. Little Colorado White Ware has a dark gray paste with white sherd temper, a white slip, and carbon paint. Designs are similar to those on Kayenta Branch Tusayan White Ware.

During the McDonald phase (early Pueblo III, A.D. 1100–1200, or 850–750 years B.P.), population increase continued in the southwestern Hopi Buttes. The Chezhincotah and Ramp sites consist of surface rooms and pithouses. The Plaza site, which contains seven habitation rooms, a plaza, a kiva, and a great kiva, may have ritually integrated several scattered communities. In the Indian Wells–Bidahochi area, the Malpais Spring site has 27 structures containing 129 rooms and two buildings much like the apparent special structures at the Plaza site.

During the Tuwiuca phase (late Pueblo III, A.D. 1200–1300, or 750–650 years B.P.), much of the area was abandoned. The population aggregated into larger sites in well-watered areas, including Homol'ovi III and IV and several settlements in the Bidahochi area. During the Pueblo IV period (A.D. 1300–1450, or 650–500 years B.P.), regional abandonments continued, and populations aggregated into clusters of large plaza-oriented communities in the Petrified Forest, Bidahochi, Homol'ovi, Silver Creek, and Upper Little Colorado areas. The largest, Homol'ovi II near Winslow, has ca. 700 rooms around three plazas containing numerous rectangular kivas. Local manufacture of pottery (Winslow and Homol'ovi orange wares) ceased in the middle Little Colorado area, with most sites in the region importing large amounts of pottery from the Hopi Mesas, Zuni, and the Upper Little Colorado. The introduction of the Kachina religion at this time is evident in the appearance of images of masked faces on pottery, rock art, and kiva murals. Puebloan people ceased to occupy the Little Colorado area shortly after A.D. 1400, but the area continued to be used for religious purposes even after the arrival of the Navajo by the eighteenth century. Many Hopi and Zuni clans trace their origins to the fourteenth-century ruins found in the region.

Kelley Ann Hays-Gilpin
Dennis Gilpin

Further Readings

Adams, E.C. (editor). 1989. The Homol'ovi Research Program: Investigation into the Prehistory of the Middle Little Colorado River Valley. *Kiva* 54(3).

Adams, E.C., and K.A. Hays (editors). 1991. *Homol'ovi II: Archaeology of an Ancestral Hopi Village, Arizona.* Anthropological Papers no. 55. University of Arizona Press, Tucson.

Bartlett, K. 1943. A Primitive Stone Industry of the Little Colorado Valley, Arizona. *American Antiquity* 8:266–268.

Breternitz, D.A. 1957. Highway Salvage Archaeology by the Museum of Northern Arizona, 1956–57. *Kiva* 23(2):8–12.

Colton, H.S. 1939. *Prehistoric Culture Units and Their Relationships in Northern Arizona.* Bulletin no. 17. Museum of Northern Arizona, Flagstaff.

Fewkes, J.W. 1898. Archaeological Expedition into Arizona in 1895. *Seventeenth Annual Report of the Bureau of Ameri-*

L

can *Ethnology for the Years 1895–1896*, pt. 2, pp. 519–742.

———. 1904. Two Summers' Work in Pueblo Ruins. *Twenty-second Annual Report of the Bureau of American Ethnology for the Years 1900–1901*, pt. 1, pp. 3–195.

Gumerman, G. 1988. *Archaeology of the Hopi Buttes District, Arizona*. Research Paper no. 49. Center for Archaeological Investigations, Southern Illinois University Press, Carbondale.

Hough, W. 1903. Archeological Field Work in Northeastern Arizona: The Museum-Gates Expedition of 1901. *Report of the United States National Museum for 1901*, pp. 279–358.

Keller, D.R., and S.M. Wilson. 1976. New Light on the Tolchaco Problem. *Kiva* 41:225–239.

Martin, P.S. 1962. Archeological Investigations in East Central Arizona. *Science* 138:826–827.

Mera, H.P. 1934. *Observations on the Archaeology of the Petrified Forest National Monument*. Technical Series no. 7. Laboratory of Anthropology, Santa Fe.

Plog, F. 1979. Prehistory: Western Anasazi. In *Southwest*, edited by A. Ortiz, pp. 108–130. Handbook of North American Indians, vol. 9, W.C. Sturtevant, general editor. Smithsonian Institution, Washington, D.C.

———. 1981. Cultural Resources Overview: Little Colorado Area, Arizona. Report prepared for Apache-Sitgreaves National Forests and Arizona Bureau of Land Management. U.S. Forest Service, Southwest Region, Albuquerque; Arizona State Office, Bureau of Land Management, Phoenix.

Stewart, Y.G. 1980. *An Archaeological Overview of Petrified Forest National Park*. Publications in Anthropology no. 10. Western Archeological Center, National Park Service, Tucson.

Little Ice Age

After the Medieval Warm Epoch (or Neo-Atlantic climatic episode), a long period of deteriorating climate after A.D. 1250 (700 years B.P.) culminated in the well-named Little Ice Age of A.D. 1550–1850 (400–100 years B.P.). The beginning of this period is not well defined, but it was probably about the sixteenth century. It is the culmination of the Neoglacial period, which covers all of the time since the Hypsithermal/Altithermal (ca. 6050–3050 B.C., or 8000–5000 years B.P.) in the terminology commonly used in North America. Throughout most of northern North America and Europe, annual temperature regimes were several degrees colder than today. In the Alps and Scandinavia, and in the mountains of western North America, glaciers reached positions more advanced in the eighteenth and nineteenth centuries A.D. than they had at any time since the end of the last major glaciation ca. 8050 B.C. (10,000 years B.P.), presumably because of a regional decrease in summer temperatures or increase in snowfall. The manifestation of the Little Ice Age beyond the areas of mountain glaciers is weak, although slight vegetation changes in forest composition in the Minnesota area and a significant depression of the tree line across the Canadian Subarctic have been attributed to the same climatic trends. The cause of this relatively short-term climatic oscillation is not known. Perhaps the Neoglacial period and its Little Ice Age represents the reversal of the insolational trend that caused the Hypsithermal, and the abrupt termination of the Little Ice Age, which coincided roughly with the Industrial Revolution, reflected the accelerated increase in atmospheric carbon dioxide related to human activities.

Well documented in Europe, the Little Ice Age was associated with the winter freezing of rivers, such as the Thames in England, reduced agricultural yields, and a southern retreat in the northern limits of agriculture in Scandinavia. In Greenland, cooling conditions leading up to the Little Ice Age may have helped bring about the demise of the Norse colony founded by Erik the Red. In Arctic Canada, worsening sea-ice conditions seem to have impeded the seasonal migration of bowhead whales into many areas and to have resulted in a widespread decline in Thule Inuit whale hunting. A cultural readaptation to the hunting of ringed seals on the winter ice during the Little Ice Age signals cultural transition to the kinds of historic Inuit cultures described by early Arctic explorers. The Little Ice Age is thought to have influenced many other cultural adaptations throughout North America.

David Morrison
H.E. Wright, Jr.

Further Readings
Grove, J.M. 1988. *The Little Ice Age*. Methuen, New York.

McGhee, R. 1970. Speculations on Climatic

Change and Thule Culture Development. *Folk* 11–12:173–184.

Little River Focus

It would be more current to use "phase" rather than "focus," but the latter is firmly entrenched in the literature. Little River focus is one of two named members of the Great Bend aspect (the other is Lower Walnut focus). Radiocarbon dates, Southwestern ceramics, and European items suggest an A.D. 1450–1700 (500–250 years B.P.) time range. Sites are concentrated in central Kansas between the Arkansas and Smoky Hill river valleys. Origins are not definitely known. One suggestion is a migration of peoples of the Washita River phase from central Oklahoma. An alternative suggestion is an in situ development from indigenous Woodland (A.D. 800–950, or 1150–1000 years B.P.) occupants through early Late Prehistoric complexes such as Pratt and Bluff Creek (A.D. 1250–1450, or 700–500 years B.P.).

Little River–focus sites consist of both large villages and small, special-purpose sites. Houses are difficult to define but appear to be round in outline and built either on the original ground surface or in shallow pits. A grass-covered, conical superstructure similar to that documented historically for the area was likely typical. "Council circles" formed by elliptical pithouses may be associated with solstice observances. Subsistence is not well documented. Horticulture, including corn and beans, is noted archaeologically, and early historic accounts suggest that it was a major subsistence activity. Elk, pronghorn, white-tailed deer, and bison were hunted, and similar accounts document the use of specialized, bison-hunting task groups. Small mammals, birds, turtles, and mussels were exploited. The predominant ceramic type is sand tempered, plain surfaced, and ovate in shape with a rounded bottom. Decoration sometimes involves clay ridges or pinched-up nodes on the neck. Lips may be diagonally incised. Some vessels are red filmed. Bone tools include bison-scapula hoes, bone awls, elk- or bison-rib shaft straighteners, and bone beads. Stone tools include small triangular points without notches; plain shafted and flanged drills; hafted knives, often with beveled edges; double-bitted axes; and end scrapers. Ground-stone tools include manos, metates, grooved mauls, shaft smoothers, and pipes. Basketry and shell spoons or scrapers also occur.

Trade materials are common. From the Southwest came Pueblo pottery, obsidian, and turquoise. Florence-A chert came from north-central Oklahoma; Alibates agatized dolomite, from the Texas Panhandle. A minority of red pipestone came from the catlinite quarries of southwest Minnesota, but most came from glacial deposits as close as northeast Kansas. Some pottery came from the Lower Loup phase (A.D. 1600–1750, or 350–200 years B.P.), some may have come from the Mississippi Valley, and some may be from the Lower Walnut focus (A.D. 1450–1750, or 500–200 years B.P.). *Olivella* shell may have come from either the Gulf or the Pacific. European material is present in small amounts. Just to the east, near Marion, Kansas, are a series of sites that are closely related to the Little River focus. They also have some ceramic and lithic characteristics that are locally distinct.

Some Little River–focus sites were visited in 1541 by Francisco Vásquez de Coronado, who used the term "Teucarea" to refer to the area. The Spanish also used the term "Quivira." In 1601, Juan de Oñate may have heard of the area as "Tancoa." Ca. 1700, part or all of the Little River–focus people may have moved to east-central Oklahoma. There, in 1719, J.-B. Bénard and Sieur de la Harpe visited the Touacara, who were also known as the Mento. Subsequent moves southward into Texas and back into southwest Oklahoma were made under the name Tawakoni and as one of the subdivisions of the modern-day Wichita tribe.

Susan C. Vehik

Further Readings

Rohn, A.H., and A.M. Emerson. 1984. *Great Bend Sites at Marion Kansas*. Publications in Anthropology no. 1. Department of Anthropology, Wichita State University, Wichita.

Vehik, S.C. 1986. Oñate's Expedition to the Southern Plains: Routes, Destinations, and Implications for Late Prehistoric Cultural Adaptations. *Plains Anthropologist* 31:13–33.

Wedel, W.R. 1959. *Introduction to Kansas Archeology*. Bulletin no. 174. Bureau of American Ethnology, Smithsonian Institution, Washington, D.C.

———. 1961. *Prehistoric Man on the Great Plains*. University of Oklahoma Press, Norman.

See also GREAT BEND ASPECT; LOWER WALNUT FOCUS

L

Locarno Beach Culture

Locarno Beach was first identified as a distinctive phase of occupation of the Fraser River delta area by Charles E. Borden in the late 1940s and early 1950s. Since then, its distribution has been extended to include the southeastern shore of Vancouver Island, the adjacent Gulf Islands, the south shore of the Strait of Juan de Fuca, and waterways and islands at the entrance of Puget Sound. Site assemblages span the years ca. 1500–500 B.C. (3450–2450 years B.P.).

An early interpretation (Borden 1951) stressed differences between Locarno Beach and other assemblages, at least some of which were demonstrably later, and suggested that there were similarities with assemblages from the Pacific Eskimo area. Borden saw little evidence for a woodworking industry and inferred the absence of such important products as dugout canoes and large splint-plank houses. His initial reconstruction depicted a people who lived in lightly constructed hide-covered dwellings, traveled in skin-covered watercraft, and subsisted on sea mammals around which their ceremonial life centered. Later research (Mitchell 1974; Matson 1992; Matson and Coupland 1995) has served to reduce considerably the uniqueness of Locarno Beach and to emphasize technological and subsistence continuities between it and the preceding (Charles/St. Mungo, ca. 2500–1500 B.C., or 4450–3450 years B.P.) and succeeding (Marpole, ca. 450 B.C.–A.D. 550, or 2400–1400 years B.P.) culture types.

Subsistence was broadly based, including fish, such as salmon (which are especially prominent at some sites), flatfish (flounder and sole), and herring; shellfish (clams, mussels, and barnacles); sea mammals (harbor seal and porpoise); land mammals (deer and wapiti); and some birds, especially waterfowl. Dog bones are relatively common, but it is not likely dogs were part of the diet. Although seasonal use of some sites has been inferred, the settlement pattern and its relation to the exploitation of seasonally available resources has not been fully worked out.

Artifact categories commonly associated with the culture type include flaked-basalt projectile points with contracting stems; quartz-crystal microblades and microcores; small utilized cryptocrystalline flakes; pebble tools; crudely fashioned slate or sandstone slab bifaces; faceted ground-slate points; nephrite or jadeite celts (often small and rectangular in plan and cross section); Gulf Island–complex items of soft stone or coal; disk-shaped labrets; small disk beads of slate, shale, or shell; notched stone sinkers; grooved stone sinkers; abrading stones (some of irregular "natural" outline, some carefully shaped); toggling harpoon heads of antler; foreshafts of antler or sea-mammal bone; unilaterally barbed bone points; bone singlepoints and bipoints; bird-bone needles; and celts made of sea mussel shell.

Distinctive features found at several sites include clay-lined pits, sometimes associated with vertically placed stone slabs and stone-slab "boxes." Their uses are not known. Two waterlogged Locarno Beach components have disclosed use of twine, cordage, and netting; basketry (mainly openwork vessels of a distinctive checker-woven wrapped twining but including burden baskets and other types of various checker, twilled, and twined constructions); and miscellaneous objects of cedar bark and wood. Among the most interesting aspects of Locarno Beach assemblages are "art" objects, which include carved antler spoon and knife handles representing small stylized humanoid figures and whales—in one case, clearly killer whales. The enigmatic Gulf Islands–complex artifacts are well made and often highly polished items of soft stone, coal, or, rarely, bone. Distinct types are discernible within the category, but their functions have not been determined. Common forms include short bars with holes through either end; small rectangular pieces of oval cross section, some with and some without paired holes; and rectangular pieces with notches sawed into each end.

A recent assessment (Matson 1992) of subsistence patterns has identified Locarno Beach as the first culture type in the Strait of Georgia region that seems to have engaged in the preservation and storage of salmon for later consumption. As such, it may represent the beginnings of the regional variant of the ethnographic Northwest Coast culture. However, some distinctive characteristics of the ethnographic pattern were not yet in evidence, including large plank-covered dwellings and social stratification. Burials, for example, provide no indication of ascribed status.

Donald H. Mitchell

Further Readings

Borden, C.E. 1951. Facts and Problems of Northwest Coast Prehistory. *Anthropology of British Columbia* 2:35–52.

———. 1970. Cultural History of the Fraser-Delta Region: An Outline. In *Archaeol-*

ogy in British Columbia, New Discoveries, edited by R.L. Carlson. *B.C. Studies* 6–7:95–112.

———. 1983. Prehistoric Art of the Lower Fraser Region. In *Indian Art Traditions of the Northwest Coast,* edited by R.L. Carlson, pp. 131–165. Simon Fraser University, Burnaby.

Matson, R.G. 1992. The Evolution of Northwest Coast Subsistence. *Research in Economic Anthropology* (Supplement) 6:367–428.

Matson, R.G., and G. Coupland. 1995. *The Prehistory of the Northwest Coast.* Academic Press, San Diego.

Mitchell, D. 1971. *Archaeology of the Gulf of Georgia Area, a Natural Region and Its Cultural Types.* Syesis, vol. 4 (Supplement no. 1).

———. 1988. Prehistory of the Coasts of Southern British Columbia and Northern Washington. In *Northwest Coast,* edited by W. Suttles, pp. 340–358. Handbook of North American Indians, vol. 7, W.C. Sturtevant, general editor. Smithsonian Institution, Washington, D.C.

Logan Creek Complex

The term "Logan Creek Complex" describes the material remains of a series of closely related Early Plains Archaic (ca. 6050–3050 B.C., or 8000–5000 years B.P.) groups that repeatedly occupied a site along Logan Creek, northeastern Nebraska. The site (25BT3) is in Burt County on the east side of the Logan Creek Valley. It was extensively excavated between 1957 and 1963 by the Nebraska State Historical Society and reexamined in 1991 by a joint University of Nebraska at Omaha–Nebraska State Historical Society team. Occupational zones are located on and within an alluvial fan. Zones A, B, C, and D (A is the uppermost) are assigned to the Logan Creek complex on the basis of similarities in artifact content. The most diagnostic artifacts are small- to medium-sized side-notched projectile points with straight or concave bases and plano-convex side-notched scrapers that usually have straight bases. Grinding is usually evident on the base and in the notches of projectile points; it is slightly less common on scrapers. Less diagnostic chipped-stone artifacts are unnotched end and side scrapers, ovoid and triangular bifacial cutting tools, and drills. Other stone tools are grinding stones, hammerstones, and scoria abraders. Lumps of ocher, possibly used as paint, and quartzite and granite glacial cobbles, often broken from exposure to fire, are common. Bone and antler tools include awls, punches, shuttles, a needle, flakers, fleshers, a fishhook, beads/tubes, and an antler hammer. Zones E and F, which are less extensively examined than Zones A through D, produced limited evidence, in the form of projectile-point fragments, that they may also be assignable to the complex if better documented. The two lowest zones, G and H, produced no diagnostic artifacts.

Hearths of several types are the most common features. Less common are small pits and isolated postholes. There was also a possible small temporary shelter or windbreak consisting of an ovoid concentration of lightly burned timbers and three associated postholes. Vertebrate faunal remains and mussel shell were abundant. There is considerable variation in dependence on these resources and in the species of each category through time. Bison bone makes up 85.7 percent of the vertebrate faunal assemblage, which included 29 identified taxonomic groupings. Zones A to F yielded the following radiocarbon ages (^{13}C corrected): 4070 B.C. ± 160, 4390 B.C. ± 120, 5070 B.C. ± 90, 5120 B.C. ± 110, 5230 B.C. ± 100, and 5400 B.C. ± 270 (6020, 6340, 7020, 7070, 7180, and 7350 years B.P.), all believed accurate for the zones assigned to the complex. The two lowest zones, G and H, are of unknown affiliation and remain undated.

The closest relationship between the Logan Creek complex and other Plains sites seems to be with the Hill site in western Iowa, which yielded both side-notched projectile points and side-notched scrapers. Other sites in western Iowa, such as the Cherokee Sewer site and the Simonsen site, also seem to be closely related. Western sites, such as the Spring Creek site in Frontier County, Nebraska, and the Hawken site and Cultural Layer 21 at Mummy Cave in Wyoming, show more general relations. All demonstrate human adaptations to less than optimum living conditions in the Plains during the dry Altithermal climatic episode.

Gayle F. Carlson

Further Readings

Anderson, D.C., and H.A. Semken, Jr. (editors). 1980. *The Cherokee Excavations: Holocene Ecology and Human Adaptations in Northwestern Iowa.*

Academic Press, New York.

Frankforter, W.D. 1959. A Pre-Ceramic Site in Western Iowa. *Journal of the Iowa Archeological Society* 8:47–72.

Frankforter, W.D., and G.A. Agogino. 1960. The Simonsen Site: Report for the Summer of 1959. *Plains Anthropologist* 5:65–70.

Kivett, M.F. 1962. Logan Creek Complex. Paper presented at the Twentieth Plains Archeological Conference, Lincoln.

Longhouses (Plateau)

When Europeans entered the Columbia Plateau in the early eighteenth century, mat longhouses were the most common form of dwelling. They were constructed of a pole framework covered by long woven mats of bark or other materials. In some instances, the structure stood over a pit up to 1 m (3.3 feet) deep. While these structures were often 18–30 m (59–98 feet) long, some were as long as 60–120 m (197–394 feet) and housed well over 100 people. When Lewis and Clark arrived at what is now Kamiah, Idaho, in the early nineteenth century they encountered several hundred warriors who lived in a single longhouse. The superstructure was sometimes heavy enough to preclude taking the structure apart easily. Often, however, the poles were light enough that the house could be taken apart and rebuilt as several small mat lodges. These structures have not been extensively studied by archaeologists. Among the earliest longhouses is one excavated in the Calispell Valley of northeastern Washington State that was 30 m (98 feet) long and is radiocarbon dated to ca. A.D. 350 (1600 years B.P.).

Why longhouses replaced pithouses as the most common house form is an important research question in Columbia Plateau prehistory. The first structures on the Columbia Plateau are semisubterranean pithouses; the first were built perhaps as early as 3550 B.C. (5500 years B.P.), and they become common in the record by 3050–2050 B.C. (5000–4000 years B.P.). After a brief hiatus at ca. 2050–1550 B.C. (4000–3500 years B.P.), pithouses were ubiquitous on the Columbia Plateau, yet they were not in widespread use by the mid-1700s. Possible explanations include the ease with which longhouses could be lengthened or shortened to accommodate changing household size and the ease with which the entire edifice could be taken down, moved, and reassembled. This would suggest that conditions on the Columbia Plateau during the last two millennia favored increasing levels of mobility and increasing flexibility in household size, but more research is needed to know with any certainty.

Kenneth M. Ames

Further Readings

Rice, H.S. 1985. *Native American Buildings and Attendant Structures on the Southern Plateau*. Reports in Archaeology and History 100–44. Archaeological and Historical Services, Eastern Washington University, Cheney.

Loseke Creek Variant

The Loseke Creek variant is distributed along the Missouri River and its tributaries from near Omaha, Nebraska, to the area of Lake Francis Case in south-central South Dakota.

The Loseke Creek settlement pattern includes villages of extensive temporal duration or frequent reoccupation. In northeastern Nebraska, excavations at the Feye site, an occupation area of 1,497 m² (1,791 square yards), disclosed 19 pits for food storage and perhaps pottery-vessel supports, five hearths, and postholes suggesting the former presence of structures. The Lawson site, a village of 2,995 m² (3,582 square yards) in size 0.4 km (0.25 mile) west of Feye, was nearly completely excavated. Features at Lawson are extramural storage pits and hearths, as well as shallow basins 1.2–1.8 m (4–6 feet) in diameter with poorly defined hearth areas, which are probably house floors. Clusters of structural remains, storage pits, and hearths at both the Feye and the Lawson sites suggest that the sites consisted of four-to-eight habitation areas, each perhaps occupied by a distinct social unit. Additional evidence for villages in the Loseke Creek variant comes from excavations at the Scalp Creek, Ellis Creek, and Arp sites, which are now flooded by Lake Francis Case in South Dakota. Temporary campsites were also integral to the settlement pattern of the Loseke Creek variant. Examples include Zone III of the Tramp Deep site, which is situated on a small intermittent stream on the south side of Lewis and Clark Lake ca. 3.2 km (2 miles) above Gavin's Point Dam; the Tabor site in a creek valley at a considerable distance from the Missouri River in the Lewis and Clark Lake area; and 39BR102, a site exposed in a cut bank of Lake Francis Case, ca. 0.8 km (0.5 mile) downstream from the Arp site.

Patterns of disposal of the dead for the Loseke Creek variant remain to be determined in detail. Data from the Eagle Creek site in northeastern Nebraska suggest that earthen mounds on elevations covering burial pits containing disarticulated human remains are probably a part of this pattern. The Loseke Creek subsistence base included hunting, gathering, and horticulture. Evidence for hunting includes the presence in sites of the bones of large mammals, including bison, deer, elk, antelope, and small mammalian forms. Hunting and butchering tools commonly occur. Projectile points are small and were probably used to tip arrows. The use of the bow and arrow is also indicated by arrowshaft smoothers. The gathering of wild-vegetable foods is indicated by plum pits at the Arp site and by handstones and grinding slabs at several sites. Hard evidence for horticulture comes from the Arp and the Lawson sites, both of which produced corn.

Although not well dated, the Loseke variant is assignable to the Late Plains Woodland period on the basis of ^{14}C dates of A.D. 450–585 (1500–1365 years B.P.) from charcoal from a level in the Rainbow site in Iowa. Associated pottery is similar to Scalp ware from the Scalp Creek site in South Dakota. The Loseke Creek variant ends with the appearance of the Initial variant of the Middle Missouri tradition ca. A.D. 950 (1000 years B.P.). Considering the possible origin of the Middle Missouri tradition in northwestern Iowa, it is interesting to note similarities between the most recent Loseke Creek–variant pottery styles and styles associated with Initial Middle Missouri.

Alfred E. Johnson

Further Readings

Grant, R.D. 1967. *Archaeological Investigations at the Arp Site, 39BR101, Brule County, South Dakota*. Archaeological Studies Circular no. 12. W.H. Over Museum, Vermillion.

Hurt, W.R., Jr. 1952. *Report of the Investigation of the Scalp Creek Site, 39GR1, and the Ellis Creek Site, 39GR2, Gregory County, South Dakota*. Archaeological Studies Circular no. 4. South Dakota Archaeological Commission, Pierre.

Kivett, M.F. 1952. *Woodland Sites in Nebraska*. Publications in Anthropology no. 1. Nebraska State Historical Society, Lincoln.

Lost Continent of Atlantis Theory

The Lost Continent of Atlantis theory refers to the myth that Native Americans are descendants of people who came from the vanished continent of Atlantis, a legendary island in the Atlantic Ocean. "Lost" Atlantis was mentioned by Plato and accepted as fact by medieval writers. Attempts to rationalize the myth after the Renaissance identified Atlantis with the Canaries, Scandinavia, Palestine, and even the Americas, and some ethnologists thought that the Basques, the ancient Italians, and the Guanches were descendants of inhabitants of the island, too. The myth was one of many speculative attempts between the sixteenth and the eighteenth centuries to account for the origin and identity of the Native Americans. Still other scholars thought that Native Americans were descendants of the Tartars, the Israelites, the Iberians, the Canaanites, the Carthaginians, or people from another lost continent, Mu.

Guy Gibbon

Further Readings

Wauchope, R. 1962. *Lost Tribes and Sunken Continents*. University of Chicago Press, Chicago.

Lost Race Theory

The Lost Race theory was a view held from the late eighteenth to the late nineteenth century that the earthen mounds of eastern North America were erected by a race of civilized White or Asian Mound Builders who had eventually disappeared or were vanquished by intruding American Indians. The view persisted even after the prominent physical anthropologist S.G. Morton concluded in his *Crania Americana* (1839) that Mound Builder skulls and the skulls of recently deceased Indians represented just one race that had two families, the "Barbarous" and the "Toltecs." The Lost Race theory is but one of many early speculations concerning the origin and identity of Native Americans.

Guy Gibbon

Further Readings

Silverberg, R. 1968. *Mound Builders of Ancient America*. New York Graphic Society, Greenwich.

Willey, G.R., and J.A. Sabloff. 1993. *A History of American Archaeology*. 3rd ed. W.H. Freeman, San Francisco.

L

See also MOUND BUILDER MYTH

Lost Terrace Site

Lost Terrace (24CH678) is, as of the mid-1990s, the only known instance when and where Avonlea-phase peoples deviated from their customary reliance on bison in the Northwestern Plains region. Lost Terrace is a single-component Late Prehistoric Avonlea-phase game-processing campsite in Chouteau County, Montana. It was discovered eroding from the left bank of the Upper Missouri River southeast of Big Sandy in 1975 in the course of a Bureau of Land Management–sponsored Montana State University floodplain reconnaissance operated from boats. Follow-up visitation in 1977 recovered diagnostic arrow points and associated artifacts and fire-broken rocks, along with the copious pulverized remains of numerous pronghorn antelope carcasses. Montana State University excavated the site in 1985–1986.

Eighty-three (minimum number of individuals) adult and subadult pronghorn antelope (*Antilocapra americana*), which had been killed elsewhere on one or more occasions by hunters using bows and arrows, were taken to Lost Terrace for meat- and hide-processing purposes during what may have been an uncommonly desperate winter ca. A.D. 950 (1000 years B.P.). Site seasonality was determined from the growth stage reached by 24 (minimum number of individuals) pronghorn fetuses at the time of their deaths. Procurement and processing by humans is suggested for a bison (*Bison bison bison*), a deer (*Odocoileus* sp.), one bobcat (*Lynx rufus*), a crow (*Corvus brachyrhynchos*), prairie dogs (*Cynomys ludovicianus*), bushytail woodrats (*Neotoma cinerea*), jackrabbits (*Lepus townsendi*), and cottontail rabbits (*Sylvilagus nuttali*). A single, stone-lined, basin-shaped fire pit, three unlined depressions, and ash-discard piles were the only features identified beneath the midden. Hundreds of pounds of fire-decomposed river cobbles, large quantities of charcoal and ash, and thousands of bone and tooth fragments dominated the midden. The lithic tool inventory included small triangular side-notched and unnotched arrow points, knives, end and side scrapers, perforators, fully grooved hammerstones, anvil stones, a sandstone shaft smoother, and unifacial and bipolar choppers. The lithic debitage included thousands of waste flakes, a dozen pebble cores, and a microblade core. Several bone awls and

Excavation of the 1,000–year-old Late Prehistoric Lost Terrace site pronghorn antelope midden along the left bank of the Upper Missouri Wild and Scenic River. (Courtesy of Museum of the Rockies/ Montana State University–Bozeman)

six polished, circular-to-ovoid, incised, and smoothed disks manufactured from mussel shell were also recovered from the midden. Obsidian points and waste flakes were fashioned from obsidian transported from the Obsidian Cliff Plateau quarries in Yellowstone National Park to the southwest in northwestern Wyoming.

Leslie B. Davis

Further Readings

Davis, L.B., and J.W. Fisher, Jr. 1988. Avonlea Predation on Wintering Plains Pronghorns. In *Avonlea Yesterday and Today: Archaeology and Prehistory*, edited by L.B. Davis, pp. 101–118. Saskatchewan Archaeological Society, Regina.

———. 1990. A Late Prehistoric Model for Communal Utilization of Pronghorn Antelope in the Northwestern Plains Region, North America. In *Hunters of the Recent Past*, edited by L.B. Davis and B.O.K. Reeves, pp. 241–276. One World Archaeology, vol. 15. Unwin Hyman, London.

Greiser, S.T. 1988. Lost Terrace Avonlea Material Culture. In *Avonlea Yesterday and Today: Archaeology and Prehistory,* edited by L.B. Davis, pp. 119–128. Saskatchewan Archaeological Society, Regina.

Lost Tribe Theory

A favorite opinion of theologically inclined writers was that Native Americans were descendants of the Ten Lost Tribes of Israel; the view became popular in the later sixteenth century and persisted into the nineteenth. Among writers favoring this interpretation were the Dominican Fray Diego Duran, who wrote shortly after the Spanish Conquest of Mexico; James Adair, an influential eighteenth-century American writer; and Lord Kingsborough, a renowned nineteenth-century antiquarian.

Guy Gibbon

Further Readings

Huddleston, L.F. 1967. *Origins of the American Indians: European Concepts, 1492–1729.* University of Texas Press, Austin.

Wauchope, R. 1962. *Lost Tribes and Sunken Continents.* University of Chicago Press, Chicago.

See also MOUND BUILDER MYTH

Lovelock Cave

Lovelock Cave (26CH18) is an open rock shelter ca. 45 m (148 feet) wide and greater than 12 m (39.4 feet) deep formed by Pleistocene Lake Lahontan in western Nevada. Large blocks of the roof fell ca. A.D. 500 (1450 years B.P.), dividing the site into a limited-access cave and an outer shelter. Human use began ca. 3050 B.C. (5000 years B.P.) and continued into the historic period as indicated by 25 radiocarbon dates. The interior cave was used only for burials and storage; all indicators of living activities are from the outer shelter.

Artifacts were discovered in Lovelock Cave by guano miners; in 1912, they were collected for display at the Lowie Museum by A.L. Kroeber's assistant, Llewyllen L. Loud. Loud returned in 1924 with Mark Harrington to obtain collections for the Heye Foundation and to record the stratigraphy for chronological information (Loud and Harrington 1929). These expeditions were the first archaeological excavations in Nevada. Subsequent studies have revised the chronology, investigated human di-

ets recorded in coprolites (fossilized feces), and examined the faunal remains for information about prehistoric use of wetland resources.

The Lovelock Cave assemblage includes more than 20,000 artifacts and faunal remains and at least 75 human burials. Surprisingly, few lithic materials were recovered, but the perishable assemblage is unusually large and diverse. It includes a cache of 11 duck decoys, numerous artifacts thought to be repair parts for duck and goose decoys, other hunting and fishing gear, baskets and basketmaking tools and raw materials, feather items possibly ceremonial in nature, blankets made of small rodent skins, dried fish, and a bone assemblage that includes a large component of water birds.

Stephanie D. Livingston

Further Readings

Ambro, R.D. 1967. Dietary-Technological-Ecological Aspects of Lovelock Cave Coprolites. *University of California Archaeological Survey Report* 70:37–47.

Clewlow, C.W., Jr. 1968. Projectile Points From Lovelock Cave, Nevada. *University of California Archaeological Survey Report* 71:89–101.

Cowan, R.A. 1967. Lake-Margin Ecologic Exploitation in the Great Basin As Demonstrated by an Analysis of Coprolites From Lovelock Cave, Nevada. *University of California Archaeological Survey Report* 70:21–35.

Follett, W.I. 1967. Fish Remains From Coprolites and Midden Deposits at Lovelock Cave, Churchill County, Nevada. *University of California Archaeological Survey Report* 70:93–116.

Grosscup, G.L. 1960. *The Culture History of Lovelock Cave, Nevada.* University of California Archaeological Survey Report no. 52.

———. 1963. Lovelock, Northern Paiute and Culture Change. *Nevada State Museum Anthropological Papers* 9:67–71.

Heizer, R.F. 1967. Analysis of Human Coprolites From a Dry Nevada Cave. *University of California Archaeological Survey Report* 70:1–20.

Heizer, R.F., and L.K. Napton. 1970. *Archaeology and the Prehistoric Great Basin Lacustrine Subsistence Regime As Seen From Lovelock Cave, Nevada.* Contribution no. 10. Archaeological Research Facility, Department of Anthropology,

University of California, Berkeley.

Livingston, S.D. 1991. Aboriginal Utilization of Birds in the Western Great Basin. In *Beamers, Bobwhites, and Blue-Points: Tributes to the Career of Paul W. Parmalee,* edited by J.R. Purdue, W.E. Klippel, and B.W. Styles, pp. 341–357. Scientific Papers, vol. 23. Illinois State Museum, Springfield.

Loud, L.L., and M.R. Harrington. 1929. *Lovelock Cave.* University of California Publications in American Archaeology and Ethnology, vol. 25, no. 1.

Napton, L.K. 1969. *Archaeological and Paleobiological Investigations in Lovelock Cave, Nevada.* Special Publication no. 2. Kroeber Anthropological Society Papers, Berkeley.

See also HUMBOLDT LAKEBED SITE

Lower Columbia River Valley Sequence

The Lower Columbia River Valley, defined to include the valley of the Columbia River downstream from Celilo Falls near The Dalles, Oregon, as well as the Willamette River drainage downstream from Willamette Falls at Oregon City, almost certainly has been inhabited for as long as the rest of North America, or for at least 11,000 years. Little direct evidence of such antiquity has been found west of the Columbia Gorge, however, probably because rising sea level between 8050 and 3050 B.C. (10,000–5,000 years B.P.) raised the level of the floodplain and sharply reduced the gradient of the river, which has modified the landforms extensively through alluvial deposition and erosion. Tidal effects extend today even to Bonneville Dam, upstream from Portland. Nearby areas, such as the Willamette Valley, however, have yielded suggestive evidence of such age in the form of Clovis fluted projectile points.

Three chronological sequences have been defined formally for the Lower Columbia Valley: for The Dalles, the Portland Basin, and the Columbia Estuary (see Table). Cultural change probably was roughly similar for these three areas. The progression from the first human population, presumably Clovis big-game hunters, to the locally distinctive Northwest Coast society living in settled existence in large villages of planked houses, is very unevenly chronicled by the known archaeological record, which is heavily biased toward the last 3,000 years. The earliest radiocarbon date for human activity is ca. 7850 B.C. (9800 years B.P.) at The Dalles, just east of the Cascade Range, where large numbers of salmon bones in an early stratum dated to ca. 5750 B.C. (7700 years B.P.) suggest that the fishing emphasis characteristic of the ethnographic Chinookan culture was in place at that early date. However, the circumstances of the find hint that fishing was opportunistic rather than systematic and fundamental to the early economy. The Dalles locality has been shown to have been intensively used from the beginning, although the record for the period 4050–1050 B.C. (6000–3000 years B.P.) is incomplete.

Downstream, in the Columbia Gorge, Portland Basin, and Columbia Estuary areas, firm dates for human occupation are not much older than ca. 1050 B.C. (3000 years B.P.), even though evidence of probable earlier human activity is plentiful. These seemingly early but undated sites appear to reflect an initial hunting emphasis, but local cultural distinctiveness is manifest in the form of stylized ground-stone tools (distinctive celts made on cobbles, shaped ovoid cobbles, and stone spheres called bolas stones). Such stylistic patterns are thought to have begun as early as 6050 B.C. (8000 years B.P.). Sites apparently older than 3,000 years have been found on surfaces above the modern floodplain. Age estimates for these sites are based primarily on projectile-point types, which include willow-leaf-shaped points probably falling between 6050 and 2050 B.C. (8000–4000 years B.P.). Other tools reported include unifacially flaked pebbles, which are nearly always present at such sites and suggest woodworking activities, and mortars and pestles and manos and metates, evidence of plant-food processing.

The Youngs River complex (ca. 6050–4050 B.C. (8000–6000 years B.P.) of the Columbia Estuary sequence, which appears to represent this poorly documented period, is characterized by shouldered and unshouldered lanceolate points, stemmed scrapers, and stone weights found at sites whose ages are only estimated based on point styles. The following Seal Island phase (ca. 4050–50 B.C., or 6000–2000 years B.P.) is associated with large corner-notched points, presumably for atlatl darts, similar to those typical of the Merrybell phase (ca. 650 B.C.–A.D. 150, or 2600–1800 years B.P.) in the Portland Basin. Smaller points, presumably for arrows, become dominant in the succeeding Multnomah (Portland Basin) and Ilwaco (Columbia Estuary) phases, and Euro-

American trade goods appear in the late eighteenth century (Multnomah 3 subphase for the Portland Basin, Historic phase for the Columbia Estuary). Key temporal markers are the adoption of the bow and arrow, evidenced by small projectile points, ca. 550–150 B.C. (2500–2100 years B.P.), and the catastrophic Cascade Landslide of ca. A.D. 1250 (700 years B.P.). The latter event occurred when a mountainside collapsed in the Columbia Gorge, temporally impounding the river, which may have broken through the natural dam, swept destructively

L

Age	Lower Columbia Valley Regions		
	Columbia Estuary	Portland Basin	The Dalles
0	Historic Phase	Multnomah 3 Subphase	Contact-Historic
500	Ilwaco 2 Subphase	Multnomah 2 Subphase	Full Protohistoric
1000		Multnomah 1 Subphase	
1500	Ilwaco 1 Subphase		
2000		Merrybell Phase	
2500			
3000			
	Seal Island Phase		Initial Protohistoric
4000		Undefined Sequence	
5000			
6000			Transitional
7000	Youngs River Complex		Final Early
8000			Full Early
9000			
			Initial Early
10,000	Undefined Sequence		
11,000			
12,000			

Cultural chronologies for three Lower Columbia Valley regions. (Prepared by R. M. Pettigrew)

through the valley downstream, and destroyed settlements in its path. The physical and cultural effects of this disaster are a topic of great research interest.

Although the archaeological record of the last 3,000 years illustrates some changes in artifacts, most fundamental lifeway patterns had probably already been established. Woodworking technology was sophisticated, salmon fishing was an economic mainstay, and the population probably resided in stable streamside villages. The developmental chronology of the rich Lower Columbia artistic tradition, largely rendered in perishable materials such as wood, remains unclear, though stylistically distinctive ground-stone tools were well established by 1050 B.C. (3000 years B.P.). Some of the biggest challenges facing Lower Columbia archaeology are tracing the basic cultural changes of earlier millennia and bringing into sharper focus the Late Prehistoric lifeway that is imperfectly reflected by early historical documents.

Richard M. Pettigrew

Further Readings

Cressman, L.S., D.L. Cole, W.A. Davis, T.M. Newman, and D.J. Scheans. 1960. *Cultural Sequences at The Dalles, Oregon: A Contribution to Pacific Northwest Prehistory*. Transactions, n.s., vol. 50, pt. 10. American Philosophical Society, Philadelphia.

Minor, R. 1983. *Aboriginal Settlement and Subsistence at the Mouth of the Columbia River*. Unpublished Ph.D. dissertation, Department of Anthropology, University of Oregon, Eugene.

Pettigrew, R.M. 1981. *A Prehistoric Culture Sequence in the Portland Basin of the Lower Columbia Valley*. Anthropological Papers no. 22. Department of Anthropology, University of Oregon, Eugene.

———. 1990. Prehistory of the Lower Columbia and Willamette Valley. In *Northwest Coast*, edited by W. Suttles, pp. 518–529. Handbook of North American Indians, vol. 7, W.C. Sturtevant, general editor. Smithsonian Institution, Washington, D.C.

Lower Loup Phase

The Protohistoric ancestors of the northern Caddoan-speaking Pawnees are identified archaeologically with the Lower Loup phase. By 1775, the Pawnees were in sustained contact with Europeans and are considered fully historic. The hypothesis of Lower Loup development from the indigenous Central Plains tradition has been repeatedly offered but does not withstand empirical testing. Ethnohistorical and traditional data suggest that the Pawnees migrated to central Nebraska from the south ca. A.D. 1600 (350 years B.P.).

About a dozen Lower Loup villages or hunting camps have been the focus of systematic excavations, most in the 1930s by Nebraska State Historical Society archaeologists. Type sites include Schuyler, Linwood, Wright, Burkett, and Barcal. Village ruins are clustered along the lower reaches of the Loup River Basin, particularly in Nance and Platte counties, and in the Platte River Valley in Colfax and Butler counties. Distribution of hunting camps extends westward to the Republican Valley, the central Platte Valley, and the Sand Hills. Lower Loup habitation sites are earthlodge villages of up to 80 lodge ruins accompanied by trails, deep cylindrical and bell-shaped storage/refuse pits, middens, and cemeteries. The density of material culture suggests that communities were occupied for at least several generations. Earthlodges were substantial circular structures 9.1–18.2 m (30–60 feet) in diameter with a narrow entry passage. Four, and occasionally six, heavy timber center posts were surrounded by wall and leaner posts. This frame was covered with grass, thatch, and a thick course of earth. Interior features included a central hearth, a storage/refuse pit or two, and sometimes a small earthen altar along the rear wall.

Lower Loup–phase ceramics bear distinctive "simple-stamped" bodies and elaborately decorated, often collared rims. Decoration normally consists of incised lines or punctates; vessel shoulders are frequently decorated. The stone industry features small unnotched triangular arrow points, knives, scrapers, modified flakes, abraders, heavy mauls, and smoking pipes. Elaborate bone artifacts include bison-scapula digging or hoeing tools, awls, flakers, arrow shaft wrenches, serrated defleshing tools, pottery paddles, and "hide grainers." European trade goods, such as kettle fragments, glass beads, gun parts, and knives, occur in increasing frequency and reach a peak in historic (after A.D. 1775) Pawnee assemblages.

Hunting camps were transitory and yield utilitarian stone tools and ceramics, tipi floors, hearths, and copious amounts of buffalo bone. Different Pawnee bands claimed exclusive hunting territories, which are reflected in lithic-acquisition patterns. Subsistence focused on bison hunting and maize (corn) agriculture. A broad spectrum of smaller mammals and birds were also hunted as secondary resources. Fish and reptiles are rare. Wild-plant foods were also collected. Lower Loup people buried their dead in individual pits within villages or, rarely, on hills overlooking villages. Burial offerings vary widely and may relate to social status.

John R. Bozell
John Ludwickson

Further Readings

Grange, R.T., Jr. 1968. *Pawnee and Lower Loup Pottery.* Publications in Anthropology no. 3. Nebraska State Historical Society, Lincoln.

Holen, S.R. 1991. Bison Hunting Territory and Lithic Acquisition Among the Pawnee: An Ethnographic and Archaeological Study. In *Raw Material Economy Among Prehistoric Hunter-Gatherers,* edited by A. Montet-White and S. Holen, pp. 399–411. Publications in Anthropology no. 19. Department of Anthropology, University of Kansas, Lawrence.

O'Shea, J.M. 1984. *Mortuary Variability: An Archaeological Investigation.* Academic Press, New York.

———. 1989. Pawnee Archaeology. *Central Plains Archaeology* 1(1):49–107.

Roper, D.C. (editor). 1989. Protohistoric Pawnee Hunting in the Nebraska Sand Hills: Archeological Investigations at Two Sites in the Calamus Reservoir. Report prepared for the Bureau of Reclamation, Great Plains Region, Grand Island, Nebraska.

Wedel, W.R. 1936. *An Introduction to Pawnee Archaeology.* Bulletin no. 112. Bureau of American Ethnology, Smithsonian Institution, Washington, D.C.

———. 1986. *Central Plains Prehistory: Holocene Environments and Culture Change in the Republican River Basin.* University of Nebraska Press, Lincoln.

———. (editor). 1979. *Toward Plains Caddoan Origins: A Symposium.* Nebraska History, vol. 60, no. 2. Lincoln.

Lower Snake River Sequence

The Lower Snake River region includes the course of the Snake River from the lower end of Hells Canyon to the confluence of the Snake and Columbia rivers and encompasses southeast Washington State, northeast Oregon, and central Idaho. In its eastern and central portions, the river flows through deep canyons. At Lewiston, Idaho, the river's elevation is ca. 320 m (1,050 feet) above sea level (asl), while its canyon walls rise more than 900 m (2,952 feet) asl. The canyons, which cut through high basalt plateaus and higher (1,500–2,500 m, or 4,920–8,202 feet) granite mountains, create a terrain that is topographically rugged and ecologically diverse. Downstream, to the west, the land is considerably lower and much more arid, particularly in the Columbia Basin. Significant subsistence resources in the region include chinook salmon, steelhead trout, antelope, elk, deer, and a range of plant resources, including lilies such as camas that were prized for their roots.

The basic cultural sequence developed for the region in 1970 (Leonhardy and Rice 1970) has remained essentially intact, except for modifications in the following summary that reflect this author's views (Ames 1991). The Lower Snake River cultural sequence is the longest well-dated sequence on the Columbia Plateau.

Windust Phase (8850–6550 B.C., or 10,800–8500 years B.P.). The Windust phase is firmly dated by radiocarbon dates on charcoal and shell. The earliest radiocarbon date on charcoal is 10,820 ± 140 B.P. (10,795 B.C. calibrated) from the Hatwai site, which is located on the Clearwater River 11.3 km (7 miles) above its confluence with the Snake River. Marmes Rock Shelter, at the confluence of the Palus and Snake rivers, has produced the major series of dates for this phase. Diagnostic Windust-phase artifacts include stemmed, bifacially flaked lanceolate projectile points that were extensively reworked and resharpened while hafted. Other common artifacts include other bifaces, cobble tools, scrapers, utilized flakes, gravers, and cores. Less common tools are hafted bone points, bone needles and awls, harpoon parts, antler wedges, abraders, small millingstones, edge-ground cobbles, beads, and ocher. One site, Pilcher Creek, has produced siltstone figurines. A wide range of subsistence resources were taken, including bison, deer, elk, antelope, and smaller animals such as rabbits. Circumstantial evidence points to plant collection and processing and fishing. Population levels were low, and no definitive habitation sites have been excavated. There is no indisputable evidence for earlier occupation in the Lower Snake River region, though very scattered evidence for the earlier Clovis culture is found to the west.

Cascade Phase (6550–3050 B.C., or 8500–5000 years B.P.). This phase was originally separated into early (6550–5050 B.C., or 8500–7000 years B.P.) and late (5050–2550 B.C., or 7000–4500 years B.P.) Cascade subphases, but this division is no longer considered necessary. The Cascade phase is distinguished from the Windust phase mainly on the basis of projectile points. By 6550 B.C. (8500 years B.P.), Windust-phase stemmed lanceolate points were replaced by willow- or laurel-leaf-shaped lanceolate points known regionally as Cascade points. They are generally ovoid in outline, with their basal third ground for hafting. Cascade points are smaller and initially more uniform than earlier point forms. After 5050 B.C. (7000 years B.P.), large corner- and side-notched points are added to the inventory. Populations remained low and scattered, though settlement and mobility patterns may have become more flexible. The diversity of mammals hunted may have decreased. Some of these changes are probably the result of the Altithermal climatic period that began ca. 6550 B.C. (8500 years B.P.).

Hatwai Phase (ca. 3050–1550 B.C., or 5000–3500 years B.P.). This unit includes portions of the late Cascade and Tucannon phases of the original culture-historic model. The Hatwai phase is marked by the appearance of relatively large semisubterranean pithouses at several sites in the Lower Snake River region, including Alpowai, Hatwai, and Hatiuhpah. While dates on houses from these sites span a lengthy period from 5500 B.P. (4387 B.C.) at Hatwai to 3640 B.P. (2021 B.C.) at Hatiuhpah, most fall between 4470 B.P. (3530 B.C.) and ca. 4000 B.P. (2884 B.C.), a period of only 650 calendar years. After ca. 2050 B.C. (4000 years B.P.), house construction declines sharply until ca. 1550 B.C. (3500 years B.P.). Important technological changes include the appearance of large, heavy food-processing tools, such as mortars and pestles, and a significant technological change in the making of hunting tools. In contrast to the generally well-made projectile points of previous periods, Hatwai-phase points required far less manufacturing effort and have a distinctively "disposable" quality. They are also less common than in other periods. Faunal remains suggest that a narrow range of animals, primarily deer, were hunted. Small mammals appear not to have been prey. There is evidence for expanded use of freshwater mussels. The appearance of large food-processing tools suggests to some researchers that there was a much greater emphasis on plant foods, particularly camas and other plants utilized for their roots, at this time. Others argue that there was a greater emphasis on fishing, but there is little evidence to support this view.

Tucannon Phase (1550–550 B.C., or 3500–2500 yers B.P.). This phase is characterized by the widespread reappearance of pithouses. These structures are generally smaller and perhaps occupied for shorter periods than those during the Hatwai phase. The general trends in technology and subsistence of the Hatwai phase continue.

Harder Phase (550 B.C.–A.D. 450, or 2500–1500 years B.P.). During this phase, people began to first utilize many of the drier portions of the Columbia Plateau, including the Columbia Basin. All portions of the region were used. There is a major expansion of the resource base to include mammals from rabbits to bison. The quantity of fish remains in archaeological deposits increases markedly, as does the presence of net weights, indicating heavier reliance on fishing, probably for salmon. Pithouses, both single ones and aggregates, are ubiquitous in the archaeological record. The bow and arrow probably enters the Plateau, a change reflected in the size of projectile points.

Piq-FAnnin Phase (A.D. 450–1720, or 1500–230 years B.P.). This late period ends with the arrival of the horse in the Plateau ca. A.D. 1720. The period displays considerable continuity with the preceding Harder phase. Regional human populations probably peaked during this period. Habitations also shifted from pithouses to mat lodges, with some of the latter more than 60 m (197 feet) long. There was some narrowing of the resource base, though fish continued to be important. One researcher has suggested that the area was visited by a smallpox pandemic in 1520, but this has not been confirmed.

Num-EDpu Phase (A.D. 1720–present). "Numipu" is the Nez Perce term for themselves. This phase includes the "ethnographic" period of the late eighteenth and nineteenth centuries as well as the modern period. Other groups whose territories include the Lower Snake River are the Palus and the Umatilla. The Palus are extinct.

Kenneth M. Ames

Further Readings

Ames, K.M. 1991. Sedentism: A Temporal Shift or a Transitional Change in Hunter-Gatherer Mobility Patterns? In *Between Bands and States*, edited by S. Gregg, pp. 108–134. Occasional Paper no. 9. Center for Archaeological Investigations, Southern Illinois University Press, Carbondale.

Leonhardy, F.C., and D.G. Rice. 1970. A Proposed Culture Typology for the Lower Snake River Region, Southeastern Washington. *Northwest Anthropological Research Notes* 4(1): 1–29.

Lower Sonoran Agricultural Complex

The Lower Sonoran Agricultural complex is one of the seven prehistoric crop complexes of North America north of Mexico. As in the others, members of the group have common geographic origins, environmental requirements, and historical associations. The many species of the Lower Sonoran Agricultural complex—cotton (*Gossypium hirsutum* var. *punctatum*); tepary bean (*Phaseolus acutifolius*); jack bean (*Canavalia ensiformis*); lima bean, also called sieva bean (*Phaseolus lunatus*); striped cushaw squash (*Cucurbita argyrosperma* ssp. *argyrosperma*, formerly classified as *C. mixta*); warty squash (*Cucurbita moschata*); and grain amaranth (*Amaranthus hypochondriacus*)—are believed to have been introduced to the Lower Sonoran Desert region of the American Southwest from various points of origin and domestication in Mexico.

Maize, or corn (*Zea mays*), and other members of the Upper Sonoran Agricultural complex were introduced to the Arizona portion of the Lower Sonoran region from Mexico by 1000 B.C. (2950 years B.P.) and were grown as supplements to the diets of the hunter-gatherer populations of the time. Some evidence of a significant component of maize in the diet occurs at at least one late site of the sort usually attributed to these hunter-gatherers, but convincing evidence of a corn-beans-squash agricultural economy in the region dates from the subsequent Pioneer period of Hohokam occupation of the Salt, Gila, and Santa Cruz river valleys of south-central Arizona. Remains of both cotton and grain amaranth have also been recovered from Pioneer contexts, suggesting that elements of the Lower Sonoran group had diffused beyond the northern border of their Mesoamerican homeland before A.D. 600 (1350 years B.P.).

Hohokam agriculture was enhanced through a variety of farming techniques designed to allow efficient exploitation of the many biological habitats of the Sonoran Desert. Cotton production, however, is thought to have been limited to those portions of the major river systems in which crops were maintained through canal irrigation. Though its fossils have not been recovered from Pioneer-period sites, the tepary bean is thought to have been established in the region at the same time as cotton. Jack beans, lima (sieva) beans, and cushaw squash are not present in Hohokam sites that date earlier than the Sedentary period (A.D. 975–1100, or 975–850 years B.P.); warty squash occurs in younger sites (Post-Classic period, A.D. 1350–1450, or 600–500 years B.P.). These data suggest continuous interaction between the Hohokam and the Mesoamerican sources of domesticates as well as gradual development of the Lower Sonoran complex.

Hohokam farmers also cultivated native wild plants, such as little barley (*Hordeum pusillium*) and century plant (*Agave* sp.), and incorporated a number of gathered wild plants in their diets (e.g., prickly pear and saguaro-cactus fruit, cholla-cactus buds, and mesquite pods). This wide range of plant foods and plant resources was probably integrated with crop plants of the Upper and Lower Sonoran complexes in various ways at various times in prehistory.

Thus, though the Hohokam may have monopolized the production and commodity value of cotton or other crops for a while, all the crop plants of the Lower Sonoran complex eventually came under cultivation by other Southwestern groups. Tepary and lima beans and cushaw squash seem to have been cultivated by Puebloan farmers on the Colorado Plateau by A.D. 900 (1050 years B.P.). Secure evidence for jack bean, grain amaranth, or cotton cultivation north or east of the Hohokam heartland, however, is dated after A.D. 1100 (850 years B.P.).

James Schoenwetter

Further Readings

Brubaker, C.L. 1992. Origin of Upland Cotton. *American Journal of Botany* 79(11):1291–1225.

Crown, P.L. 1990. The Hohokam of the American Southwest. *Journal of World Prehistory* 4(2):223–253.

Ford, R.I. 1985. Patterns of Prehistoric Food

Production in North America. In *Prehistoric Food Production in North America,* edited by R.I. Ford, pp. 341–364. Anthropological Paper no. 75. Museum of Anthropology, University of Michigan, Ann Arbor.

Kaplan, L., and L.N. Kaplan. 1988. *Phaseolus* in Archaeology. In *Genetic Resources of Phaseolus Beans,* edited by P. Gepts. Kluwer, Dordrecht.

Monro, J.M. 1987. *Cotton.* 2nd. ed. John Wiley and Sons, New York.

Schinkel, C., and P. Gepts. 1989. Allozyme Variability in the Tepary Bean, *Phaseolus acutifolius* A. Gray. *Plant Breeding* 102:182–195.

See also EASTERN AGRICULTURAL COMPLEX; UPPER SONORAN AGRICULTURAL COMPLEX

Lower Walnut Focus

"Phase" would be a more accurate term than "focus," but "focus" continues to be used. Lower Walnut focus is one of two named members of the Great Bend aspect (the other is Little River focus). Dating is poorly established, but the focus probably begins by A.D. 1450 (500 years B.P.) if not earlier and likely continues to ca. 1735–1750 (215–200 years B.P.). Sites are concentrated in south-central Kansas, especially where the Walnut River joins the Arkansas River. Origins are uncertain. One suggestion is a move down the Arkansas River by the Little River focus; a second one is a move up the Arkansas River by Arkansas River Valley Caddoans sometime after the collapse of the Spiro phase (A.D. 1450, or 500 years B.P.); and a third suggestion is an in situ development from Late Woodland (A.D. 800–950, or 1150–1000 years B.P.) populations through such early Late Prehistoric complexes as Uncas and Bluff Creek (A.D. 1250–1400, or 700–550 years B.P.).

Very few Lower Walnut sites have been excavated. Large sites that likely represent villages are known from near the mouth of the Walnut River. Extensive quarries for Florence-A (Kay County) chert along nearby Beaver Creek are also surrounded by large Late Prehistoric sites that likely represent Lower Walnut occupations. Many smaller Late Prehistoric sites in the general area reflect short-term use by Lower Walnut people. Houses were round in outline with a beehive-shaped superstructure covered with grass. Subsistence is not well documented.

Corn has been recovered archaeologically, and early historical accounts note large fields of corn. Bison were hunted, along with deer and elk. Small mammals, birds, fish, and turtles were also utilized. The predominant ceramic type was shell tempered, plain surfaced, and ovate in shape with a flat base. Decoration is rare and mostly involves diagonal lip incisions. Bone tools include bison-scapula hoes that were hafted using a system different from that of the Little River focus. The Lower Walnut hafting system resembles that used by members of the Southern Plains Village tradition. Other bone items include split-bone awls, mule-deer-tibia and bison-rib shaft straighteners, and bone beads. Stone tools include small triangular points without notches; plain-shafted and expanding-base drills; beveled-edge knives, some with hafting notches; and end scrapers. Ground-stone includes manos, celts, shaft smoothers, grooved mauls, and pipes. Trade materials include pottery and obsidian from the Southwest. Other pottery came from Caddoan groups. Red pipestone comes from an unknown source to the northeast. Some ceramics may come from the Little River focus.

It is likely that some Lower Walnut sites near the mouth of the Walnut River were visited in 1601 by Juan de Oñate. The village visited was named Etzanoa, and the residents used a Wichita word for chief. The Spanish thought the place Oñate visited was part of Quivira. Beginning in the late seventeenth century and continuing into the eighteenth, the Ouitsitas (Wichita-proper) were noted on maps as residing on the Arkansas River in the general area occupied by the Lower Walnut focus. The Bryson-Paddock site north of present-day Ponca City, Oklahoma, is likely to have been an early-eighteenth-century Wichita-proper village.

Susan C. Vehik

Further Readings

Vehik, S.C. 1986. Oñate's Expedition to the Southern Plains: Routes, Destinations, and Implications for Late Prehistoric Cultural Adaptations. *Plains Anthropologist* 31:13–33.

———. 1990. Late Prehistoric Plains Trade and Economic Specialization. *Plains Anthropologist* 35:125–145.

Wedel, W.R. 1959. *Introduction to Kansas Archaeology.* Bulletin no. 174. Bureau of American Ethnology, Smithsonian Institution, Washington, D.C.

————. 1961. *Prehistoric Man on the Great Plains.* University of Oklahoma Press, Norman.

See also GREAT BEND ASPECT; LITTLE RIVER FOCUS

Lubbock Lake

The Lubbock Lake National Historic and State Archeological Landmark (41LU1) is a 121.4-plus-ha (300-plus-acre) archaeological preserve on the Southern High Plains of Texas in an entrenched meander of Yellowhouse Draw. The site contains a cultural, faunal, and floral record within a virtually complete geological record that spans the past 11,500-plus years. It is well dated with more than 150 radiocarbon assays. More than 100 areas have been excavated in five major stratigraphic units.

Lubbock Lake was discovered in 1936 when dredging to rejuvenate local springs cut completely through the valley fill. The first archaeological investigation of the site, 1939–1941, was sponsored by the West Texas Museum (now the Museum of Texas Tech University, Lubbock). The second investigation, 1948–1951, was sponsored by the Texas Memorial Museum in Austin. The West Texas Museum conducted additional work in 1959–1960. Research resumed at Lubbock Lake under the auspices of the Museum of Texas Tech University in 1972 and has continued into the 1990s.

The valley fill is subdivided into five strata, numbered oldest (1) to youngest (5). Stratum 1 is sand and gravel alluvium. Stratum 2 includes lacustrine diatomite interbedded with marsh mud (2A) overlain by a homogeneous marsh mud (2B). Substrata 2A and 2B both have sandy aeolian and slopewash facies (2e). A marsh soil formed in the top of Stratum 2. Stratum 3 consists of lacustrine carbonate and aeolian sand. Stratum 4 contains interbedded marsh muds and alluvial sands (4A), aeolian sand (4B), and marsh mud (4m). The Lubbock Lake soil formed in upper 4B. Stratum 5 is a localized unit that includes marsh muds (5m) and two discrete layers of aeolian and slopewash sands (5A and 5B).

Five general cultural periods are recognized for the Southern High Plains, all of which are represented at Lubbock Lake: Paleoindian (9550–6550 B.C., or 11,500–8500 years B.P.), Archaic (6550–50 B.C., or 8500–2000 years B.P.), Ceramic (50 B.C.–A.D. 1450, or 2000–500

years B.P.), Protohistoric (A.D. 1450–1650, or 500–300 years B.P.), and Historic (A.D. 1650–1950s).

The Paleoindian record begins with Clovis-age occupation (ca. 9050 B.C., or 11,000 years B.P.) in Stratum 1 in deposits representing a point bar along a stream. The remains of seven species of megafauna exhibit cut lines, helical fracture surfaces, dynamic loading points, and evidence of tool use. Modified lithic tools are absent, although a Clovis point was recovered from the bonebed during the 1930s dredging operation. The point had been resharpened and was used as a butchering tool. Bone-orientation data show that bones were realigned by flowing water, but stream velocity and competency data indicate that neither the large caliche boulders recovered nor the megafaunal limb elements could have been moved by the stream.

Folsom (2A; ca. 8550 B.C., or 10,500 years B.P.), Plainview (lower 2B; ca. 8050 B.C., or 10,000 years B.P.), and Firstview (upper 2B; ca. 6650 B.C., or 8600 years B.P.) occupations are represented by a series of ancient bison kills around the margins of the ponds and marshes. They share several characteristics. Each kill was of a small cow-calf herd, and animals were butchered on the spot using both expedient lithic and bone-butchering tools. Lithic tools were either retouched or utilized amorphous flakes. Projectile points were refashioned and also resharpened for use as butchering tools. In the Folsom kills, bones from individual carcasses were stacked in small piles that represent butchering units. During Plainview and First-view times, bones were clustered or stacked in distinct concentrations with parts of more than one individual represented.

As of the mid-1990s, Lubbock Lake was the only excavated Early Archaic (6550–4550 B.C., or 8500–6500 years B.P.) site on the Southern High Plains. An ancient bison kill/butchering area on a sand ridge (2e) near the marsh dates to ca. 6050 B.C. (8000 years B.P.). Concentrations of the articulated to semiarticulated skeletal segments of several individual bison indicate the presence of butchering units. At least 28 activity areas from within aeolian (lower 4B) and marsh (3,4A, and 4m) sediments are known for the Middle Archaic (4550–2550 B.C., or 6500–4500 years B.P.). They include camps, bison (modern) kill/butchering locales, and a large oven that was probably used to process vegetal matter ca. 2850 B.C. (4800 years B.P.). The Late Archaic (2550–50 B.C., or 4500–

2000 years B.P.) is represented by at least nine occupation surfaces within aeolian sediments (upper 4B) and the A horizon of the Lubbock Lake soil. These surfaces contain scattered hearthstones from disturbed hearths, broken lithic tools, and lithic flaking debris that is

Geologic cross section of the valley-fill at Lubbock Lake. (Prepared by E. Johnson and V. T. Holliday)

concentrated in some areas and scattered in other areas. Late Archaic and Ceramic materials may be mixed in the upper A horizon of the Lubbock Lake soil, which may mean that a stable land surface existed through much of the late Holocene.

Early Ceramic (ca. 50 B.C.–A.D. 950, or 2000–1000 years B.P.) occupation is indicated by a hearth and associated camping debris that includes the remains of modern bison, lithic tools and flakes, and bone beads. For the later Ceramic (ca. A.D. 950–1450, or 1000–500 years B.P.), game-animal (modern bison, pronghorn antelope, coyote, wolf) processing stations are found in serial stratigraphic position at the edge of the marsh (lowermost 5m). For the Protohistoric period (ca. A.D. 1450–1650, or 500–300 years B.P.), both camping areas (lower 5B) and stations for processing large game animals (5m) are known. These occupations may represent the early Apache movement across the southern Plains. The aboriginal Historic period (A.D. 1650–1870s) is marked by the appearance of European trade goods and the modern horse. Camps occur along the valley margins (upper 5B). Processing stations (upper 5m) are similar to those in the Protohistoric and Ceramic periods, but they are distinctive in the inclusion of modern horse as a game animal. These occupations may represent the later Apache movement across the southern Plains. European occupation is represented by the Singer Store, a trading post located at Lubbock Lake from 1881 to 1886. Testing produced square nails, metal cans, a ginger-beer bottle, and heavy-caliber rifle shell casings that relate to this occupation and to buffalo-hunting activity. Trash dumps from the turn of the twentieth century to the 1950s attest to continued use of the Landmark by historic settlers.

Based on the Lubbock Lake data, the Southern High Plains was a grassland throughout the last 11,500 years, and neither people nor bison abandoned the region. The successive local fauna, sediments, and soils reflect changing ecosystems under pluvial to arid to mesic to semiarid conditions. The occupation of Lubbock Lake through time appears to have been by small groups of people for both economic and short-term residential uses. These hunter-gatherer peoples underwent adaptive change brought about by climatic stress and alterations to their food resources.

Eileen Johnson
Vance T. Holliday

Further Readings

Johnson, E. (editor). 1987. *Lubbock Lake: Late Quaternary Studies on the Southern High Plains.* Texas A&M University Press, College Station.

Johnson, E., and V.T. Holliday. 1980. A Plainview Kill-Butchering Locale on the Llano Estacado—the Lubbock Lake Site. *Plains Anthropologist* 25:89–111.

Lusk Complex and Projectile-Point Type

The Lusk cultural complex and projectile-point type were proposed during investigations at the Betty Greene site (48NO203) north of Lusk, Wyoming. The site was named after the landowners, Mr. and Mrs. Harris Greene, who had collected artifacts from the site. Excavations were made in 1967 under the direction of Anne Monseth Greene and Henry T. Irwin. A radiocarbon date on charcoal from the site is ca. 5050 B.C. (7000 years B.P.). The name Lusk was given to the projectile points recovered at the site, which are lanceolate and stemmed in shape with parallel-diagonal flaking. Two metates and one mano stone were found, which suggests plant utilization. A Lusk component is the youngest component at the Hell Gap site in southeast Wyoming.

George C. Frison

Further Readings

Greene, A.M. 1968. Age and Archaeological Association of Oblique Flaked Projectile Points at the Betty Greene Site, Eastern Wyoming. *Abstracts of Papers,* Thirty-Third Annual Meeting, Society for American Archaeology, Santa Fe.

Irwin-Williams, C., H.T. Irwin, G. Agogino, and C.V. Haynes, Jr. 1973. Hell Gap: Paleo-Indian Occupation on the High Plains. *Plains Anthropologist* 18(59):40–53.

L

M

Mace

A mace is a finely chipped stone object, though some were first chipped and then ground and polished. Usually fashioned on fine-grained chert, the mace has a short handle and a head that typically flares out from the handle and contains two or more projecting corners, as well as more bulbous projections on both lateral sides. In other cases, the form is embellished with additional points, projections, or spurs. Fifteen maces were discovered at the Late Prehistoric ceremonial center of Spiro in eastern Oklahoma. According to Henry W. Hamilton (1952:42), "maces are the most outstanding chipped stone artifacts found at Spiro, and must have had a great significance to the Spiro people." From their pristine condition, lack of evidence of use, and traces of painted decoration on a few, they must have had an exclusively ritual function. This contention is supported by their representation with other ritual objects on several engraved conch-shell containers from the site.

George H. Odell

Further Readings

Hamilton, H.W. 1952. The Spiro Mound. *Missouri Archaeologist,* vol. 14.

MacHaffie Site

The MacHaffie site (24JF4), first investigated by Columbia University in 1951, is an open-air, stratified, multicomponent Paleoindian (Folsom and Scottsbluff complexes) campsite that, until the 1980s, was the only widely recognized in situ Paleoindian site excavated in Montana. MacHaffie is located in Jefferson County on the northwest-facing flank of the Elkhorn Mountains at an elevation of 1,280 m (4,200 feet). It is on a peninsula within the floodplain of a perennial stream tributary to Prickly Pear Creek

Mace (Reprinted from Smithsonian Institution, Bureau of American Ethnology, Bulletin 60, Figure 156)

east of Montana City, 3 km (2 miles) southeast of Helena, and 22 km (14 miles) south of the Missouri River. Montana State University excavations in 1989–1990 suggested that the lowermost 1.2-m (4-foot) -thick alluvial unit within the 2.6-m (8.5-foot) -thick geological section encloses at least two, and possibly four, Paleoindian occupations, the uppermost two of which are of Cody-complex (Scottsbluff) affiliation. The Folsom occupation is underlain by a preceding occupation of as yet (1996) unknown Paleoindian association. Paleoindians, from 7390 B.C. ± 120 to 6150 B.C. ± 300 (9340–8100 years B.P.), exploited bison (*Bison* sp.), deer (*Odocoileus* sp.), wolf (*Canis lupus*), and jackrabbit (*Lepus* sp.), most likely in seasons other than winter, to support their stays at MacHaffie. Site selection was influenced by nearby outcrops of a high-quality chert that was utilized in substantial quantities by site occupants. The 1.4-m (4.5-foot) -thick overlying colluvium, in areas of the site not destroyed by artifact collectors, contained unstratified camp debris attributed to the Early and Middle Prehistoric Bitterroot and Pelican Lake complexes, respectively, Middle

and Late Plains Archaic (ca. 4050 B.C.–A.D. 250, or 6000–1700 years B.P.), and the Late Prehistoric period (ca. A.D. 950–1550, or 1000–400 years B.P.). Sagebrush (*Artemisia*) steppe dominated the site locally throughout the Holocene, with the valley floor itself occupied by riparian vegetation until 6330 B.C. ± 120 (8280 years B.P.).

Leslie B. Davis

Further Readings

Davis, L.B., J.P. Albanese, L.S. Cummings, and J.W. Fisher, Jr. 1991. Reappraisal of the MacHaffie Site Paleoindian Occupational Sequence. *Current Research in the Pleistocene* 8:17–20.

Davis, L.B., S.T. Greiser, J.P. Albanese, R.J. Ottersberg, G.E. Fredlund, and L.S. Cummings. 1997. Indian Creek and MacHaffie: Folsom Campsites in the Elkhorn Range, Northern Rocky Mountains. In *Folsom Archaeology and Late Pleistocene Paleoecology*, edited by M.A. Jodry and D.J. Stanford. Smithsonian Inquiry in Archaeology Series. Smithsonian Institution Press, Washington, D.C.

Forbis, R.G. 1955. *The MacHaffie Site.* Unpublished Ph.D. dissertation, Department of Anthropology, Columbia University, New York.

Forbis, R.G., and J.D. Sperry. 1952. An Early Man Site in Montana. *American Antiquity* 18:127–133.

Knudson, R. 1973. *Organizational Variability in Late Paleo-Indian Assemblages.* Unpublished Ph.D. dissertation, Department of Anthropology, Washington State University, Pullman.

Excavations in progress at the early Paleoindian MacHaffie site near Prickly Pear Creek, Upper Missouri River drainage. (Courtesy of Museum of the Rockies/Montana State University–Bozeman)

Madisonville

Madisonville (33HA36), in Hamilton County, Ohio, is a large Fort Ancient village and cemetery site on a terrace above the Little Miami River floodplain, ca. 8 km (5 miles) upstream from the Ohio River. Although it was in use by at least the fourteenth century A.D., its primary occupation was in the late sixteenth and early seventeenth centuries A.D. It is the most populous and most completely excavated Protohistoric Fort Ancient site, as well as the westernmost. When James B. Griffin (1943) first defined subareas within Fort Ancient, Madisonville was the type site for the "Madisonville focus," which was situated in the southwestern portion of the region. It also is the type site for the recently delineated late Fort Ancient "Madisonville horizon" (ca. A.D. 1450–1700, or 500–250 years B.P.).

Excavations conducted at Madisonville between 1879 and 1911 uncovered almost 1,400 burials and 1,000 large corn-storage pits. Few postmold patterns extensive enough to delineate structures were recorded, but houses seem to have been rectangular, with storage pits and burials interspersed in and around them. Subsistence included maize horticulture, hunting, fishing, and the gathering of shellfish and wild-plant resources. This is the only Fort Ancient settlement that utilized bison, and elk remains are much in evidence. Along with deer, these large mammals were important sources of meat, hides, and bone and antler tools, musical instruments, and ornaments. Food was stored and prepared in ceramic vessels, most of which were shell-tempered, and cord-marked or plain, four-handled jars with flaring rims. Chipped- and ground-stone artifacts included triangular projectile points, snub-nosed scrapers, finely made celts, and a wide variety of pipe forms. Exotic materials and artifacts found at Madisonville indicate that its residents participated in exchange networks that extended as far as the St. Lawrence Valley, western Iowa, and northern Alabama. Items made of nonlocal materials include marine-shell ornaments from the southeast, native copper ornaments, and Oneota, Iroquoian, and southeastern pipes.

European artifacts, while fairly numerous, were not large or diverse, perhaps signaling indirect contact rather than sustained direct trade. They include copper and brass scrap and small ornaments, medium-blue glass beads, parts from iron-banded kettles traded in the Northeast by Basque fishermen during the late sixteenth century, and a brass "Clarksdale" bell, which is generally associated with mid-sixteenth-century Spanish expeditions in the Southeast.

Many nonlocal items, particularly shell ornaments, were interred with burials. About half of the graves included offerings, most frequently ceramic vessels containing food. Although a strongly hierarchical social organization is not apparent in burial or settlement patterning, certain persons, probably in achieved leadership positions, such as chiefs and ritual specialists, seem to be marked by special, symbolically significant grave goods, such as distinctive stone pipes and certain types of copper and bone ornaments.

Penelope B. Drooker

M

Further Readings

Cowan, C.W. (editor). 1993. *Recent Research at the Madisonville Village Site, Hamilton County, Ohio.* Occasional Paper in Archaeology no. 1. Cincinnati Museum of Natural History, Cincinnati.

Drooker, P.B. 1996. *The View From Madisonville: Continuity and Change in Late Prehistoric–Protohistoric Western Fort Ancient Interaction Patterns.* Unpublished Ph.D. dissertation, Department of Anthropology, State University of New York, Albany.

Griffin, J.B. 1943. *The Fort Ancient Aspect: Its Cultural and Chronological Position in Mississippi Valley Archaeology.* University of Michigan Press, Ann Arbor.

Henderson, A.G., D. Pollack, and C.A. Turnbow. 1992. Chronology and Cultural Patterns. In *Fort Ancient Cultural Dynamics in the Middle Ohio Valley,* edited by A.G. Henderson, pp. 253–279. Prehistory Press, Madison.

Hooton, E.A., and C.C. Willoughby. 1920. *Indian Village Site and Cemetery Near Madisonville, Ohio.* Papers, vol. 8, no. 1. Peabody Museum of American Archaeology and Ethnology, Harvard University, Cambridge.

Magic Mountain Phase

The Magic Mountain phase is included in the Western Plains Early Archaic regional variant as defined by William B. Butler (1986). It is based on materials in Magic Mountain Zone E. Content differences from the underlying Mount Albion–phase component include the addition of six new point types and a general increase in the number of types of tools within a functional tool class. The tool assemblage is consistent with a hunting-and-gathering economy exploiting several different environments. Information gathered suggests that the Magic Mountain phase is found in the eastern foothills of the Colorado mountains and eastward some distance onto the Plains. The phase is thought to date to 3050–2550 B.C. (5000–4500 years B.P.), a span from the end of Atlantic IV (late Altithermal) to the beginning of the Sub-Boreal climatic episode.

William B. Butler

Further Readings

Butler, W.B. 1986. *Taxonomy in Northeastern Colorado Prehistory.* Unpublished

Ph.D. dissertation, Department of Anthropology, University of Missouri, Columbia.

———. 1990. Reinterpreting the Magic Mountain Site. *Southwestern Lore* 56(3):8–21.

Irwin-Williams, C., and H.J. Irwin. 1966. *Excavations at Magic Mountain: A Diachronic Study of Plains-Southwest Relationships.* Proceedings no. 12. Denver Museum of Natural History, Denver.

See also ALBION BOARDINGHOUSE PHASE; MAGIC MOUNTAIN SITE; MOUNT ALBION PHASE

Magic Mountain Site

The Magic Mountain site (5JF223) is located on Apex Creek on the western edge of the Denver Basin immediately adjacent to the foothills of the Front Range in what can be properly described as a mountain-plains transition zone. Long known as a "treasure trove" by local collectors because of an abundance of burials and surface remains, the site was formally investigated in 1959–1960 by Cynthia Irwin-Williams for her Ph.D. dissertation at Harvard University. Results of the excavations were published in 1966 under the authorship of Irwin-Williams and her brother Henry J. Irwin.

The multicomponent site, containing an abundance of projectile points and other lithic tools, has been recognized as one of the more important sites along the plains-mountain border and has long been used in interpretations of the Archaic period throughout the region. Geomorphological and other archaeological information has allowed the following reinterpretation of the stratigraphic and cultural units at the site (Butler 1986, 1990): South Platte phase (Colorado Plains Woodland), ca. A.D. 100–1000 (1850–950 years B.P.) (Stratigraphic Zones A and B); Front Range phase (Late Archaic), ca. 810 B.C.–A.D. 100 (2760–1850 years B.P.) (Zone C); Apex phase (Middle Archaic), ca. 1550–810 B.C. (3500–2760 years B.P.) (Zone D); Magic Mountain phase (Early Archaic), ca. 3050–2550 B.C. (5000–4500 years B.P.) (Zone E); Mount Albion phase (Early Archaic), ca. 4050–3050 B.C. (6000–5000 years B.P.) (Zone F). The 1,000-year gap in the sequence between 4500 and 3500 years B.P. may be resolved with new work on the site that began in 1996.

William B. Butler

Further Readings

Butler, W.B. 1986. *Taxonomy in Northeastern Colorado Prehistory.* Unpublished Ph.D. dissertation, Department of Anthropology, University of Missouri, Columbia.

———. 1990. Reinterpreting the Magic Mountain Site. *Southwestern Lore* 56(3):8–21.

Irwin-Williams, C., and H.J. Irwin. 1966. *Excavations at Magic Mountain: A Diachronic Study of Plains-Southwest Relationships.* Proceedings no. 12. Denver Museum of Natural History, Denver.

See also APEX PHASE; FRONT RANGE PHASE; MAGIC MOUNTAIN PHASE; MOUNT ALBION PHASE; SOUTH PLATTE PHASE

Mammoth/Mastodon

Mammoths (Elephantidae *Mammuthus*), mastodons (e.g., Mammutidae *Mammut*), and gomphotheres (e.g., Gomphotheriidae *Cuverionius*) in North, Central, and South America arose from one immigration (from Eurasia) of gomphotheriids (*Gomphotherium*) and mammutids (*Miomastodon*) in the Miocene and from two immigrations of elephantids (*Mammuthus meridionalis, M. primigenius*), the first in the early Pleistocene and the second in the late Pleistocene. North American cultural associations are known for *Mammuthus* (e.g., Great Plains, Basin and Range province in Arizona, Valley of Mexico) and *Mammut* (e.g., Mississippi River Valley). In South America, where neither mammoths nor mastodons occurred, cultural associations are known for gomphotheres (e.g., *Haplomastodon* in Venezuela and *Cuverionius* in Chile).

Mammuthus is aligned with *Elephas*, the Asian elephant, and, more distantly, with the African genus *Loxodonta*. With two extinct antecedent genera, these forms make up the family Elephantidae. Origin of the family is traced to late Miocene gomphotheres (ca. 6 million years ago); its arrival in North America dates to the early Pleistocene (ca. 1.9 million years ago). Elephantids have high-crowned teeth composed of transverse enamel plates that wear to produce filelike occlusal surfaces. High-crowned teeth, filelike occlusal surfaces, and horizontal jaw movements with associated skull and jaw architectures are consistent with a diet

Mammoth. (Illustration by J. J. Saunders)

of grass and a primarily grazing adaptation, a conclusion corroborated by coprolite studies. Prior to their New World extinction in the latest Pleistocene by 8050 B.C. (10,000 years B.P.), mammoths ranged from Alaska east and southward to Florida and Honduras. Their remains have been dredged from now-submerged portions of the Atlantic continental shelf. On the basis of the number of enamel plates comprising the third molars, which is expressed as an enamel-plate formula, and of enamel-plate compression expressed as plate number per 100 mm (3.9 inches) of tooth length, six species of New World *Mammuthus* are recognized. These are (with enamel-plate formulae for the upper/lower third molars, M3): *M. primigenius* (24–27/24–27), *M. meridionalis* (= *M. hayi*) (distinguished in early samples by 11 enamel plates on M3, but rapidly evolving), *M. imperator* (17–18/18–20) *M. columbi* (18–20/15–18) *M. jeffersonii* (25/24), and *M. exilis,* a dwarf form from the Channel Islands of California, distinguished from antecedent *M. imperator* by fewer plates (M3 average: 15/16) and by proportional differences associated

with the early attainment of adult size and condition. Mammoths, like modern elephantids, are inferred to have been gregarious (assemblages throughout their range comprise large numbers of individuals); sex and age ratios (females or subadults often predominate presumed catastrophic accumulations of mammoth remains) suggest a herd organization consisting of matriarchal family units. In addition, cooperative defense and rescue are behaviors possessed by both modern genera that are inferred to be general features previously possessed by mammoths as well.

Mastodons are primarily browsing proboscideans originating from gomphotheres by the early Miocene (ca. 22 million years ago). Phyletic change in mastodons was uniquely conservative and marked by little change in molar morphology; divergence is primarily recognized in the lower jaw, including a decrease in length of the symphysis and in size and persistence of the lower tusks. The earliest North American mammutid was a migrant arising from *Zygolophodon* in Eurasia. With gomphotheres, these mammutids utilized the Bering Strait during the middle Miocene (ca. 15 million years ago). Mastodon evolution culminated during the Plio-Pleistocene (ca. 3.75 million years ago) in *Mammut americanum,* known from early records in Washington and Florida. By the late Pleistocene (0.5 million years ago), the species occurred from Alaska to central Mexico, east across the United States to Florida, and northward to New Brunswick and Nova Scotia, including emergent portions of the Atlantic continental shelf. *M. americanum* was abundant in the Great Lakes region and Atlantic Canada during the latest Pleistocene from 12,050 B.C. (14,000 years B.P.) up to its extinction by 8050 B.C. (10,000 years B.P.). It occupied expansive wet areas and may have had semiaquatic habits. *Mammut americanum* possessed a broad and low cranium and simply curved upper tusks that were adapted for browsing. A short mandible contained variably persistent lower tusks. Low-crowned cheek teeth consisted of transverse crests composed of two major cusps. Transverse valleys between the crests were open and unobstructed, unlike the obstructed valleys characterizing the teeth of gomphotheres. The mammutid body was low, long, and stocky. There are no surviving close relatives, and aspects of mastodon behavior and habits remain ambiguous. Plant fossils associated with *M. americanum* link the species to pine parkland and mixed-deciduous-and-pine woodland or parkland during late Pleistocene interstadials and to deciduous forest, woodland, or savanna during interglacials. During the latest Pleistocene, *M. americanum* was associated with spruce dominance, with some fir, larch, and pine pollen, which suggests spruce forest or woodland. Small percentages of deciduous tree pollen are indicated in these latest records; grass occurs. Direct dietary information is provided by samples from *M. americanum* intestines/gut contents and teeth. Intestinal contents of a mastodon from Ohio (ca. 9550 B.C., or 11,500 years B.P.) included twigs of nonconiferous species displaying sheared ends and seeds of clover, sedges, and water-nymph. The occurrence of both twigs and herbaceous vegetation suggests that the mastodon was, at least seasonally, a selective feeder with both browsing and grazing habits.

Jeffrey J. Saunders

Further Readings

Fox, J.W., C.B. Smith, and K.T. Wilkins (editors). 1992. *Proboscidean and Paleoindian Interactions.* Baylor University Press, Waco.

Haynes, G. 1991. *Mammoths, Mastodonts, and Elephants: Biology, Behavior, and the Fossil Record.* Cambridge University Press, Cambridge.

Mead, J.I., L.D. Agenbroad, O.K. Davis, and P.S. Martin. 1986. Dung of *Mammuthus* in the Arid Southwest, North America. *Quaternary Research* 25:121–127.

Shoshani, J., and P. Tassy (editors). 1996. *The Proboscidea: Trends in Evolution and Paleoecology.* Oxford University Press, Oxford.

Mandeville

Mandeville (9CY1) is a ceremonial site in southwest Georgia that dates to the late Deptford and early Swift Creek periods. There are two mounds (A and B) and a village area. Mound A, a truncated earthen structure, was ca. 73 x 52 m (240 x 170 feet) at its base and 4.3 m (14 feet) high, while Mound B, also known as the Griffith Mound, was a burial structure 38 m (126 feet) in basal diameter and 5.5 m (18 feet) high. The final cap of Mound A is Mississippian, but aspects of the ceramics associated with the interior layers (which are not trunctated), especially tetrapods, check stamping, and complicated stamping with notched rims, indicate that they date to the late Deptford and early Swift Creek periods. A total of 23 3 x 3-m (10 x 10-foot) squares were excavated, and 10,131 sherds were recovered from a midden up to 1.1 m (3.5 feet) thick. Most of the ceramics dated to the Mississippian occupation; Woodland sherds were check stamped and complicated stamped (Betty A. Smith, personal communication). No subsurface features or structures were recorded during the excavations. Materials recovered from Mound B, including coppercovered pan pipes, copper earspools, platform pipes, tubular copper beads, and marine shell, indicate that Mandeville was a participant in an exchange network associated with Hopewellian ceremonialism in the Midwest. While mica was absent from the burial mound (Mound B), it was present in Mound A.

The Woodland occupation at Mandeville, which appears to be primarily a ceremonial presence, predates Kolomoki (ca. A.D. 250–600, or 1700–1350 years B.P.). Mandeville and Kolomoki may represent a developmental continuum of ceremonialism in South Georgia associated with an increased centralization of sociopolitical control that culminated in a protochiefdom centered on Kolomoki. Aside from individual burial mounds, there are no known late Weeden Island or Wakulla-period (both of which postdate Kolomoki) ceremonial/civic sites in Georgia or Florida. It is not until the development of Cemochechobee, a Roods-phase site north of Kolomoki, that we see the next expression of centralized sociopolical control along the lower reaches of the Chatta-hoochee River beginning at ca. A.D. 900 (1050 years B.P.).

The Mandeville site report (Keller et al. 1962) is important because it outlines the earlier stages of the development of centralized sociopolitical control in the Lower Chatta-hoochee Valley. It is interesting that, unlike Kolomoki, there were few indications of the presence of a residential village that supported the ceremonial activities that took place at the site. The village materials that were recovered are overwhelmingly from the much later Mississippian occupation of the site. This is somewhat similar to the vacant Hopewell ceremonial centers in the Midwest, which are the temporal and, to a degree, the cultural/ceremonial analogues of Mandeville.

Karl T. Steinen

Further Readings

Kellar, J.H., A.R. Kelly, and E. McMichael. 1962. The Mandeville Site in Southwest Georgia. *American Antiquity* 27:336–355.

Smith, B.A. 1975. *Re-Analysis of the Mandeville Site, 9Cla1, Focusing on Its Internal History and External Relations.* Unpublished Ph.D. dissertation, Department of Anthropology, University of Georgia, Athens.

———. 1979. The Hopewell Connection in Southwest Georgia. In *Hopewell Archaeology: The Chillicothe Conference,* edited by D.S. Brose and N. Greber, pp. 181–187. Kent State University Press, Kent.

Steinen, K.T. 1993. Sinuous Trajectory: Mandeville, Kolomoki, and the Development of Socio-Political Organization on the Gulf Coastal Plain. Paper presented at the Lamar Institute Conference on Swift Creek Culture, Macon.

See also KOLOMOKI

Mann Site

The Mann site (12PO2) is located near the confluence of the Ohio and Wabash rivers in extreme southwestern Indiana. The site served as one of the largest centers of Hopewellian habitation and ceremonialism during the latter part of the Middle Woodland period, ca. A.D. 150–500 (1800–1450 years B.P.).

Geometric earthworks and mounds were constructed on a virtually unparalleled scale. Earthen embankments define at least four geometric figures: a partial rectangular enclosure 600 m (656 yards) long and 300 m (328 yards) wide; another rectangular enclosure ca. 300 m (328 yards) square; a C-shaped enclosure 35 m (115 feet) in diameter; and a linear embankment ca. 700 m (765 yards) long. Four rectangular or loaf-shaped mounds are present, including two of the five largest Hopewell mounds in the Midwest. Remnants of at least six conical mounds 20–40 m (65.6–131 feet) in diameter are also present.

In the late nineteenth century, local antiquarians excavated several of the conical mounds and discovered human burials accompanied by Hopewellian artifacts. Among these were earspools made of native copper from the Great Lakes and beads made of marine shell from the Atlantic or Gulf coasts. Subsequent surveys and amateur mound excavations have expanded the list of exotic raw materials found at the site to include quartz, galena, Knife River chalcedony, meteoric iron, mica, obsidian, shark teeth, and steatite.

Abundant occupational debris covers as much as 40 ha (99 acres), ranking the site among the largest Middle Woodland habitations in eastern North America. James H. Kellar (1979) conducted systematic excavations (1964–1977) at four widely spaced locations in the habitation area. Extensive midden deposits and high densities of food-storage and -processing features were encountered in each case.

Most ceramic vessels were undecorated and had cord-marked or plain surfaces; a small number were decorated with Hopewellian zoned, stamped, and incised designs. One of the most distinctive features of the ceramic assemblage is the frequent occurrence of vessels decorated with impressions of elaborately carved wooden paddles. These "complicated stamped" ceramics are common in the Southeast but exceedingly rare in the Ohio Valley. Comparisons between these sherds and locally available clays indicate that they were local products rather than imports. Human-effigy figurines were also made from clay. Razor-sharp lamellar blades struck from prepared chert cores were the most common stone tool. Lowe Flared Base points probably served as spear or dart points and knives.

Agriculture was an important subsistence activity. More than 95 percent of all seeds recovered belong to cultivated species, including goosefoot (*Chenopodium* sp.), knotweed (*Polygonum erectum*), and maygrass (*Phalaris caroliniana*). Squash (*Cucurbita* sp.) was cultivated as well. Wild foods included hickory and pecan nuts. White-tailed deer dominate the faunal assemblage, accompanied by minor quantities of small mammals, birds, fish, turtles, and mussels.

More than 100 other sites in southwestern Indiana have been attributed to the Mann-phase settlement system. Most of these are small lithic scatters, which probably served as short-term hunting-and-gathering camps. Several sites contain mounds or earthworks and probably served corporate-ceremonial functions on a more limited scale. Almost 50 sites appear to represent dispersed habitations occupied by nuclear- or extended-family households. This suggests that the Mann site served as a focal point for the seasonal aggregation of otherwise dispersed social units.

Bret J. Ruby

Further Readings

Adams, W.R. 1949. *Archaeological Notes on Posey County, Indiana*. Indiana Historical Bureau, Indianapolis.

Kellar, J.H. 1979. The Mann Site and "Hopewell" in the Lower Wabash-Ohio River Region. In *Hopewell Archaeology: The Chillicothe Conference*, edited by D.S. Brose and N. Greber, pp. 100–107. Kent State University Press, Kent.

Ruby, B. 1993. *An Archaeological Investigation of Mann Phase Settlement Patterns in Southwestern Indiana*. Reports of Investigations 93–18. Glenn A. Black Laboratory of Archaeology, Indiana University, Bloomington.

See also HOPEWELL INTERACTION SPHERE; MIDDLE WOODLAND

Mano/Metate

The mano and the metate are used together as two parts of a grinding complex. The metate is the basal slab. It is always the larger of the two and may or may not have legs. Metates are often flat with a broad, slightly concave grinding surface, though deeper "trough" metates with raised sides are also common. The mano is held in the hand and pressed downward onto the metate in either a circular or a back-and-forth motion. They have been classified as "one-hand" manos, which are small and circular or square in shape; and "two-hand" manos, which are relatively long and rodlike and are characteristically used with trough metates.

Manos and metates occurred throughout North America, but they were especially prevalent in the Southwest. At Ventana Cave, for example, more than 1,300 were discovered, with some dating to well into the "Cochise culture" (Archaic) of that region (Haury 1950).

Archaeologists have traditionally shown little interest in grinding technology. As a consequence, there is not much information on it. The utility of grinding stones for reducing seeds, corn, nuts, and other vegetal materials is obvious and is supported by available ethnographies. One of the most useful of these from an archaeological perspective concerns the use, manufacture, specialization, and marketing of manos and metates among the Highland Maya of Guatemala (Hayden 1987).

The grinding of vegetal materials is not their only function, however. The Hopi say that they once used handstones for a variety of hide-working tasks, and Jenny L. Adams (1988) has demonstrated clear microscopic differences between hide-working and vegetal-working use-wear on manos. The grinding of pigments and of clay and temper for pottery making has also been observed. Analysts of function need to be aware that manos are more efficient when sharpened regularly (some estimate once a week if used every day). "Sharpening" is effected by pecking the grinding surface with a hammerstone, an activity that is certain to erase most use-wear and may, in some cases, be mistaken for it. Research into grinding technology is a nascent field that shows potential for the study of site function and the organization of technology (Schlanger 1991; Nelson and Lippmeier 1993).

George H. Odell

Further Readings

Adams, J.L. 1988. Use-Wear Analyses on Manos and Hide-Processing Stones. *Journal of Field Archaeology* 15:307–315.

Haury, E.W. 1950. *The Stratigraphy and Archaeology of Ventana Cave*. University of Arizona Press, Tucson.

Hayden, B. (editor). 1987. *Lithic Studies Among the Contemporary Highland Maya.* University of Arizona Press, Tucson.

Morris, D.H. 1990. Changes in Groundstone Following the Introduction of Maize Into the American Southwest. *Journal of Field Archaeology* 46:177–194.

Nelson, M.C., and H. Lippmeier. 1993. Grinding-Tool Design As Conditioned by Land-Use Patterns. *American Antiquity* 58:286–305.

Schlanger, S.H. 1991. On Manos, Metates, and the History of Site Occupation. *American Antiquity* 56:460–474.

Maple Sugaring

Maple sugaring is a historically observed and ethnograpically documented practice that is, as of the mid-1990s, without firm status in prehistory. If it were demonstrably prehistoric, maple sugaring could be used for modeling part of the prehistoric subsistence year in the Northeast–Great Lakes area. Routinely including sugaring as an expected spring activity could provide insights into diet and general health, particularly as an important source of calories for people whose diets might otherwise be seasonally deficient. The major difficulty in using maple sugaring as an adjunct to prehistoric research is the complex problem it presents in archaeologically recovering evidence for its presence and verifying an early presence in the relevant historic documents. It requires an unambiguous demonstration that sugar production and consumption were not only historic but prehistoric as well.

The historic pattern of Indian sugar production has been described in detail in the Northeast wherever maple trees grew in abundance. Eyewitness accounts include those of Nicolas Denys and Chrestian LeClerq in the seventeenth century and Alexander Henry's eighteenth-century descriptions of Chippewa sugaring; there are many others that extend well into the nineteenth century. The process of sugar manufacture in the eighteenth and nineteenth centuries was straightforward and consistent wherever it was found: tapping trees for their sap, bringing the sap to a central location where it was boiled to reach the proper temperature, and then working the syrup until crystallization occurred. The resulting sugar was stored in birchbark boxes for sale or for consumption throughout the spring season and sometimes even longer.

The advantages in projecting this pattern into prehistory include the possibility of interpreting certain kinds of villages or camp re-

M

Ojibwa maple-sugar making at Mille Lacs Lake, Minnesota. (Reprinted from Smithsonian Institution, Bureau of American Ethnology Bulletin 86, Plate 43)

mains as sugaring sites, identifying special suites of artifacts associated with sugaring, and abstracting settlement patterns from these data. A few sites have been identified as possible maple-sugaring stations in Michigan and Ontario; and as a pattern of prehistoric life, sugaring has been suggested for Early Woodland (ca. 800–200 B.C., or 2750–2150 years B.P.) complexes in the East as well. For none of these is the evidence clear-cut.

Debates over the feasibility of prehistoric sugaring have a long history because the ethnohistoric support for really early sugar manufacture—what would be required to firmly establish it as a native practice—is not strong. Diametrically opposite conclusions have been drawn from essentially the same documentary sources, and arguments supporting the antiquity of the practice from historic accounts are not conclusive.

Efforts to go around historic documentary data and use other kinds of evidence have been similarly inconclusive. Attempts at replication of possible sugaring techniques using aboriginal equipment have yielded insights into what was and was not possible in a prehistoric context, although they do not constitute proof of what actually occurred. Techniques for identification of sugar residues on prehistoric pottery are in their infancy.

Carol I. Mason

Further Readings

Holman, M.B. 1986. Historic Documents and Prehistoric Sugaring: A Matter of Context. *Midcontinental Journal of Archaeology* 11:125–131.

Mason, C.I. 1990. Indians, Maple Sugaring, and the Spread of Market Economies. In *The Woodland Tradition in the Western Great Lakes: Papers Presented to Elden Johnson*, edited by G. Gibbon, pp. 37–43. Publications in Anthropology no. 4. University of Minnesota Press, Minneapolis.

Pendergast, J.F. 1982. *The Origin of Maple Sugar.* Syllogeus no. 36. National Museums of Canada, Ottawa.

Quimby, G.I. 1966. *Indian Culture and European Trade Goods.* University of Wisconsin Press, Madison.

Maritime Archaic Tradition

"Maritime Archaic tradition" refers to a group of closely related cultures that occupied the northwest Atlantic Coast in the period 5550–1550/1050 B.C. (7500–3500/3000 years B.P.). "Maritime" indicates the influence the sea and its resources had on virtually all aspects of this culture; "Archaic" implies an economy based upon the hunting and gathering of these resources. The concept of the Maritime Archaic tradition was first formulated in 1968 during the excavation of a large burial site at Port au Choix in northwestern Newfoundland (Harp and Hughes 1968). A remarkably well-preserved series of human skeletons and an impressive variety of bone, antler, and ivory tools, weapons, and decorative and magico-religious objects revealed an "Indian" culture of a richness and sophistication unsuspected for far northeastern North America. Radiocarbon dates placed the Port au Choix finds, which came from one large cemetery and two smaller ones, at ca. 2050–1250 B.C. (4000–3200 years B.P.). Since the discovery of the Port au Choix cemetery, evidence of the Maritime Archaic tradition has been found over much of the far northeast and the time frame has been extended back more than 3,500 years.

Northern Branch. The first people to reach southern Labrador were clearly coastal dwellers and may have possessed some of the sophisticated elements of marine hunting technology for which their descendants are now well known. Ca. 5550 B.C. (7500 years B.P.), elaborate mound burials were being made along the coast of southern Labrador and adjacent Quebec. One of these, at l'Anse Amour in southern Labrador, contained an antler toggling harpoon, probably the oldest example of such a marine hunting weapon yet recovered from anywhere in the world. A walrus tusk and the bones of fish also suggest a maritime orientation at this early date.

Maritime Archaic people continued their northeastward expansion along the Labrador coast and by 4050 B.C. (6000 years B.P.) had established themselves well north of the tree line. These people and their distinctive way of life have become known to archaeologists as the "northern branch" Maritime Archaic. They flourished on the central and northern Labrador coasts until not long after 2050 B.C. (4000 years B.P.), when evidence of their distinctive stone tools, burial practices, longhouses, and other cultural elements begins to disappear from the archaeological record.

Although it may be a remarkable coincidence, the disappearance of Maritime Archaic

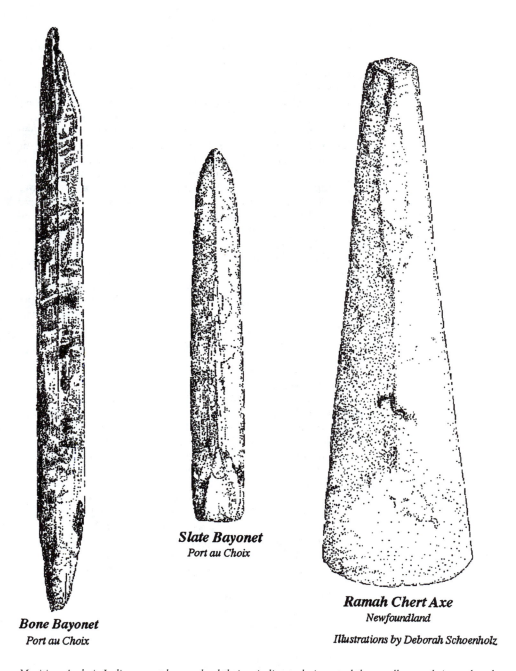

Slate Bayonet
Port au Choix

Ramah Chert Axe
Newfoundland

Illustrations by Deborah Schoenholz

Bone Bayonet
Port au Choix

Maritime Archaic Indians must have valued their grinding technique and the excellent tools it produced, for chipped and flaked tools were almost never included as grave gifts. Ground tools, like those pictured above, have been found from northern Labrador to New Jersey, many of them in graves and cenotaphs. (Drawings by Deborah Schoenholz)

culture from the north and central Labrador coasts is complemented almost perfectly by the advance of a new population southward along the coast. These people are known to archaeologists as "Paleoeskimos" and were biologically, linguistically, culturally, and historically distinct from the Maritime Archaic people. We can only imagine what each group thought of the other at the first meeting. We still have no evidence for the sort of relations that might have existed between the two groups, except to repeat the indications that if relations were marked by competition, or even conflict, the Paleoeskimos appear to have supplanted their predecessors on the Labrador coast: By ca. 1250 B.C. (3200 years B.P.), all trace of the elaborate and distinctive northern-branch Maritime Archaic culture disappears from the archaeological record.

Southern Branch. During the time that the northern-branch people were expanding northward along the Labrador coast, a "new" culture seems to have been developing along the north coast of the Strait of Belle Isle. Shortly before 4050 B.C. (6000 years B.P.), stone tools and weapons of markedly different styles and raw materials from those of their northern-branch predecessors appear. Some archaeologists believe that these artifacts mark the arrival of a new people in the Strait of Belle Isle. The southern-branch Maritime Archaic people appear to have been as fully adapted to the sea and its resources as were those of the northern branch, although no organic objects are preserved from any coastal Labrador locations. The southern-branch people also appear to have been the first humans to colonize the island of Newfoundland. Radiocarbon dates beginning ca. 3050 B.C. (5000 years B.P.) mark the progress of Maritime Archaic people from the northernmost part of the northern peninsula along both the east and west coasts and, eventually, along the southern parts of the island. Living sites of the Maritime Archaic people of Newfoundland are not unlike those of their Labrador relatives, but far better known are cemetery sites that have provided a wealth of information about the Maritime Archaic culture and the people themselves.

The site at Port au Choix in northwestern Newfoundland is probably the best example of such a cemetery. There, archaeologists found more than 60 burials containing more than 100 individuals of all ages and both sexes. With them were found not only the ground and polished stone tools and weapons known from other Maritime Archaic cemeteries, but also an almost unbelievable number and variety of bone, antler, and ivory objects—the entire assemblage in a remarkable state of preservation. The wide variety of objects—from woodworking tools of stone and walrus ivory, to harpoons and spears for the hunt, to fine carvings from stone, antler, bone, and ivory—provided a remarkable picture of a people familiar with their environment and capable of taking advantage of it; not only was their technology admirably suited to a maritime existence, their intellectual culture was also highly developed.

For some reason, however, this Maritime Archaic florescence on Newfoundland appears to have lasted only a few centuries longer than that of the northern-branch people along the Labrador coast. By ca. 1050 B.C. (3000 years B.P.), all trace of their elaborate and distinctive technology, their spectacular and informative burial practices, and, indeed, of the people themselves disappears from the island. Along the north shore of the Strait of Belle Isle, however, there is a slender thread of evidence that suggests continuity from the latest southern-branch Maritime Archaic cultures into more recent times and, just possibly, into the historic period in the form of the Inn, a people of the lower north shore and Labrador. This thread of evidence, however, remains to be followed.

James Tuck

Further Readings

Harp, E.J., and D.R. Hughes. 1968. Five Prehistoric Burials From Port au Choix, Newfoundland. *Polar Notes* 8:1–47. Baker Library, Dartmouth College, Hanover.

McGhee, R., and J.A. Tuck. 1975. *An Archaic Sequence From the Strait of Belle Isle, Labrador.* Mercury Series Paper no. 34. Archaeological Survey of Canada, National Museum of Man, Ottawa.

Tuck, J.A. 1970. An Archaic Indian Cemetery in Newfoundland. *Scientific American* 222(6):112–121.

———. 1975. *Prehistory of Saglek Bay, Labrador: Archaic and Paleo-Indian Occupations.* Publications no. 34. Archaeological Survey of Canada, Canadian Museum of Civilization, Hull.

———. 1976. *Newfoundland and Labrador Prehistory.* National Museums of Canada, Ottawa.

———. 1984. *Maritime Provinces Prehistory.* Archaeological Survey of Canada, Ottawa.

Marksville

"Marksville" is a term applied to a ceramic complex, a site, a phase, a culture, a Hopewellian horizon, and a cultural period in the Lower

Mississippi Valley that dates to ca. A.D. 100–400 (1850–1550 years B.P.). Although there is evidence of strong regional continuity with the earlier Tchefuncte culture (850–150 B.C., or 2800–2100 years B.P.), and the Marksville cultural system never became Hopewellian in a Midwestern sense, this archaeological culture is still most often considered a southern Hopewellian complex. Centered mainly in Mississippi and Louisiana, Marksville is best known from the excavation of burial mounds at sites like Marksville, Troyville, Helena Crossing, and Anderson Landing. Contact with Midwestern Hopewellian centers seems to have been sporadic, with symbols, artifact forms, and mortuary ideas adopted selectively and then often recombined with local cultural elements. Helena Crossing and Crooks are among the few sites to produce a fair amount of diagnostic Hopewellian items. In general, imported goods and raw materials are rare at this time in the Lower Mississippi Valley, with common Hopewellian objects, like platform pipes and figurines, of Marksville manufacture. Besides these two items, only prismatic blades and pottery with familiar traits, such as crosshatched rims and bird motifs, occur at most sites. These Hopewellianlike items are most often found in conical burial mounds in early Marksville components. Many mounds contain a prepared clay platform at the base and some elaborate log tombs. Earthen embankments and enclosures may have been present at some sites. There is little evidence of ranking among villages, which seem to have been occupied for relatively extended periods.

Guy Gibbon

Further Readings

Bense, J. 1994. *Southeastern Archaeology.* Academic Press, New York.

Ford, J.A. 1963. *Hopewell Culture Burial Mounds Near Helena, Arkansas.* Anthropological Papers, vol. 50, pt. 1. American Museum of Natural History, New York.

Ford, J.A., and G.R. Willey. 1940. *Crooks Site, a Marksville Period Burial Mound in La Salle Parish, Louisiana.* Anthropological Study no. 3. State of Louisiana, Department of Conservation, Louisiana Geological Survey, New Orleans.

Toth, A. 1977a. The Chronological Implications of Early Marksville Ceramics. *Southeastern Archaeological Conference Bulletin* 20.

———. 1977b. *Early Marksville Phases in the Lower Mississippi Valley: A Study of Culture Contact Dynamics.* Unpublished Ph.D. dissertation, Department of Anthropology, Harvard University, Cambridge.

———. 1979. The Marksville Connection. In *Hopewell Archaeology: The Chillicothe Conference,* edited by D.S. Brose and N. Greber, pp. 188–199. Kent State University Press, Kent.

Vescelius, G.S. 1957. Mound 2 at Marksville. *American Antiquity* 22:416–420.

See also HAVANA HOPEWELL; HOPEWELL INTERACTION SPHERE; MIDDLE WOODLAND; OHIO HOPEWELL

Marpole Culture Type

The prehistory of the Strait of Georgia region of southwestern British Columbia is divided into a chronological sequence of culture-historical units of which the Marpole culture type, generally dating to 450 B.C.–A.D. 450 (2400–1500 years B.P.), is one. The type site, Marpole (Dhrs 1, alternatively referred to as the Great Fraser Midden or the Eburne Mound), has been the focus of numerous excavations, beginning with Charles Hill-Tout and Harlan I. Smith in the late nineteenth century and continuing into the modern era. It was the location of a major village that, during its occupation, covered ca. 1.8 ha (4.5 acres) along the north shore of the Fraser River. Between 1949 and 1957, Charles E. Borden of the University of British Columbia conducted five seasons of excavation there. Comparing his assemblages with others he had excavated from the Greater Vancouver area, he identified a series of traits diagnostic of the "Marpole phase." These include unilaterally barbed antler harpoons, a preponderant use of antler in barbed-point technology, a range of flaked-stone projectile-point styles, an abundance of ground-stone knives, a heavy-duty woodworking toolkit (large celts, hand mauls, and antler wedges), and a range of personal ornaments and ritual items, including seated human figurine bowls (see Figure). Borden argued that the people to which these artifacts belonged were intruders, whose interior (Plateau) culture was in a state of transition.

Since Borden's research, many additional sites in the Strait of Georgia region have been

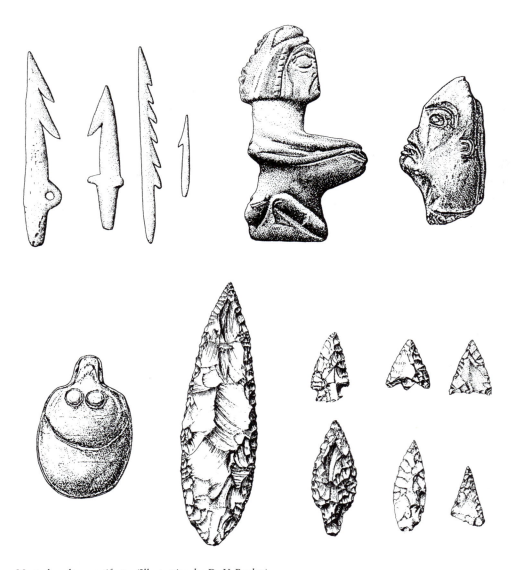

Marpole culture artifacts. (Illustration by D. V. Burley)

associated with the Marpole-culture type, firmly establishing it as a culture-historical unit. Overall site distribution during the Marpole period is bounded by the Coast Salish linguistic province, and there is little doubt that Marpole represents a developmental stage in Coast Salish culture. As to Marpole origins, early arguments for migration have been replaced by an overall consensus for continuity from the preceding Locarno Beach–culture type. Borden's material correlates for the Marpole-culture type have been generally confirmed, and, using these as a diagnostic set, archaeologists are able to differentiate Marpole components from earlier and later assemblages.

Archaeological interpretations of the Marpole period by D.H. Mitchell (1971) and D.V. Burley (1980) portray it as a complex Northwest Coast culture analogous in many respects to ethnographic peoples of the nineteenth century. Faunal analyses, technological studies, and site distributions illustrate a subsistence and settlement strategy that exploited a wide range of resources yet was dominated by the annual runs of the five species of Pacific salmon. Intensified use of this resource and the preservation of salmon through smoking and drying into stored surplus have long been assumed a foundation upon which the Northwest Coast chiefdom rested. By Marpole times, virtually all other aspects of this chiefdom were in place. Large Marpole village sites imply the historic pattern of nucleated winter settlement. Surviving house depressions on at least a few of these sites and large postholes excavated at others suggest construction of substantial multifamily dwellings. The appearance of a full woodworking toolkit indicates a concentrated use of forest resources, especially the western red cedar, for everything from clothing to canoes. This range of uses is both documented and amplified by the recovery of organic artifacts in Marpole-age waterlogged deposits, including such items as wooden splitting wedges, basketry pieces, mat fragments, and cordage. Differential treatment of the dead, as evidenced by several burials with elaborate grave inclusions, reveals a stratified society with rank based on ascription. Intentional deformation of the crania and a proliferation of objects for personal ornamentation and ritual practices may be associated with this differentiation as well. Long-range exchange networks must have been well established, for Marpole sites contain such exotics as artifacts of native copper, obsidian from Oregon, *Dentalia* shell from the outer coast of Vancouver Island, and nephrite from the Fraser Canyon. Finally, elaboration in zoomorphic and anthropomorphic representational art in stone and antler gives Marpole assemblages the cultural flamboyance so often identified as a characteristic of the Northwest Coast culture area.

While it is possible to characterize the Marpole-culture type as a homogeneous entity, one with few overall differences from the historic Coast Salish pattern, variation can be found when archaeological assemblages are compared. Quantitative analyses of these assemblages by Burley (1989) indicate Marpole is potentially divisible into discrete temporal periods based on percentage frequencies of different artifact types. Such analyses have also revealed variation along spatial lines, with differences between site assemblages from the Fraser River and those from the Gulf Islands and southern Vancouver Island. Of particular note, Fraser River assemblages incorporate a greater abundance and diversity of flaked-stone-artifact types, particularly projectile points, while those of the latter two have a tendency toward ground-stone technology. The reasons for this are unclear, though interior influences on Fraser River peoples and variation in resource-exploitation patterns between the Fraser River and the Gulf Islands are the most probable causes. Other analyses by Burley (1989) have illustrated individual correlations between a site or sites on the mainland and sites in the islands, which may indicate an overlapping settlement pattern with high mobility between groups in each of the subregions.

A review of existing radiocarbon dates for the Marpole-culture type indicates its definite appearance in the Strait of Georgia no later than 450 B.C. (2400 years B.P.). The earliest dated Marpole sites are along the Fraser River, with Marpole components identified in all other areas by 50 B.C. (2000 years B.P.). Defining a termination date is more difficult, since transition to the succeeding Gulf of Georgia–culture type is gradual. Distinguishing artifacts for the later period are beginning to appear in Marpole assemblages by A.D. 250 (1700 years B.P.). These increase in proportionate frequency after that date. Consequently, though A.D. 450 (1500 years B.P.) is commonly cited as the end of the Marpole-culture type, aspects of its distinctive assemblage may occur later.

David V. Burley

Further Readings

Borden, C.E. 1970. Culture History of the Fraser Delta Region: An Outline. In *Archaeology in British Columbia, New Discoveries,* edited by R.L. Carlson. *B.C. Studies.* 6–7:95–112.

Burley, D.V. 1980. *Marpole: Anthropological Reconstructions of a Prehistoric Northwest Coast Culture Type.* Publication no. 8. Department of Archaeology, Simon Fraser University, Burnaby.

———. 1989. *Senewèlets: Culture History of the Nanaimo Coast Salish and the False Narrows Midden.* Memoir no. 2. Royal British Columbia Museum, Victoria.

Mitchell, D.H. 1971. *Archaeology of the Gulf of Georgia Area: A Natural Region and Its Culture Types.* Syesis, vol. 4 (Supplement no. 1).

Martin, Paul Sidney (1899–1974)

Paul S. Martin began working in the Southwest in the 1920s, first in the Anasazi area and then, beginning in the 1930s, in the Mogollon region.

He is best known for his pioneering research on the Mogollon culture in west-central New Mexico and east-central Arizona. He is also remembered as the senior champion of the New Archaeology during its emergence in the early 1960s.

Martin completed his Ph.D. at the University of Chicago in 1929; his dissertation was titled *Origins and History of the Kiva in the Southwest*. After several seasons of fieldwork in Mexico at Chichen Itza, he devoted the rest of his career to Southwestern archaeology. Among his early work in the Anasazi area was the excavation of sites in the Ackman-Lowry region in Colorado shortly after he joined the staff of the Field Museum of Natural History in Chicago in 1934. Stimulated by discussions with Harold Gladwin, Emil Haury, and E.B. Sayles at the Gila Pueblo Foundation in Globe, Arizona, he decided to turn his attention to the newly discovered prehistoric culture that Haury and Gladwin had named the Mogollon culture. He set up a permanent field station at Pine Lawn, New Mexico, near the town of Reserve, and worked there from 1939 until 1955. He directed excavations at such classic sites as the SU pithouse village (Martin 1940) and Tularosa Cave.

When John B. Rinaldo joined Martin at the Field Museum in 1948, they initiated a productive professional relationship that lasted more than 25 years (e.g., Martin and Rinaldo 1950). In 1956, they moved to east-central Arizona, where they established a permanent field station at Vernon and began excavations to explore the culture history of the Little Colorado drainage in the Vernon area. By 1961, Martin had turned his attention to the Hay Hollow Valley just east of Snowflake, Arizona, where he conducted intensive research for the next 12 years. Much of this work was supported by the newly created National Science Foundation. Work in the Hay Hollow Valley began with sites such as Carter Ranch and Broken K pueblo, which became important case studies in the New Archaeology and in what came to be called "ceramic sociology." Martin's collaboration with his graduate students of that period resulted in important contributions that helped change the direction of American archaeology.

Martin's contributions were recognized by his colleagues in many ways. He was elected a fellow of the American Anthropological Association in 1926 and a fellow of the American Association for the Advancement of Science in 1950. He served as president of the Society for American Archaeology in 1965–1966 and received the Alfred V. Kidder Award from the American Anthropological Association in 1968 for outstanding contributions to American archaeology. Martin died in Tucson, Arizona.

William A. Longacre

Further Readings

Martin, P.S. 1940. *The SU Site, Excavations at a Mogollon Village, Western New Mexico, 1939*. Anthropological Series, vol. 32, no. 1. Field Museum of Natural History, Chicago.

———. 1959. *Digging Into History: A Brief Account of Fifteen Years of Archaeological Work in New Mexico*. Popular Series, Anthropology, vol. 38. Field Museum of Natural History, Chicago.

———. 1971. The Revolution in Archaeology. *American Antiquity* 36:1–8.

Martin, P.S., and J.B. Rinaldo. 1950. *Sites of the Reserve Phase, Pine Lawn Valley, Western New Mexico*. Fieldiana: Anthropology, vol. 38, no. 3. Field Museum of Natural History, Chicago.

See also BROKEN K PUEBLO; CARTER RANCH PUEBLO; MOGOLLON CULTURE AREA; PINE LAWN BRANCH; TULAROSA CAVE

Mast Forest Archaic

The end of the Ice Age brought widespread climatic changes to North America after 10,050 B.C. (12,000 years B.P.). Those changes entailed shifts in forest and grassland distributions and profound changes in their compositions. Many animal species dwindled to extinction during the early stages of this period of environmental change. North American horses, camels, mammoths, mastodons, and giant species of bison, bear, and wolf were among the most prominent of the large mammalian species to disappear, and several less prominent plant and animal species, including some songbird species, also became extinct.

All of these changes caused North American Indians to readapt to the new emerging environmental conditions. Archaeologists usually refer to the long period between the end of the Ice Age and the first appearance of ceramics, maize horticulture, and more permanent settlement as the Archaic. These developments marking the end of the Archaic do not appear simultaneously everywhere. Indeed, key attributes such as ceramics and maize horticulture do not appear at all in many parts of North America until after European contact. Consequently, the dating of the end of the Archaic varies greatly from one region to another.

Periodization of the Archaic also varies, although there is a tendency to divide it into early, middle, late, and terminal periods in various regional sequences. There is also a tendency to identify regional expressions of the Archaic by more specific labels. Thus, the Mast Forest Archaic is a variant that appeared in parts of the Northeast region during the Late Archaic period there, ca. 4000–1700 B.C. (6800–3900 ca. B.P.).

The Mast Forest Archaic was defined to cover a series of archaeological complexes found across southern New England; southern New York; westward into the Ohio River drainage of Ohio, Indiana, and Illinois; and southward along the Atlantic side of the Appalachians through Pennsylvania to as far south as North Carolina. The Mast Forest Archaic adaptation was to the temperate deciduous forest environment that ecologists often refer to as the oak-deer-maple biome. It contrasts with the Lake Forest Archaic adaptation that predominated about the same time in the maple-beech-hemlock forests around the lower Great Lakes. It also contrasts with the Maritime Archaic adaptation that predominated in northern New England and the Maritime Provinces of Canada.

The Virginia white-tailed deer and the turkey are important game animals throughout the biome, and their remains are conspicuous in sites of the Mast Forest Archaic where preservation has allowed bones to survive. Archaeologists have referred to projectile-point types known variously as narrow points, small-stemmed points, narrow-stemmed points, and small points as diagnostic of the Mast Forest Archaic. Various competing cultural terms, such as Coastal Archaic, Appalachian tradition, Taconic tradition, Piedmont tradition, and Atlantic Slope Archaic, have failed to catch on, although all or parts of them refer to all or parts of what is here called the Mast Forest Archaic. Specific archaeological complexes covered by the term at its regional core include, but are not limited to, the Squibnocket complex of southeastern New England, the River phase of eastern New York, the Lamoka phase of central New York, and the Bare Island complex of the mid-Atlantic states.

The Mast Forest Archaic should thus be thought of as a kind of adaptation, not as a well-defined single culture or period. Archaeological-site types include coastal sites in which shellfish remains are abundant. Interior camps were probably used to exploit seasonal resources such as fish runs, acorn and other mast harvesting, and deer herds. Large base camps along interior streams suggest seasonal concentrations in larger settlements for part of the year and dispersal to smaller camps at other times. Midden deposits grew at such sites as people returned to them annually in an increasingly structured pattern of seasonal movements.

Hunters used flexible spear throwers, for the bow and arrow had not yet been introduced to the region. Gatherers became ever more familiar with local plant resources, learning to anticipate the timing and location of the most productive species. People began modifying the environment by regularly burning the natural cover to produce meadows to attract deer herds and to promote the growth of favored plants. The latter eventually led to minimal, even inadvertent, forms of cultivation. Indigenous plant species, such as sumpweed, *chenopodium*, and squash, were regularly encouraged and harvested until they began to acquire botanical characteristics that they would not have developed without human intervention. Food-grinding implements found archaeologically confirm the growing importance of these and other plant resources. Neither tobacco nor smoking pipes were yet present in the region.

Regional adaptation and the regularization of seasonal movements within well-defined areas led to the increasing insulation of Mast Forest Archaic populations from one another. Local populations grew to be large enough to allow young people to find mates endogamously, and food-storage technology emerged that made local populations more self-sufficient in the long term. Both trends reduced the need or desire for contact with more distant groups. The pattern of insulation often appears to have involved segregation by river drainage. This is expressed archaeologically by increasing parochialism in the raw materials used for tool manufacture. During the Mast Forest Archaic, stone tools tended to be made of local materials, regardless of their quality. Higher-grade raw materials from across major drainage boundaries no longer made their way into the hands of local flintknappers. Boundaries that would define the exclusive cultures of later centuries were becoming established, and habits of cultivation were in place that would later facilitate the spread of maize horticulture.

Dean R. Snow

Further Readings

Fagan, B.M. 1991. *Ancient North America,* pp. 342–344. Thames and Hudson, New York.

Snow, D. 1980. *The Archaeology of New England.* Academic Press, New York.

Mathiassen, Therkel (1892–1967)

Therkel Mathiassen, pioneer Arctic archaeologist, was employed as a schoolteacher in Denmark when asked by the explorer Knud Rasmussen to join the Fifth Thule Expedition (1921–1924). As the expedition's archaeologist, Mathiassen excavated several sites in Arctic Canada, most notably Naujan. His publication *Archaeology of the Central Eskimos: The Thule Culture and Its Position Within the Eskimo Culture* (1927) was the first monograph on the subject of Arctic archaeology in North America and the first study to be based on controlled, scientific excavations. In it, Mathiassen defined the prehistoric Thule culture, which he argued was the earliest of all Eskimo cultures. He was partly right (in arguing against the inland theory of Eskimo origins) and partly wrong (for instance, in discounting Diamond Jenness's identification of Dorset culture). After the Thule expedition, Mathiassen was hired by the National Museum of Denmark. Later, he undertook fieldwork in Greenland, where he identified a Norse-influenced variant of Thule that he named Inugsuk culture.

David Morrison

Further Readings

Mathiassen, T. 1927. *Archaeology of the Central Eskimos: The Thule Culture and Its Position Within the Eskimo Culture.* Report of the Fifth Thule Expedition 1921–1924, vol. 4, nos. 1–2. Glydenclalski Boghandel, Nordisk Forlag, Copenhagen.

———. 1930a. Inugsuk: A Medieval Eskimo Settlement in Upernavik District, West Greenland. *Meddelelser om Grønland* 77:145–340.

———. 1930b. An Old Eskimo Culture in West Greenland: A Report of an Archaeological Expedition to Upernavik. *Geographical Review* 20:605–614.

———. 1931a. Ancient Eskimo Settlements in the Kangamiut Area. *Meddelelser om Grønland* 91(1).

———. 1931b. The Present Stage of Eskimo Archaeology. *Acta Archaeologia* 2(2):185–199.

———. 1934. Contributions to the Archaeology of Disko Bay. *Meddelelser om Grønland* 92(4).

———. 1958. The Sermermiut Excavations, 1955. *Meddelelser om Grønland* 161(3).

Maxon-Derby Site

The Maxon-Derby site is an early Iroquois-tradition (ca. A.D. 1000–1300, or 950–650 years B.P.) Owasco summer settlement in the Finger Lakes region of the Mohawk drainage in upper New York State. Covering ca. 1 ha (2.4 acres) of a terrace along a large stream, the village is estimated to have contained 240 people. The seven houses excavated range from almost square to oblong in shape, with the largest oblong structure measuring 8 x 18 m (26 x 59 feet). Maxon-Derby is one of a number of small loosely related Iroquois communities known for this period that lacked standardized house forms and defensive palisades. The site is important, for it displays the onset of major economic and political changes that culminated in the classic Iroquois lifeway. Among the incipient changes are the emergence of more nucleated settlements containing some multifamily dwellings that are beginning to resemble longhouses; rising population densities; and a more intensive reliance on maize agriculture. These developments coincide with what is thought to be an amelioration of climatic conditions in the Northeast.

Guy Gibbon

Further Readings

Ritchie, W.A., and R.E. Funk. 1973. *Aboriginal Settlement Patterns in the Northeast.* Memoir no. 20. New York State Museum and Science Service, Albany.

Snow, D. 1980. *The Archaeology of New England.* Academic Press, New York.

See also IROQUOIAN CULTURE

Mazama Tephra

Mazama tephra was generated by the cataclysmic eruption of Mount Mazama (now Crater

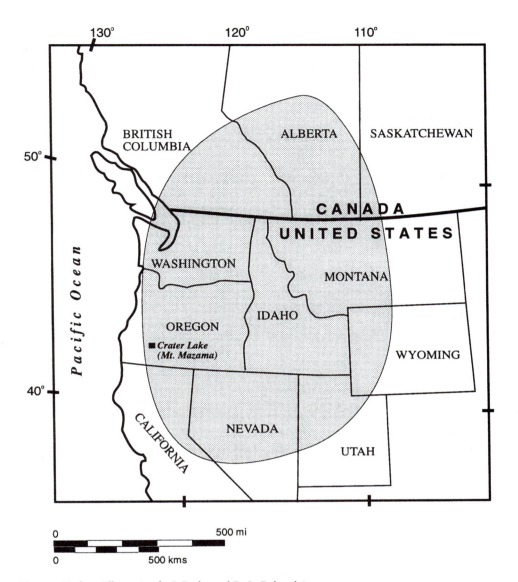

Mazama Tephra. (Illustration by J. Ryder and D. L. Pokotylo)

Lake in Oregon) ca. 4950 B.C. (6900 years B.P.). It is the most widespread late Quaternary tephra in northwestern North America and has been used by earth scientists, archaeologists, and paleobotanists to date Holocene deposits.

Mazama tephra covers an area of at least 1.7 million km^2 (656,200 square miles) and has an estimated volume of 30–38 km^3 (39,000–50,000 cubic yards). The broad plume (see Figure) probably consists of multiple lobes that reflect changing wind directions during a series of eruptions. As many as six separate layers

have been identified, and four lobes mapped in distal areas, near Crater Lake. Estimates for the duration of the eruptions range from three to as many as 100–200 years.

Mazama ash consists of a mixture of shards of volcanic glass and crystals. Crystals represent a particular suite of minerals: plagioclase, hypersthene, hornblende, augite, and apatite, although the relative proportions are not constant. The glass also has a distinctive composition—a relatively low silica and high iron and titanium content and combinations of rare earths and several other elements—that distinguishes it from other volcanic ashes.

Both physical and mineralogical characteristics vary with increasing distance downwind from the volcano. Particle size decreases from large fragments of pumice and shattered rock particles near the vent to fine ash (glass shards and crystals) at distances beyond 200 km (124 miles). Several hundred kilometers from the volcano, Mazama ash typically appears as a fine-textured layer. In dry areas, the tephra is white. In humid areas, including bogs, the tephra is a rusty, orange brown. Thickness of the primary layer varies from less than a centimeter to several centimeters, depending upon proximity to Crater Lake.

The ash layer is a discrete stratigraphic layer at sites where sedimentation by other processes was occurring ca. 5050 B.C. (7000 years B.P.). The ash is often encountered in bogs, where it forms an almost continuous layer at depths ranging from a few centimeters to several meters, and it is commonly, but not invariably, encountered in lacustrine sediments at a similar range of depths. In terrestrial environments, the ash was commonly eroded and redeposited by wind and water and, consequently, occurs as a discontinuous layer of variable thickness. At sites where wind, water, and gravitational processes were ineffective, ash survived as a surface layer until a protective cover of vegetation became established. On most land surfaces, however, Mazama ash was not preserved as a discrete layer but was eroded or washed downward into cavities in permeable substrate or mixed into the soil.

Mazama tephra is used widely as a stratigraphic marker and chronologic datum. The ash serves as a datum in palynological studies, where in some cases it fortuitously separates zones representing the early Holocene xerothermic interval and later cooler/wetter conditions. Mazama ash overlies archaeological deposits in a number of important Early-period (before 3050 B.C., or 5000 years B.P.) occupations in the Canadian Plateau, including the Gore Creek, Landels, and Drynoch sites. It also has been used to date events such as landslides, debris flows, and fluctuations of alpine glaciers.

The use of tephra as a stratigraphic marker or chronological datum requires unequivocal identification of Mazama ash. Where multiple layers of Holocene tephra may be present (e.g., Mazama, St. Helens "Y," and Bridge River in south-central British Columbia), identification of a specific tephra may require chemical, mineralogical, and physical analyses of glass and crystals.

June Ryder
David L. Pokotylo

Further Readings

Bacon, C.R. 1983. Eruptive History of Mount Mazama and Crater Lake Caldera, Cascade Range, U.S.A. *Journal of Volcanology and Geothermal Research* 18:57–115.

Powers, H.A., and R.E. Wilcox. 1964. Volcanic Ash From Mount Mazama (Crater Lake) and From Glacier Peak. *Science* 144:1334–1336.

Sarna-Wojcicki, A.M., D.E. Champion, and J.O. Davis. 1983. Holocene Volcanism in the Conterminous United States and the Role of Silicic Volcanic Ash Layers in Correlation of Latest Pleistocene and Holocene Deposits. In *Late Quaternary Environments of the United States: 2. The Holocene,* edited by H.E. Wright, Jr., pp. 52–77. University of Minnesota Press, Minneapolis.

See also EARLY PERIOD (PLATEAU)

McGraw

McGraw (33RO19) is an archaeological site in south-central Ohio located on the floodplain of the Scioto River, ca. 2 km (1.2 miles) south of Chillicothe. It was the first Middle Woodland Hopewell settlement to be recognized and excavated in this classic area of densely clustered Hopewellian ceremonial earthworks and burial mounds. Discovered and excavated in 1963 by a professional team from Case Institute of Technology, Cleveland, Ohio, McGraw proved to be a most productive sheet midden buried under riverine flood deposits. Covering an area ca. 30 x 30 m (98 x 98 feet), it yielded large quantities of typical Hopewell pottery, stone tools, and other artifacts. The ceramics led to the definition of a series of major pottery types, such as McGraw Cord-Marked and McGraw Plain, and to the recognition that these types were part of a regional ceramic tradition, whereas the typical Hopewellian pottery varieties characterized by rocker stamping, incised zoning, and crosshatched rims were part of a broader, interregional Hopewell system defined by Joseph R. Caldwell in 1964 as the Hopewell Interaction Sphere. The

McGraw flint assemblage was dominated by 233 characteristic Hopewell bladelets made of colorful Flint Ridge chalcedony.

In addition, McGraw yielded rich and varied vertebrate and molluscan faunas. Most important, the floral remains included 12-row maize intermediate between ancient pop and flint corns and Late Prehistoric eight-row Northern Flint varieties. In 1963, this discovery was considered a breakthrough, since it seemed to settle the much debated question of the economic base of Hopewell communities. Although the occurrence of maize in Middle Woodland contexts has been confirmed from other sources, the significance of this cultigen may not have been as great as originally thought. On the other hand, the recognition since the late 1980s of an Eastern Agricultural complex independent of Mesoamerican corn simply adds to the evidence that Hopewellian society relied economically to a considerable extent upon food production.

McGraw has been interpreted as a small farmstead or hamlet. A series of 10 reliable radiocarbon assays based upon charcoal samples dates McGraw to ca. A.D. 300–350 (1650–1600 years B.P.). Several similar sites have since been located in the area and in the vicinity of more distant Ohio Hopewell earthworks. Among these are the Brown's Bottom site, ca. 8 km (5 miles) south of McGraw near the Harness earthworks, and the Murphy site near the great Newark earthworks in Licking County, Ohio.

In the apparent absence of nucleated villages commensurate with the large classic Hopewell earthworks and mounds, McGraw became the interpretive linchpin for the theory that Ohio Hopewell was characterized by a reciprocal pattern of groups of food-producing hamlets or farmsteads and their specific vacant ceremonial/mortuary centers. Since the 1960s, this theory has been sharply debated, as at the meetings of the Society for American Archaeology in 1992 in a symposium entitled "Testing the Prufer Model of Ohio Hopewell Settlement Pattern."

Olaf H. Prufer

Further Readings

Blank, J.E. 1965. The Brown's Bottom Site, Ross County, Ohio. *Ohio Archaeologist* 15(1):16–21.

Caldwell, J.R. 1964. Interaction Spheres in Prehistory. In *Hopewellian Studies*, edited by J.R. Caldwell and R.L. Hall, pp. 133–143. Scientific Papers no. 12. Illinois State Museum, Springfield.

Dancey, W.S. 1991. A Middle Woodland Settlement in Central Ohio: A Preliminary Report on the Murphy Site (33Li12). *Pennsylvania Archaeologist* 61(2):37–72.

Prufer, O.H. 1964. The Hopewell Cult. *Scientific American* 211(6):90–102.

———. 1965. *The McGraw Site: A Study in Hopewellian Dynamics*. Scientific Publication, n.s., vol. 4, no. 1. Cleveland Museum of Natural History, Cleveland.

———. 1995. How to Construct a Model: A Personal Memoir. In *Ohio Hopewell Community Organization*, edited by W.S. Dancey and P.J. Pacheco. Kent State University Press, Kent.

See also HOPEWELL INTERACTION SPHERE; OHIO HOPEWELL

McKean

McKean is a Plains and Rocky Mountain region projectile-point type, as well as the name given the time period associated with this point. McKean lanceolate projectile points were first described by Richard Wheeler following his work at several sites on the northwest Plains, specifically Belle and Mule Creek rock shelters, and following William Mulloy's excavations of the McKean site. At the McKean site, Mulloy found these projectile points in the same stratigraphic position as two other types, Duncan and Hanna, and interpreted this association as indicating a range of variation in a single artifact style (see Figure). Wheeler, however, found each of these three types at different sites and named the three types separately. Not resolving this difference, George C. Frison et al. (1974) applied the term "technocomplex" to accommodate the co-occurrence of these three projectile point types but also included Mallory projectile points, which occurred with McKean lanceolates at the Scoggin site in central Wyoming.

McKean lanceolate and the other projectile-point types consistently occur at deposits radiocarbon dated to ca. 3050–1050 B.C. (5000–3000 years B.P.); hence, McKean refers to this period. For Mulloy, McKean was part of the early Middle Prehistoric period, which has come to be called the Middle Plains Archaic, the time following the Altithermal climatic episode (ca. 7050–3050 B.C., or 9000–5000 years B.P.) marked by a return to more mesic conditions.

M

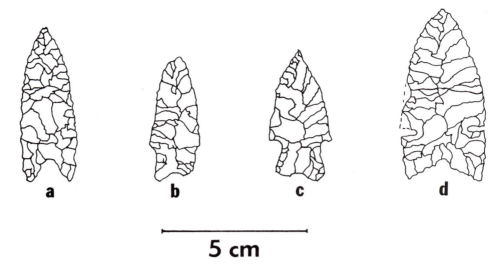

5 cm

McKean complex projectile points: a. McKean lanceolate; b. Duncan; c. Hanna; d. Mallory. (Illustration by M. Kornfeld)

During the McKean period, the southern part of the Northwest Plains culture area is marked by an increase in the use of ground-stone implements, the presence of the first securely dated stone circles, an increase in consistent use of food-processing facilities (large stone-filled hearths), and continued use of pithouses. Several of these characteristics suggest an increase in the use of plants for subsistence. Nevertheless, bison bonebeds are present in the basins, and there is evidence of procurement of mountain sheep and deer. However, the northern part of this region does not have features that can be interpreted for plant utilization, and Canadian investigators argue that big game continued to be the primary subsistence resource. The fragmentary nature of human remains found during the McKean period suggests interment of scaffold burials—a mortuary practice in which the deceased is placed on top of a wooden platform (e.g., the McKean site)—or cremation, possibly also of scaffold burials where the remains are burned (e.g., the Graham site). The only more intensive treatment of the dead is seen at the Gray site, a multiple burial complex in southeastern Saskatchewan.

Marcel Kornfeld

Further Readings

Brumley, J.H. 1975. *The Cactus Flower Site in Southwest Alberta: 1972–1974 Excavations.* Mercury Series Paper no. 6. Archaeological Survey of Canada, National Museum of Man, Ottawa.

Frison, G.C. 1991. *Hunters of the High Plains.* 2nd ed. Academic Press, San Diego.

Frison, G.C., M. Wilson, and D. Wilson. 1974. The Holocene Stratigraphic Archaeology of Wyoming: An Introduction. In *Applied Geology and Archaeology: The Holocene History of Wyoming,* edited by M. Wilson, pp. 108–127. Report of Investigations no. 10. Geological Survey of Wyoming, Laramie.

Kornfeld, M., and L.C. Todd (editors). 1985. *McKean/Middle Plains Archaic: Current Research.* Occasional Papers on Wyoming Archaeology no. 4. Office of the Wyoming State Archaeologist, University of Wyoming, Laramie.

Lobdell, J.E. 1973. *The Scoggin Site: An Early Middle Period Bison Kill.* Unpublished Master's thesis. Department of Anthropology, University of Wyoming, Laramie.

Metcalf, M.D. 1974. *Archaeological Excavations at Dipper Gap: A Stratified Butte Top Site in Northeastern Colorado.* Unpublished Master's thesis. Department of Anthropology, Colorado State University, Fort Collins.

Millar, J.F.V. 1981. Mortuary Practice of the Oxbow Complex. *Canadian Journal of Archaeology* 5:103–117.

Mulloy, W. 1954. The McKean Site in Northeastern Wyoming. *Southwest Journal of Anthropology* 10:432–460.

Syms, E.L. 1969. *The McKean Complex As a Horizon Marker in Manitoba and on the Northern Great Plains.* Unpublished Master's thesis. Department of Archaeology, University of Manitoba, Winnipeg.

Walker, E.A. 1984. The Graham Site: A McKean Cremation From Southern Saskatchewan. *Plains Anthropologist* 29(104):139–150.

Wheeler, R.P. 1952. A Note on the "McKean Lanceolate Point." *Plains Archaeological Conference Newsletter* 4(4):39–44.

———. 1954. Two New Projectile Point Types: Duncan and Hanna Points. *Plains Anthropologist* 1:7–14.

McKeithen Site

McKeithen (8CO17) is a village site of the Weeden Island culture in north-central Florida that was occupied ca. A.D. 200–750 (1750–1200 years B.P.). It was thoroughly investigated by Jerald T. Milanich and his students at the University of Florida (1976–1979) and is one of the best published examples of a Weeden Island settlement. It consists of a horseshoe-shaped occupation that includes three earthen mounds, one of which supported the residence of a probable leader and religious specialist, a precursor of later Mississippian mound use. The other two mounds were the focus of different aspects of the Weeden Island mortuary program, including the use of a charnel house and secondary interment in a burial mound. Elaborate pottery vessels in effigy forms with geometric cutouts found in mortuary contexts are reminiscent of forms found at Kolomoki in southwest Georgia. Because of its unusual (for its time) complexity of earthwork construction, cult activity, and extralocal contacts, the McKeithen site is interpreted as showing the potential of leadership in Big Man–type societies before the advent of hereditary ranking in the southeastern United States. As known ethnographically, Big Man societies are tribal formations in which local leaders achieve authority over followers by means of personal efforts and charisma.

Vernon James Knight, Jr.

Further Readings

Milanich, J.T., A.S. Cordell, V.J. Knight, Jr., T.A. Kohler, and B.J. Sigler-Lavelle.

1984. *McKeithen Weeden Island: The Culture of Northern Florida,* A.D. 200–900. Academic Press, Orlando.

McKern, Will C. (1892–1988)

Born in Medical Lake, Washington, Will Carleton McKern obtained his B.A. in anthropology from the University of California in 1917. He served in the 62nd infantry division in France and Germany during World War I, mustering out with the rank of sergeant. Following military service, he obtained a teaching appointment in 1919 at the University of Washington. His next position, as curator at Honolulu's Bishop Museum, included archaeological research on Tonga with that museum's 1919–1920 Dominick Expedition, while simultaneously, as a research associate at the Milwaukee Public Museum until 1921, he collected for Milwaukee's Oceanic holdings. From 1922 to 1925, McKern worked as assistant archaeologist at the Smithsonian Institution's Bureau of American Ethnology.

In 1925, Milwaukee Public Museum Director Samuel Barrett, the first anthropology Ph.D. at the University of California, Berkeley, appointed McKern to a curatorial position. Inaugurating a systematic archaeological research program based on excavations at major sites across central Wisconsin, McKern devised the Midwest Taxonomic Method as an explicit scientific framework for organizing the multitude of data. Ralph Linton, professor of anthropology at the University of Wisconsin, Madison, cooperated with McKern by obtaining funding and student crews for the projects; these students included Leland Cooper, John Adair, Gordon Ekholm, George Foster, William Bascom, Joffre Coe, George Quimby, and Albert Spaulding. McKern's leadership in midwestern archaeology resulted in his becoming one of the founders of the Society for American Archaeology (1935), its president (1940), and the first editor of its journal, *American Antiquity.*

In 1930, McKern became head of the Anthropology Section at the Milwaukee Public Museum; in 1943, he was named director of the museum, a post he held until his retirement in 1958. As director of the museum, McKern inaugurated the Friends of the Museum support group, popular and scientific publication series, a radio series ("Explorers' Club of the Air"), children's activities, and the construction of a six-story building, which was completed in

1963. During his tenure, he continued the acquisition of specimens from around the world in all natural-history fields and encouraged the collection of field data in ecology as well as anthropology. He advocated an open exhibit style that culminated in the great walk-through dioramas pioneered by the Milwaukee Public Museum staff. The museum's European Village Hall, which presented the anthropology of Europe through a villagelike arrangement of house fronts with "typical" rooms behind, exemplifies McKern's innovative ideas. After retirement, McKern moved to Berkeley, where he continued to publish earlier research. In 1980, he returned to Waukesha, Wisconsin, where he died in 1988.

Alice Beck Kehoe

Further Readings

Guthe, C.E. 1952. Twenty-Five Years of Archeology in the Eastern United States. In *Archaeology of Eastern United States,* edited by J.B. Griffin, pp. 1–12. University of Chicago Press, Chicago.

McKern, W.C. 1928. *Neale and McClaughry Mound Groups.* Scientific Publications, vol. 3, no. 3. Public Museum of the City of Milwaukee, Milwaukee.

———. 1930. *Kletzien and Nitschke Mound Groups.* Scientific Publications, vol. 3, no. 4. Public Museum of the City of Milwaukee, Milwaukee.

———. 1931. *A Wisconsin Variant of the Hopewell Culture.* Scientific Publications, vol. 10, no. 2. Public Museum of the City of Milwaukee, Milwaukee.

———. 1939. The Midwestern Taxonomic Method As an Aid to Archaeological Culture Study. *American Antiquity* 4(4):301–313.

———. 1945. *Preliminary Report on Upper Mississippi Phase in Wisconsin.* Scientific Publications, vol. 14, no. 3. Public Museum of the City of Milwaukee, Milwaukee.

———. 1963. *The Clam River Focus.* Publications in Anthropology no. 9. Public Museum of the City of Milwaukee, Milwaukee.

See also MIDWESTERN TAXONOMIC SYSTEM (MIDWESTERN TAXONOMIC METHOD)

Medicine Lodge Creek Site

Medicine Lodge Creek (48BH499) is a rock shelter site located along a steep bluff at the western edge of the Big Horn Mountains in northern Wyoming. Numerous rockfalls prevented Medicine Lodge Creek from degrading parts of the cultural deposits. A ca. 4-m (13-foot) -deep stratigraphic sequence of Paleoindian deposits was left intact in two areas of the site. Radiocarbon dates on charcoal are in the 8050–6050 B.C. (10,000–8000 years B.P.) range.

Except for a Cody-complex component at ca. 6050 B.C. (8000 years B.P.), the Paleoindian components represent what has come to be referred to as the Foothill-Mountain Paleoindian. There appears to have been an ecological barrier of some sort between the Plains and the foothills-mountains during Late Paleoindian times. As a result, the diagnostics (projectile points) in both areas are different. To date (1996), the Medicine Lodge Creek site has produced the longest and most complete Foothill-Mountain Paleoindian sequence along with diagnostic projectile points. However, there are not enough samples of diagnostics to propose formal projectile-point types.

George C. Frison

Further Readings

Frison, G.C. 1976. The Chronology of Paleo-Indian and Altithermal Cultures in the Bighorn Basin, Wyoming. In *Cultural Change and Continuity: Essays in Honor of James Bennett Griffin,* edited by C.E. Cleland, pp. 147–173. Academic Press, New York.

———. 1991. *Prehistoric Hunters of the High Plains.* 2nd ed. Academic Press, San Diego.

———. 1992. The Foothills-Mountains and the Open Plains: The Dichotomy in Paleoindian Subsistence Strategies Between Two Ecosystems. In *Ice Age Hunters of the Rockies,* edited by D.J. Stanford and J.S. Day, pp. 323–342. Denver Museum of Natural History, Denver; University Press of Colorado, Niwot.

Medicine Wheels

The term "medicine wheel" was initially used in archaeology around the turn of the twentieth century in reference to the Big Horn medicine wheel located near Sheridan, Wyoming. The term had been introduced, ca. 1880s, by George Bird Grinnell for small hoops in his Cheyenne ethnography, then extended to the Bighorn Mountain construction. Later archaeological research on the Plains identified other

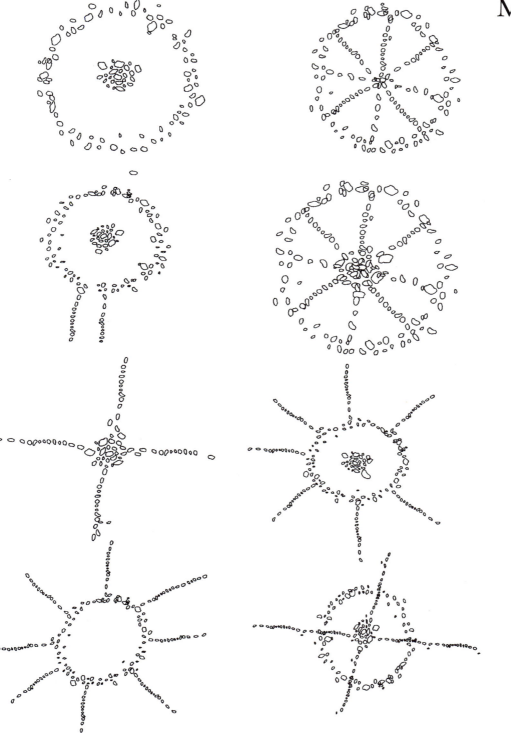

Various structural forms of medicine wheels. (Illustration by J. Brumley)

surface stone features characterized by a variety of stone-circle, cairn, and spoke configurations. Because of general similarities to the Big Horn wheel, the term "medicine wheel" was extended to describe them as well. Structures referred to as medicine wheels generally share these characteristics: (1) construction largely of unmodified natural stone; (2) a combination of at least two of the following primary components: a prominent central cairn, one or more concentric stone rings, two or more stone spokes or lines that radiate outward from a central origin point, a central cairn, or the margins of a stone ring; and (3) primary components arranged in a radially symmetrical manner.

Ca. 75 structures classifiable as medicine wheels have been identified as of the mid-1990s. All are found in the northern Plains from Wyoming and South Dakota north to the Canadian Plains of Alberta and Saskatchewan. Most medicine wheels have secondary features associated with them, such as stone tipi rings, small ancillary stone cairns, stone hearths, and anthropomorphic effigies. Medicine wheels also vary widely in size. The Big Horn medicine wheel consists of a prominent central stone cairn surrounded by a stone circle. Ca. 27 stone spokes connect the stone circle with the central cairn. The stone circle is 27 m (88.6 feet) in diameter; the central cairn, 4 m (13 feet) in diameter. In contrast, the Ellis medicine wheel in southern Alberta consists of a tipi ring–sized stone circle 5 m (16.4 feet) in diameter, from the outer wall of which 10 stone spokes radiate outward for distances of 14–19 m (46–62 feet).

The limited archaeological and ethnographic evidence available indicates medicine wheels reflect a broad range of ages, cultural associations, and functions. Several of the structures are clearly accretional; that is, they were constructed and used over long periods of time by peoples representative of several cultural complexes. Other medicine wheels clearly represent single-use events. Earliest evidence for use of medicine wheels is by Oxbow-complex peoples ca. 3050–2550 B.C. (5000–4500 years B.P.). A number of medicine wheels in the form of the Ellis wheel above date from the Late Prehistoric to the historic period. Ethnographic accounts indicate that they were constructed by the Blackfeet as memorials to prominent warriors at the time of their death. Strong evidence concerning the specific functions of other forms of medicine wheels is lacking. Available evidence indicates that most, if not all, medicine wheels reflect ceremonial activities involving large social groups. Reasonable arguments have been made that some medicine wheels specifically reflect sun-dance observances or other similar forms of ceremonialism. Evidence has also been presented suggesting a possible use of some medicine wheels as markers for astronomical events.

John Brumley

Further Readings

Brumley, J. 1988. *Medicine Wheels on the Northern Plains: A Summary and Appraisal.* Manuscript Series no. 12. Archaeological Survey of Alberta, Edmonton.

Eddy, J.A. 1977. Probing the Mystery of the Medicine Wheels. *National Geographic* 151(1):140–146.

Kehoe, A.B., and F. Thamas. 1979. *Solstice-Aligned Boulder Configurations in Saskatchewan.* Mercury Series Paper no. 48. Archaeological Survey of Canada, National Museum of Man, Ottawa.

See also BIG HORN MEDICINE WHEEL

Meighan, Clement W. (1925–1997)

Clement W. Meighan, trained at the University of California, Berkeley, before and after World War II, went to UCLA in 1954 to establish the first enduring California archaeology program at that campus. Though Meighan was also prominent in the archaeology of Chile and west Mexico, his greatest contributions have been to California prehistory. His early research focused on central California (Meighan 1950, 1953a; Meighan and Heizer 1952). His synthesis of the prehistory of the North Coast ranges was the region's first and served as the standard model for a generation (Meighan 1955a). His studies of the Borax Lake site clarified M.R. Harrington's long unclear interpretations of the Paleoindian presence in northern California (Meighan and Haynes 1968, 1970). He also did pioneering regional studies in the northern Mojave Desert (Meighan 1953b, 1955b), the Channel Islands (Meighan and Eberhart 1953; Meighan 1959c), and mainland southern California (Meighan 1954, 1959a). His excavations at Little Harbor (Meighan 1959c) were nationally influential as one of the founding studies in the ecological approach to archaeology. He also was nationally influential for his syntheses of

California prehistory (Meighan 1961, 1965) and for his explorations of the relationships between patterns of prehistoric cultures in California and elsewhere (Meighan 1959b, 1963). Meighan had been a powerful critic of claims for great human antiquity in California (Meighan 1965, 1976) and a powerful advocate for scientific management of the study of human burial remains (Meighan 1984, 1990, 1992). By founding the UCLA Archaeological Survey and helping found the UCLA Institute of Archaeology, the UCLA Obsidian Hydration Laboratory, the UCLA Rock Art Archives and Study Center, and the Society for California Archaeology, Meighan established an institutional context for research, publication, and student training that extended his impact well beyond his own research.

Joseph L. Chartkoff

Further Readings

Meighan, C.W. 1950. Excavations in Sixteenth-Century Shellmounds at Drake's Bay, California. *University of California Archaeological Survey Reports* 9:27–32.
———. 1953a. Archaeology of Sites Nap-129 and Nap-131. In *The Archaeology of the Napa Region*, edited by R.F. Heizer, pp. 315–317. Anthropological Records, vol. 12, no. 6. University of California, Berkeley.
———. 1953b. The Coville Rock Shelter, Inyo County, California. *University of California Anthropological Records* 12(5):171–224.
———. 1954. A Late Complex in Southern California Prehistory. *Southwestern Journal of Anthropology* 10:215–227.
———. 1955a. Archaeology of the North Coast Ranges, California. *University of California Archaeological Survey* 30:1–39. University of California, Berkeley.
———. 1955b. Notes on the Archaeology of Mono County. *University of California Archaeological Survey* 28:6–28. University of California, Berkeley.
———. 1959a. Archaeological Resources of Borrego State Park. *Archaeological Survey Annual Report for 1958–1959*, pp. 25–44. University of California, Los Angeles.
———. 1959b. California Cultures and the Concept of an Archaic Stage. *American Antiquity* 24:289–305.
———. 1959c. The Little Harbor Site, Catalina Island: An Example of Ecological Interpretation in Archaeology. *American Antiquity* 24:383–405.
———. 1961. The Growth of Archaeology in the West Coast and the Great Basin, 1935–1960. *American Antiquity* 27:33–38.
———. 1963. Pre-Milling Stone Cultures. *Nevada State Museum Anthropological Papers* 9:78–81.
———. 1965. Pacific Coast Archaeology. In *The Quaternary of the United States: A Review Volume for the VII Congress of the International Association for Quaternary Research*, edited by H.E. Wright and D.G. Frey, pp. 709–722. Princeton University Press, Princeton.
———. 1976. Two Views of the Manix Lake Lithic Industry. *Journal of New World Archaeology* 1(7):41.
———. 1984. Archaeology: Science or Sacrilege? In *Ethics and Values in Archaeology*, edited by E.L. Green, pp. 208–233. Free Press, New York.
———. 1990. Bone Worship. *West Virginia Archaeologist* 42(2):40–43.
———. 1992. Some Scholars' Views on Reburial. *American Antiquity* 57:704–710.
Meighan, C.W., and H. Eberhart. 1953. Archaeological Resources of San Nicolas Island, California. *American Antiquity* 19:109–125.
Meighan, C.W., and C.V. Haynes, Jr. 1968. New Studies on the Age of the Borax Lake Site. *Masterkey* 42(1):4–9.
———. 1970. The Borax Lake Site Revisited. *Science* 167:1213–1221.
Meighan, C.W., and R.F. Heizer. 1952. Archaeological Exploration of Sixteenth-Century Indian Mounds at Drake's Bay. *California Historical Society Quarterly* 31:98–108.

Mesa and Putu Sites

The Mesa (49KIR102) and Putu (49PSM027) sites provide convincing, dated evidence for a far northern Paleoindian tradition in Arctic Alaska. Their earliest radiocarbon dates have been used to support the hypothesis that Paleoindian cultures originated there rather than in mid-continental North America.

Mesa, a hunting lookout and weapon-repair camp on the northern flank of Alaska's Brooks Range in the Bering Strait region, is the

M

more securely dated of the two sites. Eleven radiocarbon dates that span the late Pleistocene–early Holocene period fall in the 9710–7780 B.C. (11,660–9730 years B.P.) range. The dates are on shallowly buried hearths associated with lanceolate Paleoindian projectile points that have heavily ground bases and basal thinning but no true flutes. They most closely resemble, but do not copy, Agate Basin and Hell Gap forms. Other tools in the assemblage include spurred gravers, hammerstones, scrapers, bifaces, and other typical Paleoindian artifacts. Absent is the core-and-blade technology characteristic of contemporary Alaskan complexes.

Putu, located 290 km (180 miles) to the east, has a single radiocarbon date of 9520 B.C. ± 500 (11,470 years B.P.) on hearth charcoal. The dated material was spatially associated with a nonfluted lanceolate-point base made with a technology similar to that at Mesa. The larger site assemblage also includes fluted points, knives, and microblades whose associations with one another, the point base, and the hearth date remain unclear.

If the radiocarbon determinations of more than 9050 B.C. (11,000 years B.P.) at Mesa and Putu do date a northern Paleoindian tradition, they challenge the widely held notion that the tradition arose in mid-continental North America. Clovis, the earliest mid-continental Paleoindian complex (9250–8950 B.C., or 11,200–10,900 years B.P.) would be too recent. In this scenario, a late glacial (9050–8350 B.C., or 11,000–10,300 years B.P.) climatic deterioration made northern Alaska uninhabitable and spurred the southward movement of these early Paleoindians to less rigorous environments in the mid-continent. At the very least, the Mesa and Putu sites demonstrate that Paleoindians once occupied the Bering Strait region and Arctic Alaska.

Guy Gibbon

Further Readings

Alexander, H.L. 1987. *Putu: A Fluted Point Site in Alaska*. Publication no. 17. Department of Archaeology, Simon Fraser University, Burnaby.

Hoffecker, J.F., W.R. Powers, and T. Goebel. 1993. The Colonization of Beringia and the Peopling of the New World. *Science* 259:46–53.

Kunz, M.L., and R.E. Reaniert. 1994. Paleoindians in Beringia: Evidence From Arctic Alaska. *Science* 263:660–662.

Mesa Verde Branch

The Mesa Verde branch is a geographically defined subarea of the larger Anasazi archaeological culture area. This regional manifestation gains its name from Mesa Verde, one of the most famous archaeological districts in the Southwest. This subarea is also referred to generically as the Four Corners region and more specifically as the northern San Juan region, since it includes those lands watered by the northern tributaries of the San Juan River. The northern San Juan region covers an area stretching from Bluff, Utah, to Durango, Colorado, and from north of Dolores, Colorado, to the San Juan River on the south.

The northern San Juan region is in the southern portion of the Colorado Plateau. Geologically, the region is characterized by flat-lying sandstone and shale sedimentary deposits that have been eroded into canyon-mesa topography. The region gets increasingly dryer and lower in elevation as one travels northeast to southwest. The headwaters of the San Juan River originate in the mountains of the San Juan Range, and its tributaries flow south or southeast to their confluences with the river. Stream flow in the tributaries becomes increasingly intermittent to the west.

Evidence of Paleoindian (10,050–8050 B.C., or 12,000–10,000 years B.P.) occupation is sparse in the Four Corners region, with only a few Clovis and Folsom points recorded, primarily in the southeastern corner of Utah. The Archaic (8050–550 B.C., or 10,000–2500 years B.P.) occupation of the region is much better represented. In 1973, Cynthia Irwin-Williams identified the Archaic-period foraging groups of the region as part of the widespread Oshara subtradition. However, it was not until the Basketmaker II period (500 B.C.–A.D. 450, or 2450–1500 years B.P.) that the San Juan Anasazi began developing a regionally distinct style of architecture and material culture. The following description focuses on the broad patterns of change that occurred during the Basketmaker and Pueblo periods in the northern San Juan region.

During the Basketmaker II period, the San Juan Anasazi began to supplement their foraging subsistence strategies with maize and squash agriculture. These early food producers occupied dispersed settlements comprising one or more pithouses. Based upon the descriptions of excavations outside Durango by Earl H. Morris and Robert F. Burgh (1954), each of these structures probably housed a single household. Storage space was created by constructing pits and cists both inside and outside the pithouses. It was not until the transitional period between Basketmaker II and III that the Anasazi began to use ceramic vessels for cooking and storage. The earliest ceramics made in the San Juan region were brown wares, suggesting a Mogollon source for their early ceramic technology.

Archaeological sites from the Basketmaker III (A.D. 450–750, or 1500–1200 years B.P.) period are quite numerous in the northern San Juan. Pithouses with circular and rectangular floor plans, 2–7 m (6.6–23 feet) in diameter, continue to serve as the primary domestic structure. Clusters of pithouses tend to be relatively small, but a few recorded sites contain 10 or more structures. The early Anasazi also constructed oversized pit structures, some of which contained upwards of 100 m^2 (120 square yards) of floor area. These Basketmaker III versions of the great kiva probably served as ritual integrative facilities for dispersed Anasazi communities. The Basketmaker III ceramic assemblage comprised primarily grey wares, some of which were decorated with black paint. Red-on-orange pottery was common in southeastern Utah during this period. Beans (*Phaseolus* sp.) were added to the agricultural complex, and the turkey was domesticated during this period as well.

The regional distribution of Anasazi population appears to have been less uniform during the Pueblo I period (A.D. 700/750–900, or 1250/1200–1050 years B.P.). Population increased in localities along the Dolores River, on Mesa Verde, and in Mancos Canyon, while other areas may have experienced short-term abandonments. On the settlement level, this period also marks the first time substantial surface architecture was used by the Anasazi, primarily in the form of rectangular rooms with slab-based foundations supporting jacal walls. The surface rooms were commonly integrated into linear or arcuate (curved) roomblocks, some of which extended more than 75 m (246 feet). Pueblo I villages achieved an unprecedented scale of population aggregation, as evidenced by McPhee village in the Dolores area, home to more than 100 households occupying arcuate roomblocks and associated pithouses. Great kivas also continued to be constructed within and between the Pueblo I villages. Red wares and orange wares continued to be manufactured in southeastern Utah, but the predominant wares made in the northern San Juan were grey wares and white wares. The emphasis on grey utility vessels and white-slipped decorated wares remained the predominant pattern in the region between ca. A.D. 700 and 1300 (1250–650 years B.P.).

During the Pueblo II period (A.D. 900–1100/1150, or 1050–850/800 years B.P.), the northern San Juan Anasazi reached their maximal geographical distribution both within and outside the region. A much wider diversity of landforms and elevational zones were occupied during the Pueblo II period than during the previous period. The majority of the Pueblo II settlements were small, unit pueblos, or "Prudden units," comprising a block of several surface rooms, with a kiva and a trash area located to the south or southeast. Surface rooms incorporated both jacal and masonry architecture, and kivas became increasingly formalized in layout and construction techniques compared to earlier Anasazi pit structures. Each unit pueblo probably belonged to a larger, localized community comprising several dispersed unit pueblos. Both great kivas and Chaco-style great houses served as community integrative facilities during the Pueblo II period. During the later Pueblo II and early Pueblo III periods, there was a notable demographic shift out of Chaco Canyon and an associated increase in population and construction around Aztec and Salmon ruins on the southern fringes of the northern San Juan region.

The ruins from the Pueblo III period (A.D. 1100/1150–1300, or 850/800–650 years B.P.) occupation of the northern San Juan have been the focus of intensive archaeological research since the late nineteenth century A.D. The increased aggregation of population resulted in the construction of the famed Mesa Verde cliff dwellings and the sprawling settlements in the nearby Montezuma Valley. Increasingly intensive agricultural strategies were used to support the aggregated villages, as evidenced by an increase in the number and scale of water-collecting and water-diversion features constructed during the period. Regional population probably reached its peak during the latter part of the period, but it declined precipitously during the last few decades of the thirteenth century. A number of factors, including increasing desiccation, scarcity of important resources (water, productive lands), and the inherent social fragility of the large Anasazi villages, eventually compelled the Anasazi to abandon the northern San Juan region by A.D. 1300 (650 years B.P.).

Michael A. Adler

M

Further Readings

Breternitz, D.A., A.H. Rohn, and E. Morris. 1974. *Prehistoric Ceramics of the Mesa Verde Region*. Ceramic Series no. 5. Museum of Northern Arizona, Flagstaff.

Brew, J.O. 1946. *Archaeology of Alkali Ridge, Southeastern Utah*. Papers, vol. 21. Peabody Museum of American Archaeology and Ethnology, Harvard University, Cambridge.

Cordell, L.S. 1984. *Prehistory of the Southwest*. Academic Press, New York.

Eddy, F.W., A.E. Kane, and P.R. Nickens. 1984. *Background and Research Directions*. Office of Archaeology and Historic Preservation, Denver.

Irwin-Williams, C. 1973. *The Oshara Tradition: Origins of Anasazi Culture*. Contributions in Anthropology, vol. 5, no. 1. Eastern New Mexico University, Portales.

Morris, E.H., and R.F. Burgh. 1954. *Basketmaker II Sites Near Durango, Colorado*. Publication no. 604. Carnegie Institution of Washington, Washington, D.C.

Prudden, T.M. 1903. Prehistoric Ruins of the San Juan Watershed in Utah, Arizona, Colorado and New Mexico. *American Anthropologist* 5(2):224–288.

Rohn, A.H. 1989. Northern San Juan Prehistory. In *Dynamics of Southwestern Prehistory*, edited by L. Cordell and G. Gumerman, pp. 149–177. Smithsonian Institution Press, Washington, D.C.

Wilshusen, R.H., and E. Blinman 1991. Pueblo I Village Formation: A Reevaluation of Sites Recorded by E. Morris on Ute Mountain Ute Tribal Lands. *Kiva* 57(3):251–269.

See also CHACO BRANCH; CLIFF PALACE; PECOS CLASSIFICATION; PUEBLO; SAND CANYON PUEBLO; YELLOW JACKET RUIN

Mica (Eastern Woodlands)

Micas are mineral silicates that crystallize into monoclinic forms characterized by nearly perfect cleavage. Because of this quality, the mineral readily separates into very thin sheets that are fairly flexible. Micas, such as muscovite, biotite, and phlogopite, differ widely in composition and range in color from colorless, to silvery, to various shades of brown and green, to black. Although present in some Late Archaic (ca. 4050–700 B.C., or 6000–2650 years B.P.) complexes, mica sheets cut into geometric and representational forms, such as human hands, bird claws, crescents, and ornaments, became highly prized exotic goods in the Early Woodland Adena (ca. 500 B.C.–A.D. 200, or 2450–1750 years B.P.) burial complex and in the widespread Middle Woodland Hopewell Interaction Sphere (ca. 1–400, or 1950–1550 years B.P.). Like Lake Superior copper, galena, and seashells, mica from mines in North Carolina and elsewhere was obtained through complex exchange networks. Mica sheets and ornaments were present as well in more recent southeastern Mississippian chiefdoms and at other Mississippian centers, such as Cahokia in Illinois.

Guy Gibbon

Further Readings

Bailey, S.W. (editor). 1984. *Micas*. Mineralogical Society of America, Washington, D.C.

Seeman, M. 1979. *The Hopewell Interaction Sphere: The Evidence for Interregional Trade and Structural Complexity*. Indiana Historical Society, Indianapolis.

Smith, C.D. 1877. *Ancient Mica Mines in North Carolina*. Washington, D.C.

See also ADENA; HOPEWELL INTERACTION SPHERE

Microblade Tradition

The Microblade tradition is an early cultural and technological tradition in northwestern North America that is defined by the presence of a microblade technology for the manufacture of cutting and piercing implements. Stone cores were shaped to produce small parallel-sided blades that were then segmented and inserted into a haft to produce projectile points or knives. The distribution of this microblade technology has formed the basis for the definition of several cultural constructs. The first was by Richard S. MacNeish (1959), who used the term as the name of a cultural tradition, the Northwest (interior) Microblade tradition, in which he included all known occurrences of the technology in Alaska, the Yukon, and interior British Columbia. The Alaskan material has since come to be called either the Denali or the Paleoarctic tradition. David Sanger (1968), who had discovered differences in technology between coastal and interior microblade and core collections from British Columbia and Washington, defined the "Plateau Microblade tradition." Knut R. Fladmark (1975) used the term "Early Coast Microblade complex" to group occurrences of microblade technology on the northern Northwest Coast. In 1979, Roy L. Carlson lumped occurrences of microblade technology in northwestern North America together, arguing that technological divergence is a natural function of distance in time and space. His "Microblade tradition" is a cultural tradition in the northern Northwest Coast and adjacent interior that has relationships north to the Arctic and south to the Columbia River.

The contiguous occurrence of microblade technology from Siberia across to Alaska and south to the Columbia River indicates that it is a unified, historical tradition. It was probably introduced into northern North America by the ancestors of the NaDene speakers (Athabascan, Tlingit, Haida, Eyak), as suggested by Donald Dumond and Charles E. Borden. It eventually spread to adjacent peoples and evolved into a variety of types based on regional differences in core-preparation techniques. This reconstructed history of the spread of the technology is supported by radiocarbon dates, which are time transgressive from north to south. It is earliest in central Alaska in the Denali complex (ca. 8550 B.C., or 10,500 years B.P.), slightly later at Ugashik on the Alaska Peninsula (ca. 8050 B.C., or 10,000 years B.P.), later still in the interior of British Columbia at Charlie Lake Cave (ca. 7550 B.C., or 9500 years B.P.) and at Namu (ca. 6550 B.C., or 8500 years B.P.), and still later on the Upper Columbia River system at Kettle Falls sometime before the Mazama ash fall of 4750 B.C. (6700 years B.P.).

Roy L. Carlson

Further Readings

Carlson, R.L. 1990. Cultural Antecedents. In *Northwest Coast,* edited by W. Suttles, pp. 60–69. Handbook of North American Indians, vol. 7, W.C. Sturtevant, general editor. Smithsonian Institution, Washington, D.C.

Carlson, R.L., and M.J. Carlson. 1990. Holocene Lithic Industries of British Columbia. In *Chronostratigraphy of the Paleolithic in North, Central, East Asia and America,* pp. 9–19. Academy of Sciences of the USSR, Novosibirsk.

Carlson, R.L., and L. Dalla Bona (editors).
1996. *Early Human Occupation in British Columbia*. University of British Columbia Press, Vancouver.

Fladmark, K.R. 1975. *A Paleoecological Model for Northwest Coast Prehistory*. Mercury Series Paper no. 43. Archaeological Survey of Canada, National Museum of Man, Ottawa.

MacNeish, R.S. 1959. A Speculative Framework of Northern North American Prehistory As of April 1959. *Anthropologia,* n.s., 1:1–17.

Sanger, D. 1968. Prepared Core and Blade Traditions in the Pacific Northwest. *Arctic Anthropology* 5(1):92–120.

Mid-Columbia River Region Sequence

The Mid-Columbia River region of the Columbia Plateau extends from the confluence of the Snake and Columbia rivers northward to the Canadian border. Cultural chronologies within the region derive primarily from archaeological projects associated with dam and reservoir development. The present chronological sequence spans the period from ca. 9300 B.C. (11,250 years B.P.) to Euro-American contact at the beginning of the eighteenth century A.D., although most radiometric dates used to define local sequences fall within the ca. 1050 B.C.–A.D. 1450 (3000–500 years B.P.) range. The regional archaeological sequence is divided into Early, Middle, and Late periods, with local units noted for specific subregions. The Kettle Falls locality at the upper boundary of the region is described in a separate entry.

Early Period (ca. 9300–4050/2050 B.C., or 11,250–6000/4000 years B.P.). Early-period occupations can be subdivided into early and late subperiods that reflect the transition from Paleoindian to post-Paleoindian (i.e., Early Archaic) traditions. The Early period has the longest temporal span of the three periods; it is also the most poorly dated and defined overall. In southern portions of the region, the early subperiod can only be inferred from surface finds of Clovis-style points and occasional Late Paleoindian lanceolate forms associated with what otherwise appear to be late subperiod assemblages. In the middle reach of the region, Clovis finds at the Richey-Roberts site date to the early subperiod. No dated sites and relatively few surface finds of Paleoindian or Late Paleoindian point styles are reported from northern portions of the region. Better documented are late subperiod components beginning with the Early Archaic Windust phase in the Lower Snake River region. Radiocarbon dates on Windust-phase occupations fall in the ca. 8850–6050 B.C. (10,800–8000 years B.P.) range in southern sections of the Mid-Columbia region. Possible coeval components, although undated, are indicated by correlative point styles at least in middle sections of this region. The final cultural tradition of the Early period is well documented throughout the region. First defined in the Lower Snake River region as the Cascade phase, coeval cultural manifestations are documented within the interval ca. 6050–2550/2050 B.C. (8000–4500/4000 years B.P.) in all parts of the Mid-Columbia region. Recognizable by common occurrences of the characteristic lanceolate, bipointed Cascade point, comparable cultural phases include Vantage, Okanagan, and Kartar. Transitions to succeeding Middle-period occupations occur somewhat earlier in the south than in the north of this region.

Middle Period (ca. 4050/2050–550/50 B.C., or 6000/4000–2500/2000 years B.P.). Changes during the transition from the Early to the Middle period are reasonably well defined throughout the region. Although relatively few sites of this period are reported for the Lower Snake River region, sufficient information was derived to define the Tucannon phase. Originally thought to appear sometime after 3050 B.C. (5000 years B.P.), more recent information suggests that this phase, and Middle-period adaptations generally, may have started as much as 1,000 years earlier (Galm et al. 1986). This transition in the Lower Snake, as in other sections of the Mid-Columbia, probably involved significant changes in economic lifestyles. Roughly coeval formulations are recognized in middle portions of the region as the Frenchman Springs phase, and the Indian Dan and Hudnut phases to the north. For some subregions, later-dating phases have also been defined, such as the Quilomene Bar phase in the Wanapum-Priest Rapids segment of the Columbia River Valley and the Chiliwist phase in the Wells Reach. A larger number of dated Middle-period components are reported in middle and northern sections of the region than to the south, although the meaning of this distribution is not entirely clear. A significant increase in off-river (especially upland steppe) distributions of Middle-period components, particularly in the northern half of the region, is apparently related to broad changes in adaptive strategies and lifeways.

Late Period (550/50 B.C.–A.D. 1700, or 2500/2000–250 years B.P.). As in preceding periods, the timing of the Late period is not synchronous across the region. The appearance of bow-and-arrow technology and an increased population density are two characteristics of the Middle-to-Late-period transition in the Mid-Columbia region. Despite many outward similarities in lifestyles, Late-period settlement is the most complex and variable of the three periods. In the south, two phases are defined for this period, the Harder phase and the succeeding Piqunin phase. Coeval phases to the north include the Cayuse phase of the middle reach of the Mid-Columbia, the Cassimer Bar phase of the Wells Reservoir area, and the Coyote Creek phase in the Chief Joseph Reach. The pattern of subdividing Late-period occupations into separate phases or subphases (i.e., Cayuse I, II, and III) is widespread and indicative of what are often subtle changes in subsistence-settlement patterns. For much of the region, these shifts are best defined ca. A.D. 1450 (500 years B.P.) and are recognizable in the form of changes in settlement strategies.

Jerry R. Galm

Further Readings

Chatters, J.C. 1986. *The Wells Reservoir Archaeological Project: 1. Summary of Findings.* Archaeological Report no. 86–6. Central Washington Archaeological Survey, Central Washington University, Ellensburg.

Galm, J.R., G.D. Hartmann, R.A. Masten, and G.O. Stephenson. 1986. *A Cultural Resources Overview of the Bonneville Power Administration's Mid-Columbia Project, Central Washington.* Reports in Archaeology and History no. 100–16. Bonneville Cultural Resources Group, Eastern Washington University, Cheney.

Leonhardy, F.C., and D.G. Rice. 1970. A Proposed Culture Typology for the Snake River Region, Southeastern Washington. *Northwest Anthropological Research Notes* 4(1):1–29.

Nelson, C.M. 1969. *The Sunset Creek Site (45KT28) and Its Place in Plateau Prehistory.* Report of Investigations no. 47. Laboratory of Anthropology, Washington State University, Pullman.

See also KETTLE FALLS SEQUENCE

Middle Missouri Tradition

A semisedentary, horticultural way of life was introduced into the northern Plains around the tenth century A.D. by peoples of the Middle Missouri tradition. This village way of life was adapted to exploiting large river floodplains for gardens, and upland grasslands for game, especially bison. The lifeway developed along the prairie-plains border and was carried deep into the High Plains along the valley of the Missouri River in North and South Dakota. The Middle Missouri tradition, originally defined by Donald J. Lehmer (1954, 1971), and refined by Lehmer and Warren W. Caldwell (1966), consisted of the early horticultural villages of southeastern South Dakota and those along the Missouri River trench as far upstream as west-central North Dakota. The tradition is, however, much more inclusive, for it also included the Mill Creek, Cambria, and Great Oasis cultures along the prairie-plains border farther east. The three variants, or subdivisions, of the Middle Missouri tradition are distinguished by geographical distribution, age, and cultural content. They are called the Initial (A.D. 900–1500, or 1050–450 years B.P.), the Extended (A.D. 1200–1500, or 750–450 years B.P.), and the Terminal (A.D. 1500–1675, or 450–275 years B.P.) variants. The Initial variant consists of two geographically separate, but closely related, divisions: an eastern division in northwestern Iowa and parts of adjoining South Dakota and Minnesota, and a western division, with villages along the Missouri River in south-central South Dakota. The Extended and the later Terminal Middle Missouri variants are confined to the Missouri Valley in North and South Dakota.

Middle Missouri sites are semipermanent, often fortified, villages located along major streams near bottomlands suitable for gardening. Subsistence was based on horticulture and on hunting and gathering, probably in about equal proportions. Maize, beans, squash, and sunflower were grown. Other, supplementary plants included sumpweed, goosefoot, and knotweed. Dwellings were long rectangular structures supported by a central ridgepole. Entryways to houses almost always faced southwest. Very little is known of burial customs. The globular, grit-tempered pottery was well made. Vessels were often elaborately decorated on the rim and shoulder, but pots more often had simple incised or cord-impressed decorations on the rim. Triangular chipped-stone projectile points, end scrapers, drills, and bifaces of varying form were common, as were bison-scapula hoes, bison-horn core-frontal scoops, bison-rib shaft wrenches, serrated fleshing tools, slotted bison-rib knife handles, and awls. L-shaped elk-antler scraper hafts, antler bracelets, and mollusk-shell beads and other ornaments occur in most sites. Grooved mauls, diorite celts, grooved shaft abraders, and other ground-stone tools were plentiful. Smoking pipes are of varying form. Luxury goods were imported from great distances: native copper from the western Great Lakes area; conch and other shells from the Gulf or Atlantic coasts, the southeastern United States, and the West Coast; and catlinite from southwestern Minnesota.

The tradition will probably ultimately be revealed to be the result of a rapid recombination of preexisting Late Woodland and, perhaps, early Great Oasis elements. Once the tradition developed, there must have been a rapid movement west into and across the High Plains to the Missouri Valley, first by the Initial-variant (ca. A.D. 900, or 1050 years B.P.) people and then by bearers of the Extended variant (ca. A.D. 1200, or 750 years B.P.). These two groups remained the pioneer gardeners in the area until the appearance of the Initial Coalescent variant ca. A.D. 1400 (550 years B.P.). The Extended variant is *not* believed to be a descendant of the Initial variant. Rather, the two variants are distinct expressions of the Middle Missouri tradition, although they probably stemmed from common antecedents.

Eastern-division phases include Cambria, Great Oasis, and the Big and Little Sioux (which are often combined and referred to as Mill Creek). Big Sioux–phase villages are on the river of the same name north of Sioux City, Iowa. Sites of the Little Sioux phase are along the Little Sioux River in northwestern Iowa. Big and Little Sioux–phase villages consist of long rectangular houses set on terraces. Most of them appear to have been built on artificial earth platforms and/or were fortified by enclosing ditches. The final disposition of the populations of the eastern division is a matter of speculation. None appear to be represented in later sites in the Middle Missouri subarea or elsewhere.

The western division was established along the Missouri River in South Dakota in the tenth century A.D. These western sites derive from those of the eastern division. Initial-variant villages occur along the Missouri Valley between the White and Cheyenne rivers. Many sites were fortified by a ditch that isolated them on a terrace spur. The center of occupation by Initial-variant peoples after A.D. 1100 was in the Big Bend area. Farther north, Lehmer believed, they came into contact with Extended-variant peoples. Many of the Initial- and Extended-variant sites in the area between the mouths of the Bad and Cheyenne rivers were fortified. Lehmer posited that the people were fortifying their villages against one another. Also according to Lehmer, Initial-variant villagers adopted a number of elements from their Extended-variant neighbors, including the technique of simple-stamped pottery.

The Extended variant occupied the Missouri Valley from about the mouth of the Bad River to the mouth of the Knife River ca. A.D. 1200–1400 (750–550 years B.P.). Sites south of the Moreau River are of the Thomas Riggs phase; those near the Heart River are principally of the Fort Yates phase; those near the Knife River are of the Nailati phase. Extended-variant communities consisted of small, dispersed, and relatively isolated villages. They were usually open in the north, and often fortified in the south, part of their range.

The Terminal variant (A.D. 1500–1675, or 450–275 years B.P.) was marked by dramatic social adaptations and brought to a close the ca. 800-year history of the Middle Missouri tradition. The variant resulted from the telescoping of the small, scattered Extended-variant villages into large, compact, heavily fortified redoubts. Sites were concentrated between the Heart and the Cannonball rivers. Long rectangular houses continued to be built for a short period, but in later sites they were displaced by circular earthlodges. This displacement began at Huff, where one of the houses was a subcircular structure supported by four center posts. This house type was derived from Coalescent sources farther downriver. In spite of the many changes in the Middle Missouri tradition, an unbroken sequence can be traced from Extended-variant villages in the northern Missouri Valley that date to ca. A.D. 1200 (750 years B.P.), through the Terminal variant, to the historic Mandan and Hidatsa Indians.

W. Raymond Wood

Further Readings

Lehmer, D.J. 1954. *Archeological Investigations in the Oahe Dam Area, South Dakota, 1950–51.* Bulletin no. 158. Bureau of American Ethnology, Smithsonian Institution, Washington, D.C.

———. 1971. *Introduction to Middle Missouri Archeology.* Anthropological Papers no. 1. National Park Service, Washington, D.C.

Lehmer, D.J., and W.W. Caldwell. 1966. Horizon and Tradition in the Northern Plains. *American Antiquity* 31(4):511–516.

Toom, D.L. 1992. Early Village Formation in the Middle Missouri Subarea of the Plains. *Research in Economic Anthropology Supplement* 6:131–191.

Middle Woodland

The term "Middle Woodland" refers to the middle period or stage of the Woodland tradition in eastern North America. Many trends that began thousands of years earlier in the Archaic period reach their climax in the Middle Woodland in some resource-rich regions. Among these were tendencies toward: (1) an increasing efficiency in harvesting a wide variety of productive and nutritious wild-food resources; (2) an increasing emphasis on the gathering and gardening of seed-bearing plants; (3) an intensification of food procurement; (4) smaller, better defined, and more circumscribed group territories; (5) more sedentary lifeways; (6) "packing" in resource-rich environments caused by increasing population sizes, group fissioning, and inward migration; (7) a sense of corporate, or "ethnic," identity; (8) increasingly conspicuous group boundary markers to legitimize a corporate right to local resources; (9) more elaborate burial rites; (10) more complex intra- and intercommunity social arrangements; and (11) increasingly formal intergroup exchange mechanisms. The most spectacular archaeological evidence of this climax is associated with the Hopewell phenomenon in the heartland of the culture area.

Middle Woodland archaeological complexes include Ohio Hopewell in southern Ohio; Havana Hopewell in the Illinois Valley and adjacent Mississippi Valley; Crab Orchard in southern Illinois; Kansas City Hopewell; Swift Creek, Copena, Deptford, Miller, and Marksville in the Southeast; Laurel in the western Upper Great Lakes; and Point Peninsula in the Northeast. Most of these complexes participated to varying degrees in what has been called the Hopewell Interaction Sphere; some in spatially peripheral areas did not participate at all.

Dates for the Middle Woodland time period vary widely across the Eastern Woodlands, for archaeologists do not agree on which traits are diagnostic of the period or stage. In addition, some events, such as the appearance of new ceramic forms, occurred at different times in different areas. For some archaeologists, the Middle Woodland is that period between 200 B.C. and A.D. 400 (2150–1550 years B.P.) when most of the Eastern Woodlands was dominated by the Hopewell culture. For others, it is defined by the presence of Middle Woodland ceramic complexes, which, according to some interpretations, ranges from ca. 300 B.C. to A.D. 300 (2250–1650 years B.P.) in the Illinois Valley, ca. A.D. 1 to 600 (1950–1350 years B.P.) in the Southeast, and ca. A.D. 1 to 900 (1950–1050 years B.P.) in the Northeast. In the southeastern Deptford and Swift Creek complexes, pottery was checked, complicated, and simple stamped. Classic Ohio Hopewell and Illinois Havana Hopewell decorated pottery had rocker-and-dentate stamp and incised designs arranged largely in zonal patterns. In general, Middle Woodland ceramic vessels tended to have more complex and sophisticated shapes and designs than the preceding Early Woodland pottery. They also had thinner walls that were more resistant to breakage when heated.

The most spectacular Hopewell ceremonial sites are in the Sciota Valley near Chillicothe, Ohio. These religious and political centers typically contain a burial mound and geometric earthwork complex that covers 4–100 ha (10 to hundreds of acres) and a sparse midden; evidence of large resident populations is lacking. Larger mounds can be up to 12 m (39.4 feet) high, 150 m (492 feet) long, and 55 m (180.4 feet) wide. Multiple mortuary structures under the mounds were often log tombs that contained the remains of skeletons that had been cremated, bundled, or interred in some other manner. Exotic raw materials and "art" objects, the diagnostic artifacts of the Hopewell Interaction Sphere, accompanied some of the burials. Included were Lake Superior copper, galena, obsidian from Wyoming, Knife River flint from North Dakota, pipestone, silver, meteoric iron, mica, chlorite, quartz crystal, petrified wood, foreign nodular flints, large and small marine shells (*Cassis, Busycon, Fasciolaria, Marginella, Oliva, Olivella*), ocean-turtle shells, alligator and shark teeth, barracuda jaws, clay figurines, platform effigy pipes, and two-dimensional representational art cut from sheets of copper or mica. Small villages where people hunted and gathered wild-food resources and tended small gardens presumably surrounded these large centers. Until the 1960s, however, the intense focus on the larger centers and their exotic contents detracted from investigations of year-round subsistence-settlement patterns. Smaller amounts of Hopewell Interaction Sphere items are found in Havana graves in Illinois and in other Hopewellian complexes. Differences in regional burial practices, ceramics, settlement patterns, and other aspects of the archaeological record suggest that these items and presumably their associated ritual practices were grafted onto local cultures.

Just what the Hopewell phenomenon represents remains a focus of investigation. Some researchers view the florescence in burial mound and earthwork construction, the elaboration of burial ceremonialism, and the presence of powerful exotic substances and manufactured items as the archaeologically visible manifestation of a climactic expression of a cosmology whose roots extend deep into the Archaic. According to this view, the spirit world had to be propitiated to ensure an abundance of food, a successful raid on a traditional enemy, and so on, and these items functioned within that process of communication. Others regard the florescence as evidence of the emergence of regional social ranking. In this view, heads of high-ranking lineages legitimized their positions, in part, by obtaining interaction-sphere symbols of power from their contemporaries in distant communities. Still another interpretation considers the aspirations of "Big Men" as responsible for moving interaction-sphere items through an extensive intertribal network. Here, a potential "Big Man" would attempt to build his own reputation and a political bloc within the segmented tribal organization by exchanging locally available items for interaction-sphere raw materials and ritual items. Presumably, aspects of all three interpretations were important to varying degrees in different Middle Woodland complexes. What seems apparent, however, is the value of viewing the Hopewell phenomenon from a social, rather than a strictly material, perspective.

Guy Gibbon

Further Readings

Brose, D.S., and N. Greber (editors). 1979. *Hopewell Archaeology: The Chillicothe Conference.* Kent State University Press, Kent.

M

Caldwell, J.R., and R.L. Hall (editors). 1964. *Hopewellian Studies.* Illinois State Museum, Springfield.

Mason, R.J. 1981. *Great Lakes Archaeology.* Academic Press, New York.

Seeman, M.F. 1979. *The Hopewell Interaction Sphere: The Evidence for Interregional Trade and Structural Complexity.* Indiana Historical Society, Indianapolis.

Smith, B.D. 1986. The Archaeology of the Southeastern United States: From Dalton to de Soto, 10,500 to 500 B.P. *Advances in World Archaeology* 5:1–92.

Steponaitus, V. 1986. Prehistoric Archaeology in the Southeastern United States 1970–1985. *Annual Review of Anthropology* 15:363–404.

See also COPENA; CRAB ORCHARD; DEPTFORD CULTURE; HAVANA HOPEWELL; HOPEWELL INTERACTION SPHERE; KANSAS CITY HOPEWELL; LAUREL CULTURE; MARKSVILLE; MILLER CULTURE; OHIO HOPEWELL; POINT PENINSULA CULTURE; SWIFT CREEK

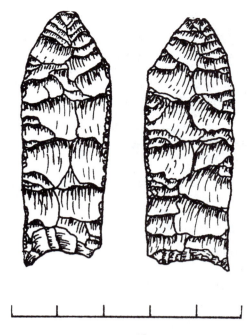

c m

Midland point from the Scharbauer site, Locality 1, the type site for the Midland complex. (Figure is based on Wendorf et al., 1955, Fig. 12–1. Redrawn by J. L. Hofman)

Midland Complex

The Midland archaeological complex was defined following discoveries at the Scharbauer site near Midland, Texas, including a human skull, animal bones, and artifacts in ancient dune deposits of uncertain late Pleistocene age, that brought considerable notoriety to the site in the late 1950s. Despite additional study at this "type site" and at other deposits in the region, and study of stratified Paleoindian assemblages at the Hell Gap site in Wyoming, the relationships between Midland and other Paleoindian complexes, especially Folsom, remain a topic of debate. Although the links between the Midland and the Folsom complexes are numerous, specific aspects of their shared chronology, technology, group composition, and archaeological taxonomy remain unresolved.

The single primary difference between Folsom and Midland assemblages is that Folsom projectile points are fluted and Midland points are not; Midland points share most other morphological and technical attributes or characteristics of Folsom points, and other elements of their tool technologies are essentially identical. These include spurred end scrapers, delicate gravers, eyed bone needles, and a pattern of use of the same lithic sources. However, there are

few stratified sites that provide a clear indication of the chronological relationship between Folsom and Midland assemblages, and, as of the mid-1990s, there were no radiocarbon dates for clearly unmixed Midland assemblages. The age is assumed top overlap with that of the Folsom complex, ca. 8800–8200 B.C. (10,750–10,150 years B.P.).

It is often assumed that Midland represents a late phase of Folsom technology when projectile-point fluting was losing popularity. This assumption is based, in part, on the fact that, while the abandonment of the fluting of projectile points by Paleoindians most likely occurred at different times and at different rates in various regions of the Plains, it was a technique that was eventually completely lost. The relationship between Midland and Folsom could reasonably be, then, a chronological or historical one, although studies in the 1980s and 1990s of the Goshen complex, an unfluted assemblage of Clovis or Folsom age in the northern Plains, demonstrate that a temporal relationship must be documented rather than simply assumed. It has also been suggested that these projectile-point types reflect the activities of two distinct, but more or less contemporary, groups and that technological aspects of projectile-point production and decisions about when to flute points may have been influenced by technological considerations, availability of special types of stone, and time constraints, among other things. A factor that might be important in deciding between these interpretations is that there are many archaeological sites, such as Shifting Sands in Texas and Hell Gap in Wyoming, where both Folsom and Midland points (or unfluted Folsom points) are found together. However, the integrity of these sites and the possibility of the mixing of remains from multiple occupations through deflation and other natural processes are generally undocumented.

The Midland and Folsom complexes are without question very similar in overall technology, economy, and, to a large extent, temporal and spatial distribution, and there are many reasonable interpretations of their relationship. Understanding this interrelationship is one of the more intriguing problems in contemporary Paleoindian research.

Jack L. Hofman

Further Readings

Agogino, G.A. 1969. The Midland Complex: Is It Valid? *American Anthropologist* 71:1117–1118.

Hofman, J.L., D.S. Amick, and R.O. Rose. 1990. Shifting Sands: A Folsom-Midland Assemblage From a Campsite in Western Texas. *Plains Anthropologist* 35:221–254.

Holliday, V.T., and D.J. Meltzer. 1993. Geoarchaeology of the Midland (Paleoindian) Site and the Age of the Midland Skull. *Current Research in the Pleistocene* 10:41–43.

Irwin-Williams, C., H.T. Irwin, G.A. Agogino, and C.V. Haynes, Jr. 1973. Hell Gap: Paleo-Indian Occupation on the High Plains. *Plains Anthropologist* 18:40–53.

Judge, W.J. 1970. Systems Analysis of the Folsom-Midland Question. *Southwestern Journal of Anthropology* 26:40–51.

Wendorf, F., and A.D. Krieger. 1959. New Light on the Midland Discovery. *American Antiquity* 25:66–78.

Wendorf, F., A.D. Krieger, C.C. Albritton, and T.D. Stewart. 1955. *The Midland Discovery*. University of Texas Press, Austin.

See also FOLSOM COMPLEX; GOSHEN COMPLEX; HELL GAP SITE; SCHARBAUER

M

Midwestern Taxonomic System (Midwestern Taxonomic Method)

Worked out in 1929, presented at an American Anthropological Association Central Section meeting in Indianapolis in 1934, and, after discussion at the 1935 Indianapolis Conference of the Committee on State Archaeological Surveys (National Research Council), published in *American Antiquity* in 1939, Will C. McKern's Midwestern Taxonomic Method was eagerly adopted in the Midwest. Alton K. Fisher, an assistant on McKern's Trempeleau (Wisconsin) site excavation in 1929, suggested to McKern that biology's classic Linneaean taxonomic system could be a model for handling a diversity of archaeological data that would challenge the simplistic stratigraphic ordering that was conventional practice in the Midwest at that time. McKern's method "dissected" assemblages of data into component traits; the degree of similarity between assemblages, a product of the number of homologues, would constitute the degree of relationship in a hierarchical system of *component* (assemblage), *focus, aspect, phase, pattern,* and *base*. Julian H. Steward (1942) attacked the method for its abjuration of chronology, seeing it in competition with the equally new Direct Historical Approach articulated by W.D. Strong (1935) on Nebraska data. McKern argued that his explicit scientific method ordered data without biasing interpretations of relationships by estimates of time or presumed ethnic correlations. This was a critical feature of the method in an era lacking radiometric procedures.

Carl E. Guthe wrote that McKern's method "was the single most constructive achievement in the eastern United States during the past 25 years. . . . It has forced into the discard practically all of the earlier working hypotheses" (Guthe 1952:9). Although the method was concerned with structuring data on the single principle of degree of similarity, it still permitted the addition of temporal and ethnic tags; the tags were, however, no longer considered defining and inherent properties of the data. In this way, McKern's Midwestern Taxonomic Method was transposed into a Midwestern Taxonomic system that remains basic to the prehistory of the region: Nomadic-Hunting and Horticultural *bases;* Woodland,

Mississippian, Archaic, and Paleoindian *patterns;* and, as a specific illustrative example, a Late Woodland *phase* containing a Northwestern Wisconsin *aspect* that includes a Clam River *focus* composed of three *component* sites, the Clam River and Spencer Lake mounds and the Fickle village, that are possibly ancestral Dakota.

Alice Beck Kehoe

Further Readings

Guthe, C.E. 1952. Twenty-Five Years of Archeology in the Eastern United States. In *Archeology of Eastern United States,* edited by J.B. Griffin, pp. 1–12. University of Chicago Press, Chicago.

McKern, W.C. 1939. The Midwestern Taxonomic Method As an Aid to Archaeological Culture Study. *American Antiquity* 4:301–313.

Steward, J.H. 1942. The Direct Historical Approach in Archaeology. *American Antiquity* 7:337–343.

Strong, W.D. 1935. *An Introduction to Nebraska Archaeology.* Miscellaneous Collections, vol. 93, no. 10. Smithsonian Institution, Washington, D.C.

See also McKern, Will C.

Migod Site

Migod (KkLn-4) at Grant Lake on the Debawnt River of the Canadian central Subarctic is the only site with a stratigraphic record spanning the entire Barrenland cultural sequence. The earliest tradition, Northern Plano (ca. 7000–4000 B.C., or 8950–5950 years B.P.), is represented by a thin cultural layer dating to 5980 B.C. ± 500 (7930 years B.P.) that contained an Agate Basin projectile point. Immediately above this layer are several Shield Archaic levels dating to ca. 4000–1750 B.C. (5950–3700 years B.P.) that contain round-based side-notched points. Above them is a thin, Pre-Dorset component that represents the southern incursion of Arctic peoples during the very cold 1500–700 B.C. (3450–2650 years B.P.) period. The Pre-Dorset occupation is followed by a range of Taltheilei-tradition occupations that lead up to European contact in the eighteenth century. Organic preservation is poor for all periods, but the richness of the site attests to its persistent importance over the millennia.

Bryan C. Gordon

Further Readings

Gordon, B.C. 1976. *Migod—8,000 Years of Barrenland Prehistory.* Mercury Series Paper no. 56. Archaeological Survey of Canada, National Museum of Man, Ottawa.

Mill Creek Quarry

The Mill Creek quarry (11U311), located in southwestern Illinois, is the main source for Mill Creek chert. This distinctive bluish-gray, coarse-textured chert derives from the Ullin limestone formation. Mill Creek chert was extremely popular during the Mississippian period (ca. A.D. 900–1400, or 1050–550 years B.P.) for the manufacture of digging implements, commonly known as spades or hoes. Exotic lithic forms, such as maces and spatulate celts, were also occasionally made from Mill Creek chert. Both the utilitarian and the exotic implements were widely exchanged throughout the central Mississippi River Valley and beyond.

The Mill Creek quarry was well known by the nineteenth century and was investigated by both the Field Museum of Natural History, Chicago, and the Smithsonian Institution, Washington, D.C. It occupies several ridges within the fairly rugged terrain of the Ozark Plateau. Early archaeologists established that the quarry covered an area of ca. 5–10 ha (12–24 acres) and was composed of hundreds of quarry depressions. A trench excavation placed through several of the pits at the turn of the century showed that shafts up to 5 m (16.4 feet) deep had been dug to extract chert, which indicates that some of the most intensive and sophisticated extractive technology in aboriginal eastern North America occurred at the quarry.

Subsequent research in the twentieth century has established that there are a number of Mill Creek chert quarries in the same area of southwestern Illinois. However, the more recent discoveries are much smaller than the main quarry. In addition, dozens of workshops scattered with hoe blanks are found throughout floodplain locations below the quarries. One small mound center, the Hale site, is also located in the Mill Creek floodplain near the main quarry.

Many archaeologists believe that the Hale site may have played an important role in the procurement of Mill Creek chert and in the production and distribution of Mill Creek chert

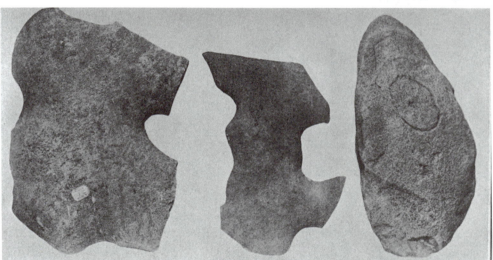

Top: Mill Creek chert nodules as they occur in the Salem limestone formation. (Reprinted from the Smithsonian Institution, Bureau of American Ethnology, Bulletin 60, Figure 65) Bottom: Examples of the flattish, irregularly shaped Mill Creek chert nodules used in the manufacture of implements. (Reprinted from the Smithsonian Institution, Bureau of American Ethnology, Bulletin 60, Figure 65)

implements. However, other mound sites farther away also have been implicated in the production of Mill Creek chert hoes. Taken together, the main Mill Creek quarry, subsidiary quarries, workshops, and mound centers make up one of the most intensive production systems found in North America.

Charles R. Cobb

Further Readings

Brown, J.A., R.A. Kerber, and H.D. Winters. 1990. Trade and the Evolution of Exchange Relations at the Beginning of the Mississippian Period. In *The Mississippian Emergence,* edited by B.D. Smith, pp. 251–280. Smithsonian Institution Press, Washington, D.C.

Cobb, C.R. 1989. An Appraisal of the Role of Mill Creek Chert Hoes in Mississippian Exchange Systems. *Southeastern Archaeology* 8:79–92.

Holmes, W.H. 1919. Handbook of Aboriginal American Antiquities. *Bureau of American Ethnology Bulletin* 60:187–194.

Phillips, W.A. 1900. Aboriginal Quarries and Shops at Mill Creek, Illinois. *American Anthropologist*, n.s., 2:37–52.

Thomas, C. 1894. *Report on the Mound Explorations of the Bureau of Ethnology.* Annual Report of the Bureau of American Ethnology, vol. 12. Smithsonian Institution, Washington, D.C.

Winters, H.D. 1981. Excavating in Museums: Notes on Mississippian Hoes and Middle Woodland Copper Gouges and Celts. In *The Research Potential of Anthropological Museum Collections,* edited by A.E. Cantwell, J.B. Griffin, and N.A. Rothschild, pp. 17–34. Annals of the New York Academy of Science, vol. 376.

Mill Iron Site

The Mill Iron site (24CT30) is located in southeast Montana a short distance from the common meeting point of Montana and North and South Dakota. The site was first tested in 1984 by a University of Wyoming field crew under the direction of George C. Frison. Diagnostic projectile points found at the site strongly resembled the Plainview type on the southern Plains and the Goshen type that was found in 1966 at the Hell Gap site in southeast Wyoming. Excavations in 1984, 1985, and 1986 produced several more projectile points and fragments, one of which refit to a point base found earlier on the surface. AMS (accelerator mass spectrometry) radiocarbon dates on charcoal fall into two groups, one ca. 9250 B.C. (11,200 years B.P.) and the other just under 9050 B.C. (11,000 years B.P.).

A nearby bison bonebed was discovered in 1987 and excavated in 1988. It contained the remains of more than 30 bison killed during the winter. The projectile points in the bonebed are of the same type as the ones found earlier. The bonebed is not believed to be the actual kill site, but one was probably nearby. Radiocarbon dates from the bonebed fall into the same two groups as the dates from the earlier excavations, which are now believed to have been in a butchering-processing area associated with the bonebed.

The Mill Iron site appears to be a component of the poorly understood Goshen complex, which was recognized in the 1960s at the Hell Gap site. The projectile points from Mill Iron are very similar to those from the Plainview type site in Texas. However, Plainview on the southern Plains is believed to be post-Folsom in age while Goshen is pre-Folsom, as indicated by radiocarbon dates from the Mill Iron and Hell Gap sites and stratigraphic evidence from the Hell Gap and Carter/Kerr-McGee sites in Wyoming. At this time, the author proposes the term "Goshen-Plainview" for the northern Plains manifestation to avoid confusing it with Plainview on the southern Plains.

George C. Frison

Further Readings

Frison, G.C. 1991. The Goshen Paleoindian Complex: New Data for Paleoindian Research. In *Clovis: Origins and Adaptations,* edited by R. Bonnichsen and K.L. Turnmire, pp. 131–151. Center for the Study of the First Americans, Oregon State University, Corvallis.

———. 1992. The Goshen Cultural Complex—Where Does It Fit in the Paleoindian Cultural Sequence? *National Geographic, Research and Exploration* 8(4):494–496.

———. (editor). 1996. *The Mill Iron Site.* University of New Mexico Press, Albuquerque.

See also GOSHEN COMPLEX; PLAINVIEW COMPLEX

Miller Complex

The Miller complex is one of the oldest archaeological manifestations in North America. Named for Albert Miller, who brought Meadowcroft Rockshelter (the type locality for this complex) to the attention of the author in 1973, the Miller complex appears to represent the pioneer population in the Upper Ohio Valley and perhaps the Northeast. Initially recognized and defined in lower and middle Stratum IIa, the basal culture-bearing lithostratigraphic unit at Meadowcroft, the Miller complex is also known from several other sites in the Cross Creek drainage of Washington County in southwestern Pennsylvania, including a series of overlapping bivouacs or short-term camps on the Mungai farm at the headwaters of Cross Creek and a quarry and lithic-reduction locus called the Krajacic site.

The dating of the Miller complex is problematic. A series of 13 stratigraphically consistent radiocarbon dates is available from the Stratum I/II interface through middle Stratum IIa at Meadowcroft. Of these, only six have clear, undeniable, and extensive artifact associations. Applying a conservative interpretation of the chronometric data, the minimum age for the Miller complex is 10,050–8050 B.C. (12,000–10,000 years B.P.). If the six deepest dates unequivocally associated with cultural materials are averaged, then the Miller complex is present at this site and in the contiguous Cross Creek drainage between ca. 12,605 and 12,005 B.C. (14,555–13,955 years B.P.). While virtually all authorities concede an age of at least 10,850 B.C. (12,800 years B.P.) for Miller, some have suggested the earlier dates may be contaminated and anomalously old. Repeated laboratory examinations, including AMS (accelerator mass spectrometry) determination, however, have consistently failed to detect any particulate or nonparticulate contaminants.

The environment of Pennsylvania at the time of the initial Miller-complex occupation is not known with any certainty. It appears that a mosaic of different periglacial habitats coexisted in Pennsylvania, with genuine tundra or steppe-tundra conditions generally occurring at the higher elevations and occasionally rather different conditions at other localities, particularly those at lower elevations. These latter settings apparently included both boreal and even limited deciduous floral elements in short-lived combinations that Stephen C. Porter (1988:19), an authority on North American late Pleistocene climates, has called "ecologically anomalous" by Holocene standards. Indeed, at the time of the first human colonization, Pennsylvania, like other parts of the Northeast, was characterized in some areas by vegetational communities with no modern analogues at all.

The same situation is apparently mirrored by compositionally heterogeneous, late Pleistocene faunal groupings. These often included now-extinct species juxtaposed with still-extant boreal and even Carolinian elements in bizarre conditions that do not exist today and, more important, have not existed for many millennia. In short, while the "fine strokes" remain to be added, the developing picture of late Pleistocene environments in Pennsylvania is more diverse and complex than previously suspected, not nearly so biotically monotonous, static, or ecologically forbidding as earlier readings would have it. Whatever its exact character, the areas of Pennsylvania and perhaps portions of Ohio that were available to their first inhabitants appear to have been amply stocked with a variety of resources susceptible to highly specialized as well as more generalized subsistence strategies.

From a technological perspective, the Miller-complex lithic-debitage sample reflects secondary and tertiary core reduction and biface thinning from late-stage manufacture and the refurbishing of finished implements. The specimens create a clear impression that an essentially curated lithic toolkit was brought to Meadowcroft by its earliest inhabitants. Curated, in this context, refers to artifacts that are "products of technologically sophisticated manufacture" that were produced from "superior quality and/or extralocal raw materials; . . . carefully . . . transported from site to site in anticipation of future use; . . . carefully maintained until discard was necessary; and . . . deposited far from the locus of primary manufacture" (Boldurian 1991:291). The site's initial populations seem to have exploited, or at least utilized through exchange, raw materials from a fairly far-flung series of quarries. These include Flint Ridge in Ohio, several Kanawha chert sources in West Virginia, the Pennsylvania jasper quarries located well to the east of the site, and the local Monongahela chert outcrops in the Cross Creek drainage. This wide-ranging procurement pattern suggests, in turn, that Custer's (1984) "serial quarry scenario"—in which quarries are proposed to have served as focal points or anchors in the seasonal rounds of mobile Paleoindian groups—may exhibit a truly venerable pedigree in eastern North America.

The inventory of flaked-stone artifacts from lower and middle Stratum IIa at Meadowcroft contains small prismatic blades that were detached from small prepared cores. Although cores themselves were not recovered at Meadowcroft, the artifact assemblage from the nearby and apparently contemporaneous Krajacic site contains a variety of the distinctive Meadowcroft-style blade implements and several small, cylindrical polyhedral cores. Recovered after the initial study of the Meadowcroft lithic assemblage had been undertaken in 1975, the Krajacic cores precisely parallel the core-reduction strategy previously posited for the Meadowcroft blades.

In 1976, a small, lanceolate biface, subsequently called the Miller Lanceolate projectile point, was found in situ on the uppermost living floor of lower Stratum IIa at Meadowcroft Rockshelter. This floor is bracketed above and below by radiocarbon assays run on charcoal from fire pits of 9350 B.C. ± 700 (11,300 years B.P.) and 10,850 B.C. ± 870 (12,800 years B.P.), respectively. This unfluted biface is the only Miller Lanceolate point thus far (1996) recovered from a directly dated stratigraphic context (though others have been recovered elsewhere in the Cross Creek drainage), and particular care must be exercised in formulating even a provisional typological definition.

Many potentially diagnostic features of the Miller biface are difficult to identify because the type specimen had been resharpened in antiquity. It therefore has undergone a considerable amount of change from its original or prototypic morphology. The prototype Miller Lanceolate almost certainly was longer. The angles of articulation between its lateral margins and base suggest that the maximum width may have been achieved toward the distal end of the biface. One fragmentary artifact from the Krajacic-site collection conforms exactly in most of its diagnostic characteristics to the Miller Lanceolate prototype. Together with the prismatic blades, the Miller type specimen is of special interest because of its great age and because it reflects its maker's sophisticated knowledge of flaked-stone-tool manufacture.

Collectively, these data suggest that the first inhabitants of eastern North America employed a technologically standardized and sophisticated, small, polyhedral core-and-blade-based industry of decidedly Eurasiatic, Upper Paleolithic "flavor." Not surprisingly, though this assemblage is presently unique in eastern North America, it reflects precisely the sort of lithic-reduction strategy that *should* be evidenced at this time. Moreover, it is not at variance technologically or chronologically with its possible Siberian prototypes.

Despite unfounded observations to the contrary, nothing in the Miller-complex lithic suite occurs in, or is apparently related to, any later cultural manifestations. Its unique blade-making technology, in particular, is unknown in later contexts. Additionally, though partially coeval at least in its later stages with Clovis, few connections between these two early cultures have been documented.

Whatever the relative clarity or opacity of our picture of Miller lithic technology, our view of the subsistence strategies of these earliest inhabitants of the eastern United States is a much darker shade of pale. Although 115,166 identifiable bones and bone fragments have been recovered from Meadowcroft Rockshelter, only 11 identifiable bone fragments and less than 11.9 g (0.42 ounces) of plant remains derive from middle and lower Stratum IIa. If all the identified faunal items from these levels represent food remains, which is highly unlikely, then these human populations exploited white-tailed deer (*Odocoileus virginianus*) and perhaps much smaller game, at least while living at the rock shelter. The meager floral remains suggest possible utilization of hickory (*Carya* spp.), walnut (*Juglans* spp.), and hackberry (*Celtis* spp.)—again, at the site itself. It is conceivable and likely that these populations may have exploited large and now-extinct Pleistocene big-game animals, notably mastodon, but there is no evidence of such predation.

In the long view, it appears that the Miller-complex populations can be tentatively characterized as generalized hunter-foragers rather than specialized hunters and, further, that despite their geographically circumscribed distribution, they represent the baseline (as of 1996) for all subsequent cultural development in both the Upper Ohio Valley and eastern North America.

J.M. Adovasio

Further Readings

Adovasio, J.M., A.T. Boldurian, and R.C. Carlisle. 1988. Who Are Those Guys? Some Biased Thoughts on the Initial Peopling of the New World. In *Americans Before Columbus: Ice Age Origins,* compiled and edited by R.C. Carlisle, pp. 45–61. Ethnology Monographs no. 12. Department of Anthropology, University of Pittsburgh, Pittsburgh.

Adovasio, J.M., J. Donahue, and R. Stuckenrath. 1990. The Meadowcroft Rockshelter Radiocarbon Chronology 1975–1990. *American Antiquity* 55:348–354.

———. 1992. Never Say Never Again: Some Thoughts on Could Haves and Might Have Beens. *American Antiquity* 57:327–331.

Adovasio, J.M., J. Donahue, R.C. Carlisle, K. Cushman, R. Stuckenrath, and P. Wiegman. 1984. Meadowcroft Rockshelter and the Pleistocene/Holocene Transition in Southwestern Pennsylvania. In *Contributions in Quaternary Vertebrate Paleontology: A Volume in Memorial to John E. Guilday,* edited by H.H. Genoways and M.R. Dawson, pp. 347–369. Special Publication no. 8. Carnegie Museum of Natural History, Pittsburgh.

Adovasio, J.M., R.C. Carlisle, K. Cushman, J. Donahue, J.E. Guilday, W.C. Johnson, K. Lord, P.W. Parmalee, R. Stuckenrath, and P. Wiegman. 1985. Paleoenvironmental Reconstruction at Meadowcroft Rockshelter, Washington County, Pennsylvania. In *Environments and Extinctions: Man in Glacial North America,* edited by J.I. Mead and D.J. Meltzer, pp. 73–110. Center for the Study of Early Man, University of Maine, Orono.

Boldurian, A.T. 1991. Folsom Technology and Organization of Lithic Technology: A View From Blackwater Draw, New Mexico. *Plains Anthropologist* 36(137):281–295.

Custer, J. 1984. *Delaware Prehistoric Archaeology: An Ecological Approach.* University of Delaware Press, Dover.

Meltzer, D.J. 1988. Late Pleistocene Human Adaptations in Eastern North America. *Journal of World Prehistory* 2(1):1–52.

Porter, S.C. 1988. Landscapes of the Last Ice Age in North America. In *Americans Before Columbus: Ice Age Origins,* compiled and edited by R.C. Carlisle, pp. 1–24. Ethnology Monographs no. 12. Department of Anthropology, University of Pittsburgh, Pittsburgh.

See also CLOVIS CULTURAL COMPLEX

Miller Culture

The Miller culture (or variant) encompasses the Middle Woodland occupations of the Tombigbee River drainage between northeastern Mississippi and eastern Alabama. Considering the broad area involved, it is unlikely that the Miller culture represents a single ethnic or cultural group. In fact, the unifying theme of the Miller culture is the occurrence and persistence of particular ceramic types (Saltillo Fabric Impressed, Baldwin Plain, and Furrs Cordmarked) throughout the Tombigbee drainage ca. 200 B.C.–A.D. 500 (2150–1450 years B.P.). The Middle Woodland mortuary ceremonialism of the Miller culture has received the greatest attention from researchers, with most of the available data derived from burial mounds at three sites in northeastern Mississippi: Bynum, Pharr, and Miller (Walling et al. 1991). Large, contemporary mound groups were evidently present as well along the southern Tombigbee.

The Bynum site is located ca. 35 km (22 miles) south of Tupelo, Mississippi. Included within an area of ca. 8 ha (20 acres) were six conical burial mounds and an early Middle Woodland (Miller I period, ca. 200 B.C.–A.D. 100, or 2150–1850 years B.P.) habitation area. Excavations in the habitation area revealed the remains of several ovoid bent-pole houses and numerous scattered postmolds and pits. A partial Marksville Incised ceramic vessel exhibiting a raptorial bird motif in the Hopewellian style was found in one pit. The excavations also produced a large ceramic sample dominated by the sand-tempered types Baldwin Plain and Saltillo Fabric Impressed. Vessels of the latter type are essentially conical in shape. The appearance of this vessel form is thought by some researchers to indicate the arrival of new populations in the region.

Excavations at the Bynum Mounds produced evidence of several types of mortuary facilities. Mound A was constructed over a low earthen platform that covered a mortuary-processing feature consisting of two pairs of parallel oak logs. The remains of an adult female, with a bicymbal copper earspool at each wrist, were located between the logs. Bynum Mound D was constructed over a small mortuary structure consisting of a rectangular canopy covering a rectangular sunken floor with a fired, circular pit near the center.

Bynum Mound B measured 4.2 m (14 feet) in height and 20 m (65.5 feet) in diameter. At the base of the mound were the remains of a large charnel house with a sunken floor; a shallow pit near the center may have served as a crematory facility. The remains of only four individuals were found within the structure, all of whom had evidently been placed within the remains of the building after it burned. Associated artifacts include 29 greenstone celts, 19 Gibson or Norton projectile points, several copper earspools, and a piece of galena. Three radiocarbon determinations suggest that Bynum Mounds A and B were essentially contemporaneous and constructed during the second century B.C.

The Pharr mound group is located ca. 90 km (56 miles) northeast of Bynum in the headwaters of the Tombigbee River. One of the largest early Middle Woodland (Miller I) sites in the Mid-South, the site includes eight conical mounds within an area of ca. 30 ha (74 acres). In contrast to Bynum, there is little evidence of an associated habitation area. The ceramic assemblage from Pharr, which consists primarily of Saltillo Fabric Impressed and Baldwin Plain, is virtually identical to that from Bynum.

Excavation of four mounds revealed similarities and important differences with Bynum. Three of the Pharr mounds were constructed over low earthen platforms that evidently functioned as mortuary-processing or ritual-display facilities. Mound E, a large earthwork with a mean diameter of more than 52 m (171 feet), had a number of associated pits, as well as a characteristic platform. In contrast to any of the Bynum earthworks, a number of ceramic vessels, both local and nonlocal, were associated with Mound E. Moreover, several distinct stages of construction and use are apparent. Among the Hopewellian artifacts found at Pharr were bicymbal copper earspools, galena, and a mica sheet. The three reliable radiocarbon determinations for Pharr all pertain to Mound E contexts and imply that construction took place in a period from the mid-first to the mid-second century A.D.

The type site of the Miller culture, the Miller site, is located ca. 55 km (180 feet) north of Bynum. Covering an area of ca. 3.5 ha (8.5 acres), it is a much smaller site than Bynum or Pharr. A pair of conical burial mounds were the most prominent features, but a habitation area with substantial midden was also present. In contrast to Bynum and Pharr, cord marking (Furrs Cordmarked) is the principal surface treatment on the sand-tempered ceramics from the site, which indicates a Miller II (ca. A.D. 100–400, or 1850–1550 years B.P.) affiliation for the earthworks. Importantly, a large collection of mixed sand- and clay-tempered ceramics, representing a later Miller III (ca. A.D. 400–1000, or 1550–950 years B.P.) occupation, was recovered from the surface of the site.

Miller Mound A was an accretional earthwork standing ca. 4.5 m (15 feet) high. Two adult primary burials were interred between two layers of clay at the base of the mound near the center. Ca. 30 individuals, all adults, were recovered from pits scattered throughout the general mound fill. At the base of Miller Mound B were a minimum of three rectangular pits extending into subsoil; a human skull and a Furrs Cordmarked jar were located in one of these. A charnel house, represented by the burned remains of a circular, bent-pole structure, was also located at the base of the mound. Other than some scraps of copper recovered from a relic hunter's pit, no characteristic Hopewellian artifacts were found in either mound. Radiocarbon evidence (four dates, all from the base of Mound B) suggests that Miller Mound B was constructed between the mid-third and the mid-fourth century A.D.

Unfortunately, very little subsistence and settlement data are available for the Miller culture. The extensive habitation remains at Bynum probably represent occupation during ritual occasions, rather than a village. The scant evidence suggests a seasonal round with semisedentary base camps and smaller hunting camps. Deer, nuts, and possibly shellfish were of particular importance to subsistence. Starchy annual seeds (e.g., *Chenopodium*) have been recovered during excavation, but their relative importance remains unclear.

Robert C. Mainfort, Jr.

Further Readings

Jenkins, N.J., and R.A. Krause. 1986. *The Tombigbee Watershed in Southeastern Prehistory*. University of Alabama Press, Tuscaloosa.

Walling, R., R.C. Mainfort, Jr., and J.R. Atkinson. 1991. Radiocarbon Dates From the Bynum, Pharr, and Miller Sites, Northeast Mississippi. *Southeastern Archaeology* 10(1):54–62.

Millingstone Horizon

The concept of a Millingstone horizon developed through the work of Robert F. Heizer, Adán E. Treganza, and, especially, William J. Wallace, from their excavations along the Los Angeles and Ventura County coastline in the 1940s and 1950s. They recognized sets of assemblages at sites along coastal terraces and up nearby canyons that contained millingstones and manos but few other kinds of artifacts. Millingstone-horizon sites typically were located in habitats where hard-seed-producing grasses and brush were locally abundant. Sites frequently included some burials, often interred beneath cairns of millingstones. Dozens of millingstones, some deliberately broken, or "killed," might overlay a single burial. Found at localities such as Malaga Cove, Arroyo

Sequit, Little Sycamore Canyon, and Topanga Canyon, Millingstone-horizon sites were thought to represent a kind of lifeway distinctive of an era dating roughly to 4050–50 B.C. (6000–2000 years B.P.), after which a different and more maritime-oriented tradition succeeded it. The millingstone-dominated assemblage was thus seen as reflecting a cultural tradition bounded in time and space, or horizon, as opposed to a specialized site type found during that era—hence, the Millingstone horizon.

More recent studies, as by Makoto Kowta (1969) at Cajon Pass, have shown that millingstone-dominated assemblages have occurred at other time periods and in other parts of the state (Haney and Whatford 1994) and as contemporaries of other types of sites in the area at the same time. The millingstone-dominated assemblage can no longer be regarded as a distinct cultural unit in one region, for, while it remains a valid analytical unit, it was developed by a number of different cultures. It also is understood to represent in some cases a special-activity site type made by cultures that created other kinds of sites from different activities. Whether any of the millingstone-dominated assemblages represent a distinctive culture type is unclear.

Joseph L. Chartkoff

Further Readings

Haney, J., and J.C. Whatford. 1994. A Preliminary Report on Milling Tool Assemblages From the Anderson Flat Archaeological Project, Lake County, California. *Proceedings of the Society for California Archaeology* 7:169–182.

Kowta, M. 1969. *The Sayles Complex: A Late Milling Stone Assemblage From Cajon Pass and the Ecological Implications of Its Scraper Planes.* Publications in Anthropology no. 6. University of California Press, Berkeley.

Warren, C.N. 1967. The Southern California Milling Stone Horizon: Some Comments. *American Antiquity* 32:233–236.

Milling Tools (California)

Milling-tool industries are distinctive features of many California prehistoric sites and are associated with the intensive processing of plant-food resources by the area's hunter-gatherer cultures. Milling tools are found in two basic sets, each with variations. The first includes millingstones (grinding slabs) and the hand stones (manos) used for grinding against the millingstone surface. In some publications, millingstones are called metates, but most writers reserve the term "metate" for the three-legged grinding slabs used in ancient Mexico. California millingstones typically are oval-shaped slabs of coarse rock measuring 60 x 30 x 10 cm (24.4 x 11.7 x 3.9 inches) and weighing 20 kg (44 lbs) or more. Manos average 15 x 10 x 5 cm (5.8 x 3.9 x 2 inches) and weigh 1–2 kg (2.2–4.4 lbs). Either type might be worn from grinding on one or both sides. Studies of wear patterns suggest that California millingstones were used with a rotary motion of the mano. In some areas of the state, bedrock exposures with milling surfaces upon them, called grinding slicks, can be found.

Mortars and pestles, the second basic set, first appeared in different parts of the state 6050–4050 B.C. (8000–6000 years B.P.), ca. 1,000–2,000 years later than millingstones, and continue to be found to some extent throughout the rest of the prehistoric period. A mortar is a stone block in which a cup-shaped depression, or mortar hole, has been worn. A well-developed mortar hole might be 20 cm (8 inches) in diameter and 15–20 cm (6–8 inches) deep, though depth can vary greatly. Some mortars are made on rough stone blocks, while others have smooth exteriors, which defines the difference between block mortars and bowl mortars. Hopper mortars are created when a basket without a bottom is placed on a stone slab. While millingstones are ground and abraded, hopper mortars show evidence of having been battered by blows from a pestle. Starting 1,500–2,000 years ago, communities in many foothill areas began to develop mortars on the horizontal surfaces of bedrock outcrops alongside permanent water sources. Typically, several mortar holes appear on the same bedrock outcrop, sometimes accompanied by grinding slicks. An outcrop at Grinding Stone State Park near Jackson in the Sierra Nevada foothills has more than 1,100 mortar holes in a single surface. The pestle is the companion of the mortar, and years ago it was not uncommon for surveyors to find pestles still sitting in bedrock mortar holes. Pestles are cylinders of basalt and similar stones and typically are 20–25 cm (8–10 inches) long and 6–8 cm (2.4–3.1 inches) in diameter. Pestles may be battered on one or both ends, while their bodies may be naturally fairly cylindrical or ground to smooth uniformity.

M

Manos and millingstones are typically associated with the processing of hard seeds, while mortars and pestles are associated with the mashing of pulpier foodstuffs such as nut, roots, and bulbs. Ethnographically, both types of tools are known to be especially associated with women's activities and have often been found as grave goods accompanying the burials of women.

Joseph L. Chartkoff

Mimbres Branch

Ranking among the greatest artistic achievements of the prehistoric Americas, Classic Mimbres pottery was used ca. A.D. 1000–1150 (950–800 years B.P.) in southwestern New Mexico, southeastern Arizona, far western Texas, and northwestern Chihuahua, Mexico. In modern times, thousands of the exquisitely decorated vessels have been plundered and dispersed unrecorded into the private art market. In the process, the original context of the pots has been largely destroyed. Despite the damage, archaeologists have been able to piece together evidence regarding several important economic and social processes within the Mimbres branch of the Mogollon culture area, including population growth, changing subsistence and mobility strategies, aggregation, abandonment, collapse, and reorganization.

This discussion is limited to the Mimbres Valley, although it was not the only area occupied by people making Mimbres pottery. The valley descends southward from an elevation of ca. 2,500 m (2,734 yards), passing through ponderosa forests, piñon-juniper-oak woodlands, and open grasslands before draining into the desert floor near Deming, New Mexico, at an elevation of ca. 1,500 m (1,640 yards). Throughout much of its 110-km (68-mile) course, the river remains a perennial source of water for drinking and irrigation. Settlement patterns in the valley changed markedly through time. The earliest recorded occupations are Late Archaic (1000 B.C.–A.D. 200, or 2950–1750 years B.P.) sites in the desert and consist of chipped-stone artifacts and occasional one-hand, circular grinding stones. Projectile points tend to be large, and bifacial tools are more common than in later periods. These sites were the base camps of highly mobile people who lived in small groups and who ate mainly wild foods. They only occasionally visited the upper portions of the valley.

The first pottery, a brown ware that was

Mimbres classic black-on-white bowl from the Galaz site. (Courtesy of the Wilford Archaeology Laboratory, University of Minnesota)

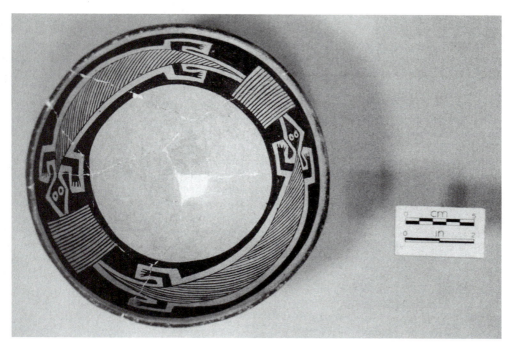

M

Mimbres classic black-on-white bowl with a highly stylized animal around the rim, from the Galaz site. (Courtesy of the Wilford Archaeology Laboratory, University of Minnesota)

followed by red-slipped and then red-on-brown types, appeared in the Early Pithouse period (A.D. 200–550, or 1750–1400 years B.P.). The red-on-brown designs are simple and typically made of a few broad lines. The settlements, most of which consist of a handful of semi-subterranean houses (pithouses) located on ridge tops high above the floodplain in the upper and middle valley, are suggestive of sedentism but may have been only winter residences. Larger villages with up to 50 houses are known, but it is unclear whether the houses were contemporary or built and abandoned sequentially. The occupants may have ranged widely, occupying temporary camps during the warm months. The houses were bean-shaped or D-shaped at first but later became circular with long rampway entrances generally facing southeast. Some houses lacked interior features, while others had a simple hearth. Burials and food-storage pits were outside the houses.

By the Late Pithouse period (A.D. 550–1000, or 1400–950 years B.P.), pottery decoration became more refined. A cream slip was added prior to the application of the red designs, and design composition was more complex. Later in the period, the firing atmosphere was converted from oxidizing to reducing, which

resulted in a black-on-white rather than a red-on-cream finish. A pronounced shift in settlement pattern occurred, with the villages moving from the ridge tops to low terraces adjacent to the floodplain of the river. Mobility may have become more restricted at this time. House shape changed from round to square, and formal hearths became common. Burials accompanied by the evolving black-on-white pottery were often placed beneath the dwelling floors.

During the Classic Mimbres period (A.D. 1000–1150, or 950–800 years B.P.), potters perfected their black-on-white technology and aesthetics to achieve the style for which the region is famous. The two variants of the style, figurative and nonfigurative, both emphasized symmetry and the complementarity of positive and negative images in apparent reference to an ideology focused on death. Humans with animal characteristics and vice versa are frequently depicted. The social context of this artistic development is unclear; there is no evidence in mortuary practices or architecture for an elite class. Yet, the quality of some of the work strongly suggests that the artists were specialists whose basic needs were supplied by some system of surplus accumulation. The Classic Mimbres period was one of rapidly increasing and aggregating population, decreasing mobility, deforestation, agricultural intensification, and the introduction of several technological innovations. The phase represents one of the earliest instances of large-scale aggregation in the American Southwest.

The transition from pithouse to pueblo appears to have been relatively abrupt, though some researchers argue otherwise, especially for outside the Mimbres Valley. The largest of the pueblos consisted of 100–250 rooms built over the ruins of pithouses from the Late Pithouse period. Interspersed among the large pueblos were smaller sites, many of which may have been seasonally occupied farmsteads. The larger pueblos had several blocks of above-ground, contiguous rooms built of unshaped masonry that were grouped around informal plazas.

Large subterranean ceremonial rooms were located either between roomblocks or on the edges of the pueblos. Other very large rooms, possibly ceremonial, were built above ground and incorporated into the roomblocks. Occupants constantly renovated and remodeled the rooms, sometimes changing their functions. Habitation rooms had hearths, while storage rooms were smaller and usually featureless. Deceased family members were interred in plazas or, more commonly, beneath the floors of habitation rooms, frequently with "killed" painted bowls inverted above the head. The dead were buried in a flexed position in small pits; as many as 50 individuals have been detected in a single room.

Classic Mimbres people may have been more dependent on agriculture than their predecessors. Classic Mimbres ruins are found along both the main river and its tributaries, a pattern different from that of the Pithouse periods when all sites were along the river. Increased settlement along tributaries seems to indicate more intensive cultivation practices, an impression echoed by the appearance of devices such as check dams, canals, and reservoirs. Botanical evidence suggests deforestation along the floodplain, most likely as a result of clearing land for fields. Some faunal analyses seem to document the disappearance of large game, although this finding is questioned by recent unpublished studies. Changes in food-processing and -storage techniques included modification of manos and metates to make grinding more efficient and the replacement of storage pits by storage rooms.

Construction of Classic Mimbres pueblos ceased at A.D. 1130 (820 years B.P.). The impeccable black-on-white pottery style, some 500 years in the making since the appearance of the first red-on-brown vessels, came to an end. The best explanation for this collapse is a generalized food-provisioning failure brought about by overpopulation and worsening climatic conditions. Small groups of people remained, reorganizing themselves to live in a less nucleated and more flexible adaptive pattern. New centers of aggregation and cultural vitality formed elsewhere, particularly 225 km (140 miles) to the south around the great site of Paquime or Casas Grandes in northwestern Chihuahua, Mexico.

During the Black Mountain phase of the Animas period (A.D. 1150–1300, or 800–650 years B.P.), a much reduced occupation continued in the Mimbres area. The small amounts of black-on-white pottery still used were of the Reserve tradition to the west and the Chupadero tradition of the Lower Rio Grande to the east. Other decorated ceramics included El Paso Polychrome of the Rio Grande area, and the Chihuahuan polychromes and textured red wares common at Casas Grandes. New adobe-walled pueblos were founded, one on the ruins of the Galaz site, a large Classic Mimbres settlement, but most sites were concentrated toward the southern end of the Mimbres Valley. Average room size nearly doubled, and storage rooms disappeared, as did obvious ceremonial rooms and farmsteads. The few existing pueblos were laid out more formally than in the past with walled plaza areas.

During the Cliff phase of the Salado period (A.D. 1300–1450, or 650–500 years B.P.), the same basic architectural and ceramic patterns persisted. Gila Polychrome ceramics were added, marking participation in the widespread Salado tradition that also affected such far-flung locations as Casas Grandes, the Gila-Salt Basin, the Tonto Basin, and the Upper Rio Grande. The Lower Rio Grande and Chihuahuan types continued with some evolution in form and design. People of this period were sedentary but did not occupy their pueblos long; whole communities appear to have moved every 25 years or less. Many previously occupied areas were left uninhabited, and occupations seem to have shifted frequently from one hydrologically favorable area to another. The option of whole-community mobility, largely foreclosed by the high levels of population in the Classic Mimbres period, had been reopened. The final prehistoric occupation of the Mimbres area was by nomadic groups, probably Apaches, who left only light artifact scatters and stone circles known as "tipi rings." In a sense, this final occupation brought the cycle of land use full circle to the ancient pattern in which Archaic hunters used the Mimbres area only occasionally.

Ben A. Nelson

Further Readings

Anyon, R., and S.A. LeBlanc. 1984. *The Galaz Ruin: A Mimbres Village in Southwestern New Mexico.* University of New Mexico Press, Albuquerque.

Blake, M., S.A. LeBlanc, and P.E. Minnis. 1986. Changing Settlement and Population in the Mimbres Valley. *Journal of Field Archaeology* 13:439–464.

Brody, J.J. 1977. *Mimbres Painted Pottery.* University of New Mexico Press, Albuquerque.

Gilman, P.A. 1987. Architecture As Artifact: Pit Structures and Pueblos in the American Southwest. *American Antiquity* 52:538–564.

Hard, R.J. 1990. Agricultural Dependence in the Mountain Mogollon. In *Perspectives on Southwestern Prehistory,* edited by P.E. Minnis and C.L. Redman, pp. 135–149. Westview Press, Boulder.

LeBlanc, S.A. 1983. *The Mimbres People: Ancient Painters of the American Southwest.* Thames and Hudson, New York.

Lekson, S.H. 1990. *Mimbres Archaeology of the Upper Gila, New Mexico.* Anthropological Papers no. 53. University of Arizona Press, Tucson.

Minnis, P.E. 1985. *Social Adaptation to Food Stress: A Prehistoric Southwestern Example.* University of Chicago Press, Chicago.

Nelson, B.A., and S.A. LeBlanc. 1986. *Short-Term Sedentism in the American Southwest: The Mimbres Valley Salado.* University of New Mexico Press, Albuquerque.

Shafer, H. 1982. Classic Mimbres Phase Household and Room Use Patterns. *Kiva* 48:17–37.

Mississippian Culture

"Mississippian" is the name given to a major cultural pattern that was established in the southern and border states of the Eastern Woodlands at A.D. 1000 (950 years B.P.) and lasted into the times of Spanish and French co-lonial contact. It is most easily identified with a particular period of time during which a critical density of maize-using economies existed in the southern portion of the Eastern Woodlands. A specific economy was not the basis for Mississippian culture, nor can this cultural pattern be attributed to a single type of political system or technology or a specific tribal culture. The pattern seems to have arisen out of the close spatial relationship of a sizable number of complex political systems that entered into economic and political interaction. Although no single material or conceptual trait has proven to be a reliable index of Mississippian culture, many of the artifacts and institutions that archaeologists have connected with this cultural pattern were a direct consequence of the population growth and economic stability brought about through the establishment of maize production. Traits such as shell-tempered pottery, platform-mound architecture, chiefdom levels of political complexity, and dependence upon maize agriculture are frequently found in this period, but by no means universally. Additionally, certain diagnostic traits, such as the use of crushed mussel shells to provide a carbonate tempering for pottery production, have a pre-Mississippian-period history extending many centuries earlier in the Ozark highlands. The extent of this cultural pattern is indicted by its attentuation into progressively less recognizable form.

James A. Brown

Further Readings

Anderson, D.G. 1994. *The Savannah River Chiefdoms: Political Change in the Late Prehistoric Southeast.* University of Alabama Press, Tuscaloosa.

Blitz, J.H. 1993. *Ancient Chiefdoms of the Tombigbee.* University of Alabama Press, Tuscaloosa.

Dye, D.H., and C.A. Cox. 1990. *Towns and Temples Along the Mississippi.* University of Alabama Press, Tuscaloosa.

Griffin, J.B. 1967. Eastern North American Archaeology: A Summary. *Science* 156:175–191.

———. 1984. Changing Concepts of the Prehistoric Mississippian Cultures of the Eastern United States. In *Alabama and the Borderlands: From Prehistory to Statehood,* edited by R.R. Badger and L.A. Clayton, pp. 40–63. University of Alabama Press, Tuscaloosa.

M

———. 1991. Comments on the Late Prehistoric Societies in the Southeast. In *Stability, Transformation, and Variation: The Late Woodland Southeast*, edited by M.S. Nassaney and C.R. Cobb, pp. 5–15. Plenum Press, New York.

Milner, G.R. 1990. The Late Prehistoric Cahokia Cultural System of the Mississippi River Valley: Foundations, Florescence, and Fragmentation. *Journal of World Prehistory* 4(1):1–44.

Morse, D.F., and P.A. Morse. 1983. *Archaeology of the Central Mississippi Valley*. Academic Press, New York.

Pauketat, T.R. 1994. *The Ascent of Chiefs: Cahokia and Mississippian Politics in Native North America*. University of Alabama Press, Tuscaloosa.

Peregrine, P.N. 1992. *Mississippi Evolution: A World-System Perspective*. Prehistory Press, Madison.

Schnell, F., V.J. Knight, Jr., and G.S. Schnell. 1981. *Cemochechobee: Archaeology of a Mississippian Ceremonial Center on the Chattahoochee River*. University Presses of Florida, Gainesville.

Smith, B.D. (editor). 1978. *Mississippian Settlement Patterns*. Academic Press, New York.

———. (editor). 1990. *Mississippian Emergence: The Evolution of Ranked Agricultural Societies in the Eastern United States*. Smithsonian Institution Press, Washington, D.C.

Steponaitis, V.P. 1983. *Ceramics, Chronology, and Community Patterns: An Archaeological Study at Moundville*. Academic Press, New York.

Williams, M., and G. Shapiro (editors). 1990. *Lamar Archaeology: Mississippian Chiefdoms in the Deep South*. University of Alabama Press, Tuscaloosa.

See also EMERGENT MISSISSIPPIAN

Modoc Rock Shelter

Modoc Rock Shelter (11R5) is a deeply stratified site located at the base of the eastern Mississippi River Valley bluffs in Randolph County, southwestern Illinois. Excavations conducted at the site between 1952 and 1956 and between 1980 and 1987 revealed ca. 9 m (30 feet) of stratified cultural deposits. Woodland- and historic-period remains appear occasionally in the upper 1 m (3.3 feet) of deposits; the lower 8 m (26 feet) of deposits represent sequential Early, Middle, and Late Archaic occupations. Based on density and diversity of artifacts and features, the period of most intensive site use occurred during the Middle and Late Archaic periods between ca. 6050 and 2550 b.c. (8000–4500 years B.P.). The sediments in the shelter consist entirely of redeposited loess in colluvial and alluvial matrices. The high calcium content of the loess ensured excellent preservation conditions for bone and shell. Lithic artifacts are also abundant. Botanical remains are limited to carbonized specimens, for the shelter environment is not sufficiently dry to promote preservation of uncarbonized plant remains and pollen.

Excavations conducted by Melvin L. Fowler of the Illinois State Museum, Springfield, in the 1950s provided a large sample of artifacts from the site (Fowler 1959). Excavation was in 0.1-, 0.15-, and 0.3-m (0.3-, 0.5-, and 1-foot) arbitrary levels. Four broad stratigraphic zones were recognized in the field and employed in subsequent analyses. The 1950s excavations and analyses were considered state-of-the-art archaeology at the time. Among the field techniques employed were the systematic recovery of artifacts through the screening of all sediments through 0.6-cm (0.25-inch) mesh and the collection of charcoal samples for radiocarbon assay. Significant results of the 1950s investigations include documentation of the antiquity of the Archaic period, with accepted radiocarbon dates indicating occupation as early as 8050 B.C. (10,000 years B.P.). The well-segregated, stratified deposits also produced a seriated sample of projectile-point types that contributed greatly to the development of regional chronological sequences through cross-typing of the point styles. The most important contribution of the 1950s excavations was the use of regional intersite comparisons and interdisciplinary analyses of lithic, faunal, and botanical remains to create an explicitly ecological interpretation of broad-scale changes in Archaic-period adaptations. The Archaic occupations at Modoc were interpreted as representing three broad adaptive strategies that were also represented in the mid-continent as a whole. An Initial period (Early Archaic, 8050–6050 B.C., or 10,000–8000 years B.P.) was characterized by generalized adaptations and nonintensive resource-exploitation strategies. This was followed by a Generalized period (Middle Archaic, 6050–3550 B.C., or 8000–

5500 years B.P.) during which populations settled into the region and adaptive strategies became more intensive but still broadly based. The Specialization period (Late Archaic, 3550–1050 B.C., or 5500–3000 years B.P.) was characterized by the specialized and intensive targeting of local environments and resources for exploitation.

Controversies developed around the interpretation of the stratigraphy and chronology of the site, as well as the use of sitewide 0.3-m (1-foot) arbitrary levels as analytical units. However, the projectile-point sequences from the site continued to be used in local and regional comparisons, and the broader ecological interpretations of the site and region were not seriously questioned. Nonetheless, some researchers took issue with specific aspects of the projectile-point sequence and claimed that the stratigraphy was either mixed or inverted. These questions remained largely unaddressed until the 1980s.

In 1980, 1984, and 1987, the Illinois State Museum and the University of Wisconsin–Milwaukee conducted additional stratigraphic excavations and analyses at Modoc with the goals of (1) documenting and sampling all natural and cultural stratigraphic units; (2) assessing the stratigraphic integrity of the site to address questions of potential stratigraphic mixing; (3) processing excavated samples through fine-scale (flotation and 0.2-cm, or 0.06-inch, water-screening) recovery techniques; (4) refining the radiocarbon chronology from the site using natural and cultural strata; (5) investigating changes in site function and use in relation to changes in local environmental conditions during the Holocene; and (6) reanalyzing a portion of the 1950s artifacts using the refined stratigraphic and chronological sequences. All goals have been met. The results, for the most part, provide refinements, rather than contradictions, of Fowler's initial site interpretations.

One of the most basic refinements is the recognition that the site is composed of two physically and stratigraphically separate rock shelters. Both contain well-defined and easily segregated cultural and natural strata (the basic "layer cake"), but local differences in deposition rates, sediment sources, and occupational histories have produced distinct chronological and stratigraphic sequences in the two shelters.

The West Shelter, excavated in 1956 and 1980, has a series of alluvial-fan sediments containing Early Archaic cultural material overlain by colluvial strata containing Middle and Late Archaic occupations. Radiocarbon assays available for the alluvial fan and the lower portions of the colluvial sediments are in the 6970–5050 B.C. (8920–7000 years B.P.) age range. Analyses of lithic and faunal density and diversity indicate that the site functioned as a short-term general habitation site ca. 6550 B.C. (8500 years B.P.). The transition from alluvial to colluvial deposition occurred at ca. 6550 B.C. (8500 years B.P.), which is near the beginning of the mid-Holocene warming and drying episode known as the Hypsithermal. This period is marked by increased deposition rates and probable use of the site as a short-term resource-extraction camp. Beginning ca. 5550 B.C. (7500 years B.P.) and continuing through the Middle Archaic period (to ca. 3050 B.C., or 5000 years B.P.), there is evidence for slower sedimentation rates and increased human occupation in the West Shelter. This part of the site probably functioned as a long-term habitation site in the local settlement system. The Late Archaic strata in the West Shelter show evidence of continued use, but activities were apparently more specialized during this period.

The Main Shelter, excavated in 1952, 1953, 1955, 1984, and 1987, has a sedimentary and occupational history similar to the West Shelter, but there are minor differences in site function through time. The Main Shelter contains no alluvial-fan sediments; the 34 major strata all consist of redeposited colluvial loess. The acceptable radiocarbon assays from this shelter establish dates for the lower two-thirds of the strata in the ca. 6580–2050 B.C. (8530–4000 years B.P.) range. As in the West Shelter, Early Archaic occupation consists of a series of short-term residential or resource-extraction camps, and sedimentation rates are highest in the ca. 6550–6050 B.C. (8500–8000 years B.P.) period. Beginning ca. 6150 B.C. (8100 years B.P.), the site shows evidence for increasingly long-term and intensive use. The Main Shelter appears to have functioned alternately as a long-term base camp and a short-term residential camp in the years 6150–4850 B.C. (8100–6800 years B.P.) (early Middle Archaic period). Between 4850 and 2750 B.C. (6800–4700 years B.P.) (middle Middle Archaic through early Late Archaic periods), the Main Shelter appears to have functioned almost continuously as a long-term habitation site or base camp in the local settlement system. The Late Archaic Titterington-phase strata (2550–1550 B.C., or 4500–3500 years B.P.) show evidence of more specialized activities that may be seasonally restricted. They primarily involve hunting, butchering, and processing of soft materials. Later occupations show evidence of only short-term use of the site.

These trends indicate a shift in overall settlement systems in the area from a residentially mobile system during the Early Archaic to a more logistically organized system during Middle and Late Archaic times. Modoc probably functioned as a base camp during the Hypsithermal climatic interval and is associated with increased floodplain deposition rates, onset of warmer and drier climatic conditions, and initial development of highly complex meandering floodplain belts with associated backwater lakes. The first use of Modoc as a long-term habitation site is directly correlated with greater amounts of aquatic species in the faunal assemblage and with the first recovery of bowfin, a species common to backwater lakes. As fluvial conditions and ground surfaces stabilized near their modern elevations during the Late Archaic period, base-camp location probably shifted west into the Mississippi River floodplain, and Modoc was used more often as a specialized hunting and processing camp. These shifts in settlement patterns and settlement-system organization have been confirmed by broad-area surveys of the Mississippi River floodplain and adjacent uplands.

Steven R. Ahler

Further Readings

Ahler, S.R. 1993. Stratigraphy and Radiocarbon Chronology of Modoc Rock Shelter, Illinois. *American Antiquity* 58:462–488.

Fowler, M.L. 1959. *Summary Report of Modoc Rock Shelter: 1952, 1953, 1955, 1956.* Reports of Investigations no. 8. Illinois State Museum, Springfield.

Styles, B.W., S.R. Ahler, and M.L. Fowler. 1983. Modoc Rock Shelter Revisited. In *Archaic Hunters and Gatherers in the American Midwest,* edited by J.L. Phillips and J.A. Brown, pp. 261–297. Academic Press, New York.

Mogollon Culture Area

Mogollon was one of four major prehistoric cultures of the American Southwest during the period from the end of the Archaic (ca. A.D. 200, or 1750 years B.P.) to the arrival of the Spanish in the summer of A.D. 1540. The Mogollon cul-

ture was defined in 1936 by Emil W. Haury, then with the Gila Pueblo Archaeological Foundation, based on extensive surveys of the mountains of east-central Arizona and west-central New Mexico in 1931 and excavations in 1933 of Mogollon Village along the San Francisco River and in 1934 of Harris Village in the Mimbres Valley. Resistance to the idea of a separate Mogollon culture and its antiquity caused Haury to establish University of Arizona archaeological field schools at Forestdale (1939–1941) and at Point of Pines (1946–1960). In 1939, Paul S. Martin of the Field Museum of Natural History, Chicago, established a field research station (1939–1954) in the Pine Lawn Reserve region of west-central New Mexico. The evidence uncovered by Haury's and Martin's field projects gave rise to Joe Ben Wheat's (1955) synthesis, which ended 20 years of debate over Mogollon legitimacy. A biennial conference, begun in 1980, reaffirms this status.

Definitions of Mogollon. In Haury's original definition Mogollon culture was characterized by true pithouses and coil-and-scraped brown pottery—polished plain (Alma Plain), red-slipped (San Francisco Red), and decorated red-on-brown (Mogollon Red-on-Brown). Haury thought that the Mogollon lost their identity after A.D. 1000 (950 years B.P.) through assimilation with the Anasazi. Erik Reed's (1950) counterinterpretation was that a separate Mogollon identity could be traced after A.D. 1000 (950 years B.P.) and, in some regions, until the abandonment of the mountains by A.D. 1400 (550 years B.P.). Distinctive characteristics of this continuity of Mogollon identity include the layout of puebo villages focusing inward on a plaza; rectangular kivas within roomblocks; primary, extended inhumation of the deceased; vertical-occipital head deformation; the three-quarter groove axe; and brown corrugated pottery often with patterned, incised, or painted designs. Researchers have embraced Reed's idea of Mogollon identity continuing well beyond A.D. 1000 (950 years B.P.). The Mogollon cannot be positively linked to a historical group. Haury suggested that the Tarahumara were an ethnographic analogue and a possible Mogollon remnant. By abandoning the mountains to take up full-time farming, the Mogollon merged archaeologically with the other pueblo farmers of the northern Southwest.

Mogollon in Time. A threefold division of Mogollon culture into Early Pithouse, Late Pithouse, and Mogollon Pueblo periods is a convenient alternative to Wheat's Mogollon 1–5 or to the extrapolation of single regional phase sequences throughout the Mogollon culture area. The Early Pithouse period begins ca. A.D. 200 (1750 years B.P.) with the addition of plain brown pottery to a Late Archaic artifact assemblage and ends in the A.D. 600s (1350–1250 years B.P.) at about the time red-on-brown decorated pottery appears. The Late Pithouse period ends with the construction of masonry pueblos, which occurred ca. A.D. 1000 (950 years B.P.) in the Mimbres Valley of New Mexico and 100–200 years later in the Arizona mountains to the west. The Mogollon Pueblo period ends with the abandonment of the mountains by A.D. 1400 (550 years B.P.). The latest tree-ring dates attributable to the Mogollon fall in the A.D. 1380s (570–560 years B.P.).

Mogollon Landscapes. The Mogollon adapted primarily to the mountain uplands and secondarily to the adjacent desert lowlands within a region bounded by major rivers: the Little Colorado on the north, the Verde on the west, and the Pecos on the east. A southern boundary in present-day Sonora and Chihuahua, Mexico, is undefined. The trait common to sites throughout this region is brown and red-slipped pottery. Subdivisions, or branches, which are less well defined than for the Anasazi, are a result of archaeologists working within the culture-history paradigm to explore isolated areas with long, continuous occupations. These areas, which are also areas of local resource abundance, include the Mimbres Valley (Mimbres branch) and the San Francisco Valley (Pine Lawn, or Cibola, branch) in New Mexico, and Point of Pines (Black River branch), San Simon Valley (San Simon branch), and Forestdale Valley (Forestdale branch) in Arizona. The Jornada branch defined in the El Paso area seems to have been a distant relative of the mountain-adapted Mogollon. Recent research in the Grasshopper area challenges the applicability of the branch construct for a Mogollon people characterized by residential mobility and flexible group membership. Meaningful geographic subdivisions may have been similar to the Western Apache band and not readily detectable in conventional archaeological data.

Early Pithouse (A.D. 200–600, or 1750–1350 yers B.P.). The Mogollon lifeway is little changed from the Late Archaic except for the addition of brown-plain pottery. Small pithouse villages located on hilltops and ridges suggest a concern with defense. Circular pithouses with a side entrance are characteristic. A large pithouse or communal structure at sites such as Bluff Village indicates a focal settlement within a dispersed, mobile community. Residential moves serve as the principal means of adjusting small populations to scattered resources. Products of hunting and gathering dominate the diet with some contribution from gardening. The Mogollon, no longer credited as the conduit for corn agriculture from Mexico, are far less committed to cultivation at this time than their Anasazi and Hohokam neighbors.

Late Pithouse (A.D. 600–1000, or 1350–950 years B.P.). This is a time of population expansion and regional differentiation. The tendency for pithouse villages like Bear Village to be located on the valley floor adjacent to land suited to cultivation suggests the growing significance of cultivation and a relaxation of previous economic and social uncertainties. Pithouses are generally rectangular with a lateral ramp entrance. A formal great kiva is present at large sites. Subsistence needs are still met through hunting, gathering, and gardening, with domesticated plants contributing in proportion to highly localized growing conditions. Residential mobility characterizes the Mogollon throughout most of their range, while in areas of greater local resources more stable settlements develop. The presence of great kivas indicates continuation of focal settlements within a dispersed community. Coresidence and multiple use of the mountains by people of different cultures indicate an increase in communication with the Anasazi and the Hohokam.

Mogollon Pueblo (A.D. 1000–1400, 950–550 years B.P.). There is continued development of regional differences through contacts with neighboring people. The most apparent change is the appearance of surface architecture and larger settlements that develop into aggregated pueblos ca. A.D. 1000 (950 years B.P.) in the Mimbres Valley, ca. A.D. 1250s (700–690 years B.P.) at Point of Pines, but not until A.D. 1300 (650 years B.P.) at Grasshopper (Reid 1989). The relatively accelerated development of the Mimbres (A.D. 1000–1150, or 950–800 years B.P.) was largely the result of contacts with people to the north and the south. Adaptation of dry-farming techniques to mountain and intermontane environments is apparent, though hunting and gathering continue as prominent components of the subsistence routine. The A.D. 1300s

(650–550 years B.P.) mark a unique moment in Mogollon prehistory, for the majority of the population live in pueblo communities of 100–800/1,000 rooms. Aggregation and a sudden population increase are products of demographic shifts on the Colorado Plateau that have brought Anasazi into the mountains to live with the Mogollon and to establish their own pueblo communities. Joint occupation of the mountains contributes to the consolidation of the Southwest pueblo farming pattern. By the mid-A.D. 1300s, agriculture cannot feed a growing population, and degraded wild-plant and -animal resources are inadequate to compensate for the shortfall. The Mogollon, now fully committed village farmers, abandon the central mountains of Arizona by A.D. 1400 (550 years B.P.) for farmland elsewhere.

J. Jefferson Reid

Further Readings

Haury, E.W. 1985. *Mogollon Culture in the Forestdale Valley, East-Central Arizona.* University of Arizona Press, Tucson.
———. 1986. The Mogollon Culture of Southwestern New Mexico. In *Emil W. Haury's Prehistory of the American Southwest,* edited by J.J. Reid and D.E. Doyel, pp. 307–404. University of Arizona Press, Tucson. This article originally published 1936 as Medallion Paper no. 20. Gila Pueblo, Globe.
Reed, E.K. 1950. Easterrn-Central Arizona Archaeology in Relation to the Western Pueblos. *Southwestern Journal of Anthropology* 6(2):120–138.
Reid, J.J. 1989. A Grasshopper Perspective on the Mogollon of the Arizona Mountains. In *Dynamics of Southwest Prehistory,* edited by L.S. Cordell and G.J. Gumerman, pp. 65–97. Smithsonian Institution Press, Washington, D.C.
Wheat, J.B. 1955. *Mogollon Culture Prior to A.D. 1000.* Memoirs of the American Anthropological Association no. 82. Memoirs of the Society for American Archaeology no. 10. Washington, D.C.

See also BEAR VILLAGE; BLACK RIVER BRANCH; BLUFF VILLAGE; FORESTDALE BRANCH; GRASSHOPPER PUEBLO; JORNADA BRANCH OF THE MOGOLLON CULTURE; MIMBRES BRANCH; PINE LAWN BRANCH; POINT OF PINES RUIN; SAN SIMON BRANCH OF THE MOGOLLON

Monitor Valley

Throughout most of the 1970s and 1980s, the American Museum of Natural History in New York conducted extensive archaeological excavations and reconnaissance in Monitor Valley, in the Great Basin uplands of central Nevada.

Excavations at Gatecliff Shelter (1970–1978) revealed more than 10 m (33 feet) of extraordinarily well-stratified deposits. They were divided into 56 geological strata and 16 cultural horizons. Primary chronological controls at Gatecliff Shelter were derived from a sequence of 47 radiocarbon dates. Several other caves and rock shelters in Monitor Valley were found to contain stratigraphic archaeological and paleoenvironmental sequences spanning the last 7,000 years.

Extensive excavations also centered on Alta Toquima (1979–1983), an unusual alpine settlement at an elevation of 3,352.8 m (11,000 feet) on Mt. Jefferson, along the western margin of Monitor Valley. More than three-dozen stone house foundations were examined, and 23 radiocarbon dates were processed on hearths from these dwellings. The earliest utilization of the Mt. Jefferson alpine zone began during the Clipper Gap phase, sometime prior to 3000 B.C. (4950 years B.P.). Utilization of Alta Toquima proper began ca. 1000 B.C. (2950 years B.P.), and people began building houses there by ca. A.D. 200 (1750 years B.P.). Roughly half of the excavated houses were initially constructed and occupied prior to A.D. 1000 (950 years B.P.). Some of the alpine dwellings continued to be used into the early Protohistoric period.

In addition, systematic and randomized archaeological surveys of the Monitor Valley area attempted to transcend obvious archaeological sites, such as Gatecliff Shelter and Alta Toquima. They examined those sources of potential information too often overlooked in traditional archaeological excavations and testing. Hundreds of specialized, "satellite sites" were located and analyzed as part of the Monitor Valley research: stone house rings, rock blinds and drive wells, petroglyph and pictograph sites, and cache localities.

David Hurst Thomas

Further Readings

Thomas, D.H. 1981. How to Classify the Projectile Points From Monitor Valley, Nevada. *Journal of California and Great Basin Anthropology* 3(1):7–43.
———. 1983a. The Archaeology of Monitor

M

1978 Gatecliff Shelter stratigraphy. (Courtesy of the National Museum of Natural History)

Valley: 1. Epistemology. *Anthropological Papers of the American Museum of Natural History* 58(1):1–194.

———. 1983b. The Archaeology of Monitor Valley: 2. Gatecliff Shelter. *Anthropological Papers of the American Museum*

1978 Gatecliff Shelter stratigraphy (Courtesy of the National Museum of Natural History)

of Natural History 59(1):1–552.
———. 1988. The Archaeology of Monitor Valley: 3. Survey and Additional Excavations. *Anthropological Papers of the American Museum of Natural History* 66(2):131–633.

———. 1994. The Archaeology of Monitor Valley: 4. Alta Toquima and the Mt. Jefferson Tablelands Complex. *Anthropological Papers of the American Museum of Natural History*.

Monks Mound

Monks Mound (11MS2), the largest Precolumbian earthen structure in the United States, towers over the Cahokia site in the Mississippi River floodplain near East St. Louis, Illinois. It is situated at the northern end of a quadrangle of smaller mounds that form the core of Cahokia, the premier settlement in this part of the valley.

Monks Mound covers ca. 7 ha (17 acres) and is ca. 30 m (98 feet) high. Construction began in the tenth century A.D. during the Emergent Mississippian period and continued into Mississippian times. The mound basically attained its final form in the twelfth century, although it was used for a long time thereafter. Its size indicates that leading members of this society were able to obtain and organize the labor needed to gather, move, and deposit great amounts of fill by hand. The number of workers at any particular time, however, did not have to be large because it took many generations before the mound reached its final dimensions.

Monks Mound has four terraces. The first extends across the south face, with a ramp projecting southward to the surrounding ground. The ramp is centrally located relative to the top of the mound, not the first terrace. The mound's west side is dominated by a lobate second terrace. Its summit is an elongated flat area offset to the east side of the mound. This surface is divided by a rise of ca. 1 m (3.3 feet) into south and north sections, called the third and fourth terraces. Additional now-destroyed mounds were once present on the third terrace's southeastern corner and the first terrace's western end. The east side of Monks Mound, dominated by two laterally projecting lobes, slopes steeply from the summit to the ground.

Several aspects of the mound's construction history have been revealed by deep cores, some of which reached the original ground surface, and excavations. Mound fill varies in color and texture, with some of it showing the highly distinctive characteristics of basket-loaded soil. The fill was laid down in layers of different thicknesses ranging up to massive homogeneous deposits. Some parts of the mound were built by forming small piles of earth that held in place subsequent deposits of fill. In several places during prehistoric and historic times, the mound fill has slumped, sometimes with a downward and lateral movement of massive blocks of earth.

It is difficult, using existing cores and excavation profiles, to link fill units with discrete mound-building events. Nevertheless, it is clear that various construction episodes supported structures, posts, and walls. Excavations in the fourth terrace encountered the remnants of an immense structure, among other features. The summit was not, however, the only heavily used part of the mound. Excavations in the southwestern corner of the first terrace found signs of multiple superimposed structures.

Flat-topped pyramidal mounds supporting important buildings were commonly constructed at major Mississippian sites in the southern Eastern Woodlands. No other mound, however, comes close to the size of Monks Mound.

George R. Milner

Further Readings

Collins, J.M., and M.L. Chalfant. 1993. A Second-Terrace Perspective on Monks Mound. *American Antiquity* 58:319–332.

Fowler, M.L. 1989. *The Cahokia Atlas: A Historical Atlas of Cahokia Archaeology*. Studies in Illinois Archaeology no. 6. Illinois Historic Preservation Agency, Springfield.

McGimsey, C.R., and M.D. Wiant. 1984. *Limited Archaeological Investigations at Monks Mound: Some Perspectives on Its Stability, Structure, and Age*. Studies in Illinois Archaeology no. 1. Illinois Historic Preservation Agency, Springfield.

Reed, N.A., J.W. Bennett, and J.W. Porter. 1968. Solid Core Drilling of Monks Mound: Technique and Findings. *American Antiquity* 33:137–148.

Skele, M. 1988. *The Great Knob: Interpretations of Monks Mound*. Studies in Illinois Archaeology no. 4. Illinois Historic Preservation Agency, Springfield.

Walthall, J.A., and E.D. Benchley. 1987. *The River L'Abbe Mission*. Studies in Illinois Archaeology no. 2. Illinois Historic Preservation Agency, Springfield.

See also CAHOKIA

M

Moore, Clarence B. (1852–1936)

World traveler, adventurer, and wealthy Philadelphia socialite, Clarence B. Moore turned his attention to Native American archaeology in the southeastern United States in the late nineteenth century. Traveling by river in his private houseboat, the Gopher, with a crew of up to eight men, he revisited previously reported sites, discovered many more, excavated more extensively than had earlier archaeologists, and amassed a large personal collection of artifacts. Many of his explorations were published in lavishly illustrated, descriptive reports. Moore is best known for his stratigraphic excavations of shell mounds along the St. John's River in Florida. A meticulous and careful observer, he demonstrated that the mounds were of human origin and confirmed earlier interpretations of their relative ages. Moore was a pioneer in viewing the southeastern archaeological record from a comparative perspective and in recognizing pattern in the geographic distribution of artifacts and sites.

Guy Gibbon

Further Readings

Moore, C.B. 1892. Certain Shell Heaps of the St. John's River, Florida, Hitherto Unexplored. *American Naturalist* 26:912–922.

———. 1894. Certain Sand Mounds of the St. John's River, Florida, pts. 1–2. *Journal of the Academy of Natural Sciences of Philadelphia* 10(1):5–103; 10(2):129–246.

———. 1896. Certain River Mounds of Duval County, Florida. *Journal of the Academy of Natural Sciences of Philadelphia* 10(4):448–502.

———. 1902. Certain Aboriginal Remains of the Northwest Florida Coast, pt. 2. *Journal of the Natural Sciences of Philadelphia* 12:127–355.

———. 1910. Antiquities of the St. Francis, White and Black Rivers, Arkansas. *Journal of the Academy of Natural Sciences of Philadelphia* 14(2):255–364.

Moorehead, Warren King (1866–1939)

W.K. Moorehead excavated widely throughout the eastern United States during the late nineteenth century and early decades of the twentieth, including sites in Ohio, Indiana, Kentucky, Maine, Georgia, Mississippi, Illinois, and Arkansas. While a student at Denison University, he began fieldwork in 1884 at excavations in southern Ohio sponsored by Frederick Ward Putnam's Peabody Museum of American Archaeology and Ethnology at Harvard University. He continued excavating around the Fort Ancient earthworks, at the Hopewell and Harness mound groups, and other sites in the area until 1897, often with little institutional support. His *Primitive Man in Ohio* (Moorehead and Fowke 1892) summarizes much of this work. He later excavated numerous sites, including Fort Ancient village sites in southern Indiana and northern Kentucky, the Etowah site in Georgia (1925–1927), Cahokia in Illinois, and rock shelters in the Ozarks. Moorehead wrote numerous articles and books, including the two-volume *The Stone Age in North America,* published in 1910. He became the first curator of the newly founded Ohio State Archaeological and Historical Society in 1894 and was director of the Department of American Archaeology at Phillips Academy, Andover, Massachusetts, from 1907 until his retirement in 1938. Although he was active throughout his career, his excavations were frequently poorly executed and documented; his reports and books, constrained by the absence of a developed interpretive framework.

Guy Gibbon

Further Readings

Guthe, C.E. 1939. Obituary. *American Antiquity* 1:65–66.

Moorehead, W.K. 1890. *Fort Ancient.* Robert Clarke, Cincinnati.

———. 1910. *The Stone Age in North America.* 2 vols. Houghton Mifflin, Boston.

———. 1922. *A Report on the Archaeology of Maine.* Publication no. 5. Department of Archaeology, Phillips Academy, Andover.

———. 1928. *The Cahokia Mounds.* Bulletin, vol. 26, no. 4. University of Illinois Press, Urbana.

———. 1931. *Archaeology of the Arkansas River Valley.* Yale University Press, New Haven.

———. 1932. *Etowah Papers.* Yale University Press, New Haven.

Moorehead, W.K., and G. Fowke. 1892. *Primitive Man in Ohio.* Putnam, New York.

Warren K. Moorehead (far left) ca. 1889 (Courtesy of the National Anthropological Archives, Smithsonian Institution, Photograph no. 11756–A)

Moresby Tradition

The Moresby tradition is the name given to the oldest dated (ca. 6550–3550 B.C., or 8500–5500 years B.P.) Lithic Stage culture on the Queen Charlotte Islands, British Columbia. The tradition is dominated by a unifacial flaked-stone industry with a well-developed microblade technology. The chosen lithic raw material is either beach pebbles or bedrock clasts of various local basalts, cherts, or argillaceous rocks. Moresby-tradition assemblages were typically formed by the production of tool flakes and microblades from prepared cores. Most such cores have well-formed conical vertical shapes, with single large, ovoid, striking platforms. Rotation among two or three platforms occurred very rarely. A variety of unifacially retouched scraperlike tools form another important part of Moresby-tradition assemblages. Most were produced by relatively rudimentary modifications of a flake edge. Others, with steep excurvate edges, were occasionally well formed. However, most retouched tools appear to have been expediently made from local beach pebbles to carry out such short-term tasks as the processing of fish or meat. The tools were then abandoned.

The Moresby tradition is best represented in the five lowest microblade-bearing components at the deeply stratified Lawn Point site on the southeastern coast of Graham Island. In excavations directed by Knut R. Fladmark in 1970, that site yielded radiocarbon dates between 5450 B.C. ± 140 and 3800 B.C. ± 110 (7400–5750 years B.P.) on charcoal samples from the second- and third-lowest components. Kasta is another Moresby-tradition site. Located on northern Moresby Island, it has radiocarbon dates of 4660 B.C. ± 95 and 3470 B.C. ± 100 (6610 and 5420 years B.P.). Another Moresbylike site ("Arrow Creek 1"), in the South Moresby Park Preserve area at the south end of Moresby Island, was investigated by a Parks Canada crew directed by Daryl Fedje. It yielded dates back to ca. 6550 B.C. (8500 years B.P.).

All known Moresby-tradition sites are associated with a prominent raised beach. Lying ca. 15 m (49 feet) above the present sea level, it was left by a higher sea-level position dating to ca. 7050–2550 B.C. (9000–4500 years B.P.). The "beachfront location" of these sites implies some interest in littoral- and marine-subsistence resources; a lack of preserved faunal remains clearly associated with Moresby-tradition occupations makes reconstructions of their subsistence practices speculative. The Queen Charlotte Islands also possessed an insular species of caribou that may have used beaches as convenient travel routes. Thus, such terrestrial faunal resources might also have been exploited by early occupants of the Queen Charlotte Islands. Sites like Lawn Point were possibly places where caribou could be strategically intercepted and the meat processed by human hunters and their families.

Knut R. Fladmark

Further Readings

Fladmark, K.R. 1982. An Introduction to the Prehistory of British Columbia. *Canadian Journal of Archaeology* 6:95–156.

———. 1986. Lawn Point and Kasta: Microblade Sites on the Queen Charlotte Islands, British Columbia. *Canadian Journal of Archaeology* 10:39–58.

———. 1989. The Native Culture History of the Queen Charlotte Islands. In *The Outer Shores*, edited by G.G.E. Scudder and N. Gessler, pp. 199–221. Queen Charlotte Islands Museum, Skidegate.

See also EARLY COAST MICROBLADE

Morris, Earl H. (1889–1956)

Earl Morris made his greatest contributions to the archaeology of the American Southwest, although he worked at Quirigua in Guatemala and supervised the excavation and reconstruction of the Temple of Warriors at Chichen Itza in Yucatan for five seasons. His formal education included an A.B. and an M.A. from the University of Colorado, which awarded him the Norlin Medal in 1931 and an honorary Doctor of Science degree in 1942. In 1953, he received the Society for American Archaeology's Alfred V. Kidder Award for outstanding contributions to Southwestern and Mesoamerican prehistory.

Growing up in New Mexico territory in the area of Farmington, Morris acquired the

Earl H. Morris. (Reprinted with permission from American Antiquity 22[4]:390)

survival skills that made him so successful in finding and excavating sites in the Four Corners country. Largely self-taught in field techniques, he began formal collections for the University of Colorado Museum when he was a student. Of importance was the painstaking excavation and restoration of the Aztec ruins in New Mexico, funded by the American Museum of Natural History in New York. This dry twelfth-century A.D. ruin produced a rich perishable material culture, including hundreds of burials. Part of the project involved reroofing the great kiva, an achievement that remains available for viewing today under the auspices of the National Park Service. From 1924 until 1956, Morris was employed by the Carnegie Institution of Washington, D.C. Besides most of the Mesoamerican work mentioned above, he worked throughout the northern Southwest. Collections at the University of Colorado Museum in Boulder and the Arizona State Museum at the University of Arizona, Tucson, are particularly rich in artifacts. Collaboration with A.E. Douglass led to a continuing interest in tree-ring dating. As of this writing (1996), the dated specimens from his Basketmaker II sites north of Durango, Colorado, remain the earliest yet recovered for that period.

Additional research along the La Plata River

exposed open sites ranging from Basketmaker III to Pueblo III. Also significant was his work in the dry caves of Canyon de Chelly, the Prayer Rock district, and other parts of northern Arizona, all of which produced a wealth of information that Morris presented in numerous articles listed in his bibliography in *American Antiquity* and *Southwestern Lore* and in monographs by this author and by Roy L. Carlson. Robert and Florence Lister have published several books, including a bibliography. A charming popular account, *Digging in the Southwest*, was written by Ann Axtell Morris.

Elizabeth Ann Morris

Further Readings

Kidder, A.V. 1957. Earl Halstead Morris 1889–1956. *American Antiquity* 22(4)390–397.

Morris, E.A. 1956. A Bibliography of Earl H. Morris. *Southwestern Lore* 22(3):40–43.

Morris, E.H. 1919. *The Aztec Ruin*. Anthropological Papers, vol. 26, pt. 1. American Museum of Natural History, New York.

———. 1921. *The House of the Great Kiva*. Anthropological Papers, vol. 26, pt. 2. American Museum of Natural History, New York.

———. 1924a. *The Aztec Ruin Annex*. Anthropological Papers, vol. 26, pt. 4. American Museum of Natural History, New York.

———. 1924b. *Burials in the Aztec Ruin*. Anthropological Papers, vol. 26, pt. 3. American Museum of Natural History, New York.

———. 1928. *Notes on Excavations in the Aztec Ruin*. Anthropological Papers, vol. 26, pt. 5. American Museum of Natural History, New York.

———. 1931. *The Temple of the Warriors*. Scribner's Sons, New York.

———. 1939. *Archaeological Studies in the La Plata District*. Publication no. 533. Carnegie Institution of Washington, Washington, D.C.

Morris, E.H., and R.F. Burgh. 1954. *Basketmaker II Sites Near Durango, Colorado*. Publication no. 604. Carnegie Institution of Washington, Washington, D.C.

Mortar and Pestle

The mortar and pestle are stone tools used together for pulverizing foodstuffs, pigments, or other substances that must be reduced to small bits or powder. The mortar is the basal stone in which a depression, which can be very deep, has been pecked. The pestle is the hand-held muller used to mash the material against the mortar in a predominantly up-and-down motion. This is in contrast to the use of a mano and metate, which are used in a rotary or back-and-forth movement. Pestles have been categorized by shape into cylindrical, conical, and bell-shaped

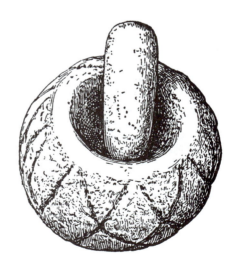

Mortar and Pestle sets (reprinted from Smithsonian Institution, Bureau of American Ethnology, Bulletin 60, Figure 25)

varieties. They may be roughly or finely abraded, but they always possess characteristic battering marks on one end. With rare exceptions, as in an engraved roller pestle from Massachusetts (Fowler 1969–1970), they are undecorated. The mortar-and-pestle combination dates to at least the Late Archaic period, for several have been found in the Indian Knoll site in Kentucky (Webb 1974). Few accounts of their use in North America exist; in Arnhem Land, Australia, however, indigenous people employed analogous objects before almost every meal for preparing vegetable foods (Peterson 1968).

George H. Odell

Further Readings

Converse, R.N. 1973. *Ohio Stone Tools.* Special Publication. Archaeological Society of Ohio, Columbus.

Fowler, W.S. 1969–1970. An Unusual Pestle Find. *Bulletin of the Massachusetts Archaeological Society* 31:26–27.

Peterson, N. 1968. The Pestle and Mortar: An Ethnographic Analogy for Archaeology in Arnhem Land. *Mankind* 6:567–570.

Webb, W.S. 1974. *Indian Knoll.* University of Tennessee Press, Knoxville.

Mortlach Aggregate

Due to problems in defining temporal, spatial, and formal content, F. Schneider and J. Kinney (1978) suggest that the term "aggregate" best describes the relationship of Mortlach materials. Sites that belong to the aggregate are found primarily in southeast Saskatchewan, northwest Montana, and northeast North Dakota. They were occupied about the time of European contact. Similar assemblages, including that of the Mortlach type site, are recognized in other parts of central and southern Saskatchewan. Mortlach aggregate sites are often identified on the basis of pottery, although Dale Walde (1994) suggests that Mortlach assemblages contain a large percentage of Plains Side-Notched points made from fused shale and Knife River flint. Virtually all Mortlach-aggregate sites are found in coulees and river valleys. The people appear to have followed a mobile plant-gathering and bison-hunting economy. There is general agreement among prehistorians that Mortlach can be affiliated with Souian speakers, either Assiniboine or Hidatsa-related.

The pottery assemblages associated with Mortlach-aggregate sites are dominated by vessels with straight and wedge-shaped rims, although other rim forms may appear. The globular vessels, probably formed using a paddle-and-anvil technique, have thin walls, compact paste, and light sand or finely crushed granite temper. Exterior surfaces may be smoothed plain, check stamped, or simple stamped; cord-roughed exteriors also appear. Pots are often decorated with dentate or cord-wrapped tool (CWT) impressions placed diagonally across the lip. A single row of discrete tool- or finger-made impressions, alone or above horizontal lines, or dentate or CWT impressions may appear on the upper part of the rim exterior. Decoration tends to be simple and sparse compared with Wascana ware vessels to the north, although W.J. Byrne (1973) does not distinguish Mortlach pottery from Wascana ware.

Mary Malainey

Further Readings

Byrne, W.J. 1973. *The Archaeology and Prehistory of Southern Alberta As Reflected by Ceramics.* Mercury Series Paper no. 14. Archaeological Survey of Canada, National Museum of Man, Ottawa.

Joyes, D.C. 1973. The Shippe Canyon Site. *Archaeology in Montana* 14(2):49–85.

Malainey, M. 1991. *Internal and External Relationships of Saskatchewan Plains Pottery Assemblages: Circa A.D. 1300 to Contact.* Unpublished Master's thesis. Department of Anthropology and Archaeology, University of Saskatchewan, Saskatoon.

Schneider, F., and J. Kinney. 1978. Evans: A Multi-Component Site in Northwestern North Dakota. *Archaeology in Montana* 19(1–2):1–39.

Walde, D.A. 1994. *The Mortlach Phase.* Unpublished Ph.D. dissertation, Department of Archaeology, University of Calgary, Calgary.

See also MORTLACH SITE

Mortlach Site

Mortlach (EcNl-1) is a stratified occupation site in the Besant Valley of southern Saskatchewan. Components from latest to earliest include Mortlach, Besant, Pelican Lake, and Sandy

Creek. This is the type site for the Besant projectile point, the Mortlach culture, and Mortlach Check Stamped pottery. Mortlach sites typically contain pottery with such a diversity of motifs, decorative techniques, and rim profiles that they are grouped as the Mortlach complex (Syms 1977) or Mortlach aggregate (Schneider and Kinney 1978). The Mortlach aggregate occupied an area ca. 804.6 km (500 miles) east-west from western Manitoba to eastern Alberta and 402 km (250 miles) north-south from Regina, Saskatchewan, to the Missouri River in Montana and North Dakota. The aggregate existed from A.D. 1520 to 1770 (430–180 years B.P.), with minor amounts of historic goods in some sites confirming its presence in the Protohistoric period. The pottery is smoothed and simple stamped with some check stamping present. Classic Mortlach Check Stamped ware has a wedge-shaped rim with flattened lip. Lips and upper parts of the rims are decorated with diagonal dentate stamps, and lower portions of the rims have cord impressions and fingernail pinches.

Ann M. Johnson

Further Readings

Malainey, M.E. 1991. *Internal and External Relationships of Saskatchewan Plains Pottery Assemblages: Circa A.D. 1300 to Contact.* Unpublished Master's thesis. Department of Anthropology and Archaeology, University of Saskatchewan, Saskatoon.

Schneider, F., and J. Kinney. 1978. Evans: A Multi-Component Site in Northwestern North Dakota. *Archaeology in Montana* 19(1–2):1–19.

Syms, E.L. 1977. *Cultural Ecology and Ecological Dynamics of the Ceramic Period in Southwestern Manitoba.* Memoir no. 12. Plains Anthropologist, Lincoln.

Wettlaufer, B.N. 1955. *The Mortlach Site in the Besant Valley of Central Saskatchewan.* Anthropological Series no. 1. Saskatchewan Museum of Natural History, Regina.

See also MORTLACH AGGREGATE

Mound Builder Myth

The term "Mound Builder" refers to a myth with roots in the late eighteenth century but popularized in the nineteenth century by explorers and armchair speculators that the numerous earthen mounds scattered throughout eastern North America were erected by a civilized race that had been displaced in the distant past by the "savage" American Indians. Suggested reasons for the myth include a lack of adequate information and conceptual frameworks, a need to create a heroic past for North America that would rival those proposed at the time for Europe, and the belief that Indians were incapable of building large mounds. Among the candidates for the vanished race were Israelites, Asians, Danes, and the Welsh. The myth was not laid to rest until Cyrus Thomas (1894) reported on the Bureau of American Ethnology's Mound Builder studies late in the century.

Guy Gibbon

Further Readings

Shetrone, H.C. 1930. *The Mound Builders.* Appleton-Century, New York.

Silverberg, R. 1968. *Moundbuilders of Ancient America: The Archaeology of a Myth.* New York Graphic Society, Greenwich.

Thomas, C. 1894. *Report of the Mound Explorations of the Bureau of Ethnology.* Smithsonian Institution, Washington, D.C.

Willey, G.R., and J.A. Sabloff. 1993. *A History of American Archaeology.* 3rd ed. W.H. Freeman, San Francisco.

Mound City

Mound City (33RO57) is an example of the large, complex geometric earthwork enclosures that are unique to Ohio Hopewell. This approximately square enclosure at Newark, Ohio, covers ca. 5.2 ha (13 acres) and contains 24 mounds. Described by Ephraim G. Squier and Edwin H. Davis (1848) in the mid-nineteenth century, the site was more intensely examined by William C. Mills (1922a, 1922b) in the early twentieth century. Excavations by the Ohio Historical Society in the 1960s (Brown and Baby 1966) reported evidence of food preparation in association with a mound and part of the embankment. Mark F. Seeman (1979) has suggested that this may be evidence of feasting and ritual in relation to the operation of a charnel house. Large enclosures like Mound City were most likely constructed over a period of time and the large burial mounds built by several generations of related people.

Guy Gibbon

Further Readings

Brown, J.A., and R.S. Baby. 1966. Mound City Revisited. Ms. on file, Department of Archaeology, Ohio Historical Society, Columbus.

Mills, W.C. 1922a. Exploration of the Mound City Group. In *Certain Mounds and Village Sites in Ohio* 3(4):245–406.

———. 1922b. Exploration of the Mound City Group. *Ohio Archaeological and Historical Quarterly* 31(4):423–584.

Seeman, M.F. 1979. Feasting With the Dead: Ohio Hopewell Charnel House Ritual As a Context for Redistribution. In *Hopewell Archaeology: The Chillicothe Conference*, edited by D.S. Brose and N. Greber, pp. 39–46. Kent State University Press, Kent.

Squier, E.G., and E.H. Davis. 1848. *Ancient Monuments of the Mississippi Valley.* Contributions to Knowledge no. 1. Smithsonian Institution, Washington, D.C.

See also OHIO HOPEWELL

Moundville

The Moundville site (ca. A.D. 1000–1550, or 950–400 years B.P.) is a large, compact settlement of Mississippian culture on the Black Warrior River of central Alabama. At the time of its heaviest residential population (A.D. 1200–1300, or 750–650 years B.P.), it took the form of a 75-ha (185-acre) village on a bluff of the river that was roughly square in plan and protected on three sides by a bastioned wooden palisade. It was at once a populous town, a political center, and a religious center, in size and complexity second only to Cahokia in Illinois. Within the enclosure, mostly bordering a central plaza, were 26 earthen mounds, the larger ones apparently supporting noble residences alternating with smaller ones that supported buildings used for mortuary and other purposes. Of the two largest mounds in the group, one, Mound A, occupies the center of the great plaza, and the second, Mound B, lies just to the north on the site's central axis. Mound B, rising to a height of 17.7 m (58 feet), is a steep pyramid with two ramps. The whole spatial arrangement gives the impression of symmetry and planning. Surrounding the plaza and the mounds is evidence of borrow pits, additional public buildings, and dozens of small houses of pole-and-thatch construction, many of which have yielded subfloor burials.

The excavated burials with their grave goods exhibit the striking differences that existed between the nobles and commoners of a stratified society. The burials also contain other rare artifacts that may be associated with particular political or religious offices. Several lines of evidence show that the center was sustained by tribute in food and labor provided by the occupants of floodplain farmsteads and minor centers that together represent an overall population of ca. 10,000 in one segment of the Black Warrior Valley. Like other Mississippian societies, Moundville's florescence was made possible by intensive maize horticulture on the floodplain, and the nobility dominated a traffic in such imported luxury goods as copper, mica, galena, and marine shell. Moundville is renowned particularly for its art in pottery, stonework, and embossed copper, for which the site is considered a benchmark in the study of Mississippian iconography.

Neither the rise of Moundville nor its eventual decline are well understood. It appears that the immediate area was thickly populated and had a few very small single-mound centers at a time just prior to the initial layout of the public architecture of the great plaza and erection of the palisade ca. A.D. 1200 (750 years B.P.). By ca. A.D. 1350 (600 years B.P.), Moundville seems to have undergone a change in use as it lost the aspect of a town, while retaining its ceremonial and political functions. A decline ensued, marked by abandonment of some mounds, secularization of others, and a decrease in the importation of prestige goods. By the 1500s, only a few portions of the site were still occupied. Despite Moundville's closeness in time to the initial European penetration of the region by DeSoto in A.D. 1540, the precise ethnic and linguistic affiliations of its inhabitants are not known.

Vernon James Knight, Jr.

Further Readings

Moore, C.B. 1905. Certain Aboriginal Remains of the Black Warrior River Valley. *Journal of the Academy of Natural Sciences of Philadelphia* 13:125–244.

———. 1907. Moundville Revisited. *Journal of the Academy of Natural Sciences of Philadelphia* 13:336–405.

Peebles, C.S. 1983. Moundville: Late Prehistoric Sociopolitical Organization in the Southeastern United States. In *The Development of Political Organization in Native North America*, edited by E.

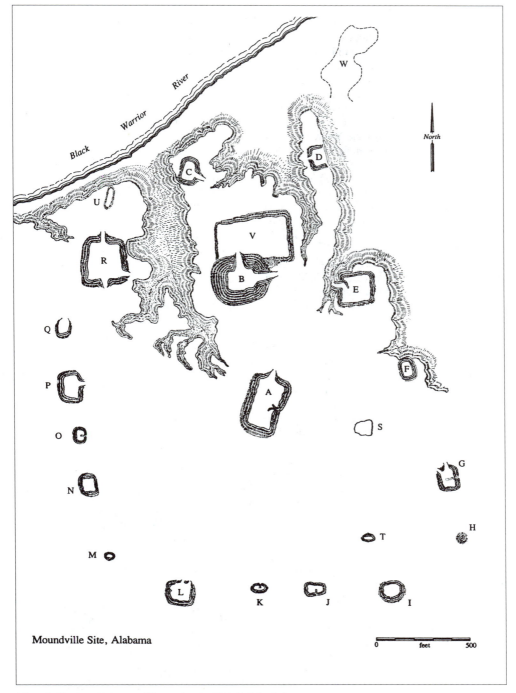

Moundville site, Alabama. (Illustration by V. J. Knight, Jr.)

Tooker, pp. 183–198. American Ethnological Society, New York.

Steponaitis, V.P. 1983. *Ceramics, Chronology, and Community Patterns: An Archaeological Study at Moundville.* Academic Press, New York.

Welch, P.D. 1991. *Moundville's Economy.* University of Alabama Press, Tuscaloosa.

Mount Albion Phase

The Mount Albion phase was originally recognized as a complex at the high-altitude Hungry Whistler and 5SL70 sites by James B. Benedict and B.L. Olson (1978). The sites are within 1.6 km (1 mile) of each other at ca. 3,048 m (10,000 feet) in the Southern Rocky Mountains just south of Rocky Mountain National Park. William B. Butler (1986) redefined Mount Albion as a phase within the Western Plains Early Archaic regional variant, which also includes the Albion Boardinghouse and Magic Mountain phases. The Mount Albion phase includes Zone F at the Magic Mountain site in the plains-mountain transition zone near Denver, which had been previously defined (Irwin-Williams and Irwin 1966) as part of the Magic Mountain complex. The Mount Albion Corner-Notched point, associated with sites of the phase, is a point similar to types MM3 and MM4 from the Magic Mountain site. The point is geographically restricted to the Continental Divide eastward for a few kilometers into the Plains, where several components are known. Other characteristics of the phase include the use of poor-quality rock types, secondary use of projectile points as hafted butchering tools, and a diversity of utilitarian implements, such as large and small ovoid bifaces, end scrapers, backed knives, flake gravers, microtools, flat metates, and cobble handstones with beveled secondary grinding surfaces. Mount Albion–phase occupation was during the later part of the Altithermal (Atlantic IV episode) and is thought to have been well established by ca. 3850–3650 B.C. (5800–5600 years B.P.) with a terminal date of ca. 3050 B.C. (5000 years B.P.). In this area the Altithermal dates to ca. 5150–3550 B.C. (7100–5500 years B.P.) (Benedict and Olson 1978). Recent research suggests that the Mount Albion phase (ca. 4050–3050 B.C., or 6000–5000 years B.P.) and the Albion Boardinghouse phase (ca. 5550–4050 B.C., or 7500–6000 years B.P.) should be considered as members of the Southern Rocky Mountain Early Archaic regional variant (ca. 5550–3050 B.C., or 7500–5000 years B.P.) for mountain-oriented cultures rather than in a Plains taxa (Butler 1986).

William B. Butler

Further Readings

Benedict, J.B., and B.L. Olson. 1978. *The Mount Albion Complex: A Study of Prehistoric Man and the Altithermal.* Research Report no. 1. Center for Mountain Archaeology, Ward.

Butler, W.B. 1986. *Taxonomy in Northeastern Colorado Prehistory.* Unpublished Ph.D. dissertation, Department of Anthropology, University of Missouri, Columbia.

Irwin-Williams, C., and H.J. Irwin. 1966. *Excavations at Magic Mountain: A Diachronic Study of Plains-Southwest Relationships.* Proceedings no. 12. Denver Museum of Natural History, Denver.

See also ALBION BOARDINGHOUSE PHASE; MAGIC MOUNTAIN PHASE; SOUTHERN ROCKY MOUNTAIN EARLY ARCHAIC REGIONAL VARIANT

Mulloy, William Thomas (1917–1978)

William Thomas Mulloy was born in Salt Lake City and received a B.A. degree from the University of Utah in 1939. He worked for the WPA (Work Projects Administration) in Louisiana excavating Crooks Mound with Arden King before joining the Montana Statewide Archaeological Survey, sponsored by the WPA, as its only professional archaeologist in 1940. There he wrote reports on sites (Hagen, Pictograph Cave, and others) previously investigated by WPA staff and supervised WPA excavations at the Billings Bison Trap and Thirty Mile Mesa.

William T. Mulloy. (Reprinted, with permission, from American Antiquity 44[3]:513)

World War II interrupted those studies. Following the war, he received an M.A. in 1948 and a Ph.D. in 1953 from the University of Chicago based primarily on his earlier WPA investigations. He joined the University of Wyoming in 1944 and worked in the late 1940s and early 1950s for the Smithsonian Institution's River Basin Surveys in Wyoming, where he excavated the McKean type site. His dissertation (Mulloy 1958) presented a cultural chronology for the northwestern Plains that is still used today (with modifications for gaps in the Pictograph Cave sequence and finer chronological control provided by radiocarbon dating). Other important work includes the definition of the Intermountain tradition and aboriginal log structures, such as conical timbered lodges. From 1949 to 1977, he taught in the Anthropology Department at the University of Wyoming. Following his participation in the Norwegian Archaeological Expedition to Easter Island and the East Pacific in 1955, he focused on that geographical area, where he was involved in excavations and architectural reconstructions while studying problems of population growth and culture change (Mulloy 1965a, 1970, 1973, 1978).

Ann M. Johnson

Further Readings

Mulloy, W.T. 1942. *The Hagen Site: A Prehistoric Village on the Lower Yellowstone.* Publications in the Social Sciences no. 1. University of Montana, Missoula.

———. 1954. The McKean Site in Northeastern Wyoming. *Southwestern Journal of Anthropology* 10(4):432–460.

———. 1958. *A Preliminary Historical Outline for the Northwestern Plains.* University of Wyoming Publications, vol. 22, no. 1. University of Wyoming, Laramie.

———. 1965a. The Fortified Village of Morongo Uta. In *Reports of the Norwegian Archaeological Expedition to Easter Island and the East Pacific: 2. Miscellaneous Papers,* edited by T. Heyerdahl and E.N. Ferdon, Jr., pp. 23–68. Monograph no. 24, pt. 2. Kon Tiki Museum; School of American Research, Santa Fe.

———. 1965b. *The Indian Village at Thirty Mile Mesa, Montana.* University of Wyoming Publications, vol. 31, no. 1. University of Wyoming, Laramie.

———. 1970. A Speculative Reconstruction of Techniques of Carving, Transporting, and Erecting Easter Island Statues. *Archaeology and Physical Anthropology in Oceania* 5(1):1–23.

———. 1973. *Preliminary Report of the Restoration of Ahu Huri a Urenga and Two Unnamed Ahu at Hanga Kio'e.* Bulletin no. 3. International Fund for Monuments, New York.

———. 1978. *The a Kiva Vai Teka Complex (with Gonzalo Figueroa).* University of Hawaii Press, Honolulu.

Slater, A.S. 1978. In Memoriam: William Thomas Mulloy. *Wyoming Contributions to Anthropology* 1:iv–vii.

Mummy Cave

Mummy Cave (48PA201) is a large rock shelter located on the North Fork of the Shoshone River in the Absaroka Range ca. 55 km (34 miles) west of Cody in northwestern Wyoming. Excavations from 1963 to 1966 disclosed 37 occupation layers within 8.5 m (28 feet) of deposits. Mummy Cave is important for its lengthy and revealing cultural stratigraphy, which is supported by a ladder of 16 radiocarbon dates. These dates document intermittent occupation of the shelter from 7280 ± 150 B.C. to A.D. 1580 ± 90 (9230–370 years B.P.) (Wedel et al. 1968). The lower three cultural strata are undated, but first use of the site probably occurred ca. 8050 B.C. (10,000 years B.P.). The excavation of Mummy Cave and rock shelters in Bighorn Canyon ca. 135 km (84 miles) to the northeast resulted in recognition of a foothill-mountain–oriented culture or tradition similar in age to, but economically different from, the High Plains Paleoindian bison-hunting culture (Husted 1969). This upland adaptation was focused on a hunting-and-gathering, or Archaic, subsistence strategy. Subsequent investigations in Wyoming and Montana have provided additional information on this still inadequately known manifestation (Frison 1992).

The Mummy Cave investigations also documented the presence of large side-notched projectile points in northwest Wyoming by 5650 B.C. (7600 years B.P.); they were also central to the recognition of an Altithermal-period continuum in foothill-mountain environments in the middle and northern Rocky Mountain area. At Mummy Cave, strata containing side-notched points truncated a succession of lanceolate point types associated with the foothill-mountain Paleoindian. Whether the early notched form represents an in situ development from the lanceolate point or arrived from elsewhere remains a question. Excavations subsequent to the Mummy Cave investigations have revealed the occurrence of these early side-notched projectiles at sites throughout Wyoming, western Montana, and southern Idaho (Greiser 1986; Frison 1992:79–88). A fully developed hunting-and-gathering Archaic lifeway is indicated, and a revised archaeological chronology for the northwestern Plains includes a sequence of side-notched points in an Early Plains Archaic period dating to ca. 6050–3050 B.C. (8000–5000 years B.P.) (Frison 1992). Other assessments of the data indicate, however, that the early side-notched point is associated more closely with foothill and mountain environments, suggesting that further revision of chronological terminology might be appropriate. Several occupation layers lie above the Paleoindian and Early Plains Archaic components, providing a continuous cultural sequence from the Paleoindian to the Late Prehistoric period. The Middle Plains Archaic stratum dating from 2470 B.C. ± 150 to 2140 B.C. ± 140 (4420–4090 years B.P.) contained many perishable items, including cordage and netting of plant fibers, coiled basketry, tubular bone smoking pipes, and other implements of animal bone and wood. A thick and extensive Late Prehistoric deposit contained an even larger inventory of fragile artifacts, including arrows; arrow-making debris of wood and feathers; a pair of fur-lined footwear; and many items of animal bone and hide, wood, and plant fibers. These two strata provide a revealing view of prehistoric material culture seldom recovered in western Plains and Rocky Mountain archaeological sites. Much remains to be learned, but Mummy Cave has been and remains pivotal in the interpretation and synthesis of western Plains and Rocky Mountain prehistory.

Wilfred M. Husted

Further Readings

Frison, G.C. 1992. *Prehistoric Hunters of the High Plains*. 2nd ed. Academic Press, San Diego.

Greiser, S.T. 1986. Artifact Collections From Ten Sites at Canyon Ferry Reservoir. *Archaeology in Montana* 27(1–2):1–190.

Husted, W.M. 1969. *Bighorn Canyon Archeology*. Publications in Salvage Archeology no. 12. River Basin Surveys.

Smithsonian Institution, Lincoln.

McCracken, H. 1978. *The Mummy Cave Project in Northwestern Wyoming*. Buffalo Bill Historical Center, Cody.

Wedel, W.R., W.M. Husted, and J.H. Moss. 1968. Mummy Cave: Prehistoric Record From Rocky Mountains of Wyoming. *Science* 160(3824):184–186.

Munkers Creek Phase

Munkers Creek is a Late Archaic cultural stage in the Flint Hills, Western Osage Plains, and Dissected Till Plains of eastern Kansas dated to ca. 3500–3000 B.C. (5450–4950 years B.P.). Sites typically are several acres in size, often stratified, and located along major river valleys. Habitation features consist of stone hearths and random isolated postholes. Diagnostic chipped-stone artifacts include large- to medium-sized lanceolate points with parallel-sided stems, long curved knives (usually with silica polish across the midsection), wasp-waisted axes, and several varieties of Clear Fork–type gouges. Ground stone is minimally represented by a small grinding slab. Modeling and firing of clay at this early date is evidenced by two small effigy human heads and a bead. The type site is the William Young site, excavated by T.A. Witty, Jr., of the Kansas State Historical Society, in the Upper Neosho River drainage. Twenty-two separate occupational levels were identified in a 1.5-m (5-foot) vertical zone.

Thomas A. Witty, Jr.

Munkers Creek phase points from the William Young site. (Illustration by T. A. Witty, Jr.)

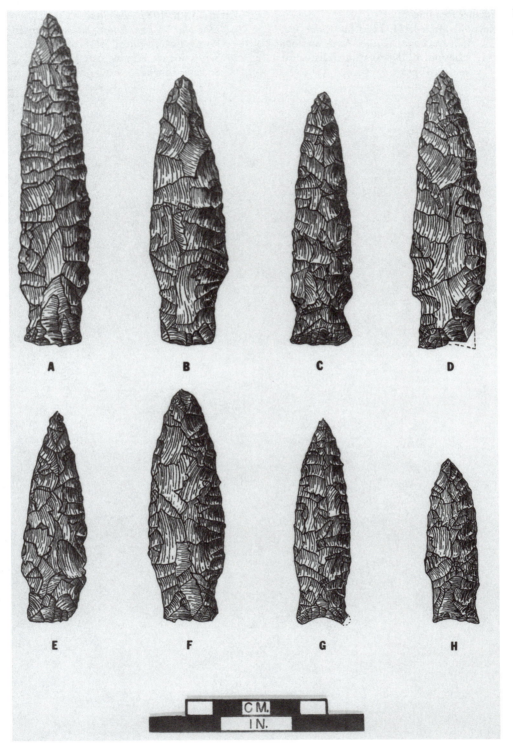

Modeled fired-clay effigy heads from the William Young site, Munkers Creek phase. (Illustration by T. A. Witty, Jr.)

Further Readings

Reynolds, J.D. 1984. *The Cow-Killer Site, Melvern Lake, Kansas.* Anthropological Series no. 12. Kansas State Historical Society, Topeka.

Witty, T.A., Jr. 1982. *The Slough Creek, Two Dog and William Young Sites, Council Grove Lake, Kansas.* Anthropological Series no. 10. Kansas State Historical Society, Topeka.

N

Naujan

The type site of Canadian Thule culture located near the modern hamlet of Repulse Bay, Northwest Territories, Naujan (MdHs-1) was excavated by Therkel Mathiassen of the Danish Fifth Thule Expedition in 1922 with the assistance of the expedition's secretary, Jacob Olsen. The site consists of the collapsed remains of 20 sod and whalebone houses as well as a large and apparently stratified midden. Employing the comparatively robust field methods of the day, Mathiassen was able to excavate 12 of the 20 houses and 60 m² (645.8 square feet) of midden to an average depth of about a meter, revealing a great range and number of ancient tools. On the basis of his finds, Mathiassen defined the prehistoric Thule culture, which we now know to be ancestral to the culture of all recent Inuit. On the basis of geological evidence, he suggested an age of ca. A.D. 950 (1000 years B.P.). Most archaeologists would now probably date the Naujan find to ca. A.D. 1250 (700 years B.P.). In 1991, the skeletal remains of approximately 30 individuals exhumed by Mathiassen were reinterred at the Naujan site.

David Morrison

Further Readings

Mathiassen, T. 1927. *Archaeology of the Central Eskimos: The Thule Culture and Its Position Within the Eskimo Culture.* Report of the Fifth Thule Expedition 1921–1924, vol. 4, nos. 1–2. Glydenclalski Boghandel, Nordisk Forlag, Copenhagen.

Nebo Hill Phase

Distributed across parts of western Missouri and eastern Kansas, the Nebo Hill phase is a distinctive regional variant of a much broader midwestern Late Archaic cultural adaptation. The Nebo Hill phase's significance once came from its suspected early Holocene age; it is now most notable for its association with the earliest pottery documented in the Midwest. The complex was described originally by J.M. Shippee based on artifacts recovered from several blufftop sites in the Kansas City area (Shippee 1957). Hallmarks of the phase include the Nebo Hill point (a distinctive, long and narrow lanceolate point with a thick biconvex or diamond-shaped cross section), three-quarter–grooved axes, ground-stone and chipped-stone celts, bifacially flaked digging tools, and rectangular and oval sandstone manos.

The Nebo Hill lanceolate point's morphological similarity to the Late Paleoindian Plains Angostura point type, which is dated to ca. 8500–6000 B.C. (10,450–7950 years B.P.), initially led Shippee to suggest an equally early age for Nebo Hill remains. This interpretation was widely accepted until the mid-1970s and early 1980s, when several sites were excavated during cultural-resource-management investigations. These sites were radiocarbon dated to ca. 2600–1000 B.C. (4550–2950 years B.P.) (Reeder 1981; Reid 1984), clearly establishing the Nebo Hill phase as much younger than originally believed. Even more surprising was the recovery of smooth-surfaced, fiber- and grog-tempered pottery from several radiometrically dated Nebo Hill components (Reid 1984), making this the earliest midwestern ceramics so far documented.

The Nebo Hill settlement pattern consists of large, artifact-rich summit or blufftop sites and smaller occupations with much lower artifact densities on tributary floodplains (Reeder

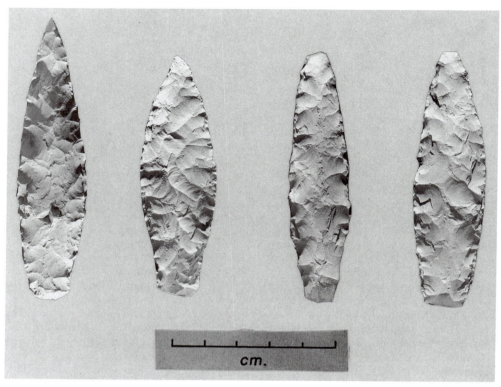

Nebo Hill projectile points from the Sohn site (23JA110), along the Little Blue River near Kansas City, Jackson County, Missouri. (Illustration by R. L. Reeder)

1981; Reid 1983). This dichotomous pattern probably reflects seasonal movement and use of different environmental zones and associated resources. Nebo Hill subsistence remains are limited due to poor preservation; however, the overall similarity of tool types in Nebo Hill sites with tool assemblages of better documented and more eastern Late Archaic Titterington and Sedalia phases suggests the presence of similar subsistence patterns. As of 1996, cultigens had not been found associated with the phase, but the frequency and diversity of tools associated with procuring and processing plant materials, such as digging tools, manos, and metates, clearly indicate vegetal resources were an integral part of Nebo Hill subsistence.

Robert L. Reeder

Further Readings

Reeder, R.L. 1981. Nebo Hill in a Riverine Environment. *Missouri Archaeologist* 42:27–42.

Reid, K.C. 1983. The Nebo Hill Phase: Late Archaic Prehistory in the Lower Missouri Valley. In *Archaic Hunters and Gatherers in the American Midwest*, edited by J.A. Brown and P.L. Phillips, pp. 11–39. Academic Press, New York.

———. 1984. Fire and Ice: New Evidence for the Production and Preservation of Late Archaic Fiber-Tempered Pottery in the Middle-Latitude Lowlands. *American Antiquity* 49(1):29–32.

Shippee, J.M. 1957. The Diagnostic Point of the Nebo Hill Complex. *Missouri Archaeologist* 19(3):42–46.

Nebraska Phase

One of five recognized divisions of the Late Prehistoric Central Plains tradition (A.D. 1000–1400, or 950–550 years B.P.), the Nebraska phase centers on the lower 32 km (20 miles) of the Platte River, Nebraska. It extends south along the Missouri River to northeast Kansas/northwest Missouri and more densely north into Dixon County, Nebraska. Elkhorn River Basin sites to the west abut a boundary with the Itskari phase in central Nebraska.

Nebraska-phase houses are square, wattle-

and-daub structures erected over housepits 0.3 to 0.9 m (1–3 feet) deep. Roofs were supported on four center posts arranged in a square around a central fire basin. Several subfloor storage/refuse pits are usually found. An entry passage emerges from the center of one wall, though cases of corner entries and entries from two adjacent walls are found. Seventy-five percent of houses are 18.6–92.9 m² (200–1,000 square feet) in area. Though clusters of up to 62 houses occur, these are likely the accumulations of solitary houses or small communities of three to 12 houses over a number of generations.

Earliest occupation was in the Lower Platte River–Weeping Water Creek vicinity, where Pennsylvanian "Nehawka" cherts and "Dakota" sandstone were magnets for settlement. Tools from these materials include single and multiple side- and side-and-base-notched projectile points, unnotched triangular projectile points or knives, drills, bifacial and beveled knives, end scrapers, and flake tools. Sandstone and scoria abraders, abraded and polished diorite celts, and other tools are also present. Bison-scapula tools are abundant only in sites north of the Platte, suggesting that either bison were more heavily exploited there than to the south or that the more acidic soils in the south destroyed bone tools. A wide variety of bone and antler tools include awls, pins, pendants, punches, fishhooks, beads, cancellous tissue abraders, antler, rib and long-bone shaft wrenches, knife handles, and deer phalange tinklers. Nebraska-phase sites have produced distinctive deer-cranium spoons, toggling harpoon heads, and (in the north) bison-horn-core-and-frontal-bone scoops. Mussel shell pendants, disk and cylindrical beads, "spoons," and scrapers are found.

Ceramics include indigenous sand- or grit-tempered globular jars with either unthickened or collared rims. The rims often have handles, tabs, nodes, or other appendages. Low-rimmed, shell-tempered jars, often with incised/trailed shoulder decoration, as well as anthropomorphic and zoomorphic effigy appendages and smoking pipes reflect influence from Mississippian sources to the south and southeast. The idea that the Nebraska phase originated from a Mississippian migration or radiation from the southeast is untrue. The earliest Nebraska-phase component, dated to A.D. 1030 (920 years B.P.) on a Platte River tributary, is similar to the Smoky Hill phase. From such pioneer settlements, the Nebraska phase expanded toward the southeast and doubtless became a medium for the diffusion of Mississippian traits. Other pioneers radiated throughout the Elkhorn River Basin. After ca. A.D. 700 (1250 years B.P.), the Nebraska phase began to contract, the dispersed populations concentrating along the Missouri River from north of Omaha to around Ponca, Nebraska. This move, analogous with hostile immigration by contemporary Initial Coalescent peoples into central South Dakota, was to interdict the export of bison products to, and the import of status symbols from, the Mississippian-period Cahokia site in Illinois by Initial Middle Missouri–tradition and Mill Creek people via the Missouri River. By A.D. 1350–1400 (600–550 years B.P.), both the Nebraska phase and Mill Creek culture had disappeared, probably because of warfare coupled perhaps with disease and environmental degradation.

John R. Bozell
John Ludwickson

Further Readings

Blakeslee, D.J. 1989. On Estimating Household Populations in Archeological Sites, With an Example From the Nebraska Phase. *Plains Anthropologist* 34(124/2):3–16.

Blakeslee, D.J., and W.W. Caldwell. 1979. *The Nebraska Phase: An Appraisal.* J and L Reprints, Lincoln.

Hotopp, J.A. 1982. Some Observations on the Central Plains Tradition in Iowa. In *Plains Indian Studies: A Collection of Essays in Honor of John C. Ewers and Waldo R. Wedel,* edited by D.H. Ubelaker and H.J. Viola, pp. 173–192. Contributions to Anthropology no. 30. Smithsonian Institution Press, Washington, D.C.

Needle

A needle is a narrow, elongated object that is pointed on one end. It usually possesses a drilled hole at the other end. Prehistoric tools of this form have rarely been interpreted as anything other than sewing implements; the analogy with modern needles is probably apt. They are usually made of bone and most often of bird bone. Needles were made throughout North America. They extend at least as far back as the Middle-Late Archaic at such locales as the Eva site in Tennessee and Riverton culture sites in Illinois. About 150 long, thin, sharp objects of copper that were round, square, or rectangular in cross-section and are thought to have been needles were unearthed in the 1930s at the Late Prehistoric Spiro site in Oklahoma. Although they lack a hole at one end, they could have functioned as sewing implements, but evidence of their use in such an activity is lacking.

George H. Odell

Further Readings

Hamilton, H.W. 1952. The Spiro Mound. *Missouri Archaeologist,* vol. 14.

Lewis, T.M.N., and M.K. Lewis. 1961. *Eva: An Archaic Site.* University of Tennessee Press, Knoxville.

Winters, H.D. 1969. *The Riverton Culture.* Reports of Investigations no. 13. Illinois State Museum and Illinois Archaeological Survey, Springfield.

Nelson, Nels C. (1875–1964)

A student of A.L. Kroeber at the University of California, Berkeley, Nels C. Nelson introduced into the American Southwest the stratigraphic method of determining temporal sequences of artifact styles. Following excavations as a student at the stratified Ellis Landing Shellmound in San Francisco Bay (Nelson 1910), he became convinced of the importance of the stratigraphic method during a visit in 1913 to stratigraphic excavations by Hugo Obermaier and Henri Breuil in French and Spanish caves. While working for the American Museum of Natural History, New York, in the Galisteo Basin of New Mexico in 1914–1916, he excavated at a series of pueblos, including a 3-m (9.8-foot)-deep midden at San Cristobel, and, employing frequency counts, described a sequence of changing pottery styles. He then used his chronology of pottery styles to date other sites from unit surface collections (Nelson 1916). His innovative approach led immediately to an emphasis on regional-chronology-building. He also introduced excavation in arbitrary and uniform metrical levels, a refinement at the time in stratigraphic excavation. Nelson (1916) later applied seriation dating developed by Leslie Spier to Southwestern masonry types; attempted to interpret excavation results in terms of a sequence of different prehistoric cultures at Mammoth Cave, Kentucky; wrote an important review of studies of the antiquity of humans in the New World (Nelson 1933); and suggested relationships between Alaska and Mongolia on the basis of excavations on the campus of the University of Alaska, an early landmark publication

Nels C. Nelson. (Reprinted with permission from American Antiquity *31[3]:394)*

in the archaeology of the interior of Alaska (Nelson 1937).

Guy Gibbon

Further Readings

Nelson, N.C. 1910. The Ellis Landing Shellmound. *University of California Publications in American Archaeology and Ethnology* 7(5):357–426.

———. 1916. Chronology of the Tano Ruins, New Mexico. *American Anthropologist* 18(2):159–180.

———. 1933. The Antiquity of Man in America in the Light of Archaeology. In *The American Aborigines, Their Origin and Antiquity,* edited by D. Jenness, pp. 85–130. University of Toronto Press, Toronto.

———. 1937. Notes on Cultural Relations Between Asia and America. *American Antiquity* 2:267–272.

Nenana Complex

The Nenana complex represents the earliest firmly dated set of archaeological remains currently (as of 1995) known in Alaska and perhaps the New World as a whole. Assemblages assigned to this complex have been recovered from several sites in central Alaska and have been dated to ca. 10,050–9050 B.C. (12,000–11,000 years B.P.). The Nenana complex is widely regarded as part of the Palaeoindian tradition and a likely Beringian progenitor of the Clovis complex. J.F. Hoffecker et al. (1993) suggest that the Nenana complex represents the initial population movement into the New World, which occurred in response to environmental changes generated by the final Pleistocene interstadial (ca. 10,050–9050 B.C., or 12,000–11,000 years B.P.).

The Nenana complex was defined by W.R. Powers and Hoffecker (1989) on the basis of several sites in the north-central foothills of the Alaska Range. Assemblages typically contain small teardrop-shaped and triangular bifacial points (Chindadn points), bifaces, end scrapers, side scrapers, wedges (*pièces esquillées*), and planes. Flake and blade-core technology are present, but the microblade technology that is so common in other Early Prehistoric industries of northern North America (e.g., Denali complex) and northeast Asia is completely absent. Although Nenana assemblages lack fluted points and are not considered part of the Clovis complex, they have been included in the Paleoindian tradition on the basis of their overall technological and typological characteristics (Haynes 1987; Goebel et al. 1991). Recent redating of major Early Palaeoindian sites in mid-latitude North America suggests that the Clovis complex falls into the 9250–8950 B.C. (11,200–10,900 years B.P.) interval and is contemporaneous with, or slightly younger than, the Nenana complex (Haynes 1991; Hoffecker et al. 1993).

Sites containing assemblages assigned to the Nenana complex have been found in the Nenana Valley, located in the north-central foothills of the Alaska Range, and in the Tanana Basin in central Alaska. Sites in the Nenana Valley include Dry Creek and Walker Road; although the lower component at Moose Creek was formerly included in the Nenana complex (Powers and Hoffecker 1989), this assemblage was subsequently dropped due to uncertainties regarding its age and typological character (Hoffecker et al. 1993). Both sites are located on south-facing promontories formed by tributary streams that have incised pre-Late Wisconsin outwash terraces. The Nenana-complex assemblages at these sites occur near the base of

loess and aeolian sand deposits that span the last 12,000 years. At Dry Creek, the Nenana occupation, which yielded a conventional radiocarbon date of 9170 B.C. ± 85 (11,120 years B.P.), underlies an assemblage containing wedge-shaped microcores and microblades (Denali complex) dated to 8740 B.C. ± 250 (10,690 years B.P.). At Walker Road, a large Nenana assemblage yielded conventional and accelerator mass spectrometry (AMS) radiocarbon dates ranging between 9870 B.C. ± 200 and 9060 B.C. ± 230 (11,820 and 11,010 years B.P.) (Powers and Hoffecker 1989).

Sites in the Tanana Basin include Chugwater, Broken Mammoth, and possibly Healy Lake. These sites, found on bedrock ridges or knobs on the north side of the Tanana River, also contain remains buried in loess and aeolian sand deposits that span the last 12,000 years. At Chugwater, an undated assemblage assigned to the Nenana complex underlies a Denali-occupation level that was radiocarbon dated to 7510–4310 B.C. (9460–6260 years B.P.) (Erlandson et al. 1991). The earliest occupation level at Broken Mammoth yielded dates of 9820–9090 B.C. (11,770–11,040 years B.P.) but no diagnostic items; an overlying level produced dates of 8320–7360 B.C. (10,270–9310 years B.P.) and a bifacial point and point fragment. Both levels have been tentatively assigned to the Nenana complex (Holmes et al. 1992). At Healy Lake, small bifacial points and microblades were recovered from the same levels, which yielded radiocarbon dates of 9140–4700 B.C. (11,090–6650 years B.P.); these levels may contain a postdepositional mixture of Nenana and Denali assemblages (Erlandson et al. 1991). Another site in the Tanana Basin, Swan Point, has produced a microblade assemblage dated to ca. 9050 B.C. (11,000 years B.P.), which suggests that the Nenana and Denali complexes could be contemporaneous or even functional variants of the same industry (Busch 1994). This problem requires further research.

There is some evidence for the Nenana complex or a related industry in northeast Asia. An assemblage containing small bifacial points (chiefly stemmed), side scrapers, and end scrapers, but lacking wedge-shaped cores and microblades, was recovered from the lowest occupation level at Ushki I in central Kamchatka (Dikov 1979). The level yielded dates of 12,350–11,650 B.C. (14,300–13,600 years B.P.). Other possibly related assemblages include Berelekh, located near the mouth of the Indigirka River in eastern Yakutia, and Bol'shoi El'gakhchan I on the Omolon River in western Chukotka (Hoffecker et al. 1993).

Faunal remains recovered from Nenana-complex sites suggest that their occupants hunted extinct late Pleistocene megafauna, such as steppe bison (*Bison priscus*), and other large and medium mammals, including wapiti (*Cervus canadensis*), sheep (*Ovis dalli*), and caribou (*Rangifer tarandus*) (Powers and Hoffecker 1989; Holmes et al. 1992). The sites in the north-central foothills of the Alaska Range may have been occupied during the fall and winter to exploit concentrations of large mammals in upland valleys during these seasons. The occupations at Dry Creek and Walker Road probably represent short-term hunting camps (Powers and Hoffecker 1989). The function and the seasonality of the Tanana Basin sites remain unclear.

John F. Hoffecker

Further Readings

Busch, L. 1994. Alaska Sites Contend As Native Americans' First Stop. *Science* 264:347.

Dikov, N.N. 1979. *Drevnie kul'tury Severo-Vostochnoi Azii*. Nauka, Moscow.

Erlandson, J., R. Walser, H. Maxwell, N. Bigelow, J. Cook, R. Lively, C. Adkins, D. Dodson, A. Higgs, and J. Wilber. 1991. Two Early Sites of Eastern Beringia: Context and Chronology in Alaskan Interior Archaeology. *Radiocarbon* 33(1):35–50.

Goebel, F.E., W.R. Powers, and N.H. Bigelow. 1991. The Nenana Complex of Alaska and Clovis Origins. In *Clovis: Origins and Adaptations,* edited by R. Bonnichsen and K. Turnmire, pp. 49–79. Center for the Study of the First Americans, Oregon State University, Corvallis.

Haynes, C.V. 1987. Clovis Origin Update. *Kiva* 52(2):83–93.

———. 1991. Geoarchaeological and Paleohydrological Evidence for a Clovis-Age Drought in North America and Its Bearing on Extinction. *Quaternary Research* 35:438–450.

Hoffecker, J.F., W.R. Powers, and T. Goebel. 1993. The Colonization of Beringia and the Peopling of the New World. *Science* 259:46–53.

Holmes, C.E., D.R. Yesner, and K.J. Crossen. 1992. The Broken Mammoth Archaeological Project, Central Tanana Valley, Alaska: Progress Update. Paper presented at the Fifty-Seventh Annual Meeting of the Society for American Archaeology, April 8–12, 1992, Pittsburgh.

Powers, W.R., and J.F. Hoffecker. 1989. Late Pleistocene Settlement in the Nenana Valley, Central Alaska. *American Antiquity* 54:263–287.

See also DENALI COMPLEX; DRY CREEK SITE; WALKER ROAD SITE

Nesikep Tradition

The Nesikep tradition was first defined in the mid-1960s as the major archaeological unit in an initial culture-historical model for south-central interior British Columbia (Sanger 1969). It was based primarily on: (1) excavations at the Nesikep Creek site, the Lehman site, and several other sites in the Lochnore Nesikep locality along the mid-Fraser River; (2) excavations at the Chase burial site in the South Thompson River Valley; and (3) surface collections from the North Thompson River Valley, the mid-Fraser River Valley, and elsewhere. The geographic extent of the Nesikep tradition was thought to include the Fraser River and its major tributaries from its confluence with the Thompson River as far north as Williams Lake, and the Thompson River and its major tributaries from its confluence with the Fraser.

As originally defined, the Nesikep tradition was a 7000-year-long (ca. 5200 B.C.–A.D. 1800, or 7150–150 years B.P.) cultural continuum representing an early population movement from central interior British Columbia that evolved into the ethnographic Interior Salish Indians of the south-central interior. The tradition is characterized by a distinctive micro-blade and prepared-core technology (until ca. 50 B.C., or 2000 years B.P.), a continuity in projectile-point styles, and a related chipping technique marked by an efficient use of raw material and a consistent preference for dark grey to black vitreous basalt. Ca. 1550 B.C. (3500 years B.P.), the semisubterranean pithouse came into use. Decorated objects were in use from the beginning of the tradition, though ethnographic Salish artwork is not evident until ca. 50 B.C. (2000 years B.P.). Ethnographic burial practices have at least a 700-year antiquity (A.D. 1100–1800, or 850–150 years B.P.). The guardian-spirit form of religion was thought to be probably very old in the Nesikep tradition and possibly present in the 5200 B.C. (7150 years B.P.) levels of the Nesikep Creek site. With regard to subsistence, the original proponent, David Sanger (1969), stated "there is nothing . . . to suggest that throughout the entire span of the Nesikep Tradition the subsistence pattern noted in early historic times (1800) did not prevail."

Fieldwork since the mid-1960s, and reevaluation of the original data from the Lochnore Nesikep locality in light of this more recent work, has led to a revised culture-historical model for the region and substantial revision of the Nesikep tradition (Stryd and Rousseau 1996). The Nesikep tradition is now thought to date ca. 5050–2550 B.C. (7000–4500 years B.P.) and to represent an interior ungulate-hunting culture that emerged from a mix of early regional cultural traditions in response to increasingly cooler and wetter environmental conditions toward the end of the Hypsithermal climatic episode. Rabbits, beaver, waterfowl, rodents, salmon, freshwater fish, small birds, turtle (in the South Thompson Valley), and plant resources supplemented the ungulate diet. There is no evidence for the intensive utilization of anadromous salmon. Freshwater mollusks, shunned by the ethnographic Interior Salish, were consumed, mostly during the latter part of the tradition. Pithouses are absent. The Nesikep tradition is thought to represent a non-Salish indigenous people who were eventually absorbed or replaced by Salish people of the Plateau Pithouse tradition, who arrived in the south-central interior starting ca. 3550 B.C. (5500 years B.P.).

There is evidence for technological and stylistic change within the Nesikep tradition, and it is anticipated that the tradition will eventually be divided into a number of named archaeological phases. At present (1996), only the Lehman phase has been defined. It comprises the later part of the Nesikep tradition and dates to ca. 4050–2550 B.C. (6000–4500 years B.P.). The interval prior to the Lehman phase is referred to as the early Nesikep tradition. The early Nesikep tradition is characterized by well-made, lanceolate, corner-notched and barbed projectile points, often with thinned bases with grinding around their edges; a high incidence of formed unifaces; a microblade technology with wedge-shaped microblade cores; antler wedges; ground rodent incisors; bone points and needles; red ocher; and small oval scrapers (formed unifaces), some with bilateral side notches. The points were frequently resharpened; large, well-barbed points represent the initial unmodified form, whereas shorter points with small barbs and shoulders are the result of repeated resharpening.

The Lehman phase appears—on the basis of continuity in projectile point, scraper, and knife styles and continuity in certain technological traits, such as heavy point-base grinding—to represent a development out of the early Nesikep tradition. Typical of the Lehman phase are thin, pentagonal projectile points with obliquely oriented, V-shaped corner or side notches (the Lehman Obliquely Notched point); lanceolate knives with straight cortex-covered bases; elliptical (or leaf-shaped) knives with prominent striking marginal retouch; "horseshoe-shaped" convex end scrapers; multidirection flake cores with medium-to-large flake scars; large but often thin direct percussion flakes; unifacially retouched flakes with cortex or retouch backing; a high incidence of fine- and medium-grained basalts; and an apparent absence of microblade technology.

Arnoud H. Stryd

Further Readings

Sanger, D. 1968. The Chase Burial Site, EeQw:1. In Contributions to Anthropology VI: Archaeology and Physical Anthropology. *National Museums of Canada Bulletin* 224:86:185.

———. 1969. Cultural Traditions in the Interior of British Columbia. *Syesis* 2:189–200.

———. 1970. The Archaeology of the Lochnore-Nesikep Locality, British Columbia. *Syesis* 3 (Supplement no. 1).

Stryd, A.H., and M.K. Rousseau. 1996. The Early Prehistory of the Mid Fraser-Thompson River Area of British Columbia. In *Early Human Occupation in British Columbia,* edited by R.L. Carlson and L. Dalla Bona, pp. 177–204. University of British Columbia Press, Vancouver.

Neville Site

The investigation of the Neville site (27HB77, 27NH38-5) by members of the New Hampshire Archeological Society in 1968 closed a puzzling several-thousand-year "gap" in northeastern prehistory between the Paleoindian and the Late Archaic periods. It established and defined the Middle Archaic cultures in the

Northeast and clarified the cultural sequence of the Late Archaic period.

The site was in Manchester on the east side of the Merrimack River at the Amoskeag Falls. Amoskeag means "fishing place" in the local Algonquian dialects; the excavation showed that fishing began shortly after the formation of the falls ca. 6050 B.C. (8000 years B.P.). At the site, 1.8 m (6 feet) of wind-blown sediments on a high river terrace enclosed the remains left by a series of people since that time. The upper levels of the site revealed artifacts characteristic of the regional Late Archaic (ca. 3050–1050 B.C., or 5000–3000 years B.P.) and Woodland (ca. 1050 B.C.–A.D. 1450, or 3000–500 years B.P.) cultures. The lowest 0.6 m (2 feet), however, contained unfamiliar forms associated with artifacts thought to belong with the Late Archaic materials above. Radiocarbon dates revealed the early Holocene age of the lower deposits, 6050–4050 B.C. (8000–6000 years B.P.). Because no cultures of that age had ever been identified in the Northeast, there was widespread skepticism about the geological and cultural integrity of the site. All began to make sense when the complexes were compared with Middle Archaic cultural assemblages from the Carolinas (ca. 6050–4050 B.C., or 8000–6000 years B.P.).

The integrity of the stratification was supported by geological, chemical, and cultural analyses, and by radiocarbon dates. The stratification of the site in essentially horizontal wind-blown sands resulted in less loss of stratigraphic information than is usual for the expedient salvage excavation methods used. However, because the site was dug in 7.6-cm (3-inch) cuts, few features were observed and recorded; consequently, interpretation of cultural activities at the site was limited.

The first people to settle on the terrace used spear blades—medium-sized, stemmed bifaces with carefully sharpened edges and tips—that were named "Neville" for the site. The rest of the toolkit included some heavy tools and flake tools in styles already ancient, including five types of flake scrapers that were not used later. High concentrations of mercury in the soil implied the catching and processing of anadromous fish. The kinds of tools, and the use-wear on them, imply activities characteristic of base camps occupied during springtime, with little big-game hunting and no hide processing.

In time, the spearhead styles changed into narrower bladed forms called "Stark." Full-

grooved axes, polished-stone spear-thrower weights, adzes, and slate knives with curved blades were added to the inventory sometime before 5050 B.C. (7000 years B.P.). All these heavy forms had previously been assigned conventionally to the Late Archaic period. By the establishment of "Merrimack"-style spear points ca. 4550 B.C. (6500 years B.P.), if not earlier, the people who fished at Amoskeag were living in the immediate area year-round. The site continued as a spring fishing camp until it was abruptly abandoned ca. 4050 B.C. (6000 years B.P.).

The next people at the site came from the west, before 3050 B.C. (5000 years B.P.). Their tools of midwestern style, made of New York State rocks, marked a distinct change from the seaboard connections of the Middle Archaic people. Seaboard cultural forms dominated again after 2550 B.C. (4500 years B.P.). Through the Late Archaic and later periods, the site was used only occasionally; the diversity and density of remains never approached those of the Middle Archaic period. The area was abandoned again in the seventeenth century A.D., when European intruders caused the native people to withdraw to the north. A second reoccupation came with the settlement of Amoskeag by British immigrants in the eighteenth century A.D. Their plow zone churned living floors, artifacts, and features of the final 3,400 years of prehistory.

The cultural sequence established at the Neville site has supported an unprecedented volume of research that has extended the inventory of Middle Archaic seasonal activities and site types and confirmed significant cultural parallels south to the Carolinas and as far north as Labrador.

Dena F. Dincauze

Further Readings

Dincauze, D.F. 1971. An Archaic Sequence for Southern New England. *American Antiquity* 36:194–198.

———. 1976. *The Neville Site: 8,000 Years at Amoskeag*. Monograph no. 4. Peabody Museum of American Archaeology and Ethnology, Harvard University, Cambridge.

Newark Earthworks

The Newark Earthworks (33LI10) are the foremost example of that class of monumental earthworks termed "Sacred Enclosures" by Ephraim G. Squier and Edwin H. Davis in their seminal *Ancient Monuments of the Mississippi Valley* (1848). Located in central Ohio in the valley of Raccoon Creek where it joins the Licking River, the earthworks are on a high, flat, glacial outwash terrace that is surrounded in part by the rolling hills of the glaciated Allegheny Plateau. Because of their size and complexity of form, the earthworks have been considered the work of the Hopewell culture (ca. 300 B.C.–A.D. 500, or 2250–1450 years B.P.), an attribution generally supported by two radiocarbon dates of A.D. 310 ± 90 and A.D. 105 ± 60 (1640 and 1845 years B.P.) from a habitation site excavated in 1980, a single date of 160 B.C. ± 80 (2110 years B.P.) from a buried soil horizon beneath the Great Circle, and two dates of A.D. 300 ± 80 and A.D. 180 ± 80 (1650 and 1770 years B.P.) from a pit feature within the octagonal enclosure (Lepper 1988, 1994). Some elements of the site may be the work of earlier mound-building peoples. In addition to being the largest complex of geometric enclosures in America, the Newark Earthworks are also the northernmost of the great Hopewellian ceremonial centers.

Squier and Davis (1848:67) wrote tellingly that the Newark Earthworks "are so complicated, that it is impossible to give anything like a comprehensible description of them." The site originally consisted of several monumental earthen enclosures of diverse form, including a large circle 336 m (1,102 feet) in diameter, a smaller circle 321 m (1,053 feet) in diameter connected to an octagon that measured ca. 186 m (610 feet) on a side, a nearly perfect square measuring 280 m (919 feet) on a side, and an oval 550 m (1,804.5 feet) in diameter. In addition, depending on whose survey one consults, there were 30–50 secondary enclosures that included small circles and semicircles ranging from 20 to 70 m (65.5–230 feet) in diameter. Much of this earthwork complex was gradually destroyed by agricultural and other activities associated with the growth of the city of Newark, Ohio. Only the Great Circle, the circle and octagon combination, and a minute portion of the square enclosure are preserved in public parks.

The large oval surrounded at least a dozen mounds, many of which yielded human bones and artifacts when they were dug through and destroyed in the nineteenth century. The Great Circle has at its center a group of conjoined mounds that was excavated in 1927. These mounds overlay the remains of a rectangular structure that may have served as a charnel house, although no human remains were recovered from the excavations. The alignments of the circle and octagon combination encode the 18.6-year-long cycle of lunar risings and settings. Whether or not these earthworks functioned as an astronomical observatory, they did bring down to earth a complex celestial choreography. A network of parallel walls 1 m (3.3 feet) high and ca. 80 m (262.5 feet) apart connected these various enclosures. One of these formal roadways extended at least 10 km (6.2 miles) to the southwest; there are indications that this "Great Hopewell Road" connected the Newark Earthworks with the center of the Hopewell world at Chillicothe, Ohio, more than 90 km (55.9 miles) away.

Surprisingly little archaeological research has been undertaken at the Newark Earthworks. As a result, it is difficult to make definitive generalizations about the prehistoric occupation of the site. There are indications that some Hopewellians did live in the immediate vicinity of the enclosures, but the circles, the octagon, and the square likely demarcated special precincts that were separated from the mundane activities of daily life.

Bradley T. Lepper

Further Readings

Hively, R., and R. Horn. 1982. Geometry and Astronomy in Prehistoric Ohio. *Archaeoastronomy* 4:S1–S20.

Hooge, P., and B.T. Lepper (editors). 1992. *Vanishing Heritage: Notes and Queries About the Archaeology and Culture History of Licking County, Ohio.* Licking County Archaeology and Landmarks Society, Newark.

Lepper, B.T. 1988. An Historical Review of Archaeological Research at the Newark Earthworks. *Journal of the Steward Anthropological Society* 18(1–2):118–140.

———. 1994. The Newark Earthworks and the Geometric Enclosures of the Scioto Valley: Connections and Conjectures. In *Hopewell Archaeology: A View From the Core,* edited by P. Pacheco. Ohio Archaeological Council, Columbus.

Salisbury, J.H., and C.B. Salisbury. 1862. Accurate Survey & Descriptions of the Earthworks, Newark, Ohio. Ms. on file, American Antiquarian Society, Worcester.

Smucker, I. 1881. Mound Builders' Works Near Newark, Ohio. *American Antiquarian* 3(4):261–270.

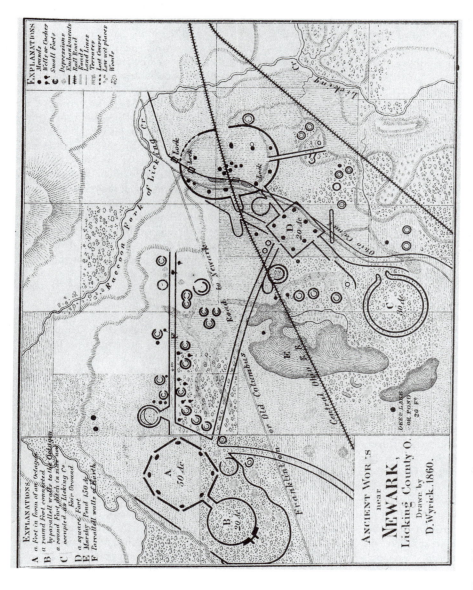

Map of the Newark Earthworks by David Wyrick published in F.W. Beer's (1866) Atlas of Licking County, Ohio. Reproduced with the permission of the Ohio Historical Society.

Squier, E., and E. Davis. 1848. *Ancient Monuments of the Mississippi Valley.* Contributions to Knowledge no. 1. Smithsonian Institution, Washington, D.C.

Thomas, C. 1894. *Report on the Mound Explorations of the Bureau of Ethnology.* Twelfth Annual Report of the Bureau of Ethnology for 1890–1891. Smithsonian Institution, Washington, D.C.

See also HOPEWELL INTERACTION SPHERE

Normative View of Culture

The "normative" conception of culture influenced archaeological research in North America during the first half of the twentieth century. According to this view, a culture is a constellation (a set) of ideas or norms shared by all members of the culture; by implication, members of the culture share similar institutions and material culture. These assumptions committed archaeologists to a search for discrete archaeological cultures identifiable by the presence of similar-appearing assemblages of artifacts and features. Processual archaeologists criticize this view because it is "mentalistic," obscures variety, assumes that differences between cultures merely reflect diversity in cultural norms (rather than, for instance, functional differences), and leads to explanations of material-culture change that stress diffusion of ideas and migration of people with different sets of norms. While processual archaeologists continue to programmatically question the value of the concept of "norm," the concept has always remained of interest to certain schools of cultural anthropology and has experienced new vitality with the inception of interpretive archaeology.

Guy Gibbon

Further Readings

Binford, L.R. 1972. *An Archaeological Perspective.* Seminar Press, New York.

Cordell, L.S., and F. Plog. 1979. Escaping the Confines of Normative Thought: A Reevaluation of Puebloan Prehistory. *American Antiquity* 44:405–429.

Norse in America

During the late tenth century A.D., the Viking-period Norse established colonies along the southwestern coast of Greenland. These colonies existed until the fifteenth century and, for much of the intervening 500 years, had a European population estimated at 3,000–5,000 people. The Norse colonies were located along the southwestern coast of Greenland, only ca. 400 km (250 miles) across Baffin Bay from the northern coast of Labrador. Two Icelandic sagas written during the thirteenth century purport to tell of Norse explorations to the west of Greenland, and European historical records make vague mentions of lands to the west. Over the past centuries, these records have stimulated a great deal of speculation regarding the nature and extent of Norse exploration in North America.

The more reliable of the two sagas relating Norse explorations from Greenland (the "Greenlanders' Saga") tells of six voyages: (1) an accidental discovery of land by a storm-driven ship captained by Bjarni Herjolfsson in the year that the Greenland colonies were established (traditional date A.D. 986); (2) an exploration voyage undertaken a few years later by Leif Eriksson, who named three new lands (from north to south: Helluland, Markland, and Vinland) and built houses in order to winter at the latter location; (3) a further exploration by Leif's brother Thorvald Eriksson, who wintered in Vinland at Leif's houses and was killed the following summer in a skirmish with natives of Markland; (4) an abortive voyage by Thorstein Eriksson to recover his brother's body, which was hindered by storms and did not sight land; (5) an attempt to colonize Vinland undertaken by Thorfinn Karlsefni (the party spent two years at Leif's houses in Vinland, traded with natives of the area, and eventually abandoned their colony after an attack by the natives); (6) a further colonization attempt by Freydis Eiriksdottir, which was abandoned after one year because of disagreement and murder.

Most scholars identify the barren unforested Helluland with Baffin Island or northern Labrador; the low forested Markland with the central coast of Labrador; and Vinland, which is described as having rich forests and even wild grapes, with the general area surrounding the Gulf of St. Lawrence. The latter identification was supported by the discovery of the only known Norse occupation site in the New World on the northern tip of the island of Newfoundland. The site was identified near the fishing village of L'Anse aux Meadows in 1960 by the Norwegian writer Helge Ingstad. Several years of excavation revealed the remains of eight turf-walled structures, including three large dwellings and several small outbuildings of the type built by the Norse in Iceland and Greenland. Artifacts recovered from the site included a large number of iron rivets that may have been used in ship repair, a small stone lamp, a soapstone spindle whorl, a bronze pin, and a few other specimens of Norse technology. The midden deposits associated with the houses were very thin, suggesting that this was not the site of a long-term habitation. The remains suggest an occupation by a few tens of people for a few years and thus are generally consistent with the picture of the Norse Vinland settlements reported in the sagas. Of course, the site cannot be identified with that of Leif Eriksson's houses, but its existence strengthens the view that the Norse Vinland can be identified with the lands around the Gulf of St. Lawrence.

The only other plausible archaeological evidence for Norse visits to temperate North America is a small chert projectile point that was recovered from the eroding Norse graveyard in western Greenland. This artifact conforms to the general style of points used by Indian peoples of southern Labrador and Newfoundland at the time of the Norse settlements. It may have reached Greenland in the body of a Norse visitor to eastern Canada.

Aside from the L'Anse aux Meadows site, only one authentic Norse artifact has been found along the eastern coast of North America. This was a Norse penny minted between A.D. 1065 and 1080, about a half-century after the Vinland voyages mentioned in the sagas. It was recovered from a prehistoric Indian occupation site on the coast of Maine; the site also produced artifacts made from a unique stone from Ramah Bay in far northern Labrador and a distinctive artifact of a type made by the Dorset-culture Paleoeskimos who occupied northern Labrador at that time. It seems plausible that the coin was brought to North America during a late-eleventh-century or twelfth-century Norse voyage to Labrador and that it reached Maine through aboriginal trade routes. A few small pieces of smelted copper have been found in Dorset Paleoeskimo sites in the region, and a voyage to Labrador (the Markland of the sagas) is recorded in an Icelandic annal for the year 1347. It seems likely that the area was visited sporadically in order to obtain timber for use in Greenland.

A number of artifacts that originated in the Greenland colonies have been found in the remains of Thule-period Inuit settlements in Arctic Canada dating to ca. A.D. 950–1450 (1000–500 years B.P.). Most of these specimens are small pieces of smelted iron, copper, or bronze, but they also include fragments of chain mail and woolen cloth as well as pieces of a bronze pot and of a bronze trader's balance. Their wide distribution throughout the eastern Arctic and as far west as the western coast of Hudson Bay reflects movement through aboriginal trade routes. The greatest concentration of such finds comes from sites on the eastern coast of Ellesmere Island in the High Arctic, an area adjacent to Greenland that may have seen direct contact between Norse and Inuit. Direct contact is also suggested by an Inuit carving that appears to represent someone in European dress. It was recovered from a Thule-period village on the south coast of Baffin Island. It has been argued that sporadic contacts and trading may have occurred between the Greenlandic Norse and the Inuit of the eastern Arctic over a period of at least two or three centuries.

Late-twentieth-century archaeological evidence confirms historical and literary hints that the Greenlandic Norse did visit North America, but it also indicates that their exploration and settlement of the New World was neither extensive nor systematic. Archaeology suggests that ca. A.D. 1000 (950 years B.P.) the Norse explored and made at least one brief attempt to establish a settlement in Newfoundland, that for at least the following century they made sporadic visits to the forested coast of Labrador, and that they probably had occasional contacts with the Inuit of the eastern Arctic.

Robert J. McGhee

Further Readings

McGhee, R. 1982. Norsemen and Eskimos in Arctic Canada. In *Vikings in the West,* edited by E. Guralnick, pp. 38–52. Archaeological Institute of America, Chicago.

———. 1984. Contact Between Native North Americans and the Medieval Norse: A Review of Evidence. *American Antiquity* 49:4–26.

Wahlgren, E. 1986. *The Vikings and America.* Thames and Hudson, New York.

Norteño Focus

Most researchers continue to use focus rather than phase to describe Norteño. Norteño occupied north-central Texas, especially the middle reaches of the Red River, the Upper Sabine

River, and the middle Brazos River, and probably dates from sometime around the mid-eighteenth century to the early part of the nineteenth century. The origin of Norteño is uncertain. Suggestions for ancestors have included the Henrietta focus of north-central Texas, the Fort Coffee phase of the Arkansas River Valley Caddo, and the Great Bend aspect of southern Kansas and northern Oklahoma. It has been argued that the focus is associated with the historic Kichai, Tawakoni-Yscani (Iscani), Caddo, or Wichita, generally. Coresidence of these groups during the historic period complicates determining the cultural, or ethnic, affiliation of precontact artifact assemblages.

Norteño sites include large midden accumulations that likely represent villages. Houses have not been defined. However, some sites have been associated with historically documented villages. Faunal studies are rare, but deer, box turtle, and turkey were the major resources at one site. Tools associated with horticultural activities are present but are not prominent. Ceramics are variable. Grit-, bone-, and shell-tempered pottery with plain surfaces predominate. Punctates and engraved designs are common. A variety of vessel forms having flat-to-round bases occur. Bone tools are not common but include awls and bison-scapula hoes. Stone tools include small triangular unnotched points; alternately beveled, diamond-shaped and two-edged knives; end scrapers; and expanding-base drills. Ground stone includes celts, pipes, shaft smoothers, and grinding implements. European-made objects are common and include glass beads, gun parts, bullets and lead balls, iron axes and wedges, metal knives, arrow points, and awls, horse trappings, and brass bells and tinklers. European trade items are common. Southwestern trade items are apparently infrequent and involve mostly turquoise. Red pipestone, Florence-A chert (north-central Oklahoma), Alibates agatized dolomite (Texas Panhandle), and Edwards chert (central Texas) reflect trade with other Plains areas. Novaculite (Ouachita Mountains), conch shell, and Caddoan ceramics reflect contacts to the east. Oliva shell may be of Pacific or Gulf origin. However, the Caddoan material may reflect on-side residence by Caddoan groups.

Susan C. Vehik

Further Readings

Duffield, L.F., and E.B. Jelks. 1961. *The Pearson Site*. Archaeology Series no. 4. Department of Anthropology, University of Texas, Austin.

Harris, R.K., I.M. Harris, J.C. Blaine, and J. Blaine. 1965. A Preliminary Archeological and Documentary Study of the Womack Site, Lamar County, Texas. *Bulletin of the Texas Archeological Society* 36:287–363.

Jelks, E.B. (editor). 1967. The Gilbert Site. *Bulletin of the Texas Archeological Society* 37:1–248.

Northern Archaic Tradition

The Northern Archaic tradition is a taxonomic entity that accommodates a number of middle-to-late Holocene assemblages from northwestern North America that contain side-notched projectile points of continental North American aspect. Northern Archaic projectile weapons presumably were delivered by hand or with a throwing board rather than with a bow. Most Northern Archaic sites are located in the interior Boreal Forest and uplands of Alaska and northwestern Canada west of the Mackenzie River. Other characteristic artifacts include a variety of lanceolate points; large bifaces that presumably functioned as knives; numerous and diverse end scrapers, side scrapers, and utilized flakes; boulder spalls; and tabular schist bifaces. Of rarer occurrence are stemmed projectile points; burins of diverse forms; large edge-notched pebbles that are variously interpreted as axes, net sinkers, or killing clubs; choppers and other heavy cobble implements; stone wedges (*pièces esquillées*); and ground-slate and schist fragments, often worked to no readily apparent standardized shape. Although rarely preserved in the acidic interior soils, the occasional bone or antler artifact fragment suggests considerable skill in shaping hard organics and reminds us of a dimension of Northern Archaic technology that is rarely preserved in sites.

Microblades and microblade cores of ultimate Asiatic derivation, a prominent feature in some earlier and even contemporary northwest North American inventories, are not typical of the Northern Archaic technology. Some of the largest or best controlled Northern Archaic assemblages, for example Onion Portage on Alaska's Kobuk River (Anderson 1988), lack microblades entirely. Nevertheless, microblades occur in association with typical Northern Archaic tools at a modest number of sites, leading some to suggest that their association is the result of cultural contact and occasional technological acculturation with microblade-using technologies. Others believe that mechanical admixture of discrete inventories in the typically shallow and often disturbed interior sites provides a more reasonable explanation for these hybrid industries. Clearly, the basic Northern Archaic lithic-reduction strategy generated flakes, often fairly regular flake blades, rather than microblades.

Poor preservation of organics may explain the virtual absence of art from Northern Archaic assemblages. We know nothing about Northern Archaic burial practices or the physical characteristics of the populations that generated the tradition. Also, due to poor bone preservation, primary data on subsistence activities are very meager. A generalized strategy based on large- and small-game hunting, fishing, and the taking of birds is indicated by the meager evidence, which consists of small amounts of highly fragmented and calcined bone that appears to have been routinely burned, perhaps after boiling to render bone grease. Caribou, moose, mountain sheep, hare, beaver, muskrat, and the like have been identified in site faunas. Hunters of the early Taye Lake phase in southern Yukon also took bison.

Settlement-pattern data are also meager. Several excavated sites are fairly large and rich by interior standards and were occupied over a substantial span of years, suggesting that small bands of Northern Archaic hunters returned repeatedly to the same locations on their yearly rounds. Group size was probably fairly small and populations highly mobile, although perhaps less so than later inhabitants in some of the same areas. Simple ash- and bone-filled hearths, lacking outlining or paving stones, are fairly common, but only a few sites have yielded evidence for dwellings in the form of tent rings or shallow pit foundations for semisubterranean houses. Ground caches are rare or absent.

Northern Archaic sites appear to be the oldest in northwestern Alaska. Tuktu in the Brooks Range has been dated to ca. 4550 B.C. (6500 years B.P.), while the Palisades-Portage sequence at Onion Portage on the Kobuk River is dated by 16 radiocarbon dates to 3850–2150 B.C. (5800–4100 years B.P.), with the possibly derivative Itkillik complex making a brief appearance ca. A.D. 550 (1400 years B.P.). The long-lived Taye Lake phase in southern Yukon appears significantly younger; it is dated to 3050/2550 B.C.–A.D. 650 (5000/4500–1300

years B.P.). Radiocarbon dates on Northern Archaic material are compatible with a south and eastward spread of people from northern Alaska through interior Alaska to the southern Yukon.

Most workers recognize the strong probability that the respectably old side-notched projectile points characteristic of the Northern Archaic are genetically connected to even older notched points that first appear in the early Holocene (7050–5550 B.C., or 9000–7500 years B.P.) in continental North America. Prototypes for this characteristically North American implement form are lacking in the north and adjacent Asia. Various scenarios involving diffusion of technology or migration of peoples have been advanced to explain the presence of these projectile points. As for the Northern Archaic technology as a whole, some would root it in antecedent early Holocene, northwest North American technologies, such as the American Paleoarctic or the Northern Cordilleran Plano, while others, perhaps a minority, see it as imported as a complex without local antecedents by migration from the south and east. As of the mid-1990s, the typological evidence for all of these positions was weak, although it should be noted that few convincing typological connections can be demonstrated with antecedent, contemporary, or later coastal technologies. Northern Archaic peoples appear to have been adapted to, or at least tolerant of, the harsh, sparse, Boreal Forest environment as opposed to the northern tundras and coasts. A number of workers believe that the Northern Archaic technology was produced, at least in part, by the ancestors of the modern Athapaskans; that is, that Northern Archaic peoples spoke Nadene (or proto-Nadene) languages. In southern Yukon, the Taye Lake phase seems to evolve smoothly into the Late Prehistoric Aishihik phase, which dates after ca. A.D. 650 (1300 years B.P.). The Aishihik phase is, in turn, clearly ancestral to the ethnographic southern Tutahone.

The most complete evidence for the chronology and internal development of the Northern Archaic tradition comes from the Palisades and Portage complexes at the beautifully stratified and well-dated Onion Portage site on the Kobuk River, with related Palisades material in an unusual, near-coastal setting at Cape Krusenstern. The possibly older Tuktu complex in Anaktuvuk Pass differs from typical assemblages in its possession of a well-developed microblade industry, and contains, according to Douglas Anderson (1988), materials typical of several chronologically discrete Northern Archaic complexes at Onion Portage, where microblades are conspicuously absent. A number of other Alaskan collections, often small, undated, or of problematical status, might also be assigned to the Northern Archaic. The fairly well-documented Taye Lake complex in southern Yukon appears to be strikingly similar to Palisades at Onion Portage and to be related to the Old Chief complex in northern Yukon. Northern Archaic affinities might also be suggested for the Julian and Mackenzie complexes in the Fisherman's Lake area, southern Mackenzie district.

William B. Workman

Further Readings

Anderson, D. 1988. *Onion Portage: The Archaeology of a Stratified Site From the Kobuk River, Northwest Alaska.* Anthropological Papers of the University of Alaska, vol. 22, nos. 1–2. University of Alaska Press, Fairbanks.

Clark, D.W. 1981. Prehistory of the Western Subarctic. In *Subarctic*, edited by J. Helm, pp. 107–129. Handbook of North American Indians, vol. 6, W.C. Sturtevant, general editor. Smithsonian Institution, Washington, D.C.

———. 1991. *Western Subarctic Prehistory.* Canadian Prehistory Series. Canadian Museum of Civilization, Hull.

Workman, W.B. 1977. The Prehistory of the Southern Tutahone Area. In *Problems in the Prehistory of the North American Subarctic: The Athapaskan Question,* edited by J.W. Helmer, J. Van Dyke, and F.J. Kense, pp. 46–61. Archaeological Association, University of Calgary, Calgary.

———. 1978. *Prehistory of the Aishihik-Kluane Area, Southwest Yukon Territory.* Mercury Series Paper no. 74. Archaeological Survey of Canada, National Museum of Man, Ottawa.

Northern (Canadian) Plateau

The Northern (or Canadian) Plateau covers the intermountain zone of south-central British Columbia and north-central Washington State, an area inhabited at contact (ca. A.D. 1808) by groups speaking Interior Salish or Athapaskan languages. Kootenay-speaking peoples also dwelled on the eastern periphery of the Northern Plateau. The margins of the Northern Plateau are marked by the Coast Range on the west, the Columbia Mountains on the east, a line ca. 65 km (40 miles) below the international border on the south, and roughly 52°30' north latitude. The area consists of gently rolling uplands of low relief, measuring 1,300–1,700 m (4,263–5,577 feet) in elevation, separated by deeply incised river and lake valleys, and intermittent highlands and mountain ranges rising to 2,500 m (8,202 feet). Most of the area lies within the Fraser River drainage basin. The southern portion is drained by the middle and upper reaches of the Columbia River, and the western edge of the Chilcotin Plateau in the northwest by streams flowing through the Coast Mountains, which empty directly into the sea.

The alternating highlands and river valleys show altitudinal zonation of flora and fauna and a rich diversity of local habitats, ranging from semiarid to alpine. The entire area is in the rain shadow of the Coast Mountains and has an average annual precipitation of 25–30 cm (10–12 inches). Six "biogeoclimatic" zones, characterized by distinctive vegetation, soils, topography and climate, are present. The Ponderosa Pine–Bunchgrass zone covers hot, dry valley floors south of 51°31' north latitude. To the north, the Caribou Aspen–Lodgepole Pine zone predominates. Throughout the area, middle elevations to 1,350 m (4,428 feet) support the Interior Douglas Fir zone, and a Western Hemlock zone appears above it in moister eastern regions. The Engelmann Spruce–Subalpine Fir zone occurs at subalpine elevations, and Alpine Tundra is present above the tree line.

Northern Plateau native groups at contact had a generally riverine focus, with a semisedentary winter pithouse village settlement pattern and subsistence relying primarily on salmon, ungulates, and wild roots. Their variable degrees of sedentism and population density seem related to proximity and access to salmon-bearing drainage systems. The ethnographic subsistence-settlement pattern extends back in time to 2050–1050 B.C. (4000–3000 years B.P.).

Archaeological investigations of the Northern Plateau began in 1877, when George Dawson recorded archaeological and ethnographic sites while conducting geological surveys. The first intentional research was carried

N

out by Harlan Smith for the American Museum of Natural History's Jesup North Pacific Expedition from 1897 to 1899. However, systematic excavations did not occur until the late 1950s. The period since the late 1960s has been one of expanded research activity. Archaeological investigations have been conducted in most regions of the Northern Plateau to document the presence of archaeological material, and growing effort has been directed to a further understanding of basic problems, such as culture history, prehistoric cultural ecology, and regional subsistence-settlement studies.

The Fraser and Columbia river basins demarcate two archaeological subareas distinguished by environment and culture history. The major difference is in anadromous fish resources, with salmon runs in the middle and Upper Columbia drainage considerably less dense than those in the Fraser River system. Within these two subareas, a number of archaeological regions are identified on the basis of artifact inventories and adaptations to local environments. Notwithstanding the local and regional sequences, Northern Plateau prehistory can be partitioned into three main periods—Early period (ca. 9050–5050 B.C., or 11,000–7000 years B.P.); Middle period (ca. 5050–1550 B.C., or 7000–3500 years B.P.); and Late period (ca. 1550 B.C.–A.D. 1750, or 3500–200 years B.P.)—that monitor changes from initial occupation by mobile foraging groups to the development of a riverine adaptation that culminates in the semisedentary way of life observed at contact.

David L. Pokotylo

Further Readings

Fladmark, K.R. 1982. An Introduction to the Prehistory of British Columbia. *Canadian Journal of Archaeology* 6:95–156.

Richards, T.H., and M.K. Rousseau. 1987. *Late Prehistoric Cultural Horizons on the Canadian Plateau.* Publication no. 16. Department of Archaeology, Simon Fraser University, Burnaby.

Stryd, A.H., and M.K. Rousseau. 1996. The Early Prehistory of the Mid Fraser-Thompson River Area of British Columbia. In *Early Human Occupation in British Columbia*, edited by R. Carlson and L. Dalla Bona, pp. 177–204. University of British Columbia Press, Vancouver.

Northern Cordilleran Tradition

The "Northern Cordilleran" concept proposed by D. Clark (1983) can be traced to the Cordilleran tradition of Richard S. MacNeish (1959, 1964), but it is more limited in its geographic scope though both incorporate evidence from northwestern Canada. MacNeish envisioned the Cordilleran as a Paleowestern tradition distinguishable from the Plano tradition, which it both overlapped and preceded temporally and from which it was largely separate in space.

Few archaeologists accepted this poorly defined entity, which was purportedly characterized by prismatic blades (but no microblade industry), leaf-shaped projectile points and knives, and flake burins. It was almost wholly undated but had a proposed antiquity of 10,050–6050 B.C. (12,000–8000 years B.P.) to even 12,050 B.C. (14,000 years B.P.). Nevertheless, by the 1970s, some archaeologists theorized that the prehistory of the western Subarctic prior to the Northern Archaic tradition, which began ca. 4000 B.C. (5950 years B.P.), could not all be subsumed within the microblade-using American Paleoarctic tradition, which began ca. 8600 B.C. (10,550 years B.P.). The Plano tradition, to consider a more established alternative to the Northern Cordilleran, did not offer a fully satisfactory alternative explanation of this additional diversity in the north because of inexact typological correspondences and the purported age of Northern Plano points (which often turned out to date to less than 50 B.C., or 2000 years B.P.), and because the term "Plano" implies migration from the Plains or at least an archaeological development that diffused northward.

By the beginning of the 1980s, several components characterized by lanceolate points but lacking microblades had been discovered in the territory stretching from Great Bear Lake, Northwest Territories, to the Bering Strait. Examples are Acasta, Northwest Territories; Basal Canyon, Yukon; and Mesa, Alaska. All three of these components have been radiocarbon dated to 7000–5000 B.C. (8950–6950 years B.P.). To this list of dates might be added northern fluted points, those found both with and without associated microblades, which are poorly dated to 9000–7000 B.C. (10,950–8950 years B.P.); Flint Creek of the northern Yukon, one of MacNeish's original Cordilleran components, that has been more recently dated to 7800 B.C. (9750 years B.P.) (Cinq-Mars et al. 1991); and the Chindadn component of Healy Lake, which has been roughly dated to 9000–7000 B.C. (10,950–8950 years B.P.) and in which microblades are relatively scarce. Earlier authors generally had little to say about the place of these complexes in North American prehistory.

In addition to the theories noted above, there is still another explanation. Evidence from this period has also come from several sites in the Tanana drainage in Alaska. These early occupations are not only nonmicroblade but also premicroblade in the sense that they predate the Paleoarctic tradition as defined around its core feature, a microblade industry based on wedge-shaped cores. It has been termed the Nenana complex (Gobel et al. 1991; Hoffecker et al. 1993), though the term "complex" is unnecessarily restrictive since related material is known and dated from several sites. An alternative explanation is that the so-called Northern Cordilleran complexes of a later period are derived from northern antecedents, specifically from the Nenana complex and any conjoiners of 9300–9000 B.C. (11,250–10,950 years B.P.) that occupied the region then known as Beringia. Broadly interpreted in the sense of a tradition, Nenana may be viewed as an early part of a Northern Cordilleran tradition. As of 1996, archaeologists working with Nenana material had refrained, in print, from relating Nenana to any of the more recent nonmicroblade complexes, while at the same time they had proposed that Nenana is closely related to the initial late Pleistocene occupation of Beringia and to ancestral Clovis (fluted-point Paleoindian).

One likely scenario is that a spread of Asian microblade technology or people (the Dyuktai culture) from Siberia into Alaska progressively replaced Nenana technology or people (e.g., early Northern Cordilleran). This would have occurred on a more or less west-to-east time slope (Clark 1983, 1991a, 1991b). The spread of the early microblade industry, termed the American Paleoarctic in North America, slowed in the western Yukon and stalled in some areas where the Northern Cordilleran would have persisted well into the Holocene. In the north at Engigstiack, for instance, where the Flint Creek component is dated at 7800 B.C. (9750 years B.P.), there is no evidence of any preceding or succeeding Paleoarctic occupation. There was a later Paleoarctic occupation of the southern Yukon ca. 5000 B.C. (6950 years B.P.) that eventually extended eastward to the southwestern Mackenzie district. Elsewhere in western Mackenzie and northern Alberta, late assemblages containing microblades are suggestive of technological diffusion rather than migration. By that time, American Paleoarctic microblade technology had waned in many areas of interior Alaska. It was succeeded by complexes characterized by lanceolate points, which are found from the Susitna Valley in the south northward and across the Brooks Range. This author (Clark 1991a, 1991b) has interpreted this occurrence as a reexpansion of late Northern Cordilleran technology and perhaps peoples. An alternative explanation, which does not appear to fit the data, is that these assemblages are simply task-specific Paleoarctic assemblages that for functional reasons lack microblades.

The later Northern Archaic tradition may be seen primarily as a development out of this proposed late Northern Cordilleran base ca. 4050 B.C. (6000 years B.P.). The premise that the Northern Archaic is not directly sequential to the Paleoarctic has not been generally accepted by prehistorians, nor has that of a Northern Cordilleran, especially one that is, in its varied aspects, both antecedent to the American Paleoarctic and in some ways responsible for its demise. The varied, nonhomogeneous evidence brought together under this label is a congeries of data assembled for the bearing it has on certain models of northwestern North American prehistory.

Donald W. Clark

Further Readings

Cinq-Mars, J., C.R. Harington, D.E. Nelson, and R.S. MacNeish. 1991. *Engigstiack Revisited: A Note on Early Holocene AMS Dates From the "Buffalo Pit,"* edited by J. Cinq-Mars and J.-L. Pilon. Occasional Paper no. 1. Canadian Archaeological Association.

Clark, D.W. 1983. Is There a Northern Cordilleran Tradition? *Canadian Journal of Archaeology* 7(1):23–48.

———. 1991a. The Northern (Alaska-Yukon) Fluted Points. In *Clovis: Origins and Adaptations*, edited by R. Bonnichsen and K. Turnmire, pp. 35–48. Center for the Study of the First Americans, Oregon State University, Corvallis.

———. 1991b. *Western Subarctic Prehistory*. Canadian Prehistory Series. Canadian Museum of Civilization, Hull.

Goebel, T., W.R. Powers, and N. Bigelow. 1991. The Nenana Complex of Alaska and Clovis Origins. In *Clovis: Origins and Adaptations*, edited by R. Bonnichsen and K. Turnmire, pp. 49–79. Center for the Study of the First Americans, Oregon State University, Corvallis.

Hoffecker, J.F., W.R. Powers, and T. Goebel. 1993. The Colonization of Beringia and the Peopling of the New World. *Science* 259:46–53.

MacNeish, Richard S. 1959. Man Out of Asia, As Seen From the Northwest Yukon. *Anthropological Papers of the University of Alaska* 7(2):41–70.

———. 1964. Investigations in Southwest Yukon: Archaeorical Excavations, Comparisons, and Speculations. *Papers of the Robert S. Peabody Foundation for Archaeology* 6(2 xii):199–488.

Northern Great Basin Wetland and Lakeside Adaptations

The high desert of the northern Great Basin is a region of hydrological contrasts. Some of the enclosed basins in the region are extremely dry, while others contain extensive systems of streams, marshes, and lakes. The "wet" basins include Harney Basin, Warner Valley, the Lake Abert–Chewaucan Marsh Basin, and Silver Lake Valley in Fort Rock Basin, all in Oregon. These wetland areas contain many plant and animal resources and, based on archaeological evidence, have been used by human populations of the region since the early Holocene. The intensity of use varied over time and is correlated to some degree with environmental changes that affected the amount of effective moisture in the region.

The Klamath (on the western periphery of the northern Great Basin) and the Wada'tika Northern Paiute (Harney Basin) used wetland resources and provide ethnographic models for considering archaeological evidence (Aikens and Greenspan 1988; Oetting 1989). Both groups employed tethered settlement-subsistence systems, with lowland winter villages and seasonal dispersal of family groups. The Klamath were more sedentary, maintaining winter villages near wetlands. There, large semisubterranean pithouses were reoccupied annually by the same families. The economy focused on fish and wokas (pond lily seeds) and included marsh/meadow root crops (camas, wapato,

tule, cattail), waterfowl, and aquatic mammals. The Wada'tika used less substantial winter villages with brush-and-pole wickiups. Village locations and residents might vary annually. Families were mobile much of the year, hunting and moving about to harvest scattered seed and root resources. Wetland resources included waada seeds (a lakeside chenopod), camas and other roots, waterfowl, nearby grasslands (giant wildrye, Indian rice grass, blazing star), and terrestrial mammals drawn to the wet meadows and marshes.

Clovis and stemmed points found on old shorelines indicate that resources from lake and marsh locales were utilized in the early Holocene. However, the first intensive use of the wetlands coincided with the Neopluvial, a period of increased moisture marking the beginning of the Medithermal (2550 B.C., or 4500 years B.P.), and continued until Late Prehistoric times.

Large sites with diverse faunal, botanical, and artifact assemblages begin to appear ca. 2550 B.C. (4500 years B.P.) in and near lake, marsh, and riverine settings in the region. Some also contain circular depressions or rock rings of varying sizes. Such sites are found in all of the wet basins but are not present in neighboring basins that lack wetlands (Weide 1978; Aikens 1993). Cultural assemblages include remains of fish, waterfowl, and aquatic and shoreline plants, as well as artifacts such as fishhooks, net or line weights, and large numbers of groundstone tools (Greenspan 1990; Aikens 1993). Excavations in the depressions and rock rings have demonstrated that many were houses (pithouses or wickiups) (Oetting 1989; Musel 1992).

There are more than 300 archaeological sites, including 76 with houses, in the Lake Abert–Chewaucan Marsh Basin alone (Oetting 1989). Settlement-pattern studies have found that sites older than 50 B.C. (2000 years B.P.) were located in diverse settings across the basin, but sites less than 50 B.C. (2000 years B.P.) were primarily situated near wetland areas. All of the pithouse-village sites were located adjacent to wetlands. Some of these villages were occupied by 2050 B.C. (4000 years B.P.), but most were used after 50 B.C. (2000 years B.P.). Similar settlement locations have been observed in Warner Valley, where the basin lakes and marshes are bordered by pithouse villages and large processing sites (Weide 1968; Cannon et al. 1990). Faunal remains at the processing sites include clamshells, eggshells, and fish, toad, and terrestrial mammal bones. Sites on the shores of Silver Lake and along now-dry overflow channels to the north yielded fish and toad bones; freshwater snail shells; seeds of waada, goosefoot, and sedges; and fishhooks, gorges, and stone net sinkers (Aikens and Jenkins 1994). Housepits at these sites contained living floors, hearths, and storage pits and date to 2930 B.C.–A.D. 1250 (4880–700 years B.P.) in Harney Basin. Large sites with high densities of artifacts are located on the edges of Malheur Lake, Blitzen Marsh, and Diamond Swamp (Aikens and Greenspan 1988; Oetting 1990). Several types of net sinkers are found in the diverse artifact assemblages. Test excavations have revealed a variety of faunal remains, with several species of fish, aquatic mammals, and some waterfowl. Several sites dating to 1305 B.C.–A.D. 1470 (3255–480 years B.P.) have housepits with living floors and other features (Musil 1992).

The locations of these sites near wetlands, the presence of specialized artifacts, and direct evidence from faunal and floral remains suggest that subsistence pursuits were focused on the varied plant and animal resources of the adjacent wetlands. The larger multiple-activity sites with house features have been interpreted as annually reoccupied (semisedentary) winter villages. Although wetland resources were a primary economic focus of these populations, they were not the exclusive economic focus of the people. Archaeological research in the uplands around Warner Valley and Silver Lake Valley has found pithouse-village sites in upland settings near extensive plant-gathering areas, suggesting that while the lowland lakes were the main focus of subsistence activity during some parts of the year, upland root and seed plant plots were an important secondary focus of activity, especially in late spring and summer.

Settlement-subsistence patterns changed between A.D. 950 and 1650 (1000–300 years B.P.). Sites dating to this late period in Warner Valley and the Harney Basin suggest a more mobile settlement system, based on less substantial and less diverse artifact assemblages and smaller, less labor-intensive houses (shifting from pithouses to wickiups) (Weide 1968; Musil 1992). These have been interpreted as adaptive responses to increasing aridity, with groups coping by becoming more mobile, using a wider variety of resources, and covering a wider area to secure those resources. Others, emphasizing social factors, suggest that groups

adapted to wetlands resources withdrew from the region because of the changing environment, leaving the basins open to more desert-adapted people, or were forced to withdraw because of increasing pressure from these groups (Aikens and Witherspoon 1986; Oetting 1989).

The Great Basin has traditionally been viewed as an arid wasteland populated by small, hardy bands of hunter-gatherers who moved constantly over the landscape to obtain scattered, unpredictable food resources. The discovery of large, possibly semisedentary sites and specialized economic adaptations focused on Great Basin wetland settings initially surprised archaeologists. Such evidence, however, simply reaffirms that Great Basin peoples made effective use of the resources available in their home territories.

Albert C. Oetting

Further Readings

Aikens, C.M. 1993. *Archaeology of Oregon.* 2nd ed. Oregon State Office, Bureau of Land Management, Portland.

Aikens, C.M., and R.L. Greenspan. 1988. Ancient Lakeside Culture in the Northern Great Basin: Malheur Lake, Oregon. *Journal of California and Great Basin Anthropology* 10(1):32–61.

Aikens, C.M., and D.L. Jenkins (editors). 1994. *Archaeological Researches in the Northern Great Basin: Fort Rock Archaeology Since Cressman.* Anthropological Papers no. 50. Department of Anthropology and State Museum of Anthropology, University of Oregon, Eugene.

Aikens, C.M., and Y.T. Witherspoon. 1986. Great Basin Numic Prehistory: Linguistics, Archaeology, and Environment. In *Anthropology of the Desert West: Essays in Honor of Jesse D. Jennings,* edited by C.J. Condie and D.D. Fowler, pp. 7–20. Anthropological Papers no. 110. University of Utah Press, Salt Lake City.

Cannon, W.J., C.C. Creger, D.D. Fowler, E.M. Hattori, and M.F. Ricks. 1990. A Wetlands and Uplands Settlement-Subsistence Model for Warner Valley, Oregon. In *Wetland Adaptations in the Great Basin,* edited by J.C. Janetski and D.B. Madsen, pp. 173–182. Occasional Papers no. 1. Museum of Peoples and Cultures, Brigham Young University, Provo.

N

Greenspan, R.L. 1990. Prehistoric Fishing in the Northern Great Basin. In *Wetland Adaptations in the Great Basin,* edited by J.C. Janetski and D.B. Madsen, pp. 207–232. Occasional Papers no. 1. Museum of Peoples and Cultures, Brigham Young University, Provo.

Musil, R.R. 1992. *Adaptive Transitions and Environmental Change in the Northern Great Basin: A View From Diamond Swamp.* Unpublished Ph.D. dissertation, Department of Anthropology, University of Oregon, Eugene.

Oetting, A.C. 1989. *Villages and Wetlands Adaptations in the Northern Great Basin: Chronology and Land Use in the Lake Abert-Chewaucan Marsh Basin, Lake County Oregon.* Anthropological Papers no. 41. Department of Anthropology, University of Oregon, Eugene.

———. 1990. *The Malheur Lake Survey: Lacustrine Archaeology in the Harney Basin, Central Oregon.* Heritage Research Associates Report no. 96 to Malheur National Wildlife Refuge, U.S. Fish and Wildlife Service. Heritage Research Associates, Eugene.

Weide, M.L. 1968. *Cultural Ecology of Lakeside Adaptation in the Western Great Basin.* Ph.D. dissertation, Department of Anthropology, University of California, Los Angeles.

———. 1978. On the Correspondence Between Villages and Wetlands in the Great Basin. *Journal of California Anthropology* 5(2):289–292.

Northern Plano Culture

Related to the Plano culture of the Plains to the south, specifically Agate Basin, Northern Plano is, as of the mid-1990s, best known from sites in the southern Keewatin district of the Northwest Territories. There is also evidence from southeastern Manitoba of a related cultural adaptation to the boreal resources of the western margins of the Canadian Shield, which was progressively being freed of ice and water impediments to human colonization. The Northern Plano culture dates to ca. 7050–6050 B.C. (9000–8000 years B.P.) (Gordon 1996). Technological, settlement-pattern, and inferred-subsistence evidence suggests that the Northern Plano people, as well as related peoples in Manitoba and environs, were the ancestors of the subsequent Shield culture. This adaptation to latitudinal tundra, lichen-woodland, and Boreal Forest vegetation provinces would have required certain archaeologically invisible technologies such as portable watercraft, snowshoes, and sleds and/or toboggans.

While Northern Plano projectile points are indistinguishable from those on the Plains, the rest of the toolkit differs in a number of respects, with chipped- and ground-stone adzes, a distinctive flat scraping tool called a *chi thos*, wedges (multipurpose slotting-scraping burins), and other categories of tools either absent or rare on the Plains. The burination of broken projectile points in order to resharpen scraping and slotting edges and corners is another characteristic northern trait. Unlike in the Plains, the practice of cooking with heated rocks was common. However, other than small calcined fragments, bone preservation is lacking, and, as with most human occupation of the Canadian Shield, subsistence must be inferred from settlement-pattern evidence. For example, major sites are situated at caribou-herd river and lake crossings, with locations varying from favorable ambush topography, to high-banked river-crossing constrictions, to highland locales with broad vistas of the countryside. Single-family-tent floors, 4–5 m (13.1–16.4 feet) in diameter and demarcated by weight stones, hearth floors, and chipped detritus concentrations, have been recorded. Frequently associated with sites are swifts and rapids that to this day are rich in schools of lake trout and grayling. Sites were occupied in the summer in proximity to caribou calving grounds and migration routes. There is some settlement-pattern evidence to suggest that, by late summer, people would have followed the caribou herds to their wintering grounds in the forest of southeastern Mackenzie district and adjacent Saskatchewan.

To date (1996), there is little evidence for contacts with other bands as would be reflected in the presence of exotic lithics with known geological sources. Ubiquitous quartzite cobbles were the dominant raw materials for tool manufacture. If the movement between summer caribou calving grounds in northeastern Keewatin district to caribou wintering grounds to the southeast is an accurate interpretation of the evidence, then the hunting ranges of individual bands were exceptionally extensive. Eventual sourcing of a range of quartzites, basalts, and cherts will likely throw light on intraband relationships.

The general transformation of Northern Plano culture into early Shield culture in the western Canadian Shield is seen as a progressive adaptation to the forested and interconnected waterways of the region beginning ca. 7050 B.C. (9000 years B.P.). Some archaeologists speculate that another major change involved the replacement of the thrusting spear by spear thrower-weapon technology, which appears to have been developed in southeastern North America prior to 8050 B.C. (10,000 years B.P.).

J.V. Wright

Further Readings

Gordon, B.C. 1981. Man-Environment Relationships in Barrenland Prehistory. *Musk-Ox* 28:1–19. Institute for Northern Studies, University of Saskatchewan, Saskatoon.

———. 1996. *People of Sunlight, People of Starlight: Barrenland Archaeology in the Northwest Territories of Canada.* Mercury Series Paper no. 154. Archaeological Survey of Canada, Canadian Museum of Civilization, Hull.

Wright, J.V. 1976. *The Grant Lake Site, Keewatin District, N.W.T.* Mercury Series Paper no. 47. Archaeological Survey of Canada, National Museum of Man, Ottawa.

See also SHIELD CULTURE

Northwest Coast Culture Area

Although all culture-area schemes have readily recognized the distinctiveness of the Northwest Coast of North America, there has been less agreement about its boundaries as a culture area. Its eastern edge is consistently put at the Coast/Cascade Mountain ranges (with the territories of the Nishga and Gitksan peoples along the "interior" reaches of the Nass and the Skeena rivers an exception), and its northern edge at the Copper River in Alaska. To the south, however, the position of the tribes of northwest California has been equivocal. Included by A.L. Kroeber and by Philip Drucker (Drucker 1963, 1965), they were omitted in the later survey edited by Wayne Suttles (Suttles 1990). We have followed this more recent practice and extend the border of the culture area only as far south as the Oregon seaboard.

The region is environmentally distinctive. It is a relatively narrow coastal strip that is well watered by the prevailing westerlies, which are forced to discharge copious amounts of moisture as they lift over the backdrop of high mountains. Abundant rain and mild winter temperatures provide for lush vegetation—a true temperate rain forest carpets the land from saltwater shoreline to high up mountain slopes. The southern third of the coast borders directly on the open Pacific Ocean. Shelter here is provided only by the occasional river estuary or bay. The northern two-thirds is largely archipelago and, as a result, is distinguished by its long, protected waterways. Channels wind among the islands, and fjords reach deep into the coastal mountains.

The dense coastal forest was home to comparatively few plants and animals that were of importance to the region's human occupants, with the western red cedar being the notable exception. It was valued for its bark (the fibers were used for cordage, mats, and clothing) and for its long-lasting and easily split and carved wood, from which canoes, houses, boxes, commemorative poles, masks, and many other items of the distinctive Northwest Coast material culture were produced. Berries (cranberry, Oregon grape, salal, huckleberry, and salmon berry) were present at the edge of the forest, in river floodplains, and in clearings caused by periodic fires. Such areas also supported a population of coast deer. Goats were on mainland mountain slopes; elk herds were present on island and mainland heights and seasonally on lowland prairies. The principal subsistence resources, however, came not from the land but from the sea and the many rivers and streams that flowed in or through this area of great precipitation. From the sea came sea mammals (seal, porpoise, and whale), fish (cod, rockfish, salmon, herring, and halibut), and a host of waterfowl; from the beaches, intertidal invertebrates (clams, mussels, abalone, crabs, sea urchin, and sea cucumber); and from the rivers, salmon (the most important resource) and eulachon.

All but the southernmost portion of the coast and a few isolated refugia were deeply buried in ice during the Wisconsin glaciation (ca. 150,000–12,000 years B.P.). Glaciers did not substantially withdraw until ca. 11,000–10,000 B.C. (12,950–11,950 years B.P.). Subsequent warming saw a general rise of sea level and drowning of what had been in places a broad coastal plain. Vegetation, at first dominated by pine forest, gave way to mixed stands of hemlock, fir, and cedar. Something approaching modern conditions was reached during the

Table 1. Northwest Coast regional sequences. (Table by D. H. Mitchell)

B.P.	Southeast Alaska	Kitselas Canyon	Fraser River Canyon	The Dalles	Portland Basin	Columbia Estuary	Willamette Valley	Southern Northwest Coast
200								
500	Late Period	?	Canyon					Formative
1000		Kleanza					Late Archaic	
2000			Skamel					Late Archaic
3000	Middle Period	Paul Mason / Skeena	Baldwin					
4000		Gitaus					Middle Archaic	Middle Archaic
5000		Bornite	Charles					
6000								
7000			Old Cordilleran					
8000	Early Period						Early Archaic	Early Archaic
9000								
10,000								
12,000							Paleoindian	Pre-Archaic

5000–2000 B.C. (6950–3950 years B.P.) period.

Characteristics of the distinctive culture that was using this environment at the time of contact (ca. A.D. 1780) can be summarized as follows:

1. Subsistence was based largely on marine, foreshore, and riverine resources, with river-run Pacific salmon of special importance.
2. A wide range of devices and techniques

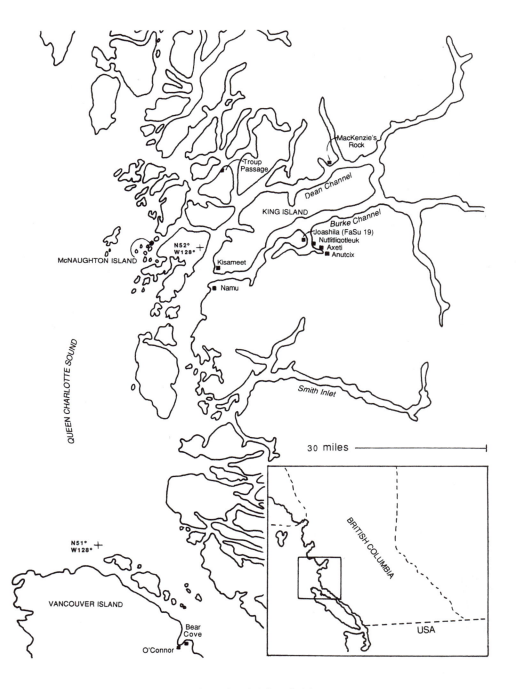

Central British Columbia Coast. (Drawn by Deborah Schoenholz)

existed for harvesting these resources, including spears, harpoons, gaffs, weirs, and traps and nets of many kinds. Special devices were used at specific kinds of locations for specific purposes.

3. There was an efficient preservation technology based mainly on drying and/or smoking that permitted at least short-term storage of seasonally plentiful fish, shellfish, and fruit. Sea mammal and fish oils were important additions to the dried-food diet. They were rendered and available for somewhat longer-term storage.

4. Many prominent items of material culture came from the cedar tree. Roots were used for basket manufacture and heavy cordage; bark fibers for lighter cordage, mats, and clothing; and trunk wood shaped by adzing or splitting to form posts, beams, and roof and wall planks for the large houses. Cedar planks were formed into back rests, lounging platforms, and storage and cooking boxes. Cedar and other woods were carved to form rattles, bowls, and dishes. Larger carved products included graceful and ornamental dugout canoes—some of considerable size, and, in at least the central and northern parts of the coast, sculptured figures and columns.

5. Settlements were seasonal, with the pattern usually involving winter residence in a village of 400–500 occupants and spring, summer, and fall dispersal to smaller villages and camps at various resource locations. However, there was great variation in the seasonal settlement pattern, with some very large aggregations occurring where resources were particularly rich.

6. Societies were kin based at what is best seen as a tribal level of organization (local groups, social units that shared a common winter village, were politically autonomous), but, unusual for tribal societies, economic classes were also present, as was the institution of slave labor.

7. Ceremonial life was rich and intimately connected with economic and religious activities. Masked or costumed dancers figured prominently at occasions marking important events in the lives of upper-class villagers. They also performed at cycles of religion-based winter dances in portions of the central and northern coast. A special form of ceremonial feast common to the same areas is usually referred to as the potlatch. It involved distribution of wealth and food to guests assembled to witness some action of the host, such as the assumption of an inherited or otherwise acquired name or "title," the completion of a new house, or the launching of a new canoe.

8. While there was much variation in emphasis, decoration and ornamentation of objects, even utilitarian objects, were

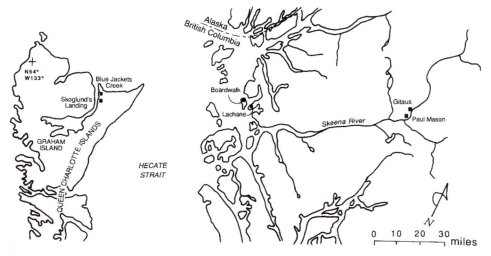

Queen Charlotte Islands/Skeena River. (Drawn by Deborah Schoenholz)

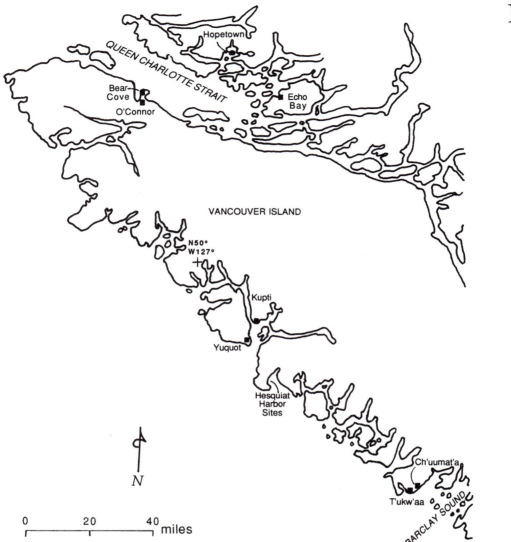

South Central British Columbia Coast/West Coast Vancouver Island. (Drawn by Deborah Schoenholz)

common. The exuberance of the northern Northwest Coast art style is well known.

Hypotheses about the origins of this distinctive area culture type dominated early works on the prehistory of the Northwest Coast. The earliest systematic excavations were those at the turn of the century by Charles Hill-Tout (1895) and Harlan Smith (1903, 1907), whose work on the coast concentrated on sites in Salishan territory in the Lower Fraser River Valley and southeastern Vancouver Island. Smith's explorations here and in the adjacent interior of British Columbia led him to view similarities between middle and Lower Fraser River assemblages as evidence of diffusion or migration from the interior to the coast—thus suggesting an interior origin for Northwest Coast culture and the mouth-of-the-Fraser-Salishan location for the earliest appearance of the distinctive coastal culture. These themes were reasserted by Kroeber (1923, 1939) in the 1920s and 1930s, and, although little or no further work had been done in the Salishan area, remained evident in

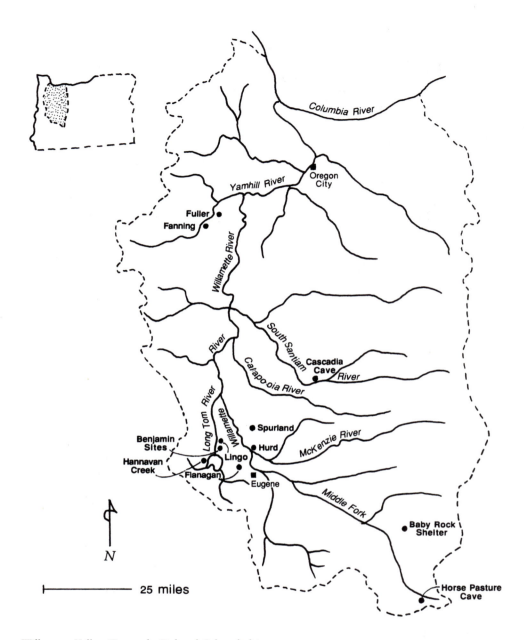

Willamette Valley. (Drawn by Deborah Schoenholz)

interpretations of data collected by Duncan Strong, W.E. Schenck, and Julian Steward (1930) at the Dalles-Deschutes area of the Lower Columbia River and by Drucker (1943) on the northern coast of British Columbia in the decade preceding World War II.

When archaeological research resumed after the wartime hiatus, it was once again situated primarily in the Coast Salish area. In the

late 1940s and early 1950s, the University of British Columbia's Charles E. Borden (1950, 1951) outlined a series of phases based on excavations at several sites in the Lower Fraser River area, and Arden King (1950) of the University of Washington proposed a different set derived mainly from excavations at the Cattle Point site on San Juan Island. Both initially saw their results as supporting an interior (or at least "island") source for significant Northwest Coast characteristics, although King also thought some were more likely of Alaskan origin. In the 1950s, Borden (1951) and Drucker (1958) further emphasized this latter derivation. They developed a model of culture history that saw coastal Alaskan and interior "streams" of culture melding at the mouth of the Fraser River to form the Salishan variant of Northwest Coast culture.

By the 1960s and 1970s, nearly all major parts of the Northwest Coast saw projects under way that were to result in a different interpretation of past events. As significant parts of the record were filled in, the prevailing view was that Northwest Coast culture had largely developed in place. From origins, attention has since shifted to questions about the causes of those changes in the past that seemed to lead to the area culture type. Explanations at first favored what were seen as important shifts in environmental conditions, but since the late 1980s they have emphasized the role of innovations in harvesting and in preservation technology.

The broad outlines of Northwest Coast prehistory are becoming more distinct, although the gaps in our knowledge of time and space variants are still large. The record begins on the southern part of the coast with surface evidence of a "Clovis" presence from Puget Sound south. This is soon supplanted by assemblages of the Old Cordilleran form with their leaf-shaped points and crude pebble and flake tools. People bearing this culture seem to have colonized the central coast by ca. 5050 B.C. (7000 years B.P.), within 2,000–3,000 years of the retreat of glacial ice. Those few sites where conditions have preserved some organic materials disclose at least seasonal use of a wide range of land and marine shoreline and riverine resources. They also suggest the presence of at least a rudimentary woodworking industry.

The north coast had a different early history. Entry, perhaps as early as 8050 B.C. (10,000 years B.P.), seems to have been from the north and by a culture characterized by microblade technology. These northern assemblages also display a prominent emphasis on unifacial stoneworking. Bifaces are rare but not unknown.

Evidence of these early north and central and south coast traditions lasts until ca. 3500 B.C. (5450 years B.P.). After this date, large shell middens increasingly dominate the archaeological record. Such sites provide significantly better conditions for preservation of organic materials, a situation that is at least partly responsible for a noticeable increase in "richness" of Northwest Coast assemblages after ca. 3500–3000 B.C. (5450–4950 years B.P.). But the widespread use of stone-grinding technology also contributes to this impression.

By ca. 1500–1000 B.C. (3450–2950 years B.P.), salmon had become the preeminent subsistence resource, and there are signs that fish were by then being dried and stored for later consumption. Investigations on various parts of the coast record that, within the period 500 B.C.–A.D. 500 (2450–1450 years B.P.), cultures of

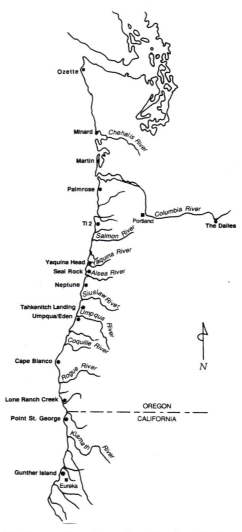

Washington Open Ocean Coast/Southern Northwest Coast. (Drawn by Deborah Schoenholz)

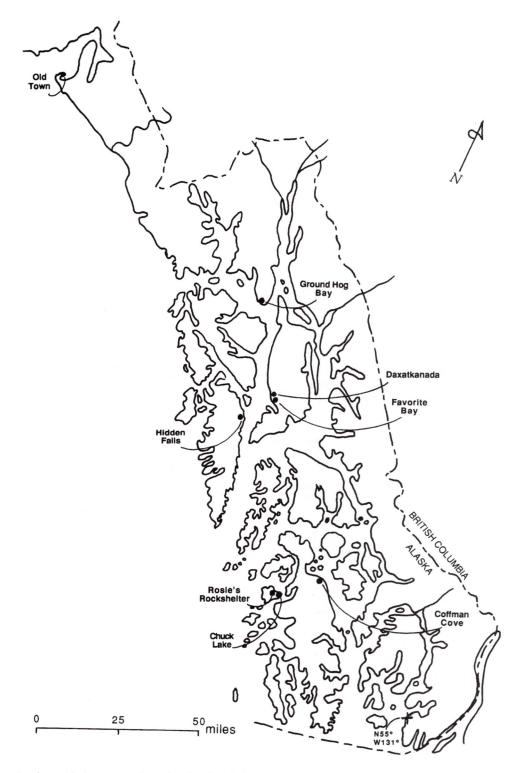

Southeast Alaska. (Drawn by Deborah Schoenholz)

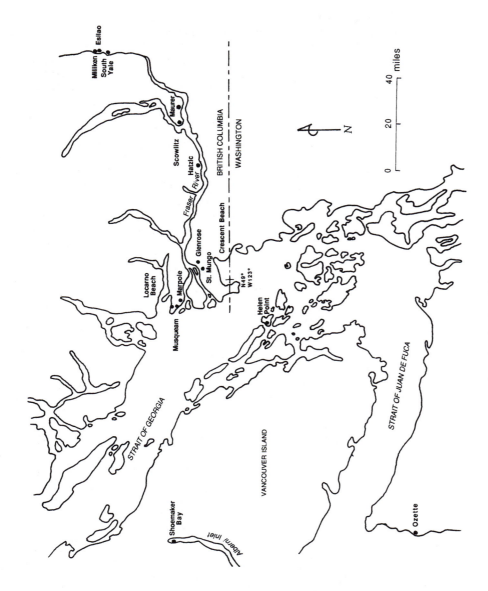

Strait of Georgia/Fraser River Valley. (Drawn by Deborah Schoenholz)

essentially historic form were in place. Assemblages attest to virtually all characteristics outlined earlier as distinctive of the Northwest Coast culture area.

Donald H. Mitchell

Further Readings

Borden, C.E. 1950. Preliminary Report on Archaeological Investigations in the Fraser Delta Region. *Anthropology in British Columbia* 1:13–27.

———. 1951. Facts and Problems of Northwest Coast Prehistory. *Anthropology in British Columbia* 2:35–52.

Drucker, P. 1943. *Archaeological Survey on the Northern Northwest Coast*. Bulletin no. 133. Bureau of American Ethnology, Smithsonian Institution, Washington, D.C.

———. 1958. Sources of Northwest Coast Culture. In *New Interpretations of Aboriginal American Culture*, edited by B. Meggers, pp. 59–81. Anthropological Society of Washington, Washington, D.C.

———. 1963. *Indians of the Northwest Coast*. Natural History Press, Garden City.

———. 1965. *Cultures of the North Pacific Coast*. Chandler, San Francisco.

Hill-Tout, C. 1895. *Later Prehistoric Man in British Columbia*. Transactions of the the Royal Society of Canada, ser. 2, vol. 1.

King, A. 1950. *Cattle Point: A Stratified Site on the Southern Northwest Coast*. Memoirs no. 7. Society for American Archaeology, Menasha.

Kroeber, A.L. 1923. American Culture and the Northwest Coast. *American Anthropologist* 25:1–20.

———. 1939. *Cultural and Natural Areas of Native North America*. Publications in American Ethnology, vol. 32. University of California, Berkeley.

Matson, R.G., and G. Coupland. 1995. *The Prehistory of the Northwest Coast*. Academic Press, San Diego.

Smith, H.I. 1903. *Shell-Heaps of the Lower Fraser River, British Columbia*. Publications of the Jesup North Pacific Expedition, vol. 2, pt. 4. E.J. Brill, Leiden.

———. 1907. *Archaeology of the Gulf of Georgia and Puget Sound*. Publications of the Jesup North Pacific Expedition, vol. 2, pt. 6. E.J. Brill, Leiden.

Strong, W.D., W.E. Schenck, and J. Steward. 1930. *Archaeology of the Dalles-Deschutes Region*. Publications in American Archaeology and Ethnology, vol. 29. University of California, Berkeley.

Suttles, W. (editor). 1990. *Northwest Coast*. Handbook of North American Indians, vol. 7, W.C. Sturtevant, general editor. Smithsonian Institution, Washington, D.C.

Northwest Microblade Tradition

The Northwest Microblade tradition was the first distinctive northern interior North American archaeological entity to be recognized, although not by that name, when Nels C. Nelson (1935) drew attention to the similarities between the Alaskan Campus-site microblade cores and Asian microblade industries. Following further finds of microblade assemblages in the western Subarctic, most of them in the southern Yukon and the southwest Mackenzie district, Richard S. MacNeish wrote in 1954 that "in interior northwest North America . . . there was a series of related sites with a distinctive cultural pattern," which before long he called the "Northwest Microblade tradition" (see also MacNeish 1964).

The core trait is the microblade industry, which remains distinct from the Arctic Small Tool tradition as well as from Plateau, Pacific coastal, and early eastern Siberian microblade traditions, none of which was well known in 1954. The cores tend to be wedge-shaped and often are similar to the Denali type characteristic of the Paleoarctic tradition in Alaska. Generalized biface knives, leaf-shaped points, end scrapers, flake burins, graver spurs, and notched pebbles (sinkers and choppers) are present; in some components, split cobble tools, notched spear points, and knives are also common. However, the component assemblages varied to the point that some investigators wondered whether the tradition had integrity. Moreover, it was poorly dated, though the age of most components evidently falls between 3050 and 50 B.C. (5000–2000 years B.P.). Definition of the Northwest Microblade tradition has remained essentially static since 1964, although, in retrospect, its range has been expanded eastward to include nearly all of the western Mackenzie district and northern Alberta (not distinguishing between it and late or derivative Paleoarctic assemblages). The construct has not been revised in any acceptable manner to take into account information that has become available from a greater geographic range and from microblade components dated considerably earlier than those originally reported by MacNeish. Instead, alternative constructs have been proposed that account for the evidence to varying degrees. Used selectively, these replace the Northwest Microblade tradition construct. However, some archaeologists still use this tradition in classifying assemblages from the western Mackenzie district. Key questions also surrounded the interpretation of some of the data subsumed in the Northwest Microblade tradition, such as the differential association of microblades with notched points.

Since 1970, most northwestern Subarctic components that lacked microblades but contained notched points have been reassigned to the Northern Archaic tradition, a construct whose definition by D. Anderson (1968) postdates MacNeish's era of northern fieldwork. It may be noted, though, that MacNeish had subdivided the Northwest Microblade into several phases, one of which, Taye Lake (2050 B.C.–A.D. 450, or 4000–1500 years B.P.), has notched points. In a climate that recently had seen the development of new tradition constructs, especially the Denali complex and the American Paleoarctic tradition, which both date to ca. 50 B.C.–A.D. 950 (2000–1000 years B.P.), to account for an early Alaskan microblade industry, discussion centered on the validity of assemblages characterized by both microblades and notched points such as were reported by MacNeish.

With "pure" microblade assemblages interpretable as late expressions of Denali or the Paleoarctic, and with the "pure" notched-point assemblages assigned to the Northern Archaic, all that is left to account for in the Northwest Microblade tradition are those assemblages with what seem to be hybrid or amalgamated technologies. Much archaeological interpretation since 1975 views these assemblages as an aspect of the Northern Archaic influenced by its microblade-using antecedents. Some specialists, though, hold out for the technological purity of the Northern Archaic and assign the combined microblade and technology to a Late Denali phase or culture (Dixon 1985). Late Denali is not fundamentally different from the Northwest Microblade tradition in age, distribution, or technological makeup, though it is more westerly in its primary focus. Given the lack of consensus on defining the major lineages of northwestern Subarctic prehistory, especially in Alaska, a revised Northwest Microblade construct would hardly be any less valid than some of the proposed alternatives.

There remains, though, serious concern over the suitability of classifying and viewing regional prehistory in terms of a single technology. This may be especially so for the western Mackenzie district and adjacent areas, where it is tempting to impose this classificatory convenience on an almost one-of-a-kind series of local assemblages all characterized by the production of microblades and found from Great Bear Lake west into the northern Yukon and from the Mackenzie delta south into northern Alberta. Another problem in identifying site affiliation lies in technological visibility (or invisibility). Given the often small size of some of the samples and the presumed task-specific or seasonal nature of some sites, culture index artifacts may be variously present at a particular site. Assemblages of a single culture could be characterized by microblades, microblades and side-notched points, or by notched points alone.

In the relevant literature, William B. Workman (1978) reviews MacNeish's original (1964) periodization of southwest Yukon prehistory. In presenting his own revised scheme, Workman avoids using the term "Northwest Microblade tradition," though his synthesis accordingly lacks broader regional reference. Donald W. Clark (1991) also avoids the term in his summary of western Subarctic prehistory, although the archaeological components are covered by an alternative taxonomy. In MacNeish's 1964 work, description is by component phases, usually without reference to the tradition, but a summary statement of what the Northwest Microblade tradition is about appears there in Figure 84a and on pages 345–346 and 380–381.

Donald W. Clark

Further Readings

Anderson, D.D. 1968. A Stone Age Campsite at the Gateway to America. *Scientific American* 218(6):24–33.

Clark, D.W. 1991. *Western Subarctic Prehistory.* Canadian Prehistory Series. Canadian Museum of Civilization, Hull.

Clark, D.W., and R.E. Morlan. 1982. Western Subarctic Prehistory: Twenty Years Later. *Canadian Journal of Archaeology* 6:79–93.

Dixon, E.J. 1985. Cultural Chronology of Central Interior Alaska. *Arctic Anthropology* 22(1):46–66.

MacNeish, R.S. 1954. The Pointed Mountain Site Near Fort Liard, N.W.T., Canada. *American Antiquity* 19(3):234–253.

———. 1964. Investigations in Southwest Yukon: Archaeological Excavations, Comparisons, and Speculations. *Papers of the Robert S. Peabody Foundation for Archaeology* 6(2 xii):199–488.

Nelson, N.C. 1935. Early Migration of Man to America. *Natural History* 35(4):356.

Workman, W.B. 1978. *Prehistory of the Aishihik-Kluane Area, Southwest Yukon Territory.* Mercury Series Paper no. 74. Archaeological Survey of Canada, National Museum of Man, Ottawa.

Northwestern California

Northwestern California includes three major and distinct geomorphological provinces. The North Coast ranges stretch 300 km (186 miles) from Marin County to Humboldt County. Formed mainly of mid-Cenozoic and later deposits, they are not especially lofty but provide considerable local ecological variability with peaks up to 2,000 m (6,562 feet). Downcut by many small streams and rivers, mostly on the ocean (west) side, they separate the Sacramento River Valley from the coast and provide a partial rain shadow. As a result, their eastern slopes are drier than those on the western side. The Klamath Mountains form a different geological province. Once an extension of the Sierra Nevada, they were realigned east-west by the tectonic forces that created the Cascade ranges and now parallel the California-Oregon border. The Klamath River system is the major drainage through these ranges in northwestern California. The last province is the coastal strip. It extends for 400 km (248 miles) from Marin County to the Oregon border. Ecologically complex with patchworks of rocky and sandy shores, estuaries, lagoons and stream mouths, grassy terraces, chaparral-covered hillsides, oak-filled valleys, and redwood forests, the narrow coastal strip enjoyed climatic constancy during the year because of the ocean's influence. The region saw a florescence of cultural development at its northern end, which is the southern extremity of the Northwest Coast region, and in its southern area, where it adjoined central California and the Bay region.

Northwestern California remains one of the least studied parts of the state. L.L. Loud's (1918) report on excavations at the Gunther Island site established a model for late prehistory along the northwestern California Coast. Only a handful of other major excavations have

been conducted in that region. While a more substantial sequence of regional cultures can be defined, much of the earlier prehistory remains an unevenly integrated and incomplete patchwork. The Coast ranges are somewhat better known. The first excavation of a stratified site was C.W. Meighan's (1955) study at CA-Men-500. Since then, a series of cultural-resource-management projects has helped outline cultural sequences in the northern and southern parts of the North Coast ranges that link M.R. Harrington's (1948) Paleoindian discoveries at Borax Lake, which date to ca. 10,000–9000 B.C. (11,950–10,950 years B.P.) with ethnographically known cultures nearly 12,000 years later (Frederickson 1974). The Klamath Mountains are less well known than the coastal area. The few studies published refer primarily to the Protohistoric period (Eidsness 1985; Chartkoff 1991). The most substantial regional model is David Fredrickson's (1984), which is summarized here and linked with the more general Joseph L. Chartkoff and Kerry K. Chartkoff (1984) framework.

A Paleoindian presence in northwestern California is demonstrated at the Borax Lake site (Meighan and Haynes 1970). Finds of fluted points have also been made in Shasta County (Beck 1970), Humboldt County and Mendocino County. Northwestern California shows essentially continual human use for at least the past 12,000 years. The Borax Lake site is also the primary locale of the next period, named the Post pattern after the site's owner (ca. 10,050–6050 B.C., or 12,000–8000 years B.P.). It may be represented, too, at the Mostin site on Kelsey Creek, also in Lake County. Other contemporary traces are suggested at Laguna de Santa Rosa in Sonoma County, at Warm Springs Creek in Sonoma County, and at Bodega Bay (Fredrickson 1984:485–524). This phase is equivalent to the Early Archaic in the Chartkoff and Chartkoff model (Fredrickson 1984 uses the term "Lower Archaic" for the subsequent Borax Lake pattern, 6050–1050 B.C., or 8000–3000 years B.P.). Post-pattern sites are associated with diversified aquatic-edge adaptations in which varied hunting, fishing, and fowling practices were most important. A specialized plant-processing technology, such as milling tools, and systematic shellfish collecting were absent. Post-pattern artifacts include a few large, leaf-shaped projectile points, some with a certain amount of basal fluting that may be linked with the earlier Paleoindian era. Several crescentic chipped-stone pieces are known for this period. Reflected are tiny groups with generalized foraging adaptations having a marshland focus and little specialized technology. Lacking are campsites of continuing occupation, architecture, cemeteries, evidence of regional exchange, and ritual activity.

The next era defined by Fredrickson is the Borax Lake pattern (6050–1050 B.C., or 8000–3000 years B.P.). It is more widely spread throughout the North Coast ranges, even though the Borax Lake site is again a primary example. The Borax Lake pattern occurs from Sonoma to Humboldt counties and represents what Chartkoff and Chartkoff (1984) term the Middle and Late Archaic periods for northwestern California. Early Borax Lake–pattern sites are similar across the region, while later Borax Lake sites are more varied. Nevertheless, they contain many common features. Projectile points are large and triangular, with wide stems, some bifurcated. Millingstone and manos are common in Borax Lake–pattern assemblages. The mortar and pestle, sometimes with bowl mortars and sometimes with hopper mortars, appear later during the era. D.L. True and others saw important parallels in these materials with Encinitas-tradition materials from southern California, both of which they regard as part of the Millingstone horizon (True et al. 1979). Without implying historical connections, they suggest that the Borax Lake pattern, like the Encinitas tradition, reflects a diversified foraging lifeway by family- and band-sized units. In contrast with the earlier Post pattern, Borax Lake–pattern economies emphasized the use of hard seeds and, later, acorns, supplemented by varied animal and other plant resources. Settlement changed frequently during the year and shifted seasonally between the highlands in the summer and the lowland valleys in the winter. Modest amounts of exchange occurred, most evident in obsidian. The Clear Lake obsidian sources were mainly used in southern and central areas, while at the northern end Siskiyou County sources were important. Chert, apparently from local sources, also was widely used.

In the central and northern parts of northwestern California, the Borax Lake pattern persisted into Chartkoff and Chartkoff's early Pacific period (2050–550 B.C., or 4000–2500 years B.P.) and possibly into the middle Pacific period (550 B.C.–A.D. 450, or 2500–1500 years B.P.) with few major changes beyond the shifting of seasonal camps as climatic changes caused resource distributions to change. In the southern area, the Borax Lake pattern gave way during the early Pacific period ca. 1050–550 B.C. (3000–2500 years B.P.) to what Fredrickson calls the Berkeley pattern. Several writers have associated the Berkeley pattern with the appearance of the ancestors of ethnographically known peoples of the area, such as Pomoans in Sonoma County (Fredrickson 1974) and Coast Miwok in Napa County (Werner 1980; Whistler 1980). In Berkeley-pattern assemblages, earlier point types are replaced by shouldered, lanceolate, and contracting-stem types. Millingstones are replaced by bowl mortars and pestles. Distinctive split-beveled *Olivella* shell beads appear. The great abundance of points and the reduced occurrence of mortars and pestles suggest a greater emphasis on hunting, which may, in turn, reflect either ethnic change, or environmental change, or both. The Berkeley pattern goes no farther north than southern Lake County; why similar changes are not found farther north is not known.

Between A.D. 450 and 750 (1500–1200 years B.P.), these patterns give way to the final prehistoric traditions for the region. The Gunther pattern refers to these traditions in the northern areas, which essentially span Humboldt and Del Norte counties. The Augustine pattern refers to the other parts of northwestern California. Fredrickson (1984) groups both into an Emergent period (A.D. 450–1850, or 1500–100 years B.P.). In the Chartkoff and Chartkoff framework, they fall within the late Pacific (A.D. 450–1450, or 1500–500 years B.P.) and final Pacific (A.D. 1450–1769, or 500–181 years B.P.) periods. In all cases, historically known cultures are associated with these patterns.

The Gunther pattern stems from Loud's (1918) excavations at CA-Hum-67, the Gunther Island site, in Humboldt Bay at Eureka. Some other major village sites include Patrick's Point (Elsasser and Heizer 1966), Tsurai at Trinidad Bay (Heizer and Mills 1952), Tsahpek at Stone Lagoon (Moratto 1970), and Point St. George at Crescent City (Gould 1966). The Gunther pattern reflects a regional florescence based on intensive sea-mammal hunting and salmon fishing, a subsistence emphasis supplemented by diversified plant harvesting and land-mammal hunting. The artifact assemblage is equally distinctive. Small projectile points, notably the Gunther Island Barbed type, predominate, with large numbers of bone harpoon barbed points, both large and small, associated, respectively, with sea-mammal hunting and salmon spearing. Notched-pebble net weights are abundant, as are varied beads of clamshell, *Olivella, Dentalium* (presumed from Puget Sound), steatite, and bone. Steatite was also used in the manufacture of bowls, pipes, and figurines. Antler wedges and stone-bladed adzes indicate extensive woodworking. Historic peoples in the area had long built large dugout canoes capable of ocean as well as river travel. Bone awls reflect the superb basketmaking of the area; elaborate flanged pestles, food processing. Gunther sites indicate extensive regional exchange networks in which many types of raw materials moved in quantity. Permanent villages with substantial plank or pithouses form major village sites at key coastal and riverine locations.

The more widely distributed Augustine pattern represents a less intense focus on ocean and river resources and more influence from neighboring areas. To the south, similarities with Bay area and Delta cultures can be seen. In the central and northeastern areas, the sharing of traits with Sacramento Valley communities is evident. Many different ethnic groups, speaking languages of at least four separate families, produced Augustine-pattern assemblages, so variation is to be expected. In contrast to the Gunther pattern, the Augustine pattern has been defined from dozens of sites. Mostly of modest size, the sites appear in an area that extends from Shasta and Trinity reservoirs (in Shasta and Trinity counties, respectively; Smith and Weymouth 1952; Treganza 1959) to Napa and Sonoma counties (Bennyhoff 1977; Baumhoff 1980). Augustine-pattern sites yield small, triangular projectile points of chert and obsidian, such as Gunther Island Barbed, and basal-notched, corner-notched, and desert side-notched points. Well-fashioned tapered pestles were used with basket-hopper mortars. Large chert bifaces were common, as were ground-stone pieces in a variety of forms called "charmstones." Beads of magnesite, clamshell disks, spire-lopped *Olivella,* and pinenut shells were abundant. Abalone (*Haliotis*) shell pendants and gorgets were also popular.

William R. Hildebrandt (1981) recognized two fundamentally different adaptive strategies in the region that distinguish Gunther-pattern from Augustine-pattern societies. Gunther-pattern subsistence was based on a "pursuer" strategy that concentrated on a few key resources whose presence at particular places at particular times was highly predictable—in this case, sea mammals and salmon. Augustine communities followed a "searcher" strategy in which a diverse array of resources spread across a variety of habitats within a territory was exploited. The patterns, he thought, reflected differences in the occurrence of resources within the region. Only in the northwestern coastal zone of Humboldt and Del Norte counties were key resources abundant and reliable enough to allow large surpluses to be harvested at one location. As a result, it was only there that village sedentism reached its greatest development. The variation and dispersal of resources elsewhere, while still allowing large populations to be supported, required group size to remain small and groups to relocate several times during the year. Group size varied from season to season. This idea suggests the distinction Cleland (1976) drew between focal and diffuse economies. While Augustine cultures represent the richest developments of their areas, the Gunther pattern represents the cultural climax for northwestern California as a whole.

Joseph L. Chartkoff

Further Readings

Baumhoff, M.A. 1980. The Evolution of Pomo Society. *Journal of California and Great Basin Anthropology* 2(2):175–182.

Beck, J.L. 1970. The Fluted Point Tradition in the Far West. Paper presented at the Annual Meeting of the Society for California Archaeology, Asilomar.

Bennyhoff, J.A. 1977. *Ethnogeography of the Plains Miwok.* Publications no. 5. Center for Archaeological Research at Davis, University of California, Davis.

Chartkoff, J.L. 1991. The Collord Site (CA-Sis-515): A Proto-Karok Village at Happy Camp. *Proceedings of the Society for California Archaeology* 4:23–43.

Chartkoff, J.L., and K.K. Chartkoff. 1984. *The Archaeology of California.* Stanford University Press, Stanford.

Cleland, C.E. 1976. The Focal-Diffuse Model: An Evolutionary Perspective on the Prehistoric Cultural Adaptations of the Eastern United States. *Midcontinental Journal of Archaeology* 1:59–76.

Eidsness, J.P. 1985. *Prehistoric Archaeology Within Chimariko Territory, California.* Unpublished Master's thesis. Department of Anthropology, Sonoma State University, Rohnert Park.

Elsasser, A.B. 1986. Archaeology on Gunther Island (Site Hum-67). In *A New Look at Some Old Sites,* edited by F.A. Riddell, pp. 49–54. Archives of California Prehistory, vol. 6. Coyote Press, Salinas.

Elsasser, A.B., and R.F. Heizer. 1964. Archaeology of Hum-67, the Gunther Island Site in Humboldt Bay, California. *University of California Archaeological Survey Reports* 62:5–122.

———. 1966. Excavation of Two Northwestern California Coastal Sites. *University of California Archaeological Survey Reports* 67:1–149.

Fredrickson, D.A. 1974. Cultural Diversity in Early Central California: A View From the North Coast Ranges. *Journal of California Anthropology* 1(1):41–54.

———. 1984. The North Coastal Region. In *California Archaeology,* edited by M.J. Moratto, pp. 471–528. Academic Press, New York.

Gould, R.A. 1966. *Archaeology of the Point St. George Site and Tolowa Prehistory.* Publications in Anthropology no. 4. University of California, Berkeley.

Harrington, M.R. 1948. *An Ancient Site at Borax Lake, California.* Papers no. 16. Southwest Museum, Los Angeles.

Heizer, R.F., and J.E. Mills. 1952. *The Four Ages of Tsurai: A Documentary History of the Indian Village on Trinidad Bay.* University of California Press, Berkeley.

Hildebrandt, W.R. 1981. *Native Hunting Adaptations on the North Coast of California.* Unpublished Ph.D. dissertation, Department of Anthropology, University of California, Davis.

Loud, L.L. 1918. Ethnogeography and Archaeology of the Wiyot Territory. *University of California Publications in American Archaeology and Ethnology* 14(3):221–437.

Meighan, C.W. 1985. Archaeology of the North Coast Ranges, California. *University of California Archaeological Survey Report* 30:1–39.

Meighan, C.W., and C.V. Haynes. 1970. The Borax Lake Site Revisited. *Science* 167(3922):1213–1221.

Moratto, M.J. 1970. *Tsahpekw: An Archaeological Record of 19th Century Acculturation Among the Yurok.* R.E. Schenck Memorial Archives of California Archaeology no. 7. San Francisco State University, San Francisco; Society for California Archaeology, Asilomar.

———. 1984. *California Archaeology.* Academic Press, New York.

Smith, C.E., and W.D. Weymouth. 1952. Archaeology of the Shasta Dam Area, California. *University of California Archaeological Survey Reports* 18:1–35, 43–49.

Treganza, A.E. 1959. Salvage Archaeology in the Trinity Reservoir Area—Field Season 1958. *University of California Archaeological Survey Reports* 46:1–32.

True, D.L., M.A. Baumhoff, and J.E. Hellen. 1979. Milling Stone Cultures in Northern California: Berryessa I. *Journal of California and Great Basin Anthropology* 1(1):124–154.

Werner, R.H. 1980. Archaeological Investigations at CA-Lak-395, Detert Reservoir, Lake County, California. Ms. on file, Anthropological Studies Center, Sonoma State University, Rohnert Park.

Whistler, K.A. 1980. *Pomo Prehistory: A Case for Archaeological Linguistics.* Anthropological Studies Center Manuscripts S-2107. Sonoma State University, Rohnert Park.

Norton Culture

The original Norton assemblage was discovered in 1948 by J.L. Giddings at Cape Denbigh in Norton Bay of Norton Sound, Alaska, where it lay stratigraphically above deposits of the Denbigh Flint complex and below those of later prehistoric Eskimos designated as Nukleet culture. Although he named the new culture for that region, Giddings noted that similar remains had been recognized nearly a decade earlier near the Ipiutak site at Point Hope, where it was called Near Ipiutak (Giddings 1964). The Norton Bay finds were later radiocarbon dated to ca. 500 B.C.–A.D. 500 (2450–1450 years B.P.). Since then, comparable assemblages have been reported from extreme northwestern Canada on the northeast, around coastal Alaska to the Ugashik River drainage on the Bering Sea slope of the Alaska Peninsula on the southwest, and in the interior coastal hinterland on a number of rivers in between. First appearances date uniformly to a century or two after 500 B.C. (2450 years B.P.). Giddings and others, especially archaeologists working in north Alaska, have tended to refer to all of these assemblages simply as Norton culture without finer distinction, despite some regional and temporal variations.

Norton sites are especially plentiful on the American coast of the Bering Sea and along the lower reaches of the Kuskokwim and Yukon rivers, with sites also along streams draining into Bristol Bay; they represent the earliest known human occupations of some offshore islands, such as Nunivak. In this Bering Sea region, the earliest Norton remains give rise to later, related variants in an evolutionary progression that continues without interruption until ca. A.D. 950 (1000 years B.P.), but north of the Seward Peninsula Norton cultures disappear before A.D. 450 (1500 years B.P.).

Norton assemblages commonly include plentiful ceramics in the form of well-fired pottery that is commonly fiber tempered, most frequently check stamped, sometimes linear or diamond stamped, with plain ware becoming more frequent through time in some southern regions. Shapes are few, with pots displaying interior deposits that mark them consistently as cooking vessels. Stone implements are chipped, commonly volcanic or silicified sedimentary rocks, with projectile blades often weakly stemmed or basally contracting, apparently for insertion into organic projectile heads. Some bipointed end blades in cryptocrystalline silicates or silicified sedimentary rock appear, and asymmetric side blades in comparable materials are plentiful. Small chipped adzes of igneous or silicified rocks have polished bits; there are some polished burinlike implements, but chipped burins are absent. Polished slate is rare but increases through time. Preservation is often poor in Norton sites, so that organic artifacts are less well known, but those of caribou antler include arrow or dart bases and simple toggling harpoon heads, which are often rudimentary, self-armed, and with an open socket. Basketry and twined matting are reported from some favorable locations. Art is almost uniformly absent, although Giddings believed that some rather simple engraved antler pieces from Burial 4 at Battle Rock, north of Cape Krusenstern on the Chukchi Sea, pertained to an early aspect of Norton.

Houses were semisubterranean, single-room structures with a central fireplace and a sloping entrance passage that entered at floor level. Villages of substantial size are more common south of the Bering Strait. The coastal locations of many villages, the presence of harpoon parts and seal bones in coastal sites, and the find in Near Ipiutak context at Point Hope

of larger harpoon heads apparently for whaling—all combine to indicate a significant interest in hunting along the seacoast and in open water. But the heavy presence of sites on river systems emptying on the Bering Sea, along with plentiful notched stones interpreted as fishnet sinkers and a preponderance of land-mammal bones, mark the people at least equally, and possibly predominantly, as inland fishers and hunters, a fact that heavy use of antler for organic artifacts substantiates. Ivory and sea-mammal bone are generally less common.

Although Norton remains have never been reported from the Chukchi Peninsula or the Asian coast of the Bering Sea, correspondences in ceramics and some stone artifacts have been noted with interior Siberian Neolithic cultures. The origin of Norton culture itself is unclear. While the pottery is Asian in derivation, numerous stone-artifact correspondences with the Denbigh Flint complex of the earlier Arctic Small Tool tradition bespeak American as well as Asian elements. Some commentators stress apparent southern Alaskan traits, such as oil lamps and polished slate.

The disappearance of Norton culture north of the Seward Peninsula comes before A.D. 450 (1500 years B.P.), with the appearance of the not altogether dissimilar, but distinctive, Ipiutak culture. In the south, it comes ca. A.D. 1000 (950 years B.P.), with the abrupt change toward recent prehistoric Eskimo culture. This latter change is marked by a sudden, increased reliance on slate grinding as opposed to stone chipping, a sharp change in form and paste of ceramics, and the appearance of the cold-trap entrance on semisubterranean houses. Despite these drastic changes, continuity from late Norton assemblages into those of the succeeding Late Prehistoric period is recognizable enough in favorable sites to suggest that the change did not involve a complete population replacement.

Don E. Dumond

Further Readings

Giddings, J.L. 1964. *The Archeology of Cape Denbigh.* Brown University Press, Providence.

Shaw, R.D., and C.E. Holmes (editors). 1982. The Norton Interaction Sphere: Selected Papers From a Symposium. *Arctic Anthropology*, vol. 19, no. 2.

See also NORTON TRADITION

Norton Tradition

"Norton" is a tradition defined by D.E. Dumond (1977) to include Alaskan assemblages known commonly as Choris culture (1050–550 B.C., or 3000–2500 years B.P.), Norton culture (550 B.C.–A.D. 950, or 2500–1000 years B.P.), and Ipiutak culture (A.D. 50–950, or 1900–1000 years B.P.) as part of a summary of Arctic prehistory. The conceptualization drew attention to similarities in ecology and artifacts among the three cultures. The formulation stressed the identity of Choris and Norton ceramics and chipped-stone side blades (while not minimizing the distinctiveness of other artifacts) as well as the close similarity of Norton and Ipiutak stone implements (while noting that Ipiutak lacked ceramics and Norton seemed to lack art). On a practical level, the newly defined unit recognized the inability of fieldworkers to distinguish small archaeological sites of the three cultures in regions such as the Brooks Range of northern Alaska. The concept also provided a framework for organizing the specifically Norton-culture assemblages around the American side of the Bering Sea, where local sequences had been defined as two to three sequential and related, but recognizably different, phases or complexes.

As defined, the Norton tradition was used by Dumond in the reconstruction of Eskimo prehistory to subsume the coastal and near-coastal assemblages of Alaska dating from shortly after 1000 B.C. (2950 years B.P.) to a time near A.D. 950 (1000 years B.P.). These assemblages mark the first definitive shift toward establishment of permanent settlements on the seacoast. In the reconstruction, the Alaskan Norton tradition was balanced in the eastern Arctic by a Dorset tradition of coastal dwellers of about the same period. Both of these traditions were conceived of as having a greater (in the case of Dorset) or lesser (Norton) proportion of their origin in the earlier Arctic Small Tool tradition, which began ca. 2550 B.C. (4500 years B.P.) and was defined, as had been customary, to include both Alaska assemblages related to the Denbigh Flint complex and Pre-Dorset assemblages of the eastern region. Norton and Dorset traditions were both eclipsed by the spread of recognizable Late Prehistoric Eskimos bearing a culture of what was defined as the Thule tradition between A.D. 450 and 1050 (1500–900 years B.P.).

Don E. Dumond

Further Readings

Dumond, D.E. 1977. *The Eskimos and Aleuts.* rev. ed., 1987. Thames and Hudson, London.

———. 1982. Trends and Traditions in Alaskan Prehistory: The Place of Norton Culture. *Arctic Anthropology* 19(2):39–52.

See also NORTON CULTURE

Notched Piece

A notched piece consists of chipped stone in which an indentation has been retouched on a side or end. Since indentations of this nature were made on flakes, blades, blocky fragments, and even cores; the name used here includes all of these technological blank forms. Notched pieces, occasionally called "notches" or "notched scrapers," are common throughout North America, though they have not always been distinguished as a typological class. Where they have been, as in areas A and B of the Archaic Black Earth site in southern Illinois (Jefferies and Butler 1982), they form a moderately frequent constituent of the tool assemblage. A distinction is occasionally made between a notched flake and a "spokeshave," as in the Normandy Reservoir Project in Tennessee (Faulkner and McCollough 1973:82). In this case, the spokeshave possesses one or more multiple-blow notches that are broader and deeper than those of the notched flake. The overall function of the notched piece has not been established, since large samples of them have never been microscopically examined for use-wear. The tool itself was probably multifunctional. The purpose of the notch might have been to shave a rounded elongated object with small diameter, such as an arrow shaft; to shape the piece for the isolation of a projecting part, which would subsequently be utilized; or to prepare purchase for a hafting device. It is no surprise, then, that W. James Judge (1973:107) found a large amount of variation in notch width in his sample of Paleoindian notched pieces from New Mexico. Because of the generalized use of the notched piece, it was present throughout the prehistoric period in North America.

George H. Odell

Further Readings

Faulkner, C.H., and M.C.R. McCollough. 1973. *Introductory Report of the Normandy Reservoir Salvage Project: Environmental Setting, Typology, and Survey.* Normandy Archaeological

Project, vol. 1. Report of Investigations no. 11. Department of Anthropology, University of Tennessee, Knoxville.

Jefferies, R.W., and B.M. Butler (editors). 1982. *The Carrier Mills Archaeological Project: Human Adaptation in the Saline Valley, Illinois,* vol. 1. Research Paper no. 33. Center for Archaeological Investigations, Southern Illinois University, Carbondale.

Judge, W.J. 1973. *Paleoindian Occupation of the Central Rio Grande Valley in New Mexico.* University of New Mexico Press, Albuquerque.

Numic Expansion

Numic expansion is the subject of a hypothesis that the ethnographic distribution of Numic-speaking peoples is the result of a relatively recent and rapid dispersal from a homeland in southeastern California that proceeded simultaneously northward and eastward across the Great Basin and into adjoining portions of Oregon, Idaho, Wyoming, Colorado, New Mexico, and Arizona. Commonly termed the "Numic spread," the hypothesis was suggested initially by Sydney M. Lamb (1958), who employed it to explain the striking fanlike distribution of Numic languages, within which the three branches of Numic (southern, central, and western) occupy roughly equal wedges and are anchored at the base of the fan, which is situated just south of Owens Valley, California. Lamb and others, such as A.L. Kroeber, recognized that the major divisions and subdivisions within Numic formed relatively late in time, probably in the second millennium A.D. Lamb argued that Numic had split into the three branches while still in southeastern California, shortly after which something had triggered rapid Numic expansion north and east into the Great Basin beginning ca. A.D. 950 (1000 years B.P.). This produced two languages in each Numic branch, an older, prespread language (southern: Kawaiisu, central: Panamint, northern: Mono) occupying a small area near the base of the fan and a more recent, "postspread" language (southern: Southern Paiute/Ute, central: Shoshone, northern: Northern Paiute) occupying the much larger outer part of the fan. A number of investigators have provided support for that account (Goss 1968; Madsen 1975; Miller 1986). The linguistic data used to construct the model indicate that the Numic

expansion was rapid but do not provide firm evidence for the amount of time needed to complete the spread. Computer simulations (Young and Bettinger 1992), however, suggest that the ethnographic distribution of Numic was attained about 600 years after the spread began, which is a reasonable estimate. Alternative accounts have been presented by other archaeologists who variously propose Numic homelands north of the Great Basin (Taylor 1961), in southwestern Utah/northwestern Arizona (Gunnerson 1962), and in the central Great Basin (Aikens and Witherspoon 1986). None of these alternatives satisfactorily accounts for the distinctive fan-shaped distribution of Numic languages or for a variety of other evidence provided by mythology, plant and place names, and orientation of dialect boundaries, all of which favor the Lamb model.

Culture, climate, and demography have all been proposed as causes of the spread. One hypothesis (Grayson 1994) equates Numic expansion with a recolonization of the Great Basin as climate improved following the mid-Holocene Altithermal warm/dry period during which the Great Basin was abandoned. According to this hypothesis, Numic expansion began ca. 2550 B.C. (4500 years B.P.). An alternative hypothesis links the process to more recent episodes of climatic deterioration (A.D. 1250, or 700 years B.P.) that forced the withdrawal of established marsh-adapted hunter-gatherers in western Nevada and horticulturalists in Utah and southern Nevada (Aikens and Witherspoon 1986). The withdrawal cleared the field for Numic expansion out of central Nevada. Still other hypotheses favor cultural rather than climatic explanations. One of these proposes that Numic peoples were culturally predisposed to warlike and aggressive behavior, which permitted them to expand their territory at the expense of their neighbors (Sutton 1986).

In contrast to these relatively simple accounts, Robert L. Bettinger and M.A. Baumhoff (1982) propose a more complex model that links the Numic spread to adaptive shifts in the Numic homeland that resulted in the development of a novel and competitively superior hunter-gatherer strategy. They join the diet-breadth and patch-choice models of optimal-foraging theory to deduce a theoretical continuum of hunter-gatherer strategies that differ with respect to population, settlement, and subsistence in which traveler strategies represent one extreme and processor strategies the other.

In the traveler-processor model, as population increases from low densities (the traveler situation) to high densities (the processor situation), diet breadth, diet cost, and amount of time spent in individual resource patches (e.g., piñon groves) increase while the amount of time spent traveling between highly productive patches decreases. The model has important implications for competitive expansion because processor strategists can gain footholds in territories utilized by traveler strategists by occupying small, unused, and thus uncontested, tracts and by occupying more favored locations, where, by virtue of their more generalized subsistence patterns and more stable residential patterns, they generally concentrate in greater numbers than traveler strategists who might contest for access to the same place. Bettinger and Baumhoff argue that this happened in the Numic case. They hold that, through the use of low-quality plant resources, such as seeds, early Numic-speaking peoples living in southeastern California developed a costly, but highly effective, processor strategy capable of sustaining a relatively high population density. With this processor strategy firmly entrenched by A.D. 1000 (950 years B.P.), aboriginal groups in southeastern California were preadapted for expansion into adjacent parts of the Great Basin then occupied by Prenumic groups embracing traveler strategies. They argue further that early Numic peoples subsequently used this adaptation to expand their territory within the Great Basin through the displacement of Prenumic peoples whose adaptation was more selective in its use of high-quality resources, such as mountain sheep. Prenumic selectivity produced calories at relatively low cost, but it was less efficient than the Numic strategy in extracting calories from low-quality resources and so produced fewer calories per unit of territory. These relationships resulted in an important competitive asymmetry: Numic peoples competed for all the Prenumic resources, but Prenumic peoples competed for only a fraction of the Numic resources and ignored all the higher-cost resources upon which the Numic strategy ultimately rested. Because of this, Prenumic peoples were powerless to deflect the spread of the Numic adaptation.

The Numic spread has proven difficult to document archaeologically. Numic-style ceramics (conical, coil-scrape plain wares), for example, seem to appear later in time as one moves from southwest to northeast in the Great

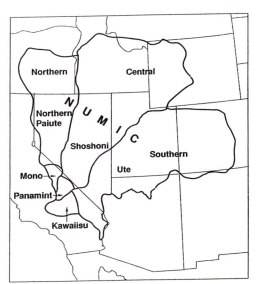

Numic expansion. (Illustration by R. L. Bettinger)

Basin, as predicted, but dating is imprecise and heavily reliant on "guess dates" for the appearance of ceramics in the Numic homeland. Bettinger and Baumhoff suggest that observed changes in seed-procurement technology, settlement pattern, and ritual hunting behavior are more appropriate measures but cite limited evidence to support this. Investigators have attempted to link Late Prehistoric adaptive shifts in various parts of the Great Basin to the spread but have found it difficult to eliminate the possibility that they result from local changes within existing systems.

Robert L. Bettinger

Further Readings

Aikens, C.M., and Y. Witherspoon. 1986. Great Basin Numic Prehistory: Linguistics, Archaeology, and Environment. *University of Utah Anthropological Papers* 110:7–20.

Bettinger, R.L., and M.A. Baumhoff. 1982. The Numic Spread: Great Basin Cultures in Competition. *American Antiquity* 47:485–503.

———. 1983. Return Rates and Intensity of Resource Use in Numic and Prenumic Adaptive Strategies. *American Antiquity* 48:830–884.

Fowler, C.S. 1972. Some Ecological Clues to Proto-Numic Homelands. In *Great Basin Culture Ecology: A Symposium,* edited by D.D. Fowler, pp. 105–121.

Publications in the Social Sciences no. 8. Desert Research Institute, Reno.

Goss, J.A. 1968. Culture-Historical Inference From Utaztekan Linguistic Evidence. In *Utaztekan Prehistory*, edited by E.H. Swanson, Jr., pp. 1–42. Occasional Papers no. 22. Idaho State University Museum, Pocatello.

Grayson, D.K. 1994. Chronology, Glottochronology, and Numic Expansion. In *Across the West: Human Population Movement and the Expansion of the Numa,* edited by D.B. Madsen and D.R. Rhode, pp. 20–23. University of Utah Press, Salt Lake City.

Gunnerson, J.H. 1962. Plateau Shoshonean Prehistory: A Suggested Reconstruction. *American Antiquity* 28(1):41–45.

Kroeber, A.L. 1959. Ethnographic Interpretations: Recent Ethnic Spreads. *University of California Publications in American Archaeology and Ethnology* 47:259–281.

Lamb, S.M. 1958. Linguistic Prehistory in the Great Basin. *International Journal of American Linguistics* 24(2):95–100.

Leland, J. 1986. Population. In *Great Basin,* edited by W.L. D'Azevedo, pp. 608–619. Handbook of North American Indians, vol. 11, W.C. Sturtevant, general editor. Smithsonian Institution, Washington, D.C.

Madsen, D.B. 1975. Dating Paiute-Shoshoni Expansion in the Great Basin. *American Antiquity* 40:82–86.

Miller, W.C. 1966. Anthropological Linguistics in the Great Basin. In *Current Status of Anthropological Research in the Great Basin: 1964,* edited by W.L. D'Azevedo, pp. 75–112. Social Sciences and Humanities Publications no. 1. Desert Research Institute, Reno.

———. 1986. Numic Languages. In *Great Basin,* edited by W.L. D'Azevedo, pp. 98–106. Handbook of North American Indians, vol. 11, W.C. Sturtevant, general editor. Smithsonian Institution, Washington, D.C.

Sutton, M.Q. 1986. Warfare and Expansion: An Ethnohistoric Perspective on the Numic Spread. *Journal of California and Great Basin Anthropology* 8(1)65–82.

Taylor, W.W. 1961. Archaeology and Language in Western North America. *American Antiquity* 27:71–81.

Young, D.A., and R.L. Bettinger. 1992. The Numic Spread: A Computer Simulation. *American Antiquity* 57(1):85–99.

Nunguvik and Saatut Sites

The most important Dorset sites in the Pond Inlet area of northern Baffin Island, Nunguvik and Saatut are both situated on Navy Board Inlet. They were apparently inhabited by the same people at different times of the year: Nunguvik, mostly in winter and spring; Saatut, mostly in late summer and fall as a fishing and seal-hunting camp. Dorset people inhabited the Nunguvik site almost continuously from ca. 400 B.C. (2350 years B.P.) until the arrival of the first Thule people. The midpoints on two radiocarbon dates from the earliest Thule house and the latest Dorset house are A.D. 1095 and 1090 (855 and 860 years B.P.), respectively. Thule fire-making artifacts were found in a Dorset house. The fact that sea level has changed very little during the first and second millennia A.D. allows the sort of continuous habitation seen particularly at Nunguvik. Occupations are thus superimposed, and much is deeply buried in the permafrost. Organic preservation is good; not only stone tools have been found but also many tools with wooden handles.

In contrast to most other Dorset sites, Nunguvik and Saatut are characterized by the importance of caribou bone in the tool industry. The bones used include mostly metatarsals, ribs, radial-ulnas, scapulas, and antler. The debitage suggests that bone tools were mostly made at Nunguvik but used at Saatut, where most of the food consumed was seal and fish. At Nunguvik, caribou bone outnumbers that of seal by three or four to one. Among the most interesting finds at Nunguvik and Saatut are wooden skis, kayak parts, and kayak models. Traditionally, Dorset people were thought to lack boats of any sort, but this no longer appears to be tenable.

Guy-Marie Rousseliere

Further Readings
Rousseliere, G.-M. 1968. *Reconnaissance archeologique dans la region de Pond Inlet, Territories du Nord-Ouest.* Universite Laval, Quebec.

Nuts

Nuts have been an important food resource throughout North American prehistory. They are highly nutritious and can be readily harvested and stored. Hickory, walnut, piñon, and hazelnut are oily nuts with a high caloric content and excellent protein value. They provide comparable quantities of protein at twice the caloric contribution of lean venison and are good sources of phosphorus, iron, thiamine, and riboflavin. Many of these nuts are easily processed. Hickory nuts, for example, can be processed by simply pounding the shells and meats on a mortar or a large rock and then boiling the whole mass. The nut shells sink to the bottom, and the oils and meat rise to the surface where they can be skimmed off. The oils can be stored and used as a butter, cooking oil, or milk to mix with gravies or soups. The meats can be eaten raw, ground into flour for nut breads, or combined with grains and fruits to make breads that can be eaten fresh or dried for storage. Acorns, which are starchy, nonoily nuts, provide only a little more than half of the caloric contribution and only about one-third of the protein of the oily nuts and lesser quantities of all of the other vitamins and minerals. Red and black acorns require some leaching to remove tannin from the nut meats before they are edible. White oak and burr oak would have been common prehistorically on the terraces and prairies/savannas of the mid-continent, and their nuts do not require leaching to be edible.

Different patterns of nut use emerged in North America because of resource availability and cultural preference. Nuts played an especially important economic role in the Eastern Woodlands, California, and the Great Basin. In the Eastern Woodlands, the most important nuts were hickory nuts and black walnuts and, to a lesser extent, acorns and hazelnuts. The first signs of heavy nut use appear in Early Archaic (ca. 8000–6000 B.C., or 9950–7950 years B.P.) sites in Tennessee, Illinois, Missouri, and throughout the Eastern Woodlands when postglacial climates moderated and modern vegetation patterns emerged. Even when cultivated plants were incorporated into the economy of the Eastern Woodlands, nuts continued to be an integral part of the diet. Acorns occur in low quantities in archaeological sites in the midwestern United States. Their low frequency might be due to the difficulty of processing them or to the fact that their shell is thin and less likely to be preserved after charring than the dense shells of hickory or walnut. In central California, however, populations focused on acorn gathering in conjunction with hunting, fishing, and gathering at least from 3000 B.C. (4950 years B.P.) to historic times (sixteenth century A.D.). Prehistoric inhabitants of the Great Basin in Utah, Nevada, and Idaho focused on piñon, locating sites with respect to prime piñon habitat. They were particularly heavily used there after 4000 B.C. (5950 years B.P.) and formed a staple of this very stable adaptation after A.D. 400–500 (1550–1450 years B.P.).

Constance Arzigian

Further Readings

Munson, P.J. (editor). 1984. *Experiments and Observations on Aboriginal Wild Food Utilization in Eastern North America.* Prehistoric Research Series, vol. 6, no. 2. Indiana Historical Society, Indianapolis.

Obsidian

Obsidian is a natural form of glass created by volcanic eruption. When molten lava cools very quickly, it turns into glassy obsidian. Obsidian was highly prized as a material for making chipped-stone tools, such as projectile points, knives, and many forms of scraping tools, for its glassy structure allows very sharp edges to be produced. Western North America, the most tectonically active part of the continent, has seen the most volcanic activity and, therefore, has the greatest number of obsidian outcrops. More than 100 obsidian sources have been identified in and around California alone. Most of these sources were used prehistorically, though about a dozen sources provided most of the supply.

Two characteristics make obsidian a particularly valued material for archaeological study. It interacts with oxygen to develop a hydration rind that grows thicker over time, making it possible to determine the ages of obsidian artifacts. In addition, every obsidian flow possesses a unique combination of trace elements, making it possible to determine from what source the material used to make obsidian artifacts was taken. These characteristics have shed invaluable light on patterns of prehistoric trade and exchange in addition to being important aids in dating the past.

Obsidian Hydration. Compared with other lithic raw materials, obsidian is unique in its capacity to indicate an artifact's age from the material itself. This capacity reflects the process of obsidian hydration. When obsidian is freshly flaked, the exposed surfaces begin to react with moisture in the air or ground, a process called obsidian hydration. This process produces an oxidized zone, or hydration rind, at the newly exposed surface. Over time, the rind penetrates deeper into the body of the artifact. Rind thickness can be measured by cutting a thin section through the artifact, mounting the section on a slide, and observing the specimen through a microscope with a built-in micrometer scale. In general, the thicker the rind, the more ancient the artifact.

This process was first applied to archaeology by Donovan Clark of the University of California, Berkeley, in the late 1950s. Clark originally assumed a uniform hydration rate for all obsidian, allowing it to serve as an alternative, and much less expensive, dating method to radiocarbon assays. Further research revealed that hydration rates were affected by many factors, chief among them being the obsidian source, groundwater conditions, ambient air and ground temperature, and whether the artifact was buried or found on the ground's surface. In general, surface artifacts have proven unreliable, buried artifacts from different sources yield different hydration rates in the same site, and obsidian from the same source can yield different hydration rates at different sites. The method remains useful for the study of large numbers of obsidian specimens from the same site when source can be controlled, for large numbers of specimens can indicate strong patterns of relative chronology. When those hydration patterns can be linked to calendar dates through additional chronometric means, such as radiocarbon, the result can be a powerful aid in charting patterns of regional culture change over time and space.

Obsidian Sourcing. Obsidian possesses properties that allow researchers to determine the specific source from which an individual artifact's material originated. This ability allows archaeologists to reconstruct ancient routes of trade and exchange along which goods moved between early cultures. Lava, the material from which obsidian originates, contains up to 50 trace mineral elements (minerals each composing less than 1 percent of the stone), most in quantities of a few parts per million. The procedures of neutron activation analysis and X-ray fluorescence allow the identification of trace elements and the counting of parts per million in the specimen of each trace element. Every obsidian deposit has a unique pattern of percentages in parts per million contributed by different trace elements. By studying the trace-element composition of obsidian pieces (artifacts, waste flakes, and unused material) found in a site, analysts can determine specimens that came from the same source. For example, analysis of trace elements in samples from each of the more than 100 known sources in and near the present-day state of California has allowed the connection of obsidian found in archaeological sites with specific sources. Resulting patterns show the importance of different sources to regional cultures and how preferences changed over time and for different functions. Many obsidian artifacts have been found archaeologically more than 500 km (310 miles) from their sources, with the beginnings of obsidian exchange starting as early as Paleoindian times (ca. 9200 B.C., or 11,150 years B.P.).

Joseph L. Chartkoff

Further Readings

Clark, D.L. 1964. Archaeological Chronology in California and the Obsidian Hydration Method: Part 1. *Archaeological Survey Annual Report* 62:139–225. University of California, Los Angeles.

Michels, J.W., and I.S.T. Tsong. 1980. Obsidian Hydration Dating: A Coming of Age. *Advances in Archaeological Method and Theory* 3:405–444.

Obsidian Cliff Plateau Quarries

The often-mentioned but not well-known Obsidian Cliff lithic source (48YE433) in Yellowstone National Park was systematically surveyed for the first time in 1989 by Montana State University under National Park Service sponsorship. The surface of this 180,000-year-old flow within the Yellowstone Rhyolite Plateau of northwestern Wyoming was collected and quarried periodically from at least 9050 B.C.–A.D. 1650 (11,000–300 years B.P.) by Rocky Mountain and Plains hunter-gatherers. Surface examination was facilitated by the extensive burnoff by the Wolf Creek fire in 1988 of dog hair–thick lodgepole pine and heavy duff ground cover. The survey identified and documented 59 spatially discrete quarry entries into bedrock and initial-stage workshop activity areas within the perimeter of the 14.5-km² (5.6-square-mile) plateau. The quarry features vary in form, depth, and scale. They range from single ovoid pits on flat surfaces and hillsides to multiple intersecting depressions that occupy large areas, some 250 m (825 feet) in length. Winding linear trenches were formed by the persistent quarrying of bedrock elsewhere on the plateau. The source-specific geochemistry of geological and archaeological obsidian specimens collected from the Obsidian Cliff plateau during the survey, as determined by X-ray fluorescence, is internally highly homogeneous irrespective of color and textural variability. Obsidian from Obsidian Cliff has been recognized in sites of Hopewell affiliation as far east as Ohio, northward into the southern Canadian Plains, and westward into the state of Washington. This obsidian was accessed and used differentially by indigenous hunter-gatherers by 9050 B.C. (11,000 years B.P.) and was traded widely. On those grounds, the Obsidian Cliff plateau was designated a National Historic Landmark in 1996 by the National Park Service.

Leslie B. Davis

Further Readings

Davis, L.B., S.A. Aaberg, and A.M. Johnson. 1992. Archaeological Fieldwork at Yellowstone's Obsidian Cliff. *Park Service: A Resource Management Bulletin* 12(2):26–27.

Davis, L.B., S.A. Aaberg, and J.G. Schmitt. 1995. *The Obsidian Cliff Plateau Prehistoric Lithic Source, Yellowstone National Park, Wyoming*. Selections From the Division of Cultural Resources no. 6. National Park Service, Rocky Mountain Region, Denver.

Ocean Bay Tradition

Ocean Bay is an early maritime tradition found along the north Pacific coast of Alaska on Kodiak Island, the adjacent Alaska Peninsula, parts of outer Cook Inlet, and probably Prince William Sound—the historic Pacific Eskimo area. On the basis of a small assemblage from

Prehistoric obsidian quarry of the linear trench type discovered on the Obsidian Cliff Plateau in Yellowstone National Park during the 1989 archaeological survey, following the 1988 Wolf Creek fire. (Courtesy of Museum of the Rockies/Montana State University–Bozeman)

Ocean Bay on Sitkalidak Island, Kodiak Island group, it was recognized in 1963 as a distinct entity older than any phase previously known in the regional sequence.

The best-documented assemblages date from ca. 5050 to 2050 B.C. (7000–4000 years B.P.) in calibrated radiocarbon years. Two sites on Kodiak also are dated to the next earlier millennium but have yielded too few artifacts for accurate characterization. It is anticipated that the tradition has strong ties with Anangula (Aleutian Islands) and the Paleoarctic-related Ugashik Narrows complex of the Alaska Peninsula ca. 7050–6050 B.C. (9000–8000 years B.P.). Circumstances suggest that these are the earliest maritime and partially maritime cultures in the region. In turn, a transition from Ocean Bay to the Kachemak tradition on Kodiak ca. 1550–1450 B.C. (3500–3400 years B.P.) is expected on the basis of close late Ocean Bay (Ocean Bay II) and Early Kachemak dates and technological sharing. To date (1996), though, derivation of the one from the other remains to be adequately demonstrated. There is, instead, slight but tantalizing evidence from P. Hausler-Knecht's excavations at the Rice Ridge site for an assemblage in this time range that is part Ocean Bay II and part Arctic Small Tool tra-

dition (ASTt) in its technological affiliation. But the ensuing Early Kachemak phase (at other sites) is absolutely unrelated to the early Denbigh Flint phase of the ASTt. However, off Kodiak on the Pacific side of the Alaska Peninsula, the Takli Alder phase, which begins essentially as a local form of Ocean Bay II, changes into a Kachemak tradition–related culture ca. 1050 B.C. (3000 years B.P.) (though not fully Kachemak as found on Kodiak and outer Cook Inlet). Thus, for Kodiak and Cook Inlet, prehistorians face the concomitant problems of explaining the end of the Ocean Bay tradition and the origins of the Kachemak tradition. The answer may lie in a scarcely investigated site (49AFG088) located at the mouth of the Afognak River. The 49AFG088 assemblage, known from three small test pits and a surface collection, has technological attributes of both the Ocean Bay and Kachemak traditions.

Earliest Ocean Bay technology, during Ocean Bay I times, featured bifacially flaked projectile points and knives, a microblade industry, and a few larger blades. The microblades were inserted into plain, bilaterally slotted, slender bone shafts (points). Ground-slate tools were developed by Ocean Bay people ca. 3050 B.C. (5000 years B.P.). Then bone-working techniques of sawing and scraping were applied to slate to produce blanks for ground-slate points and pointed knives (some blanks also were chipped) in a range of sizes and styles. This event defines the beginning of Ocean Bay II. Often there are parallel forms in flaked chert and ground slate, though, at some localities, ground-slate tools almost completely superseded flaked stone. With local exceptions, ground slate became the dominant lithic technology of the North Pacific area from Kodiak Island eastward and southward. Some Ocean Bay flaked-chert tips are so tiny that they would be identified as arrow tips were it not for the fact that the bow and arrow is not known to have been used in early North America and was little used later by maritime hunters from their small skin boats.

A slate-tool factory that probably was also a salmon-fishing and -processing site is located on Afognak Island (Kodiak group); the evidence of slate processing at many other sites is minimal, though finished tools are abundant. In this case, good-quality slate, found on only certain parts of Kodiak, was at hand at the mouth of the Afognak River. Concomitantly, boulder flakes (spalls), used mainly for saws but in some cases as hide scrapers, were abundant at the Afognak site and uncommon elsewhere. Evidently, there was local industrial specialization and trade in utilitarian objects, such as slate blades, and partial differentiation of work areas.

Barbed harpoon heads, stone lamps, and delicate eyed needles were used throughout the sequence. The harpoons are largely of a single format—with line guard but no line hole—that varies greatly in size. No toggle harpoon heads have been recovered. The broad, semilunar ulu butchering knife appeared only late in Ocean Bay II. Small notched pebbles, which were probably net sinkers, and grooved cobble weights also appeared late in the tradition but are not abundant. Nor are there labrets (lip plugs) except in the late Takli Alder phase of the adjacent mainland. All of these artifact classes became common in the succeeding Kachemak tradition after 2050 B.C. (4000 years B.P.) and in some cases after 1050 B.C. (3000 years B.P.). Compared with later regional prehistory, the Ocean Bay tradition's technological development looks incomplete; still, it represents a highly successful culture wholly maritime in its economy and orientation.

A wide range of shellfish, fish, and sea mammals were exploited. Whale bones recovered from Ocean Bay deposits provide circumstantial evidence for whaling. In contrast to the later diet of the peoples of Kodiak, sea otters evidently were consumed in abundance, judging from the frequent recovery of cooked cranial fragments by Hausler-Knecht at Chiniak (Rice Ridge site).

Only a few fragments of human skeletal elements have been recovered, and the biological relationships of Ocean Bay people to Eskimos and Indians remains to be determined. The technology suggests relationships with the peoples of the Aleutian Islands, the Alaska Peninsula, and, in the opposite direction, with southeastern Alaska, the last especially in Ocean Bay II times.

Donald W. Clark

Further Readings

Clark, D.W. 1979. *Ocean Bay: An Early North Pacific Maritime Culture.* Mercury Series Paper no. 86. Archaeological Survey of Canada, National Museum of Man, Ottawa.

———. 1992. "Only a Skin Boat Load or Two": The Role of Migration in Kodiak Prehistory. *Arctic Anthropology* 29(1):2–17.

Clark, G.H. 1977. *Archaeology on the Alaska Peninsula: The Coast of Shelikof Strait 1963–1965.* Anthropological Papers no. 13. Department of Anthropology, University of Oregon, Eugene.

Dumond, D.E. 1981. *Archaeology on the Alaska Peninsula: The Naknek Region, 1960–1975.* Anthropological Papers no. 21. Department of Anthropology, University of Oregon, Eugene.

Oswalt, W.H. 1955. Prehistoric Sea Mammal Hunters at Kaflia, Alaska. *Anthropological Papers of the University of Alaska* 4(1):23–61.

Ocmulgee Site

The term "Ocmulgee site" has several archaeological referents: (1) a group of sites located near Macon, Georgia, that were excavated by federal relief program archaeologists during the Great Depression; (2) the Ocmulgee National Monument, which includes two geographically separated sites, Lamar (9BI2) located southwest of Macon and Macon Plateau (9BI1); and (3) the Macon Plateau site itself, which is described in this entry.

The Macon Plateau site is situated on a relatively flat section of upland hills (the Macon

Plateau) that border the broad floodplain of the Ocmulgee River at Macon. Large-scale excavations, employing hundreds of workers at their peak, were conducted at the site between 1933 and 1942. Thousands of meters of trenches, thousands of square meters of block units, and portions of eight earth mounds were excavated, making the Macon Plateau site one of the most extensively excavated sites in the southeastern United States.

The Macon Plateau was occupied at various times during the Paleoindian, Archaic, and Woodland periods. The major occupation, known as the Macon Plateau phase, occurred ca. A.D. 950–1150 (1000–800 years B.P.) during the Early Mississippian period. Following a hiatus of ca. 500 years, the Plateau was again occupied briefly by Creek Indians (Ocmulgee Fields phase, ca. A.D. 1675–1725) and English traders, who built a stockaded trading post. The Macon Plateau phase at the Macon Plateau site includes eight earth mounds and subsurface features distributed over an area of at least 70 ha (173 acres). Most, if not all, mounds were of the platform type. Mound A, the largest, measures 15 m (49 feet) high and 91 m (298.5 feet) square at the base. The two most well-known features at the site are the Macon Earth Lodge and the Mound D ridged field. The former is a 13-m (42.6-foot) -diameter circular structure with a long entrance passage and distinctive interior furnishings of molded clay. There is some controversy regarding whether the structure was earth covered or not. The second feature is a 16 x 18-m (52.5 x 59-foot) section of aboriginal ground surface preserved beneath Mound D. Low, close-spaced, parallel ridges that cover the entire area are generally identified as the ridges and furrows of a cultivated field.

At 70 ha (173 acres), the Macon Plateau site is one of the largest Mississippian sites known. There is some question, however, whether the site represents a single architecturally integrated settlement. Distances between some mounds are exceptionally large, ranging between 250 and 350 m (820 and 1,148 feet), and ceramic evidence suggests that mounds at the southern end of the site were constructed and abandoned before those at the northern end were begun. The Macon Plateau phase is generally considered the archaeological remains of an Early Mississippian population that migrated into central Georgia from the Tennessee River Valley. Pottery types, platform mounds, and other artifact types resemble forms present in eastern Tennessee phases, such as Hiwassee Island, and differ greatly from those characteristic of the Late Woodland period (ca. A.D. 450–950, or 1500–1000 years B.P.) in central Georgia. The opposite view, that the Macon Plateau phase developed in central Georgia from Late Woodland antecedents, is held by some archaeologists.

David J. Hally

Further Readings

Fairbanks, C.H. 1956. *Archaeology of the Funeral Mound, Ocmulgee National Monument, Georgia.* Archaeological Research Series no. 3. National Park Service, Washington, D.C.

Hally, D.J. (editor). 1993. *Ocmulgee Archaeology, 1936–1986.* University of Georgia Press, Athens.

Ohio Hopewell

The people who left the remarkable cultural remains called Ohio Hopewell flourished in all but one of the major river valleys of southern Ohio from ca. 100 B.C. to A.D. 450 (2050–1500 years B.P.). Named in honor of its major site, this culture was built upon knowledge and traditions that had grown in the area over many centuries. It also contained elements of behavior shared by contemporary groups of peoples who lived in scattered sections of eastern North America from Canada to Florida. Some cultural values were shared that fostered the use of exotic materials and/or of specific objects or architectural forms as socially recognized symbols. Each group interpreted these values within its own ecological, social, political, and historical setting. A widely shared art style was carried out in a variety of media, including stone, clay, metals, bone, and other perishable materials. Naturalistic, conventional, abstract, and geometric forms occur. Local interpretations of this style help define both regional and subregional geographic units and probable levels of intergroup contacts. Artifacts whose patterns of attributes and spatial distribution have also been used to define spatial units include prismatic flint blades, bicymbal ear ornaments, celts, panpipes, pipes, and ceramics. The attempts to define time sequences have been less successful. The quantity, quality, and lavish intensity found in the concentrations of Ohio Hopewell artifactual and structural remains distinguish this culture among its contemporaries, and the designation "Hopewell" has frequently been extended to groups outside Ohio.

The acquisition of exotic raw materials and, to a lesser extent, exotic objects is a signature of Ohio Hopewell. Copper, mica, and marine shell are relatively widespread. Added to the inventory are more rare occurrences of obsidian, tiny bits of gold, somewhat more silver, galena, and a wide variety of fine flints and stones. These arrived in Ohio through a mix of contacts, each material likely in its own trajectory. Personal travel, formal and informal gifts, direct and indirect barter, and other personal and group activities were carried on through time. Technical studies have identified the original geographic source of some raw materials, but the type and duration of the contacts involved are not yet clearly defined. In any case, it is clear that whatever their form, these contacts resulted in accumulation of nonperishable artifacts and materials in Ohio while few such objects from Ohio are found elsewhere. The great majority of the recorded objects and raw materials, both local and exotic, were elements of arranged deposits, small to vast in size and not directly associated with human remains. The arrangement of these deposits was undoubtedly part of events occurring in a cyclic cultural calendar as well as those from the life cycles of families and individuals. Funeral or memorial events are represented in the individual and group tombs found in demarcated areas of the major sites and in the more numerous small sites.

Hopewellian groups set aside spaces, apparently for ritual, ceremonial, or other special purposes. In Ohio, such spaces vary in size and complexity. At the simple end, a prepared ca. 15.2 x 15.2-m (50 x 50-foot) floor was enclosed by a light screen or fence at Shetrone Mound 17 at the Hopewell site. Multiroomed, carefully designed great houses occur, including at least two at the Hopewell and Seip sites and single instances at Porter, Harness, and other sites. At the far end of the scale are the literally miles of earthen and stone walls that make up the various plan forms seen in the series of enclosures at sites such as Fort Ancient, Portsmouth, Hopewell, and Newark. Other smaller, but still impressive, conjoined enclosures occur, particularly among the groups of sites near Chillicothe and in the Miami valleys. These sites all demonstrate sophisticated engineering and surveying skills. The geographic concentration of such sites is a unique aspect of Ohio Hopewell.

Large wooden structures and their smaller counterparts were eventually covered with carefully constructed mounds. Since some sites were used for generations, the numbers of mounds present often became quite large. An example is the Hopewell site, with at least 40 mounds. Not all mounded areas included tombs. Small burned work areas, prepared floors with few features, deposits of artifacts, relatively empty wooden structures, and enigmatic features were also mounded over. At the major sites with

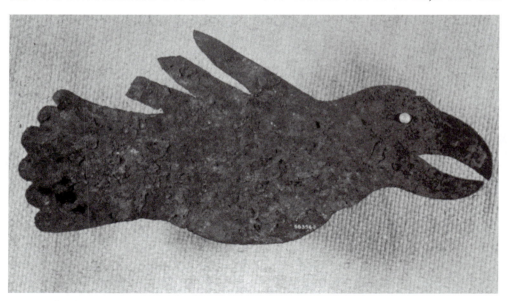

Copper effigy breastplate, Ohio. (Illustration by N. B. Greber)

extensive enclosures and mounded areas, such as Turner, Fort Ancient, Seip, Hopewell, and Newark, the complex of artifactual and structural remains is most likely the material residue of intertwined civic, religious, and secular activities.

The subsistence base that supported or allowed this cultural florescence likely includes gathering wild flora and fauna, hunting, and gardening. The starchy and oily seeds of the Eastern Agricultural complex are present. Directly (accelerator mass spectrometry, or AMS) dated corn came from an apparently ritual or ceremonial context at Edwin Harness; however, based on limited skeletal studies, corn was not a major Hopewellian food item. The local settlement pattern is still debated but appears to have been based on regular movements of at least substantial segments of the societies in a relatively limited area. Larger gatherings may have been seasonal, but the largest were most likely based on a longer, culturally determined cycle. Changes in local patterns over five centuries are a distinct possibility. The major enclosure sites themselves tend to occur within or near the boundaries of the glacial advances; that is, in areas containing the greatest number of varied ecological niches. At least in Ross County, which holds the greatest number of such niches in the central Ohio River Valley, small Hopewell occupations are commonly found as part of multicomponent sites along old oxbow levees or other similar locations used through millennia. The physical environment of the unglaciated Hocking River Valley of southeastern Ohio differs from that of its neighbors. The cultural remains in the Hocking Valley during this time period are not typical Ohio Hopewell but are closer to those found in areas south of the Ohio River adjacent to the Ohio Hopewell core.

The social organization that initiated and supported the great engineering and artistic achievements in Ohio has been variously reconstructed in general and professional publications spanning more than 200 years. Based on the clothing, regalia, and objects found in groups of tombs, the societies valued leadership and public display recognizing this leadership. However, the specific symbols of leadership tend to vary from site to site. Group membership at the clan or similar level of organization appears to have been important. Large social units pooled resources for some social purposes, such as great ceremonies or earthwork con-

O

Bobwhite effigy pipe, Ohio. (Illustration by N. B. Greber)

structions. The composition of these large groups varied as polities of varying sizes and complexity waxed and waned within the several river valleys. Their relationships with each other were closely tied to the varying prestige of local leaders, whose duties, privileges, and leadership authority rested upon general social customs, persuasion, and individual abilities.

All major sites and most minor ones have been impacted both by the great changes in land use that began with the introduction of modern farming in the 1780s and by formal archaeological excavations from the early 1800s to the present. Museum archives are an essential part of the database, which is growing through academic and culture-resource-management fieldwork and new laboratory studies. The sources cited below, and their bibliographies, will lead readers to the extensive literature of original data and interpretations of a major North American cultural florescence as seen in Ohio Hopewell.

N'omi B. Greber

Further Readings

Brose, D.S., and N. Greber (editors). 1979. *Hopewell Archaeology: The Chillicothe Conference.* Kent State University Press, Kent.

Caldwell, J., and R. Hall (editors). 1964. *Hopewellian Studies.* Scientific Papers no. 12. Illinois State Museum, Springfield.

Greber, N. 1991. A Study of Continuity and Contrast Between Central Sciota Adena and Hopewell Sites. *West Virginia Archeologist* 43(1–2):1–26.

Pacheo, P.J. (editor). 1994. *A View From the Core: A Synthesis of Ohio Hopewell Archaeology.* Proceedings of a conference sponsored by the Ohio Archaeological Council, November 19–20, 1993, Chillicothe.

Riley, T.J., G.R. Walz, C.J. Bareis, A.C. Fortier, and K.E. Parker. 1994. Accelerator Mass Spectrometry (AMS) Dates Confirm Early *Zea Mays* in the Mississippi River Valley. *American Antiquity* 59:490–498.

Seeman, M.F. 1979. *The Hopewell Interaction Sphere: The Evidence for Interregional Trade and Structural Complexity.* Prehistory Research Series, vol. 5, no. 2. Indiana Historical Society, Indianapolis.

Silverberg, R. 1968. *Mound Builders: The Archaeology of a Myth.* New York Graphic Society, Greenwich.

Smith, B.D. 1992. *Rivers of Change.* Smithsonian Institution Press, Washington, D.C.

Squier, G.E., and E.H. Davis. 1973 [1848]. *Ancient Monuments of the Mississippi Valley.* Contributions to Knowledge no. 1. Smithsonian Institution, Washington, D.C. Reprinted 1973 with an introduction by J.B. Griffin as *Antiquities of the New World: Early Explorations in Archaeology,* vol. 2. Published for the Peabody Museum of American Archaeology and Ethnology, Harvard University, Cambridge, by A.M.S. Press, New York.

Okanagan Valley Sequence

The Okanagan Valley extends northward ca. 250 km (155 miles) from the confluence of the Okanagan and Columbia rivers in north-central Washington State to headwaters in British Columbia. Historically, the valley was occupied by the Interior Salish-speaking Okanagan people. The valley can be divided on the basis of physiographic, ecological, and cultural variation into northern and southern portions, with the division at Okanagan Falls near the international border. Okanagan Falls posed a major barrier to the upstream runs of salmon. As a result, inhabitants in the northern areas developed extracommunity interaction relationships with groups to the north and south to acquire this storable food resource, which allowed them to maintain a semisedentary winter village settlement pattern.

As might be expected, the archaeological record discloses that the northern and the southern portions of the Okanagan Valley developed along different lines, although at the start they may have been quite similar. The north came to resemble contemporaneous phases in the Thompson River and Western Shuswap Lakes region, while the south was similar for a long period to middle Columbia River sequences. Despite these differences, a common set of four phases originally defined for the Wells Reservoir, situated at the confluence of the Okanagan and Columbia rivers, has been proposed for the entire valley system (Grabert 1974). Subsequent work (Copp 1979) at the McCall site in the north Okanagan Valley has allowed refinement of the third phase.

Okanagan Phase. This phase is poorly known and of a provisional nature; its characteristics are known from several small and putatively early assemblages in the Okanagan Valley. They share a high proportion of flake tools, a few large leaf-shaped and stemmed points, and some large, crude, leaf-shaped bifaces (preforms). Most of these items are made of basalt. Fragments of mussel shell are the only known faunal remains. From their geographic and stratigraphic positions, site components of this phase are placed in time from ca. 6000 to 4000 B.C. (7950–5950 years B.P.).

Indian Dan Phase (4000–1000 B.C., or 5950–2950 years B.P.). Large basal-notched stemmed points (some of which bear distinct barbs), medium and large leaf-shaped points, millingstones, pestles, and numerous flake tools distinguish the phase. Sites are in open locations or rock shelters. Earth ovens are occasionally present. Faunal remains include mussel shells, fish bones, and bones of land mammals.

Chiliwist Phase (1000 B.C.–A.D. 1100, or 2950–850 years B.P.). Chiliwist provides the earliest evidence for pithouses in the south Okanagan. These are steep-walled, deep, circular housepits commonly grouped as small settlements. Other characteristics of the phase include large leaf-shaped points; medium-sized, barbed, basal-notched stemmed points; microblades; ground-stone celts; millingstones; and the occasional bone artifact. Raw materials other than basalt are prominent in the flaked-stone industry. Salmon and other fish remains, along with mussel shell, are abundant. Mammal bone consists mainly of ungulates: elk, deer, and mountain sheep.

The Chiliwist phase has been divided into three subphases. Subphase III, which begins ca.

A.D. 100 (1850 years B.P.), is simply a 1,000-year void in the record. Subphases I (1000–400 B.C., or 2950–2350 years B.P.) and II (400 B.C.–A.D. 100, or 2350–1850 years B.P.) are distinguished from each other by the presence in the first of microblades and in the second of points similar to, but smaller than, those of the prior subphase. A late Subphase II shift in dominance from wide-necked to narrow-necked points is thought to have resulted from the introduction of the bow and arrow, which largely replaced the atlatl.

Cassimer Bar Phase (A.D. 1100–1800, or 850–150 years B.P.). The identifying characteristics of this phase are a wide variety of small projectile points, including corner-notched and side-notched forms; millingstones; carved steatite items; and bone-composite toggling harpoon heads. Geometric or zoomorphic designs decorate some bone and stone artifacts. Housepits are circular or ovoid, shallow, and saucer shaped, but there are also rectangular mat-lodge depressions. At least some burials are in wood-lined cysts. Bones of large ungulates predominate among faunal remains, but, when compared with earlier phases, there are also increased numbers of freshwater mussel shell and fish bone.

The most obvious differences between the southern and the northern segments of the Okanagan Valley are the presence in the north of a lengthy tradition of side-notched points and an affluent appearance to northern assemblages that is mainly the result of a greater number of ornamental items. The enduring differences have been considered evidence of northern stability, which, in turn, has been attributed to a less severe climatic impact in the north than in the south during the warm/dry Altithermal climatic period (ca. 5550–2050 B.C., or 7500–4000 years B.P.).

Donald H. Mitchell
David L. Pokotylo

Further Readings

Copp, S. 1979. *Archaeological Excavations at the McCall Site, South Okanagan Valley, British Columbia.* Unpublished Master's thesis. Department of Archaeology, Simon Fraser University, Burnaby.

Grabert, G.F. 1974. *Okanagan Archaeology: 1966–67.* Syesis, vol. 7 (Supplement no. 2).

Old Bering Sea/Okvik Culture

The earliest evidence for an Eskimo type of maritime adaptation with a fully developed technology for hunting seal, walrus, and whale from the ice and in open leads began ca. 150–50 B.C. (2100–2000 years B.P.). The cultural assemblage of this time period (Old Bering Sea/Okvik) continued to A.D. 700 (1250 years B.P.), when it was replaced by the Birnirk and Punuk cultures. The Old Bering Sea/Okvik culture appears to have been essentially Asiatic in origin. While the capture of whales was an important part of the maritime subsistence pattern, other resources, such as land mammals, particularly caribou and reindeer, birds, and fish, were not disregarded.

Given the culture's emphasis on the resources of the sea, sites of the Old Bering Sea/Okvik culture are found on promontories or high beaches that overlook the leads in the ice that formed in early spring and through which migrating whales made their way from the Pacific Ocean to the Arctic Ocean. Houses were semisubterranean structures with horizontally laid log walls, stone floors, and timbered ceilings; they were covered over with sod and earth. Entry passages were lower than the house floor to prevent heat loss. Hunting implements included those for sea mammals (toggling harpoons, seal darts and throwing boards, lances, floats, paddles, and boats [kayak and umiak]), land mammals (bow and arrow and spears), birds (multipronged bird spears used with throwing boards), and fish (leisters, fishhooks, and line weights). Snow goggles were worn to reduce the glare from snow and ice. Well-insulated clothing of caribou or seal skin was tailored to ward off the cold. In terms of a domestic toolkit, there were ground-slate knives fitted with bone or wooden handles for both men and women; ground-stone adzes; chipped-stone scrapers and drills; and bone or ivory needles, needle cases, drills, skin scrapers, mattocks, and picks. Tools were often made up of several parts and several different kinds of materials. The harpoon for securing walrus and whale consisted of a shaft of wood with a bone or ivory ice pick at one end, and a socket piece, a foreshaft, and a harpoon head of walrus ivory or bone at the other. Pottery lamps and cooking pots with a linear or check-stamp surface treatment completed the domestic inventory. While dogs have been reported from Old Bering Sea/Okvik sites, there is no indication that dog traction was used. Small hand-pulled sleds were used by individual hunters on the land and on the sea ice.

The decorative style of the Old Bering Sea/

O

Okvik culture, as seen in elaborate ivory carvings of animal and human figurines as well as engraved and carved items used in hunting, for personal adornment, clothing, and containers, is most distinctive. Mythic animals of the land and sea, and motifs composed of circle-dog, spurred lines, and inverted V and Y figures, completely cover the surfaces of harpoon heads, throwing-board weights, wooden box parts, carrying-bag handles, and the like. The function of this elaborate art style is unknown; it appears on items associated with everyday activities as well as on those associated with hunting or burial, suggesting that art and, by inference, religion were involved in all aspects of life.

Although Old Bering Sea and Okvik cultural expressions have been grouped as a single archaeological phase, there are some differences in their specific art styles and in the distributions of their settlements. The Old Bering Sea art style is more curvilinear, with elements flowing gracefully into one another. The Okvik art style is more static, with an emphasis on the zonation of geometric elements. In terms of settlement distribution, Okvik sites are restricted to St. Lawrence Island and the eastern extremity of the Chukchi Peninsula. Old Bering Sea sites extend from Cape Baranov on the East Siberia Sea to the village of Enmylen on the south coast of the Chukchi Peninsula and to St. Lawrence Island. There are also traces of the Old Bering Sea culture at locations along the coast of the Alaskan mainland.

While the derivation of the Old Bering Sea/Okvik culture from the earlier Norton culture of Alaska and the Neolithic cultures of Asia seems probable, the first indication of a marked cultural elaboration based upon an intensified use of natural resources through a well-organized social collective appears during the Old Bering Sea/Okvik cultural phase. Such social structural changes were to be elaborated in the succeeding cultural phases, Birnirk and Punuk, and paralleled in the contemporary Ipiutak cultural complex at Point Hope on the Alaskan mainland.

Robert E. Ackerman

Further Readings

Dumond, D. 1987. *Eskimos and Aleuts.* Thames and Hudson, New York.

Fagan, B. 1991. *Ancient North America,* pp. 164–167. Thames and Hudson, New York.

Old Copper Culture

When pioneering Europeans cleared the forests and plowed the fields in the Upper Midwest, large numbers of copper artifacts unexpectedly turned up in addition to the usual chipped-flint projectile points and ground-stone axes made familiar by previous finds in states to the east and south. Because the Indians known to the pioneers rarely possessed metal other than what they had acquired from the Europeans themselves, the newly unearthed copper objects were assumed to be prehistoric and possibly the products of a mysterious, vanished race. The idea of prehistoric Indian authorship eventually prevailed, and the objects of speculation were assigned to an "Old Copper culture."

When archaeologists eventually learned more about the geographical and temporal ranges of the copper artifacts, it became clear that they were more widespread than originally thought and that they had been produced by more than one people or culture. Native copper beads, hair tubes, awls, and fishhooks, for example, are known to have been made for thousands of years and to occur on archaeological sites over a good part of eastern North America. Apparently, the excellent, nearly pure native copper of the Lake Superior Basin had become a long and widely demanded trade commodity, both as a raw material and as finished artifacts. Nevertheless, the idea of an ancient copper-using culture in Wisconsin and the Upper Midwest persisted despite the subtraction from its unique inventory of the space- and time-transgressing awls, gorges, fishhooks, and other items.

Old Copper is defined by a suite of copper implements that dates to the Middle or (depending on one's preferred definitions) Late Archaic period, 3000–1000 B.C. (4950–2950 years B.P.). Most of these implements are concentrated in eastern Wisconsin, but many have also been found in adjoining parts of Michigan, Minnesota, Iowa, Illinois, and Ontario. Some astonishingly rich burial caches of the same kinds of artifacts have been found, too, in southwestern Quebec. Included in this suite of implements are varieties of tanged (stemmed) and socketed spear points that often exhibit ridged blade backs and faceted or beveled edges and that often were originally secured to their hafts with rivets; tanged asymmetrical knives (similar but usually smaller, blunter forms are common in later contexts); crescentic knives with and without paired right-angle tangs that resemble the Eskimo women's knife, or ulu; thin

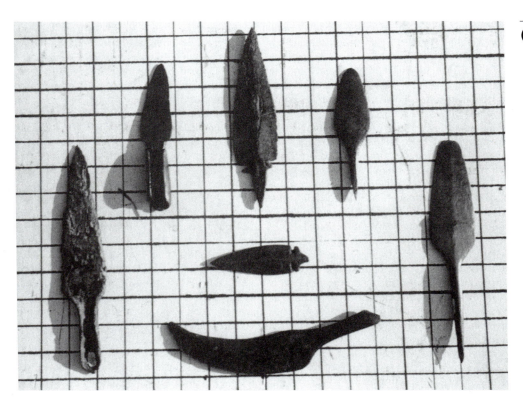

Old Copper Culture artifacts. Background ruled in one-inch squares. (Courtesy of the Wilford Archaeology Laboratory, University of Minnesota)

crescents of uncertain function, adzes, and socketed axe blades that in many cases are actually adze bits. Tanged and barbed harpoons, even toggle-head harpoons, have occasionally been found. In association often are awls and other usually small and simple tools that are not easily distinguished from later examples. Some of the tanged projectile points, including those with curiously multinotched stems, as well as the crescentic, or semilunar, knives, are duplicated far to the east in ground slate in the Maritime Archaic and in related cultures of the Lake Forest Archaic Laurentian tradition. All of these ancient metal artifacts were made by heating and hammering native copper procured from glacial gravel deposits or from the rich mother lodes in the Lake Superior Basin.

Although Archaic copper tools have been recovered at many archaeological localities, no single-component or stratified multicomponent village sites are known to date (1996). Certain levels in a few rock shelters have been proclaimed "Old Copper without the copper," but these identifications are regarded with prudent skepticism by many archaeologists. However,

three burial sites (Osceola, Oconto, and Reigh), all in Wisconsin, have been especially productive of artifacts and information, in spite of being seriously disturbed before proper excavation could be undertaken. These sites produced evidence of multiple forms of inhumation: from bundle burials and cremations to flexed and extended burials, and from individual interments to an ossuary, or mass grave. Some of the stone tools accompanying the copper, including the projectile points, are sufficiently different from site to site to argue against the notion of common authorship by one people at one particular time. Bannerstones were found at Osceola only; a sandal-sole shell gorget is unique at Reigh. Some of these discrepancies, including the presence or absence of certain copper items such as "spuds" or socketed axes, may be functions of inadequate sampling. But there are enough differences to indicate that probably more than one archaeological culture is represented in the "Old Copper" syndrome and that a considerable period of time is represented as well. Tracing out these complications has proven difficult.

Even though information remains more limited than archaeologists would like, it has become increasingly clear that the designation "Old Copper culture" should be understood to mean the material remains of probably several different societies that shared a common primitive metallurgy for something like 2,000 years during the Middle to Late Archaic periods in the western Great Lakes. These societies may not even have shared the same notions of implement style. When the first attempts were made at radiometrically dating the Old Copper culture at the Oconto site in northeastern Wisconsin, the radiocarbon method was subject to sources of error that have since come under much better control. Unfortunately, the first assays produced dates far in excess of the likely age of the site, as later demonstrated by geochronological studies and by radiocarbon dates from other sites. Doubtless the first attempts at fabricating implements from native copper began long before the establishment of the Oconto and other excavated cemeteries, but it appears that the 3000–1000 B.C. (4950–2950 years B.P.) period roughly encompasses most of the tenure of the "Old Copper culture."

Ronald J. Mason

Further Readings

Fogel, I.L. 1963. The Dispersal of Copper Artifacts in the Late Archaic Period of Prehistoric North America. *Wisconsin Archeologist* 44(3):129–180.

Mason, R.J. 1981. *Great Lakes Archaeology*. Academic Press, New York.

Ritzenthaler, R. (editor). 1957. The Old Copper Culture of Wisconsin. *Wisconsin Archeologist* 38(4):185–329.

See also LAKE FOREST ARCHAIC; LAURENTIAN ARCHAIC; MARITIME ARCHAIC TRADITION

Old Cordilleran Tradition

The term "cordilleran" or "cordillerian"—pertaining to mountains or a mountain range—is part of the name of several similarly defined cultural constructs used in the explanation of the early prehistory of northwestern North America. B. Robert Butler and Richard S. MacNeish, who were corresponding with each other, both began using the term ca. 1958. MacNeish (1959) defined the "Cordillerian tradition" as the second earliest cultural tradition in the Yukon with extensions from the Yukon coast south to the Columbia River; it was considered immediately post-Paleoindian. Assemblages contained large lenticular "lermalike" bifaces, various types of pebble tools, crude blades, burins of several types, fish gorges, slab choppers, and scalelike scrapers. The tradition was identified at components of the Flint Creek phase on the Firth River and at the Klondike site near Fort Liard. The early assemblages from the Milliken site on the Fraser River and from sites at Five Mile Rapids on the Columbia River were considered to be extensions of this tradition.

In 1983, Donald W. Clark, who had reviewed the Yukon and Alaskan evidence, renamed the tradition in this region the "northern Cordilleran" and included it with pre-Denali, Paleoindian complexes from Alaska, such as Putu, Nenana, the Mesa site complex, and undated assemblages from Batza Tena. Defined in this manner, it is a variant and potential ancestor of more southerly Paleoindian cultures, such as Clovis, even though temporal precedence in the north has not been satisfactorily demonstrated.

In 1961, Butler formalized his use of the term by defining the "Old Cordilleran Culture" as a "tradition characterized by a leaf-shaped point and blade complex, along with a generalized assortment of cutting, chopping, and scraping implements . . . a generalized hunting-fishing-gathering economy . . . (that became) a maritime tradition on the Northwest Coast . . . "; he considered it contemporaneous with Paleoindian traditions, such as Clovis. Butler called the generalized leaf-shaped points "Cascade points." He hypothesized that this cutlure extended along the Pacific cordilleras from North to South America, with its earliest occurrences in the northern interior rather than on the coast. Some of the same site assemblages that MacNeish had used were included as components of the Old Cordilleran culture.

It has since been conclusively demonstrated that the artifact complex on which this construct was based is not the earliest complex in the interior parts of the Pacific Northwest, but was preceded there by complexes belonging to both the Fluted Point and the Stemmed Point traditions; and that the leaf-shaped points and associated pebble tools belong to an early coastal tradition and not to an old interior cordilleran tradition. For these reasons, the concept has been replaced in some usages by the term "Pebble Tool" tradition.

Roy L. Carlson

Further Readings

Butler, B.R. 1961. *The Old Cordilleran Culture in the Pacific Northwest.* Occasional Papers no. 5. Idaho State College Museum, Pocatello.

Carlson, R.L. 1990. Cultural Antecedents. In *Northwest Coast,* edited by W. Suttles, pp. 60–69. Handbook of North American Indians, vol. 7, W.C. Sturtevant, general editor. Smithsonian Institution, Washington, D.C.

Clark, D.W. 1983. Is There a Northern Cordilleran Tradition? *Canadian Journal of Archaeology* 7(18):23–48.

MacNeish, R.S. 1959. A Speculative Framework of Northern North American Prehistory As of April 1959. *Anthropologia,* n.s., 1:1–17.

See also PEBBLE TOOL TRADITION; STEMMED POINT TRADITION

Bonnichsen, R., and M.H. Sorg (editors). 1989. *Bone Modification.* Center for the Study of the First Americans, Institute for Quaternary Studies, University of Maine, Orono.

Hoffecker, J.F., W.R. Powers, and T. Goebel. 1993. The Colonization of Beringia and the Peopling of the New World. *Science* 259:46–53.

Irving, W.N., and C.R. Harrington. 1973. Upper Pleistocene Radiocarbon-Dated Artifacts From the Northern Yukon. *Science* 179:335–340.

Morlan, R.E. 1978. Early Man in Northern Yukon Territory: Perspectives As of 1977. In *Early Man in America,* edited by A.L. Bryan, pp. 78–95. Occasional Paper no. 1. Department of Anthropology, University of Alberta, Edmonton.

See also BONE MODIFICATION

Old Crow Flats

Now mainly of interest in the history of archaeology, Old Crow Flats (MkV1-12) was widely thought in the 1970s to contain cultural bone dating as early as 80,000–30,000 years B.P. Located on the Porcupine River in the Old Crow Basin along the northern Yukon-Alaska border, the site is a rich, redeposited bonebed containing the remains of mammoth, horses, caribou, and other late Pleistocene animals. An apparently well-made caribou bone flesher with a bone apatite radiocarbon date of 25,000 B.C. ± 3000 (26,950 years B.P.), and many mammoth and other bones that were thought to have been deliberately flaked or fragmented when green, were identified in the bed. Critics have convincingly argued that the specimens represent naturally fractured bone and artifacts of Holocene age (8000 B.C., or 9950 years B.P., to the present). On the positive side, the controversy spurred important investigations of the nature of cultural and natural bone modification.

Guy Gibbon

Further Readings

Bonnichsen, R. 1978. Critical Arguments for Pleistocene Artifacts From the Old Crow Basin, Yukon: A Preliminary Statement. In *Early Man in America,* edited by A.L. Bryan, pp. 102–118. Occasional Paper no. 1. Department of Anthropology, University of Alberta, Edmonton.

Old Women's Phase

Old Women's phase is a designation for Late Prehistoric and Protohistoric manifestations in southern Alberta and occasionally Montana, except for the One Gun phase. The name is taken from the Old Women's Buffalo Jump, ca. 80.5 km (50 miles) south of Calgary, Alberta. Buffalo jumps, where bison were stampeded over steep slopes or cliffs, are prominent communal kill sites in this phase. Sites often consist of multiple strata below the precipice and contain a surfeit of bone. Enormous processing areas for butchering and preparation of hides and pemmican (a mixture of dried meat, bone grease, and berries) may be located near the kill (Brink and Dawe 1989). Increasing human population levels and sedentism apparently resulted from the increasing perfection of bison drives during Old Women's times.

The principal diagnostics of the phase are small arrow points. For the Old Women's Buffalo Jump, the points have been arranged in an unbroken typological series starting ca. A.D. 600–700 (1350–1250 years B.P.) when arrows are generally considered to have replaced the larger atlatl darts of the Middle Prehistoric (Forbis 1962). The arrow points are known variously as Plains or Prairie Side-Notched (Kehoe 1973). Local lithic raw materials are common and include silicified wood and cherts, including small black pebbles split by means of bipolar percussion techniques. Exotic lithics from Knife River in North Dakota and the Madison formation in Montana indicate extensive trade or movement outside the immediate area. When pottery is present in the Old Women's phase, it belongs to the Saskatchewan Basin complex, with its closest relationships to the east (Byrne 1973). Aceramic sites may be attributed to the Old Women's phase simply on grounds of projectile point types or Late Prehistoric age.

Brian O.K. Reeves (1983:20, 47) sees the origins of early Old Women's in the Besant phase of his Napikwan tradition and regards the Besant–Old Women's transition as complete at A.D. 750–780 (1200–1170 years B.P.). He distinguishes it from the Avonlea phase of his Tunaxa tradition. Small, delicate side-notched arrow points—the distinctive hallmark of Avonlea—appear at A.D. 200 (1750 years B.P.). In Reeves's scenario (1983:20), they influenced "Early" Old Women's ca. A.D. 1200 (750 years B.P.) to produce "Late" Old Women's. William J. Byrne (1973:470) suggests that the origins of Old Women's lie in an amalgam of Besant and Avonlea "before and after 850 A.D." However, as noted earlier, the first arrow points in the Old Women's series are earlier than this, and some of the arrow points extend well back into the Middle Prehistoric (ca. 3000 B.C.–A.D. 150, or 4950–1800 years B.P.).

Reeves's postulated linkages of Old Women's to various historic tribes—Blackfoot, North Peigan, Blood, Atsina, and Gros Ventre—remain controversial, since the point types are widespread in North America, and other phase attributes are not known to be tribe specific. The phase ends with the arrival of European trade goods during the Protohistoric (ca. A.D. 1700, or 250 years B.P.), when Algonquian-speaking groups almost certainly dominated much of southern Alberta.

Richard G. Forbis

Further Readings

Brink, J., and B. Dawe. 1989. *Final Report on the 1985 and 1986 Field Season at Head-Smashed-In Buffalo Jump, Alberta.* Manuscript Series no. 16. Archaeological Survey of Alberta, Edmonton.

Byrne, W.J. 1973. *The Archaeology and Prehistory of Southern Alberta As Reflected by Ceramics.* Mercury Series Paper no. 14. Archaeological Survey of Canada, National Museum of Man, Ottawa.

Forbis, R.G. 1962. *The Old Women's Buffalo Jump, Alberta.* Contributions to Anthropology, 1960, pt. 1:56–123. Bulletin no. 180. National Museum of Man, Ottawa.

Kehoe, T.F. 1973. *The Gull Lake Site: A Prehistoric Bison Drive Site in Southwestern Saskatchewan.* Publications in Anthropology and History no. 1. Public Museum of the City of Milwaukee, Milwaukee.

Reeves, B.O.K. 1983. *Culture Change in the Northern Plains: 1000 B.C.–A.D. 1000.* Occasional Paper no. 20. Archaeological Survey of Alberta, Edmonton.

See also CLUNY EARTHLODGE VILLAGE

Olivella (California)

Olivella biplicata, the purple olive snail, is a small shoreline marine shell found from Vancouver to Baja California. Prehistoric Californians harvested the shells to use for bead manufacturing. With one end ground off and the other naturally open, whole shells could be strung or sewn on clothing as ornaments. Alternatively, shells were broken into pieces; the fragments were given holes by drilling; and the drilled pieces were shaped into squares or disks and strung on cords to make long strings of beads. *Olivella* shell beads were widely used throughout California, especially in the Late period (A.D. 500–1850, or 1450–100 years B.P.) both as decorations and as shell bead money.

Joseph L. Chartkoff

See also SHELL MONEY (CALIFORNIA)

Olsen-Chubbuck Site

Olsen-Chubbuck (5CH1) is a carefully excavated Folsom kill site near the town of Kit Carson in east-central Colorado. The now classic report by Joe Ben Wheat (1972) graphically demonstrated how a wide variety of detailed information could be extracted from a bonebed. Radiocarbon dated to ca. 8050 B.C. (10,000 years B.P.) on bone collagen, the kill took place in late summer or early fall when ca. 200 bison (*Bison occidentalis*) were stampeded down a steep hillside into a deep, long, and narrow arroyo ca. 3 m (10 feet) wide and 2 m (6.6 feet) deep in an apparently efficient and rapid multifamily operation. Wheat skillfully reconstructed the composition of the herd, which included animals of all ages and both sexes, and the pattern of the butchery process. Included among the more than 60 artifacts recovered were fluted and "unfluted" Folsom projectile points, flake knives and scrapers, and cobbles for breaking bone. The variety of raw materials used to make flaked tools supports the notion that Paleoindian bands roamed vast territories in their search for game.

Guy Gibbon

Further Readings

Frison, G.C. 1991. *Prehistoric Hunters of the High Plains.* 2nd ed. Academic Press, San Diego.

Wheat, J.B. 1967. A Paleoindian Bison Kill. *Scientific American* 216:44–52.

———. 1972. *The Olsen-Chubbuck Site: A Paleo-Indian Bison Kill.* Memoir no. 26. Society for American Archaeology, Washington, D.C.

See also FOLSOM COMPLEX

One Gun Phase

The One Gun phase reflects a Protohistoric-period intrusion of an archaeological complex into southern Alberta and immediately adjacent portions of Saskatchewan. The prehistoric record at this time is dominated by various manifestations of the Old Women's phase, which appears to develop locally out of even earlier indigenous archaeological occupations. Sites of the Old Women's phase constitute the major archaeological presence throughout much of the Late Prehistoric and Protohistoric periods, and well into the historic period. For a brief era, ca. A.D. 1725–1750, there is a coeval presence, the One Gun phase, which appears to reflect the arrival of a group of people that trace their ancestry to the Middle Missouri Plains Village farmers of North and South Dakota.

The strongest evidence for this intrusion is found at the Cluny site on the banks of the Bow River ca. 80.5 km (50 miles) downstream from Calgary, Alberta. The site consists of the remains of what appears to be a Middle Missouri–style fortified earthlodge village made up of 11 "house" depressions, a palisade, and a semicircular fortification ditch. While a number of construction details are unusual when compared to contemporary sites in the Dakotas, the entire complex is completely foreign to the traditional archaeological record of Alberta and Saskatchewan; it is clearly reminiscent of sev-

enteenth- and eighteenth-century Middle Missouri sites.

Evidence for the Middle Missouri connection is strengthened by associated artifacts, particularly pottery. The local ceramic tradition, the Saskatchewan Basin complex, first appears ca. A.D. 200 (1750 years B.P.), and persists to the early 1800s. However, the One Gun phase embodies very different ceramic materials. The Cluny-complex ware features many characteristics also reminiscent of Middle Missouri ancestry, including check and simple stamping on the bodies, squat and globular vessel forms, frequent use of an S-shaped neck profile, and linear dentate stamp and fine-line incision decorations on the lips and collars. As for other intrusive associated artifact types, pitted handstones, grinding slabs, and scapula knives represent items seemingly unique to One Gun occupations.

While the Cluny site apparently reflects a unique site unit intrusion, other aspects of the One Gun phase are much more prevalent in the region. Cluny-complex pottery is found in many Protohistoric occupations, frequently in association with Old Women's–phase assemblages as a minor component in a ceramic inventory dominated by Saskatchewan Basin complex materials. In Saskatchewan in particular, the mixing of ceramic traditions is more evident than in Alberta, and suggestions have been made that there is an actual fusion of the cultures in that region that is sometimes called Mortlach or Mortlach Aggregate.

Regardless of local variations, what does seem evident is that sometime in the early 1700s a migrant group made its way across the watershed between the Missouri Basin and the Saskatchewan River drainage. After a short-lived attempt to reconstruct a familiar way of life in an alien environment, the intruders were assimilated or eliminated by the local population and disappeared as a distinct culture. Ethnic identification of these people is tenuous at best, but there is some reason to suggest that they were Siouan speakers, possibly representing a Hidatsa splinter group.

William J. Byrne

Further Readings

Byrne, W.J. 1973. *The Archaeology and Prehistory of Southern Alberta As Reflected by Ceramics.* Mercury Series Paper no. 14. Archaeological Survey of Canada, National Museum of Man, Ottawa.

———. 1978. An Archaeological Demonstration of Migration on the Northern Great Plains. In *Archaeological Essays in Honor of Irving B. Rouse*, edited by R.C. Dunnell and E.S. Hall, Jr., pp. 247–274. Mouton, The Hague.

Forbis, R.G. 1977. *Cluny: An Ancient Fortified Village in Alberta.* Occasional Paper no. 4. Department of Archaeology, University of Calgary, Calgary.

Vickers, J.R. 1994. Cultures of the Northwestern Plains: From the Boreal Forest Edge to Milk River. In *Plains Indians, A.D. 500–1500,* edited by K.H. Schlesier, pp. 3–33. University of Oklahoma Press, Norman.

Oneota disc pipe made of catlinite. (Courtesy of the Wilford Archaeology Laboratory, University of Minnesota)

Oneota

Oneota is a widespread, Late Prehistoric, Upper Mississippian archaeological culture centered in southern Wisconsin and Minnesota, Iowa, and parts of northern Illinois. Although the date and place of origin of the culture remain obscure, Oneota people apparently expanded southward and southwestward throughout much of the Prairie Peninsula after ca. A.D. 1200 (750 years B.P.). Radiocarbon dates indicate that the culture was present in at least some areas of the southern half of Wisconsin by A.D. 1000 (950 years B.P.). The Oneota economy was seemingly focused on maize agriculture and seasonal bison hunts, although a wide range of other food resources were eaten. Burial mounds were constructed at some early villages, but later villages are associated with cemetery burial in which individuals were, for the most part,

Oneota ceramic vessel from the Rushford site (21FL9), Fillmore County, Minnesota. (Courtesy of the Wilford Archaeology Laboratory, University of Minnesota)

laid on their back in an extended position. House type and size seem to have varied widely through space and time. At least some villages were surrounded by palisades and other possible defensive structures. Oneota components at sites are most easily identified by the presence of globular, shell-tempered jars with strap handles and geometric motifs, at least some of which are thought to represent hawk symbolism. The ancestors of the Winnebago, Oto, Ioway, Missouri, and Osage, which are grouped together as the Chiwere Sioux, are generally considered the primary producers of the remains archaeologists refer to as Oneota culture.

Guy Gibbon

Further Readings

Benn, D.W. 1989. Hawks, Serpents, and Bird-Men: Emergence of the Oneota Mode of Production. *Plains Anthropologist* 34(125):233–260.

Brown, J.A., and D.L. Asch. 1990. Cultural Setting: The Oneota Tradition. In *At the Edge of Prehistory: Huber Phase Archaeology in the Chicago Area*, edited by J.A. Brown and P.J. O'Brien, pp. 145–154. Published for the Illinois Department of Transportation by the Center for American Archeology, Kampsville.

Gibbon, G.E. 1972. Cultural Dynamics and the Development of the Oneota Lifeway in Wisconsin. *American Antiquity* 37:166–185.

———. (editor). 1982. *Oneota Studies.* Publications in Anthropology no. 1. University of Minnesota Press, Minneapolis.

Henning, D.R. 1970. Development and Interrelationships of Oneota Culture in the Lower Missouri River Valley. *Missouri Archaeologist* 32(1–4):1–180.

Mason, R.J. 1993. Oneota and Winnebago Ethnogenesis: An Overview. *Wisconsin Archeologist* 74(1–4):347–368.

Overstreet, D.F., and P.B. Richards (editors). 1992. *Archaeology at Lac des Puans, the Lake Winnebago Phase, a Classic Horizon Expression of the Oneota Tradition in East-Central Wisconsin.* Reports of Investigations no. 280. Great Lakes Archaeological Research Center, Milwaukee.

Sasso, R.J. 1993. La Crosse Region Oneota Adaptations: Changing Late Prehistoric Subsistence and Settlement Patterns in the Upper Mississippi Valley. *Wisconsin Archeologist* 74(1–4):246–290.

Wedel, M.M. 1959. Oneota Sites on the Upper Iowa River. *Missouri Archaeologist* 21(2–4).

O

Oshara Tradition

The Oshara tradition was first defined in the early 1970s by Cynthia Irwin-Williams as a regional manifestation of the Picosa culture. It was intended to be an interpretive framework for understanding Archaic and subsequent cultures in the northern Southwest. This enduring concept was based on surveys and excavations carried out primarily in the Arroyo Cuervo region of northwestern New Mexico under the general auspices of the Anasazi Origins Project (AOP). Interdisciplinary research in the Arroyo Cuervo under Irwin-Williams's guidance was one of the first problem-oriented studies undertaken in the Southwest that dealt with preceramic sites, which frequently had been ignored as unimportant. The ultimate goal of the AOP was to define the origins of agriculture in the Southwest and to examine the trajectory taken in subsequent Anasazi Puebloan formations. In order to do this, it was necessary to find an unbroken sequence of cultural development that led to the earliest phases of recognizable Anasazi culture. Arroyo Cuervo contained such a sequence, and Irwin-Williams defined several phases, which encompassed the Oshara tradition.

The earliest Oshara manifestations postdate the Paleoindian period. Irwin-Williams termed these the Jay and the Bajada phases and dated them to ca. 5500–3200 B.C. (7450–5150 years B.P.). During these phases, subsistence was based on extensive mixed foraging and hunting, and a wide range of locally available plants and animals were exploited. The basic social units were small nomadic bands that operated on a relatively unstructured annual round. During the subsequent San Jose phase (ca. 3200–1800 B.C., or 5150–3750 years B.P.), climatic amelioration occurred, and technological improvements in food processing permitted more intensive and efficient use of resources. This was coupled with a regional population increase, although the basic social or annual economic structure remained unchanged. In the Armijo phase (ca. 1800–800 B.C., or 3750–2750 years B.P.), a major economic alteration, the introduction of limited maize agriculture, occurred. This made possible a small seasonal surplus and permitted a seasonal pattern of aggregation to develop. The new resource initially contributed more toward increased complexity in socioceremonial interaction than it did to the actual economic structure: Although agriculture was an economic element, it was not initially a major subsistence variable. During the succeeding En Medio phase (ca. 800 B.C.–A.D. 400, or 2750–1550 years B.P.), which includes the Basketmaker II period, and the Trujillo phase (ca. A.D. 400–600, or 1550–1350 years B.P.), or early Basketmaker III, fully seasonal annual economic and socioceremonial cycles developed. Irwin-Williams interpreted these changes as the result of a structured widening of the resource base in response to increased population. The Trujillo phase is essentially a transition between the Archaic and the Anasazi periods, and the last two phases of the Oshara tradition represent local Anasazi developments. The Sky Village (ca. A.D. 600–700, or 1350–1250 years B.P.), or late Basketmaker III, and the Loma Alta (ca. A.D. 700–850, or 1250–1100 years B.P.), or Pueblo I, phases witnessed the formation of semisedentary agriculturally dependent villages. These were initiated partly as a response to continuing population growth and local environmental hardships. Subsequent developments followed continuing Anasazi patterns to their culmination with historic Pueblo groups. Irwin-Williams (1973:18) summarized the Oshara tradition as representing long-term progress toward sedentarism that seems to have been the result of cultural adjustment to a number of complex and interacting elements, principally climatic change, population increase, and the introduction and development of new subsistence and processing technologies.

Each of these phases is composed of a specific constellation of sites, artifacts, and locational variables. In Arroyo Cuervo, base camps and at least two types of specific-activity sites have been recognized: isolated hunting and/or gathering camps and quarry-workshop camps. In addition, scattered chipping areas and isolated projectile points occurred. Toward the end of the Archaic (during the Armijo phase), Irwin-Williams recognized a new settlement type represented by the pattern of seasonal aggregation described above. This is best illustrated by Armijo rock shelter. Such sites are much larger than earlier ones. Finally, during the terminal Archaic phases (En Medio and Trujillo), small seasonal sites located on sand dunes became important. Site location figures prominently in Irwin-Williams's scheme, and several microhabitats were differentially used through time.

One of the most controversial aspects of the Oshara tradition has been the proposal that agriculture was, after initial stimulus from Mesoamerica, essentially a long-term in situ development in the northern Southwest. Irwin-Williams believed that initial experimentation with maize agriculture commenced during the Armijo phase and that this economic strategy gradually assumed a more significant role. Ultimately, it established the economic foundation for the development of Anasazi culture. This

Sheep Camp Shelter, near Chaco Canyon, New Mexico. Evidence for the use of cultigens (corn and squash) in a Late Archaic (ca. 100–1000 B.C.) context was discovered at this site. The project was conducted by the University of Kansas with NSF funding. (Courtesy of A. H. Simmons)

Close-up of carbonized corn cob found in Oshara tradition pit dating to ca. 700–1000 B.C. (Courtesy of A. H. Simmons)

position went unchallenged for several years, but in the 1980s several researchers began to question some of the assumptions and databases for presumed "early" (i.e., Armijo phase) agriculture in the Southwest (Berry 1982, 1985; Minnis 1985; Wills 1988; Matson 1991). A new model of relatively late and often accelerated agricultural development was proposed as an alternative to the scenario envisioned by the Oshara tradition (Berry 1982, 1985). However, even more recent research into the issue, using modern data recovery methods and direct AMS (accelerated mass spectrometry) dating of cultigens, tends to support the initial Oshara model. These new excavations include sites in northwestern New Mexico (Simmons 1986), southern Arizona (Fish and Miksicek 1986; Huckell 1995), and southern New Mexico (Upham et al. 1987; Tagg 1996). It now seems that some form of agriculture was practiced in portions of the Southwest by ca. 1500 B.C. (3450 years B.P.) if not earlier (Simmons 1989:59–60; Wills 1995:215). Thus, Irwin-Williams's original position appears largely vindicated.

It was not Irwin-Williams's original intention that the Oshara tradition be applied to areas outside of the Arroyo Cuervo. This, how-ever, is exactly what happened, and Osharalike sites are now known from several areas in the northern Southwest. The "Oshara tradition" concept has been modified and refined and continues to provide a useful framework from which to evaluate Archaic cultures of the northern Southwest. While some researchers have criticized the conceptual basis of the tradition, it was a pioneering attempt to bring order into what had previously been a neglected, but significant, aspect of Southwestern prehistory. As such, the Oshara tradition has earned a permanent position in the history of Southwestern archaeology.

Alan H. Simmons

Further Readings

Berry, M. 1982. *Time, Space, and Transition in Anasazi Prehistory.* University of Utah Press, Salt Lake City.

———. 1985. The Age of Maize in the Greater Southwest: A Critical Review. In *Prehistoric Food Production in North America*, edited by R. Ford, pp. 279–307. Anthropological Papers, vol. 75. Museum of Anthropology, University of Michigan, Ann Arbor.

Fish, A.L., and C. Miksicek. 1986. Early Corn Remains From Tumamoc Hill, Southern Arizona. *American Antiquity* 51:563–572.

Huckell, B. 1995. *Of Marshes and Maize: Preceramic Agricultural Settlement in the Cienga Valley, Southeastern Arizona.* Anthropological Papers no. 59. University of Arizona Press, Tucson.

Irwin-Williams, C. 1967. Picosa: The Elementary Southwestern Culture. *American Antiquity* 32:441–457.

———. 1968. Archaic Cultural History in the Southwestern United States. *Eastern New Mexico University Contributions in Anthropology* 1:48–54.

———. 1973. The Oshara Tradition: Origins of Anasazi Culture. *Eastern New Mexico University Contributions in Anthropology* 5(1):1–30.

———. 1977. Black Boxes and Multiple Working Hypotheses: Reconstructing the Economy of Early Southwest Hunters. *Kiva* 42:285–299.

———. 1979. Post-Pleistocene Archaeology, 7000–2000 B.C. In *Southwest,* edited by A. Ortiz, pp. 31–42. Handbook of North American Indians, vol. 9, W.C. Sturtevant, general editor. Smithsonian Institution, Washington, D.C.

———. 1985. Review of *Time, Space, and Transition in Anasazi Prehistory*, by M. Berry. *Kiva* 51:44–48.

Irwin-Williams, C., and C.V. Haynes. 1970. Climatic Change and Early Population Dynamics in the Southwestern United States. *Quaternary Research* 1:59–71.

Irwin-Williams, C., and S. Tompkins. 1968. *Excavations at En Medio Shelter, New Mexico.* Contributions in Anthropology, vol. 1, no. 2. Eastern New Mexico University, Portales.

Matson, R. 1991. *The Origins of Southwestern Agriculture.* University of Arizona Press, Tucson.

Minnis, P. 1985. Domesticating People and Plants in the Greater Southwest. In *Prehistoric Food Production in North America,* edited by R. Ford, pp. 309–340. Anthropological Papers, vol. 75. Museum of Anthropology, University of Michigan, Ann Arbor.

Simmons, A. 1986. New Evidence for the Early Use of Cultigens in the American Southwest. *American Antiquity* 51(1):73–89.

———. 1989. The Unknown Archaeology of the Southwest. Chapter 5 in *Human Adaptations and Cultural Change in the Greater Southwest: An Overview of Archaeological Resources in the Basin and Range Province,* edited by A.H. Simmons, with contributions by A. Stodder, D. Dykeman, and P. Hicks, pp. 39–74. Research Series no. 32. Arkansas Archeological Survey, University of Arkansas, Fayetteville.

Tagg, M. 1996. Early Cultigens From Fresnal Shelter, Southeastern New Mexico. *American Antiquity* 61:311–324.

Upham, S., R. MacNeish, W. Galinat, and C. Stevenson. 1987. Evidence Concerning the Origin of Maiz de Ocho. *American Anthropologist* 89:410–419.

Wills, W.H. 1988. *Early Prehistoric Agriculture in the American Southwest.* School of American Research Press, Santa Fe.

———. 1995. Archaic Foraging and the Beginning of Food Production in the American Southwest. In *Last Hunters, First Farmers,* edited by T.D. Price and A.B. Gebauer, pp. 215–242. School of American Research Press, Santa Fe.

See also PICOSA

Oxbow Complex

The Oxbow complex derives its name from the Oxbow Dam site located in southeastern Saskatchewan where it was first identified and described (Nero and McCorquodale 1958). The complex is characterized by a distinctive form of side-notched, concave-based projectile point of the same name, whose size suggests that it was used with the atlatl. Accepted radiocarbon dates for the Oxbow complex range from ca. 2750 to 1050 B.C. (4700–3000 years B.P.).

Oxbow-complex sites are most abundant within the plains and parkland of southern Saskatchewan, Canada, and are found to a lesser extent throughout adjoining areas of Alberta, Manitoba, Montana, and North Dakota. Known Oxbow-complex sites are generally small camps, but individual and mass human burial sites are known as well. Faunal remains from campsites indicate an almost exclusive subsistence reliance on bison hunting, although to date (1996) no communal kills attributable to Oxbow-complex peoples have been discovered. The Gray burial site near Swift

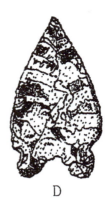

A   B   C   D

Oxbow complex projectile points from the Long Creek (A, B) and Moon Lake (C) sites in Saskatchewan, and the King site (D) in northern Montana. (Drawn by J. Brumley, A–C redrawn from Dyck 1983)

Current, Saskatchewan, is a mass burial where more than 100 Oxbow-complex burials were excavated. Individual burials were primarily secondary in nature and interred intermittently over the entire temporal range of the complex. Burial sites containing but a single interment are also known from Saskatchewan. Present (1996) evidence indicates that Oxbow-complex peoples were the first to construct and use certain varieties of medicine wheels that were then further added to and used by later cultural complexes. There is also limited evidence for the construction of tipi rings by Oxbow-complex peoples.

Characteristic campsite assemblages consist primarily of heat-fractured or fire-cracked rock, chipped-stone debitage, and butchered faunal remains. Simple and well-made chipped-stone-tool forms include pebble and cobble cores, marginally retouched pieces of debitage, plano-convex end scrapers, unifacial and bifacial knives, unifacial flake perforators, projectile points, and lanceolate-projectile-point preforms. Bone, shell, and ground-stone items from both Oxbow-complex camp and burial sites include bone awls, drilled-shell gorgets, drilled-shell beads, bone beads, and grooved-stone mauls. Beads and copper crescents of native copper from the Great Lakes area are rare finds at several Oxbow sites that attest to long-range trade and, perhaps, other forms of relationships.

Several models of Oxbow interaction with other complexes have been proposed. Many researchers suggest that Oxbow developed out of an earlier local complex generally referred to as the Mummy Cave complex. The Oxbow and McKean complexes are also, in part, temporally and spatially contemporaneous, with Oxbow and McKean materials found together at some sites. This has led some researchers to suggest that McKean developed out of Oxbow. More recent research (Dyck 1983; Epp and Dyck 1983) indicates that McKean and Oxbow represent neighboring peoples with different cultural traditions and that sites with materials from both complexes reflect stratigraphic mixing and/or interaction between their members.

John Brumley

Further Readings

Dyck, I. 1983. *The Harder Site: A Middle Period Bison Hunters Campsite in the Northern Great Plains.* Mercury Series Paper no. 67. Archaeological Survey of Canada, National Museum of Man, Ottawa.

Epp, H.R., and I. Dyck. 1983. *Tracking Ancient Hunters: Prehistoric Archaeology in Saskatchewan.* Saskatchewan Archaeological Society, Regina.

Nero, R.W., and B.A. McCorquodale. 1958. Report on an Excavation at the Oxbow Site. *Blue Jay* 16(2):82–92.

P

Pacific Salmon

Pacific salmon is a resource harvested by human populations of the continent's west coast and Pacific drainage Arctic and Subarctic for at least the last 8,000 years. Pacific salmon (*Oncorhychus*) comprise five distinct species. These are (with average weights): sockeye (*O. nerka*), 2.8 kg (6.2 lbs); pink (*O. gorbuscha*), 2.2 kg (4.8 lbs); coho (*O. kisutch*), 3.2 kg (7.1 lbs); chum (*O. keta*), 5.3 kg (11.7 lbs); and chinook (*O. tschawytscha*), 5.8 kg (12.8 lbs). All spend the early part of life in streams or lakes, the majority of their time in distant ocean feeding grounds, and the final months before death in returning to spawn at their freshwater birthplace. Dissimilarity in cohort population size and the difference in the age at return (cycles range from two to eight years and differ even within a species) combine to produce considerable annual variation in numbers reappearing to spawn. The big sockeye runs of the Pacific Northwest's major river systems were especially important in sustaining large human populations, but, overall, the more widely distributed chum were likely more significant. Salmon were a seasonally harvested resource (peak spawning activity is usually in the late summer or fall) taken by a wide variety of techniques from baited troll hooks and harpoons to dip nets and traps. Weirs and traps were among the most productive means. Most of the harvest was stored for winter consumption, with drying and smoking the most common preservation techniques. Dried salmon is highly nutritious: ca. 100–150 g (3.5–5.3 ounces) will provide an adult's daily requirement for protein.

Donald H. Mitchell

Further Readings

Foerster, R.E. 1968. *The Sockeye Salmon,* Oncorhynchus nerka. Bulletin no. 162. Fisheries Research Board of Canada, Ottawa.

Groot, C., and L. Margolis (editors). 1991. *Pacific Salmon Life Histories*. University of British Columbia Press, Vancouver.

Packrat Middens

Packrat middens are refuse accumulations gathered by species of the rodent genus *Neotoma*. Packrats, or woodrats, possess an acquisitive behavioral trait: They collect large amounts of plant debris that they then transport back to their den. Modern middens are loose piles of vegetal debris and fecal pellets. Ancient middens are usually gray-to-brown masses thoroughly saturated with dehydrated urine; they possess the consistency and mass of an unfired adobe brick. These solidified packrat middens may be less than a century to more than 50,000 years old. Because they are preserved by mummification, they occur in North America only in rock shelters or caves in the more arid portions of the western part of the continent. Packrat middens are analyzed by dissolving carefully selected samples in water. Plant fragments are then captured on sieves. After drying, the material is identified. This process yields a list of the plant species that grew within the limited foraging range of the rat. The plant remains and fecal pellets are also ideal material for radiocarbon dating. Since sources of paleoenvironmental data are limited in deserts, the discovery of the scientific potential of middens in the 1960s has led to a revolution in the understanding of the climatic and ecological history of the American West.

W. Geoffrey Spaulding

Further Readings

Betancourt, J.L., P.S. Martin, and T.R. Van Devender (editors). 1990. *Packrat Middens: The Last 40,000 Years of Biotic Change*. University of Arizona Press, Tucson.

Jaroff, L. 1992. Nature's Time Capsules. *Time* 139(14):61.

Van Devender, T.R., R.S. Thompson, and J.L. Betancourt. 1987. Vegetation History of the Deserts of Southwestern North America: The Nature and Timing of the Late Wisconsin-Holocene Transition. In *North America and Adjacent Oceans During the Last Deglaciation*, edited by W.F. Ruddiman and H.E. Wright, Jr., pp. 323–352. Geological Society of America, Boulder.

Paddle-and-Anvil Technique

The paddle-and-anvil technique is a method of consolidating and thinning the walls of ceramic vessels. Jars built up by coils or slabs were thinned by striking the exterior surface with a paddle. An anvil, or support, was held against the interior surface to absorb the blow and shape the body. Paddles were usually wrapped with cord or carved with simple geometric designs like checks. An imprint of the cords or carved designs was left on the vessel's surface when it was struck. In the Eastern Woodlands, a diagnostic trait of many Woodland-tradition ceramic vessels is the presence of cord marking over the exterior body surface. In some archaeological complexes, paddle impressions were smoothed over to leave a plain surface that was then decorated by other kinds of stamps or tools.

Guy Gibbon

Further Readings

Sheppard, A.O. 1956. *Ceramics for the Archaeologist*. Publication no. 609. Carnegie Institution of Washington, Washington, D.C.

Paleoarctic Tradition

The concept of an American Paleoarctic tradition was first applied by Douglas D. Anderson to the Akmak and Kobuk components at On-ion Portage in Alaska in 1968. These components, which contain wedge-shaped microblade cores and burins, lay at the base of a deeply buried sequence. Bifaces are also assumed to be part of the Paleoarctic tradition toolkit. While they are absent from Kobuk, this was ascribed to the small size of the assemblage. Anderson saw similarities with Siberian collections in both assemblages and noted that neither bore any resemblance to Paleoindian assemblages as then understood. Taking them to be indigenous developments out of a Siberian base, he placed both within the "American Paleo-Arctic Tradition." While the original use of the concept was restricted to Arctic components, the term has subsequently been extended geographically into the Subarctic to encompass somewhat similar core-burin assemblages. The concept remains somewhat variable and informal, and the word "American" is frequently dropped. Nonetheless, the reference is always to assemblages on the American side of the Bering Strait.

Frederick Hadleigh West

Further Readings

Anderson, D.D. 1969. A Stone Age Campsite at the Gateway to America. *Scientific American* 218(6):24–33.

———. 1970. *Akmak: An Early Archaeological Assemblage From Onion Portage, Northwest Alaska*. Acta Arctica, Fasc. 16. Copenhagen.

———. 1988. *Onion Portage: The Archaeology of a Stratified Site From the Kobuk River, Northwest Alaska*. Anthropological Papers, vol. 22, nos. 1–2. University of Alaska Press, Fairbanks.

Paleoindian

H.M. Wormington (1957:3) used the term "Paleo-Indian" as "a designation for the oldest inhabitants" of the New World, although she said that it "is an undesirable term if we give it racial connotations." In her classic 1957 study, "Paleo-Indian" referred "to people who hunted animals which are now extinct, to the people who occupied the western United States prior to about 6,000 years ago, and to the makers of the fluted points of the eastern United States" (Wormington 1957:3). G.R. Willey and P. Phillips (1958:112–113) expressed concern over the term "Paleoindian" or "Lithic stage," arguing that it was being used indiscriminately, particularly in the east, to refer to all cultures that are reasonably early and not Archaic. Willey (1966:38) preferred the term "Big-Game Hunting tradition" but accepted Paleoindian as a "perfectly good term." J.D. Jennings (1989) uses the term "Classic Paleoindian" as a division of the Early Cultures that is separate from his Archaic stage. Included among the Classic Paleoindians are the Clovis culture, the Dalton horizon, the Folsom culture, Western desert sites, and the Plano cultures. Since the mid-1970s, most authors have adopted the term "Paleoindian" in addressing New World cultures before ca. 8,000 years ago. All admit there are problems with its usage.

George C. Frison

Further Readings

Jennings, J.D. 1989. *Prehistory of North America*. 3rd ed. Mayfield, Mountain View.

Willey, G.R. 1966. *An Introduction to American Archaeology*, vol. 1. Prentice-Hall, Englewood Cliffs.

Willey, G.R., and P. Phillips. 1958. *Method and Theory in American Archaeology*. University of Chicago Press, Chicago.

Wormington, H.M. 1957. *Ancient Man in North America*. Popular Series no. 4. Denver Museum of Natural History, Denver.

Paleolith

A paleolith is a stone implement made during the Paleolithic period, which in the Old World extends from the age of the oldest known stone implement to the end of the Pleistocene Ice Age, or from ca. 2.5 million to 10,000 years B.P. (8050 B.C.). In the latter half of the nineteenth century, some North American archaeologists, stimulated by Boucher de Perthes's discovery of stone implements in Ice Age gravels in France, by the implications of Charles Darwin's popular new theory of evolution, and by the desire to prove a great antiquity for the first people in the Americas, claimed that they had found paleoliths in the New World, too. These were in general roughly hewn implements, such as choppers, that "looked" old because of the crudeness of their form. An example is Charles C. Abbott's discovery of "paleoliths" made of argillite in the Trenton Gravels of New Jersey (Abbott 1876). Abbott's belief that they dated to glacial times was supported by professional archaeologists, such as Frederick Ward Putnam,

who were committed to proving that people were in the New World before the end of the Ice Age. An examination of the Trenton Gravel and other purported "paleoliths" by William Henry Holmes demonstrated that they were most likely crude stone implements, such as hastily fashioned quarry preforms and rejects of the manufacturing process, that had been made by more recent people (Holmes 1892). Besides spurring innovations in lithic analysis, these claims were also responsible, in part, for a more rigorous examination of the geomorphic context of archaeological deposits. The word "paleolith" in North American archaeology is a vestige of these early debates about the antiquity of the first people in the Americas.

Guy Gibbon

Further Readings

Abbott, C.C. 1876. The Stone Age of New Jersey. *Annual Report of the Smithsonian Institution for 1875,* pp. 246–380.

Haynes, H.W. 1889. The Prehistory of North America. In *Narrative and Critical History of America*, edited by J. Winsor. Houghton Mifflin, Boston.

Holmes, W.H. 1892. Modern Quarry Refuse and the Paleolithic Theory. *Science* 20:295–297.

Richards, H.G. 1939. Reconsideration of the Dating of the Abbott Farm Site at Trenton, New Jersey. *American Journal of Science* 237(5):345–354.

Willey, G.R., and J.A. Sabloff. 1993. *A History of American Archaeology*. 3rd ed. W.H. Freeman, New York.

See also ABBOTT, CHARLES C.; HOLMES, WILLIAM HENRY; PUTNAM, FREDERICK WARD

Panpipe

A panpipe is an ancient musical instrument that was played like a harmonica. It consists of a series of three or four contiguous hollow tubes made of cane, reed, or bone often held in place by interior packing material, such as cordage, sinew, or inner tree bark. The tubes were commonly covered with a thin sheet of copper, although meteoric iron and silver were also occasionally employed. The metal had holes near its periphery for fastening it into place. In North America, these objects have been found almost exclusively in Middle Woodland cultural deposits. Although panpipes are most widely associated with the famous Hopewell sites of Ohio, such as the Hopewell, Harness, and Turner mound groups, Mark F. Seeman (1979) has documented their occurrence in several other locales throughout midwestern and southeastern North America. They have most frequently been discovered in mortuary context, although Beth A. Cree (1992) has reported one found at the New Castle site in Indiana unassociated with burial activity.

George H. Odell

Further Readings

Cree, B.A. 1992. Hopewell Panpipes: A Recent Discovery in Indiana. *Midcontinental Journal of Archaeology* 17:3–15.

Griffin, J.B., R.E. Flanders, and P.A. Titterington. 1970. *The Burial Complex of the Knight and Norton Mounds in Illinois and Michigan.* Memoir no. 2. Museum of Anthropology, University of Michigan, Ann Arbor.

Seeman, M.F. 1979. *The Hopewell Interaction Sphere: The Evidence for Interregional Trade and Structural Complexity.* Prehistoric Research Series, vol. 5, no. 2. Indiana Historical Society, Indianapolis.

Papagueria

The Papagueria (the land of the Papagos) covers southwestern Arizona and the northwesternmost tip of Sonora, Mexico. There are no permanent flowing rivers or streams in the region. Precipitation ranges from ca. 25.4 cm (10 inches) annually at its eastern edge to 7.6 cm (3 inches) at Yuma, Arizona, on the Colorado River.

Aboriginal subsistence practices in the Papagueria depended upon both farming and foraging for wild foods. Agriculturalists practiced *ak chin* (floodwater) agriculture, in which fields were carefully placed so that storm runoff would flow over them. In the Papagueria, the frequency of areas suitable for this technique tends to decline from east to west, following the rainfall gradient. In the eastern portion of the region, modern Tohono O'odham (Papagos) built elaborate systems of dams, reservoirs, and canals to capture runoff water and to distribute it over wide areas. Late Prehistoric peoples in the region probably did the same. Wild-plant foods were a significant part of the diet in all time periods. Two of the most important wild foods were the fruit of the saguaro cactus and the beans of the mesquite bush.

Most information on the Paleoindian and Archaic periods in the Papagueria comes from the site of Ventana Cave, where Emil W. Haury (1950) found stratified deposits dating from the late Pleistocene to the present. The earliest Hohokam villages date to the Snaketown phase (A.D. 650–750, or 1300–1200 years B.P.) and appear in the Santa Rosa wash drainage. Earlier Pioneer-period (A.D. 300–650, or 1650–1300 years B.P.) pottery types have been found at scattered locations in the Papagueria, but to date (1996) there is no evidence of villages for this period. During the Colonial (A.D. 750–1000, or 1200–950 years B.P.) and Sedentary (A.D. 1000–1150, or 950–800 years B.P.) periods, small Hohokam pithouse settlements existed throughout the area of the modern Tohono O'odham nation. The artifact assemblage in these sites is typically Hohokam, with effigy palettes, stone bowls, and serrated projectile points. Painted ceramics are Phoenix Basin Hohokam Red-on-buff types, but they never exceed 5 percent of any sample. Julian D. Hayden (1972) has traced a prehistoric shell-trade route from the Papagueria to the Gulf of California. Some researchers argue that Papagueria villages specialized in making jewelry for trade into the Phoenix Basin (Doelle 1980; McGuire and Schiffer 1982).

In the Classic period (A.D. 1150–1450, or 800–500 years B.P.), there was an expansion of population. More sites are known for this period than all previous periods combined. Pithouse villages along the east and west flanks of the Baboquivari Mountains include platform mounds, and a new site type, *cerros de trincheras*, appears. These latter sites are isolated volcanic hills covered with terraces, walls, and, sometimes, domestic compounds. Most were probably hillside villages put in these locations for defensive reasons. There is a dramatic shift in ceramics, with Tucson Basin Red-on-brown types replacing Phoenix Basin Hohokam Red-on-buff types. The historic occupants of the region, the Tohono O'odham, lived in scattered villages and practiced *ak chin* agriculture. The Spanish never successfully missionized the Papagueria, and the Tohono O'odham lived outside of effective European domination until the 1880s. Today, the Tohono O'odham continue to live in the desert land of their prehistoric ancestors.

Randall H. McGuire

Further Readings

Castetter, E.F., and W.H. Bell. 1942. *Pima and Papago Indian Agriculture*. University of New Mexico Press, Albuquerque.

Doelle, W.H. 1980. *Past Adaptive Patterns in the Western Papagueria: An Archaeological Study of Non-Riverine Resource Use*. Unpublished Ph.D. dissertation, Department of Anthropology, University of Arizona, Tucson.

Goodyear, A.C., III. 1975. *Hecla II and III: An Interpretive Study of Archaeological Remains From the Lakeshore Project*. Anthropological Research Papers no. 9. Arizona State University Press, Tempe.

Haury, E.W. 1950. *The Stratigraphy and Archaeology of Ventana Cave*. University of Arizona Press, Tucson.

Hayden, J.D. 1972. Hohokam Petroglyphs of the Sierra Pinacate, Sonora, and the Hohokam Shell Expeditions. *Kiva* 37:74–84.

Huckell, B.B. 1979. *The Cornet Real Project: Archaeological Investigations on the Luke Range, Southwestern Arizona*. Archaeological Series no. 129. Arizona State Museum, University of Arizona, Tucson.

Masse, W.B. 1980. *Excavations at Gu Achi*. Publications in Archaeology no. 12. Western Archaeological Center, National Park Service, Tucson.

McGuire, R.H. 1992. On the Outside Looking In: The Concept of Periphery in Hohokam Archaeology. In *Exploring the Hohokam*, edited by G.J. Gumerman, pp. 347–383. University of New Mexico Press, Albuquerque.

McGuire, R.H., and M.B. Schiffer. 1982. *Hohokam and Patayan: The Archaeology of Southwestern Arizona*. Academic Press, New York.

Nabhan, G.P. 1979. The Ecology of Floodwater Farming in Arid Southwestern North America. *Agro-Ecosystems* 5:245–255.

Withers, A.M. 1973. *Excavations at Valshni Village, Arizona*. Arizona Archaeologist no. 7. Arizona Archaeological Society, Phoenix.

Parker, Arthur Caswell (1881–1955)

A Seneca Indian as well as a friend and former student of Fredrick Ward Putnam, A.C. Parker concentrated upon Iroquoian archaeology in the interior of New York State, where he became

Arthur C. Parker. (Reprinted with permission from American Antiquity 21[3]:291)

state archaeologist in 1906. Parker received his formal education at Dickinson Seminary in Williamsport, Pennsylvania, in preparation for the ministry. He was an archaeological assistant at the American Museum of Natural History in New York (1900–1903) before serving his apprenticeship as a field archaeologist for the Peabody Museum of American Archaeology and Ethnology of Harvard University under the direction of Putnam. Parker later received honorary degrees from various institutions, such as a doctorate in 1940 from Union College. His report on the Ripley site (1907) was an expression of an early-twentieth-century interest in reconstructing the lifeways of the inhabitants of sites from ethnographic information. As early as 1916, he used the direct-historical approach to relate prehistoric village sites to historic Iroquoian tribes. In *The Archaeological History of New York* (1922), he recognized four major periods: a Mound Builder; an Eskimolike; an "Algonquian" with Eskimo influence; and an Iroquoian. Parker was a member of an early pan-Indian group, the Society of American Indians.

Guy Gibbon

Further Readings

Hertzberg, H.W. 1978. Arthur C. Parker, Seneca, 1881–1955. In *American Indian*

Intellectuals, edited by M. Liberty, pp. 128–138. Papers of the American Ethnological Society Spring Symposium, March 31–April 1, 1976, Atlanta. West Publishing, St. Paul.

———. 1979. Nationality, Anthropology and Pan-Indianism in the Life of Arthur C. Parker (Seneca). *Proceedings of the American Philosophical Society* 123:47–72.

Parker, A.C. 1907. *Excavations in an Erie Indian Village and Burial Site at Ripley, Chataqua County, New York*. Bulletin no. 117. New York State Museum, Albany.

———. 1916. The Origins of the Iroquois As Suggested by Their Archaeology. *American Anthropologist* 18:479–507.

———. 1922. *The Archaeological History of New York*. Bulletin nos. 235–238. New York State Museum, Albany.

Ritchie, W.A. 1956. Arthur Caswell Parker—1881–1955. *American Antiquity* 21:293–295.

Parkhill Cultural Complex

The Parkhill complex, which is also referred to as a phase, is one of three Early Paleoindian "cultures" recognized in the Lower Great Lakes region. The other two are called Gainey and Crowfield. Each of these complexes is characterized, in part, by a distinctive type of fluted projectile point, which together are regarded as representing a typological and temporal series. From earliest to latest, these point types (and the complexes they represent) are Gainey (Gainey), Barnes (Parkhill), and Crowfield (Crowfield). Unfortunately, this presumed succession of "cultures" has not been corroborated by radiocarbon dating. It is inferred instead from the spatial distribution of the three point types, which occur largely on different sites, suggesting that they were made and used by different groups of people; and from their close technological and stylistic relationships, which suggest that they represent a temporal series. The possibility that these point types distinguish different cultures is supported by their associated lithic assemblages, which appear to have different toolkit contents and patterns of raw material use.

The Barnes point type was first recognized at the site of that name in Michigan. The cultural complex associated with the Barnes point was named after the Parkhill site in southwestern Ontario, for Parkhill produced larger samples of both points and other types of tools than the Barnes site did. In addition to occurring in both southern Michigan and Ontario, the Parkhill complex may also be present south of the Great Lakes in northern Ohio, northwestern Pennsylvania, and western New York, for a small number of sites and isolated discoveries of Barnes-type points have been reported from these areas. Barnes points, or points similar to this type, have also been reported from a much larger region that extends from Wisconsin to southern New England. It is not known whether these points identify the distribution of the Parkhill complex itself or of several other distinct, albeit closely related, cultural groups. Similarly, the relationship of the Barnes point type, and the culture that produced it, to point types in the southeastern United States remains unknown.

Age. As of the mid-1990s, the Parkhill complex had not been radiocarbon dated. However, since the Barnes point type is technologically more developed than Gainey, the latter presumably being closer to Clovis in this regard, and since no Parkhill sites in Ontario have been found below the lake level of the Main stage of glacial Lake Algonquin, it is inferred that the complex dates between 8450 B.C. (10,400 years B.P.) (the terminal date for Lake Algonquin) and ca. 9050 B.C. (11,000 years B.P.) (the date of initial occupation of the province by Clovis and/or Gainey people). This age span is supported indirectly by paleoecological data from the Fisher site in south-central Ontario. Fisher is associated with a glacial lake strandline that can be dated by correlation with the late glacial pollen (vegetation) record.

Subsistence. To date (1996), no faunal evidence for the subsistence of Parkhill complex people has been found. However, the presumed association of numerous sites with glacial Lake Algonquin has been interpreted as possibly reflecting an interest in large game, such as caribou, whose movements may have been directed or concentrated by the large water body. Usewear study of informal tools from the Fisher site provides evidence for the butchering of large animals and the working of bone, antler, and skins presumably from those animals. Somewhat unexpectedly, that study also produced evidence for the butchering of fish. Thus, an interest in fishing, perhaps during spawning periods, may have prompted Early Paleoindian people to occupy lakeside habitats.

Community Patterning. Although the Parkhill complex is much better known in

Selected examples of Barnes-type fluted projectile points and preforms from the Fisher site, Ontario, Canada (a, b, f: complete points, finished except for lateral and basal grinding. Specimen (a) exhibits a marked constriction ("fishtail") near the base, an attribute that is diagnostic (although not always present) on Barnes-type points of the Parkhill complex. Note the divergent flute scar on specimen (b) and multiple flute scars on specimen (f); c: base of unfinished point. Note the remnants of the basal platform (nipple) used for fluting; d, e: bifacially worked preforms. From its size and shape, specimen (e) was apparently intended to be a point preform. (Courtesy of the Royal Ontario Museum)

Ontario than the Gainey or Crowfield complexes, only a few Parkhill-complex sites have been excavated extensively. These are the Parkhill site itself and the nearby Thedford II site, both of which are in southwestern Ontario, and the Fisher site, which is ca. 175 km (108.5 miles) to the northeast in south-central Ontario. Thedford II may have been a short-term, single-event occupation by a group of several families who arranged their individual camps around a central, communally used work area. The Parkhill and Fisher sites are much larger and more complex. They may represent repeated occupations by small groups of families or, less likely, single occupations of larger aggregations of families or bands.

Settlement Patterning. Many Parkhill-complex sites are presumed, largely on the basis of geographic proximity, to have been associated with glacial Lake Algonquin. However, only the Fisher site has been studied in detail geologically and shown to be associated with one or possibly two strandlines of a lake (either Algonquin or another lake) dating to ca. 9250–8650/8450 B.C. (11,200–10,600/10,400 years B.P.). A dozen or so much smaller sites, primarily in southwestern Ontario, that are not associated with a glacial lake are thought to be small, interior hunting camps. These sites may have been occupied in the winter months. The few excavations conducted on these sites have not been reported in any detail.

In Ontario, Parkhill-complex people made preferential use of a type of chert that is restricted to a small area in the southern Georgian Bay region of the province. The chert is from the Fossil Hill Formation and is sometimes referred to as Collingwood chert. It constitutes 75–85 percent of individual lithic assemblages at distances as far as 200 km (124 miles) from the chert source. It may have been used over an area of ca. 25,000 km² (9,650 square miles) in southern and south-central Ontario. Evidence that the chert was obtained directly from the source area, rather than indirectly by trade, indicates that Parkhill-complex people moved periodically between the southern Georgian Bay region (where the chert source area is located) and extreme southwestern Ontario. Since chert would have been accessible only during the snow-free seasons of the year, Parkhill-complex people may have visited the southern Georgian Bay region only during the warmer months of the year, occupying extreme southwestern Ontario during the winter. The implication of

repeated visits between different regions of the province also suggests that band movements may have occurred, at least for a short period, within a more or less well-defined geographic range or territory. This form of land use may contrast with that of earlier Paleoindian groups in the Great Lakes region, such as Clovis or Gainey people. Research in the late 1970s and 1980s (Kirby 1986; Storck and von Bitter 1989) suggested that Early Paleoindian people obtained chert in the southern Georgian Bay region through special task groups that visited the geologic source in the uplands for only short periods, during which time the band as a whole lived at base camps situated elsewhere, perhaps in areas with more subsistence resources. The Fisher site, located ca. 25 km (15.5 miles) east of the chert source area in a lowland environment and adjacent to a glacial lake, may have been such a base camp. Recently (Storck and von Bitter 1994), ongoing research in the chert source area is reevaluating the interpretation that Fossil Hill Formation chert was obtained by special task groups and, secondly, the assumption that the chert may have been preferred solely because of its physical properties for tool manufacture. An alternative hypothesis is being tested: that unique or seasonally concentrated biological resources in the chert source area may have led Early Paleoindians to discover the chert source and continue using it over a lengthy period of time.

Peter L. Storck

Further Readings

Deller, D.B., and C.J. Ellis. 1992a. The Early Paleo-Indian Parkhill Phase in Southwestern Ontario. *Man in the Northeast* 44:15–54.

———. 1992b. *Thedford II: A Paleo-Indian Site in the Ausable River Watershed of Southwestern Ontario.* Memoir no. 24. Museum of Anthropology, University of Michigan, Ann Arbor.

Kirby, M. 1986. Field Manual: Prehistoric Archaeology of the Beaver Valley. 3 vols. Unpublished report on file with the Regulatory and Operations Group, Ontario Ministry of Culture, Tourism, and Recreation, Toronto.

Storck, P.L., and P. von Bitter. 1989. The Geological Age and Occurrence of Fossil Hill Formation Chert: Implications for Early Paleoindian Settlement Patterns. In *Eastern Paleoindian Lithic Resource*

Use, edited by C.J. Ellis and J.C. Lothrop, pp. 165–189. Westview Press, Boulder.

———. 1994. The Significance of the Niagara Escarpment in Early Paleo-Indian Land-Use and Subsistence During the Late Pleistocene. In *Leading Edge '94: A Conference Linking Research, Planning, and Community in the Niagara Escarpment*, pp. 144–149. Ontario Ministry of Environment and Energy, Toronto.

Storck, P.L. (with contributions by B.E. Eley, Q.H.J. Gwyn, J.H. McAndrews, A. Nolin, A. Stewart, J. Tomenchuk, and P. von Bitter). 1997. *The Fisher Site: Archaeological, Geological, and Paleobotanical Studies at an Early Paleo-Indian Site in Southern Ontario.* Royal Ontario Museum, Toronto; Museum of Anthropology, University of Michigan, Ann Arbor.

Wright, H.T., and W.B. Roosa. 1966. The Barnes Site: A Fluted Point Assemblage From the Great Lakes Region. *American Antiquity* 31:850–860.

Parkin Site

Parkin (3CS29) is an archaeological site and state park located in Parkin, Arkansas, 80.5 km (50 miles) west of Memphis that dates to the mid-sixteenth century A.D. Parkin measures ca. 7 ha (17.3 acres) in area and has a midden up to 3 m (9.8 feet) deep. Prominent features include seven mounds, the largest of which is 6.5 m (21.3 feet) high. Another prominent feature is a large ditch, or "moat," that surrounds the rectangular-shaped site on three sides. The St. Francis River borders the site on the fourth side.

The Parkin site is the largest of 21 similar sites clustered in the Parkin phase. It is strategically located at the junction of two rivers in a convenient position for receiving tribute from other known Parkin-phase sites. Each site, whose economy was based on corn and bean agriculture, is located within regions of very productive soils and near water. Each site also appears to have been fortified. Typical artifacts include Nodena arrow points for hunting and warfare, Parkin Punctated and Barton Incised pottery cooking jars, end scrapers for hide preparation, chisels and adzes for woodworking, stone hoes, and bone fishhooks. Exotic pottery includes the rare "headpot," a bottle shaped like a human head that may represent a deceased paramount chief.

The Parkin site was probably the capital of the province of Casqui, which was first visited by Spanish explorer Hernando de Soto on St. John's day, 1541. A high cross was raised on the large mound, and several of the inhabitants were baptized during a period of diplomacy that resulted in the two armies of Spain and Casqui combining to attack the neighboring province of Pacaha. Two artifacts representative of this interaction have been recovered from the site: a sixteenth-century brass "Clarksdale-style" bell and a sixteenth-century chevron-type bead. Excavations are ongoing at the site, and displays of typical Protohistoric artifacts found at the site are on exhibit at the visitor center.

Dan F. Morse

Further Readings

Morse, D., and P. Morse. 1987. *Archeology of the Central Mississippi Valley.* Academic Press, New York.

Morse, P.A. 1981. *Parkin: The 1978–1979 Archeological Investigations of a Cross County, Arkansas Site.* Research Series no. 13. Arkansas Archeological Survey, Fayetteville.

Parowan Valley

The largest documented Fremont community was located in the Parowan Valley of south-central Utah a few miles north of Cedar City on the lower reaches of Red Creek. In 1851, Brigham Young described the remains, now called the Paragoonah site, as "120 . . . dirt lodges" or mounds spread over an area "two miles long and one wide" (3.2 x 1.6 km). The Paragoonah ruins were repeatedly visited by explorers and archaeologists over the next 125 years: H.C. Yarrow of the U.S. Geological Survey in 1872; Edward Palmar in 1877; Henry Montgomery of the University of Utah and Don Maguire in 1893; Neil Judd of the Smithsonian Institution in 1916 and 1917; and researchers from UCLA between 1954 and 1960. Each excavated portions of the site, with the number of mounds dwindling from 400 documented by Yarrow to 32 mapped in 1954 by UCLA. Only a few had not been trenched by locals, and few intact mounds remain.

An unknown number of mounds were also present at the south end of Parowan Valley near the towns of Parowan and Summit. UCLA spent four seasons between 1960 and 1964 excavating the Parowan and Evans mounds, and Southern Utah State College from Cedar

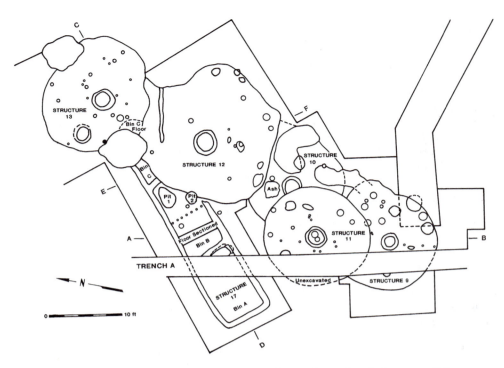

Plan map of overlapping houses in Area A at Mediam Village at the south end of Parowan Valley. (Redrawn by J. C. Janetski from Marwitt, 1970)

City dug sporadically for several years between 1964 and 1970 at both Evans and Median Village, also near Summit. The University of Utah excavated at Median Village and the Evans Mound between 1968 and 1973. Despite the many years of excavation, few detailed reports have appeared on Parowan sites. Important exceptions are those by the University of Utah (Marwitt 1970; Berry 1974; Dodd 1982). Others described their findings in preliminary fashion (Judd 1926; Meighan et al. 1956; Alexander and Ruby 1963).

The significance of Parowan Valley in the context of Fremont studies lies in the realm of demographics and ideology. Although the total number of houses and certainly the number occupied at any one time will never be known, it is worth pointing out that Judd (1926:69) found "43 quadrangular dwellings, 3 circular rooms, and numerous court shelters" on the "big mound" alone. Marwitt (1970:10) excavated 17 structures at Median Village where no visible mound was present, and Dodd (1982) described at least 30 structures at the Evans Mound. Given the small sample of the original number of mounds represented by these excavations, and the fact that many structures were not associated with mounds, the size of the Parowan Valley Fremont community must have been significant, even when contemporaneity issues are considered.

Insights into Fremont ideology and perhaps social status come from two burials rich in grave goods, a rarity in Fremont sites. One is from the Evans Mound (Pecotte 1982:117), and the other from Paragoonah (Meighan et al. 1956:82). The Paragoonah burial was a flexed male apparently buried with a garment decorated with weasel and bird skins. The burial pit was sealed with a clay cap 2.5–20.3 cm (1–8 inches) thick. The Evans burial was a male, too, with the remains (probably skins also) of a great horned owl and nine magpies. Other artifacts thought to be associated with the burial are bone tools, seven ceramic vessels, and a metate with seven arrow points arranged in a geometric design on the surface.

Joel C. Janetski

Further Readings

Alexander, W., and J.W. Ruby. 1963. 1962 Excavations at Summit, Utah: A Progress Report. In *1962 Great Basin Anthropological Conference*, pp. 17–32. Anthropological Papers no. 9. Nevada State Museum, Carson City.

Berry, M.S. 1974. *The Evans Mound: Adaptations in Southwestern Utah*. Unpublished Master's thesis. Department of Anthropology, University of Utah, Salt Lake City.

Dodd, W.A., Jr. (editor). 1982. *Final Year Excavations at the Evans Mound Site*. Anthropological Papers no. 106. University of Utah Press, Salt Lake City.

Judd, N.J. 1926. *Archaeological Observations North of the Rio Colorado*. Bulletin no. 82. Bureau of American Ethnology, Smithsonian Institution, Washington, D.C.

Marwitt, J.P. 1970. *Median Village and Fremont Culture Regional Variation*. Anthropological Papers no. 95. University of Utah Press, Salt Lake City.

Meighan, C.W., N.E. Coles, F.D. David, G.M. Greenwood, W.M. Harrison, and E.H. MacBain. 1956. *Archaeological Excavations in Iron County, Utah*. Anthropological Papers no. 25. University of Utah Press, Salt Lake City.

Montgomery, H. 1894. Prehistoric Man in Utah. *Archaeologist* 2:227–343.

Pecotte, J.K. 1982. Human Skeletal Remains. Appendix. In *Final Year Excavations at the Evans Mound Site*, edited by W.A. Dodd, Jr., pp. 11–119. Anthropological Papers no. 106. University of Utah Press, Salt Lake City.

Patayan Culture Area

Of all the prehistoric cultural areas or cultural groups in the Southwest, the Patayan is the least understood and has one of the most controversial chronologies. The term "Patayan" comes from a Walapai term meaning "old people." It was adopted by H.S. Colton (1945) in an effort to avoid the assumption that the archaeological record was definitively linked to the ethnohistoric Pai groups. This caution by Colton signifies the confusion concerning this culture area. It has generally been ignored by most Southwestern archaeologists, who favor research in Hohokam, Anasazi, Mogollon, Salado, or Sinagua areas. Most recent work is a result of cultural-resource-management (CRM) investigations, which are often linear surveys for power lines or water service. The chronological sequence for the Patayan, derived mainly from M.J. Rogers's (1945) Yuman chronology and

recently defended by M.R. Waters (1982) is generally accepted to be as follows: Patayan I (A.D. 700–1000, or 1250–950 years B.P.), Patayan II (A.D. 1000–1500, or 950–450 years B.P.), and Patayan III (A.D. 1500 to the historic period). The area occupied in Patayan III, the final period in the Patayan culture series, is generally designated as that area west of the Hohokam region, north to the Grand Canyon, south into some point in Baja California Norte, and west to San Diego Bay at the Pacific Ocean (see Figure). This is an environmentally diverse region. Historically, it was occupied by Pai or Yuman speakers, most of whom followed a hunter-gatherer lifeway but some of whom practiced floodwater agriculture. This environmental and cultural diversity makes an understanding of the area difficult.

Early Research. Early researchers, such as Colton, M.J. Harner (1958), M.J. Rogers (1945), and A.H. Schroeder (1952, 1953, 1957, 1975, 1979), agreed on little concerning the character of the culture area, particularly its dimensions and material-culture attributes. Rogers found that the oldest material culture consisted of lithic artifacts that were probably Paleoindian in age but included few of the better known artifacts associated with Clovis or Folsom sites. The later ceramic assemblages (after A.D. 500, or 1450 years B.P.) were composed of paddle-and-anvil-formed vessels with some decoration. These assemblages shared few similarities with Hohokam ceramic assemblages to the east. From the few early excavations, architectural diversity seemed to be the norm, with stone-walled structures and pithouses lined with timbers in the north and earth pithouses in the south.

In 1925, Rogers excavated a stratified trail shrine (SDM C-1) in eastern Imperial County, California, that contained Patayan I and II ceramics (see Figure). The Patayan I material was recovered in association with Hohokam Santa Cruz Red-on-buff sherds. Based on this and work throughout the Colorado and Yuma deserts, he formulated a tripartite ceramic sequence (Yuman I, II, III) for developments in the Lower Colorado River Valley. However, this created confusion with Colton's ceramic sequence in the north. As mentioned above, Rogers's (1945) Yuman sequence, based on ceramic cross-dating, remains relatively the same. Rogers thought that Yuman I began before the Hohokan Santa Cruz phase by A.D. 800 (1150 years B.P.) and ended sometime before the production of

P

Casa Grande Red-on-buff at A.D. 1050 (900 years B.P.). He dated the Yuman II from after this date until the Spanish entrance into the Southwest in the 1500s (Waters 1982). Chronometric dating since Rogers's original scheme was proposed has supported his framework. Given this and the other cultural issues mentioned above, the cultural term "Patayan" and the Patayan chronology are used throughout the region.

In the 1950s, Schroeder, based on work in the Lower Colorado River Valley and an examination of Rogers's ceramic type collections, completely revised the ceramic typology and questioned Rogers's chronology. Founded on Schroeder's work, the term "Hakataya" was adopted at the 1956 Pecos Conference to include the culture area of the Upper and Lower Colorado River and adjacent areas. Traits associated with this area included hunting and gathering, floodwater agriculture, stone-lined roasting pits, paddle-and-anvil ceramics of varying paste composition, ceramic-vessel food storage, mortars and pestles, percussion-flaked chopping tools rather than hafted ground-stone axes, temporary circular shelters rarely observable in the archaeological record, housing of variable form and composition, a dominance of cremation, and rock shrines and trail markers. Most archaeologists today agree

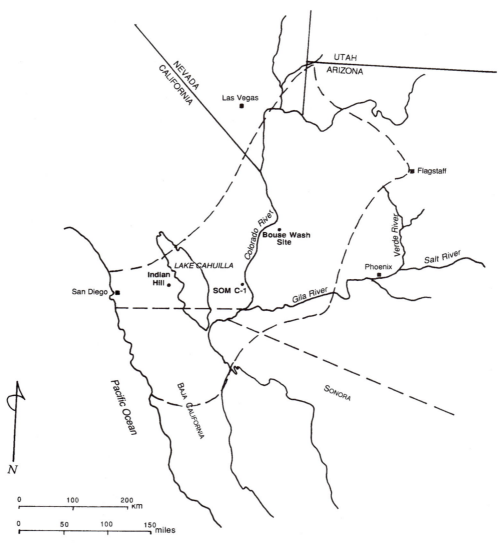

Patayan culture area. (Illustration by M. S. Shackley)

that these are important cultural attributes in this region. It is also apparent, however, that the "Hakataya" concept contains too much cultural variability and that some of this variability should be included in the Salado and Sinagua cultural areas. Hakataya has generally been rejected in favor of Patayan for the region included in the Figure.

Also in the 1950s, Harner excavated a stratified walk-in well in western Arizona at Bouse Wash (see Figure). He defined three phases that generally correlate with Rogers's chronology: Bouse phase 1, Bouse phase 2, and Moon Mountain phase. Bouse phase 1 contained mainly Rogers's Patayan (Yuman) I material underneath Santa Cruz Red-on-Buff ceramics. Bouse phase 2 was associated with Gila Red and Verde Black-on-Grey sherds dating, according to Harner, to A.D. 1000–1300 (950–650 years B.P.). The Moon Mountain levels contained what Rogers would consider Patayan (Yuman) III attributes, including Lower Colorado Buffware and stuccoing. Harner dated this level to A.D. 1300–1700 (650–250 years B.P.).

Recent Research and Synthesis. Recent archaeological research in the Patayan culture area has rarely focused, at least directly, on cultural chronological problems. An exception is the work of Michael Waters (1982, 1983), who spent considerable time in the 1980s investigating the chronological problems of the Lowland Patayan. This work focused on the consequences for Patayan lifeways of the lacustrine history of Lake Cahuilla, a sporadically filled Holocene lake in the Salton Trough in the Colorado Desert. Waters also reevaluated Rogers's ceramic chronology (see Figure). Lake Cahuilla filled four to six times between A.D. 700 and 1600 (1250–350 years B.P.). Each filling caused consequent occupation of the shoreline by ceramic-producing Patayan groups. It appears that the lake fillings actually contributed to the population of southwestern California by Patayan groups after after A.D. 700 (1250 years B.P.); by A.D. 1300 (650 years B.P.), the Patayan occupation of this area was firmly established. With each drying period, pulses of occupation occurred to the west and to the east of the lake. Importantly, the lake strand chronology generally demarcated the Lowland Patayan tripartite chronology, although now it appears that there may have been more lake fillings. The Patayan I period (A.D. 700–1000, or 1250–950 years B.P.) is defined by five ceramic types. They have been found at least in western Arizona, southeastern California, northern Baja California, the Sierra Pinacate of northern Sonora, and on the eastern shoreline of Lake Cahuilla. Patayan components are generally small scatters of artifacts in the lower levels of lakeshore sites.

The Patayan II period (A.D. 1000–1500, or 950–450 years B.P.) exhibited important changes in ceramic style and technology. A great eastern movement also occurred into southwestern Arizona, and occupation expanded around the entire shoreline of Lake Cahuilla. The number and size of sites increased, and there is good indication that occupation occurred with some frequency all the way west to the coast. Similar population changes were occurring in the northern portion of the culture. The Patayan III period (A.D. 1500 to the historic period) exhibited the greatest changes in ceramic style and composition, and the entire area was now intensively occupied (see Figure). This was the period just before contact of the Pai or Yuman occupation. Logistic organization, floodwater agriculture, and large village aggregations became firmly established during this time.

While not specifically focused on the problem of Patayan prehistory, the recent excavation of Indian Hill rock shelter (Donald 1992) in far eastern San Diego County, California, provides some important verification of settlement expansion west of Lake Cahuilla. This rock shelter contains a deep midden that, while not geologically stratified, does exhibit considerable change from a Late Archaic occupation at the base to Patayan III material at the top. Patayan ceramics were associated with a date of 1210 ± 75 B.P. (A.D. 687–938 [UCR-2439]), and the Patayan II ceramic type Tumco Buff was common in the site. Additionally, radiocarbon dates earlier than A.D. 900 (1050 years B.P.) have been obtained from ceramic-bearing levels in sites in western San Diego County near the coast, although the vast majority of Late Prehistoric sites in this area date after A.D. 1300 (650 years B.P.), the Patayan III period.

The Patayan culture area presents a number of unresolved research problems. Still, the promise of a greater understanding of hunter-gatherer lifeways and social organization in diverse environments is very great. It even appears that it will be possible to track the spread of the Patayan in the archaeological record, an accomplishment difficult to achieve in many areas of North America.

M. Steven Shackley

Further Readings

Colton, H.S. 1945. The Patayan Problem in the Colorado River Valley. *Southwestern Journal of Anthropology* 1(1):114–121.

Harner, M.J. 1958. Lowland Patayan Phases in the Lower Colorado River Valley and Colorado Desert. *University of California Archaeological Survey Report* 42:93–97.

McDonald, A.M. 1992. *Indian Hill Rockshelter and Aboriginal Cultural Adaptation in Anza-Borrego Desert State Park, Southeastern California.* Unpublished Ph.D. dissertation, University of California, Riverside. University Microfilms, Ann Arbor.

McGuire, R.H., and M.B. Schiffer (editors). 1982. *Hohokam and Patayan: Prehistory of Southwestern Arizona.* Academic Press, New York.

Rogers, M.J. 1945. An Outline of Yuman Prehistory. *Southwestern Journal of Anthropology* 1:167–198.

Schroeder, A.H. 1952. *The Excavations at Willow Beach, Arizona, 1950.* National Park Service, Southwest Region, Santa Fe.

———. 1953. The Problem of Hohokam, Sinagua, and Salado Relations in Southern Arizona. *Plateau* 26(2):75–83.

———. 1957. The Hakataya Cultural Tradition. *American Antiquity* 23:176–178.

———. 1975. *The Hohokam, Sinagua and Hakataya.* Reprinted. Occasional Paper no. 3. Imperial Valley College Museum. Originally published 1960, Archives of Archaeology no. 5. Society for American Archaeology, Washington, D.C.

———. 1979. Prehistory: Hakataya. In *Southwest,* edited by A. Ortiz, pp. 100–107. Handbook of North American Indians, vol. 9, W.C. Sturtevant, general editor. Smithsonian Institution, Washington, D.C.

Waters, M.R. 1982. The Lowland Patayan Ceramic Tradition. In *Hohokam and Patayan: Prehistory of Southwestern Arizona,* edited by R.H. McGuire and M.B. Schiffer, pp. 275–298. Academic Press, New York.

———. 1983. Late Holocene Lacustrine Chronology and Archaeology of Ancient Lake Cahuilla, California. *Quaternary Research* 19:373–387.

Pavo Real

From June 1979 to January 1980, the Texas State Department of Highways and Public Transportation excavated Pavo Real (41BX52), a multicomponent site on the east bank of Leon Creek in northwest San Antonio, Bexar County, Texas. A discrete Paleoindian component that contains both Clovis and Folsom artifacts was isolated by alluvial gravel deposits 50–70 cm (19.5–27.3 inches) below the present ground surface. The artifact assemblage, which consists only of pieces of chert, includes several of the major tool and debitage categories found at other Early Paleoindian sites and evidence of a blade-making industry. Materials from the assembly date to ca. 9550–8050 B.C. (11,500–10,000 years B.P.). Diagnostic artifacts include two Clovis points, seven points from the Folsom occupation, and six Folsom preforms. Scrapers of several kinds are the most numerous stone tool. The majority are end scrapers, some of which have beaks or trimmed lateral edges, or both. There are also side scrapers, and trimmed or use-modified flakes and blades. Among the debitage categories are biface fragments, depleted cores, initial blades, and the first core tablets found in an Early Paleoindian component. The debitage sample contains ca. 15,000 specimens.

Preliminary analysis of the assemblage permits some observations about Early Paleoindian lithic technology in south-central Texas and how it compares with contemporary technologies in other parts of the country. At Pavo Real, toolmakers exploited Edwards chert that was immediately available and abundant but of variable quality. The large amount of debitage, including cores, cortex flakes, and shatter spall, and the natural presence of some of this material at the site indicate that Pavo Real was a quarry workshop as well as a campsite. In addition to the pressure flaking and fluting of projectile points, the stone-tool technology (including the blade industry) was apparently based on hard- and soft-hammer direct percussion. Of particular interest is the core/blade assemblage, which was among the first documentation of an Early Paleoindian technology that is now known to be widespread. While very similar to other Early Paleoindian core/blade assemblages, it does not contain all the elements of the blade industry. Since the Paleoindian material assemblage at Pavo Real is a mixture of Clovis and Folsom components, one of the more critical aspects of the analysis will be the separation of Folsom from Clovis artifacts.

Two apparent hearths were found at Pavo Real. Each was a small circular area, 30–40 cm

(11.7–15.6 inches) in diameter, that consisted of burned soil, flecks of charcoal, and small burned pebbles. In apparent association with one hearth were three beaked scrapers and two large flakes with trimmed edges. The only faunal remains recovered were a bison tooth and three small unidentifiable bone fragments. Based on the number and variety of tools present, as well as the patterning of features and artifacts concentrations, it is believed that Pavo Real represents a multiple-activity, repeatedly occupied seasonal encampment and workshop. Proximity to water and an abundant chert source were probably critical factors in selecting this location, as was a high bluff directly opposite that could have served as a bison jump.

Glenn T. Goode
Jerry Henderson

Pebble Tool Tradition

The Pebble Tool tradition is the basal cultural tradition of the Northwest Coast north of the Strait of Juan de Fuca. This term was first used in this region by Charles E. Borden in the late 1960s. He was attempting to place large assemblages of unifacial pebble (cobble in the geological sense) tools from terracelike formations at the South Yale site on the Fraser River in British Columbia into a broader cultural context by comparing them with the Paleolithic pebble tool industries of Asia. The local manifestation on the Fraser River was called the Pasika complex, a complex in which bifacial technology was thought to be absent. In 1979, Roy L. Carlson provisionally divided the Pebble Tool tradition into an early segment in which bifaces are absent and a late one in which they are present. Subsequent work by Shawn D. Haley on the original collections from the type site at South Yale showed that bifacial trimming flakes are present in the assemblages and that the tools occur in eolian sediments overlying glacial terraces rather than in the terraces themselves. Radiocarbon dates from the same site in the 4050–2050 B.C. (6000–4000 years B.P.) range indicate: (1) that areas of concentration of pebble tools with minimal evidence of bifacial technology are best interpreted as special-use areas; (2) that these date to the same time period as assemblages in which there are both pebble tools and bifaces; and (3) that they are not early primitive industries. As such, there is not an early segment of the tradition that predates the introduction of bifacial technology.

The Pebble Tool tradition now redefined as coincident with what was the late segment is recognizable artifactually by the occurrence of pebble tools, leaf-shaped bifacial points and knives, and simple flake tools in components on the coast of British Columbia that predate the appearance of a microblade technology at ca. 6650 B.C. (8500 years B.P.).

The Pebble Tool tradition is time transgressive down the coast, with younger, dated components at the Bear Cove site on northern Vancouver Island, the Milliken site in the Fraser Canyon, and the Old Cordilleran component at the Glenrose Cannery site near the mouth of the Fraser River. South of the Strait of Juan de Fuca, the Olcott complex in western Washington State and the full early component at Five Mile Rapids on the Columbia River mark the spread of the tradition to coastal and upriver regions where it succeeds earlier fluted- and stemmed-point complexes. Microblade technology is also time transgressive down the coast and is added to the lithic technology of sites after 6650 B.C. (8500 years B.P.). The Pebble Tool tradition centers in the territories occupied historically by speakers of the Coast Salish and Wakashan languages and probably represents the ancestors of these peoples.

Roy L. Carlson

Further Readings

Borden, C.E. 1969. Early Population Movements From Asia into Western North America. *Syesis* 2(1–2):1–13.

Carlson, R.L. 1979. The Early Period on the Central Coast of British Columbia. *Canadian Journal of Archaeology* 3:211–228.

———. 1990. Cultural Antecedents. In *Northwest Coast*, edited by W. Suttles, pp. 60–69. Handbook of North American Indians, vol. 7, W.C. Sturtevant, general editor. Smithsonian Institution, Washington, D.C.

Carlson, R.L., and L. Dalla Bona (editors). 1996. *Early Human Occupation in British Columbia.* University of British Columbia Press, Vancouver.

Haley, S.D. 1987. *The Pasika Complex: Cobble Reduction Strategies on the Northwest Coast.* Unpublished Ph.D. dissertation, Department of Archaeology, Simon Fraser University, Burnaby.

See also MICROBLADE TRADITION

Pecos Classification

Prehistoric archaeologists use a variety of chronological frameworks to organize their knowledge of the past. In the northern portion of the American Southwest, including the Four Corners, where Arizona, New Mexico, Colorado, and Utah meet, the best-known framework is the Pecos Classification. This chronology, which applies specifically to the region's prehistoric Pueblo, or Anasazi, inhabitants, consists of time-and-culture units that are designated Basketmaker II and III and Pueblo I through V. The time period covered extends from the early centuries B.C. through the historic period. The Pecos Classification was developed in 1927 at a meeting, held at the ruins of Pecos Pueblo, New Mexico (hence the name), that was attended by the leading Southwestern archaeologists of the day.

As initially defined, the Pecos Classification was a summary of stages in the development of Pueblo culture. Only some of the key changes in culture are mentioned here, including modifications since 1927. Basketmaker I was a postulated preagricultural stage with an economy based on the gathering of wild-plant foods and the hunting of animals; units from Basketmaker II onward were agricultural. In other words, the Basketmaker I/Basketmaker II transition was based on a change in the subsistence economy. Basketmaker I was later dropped from the sequence, when it was realized that the preagricultural, hunting-and-gathering stage was already covered under the term "Archaic." Basketmaker II was characterized by the weaving of baskets and sandals, by the construction of pithouses (semisubterranean earthlodges), and by the cultivation of corn. The shift from Basketmaker II to Basketmaker III was marked by a technological change, the addition of pottery to the artifact assemblage. Pithouses became more substantial, and settlements took on a "front orientation" in which the pithouse was placed to the southeast of an alignment of storage (later habitation) rooms; trash was dumped on a midden to the southeast of the pithouse. The transition from Basketmaker III to Pueblo I saw the development of simple, above-ground masonry structures that were used initially for storage and later for storage and habitation; pithouses continued to be used as well. Cranial deformation, the flattening of the back of the skull of babies caused by strapping them to a relatively hard cradle board, was introduced during Pueblo I. Also, a distinctive decoration called neck-banding appeared on pottery vessels used for cooking and storing foods; pots were made using coils of clay, and neck-banding was produced by not smoothing over, and in fact accentuating, the coils located just below the rim of the vessel. Pueblo II saw further development in masonry architecture, the use of a decorative technique of corrugation over the entire outer surface of some pottery vessels, and the geographic expansion of population into new areas. The pithouse had by this time developed into the kiva, a subterranean or semisubterranean structure with attributes that were clearly of ceremonial significance, though the structures no doubt continued to be used for domestic activities between ceremonies.

Pueblo III was recognized by the originators of the Pecos Classification as a peak in cultural development. It was characterized by a heightened artistic expression and by the concentration of population into large communities. Villages lost their front orientation and were now roomblocks arranged around plazas that often contained kivas. Although some areas were abandoned early in Pueblo III, regional population was probably at an all-time high. Pueblo IV was accompanied by a contraction of the area inhabited by Puebloan groups and by the further concentration of population into large communities. Pueblo V refers to the historic period, which began when missionaries and settlers from the Spanish colony of Mexico established a permanent presence in the Southwest.

As should be apparent from this summary, the criteria used to define the units of the Pecos Classification change from one portion of the sequence to another. The units were initially defined as stages of development. Thus, the framework included the possibility of spatial variation in the pace of change, with some areas entering a new stage earlier than others. On the other hand, because the Pecos Classification is a simplified, "normative" description of prehistoric culture, it cannot account for variation between areas that were at the same stage of development. To deal with this spatial variation, archaeologists have developed "phase" sequences that apply to small areas. Except for Pueblo V, the calendrical dating of the stages was based at first entirely on conjecture. Since 1927, however, tree-ring dating (dendrochronology) has made it possible to assign calendar dates to the units and thus to treat them as time periods. One version of the dated sequence is as follows: Basketmaker II (500 B.C.–A.D. 500, or 2450–1450 years B.P.), Basketmaker III (A.D. 500–700, or 1450–1250 years B.P.), Pueblo I (A.D. 700–900, or 1250–1050 years B.P.), Pueblo II (A.D. 900–1100, or 1050–850 years B.P.), Pueblo III (A.D. 1100–1300, or 850–650 years B.P.), Pueblo IV (A.D. 1300–1600, or 650–350 years B.P.), and Pueblo V (A.D. 1600–1900, or 350–50 years B.P.). Archaeologists use the Pecos Classification as a sequence of both developmental stages *and* time periods. As a result, the reader may have to decide which is being referred to in a given context. This is one limitation in the use of the Pecos Classification. Another is the implication that culture change occurs in stepwise fashion; that is, at the boundaries between stages or periods. This problem can be overcome by relying, when possible, on the dating of specific prehistoric events—for example, by using tree-ring dates to show that a house was built in a particular decade.

The Pecos Classification has survived as a useful chronological tool for more than 60 years. It is particularly appropriate for broadscale comparisons. If an archaeologist refers to a "Pueblo I site," the knowledgeable listener has a general idea of what the site is like and how old it is. On the other hand, if one wishes to study the details of Puebloan prehistory, the Pecos Classification must be supplemented, or replaced, by more sensitive chronological tools.

Richard Ahlstrom

Further Readings

Ambler, J.R. 1977. *The Anasazi: Prehistoric People of the Four Corners Region*. Museum of Northern Arizona, Flagstaff.

Cordell, L.S. 1979. Prehistory: Eastern Anasazi. In *Southwest*, edited by A. Ortiz, pp. 131–151. Handbook of North American Indians, vol. 9, W.C. Sturtevant, general editor. Smithsonian Institution, Washington, D.C.

Kidder, A.V. 1927. Southwestern Archeological Conference. *Science* 66(1716): 489–491.

———. 1928. Southwestern Archaeological Conference. *American Anthropologist* 30(1):172.

Plog, F. 1979. Prehistory: Western Anasazi. In *Southwest*, edited by A. Ortiz, pp. 108–130. Handbook of North American Indians, vol. 9, W.C. Sturtevant, general editor. Smithsonian Institution, Washington, D.C.

Pecos Pueblo

Pecos Pueblo's (LA625) significance derives both from its prominence as a major trade center between the Eastern Pueblos and the Plains, and its association with A.V. Kidder and the early development of American archaeology. The site is located on a narrow mesilla in the Upper Pecos Valley, just below the terminus of the southern Rocky Mountains in New Mexico. The town was strategically situated to control access between the northern Rio Grande Valley and the southern High Plains. Although the Upper Pecos Valley had been a major cultural crossroads for nearly 10,000 years, by the fifteenth century A.D. settlement appears to have been concentrated at the site of Pecos itself. The abandonment of other pueblos in the area and the aggregation of population at Pecos may have been a response to incursions by nomadic Plains groups during this period. The town's defensive posture is reflected in its elevated position and the low wall constructed around the site, which is a feature in this region unique to Pecos.

By the middle of the fifteenth century A.D., Pecos had developed stable trade relations with its Plains neighbors. Sixteenth-century Spanish documents record the annual visits of Plains bison-hunters to Pecos to exchange meat and hides for agricultural produce and craft items. In turn, bison hides and other Plains products were traded throughout the Southwest. These connections linked Pecos into a series of expanding regional networks of economic interaction and political integration during the fifteenth and sixteenth centuries.

By the time of European contact, Pecos was a large, consolidated, and powerful town that continued to be of great economic and strategic importance to the early Spanish colony. To the clergy, it was the eastern outpost of Spanish Catholicism, while secular leaders vied for control of its lucrative hide trade. Later, as raids by nomadic groups increased, Pecos became an important defensive outpost that protected Spanish and native settlements along the Rio Grande. The town's population and power waned during the eighteenth century due to factionalism, disease, famine, and the increasing devastation caused by Comanche raiding. Pecos's position as a major trade center and frontier outpost was eventually eclipsed by Taos Pueblo and expanding Hispanic settlements in the Upper Pecos Valley. In A.D. 1838, a small remnant population abandoned the town and went to live with their Towa-speaking kin at Jemez.

Kidder identified at least three distinct Pueblo occupations at Pecos that date from the site's initial settlement in the fourteenth century A.D. through its final abandonment in the nineteenth. Also present at the site are the remains of at least three colonial churches. The convento, which was the cloistered living quarters of the Franciscan priests, and the church that continue to dominate the southern end of the mesilla were built in the eighteenth century atop the ruins of a much grander seventeenth-century complex that was destroyed during the Pueblo revolt of A.D. 1680. Other colonial-period structures associated with the Pueblo include the Presidio and Casas Reales. Several shrines and petroglyph sites have been located in the vicinity of the Pueblo, along with small campsites attributed to nomadic Apache traders. The nearby ruins of Forked Lightning and Loma Lothrap are thought to represent closely related ancestral sites.

The most comprehensive excavations at Pecos Pueblo were conducted by Kidder between 1915 and 1929. The Pecos project, sponsored by Phillips Academy in Andover, Massachusetts, was unprecedented in American archaeology for its duration and scale, careful planning and organization, and use of multidisciplinary specialists. It quickly became the model for large site excavations throughout the New World. Kidder's use of stratigraphic techniques, combined with his seriation of the ceramic sequence at the site, set the standard for cultural-historical reconstructions throughout the Southwest. His results and interpretations, which are reported in a series of comprehensive monographs, form the core of our understanding of the late prehistory of the Eastern Pueblos.

Judith A. Habicht-Mauche

Further Readings

Bandelier, A.F.A. 1881. A Visit to the Aboriginal Ruins in the Valley of the Rio Pecos. *Papers, American Series* 1(2):37–135. Archaeological Institute of America, Cambridge.

Gunnerson, J.H., and D.A. Gunnerson. 1970. Evidence of Apaches at Pecos. *El Palacio* 76(3):1–6.

Hayes, A.C. 1974. *The Four Churches of Pecos.* University of New Mexico Press, Albuquerque.

Hewett, E.L. 1904. Studies of the Extinct Pueblo of Pecos. *American Anthropologist* 64(4):426–439.

Hooten, E.A. 1930. *The Indians of Pecos Pueblo.* Papers of the Phillips Academy Southwestern Expedition no. 4. Yale University Press, New Haven.

Kessell, J.P. 1979. *Kiva, Cross, and Crown.* National Park Service, Washington, D.C.

Kidder, A.V. 1924. *An Introduction to the Study of Southwestern Archaeology, With a Preliminary Account of the Excavations at Pecos.* Papers of the Phillips Academy Southwestern Expedition no. 1. Yale University Press, New Haven.

———. 1932. *The Artifacts of Pecos.* Papers of the Phillips Academy Southwestern Expedition no. 6. Yale University Press, New Haven.

———. 1958. *Pecos, New Mexico: Archaeological Notes.* Papers, vol. 5. Robert S. Peabody Foundation for Archaeology, Phillips Academy, Andover.

Kidder, A.V., and C.A. Amsden. 1931. *The Pottery of Pecos: 1. The Dull-Paint Wares.* Papers of the Phillips Academy Southwestern Expedition no. 5. Yale University Press, New Haven.

Kidder, A.V., and A.O. Shepard. 1936. *The Pottery of Pecos: 2. The Glaze Paint, Culinary, and Other Wares.* Papers of the Phillips Academy Southwestern Expedition no. 7. Yale University Press, New Haven.

Schroeder, A.H. 1979. Pecos Pueblo. In *Southwest,* edited by A. Ortiz, pp. 430–437. Handbook of North American Indians, vol. 9, W.C. Sturtevant, general editor. Smithsonian Institution, Washington, D.C.

Stubbs, S.A., B.T. Ellis, and A. Dittert. 1957. "Lost" Pecos Church. *El Palacio* 64(3–4):69–73.

See also KIDDER, ALFRED V.

Pelican Lake

The name "Pelican Lake" was first used by Boyd Wettlaufer (1955) for materials excavated at the Mortlach site in south-central Saskatchewan. He described four Pelican Lake components at the site, three of which exhibited a characteristic point type. Since then, the name has been applied to sites scattered over practically the entire area from Canada's Red River Valley south to the Arkansas River and from the Continental Divide east to the Mississippi River. Indeed, the reported presence of Pelican Lake sites in any part of the region seems a function of intensity of archaeological fieldwork. Depending on the authority cited, Pelican Lake assemblage dates cluster between 1050 B.C. and A.D. 500 (3000–1450 years B.P.) (Frison 1992:101–111), which places them in the late Middle Prehistoric period (Foor 1981). Major types of artifact assemblages within this group have been interpreted as kill sites (Reeves 1978), campsites (Brumley et al. 1981), quarry sites (Davis 1982), and burials (Frison and Van Norman 1985). Archaeologists have inferred that Pelican Lake peoples gained their subsistence through hunting, gathering, and fishing. The major unifying feature of Pelican Lake components is the presence of relatively large corner-notched projectile points that were probably propelled by dart throwers. Earlier corner-notched artifacts that were presumably used as projectiles are found to the east, but the relationship between their makers and the Pelican Lake people is obscure.

Much research has focused on the Pelican Lake people's successors, who left assemblages characterized by the presence of Besant, Avonlea, and the smaller Head-Smashed-In corner-notched projectile point types, among others (Duke 1991). At one time, Brian O.K. Reeves (1983:17–19) hypothesized that Avonlea assemblages were left by descendants of Pelican Lake peoples. In his original classification, he grouped Pelican Lake and the later Avonlea assemblages within the more general Tunaxa tradition. Many archaeologists divide the assemblage class Pelican Lake into subclasses. Reeves (1983:76) originally proposed eight divisions, with each corresponding to regional differences in point form and artifact assemblage attributes. More recently, I. Dyck (1983:105) and J.B. Brumley and B.J. Dau (1988) have subdivided Pelican Lake assemblages into two regional groups on the basis of differences in projectile-point form. Brumley and Dau have proposed that the different point forms reflect different social organizations. Artifact assemblages of the first type are characterized by the presence of points with a straight base and by location in southeast and south-central Alberta. Most of the points are chipped from types of stone found locally, and, if stone from outside the area is used, it is often Knife River flint (Brumley and Dau 1988:34). Brumley and Dau report that dates associated with these assemblages tend to be earlier than those associated with the second. The second assemblage type has relatively large corner-notched projectile points

with concave bases. These assemblages are found in north and central Montana and the higher elevations of southern Alberta, and points are chipped from stone found in Madison limestones, Avon chert, or porcellanite. The significance of these differences is not clear, but Brumley and Dau (1988:26) believe that descendants of the people leaving the first type of assemblage ultimately made and used the relatively small Head-Smashed-In corner-notched and Avonlea arrow points, while those associated with the second type made and used points of the Highwood complex.

Thomas A. Foor

Further Readings

Brumley, J.H., and B.J. Dau. 1988. *Historical Resource Investigations Within the Forty Mile Coulee Reservoir*. Manuscript Series no. 13. Archaeological Survey of Alberta, Edmonton.

Brumley, J., B.J. Dau, M. Green, L. Heikkla, M. Quigg, C. Rushworth, and S. Saylor. 1981. Archaeological Salvage Investigations Conducted in 1979 and 1980. Cyprus Hills Provincial Park. Ms. on file, Archaeological Survey of Alberta, Edmonton.

Davis, L.B. 1982. Archaeology and Geology of the Schmitt Chert Mine, Missouri Headwaters. *Guidebook for Field Trip*. Presented at the Thirty-Fifth Annual Meeting of the Geological Society of America, Montana State University, Bozeman.

Duke, P. 1991. *Points in Time: Structure and Event in a Late Northern Plains Hunting Society*. University Press of Colorado, Niwot.

Dyck, I. 1983. The Prehistory of Southern Saskatchewan. In *Tracking Ancient Hunters*, edited by H.T. Epp and I. Dyck, pp. 63–139. Saskatchewan Archaeological Society, Regina.

Foor, T.A. 1985. Archaeological Classification in the Northwestern Plains Region. *Plains Anthropologist* 30(108):123–1135.

Frison, G.C. 1992. *Prehistoric Hunters of the High Plains*. 2nd ed. Academic Press, New York.

Frison, G.C., and Z. Van Norman. 1985. The Wind River Canyon Burial and Cache. *Archaeology in Montana* 26(2):43–52.

Reeves, B.O.K. 1978. Head-Smashed-In: 5000 Years of Bison Jumping in the Alberta Plains. In *Bison Procurement and Utiliza-*

tion: A Symposium, edited by L.B. Davis and M.C. Wilson, pp. 151–174. Memoir no. 14. Plains Anthropologist, Lincoln.

———. 1983. *Culture Change in the Northern Plains, 1000 B.C. to A.D. 1000.* Occasional Paper no. 20. Archaeological Survey of Alberta, Edmonton.

Wettlaufer, B. 1955. *The Mortlach Site in the Besant Valley of Central Saskatchewan.* Anthropological Series no. 1. Saskatchewan Department of Natural Resources, Regina.

Period

A period is an interval of calendrical time that brackets specific cultural phenomena, such as the existence of Paleoindian or Archaic societies; the concept allows archaeologists to designate Paleoindian and Archaic periods. Periods usually pertain to wide areas and are frequently subdivided with labels like *early, middle,* and *late* or with names such as *Pioneer, Colonial, Sedentary,* and *Classic,* which are the periods for the Hohokam cultural tradition of the Southwest. Although the concepts "period" and "stage" are often used together, some archaeologists prefer period to stage schemes because they do not presuppose development or evolutionary advance.

Guy Gibbon

Further Readings

Rowe, J.H. 1962. Stages and Periods in Archaeological Interpretation. *Southwestern Journal of Archaeology* 18:40–54.

Petroglyph

A petroglyph is a rock-cut design or image made by pecking, incising, abrading, scratching, or otherwise engraving a figure on a rock in the landscape. Pecking with stone chisel and/or hammerstone was the most commonly employed technique. Petroglyphs were frequently cut through rock surfaces darkened by "desert varnish," or patina, a thin accretion of manganese and iron oxides, clay minerals, and other elements, so that the resulting imagery contrasted with the rock surface on which it was made.

Polly Schaafsma

Further Readings

Grant, C. 1967. *Rock Art of the American Indian.* Thomas Y. Crowell, New York.

Wellman, K. 1979. *A Survey of North American Rock Art.* Akademische Druck-u. Verlagsanstalt, Graz, Austria.

See also ROCK ART

Phase

"Phase" is a widely used term in North American archaeology generally defined as a spatial-temporal segment of an archaeological culture sufficiently distinctive in its traits to distinguish it from other phases of the same or other archaeological cultures. Phases are constructed by linking similar components from more than one site and are, in turn, the building blocks of archaeological cultures, traditions, and stages in cultural-historical syntheses. They span brief intervals of time and are restricted to localities or regions. The concept enables archaeologists to establish regional contemporaneity among components and to examine the lifeways of communities within cultures. A phase in this sense is roughly comparable to a focus in the Midwestern Taxonomic system, although a focus is a pure taxonomic unit lacking spatial-temporal connotations. The term has also been used to refer to a grouping of aspects in the Midwestern Taxonomic system.

Guy Gibbon

Further Readings

Willey, G.R., and P. Phillips. 1958. *Method and Theory in American Archaeology.* University of Chicago Press, Chicago.

See also MIDWESTERN TAXONOMIC SYSTEM (MIDWESTERN TAXONOMIC METHOD)

Phillips Spring

The Phillips Spring site (23HI216), discovered in 1973, is upstream from Rodgers Shelter and near the center of the Pomme de Terre River Valley in northern Hickory County, Missouri. Systematic excavations of the site, an active artesian spring, began in 1974 and continued in the years 1976–1978. The initial investigation was an attempt to locate another late Pleistocene (ca. 40,000–10,000 years B.P.) or Holocene (since ca. 8050 B.C., or 10,000 years B.P.) palynological record that might coincide with the prehistoric habitations in the valley and to provide direct evidence of middle Holocene environmental and climatic conditions in the western Ozark Highland. Ultimately, these goals were largely satisfied. Along the way, even more impressive discoveries were made, including that of potential ancient cultigens (*Cucurbita pepo* [pepo squash] and *Lagenaria siceraria* [bottle gourd]). The unimpeachable, deeply stratified contexts of these discoveries at Phillips Spring extended the record of plant husbandry for the Archaic of the Eastern Woodlands of North America to a date earlier than 2250 B.C. (4200 years B.P.). Even more significant, they were a catalyst in reformulations of the Archaic as a period of dynamic adaptation and experimentation.

Phillips Spring is a deep, finely stratified archaeological site with exceptional preservation of normally perishable, uncarbonized plant remains. Under these sediments is an equally important, older alluvial record for the late Pleistocene and early Holocene that contains scattered pollen layers. Its remarkable organic preservation stems from the anaerobic environment created by the spring itself. The site contains the best-defined, radiocarbon-dated sequence of Holocene alluvial cut-and-fills in the valley. Just above bedrock is a Late Wisconsin Boreal Forest assemblage dominated by jack pine that dates to ca. 13,050 B.C. (15,000 years B.P.). Unlike other artesian springs in the valley, Phillips does not contain a Pleistocene bonebed.

The archaeology of Phillips is dominated by Late Archaic Sedalia-phase (ca. 2550–650 B.C., or 4500–2600 years B.P.) encampments that probably represent base camps. Subterranean food-storage facilities were dug, and large, oval basins were used as steaming pits for communal cooking. Adzes dominate the tool assemblage, but simple ground-stone tools and a variety of hafted chipped-stone points are present, too. The adzes have been referred to as "Sedalia diggers," but they are clearly heavy duty woodworking tools. At least one broken Nebo Hill lanceolate of seemingly nonlocal material was found along with an occasional wooden tool. Subsequent habitations include Middle and Late Woodland encampments that generally have larger-sized storage pits; one well-defined oval house and a distinctively local, hematite-tempered ceramic are present.

The Phillips Spring site is now beneath the waters of Harry S. Truman Lake, a federal impoundment.

Marvin Kay

Further Readings

Chomko, S.A. 1978. Phillips Spring, 23HI216: A Multicomponent Site in the Western Missouri Ozarks. *Plains Anthropologist* 23(81):235–255.

Chomko, S.A., and G.W. Crawford. 1978. Plant Husbandry in Prehistoric Eastern North America: New Evidence for Its Development. *American Antiquity* 43:405–408.

Haynes, C.V., Jr. 1985. *Mastodon-Bearing Springs and Late Quaternary Geochronology of the Lower Pomme de Terre Valley, Missouri*. Special Paper no. 204. Geological Society of America, Boulder.

Kay, M. 1983. Archaic Period Research in the Western Ozark Highlands, Missouri. In *Archaic Hunters and Gatherers in the American Midwest*, edited by J.L. Phillips and J.A. Brown, pp. 41–70. Academic Press, New York.

———. 1986. Phillips Spring: A Synopsis of Sedalia Phase Settlement and Subsistence. In *Foraging, Collecting, and Harvesting: Archaic Period Subsistence and Settlement in the Eastern Woodlands*, edited by S.W. Neusius, pp. 275–288. Occasional Paper no. 6. Center for Archaeological Investigations, Southern Illinois University, Carbondale.

Kay, M., F.B. King, and C.K. Robinson. 1980. Cucurbits From Phillips Spring: New Evidence and Interpretations. *American Antiquity* 45:806–822.

King, F.B. 1985. Early Cultivated Cucurbits in Eastern North America. In *Prehistoric Food Production in North America*, edited by R.I. Ford, pp. 73–98. Anthropological Paper no. 75. Museum of Anthropology, University of Michigan, Ann Arbor.

Smith, B.D. 1992. *Rivers of Change: Essays on Early Agriculture in Eastern North America*. Smithsonian Institution Press, Washington, D.C.

Pick

The pick is an elongated stone object whose function has long eluded archaeologists. One reason for the quandary is that at least two different types of picks have been distinguished in North America. The first is a rough chipped and/or pecked variety, such as those excavated from the Eva site in Tennessee, where they occurred throughout the Archaic period. Since both ends show signs of battering, they appear to have been made to pound or peck. The second variety has been called a "ceremonial pick" or, occasionally, a "chisel." It was typically made of slate, though a variety of materials, including hard igneous stones and cannel coal, are represented. This variety of pick was always handsomely crafted by grinding and polishing. At least one of the ends was usually fashioned into a narrow transverse bit, a feature that has allowed its interpretation as a chisel. However, neither end typically shows much use-wear and most exhibit no wear at all; hence, the inference that they were "ceremonial" items.

The center of pick distribution is Ohio, but picks occur throughout the Eastern Woodlands and northward into Ontario. The type is rare, but they appear to have been manufactured in both the Middle and Late Woodland period. There is an apparent hiatus in their manufacture throughout the last few centuries before European contact in the seventeenth century. This may be illusory, for a few ethnographic accounts of them exist, and rare ethnographic examples can be seen in museums. Most picks were discovered and recorded early in the history of archaeological endeavor. In the most comprehensive study of this tool type to date, John R. Halsey (1984) argued that they functioned as the blade of a tomahawk.

George H. Odell

Further Readings

Converse, H.N. 1978. *Ohio Slate Types*. Special Publication. Archaeological Society of Ohio, Columbus.

Halsey, J.R. 1984. The Ceremonial Pick: A Consideration of Its Place in Eastern Woodlands Prehistory. *Midcontinental Journal of Archaeology* 9:43–62.

Lewis, T.M.N., and M.K. Lewis. 1961. *Eva: An Archaic Site*. University of Tennessee Press, Knoxville.

Picosa

"Picosa" is a concept developed in the 1960s by Cynthia Irwin-Williams in an attempt to bring order to pre-Puebloan cultural developments in the southwestern United States, for these developments had not until then received adequate attention. Her contribution is significant, since it signaled an early effort to understand what she termed the "elementary southwestern culture."

Picosa is an acronym derived from letters in Pinto Basin (PI), Cochise (CO), and San Jose (SA), each a relevant archaeological culture. Irwin-Williams defined it as a continuum of similar preceramic cultures that existed in the Southwest prior to Puebloan developments and essentially includes what would be termed the "Archaic" of the region. The area covered by Picosa is large and is composed of three separate but interacting Archaic traditions. These are the Pinto-Amargosa complex of California, southern Nevada, and western Arizona; the Chiricahua and San Pedro phases of the Cochise culture of southeastern Arizona and southwestern New Mexico; and a wide range of poorly documented remains grouped as San Jose, Zobo, Santa Ana, and Atrisco from northwestern New Mexico, northeastern Arizona, southeastern Utah, and central and southwestern Colorado. Picosa is based on a constellation of similar traits in dwellings, subsistence, burial practices, ornamentation, and typology/technology. Various forms of presumably diagnostic projectile points are important in defining specific regional variations.

Irwin-Williams believed that the Southwestern Archaic (6000/5500 B.C.–A.D. 400, or 7950/7450–1550 years B.P.) was best examined at two levels. The first was integrative and linked the Southwest Archaic to generalized Archaic patterns throughout North America. In this sense, Picosa has similarities to the "Desert culture" defined by Jesse Jennings (1957, 1964). The second was isolative and identified cultural traits that set one geographic region apart from another. At this level, specific traits and patterns distinguished the Southwest and regions within it from other geographic areas. As an integrative concept, Picosa represented the initial period of formation when the Southwest emerged as a discrete culture area. Irwin-Williams thought that this was the result of a cultural synthesis of uniform developments originating as early as 8000 B.C. (9950 years B.P.). Of particular importance here was the idea that later Puebloan Anasazi developments derived from the Oshara tradition, a discrete Picosa manifestation defined for northwestern New Mexico. Based on excavations and surveys in that area, Irwin-Williams believed that some of the earliest evidence for agriculture in the Southwest first occurred within the Oshara tradition and that subsequent Anasazi origins were the ultimate result.

The "Picosa" concept is significant because, although based on a cultural-historical perspective, it was an early attempt to interject

Top: LA 18091, south of Farmington, New Mexico. This site yielded macrobotanical remains of corn in a Late Archaic context. Illustrated is one of the buried storage pits. The site was excavated as part of the ADAPT I project, funded by the Alamito Coal Company and conducted by the Navajo Nation Cultural Resource Management Program. (Courtesy of A. H. Simmons) Bottom: LA 18103. Another site from the ADAPT I project that contained evidence of Archaic use of corn in the form of pollen from the illustrated hearth. The site dates to ca. 1700–2000 B.C. (Courtesy of A. H. Simmons)

interpretation into an area that had largely been characterized by descriptive studies. Picosa has been criticized by some contemporary archaeologists as simplistic. It was, however, an important first step in recognizing that preceramic sites in the Southwest, often overshadowed by spectacular Puebloan remains, are more complex than first believed. Such sites contain information directly relevant to a variety of important research issues, including the origins of agriculture and hunter-gatherer adaptations.

Alan H. Simmons

Further Readings

Irwin-Williams, C. 1967. Picosa: The Elementary Southwestern Culture. *American Antiquity* 32:441–457.

———. 1968. Archaic Cultural History in the Southwestern United States. *Eastern New Mexico University Contributions in Anthropology* 1:48–54.

———. 1973. The Oshara Tradition: Origins of Anasazi Culture. *Eastern New Mexico University Contributions in Anthropology* 5(1):1–30.

———. 1977. Black Boxes and Multiple Working Hypotheses: Reconstructing the Economy of Early Southwest Hunters. *Kiva* 42:285–299.

———. 1979. Post-Pleistocene Archaeology, 7000–2000 B.C. In *Southwest*, edited by A. Ortiz, pp. 31–42. Handbook of North American Indians, vol. 9, W.C. Sturtevant, general editor. Smithsonian Institution, Washington D.C.

Irwin-Williams, C., and C.V. Haynes. 1970. Climatic Change and Early Population Dynamics in the Southwestern United States. *Quaternary Research* 1:59–71.

Irwin-Williams, C., and H.J. Irwin. 1966. *Excavations at Magic Mountain*. Proceedings no. 12. Denver Museum of Natural History, Denver.

Irwin-Williams, C., and S. Tompkins. 1968. *Excavations at En Medio Shelter, New Mexico*. Contributions in Anthropology, vol. 1, no. 2. Eastern New Mexico University, Portales.

Jennings, J. 1957. *Danger Cave*. Anthropological Papers no. 27. University of Utah

Pictograph Cave, Montana, as it appeared in 1964. (Photograph by A. M. Johnson)

An excavated 400–year-old Late Prehistoric tipi ring at the Pilgrim habitation site in the Limestone Hills, Upper Missouri River drainage. (Courtesy of Museum of the Rockies/Montana State University–Bozeman)

Press, Salt Lake City.

──────. 1964. The Desert West. In *Prehistoric Man in the New World*, edited by J. Jennings and E. Norbeck, pp. 149–174. University of Chicago Press, Chicago.

See also OSHARA TRADITION

Pictograph Cave

Pictograph Cave (24YE1) (see Figure) is a large dry rock shelter 16 km (10 miles) east of Billings, Montana, that was excavated by the WPA (Works Progress Administration) between 1937 and 1940. It derives its name from numerous pictographs on the back walls that represent shield-bearing warriors, V-shouldered anthropomorphs, animals, birds, horses, and flintlock guns, all in black, red, and white colors. Numerous perishable artifacts were recovered during excavation, including cord, whistles, basketry, moccasins, fire drills, arrow shafts and bow fragments, game counters, and shell and bone beads. These artifacts provide a rare glimpse into prehistoric material culture. Occupations dating from Late Paleoindian to historic times (9000 B.C.–A.D. 1700s, or 10,950–250/150 years B.P.) (rock-art guns) were identified and

formed the cornerstone of the first cultural chronology for the northwestern Plains (Mulloy 1958). Pictograph Cave is a Montana state park.

Ann M. Johnson

Further Readings

Mulloy, W.T. 1958. *A Preliminary Outline for the Northwestern Plains*. University of Wyoming Publications, vol. 22, no. 1. University of Wyoming Press, Laramie.

Pilgrim Site

The Pilgrim site (24BW675) is an open-air, repeatedly occupied, multicomponent habitation site located in a limestone-ridge-bounded arid grassland basin inside the Limestone Hills in west-central Montana. It is west of the Townsend Basin and east of the Elkhorn Mountains in Broadwater County. The site was investigated by Montana State University in 1979–1982 as an impact mitigative response to ongoing site disturbance by military training and maneuver activities. Forty (55 percent) of the identified tipi rings, two exterior hearths, and a rockpile were excavated. This 12-ha (30-acre) campsite was occupied seasonally from the late Middle Prehistoric period (Pelican Lake phase) into the Late Prehistoric period (Avonlea and Late Plains); that is, from ca. 1400 B.C. to A.D. 1450 (3350–500 years B.P.). Subsistence support was provided partly by the procurement of bison (*Bison bison bison*), pronghorn antelope (*Antilocapra americana*), and deer (*Odocoileus* sp.). However, site selection and seasonality may have been driven by the short-term availability of locally abundant plant species, especially wild parsley (*Musineon divaricatum*) and bitterroot (*Lewisia rediviva*), which were ready for gathering in the spring. Thirty-eight other plant species available in the spring would also have been resource attractions. Of 75 plant species growing on the site, 60 percent are known to have been eaten or used for ritual, medicinal, or industrial purposes by later Native Americans who frequented the Northern Rockies and northern Plains.

Leslie B. Davis

Further Readings

Aaberg, S.A. 1983. Plant Gathering As a Settlement Determinant at the Pilgrim Stone Circle Site. In *From Microcosm to Macrocosm: Advances in Tipi Ring Investigation and Interpretation*, edited by L.B. Davis, pp. 279–303. Memoir no. 19. Plains Anthropologist, Lincoln.

Davis, L.B. 1983. Stone Circles in the Montana Rockies: Relict Households and Transitory Communities. In *From Microcosm to Macrocosm: Advances in Tipi Ring Investigation and Interpretation*, edited by L.B. Davis, pp. 235–278. Memoir no. 19. Plains Anthropologist, Lincoln.

Pin

The pin is a relatively long, pointed metapodial bone of elk or deer. Pins have been discovered at several Middle Woodland inhumations, including the Bedford, Klunk, and Elizabeth mound groups in the Lower Illinois Valley. With few exceptions, pins have been reported only from central tombs, where they appear to have been part of the ritual paraphernalia. They probably fixed vegetal matting to the top or sides of these tombs.

George H. Odell

Further Readings

Leigh, S.R. 1988. Comparative Analysis of the Elizabeth Middle Woodland Artifact Assemblage. In *The Archaic and Wood-*
land Cemeteries at the Elizabeth Site in the Lower Illinois Valley, edited by D. Charles, S. Leigh, and J. Buikstra, pp. 191–217. Research Series, vol. 7. Center for American Archeology, Kampsville.

Perino, G.H. 1968. The Pete Klunk Mound Group, Calhoun County, Illinois: The Archaic and Hopewell Occupations. In *Hopewell and Woodland Site Archaeology in Illinois*, pp. 9–128. Bulletin no. 6. Illinois Archaeological Survey, University of Illinois Press, Urbana.

Pine Lawn Branch

The concept of the Mogollon cultural tradition is closely tied to the Pine Lawn Valley of west-central New Mexico and the archaeological research conducted there over two decades by the Field Museum of Natural History, Chicago. Between 1939 and 1957, a small roadside guest ranch called Pine Lawn was the headquarters for archaeological investigations led by Paul S. Martin and John B. Rinaldo. That fieldwork produced some of the "classic" studies in Southwestern archaeology, including analyses of the beginnings of agriculture, the initial formation of village communities, temporal changes in ceramic design and technology, and the abandonment of local regions. When the Field Museum moved its operations from the Pine Lawn Valley to eastern Arizona in the late 1950s, it had established a detailed cultural sequence spanning nearly 3,000 years based on excavations at a variety of sites. Many of the approaches developed during the Pine Lawn investigations, such as the application of "cultural ecology" as an explanatory framework, formed the basis for "New Archaeology" studies associated with Field Museum research in eastern Arizona during the 1960s.

The sequence of the Pine Lawn "branch" of the Mogollon cultural tradition has two major prehistoric periods, the preceramic (or Archaic) and the ceramic. Most of the Field Museum research concentrated on the ceramic period, within which five sequential phases were defined. Chronological ambiguity haunted this sequence, in part because very few chronometric dates were available until the 1980s, and in part because the systematics used to define various periods were often unclear. William Bullard presented a devastating critique of the Field Museum chronology in 1962 that called into question most of the phase dating but offered few convincing alternatives. As a result, the basic phase series continues to be used, but exact dating of these intervals remains imprecise.

The earliest ceramic phase is called Pine Lawn and is represented in the Field Museum excavations primarily by the SU and Promontory sites. In addition to the beginning of ceramic-vessel manufacture, the Pine Lawn phase is characterized by two major technological changes. These are the construction of large, semisubterranean pithouses with massive timber and earthen superstructures and the first appearance of rectangular manos and trough metates in the milling assemblage. Together they indicate a dramatic increase in sedentism compared to the preceding Archaic occupation of the area. Researchers generally agree that agricultural intensification was a key feature in this development. Originally, the Pine Lawn phase was dated at ca. 300 B.C.–A.D. 500 (2250–1450 years B.P.), but recent chronological data from projects conducted by the Museum of New Mexico and the University of New Mexico suggest a much more abbreviated interval, ca. A.D. 450–550 (1500–1400 years B.P.) (Cordell 1984).

The Pine Lawn phase is followed by the Georgetown phase, which is usually lumped with the succeeding San Francisco phase in most discussions of the region, for it has proven difficult to separate them based on the original phase criteria. Together they represent the period ca. A.D. 550–900 (1400–1050 years B.P.), although there are very few chronometric data from these phases. Among the notable characteristics of these two phases are the beginning of decorated pottery types and a shift to smaller pithouses. There are some suggestions that the region around the Pine Lawn Valley may have experienced a decline in population at this time, possibly in response to rapid population aggregation in areas such as the Mimbres Valley to the south. Key excavated sites include Turkey Foot Ridge and Starkweather Ruin.

The interval from ca. A.D. 900 to 1000 (1050–950 years B.P.) is associated with the Three Circle phase, which is distinguished primarily by two decorated ceramic types, Three Circle Red-on-white and Mimbres Boldface Black-on-white. Excavated data for this phase from the Pine Lawn Valley proper are extremely limited, consisting mostly of potsherds and a few pithouses. Although the Turkey Foot Ridge site is generally associated with the Three Circle phase, there are other representative sites in the Pine Lawn region, including Luna Village and the Jewett Gap site. Pithouses continued to be fairly small, averaging less than 20 m² (26 square yards) in floor area, but some settlements, such as Luna Village, may have had up to 100 individual houses and large, unroofed communal structures. Agriculture was important, but it is impossible to say whether it was more important than in earlier phases.

The Reserve phase is dated at ca. A.D. 1000–1150 (950–800 years B.P.), although recent research suggests that this may be too early. The Reserve phase is associated with two important cultural changes. First, surface architecture in the form of rectangular rooms built of stone and jacal becomes prominent. Consequently, the Reserve phase is thought to reflect a pan-Southwestern phenomenon known as the "pithouse to pueblo transition." However, pithouses remain a fundamental part of the settlement pattern, and, thus, the surface rooms are actually more of an addition than a replacement. Second, the ceramic assemblage found in Reserve-phase sites is clearly part of the Cibola tradition found mostly north and west of the Pine Lawn Valley, in contrast to the affiliations with the Mimbres tradition to the south that characterized earlier ceramic phases. Field Museum archaeologists interpreted this shift as the result of immigration by northern populations, but the exact meaning of the change in nonlocal ceramics is unclear. In several places, there appear to have been dispersed communities of small hamlets centered around a single, large communal building.

The Tularosa phase (ca. A.D. 1150–1300, or 800–650 years B.P.) is usually considered the last major cultural phase in the Pine Lawn sequence. During this time period, local populations apparently aggregated into large masonry pueblos that were often built around a communal house or structure. Ceramic types continue to reflect a northern connection, and the densest Tularosa-phase populations appear to have been north of the Pine Lawn Valley. Higgins Flat Pueblo is the major Tularosa-phase site excavated by the Field Museum. More recently, the University of Texas has conducted extensive excavations at the WS Ranch site south of the Pine Lawn Valley. A little known and poorly understood aspect of the Tularosa phase is the widespread distribution of small cliff dwellings throughout the Mogollon Highlands. The Field Museum excavated some of these, but their relationship to larger settlements is unknown and largely unexamined.

P

The prehistoric occupation of the Pine Lawn area is thought to have ended by ca. A.D. 1300 (650 years B.P.), although it seems likely that regional populations made extensive use of the abundant natural resources through hunting and gathering. No convincing explanations of why local populations left this resource-rich area of relatively high precipitation have been suggested. Radiocarbon dates and material culture indicate that Apache use of the area was intensive by the A.D. 1700s and continued through the late 1800s. Many prehistoric sites were reoccupied by Apache groups, a potential source of disturbance that archaeologists are only recently confronting.

W.H. Wills

Further Readings

Bullard, W., Jr. 1962. *The Cerro Colorado Site and Pit House Architecture in the Southwestern United States Prior to A.D. 900.* Papers, vol. 44, no. 2. Peabody Museum of American Archaeology and Ethnology, Harvard University, Cambridge.

Cordell, L.S. 1984. *Prehistory of the Southwest.* Academic Press, San Diego.

Martin, P.S. 1943. *The SU Site, Excavations at a Mogollon Village, Western New Mexico: Second Season 1941.* Anthropological Series, vol. 32, no. 2. Field Museum of Natural History, Chicago.

Martin, P.S., and F. Plog. 1973. *The Archaeology of Arizona.* Doubleday Natural History Press, New York.

Martin, P.S., J.B. Rinaldo, E.A. Bluhm, and H.C. Cutler. 1956. *Higgins Flat Pueblo, Western New Mexico.* Fieldiana: Anthropology, vol. 45. Field Museum of Natural History, Chicago.

Wheat, J.B. 1955. *Mogollon Culture Prior to A.D. 1000.* Memoir no. 82. American Anthropological Association, Menasha; Memoir no. 10. Society for American Archaeology, Washington, D.C.

Wills, W.H. 1989. Patterns of Prehistoric Agriculture in West-Central New Mexico. *Journal of Anthropological Research* 45(1):139–157.

Pinson Mounds Site

The largest Middle Woodland site in the Southeast, Pinson Mounds (40MD1) is located ca. 20 km (12 miles) south of Jackson, Tennessee, on the South Fork of the Forked Deer River. Occupying a relatively level tableland on the bluffs overlooking the river bottomland, the site consists of at least 12 extant mounds, a geometric enclosure, and associated ritual-activity localities within an area of ca. 160 ha (395 acres). In addition to its large size and the immense volume of earthwork fill represented (more than $100,000 \text{ m}^3$, or 130,800 cubic yards), the presence of five large rectangular platform mounds of Middle Woodland age underscores the unique nature of the site. These earthworks range in height from 2.5 to 22 m (8–72 feet).

Excavations on Ozier Mound (Mound 5) provided the first unequivocal evidence for the construction of rectangular platform mounds during the Middle Woodland period (ca. 200 B.C.–A.D. 400, or 2150–1550 years B.P.). This ramped earthwork, ca. 10 m (33 feet) tall, was constructed in at least six stages, with the summit of each stage covered with pale yellow sand. Mica, copper, and nonlocal microblades were found in association with the uppermost summit, linking this locality with other ritual-activity areas elsewhere within the site.

Although few earthworks at Pinson Mounds were constructed specifically for interment, partial excavation of the northern Twin Mound (Mound 6) provided a rare opportunity to view a large, undisturbed Middle Woodland burial mound. At the base of the mound, four log and/or fabric-covered tombs containing the remains of 16 individuals were excavated. Several individuals wore freshwater pearl necklaces and fiber headdresses decorated with copper ornaments. A pair of engraved rattles cut from human parietals and decorated in the classic Hopewellian style were found at the knees of an elderly male.

This mound exhibited unusually complex stratigraphy. First, a layer of puddled clay was placed over the tombs and associated features. A circular, flat-topped primary mound covered with alternating bands of multicolored earth was then built over the area containing tombs. Numerous sharpened wooden poles were driven into the surface of the primary mound. Surrounding the primary mound was a low, sand-covered platform, which was separated from the primary mound by a narrow walkway. Several distinctive layers of fill were subsequently added to bring the northern Twin Mound to its final height of ca. 7 m (23 feet). Four radiocarbon dates indicate that the mound was constructed ca. A.D. 100 (1850 years B.P.).

As was the case with most large Middle Woodland ceremonial sites, Pinson Mounds was not built by a single small village or group of villages. Ceramic evidence suggests that individuals from as far away as southern Georgia and Louisiana participated in rituals at Pinson Mounds. This is best documented at a locality designated the Duck's Nest Sector, a ritual-activity area dating to ca. A.D. 300 (1650 years B.P.) at which numerous examples of nonlocal pottery were found. These include limestone-tempered wares from the Tennessee River Valley, Swift Creek Complicated Stamped from southern Georgia, McLeod Simple Stamped from the Mobile Bay area, and several other types with no known counterparts.

Robert C. Mainfort, Jr.

Further Readings

Mainfort, R.C., Jr. 1988. Middle Woodland Ceremonialism at Pinson Mounds, Tennessee. *American Antiquity* 53:158–173.
Mainfort, R.C., Jr., and R. Walling. 1992. 1989 Excavations at Pinson Mounds: Ozier Mound. *Midcontinental Journal of Archaeology* 17(1):112–136.

Pipe

The origin of aboriginal pipe smoking in the Americas is unclear, but it does not appear to date farther back in time in North America than the Middle Woodland period, ca. 2,000 years ago. The earliest paleobotanical remains of tobacco date to this period, as well as an extensive array of stone pipe bowls. Usually found in graves, they were meticulously manufactured into a variety of shapes and fitted with an appropriate stem of reed or cane. Shapes included platform pipes and effigy forms that commonly depict animals. The names of types of platform pipes often refer at least in part to the place of their initial recovery in Ohio or Illinois, such as Bedford, Tremper A and B, and Hopewell 17.

Smoking continued through the later Late Woodland and Mississippian periods, with its attendant paraphernalia becoming even more elaborate through time. The Utz site, a Late Prehistoric Oneota-affiliated habitation in Missouri, for example, yielded more than 200 fragments of different pipes made from catlinite, limestone, shale, granite, hematite, and greenstone. In the Mississippi drainage, a "Cahokia style" of pipe-bowl making, characterized by

large human figures accompanied by ceremonial regalia and abundant ritual symbolism, developed. Often made from reddish bauxite or a stone known as "fire-clay," figure-pipes have been recovered from several localities in the American Bottom and nearby regions. A particularly impressive array of stone pipe bowls, most of which are in the form of human and animal effigies, and a large double-stemmed "T," were recovered from the Craig Mound at the Spiro site in Oklahoma.

George H. Odell

Top: A variety of pipe forms made of stone and clay. (Courtesy of the Wilford Archaeology Laboratory, University of Minnesota) Bottom: Effigy pipe. (Courtesy of the Wilford Archaeology Laboratory, University of Minnesota)

P

Further Readings

Emerson, T.E. 1982. *Mississippian Stone Images in Illinois*. Circular no. 6. Illinois Archaeological Survey, University of Illinois Press, Urbana.

Hamilton, H.W. 1967. *Tobacco Pipes of the Missouri Indians*. Memoir no. 5. Missouri Archaeological Society, Columbia.

McGuire, J.D. 1897. Pipes and Smoking Customs of the American Aborigines. *Annual Report of the Board of Regents, Smithsonian Institution, Report of U.S. National Museum*, pt. 1, pp. 351–645.

Seeman, M.F. 1977. Stylistic Variation in Middle Woodland Pipe Styles: The Chronological Implications. *Midcontinental Journal of Archaeology* 2:47–66.

Pismo Clam

The Pismo Clam (*Tivela stultorum*) is a surf-zone shellfish that once was abundant from above Monterey to Baja California. It was heavily harvested prehistorically for both its meat and its shell. In the last 1,000 years of California prehistory (ca. A.D. 770–1769, or 1180–181 years B.P.) clamshell was the most favored material for the making of beads.

Joseph L. Chartkoff

Pithouse

Pithouses, pit structures, or more generally semisubterranean structures include some of the oldest relatively permanent dwellings in the world. Among some groups, they have also remained an important type of housing into the very recent past. Various forms of pithouses are found archaeologically and in recent use in North America.

The defining characteristic of pithouses is the excavation of the floor below the ground. Most pithouses also have an earth covering on their roofs and walls. The most common forms are round or rounded, but rectangular or more complicated multilobed shapes also occur. From the pit base, walls generally extend up to or, more common, well above ground level. Posts in the house interior, along the walls themselves, or in both positions support a roof. Entry is via a ladder through an opening in the roof or through a ramp or doorway. The superstructure usually consists of a stout wooden skeleton covered with an organic filler, such as smaller logs and twigs or bark; the structure is then capped with dirt. In this respect, the pithouse is generally a form of earthlodge with a subterranean floor and walls that extend partially underground. The placement of the structure in the ground, combined with the earthen cap, provides excellent insulation against both heat and cold.

Excavation of the pit and collection of beams strong enough to support the weight of the roof represents a substantial investment in time and labor. The structures vary dramatically in both diameter and depth. Large, deep houses, such as those of some of the Salish-speaking peoples of interior British Columbia in the late nineteenth century, housed as many as 30 occupants in a dwelling 7 m (23 feet) or more across at floor level and dug more than 1 m (3.3 feet) deep. Other examples of pit structures are much smaller in diameter, shallower, or both. The earliest dwellings recognized in southern Arizona, which date to ca. 800–700 B.C. (2750–2650 years B.P.), are on the average ca. 3 m (10 feet) across and 10 cm (4 inches) deep.

Archaeologists in North America and elsewhere often suggest that pithouses provide evidence of sedentism. Recent research, however, has complicated this view. The close contact between the wood and the surrounding dirt makes pithouses susceptible to rapid decay and vermin infestation, so they generally do not remain in use without substantial repair or rebuilding much longer than 10–15 years. Furthermore, the simplicity of pithouse construction generally produces a single central room. This makes remodeling for extra interior storage or to accommodate changes in the number of occupants difficult. In contrast, surface architecture easily permits rooms to be added and remodeled. Probably because of these factors, most historic pithouses were used by populations who were sedentary and reliant on stored foods for only part of the year, particularly winter. At other times, they moved and usually lived in less substantial houses. Thus, pithouses typically appear to be associated with a heavy investment in a location and *seasonal* sedentism, but with populations that were mobile at other times of the year.

Within North America, widely recognized pithouse architecture was common in broad areas. One ran from the Aleutian Islands (in fact, it extended west into an ancient pithouse tradition in Siberia) through much of coastal Arctic Canada. This area also extended south in interior Alaska, interior British Columbia,

Reconstruction of a pithouse (From Frank H.H. Roberts, Jr. 1939. "Archeological Remains in the Whitewater District, Eastern Arizona." Part I. House Types; fig. 28. Bulletin 121, Bureau of American Ethnology, Smithsonian Institution)

down into the Columbia Plateau region of the United States, and into interior California. The earliest pithouses date to earlier than 2050 B.C. (4000 years B.P.) in some of these regions, though the most substantial structures were made more recently than ca. A.D. 1 (1950 years B.P.). In some regions, pithouses remained the primary winter dwellings well into the nineteenth century.

The other major area known for pithouses is in the American Southwest, extending into Mexico. Here again the earliest semisubterranean structures date to 2050 B.C. (4000 years B.P.) or earlier. In much of the Southwest, pithouses were superseded by surface architecture around the start of the second millennium A.D. Among many of the Southwestern Pueblo peoples, pithouses took on a specialized ceremonial role (often referred to by the Hopi word "kiva"), which they retain even now. The religious significance of the underworld or emergence is widespread, and pit structures often remain in use for ceremonial purposes after their domestic functions are abandoned. They even served as a rallying point of a mid- to late-nineteenth-century revitalistic movement among California native peoples.

In the major river valleys of the eastern Plains, a third area was characterized by large earth-covered dwellings, generally called "earthlodges." This architecture dates from ca. A.D. 1000 (950 years B.P.) to the late nineteenth century and is variable across time and space. Some of the lodges were partly underground and were, in fact, large pithouses.

Although less widely recognized, Native Americans in many other areas used pithouses or at least structures that graded into pithouse forms. These include scattered archaeological examples from the eastern and midwestern United States in contexts ranging from the Late Archaic through Late Woodland and Mississippian periods. Historic dwellings, such as the winter houses of some Southeastern native groups and the hogans of the Navajo of the Southwest, sometimes had sunken floors, though these house styles are not generally classified as pithouses.

Thomas R. Rocek

Further Readings

Cameron, C.M. 1990. The Effect of Varying Estimates of Pit Structure Use-Life on Prehistoric Population Estimates in the American Southwest. *Kiva* 57:155–166.

Farwell, R.Y. 1981. Pit House: Prehistoric Energy Conservation? *El Palacio* 87:43–47.

Gilman, P.A. 1987. Architecture As Artifact: Pit Structures and Pueblos in the American Southeast. *American Antiquity* 52:538–564.

Lekson, S.H. 1988. The Idea of the Kiva in Anasazi Archaeology. *Kiva* 53:213–234.

McGuire, R.H., and M.B. Schiffer. 1983. A Theory of Architectural Design. *Journal of Anthropological Archeology* 2:277–303.

Nabokov, P., and R. Easton. 1989. *Native American Architecture*. Oxford University Press, New York.

Ray, V.F. 1939. *Cultural Relations in the Plateau of Northwestern America*. Publications of the Frederick Webb Hodge Anniversary Publication Fund, vol. 3. Southwest Museum, Los Angeles.

Roberts, F.H.H., Jr. 1939. *Archeological Remains in the Whitewater District, Eastern Arizona: 1. House Types*. Bulletin no. 121. Bureau of American Ethnology, Smithsonian Institution, Washington, D.C.

Spencer, R.F. 1959. *The North Alaskan Eskimo: A Study in Ecology and Society*. Bulletin no. 171. Bureau of American Ethnology, Smithsonian Institution, Washington, D.C.

Waterman, T.T., (and collaborators). 1921. *Native Houses of Western North America*. Indian Notes and Monographs no. 11. Museum of the American Indian-Heye Foundation, New York.

Pithouses (Plateau)

Semisubterranean structures, or pithouses, are widespread on the North American Plateau, where winter temperatures descend substantially below freezing for prolonged periods of time and where climates are relatively dry. In their most developed form, pithouses are associated with seasonal (winter) sedentism, logistical mobility, stored foods, and substantial effort in their construction. However, in some smaller, shallower examples, which may be transitional from simpler shelters with scooped-out floors, these relationships may be less apparent. There is a debate over whether early pithouses on the Plateau were used by broad-spectrum foragers for a single season or were occupied by hunters who had already specialized in the exploitation of a few species. Pithouses tend to occur only where resources are rich enough to make seasonal sedentism possible. Otherwise, the effort involved in constructing them was likely too great for short-term occupations associated with the exploitation of sparse resources,

as in the Boreal Forests. A distinction is often made between pithouses (structures still standing) and housepits (where only the house depression is left).

The earliest pithouses are located in northeast California and on the Plateau where they date to ca. 3550 B.C. (5500 years B.P.). Independent studies indicate that they do not seem to have been used very much between 2050 and 1550 B.C. (4000–3500 years B.P.). This period was followed by a florescence in their use from ca. 1550 B.C. to A.D. 1800 (3500–150 years B.P.), after which they are widely replaced by log cabins. On the Canadian Plateau, the earliest housepit has been dated to 2550 B.C. (4500 years B.P.) at the Baker site, near Kamloops.

In the most developed forms of pithouses, earth is first removed from the area to be used as the inside of the structure, typically to a depth of 30–200 cm (12–78 inches). A frame of poles is then erected over the pit to serve as the roofing superstructure. Additional poles are added to fill in gaps, after which coverings of bark, reed mats, pine needles, and/or skins are added. Earth is then either banked up around the base of this roof or spread over the entire roof. Although James A. Teit's (1900) illustration of a historic pithouse (see Figure) has become the stereotyped architectural image of Plateau pithouses, archaeological research and ethnographic comparisons show considerable architectural variation both within and between regions. Many of these variations are likely due to size differences (ranging from 3-m, or 10-foot, diameters lacking internal supports to large corporate residences more than 20 m, or 65.5 feet, in diameter). Entrance was typically through the smoke hole in the roof down a log ladder; however, this also varied according to size, with side entrances used in smaller houses and probably also in the largest houses. Pithouses could also be flat-topped, as in the Southwest, conical, square, or round. Numerous internal-post-support arrangements were also possible.

A wide range of social and economic organizations characterized pithouse life, from communal to hierarchical. Smaller pithouses tended to have shorter use-lives, whereas larger corporate residences, such as those at the Keatley Creek site in British Columbia, were sometimes owned and maintained by the same corporate group for over a thousand years.

Cross-cultural analysis has shown that pithouses were densely occupied, with an average space of only 2–3 m^2 (2.4–3.6 square yards) per person. Such densities were likely maintained to maximize the use of body heat in order to stay warm throughout severe winters. Most accounts indicate that pithouse residents were eager to leave as early as possible in the spring.

Brian Hayden

Further Readings

Ames, K. 1991. Sedentism: A Temporal Shift or a Transitional Change in Hunter-Gatherer Mobility Patterns? In *Between Bands and States*, edited by S. Gregg, pp. 109–134. Southern Illinois University Press, Carbondale.

Chatters, J. 1989. Resource Intensification

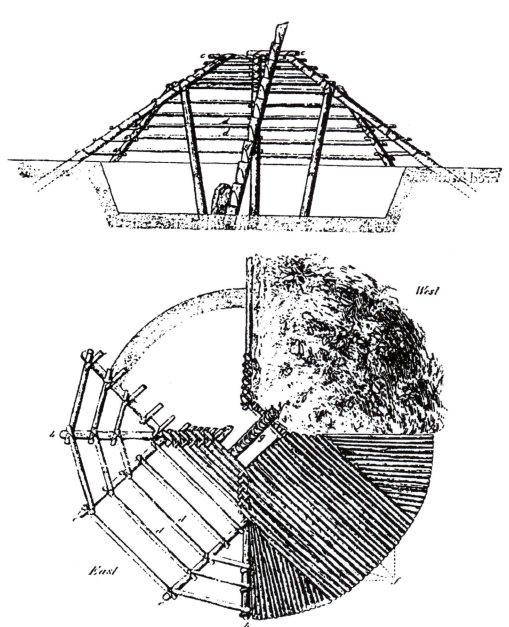

Schematic illustration of historic pithouse architecture typical of the Canadian Plateau. (Redrawn by B. Hayden from James Teit, 1900)

and Sedentism on the Southern Plateau. *Archaeology in Washington* 1:3–19.

Teit, J.A. 1900. The Thompson Indians of British Columbia. *Memoirs of the American Museum of Natural History, Jesup North Pacific Expedition* 2(4):163–392.

See also CLASSIC LILLOOET CULTURE

Pitted Stone

Pitted stones, also referred to as "cupstones" or "nutting stones," are a hard stone implement, often sandstone, in which a shallow depression has been pecked on one or more of its flat surfaces. The depression may have been formed by cracking nutshells, though this activity lacks adequate confirmation through ethnographic examples or published experimentation. Wear from pitting is frequently associated with pounding wear on an end or side of the implement, suggesting the tool was used for general percussive purposes. This is a common implement found throughout the continent. It dates to well into the Archaic period, as at the Modoc Rock Shelter in Illinois, and extends through the Woodland period, as at the Albertson site in Arkansas.

George H. Odell

Further Readings

Converse, R.N. 1973. *Ohio Stone Tools*. Special Publication. Archaeological Society of Ohio, Columbus.

Dickson, D.R. 1991. *The Albertson Site: A Deeply and Clearly Stratified Ozark Bluff Shelter*. Research Series no. 41. Arkansas Archeological Survey, Fayetteville.

Fowler, M.R. 1959. *Summary Report of Modoc Rock Shelter*. Report of Investigations no. 8. Illinois State Museum, Springfield.

Ritchie, W.A. 1929. *Hammerstones, Anvils, and Certain Pitted Stones*. Researches and Transactions, vol. 7, no. 2. New York State Archaeological Association, Rochester.

Plains

The Plains area has been variously defined, but the most current conceptualization is that of Waldo R. Wedel (1961:Map 1); Plains archaeologists rarely deviate significantly from his boundaries. There are five recognized archaeological subareas of the Great Plains: the Middle Missouri, and the northwestern, northeastern, central, and southern Plains.

The Middle Missouri subarea comprises the valley of the Missouri River between the mouth of the White River in southeastern South Dakota and that of the Yellowstone River in western North Dakota. This subarea is significant only to the Late Prehistoric peoples of the Plains Village tradition (ca. A.D. 900–1886, or 1050–64 years B.P.), when it was intensively occupied by horticultural town dwellers. Previous to that time, the Missouri Valley provides only an approximate boundary between the people that lived in the northeastern and the northwestern Plains.

The northwestern Plains, extending from southeastern Alberta to southeastern Wyoming east of the Rocky Mountains, is generally the most arid part of the Plains. Historically, it was the home of many nomadic bison hunters. The northeastern Plains consists largely of that part of North and South Dakota east of the Missouri River and of adjoining eastern and northern grasslands. The central Plains embraces most of eastern Nebraska and north-central Kansas. The southern Plains is composed of central and southern Kansas, most of western Oklahoma, and the Texas Panhandle and environs.

W. Raymond Wood

Further Readings

Wedel, W.R. 1961. *Prehistoric Man on the Great Plains*. University of Oklahoma Press, Norman.

Plains Village Tradition

The concept of the "Plains Village tradition" was first presented in detail by Donald J. Lehmer in a monograph describing his excavations at the Dodd village site in central South Dakota (Lehmer 1954). He argued that all of the village cultures of the central and northern Plains represented a single basic configuration he initially called the Plains Village pattern. The core of the pattern was a set of shared characteristics: The village groups depended about equally on hunting and gardening; built semisedentary villages on terraces along major streams; lived in earthlodges with covered entry passages; stored goods in bell-shaped and straight-sided cachepits in and near the houses; made grit-tempered pottery with paddle-marked walls and cord- or tool-impressed embellishments; used small triangular arrow points and a wide range of chipped stone; and had a large inventory of bone tools, including hoes and hide-dressing tools.

The tradition is divided into three subtraditions: Central Plains, Middle Missouri, and Coalescent. It spanned the period from ca. A.D. 900 to 1886 (1050–64 years B.P.). The Central Plains tradition is composed of the Upper Republican, Nebraska, and related variants. The roughly contemporaneous Middle Missouri tradition includes the Anderson, Grand Detour, Thomas Riggs, Fort Yates, Huff, and related phases. The Coalescent tradition grew out of a coalescence of the preceding two traditions. The Coalescent was directly attributable to the historic Mandan, Hidatsa, Arikara, and Pawnee, and their Protohistoric antecedents. Each of the three traditions was further subdivided into variants that, useful initially, are losing their usefulness as knowledge of Plains prehistory continues to grow.

W. Raymond Wood

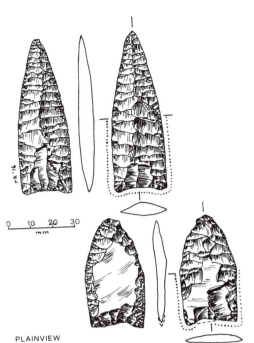

PLAINVIEW

Plainview projectile point. (Illustration by R. Knudson)

Further Readings

Lehmer, D.J. 1954. *Archeological Investigations in the Oahe Dam Area, South Dakota, 1950–51.* Bulletin no. 158. Bureau of American Ethnology, Smithsonian Institution, Washington, D.C.

———. 1971. *Introduction to Middle Missouri Archeology.* Anthropological Papers no. 1. National Park Service, Washington, D.C.

Lehmer, D.J., and W.W. Caldwell. 1966. Horizon and Tradition in the Northern Plains. *American Antiquity* 31:511–516.

See also CENTRAL PLAINS TRADITION; COALESCENT TRADITION; MIDDLE MISSOURI TRADITION

Plainview Complex

The Plainview complex is a 10,000-year-old set of Late Paleoindian sites and assemblages in the southern High Plains of North America that reflects a specific flaked-lithic-production system associated with a lanceolate projectile point form and a big-game-hunting subsistence pattern. Historically, the term "Plainview" has been used to refer to any and almost all unfluted lanceolate points found on the High Plains in the period understood to represent the immediate post-Folsom big-game hunters. This use of the term is inaccurate and misleading.

In the 1920s, cousins Harold Andersen and Bert Mountain made extensive surface collections of fluted and unfluted lanceolate flaked-stone projectile points in Yuma County, Colorado. Some of these specimens are now labeled Clovis, Folsom, Milnesand, Plainview, Firstview, Agate Basin, and Scottsbluff. In the 1920s and 1930s, the unfluted points were called "Yumas." On some of those wind-blown sites, Yumas were found in surface association with fluted points. After the discovery of the Folsom site in 1926, the search for successors to Folsom took note of the eastern Colorado fluted point–Yuma associations. Researchers expected to find sites representing a post-Folsom cultural adaptation distributed as widely as Folsom was then assumed to be distributed. In the mid-1940s, a buried Yumalike site was found in Plainview, Texas, and the ambiguities attached to the "Yuma" label were simply transferred to what became the "Plainview" label.

The Plainview complex is named after the archaeological attributes exhibited at the Plainview site (41HA1) in Plainview. The site was identified in 1944, excavated in 1945, and almost immediately described in a widely distributed publication (Sellards et al. 1947). The site assemblage was characterized by unfluted lanceolate projectile points made of fine cryptocrystallines available only in selected outcrops across or even outside the southern Plains. The points were flaked using what is now recognized as a Sudplano-reduction technology. The Sudplano technology apparently involved prepared polyhedral core and specialized flake production, with patterned use of several types of flakes as preforms. Long bladelike flakes were shaped in a series of thinning reductions, the last of which used regular pressure flaking that resulted in parallel-collateral patterning; the final projectile point had a rounded diamond cross section. Thin flakes produced during core reduction were shaped into tools with no major cross-section reduction. Edge shaping was used to take advantage of the thick-flake bulb remnant to shape a strong point tip, and the thin-flake cross section was easily shaped into a narrow-width haft. This *direct thin-flake manufacture* resulted in smooth tool faces that

Clovis projectile point. (Illustration by R. Knudson)

reflect the original flat ventral (and sometimes also dorsal) flake preform face. What were produced were "unfluted Folsoms."

Between these two extremes at the Plainview site were preforms that were neither long and strong enough (not bladelike enough) to reduce serially to achieve patterned facial flaking and a strong cross section nor thin enough to just edge-shape into a tool form. The resulting "in between" points were ambiguous in that they had a lanceolate form, sometimes had tendencies toward patterned facial flaking, sometimes had a remnant of the original flake preform face, were not fluted, and were neither obviously thin-flake nor strongly stylized lanceolate tools. Many Paleoindian flaked-stone projectile points, when encountered in archaeological collections, have simply been labeled "Yuma" or "Plainview" because they appear similar to these forms. When looked at in terms of the assemblage in which they were found, however, their lack of patterned concordance with "Plainview" is noticeable.

Identifying a Plainview "complex" implies that the various bits of archaeological evidence found within assemblages at particular sites have a connection that forms, in toto, a distinctive complex. The utility of the "complex" concept is that some form of prehistoric cultural patterning underlies artifact patterning. The implications of these ideas have not been explicitly explored, however, for the Plainview "complex." While there must be some sharing of traits to justify inclusion within a complex, just what combinations of shared traits fall within the Plainview "complex" has not been well defined. This is a critical issue, for assemblages assigned to the "complex" do not share all traits in common.

Current research (Knudson 1983; Knudson et al. 1997) indicates that the Plainview-complex nexus most likely consists of shared Sudplano technology, selection of fine cryptocrystalline flaking material, predominance of an unfluted lanceolate projectile-point form complemented by an apparent social investment in some highly reduced parallel-collateral flaked points, probable specialization of knapping artisans, use of bipolar technology for pragmatic tool production, lack of ground-stone-tool-manufacturing technology, frequent use of (either hunts or natural) large game kills for subsistence, and use of the southern High Plains ca. 8050 B.C. (10,000 years B.P.).

The smallness of the Plainview site assemblage and the apparent heavy-use damage of many of its artifacts, and the single short-term bison kill that resulted in its deposition, make this assemblage an equivocal basis for defining a point type or an archaeological complex. Still, its use as a reference point since the mid-1940s means that it is not going to go away. The responsible response, then, is to use this information to reflect as much prehistoric reality as possible.

No intensive investigation has been conducted to support a multisite Plainview complex membership, as the complex has been defined here. Direct thin-flake projectile-point manufacture is evident at the Folsom (New Mexico), Midland (Texas), Milnesand (Texas), Jurgens (Colorado), Olsen-Chubbuck (Colorado), Lubbock Lake (Texas), Lindenmeier (Colorado) Folsom level, and Bonfire Shelter (Texas) sites; it may be present at Blackwater Draw. It is infrequent in northern Plains Paleoindian assemblages. It is present in the Midland level at Hell Gap but does not appear to have been a popular technique at that site over time. Most of the above assemblages date prior to or around 8050 B.C. (10,000 years B.P.) and are associated with High Plains big-game hunting, use of high-quality cryptocrystalline, and apparently flintknapping specialization. Undoubtedly, it is not archaeologically useful to identify all of the sites mentioned above as part of a Plainview complex. Nonetheless, all of those assemblages merit more detailed investigation of their organizational and distributional variability in order to identify archaeologically and perhaps culturally significant interrelationships. Data current to the mid-1990s suggest that the strongest candidates for a "Plainview complex" are Plainview, Bonfire Shelter, Midland, Milnesand, Lubbock Lake, Olsen-Chubbuck, and Jurgens. Since technology is more culturally conservative than style, it merits precedence in defining the Plainview complex. The relationship of this technology with changing Pleistocene/Holocene (ca. 8050 B.C., or 10,000 years B.P.) climatic regimes, with plant, animal, and human ecologies, and with contemporary tool technologies and styles merits more detailed investigation.

Ruthann Knudson

Further Readings

Bell, R.E. 1958. *Guide to the Identification of Certain American Indian Projectile Points*. Special Bulletin no. 1. Oklahoma Anthropological Society, Norman.

Johnson, E. (editor). 1987. *Lubbock Lake: Late Quaternary Studies on the Southern High Plains*. Texas A&M University Press, College Station.

Knudson, R. 1983. *Organizational Variability in Late Paleo-Indian Assemblages*. Report of Investigations no. 60. Laboratory of Anthropology, Washington State University, Pullman.

Knudson, R., E. Johnson, and V.T. Holliday. 1997. The 10,000-Year-Old Lubbock Flaked Stone Assemblage From the Lubbock Lake Landmark, Texas. *Plains Anthropologist*.

Sellards, E.H., G.L. Evans, and G.E. Meade, with A.D. Krieger. 1947. Fossil Bison and Associated Artifacts From Plainview, Texas. *Bulletin of the Geological Society of America* 58:927–954.

Suhn, D.A., and E.B. Jelks (editors). 1962. *Handbook of Texas Archeology: Type Descriptions*. Special Publication no. 1. Texas Archeological Society, Austin. Bulletin no. 4. Texas Memorial Museum, Austin.

Wormington, H.M. 1957. *Ancient Man in North America*. 4th rev. ed. Popular Series no. 4. Denver Museum of Natural History, Denver.

See also PLAINVIEW SITE

Plainview Site

The Plainview bison-kill site (41HA1) was identified in 1944 by Glen Evans and Grayson Meade on private property within the community of Plainview along Running Water Creek Valley in the Texas Panhandle. The University of Texas Bureau of Economic Geology and Texas Memorial Museum collaborated on excavating most (ca. 55.7 m^2, or 600 square feet), of the site during the summer of 1945. Several professional and avocational archaeologists collected material after its initial professional excavation into the mid-1960s. The Plainview site was designated a National Historic Landmark in 1964.

Thirty flaked-stone tools are known to have come from the site's main bonebed, including 20 complete or partial projectile points and 10 flake tools. An additional seven or more points or point fragments and two or more flake tools have been found in the vicinity of the

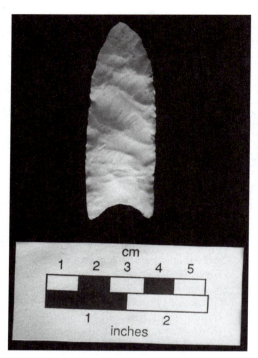

Plainview projectile point. (Courtesy of the Wilford Archaeology Laboratory, University of Minnesota)

main bonebed. The flaked-stone tools were associated with the skeletal remains of more than 100 *Bison taylorii*. Together, they probably represent a mid- to late-summer kill that had accumulated in the creek channel (now a sand and gravel layer). Freshwater shell collected from the site in 1953 was originally determined to date to 7220 B.C. ± 500 (9170 years B.P.), and bone collected in 1955 (after having been exposed for 10 years) produced a date of 5150 B.C. ± 160 (7100 years B.P.). The Lamont analysis was subsequently recalibrated to 7850 B.C. ± 500 (9800 years B.P.), and a split sample of bone apatite from 1945-excavated bone yielded ages of 8250 B.C. ± 400 (10,200 years B.P.) and 7910 B.C. ± 180 (9860 years B.P.).

All recovered Plainview-site tools reflect heavy use (breakage, edge damage), and most of the projectile points appear to have been reworked and used heavily as knives. The site is the remainder of a major bison-butchering episode, and most of the recovered artifacts appear to have exhausted their usefulness or to have been lost in the butchering process. No debitage was recovered during the excavations or from the plaster-jacketed blocks of site material that were reexcavated at the University of Texas in 1980. There is no evidence that cobble tools were present in the site accumulation, and there has been no evaluation to identify bone cut marks or possible bone-tool use at the site.

Plainview-site lithic technology probably involved prepared polyhedral cores and specialized flake production, with patterned use of several types of flakes as preforms. The bifaces are fine cryptocrystalline materials that probably all outcrop at least 161 km (100 miles) from the site. The biface-production system (Sudplano) was complemented by bipolar reduction of local gravels to produce pragmatic tools. Probably only one or two individuals flaked all the points. Stabbing projections and long, straight bifacial or unifacial cutting edges dominate the collection, with few short, strongly curved edges (e.g., scrapers). Points/ knives made directly on thin flakes exhibit little stylization; in contrast, those reduced several times have final parallel-collateral facial pressure flaking and a rounded diamond cross section. Plainview point/knife bases usually are shallowly concave with strong proximal thinning; one tool exhibits slight shoulders. The Plainview-site collection exhibits flaked-stone technical conservation and efficiency, with style a secondary consideration of skilled artisans.

Ruthann Knudson

Further Readings

Guffee, E. 1979. *The Plainview Site: Relocation and Archeological Investigation of Late Paleo-Indian Kill Site in Hale County, Texas.* Archeological Research Laboratory, Llano Estacado Museum, Plainview.

Holliday, V.T. (editor). 1986. *Guidebook to the Archaeological Geology of Classic Paleoindian Sites on the Southern High Plains, Texas and New Mexico.* Department of Geography, Texas A&M University, College Station.

Knudson, R. 1983. *Organizational Variability in Late Paleo-Indian Assemblages.* Report of Investigations no. 60. Laboratory of Anthropology, Washington State University, Pullman.

Sellards, E.H., G.L. Evans, and G.E. Meade, with A.D. Krieger. 1947. Fossil Bison and Associated Artifacts From Plainview, Texas. *Bulletin of the Geological Society of America* 58:927–954.

See also PLAINVIEW COMPLEX

Plaquemine Culture

Plaquemine is a division of the Mississippian cultural tradition that extended over a large portion of the Eastern Woodlands of the United States in the second millennium A.D. The first description (Quimby 1951) of this culture was based on excavations at the Medora site in West Baton Rouge Parish, Louisiana. The Plaquemine culture is now known to have covered much of the southern portion of the Lower Mississippi Valley. At its peak, it extended over a large portion of Louisiana, Mississippi, and Arkansas. The geographical shape of its distribution is a large triangle, with the Mississippi River delta representing its base and Greenville, Mississippi, in the central Yazoo Basin, its apex. Plaquemine had its roots in the earlier Coles Creek culture (A.D. 700–1200, or 1250–750 years B.P.), but it was also influenced by the Caddoan culture to the west. It began ca. A.D. 1200 (750 years B.P.) and continued in certain regions until the late seventeenth century.

In the eastern portion of its distribution, Plaquemine has been described as a blend of two very different cultural developments. Jeffrey P. Brain (1989) described it as a hybridization—"Mississippianized" Coles Creek, neither one nor the other, but a product of both. Plaquemine clearly represents a florescence in activities at major mound centers. Many of the earlier Coles Creek–culture ceremonial sites continued to be occupied, but the pyramidal platform mounds were expanded until they became imposing edifices. Not only were thick mantles of earth added to the existing Coles Creek mounds, but many additional mounds were constructed at these centers. Smaller Plaquemine mound centers usually had only a couple of mounds that surrounded an open plaza. The larger Plaquemine centers, however, characteristically had a dominant mound surrounded by several small mounds. Major sites, like Winterville and Lake George in the Lower Yazoo Basin, contained between 15 and 30 mounds. There is no evidence for large populations at these centers. Whereas major Mississippian mound sites to the north often had dense populations, Plaquemine centers were not heavily occupied. Most people appear to have resided in the surrounding countryside, while only a small residential population was present at the principal centers to cater to the nobles and their extended families. These chiefly compounds had heavy usage only during ritual events that affected all or major parts of the society.

Plaquemine sites have been found in the loess bluffs of Mississippi as well as in the alluvial valley of the Mississippi River. In the hills, these sites occur along the valleys of secondary and tertiary streams that are tributaries to the Mississippi, and on the tops of the hundreds of little hills that exist in the region. In the Mississippi alluvial valley, Plaquemine sites are typically found on the well-drained soils of natural levees, which are excellent locations for people who practiced agriculture. In the Natchez Bluffs region, settlement patterns changed markedly in the transition from Coles Creek to Plaquemine culture A.D. 1000–1200 (950–750 years B.P.). In addition to the expansion of the major centers like Anna and Emerald, an increase in the number of smaller sites occurred at this time. This increase is believed to reflect a burgeoning population, one that apparently took advantage of a new and better subsistence base. Undoubtedly, there were differences between the relative importance of agriculture and hunting and gathering in various regions. In general, however, Plaquemine culture was an agrarian economy in which the bulk of the population lived in small sedentary farmsteads or hamlets (several households in close proximity), where they grew crops of maize, beans, and squash. Nearby small mound centers are believed to have been the chiefly compounds of secondary chiefs who were probably matrilineally related to the principal leaders at the major Plaquemine mound centers.

By A.D. 1350 (600 years B.P.), Plaquemine culture had reached its zenith and attained its greatest geographical extent. It subsequently began to decline. The actual reasons for its decline are not known, but it is evident that many of the major sites, like Winterville and Lake George, were subjected to strong influences from the north. This is seen particularly in the realm of ceramic technology, as Plaquemine material culture, particularly pottery, became more like that found on Mississippian-culture sites in the central portion of the Mississippi Valley. Plaquemine culture did not actually end, but its domain shrank. Parts of former Plaquemine territory, like the Tensas Basin in Louisiana and all of the Yazoo Basin in Mississippi, eventually became Mississippian territory. Only the Natchez Bluffs region, the home of the historic Natchez Indians, and regions to the south resisted Mississippian cultural influences.

Plaquemine culture, although constantly changing, can still be recognized as Plaquemine throughout the Foster (A.D. 1350–1500, or 600–450 years B.P.) and Emerald (A.D. 1500–1680, or 450–270 years B.P.) phases of the Natchez Bluffs region. Major demographic changes occurred in this region in the late seventeenth and early eighteenth centuries, but the people were still basically of the Plaquemine culture. The Natchez Indians still continued to use the same sites as their Plaquemine ancestors had, including mound and nonmound settlements, but occupation was not as intense because of population decrease, and there was

The Anna (top) and Emerald (bottom) sites. (Illustration by I. W. Brown)

only a semblance of the mound-building activity that had occurred earlier.

Ian W. Brown

Further Readings

Brain, J.P. 1989. *Winterville: Late Prehistoric Culture Contact in the Lower Mississippi Valley*. Archaeological Report no. 23. Mississippi Department of Archives and History, Jackson.

Brown, I.W. 1985. Plaquemine Architectural Patterns in the Natchez Bluffs and Surrounding Regions of the Lower Mississippi Valley. *Midcontinental Journal of Archaeology* 10(2):251–305.

Quimby, G.I. 1951. *The Medora Site, West Baton Rouge Parish, Louisiana*. Anthropological Series no. 24, pt. 2. Field Museum of Natural History, Chicago.

Williams, S., and J.P. Brain. 1983. *Excavations at the Lake George Site, Yazoo County, Mississippi, 1958–1960*. Papers, vol. 74. Peabody Museum of American Archaeology and Ethnology, Harvard University, Cambridge.

See also Coles Creek Culture

Plateau Culture Area

The Plateau culture area includes portions of British Columbia, Washington State, Oregon, Idaho, and western Montana. It corresponds physiographically to the region between the Cascade and Coast ranges of the Rocky Mountain Cordillera and the Pacific Coast. To the south, it is bordered by the Great Basin; to the north, by the Subarctic. The Plateau is dominated by two great rivers, the Fraser, which drains much of interior British Columbia, and the Columbia, which drains parts of southern British Columbia and most of the region in the United States. The Plateau is usually divided into northern and southern subareas. This boundary corresponds roughly to the Canada-United States international border.

The region displays a number of repeating natural patterns and gradients that are important for understanding its prehistory. Local conditions can significantly modify these regional patterns.

The Cascade-Coast Range mountain system forms the Northwest's major mountain axis. The Cascades extend from Mt. Lassen in northern California to south-central British Columbia. The Coast Range begins north of the Fraser River and ends with the Mt. Saint Elias Range of southern Alaska. The eastern slopes of this system merge into the intermontane plateau, which is actually a complex of plateaus and mountains. There are two major plateaus, the Northern (or Canadian) Plateau of British Columbia, and the Columbia Plateau of Washington State. These are separated by the Okanagan Highlands, a range of low, rolling mountains that lie across the international border. The Northern Plateau is actually composed of several lesser plateaus and uplands, flanked by several north-south-trending mountain ranges. Thus, the topography on the Northern Plateau is not uniform. In contrast, the Columbia Plateau is quite uniform. It is composed of enormous basalt flows. The Columbia Plateau is lowest in the west, where it meets the Cascades. It starts below 152 m (500 feet) above sea level and rises slowly eastward to 914 m (3,000 feet) or more where it abuts the Northern Rockies. A southern segment of the Columbia Plateau extends south and east through southern Idaho, where it is deeply dissected into great canyons.

The Canadian and Northern Rockies form the eastern edge of the region, while the Blue Mountains border the southern Columbia Plateau in central Oregon, and the basin and range physiographic province border the Columbia Plateau in southern Idaho. While the Rockies and the Blue Mountains are included here, the basin province is not. The Rockies in this area rarely exceed 3,658 m (12,000 feet), though peaks between 2,743 and 3,048 m (9,000–10,000 feet) are common. However, these mountains were heavily glaciated in the north, and there were ice caps in the south. The more southerly mountains are also deeply dissected and heavily vegetated. The Blue Mountains are a moderately high complex of alpine mountains and basalt plateaus in northwestern Oregon.

The Plateau is drained by its two great rivers and by many lesser systems. The Fraser and the Columbia have vast interior drainage basins, and it was on these two rivers and their tributaries that most Plateau peoples caught their salmon. These two rivers both flowed west through narrow gorges to enter the sea. The few places where rivers broke through the mountains were the sites of major aboriginal fisheries.

A cold grassy steppe covers the Columbia Plateau between the Blue Mountains to the south and the Okanagan Highlands to the north. Rainfall is low, winters cold, and summers hot. The dominant vegetation is sagebrush, rabbit brush, and bunch grasses. Trees and shrubs are found along water courses. The Plateau forest extends north from the Columbia River to the Boreal Forest in northern British Columbia. This zone contains a variety of forests and open parks and meadow lands. The winters are cold, summers are cool and moist. However, local rainshadows and variations in altitude create a more complex mosaic than this description suggests. Alpine meadows above the tree line are important local environments. The variations in topography along the eastern edge of the intermontane plateau from central British Columbia to southwestern Idaho create a complete ecological situation that is more obvious in the south, where the steppe merges into the forest.

Common large land mammals throughout the Northwest include deer, elk, mountain sheep, black bear, and grizzly bear. Mammals with a more limited distribution are antelope and bison on the Plateau steppe, and moose and caribou in the Plateau forest. The six species of anadromous salmon and trout were the major riverine resources, but other important fish include minnows and sturgeon. The steppes and meadows of the Plateau support a series of important plants whose roots and bulbs were significant in the aboriginal diet, particularly as winter stores. The most important of these are camas, balsamroot, bitterroot, biscuitroot, and Indian potato. The distribution of these plants is controlled by effective moisture and soil conditions, but at least one of them is available in most areas of the Plateau.

Archaeological research on the Plateau is almost entirely a post–World War II development. Some work was done in the first half of the century, but the postwar boom in development, dam construction, logging, and road building fueled an explosive growth in our knowledge of the region. This research has been guided by some basic research questions: (1) What is the cultural chronology of the area, which involves establishing a firm chronological framework of changes in prehistoric Plateau cultures? (2) When was the region first inhabited and what are the relations between those first inhabitants and subsequent people in the region and those in adjacent regions? (3) How has the subsistence economy of the Plateau changed during prehistory—particularly, when and why did salmon consumption and storage

become central to the area's subsistence? (4) When and why did semisedentism develop on the Plateau, what was the nature of that semisedentism, and what were the causal relationships between semisedentism and subsistence and technological changes? (5) What are the causal relationships between environmental changes and changes in Plateau cultures? (6) How are the prehistoric cultures of the Plateau linked to historic ones?

The archaeological record of the Plateau spans a minimum of 11,500 radiocarbon years. A cache of Clovis material at the Richey-Roberts site near Wenatchee, Washington, is presently (1996) the oldest indisputable evidence (based on tool form and technology) of human occupation in the area. Although regional and local culture-historical archaeological sequences now exist for most parts of the Plateau, three major periods in prehistory can be defined: Early (ca. 9550–5050 B.C., or 11,500–7000 years B.P.), Middle (5050–2550 B.C., or 7000–4500 years B.P.), and Late (2550/2050 B.C.–ca. A.D. 1720, or 4500/4000–230 years B.P.). The historic period in the Columbia Plateau commenced ca. A.D. 1720 with the introduction of the horse, although direct contact did not occur until 1805; historic contact in the Northern Plateau occurred in 1808. The three periods show a trend from initial occupation by highly mobile foragers to increasing diversification in the subsistence economy that culminates in the intensive harvesting and storage of anadromous salmon, ungulates, and roots, and a winter-pithouse-village settlement pattern by 2550/2050 B.C. (4500/4000 years B.P.).

Kenneth M. Ames
David L. Pokotylo

Further Readings

Ames, K.M. 1988. Early Holocene Forager Mobility Strategies on the Southern Columbia Plateau. In *Early Human Occupation in Western North America*, edited by J.A. Willing, C.M. Aikens, and J. Fagan, pp. 325–369. Anthropology Papers no. 21. Nevada State Museum, Carson City.

Brauner, D.R. 1976. Alpowai: The Culture History of the Alpowa Locality. Unpublished Ph.D. dissertation, Department of Anthropology, Washington State University, Pullman.

Leonhardy, F.C., and D.G. Rice. 1970. Proposed Culture Typology for the Lower

Snake River Region, Southeastern Washington. *Northwest Anthropological Research Notes* 4(1):1–29.

Richards, T.H., and M.K. Rousseau. 1987. *Late Prehistoric Cultural Horizons on the Canadian Plateau*. Publication no. 16. Department of Archaeology, Simon Fraser University, Burnaby.

Stryd, A.H., and M.K. Rousseau. 1996. The Early Prehistory of the Mid Fraser-Thompson River Area of British Columbia. In *Early Human Occupation in British Columbia*, edited by R. Carlson and L. Dalla Bona, pp. 177–204. University of British Columbia Press, Vancouver.

Plateau Microblade Tradition

The Plateau Microblade tradition (PMT) is found in south-central interior British Columbia and the Columbia Plateau of northern Washington State. Although the characteristic wedge-shaped microblade cores are not unique to the PMT, the core-reduction sequence is distinctive. PMT characteristics include microcores made from small split nodules, striking platforms flaked and ground only at the core edge, a single fluted face, and core rejuvenation by removal of the fluted face. The stone used reflects local availability, primarily obsidian in central British Columbia; vitreous basalt, chert, and chalcedony in southern British Columbia; and chalcedony and jasper in the Columbia Plateau. Although microblade technologies occur earlier in the Subarctic and the northern Northwest Coast, too many technological differences exist to directly derive the PMT from either of these areas.

In the Canadian Plateau, the PMT first appears at 6450 B.C. (8400 years B.P.) and is present at two of the three sites securely dated to the Early Prehistoric period (9050–5050 B.C., or 11,000–7000 years B.P.), Landels and Drynoch Slide. Most Early and Middle (5050–2550 B.C., or 7000–4500 years B.P.) Prehistoric-period microlithic sites occur in the valleys of

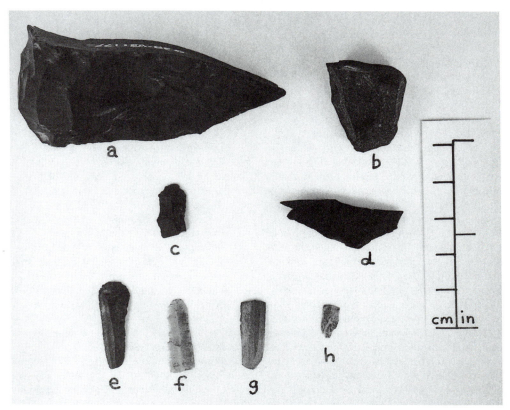

Wedge-shaped microcore and associated products: a) microcore; b) microcore fragment (fluted face); c) microcore preparation flake; d) microcore rejuvenation flake; e) microblade; f) microblade proximal fragment; g) microblade medial fragment; h) microblade distal fragment. (Illustration by S. Greaves)

the mid-Fraser and the Thompson rivers. The prevailing view of the PMT is based on the Lehman, Lochnore, and Nesikep sites along the Fraser River, but stratigraphy at these sites is complex, and dating is problematic. Single-component Middle Prehistoric-period sites are rare, and microblades are commonly found in association with large projectile points assumed to date to at least 2550 B.C. (4500 years B.P.). The few single-component microlithic sites suggest the use of portable dwellings in short-term settlements, a foraging subsistence strategy, and a generalized subsistence base. The PMT is most typical of assemblages dated to 5050–1550 B.C. (7000–3500 years B.P.); it declines considerably after 1550 B.C. (3500 years B.P.). However, this view has yet to resolve problems in dating components with microlithic artifacts, as well as the problem of the early research emphasis on major river-valley bottoms where the tradition was not present after ca. 1550 B.C. (3500 years B.P.).

In several areas of the Canadian Plateau, the PMT persists well into the Late Prehistoric period (ca. 2550 B.C.–A.D. 1808, or 4500–142 years B.P.). Microlithic technology probably continued to 50 B.C.–A.D. 350 (2000–1600 years B.P.) in north-central British Columbia, where it is evident in several pithouse sites, including Natalkuz Lake, Tezli, Ulkatcho, and Anahim Lake. Surface sites with microcores and microblades in the southern interior uplands may also reflect Late Prehistoric use.

Microblade technology occurs in the Columbia Plateau as early as 5050 B.C. (7000 years B.P.), but the few sites found have much smaller numbers of microlithic artifacts. The technology is identical to that in the Canadian Plateau, except for the use of chalcedony and jasper. The PMT on the Columbia Plateau appears to be restricted to 3050–2050 B.C. (5000–4000 years B.P.) and is associated with artifact assemblages distinct from those of the Canadian Plateau. This suggests that the PMT was added to the indigenous material culture, rather than brought south by an expanding population.

The PMT has been linked to the migration of Athapaskan-speaking people into the Canadian Plateau. However, Late Prehistoric sites clearly affiliated with Athapaskans lack microblades, and sites with microblades do not contain artifactual evidence identified as Athapaskan. The antiquity and geographic range of the PMT are too great to be associated with any one ethnic group.

Microblade function is more a topic of informed speculation than systematic research. Suggested uses of microblades include hafted engraving tools and side-slotted barbs in projectile shafts. Use-wear studies show that microblades were used in tasks relating more to food processing and tool and utensil construction than to food procurement. Microblade usage differed regionally and perhaps chronologically as well.

The Plateau Microblade tradition remains a controversial concept. It disappeared in most of the Canadian Plateau by 1550 B.C. (3500 years B.P.). However, some well-dated components indicate that the PMT may have lasted well into the period of pithouse occupation. Although the lack of well-dated sites remains problematic, the most recent research (Greaves 1991) indicates considerable variability in the use and spatial distribution of microlithic technology in the Plateau.

Sheila Greaves

Further Readings

Greaves, S. 1991. *The Organization of Microcore Technology in the Canadian Southern Interior Plateau.* Unpublished Ph.D. dissertation, Department of Anthropology and Sociology, University of British Columbia, Vancouver.

Richards, T., and M.K. Rousseau. 1987. *Late Prehistoric Cultural Horizons on the Canadian Plateau.* Publication no. 16. Department of Archaeology, Simon Fraser University, Burnaby.

Sanger, D. 1968. Prepared Core and Blade Traditions in the Pacific Northwest. *Arctic Anthropology* 5:92–120.

Stryd, A.H., and M. Rousseau. 1996. The Early Prehistory of the Mid Fraser-Thompson River Area of British Columbia. *In Early Human Occupation of British Columbia*, edited by R. Carlson and L. Dalla Bona, pp. 177–204. University of British Columbia Press, Vancouver.

Plateau Pithouse Tradition

The Plateau Pithouse tradition (PPT) commenced ca. 3550–3050 B.C. (5500–5000 years B.P.) in the Fraser River and Thompson River drainage areas on the Canadian Plateau. The PPT represents a river-oriented adaptive pattern resulting from movement of south Coast Salishan-speaking peoples up the Fraser River, and possibly Columbia River, drainages into southern interior British Columbia to utilize increasing salmon resources at the onset of cooler and wetter climatic conditions. It includes the Lochnore phase, the Shuswap horizon, the Plateau horizon, and the Kamloops horizon.

Lochnore Phase (ca. 3550/3050–1550 B.C., or 5500/5000–3500 years B.P.). Lochnore-phase residential and field encampment sites are often small to medium sized and fairly deeply buried; contain medium-to-high-density scatters of lithics, bone, and freshwater mussel shell; and suggest relatively short-term occupation episodes. Some of the larger residential encampments indicate repeated occupations. Many sites are situated on the edges of upper river terraces along main river valley bottoms, especially at or near junctures of major tributary creek valleys, and in mid-altitude valleys beside small lakes and streams.

Lithic assemblages include leaf-shaped, lanceolate, unbarbed projectile points with wide side notches, heavy basal-edge grinding, and pointed or convex bases; unnotched leaf-shaped points and bipoints; unnotched leaf-shaped points with straight basal margins; oval bifaces; round and oval scrapers; side scrapers; microblade technology at some sites; edge-battered cobbles; unifacial cobble choppers; notched flattened pebbles (net sinkers); and a predominant use of fine-grained-to-vitreous basalts for lithic tool manufacture. Bone and antler items include bone-splinter unipoints and antler flakers, wedges, and unilaterally barbed points. Also present are worked rodent incisors, drilled animal-tooth and eagle-claw pendants, and marine shell beads.

Lochnore-phase faunal assemblages suggest a generalized subsistence economy characterized by a broad-spectrum foraging strategy that included deer, elk, beaver, migratory fowl, freshwater fish, anadromous salmonoids, turtles, and freshwater mussels. The Lochnore-phase adaptive pattern best fits the "forager" end of the "forager-collector" subsistence-settlement strategy continuum, with a slight tendency toward a "collector" pattern.

Housepits were small (ca. 4–5 m, or 13–16.4 feet, in diameter), shallow (30–40 cm, or 11.7–16.4 inches, deep), and had light roof superstructures. Although pithouses were used as early as 2550 B.C. (4500 years B.P.) in the south Thompson River Valley, they likely appeared initially between 3550 and 3050 B.C.

(5500–5000 years B.P.). Numerous sites with artifact assemblages dating to this period are identical to those found in early south Thompson houses, and similar houses were also being used on the nearby Columbia Plateau and south coast at the same time. However, housepits predating 2550 B.C. (4500 years B.P.) on the Canadian Plateau have yet to be confirmed by archaeological investigations.

Shuswap Horizon (1550–450 B.C., or 3500–2400 years B.P.). Shuswap-horizon sites are located within main valley bottoms or large tributary valleys beside or near rivers and lakes. Housepits are fairly deep, medium to large (7–20 m, or 23–65.6 feet, in diameter) depressions lacking raised earth rims, reflecting one or two major occupational episodes, and have hearths, storage and cooking pits, and flexed burials in pits within housepit floors. Other characteristics include a variety of distinctive stemmed, basally indented, and corner-removed point styles; key-shaped formed unifaces; small "thumbnail" scrapers and convex-edged hide scrapers with straight proximally tapered lateral margins; split-cobble tools; and high frequencies of utilized and unifacially retouched flake tools. Lithic assemblages generally display overall relative simplicity in composition, technological proficiency, and sophistication, and a fairly heavy reliance on the use of locally obtained, fair-to-good-quality lithic raw materials. A well-developed bone-and-antler industry is also present.

Faunal remains include elk, deer, mountain sheep, black bear, beaver, muskrat, striped skunk, porcupine, marmot, domestic dog, wolf, red fox, snowshoe hare, several waterfowl species, freshwater mussels, freshwater fish, and anadromous salmonoids. The people of the Shuswap horizon were clearly engaged in a logistically organized "collector" adaptive strategy, but they tended more toward a "forager" pattern than people in the later Plateau and Kamloops horizons. During the Shuswap horizon, overall residential-group mobility steadily decreased, and the mobility of small task-specific groups increased, relative to the Lochnore phase. A steady population increase is evident throughout the Shuswap horizon.

Plateau Horizon (450 B.C.–A.D. 750, or 2400–1200 years B.P.). Most Plateau-horizon residential sites are situated near salmon-fishing stations and areas where important floral resources were abundant and easily accessible. A high degree of site-type variability suggests that specific task groups engaged in a relatively wide spectrum of specific and varied economic activities. Although sizes of pithouse villages vary, most are significantly larger than those of the Shuswap horizon, and almost all indicate continuous reoccupation for fairly long periods of time. Housepits are typically small (5–7.5 m, or 16.4–24.6 feet, in diameter) and lack raised earth rims. Numerous storage-pit features within and near winter villages were used to store primarily dried salmon, which indicates a heavy reliance on this commodity during winter months. Numerous small field camps and resource-extraction locations (notably, root-processing sites) have been identified in mid- and high-altitude areas.

Projectile points are typically barbed and have either corner or basal notches. Basally notched forms are more common ca. 450–50 B.C. (2400–2000 years B.P.); corner-notched forms, ca. 50 B.C.–A.D. 750 (2000–1200 years B.P.). An overall reduction in point size is evident throughout the Plateau horizon. Convex-shaped chipped-stone end scrapers and "key-shaped" formed unifaces are more common during this horizon than in the preceding Shuswap horizon. Task-specific artifact types, such as digging-stick handles, well-made bifaces, and several types of specialized formed unifaces, are common.

Archaeological data clearly indicate that the typical Plateau-horizon adaptive pattern leaned heavily toward the "collector" type of subsistence and settlement strategy and toward more logistical organization than in the preceding Shuswap horizon and ensuing Kamloops horizon.

Kamloops Horizon (A.D. 750–1750, or 1200–200 years B.P.). Kamloops-horizon sites are found in the same environmental contexts as Plateau-horizon sites, but they are less common in upland areas. Housepits range from 6 to 20 m (19.7–65.6 feet) in diameter and are usually oval, circular, rectangular, or square in plan, and most always have prominent raised earth rims. Side entrances are sometimes evident. Projectile points are typically small, triangular, side-notched forms referred to as Kamloops Side-Notched. A variety of formed chipped-stone tools are common, including well-made scrapers, gravers, and perforators.

The people participating in the Kamloops horizon were engaged in a "logistical-collector" subsistence and settlement pattern, but it was less logistically organized than the pattern of the preceding Plateau horizon. Although regional population density was fairly high during this horizon, it was probably not as great as during the Plateau horizon.

Mike K. Rousseau

Further Readings

Richards, T., and M. Rousseau. 1987. *Late Prehistoric Cultural Horizons on the Canadian Plateau.* Publication no. 16. Department of Archaeology, Simon Fraser University, Burnaby.

Stryd, A.H., and M.K. Rousseau. 1996. The Early Prehistory of the Mid Fraser-Thompson River Area of British Columbia. In *Early Human Occupation in British Columbia*, edited by R.L. Carlson and L. Dalla Bona, pp. 177–204. University of British Columbia Press, Vancouver.

Plateau Root Foods

Root foods supplemented by other plants were important Plateau (interior parts of southwest Canada and northwest United States) resources throughout prehistory, accounting for 30–50 percent or more of the annual diet during the ethnographic period (early A.D. 1800s before the region's native economies were impacted by European systems). Edible wild roots, or geophytes, are perennial plants that bear underground buds known as bulbs, corms, tubers, taproots, or rhizomes. Most edible geophytes in the Plateau are as nutritious as potatoes, but they require about four years to reach edible size.

The importance of root foods in the Plateau is partly due to the paucity of seed and nut crops but principally to root foods, abundance and widespread occurrence. Camas (*Camassia quamash*), the most widely used geophyte in the Columbia Plateau, grows well in wet meadows, from low-elevation grasslands to forested montane country. Other important geophytes with wide ecological amplitudes throughout the Plateau area include biscuitroot (*Lomatium* spp.) and other parsley-family plants; balsamroot (*Balsamorhiza sagittata*) and other composite-family plants; purslane-family plants, including bitterroot (*Lewisia rediviva*) and Indian potato (*Claytonia lanceolata*); and lily-family plants, such as onion (*Allium* spp.), sego lily (*Calochortus* spp.), glacier lily (*Erythronium grandiflorum*), yellow fritillary (*Fritillaria pudica*), and wild hyacinth (*Brodiaea douglasii*).

Archaeological data from the Calispell Valley in northeastern Washington show that camas was regularly used by 3550 B.C. (5500 years B.P.) and was a staple by 1550 B.C. (3500 years B.P.). Biscuitroot, second in importance to camas, was used extensively in drier regions. In the Columbia Plateau, its charred remains have been recovered at sites dated to 2750 B.C.–A.D. 950 (4700–1000 years B.P.). Bitterroot, the third most important geophyte during the ethnographic era, was undoubtedly used during the prehistoric era, although it has not been archaeologically documented. Charred remains of onions and lily- and composite-family plants were recovered from earth ovens in Upper Hat Creek Valley in southern interior British Columbia dating to the last 2,000 years. The Potato Mountain site in south-central interior British Columbia yielded Indian potatoes in earth ovens postdating 550 B.C. (2500 years B.P.). Wild hyacinth corms are reported from sites dated to 2850 B.C.–A.D. 1350 (4800–600 years B.P.) at Kettle Falls in northeast Washington State.

Geophytes were usually dug with antler-

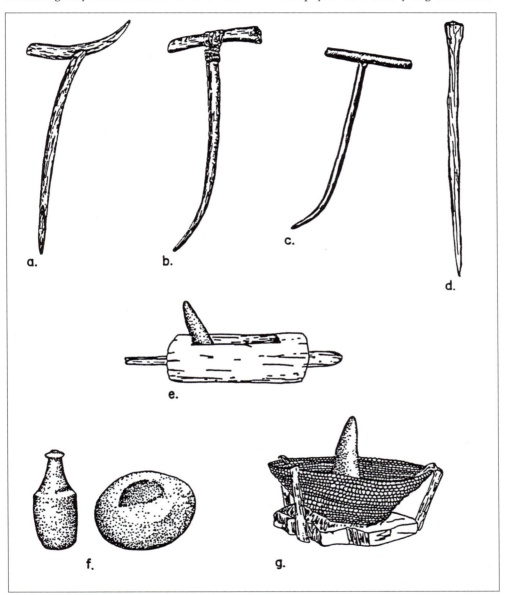

Plateau digging sticks and root processing tools: a-d) digging sticks; e) wooden mortar and stone pestle; f) stone mortar and pestle; g) basket, hopper-mortar base, and stone pestle. (Drawn by A. V. Thoms)

handled, hardwood digging sticks; then they were cooked in earth ovens and pulverized using pestles and mortars (see Figure). Mashed roots were often made into cakes, which were dried and stored, or whole roots were hung from rafters. During the ethnographic period, an individual family typically dug, processed, and stored as much as two metric tons of roots for annual use. In the Calispell Valley, probable camas-storage-pit features range from 0.45 to ca. 20 m^3 (0.6–26.2 cubic yards).

Digging sticks, pestles, and earth ovens were in use by 4550–3550 B.C. (6500–5500 years B.P.) in the Plateau, but a significant increase in their numbers after 2550 B.C. (4500 years B.P.) marks the onset of geophyte intensification. Large earth ovens may not have been commonplace until 1550 B.C. (3500 years B.P.) on the Columbia Plateau and 550 B.C. (2500 years B.P.) on the Canadian Plateau, well after the onset of the winter-pithouse-village pattern but prior to the widespread occurrence of large village sites ca. 50 B.C. (2000 years B.P.). Earth ovens are present at both special-processing and village sites throughout the Plateau. Pestles and mortars are mainly found on the Columbia Plateau. They are common at both special-processing and village sites but have a higher incidence in the latter, suggesting that cooked roots were routinely transported to villages for processing into cakes. The most common tools at camas-processing sites in the Calispell Valley were large cobble and flake tools, and tabular knives possibly used to construct drying racks, mat coverings, and perhaps sacks to hold the roots while they cooked. Base processing camps in Upper Hat Creek Valley and Scheidam Flats in south-central British Columbia are characterized by intensive lithic-reduction activities and expedient tool production.

Alston V. Thoms

Further Readings

Hunn, E.S. 1990. *Nch'i-Wana "The Big River": Mid-Columbia Indians and Their Land.* University of Washington Press, Seattle.

Pokotylo, D.L., and P. Froese. 1983. Archaeological Evidence for Prehistoric Root Gathering on the Southern Interior Plateau of British Columbia: A Case Study From Upper Hat Creek Valley. *Canadian Journal of Archaeology* 7(2):127–157.

Thoms, A.V. 1989. *The Northern Roots of Hunter-Gatherer Intensification: Camas and the Pacific Northwest.* Unpublished Ph.D. dissertation, Department of Anthropology, Washington State University, Pullman.

Turner, N.J. 1978. *Food Plants of British Columbia Indians: 2. Interior Peoples.* Handbook no. 36. British Columbia Provincial Museum, Victoria.

Plateau Ungulates

The Columbia-Fraser Plateau comprises that area of northwestern North America bounded on the west by the Cascade Range of Oregon and Washington and the Coast Mountains of British Columbia, and on the east by the Rocky Mountains. The southern boundary lies just north of central Oregon and central Idaho. This approximately triangular area is drained by the Columbia and Fraser rivers, hence the name, though locally it is referred to simply as the Plateau. Nine ungulate species are known in the Plateau, although only six seem to have been regularly utilized by prehistoric humans. Mule deer (*Odocoileus hemionus*) and white-tailed deer (*O. virginianus*) are the most frequently represented ungulates in archaeofaunal collections from this area. Bison (*Bison bison*) and pronghorn antelope (*Antilocapra americana*) are found in collections from the Columbia Plateau, while mountain or bighorn sheep (*Ovis canadensis*) and wapiti (*Cervus elaphus*) are present in collections throughout the Plateau. Remains of caribou (*Rangifer tarandus*) and mountain goats (*Oreamnos americanus*) occur in sites in northern Washington State and south-central British Columbia and seem to represent locally available animals. Remains of moose (*Alces alces*) represent items traded into the area from northern British Columbia. The last three taxa are seldom represented in collections, perhaps because they were relatively rare in the area during prehistoric times.

Remains of wapiti and white-tailed deer are fairly common in sites in the Columbia Basin where these taxa have not been historically reported. Bison, bighorn sheep, and pronghorn antelope were locally extinct over much of the Columbia Plateau by the early historic period (ca. A.D. 1800).

During the last 3,000–4,000 years, wapiti and bison occurred in isolated population pockets along the Lower Snake River of southeastern Washington, and bison also may have occurred in several pockets in the presently arid Columbia Basin of east-central Washington.

Remains of bighorn sheep dominate two collections from rock shelters in the Channeled Scablands of east-central Washington, and pronghorn antelope dominate a collection from the mouth of the Snake River in what is today the most arid part of Washington State. Throughout the Holocene (8050 B.C., or 10,000 years B.P., to the present), collections from the Lower Snake River tend to have more wapiti and pronghorn-antelope remains than bighorn-sheep remains, whereas collections from north-central Washington have more bighorn-sheep remains than wapiti remains and fewer pronghorn remains than collections from the Lower Snake. In the Lillooet region along the mid-Fraser River of south-central British Columbia, mule-deer and bighorn-sheep remains constitute the most abundant ungulate species found in housepit sites spanning the last 3,000 years (ca. 1200 B.C.–A.D. 1800, or 3150–150 years B.P.).

Relative abundances of ungulates fluctuated through time. Along the Lower Snake River of southeastern Washington, summed samples of pronghorn-antelope and bison remains are more abundant in the period 4050–50 B.C. (6000–2000 years B.P.) than summed samples of elk, deer, and bighorn sheep; the latter three taxa are more abundant than the former two before and after this time period. Remains of bighorn sheep decline in abundance after 50 B.C. (2000 years B.P.) in collections from the Upper mid-Columbia River in north-central Washington, whereas those of pronghorn antelope increase. These fluctuations in abundances probably reflect climatic changes during the Holocene, as there is little evidence for marked changes in hunting strategies that cannot be parsimoniously ascribed to changing availability of ungulate taxa. Similarly, geographic variation in the abundances of ungulate taxa during particular time periods probably reflects climatic and/or environmental differences.

Ethnographically, ungulates were hunted at all times of the year, but the greatest efforts were made in the fall months. Based on analyses of dental-eruption sequences and other data, this also seems to be the season when most ungulates were killed by prehistoric human hunters. Butchering of ungulates depended in part on the size of the carcass, as is evident from cut marks made by stone tools. Marrow was regularly extracted from limb bones, as indicated by the typically broken condition of the bones and the presence of hammerstone impact notches on many specimens. Ulnae, scapulae,

and metapodials were often made into a variety of perforating tools; antlers were made into digging-stick handles and wedges; and ungulate incisors were occasionally made into pendants.

R. Lee Lyman

Further Readings

Langemann, E.G. 1987. *Zooarchaeology of the Lillooet Region, British Columbia.* Unpublished Master's thesis. Department of Archaeology, Simon Fraser University, Burnaby.

Lyman, R.L. 1992. Influences of Mid-Holocene Altithermal Climates on Mammalian Faunas and Human Subsistence in Eastern Washington. *Journal of Ethnobiology* 12:37–62.

Lyman, R.L., and S.D. Livingston. 1983. Late Quaternary Mammalian Zoogeography of Eastern Washington. *Quaternary Research* 20:360–373.

Platform Mounds (Southwest)

Platform mounds are artificially raised hills upon which ceremonial activities took place and buildings were built. In the southwestern United States, they are found only in the Hohokam and Salado culture areas of south-central Arizona. The first platforms were ca. 1 m (3 feet) high while later ones were a little over 3 m (10 feet) tall. Platform mounds have been variously interpreted as priest temples, house mounds, and pyramids. Early excavations by Jesse W. Fewkes (1912) at Casa Grande in Arizona demonstrated that mounds were raised areas that supported buildings on their summits. Debate ensued in the late 1980s following the excavation of structures in river basins on the fringes of the Hohokam culture area over whether all mounds were really the ruins of multistoried pueblos or artificial hills. More recent investigations conducted during the 1970s and 1980s in the Gila and Salt drainages of Arizona condition our present-day concept of the Southwestern platform mound (Doyel 1974; Gregory and Abbott 1988).

Edwin N. Ferdon, Jr., (1955) observed six features of most Hohokam platform mounds. These features appear to be attributes of the traditional Mesoamerican method of platform and pyramid building, for the idea of platform mounds almost certainly came from the south. They had a massive rectangular retaining wall enclosing and filled with earth and trash. Various buildings were constructed on top of the platform, which was enclosed by a compound wall. Enlargement of the platform occurred by covering over the original surface and adding a new facing. When buildings on the mound top were destroyed, they were replaced by new buildings that were superimposed on the remains of old ones. However, because of their long use in the Hohokam area, wide variation exists in what has been identified as a platform mound. Architecturally, mounds that were irregular rather than rectangular in plan and that were constructed by filling ground-level rooms also are considered platform mounds. The first mounds were low, raised round dance platforms that were filled with earth and trash and then capped. They are known from the site of Snaketown in the middle Gila River Valley, Arizona, and were built as early as A.D. 700 (1250 years B.P.). The last mounds to be constructed, sometime between A.D. 1200 and 1300 (750–650 years B.P.), were large irregular platforms formed from fill-in rooms, with buildings constructed on top as well as along their base. Platform mounds in peripheral Hohokam areas, such as the Tucson Basin and the Salado area of the Tonto Basin, have less architectural variation. It appears that there are no early dance platforms in these areas and that all mounds were constructed after A.D. 1200 (750 years B.P.).

Scholars have consistently associated platform mounds with ceremony and status by equating them with truncated pyramids in Mexico. Ferdon suggested that, as with Mexican pyramids, platform mounds indicate the presence of a class-structured society with strong central authority. The size and central position of buildings on top of platform mounds led Frank H. Cushing in 1890 to assume that they were the abodes of priests and that commoners occupied the less conspicuous neighboring buildings. Excavations in the 1970s and 1980s and analyses of buildings on top of platform mounds have focused on the role of their inhabitants. David E. Doyel (1974) has suggested that the mounds represent a focus of panvillage integration and cooperation, for a substantial amount of effort was necessary for mound construction. He has speculated that the people living on the mound possessed specialized information regarding ritual and the scheduling of important activities. They could also act to sanction or promote cooperation in labor. David A. Gregory and Fred L. Nials (1985) have suggested that the distribution of platform mounds at periodic intervals along canal systems is evidence of the labor-coordinating efforts of these mound occupants.

Platform mounds were abandoned in the Southwest with the retreat of societies from the Hohokam and Salado culture areas sometime after A.D. 1400 (550 years B.P.).

Owen Lindauer

Further Readings

Doyel, D.E. 1974. *Excavations in the Escalante Ruin Group, Southern Arizona*. Arizona State Museum Series no. 37. University of Arizona, Tucson.

Ferdon, E.N., Jr. 1955. *A Trial Survey of Mexican-Southwestern Architectural Parallels*. Monograph no. 11. School of American Research Press, Santa Fe.

Fewkes, J.W. 1912. *Casa Grande, Arizona*. Twenty-Eighth Annual Report of the Bureau of American Ethnology. Smithsonian Institution, Washington, D.C.

Gregory, D.A., and D.R. Abbott. 1988. Stages of Mound Construction and Architectural Details. In *The 1982–1984 Excavations at Las Colinas, the Mound 8 Precinct*, edited by D.A. Gregory, pp. 9–50. Archaeological Series no. 162, vol. 3. Cultural Resource Management Division, Arizona State Museum, University of Arizona, Tucson.

Gregory, D.A., and F.L. Nials. 1985. Observations Concerning the Distribution of Classic Period Hohokam Platform Mounds. In *Proceedings of the 1983 Hohokam Symposium*, edited by A.E. Dittert and D.E. Dove, pp. 373–388. Occasional Paper no. 2. Arizona Archaeological Society, Phoenix.

Hammack, L.C., and A.P. Sullivan (editors). 1981. *The 1968 Excavations at Mound 8, Las Colinas Ruins Group, Phoenix, Arizona*. Archaeological Series no. 154. Cultural Resource Management Divison, Arizona State Museum, University of Arizona, Tucson.

Haury, E.W. 1976. *The Hohokam: Desert Farmers and Craftsmen*. University of Arizona Press, Tucson.

Hayden, J.D. 1957. *Excavations, 1940, at University Indian Ruin*. Technical Series no. 5. Southwestern Monuments Association, Gila Pueblo, Globe.

Lindauer, O. 1992. Architectural Engineering and Variation Among Salado Platform

Mounds. In *Proceedings of the Second Salado Conference*, edited by R.C. Lange and S. Germick, pp. 50–56. Occasional Paper. Arizona Archaeological Society, Phoenix.

Rice, G.E. 1991. Variability in Development of Classic Period Elites. In *A Design for Salado Research*, edited by G.E. Rice. Monograph Series no. 1. Anthropological Field Studies no. 22. Office of Cultural Resource Management, Arizona State University, Tempe.

Platform Pipe

Platform pipe is the generic name for a category of smoking pipe that includes varieties known as the effigy platform pipe and the plain platform pipe. The platform pipe is a characteristic artifact of the Middle Woodland period in the eastern United States and, in particular, of the middle Middle Woodland or Hopewellian phases of the Havana tradition of the Illinois and northern Mississippi river valleys and of the Ohio Valley Scioto tradition. The concept of the platform pipe and platform pipes themselves circulated between and beyond these areas as part of the exchanges defining the Hopewellian Interaction Sphere of the period 100 B.C.–ca. A.D. 350 (2050–1600 years B.P.).

Platform pipes were typically made of Ohio pipestone, an argillaceous ironstone varying in color from gray to red, although some were made of limestone or other materials. Platform pipes take their name from a 0.6-m (0.25-inch) -thick, rectangular base upon which sits the bowl containing the tobacco or other smoking material and within which was drilled a fine-diameter hole for the passage of smoke from the bowl. On plain platform pipes, the bowl was formed within a cylindrical or jarlike projection rising from and centered on the platform. Effigy platform pipes were called thus because the bowl for the smoking material was fashioned into the head or the body of an animal seated upon the platform and facing the smoker.

Despite the absence of convincing evidence that platform pipes were ever attached to wooden stems, the flat and tabular character of the pipe platform continues to inspire speculation that Hopewellian platform pipes lie somewhere in the background of the long, flat wooden stems used on certain sacred pipes by historic Indian peoples of the northern Mississippi Valley and prairie borders of the Plains area. A compromise argument holds that plain platform pipes were not themselves attached to wooden stems but came to be made in Middle Woodland times as scaled-down representations in stone of Early Woodland smoking devices. These devices did have long, flat wooden

Plain platform pipe, Hopewellian, made of steatite, 4¹/₈" in length and 1⁷/₈" in width. (Courtesy of the Wilford Archaeology Laboratory, University of Minnesota)

Platform pipe in the form of a raven effigy, Hopewellian, made of mottled Ohio pipestone. (Illustration by R. L. Hall)

stems. They are thought to have been slat-shafted wooden atlatls or spear throwers of the single-hole variety that doubled as tube pipes on ritual occasions, when short sections of cane were inserted into the hole. The flat-stemmed sacred pipes of recent times would thus be descended not directly from platform pipes but from a shared prototype.

The most famous series of platform pipes is a collection of 136 discovered in 1915 during the excavation of a Hopewellian mound on the W.D. Tremper farm in Scioto County, Ohio (Mills 1916). This series included pipes of both the effigy and plain type that were made from Ohio pipestone, which is available in outcroppings on the east bank of the Scioto River and elsewhere in Scioto County. The animals represented among the effigies include bear, mountain lion, wildcat, raccoon, porcupine, opossum, beaver, otter, dog, rabbit, mink, deer, fox, wolf, squirrel, turtle, toad, eagle, hawk, parakeet, owl, heron, crane, quail, kingfisher, bluejay, and crow.

Robert L. Hall

Further Readings

Hall, R.L. 1983. The Evolution of the Calumet-Pipe. In *Prairie Archaeology: Papers in Honor of David A. Baerreis*, edited by G.E. Gibbon, pp. 37–52. Publications in Anthropology no. 3. University of Minnesota Press, Minneapolis.

Mills, W.C. 1916. Exploration of the Tremper Mound. *Ohio State Archaeological and Historical Quarterly* 16(3):262–398.

Seeman, M.F. 1977. Stylistic Variation in Middle Woodland Pipe Styles. *Midcontinental Journal of Archaeology* 2(1):47–66.

Plummet

A plummet is an elongated stone object of enigmatic origin and function. Commonly manufactured from hematite, it was finely ground to a shape that often resembled a teardrop. A rope or cord was apparently passed through a hole or wound around a groove near one end. It has been suggested that plummets were used as bolas or fishnet weights. The beauty and craftsmanship of these items make these uses unlikely, however, for they could easily have become lost during mundane tasks like these.

Several plummets have been recovered from large Late Archaic settlements, such as Jaketown in central Mississippi and Poverty Point in northeast Louisiana, and the Late Archaic period (ca. 3050–850 B.C., or 5000–2800 years B.P.) is considered to be the florescence of this type. Their manufacture continued into the

Middle Woodland period (ca. 450 B.C.–A.D. 450, or 2400–1500 years B.P.), judging from their association with materials of this date at sites like Synders Village in the Mississippi Valley in Illinois. Plummets have even been unearthed at the Late Prehistoric Spiro Mound in Oklahoma, where their surfaces were decorated with animal designs—in particular, turtles, snakes, and anthropomorphic figures. Several varieties of plummets are known and have been classified into types, such as Godar Drilled, Elm Point, Gilcrease Grooved, and Synders Grooved. These types seem to have some integrity, for each tends to cluster within a specific span of time.

George H. Odell

Further Readings

Ford, J.A., P. Phillips, and W.H. Haag. 1955. *The Jaketown Site in West Central Mississippi.* Anthropological Papers, vol. 45, pt. 1. American Museum of Natural History, New York.

Perino, G. 1961. Tentative Classification of Plummets in the Lower Illinois River Valley. *Central States Archaeological Journal* 8:43–56.

Point of Pines Ruin

Point of Pines Ruin (Arizona W:10:50) is a large Mogollon, or Mountain Pueblo, site located in the Point of Pines region of Arizona on the San Carlos Apache Reservation, ca. 96.6 km (60 miles) east of Globe, Arizona. A total of 111 rooms were excavated there during the 1940s and 1950s by the University of Arizona archaeological field school under the direction of Emil W. Haury (Haury 1989). The site is dated through its pottery and by the tree-ring dating (dendrochronology) of room beams. Phases represented include late Tularosa (A.D. 1200–1275, or 750–675 years B.P.), Pinedale (A.D. 1275–1325, or 675–625 years B.P.), Canyon Creek (A.D. 1325–1400, or 625–550 years B.P.), and Point of Pines (A.D. 1400–1450, or 550–500 years B.P.).

During the Pinedale and Canyon Creek phases, Point of Pines was the largest pueblo of the region. At its peak, it was a stone masonry community of ca. 800 contiguous ground-floor rooms arranged in a roughly rectangular block ca. 275 m (300 yards) long and 100 m (109 yards) wide. It had a large rectangular great kiva for ceremonies, two plazas, and a surrounding wall. The people hunted, gathered, and farmed

for a living. Their environment was a grassland plain at an altitude of ca. 1,829 m (6,000 feet). Nearby ponderosa pine, juniper, and piñon provided wood for roof beams and fires. Animal life was abundant, with deer, antelope, bighorn sheep, rodents, and turkeys providing meat. Useful wild plants included walnuts, acorns, piñon nuts, yucca, and cactus. The people grew corn, beans, squash, gourds, and cotton.

Ca. A.D. 1265–1300 (685–650 years B.P.), a group of immigrants moved into the already established pueblo and built a block of ca. 70 rooms, 21 of which have been excavated. Pithouses found under the surface rooms may have served as temporary housing for the immigrants as they built their more permanent homes. These foreigners at Point of Pines have been called the Maverick Mountain people. Their material culture is markedly different from that of the Point of Pine natives, and their masonry rooms were larger and less square than the other rooms of the site. Their D-shaped kiva and decorated pottery styles suggest that they were Kayenta Anasazi, whose original home was located to the north. Ca. 1300 (650 years B.P.), a fire broke out that destroyed the Anasazi community at Point of Pines. Of the 21 Maverick Mountain rooms excavated, 18 were burned. It is uncertain whether this fire was accidental or set on purpose by, perhaps, unhappy hosts. Several skeletons of individuals who lost their lives in the fire were found in one room (Haury 1958, 1989; Lindsay 1987).

During the Point of Pines phase (A.D. 1400–1450, or 550–500 years B.P.), several small villages were built on top of and just outside the ruins of the earlier Point of Pines site (Wendorf 1950; Wasley 1952). Whatever advantage there had been to aggregation during the Tularosa, Pinedale, and Canyon Creek phases no longer applied. By A.D. 1450 (500 years B.P.), even these small late sites were abandoned, and the whole Point of Pines region was deserted by Pueblo peoples and not reoccupied until some later time by the Apaches.

Julia C. Lowell

Further Readings

Haury, E.W. 1958. Evidence at Point of Pines for a Prehistoric Migration From Northern Arizona. In *Migrations in New World Culture History*, edited by R.H. Thompson. University of Arizona Press, Tucson.

———. 1989. *Point of Pines, Arizona: A His-*

tory of the University of Arizona Archaeological Field School. Anthropological Papers no. 50. University of Arizona Press, Tucson.

Lindsay, A.J. 1987. Explaining an Anasazi Migration to East Central Arizona. *American Archeology* 6(3):190–198.

Wasley, W.W. 1952. *The Late Pueblo Occupation at Point of Pines, East-Central* Arizona. Unpublished Master's thesis. Department of Anthropology, University of Arizona, Tucson.

Wendorf, F. 1950. *A Report on the Excavation of a Small Ruin Near Point of Pines, East Central Arizona.* University of Arizona Bulletin, vol. 21, no. 3. Social Science Bulletin no. 19. University of Arizona Press, Tucson.

See also BLACK RIVER BRANCH; KAYENTA BRANCH

Point Peninsula Culture

The noun "Point Peninsula" denominates a tradition or cultural continuity identifiable over a considerable span of time (at least 250 B.C.–A.D. 650, or 2200–1300 years B.P.), depending on the definition used). It is also the name of a geographically and temporally bounded cultural isolate of that tradition within the Middle Woodland period of northeastern North America (ca. 250 B.C.–A.D. 650, or 2200–1300 years B.P.).

Divided into a number of temporal-geographical phases (e.g., Canoe Point, Kipp Island), the Point Peninsula tradition is best known in New York, southern Ontario, and neighboring parts of Quebec and New England. In the second usage, Point Peninsula is the premier eastern exemplar of the Lake Forest, or "Middle Tier," cultures of the Middle Woodland period in the Great Lakes–St. Lawrence River drainage basin. Contemporaneous and more westerly distributed Middle Tier cultures include Saugeen in western lower Ontario, which some archaeologists suggest is an early phase of Point Peninsula, especially if some controversial early radiocarbon dates are accepted; and the Nokomis and North Bay cultures in Wisconsin. Related is the "Northern Tier" Laurel culture of eastern Saskatchewan, Manitoba, Ontario, and northern Minnesota and Upper Michigan. Partly coeval "Southern Tier" Middle Woodland cultures are much more

distinctly Hopewellian or Hopewell influenced. One of these, Squawkie Hill, in western New York, is nevertheless strongly affiliated, particularly in its ceramics, with Point Peninsula. Unlike the western representatives of the Middle Tier and Northern Tier Middle Woodland cultures, whose tenures initiated pottery making in their respective areas, Point Peninsula ceramics in the east were preceded by the much rarer Vinette I ware of the regional Early Woodland period (ca. 850–150 B.C., or 2800–2100 years B.P.).

Befitting its far-flung ties, Point Peninsula shares many traits with other Middle Tier and Northern Tier contemporaries. These are especially salient in the pottery. The surface finish of Point Peninsula vessels, before decoration was applied, tended to be plain or smoothed. But cord-marked-surface finishing became increasingly popular in late Point Peninsula time, especially if its tenure is extended to incorporate the clearly related Hunter's Home phase that chronologically falls in the early part (ca. A.D. 450–750, or 1500–1200 years B.P.) of the succeeding Late Woodland period. Similarly, pots tended to become larger through time, and pointed or conoidal bases became rounder as more globular shapes came to predominate. Decoration included various combinations of stamping with plain, sinuous (pseudo-scallop shell), or tooth-edged (dentate) tools. These were discretely impressed, applied in a continuous ("push-pull" or "stab-and-drag") fashion, or imposed in a walked (rocker-stamped) style, singly or in combination. With time, stamping with a cord-wrapped dowel eclipsed and then replaced these earlier techniques. Not only do relative frequencies vary among Point Peninsula phases, but they can often be used through the method of seriation to help order clusters of sites in sequence.

Point Peninsula projectile points include stemmed, pentagonally shaped, and corner-notched forms, as well as large triangular ones called Levanna points that are most common on Kipp Island and later sites. A well-developed bone-and-antler industry produced unilaterally and bilaterally barbed spear points; knives or daggerlike implements; harpoons of both unilaterally multibarbed (and tanged) and antlertine toggle-head varieties; clothing and hair(?) pins, awls, and tool handles. Finely crafted hair combs of moose antler, many beautifully embellished with incised geometric designs, have been recovered from some sites. Polished slate pendants, varieties of shell beads, beaver incisor chisels and draw-knives (crooked knives), and smoking pipes of platform and, more common, elbow styles are other important elements of the Point Peninsula inventory.

Notwithstanding unmistakable signs of influence from the potent cultural realm of the Hopewell-inspired societies to the south and west, Point Peninsula and its other Lake Forest counterparts exhibit a high degree of independent development and a configurational integrity uniquely their own. With a subsistence base largely predicated on the Archaic pattern (that is, a preagricultural pattern based on hunting, fishing, and plant collecting), notwithstanding the addition of pottery and, thus, new methods of food processing, Point Peninsula exhibits strong continuities with the succeeding Owasco cultures and, through them, an ancestral role in the genesis of the Iroquoian cultural pattern of later prehistory and history.

Ronald J. Mason

Further Readings

Mason, R.J. 1981. *Great Lakes Archaeology.* Academic Press, New York.

Ritchie, W.A. 1969. *The Archaeology of New York State.* rev. 2nd ed. Natural History Press, Garden City.

Spence, M.W., R.H. Pihl, and C.R. Murphy. 1990. Cultural Complexes of the Early and Middle Woodland Periods. In *The Archaeology of Southern Ontario to A.D. 1650,* edited by C.J. Ellis and N. Ferris, pp. 125–169. Occasional Publications no. 5. London [Ontario] Chapter, Ontario Archaeological Society, London.

Pointed Mountain/Fisherman Lake

Fisherman Lake is an area of special archaeological interest in the Upper Mackenzie River drainage in the southwestern corner of the Canadian Northwest Territories. A total of 154 archaeological sites have been recorded. The 10 excavated between 1952 and the early 1970s reveal a long and problematic history of human occupation. Unfortunately, much of the work remains unpublished. The single most important site is Pointed Mountain (JcRx-2), type site of R.S. MacNeish's Northwest Microblade tradition.

David Morrison

Further Readings

MacNeish, R.S. 1954. The Pointed Mountain Site Near Fort Liard, Northwest Territories, Canada. *American Antiquity* 19:234–253.

Millar, J. 1981. Interaction Between the Mackenzie and Yukon Basins During the Early Holocene. In *Networks of the Past,* edited by P. Francis, F. Kense, and P. Duke, pp. 259–294. Archaeological Association, University of Calgary, Calgary.

Pomona Phase

Dating to A.D. 950–1350 (1000–600 years B.P.), sites of the Pomona phase are distributed along the main drainages and the tributary streams of eastern Kansas and western Missouri. Except for a frontier zone of overlap in northeastern Kansas, the phase's western and northern boundaries seemingly correspond to the distri-

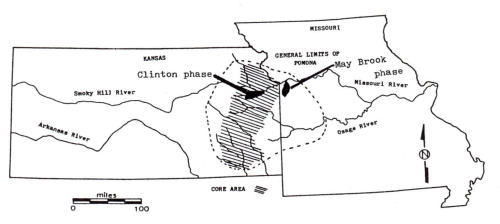

Distribution of the Pomona phase in eastern Kansas and western Missouri. (Redrawn by A. Johnson from K. L. Brown, 1984. Pomona: A Plains Village Variant in Eastern Kansas and Western Missouri. Unpublished Ph.D. dissertation, Department of Anthropology, University of Kansas, Lawrence, Kansas)

bution of the Central Plains tradition and the Steed-Kisker phase. Pomona settlements were dispersed and included several site types: villages, isolated dwellings, campsites, and special-purpose sites, such as butchering stations. Houses were lightweight surface structures formed by lacing saplings together and covering the frame, at least partly, with daubing clay. The small amount of enclosed floor space suggests that they were nuclear-family dwellings, and the frequent absence of an interior hearth suggests seasonal occupation. The presence of larger houses with multiple hearths in a Plains Late Woodland complex (ca. A.D. 750–1000, or 1200–950 years B.P.) believed ancestral to Pomona may indicate, by contrast, fall-winter extended-family congregations.

Pomona pottery consists of small globular jars with exterior overall cord marking and grog or shale temper. Rims are direct, and textured decorations are rare. Hunting was accomplished with the bow and arrow, with arrows tipped with small triangular points. Agriculture was practiced, as demonstrated by finds of charred corn at several sites. Utilitarian artifacts, such as scraping tools, knives, drills, and grinding implements, mirror those from contemporaneous central Plains–area complexes.

The Pomona phase seems clearly derived from earlier eastern Plains Late Woodland developments, with continuity obvious in ceramics, styles of projectile points, settlement patterns, and architectural forms. Historic tribal descendants of the phase have not been identified with certainty, although a recent argument of continuity to the Kansa has been offered (Johnson 1991:57–66).

Alfred E. Johnson

Further Readings

Blakeslee, D.J., and A.H. Rohn. 1986. *Man and Environment in Northeastern Kansas: The Hillsdale Lake Project*. Report prepared for the Kansas City District, U.S. Army Corps of Engineers, Kansas City, Missouri, in fulfillment of Contract no. DA-CW41-76-C-0162 by the Department of Anthropology, Wichita State University, Wichita.

Brown, K.L. 1984. *Pomona: A Plains Village Variant in Eastern and Western Missouri*. Unpublished Ph.D. dissertation, Department of Anthropology, University of Kansas, Lawrence.

Johnson, A.E. 1991. Kansa Origins: An Alternative. *Plains Anthropologist* 36(133):57–66.

Ponca Fort

In the closing years of the eighteenth century A.D., the Ponca Indians built a fortified earthlodge village on a hilltop overlooking the valleys of the Missouri River and the Ponca Creek in Knox County, northeastern Nebraska. The Ponca Fort site, occupied between ca. 1790 and 1800 (160–150 years B.P.), is the only Ponca village yet identified and excavated; it was excavated in 1936 and 1937 by Perry Newell for the Nebraska State Archaeological Survey. The Ponca were in close contact with Spanish and other traders while they lived there. Numerous excavations in the village and cemetery areas have provided a wide range of Euro-American trade goods and native-made artifacts that confirm Ponca Fort's dating by early traders and by later ethnographers, especially James O. Dorsey. Most of the ceramics, however, are identified as Stanley Braced Rim ware, a pottery normally associated with Protohistoric Arikara peoples. Skeletal analysis reveals the Ponca Fort cemetery population best aligns with the Omaha, from whom they had separated perhaps a century earlier. However, two female skulls classify unambiguously as Arikara (Jantz 1974:12) and indicate who may be responsible for the pottery. The Ponca continued to live in the same general area after the village was abandoned.

Because so much of the assemblage had been modified by Euro-American displacements, prehistoric antecedents for the historic Ponca remain obscure. One hypothesis, rapidly losing favor, suggests the Redbird phase in northeastern Nebraska, which dates to ca. A.D. 1550–1650 (400–300 years B.P.).

W. Raymond Wood

Further Readings

Dorsey, J.O. 1884. Omaha Sociology. *Annual Report of the Bureau of American Ethnology* 3(1881–1882):205–370.

Jantz, R.L. 1974. The Redbird Focus: Cranial Evidence in Tribal Identification. *Plains Anthropologist* 19(63):5–13.

Wood, W.R. 1960. *Nắⁿza: The Ponca Fort*. Archives of Archaeology no. 3. Society for American Archaeology, Washington, D.C.

See also REDBIRD PHASE

Port Moller

Port Moller lagoon is the largest embayment on the Bering Sea coast of the Alaska Peninsula. It is important archaeologically because of the Hot Springs village site (XPM-012) that is located on a headland ca. 10 km (6.2 miles) southeast of the lagoon's entrance. This site, which covers ca. 60,000 m² (71,760 square yards), is one of the largest sites known in the Lower Alaska Peninsula area. It is named after the hot springs between two areas of house depressions.

The site was first tested by Edward Weyer in 1928 (Weyer 1930). Larger excavations were carried out in 1960 by a joint U.S.-Japanese team, and, during the 1970s, additional excavations were carried out under the direction of Hiroaki and Atsuko Okada (Okada and Okada 1974; H. Okada 1980). It proved to be a large village of Alaska Peninsula people with noncontinuous occupation ca. 1500 B.C.–A.D. 1500 (3450–450 years B.P.). More than 200 shallow house depressions cover the site. These semisubterranean dwellings had internal hearths and clay-lined and stone-lined storage pits. Thick midden deposits appear over much of the site. They reflect the many years of occupation and provide excellent bone and other organic material preservation. Residents undoubtedly exploited the rich lagoon fauna, especially salmon, as well as Bering Sea coast fauna, including large whales. Land mammals of continental Alaska, such as caribou, bear, and wolf, are also represented in the fauna collections. Several human burials were found, some of which were associated with house depressions. Red ocher was commonly used to cover these burials.

Major artifact classes include stone net weights, chipped-stone projectile points, knives, scrapers, and drills; bone harpoon and dart heads, wedges, picks, and adze heads; and bone and ivory ornaments and jewelry. While the chipped-stone assemblage resembles that of the Aleutian tradition, much of the bone assemblage more closely resembles that of other mainland Alaskan-Kodiak Island sites.

Allen P. McCartney

Further Readings

Okada, H. 1980. Prehistory of the Alaska Peninsula As Seen From the Hot Springs Site, Port Moller. In *Alaska Native Culture and History*, edited by Y. Kotani and W. Workman, pp. 103–112. Senri Ethnological Series no. 4. Osaka.

Okada, H., and A. Okada. 1974. *The Hot Springs Village Site: Preliminary Report on the 1972 Excavations at Port Moller, Alaska*. Hiratsuka, Tokyo.

Weyer, E.M. 1930. *Archaeological Materials From the Village Site at Hot Springs, Port Moller, Alaska*. Anthropological Papers, vol. 31, pt. 4. American Museum of Natural History, New York.

Workman, W.B. 1966. Prehistory at Port Moller, Alaska Peninsula, in Light of Fieldwork in 1960. *Arctic Anthropology* 3(2):132–147.

See also ALEUTIAN TRADITION

Pottery (California)

The manufacture of pottery artifacts from tempered clay that has been fired is a distinctive feature of later prehistoric cultures in much of the eastern two-thirds of North America. Pottery has been especially prized by archaeologists for its survival in sites and because it possesses distinctive features of style that make it a valuable tool for identifying cultures. Most prehistoric California cultures did not manufacture pottery regularly, but there are important exceptions. Southeastern California, in particular, had a substantial pottery-making tradition, and recent discoveries (Chartkoff and Chartkoff 1984; Moratto 1984) show the existence of some pottery in other parts of the state. Why pottery-making did not become more widespread is a question that remains to be answered. In southeastern California, the regular use of pottery vessels for cooking, storage, and transportation of food and water began by at least A.D. 1000 (950 years B.P.).

Joseph L. Chartkoff

Further Readings

Chartkoff, J.L., and K.K. Chartkoff. 1984. *The Archaeology of California*. Stanford University Press, Stanford.

Moratto, M.J. (editor). 1984. *California Archaeology*. Academic Press, New York.

Poverty Point Culture

The Poverty Point culture refers to a regional manifestation centered in the Lower Mississippi Valley that developed during the second millennium B.C., reached its zenith ca. 1000 B.C. (2950 years B.P.), and by 600 B.C. (2550 years B.P.) had disappeared from the archaeological record of the region. It is distinguished from contemporaneous Late Archaic cultures by the presence of significant amounts of nonlocal lithic and other exotic materials in typical site collections and by the construction of mounds and other earthworks at larger sites. The culture's name is taken from the type site, Poverty Point (16WC5), an earthwork complex located in northeast Louisiana. The Poverty Point culture likely encompasses the remains of a number of prehistoric societies linked through economic and possibly political relationships. These societies are represented by clusters of sites in southeast Arkansas, the Yazoo Basin of Mississippi, northeast and central Louisiana, and the central Gulf Coast.

Although regional differences exist, sites of the Poverty Point culture share a material-culture assemblage that includes distinctive stemmed and notched projectile-point types, a microlithic stone-tool industry, a uniquely high representation of nonlocal stone used for chipped-stone-tool manufacture, steatite and sandstone vessels, ground-stone artifacts, such as plummets, bar gorgets, perforated boat-stones, and pipes, lapidary objects (beads, zoomorphic figures), native copper, and "Poverty Point Objects," which are fashioned clay objects used in earth-oven cookery. Fiber-tempered or untempered pottery, though apparently not a significant part of the material culture, is associated with some sites.

The distribution of these items in the Lower Mississippi Valley is interpreted to reflect an increased emphasis on exchange relations among participating populations. However, the mechanisms by which this exchange occurred are not well understood. There is clearly an increased intensity or regularity of trade of durable materials compared with preceding Late Archaic (ca. 3000–1500 B.C., or 4950–3450 years B.P.) societies. Nonlocal raw materials are represented in Poverty Point collections in much greater quantities than in preceding and subsequent cultures. Stone was acquired from Alabama, the Tennessee River Valley, the Midwest, southwestern Arkansas, and the Ozarks. Some tool classes were preferentially made from certain materials: More than 75 percent of the distinctive corner-notched Motley point are made from gray cherts from Tennessee and the Midwest, while Southern Appalachian sources of steatite, used for making bowls, are indicated by

trace-element analyses. Other raw materials acquired from afar include slate, galena, magnetite, hematite, greenstone, copper, and a soft red stone similar to catlinite. Although the presence of raw materials from nonlocal sources is a hallmark of Poverty Point components, no site has produced a greater quantity or variety of artifacts made from them than the Poverty Point site.

Poverty Point sites exhibit considerable variability. Several relatively large sites are interpreted as having served as regional centers. They are distinguished by the presence of public architecture, including mounds or embankments of earth or shell. At the Poverty Point site, earthwork construction reached an unprecedented scale and complexity, with several large mounds and a series of six concentric semi-elliptical ridges with an outer diameter of ca. 1,200 m (1,312 yards) in the central precinct. Other sites interpreted as having served as regional centers include the Jaketown site in the Yazoo Basin, Caney Island in central Louisiana, and the Claiborne site at the mouth of the Pearl River in Hancock County, Mississippi. Although smaller in scale than the Poverty Point site, each dominates the local settlement pattern. A number of other sites that presumably served a local integrative function have small mounds of probable Poverty Point age. At the lower end of the regional settlement hierarchies are residential settlements and special-purpose sites as small as 0.4–0.8 ha (1–2 acres) in size. While the archaeological deposits encountered at investigated sites vary considerably, well-developed middens at some settlements suggest long-term, if not sedentary, occupations.

Subsistence data are presently meager. Settlement locations imply a riverine or coastal estuarine adaptation. Faunal remains collected during excavation at the J.W. Copes site, a small hamlet near the Poverty Point site, point to a broad spectrum of exploited species but a rather narrow reliance on fish and deer. Floral remains indicate a reliance on nuts found in bottomland hardwood forests, supplemented by the cultivation of squash; as of the mid-1990s, there was no evidence for the use of seedy species of the Eastern Agricultural complex.

A number of interpretive issues guide Poverty Point research. One controversial issue is the nature and scale of sociopolitical organization. The apparent settlement hierarchy suggested by the presence of distinctive centers and the quantities of nonlocal resources point to

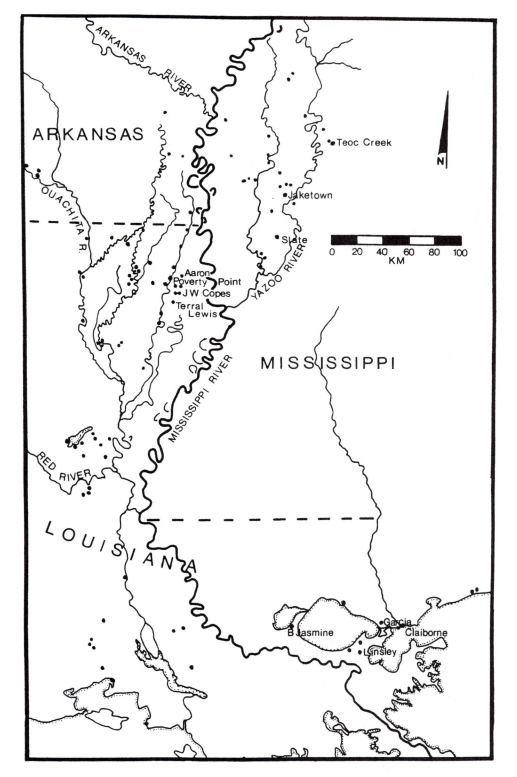

Distribution of Poverty Point components in the Lower Mississippi Valley. (Illustration by H. E. Jackson)

greater integration than is suggested by the earlier Late Archaic record (Gibson 1974). Site clusters have been interpreted as representing chiefdoms, with the Poverty Point site perhaps having paramount control over the entire system. Corroborative archaeological evidence for the presence of an elite social stratum is lacking. An alternative model views the Poverty Point system as comprising multiple trading partnerships, maintained by individuals, that link otherwise independent societies; the increased intensity of exchange was facilitated by periodic aggregations of the traders at the regional centers (Jackson 1991).

Resolution of the question of organization hinges, in part, on an understanding of the nature of occupation at the large centers. Two alternative interpretations await adequate evaluation with excavated data. The large centers, Poverty Point in particular, have been interpreted as having supported permanent resident populations, in essence as being prehistoric towns. The capacity to support a large "urban" populace implies a relatively high level of sociopolitical integration (Gibson 1974). Alternatively, it is possible that only a small resident population inhabited the centers year-round, with the population swelling periodically when people gathered there for trade and ritual participation. Superordinate political control in such a scenario could be temporary and perhaps codified in ritual activity (Jackson 1991).

A final issue is the identification of factors leading to the emergence of this distinctive cultural complex. Early interpretations evoked external influences and even migration as likely stimuli. However, each of the culture's major characteristics—earthwork construction, stone lapidary, and exchange of exotics over long distances—has Middle and earlier Late Archaic antecedents. It is likely that models of the culture's development ultimately will be grounded in local cultural, and perhaps human ecological, dynamics.

H. Edwin Jackson

Further Readings

Bryd, K.M. (editor). 1991. *The Poverty Point Culture: Its Local Manifestations, Subsistence Practices, and Trade Networks.* Geoscience and Man, vol. 29. Museum of Geosciences, Louisiana State University, Baton Rouge.

Ford, J.A., and C.H. Webb. 1956. *Poverty Point: A Late Archaic Site in Northeast Louisiana.* Anthropological Papers, vol. 46, pt. 1. American Museum of Natural History, New York.

Gibson, J.L. 1974. Poverty Point: The First American Chiefdom. *Archaeology* 27:96–105.

Jackson, H.E. 1991. The Trade Fair in Hunter-Gatherer Interaction: The Role of Intersocietal Trade in the Evolution of Poverty Point. In *Between Bands and States*, edited by S.A. Gregg, pp. 265–286. Occasional Papers no. 9. Center for Archaeological Investigations, Southern Illinois University, Carbondale.

Webb, C.H. 1982. *The Poverty Point Culture.* 2nd ed. Geoscience and Man, vol. 17. Museum of Geosciences, Louisiana State University, Baton Rouge.

See also POVERTY POINT OBJECTS; POVERTY POINT SITE

Poverty Point Objects

Poverty Point objects (or P.P.O.s) are hand-modeled baked-clay objects used in earth-oven cookery in the Lower Mississippi Valley during the Poverty Point period. They are similar in form to ones distributed from eastern Missouri south to the Gulf of Mexico, along the Florida Panhandle, and on the south Atlantic seaboard. P.P.O.s are generally poorly fired, with colors ranging from buff to dark red. Pastes, typically containing significant amounts of silts and sands, vary locally; objects made in the Mississippi Valley tend to be made from silty to fine sandy clay, while those made along the Gulf Coast are from coarse sandy clays.

The majority of P.P.O.s can be sorted into recurring typological categories. Basic shapes include biconical, spherical, discoidal, cylindrical, ellipsoidal, flattened or "biscuit" shaped, and rectangular; they are sometimes modified by grooves, twists, or designs applied by incision or punctation. Among the most common types found are cylindrical-grooved, biconical-plain, biconical-grooved, cross-grooved, and grooved and ungrooved melon shapes. Objects with punctated or incised designs are uncommon, as are conoidal, pyramidal, tetrahedral, and mushroom-shaped ones. Sizes of the objects vary, though most are smaller than a tennis ball and weigh between 50 and 80 g (1.8–2.8 ounces).

Attempts to identify chronological trends in the morphological variation of these objects have met with little success. Larger, relatively simple objects appear as early as 2000 B.C. (3950 years B.P.), while small biconical P.P.O.s persist into the subsequent Tchefuncte period, after 700 B.C. (2650 years B.P.).

The archaeological contexts in which the P.P.O.s are found, as well as replicative experiments, suggest that they were employed in earth-oven cookery. Pits were lined with objects, and fires were built on top. Once the P.P.O.s were heated, food was placed in the pit. The heat radiated by the objects roasted the food. Experiments suggest that differences in shape result in different thermal properties, permitting some control over temperature and cooking duration. Prior to experimentation, it had been suggested that the objects could have been used in a way analogous to hot-rock boiling. This is unlikely since the characteristic light firing rendered them porous and erodable, and significant amounts of grit would be added to cooking water if they were used in this fashion.

H. Edwin Jackson

Further Readings

Gibson, J.L. 1975. Fire Pits at Mount Bayou (16CT35), Catahoula Parish, Louisiana. *Louisiana Archaeology* 2:201–218.

Webb, C.H. 1982. *The Poverty Point Culture.* 2nd ed. Geoscience and Man, vol. 17. Museum of Geosciences, Louisiana State University, Baton Rouge.

See also POVERTY POINT CULTURE; POVERTY POINT SITE

Poverty Point Site

The Poverty Point site (16WC5), located on the eastern slope of Macon Ridge in Madison Parish, northeast Louisiana, is a large earthwork complex that serves as the type site of the Poverty Point culture. It consists of several large mounds and six semielliptical ridges. Its large overall size and the scale of earthen construction are unmatched by contemporaneous North American archaeological sites. Initial construction, consisting of land modification to form the plaza area, began in ca. 1500 B.C. (3450 years B.P.), and the site reached its final form in ca. 1000 B.C. (2950 years B.P.). Despite perennial archaeological interest in the site, it continues to elude satisfactory interpretations regarding function, size of resident population, and construction history.

While the most obvious features of the site have long been recognized by investigators, the late-twentieth-century understanding of its configuration has benefited considerably by research during the 1980s. The central feature is a 25-m (82-foot) -high Mound A, a complexly shaped mound that some believe resembles a bird. As described by James A. Ford (Ford and Webb 1956:14), the summit is ca. 5 m (16.4 feet) in diameter, with narrow ridges descending north and south from it in a steplike fashion. The western flank is steep, while on the eastern flank an apparent ramp leads down to a platform 8 m (26.2 feet) above ground level.

Two other mounds, a 6.5-m (21.3-foot) high conical mound north of Mound A and a low, 1.5-m (5-foot) -high flat-topped mound near the northeast corner of the plaza, are also part of the central earthwork complex. A third small mound in the southwest corner of the plaza may be of Poverty Point age, but it is in the midst of the few concentrations of post–Poverty Point materials on the site.

Abutting Mound A on its eastern edge are six concentric, semielliptical ridges that are interrupted by four to five openings, at least some of which suggest aisles. The ridges terminate at the bluff edge. The ridges, which range in diameter from 1,200 m (1,312 yards) for the outermost to nearly 600 m (656 yards) for the innermost, encompass a 14-ha (34.6-acre) plaza area. Although difficult to estimate because of extensive historic cultivation, the ridges were probably ca. 2 m (6.6 feet) higher than the swales that separated them. Each ridge is made up of loaded earth interspersed with midden lenses, which suggests that they were used as residential areas. In the southwestern sector, an additional long ridge was constructed perpendicular to the concentric ridge complex. It crossed the six ridges and extended southwesterly another 90 m (295.3 feet) beyond the enclosure.

Earthwork construction extends beyond the central precinct. Both the 16-m (52.5-foot) -high Motley Mound, which is 2.4 km (1.5 miles) north of Poverty Point, and the more modest, conical Lower Jackson Mound, which is 2.8 km (1.7 miles) south of the main complex, are also considered part of the overall configuration based on apparent north-south alignments and near equal spacing.

Unresolved issues include the development of a site-construction chronology and a data-grounded interpretation of the nature of the occupation, whether sedentary or intermittent. Both will require more excavation and systematically collected chronometric dates. Regarding the latter, midden development on ridge surfaces and high artifact density imply extensive use of the site and have been interpreted as some evidence for a large permanent resident population. However, evidence for substantial residential architecture remains undocumented.

H. Edwin Jackson

Further Readings

Bryd, K.M. (editor). 1991. *The Poverty Point Culture: Its Local Manifestations, Subsistence Practices, and Trade Networks.*

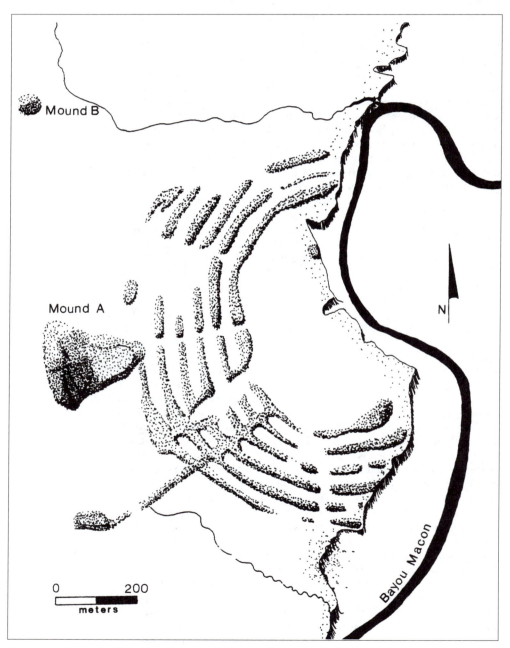

The Poverty Point site, West Carroll Parish, Louisiana. (Illustration by H. E. Jackson)

Geoscience and Man, vol. 29. Museum of Geosciences, Louisiana State University, Baton Rouge.

Ford, J.A., and C.H. Webb. 1956. *Poverty Point: A Late Archaic Site in Northeast Louisiana.* Anthropological Papers, vol. 46, pt. 1. American Museum of Natural History, New York.

Webb, C.H. 1982. *The Poverty Point Culture.* 2nd ed. Geoscience and Man, vol. 17. Museum of Geosciences, Louisiana State University, Baton Rouge.

See also POVERTY POINT CULTURE; POVERTY POINT OBJECTS

Powell, John Wesley (1834–1902)

Renowned explorer, ethnologist, geologist, and administrator, John Wesley Powell is best known for his pioneer classification of Native American languages and his geological surveys (1867–1879) of the Rocky Mountain region and the canyons of the Green and Colorado rivers, during which he became the first person to descend the Grand Canyon rapids of the Colorado in a boat (1869). Appointed professor of geology in 1865 at Illinois Wesleyan University and later at Illinois Normal College (now Illinois State), he became the first chief of the U.S. Bureau of American Ethnology (BAE) (1879–1902). Although he was committed at the BAE to ethnological and linguistic studies, his own earlier excavations, conducted while he was a major in the Union Army near Nashville, of a mound in Illinois and a cemetery in Tennessee had convinced him that the ancestors of Native Americans had built the mounds scattered across the eastern United States. When directed by Congress in 1881 to investigate "the Mound Builders and prehistoric mounds," he set up an archaeological division of the BAE under the eventual supervision of Cyrus Thomas that systematically undermined the Mound Builder myth. Under Powell's direction, the BAE established the empirical foundations of archaeology in the United States on a broad geographical scale and became the leading center of anthropological research in North America.

Guy Gibbon

Further Readings

Darrah, W.C. 1951. *Powell of the Colorado.* Princeton University Press, Princeton.

Fowler, D.D., and C.S. Fowler (editors).
1971. *Anthropology of the Numa: John Wesley Powell's Manuscripts on the Numic Peoples of Western North America, 1868–1880.* Smithsonian Institution Press, Washington, D.C.

Judd, N.M. 1967. *The Bureau of American Ethnology.* University of Oklahoma Press, Norman.

See also MOUND BUILDER MYTH; THOMAS, CYRUS

Pratt Complex

Although often mentioned, the Pratt complex is not well known. Sites are in west-central Kansas and extend from just south of the Smoky Hill River, across the Arkansas River valley, and into the upper reaches of the Ninnescah River Valley. The complex probably dates to ca. A.D. 1300–1400 (650–550 years B.P.). Its origins are uncertain. Some researchers argue for a migration by Washita River–phase people from central Oklahoma. Others suggest an in situ development. Regardless, Pratt has material-culture similarities with both the central and southern Plains Village traditions. The Pratt complex may be ancestral to the Great Bend aspect, especially the Little River focus.

Large village sites are thought to exist, although the best documented is the Lewis site, a hunting station consisting of only one complete house and parts of three other houses. Houses are circular with a central hearth. Subsistence is not well documented. Maize has been recovered, as have plum pits and berry seeds. Bison and deer were hunted. Ceramics include plain, cord-marked, and simple-stamped surfaces on sand-tempered vessels, although a few sherds have plain surfaces and shell temper. Vessels have diagonal incised lines on the lip and appliqué decoration on the neck. Vessel form is globular. Bone tools include bison-tibia digging-stick tips, bison-scapula hoes, perforators, and split-bone awls. Stone tools include small triangular side-notched projectile points; end scrapers; plain-shafted and expanding-base drills; alternately beveled, diamond-shaped knives; and two-edged, alternately beveled hafted knives. Ground-stone tools include shaft smoothers, pipes, grooved mauls, and grinding stones. Materials obtained through trade include Southwestern ceramics, turquoise, obsidian, and *Olivella* shell. Alibates agatized dolomite from the Texas Panhandle and Florence-A chert from north-central Oklahoma also may have been obtained through trade.

Susan C. Vehik

Further Readings

O'Brien, P.J. 1984. *Archeology in Kansas.* Public Education Series no. 9. Museum of Anthropology, University of Kansas, Lawrence.

Wedel, W.R. 1959. *Introduction to Kansas Archaeology.* Bulletin no. 174. Bureau of American Ethnology, Smithsonian Institution, Washington, D.C.

Witty, T. 1978. Along the Southern Edge: The Central Plains Tradition in Kansas. In *The Central Plains Tradition,* edited by D.J. Blakeslee, pp. 56–66. Report no. 11. Office of the State Archaeologist, University of Iowa, Iowa City.

Pre-Clovis

The term "pre-Clovis" refers to potential human occupation of the Americas prior to the unequivocal Clovis occupation of 9550–8850 B.C. (11,500–10,800 years B.P.). Proponents of a pre-Clovis occupation of the New World believe that there were a number of human migrations across Beringia throughout the Pleistocene and that both coastal and inland routes were possible.

Those who remain unconvinced of a pre-Clovis occupation of the New World claim that there is no indisputable evidence of pre-Clovis-age sites. They contend that the evidence from purported pre-Clovis sites is flawed, arguing that (1) the associations of human artifacts and early dates are inconclusive; (2) the deposits are mixed or disturbed, which has led to errors in interpreting stratigraphy; (3) radiocarbon dates are contaminated; or (4) the reported artifacts are the result of natural geological processes.

There are many purported pre-Clovis sites and many pieces of evidence. Most have been discarded as too problematic or inconclusive, even by the most ardent defenders of the existence of pre-Clovis cultures. A few key sites continue to be mentioned, however, when the pre-Clovis issue is discussed.

Two Arctic sites that are often mentioned are Old Crow Flats and Bluefish Caves. At Old Crow Flats in the Yukon, carved-bone tools and radiocarbon dates on bone have supported the possibility that early hunters roamed the Yukon-Alaskan borderlands ca. 25,050 B.C.

(27,000 years B.P.). However, recent redating of the bones, using the precision of accelerator mass spectrometry, indicates that what was once believed to be the best evidence for pre-Clovis occupation in the Arctic is actually less than 2,000 years old. At Bluefish Caves, 64.3 km (40 miles) southwest of Old Crow Flats, archaeologist Jacques Cinq-Mars reported ancient bone and stone tools, animal bones with cut marks made by stone knives during butchering, and the bones of extinct horse and mammoth dated between 13,050 and 11,050 B.C. (15,000–13,000 years B.P.). Nevertheless, skeptics remain unconvinced; they suspect that the caves' sediments were mixed by repeated cycles of freezing and thawing.

The pre-Clovis site containing the oldest evidence is Calico near Barstow, California. There, in the Mojave Desert, Ruth Simpson and her colleagues found hundreds of what they believe are flaked-stone tools in 100,000–600,000-year-old deposits. These finds are still hotly debated by skeptics who claim that the flaked stones were chipped by geological forces rather than by humans. In the San Diego region, George Carter spent decades recovering thousands of flaked stones from excavations of suspected human campsites and hearths. Geologically, the deposits range in age from 80,000 to more than 120,000 years B.P. Like the material from Calico, however, there is heated debate whether Carter's flaked stones, his ancient campsites, and the burned hearthlike areas are really the remains of human activity or of natural geological forces. Another site, the Meadowcroft Rockshelter in southwestern Pennsylvania, is also under fire from skeptics who question the accuracy of early radiocarbon dates that suggest that ancient hunters used the site between 12,550 and 12,050 B.C. (14,500–14,000 years B.P.). A more recently discovered U.S. pre-Clovis candidate is a site Richard S. MacNeish is excavating in southeastern New Mexico. His Orogrande Cave (also called Pendejo Cave) contains a long and well-stratified sequence of extinct animal and plant remains that extends back nearly 40,000 years. Eight human palm prints etched in fire-hardened clay, human hairs, chipped stones, and hundreds of broken animal bones have convinced MacNeish and others of the cave's long record of human occupation, which spans more than 30,000 years. Skeptics, however, remain unconvinced of the association of human remains with the site's early radiocarbon dates.

Central America also has pre-Clovis sites. At the El Bosque site in Nicaragua, Alan L. Bryan, Richard Morlan, William Irving, and Ruth Gruhn during their 1975 excavation discovered extinct animal bones, chipped stones, and large blackened areas with river-pebble concentrations they believe to be ancient fire hearths. Radiocarbon ages show the deposits to date to 28,050–16,050 B.C. (30,000–18,000 years B.P.), but skeptics consider the blackened areas the remains of natural brush fires and the chipped stones works of nature, not of humans. At Valsequillo, MacNeish, Juan A. Camacho, and Cynthia Irwin-Williams found 19,050 B.C. (21,000 years B.P.) animal bones in association with unifacial stone implements they believe were of human origin. Skeptics claim that the implements are not human-made tools, are not associated with the extinct animal bones, and are not stratigraphically associated with the radiocarbon date.

At the southern tip of South America at Monte Verde in Chile, Tom E. Dillehay has excavated a campsite containing wooden, bone, and stone artifacts, and the remains of seven mastodons dated between 11,050 and 10,550 B.C. (13,000–12,500 years B.P.). Skeptics agree on the importance of the site, yet they suspect that the dated samples were contaminated. Two other important pre-Clovis sites in South America are Pikimachay in Peru and Pedra Furada in Brazil. In the bottom deposits of Pikimachay, MacNeish found extinct sloth and horse bones, broken river cobbles, charcoal, and fist-sized pieces of volcanic tufa rock that he believes were chipped by humans. Radiocarbon dates range from 23,050 to 14,050 B.C. (25,000–16,000 years B.P.), yet skeptics remain unconvinced by the dates and do not believe that the tufa rock and river cobbles were broken by humans. The final South American location is the rock-shelter site of Boqueirão da Sitio da Pedra Furada, where Nième Guidon began working in the early 1980s. She has found ancient pictographs, hundreds of chipped and broken stones, and areas she thinks are fire hearths. Seventeen radiocarbon dates suggest the deposits range in age from 28,050 to 3050 B.C. (30,000–5000 years B.P.). Skeptics have suggested, however, that the chipped and broken stones may be of natural origin and the hearth areas burned by ancient grass fires.

Of the current pre-Clovis sites, remains from Monte Verde, Meadowcroft, and Pedra Furada are slowly becoming accepted by a growing number of skeptics. Nevertheless, pre-Clovis sites will continue to capture the imagination and curiosity of scientists and laypersons alike because they remain one of our best unresolved mysteries.

Vaughn M. Bryant, Jr.

Further Readings

Bonnichsen, R., and D.G. Steele. 1994. *Method and Theory for Investigating the Peopling of the Americas.* Center for the Study of the First Americans, Oregon State University, Corvallis.

Bryan, A.L. 1986. *New Evidence for the Pleistocene Peopling of the Americas.* Center for the Study of Early Man, University of Maine, Orono.

Carlisle, R.C. 1988. *Americans Before Columbus: Ice-Age Origins.* Ethnology Monographs no. 12. Department of Anthropology, University of Pittsburgh, Pittsburgh.

Carter, G.F. 1980. *Earlier Than You Think: A Personal View of Man in America.* Texas A&M Press, College Station.

Chrisman, D., R.S. MacNeish, J. Mavalwala, and H. Savage. 1996. Late Pleistocene Human Friction Skin Prints From Pendejo Cave, New Mexico. *American Antiquity* 61:357–376.

Dillehay, T.E., and D.J. Meltzer. 1991. *The First Americans: Search and Research.* CRC Press, Boca Raton.

Fagan, B.M. 1987. *The Great Journey: The Peopling of Ancient America.* Thames and Hudson, New York.

Irwin-Williams, C. 1969. Comments on the Associations of Archaeological Materials and Extinct Fauna in the Valsequillo Region, Puebla, Mexico. *American Antiquity* 34:82–83.

Pre-Dorset

Pre-Dorset refers to a major culture-chronological subdivision of eastern Arctic prehistory. Precise definition of this term, however, is complicated because the label "Pre-Dorset" has, historically, been used in several different ways to refer to very different conceptual phenomena. In its original and, in many ways, its broadest definition, the term refers to the eastern Arctic manifestation of the Arctic Small Tool tradition (ASTt). In other words, Pre-Dorset can be viewed as the eastern Arctic equivalent of the western Arctic Denbigh Flint complex. As originally proposed by Henry Collins (1954), it subsumes all those archaeological assemblages from the eastern Arctic dating to ca. 2550–1050 B.C. (4500–3000 years B.P.) that are characterized by the very small size of most, if not all, of their associated artifacts; microblades, some exhibiting further retouch, struck from an assortment of prepared microcore forms; a variety of often finely finished, parallel-sided, expanding- or contracting-stemmed, or triangular end blades, bifaces, and/or knives; flaked burins; burin spalls (occasionally retouched); bifacial and/or unifacial ovate or crescentic side blades; various end- and side-scraper forms; small ovate or circular stone lamps, which are commonly, though not exclusively, made of soapstone; and, where the state of organic preservation permits, a range of open-socketed toggling or tang-based nontoggling harpoon head forms; lance heads; unilateral and bilateral barbed darts; bone, ivory, antler, or wood knife handles; and bone or ivory sewing needles.

As additional research was carried out throughout the eastern Arctic, it became increasingly apparent that the Arctic Small Tool tradition in the eastern Arctic was considerably more heterogeneous than the ASTt in the western Arctic. Much of this variation appeared, on first consideration, to be geographically based (Maxwell 1985). Assemblages perceived to be distinctive stylistic variants of the ASTt from High Arctic Canada and northeastern Greenland were grouped together and identified as belonging to the Independence I culture. Similarly, artifact assemblages characterized by several distinctive technological attributes, such as the extensive polishing of burins, bifaces, and end blades made from a local variety of siliceous shale, recovered from western Greenland were identified as belonging to the Saqqaq (or Sarqaq) culture. ASTt assemblages from the west-central and east-central Canadian Arctic that were stylistically not directly comparable to either Independence I or Saqqaq were identified as belonging to the Pre-Dorset culture. From this perspective, the term "Pre-Dorset" refers to a distinctive regional variant of the ASTt in the Canadian eastern Arctic. The Pre-Dorset culture is, in this narrow sense of the term, regarded as being contemporaneous with the Independence I and Saqqaq cultures and, apart from sharing a common ancestor, to have developed independently from them.

It has been hypothesized (Maxwell 1985) that the expansion of the Arctic Small Tool tradition from the Bering Strait region into the eastern Arctic occurred along two separate routes. One route extended in a northeasterly direction through islands in the Canadian High Arctic and into northeastern Greenland. ASTt groups that followed this path are believed to have developed into the Far Northern Independence I culture. The second migration route followed by bearers of the ASTt is thought to have extended along the Canadian Arctic mainland coast, including the "low Arctic islands," as far east as the rugged east coasts of Baffin Island and Labrador. Groups who followed this route are thought by some to have been the ancestors of the Pre-Dorset culture. Proponents of the preceding scenario have suggested that members of the more northerly Independence I culture continued to expand along the east coast of Greenland. In the course of this secondary expansion, elements of the Independence I culture are thought to have undergone a series of minor technological and stylistic changes that led to the emergence of what has come to be called the Saqqaq culture.

In High Arctic Canada, the Independence I culture is hypothesized (McGhee 1976) to have died out by ca. 1800 B.C. (3750 years B.P.). Supporters of this position suggest that some centuries after the local disappearance of the Independence I culture in the Canadian Far North, the High Arctic archipelago was reoccupied by a secondary northward expansion of the Pre-Dorset culture. Farther to the south—in the east-central Canadian Arctic—the Pre-Dorset culture is thought to have flourished in the Foxe Basin and Hudson Strait area, an ecologically stable and productive region that has been called the core area of eastern Arctic Paleoeskimo cultural development. It has been suggested that human occupation in the core area was more or less continuous over the past ca. 4,500 years and that in the period ca. 2550–1050 B.C. (4500–3000 years B.P.) a series of in situ technological and economic changes in the Pre-Dorset culture led to the local emergence of the late Arctic Small Tool tradition Dorset culture (Taylor 1968; Maxwell 1985).

The view that Pre-Dorset constitutes a regional variant of the Arctic Small Tool tradition contemporary with, but distinct from, the Independence I and Saqqaq cultures has been challenged by a growing corpus of radiometric and typological evidence (Groennow 1988; Helmer 1991). It is becoming increasingly apparent that many of the stylistic attributes used to distinguish the Independence I culture from the Pre-Dorset and the Saqqaq cultures, such as edge-serrated bipointed end blades and bifaces, are not, in fact, unique to assemblages from the Canadian High Arctic and northeastern Greenland but also characterize the earliest Pre-Dorset and Saqqaq assemblages (dating to ca. 2550–1900 B.C., or 4500–3850 years B.P.) recovered from the east-central Canadian Arctic and West Greenland. Similarly, specific typological elements of the Pre-Dorset and Saqqaq cultures associated with assemblages dating to ca. 1900–1450 B.C. (3850–3400 years B.P.) in the Canadian Arctic share a fair degree of similarity. In fact, much of what has been recognized as evidence of spatial/cultural variability in the eastern Arctic branch of the ASTt is coming to be regarded as evidence of temporal stylistic change; that is, Independence I and Pre-Dorset are now being regarded as chronological stages of the ASTt in the eastern Arctic and not as distinct, largely contemporary cultural/spatial variants. The only exception to this trend appears to be the later period (ca. 1450–1050 B.C., or 3400–3000 years B.P.) of the Saqqaq culture in West Greenland and on east-central Ellesmere Island in the Canadian High Arctic (Schledermann 1990), where convincing evidence of the in situ development of a unique local variant of the ASTt, distinct from contemporary late manifestations of Pre-Dorset in the Canadian Arctic, appears to be holding up to intensive scrutiny.

J.W. Helmer's (1994) recent, though not universally accepted, definition of Pre-Dorset views this taxon as a cultural tradition encompassing the entire range of material, cultural, economic, and social variability—both spatial and temporal—inherent in all eastern Arctic manifestations of the Arctic Small Tool tradition. Helmer (1994) has suggested that the Pre-Dorset cultural tradition also be tentatively subdivided into four chronological episodes or cultural horizons—Initial, Early, Middle, and Late Pre-Dorset—based on the preliminary recognition of continuities and/or changes in material culture, economic adaptations, and settlement patterns. Considerably more detailed analysis of the patterning and variability of archaeological data pertaining to this important episode in eastern Arctic culture history must be undertaken, however, before the temporal and spatial dynamics of Pre-Dorset culture history can be more fully understood.

James W. Helmer

Further Readings

Collins, H. 1954. Archaeological Research in the North American Arctic. *Arctic* 7(3–4): 296–306.

Groennow, B. 1988. Prehistory in Permafrost: Investigations at the Saqqaq Site Qeqetasussuk, Disco Bay, West Greenland. *Journal of Danish Archaeology* 7:24–39.

Helmer, J.W. 1991. The Palaeo-Eskimo Prehistory of the North Devon Lowlands. *Arctic* 44(4):301–317.

———. 1994. Resurrecting the Spirit(s) of Taylor's Carlsberg Culture: Cultural Traditions and Cultural Horizons in Eastern Arctic Prehistory. In *Threads of Arctic Prehistory: Papers in Honour of William E. Taylor Jr.*, edited by D. Morrison and J.-L. Pilon, pp. 15–34. Mercury Series Paper no. 149. Archaeological Survey of Canada, Canadian Museum of Civilization, Ottawa.

Maxwell, M.S. 1973. *Archaeology of the Lake Harbor District, Baffin Island, Canada.* Mercury Series Paper no. 6. Archaeological Survey of Canada, Canadian Museum of Man, Ottawa.

———. 1976. *Eastern Arctic Prehistory: Paleoeskimo Problems.* Memoir no. 31. Society for American Archaeology, Washington, D.C.

———. 1984. Pre-Dorset and Dorset Prehistory of Canada. In *Arctic*, edited by D. Damas, pp. 359–368. Handbook of North American Indians, vol. 5, W.C. Sturtevant, general editor. Smithsonian Institution, Washington, D.C.

———. 1985. *Prehistory of the Eastern Arctic.* Academic Press, New York.

McGhee, R. 1976. Paleoeskimo Occupations of Central and High Arctic Canada. In *Eastern Arctic Prehistory: Paleoeskimo Problems*, edited by M.S. Maxwell, pp. 15–39. Memoir no. 31. Society for American Archaeology, Washington, D.C.

Schledermann, P. 1990. *Crossroads to Greenland: 3,000 Years of Prehistory in the Eastern High Arctic.* Komatik Series no. 2. Arctic Institute of North America, Calgary.

Taylor, W.E., Jr. 1968. *The Arnapik and Tyara Sites: An Archaeological Study of Dorset Culture Origins.* Memoir no. 22. Society for American Archaeology, Washington, D.C.

P

Primary Forest Efficiency

"Primary forest efficiency" is a concept proposed by Joseph R. Caldwell in the late 1950s to partly explain the pattern of development of Archaic cultures in the Eastern Woodlands (Caldwell 1958). According to the concept of primary forest efficiency, Archaic peoples learned over the millennia how to ever more efficiently and skillfully exploit a wider and wider spectrum of natural food resources in their generous woodland environment. The result was the establishment of cyclical seasonal procurement schedules that focused on the harvesting of foods that were abundant, nutritious, and relatively easy to gather or capture. By the Late Archaic period (ca. 4000 B.C., or 5950 years B.P.), this lifeway had led in some areas to optimally adapted, dense populations living in permanent settlements. Accompanying this gradual in situ trend were a diversification of types of tools to capture and process the new broad-spectrum food resources, such as crushing and grinding implements, a broadened range of raw materials for tool manufacture, and ever more complex social organizations. This "natural" lifeway was eventually eclipsed in Caldwell's formulation by the establishment of food production as an economic basis early in the Woodland period (ca. 1050–50 B.C., or 3000–2000 years B.P.). Jesse D. Jennings later suggested that the concept could be broadened to the North American Archaic in general (Jennings 1989). In his terms, Eastern Woodlands primary forest efficiency is a geographically restricted example of "Archaic efficiency."

Images evoked by the concept of primary forest efficiency include "settling in," a "complete and harmonious" adjustment, a "diffuse (as compared to a focal) adaptation," and "learners" versus "know-it-alls" in efficiency of resource exploitation. In contemporary terms, primary forest efficiency is similar to an optimal foraging strategy. Although an insightful explanation of some trends in the Archaic period in the Eastern Woodlands, the concept is most likely inadequate as an explanation of all cultural developments in the period. Population growth, diffusion of innovations, climatic and landscape changes, increasing intergroup interaction, the logic of cultural development, stress on available resources, and the fluctuating productivity of the Eastern Woodlands itself were probably of equal, and at times greater, importance in the history of specific Archaic cultures.

Guy Gibbon

Further Readings

Caldwell, J.R. 1958. *Trend and Tradition in the Prehistory of the Eastern United States*. Illinois State Museum, Springfield.

Jennings, J.D. 1989. *The Prehistory of North America*. 3rd ed. Mayfield, Mountain View.

Prince Rupert Harbor

Rupert Harbor is located on the north coast of the British Columbia mainland between the mouths of the Skeena and the Nass rivers. During the eighteenth and nineteenth centuries, its sheltered waters were the heart of Coast Tsimshian territory and the locale for their principal towns. The harbor's location provided access to salmon (*Oncorhynchus* spp.) runs on both rivers, to spring eulachon (*Thaleichthys pacificus*) runs on the Nass, and to a range of rich littoral, marine, and terrestrial environments. Extensive excavations of 10 of the harbor's massive shell middens and smaller excavations of several of its other middens have produced one of the largest bodies of archaeological data for the northern Northwest Coast. These data, including more than 120 radiocarbon dates, are the basis for a chronology that spans the last 6,000 calendar years. This chronology, which is central to our understanding of the archaeology and culture history of the entire northern Northwest Coast, is as follows:

Pre-3050 B.C. (5000 years B.P.). While most of the excavated sites in the harbor were first occupied sometime after 3050 B.C. (5000 years B.P.), some may have been occupied before this date. Several have water-logged basal deposits, suggesting that they were initially occupied during a period of lowered sea levels that dates in this area between 6050 and 3050 B.C. (8000–5000 years B.P.). Possible pre-3050 B.C. (5000 years B.P.) components have few artifacts or faunal remains. Microblades and microblade cores, the temporally diagnostic artifacts of the pre-3050 B.C. (5000 years B.P.) period on the northern Northwest Coast, have yet to be recovered or recognized in Prince Rupert Harbor.

3050–2050 B.C. (5000–4000 years B.P.). Several sites have assemblages dating to this period. However, they do not differ in any distinctive way from small, younger assemblages in the harbor. By the end of the millennium, at least two of the largest sites (Boardwalk and Lachane) may have achieved their maximum areal extent. There is no direct evidence of structures or other permanent features. Faunal remains indicate that deer, salmon, flatfish, seals, and birds were among the species utilized. The absence of small-boned creatures like herring and eulachon may reflect sampling biases rather than subsistence practices. Recovered subsistence equipment includes bone barbs and points, harpoons, and ground-slate points. Net weights and harpoon valves are absent, though this again may be a function of sampling bias.

2050–1050 B.C. (4000–3000 years B.P.). Several important developments appear in the harbor during this period: (1) the practice of midden burial, which was ubiquitous on the Northwest Coast ca. 2050 B.C.–A.D. 750 (4000–1200 years B.P.), begins, with more than 230 inhumations recovered in excavations in the harbor; (2) some burials are in wooden boxes reminiscent of historic food-storage boxes, which suggests that food storage may have become economically significant during this period; (3) the condition of some skeletons points to endemic warfare by the end of the millennium; (4) net weights and harpoon valves appear in deposits, which may point to an expansion of fishing, though sampling bias may explain their absence earlier.

1050–50 B.C. (3000–2000 years B.P.). There is strong evidence for the presence of multihouse, multirow plank-house villages by the early centuries of this millennium, including surface depressions left by the structures and what are probably superimposed house floors. Midden burials occur in dense clusters (cemeteries) in dump areas directly associated with residential areas, which suggests the presence of relatively long-lived households or kin groups. There is also clear evidence for the procurement, storage, and transport of salmon and eulachon and the intensive exploitation of marine environments. The latter evidence includes the intense occupation of strategically located islands that, while marginal residential localities, provided access to rich littoral and pelagic habitats. Storage facilities are associated with evidence for the exploitation of a wide range of fish, birds, and territorial and marine mammals. Both grave goods and burials point to the presence of social stratification and slavery at this time, as well as at least part-time specialists in copper metallurgy. Deposits of the age contain increased numbers of ground-stone tools, particularly those associated with heavy woodworking and carpentry, and the first objects clearly displaying elements of the Northwest Coast art style.

50 B.C.–A.D. 950 (2000–1000 years B.P.). This millennium is characterized by a number of dramatic changes: (1) the practice of midden burial ends by ca. A.D. 650 (1300 years B.P.); (2) many sites, including those that had been occupied since at least 3050 B.C. (5000 years B.P.), are abandoned, perhaps more than once; (3) patterns of site utilization change, with residential areas now being used as dumps, sometimes after a period of abandonment, and dumps now being used as residential areas; (4) the small island sites that were intensively utilized during the previous millennia are abandoned; and (5) while some locations are abandoned, others begin to be used, at least seasonally, for the first time. Despite these shifts, multirowed villages of small rectangular houses continued to be built in the harbor. There is also no evidence for significant shifts in subsistence or major breaks in material culture.

A.D. 950–1450 (1000–500 years B.P.). The history of this period is difficult to reconstruct, for the upper levels of many of the harbor's excavated middens have sustained significant damage. However, a number of sites that were abandoned during the previous millennium were reoccupied as residential sites, and at least one seasonal site became a residential site. Artifacts from the upper levels and surfaces of these middens are identical in style and workmanship to those in ethnographic collections made from the northern Northwest Coast. The ethnohistorical record suggests that at least some of the Coast Tsimshian tribes that occupied the harbor at contact in the eighteenth century A.D. had moved to the harbor from the Lower Skeena River. The move occurred perhaps during this period.

The evidence summarized here clearly indicates that basic features of historic northern Northwest Coast culture were present in Prince Rupert Harbor by 1050–50 B.C. (3000–2000 years B.P.), if not somewhat earlier. These features include multihouse plank-house villages, reliance on stored salmon supplemented by a diverse array of other fresh and stored food resources, seasonal movement away from the principal residence, social stratification and slavery, households with extended time depth, warfare, and Northwest Coast art. Changes after 50 B.C. (2000 years B.P.) including cessation of midden burial, residential instability, and settlement-pattern shifts, suggest the presence of important regional events that are not fully understood.

Kenneth M. Ames

Further Readings

Cybulski, J. 1990. Human Biology. In *Northwest Coast*, edited by W. Suttles, pp. 52–59. Handbook of North American Indians, vol. 7, W.C. Sturtevant, general editor. Smithsonian Institution, Washington, D.C.

MacDonald, G.F., and R.I. Inglis. 1981. An Overview of the North Coast Prehistory Project (1966–1980). *BC Studies* 48:37–63.

Pryor Stemmed-Lovell Constricted

Pryor Stemmed and Lovell Constricted are two Late Paleoindian (ca. 6350–5850 B.C., or 8300–7800 years B.P.) projectile-point types known from foothill and mountain locations in Wyoming and southwestern Montana. Both were defined from specimens recovered during excavation of rock shelters in Bighorn Canyon in northern Wyoming and in adjacent Montana (Husted 1969). Pryor Stemmed points usually have a stem with a weakly concave base; shoulders vary from prominent to a simple angle between the stem and blade edges. The type is characterized by alternate beveling of the blade edges (Husted 1969:Figure 23; Frison 1992:Figure 2.35). Lovell Constricted points are lanceolate with a constriction of the lateral edges near the proximal end; blade edges may expand weakly or flare sharply above the constriction (Husted 1969:Figures 9, 20).

Pryor Stemmed is the better known of the two. A cultural complex representing small groups with a strong gathering orientation has been defined for the type (Frison and Grey 1980). The complex appears to be concentrated in the Bighorn and Pryor mountain area, but Pryor Stemmed points or something very similar have been found in the Pathfinder and Seminoe reservoir areas in south-central Wyoming and the Hartville Uplift near Guernsey in the southeastern part of the state (Davis 1991). Lovell Constricted is less well known but appears to have a more westerly distribution in the Absaroka Range on the west side of the Big Horn Basin and the Beartooth Mountains immediately to the north. Lovell Constricted points were recovered from strata immediately beneath deposits containing Pryor Stemmed points at two sites in Bighorn Canyon. However, vertical separation was minimal, and radiocarbon dates for the two overlap (Frison 1992:Tables 2.3, 2.5 and 2.10). Little, if any, time separates the two types, which suggests

Lovell Constricted (left) and Pryor Stemmed (right) points. These are type specimens from the Sorenson site, Wyoming. (Adapted by W. M. Husted from Husted 1969, figures 9 and 10)

contemporaneous or nearly coeval groups occupying adjacent territories. W.M. Husted (1969:83) postulated a mountain-adapted culture distinct from the Plains Paleoindian and suggested that the early Bighorn Canyon components, including Pryor Stemmed and Lovell Constricted, were related to this mountain-oriented manifestation. G.C. Frison (1992:71, 74) includes Pryor Stemmed and Lovell Constricted in a foothill-mountain Paleoindian category distinct from the Plains Paleoindian.

The origin and the fate of the two point types remain problematic. The most likely source appears to be earlier foothill-mountain Paleoindian complexes in the northern Wyoming–southern Montana area. Large side-notched projectile points truncate a continuum of lanceolate projectiles ending with Lovell Constricted points at stratified sites in the Absaroka Range. Whether the abrupt change represents a simple linear development or an ingress of unrelated people is conjectural. Whatever the answers, Pryor Stemmed and Lovell Constricted represent a phase or phases of an Archaic way of life that was to continue for another 6,000 years in the western Plains–Rocky Mountain area until ca. A.D. 450 (1500 years B.P.).

Wilfred M. Husted

Further Readings

Davis, D.P. 1991. Pryor Stemmed Tools: Twisted Technology on the High Plains. *Wyoming Archaeologist* 34(1–2):1–13.

Frison, G.C. 1973. Early Period Marginal Groups in Northern Wyoming. *Plains*

Anthropologist 18(62):300–312.

———. 1992. *Prehistoric Hunters of the High Plains.* Academic Press, San Diego.

Frison, G.C., and D.C. Grey. 1980. Pryor Stemmed: A Specialized Paleo-Indian Ecological Adaptation. *Plains Anthropologist* 25(87):27–46.

Husted, W.M. 1969. *Bighorn Canyon Archeology.* Publications in Salvage Archeology no. 12. River Basin Surveys. Smithsonian Institution, Lincoln.

Pueblo

Pueblo is a Spanish word for village. Native Americans in New Mexico and Arizona who traditionally lived in apartment-style dwellings

are known as the Pueblo people. In archaeology, pueblo has come to mean the architecture associated with these people and their ancestors, who are known as the Mogollon and the Anasazi. It is this last use of the term "pueblo" that is addressed here, with an emphasis on Anasazi pueblos.

A pueblo is a substantial, above-ground structure that includes living quarters. Most pueblos have contiguous rectangular rooms, and some have hundreds of rooms and multiple stories. Many early pueblos were made primarily of jacal (sticks and mud or adobe), while later pueblos were more often made of masonry and/or adobe, although construction varied across time and space. Classic Chacoan pueblos had elaborate patterned masonry, with stone

Cliff Palace, a cliff dwelling at Mesa Verde in southwest Colorado. This thirteenth-century pueblo contained approximately 220 rooms and 23 kivas. The illustration of the intact and partially reconstructed structure shows rectangular multi-story surface rooms, round kivas supported by retaining walls, and a square tower. (Drawing by Regan Giese; courtesy of M. Hegmon)

veneers and rows of small and large blocks. Later pueblos in both Chaco Canyon and southwest Colorado were made of substantial, though less elaborate, blocky masonry. Classic Mimbres pueblos were made of cobbles held together with adobe, although later pueblos in the Mimbres area, in southwest New Mexico, were made almost entirely of adobe.

Before pueblos, people lived primarily in subterranean pit structures. The development of pueblos in many, though not all, parts of the northern Southwest occurred in the period A.D. 750–900 (1200–1050 B.P.), when people began building rows of jacal surface rooms with pit structures in front. This change, a milestone in Southwestern prehistory, is known as the pithouse-to-pueblo transition. With pueblo architecture, people could make bigger, more complex, and more specialized structures. They could add on rooms as necessary and mark out what appear to be private spaces, such as storage rooms attached to habitation rooms. By this time, most people were probably living in their pueblo sites year-round, possibly using the surface rooms more in summer and the pit structures more in the winter. Although many pueblo sites are small, the first aggregated villages, which probably housed hundreds of people, appeared by the ninth century A.D.

Before A.D. 1300 (650 years B.P.), most pueblo architecture in the Southwest, both large and small, was based on a unit—sometimes called a unit pueblo or Prudden unit—that consisted of six–eight surface rooms, a pit structure, and sometimes a trash midden (Chacoan and Mogollon sites are exceptions). This oft-repeated architectural unit appears to have been associated with a fundamental social unit in prehistoric pueblo life. This unit consisted of perhaps several households that lived in the surface rooms and shared the pit structure or perhaps an extended household that shared the whole suite. These pueblo sites were occupied for fairly short periods of time, generally 10–50 years.

Ca. A.D. 1300 (ca. 650 years B.P.), people abandoned much of the northern Southwest and moved south, many settling in large pueblos along the Little Colorado River and the Rio Grande. These pueblos lack unit-type architecture. They appear instead to have been organized around a few large kivas or plazas that may have been shared by many members of the community. This new form of organization may have provided more social stability, because

many of these large pueblos were occupied for longer periods than were earlier pueblos. Modern Pueblo people can trace their ancestry back to some of these large pueblos.

Michelle Hegmon

Further Readings

Gilman, P.A. 1987. Architecture As Artifact: Pit Structures and Pueblos in the American Southwest. *American Antiquity* 52:538–564.

Hill, J.N. 1970. *Broken K Pueblo: Prehistoric Social Organization in the American Southwest.* Anthropological Papers no. 18. University of Arizona Press, Tucson.

Lekson, S. 1986. *Great Pueblo Architecture of Chaco Canyon, New Mexico.* Reprinted, University of New Mexico Press, Albuquerque. Originally published 1984, Publications in Archaeology no. 18B, National Park Service, Albuquerque.

Mindeleff, V. 1989. A Study of Pueblo Architecture, Tusayan and Cibola. Reprinted, Smithsonian Institution Press, Washington, D.C. Originally published 1891, in the *Eighth Annual Report of the Bureau of Ethnology to the Secretary of the Smithsonian Institution, 1886–1887,* pp. 13–228. GPO, Washington, D.C.

Plog, F.T. 1974. *The Study of Prehistoric Change.* Academic Press, New York.

Prudden, T.M. 1903. The Prehistoric Ruins of the San Juan Watershed in Utah, Arizona, Colorado, and New Mexico. *American Anthropologist* 5(2):224–288.

Pueblo Bonito

The largest building in Chaco Canyon in northwestern New Mexico and probably the largest building in North America at the time that it was occupied, Pueblo Bonito (LA226) covers almost 0.8 ha (2 acres), stood four stories high in some sections, and contained an estimated 695 rooms, 33 kivas, and three great kivas. The immense D-shaped structure was built in a series of construction stages between the early A.D. 900s and at least the late A.D. 1000s (1050–850 years B.P.). In addition to the visible portions of the pueblo, there is a buried complex of foundations and partly completed and razed walls extending from the eastern side of Pueblo Bonito to the east/southeast for at least 150 m (164 yards). Built in the A.D. 1070s, this "foundation complex" appears to represent two or more

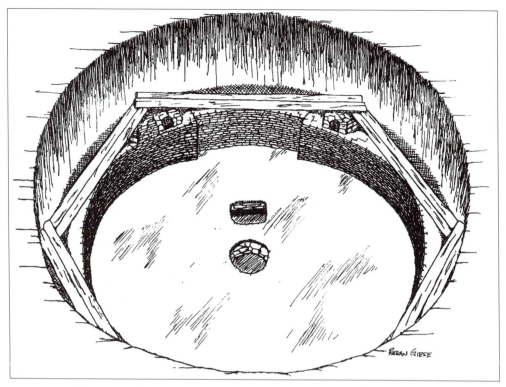

Kiva L at Pueblo Bonito in Chaco Canyon, built in the mid-eleventh century A.D. *Illustration shows the central fire pit, the opening of a sub-floor ventilator behind the fire pit, masonry walls, a bench with pilasters and beams from a cribbed roof. (Drawing by Regan Giese, after Judd 1922: Plate 60; courtesy of R. Giese)*

large additions to the structure that were planned and begun but abandoned before the additions could be finished. If completed, these additions might have doubled the size of the structure. Various excavation projects within the pueblo and outside the curving back wall have revealed the presence of an earlier structure beneath the oldest portions of the current structure.

Two large rectangular mounds stand ca. 15 m (49 feet) south of the long, straight front wall of the pueblo. Both are surrounded by masonry walls more than 2 m (6.6 feet) high. The rubble, trash, and sand fill of both masonry enclosures shows clear stratigraphic breaks at the level of the wall tops. Considerable deposition of trash and construction debris had taken place prior to the construction of the masonry enclosures, probably during the last quarter of the twelfth century, and deposition continued after the construction of the enclosures. The mounds appear to have been covered with a level prepared surface, however, at the time that the enclosures were built.

The load-bearing walls of Pueblo Bonito are massive and were usually built in the core-and-veneer technique, in which a masonry or rubble core is faced on both sides with well-coursed and shaped facing stones. The "built to last" quality of Pueblo Bonito and the other canyon great houses is evident from the fact that many rooms in these structures were standing, roofed, and habitable 700 years after the site was abandoned in the late A.D. 1100s. Labor investment in Pueblo Bonito was considerable but not beyond the capabilities of a society at a relatively simple level of organization. Probably the most "expensive" aspect of Pueblo Bonito was the relatively lavish use of wood, a very costly-to-acquire building material in the treeless San Juan Basin.

Excavations in Pueblo Bonito in the early twentieth century yielded large numbers of items of material wealth. Hundreds of whole ceramic vessels were found cached in store-rooms and entombed with burials. Large numbers of turquoise and shell items were recovered, and normally perishable items, such as cotton textiles and baskets, were found preserved by the protective mass of the building. Because these excavations were carried out prior to the development of modern excavation standards, however, archaeologists have been unable to determine from existing records how many families lived in Pueblo Bonito at any one time or what functions, other than domestic ones, the building may have had.

Lynne Sebastian

Further Readings

Judd, N.M. 1925. Archaeological Investigations at Pueblo Bonito, New Mexico. *Smithsonian Miscellaneous Collections* 77(2):83–91.

———. 1954. *The Material Culture of Pueblo Bonito*. Miscellaneous Collections, vol. 138, no. 1. Smithsonian Institution, Washington, D.C.

———. 1964. *The Architecture of Pueblo Bonito*. Miscellaneous Collections, vol. 147, no. 1. Smithsonian Institution, Washington, D.C.

Lekson, S.H. 1984. *Great Pueblo Architecture of Chaco Canyon, New Mexico*. University of New Mexico Press, Albuquerque.

Pepper, G.H. 1905. Ceremonial Objects and Ornaments From Pueblo Bonito, New Mexico. *American Anthropologist* 7:183–197.

———. 1909. The Exploration of a Burial Room in Pueblo Bonito, New Mexico. In *Putnam Anniversary Volume: Anthropological Essays Presented to Frederick Ward Putnam in Honor of His Seventieth Birthday*, edited by F. Boas, pp. 196–252. Strechert, New York.

———. 1920. *Pueblo Bonito*. Anthropological Papers, vol. 27. American Museum of Natural History, New York.

Puget Lowland Sequence

Twelve thousand years ago, the Puget lowland lay under glacial ice. The bays, inlets, sand spits, ash falls, mudflows, and extensive deltas and floodplains encompassing the modern lowland landscape are the result of the interaction of postglacial erosional and depositional processes. The very constancy of these processes influenced and defined human cultures in the region. The material resources developed for use by humans may have been selected for their adaptability to this perpetually changing topography. The local impacts of these processes have complicated the location and interpretation of the archaeology in the area.

After melting glacial waters inundated the Puget lowland, tundra grasses and shrubs invaded the bare land. Many areas were swampy, and peat formed in low-lying places. Mammoth, mastodon, bison, elk, caribou, and humans entered the area as soon as the ice melted (by ca. 9050 B.C., or 11,000 years B.P.). Signs of a human presence come from glacial outwash uplands and from lakeshores formed by lateral and terminal moraines in the foothills of the Cascade and Olympic mountains. These signs are a few Clovis points and other tools of flaked stone and shaped bone associated with the hunting of extinct megafauna.

By 6050 B.C. (8000 years B.P.), most of the large elephants had become extinct, and the regional vegetation was changing to mixed forest and prairie, with the forests containing both deciduous and evergreen species. Puget Sound diminished to a series of channels. Due to erosional processes since ca. 4050 B.C. (6000 years B.P.), evidence for human presence along Puget Sound shores remains scarce. However, a number of sites along lakes in the interior uplands and mountain ranges indicate that people were increasing in numbers and initiating development of local terrestrial resources, such as camas. Flaked-stone tools found in the Cascade foothills readily fit tool sequences developed for the Columbia Plateau of eastern Washington State. Cultural similarities between these areas may reflect both interaction and comparable environments.

Between 4050 and 550 B.C. (6000–2500 years B.P.), the landscape changed from a predominantly terrestrial lowland to an inland sea with shoreline elevations 12.2 m (40 feet) or more above present ones. As the brackish interior channels again became Puget Sound, changes in landforms were accompanied by a cultural shift from terrestrial to marine resources. Tectonic events resulting in local faulting, ash falls, and mudflows occurred frequently.

Salmon and shellfish became available wherever the topography was favorable. Shoreline sites can be identified from shell deposits. The northwest forests of cedar, hemlock, and fir were established. Cedar became the primary material for artifact manufacture; salmon, the major food resource. The major salmon-procurement technique after 1050 B.C. (3000 years B.P.) involved the use of intertidal and stream-channel nets and traps made of cedar. Evidence for these resources is extensive. The shells of bivalves and univalves were used as foundation and drainage material in the construction of large cedar houses. The shell middens formed excellent environments for preservation of faunal remains. Shoreline sites often were associated with overbank deposits in anaerobic environments, presenting a wealth of otherwise perishable plant remains and woven and carved items.

Finely crafted adzes and celts of stone and splitting wedges of antler were developed for woodworking. These tools were used to manufacture planks, poles, and seagoing vessels. The ground-stone technique extended to the manufacture of slate knives and projectile points. Distinct local styles of flaked-stone tools appear only in the San Juan Islands and the Cascade foothills. Stone-tool sequences for the region often refer to relationships to the north and the Columbia Plateau, possibly indicating extensive contact with those regions.

Sea levels stabilized to current elevations ca. A.D. 750 (1200 years B.P.). With this came the fully developed lowland culture that was to last until non-Indian settlement of the Northwest. That culture was tied to management of resources developed since glacial times: salmon, shellfish, cedar, and camas. A population with a density comparable to, or even greater than, that in other temperate regions of the world utilized this network of resources. Salmon management extended from shoreline traps to mountain spawning streams. Shellfish beds were owned, tended, and reseeded. Shellfish were a major trade item across the Cascade Range. Trunk wood, roots, or bark of the cedar tree were used in the construction of all housing, water transport, and fish traps, as well as in the manufacture of baskets and boxes, clothing and utensils, ceremonial objects, and works of art. Harvesting of local plants continued, and ownership of fields was assigned. Forests were selectively burned to maintain open areas for camas, berries, and other plants, as well as browse for deer and elk. Hunting of land and sea mammals continued as before.

In the A.D. 1600s, new products were introduced in increasing quantity, but there was little face-to-face contact between lowland Indians and non-Indian peoples until the late 1700s.

The strongest impact resulted from the British and U.S. fur trade in the early 1800s. A variety of items, including metal, cloth, and firearms, were traded for furs. Sea otter, beaver, ermine, and seal were all hunted for their skins in such quantities that the animals became extinct in some locations.

From the earliest contacts, the Indians were exposed to European diseases that resulted in heavy population losses that severely affected the conduct of the Indian way of life. The greatest changes came after treaties in the 1850s, when settlers entered the Northwest. Most tribes were relocated away from traditional areas and grouped together on reservations. While the changes were devastating, a cultural core of traditional Indian beliefs and practices has persisted. A continuously expanding picture of the cultural base for the region may be developed by observing that continuity in a modern context. The continuity reflects the nature of the Puget lowland cultural base, which is a product of the interplay between a changing landscape and ever-changing situations and viewpoints.

Astrida R. Blukis Onat

Further Readings

Blukis Onat, A.R. (editor). 1992. *Development of Complex Maritime Societies on the Pacific: West Coast of North America*. Simon Fraser University Press, Burnaby.

Borden, C.E. 1975. *Origins and Development of Early Northwest Coast Culture to About 3000 B.C.* Mercury Series Paper no. 45. Archaeological Survey of Canada, National Museum of Man, Ottawa.

Kirk, R., with R.D. Daugherty. 1978. *Exploring Washington Archaeology*. University of Washington Press, Seattle.

Punuk Culture

The Punuk-culture phase, known primarily from sites on St. Lawrence Island, Alaska, dates between the sixth and fourteenth centuries A.D. As a cultural phase, it overlaps Birnirk and is a continuance of the maritime adaptation established during the Old Bering Sea/Okvik culture complex (ca. 50 B.C.–A.D. 700, or 2000–1250 years B.P.). Punuk sites are frequently found next to or overlying earlier Old Bering Sea/Okvik sites, but they are considerably larger in area and more numerous. Large mounds created by repeated house-building episodes can be noted for some distance offshore and indicate larger population aggregates than earlier. Massive amounts of whalebone are present in these sites, indicating that the Punuk Eskimo had perfected the technology for whale hunting and developed the necessary social structure for its implementation.

Harpoon heads for seal, walrus, and whale hunting are the most temporally diagnostic items in the cultural assemblage. These feature an offset line hole and asymmetric spur to cause the harpoon head to turn perpendicular to the entry wound and thus more effectively secure an animal diving under ice floes. The harpoon heads were secured to foreshafts by open or closed sockets, and end-blade slots rather than side-blade slots held ground-stone blades. Decoration was by deep incision (probably using metal tools) and consisted of Y figures, spurred lines, crossbars, and dot and circle-dot motifs. The circle-dot motif created the impression of eyes and, in this regard, carried forward the animal art style of the Old Bering Sea/Okvik phase. The incisions were filled in with red pigment.

Other aspects of the maritime assemblage include sealing darts with throwing boards, throwing and thrusting harpoons, and chipped- and ground-stone lances; floats, paddles, and two kinds of boat (the single-person *kayak* and the multiple-person *umiak*); multipronged bird spears cast with a throwing board; bolas and fishing equipment. The small boat sledge with ivory runners used to move the umiak over ice floes is the only sledge type noted. There is evidence for baleen toboggans, but these do not appear to be very large and may have been used to transport meat. Dogs were present, but there is no evidence for the use of dog traction; dog sledges do not appear until Late Prehistoric times (ca. 1500 to European contact in the eighteenth century A.D., or 550–200 years B.P.).

Land hunting was also important, for there were reinforced bows with sinew or cable backing, wrist guards, and a variety of antler or bone arrow-point forms: blunts for birds and small mammals, and single or multiple barbed for larger game.

Domestic tools included sand-tempered, largely undecorated pottery in a variety of vessel forms; ground-stone knife blades (women's and men's forms) fitted into handles of wood or ivory; scrapers and adze blades fitted into antler or bone sleeves; bone and stone drills and bone or ivory needles and needle cases that were often highly decorated; bag handles, wooden trays, and spoons of bone or ivory. Decorative items in the cultural inventory included combs, belt fasteners, pendants, buttons, brow bands, and ivory chains. Toys included kayaks made of ivory or wood, small wooden bows and arrows, ivory or bone-bird figures, sledges, tops, and dolls.

House forms in the early part of the Punuk phase (A.D. 850–1200, or 1100–750 years B.P.) were similar to the semisubterranean Old Bering Sea/Okvik (ca. 50 B.C.–A.D. 700, or 2000–1250 years B.P.) type. Foundations were formed by horizontally laid logs with corner post support. The upper part of the structure was a crib-work construction covered with sod. In late Punuk, boulders, walrus and whale skulls, and whale vertebrae made up the walls. Whale ribs served as vertical support posts.

Plate armor of long narrow strips of bone with lashing holes to tie the bone plates together over a hide garment makes its first appearance during the Punuk phase. Large multibarbed arrows, labeled "war arrows" by the Eskimo of St. Lawrence Island, also appear for the first time. The presence of armor with a developed archery complex (cable-backed bow, wrist guards, new arrowhead types) and evidence for larger population aggregates suggest that competition for resources, trade routes, or prized village locations may have resulted in armed conflict. Societal forms were undoubtedly more complex, with a warrior class or status in addition to the status accruing to those who were boat captains or members of whaling crews.

The Punuk phase on St. Lawrence Island continued into the Late Prehistoric era, where it is marked as well with an emphasis on whale and walrus hunting. On the Siberian and Alaskan mainland, Punuk merged with the Thule culture, which had developed out of a Birnirk base. Like Punuk, Thule emphasized the hunting of whales.

Robert E. Ackerman

Further Readings

Ackerman, R.E. 1984. Prehistory of the Asian Eskimo Zone. In *Arctic*, edited by D. Damas, pp. 106–118. Handbook of North American Indians, vol. 5, W.C. Sturtevant, general editor. Smithsonian Institution, Washington, D.C.

Collins, H.B. 1937. *The Archeology of St. Lawrence Island.* Miscellaneous Collections, vol. 96, no. 1. Smithsonian Institution, Washington, D.C.

See also Birnirk Culture; Birnirk Phase; Old Bering Sea/Okvik Culture; Thule Culture

Purgatoire Phase

The concept "Purgatoire phase" developed from archaeological research on the Apishapa phase conducted in a restricted military reservation in southeastern Colorado at the Pinon Canyon Maneuver site. Archaeological investigations of the 98,420-ha (380-square-mile) army mechanized training facility located on the west side of the Purgatoire River in Las Animas County recorded ca. 2,300 sites, of which 270 contain Middle Ceramic components defined by the presence of vertical stone-slab architecture and projectile points; 90 of these sites were assigned to the Apishapa phase (Andrefsky 1990). Analysis of "Apishapa" sites (Purgatoire phase) in the Pinon Canyon region of the Purgatoire River presents interesting differences in site setting, architecture, and artifact-assemblage composition compared to Apishapa sites in the Apishapa Canyon on the Arkansas River, farther north on Turkey Creek, and along the east and west sides of the Purgatoire River itself. Pinon Canyon sites consist of only one fortified village and two defensible aggregates; most of the other sites are unfortified enclosures on the mid-reaches of tributary arroyos to the Purgatoire River. Chaquaqua Plateau Apishapa sites are generally located on high defensible positions, with the majority of unfortified enclosure sites located in the vicinity of fortified sites. Apishapa Canyon sites tend to occur on high overlooks, but only one site is fortified; other sites occur on upper terraces or at the base of the canyon. Apishapa sites along the Arkansas River occur on bluffs overlooking the valley.

Pinon Canyon architecture is similar to that of sites on the Chaquaqua Plateau, although the plateau sites lack definable entranceways and rarely have central hearths. The Pinon Canyon sites also lack the stone roof supports found at Apishapa sites in the Apishapa Canyon. Arkansas River sites also incorporated pithouses with stone-slab linings and earthlodges with juniper posts and horizontal stone but no vertical stone slabs.

Tool assemblages also vary, with the northern Apishapa Canyon and Turkey Creek assemblages dominated by side-notched projectile points and cord-marked pottery. Pinon Canyon sites lack ceramics and are dominated by corner-notched projectile points. Although rare, ceramics do occur on the Chaquaqua Plateau, but corner-notched projectile points dominate the assemblage. There is a strong correlation between side-notched points and the presence of ceramics on stone-slab architectural sites assigned to the Apishapa phase, while Purgatoire-phase sites of the Pinon Canyon Maneuver site and the Chaquaqua Plateau generally lack cord-marked ceramics and contain corner-notched points.

The dated sites for the Purgatoire phase in the Pinon Canyon area generally cluster around A.D. 1000 (950 years B.P.). There are also significant differences between the Purgatoire-phase and Antelope Creek sites, with Pinon Canyon sites lacking the bone horticultural tool complex, ceramics, side-notched points, and trade items associated with Antelope Creek–phase sites.

Steven L. De Vore

Further Readings

Andrefsky, W., Jr. (editor). 1990. *Introduction to the Archaeology of Pinon Canyon, Southeastern Colorado.* 5 vols. Larson-Tibesar Associates, Laramie. Report (Contract no. CX 1200-7-8054) submitted to the National Park Service, Washington, D.C.

Chomko, S.A., S.L. De Vore, and L.L. Loendorf. 1990. Apishapa Phase Research at the Pinon Canyon Maneuver Site, Southeastern Colorado. Ms. on file, National Park Service, Denver.

See also Antelope Creek Phase; Apishapa Phase

Putnam, Frederick Ward (1839–1915)

An ichthyologist by training, Frederick Ward Putnam became interested in the Mound Builder problem, testing mounds in central Indiana as early as 1871–1872. Upon becoming curator of Harvard University's Peabody Museum of American Archaeology and Ethnology (1875–1909), he focused his interests on archaeology and general anthropology, excavating at the Madisonville cemetery, the Turner, Marriott, and Harness mounds, and at the Great Serpent mound (Putnam 1890), among others, in the Ohio Valley. He also conducted extensive excavations in the Nashville Basin in

Frederick W. Putnam. (Courtesy of the National Anthropological Archives, Smithsonian Institution, Photograph No. 64–D)

Tennessee (Putnam 1878) and analyzed and published collections from southern California and the New Mexico pueblos obtained by the Wheeler Geographical Expedition. He sponsored and encouraged other mound excavations in Ohio, Illinois, Wisconsin, Michigan, and other eastern states as well as "paleolithic" research, including Charles C. Abbott's explorations of the Trenton gravel deposits, for he was intent on proving the great antiquity of early man in the New World. He was one of the first to encourage the preservation of major prehistoric monuments, helping raise funds for the purchase and restoration of the Great Serpent mound in Ohio.

Putnam has been called the "professionalizer of American archaeology" for his contributions as an administrator, educator, excavator, and founding father of several North American museums and departments of anthropology. As Peabody Professor of American Archaeology and Ethnology at Harvard (1887–1909), the first such university teaching position in the United States, he began the training of a generation of professional archaeologists in surveying and mapping, digging, recording stratigraphic cross sections, and the careful plotting and recording of finds. (The first doctorate in prehistoric archaeology in the United States was granted at Harvard in 1894.) Besides guiding the Peabody Museum to prominence as one of the leading anthropology institutions in the United States, he was secretary of the American Association for the Advancement of Science for 25 years; he helped found the Field Museum of Natural History in Chicago, the Anthropology Department of the American Museum of Natural History in New York, and the Department of Anthropology at the University of California, Berkeley; and he was in charge of the anthropology building and exhibit at the 1892 Exposition in Chicago.

Guy Gibbon

Further Readings

Mark, J. 1980. *Four Anthropologists: An American Science in Its Early Years.* Science History, New York.

Putnam, F.W. 1878. Archaeological Explorations in Tennessee. *Reports of the Peabody Museum of American Archaeology and Ethnology* 2(2):305–360.

———. 1886. *On Methods of Archaeological Research in America.* Circular no. 5 (49, 89). Johns Hopkins University Press, Baltimore.

———. 1890. The Serpent Mound of Ohio. *Century Illustrated Magazine* 39:871–888.

Willey, G.R., and J.A. Sabloff. 1976. *A History of American Archaeology.* 2nd ed. W.H. Freeman, San Francisco.

See also ABBOTT, CHARLES C.

Q

Quartz Crystals (California)

Natural quartz crystals were utilized in certain prehistoric California cultures for ritual purposes. The best-documented use occurs in the central California Delta during the Early Horizon (4550–550 B.C., or 6500–2500 years B.P.) (Beardsley 1954) or Windmiller culture (Ragir 1972). There, quartz crystals were commonly placed with burials as grave offerings, often in association with charmstones, bird-bone whistles, and other ritual objects. D.D. Fredrickson tentatively associates them with "shaman's kits" (Fredrickson 1973). M.J. Moratto (1984:206) notes that quartz crystals occur naturally in the Sierra Nevada foothills and suggests that Windmiller people may have spent summers in the Sierras and winters in the Central Valley lowlands, which would have provided them with ready access to supplies of crystals. B.A. Gerow (1968:109–110) notes that Bay sites contemporary with Windmiller, such as CASMa77, show relatively few quartz crystals or other Sierran materials with burials, even though the cultures were generally similar. This difference may simply reflect the greater distance of the Bay from the Sierran foothills. Windmiller-period sites in the Sierras have yielded burials with quartz crystals in association, such as in the ossuaries at Winslow Cave and Pinnacle Peak Cave. Later periods throughout the region show discontinuation of the use of quartz crystals with grave offerings. Another region shows a still different use of quartz crystals. Newberry Cave, excavated by G.A. Smith (Smith et al. 1957), had an Amargosa-period (2050 B.C.–A.D. 450, or 4000–1500 years B.P.) component that featured a number of ritual artifacts including quartz crystals, but no burials were involved. Smith suggested that the crystals were associated with hunting magic.

Joseph L. Chartkoff

Further Readings

Beardsley, R.K. 1954. *Temporal and Areal Relationships in Central California Archaeology.* Archaeological Survey Reports, vols. 24–25, pts. 1–2. University of California, Berkeley.

Fredrickson, D.D. 1973. *Early Cultures of the North Coast Ranges, California.* Unpublished Ph.D. dissertation, Department of Anthropology, University of California, Berkeley.

Gerow, B.A. 1968. *An Analysis of the University Village Complex With a Reappraisal of Central California Archaeology.* Stanford University Press, Stanford.

Moratto, M.J. (editor). 1984. *California Archaeology.* Academic Press, New York.

Ragir, S.R. 1972. *The Early Horizon in Central California Prehistory.* Contributions no. 15. Archaeological Research Facility, Department of Anthropology, University of California, Berkeley.

Smith, G.A., W.C. Schuiling, L. Martin, R. Sayles, and P. Jillson. 1957. *The Archaeology of Newberry Cave, San Bernardino County, California.* San Bernardino County Museum Association, San Bernardino.

Quebec's Subarctic Region

Quebec's Subarctic region extends from 56° to 49° north latitude and encompasses the southern half of the Hudson Bay drainage basin, the James Bay drainage basin, and nearly all of the Laurentidian Plateau and the north shore of the

St. Lawrence River, as well as the southern half of Labrador. Covering an area of 1,300 x 800 km (806 x 496 miles), it constitutes more than half the total area of the province. Its vegetation is dominated by black spruce, which decreases in density from south to north. At the southern border, fir tends to replace spruce, while forest tundra begins at the region's northern limit.

During the Late Wisconsin stage of the Quaternary, the melting of the Laurentide ice sheet occurred at different times in the subregions. In the eastern part, the shores of the St. Lawrence and the Labrador coast were free of ice ca. 9050 B.C. (11,000 years B.P.), while in the western part the coast of Hudson Bay emerged ca. 5550 B.C. (7500 years B.P.). The ice sheet totally disappeared from the landscape in the north-central part of the region ca. 3550 B.C. (5500 years B.P.). As far as postglacial sea levels are concerned, the maximum levels registered on the eastern (Goldthwait Sea) and western (Tyrrell Sea) coasts reached 135 m (443 feet) and 250 m (820 feet), respectively. Floral and faunal life spread rapidly as the land became gradually free of ice and water. It seems likely that humans could have been present as early as 7550 B.C. (9500 years B.P.) on the east coast, by 4550 B.C. (6500 years B.P.) on the western shore and in the south-central part of the Subarctic, and by 3050 B.C. (5000 years B.P.) in the north-central part of the region. Only about 20 percent of the Subarctic area has benefited from some form of archaeological research: the coastal areas in the east, the basins of some rivers in the west (in response to hydroelectric development), and the banks of three major interior lakes.

The earliest remains, found on the continental side of the Strait of Belle Isle (Quebec and Labrador), have been dated to 6850 B.C. (8800 years B.P.). They can be compared to Early Archaic assemblages, though some researchers believe they could date to the Late Paleoindian period. These hunters came from southern coastal areas and not from the interior via the St. Lawrence River. Living in what is known to have been the warmest phase since the end of the glaciation, this new population produced tools adapted to the exploitation of both marine and land animals. These assemblages have been coined "Maritime Archaic" and extended in time until 2050 B.C. (4000 years B.P.). Artifacts of this period have been identified in sites along the north shore of the St. Lawrence and the Labrador coast. Ca. 4050 B.C. (6000 years B.P.),

some Maritime Archaic groups progressed inland less than 300 km (186 miles) to hunt migrating caribou that were grazing around the large interior lakes. At that time, the climate was cooler than during the preceding phase but still warmer than today; it remained so until ca. 1050 B.C. (3000 years B.P.). After 2050 B.C. (4000 years B.P.), some people migrated from the east toward the north-central and the northwestern parts of the Subarctic region. Indeed, the oldest remains found in the Caniapiscau Lake area in the northern James Bay and Hudson Bay drainage basins date to 1550–1250 B.C. (3500–3200 years B.P.); some of the tools of this period are related to ones associated with the Maritime Archaic.

In the southwestern part of the Subarctic near the Abitibi-Témiscaminge area, the St. Maurice River, and the Lake St. John drainage basins, it seems probable that early sites (4050–3050 B.C., or 6000–5000 years B.P.) will be found in the near future, since remains of Laurentian Archaic affinity have been collected in these areas. Some remains located in the Lake Mistassini area could date to this period, too.

All of the Subarctic region was inhabited by 1050 B.C. (3000 years B.P.): Paleoeskimos occupied the coastal areas of Hudson Bay (since 1750 B.C., or 3700 years B.P.) and northern Labrador (since 1850 B.C., or 3800 years B.P.), while Indian groups lived inland and in the coastal areas of the St. Lawrence River and James Bay. After 550 B.C. (2500 years B.P.), regional differences become more perceptible, and the number of sites increases. The groups of that period seem to have developed territorial and technological particularities and to have formed exchange relations with other groups to obtain certain goods such as stone, especially Mistassini quartzite and Ramah chert, for lithic toolmaking. In the southern part of the Subarctic, Early to Late Woodland artifacts indicate some relationship with the Laurentian area and the Northeast. Indeed, certain pottery sherds excavated from these sites are made of local clay, demonstrating that the artisans had an intimate knowledge of the area.

The size of local Indian groups depended upon the availability of animal resources. Over the years, caribou seems to have been the major animal resource, and human groups adapted to its natural fluctuations. When caribou were numerous, human families tended to form large groups (40–50 persons) that stayed together most of the year. During periods when caribou were scarce, human families formed small groups (less than 20 persons) and moved around more often so as to exploit sedentary animals, such as beaver, hare, and porcupine. Fish have always been considered a main staple, too.

Inuit groups occupied the shores of Hudson Bay and Labrador during the first centuries of their arrival in the eastern Arctic. Pre-Dorset or Independence sites have been found in the area of Kuujjuaraapik (Great Whale River on the eastern coast of Hudson Bay) and Thalia Point (on the coast of northern Labrador). Dorset and Thule sites are more numerous and indicate a continuous presence since 850 B.C. (2800 years B.P.). Some Dorset remains have also been located on inland lakes in the northernmost part of the area.

Contact with Europeans occurred at different times in different areas. In the first half of the sixteenth century, local groups (Montagnais Indians) living on the eastern coast met Jacques Cartier and Basque fishermen. On the western coast, Cree Indians met Henry Hudson in 1611 in the southern part of James Bay. During the seventeenth century, the influence of fur trading was significant only for those Subarctic groups in contact with southerly Indian groups directly involved in the trade. During the eighteenth century, all inland groups began to participate, to different degrees, in the fur trade and, consequently, modified their traditional technology. The Inuit began trading mainly during the nineteenth century. The influence of fur trading on the social organization of these groups was most prominent during the nineteenth and twentieth centuries.

Daniel Chevrier

See also DORSET CULTURE; MARITIME ARCHAIC TRADITION; THULE CULTURE

Queen Charlotte Strait Sequence

Queen Charlotte Strait lies between the northern portion of Vancouver Island and the mainland in the central part of the British Columbia coast. Its eastern end is an extensive archipelago with fjords and channels running deep into the coast mountains and south toward the Strait of Georgia. At contact, this was the home of the Kwakwaka'wakw (Southern Kwakiutl). Aspects of their late nineteenth–early twentieth century culture were exhaustively recorded by George Hunt and reported by Franz Boas (1909, 1921), but compara-tively little is known about the precontact occupation of Kwakwak'wakw territory. Excavations at three sites in the vicinity of Hardy Bay on Vancouver Island and at eight sites in the eastern islands indicate that at least three distinct culture types were present during the past 8,000 years. There may be a fourth, but it is known only from burial assemblages at one site and the latter part of a component at another site. These culture types are described below.

Old Cordilleran Culture Type. One component at the Bear Cove site in Hardy Bay, dating from ca. 6000 B.C. (7950 years B.P.), is of this widespread, early Pacific Northwest form. The assemblage includes well-made leaf-shaped flaked-stone points; crude unifacial pebble and primary flake tools, including many based on cortex spalls; and flaked-stone bifaces. Rockfish are the chief fish remains, with salmon a distant second. Dolphins and porpoise are especially prominent among the identified mammal bones.

Obsidian Culture Type. This culture type spans at least the 2800–500 B.C. (4750–2450 years B.P.) period and is known from four components (Echo Bay I, Hopetown I, and parts of O'Connor II and Bear Cove III). It is distinctive for an abundance of obsidian microflakes, most of which were produced by bipolar techniques. Other stone tools characteristically include leaf-shaped points, hammerstones, and irregularly shaped abraders. Ground-stone implements are rare. Bone artifacts include composite toggling harpoon valves, bipoints, single points, spatulates, and deer-ulna awls or knives. Shell from sea mussel (*Mytilus californianus*) was shaped to form knives and celts. There is a small fragment of a native copper object from Hopetown I formed of several pieces flattened and fused by hammering. Faunal data suggest a broad-based subsistence pattern without a dependence on any one resource. Land mammals, especially coast deer, were evidently more important than sea mammals, such as porpoise and harbor seal, but they do not dominate the total diet. Of the fish, salmon are most prominent, although they are generally less than 50 percent of the category. Herring, ratfish, dogfish, and rockfish remains are all present in significant numbers, but the first becomes insignificant if edible flesh is calculated. A wide range of birds was taken in similar magnitudes, including ducks, loons, gulls, eagles, and grebes. Among shellfish, butter clams, littleneck clams, horse clams, whelks, and barnacles were particularly notable.

Q

Queen Charlotte Strait Culture Type. Components of the most recent phase of precontact occupation, which dates from sometime after 500 B.C. (2450 years B.P.), are found at all 11 of the area's excavated sites. Flaked-stone artifacts are rare. More common are items in the ground- or pecked-and-ground-stone categories: celts, flat-topped hand mauls, hammerstones, stone discs, and both irregular and shaped abrasive stones. Especially prominent are artifacts of bone: unilaterally barbed nontoggling harpoon points, composite toggling harpoon valves (also made of antler), bipoints, single points, awls, deer-ulna awls, bark beaters, spindle whorls, and blanket or hair pins. Tools made from sea mussel include celts and knives. There are marked differences in major categories of faunal remains from the preceding culture type. The patterns for birds and shellfish are similar, but emphasis has shifted strongly from mammals to sea mammals, particularly harbor seal, sea lion, and porpoise. Salmon is the predominant fish.

The burial assemblages mentioned earlier, dating from ca. A.D. 350 (1600 years B.P.), and material from the upper levels of O'Connor II may represent a fourth form for the area or may simply be an earlier variant of the Queen Charlotte Strait culture type. Aspects of these assemblages resemble most closely the contemporaneous Marpole culture of the Strait of Georgia.

One interpretation of the differences between the Obsidian and Queen Charlotte Strait culture types is that they reflect replacement of an earlier Salishan way of life by the Wakashan culture that was present at contact. However, too little work has been done in this region to make definitive statements about its culture history.

Donald H. Mitchell

Further Readings

Boas, F. 1909. *The Kwakiutl of Vancouver Island.* Publications of the Jesup North Pacific Expedition, vol. 5, pt. 2. E.J. Brill, Leiden.

———. 1921. *Ethnology of the Kwakiutl.* Annual Report of the Bureau of American Ethnology, vol. 35, pts. 1–2. Smithsonian Institution, Washington, D.C.

Carlson, C. 1979. The Early Component at Bear Cove. *Canadian Journal of Archaeology* 3:177–193.

Chapman, M.W. 1982. Archaeological Investigations at the O'Connor Site, Port Hardy. In *Papers on Central Coast Archaeology,* edited by P. Hobler, pp. 65–132. Publication no. 10. Department of Archaeology, Simon Fraser University, Burnaby.

Mitchell, D. 1988. Changing Patterns of Resource Use in the Prehistory of Queen Charlotte Strait, British Columbia. In *Prehistoric Economies of the Pacific Northwest Coast,* edited by B.L. Isaac, pp. 245–290. Research in Economic Anthropology Supplement no. 3. JAI Press, Greenwich.

———. 1990. Prehistory of the Coasts of Southern British Columbia and Northern Washington. In *Northwest Coast,* edited by W. Suttles, pp. 340–358. Handbook of North American Indians, vol. 7, W.C. Sturtevant, general editor. Smithsonian Institution, Washington, D.C.

R

Rancheria

Spanish for "groups of huts," the word "rancheria" is used to describe the settlement patterns of historic Piman-speaking groups of southern Arizona and northern Mexico. Although poorly defined, a rancheria is usually considered a village made up of widely scattered individual structures occupied by independent families. Early archaeologists working in the Southwestern United States, such as Emil W. Haury, applied this term as well to Hohokam settlement patterns, in particular to structures in pre-Classic Hohokam phases. In archaeological situations, a rancheria is a site whose structures do not appear to be either aggregated or arranged in a pattern. Instead, houses seem to be scattered randomly over the landscape, with no clear arrangement with respect to streets, plazas, or other features, such as trash mounds.

Reevaluation of the settlement structure of Hohokam sites has revealed considerable patterning, however, to the distribution of structures and their associated features. A particularly important example is David R. Wilcox's work at the large site of Snaketown (Wilcox et al. 1981). His research indicates that individual economic units, probably extended families, occupied a series of structures with entries opening onto a common courtyard. A number of these household clusters, or courtyard groups, occurred in complexes associated with work areas and sometimes cemeteries. These larger complexes of courtyard groups were, in turn, patterned in their arrangement around larger communal features, such as plaza areas, trash mounds, and ballcourts, although they are all sometimes separated by several hundred meters.

Because pre-Classic Hohokam sites are now known to have been highly patterned in layout and organization, most archaeologists working in the Hohokam area no longer use the term "rancheria."

Patricia L. Crown

Further Readings

Haury, E.W. 1945. *The Excavation of Los Muertos and Neighboring Ruins in the Salt River Valley, Southern Arizona.* Papers, vol. 25, no. 1. Peabody Museum of American Archaeology and Ethnology, Harvard University, Cambridge.

———. 1976. *The Hohokam: Desert Farmers and Craftsmen.* University of Arizona Press, Tucson.

Sires, E.W. 1984. *Hohokam Architecture and Site Structure: Hohokam Archaeology Along the Salt-Gila Aqueduct Central Arizona Project: 9. Synthesis and Conclusions,* edited by L. Teague and P. Crown, pp. 115–139. Archaeological Series no. 150. Arizona State Museum, University of Arizona, Tucson.

Wilcox, D.R., T.R. McGuire, and C. Sternberg. 1981. *Snaketown Revisited.* Archaeological Series no. 155. Arizona State Museum, University of Arizona, Tucson.

See also HOHOKAM CULTURE AREA; SNAKETOWN

Range Site

The Range site (11S47) is a multicomponent location situated in the American Bottom segment of the central Mississippi River Valley of southwestern Illinois. The various occupations, ranging in age from the Middle Archaic (6000–3000 B.C., or 7950–4950 years B.P.) through the

Mississippian periods, covered a 10-ha (25-acre) area of an abandoned Mississippi River oxbow point bar known locally as Prairie Lake.

Extensive excavations occurred (1978–1981) at this site as part of the FAI-270 Archaeological Mitigation Project prior to the construction of Interstate 255. This work was conducted by the Department of Anthropology at the University of Illinois Champaign-Urbana, under the auspices of the Illinois Archaeological Survey for the Illinois Department of Transportation and the Federal Highway Administration.

A 4.5-ha (11-acre) area of the site systematically exposed between 1978 and 1981 resulted in the delineation and excavation of more than 5,500 prehistoric features, including more than 600 prehistoric structures. The earliest features were associated with a series of five Late Archaic (3000–600 B.C., or 4950–2550 years B.P.) occupation areas. While Early (600–150 B.C., or 2550–2100 years B.P.) and Middle (150 B.C.–A.D. 300, or 2100–1650 years B.P.) Woodland materials were recovered from the surface and in later feature fills, no subsurface features were identified. An intense utilization of this landscape was initiated by the Late Woodland, ca. A.D. 600 (1350 years B.P.), and persisted until the early Mississippian, ca. A.D. 1100 (850 years B.P.).

The Late Woodland–through–Mississippian utilization of this locale consisted of a series of 28 discontinuous occupational episodes delineated on the basis of the feature distribution. This sequence of settlements serves to document the emergence of Mississippian society in the American Bottom at a single locale. The nine Late Woodland Patrick-phase (A.D. 600–800, or 1350–1150 years B.P.) occupations range in size from scattered households to a small aggregated village of 30 structures distributed about a community square. These communities are suggestive of a system of shifting settlements indicative of tribal-level societal organization in which there is a constant fusion and fission of settlements.

The 11 communities associated with the initial part of the Emergent Mississippian period (Dohack [A.D. 800–850, or 1150–1100 years B.P.] and Range [A.D. 850–900, or 1100–1050 years B.P.] phases) are also small aggregated communities. In contrast with its Late Woodland antecedents, these villages are characterized by three types of features that accentuate the center of each community square: a

Range site excavations. Early Mississippian nodal community (wall trench houses and circular sweatlodges) and Emergent Mississippian community with four central pits and posts. (Illustration by J. E. Kelly)

Range site, excavations in progress, view to the south toward the Prairie Lake Meander and Bluffs. (Illustration by J. E. Kelly)

large square structure, quadripartite arrangement of four pits about a central post, and a central post. Considerable symbolism and societal implications are embodied in these central facilities that serve to integrate the various segments of these societies.

By the latter half of the Emergent Mississippian, the populations in the area had nucleated into a large village of more than 200 structures. This village began during the George Reeves phase (A.D. 900–950, or 1050–1000 years B.P.) with a dual division of two large plazas. The configuration of structures and courtyards flanking the southern plaza area provides the initial evidence for societal ranking within the region. The overall arrangement represents an important precursor to the later configuration at Cahokia 20 km (12.5 miles) to the north. The three types of central facilities described for the earlier Emergent Mississippian villages are arranged so as to accommodate spatial divisions within the community. Another segment of the village to the north is characterized by structures distributed about a secondary plaza. During the subsequent Lindeman phase (A.D. 950–1000, or 1000–950 years B.P.), the village was eventually reorganized around this plaza. By the end (A.D. 1000, or 950 years B.P.) of the occupation, the community had dispersed

perhaps into the nearby mound center at the Pulcher site.

The Mississippian habitation dating to the Lindhorst (A.D. 1000–1050, or 950–900 years B.P.) and early Stirling (A.D. 1050–1100, or 900–850 years B.P.) phases consists of three small farmsteads and a nodal community with circular sweat lodges and a large building that served to integrate the local farming populations.

The final prehistoric utilizations of the site consist of two Mississippian cemeteries and two small Oneota, Vulcan phase (A.D. 1400–1500, or 550–450 years B.P.), households. The Oneota component is the latest prehistoric occupation in the region and consists of at least one single-post longhouse and associated pits.

John E. Kelly

Further Readings

Kelly, J.E. 1990. The Range Site Community Patterns and the Mississippian Emergence. In *The Mississippian Emergence*, edited by B.D. Smith, pp. 67–112. Smithsonian Institution Press, Washington, D.C.

Kelly, J.E., S.J. Ozuk, and J.A. Williams. 1990. *The Range Site 2: The Emergent Mississippian Dohack and Range Phase Occupations*. American Bottom Archaeology FAI-270 Site Reports, vol. 20.

University of Illinois Press, Urbana.

Kelly, J.E., A.C. Fortier, S.J. Ozuk, and J.A. Williams. 1987. *The Range Site: Archaic Through Late Woodland Occupations.* American Bottom Archaeology FAI-270 Site Reports, vol. 16. University of Illinois Press, Urbana.

Rattle

The most common prehistoric rattles are made of turtle shell through which a hole was drilled for a handle and for the insertion of quartz pebbles or other percussive materials. By ethnographic analogy, they are considered implements used in dances and ceremonies. Rattles have been found in Archaic sites in the mid-continent and the Northeast, such as at Carlston Annis and Indian Knoll in Kentucky, Riverton in Illinois, Eva in Tennessee, and Lamoka Lake in New York. An excellent comparison of Archaic rattles can be found in H.D. Winters (1969:74–79), who distinguished among Indian Knoll, Iroquois, Seneca, and Shawnee types and plotted the distribution of each type. Employment of rattles extended, as Winters's types suggest, past the Archaic and into the historic period. The apparent remains of an unusual copper-covered wood or gourd rattle were unearthed in 1949 at the early Caddoan Harlan site in the fill of Mound 1B. All that remained of this badly disintegrated object was a cluster of 15 small pebbles associated with organic and copper stains and fragments of sheet copper (Bell 1972:242). A carved-cedar turtle recovered from the nearby Spiro site has also been interpreted as a rattle.

George H. Odell

Further Readings

Bell, R.E. 1972. *The Harlan Site, Ck-6, A Prehistoric Mound Center in Cherokee County, Eastern Oklahoma.* Memoir no. 2. Oklahoma Anthropological Society, Oklahoma City.

Winters, H.D. 1969. *The Riverton Culture.* Reports of Investigations no. 13. Illinois State Museum and Illinois Archaeological Survey, Springfield.

Reburial Issue

The reburial issue is part of a broader international problem relating to repatriation, or the return of cultural properties to nations, indigenous peoples, and ethnic groups who claim them. Within North America, this has been largely focused on demands of American Indians for proper treatment and disposition of human remains, funerary goods, and sacred objects of their ancestors. The issue is complex. On the surface, the issue seems entirely polarized, but there is actually a continuum of opinion among both American Indians and archaeologists.

Many American Indians argue that excavation, study, and curation of human remains

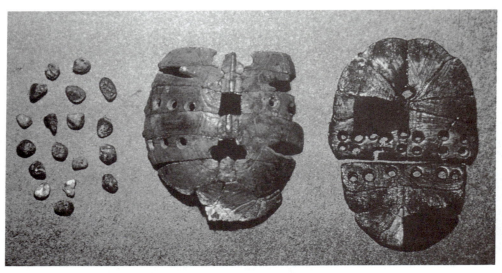

Turtle shell rattle from the Synders site, Calhoun County, Illinois. (Courtesy of the Wilford Archaeology Laboratory, University of Minnesota)

Medicine man and Sioux at Crow Creek reburial, 1981. (Photograph by L. J. Zimmerman)

is sacrilegious or, at the very least, disrespectful to the dead and spiritually dangerous. Many see the issue as a form of scientific colonialism by the dominant society. Some demand no archaeological excavation or study and the complete return of all remains in existing collections. Others are more willing to compromise, realizing that potentially valuable information is provided by the remains.

Many archaeologists and physical anthropologists argue that some of these demands are a violation of academic freedom and that remains from prehistoric sites are a universal cultural heritage. Valuable information regarding social structure, diet, genetics, and disease patterns, for example, will be lost if remains are not studied or are made unavailable for future study. Other archaeologists have been more willing to compromise and have actively participated in repatriation and reburial and the development of ethics codes for the treatment of human remains.

This issue has been debated and discussed since the late 1960s. Responses from archaeologists have ranged from the passage of resolutions or policy statements against reburial to work on legislation that represents compromises. Many states have passed laws concerning reburial, and nationally the issue has been dealt with by Public Law 101–601, the Native American Graves Protection and Repatriation Act (NAGPRA). NAGPRA requires that federal agencies and museums receiving federal funding inventory their holdings and work with tribes to determine if repatriation is appropriate.

Some legal matters are yet to be resolved, especially in cases in which the federal government is not involved and materials are held privately. Broader issues remain regarding archaeological ethics and Indian-archaeologist relationships, "control" of the past, and epistemological differences about how the past is known.

Many archaeologists and American Indians are hopeful that if these issues can be resolved, the two groups can work together for a more complete understanding of the prehistoric North American past and for legislation that will provide greater protection for archaeological sites.

Larry J. Zimmerman

Further Readings

Davidson, G.W., and L.J. Zimmerman (editors). 1990. Human Remains: Contemporary Issues. Special edition of *Death Studies*, vol. 14, no. 6.

Echo-Hawk, W. (editor). 1992. Repatriation of American Indian Remains. Special edition of *American Indian Culture and Research Journal*, vol. 16, no. 2.

Hubert, J. 1991. After the Vermillion Accord: Developments in the "Reburial Issue." *World Archaeology Bulletin* 5:113–118.

Price, H.M., III. 1991. *Disputing the Dead: U.S. Law on Aboriginal Remains and*

Grave Goods. University of Missouri Press, Columbia.

Quick, P. McW. 1986. *Proceedings: Conference on Reburial Issues, Newberry Library, Chicago, June 14–15, 1985.* Society for American Archaeology, Washington, D.C.

Red Paint Culture

The Red Paint culture of Maine came to light in the late nineteenth century when unique artifacts were plowed up with red ocher near Lake Alamoosook in Orland. C.C. Willoughby of the Peabody Museum of American Archaeology and Ethnology at Harvard University visited the area in 1892 and discovered cemeteries with ocher-filled graves that contained diverse tools and ornaments unlike those then known from other prehistoric sites in Maine (Willoughby 1898). Willoughby (1898:3) exhibited his work at the 1893 World's Columbian Exposition in Chicago, where he attracted the attention of Warren K. Moorehead, who was exhibiting the results of his work on Ohio burial mounds. Moorehead later did extensive fieldwork in Maine for the newly established (1901) Robert S. Peabody Foundation for Archaeology at Phillips Academy in Andover, Massachusetts. He excavated an estimated 440 graves at a dozen cemeteries in the years 1912–1920 (Moorehead 1922:13).

More than 30 cemeteries have been discovered to date (Bourque 1995). They cluster between Merrymeeting Bay, Maine, and Grand Lake on the St. John River in southwestern New Brunswick. Nearly all are within 80.5 km (50 miles) of the coast. Typical grave furnishings include plummets, adzes, gouges, stemmed points, and ground-slate bayonets. Some plummets and other stone figurines represent abstract forms and animals, primarily marine mammals.

Willoughby (1898:50–52; 1909) was the first to appreciate the antiquity of the cemeteries, but he anachronistically linked them to the historic Beothuk, or "Red Indians," of Newfoundland. In 1913, Moorehead (1913:39–41) published "The Red Paint People of Maine," which supported Willoughby's assertion that the cemeteries predated the arrival of the region's historic Algonquian-speaking peoples. His claim was attacked by D.I. Bushnell, Jr., (1913, 1915) and C.B. Moore (1914, 1915). Uncertainty about the age and cultural affiliation of the cemeteries continued until J.H. Rowe (1940:14–18) presented stratigraphic evidence for the great age of artifacts typically found in the graves, including ground-slate bayonets and plummets.

New fieldwork beginning in the late 1960s revived interest in the cemeteries. In 1968, J.A. Tuck (1971, 1976) excavated a spectacular Late Archaic (4050–1550 B.C., or 6000–3500 years B.P.) "red paint" cemetery at Port au Choix in northern Newfoundland. Elaborating upon a theme initiated by D.S. Byers (1959:252; 1962) and reiterated by E. Harp, Jr. (1963), Tuck posited a "whole cultural tradition" (Goggin 1949:17) for the entire coastal region from Maine to northern Labrador. He named it the Maritime Archaic tradition (Tuck 1971:350–357). In Tuck's view, the technology and mortuary practices of this tradition indicated a strong maritime hunting orientation. D. Sanger's excavation at the elaborate Cow Point cemetery on Grand Lake in New Brunswick led him to disagree with Tuck. He suggested instead that the Laurentian tradition was responsible for the Maine cemeteries, which he referred to as the Moorehead Burial tradition (Sanger 1973:128–136).

B.J. Bourque's (1975, 1976, 1983, 1992) thesis research, completed in 1971, and subsequent excavations at the Turner Farm site on North Haven Island, Maine, caused him to hypothesize that the cemeteries were a mortuary expression of a particular Late Archaic culture he called the Moorehead phase (2550–1850 B.C., or 4500–3800 years B.P.) (Willey and Phillips 1958:626–628). The Turner Farm site contained no mortuary remains, but its linkage to the cemeteries is obvious in the stone and bone tools, many of which strongly resemble specimens recovered from the nearby Nevin Red Paint cemetery excavated by D.S. Byers (1979) in the 1930s. Bourque (1975:40, 1976:25–26) rejected the Laurentian tradition as ancestral to the Moorehead phase. It has subsequently become apparent that it developed locally from what W.A. Ritchie originally named the "Small Stemmed Point tradition" (Ritchie 1969:216–219; Bourque 1995). It also now seems clear that while Late Archaic peoples on both sides of the Gulf of St. Lawrence exchanged stone artifacts and shared many patterns of behavior, their cultures did not arise as one unified tradition (Bourque 1995).

As the age (ca. 2550–1850 B.C., or 4500–3800 years B.P.) and cultural origins of the Moorehead phase came into focus during the

1970s, so did its settlement and subsistence patterns. Rowe's (1940:16–17) early work had demonstrated that swordfish were among the species hunted by these people. Excavations at the Turner Farm site revealed that swordfish hunting had begun as early as 3050 B.C. (5000 years B.P.) among peoples identified as belonging to the Small Stemmed Point tradition (Bourque 1983:63; 1995). Faunal and artifactual evidence from the Turner Farm site and from the Seabrook Marsh site in New Hampshire suggested that marine species, especially swordfish and cod, became particularly important resources by the beginning of the Moorehead phase (Robinson 1985; Bourque 1995). Still, deer bone was also abundant at the Turner Farm site, leaving in doubt the relative importance of marine and terrestrial protein sources. This ambiguity has been clarified through the analysis of stable isotopes in human bone from the Nevin site, where bone preservation is excellent because the cemetery was subsequently covered by shell midden (Bourque and Krueger 1991). The Nevin population appears to have been as maritime, or nearly so, as that of Port au Choix.

Among the more interesting artifacts of the Moorehead phase are ground-slate bayonets, some of which are richly decorated and reach lengths of more than 30 cm (30.4 inches) (Sanger 1973:186–188). Occurring in several distinct styles, they differ from the broad, short, utilitarian-looking forms found in Laurentian-tradition contexts to the west. Virtually identical forms have, however, been found in Newfoundland and Labrador contexts. These may have been traded reciprocally for flaked points uncovered in Maine's Red Paint cemeteries that are made of Ramah chert, a visually striking raw material from northern Labrador. Other exotics include large stemmed points made of raw materials from the Lake Champlain Basin. The origin of ground-slate technology in the Northeast remains unclear, as does the nature of contacts across the Gulf of St. Lawrence between 2550 and 1850 B.C. (4500–3800 years B.P.). A final uncertainty surrounds the sudden disappearance of the cultures responsible for the cemeteries in both regions ca. 1850–1550 B.C. (3800–3500 years B.P.). In Maine, they were replaced by immigrants of the Susquehanna tradition, who moved in from the south. In the north, Paleoeskimo cultures came to prevail over much of the domain of the Maritime Archaic tradition.

The Moorehead phase represents a cultural florescence along the central and eastern Maine coastal zone beginning ca. 2550 B.C. (4500 years B.P.). It involved maritime hunting, elaborate mortuary ritual, and long-distance exchange. Its origins apparently lie in earlier Archaic populations of the New England region. Its sudden disappearance ca. 1850 B.C. (3800 years B.P.) may have been brought about by changing oceanographic conditions in the Gulf of Maine.

Bruce J. Bourque

Further Readings

Bourque, B.J. 1975. Comments on the Late Archaic Populations of Central Maine: The View From the Turner Farm. *Arctic Anthropology* 12(2):35–45.

———. 1976. The Turner Farm Site: A Preliminary Report. *Man in the Northeast* 11:21–30.

———. 1983. The Turner Farm Archaeological Project. *National Geographic Society Reports*, pp. 59–65.

———. 1992. *Prehistory of the Central Maine Coast*. Garland, New York.

———. 1995. *Diversity and Complexity in Prehistoric Maritime Societies: A Gulf of Maine Perspective*. Plenum Press, New York.

Bourque, B.J., and H.W. Krueger. 1991. Dietary Reconstruction of Prehistoric Maritime Peoples of Northeastern North America: Faunal vs. Stable Isotope Approaches. Paper presented at the Annual Meeting of the Canadian Archaeological Association, St. John's, Newfoundland.

Bushnell, D.I., Jr. 1913. The Red Paint People. *American Anthropologist* 15:707–710.

———. 1915. The Red Paint People II. *American Anthropologist* 17:207–209.

Byers, D.S. 1959. The Eastern Archaic: Some Problems and Hypotheses. *American Antiquity* 24:233–256.

———. 1962. New England and the Arctic. In *Prehistoric Cultural Relations Between the Arctic and Temperate Zones of North America*, edited by J.M. Campbell, pp. 143–153. Technical Paper no. 11. Arctic Institute of North America, Montreal.

———. 1979. *The Nevin Shellheap: Burials and Observations*. Papers, vol. 9. Robert S. Peabody Foundation for Archaeology, Phillips Academy, Andover.

Goggin, J. 1949. Cultural Traditions in Florida Prehistory. In *Florida Indian and*

His Neighbors, edited by J.W. Griffin. Rollins College, Winter Park.

Harp, E., Jr. 1963. Evidence of Boreal Archaic Culture in Southern Labrador and Newfoundland. *National Museums of Canada Bulletin* 193(1):184–261.

Moore, C.B. 1914. The Red Paint People of Maine. *American Anthropologist* 16:137–139.

———. 1915. The Red Paint People II. *American Anthropologist* 17:209.

Moorehead, W.K. 1913. The Red Paint People of Maine. *American Anthropologist* 15:33–47.

———. 1922. *A Report on the Archaeology of Maine.* Andover Press, Andover.

Ritchie, W.A. 1969. *The Archaeology of Martha's Vineyard.* Natural History Press, Garden City.

Robinson, B.S. 1985. *The Nelson Island and Seabrook Marsh Sites: Late Archaic, Marine Oriented People on the Central New England Coast.* Occasional Publications in Northeastern Anthropology no. 9. Department of Anthropology, Franklin Pierce College, Rindge.

Rowe, J.H. 1940. *Excavations at the Waterside Shell Heap, Frenchman's Bay, Maine.* Papers, vol. 1, no. 3. Excavators Club, Cambridge.

Sanger, D. 1973. *Cow Point: An Archaic Cemetery in New Brunswick.* Mercury Series Paper no. 12. Archaeological Survey of Canada, National Museum of Man, Ottawa.

———. 1975. Culture Change As an Adaptive Process in the Maine-Maritime Region. *Arctic Anthropology* 7(2):60–75.

Tuck, J.A. 1971. An Archaic Cemetery at Port au Choix, Newfoundland. *American Antiquity* 36:343–358.

———. 1976. *Ancient People of Port au Choix: The Excavation of an Archaic Indian Cemetery in Newfoundland.* Newfoundland Social and Economic Studies no. 17. Memorial University of Newfoundland, St. John's.

Willey, G.R., and P.B. Phillips. 1958. *Method and Theory in American Archaeology.* University of Chicago Press, Chicago.

Willoughby, C.C. 1898. *Prehistoric Burial Places in Maine.* Archaeological and Ethnological Papers, vol. 1, no. 6. Peabody Museum of American Archaeology and Ethnology, Harvard University, Cambridge.

———. 1909. Pottery of the New England Indians. In *Putnam Anniversary Volume: Anthropological Essays Presented to Frederick Ward Putnam in Honor of His Seventieth Birthday,* edited by F. Boas, pp. 83–101. Stechert, New York.

See also MARITIME ARCHAIC TRADITION

Red Wing Locality

The Red Wing locality is a dense concentration of Native American village and mound sites along the Mississippi River in Goodhue County, Minnesota, and Pierce County, Wisconsin. The locality encompasses ca. 15,022 ha (58 square miles) and contains more than 2,000 mounds and earthworks, eight major villages, and numerous smaller sites that date between the tenth and thirteenth centuries A.D. These sites are associated with the emergence of corn horticulture in the Upper Mississippi River Valley and are related to the complex Mississippian cultures of the lower Midwest, most notably the premier site of Cahokia and other sites on the American Bottom of southwestern Illinois ca. 805 km (500 miles) downriver.

The physical setting of the locality is a complex mosaic of dissected uplands, glacial outwash terraces, stream deltas, recent floodplain features, and deposits associated with Lake Pepin (see Figure). The diverse combination of environmental zones, particularly the large expanses of arable land in the Cannon River delta, made this region particularly attractive to ancient settlers (Dobbs and Mooers 1991). Similarly, the Mississippi and the Cannon rivers were key transportation links along a north-south and east-west axis.

Lake Pepin, which has been steadily infilling since ca. 7050 B.C. (9000 years B.P.), appears to have played a key role in the human use of this landscape. By ca. 50 B.C. (2000 years B.P.), the head of the lake was north of the Cannon junction; by ca. A.D. 950 (1000 years B.P.), it was slightly south of the mouth of the Cannon. The movement of the lake may have dramatically influenced cultural events as the landscape was transformed from one dominated by the lake into an area of backwater swamps and sloughs and the main river channel (Dobbs and Mooers 1991).

Two distinct archaeological cultures are

present within the locality. The Silvernale phase (ca. A.D. 1150–1250, or 800–700 years B.P.) (Wilford 1945) is characterized by rolled-rim ceramics and other artifacts clearly related to Mississippian cultures to the south. There is also a widespread Oneota presence (ca. A.D. 1300–1650, or 650–300 years B.P.) within the locality that has not yet been defined as a phase, but the associated ceramics are most clearly related to the Blue Earth series. The temporal and cultural relationships between these two cultures remain problematic. For example, Silvernale materials are always found on sites that also contain Oneota materials (e.g., Bryan, Silvernale, Mero/Diamond Bluff), but there are Oneota sites (e.g., Adams, Double) that do not contain Silvernale materials.

Although the locality contains one of the most extensive concentrations of mounds and earthworks in the Upper Mississippi Valley, many groups are largely destroyed. Fortunately,

extensive surveying efforts in the 1880s by T.H. Lewis of the Northwestern Archaeological Survey have allowed a reconstruction of the configuration of these groups (Dobbs 1992b). The majority of mounds were associated with the major village sites, although smaller groups situated on the bluff tops overlooking the river were common, too. While most mounds in the locality were conical in form, a few effigy mounds were present, including snakes, animals, and at least one bird form, and one flat-topped pyramidal mound was associated with the Energy Park site. A boulder outline of a bird effigy was present in Pierce County, and several stone cairns described as more than 3 m (10 feet) high were on bluffs overlooking Spring Creek.

The major villages in the Red Wing locality are large and situated on high, glacial outwash terraces overlooking major streams. Each village was surrounded by a group of

Silvernale vessel from Feature 450 at the Bryan site. A series of calibrated radiocarbon dates indicate a date of A.D. 1189–1224 at 1 standard deviation for the vessel. Grit-tempered, Plains-like ceramics were found stratigraphically below the vessel. (Photograph by Sylvia Horwitz. Courtesy of the Institute for Minnesota Archaeology)

Complete vessel from Feature 513 at the Bryan site. (Photograph by Sylvia Horwitz. Courtesy of the Institute for Minnesota Archaeology)

mounds on its landward side. The villages are concentrated along the Cannon River, in the valley of Spring Creek, on Prairie Island, and on terraces overlooking the Mississippi River.

The Cannon River villages include Silvernale, Bryan, Energy Park, and Belle Creek. Of these, Bryan has been the most extensively investigated. The presence at this site of an extensive palisade, several different house types, including square postmold structures and shallow basins, and thousands of refuse pits has been documented (Dobbs 1989). Ceramic evidence indicates that there was direct contact between Bryan and sites to the west, including most probably the Cambria site. High-precision radiocarbon dating indicates that the occupation at Bryan was intense and relatively short lived, with the most expansive period of occupation probably occurring ca. A.D. 1190–1223 (760–727 years B.P.) (Dobbs 1992a). These dates are consistent with the calibrated chronology for the Stirling phase at Cahokia.

A series of smaller, and perhaps later,

Oneota sites are clustered in Spring Creek Valley immediately north of Bryan. A group of petroglyphs has also been recorded along Spring Creek.

The Bartron site is situated on Prairie Island, a low outwash feature bounded by the Vermillion and the Mississippi rivers. Bartron appears to contain both Oneota and Silvernale elements; a basin-style house has been identified there (Gibbon 1979). Prairie Island also contains numerous mound groups, many of which may be associated with Late Woodland (ca. A.D. 400–1100, or 1550–850 years B.P.) rather than Oneota or Silvernale cultures. Several small Late Woodland sites have been identified on the island.

The Mero (Diamond Bluff) complex is on a 1,524-m (5,000-foot) -long terrace overlooking the confluence of the Trimbelle and the Mississippi rivers. This terrace was covered with more than 600 mounds. There are also two major Silvernale/Oneota sites on the terrace and at least three smaller Woodland sites. The

Diamond Bluff site is the best known of these. Excavations at the site have identified semisubterranean houses, thousands of refuse pits, and Oneota-style pottery associated with burials in one effigy mound (Maxwell 1950; Wendt and Dobbs 1989). Several other Late Woodland sites have been identified in the adjacent floodplains and on terraces to the north.

The Adams site is southeast of the Mero complex and overlooks the Mississippi River. Adams contains only Oneota materials and is characterized by the presence of large midden deposits rather than deep trash pits. These middens were used during different seasons, as documented by the massive deposits of freshwater shell in some and large mammal bone in others. Geomorphological evidence indicates that Lake Pepin was adjacent to the site during its occupation.

The Red Wing locality was the northernmost node in a complex of interaction along the Mississippi and Missouri drainages during the twelfth and thirteenth centuries A.D. The relationship between the locality, situated on the northern frontier of Mississippian culture, and the American Bottom in the Mississippian

heartland has been debated for many years (Griffin 1961; Gibbon 1974; Stoltman 1986, 1991; Gibbon and Dobbs 1991). Although the debate is far from resolved, it now appears that developments in the Red Wing locality paralleled those in the American Bottom. An emerging model of events at the locality incorporates the complex landform changes created by Lake Pepin and the dynamic cultural changes that occurred in the region ca. A.D. 900–1300 (1050–650 years B.P.). In this model, the locality emerges in the tenth century as the center place for indigenous groups during the Late Woodland coincident with the movement of Lake Pepin south of the confluence of the Cannon and the Mississippi. During the eleventh century, the economy and material culture of these groups were rapidly transformed as corn horticulture and other Mississippian elements were locally adopted. The florescence of the locality occurred between ca. A.D. 1150 and 1250 (800–700 years B.P.), probably linked, in part, to internal developments within the American Bottom and the expansive character of the Stirling phase. The Silvernale phase itself may represent powerful local families who were

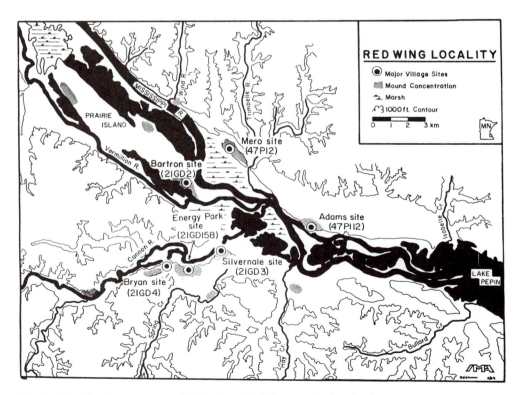

The Red Wing locality. (Courtesy of the Institute for Minnesota Archaeology)

emulating more southerly Mississippian groups. After A.D. 1250 (700 years B.P.), the intense settlement and activity at the locality waned, and a series of distinct regional Oneota cultures emerged. For whatever reason, there appears to be relatively little settlement at the locality between ca. A.D. 1300 and 1650 (650–300 years B.P.), when Santee Dakota groups began settling in the area.

Clark A. Dobbs

Further Readings

Dobbs, C.A. 1989. *Cataloging and Preliminary Analysis of Archaeological Materials Obtained From the Bryan Site (21GD4), Goodhue County, MN.* Reports of Investigations no. 63. Institute for Minnesota Archaeology, Minneapolis.

———. 1992a. *A Pilot Study of High Precision Radiocarbon Dating at the Red Wing Locality: Final Report Submitted to the National Science Foundation for NSF Project BNS-9011744.* Reports of Investigations no. 228. Institute for Minnesota Archaeology, Minneapolis.

———. 1992b. Recreating Vanished Mound Groups in the Upper Mississippi River Valley (U.S.A.): Integrating Historic Documents, CADD, and Photogrammetric Mapping. In *Computing the Past: Computer Applications and Quantitative Methods in Archaeology,* edited by J. Andresen, T. Madsen, and I. Scollar. Aarhus University Press, Denmark.

Dobbs, C.A., and H. Mooers. 1991. *Phase I Archaeological and Geomorphological Study of Lake Pepin and the Upper Reaches of Navigation Pool 4, Upper Mississippi River, Pierce and Pepin Counties, Wisconsin, and Goodhue and Wabasha Counties, Minnesota.* Reports of Investigations no. 44. Institute for Minnesota Archaeology, Minneapolis.

Gibbon, G.E. 1974. A Model of Mississippian Development and Its Implications for the Red Wing Area. In *Aspects of Upper Great Lakes Anthropology,* edited by E. Johnson, pp. 129–137. Minnesota Prehistoric Archaeology Series no. 11. Minnesota Historical Society, St. Paul.

———. 1979. *The Mississippian Occupation of the Red Wing Area.* Minnesota Prehistoric Archaeology Series no. 13. Minnesota Historical Society, St. Paul.

Gibbon, G.E., and C.A. Dobbs. 1991. The Mississippian Presence in the Red Wing Area, Minnesota. In *New Perspectives on Cahokia: View From the Periphery,* edited by J.B. Stoltman, pp. 281–305. Prehistory Press, Madison.

Griffin, J.B. 1961. Some Correlations of Climatic and Cultural Change in Eastern North American Prehistory. *Annals of the New York Academy of Science* 95:710–717.

Maxwell, M.S. 1950. A Change in the Interpretation of Wisconsin's Prehistory. *Wisconsin Archeologist* 33:427–443.

Stoltman, J.B. 1986. The Appearance of the Mississippian Cultural Tradition in the Upper Mississippi Valley. In *Prehistoric Mound Builders of the Mississippi Valley,* edited by J.B. Stoltman, pp. 26–34. Putnam Museum, Davenport.

Wendt, D., and C.A. Dobbs. 1989. A Reevaluation of the Mero (Diamond Bluff) Site Complex. *Wisconsin Archeologist* 70(3):281–309.

Wilford, L.A. 1945. Three Village Sites of the Mississippi Pattern in Minnesota. *American Antiquity* 11:32–40.

Redbird Phase

The Redbird phase is a Late Prehistoric Plains Village–pattern manifestation in north-central and northeast Nebraska, with semipermanent earthlodge villages along Ponca Creek and the lower Niobrara River Basin in Holt and Knox counties. Other villages may exist in the upper part of the Elkhorn drainage, especially in Antelope County. Hunting camps occur along the central Niobrara as far west as the mouth of the Snake River in the Sand Hills of Cherry County. Type sites are Redbird I, Redbird II, Wirth, and Minarik. Although radiocarbon samples have not been run, ceramics and architecture suggest the phase existed from A.D. 1550 until ca. 1650 (400–ca. 300 years B.P.). Redbird affinities lie most closely with Extended Coalescent taxa of South Dakota and the Lower Loup phase of central Nebraska, which suggest Pawnee or Arikara ancestry. Redbird people may also be the Protohistoric ancestors of the Siouan-speaking Ponca.

Settlements were small, unfortified hamlets of several houses set on terraces and ridges overlooking stream valleys. Dwellings were circular earthlodges with four or six centerposts, wall posts, and an entry passage on the south or east wall. Interior and exterior features include deep undercut storage and trash facilities, hearths, basins, and posts suggesting racks. The few burials are single extended interments within the village or on surrounding hilltops. Grave offerings were modest. Subsistence focused on maize horticulture, gathering wild plants and shellfish, fishing, as well as hunting bison, deer, and smaller mammals, and birds.

Pottery is divided into either Evans (direct rims) or McKay ware (thickened or collared rims). Vessels are thin and globular with simple-stamped bodies and wide mouths. Decoration was applied by trailing, incising, punctating, or finger-decorating and involved geometric designs applied to lips, rims, or shoulders. Oneota pottery was occasionally traded into Redbird villages. Chipped-stone tools include triangular side- and unnotched projectile points, pointed or ovate knives, end scrapers, drills, and choppers. Ground- or pecked-stone tools include grooved mauls, hammerstones, sandstone or clinker abraders, and incised catlinite. Bison-scapula digging tools are the most common bone implement. Others include ulna picks, deer or antelope metapodial awls, cancellous-tissue abraders, rib awls, antler-tine flakers, and beads. Euro-American manufactured trade goods were recovered from one burial, but the interment may be an intrusive nineteenth-century Ponca person.

John R. Bozell
John Ludwickson

Further Readings

Jantz, R.L. 1974. The Redbird Focus: Cranial Evidence in Tribal Identification. *Plains Anthropologist* 19(63):5–13.

Ludwickson, J., D.J. Blakeslee, and J.M. O'Shea. 1987. *Missouri National Recreational River: Native American Cultural Resources*. Publications in Anthropology no. 3. Department of Anthropology, Wichita State University, Wichita.

Wood, W.R. 1965. *The Redbird Focus and the Problem of Ponca Prehistory*. Memoir no. 2. Plains Anthropologist, Lincoln.

Retouch

The most useful operational definition of retouch is simply "the intentional secondary modification of flint"; that is, the modification of a piece of stone after it has been removed from its core; or, if the piece of stone is itself a core or nodule, the removal of a flake from a core or nodule. This definition of retouch generally corresponds with those given by D.E. Crabtree (1972:89) and M. Brezillon (1968:106–107), though J. Tixier (1974:19) curiously includes utilization retouch with his definition, almost as an afterthought. Although seemingly straightforward, the definition requires clarification since it includes modification of stone that is usually not considered retouch by most archaeologists, such as blows to a core to produce flakes. Because, for interpretive purposes, it is useful to distinguish cores from other kinds of pieces of stone, this kind of modification can be considered at most a special case of "retouch."

The definition presupposes, too, that analysts can distinguish intentional retouch from other forces that cause fracture to stone, such as use, excavation and laboratory damage, plowing, and the "spontaneous retouch" that sometimes occurs on the distal end of a flake during its removal (Newcomer 1976). To acquire the skill to distinguish intentional from nonintentional retouch, archaeologists must meticulously examine thousands of pieces of "worked" stone of different kinds. The alternative is the commingling of purposefully shaped pieces and those that became that way through other means. The definition also includes all sizes of removals, from a 2-mm (0.08-inch) scar on a graver to a 2-cm (0.8-inch) scar on a biface. Thus, a flintknapper could retouch an edge by a hammerstone, billet, or pressure flaker. The rationale is that, since fracture size is a continuous variable, divisions along the dimension are only arbitrary.

Prehistoric people retouched stone tools for a variety of reasons. Stone was shaped to fit an intended function or to prepare it for a specific hafting device, to sharpen an edge, or to blunt an edge so that the stone tool could be safely grasped in the hand. In developing typologies to aid in interpreting stone assemblages in sites, archaeologists tend to focus on retouch that shapes a stone to fit an intended function. Because there are many other reasons for retouching a tool, this typological focus often obscures other, perhaps more important, activities that took place at these sites.

George H. Odell

Further Readings

Brezillon, M. 1968. *La Denomination des Objets de Pierre Taillee*. Gallia Prehistoire, Supplement no. 4. Centre

National de la Recherche Scientifique, Paris.

Crabtree, D.E. 1972. *An Introduction to Flint-working*. Occasional Paper no. 28. Idaho State University Museum, Pocatello.

Newcomer, M. 1976. Spontaneous Retouch. In *Second International Symposium on Flint*, edited by F. Engelen, pp. 62–64. Nederlandse Geologische Vereniging, Maastricht.

Tixier, J. 1974. *Glossary for the Description of Stone Tools*, translated by M. Newcomer. Special Publication no. 1. Newsletter of Lithic Technology, Washington State University, Pullman.

Retouched Piece

"Retouched piece" is a catch-all, typotechnological classification used for nonbifacial chipped-stone implements that possess some, usually limited, retouch on one or more sides but that cannot be placed in a more specific category. According to this definition, a retouched piece can be fabricated on a flake, a blocky fragment, or a blade, though many archaeologists prefer to separate the type further by blank form. Although this type is ubiquitous in North America and occurs throughout prehistory, not all archaeologists have employed it. Where it has been used, it forms a major component of chipped-stone assemblages. In the Illinois Valley, for example, retouched pieces constituted 35 percent and 16 percent, respectively, of the Early and Middle Archaic type collections of the Campbell Hollow site. The numerical importance of the type in the region continued through the Mississippian Hill Creek occupation, in which, at 22 percent, it formed the most frequently represented tool type (Odell 1985a, 1985b).

George H. Odell

Further Readings

Odell, G.H. 1985a. Hill Creek Site Lithic Analysis. In *The Hill Creek Homestead: A Late Mississippian Settlement in the Lower Illinois Valley*, edited by M. Connor, pp. 55–114. Research Series, vol. 1. Center for American Archeology, Kampsville.

———. 1985b. Lithic Assemblage. In *The Campbell Hollow Archaic Occupations: A Study of Intrasite Spatial Structure in the Lower Illinois Valley*, edited by C.R. Stafford, pp. 37–52. Research Series, vol. 4. Center for American Archeology, Kampsville.

Rice Lake Site

Rice Lake is located in southern Ontario, 20 km (12.5 miles) north of Lake Ontario. The Rice Lake (Serpent Mounds) site (BbGm-2), which was occupied primarily in the Middle Woodland and early Late Woodland periods (ca. 350 B.C.–A.D. 1250, or 2300–700 years B.P.), is on its northern shore. The Middle Woodland occupants, the Point Peninsula people, exploited the area's abundant fish, shellfish, wild rice, nut, and deer resources; they accumulated a shell midden that extended 100 m (328 feet) along the shore. The seriation of ceramics from this midden has led to the definition of a basic sequence of ceramic change for Point Peninsula in Ontario.

A cluster of nine mounds lies 45 m (148 feet) northeast of the Rice Lake site. One, Mound E, is known as the Serpent Mound because of its vaguely sinuous shape, though this is probably only an accidental effect of the blending of three successive mounds. Excavations uncovered the remains of at least 74 individuals. With some exceptions, they fall into two categories that probably reflect a rank distinction in the society. The first category is composed of generally disarticulated and incomplete burials in the fill of the mound. They are sometimes cremated and have few grave offerings. The second category is composed of partly or fully articulated skeletons in pits in the mound floor. These burials are associated with more elaborate grave offerings, including numerous marine shell beads, some beads of native copper and silver (the latter from the Cobalt area, 400 km, or 248 miles, to the north), masks made from wolf and bear facial bones, fossil horn corals, loon beaks, and a bear canine. The ceramics from the mound fill, the grave items, and two radiocarbon dates indicate an age range for the mound of ca. A.D. 100–250 (1850–1700 years B.P.). The age range relates the mound to the shell midden, to other Point Peninsula burial mounds in the region, and, ultimately, to the Squawkie Hill phase of New York and the widespread Hopewell Interaction Sphere. Two other mounds, G and I, each covered a mass of human bone. Nineteen individuals were present in the excavated portion of Mound G and 42 in Mound I, which was completely excavated. Most were secondary burials; there were no grave offerings. These mounds probably date late in the Middle Woodland occupation (ca. A.D. 300–600, or 1650–1350 years B.P.).

Three ossuary mounds, each holding mass secondary burials of 15 to 29 individuals, are located ca. 50 m (164 feet) north of the mounds. Associated ceramics and radiocarbon dates indicate an early Late Woodland affiliation with the Pickering phase (A.D. 900–1250, or 1050–700 years B.P.) of the Early Ontario Iroquois stage. Similar pottery occurs in the surface layer of the lakeshore midden, which overlies the shell and its associated Point Peninsula pottery.

Archaeological investigations at the Rice Lake site have led to the seriation of Point Peninsula ceramics, the linking of mound burial in southern Ontario to Point Peninsula and to Hopewellian influence, the identification of rank differentiation in local societies, and the definition of an early expression of mass secondary (ossuary) burial. Of equal significance, however, is the detailed information that has been attained on skeletal morphology, dentition, and pathology. Comparison of the mound and the pit series with each other and with later collections has established a sequence of morphological continuity from the Middle Woodland Point Peninsula people to the prehistoric Huron of Ontario.

Michael W. Spence

Further Readings

Anderson, J.E. 1968. *The Serpent Mounds Site Physical Anthropology.* Art and Archaeology Occasional Papers no. 11. Royal Ontario Museum, Toronto.

Johnston, R.B. 1968. *The Archaeology of the Serpent Mounds Site.* Art and Archaeology Occasional Papers no. 10. Royal Ontario Museum, Toronto.

———. 1979. Notes on Ossuary Burial Among the Ontario Iroquois. *Canadian Journal of Archaeology* 3:91–104.

Spence, M.W., R.H. Pihl, and J.E. Molto. 1984. Hunter-Gatherer Social Group Identification: A Case Study From Middle Woodland Southern Ontario. In *Exploring the Limits: Frontiers and Boundaries in Prehistory,* edited by S. De Atley and F. Findlow, pp. 117–142. BAR International Series 223. British Archaeological Reports, Oxford.

Spence, M.W., R.H. Pihl, and C.R. Murphy. 1990. Cultural Complexes of the Early and Middle Woodland Periods. In *The Archaeology of Southern Ontario to A.D. 1650,* edited by C. Ellis and N. Ferris, pp. 125–169. Occasional Publications no. 5. London [Ontario] Chapter, Ontario Archaeological Society, London.

R

Richey Clovis Cache

The Richey Clovis cache (45DO432) is but one archaeological feature at a Clovis encampment of undetermined size in the Columbia River Valley, Douglas County, central Washington State. The implement cache lay within a shallow, oval pit with approximate dimensions of 1 x 1.5 m (3.3 x 4.9 feet). Fifty-seven large flaked-stone and bone artifacts were removed from it by various excavators in 1987, 1988, and 1990. Twenty-four of these objects were collected by farm workers when they discovered the site; their positions within the feature are not known exactly. A second archaeological feature, also thought to be a cachepit, was observed nearby. Its principal contents were two flaked stone tools: a utilized prismatic blade and a side scraper.

The inventory of artifacts in the Richey Clovis cache is impressive by any standard. It includes 14 Clovis fluted points, only one of which is a servicable projectile point; eight bifacial knives; seven fluted-point preforms, which also served as knives; four side scrapers; three prismatic blades used as cutting instruments; three adzes or celts; two delicate engraving tools; two flake knives; a cursorily shaped stone slab (implement blank); and at least 13 bi-beveled rods of mastodont or mammoth limb bone. The total weight of flaked-stone tools is ca. 5 kg (11 lbs). All of the stone tools exhibit evidence of use and resharpening. Despite their large size and select raw materials, it is likely that most tools were employed in killing and processing animals, if not for other purposes. The function of the sets of bi-beveled bone rods is unknown. It has been suggested that they were foreshafts or hafts for fluted points; however, other lines of evidence indicate that they may have been shoes to protect sled runners. Two of the rods bear decorative patterns of incising upon one of their faces. Similar patterns of incisions are known in Epi-Paleolithic and late Paleolithic cultures in Eurasia that date to ca. 11,000–8000 B.C. (12,950–9950 years B.P.). The origins of many of the raw materials used by the site's occupants appear to be local. Some stone varieties, such as chalcedony and obsidian, however, may lie several hundred kilometers south in the Great Basin of Oregon.

The absolute age of the Richey Clovis cache has not been established. Based upon trace-element studies and geological evidence, the ancient occupation is thought to postdate volcanic ash falls that are known to have occurred 11,200 years ago. Much exploration remains to be done at this first Clovis site to be recorded for Washington State, and basic data remain to be assembled. In response to demands by Native Americans and others, a moratorium on additional archaeological fieldwork was effected in 1990; a generation must pass before a fuller understanding of this unique discovery is gained.

Richard Michael Gramly

Further Readings

Gramly, R.M. 1993. *The Richey Clovis Cache.* Persimmon Press, Buffalo.

Mehringer, P.J., and F.F. Foit, Jr. 1990. Volcanic Ash Dating of the Clovis Cache at East Wenatchee, Washington. *National Geographic Research* 6(4):495–503.

Ridged-Field Agriculture
Ridged or raised fields were constructed by mounding earth with hoes, spades, or digging sticks into large linear ridges and planting crops on top of them. This labor-intensive agricultural technique was widely used in Latin America and Oceania and is frequently, but not always, associated with complex societies. Common functions of ridged fields included wetland reclamation, frost drainage, erosion control, and weed control. In some regions, ridged-field agriculture was employed to cultivate grasslands.

In North America, prehistoric ridged fields occur in the midwestern and southeastern United States. Many "garden beds," some apparently extending over many acres, were reported from Wisconsin and the lower peninsula of Michigan in nineteenth- and early-twentieth-century survey reports. These fields most commonly occurred in upland settings and may have functioned to promote frost drainage. They also could have served as a means of cultivating the widespread prairies and savannas that crossed the area. The primary crop appears to have been maize, but squashes and seed crops were probably grown, too. While early investi-

gators speculated that the fields were built by the mythical "Mound Builders," some in Wisconsin and eastern Iowa were definitely associated with the Late Prehistoric Oneota culture, and Late Woodland societies may have constructed the ridged fields in Michigan. Striking examples of extensive, well-preserved, buried ridges were recently uncovered (Gallagher et al. 1985) within a bluff-base alluvial fan at the Sand Lake Oneota site in the Upper Mississippi Valley of southwestern Wisconsin (see Figure). Middle Mississippian (ca. A.D. 1000–1400, or 950–550 years B.P.) societies also constructed ridged fields. Among the better-documented fields are those at the Texas site in central Illinois, at Fort Center in Florida, and at Macon in Georgia. Possible fields occur in aerial photographs of the American Bottom, a center of Middle Mississippi culture in the Mississippi Valley, but, into the mid-1990s, they had not been confirmed by fieldwork. Many upland fields have been destroyed by modern cultivation or urban expansion, but extensive fields probably still exist within the floodplains of the Mississippi River and in other buried deposits.

Charles R. Moffat

A buried ridged field at the Sand Lake site (47Lc–44), La Crosse, Wisconsin. Courtesy of Dr. James Gallagher, University of Wisconsin at La Crosse.

Further Readings

Denevan, W.M. 1970. Aboriginal Drained Field Cultivation in the Americas. *Science* 169:647–654.

Gallagher, J.P., R.F. Boszhardt, R.F. Sasso, and K. Stevenson. 1985. Oneota Ridged Field Agriculture in Southwestern Wisconsin. *American Antiquity* 50:605–612.

Moffat, C.R. 1979. Some Observations on the Distribution and Significance of the Garden Beds of Wisconsin. *Wisconsin Archeologist* 60:222–248.

Riley, T.J., C.R. Moffat, and G. Freimuth. 1981. Prehistoric Raised Fields in the Upper Midwestern United States: An Innovation in Response to Marginal Growing Conditions. *North American Archaeologist* 2:101–116.

See also LATE WOODLAND; MISSISSIPPIAN CULTURE; ONEOTA

Rio Grande Branch

The Rio Grande branch of the Anasazi, as examined here, includes the middle and northern Rio Grande Valley and the surrounding mountains, an area that extends from Socorro in the south to the New Mexico border in the north. A general temporal scheme for the area was developed in the 1950s (Wendorf and Reed 1955). Everything before ca. A.D. 600 (1350 years B.P.) was lumped into a Preceramic period, which includes Paleoindian and Archaic remains. A Developmental period (A.D. 600–1200, or 1350–750 years B.P.) was subdivided into early, middle, and late phases 100–300 years in length. A Coalition period (A.D. 1200–1325, or 750–625 years B.P.) was subdivided into early and late phases 50 and 75 years in length, respectively. A Classic period (A.D. 1325–1600, or 625–350 years B.P.) was subdivided into early, middle, and late phases of 75, 150, and 50 years in length, respectively. These periods and phases are useful for general discussions and comparisons of areas, but less so for identifying short-term organizational or settlement changes. Most sites are dated on the basis of ceramic types, and, given the state of ceramic dating, major refinement of this scheme is a long way off.

Paleoindian and Archaic populations visited and inhabited the Rio Grande area in sparse numbers. Projectile-point styles representing these occupants indicate that the area was visited at least for hunting, and the presence of Archaic campsites indicates seasonal or even longer-term use of the area. Preceramic pithouses appeared in the Albuquerque area as early as 1000 B.C. (2950 years B.P.), and, although pithouses were less common than above-ground structures during Anasazi times, they never completely disappeared.

The Developmental period, which encompasses Basketmaker III, Pueblo I, Pueblo II, and part of Pueblo III in the Pecos classification, subsumes much architectural variability in a 600-year period. Pithouses, often grouped into villages of several pithouses, activity areas, and storage cists were the common form of habitation throughout the A.D. 800s. In the late A.D. 800s or early A.D. 900s, above-ground adobe or masonry structures appeared. Subsistence remains in the early sites indicate that hunting, gathering, and agriculture were important sources of food. Early habitation sites are rare. Their scarcity could be the result of both sparse population and burial of sites, as many habitations were at lower elevations in proximity to water; most were also close to arable land, indicating the probable importance of agriculture in the diet. Architectural heterogeneity continues into the 1000s and 1100s, with pithouses, adobe surface structures, and stone masonry surface structures all present. Habitation sites increased in number and size, indicating a probable population increase in some areas. Although Developmental-period sites of up to 100 rooms have been found in the Santa Fe area, sites of eight to 12 rooms are more common. Also in the 1000s and 1100s, black-on-white ceramics were manufactured locally rather than brought in from areas north and west of the Rio Grande Valley. This local ware, Kwahe'e Black-on-white, is characterized by mineral paint with designs reminiscent of those on pottery from the west. Subsistence continued to be diverse during the latter part of the Developmental period.

The Coalition period was one of increasing population size and aggregation in the Rio Grande area. Higher elevations in the Taos, Gallina, and Pajarito Plateau areas were the loci of rapid increases in population size and population aggregation, probably due, in part, to climate. By the mid-1200s, almost all of the population in the Taos area was aggregated into large pueblos. A lower percentage of the Pajarito population was aggregated at this time, but the shift from small habitations to larger pueblos of 50–300 rooms arranged around a central plaza was a dominant feature during the mid- to late 1200s in the higher elevations. Only in the Gallina area was population in the higher elevations less aggregated (probably less than 30 percent); in contrast to Taos and Pajarito, the area was abandoned by A.D. 1300 (650 years B.P.). Population and aggregation in the Santa Fe area increased during the period, more in the northern areas of the middle Rio Grande than in the southern areas. Architecturally, building materials and styles of above-ground structures varied widely. Pithouses were rare, and kivas became more common, especially in the larger aggregated habitations. Santa Fe Black-on-white was the predominant painted ware marking the Coalition period. It differed from Kwahe'e Black-on-white in that its makers used carbon paint, but they did retain many of the Kwahe'e designs. Subsistence became more focused on agriculture, with agricultural features, such as terraces, grid gardens, and check dams, increasing. Settlement systems were reorganized to better accommodate agriculture among aggregated populations: Some agricultural fields were now at a greater distance from the habitation areas than earlier when population density was lower and people relied less on agriculture. Field houses were established in which people resided temporarily to tend fields rather than travel back and forth between fields and home. In addition, with increasing population and probable increases in conflict over arable land, field houses were a way of staking claim to land.

The Classic period was one of major population decline in some areas, population increase in others, and a continuation of aggregation into larger pueblos, even where population was declining. Large pueblos with multiple plazas and numerous kivas abound in the Chama, Taos, Pajarito Plateau, Jemez, Santa Fe, Pecos, Galisteo Basin, Albuquerque, and Salinas areas. Eventually, all of these areas lost most of their population during the period, with the decline on the Pajarito Plateau appearing to have begun earlier than among the other higher-elevation, northern areas. The number of field houses continued to increase, as did distances from aggregated pueblos to them. Numerous gravel mulch and grid gardens appeared in the Chama area as the population attempted to take advantage of agricultural locations while mitigating temperature and water problems. In the early A.D. 1300s, there was a radical change in ceramic technology, evidenced by the production of glaze-paint ceramics. Glaze-production centers have been identified in the Galisteo Basin, Pecos, Salinas, and perhaps Pajarito Plateau areas. Black-on-white ceramics continued to be produced in the northern areas, especially the Chama Valley (the "biscuit" wares—Abiquiu Black-on-gray and Bandelier Black-on-gray) and in the Jemez Mountains (Jemez Black-on-white).

Janet D. Orcutt

Further Readings

Biella, J.V., and R.C. Chapman (editors). 1977. *A Survey of Regional Variability.* Archeological Investigations in Cochiti Reservoir, New Mexico, vol. 3. Office of Contract Archeology, University of New Mexico, Albuquerque.

———. 1979. *Adaptive Change in the Northern Rio Grande Valley.* Archeological Investigations in Cochiti Reservoir, New Mexico, vol. 4. Office of Contract Archeology, University of New Mexico, Albuquerque.

Cordell, L.S. 1979. *Cultural Resources Overview of the Middle Rio Grande Valley.* GPO, Washington, D.C.

———. 1989. Northern and Central Rio Grande. In *Dynamics of Southwest Prehistory,* edited by L.S. Cordell and G.J. Gumerman, pp. 293–335. Smithsonian Institution Press, Washington, D.C.

Crown, P.L. 1991. Evaluating the Construction Sequence and Population of Pot Creek Pueblo, Northern New Mexico. *American Antiquity* 56(2):291–314.

Dickson, D.B., Jr. 1979. *Prehistoric Pueblo Settlement Patterns: The Arroyo Hondo New Mexico Site Survey.* Arroyo Hondo Archaeological Series, vol. 2. School of American Research Press, Santa Fe.

Orcutt, J.D. 1991. Environmental Variability and Settlement Changes on the Pajarito Plateau, New Mexico. *American Antiquity* 56(2):315–332.

Preucel, R.W., Jr. 1990. *Seasonal Circulation and Dual Residence in the Pueblo Southwest: A Prehistoric Example From the Pajarito Plateau, New Mexico.* Garland, New York.

Stuart, D.E., and R.P. Gauthier. 1981. *Prehistoric New Mexico Background for Survey.* Historic Preservation Bureau, Department of Finance and Administration, Santa Fe.

Wendorf, F., and E.K. Reed. 1955. An Alternate Reconstruction of Northern Rio Grande Prehistory. *El Palacio* 62:131–173.

Woosley, A.I. 1986. Puebloan Prehistory of the Northern Rio Grande: Settlement, Population, Subsistence. *Kiva* 51:143–164.

Ritchie, William A. (1906–1995)

A prodigious fieldworker and prolific writer, William "Bill" Augustus Ritchie was primarily responsible for establishing the cultural-historical and methodological foundations of northeastern prehistory between the 1930s and the mid-1960s. He was one of the first individuals in the Northeast to recognize the importance of stratigraphy as an essential interpretive tool in archaeology, to effectively synthesize the prehistory of a single state, to systematically apply the Midwestern Taxonomic Method to a large corpus of material, to apply geochronological methods of dating Paleoindian occupations, to develop state antiquities legislation and to instigate comprehensive salvage programs, to apply settlement-pattern analysis to a large region, and to describe cultural units as adaptive systems functioning within a natural environment. In addition, in the 1930s he almost single-handedly developed the concept of an early North American Archaic horizon.

Although Ritchie was always concerned most basically with describing cultures and establishing cultural sequences, his shifting interests reflect the rapid changes that were transforming North American archaeology throughout his career. During his early years at the Rochester Municipal Museum in New York State (1924–1949), where he eventually became curator of anthropology, he was concerned primarily with historical reconstruction, the basic goal of archaeology at that time. At first, he applied the classificatory scheme developed by his mentor, Arthur C. Parker, the museum director, which placed material into an "Algonquian-Iroquois" dichotomy. In the mid-1930s, he shifted with vigor to the use of the then popular Midwestern Taxonomic Method, as is evident in his "A Perspective of Northeastern Archaeology" (1938) and in his first major synthesis, *The Pre-Iroquoian Occupations of New York State* (1944). The latter work, his doctoral dissertation at Columbia University, was awarded the A. Cressy Morrison Prize of the New York

William A. Ritchie. (Reprinted with permission from American Antiquity *52[3]:450)*

Academy of Sciences (1944) and is considered a classic of early 1940s archaeology.

In 1949, Ritchie left Rochester to become state archaeologist at the New York State Museum in Albany, where he remained until his retirement in 1971. By the late 1950s, he had altered his field strategies to accommodate settlement-pattern analyses, and in the 1960s he adopted a cultural-ecological perspective, which is reflected in his second major synthesis and seminal work, *The Archaeology of New York State* (1965).

During his long and productive career, Ritchie conducted major excavations at more than 75 sites, including Lamoka Lake, Levanna, Geneva, Robinson, Oberlander, Wickham, Vinette, Frontenac Island, Canandaigua, Castle Creek, Brewerton, and Reagen. Besides his archaeological focus, he was a trained physical anthropologist and paleopathologist, prepared exhibits in the Anthropology Halls at the Rochester Museum, and taught courses at nearby colleges and universities. He was president of the Society for American Archaeology (1956–

1957) and was an assistant or associate editor of that organization's journal from 1935 through 1955. Among other honors, Ritchie was appointed a research associate of the Section of Man at the Carnegie Museum of Natural History in Pittsburgh in 1973.

Guy Gibbon

Further Readings

Funk, R.E. 1971. William A. Ritchie: A Valediction. *Bulletin of the New York State Archaeological Association* 52:13–21.

Funk, R.E., and C.F. Hayes, III. 1977. *Current Perspectives in Northeastern Archeology: Essays in Honor of William A. Ritchie.* Researches and Transactions, vol. 17, no. 1. New York State Archaeological Association, Rochester.

Ritchie, W.A. 1932. The Lamoka Lake Site: The Type Station of the Archaic Algonkin Period in New York. *Researches and Transactions of the New York State Archaeological Association* 7(4):79–134.

———. 1938. A Perspective of Northeastern Archaeology. *American Antiquity* 4:94–112.

———. 1944. *The Pre-Iroquoian Occupations of New York State.* Memoir no. 1. Rochester Museum of Arts and Sciences, Rochester.

———. 1946. Archaeological Manifestations and Relative Chronology in the Northeast. In *Man in Northeastern North America,* edited by F. Johnson, pp. 96–105. Papers, vol. 3. Robert S. Peabody Foundation for Archaeology, Phillips Academy, Andover.

———. 1965. *The Archaeology of New York State.* Natural History Press, Garden City.

———. 1969. *The Archaeology of Martha's Vineyard: A Framework for the Prehistory of Southern New England: A Study in Coastal Ecology and Adaptation.* Natural History Press, Garden City.

River Snails

The durable shells of a few species of freshwater river snails were sometimes modified by Precolumbian native peoples of the American Midwest to serve as decorative items. The onyx rocksnail (*Leptoxis praerosa,* formerly *Anculosa praerosa*), once a common inhabitant of the central Ohio River, seems to have been the freshwater snail shell favored for exchange outside of its native range. The rocksnail has an attractive, nearly spherical shell ca. 1 cm (0.4 inches) in height. Aboriginal shell workers flattened the aperture side by grinding a facet that would permit a string or a sinew thread to pass between the exposed whorls to allow the shell to be pulled tightly against a fabric or leather base. These *Leptoxis* "embroidery" shells have been recovered in mortuary contexts throughout much of the midwestern United States up to 805 km (500 miles) from their source area *Leptoxis* beads first appear ca. 6000 B.C. (7950 years B.P.) at the Modoc Rock Shelter in Illinois. They seem particularly abundant in some Middle Archaic (ca. 4000 B.C., or 5950 years B.P.) sites, such as Elizabeth in Illinois where the patterned distribution of beads with burials appeared to outline waist belts or sashes. In Middle Woodland (ca. A.D. 300, or 1650 years B.P.) ritual context at the Turner site in southwestern Ohio, *Leptoxis* beads were found by the thousands. Shells of other freshwater taxa, such as *Pleurocera, Campeloma,* and *Lithasia,* were infrequently used for decorative purposes but were of some significance as a food item. In general, freshwater snail shells never seem to have acquired the popularity of some marine species, like the common Atlantic marginella (*Marginella apicina*), the shells of which were used in large numbers in the Midwest for embroidery beads.

James L. Theler

Further Readings

Albertson, D.G., and D.K. Charles. 1988. Archaic Mortuary Components. In *The Archaic and Woodland Cemeteries at the Elizabeth Site in the Lower Illinois Valley,* edited by D.K. Charles, S.R. Leigh, and J.E. Buikstra, pp. 29–40. Research Series, vol. 7. Center for American Archeology, Kampsville.

Fowler, M.L. 1959. *Summary Report of Modoc Rock Shelter 1952, 1953, 1955, 1956.* Report of Investigations no. 8. Illinois State Museum, Springfield.

Klippel, W.E., and D.F. Morey. 1986. Contextual and Nutritional Analyses of Freshwater Gastropods From Middle Archaic Deposits at the Hayes Site, Middle Tennessee. *American Antiquity* 51:799–813.

Van Dyke, A.P., D.F. Overstreet, and J.L. Theler. 1980. Archaeological Recovery at 11-RI-337, an Early Middle Woodland Shell Midden in East Moline, Illinois.

Wisconsin Archeologist 61(2):125–265.

Willoughby, C.C., and E.A. Hooton. 1922. *The Turner Group of Earthworks, Hamilton County, Ohio.* Papers, vol. 8, no. 3. Peabody Museum of American Archaeology and Ethnology, Harvard University, Cambridge.

Roberts, Frank H.H., Jr. (1897–1966)

Frank Harold Hanna Roberts, Jr., had an active and distinguished career in the Bureau of American Ethnology (BAE) at the Smithsonian Institution, Washington, D.C., where he became a leader in the development of Southwestern and Paleoindian archaeology and of nationwide salvage programs. Although his activities as an archaeologist were numerous and diverse, they can be separated into three fairly clear periods of concentration: work in the Southwest on Pueblo and Basketmaker sites in the years 1921–1933, a concern with Paleoindian sites and problems in the years 1934–1944, and full-time administrative responsibilities from 1945 until poor health forced him to retire in 1964—after which he continued to serve as a part-time administrator until his death in 1966.

Roberts's first fieldwork experience was in the Piedra-Pagosa region of the Upper San Juan River Basin in southwestern Colorado in the years 1920–1923 while he was assistant curator of archaeology at the State Historical and Natural History Society of Colorado and an instructor at the University of Denver. He continued his education at Harvard University in 1924, where he was an assistant in anthropology in 1925–1926. His doctoral dissertation, *The Ceramic Sequence in the Chaco Canyon, New Mexico, and Its Relations to the Cultures of the San Juan Basin,* was based upon materials provided by his participation in a National Geographic Society expedition under the direction of Neil M. Judd in 1926 to Pueblo Bonito. Roberts joined the BAE in 1926, serving as a staff archaeologist to 1944. He became assistant chief in 1944, associate director in 1947, and director of the BAE from 1957 until his retirement in 1964. His work in the Southwest for the BAE until 1933 included investigations of sites dating primarily to the last 2,000 years in Texas, New Mexico, Colorado, and Arizona. In 1927, he participated in the first Pecos Conference at Pecos Pueblo, where he took a major role in formulating the "Pecos Classification," a new outline of culture sequences for South-western archaeology that established the numbered sequences of Basketmaker-Pueblo cultures.

Although Roberts's interest in the problem of the early peopling of the New World was stimulated as early as 1927 by a visit to the Folsom excavations in New Mexico, his commitment to Paleoindian studies was not solidified until 1934, when he visited and tested the Lindenmeier site in northern Colorado, where Folsom points had been found. He started extensive excavations at the site in 1935 that continued through 1940. In the years 1934–1944, he also visited or tested other possible early sites in Colorado, Wyoming, Iowa, Arizona, Nebraska, and Saskatchewan. Among the sites tested were San Jon in eastern New Mexico (1941) and Agate Basin in Wyoming (1942). Roberts became the foremost Paleoindian scholar during this period.

During his administrative years (1945–1966), Roberts helped organize the nationwide River Basin Surveys program, one of the largest and most successful single archaeological efforts ever undertaken by the U.S. government. The River Basin Survey, of which he became director at its inception in 1945, remained his chief interest for the remainder of his life.

Roberts was a member of numerous committees and boards, a consultant, and an officer in a variety of organizations. With A.V. Kidder and A.L. Kroeber, he helped establish the Society for American Archaeology in 1934 and became president of that organization in 1950. He was elected president of the Anthropological Society of Washington (1936–1937) and of the Washington Academy of Science (1949); he was vice president of the American Anthropological Association (1944), vice chairman of the Division of Anthropology and Psychology of the National Research Council (1946), and vice president of the American Association for the Advancement of Science (1952). Roberts was also associate editor of *American Anthropologist* (1932–1944) and representative of the American Anthropological Association on the National Research Council (1935–1937, 1939–1941, and 1947–1949), and he represented the United States on the International Commission for Historic Sites and Monuments (1939–1943). Among his numerous awards were the Viking Fund Medal and Award (1951) and honorary Doctor of Laws degrees from the universities of New Mexico (1957), Colorado (1959), and Denver (1962).

Guy Gibbon

R

Further Readings

Judd, N.M. 1966. F.H.H. Roberts, Jr., 1897–1966. *American Anthropologist* 68:1226–1232.

Roberts, F.H.H., Jr. 1929. *Shabik'eshchee Village: A Late Basketmaker Site in the Chaco Canyon, New Mexico.* Bulletin no. 992. Bureau of American Ethnology, Smithsonian Institution, Washington, D.C.

———. 1931. *The Ruins of Kiatuthlanna, Eastern Arizona.* Bulletin no. 100. Bureau of American Ethnology, Smithsonian Institution, Washington, D.C.

———. *The Village of the Great Kivas on the Zuñi Reservation, New Mexico.* Bulletin no. 111. Bureau of American Ethnology, Smithsonian Institution, Washington, D.C.

———. 1935a. *A Folsom Complex: Preliminary Report on Investigations at the Lindenmeier Site in Northern Colorado.* Miscellaneous Collections, vol. 94, no. 4. Smithsonian Institution, Washington, D.C.

———. 1935b. A Survey of Southwestern Archaeology. *American Anthropologist* 37:1–33.

———. 1936. *Additional Information on the Folsom Complex.* Miscellaneous Collections, vol. 95, no. 10. Smithsonian Institution, Washington, D.C.

———. 1937. Archaeology in the Southwest. *American Antiquity* 3:3–33.

———. 1939. *Archaeological Remains of the Whitewater District, Eastern Arizona.* Bulletin no. 121. Bureau of American Ethnology, Smithsonian Institution, Washington, D.C.

———. 1940. Developments in the Problem of the North American Paleo-Indian. In *Essays in Historical Anthropology in North America,* pp. 51–116. Miscellaneous Collections, vol. 100. Smithsonian Institution, Washington, D.C.

Stephenson, R.L. 1967. Frank H.H. Roberts, Jr., 1897–1966. *American Antiquity* 32:84–94.

Rock Art

The term "rock art" refers to designs inscribed on cliffs, boulders, bedrock, or any natural rock surface within a landscape context. Rock paintings and drawings made with paints or dry pig-

Petroglyph carved by early eighteenth-century Navajos, northwestern New Mexico. (Photograph by Curtis Schaafsma)

ments are sometimes referred to as pictographs. Figures pecked, incised, abraded, scratched, or otherwise cut into rock are called petroglyphs (see Figure 1). These images, derived from culturally defined repertoires of signs and symbols executed in implicitly or explicitly culturally prescribed ways, express past ideologies—nonmaterial values, beliefs, and worldviews of the authoring group. Indian rock art in North America dates from ca. 2050 B.C. (4000 years B.P.) or earlier through the twentieth century A.D. Garrick Mallery's *Picture-Writing of the American Indians* (1893) provides some of the earliest notations of rock art from various locations in the Americas. More specifically focused on rock art from given regions are a few major early-twentieth-century works, such as Julien H. Steward's "Petroglyphs of California and Adjoining States" (1929). Although early archaeologists often referenced its presence and described rock art near habitation sites, rock art was only occasionally a focus of study until the 1960s. Since that time, interest in this subject as an archaeological resource has increased considerably, and research directions have expanded. Noteworthy overviews of North American rock art include *Rock Art of the American Indian* (1967) by Campbell Grant and *A Survey of North American Indian Rock Art* (1979) by Klaus F. Wellmann.

Preliminary research has necessarily been preoccupied with problems of taxonomy and dating. Like other art, rock-art imagery is patterned in regard to style and content. Rock-art styles, in turn, conform to specific cultures and time periods and constitute shared visual systems with meaning to the members of a given culture or social group. Technological advances promise assistance in the difficult problem of dating rock art. Accelerator radiocarbon studies and analysis of patina formation on petroglyphs may make absolute dating of rock art possible. Traditional methods of dating rock art or relating it to a particular cultural framework include associating rock art with datable habitation sites and comparative studies of imagery between those in rock art and those on datable artifacts, such as ceramics. Where different styles occur on the same rock, relative dating of figures and styles can be established through studies of superimpositions and differences in the degree of patina, or "desert varnish," accumulation and weathering.

Among tribal peoples, images were made on rocks for a variety of reasons. In many cases, rock art had to do with economic, social, and religious issues, and even protective magic. In some cases, it was made with the intent of manipulating supernatural forces to advantage. Rock art may designate shrines where communication with the supernatural was possible or otherwise important localities in the landscape such as sites where important mythical events took place. Some rock art of North American hunter-gatherers emphasizes shamanic themes. Ethnohistorically, rock art has been made in the context of vision quests, puberty, and curing ceremonies; in the context of increase rites and requests for game; to mark social boundaries and land-usage rights; to document important events; and to represent status objects. These functions have implications for prehistoric behavior as well and are the focus of rock-art studies in the American West.

Polly Schaafsma

Warrior bearing star decorated shield, Rio Grande Pueblo, A.D. 1325–1680, Socorro County, New Mexico. (Illustration by P. Schaafsma)

Further Readings

Cole, S.J. 1990. *Legacy on Stone: Rock Art of the Colorado Plateau and the Four Corners Region.* Johnson Books, Boulder.

Dorn, R.I. 1983. Cation-Ratio Dating: A New Rock Varnish Age-Determination Technique. *Quaternary Research* 20:49–73.

Grant, C. 1967. *Rock Art of the American Indian.* Thomas Y. Crowell, New York.

Heizer, R.F., and M.A. Baumhoff. 1962. *Prehistoric Rock Art of Nevada and Eastern California.* University of California Press, Berkeley.

Mallery, G. 1893. *Picture-Writing of the American Indians.* Tenth Annual Report of the Bureau of Ethnology, 1888–1889. 2 vols. Washington, D.C.

Schaafsma, P. 1980. *Indian Rock Art of the Southwest.* School of American Research, Santa Fe; University of New Mexico Press, Albuquerque.

———. 1985. Form, Content, and Function: Theory and Method in North American Rock Art Studies. In *Advances in Archaeological Method and Theory,* vol. 8, edited by M. Schiffer, pp. 237–277. Academic Press, New York.

Steward, J.H. 1929. Petroglyphs of California and Adjoining States. *University of California Publications in American Archae-*

ology and Ethnology 24:47–238.

Turpin, S. (editor). 1994. *Shamanism and Rock Art in North America*. Special Publication no. 1. Rock Art Foundation, San Antonio.

Wellmann, K.F. 1979. *A Survey of North American Indian Rock Art*. Akademische Druck, Verlagsanstalt, Graz.

See also PETROGLYPH

Rock Art (California)

Rock art involves cutting (petroglyphs) or painting (pictographs) figures or designs on rock faces. California has one of the greatest assemblages of rock art in North America. Hundreds of recorded sites include hundreds of thousands of individual depictions. Petroglyphs greatly outnumber pictographs, due at least partly to preservation, for relatively few rock-art sites occur in protected locations where delicate paintings might survive (Painted Caves State Park near Santa Barbara is an example). Most occur on canyon walls or outcrop surfaces (Grinding Rock State Park near Jackson has unusual horizontal petroglyphs). Because most examples occur in isolation, the dating of rock art is generally problematic. Most California designs are geometric, though a variety of humanlike (anthropomorphic) and animal-like (zoomorphic) examples are known. Some examples may have astronomical significance. Many are assumed to reflect shamanistic or other religious activities, but firmly supported interpretations are usually difficult to establish. Systematic studies have examined regional and temporal styles and their significance (Heizer and Baumhoff 1962; Heizer and Clewlow, Jr. 1973; Hudson and Underhay 1978).

Joseph L. Chartkoff

Further Readings

Grant, C. 1966. *The Rock Paintings of the Chumash*. University of California Press, Berkeley.

Heizer, R.F., and M.A. Baumhoff. 1962. *Prehistoric Rock Art of Nevada and Eastern California*. University of California Press, Berkeley.

Heizer, R.F., and C.W. Clewlow, Jr. 1973. *Prehistoric Rock Art of California*. Ballena Press, Ramona.

Hudson, T., and E. Underhay. 1978. *Crystals in the Sky: An Intellectual Odyssey Involving Chumash Astronomy, Cosmology and Rock Art*. Anthropological Papers no. 10. Ballena Press, Socorro.

Lee, G., and W.D. Hyder. 1990. Relative Dating and the Rock Art of Lava Beds National Monument. *Proceedings of the Society for California Archaeology* 3:195–205.

Whitley, D.S., and R.I. Dorn. 1987. Rock Art Chronology in Eastern California. *World Archaeology* 19:150–164.

Rodgers Shelter

Discovered in 1962, excavated in the 1960s and 1970s, and listed on the National Register of Historic Places, Rodgers Shelter (23BE125) in south Benton County, Missouri, is among the prime archaeological sites of the Ozark Highland. It and related archaeological and paleontological sites of the Lower Pomme de Terre River Valley are now submerged beneath the waters of Harry S. Truman Lake, a federal impoundment. Rodgers Shelter is a multilayered, deep site. Deposits exceed 9 m (29.5 feet) in depth and occur within four major strata radiocarbon dated between 8550 B.C. and A.D. 1150 (10,500–800 years B.P.). The site consists of two adjacent areas at the base of a rocky hill slope and bluff line: the protected area beneath the south-facing rock overhang and the adjoining alluvial terrace that is further subdivided by a gully. The combination of a complex, nearly continuous sedimentary record for most of the postglacial epoch, the quality of organic preservation, especially of animal remains, and extensive excavation of the shelter area and the terrace immediately to its south make Rodgers Shelter a natural laboratory for the study of human adaptation to changing postglacial landscapes.

Rodgers Shelter is in an especially opportune location for documenting changes in human adaptation, climate, and environment over thousands of years. These changes were generally accompanied by shifts in the composition of the ecotone that spans the western flank of the Ozark Highland, where Rodgers Shelter is. Today, this ecotone marks the transition from the central Plains tall-grass prairies on the west to the eastern deciduous, oak-hickory forests of the Ozark Highland. Most dramatic were changes that accompanied the postglacial climatic extremes of the middle Holocene (ca. 6550–1850 B.C., or 8500–3800 years B.P.). When compared with records from midwestern archaeological sites to the east, such as Graham Cave on the Loutre River in Montgomery County, Missouri, Modoc Rock Shelter in the Mississippi Valley of Illinois, and Koster on a small tributary of the Illinois River in west-central Illinois, the middle Holocene is revealed to have had a steeper, or more pronounced, climatic and environmental gradient than is present today for the Ozarks and the Mississippi Valley. The Rodgers Shelter locale experienced progressively more severe, long-term drought in the middle Holocene than did areas to the east.

Postglacial habitation of Rodgers Shelter reflects the dynamics of an evolving riverine landscape within an environmentally and climatically changing region. The basal encampments were by Dalton foragers. They lived beneath the shelter overhang on a much higher bedrock bench than exists now, near an actively aggrading floodplain. Middle and late Holocene groups reoccupied the site when it was less prone to being flooded out. As environmental conditions declined during the middle Holocene, however, site use became less frequent, or the site was simply abandoned for periods of up to 1,500 years or so. During this time, the first documented experimentation with domesticated plants began, and there was a greater reliance on aquatic food resources that continued into the late Holocene.

Marvin Kay

Further Readings

Haynes, C.V., Jr. 1985. *Mastodon-Bearing Springs and Late Quaternary Geochronology of the Lower Pomme de Terre Valley, Missouri.* Special Paper no. 204. Geological Society of America, Boulder.

Kay, M. 1983. Archaic Period Research in the Western Ozark Highlands, Missouri. In *Archaic Hunters and Gatherers in the American Midwest,* edited by J.L. Phillips and J.A. Brown, pp. 41–70. Academic Press, New York.

McMillan, R.B., and W.E. Klippel. 1981. Post-Glacial Environmental Change and Hunting-Gathering Societies of the Southern Prairie Peninsula. *Journal of Archaeological Science* 8:215–245.

Wood, W.R., and R.B. McMillan (editors). 1976. *Prehistoric Man and His Environments: A Case Study in the Ozark Highland.* Academic Press, New York.

Rogers, David Banks (1868–1954)

David Banks Rogers defined the first significant regional sequence of cultures in California archaeology. Employed at the Santa Barbara Museum of Natural History in the 1920s, Rogers excavated a number of coastal sites in the vicinity. The results, described in his *Prehistoric Man of the Santa Barbara Coast* (1929), allowed him to define three successive periods in the region's culture sequence: the Oak Grove culture, the Hunting culture, and the Canalino culture. Rogers's arrangement of these three episodes in relative chronological order is still regarded as fundamentally valid, though absolute dates could not be assigned until radiocarbon assays became available two decades later.

In Rogers's scheme, the Oak Grove culture (6050–2050 B.C., or 8000–4000 years B.P.) represented the first permanent tradition along the Santa Barbara coast. Oak Grove sites reflect exploitation of land-based resources, especially the acorns of the coastal live oak (*Quercus agrifolia*), which flourished in coastal canyons, and various species of hard-seed–producing chaparral brush and annual bunch grasses, which blanketed the coastal hills. Oak Grove sites contain many milling tools, including mortars and pestles, which are associated with acorn processing, and millingstones and manos, which are associated with the grinding of hard seeds. Core tools and heavy flake scrapers were also abundant, but projectile points and ornamental artifacts were scarce. Rogers associated Oak Grove sites with hilltop locations.

The subsequent Hunting culture (2050 B.C.–A.D. 450, or 4000–1500 years B.P.) was interpreted by Rogers as a shift in settlement to seashore locations and coastal estuaries and a shift in economy away from acorns and hard seeds toward game and fish, particularly deer and pinnipeds (seals and sea lions). Hunting-culture sites contain fewer milling tools and heavy core industries than earlier sites, but they do contain more projectile points and chipped-stone tools associated with butchering and scraping.

Canalino-culture sites (A.D. 450–1770, or 1500–180 years B.P.) were viewed by Rogers as evidence of the emergence of a tradition described ethnographically in studies of the Chumash Indians of the Santa Barbara region. The Canalino lived in coastal sedentary villages, some of which were reckoned later to have populations of 1,000–1,500, with diversified economies that relied heavily on maritime resources. They built distinctive seagoing wood-plank canoes in which they traveled regularly between the northern Channel Islands (Santa Cruz, San Miguel, Santa Rosa, San Nicolas) and the mainland. They also made trading expeditions to Santa Catalina Island to acquire steatite (soapstone), with which they carved a wide range of utilitarian and ornamental objects: bowls, frying griddles (comals), smoking pipes, large tube beads, whale effigies, and models of canoes, among others. Extensive cemeteries with marked differences in grave goods among the burials suggested ranked societies, a system that flourished until the Spanish conquest.

Joseph L. Chartkoff

Further Readings

Arnold, J.E. 1987. *Craft Specialization in the Prehistoric Channel Islands, California.* Publications in Anthropology no. 18. University of California Press, Berkeley.

Erlandson, J.M., and R.H. Colton (editors). 1991. *Hunter-Gatherers of Early Holocene Coastal California.* Perspectives in California Archaeology, vol. 1. Institute of Archaeology, University of California, Los Angeles.

Glassow, M.A. 1977. An Archaeological Overview of the Northern Channel Islands, California. Ms. on file, Western Archaeological Center, National Park Service, Tucson.

King, C.D. 1981. *The Evolution of Chumash Society: A Comparative Study of Artifacts Used in Social System Maintenance in the Santa Barbara Channel Region Before A.D. 1804.* Unpublished Ph.D. dissertation, Department of Anthropology, University of California, Davis.

Olson, R.L. 1930. Chumash Prehistory. *University of California Publications in American Archaeology and Ethnology* 28(1):1–22.

Rogers, D.B. 1929. *Prehistoric Man of the Santa Barbara Coast.* Santa Barbara Museum of Natural History, Santa Barbara.

Warren, C.N. 1968. Cultural Tradition and Ecological Adaptation on the Southern California Coast. In *Archaic Prehistory in the Western United States,* edited by C. Irwin-Williams, pp. 1–14. Contributions in Anthropology, vol. 1, no. 3. Eastern New Mexico University, Portales.

Malcolm J. Rogers. (Reprinted with permission from American Antiquity *26[4]:532)*

Rogers, Malcolm J. (1890–1960)

Malcolm Jennings Rogers, employed by the San Diego Museum of Man for more than 30 years, pioneered the archaeology of southern California's deserts and established the first models of that region's culture sequences. His fieldwork extended from the coast to the Colorado River and from Death Valley to the Mexican border. He defined several major cultural phases, most notably the San Dieguito, Amargosa, and Yuman. In identifying Anasazi ceramics in the Mohave Sink and especially at the Halloran Springs turquoise-mining area, he drew attention to connections between California and the Southwest. Rogers worked mainly before the development of effective dating methods and environmental reconstructions; his definitions of culture sequences and their ages have been often revised, even by himself, but his basic framework continues to be widely used.

Joseph L. Chartkoff

Further Readings

Moratto, M.J. (editor). 1984. *California Archaeology.* Academic Press, New York.

Rogers, M.J. 1929. *Report on an Archaeological Reconnaissance in the Mohave Sink Region.* Papers no. 1. San Diego Museum of Man, San Diego.

———. 1939. *Early Lithic Industries of the Lower Basin of the Colorado River and Adjacent Desert Areas.* Papers no. 3. San

Diego Museum of Man, San Diego.

———. 1945. An Outline of Yuman Prehistory. *Southwestern Journal of Anthropology* 1(2):167–198.

———. 1958. San Dieguito Implements From the Terraces of the Rincon-Patano and Rillito Drainage System. *Kiva* 24(1):1–23.

———. 1966. *Ancient Hunters of the Far West*. Union-Tribune Publishing, San Diego.

Warren, C.N. 1984. The Desert Region. In *California Archaeology,* edited by M.J. Moratto, pp. 339–430. Academic Press, New York.

Ruin Island Phase

Ruin Island is the pioneering phase of Thule culture in the Smith Sound–Kane Basin region of the eastern High Arctic. It was designated the Ruin Island phase after the small island off the coast of northwest Greenland where its remains were first identified by the Danish archaeologist Erik Holtved in the 1930s (Holtved 1944). The phase is defined in the eastern High Arctic by a distinctive style of family dwelling made of sod, stone, and whale bone with a kitchen offshoot built off a front corner of the main room, by the use of large communal structures in winter settlements, and by a particular constellation of western-related artifact traits that serve to distinguish it from other early Thule-culture manifestations in the eastern Arctic. Radiocarbon dating of materials from Ruin Island house ruins in eastern Ellesmere Island, Canada, have indicated a late twelfth or early thirteenth century A.D. period of occupation for the phase. A comparative analysis of house forms and selected artifact traits, such as harpoon heads, arrowheads, clay pottery, and needle cases, indicates a strong relationship to Punuk-influenced early Western Thule–culture sites in western Alaska rather than to north Alaska, which has generally been considered the source area for Canadian Thule culture. Analysis of faunal remains from winter-house ruins shows that the early Thule-culture residents of the eastern High Arctic survived on a diet of sea mammal resources (seals, walrus, and whales) supplemented by musk-ox, arctic hare, arctic fox, and birds such as eiders, geese, gulls, and ravens.

Karen McCullough

Further Readings

Holtved, E. 1944. Archaeological Investigations in the Thule District: I and II. *Meddelelser om Grønland* 141(1):308 and 141(2):184.

McCullough, K.M. 1989. *The Ruin Islanders: Early Thule Culture Pioneers in the Eastern High Arctic*. Mercury Series Paper no. 141. Archaeological Survey of Canada, Canadian Museum of Civilization, Hull.

Schledermann, P., and K.M. McCullough. 1980. Western Elements in the Early Thule Culture of the Eastern High Arctic. *Arctic* 33:833–841.

R

S

Salado Horizon

Salado is an archaeological horizon in the low deserts of the American Southwest that persisted from the late thirteenth century to the mid-fifteenth century A.D. It is defined by the appearance of Gila Polychrome in the Late Prehistoric phases of eight archaeologically defined areas that extend from the Phoenix Basin on the west to the Rio Grande on the east (see Table). Despite its importance to the definition of the Salado horizon, the Gila Polychrome style also occurs in areas well beyond that commonly assigned to the Salado horizon (see Map).

Gila Polychrome, unlike other Southwestern wares, was manufactured in many different local areas, and has the greatest spatial distribution of any Southwestern ceramic type. Gila Polychrome is closely related to Pinto and Tonto Polychrome types, which collectively are called either Roosevelt Red wares or Salado Polychrome. Pinto Polychrome appears ca. A.D. 1270–1280 (680–670 years B.P.); Gila Polychrome, shortly after A.D. 1300 (650 years B.P.). Some researchers have argued that Gila Polychrome was present for several centuries in northern Mexico before its first appearance in the Southwest, but John C. Ravesloot and Jeffrey S. Dean make an excellent case for a uniform A.D. 1300 (650 years B.P.) beginning date in all areas (Dean and Ravesloot 1993).

Another characteristic of the Salado horizon is a general tendency to enclose communities with a compound wall, although the morphology of these compounds varies considerably from the Hohokam area on the west to the Mimbres region on the east.

In general, however, the Salado horizon cannot be defined as a package of widely co-occurring traits. In an excellent review of Salado

research, Ben A. Nelson and Steven A. LeBlanc observe that the appearance of Gila Polychrome in the Southwest is associated with other changes in local patterns (settlement patterns, architecture, burial practices, ceramics) but that the nature of these changes is not the same in all places (Nelson and LeBlanc 1986).

Winifred J. and Harold S. Gladwin first introduced the term "Salado" in 1930 to refer to Classic-period (A.D. 1100–1450, or 850–500 years B.P.) archaeological components in the Tonto Basin of central Arizona. Usage broadened in the ensuing decades, however, as archaeologists working in the Salt and Gila basins sought to explain the changes that took place in the architecture, ceramic styles, and burial practices of the Hohokam at ca. 1100 (850 years B.P.). Feeling that the changes were too sudden to be part of an indigenous Hohokam development, archaeologists formulated the "Salado Migration" hypothesis, which proposes that, from A.D. 1100 to 1300 (850–650 years B.P.), the Salado influenced the Hohokam indirectly through long-distance contacts and that at ca. A.D. 1300 (650 years B.P.) they migrated into the Hohokam region, where they assumed a dominant role in Hohokam society.

As described by Emil W. Haury (1945), the Salado migration was triggered by the abandonment of portions of the Colorado Plateau in the late thirteenth century. He suggested that people from the Kayenta and the Four Corners areas moved into the Little Colorado Valley and southward into the Mogollon region. The resulting population pressure in turn prompted the Salado, a mixture of Mogollon and Anasazi people living in the Tonto Basin who had perfected an adaptation to the desert environment, to migrate into the Hohokam region, taking

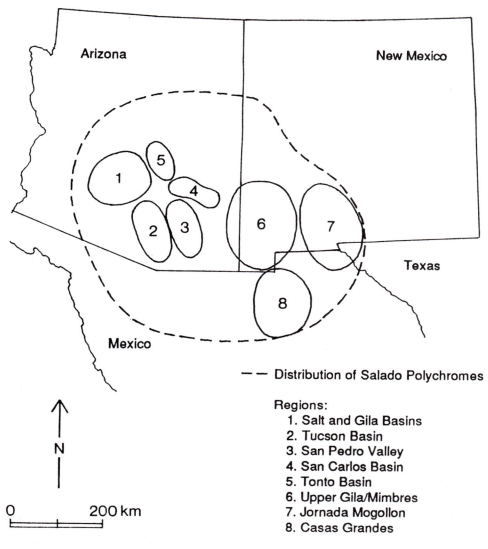

Distribution of Salado Polychromes

Regions:
1. Salt and Gila Basins
2. Tucson Basin
3. San Pedro Valley
4. San Carlos Basin
5. Tonto Basin
6. Upper Gila/Mimbres
7. Jornada Mogollon
8. Casas Grandes

The Salado horizon extends across eight archaeological regions of the southwestern United States and northern Mexico. (Courtesy of G. E. Rice)

with them Puebloan traits, such as polychrome ceramics, walled compounds, and inhumation practices. At the close of the Civano phase (ca. A.D. 1450, or 500 years B.P.), the Salado purportedly moved east into the San Pedro Valley and southwestern New Mexico, from where they eventually reached the site of Casas Grandes in northern Mexico (not to be confused with the singular Casa Grande in Arizona).

The migration hypothesis has drawbacks. First, the excavation of more Hohokam sites has demonstrated that the Civano phase had well-established antecedents in the earlier Hohokam phase. Second, estimates of prehistoric population sizes indicate that an area as small as the Tonto Basin could not have supported an out-migration of enough people to dominate the Hohokam region while still retaining a sizable population.

Another group of hypotheses treats the Salado horizon as an interregional reaction to the development of a complex society within either the Casas Grandes area of northern Mexico or the Hohokam area of southern Arizona. These hypotheses are based on the recognition that complex societies do not operate in isolation. Their leaders are interested in distant areas that can provide them with exotic items, which they use to symbolize their importance to their followers, and perhaps even laborers, which they use to increase the productivity of their own society. The trade requirements of a complex society can stimulate changes well beyond its borders, too, with people in distant locations adjusting their settlement patterns or economies to improve the efficiency of their participation in the trade network. They may even copy material-culture styles of the complex society to demonstrate their own importance.

Rex E. Gerald (1976) and, subsequently, Glen E. Rice (1990) suggest that the Salado horizon is a regional influence of complex social groups among the Classic-period Hohokam (A.D. 1100–1450, or 850–500 years B.P.). The rooms built on top of platform mounds are considered elite residences and evidence that the Classic-period Hohokam were organized as a number of competing chiefdoms. According to this model, Gila Polychrome vessels were used by the elite as a symbol of their wealth and importance, and the style was copied in distant regions by social groups seeking to emulate them. Nelson and LeBlanc propose a similar model, but from the perspective of Casas Grandes. In their model, the wealth and prestige of a Mesoamerican-style center in northern Mexico attracted people from across the South-

S

west. As they returned from Casas Grandes, they brought with them new ideas about material culture and social organization.

One critical problem with these models is a lack of evidence that the use of Gila Polychrome was ever limited to an elite. Use-wear on the vessels suggests that many were used for practical purposes; in addition, the vessels are found in different contexts at sites of different sizes.

Patricia L. Crown (1994) approaches the Salado issue by concentrating only on Salado polychromes. She suggests that these styles were associated with the spread of a religious cult concerned with weather control, water, and fertility. Among the motifs used to decorate Salado Polychrome vessels is a recurring suite of icons that represent snakes (see Illustration), horned serpents, parrots and other birds, humans, masked beings, eyes, flowers, stars, clouds, and the sun. Although their meaning in fourteenth-century Southwestern societies cannot be determined, they co-occur in patterns that demonstrate that they were part of a symbolic system related to a unified set of beliefs. Furthermore, because most Salado polychromes were apparently made for household use rather than for special ceremonies (for instance, they do not occur predominantly in burials), the beliefs associated with the icons were most likely shared by a large community of believers. In ethnographically documented cases, cults that

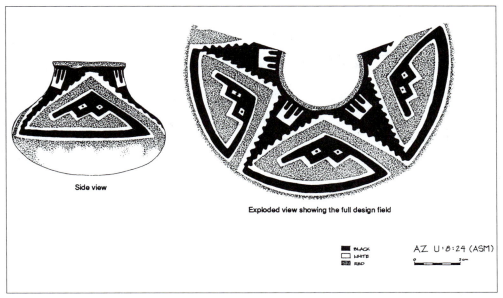

Side view

Exploded view showing the full design field

BLACK
WHITE
RED

AZ U:8:24 (ASM)

Serpent motif on a Tonto polychrome jar from Tonto Basin, Arizona (Site AZ U:8:24 [ASM], Specimen Number 19039). (Courtesy of G. E. Rice)

	Tucson Basin, San Pedro River, San Carlos Basin	Salt and Gila Basins	Tonto Basin	Upper Gila/ Mimbres	Jornada Mogollon	Casas Grandes (Mexico)
A.D.1500	Spanish Entrada	Spanish Entrada	Spanish Entrada	Spanish Entrada	Spanish Entrada	Spanish Entrada
A.D.1450	(abandoned ?)	(abandoned ?)	(abandoned)	(abandoned)	(abandoned)	Diablo
A.D.1400		El Povoron (recently defined)				
A.D.1350	Tucson Phase	Civano Phase	Gila Phase	Cliff Phase	El Paso	Paquime
A.D.1300						
			Roosevelt			
A.D.1250	Tanque Verde	Soho		Black Mountain	Dona Ana	Buena Fe
			Miami/Hardt (recently defined)			
A.D.1200						

▭ Phases assigned to the Salado Horizon.

▭ Phase linked to discussions of the Salado Horizon (and once associated with the migration hypothesis).

The place of the Salado horizon in the culture history of the American Southwest. (Courtesy of G. E. Rice)

are open to all members of a society tend to be concerned with the fertility of the earth and the well-being of the community. Salado-like icons are still important in modern Puebloan religion and are very similar to iconographic systems in use in Mesoamerica at the time of the Spanish conquest (A.D. 1519). In both cases, for which written documentation exists concerning the meaning of icons, the icons are part of a belief system having to do with weather control and fertility.

Crown links the fourteenth-century success of the cult to the same events that Haury cites in the migration model, such as the wholesale abandonment of the Kayenta area in the late thirteenth century and the establishment of Kayenta communities in the Mogollon region. In this model, the tensions generated by the forced mingling of different groups were offset by a shared belief system, a possibility that has archaeological support, for Salado polychromes appear first in those parts of the Mogollon area that were settled by Kayenta migrants, and the Salado Polychrome styles are derived from a mixing of Kayenta and Mogollon styles.

The cult hypothesis is an elegant and well-supported explanation of the appearance and distribution of Salado polychromes. Part of

Crown's success in providing a plausible resolution of this problem lay in her decision to limit investigation to ceramics. The initial statement of the Salado-migration hypothesis drew together a large body of data ranging from platform mounds and compounds to burial practices and ceramics. It is not clear, however, that a single model should be sought to explain all of these disparate phenomena.

Glen E. Rice

Further Readings

Crown, P.L. 1994. *Ceramics and Ideology: Salado Polychrome Pottery.* University of New Mexico Press, Albuquerque.

Dean, J.S., and J.C. Ravesloot. 1993. The Chronology of Cultural Interaction in the Gran Chichimeca. In *Culture and Contact, Charles C. DiPeso's Gran Chichimeca*, edited by A. Woosley and J. Ravesloot, pp. 83–103. University of New Mexico Press, Albuquerque.

Doyel, D.E., and E.W. Haury. 1976. The 1976 Salado Conference. *Kiva* 42(1).

Gerald, R.E. 1976. A Conceptual Framework for Evaluating Salado and Salado-Related Material in the El Paso Area. *Kiva* 42(1):65–70.

Gladwin, W., and H.S. Gladwin. 1930. *Some Southwestern Pottery Types, Series I.* Medallion Papers no. 8. Gila Pueblo, Globe.

Haury, E.W. 1945. *The Excavation of Los Muertos and Neighboring Ruins in the Salt River Valley, Southern Arizona.* Papers, vol. 24, no. 1. Peabody Museum of American Archaeology and Ethnology, Harvard University, Cambridge.

Nelson, B.A., and S.A. LeBlanc. 1986. *Short-Term Sedentism in the American Southwest: The Mimbres Valley Salado.* Maxwell Museum of Anthropology Publication Series. Maxwell Museum of Anthropology and University of New Mexico Press, Albuquerque.

Reid, J.J., B.K. Montgomery, M.N. Zedono, and M.A. Neuport. 1992. The Origin of Roosevelt Red Ware. In *Proceedings of the Second Salado Conference, Globe, Arizona, 1992,* edited by R.C. Lange and S. Germick, pp. 212–215. Arizona Archaeological Society, Phoenix.

Rice, G.E. (editor). 1990. *A Design for Salado Research.* Anthropological Field Studies no. 22. Department of Anthropology, Arizona State University, Tempe.

Salmon River–Clearwater River Sequences

The Salmon and Clearwater rivers of west-central Idaho drain a region of mountainous terrain and coniferous forests along the eastern periphery of the Columbia Plateau. The two rivers are major tributaries of the Lower Snake River, which drains into the Columbia River. At European contact in the eighteenth century A.D., the Clearwater-Salmon basins coincided with the territory of the Nez Perce Indians. Salish speakers used the upper reaches of the Clearwater River, and Northern Shoshone occupied upper areas of the Salmon River, including the Middle Fork Salmon River. Historically, the salmon, ungulate (mountain sheep, deer, elk, and bison), and root resources in the Clearwater and Salmon river basins supported relatively dense human populations and large seasonal aggregations of horse-mounted people. Separate cultural chronologies recently proposed for each basin outline long-term changes in settlement features and artifact assemblages that are thought to reflect shifts in subsistence and social organization (Hackenberger 1988; Reid 1991; Sappington 1994).

Comparisons of Late Prehistoric housepits along the middle Snake, Salmon, and Middle Fork Salmon rivers help illustrate the effects of human population growth and resource fluctuations on the development of complex hunting-and-gathering societies in the region prior to adoption of the horse. Large housepits (5–10 m, or 16.5–33 feet, in diameter) in small clusters along the middle Snake and Lower Salmon rivers may reflect extended families and multi-season or -year residential bases of small groups of collectors who stored predictable resources. Small housepits (3–4 m, or 10–13 feet, in diameter) in small and large clusters along the middle Salmon and the Middle Fork Salmon rivers suggest nuclear families and single-season or -year residence of more mobile groups using abundant, but highly unpredictable, resources. Total numbers of housepit features in the region (ca. 1,400) and estimates of the length of short-duration occupation suggest very small pre-horse regional populations. If house features were occupied for longer than expected (100-plus years each), or many more burial houses exist, or both, then higher population densities were the norm.

Salmon River Sequence. The Salmon River sequence emphasizes local hunting adaptations and the influence of Great Basin cultural traditions, which is reflected in the predominance of Great Basin projectile-point types in archaeological components. Early Prehistoric (pre-3050 B.C., or 5000 years B.P.) and Protohistoric (A.D. 1450–1750, or 500–200 years B.P.) sites are not well documented. Four phases are defined: Shoup (3050–1050 B.C., or 5000–3000 years B.P.), with large side-notched points; Big Creek (1050–50 B.C., or 3000–2000 years B.P.), with large corner-notched and stemmed points; Owl Creek (50 B.C.–A.D. 950, or 2000–1000 years B.P.), with large and small corner-notched points; and Corn Creek (A.D. 950–1450, or 1000–500 years B.P.), with house features, ceramics, and small side-notched, and large and small corner-notched, points.

In the Shoup and Weis rock shelters, and the Redfish overhang, early radiocarbon dates extend from 10,460 B.C. ± 115 (12,410 years B.P.) (shell in alluvial deposit) to 3650 B.C. ± 230 (5600 years B.P.). A variety of large lanceolate, stemmed, leaf-shaped, and side-notched and corner-notched points from these sites and the Cooper's Ferry site reflect the early influence of Great Plains, Columbia Plateau, and Great Basin lithic traditions.

S

Intense use of Big Creek Cave by 1250 B.C. (3200 years B.P.), and the Pinto Stemmed and Elko Corner-Notched points that characterize the Big Creek phase, represent the presence or influence of Great Basin peoples. Mountain sheep dominate the faunal remains recovered from this site and from later components in sites along the middle Salmon and the Middle Fork Salmon rivers, although deer and elk remains have also been recovered. Upland sites with components that may be attributed to the Big Creek phase are situated in prime areas for summer hunting and the procurement of white-bark-pine nut. Artifact deposition at Coyote Springs on Cold Mountain and Sheepeater Battle Ground on the Upper Middle Fork Salmon River appears to double by ca. 550 B.C. (2500 years B.P.). Excavations at Dagger Falls (a major historic salmon-spearing station) yielded very high frequencies of Elko-type points. These finds and associated pollen remains suggest increased use of uplands during a warm, dry period ca. 550 B.C. (2500 years B.P.) that corresponds with the Big Creek phase.

During the Corn Creek phase, house features appear at ca. A.D. 750 (1200 years B.P.) at the Corn Creek site. Relatively intense occupation, including the only documented human burial in the drainage, continued until ca. A.D. 1450 (500 years B.P.). Occupations of nearby Big Creek Village began by 50 B.C. (2000 years B.P.); however, relatively intensive occupation with house features occurred only between the Late Owl Creek and the Corn Creek phases. Fourteen radiocarbon dates for small, shallow house features from the middle Salmon and the Middle Fork Salmon are in the A.D. 750–1150 (1200–800 years B.P.) range. The house features (3–4 m, or 10–13 feet, in diameter and 20–50 cm, or 8–19. 5 inches, deep) may correspond with a warm, dry period of increased ungulate availability in forested valleys. The houses may represent the first regular year-round settlement of the Middle Fork Salmon River Basin by the Numic-speaking people, who are ancestral to the Northern Shoshone. The Middle Fork area is also significant for the large numbers of Protohistoric rock-ring sites affiliated with the Northern Shoshone; however, these rock rings have probably all been destroyed. Small bison jumps south of Challis along the more arid Upper Salmon River contain Late Prehistoric and Protohistoric components.

In addition to point types and house forms, pictographs, talus pits, and pottery indicate the Late Prehistoric and Protohistoric presence of people with Great Basin cultural traditions. Pictographs on rock faces of overhangs and shelters in the Salmon River Basin commonly portray human and animal stick figures, and dots and dashes, in red paint. They depict elk, deer, mountain sheep, dogs, bows, and, at least in one instance, a mounted horseman with a possible rifle. Talus pits, which may have served as hunting blinds or meat caches, or both, are also numerous in prime big-game ranges within the river valleys. Undecorated brown and gray pottery sherds in several Corn Creek–phase components at sites along the middle Salmon and Middle Fork Salmon rivers may mark the presence of Northern Shoshone peoples. This ceramic technology may also reflect the preparation of mush from pine nuts.

Clearwater River Sequence. The Clearwater River chronology acknowledges the continued influence of Columbia Plateau traditions from the Early Prehistoric Windust and Cascade phases to the Protohistoric period, but it also identifies unique local developments in the last 6,000 years. These developments include major changes in subsistence and settlement during three archaeological phases, the Hatwai (4050–1050 B.C., or 6000–3000 years B.P.), the Ahsahka (1050 B.C.–A.D. 1450, or 3000–500 years B.P.), and the Kooskia (A.D. 1450–1750, or 500–200 years B.P.).

During the Hatwai phase, a major change in settlement is marked by early rectangular and later round housepit features excavated at the Hatwai site (3950–2850 B.C., or 5900–4800 years B.P.). The appearance of these first "homesteads" correlates with more evidence for dependence on early-spring root resources of the lower river valley, such as various species of *Lomatium*, and increased evidence for summer fishing and fall hunting of deer and elk in the upper reaches of the Clearwater Basin.

The Ahsahka phase is characterized by the increased frequency and size of circular and oval housepits. This development of hamlet-like settlements is associated with relatively more numerous bison remains, northern Great Plains–style (Avonlea) arrow points that mark the introduction of the bow, and widespread use of net sinkers that represents more intensive harvesting of salmon and sucker.

In the Protohistoric Kooskia phase, a shift from housepits to larger longhouses with shallow floor basins occurs. Excavations at the Ahsahka Fish Hatchery provide the only archaeological evidence in the region for ethno-historic longhouses constructed of easily transportable poles and mats. Shallow-basin longhouses are difficult to recognize and date precisely. Therefore, the extent to which a shift to larger, mobile house forms was due to settlement reconfiguration resulting from pre-A.D. 1700 epidemics, subsistence changes made possible by the post-A.D. 1700 adoption of the horse, or both, remains undetermined.

The Clearwater and Salmon river archaeological sequences document significant environ-

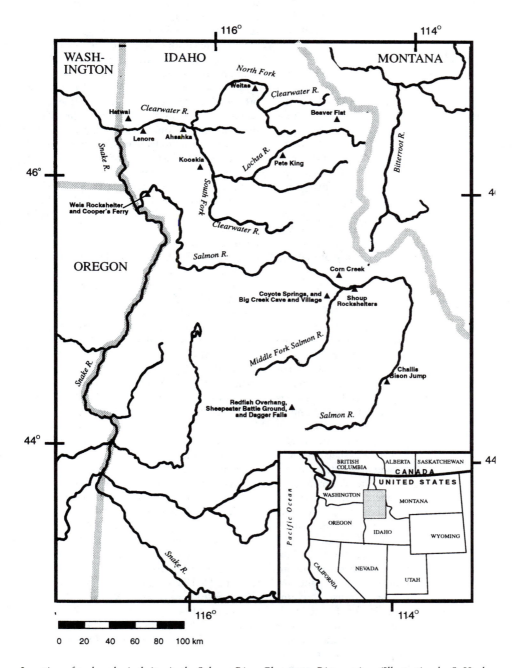

Location of archaeological sites in the Salmon River-Clearwater River region. (Illustration by S. Hackenberger and R. L. Sappington)

mental and cultural changes in the Snake River tributary region. Further development and comparison of these sequences is important for increasing our understanding of different adaptations of peoples with Plateau or Great Basin cultural traditions on the eastern margin of the Columbia Plateau.

Steven Hackenberger
Robert L. Sappington

Further Readings

Hackenberger, S. 1988. *Cultural Ecology and Evolution in Central Montane Idaho.* Unpublished Ph.D. dissertation, Department of Anthropology, Washington State University, Pullman.

Reid, K.C. (editor). 1991. *An Overview of Cultural Resources in the Snake River Basin: Prehistory and Paleoenvironments.* Project Report no. 13. Center for Northwest Anthropology, Washington State University, Pullman.

Sappington, R.L. 1994. *The Prehistory of the Clearwater River Region.* Anthropological Reports no. 95. University of Idaho, Moscow.

Salt

Traditional explanations of the importance of sodium chloride in the human diet have focused on the need of this mineral for the maintenance of human life. Whether human craving for salt is a reflection of real biological needs, a kind of addiction, or merely an acquired habit, there is no doubt that people consider it of great importance. For example, during the Spanish invasion of the East, the Gentleman of Elvas (1557 [1851:55]) reported, "There was such a want of salt also, that often times, in many places, a sick man having nothing for his nourishment, and was wasting away to bone, . . . he would say: 'Now, if I had but a slice of meat, or only a few lumps of salt, I should not die.'" Modern studies suggest that while it is easy for humans to become habituated to sodium chloride, real dietary needs are easily met by normal human diets. The "Bunge hypothesis," that sodium chloride is needed by agriculturalists to counteract increased porassium intake (Bunge 1873, 1874), is no longer completely credible (Kaunitz 1956:1141; Dauphinee 1960). Organized salt production did commonly begin in the time during which horticulture was adopted, but other causes, such as replacement of warm-sea-

son perspiration losses, may be enough to account for increased salt requirements.

Of salt's attractiveness as a seasoning there can be no doubt. While a dietary role for salt cannot be ruled out, its use seems often to be of the same character as the other components still used today to make cheap food tasty: sugar and fat. All of these are substances for which "natural" human life rarely provided an excess and for which we have not evolved well-developed satiation responses. The attractiveness of salt, for whatever purposes, is so great that it should be no surprise that, in many state-level societies, its production and distribution are a state monopoly. Salt is used worldwide in the expression of relations of domination; however, its use in North America appears to lack most of these social elements. Salt production in Mississippian societies (A.D. 900–1500, 1050–450 years B.P.) appears to have been carried out on a largely household basis by transient producers (Muller 1984).

Jon Muller

Further Readings

Bunge, G. 1873. Uber die Bedeutung des Kochsalzes und das Verhalten der Kalisalze in menschlichen Organismus. *Zeitschrift für Biologie* 9:104–142.

———. 1874. Ethnologischer Nachtrag zur Abhandlung über die bedeutung des Kochsalzes und das Verhalten der Kalisalze in menschlichen Organismus. *Zeitschrift für Biologie* 10:111–132.

Dauphinee, J.A. 1960. Sodium Chloride in Physiology, Nutrition and Medicine. In *Sodium Chloride: The Production and Properties of Salt and Brine,* edited by D. Kaufmann, pp. 382–453. Reinhold, New York.

Gentleman of Elvas (Fidalgo deluas). 1557. *Relaçam verdadeira dos trabalhos q ho gouemador dö Fernãdo de souto e centos fidalgos portugueses passarom no descubrimeto da prouincia da Frolida. Agora nouaméte teita per hú fidalgo Deluas.* Evora. Reprinted 1851, Hakliyt Society, London.

Kaunitz, H. 1956. Causes and Consequences of Salt Consumption. *Nature* 178(4543): 1141–1144.

Muller, J. 1984. Mississippian Specialization and Salt. *American Antiquity* 49(3):489–507.

See also GREAT SALT SPRING

San Pedro Valley Clovis Sites
(Lehner and Murray Springs)

A mammoth skeleton and eight associated Clovis points at Naco, Arizona, discovered in 1950 was the fourth known buried site of the Clovis culture, the earliest clearly defined culture in the New World (Haury et al. 1953). While Emil W. Haury of the Arizona State Museum, Tucson, was excavating the Naco site in 1952, Edward Lehner reported the occurrence of more mammoth bones at his property on the San Pedro River 19.3 km (12 miles) to the west. This eventually led to the excavation of the now famous Lehner Clovis site. Scientific results at Lehner included the first Clovis fire hearths, the first radiocarbon dates for the culture, and the first possible association with extinct tapir, in addition to 13 Clovis points and eight other artifacts in association with the bones of nine mammoths (Haury et al. 1959). The bones of horse (*Equus*), bison (*Bison*), and tapir (*Tapirus*), in addition to those of the mammoths, were studied by John F. Lance (1959).

The early geological work was conducted by Ernst Antevs (1959), who described the detailed stratigraphy of the site and demonstrated that the kill had taken place in and along a small creek called Mammoth-Kill, a tributary, now buried, of the San Pedro River.

The deposit directly overlying the channel sands of Mammoth-Kill Creek and the adjacent banks is a black organic clay referred to as the "black mat." It probably represents an algal mat formed in a wet meadow or cienega where the water table stood at the surface and supported a lush local flora.

In 1963, palynological and geochronological investigations at the site (Mehringer, Jr., and Haynes, Jr. 1965) resulted in a better understanding of the paleoenvironment of the past 11,000 years. In one stratigraphic trench, another mammoth skeleton was revealed in the channel sands of Mammoth-Kill Creek. In subsequent years, two other Clovis sites, the Escapule and the Murray Springs sites, were discovered and excavated with the support of the National Geographic Society (Haynes, Jr., and Hemmings 1969; Hemmings 1970; Haynes, Jr. 1973, 1974, 1976). The discovery of clearly defined kill, butchering, and camping areas at the Murray Springs Clovis site suggested that similar activity areas should also occur 19.3 km (12 miles) to the south at the Lehner site. These areas should be upslope from the buried channel of Mammoth-Kill Creek.

With the objectives of testing this possibility and excavating the mammoth found in 1963, new excavations were begun in 1974. The Lehner Clovis site was reopened after 18 years of rest by moving up to 2 m (6.6 feet) of culturally sterile overburden with mechanical equipment. The first area cleared, Area B, was west of the 1963 stratigraphic Trench 2 and east of the 1954–1955 excavations of Haury and others (1959), which is referred to here as Area A. After careful exposure, the black mat (Unit F_2) directly overlying the Clovis-occupation surface was removed by hand with trowels, brushes, and dental picks.

Mammoth bones exposed by Trench 2 in 1963 were the first paleontological specimens to be uncovered. They were on and in the upper part of channel sands and gravels of Mammoth-Kill Creek (Unit F_1). Ribs, leg bones, and mandibles representing two young mammoths were found in association with one chert flake and scattered lumps of charcoal.

Exavations to the south and west in Area B showed more evidence of human occupation of the south bank of the ancient creek. The ancient ground surface, which contains several irregular depressions, rises gently but irregularly to the south. Scattered over this surface were two unifacial tools, two fragments, a utilized flake, 27 flakes, numerous bone fragments, and charcoal lumps. An oval-shaped depression, the closed part of which measures 2 x 4 m (6.6 x 13 feet), in the middle of Area B contained a concentration of charcoal, charred and calcined bone fragments, and several flakes and tool fragments. Around this depression were numerous broken bones of a young mammoth, bison, jackrabbit, tortoise, and bear. The feature is obviously a hearth or roasting pit. Eighteen red and gray chert flakes concentrated at the western part of Area B are unifacial edge-sharpened flakes that very likely came from the large flake side scraper (No. 3) found farther west (Area A) in the 1954 excavations.

Trench 7, excavated with a backhoe to provide a stratigraphic profile, revealed the black mat to extend 37 m (121 feet) farther south. To test the possibility that the occupation extended in this direction, a 6-m (20-foot) -wide area was cleared eastward from the trench, thus extending Area B southward. Hand excavation of the black mat in the northern half of this area revealed scattered charcoal and bones, some charred, of bison, horse, camel, jackrabbit, and garter snake. The split camel bones are possible evidence of Clovis utilization of this species. Smaller animals have long been suspected of being a part of the Clovis diet, so this evidence is reassuring in that regard.

Several fragments, some matching, of fine-grained igneous rock came from near the center of Area B. They were found several centimeters above the Clovis occupation surface and at the base of the gray silt (Unit F_3) that overlies the black mat. A concentration of charcoal occurred within the black mat in this area. This unexpected post-Clovis occupation may represent the Sulphur Spring phase of the Cochise culture and adds to the importance of the Lehner site. It suggests that the early Cochise stage is a different culture of later age.

Excavations in Area C were done in 1975 because a probe of the strata with a soil auger had found bone fragments in association with the buried black mat. While no definite artifacts were found in this area, there were a few bone and tooth fragments scattered on the Clovis occupational surface, the basal contact of Unit F_2. Some of these proved to be teeth and jaw fragments of a juvenile mastodon (*Mammut americanum*), the first reported occurrence for Arizona. Further excavation revealed these remains to be part of Unit Z and, therefore, at least 30,000 years older than Clovis. They were exposed by erosion during the incision of the F_1 channel and, therefore, were probably exposed during occupation of the site by Clovis people (Mead et al. 1979).

A few meters (ca. 7 feet) west of the mastodon are the remains of a cylindrical hole ca. 60 cm (23.4 inches) in diameter and 62 cm (24.2 inches) deep that extended from Unit F_3 through F_2 and into Unit Z. Although associated artifacts were lacking, it is probably a prehistoric well of the Cochise culture. Similar wells of Cochise age were found at Murray Springs.

The preliminary result of radiocarbon dating 21 charcoal samples collected from the Clovis living floor indicates that the occupation took place at ca. 9050 B.C. ± 100 (11,000 years B.P.). Two dates of 7950 B.C. ± 80 and 7910 ± 80 (9900 and 9860 years B.P.) indicate that the Cochise occupation took place ca. 1,000 years later and is thus similar in age to the Sulphur Spring occupation at Double Adobe, Arizona (Waters 1986).

From the 1974–1975 excavations of the Lerner site, it is apparent that: (1) Clovis game-processing and roasting areas extend southward from Mammoth-Kill Creek; (2) small vertebrates as well as large were utilized; (3) the Clovis occupation occurred at essentially the same time as at Murray Springs and elsewhere in southwestern North America; (4) Cochise people occupied the site ca. 7750 B.C. (9700 years B.P.); and (5) mastodons lived in southeastern Arizona sometime before 28,050 B.C. (30,000 years B.P.).

The Clovis site at Murray Springs is located 17 km (10.5 miles) north of the Lehner Clovis site. It is on Curry Draw, a tributary of the Upper San Pedro River in southeastern Arizona. The site, on the riparian preserve of the Bureau of Land Management, is unique in that it contains three distinct activity areas where a band of Clovis hunters killed a mammoth and several bison and occupied a small campsite during at least two brief visits in ca. 9050 B.C. (11,000 years B.P.) (Haynes, Jr. 1968, 1973, 1974, 1976, 1978, 1979, 1980; Hemmings 1970).

The buried occupation surface is clearly displayed in the arroyo walls as an erosional contact at the base of a distinctive black organic mat. The mat preserved artifacts and bones of extinct animals in their original position, and mammoth tracks, just as they were left.

On a tributary to Curry Draw and under as much as 3 m (9.8 feet) of Holocene alluvium, the occupation floor in Area 3 contains the skeleton of a younger adult female mammoth. Artifacts located around the skeleton include a Clovis projectile point and fragments of two more, a flake knife, a broken biface, a broken blade, and several thousand bifacial thinning flakes, mostly in distinct piles or concentrations. An Upper Paleolithiclike shaft straightener made of mammoth bone (Haynes, Jr., and Hemmings 1968) occurred 10 m (32.8 feet) southeast of the mammoth skeleton and near a shallow well probably excavated by mammoths during a drought (Haynes, Jr. 1991).

Centered ca. 30 m (98.4 feet) northwest of the mammoth skeleton was a shallow-basin hearth among the remains of 13 bison skeletons in Areas 4 and 5. Scattered among the bison bones were seven damaged Clovis points, three blades, four bifaces in various stages of completion or breakage, and a unifacial tool with a pressure-flaked cutting edge and a true burin at the distal end. Hundreds of resharpening and bifacial-thinning flakes occurred in distinct clusters. The skeletal remains of a horse at the west end of Area 5 may have been a Clovis kill (Hemmings 1970).

The Clovis hunters's campsite, located on higher ground between Curry Draw and the tributary passing through Area 3, extends from 50 to 150 m (164–492 feet) southwest of the mammoth kill and is buried by up to 30 cm (11.7 inches) of very bioturbated (severely disturbed by living things such as tree roots, gophers, worms, and the like) slope-wash alluvium. While hundreds of flakes and tools are mixed vertically, the lateral dispersion was much less than expected considering the 11,000 years of bioturbation that the occupation surface has suffered. Artifacts in the campsite included six Clovis point bases, four end scrapers, a biface and a biface fragment, seven flake tools or knives (one with three graver spurs), and a multiple-use blade tool.

Two impact-fracture flakes found in the campsite fit impact fractures on the tips of two Clovis points, one from the bison-kill area and the other from a Clovis-point midsection found on the surface between the mammoth kill and the camp. Lithic source areas include Arizona's Petrified Forest 250 km (155 miles) to the north, an obsidian locality near Morenci 130 km (81 miles) to the northeast, and a chalcedony locality near St. David 25 km (15.5 miles) to the north. Several local sources have yet to be discovered.

Four confirmed Clovis sites (Naco, Lehner, Escapule, and Murray Springs) plus two probable Clovis sites (Leikem and Navarrete) make the San Pedro Valley host to the largest concentration of in situ Clovis sites known. All occur in similar stratigraphic context on the same erosional surface covered by the black mat and are radiocarbon dated at 9030 B.C. ± 50 (10,980 years B.P.). Some bifacial-thinning flakes in a cluster at Murray Springs contain stripes that match those in one of the Naco Clovis points. This and other factors suggest that the Clovis occupation of the San Pedro Valley may have been by a single band that spent a single year or less there before moving on. The valley appears to have been left without human habitation until the arrival of the Sulphur Springs people 500–1,000 years later.

C. Vance Haynes

Further Readings

Antevs, E. 1959. Geologic Age of the Lehner Mammoth Site. *American Antiquity* 25:31–34.

Haury, E.W., E. Antevs, and J.F. Lance. 1953. Artifacts With Mammoth Remains, Naco, Arizona. *American Antiquity* 19:1–24.

Haury, E.W., E.B. Sayles, and W.W. Wasley. 1959. The Lehner Mammoth Site. *American Antiquity* 25:2–30.

Haynes, C.V., Jr. 1968. Preliminary Report on the Late Quaternary Geology of the San Pedro Valley, Arizona. In *Southern Arizona Guidebook*, vol. 3, pp. 79–96. Arizona Geological Society, Tucson.

———. 1973. Exploration of a Mammoth-Kill Site in Arizona. *National Geographic Society Research Reports, 1966 Projects*, pp. 125–126.

———. 1974. Archaeological Excavations at the Clovis Site at Murray Springs, Arizona, 1967. *National Geographic Society Research Reports, 1967 Projects*, pp. 145–147.

———. 1976. Archaeological Investigations at the Murray Springs Site, Arizona, 1967. *National Geographic Society Research Reports, 1968 Projects*, pp. 165–171.

———. 1978. Archaeological Investigations at the Murray Springs Sites, Arizona, 1969. *National Geographic Society Research Reports, 1969 Projects*, pp. 239–242.

———. 1979. Archaeological Investigation at the Murray Springs Clovis Site, Arizona, 1970. *National Geographic Society Research Reports, 1970 Projects*, pp. 261–267.

———. 1980. Archaeological Investigations at the Murray Springs Clovis Site, Arizona, 1971. *National Geographic Society Research Reports* 12:347–353.

———. 1991. Geoarchaeological and Paleohydrological Evidence for a Clovis Age Drought in North America and Its Bearing in Extinction. *Quaternary Research* 35(3):438–450.

Haynes, C.V., Jr., and T.E. Hemmings. 1969. The Escapule Mammoth and Associated Projectile Points, San Pedro Valley, Arizona. *Journal of the Arizona Academy of Science* 5:184–188.

Hemmings, T.E. 1970. *Early Man in the San Pedro Valley, Arizona.* Unpublished Ph.D. dissertation, Department of Anthropology, University of Arizona, Tucson.

Lance, J.F. 1959. Faunal Remains From the Lehner Mammoth Site. *American Antiquity* 25:35–42.

Mead, J.I., C.V. Haynes, and B.B. Huckell.

S

1979. A Late Pleistocene Mastodon (*Mammut americanum*) From the Lehner Site, Southeastern Arizona. *Southwestern Naturalist* 24:231–238.

Mehringer, P.J., Jr., and C.V. Haynes, Jr. 1965. The Pollen Evidence for the Environment of Early Man and Extinct Animals at the Lehner Mammoth Site, Southeastern Arizona. *American Antiquity* 31:17–23.

Waters, M.R. 1986. The Sulphur Spring Stage and Its Place in New World Prehistory. *Quaternary Research* 25:251–256.

San Simon Branch of the Mogollon

San Simon is the most southwestern branch of the Mogollon culture in the American Southwest. It lies primarily in southeastern Arizona with its geographical boundaries roughly defined by the Gila River to the north, the New Mexico-Arizona state line to the east, the San Pedro River to the west, and an unknown boundary south of the international border in Sonora, Mexico. Most of this area is occupied by three northwest-southeast-trending valleys; these are, from west to east, the San Pedro, Sulphur Springs, and San Simon. Desert grasslands dominate this region, which is transected by narrow mountain ranges and the riverine zones.

The San Simon branch, as originally defined, dates from ca. A.D. 450 to 1150 (1500–800 years B.P.). As in other Mogollon branches, it appears to have developed from a local Archaic population base belonging to the Cochise culture. Late developments in the Archaic populations, notably the introduction of maize horticulture and the construction of small pithouses, immediately preceded the emergence of the San Simon branch, an event that is recognizable primarily by the addition of ceramics. At ca. A.D. 1150 (800 years B.P.), house types change to contiguous above-ground structures, and ceramic types change as well. These changes traditionally mark the end of the Mogollon culture and, therefore, of its San Simon branch.

Edwin B. Sayles (1945) developed the basic description and chronological subdivisions for the San Simon branch. His research incorporated large-scale reconnaissance survey and excavations at two type sites, Cave Creek Village and the San Simon Village, both of which are in the San Simon Valley. Excavation involved well over 50 houses, burials, and a ballcourt at the San Simon Village. He defined

six phases that are organized into three periods. They are (dates are approximate):

Late period
    Encinas phase   A.D. 875–1150
                          (1075–800 years B.P.)
    Cerros phase
Intermediate period
    Galiuro phase   A.D. 600–874
                          (1350–1076 years B.P.)
    Pinaleno phase
    Dos Cabezas phase
Early period
    Penasco phase   A.D. 450–599
                          (1500–1351 years B.P.)

Although house forms, burial practices, stone tools, and other artifacts help identify the San Simon branch and its phases, ceramic typology plays a central role in their identification. San Simon–branch ceramics are brownwares whose technology, morphology, and decorative techniques are part of the Mogollon tradition. The vessels associated with the earliest phase, Penasco, are either plain (Alma plain) or red slipped (San Francisco Red). These types dominate the assemblage throughout the sequence. An associated bichrome type defines each of the remaining five phases. Painted types have red paint and, except Cerros Red-on-white, employ an unslipped brown background. Decorations typically, and especially in the Intermediate period, occupy the interior of bowls, where they emphasize rectilinear elements; the decorative field is sometimes divided into quarters.

Domestic architecture is primarily based on shallow pithouses whose shape and plan change through time. Similar to the Late Archaic, Early-period San Simon pit structures are generally small (2–3 m, or 6.5–10 feet, in diameter), roughly circular to oval in shape, and lack a ramped entry. Intermediate- and Late-period structures are generally larger, rectilinear in shape, and possess a ramped entry way. A major trend from the Intermediate period through the Late period is a shift from rounded to square corners. Patricia A. Gilman's (1991) survey and excavation in the San Simon Valley add a house type to Sayles's original description. She found that the architectural sequence culminated in shallow, detached, rectilinear structures delineated by upright slabs at the end of the Late period (perhaps A.D. 1050–1150, or 900–800 years B.P.). The only occurrence of public architecture is a ballcourt at the San Simon Village.

Burial customs also change through time. Flexed pit burials, typical in the Early and Intermediate periods, were replaced by extended burials in the Late period. Cremation was added to the burial practices in the Encinas phase.

Compared with other regions in the Southwest, the San Simon branch has not attracted much research. As a result, the organization of its settlement, social, and subsistence systems is only sketchily known. Gilman suggests, based on her excavations at the Timber Draw site, that San Simon pithouse sites may have been occupied seasonally. This hypothesis raises a host of questions concerning the mix of gathering, hunting, and horticulture that was practiced, the size and composition of the territory that was occupied, and the social organization of these people.

Other questions concern the interaction of the branch with surrounding regions and its chronological and geographical boundaries. For Sayles, the San Simon branch emerges as a cultural entity in the Early period, is best defined in the Intermediate period, and looses much of its distinctiveness in the Late period. Curiously, the Late-period San Simon branch incorporates goods and traits from *both* the Mimbres branch to the east and the Hohokam culture to the west. Cerros Red-on-white mirrors Three Circle Red-on-white from the Mimbres branch, and, during the Encinas phase, Mimbres Black-on-white becomes a common intrusive. At the end of the Late period at the Timber Draw site, Gilman found, the most common painted ceramic was Mimbres Black-on-white. From the west, elements of Hohokam culture in the San Simon branch include the ballcourt at San Simon Village, cremations, stone palettes, carved-stone vessels, clay figurines, and shell jewelry, most notably *Glycymeris* shell bracelets. These traits and exchange items demonstrate interaction with the Hohokam, use of Hohokam ritual items, and, perhaps, evidence for inclusion of some villages in the Hohokam regional system, particularly during the Late period.

In southeastern Arizona, the distribution of culture traits and exchange items shows important shifts through time that rarely form simple patterns corresponding to river drainage. The result has been scholarly disagreement over the time and space boundaries of the San Simon branch. Sayles ended the branch with the transition to contiguous above-ground structures. Nonetheless, evidence for cultural continuity from the pithouse villages to these post-A.D.

1150 (800 years B.P.) "pueblo" sites can be found. Paralleling a pan-Mogollon tendency for researchers to include late surface structure sites as Mogollon, the San Simon label could be applied until regional abandonment in ca. A.D. 1450 (500 years B.P.).

The spatial boundaries of the San Simon branch have also been subjected to revision. Sayles suggested that the branch included pithouse villages in three major valleys. However, pithouse villages in the two western valleys—San Pedro and Sulphur Springs—have been assigned by various researchers to either the Dragoon, O'otam, or Hohokam cultures (Sayles 1945; Bronitsky and Merritt 1986). Recent interpretations tend to place the San Pedro Valley within the province of the Hohokam culture, to view the Sulphur Springs Valley as a transition zone, and to regard the San Simon Valley as the heartland of the branch (Bronitsky and Merritt 1986; Douglas 1987). Yet, even in the San Simon Valley, the early Mogollon pattern differs little from the early Hohokam pattern to the west, and, by the Late period, the mixture of Mimbres and Hohokam items and traits in the San Simon Valley makes tidy delineations impossible. In brief, the San Simon branch represents a reasonable beginning point for understanding regional patterns, but the spatial and temporal cultural mosaic found in southeastern Arizona belies any simplistic rendering.

John E. Douglas

Further Readings

Bronitsky, G., and J.D. Merritt. 1986. *The Archaeology of Southeast Arizona: A Class I Cultural Resource Inventory.* Cultural Resource Series Monograph no. 2. Arizona State Office, Bureau of Land Management, Phoenix.

Douglas, J.E. 1987. Late Prehistoric Archaeological Remains in the San Bernardino Valley, Southeastern Arizona. *Kiva* 53(1):35–52.

Gilman, P.A. 1991. Changing Land Use and Pit Structure Seasonality Along the San Simon Drainage in Southeastern Arizona. In *Mogollon V*, edited by P.H. Beckett, pp. 11–27. COAS, Las Cruces.

Sayles, E.B. 1945. *The San Simon Branch: Excavations at Cave Creek and the San Simon Valley.* Medallion Paper no. 34. Gila Pueblo, Globe.

See also MOGOLLON CULTURE AREA

Sand Canyon Pueblo

Sand Canyon pueblo (5MT765) is a large, late-thirteenth-century A.D. ancestral Puebloan ruin in southwestern Colorado. Research by the Crow Canyon Archaeological Center has included intensive excavations, involving ca. 15 percent of the architecture of the main ruin, and archaeological survey, testing, and environmental reconstruction in the surrounding locality. Architecture in the main Sand Canyon pueblo area includes an estimated 420 rooms, 90 kivas, 14 towers, a central plaza, a great kiva, a large D-shaped building, and a site-enclosing wall. The site is one of the best dated in the Mesa Verde region, with accurate construction dates (to the year) of specific architectural units inferred from tree-ring date clusters. Information current to the mid-1990s indicates that the entire site was built, used, and abandoned between A.D. 1250 and 1290 (700–660 years B.P.), a time period corresponding to the permanent movement of Puebloan peoples out of the region.

Various explanations for the formation of large thirteenth-century towns have been proposed, but the investigation of Sand Canyon pueblo is the first in the Mesa Verde region to test these theories using current methods. One theory is that the large towns represent an aggregation of formerly dispersed populations into centralized communities, perhaps for defensive purposes. In this case, one might expect the towns to be made up of concentrations of normal domestic architecture, possibly grouped in defensive locations. Another theory is that the large sites were not primarily domestic habitations but specialized ritual centers that served an outlying, dispersed community. If this were the case, one would expect to be able to identify an outlying contemporary population and to find primarily special-function architectural forms in the central site.

Research at Sand Canyon pueblo and in the surrounding locality has failed to support either theory. What has emerged is a site reconstruction that included both a domestic population concentrated in the eastern portion and a special-function area with community-based civic architecture in the western area. Although the site location and the presence of an enclosing wall could be considered defensive, excavations have identified access points that probably promoted movements of people in and out of the center of the town. The possible dual-function layout of the site is suggestive of an earlier settlement form especially prevalent in north-western New Mexico known as Chacoan communities. Sand Canyon pueblo is different in that there does not seem to have been much of an outlying population, and the functional differentiation is expressed by a dual division of the site itself. This pattern has not been identified in later prehistoric or historic Puebloan settlements.

The dramatic shift in settlement pattern exhibited at Sand Canyon pueblo, its relative brevity, evidence of some traumatic abandonment events, the leaving of large assemblages of usable artifacts, and the loss of certain components of symbolism have led to speculations about the origins and demise of this special cultural expression. One speculation is that a religious revivalist movement (specifically Chacoan) swept through the Mesa Verde region in the mid-thirteenth century, and, although it incorporated a substantial population, it failed to mature into a viable cultural alternative. This failure may have contributed to the decision to abandon the region in favor of cultural developments to the south.

Bruce A. Bradley

Further Readings

Bradley, B.A. 1993. Planning, Growth, and Functional Differentiation at a Prehistoric Pueblo: A Case Study From SW Colorado. *Journal of Field Archaeology* 20:23–42.

———. 1992. Excavations at Sand Canyon Pueblo. In *The Sand Canyon Archaeological Project: A Progress Report,* edited by W.D. Lipe, pp. 79–97. Occasional Papers no. 2. Crow Canyon Archaeological Center, Cortez.

Lipe, W.D. (editor). 1992. *The Sand Canyon Archaeological Project: A Progress Report.* Occasional Papers no. 2. Crow Canyon Archaeological Center, Cortez.

Sand Lake Site

Sand Lake (47Lc44) is an early fifteenth century A.D. Oneota village and agricultural field site located ca. 16 km (10 miles) north of La Crosse in western Wisconsin. The stratified site lies on an alluvial fan in a floodplain at the mouth of Sand Lake Coulee, a small tributary along the eastern margin of the trench of the Mississippi Valley. The field portion of the site consists of a series of superimposed ridged fields or garden-bed plots buried under repeated episodes of al-

Cross-section through three buried Oneota agricultural ridges at the Sand Lake site (47Lc44).(July 1984 photograph by R. F. Sasso)

luvial deposition. The initial set of agricultural ridges was constructed ca. A.D. 1420 (530 years B.P.) using black floodplain soils with very high organic content. The construction and use of these initial ridges were followed by their burial, to varying depths, under lightly colored alluvial sediments that originated in an upland ravine north of the site. During the Oneota occupation, these lighter alluvial sediments became incorporated into the ridges when they were rebuilt. The pattern of ridge construction, use, sedimentation, and reconstruction was repeated a minimum of 10 times over a period believed to have lasted between 10 and 50 years. After the Oneota abandoned cultivation on the site, the alluvial fan became the site of a major village.

Intensive investigations under the direction of James P. Gallagher were conducted at Sand Lake by the Mississippi Valley Archaeology Center at the University of Wisconsin-La Crosse between 1982 and 1986. Excavation yielded a quantity of data that provide expanded insights into the nature of fifteenth-century Oneota cultivation practices. Well-preserved remains of several cultigens were recovered, including corn kernels and cobs, beans, squash, tobacco, and commensal plants, such as goosefoot, amaranth, and panic grass. Deposits of charcoal and habitation garbage at the site indicate that village waste was dumped into the fields, a prac-

tice that created what appear to be compost features. Bison- and elk-scapula hoe blades were recovered, as were fragments of scapulae that apparently broke off hoes during cultivation. One elk antler fragment has been worked into a similarly shaped hoe blade. The Oneota at Sand Lake primarily constructed long linear or curvilinear ridges that typically measure 90–220 cm (35–85 inches) wide x 20–35 cm (8–14 inches) high. They also apparently created at least a few small circular features known as corn hills. In certain areas of the site, even smaller conical features were encountered along the surfaces of several ridges. These, which measure ca. 20 cm (8 inches) in diameter, have been interpreted as the actual planting locations along the margins of the ridgetops (Gallagher 1992:115–116).

A variety of typical Oneota artifacts were recovered from both ridged-field and habitation contexts, including unnotched triangular projectile points, end scrapers, bone tools, and sandstone abraders. Shell-tempered earthenware ceramics indicate that the site was occupied during a cultural transition known locally as the Pammel Creek phase. A suite of five radiocarbon dates was obtained for ridged-field and habitation contexts (Sasso et al. 1985:95–97).

The Sand Lake site is one of the only prehistoric agricultural sites to be intensively excavated in eastern North America. Investigations at this site have added greatly to our understanding of Oneota subsistence and economy and have provided especially important data on the adaptation of Oneota culture to the changing physical and social environment of the Late Prehistoric Upper Midwest. In a broader sense, these studies have demonstrated the enormous archaeological potential of relict agricultural sites for providing significant insights into prehistoric agricultural practices and cultural development.

Robert F. Sasso

Further Readings

Boszhardt, R.F., T.W. Bailey, and J.P. Gallagher. 1985. Oneota Ridged Fields at the Sand Lake Site (47Lc44), La Crosse County, Wisconsin. *Wisconsin Archeologist* 66(1):47–65.

Gallagher, J.P. 1982. Prehistoric Field Systems in the Upper Midwest. In *Late Prehistoric Agriculture: Observations From the Midwest,* edited by W.I. Woods, pp. 95–135. Studies in Illinois Archaeology no. 8. Illinois Historic Preservation Agency, Springfield.

Gallagher, J.P., and R.F. Sasso. 1987. Investigations into Oneota Ridged Field Agriculture on the Northern Margin of the Prairie Peninsula. *Plains Anthropologist* 32(116):141–151.

Gallagher, J.P., R.F. Boszhardt, R.F. Sasso, and K. Stevenson. 1985. Oneota Ridged Field Agriculture in Southwestern Wisconsin. *American Antiquity* 50: 605–612.

———. 1987. Floodplain Agriculture in the Driftless Area: A Reply to Overstreet. *American Antiquity* 52:398–404.

Sasso, R.F., R.F. Boszhardt, J.C. Knox, J.L. Theler, K.P. Stevenson, J.P. Gallagher, and C. Stiles-Hanson. 1985. *Preshistoric Ridged Field Agriculture in the Upper Mississippi Valley.* Reports of Investigation no. 38. Mississippi Valley Archaeology Center, La Crosse.

Sandia Cave

Sandia Cave (LA 39937) is located in Las Huertas Canyon in the Sandia Mountains of New Mexico. It is a tunnel-like cavern in limestone ca. 138 m (151 yards) in length and 3 m (9 feet) in diameter. The cave was found by Boy Scouts in 1935. Early excavations were carried out by Wesley Bliss (1940) and Frank Hibben (1941, 1957), both associated with the University of New Mexico. The site has long been a subject of controversy. Who was the original excavator? What is its chronological age? Are "Sandia Points" possibly knives? Is their presence under the yellow ocher a true indicator of age? Were they later placed there by either Agate Basin or Folsom occupants of the cavern?

Top: Unfluted Folsom-shaped point embedded in debris from Sandia Cave, after Hibben 1941. Bottom: Dr. George Agogino looks up Las Huertas Canyon from the mouth of Sandia Cave. (Both reprinted from Sandia Cave: A Study in Controversy. *Courtesy of Eastern New Mexico University Paleo-Indian Institute)*

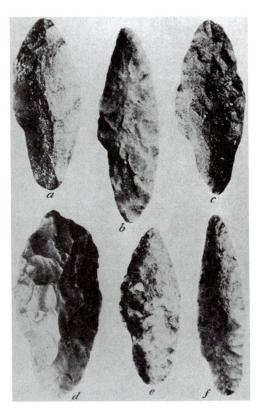

Sandia points (knives), after Hibben 1941. (Reprinted from Sandia Cave: A Study in Controversy. *Courtesy of Eastern New Mexico University Paleo-Indian Institute)*

In 1975, George A. Agogino became interested in these questions. He and a graduate student, Dominique Stevens, wrote a monograph, *Sandia Cave: A Study in Controversy* (Stevens and Agogino 1975), that reviewed conflicting viewpoints regarding the excavation and interpretation of the cavern. Later, C. Vance Haynes and Agogino conducted intermittent research for nearly 20 years within the cavern in an attempt to resolve these problems. Their research resulted in a Smithsonian monograph, "Geochronology of Sandia Cave" (Haynes and Agogino 1986) that tried to answer some of the cultural-stratigraphic conflicts. The possibility exists that Sandia points are knives that were used by a later culture to cut ocher; they could then have been stored under the ocher deposit. This interpretation questions the existence of a valid Sandia culture.

Sandia Cave is difficult to excavate. Many of the artifacts are in strata as hard as cement. The presence of ocher requires the use of dust masks at all times, and the narrowness of the cavern makes excavations difficult. Since the mouth of the cavern is so small, artificial light is necessary even a short distance from the opening. It is, perhaps, due to these difficulties that the stated position of artifacts, bones, and strata often conflict from one publication to another. The post-ocher sequence lacks a Clovis horizon, but it does include Folsom artifacts and those of a number of other Paleoindian cultures. However, no channel flakes were found, which suggests that Folsom people never used the cavern as a base camp. They probably entered the cavern briefly for ocher. Haynes believes that his geochronological studies of the cavern show that the Sandia artifacts can be no older than 12,050 B.C. (14,000 years B.P.). They are, according to this interpretation, most likely more recent than that date. The idea that post-ocher cultures, seeking ocher, could afterward place the Sandia knives beneath the ocher is a valid option. In addition, Haynes thinks that the Sandia level "is not a primary sedimentary deposit but . . . a bioturbated mixture of deposits" (Haynes and Agogino 1986:29).

The story of Sandia Cave is not completed. Perhaps additional work at the Lucy site might provide much needed answers. The Lucy site has yielded Sandia knives and also has an ocher level (Roosa 1957). If the Sandia culture is a valid concept, other Sandia sites will appear in time. Their investigation will clear up questionable conclusions made by the original excavators.

George A. Agogino

Further Readings

Agogino, G. 1963. The Paleo Indian, Relative Age and Cultural Sequence. *Great Plains Journal* 3(1):17–24.

Agogino, G., and I. Rovner. 1964. Paleo-Indian Traditions: A Current Evaluation. *Archaeology* 17(4):237–243.

Beyers, D.S. 1942. Concerning Sandia Cave. *American Antiquity* 7:408–409.

Bliss, W.L. 1940. A Chronological Problem Present at Sandia Cave. *New Mexico Magazine* 5(3):200–201.

Haynes, C.V., and G. Agogino. 1970. Radiocarbon Dating of Sandia Cave, New Mexico. *National Geographic Society Research Reports, 1961–1962,* pp. 121–122.

———. 1986. Geochronology of Sandia Cave. *Smithsonian Contributions to Anthropology* 32:1–32.

Hibben, F.C. 1941. *Evidences of Early Occupation in Sandia Cave, New Mexico, and Other Sites in the Sandia-Manzano Region*. Miscellaneous Collections, vol. 99, no. 23. Smithsonian Institution, Washington, D.C.

———. 1957. Comments on Radiocarbon Dates From Sandia Cave, Correction. *Science* 125(3241):235.

Roosa, W.B. 1957. The Lucy Site in Central New Mexico. *American Antiquity* 19:280–281.

Stevens, D., and G. Agogino. 1975. *Sandia Cave: A Study in Controversy*. Eastern New Mexico University Press, Portales.

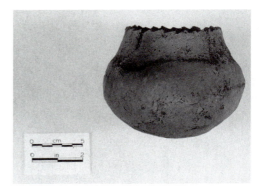

Sandy Lake pottery vessel. (Courtesy of the Wilford Archaeology Laboratory, University of Minnesota)

Sandy Lake

Originally defined in 1964 by Leland Cooper and Elden Johnson as a Late Woodland ceramic ware distributed throughout the mixed hardwood forests of northwestern Wisconsin and northern Minnesota, the term "Sandy Lake" is also used to refer to the archaeological complex or complexes of the people who made the ware. As a ware, Sandy Lake ceramics are characterized by cord-marked globular jars with shell temper or, increasingly to the north, grit temper (see Figure). Rims are generally vertical and fairly straight. Decoration, when present, usually consists of notching or punctates on the lip, upper rim interior, or inner neck surface. Some vessel surfaces are plain, simple stamped, or check stamped. Both utilitarian and smaller mortuary-vessel forms are known. Recent distributional studies expand the main range of the ware to the Thunder Bay–Nipigon area of Ontario westward to southeastern Manitoba and across eastern North Dakota, although the Mississippi headwaters region in Minnesota remains the area of greatest concentration for the ware (Gibbon 1994).

Sandy Lake is less clearly defined as an archaeological culture or complex. Johnson believed that the names of wares should not be applied to the complexes of which they are a part, for, among other reasons, wares can span linguistic and cultural boundaries. Subsequently, D.H. Birk (1979) proposed the Ojibwa word *Wanikan* (wild-rice gatherer) for the archaeological culture of the makers of Sandy Lake ware and provided a list of likely accompanying traits that included ricing features, small triangular projectile points, low conical burial mounds, and primary flexed interments with mortuary vessels. He also suggested a time range for the culture of A.D. 1000–1700 (950–250 years B.P.). Guy Gibbon (1994) later proposed that the Dakota word *Psinomani* (wild-rice gatherer) be applied to the archaeological complex found at those sites in the southern portion of the ware's range where temper was predominantly shell. According to this interpretation, the complex is the archaeological remains of the eastern Sioux, and its emergence was part of the structural transformation that produced Oneota, Mill Creek, and other horticultural groups to the south. The *Psinomani* were forest-edge dwellers who hunted bison in the northeastern prairies and harvested wild rice in the adjacent mixed hardwood forests. Presumably other, perhaps even Algonquian-speaking, people made Sandy Lake pottery in other portions of its range.

Guy Gibbon

Further Readings

Birk, D.A. 1979. Sandy Lake Ceramics. In *A Handbook of Minnesota Prehistoric Ceramics*, edited by S.F. Anfinson, pp. 175–182. Occasional Publications in Minnesota Archaeology no. 5. Minnesota Archaeological Society, Fort Snelling.

Cooper, L., and E. Johnson. 1964. Sandy Lake Ware and Its Distribution. *American Antiquity* 29:474–479.

Gibbon, G. 1994. Cultures of the Upper Mississippi River Valley and Adjacent Prairies in Iowa and Minnesota. In *Plains Indians, A.D. 500–1500*, edited by K.H. Schlesier, pp. 128–148. University of Oklahoma Press, Norman.

Peterson, L.A. 1986. *An Attribute Analysis of*

Sandy Lake Ware From Norman County and North Central Minnesota. Unpublished Master's thesis. Department of Anthropology, University of Nebraska, Lincoln.

Saqqaq Culture

Saqqaq is a Greenlandic Paleoeskimo culture belonging to the Arctic Small Tool tradition. Dating to ca. 2400–800 B.C. (4350–2750 years B.P.), it represents the earliest known culture in a large area comprising almost all of Greenland except the northernmost part of the country, where the Independence I culture is found (ca. 2500–2000 B.C., or 4450–3950 years B.P.).

First defined by Danish archaeologists Helge Larsen and Jørgen Meldgaard (1958), Saqqaq is characterized by a variety of stone tools made in particular from *killiaq,* a gray silicified slate (formerly *angmaq*) found in great quantities in the Disko Bugt area. Colored varieties of agate and quartz crystal were also used to make small tools. Tools are primary bifaces, and facial grinding is frequent. Defining tools are spalled burins ground on both sides; small triangular ground harpoon blades; slender projectile points with tapering stems; and relatively large asymmetrical knife blades. A typical Saqqaq stone-tool sample also includes ground saw blades, triangular end scrapers, side scrapers, drill points, adzes, and microblades. Recent excavations of permafrozen culture layers at the Qajaa and Qeqertasussuk sites in the Disko Bugt have yielded comprehensive information on bone and wooden artifacts. Tanged harpoon heads with a distal barb and toggling harpoon heads exactly like the finds from the Canadian Pre-Dorset culture have been found, as well as hafted hand tools, lances, bird spears, bows and arrows, and a variety of ladles and bowls. In the deepest permafrost layers at Qeqertasussuk, evidence of kayaks (frames and oars) and skin garments (including a kamik) have been found, and four human bones and hair tufts that are the earliest-known human remains in the eastern Arctic. Other important Saqqaq sites are Saqqaq and Sermermiut in the Disko Bugt, Akia and Nipisat in the Sisimiut district, and Nuunnguaq and Itinnera in the Nuuk district. Recent surveys in the Thule area, Ellesmere Island, and east Greenland have yielded several new sites.

Analyses of faunal material and site location of the Saqqaq culture show an extremely broad-spectrum subsistence economy. In some areas, Saqqaq sites are more numerous than Thule-culture sites and cover all ecological zones from the outer coast to the inner fjords. Exploitation of 45 different animal species, marine and terrestrial, was documented at the Qeqertasussuk site (Grønnow 1994), which was used year-round. In contrast, the Itinnera site in the innermost Godthåbsfjord (Nuuk) was a specialized summer caribou-hunting camp. Traces of dwellings vary from diffuse tent rings, some with a central hearth, to substantial midpassage structures with elevated platforms on each side of the floor along the midpassage. Small caches containing complete tools have been found inside the dwellings, and characteristic "dumps" of fire-cracked stones and debitage from the clearing of the dwellings are found outside.

Detailed typological/chronological studies have been made only in the Disko Bugt and Sisimiut districts. The Saqqaq tool inventory shows remarkably little stylistic change. Burins become gradually more slender through time, and facial grinding of projectile points seems to increase in the youngest part of the culture. Raw-material preferences also change through time but in different ways on a regional scale. There are significant geographical variations in material, but detailed studies of these variations are lacking.

Bjarne Grønnow

Further Readings

Grønnow, G. 1994. Qeqertasussuk: The Archaeology of a Frozen Saqqaq Site in Disko Bugt, West Greenland. In *Threads of Arctic Prehistory: Papers in Honour of William E. Taylor, Jr.,* edited by D. Morrison and J.-L. Pilon, pp. 197–238. Mercury Series Paper no. 149. Archaeological Survey of Canada, Canadian Museum of Civilization, Hull.

Larsen, H., and J. Meldgaard. 1950. Paleo-Eskimo Cultures in Disko Bugt, West Greenland. *Meddelelser om Grønland* 161(2).

Møbjerg, T. 1986. A Contribution to Paleoeskimo Archaeology in West Greenland. *Arctic Anthropology* 23(1–2):19–56.

Scharbauer

The Scharbauer site is located in the bottom of Monahans Draw near the southern edge of the Llano Estacado, ca. 10 km (6.2 miles) southwest of Midland, Texas. The site is of particular interest because a fossilized human calva, a rib, and a few other bone scraps were discovered there in June 1953 by amateur archaeologist Keith Glasscock. It is also important because the locality was repeatedly used as a camp by groups with Midland projectile points. The human remains apparently had been exposed recently and were mostly on the surface of a gray-colored aeolian sand informally named the Gray Sand. Near the human remains were two projectile points. In size, outline, and workmanship, these Midland points resemble the Folsom type; however, they are thinned and unfluted.

The margins of Monahans Draw are defined by a carborate bedrock with an overlying mantle of dark red aeolian sand covered by a thin veneer of tan-colored sand. Bunch grass, low bushes, and mesquite trees grow on the tan sand. In several areas along the north side of the draw, wind deflation has removed the vegetation and hollowed out shallow depressions, exposing the underlying dark red sand. On the surface of this red sand, there are several clusters of archaeological materials, including some Folsom artifacts.

One of these wind-deflated areas is in the bottom of Monahans Draw, and it is here that the human remains were found. The west end of the "blowout" is floored by a white calcareous sand named the White Sand. The eroded surface of this White Sand was littered with numerous bones of late Pleistocene animals, mostly horse of two varieties (*Equus* sp. and *Asinus conversidens*), as well as mammoth, dire wolf, camel, and extinct brocket or antelope (either *Mazama* or small and large *Capromeryx*), rabbits, and rodents. Shells of several aquatic and terrestrial species of invertebrates were also present. A sample of these shells from within the white calcareous sand yielded a ^{14}C date of 11,450 B.C. ± 1200 (13,400 years B.P.), and bone from the same unit gave a ^{14}C date of 6720 B.C. ± 600 (8670 years B.P.). This last date has been rejected as too young for the associated fauna. One flake found just below the surface of the White Sand was the only artifact recovered, although one horse femur found on the surface had traces of cut marks that may have been of human origin. At the east end of this "blowout," the surface consists of two sandy units: the Gray Sand on which the human remains were found and a dark red sand. Excavations disclosed a complex stratigraphic sequence, with the White Sand at the base, followed by the Gray Sand, the Red Sand, and finally the Tan Sand. The White Sand included both lacustrine and fluvial components and was more than 2 m (6.6 feet) thick. It is separated from the overlying Gray Sand by an unconformity indicating a period of erosion. The Gray Sand is believed to be a fossil dune consisting of materials blown from the surface of the White Sand and mixed with occasional grains of a dark red sand.

The Gray Sand was divided into two superimposed beds. The lower unit (Bed A) had a maximum thickness of 50 cm (19.5 inches), was pale orange in color, and contained numerous pebble-sized clods of the White Sand. No archaeology was found in this bed. Unconformably overlying Bed A was a grayish-orange calcareous sand (Bed B). It was near the base of this deposit that the human remains presumably were eroding. Bed B had a maximum thickness of 2 m (6.6 feet) and contained cultural material throughout, including fragments of Midland points, scrapers, and broken bones, some of which were burned. Among the identified bones present were those of horse, bison, the small *Capromeryx* antelope (the latter was burned), rabbits, and other rodents. In 1994, this author reexamined the bones recovered during the 1955 excavations and discovered a fragment of the left maxilla from another human skull. This fragment was found in the Gray Sand; all of the cavities in the bone were filled with Gray Sand, and the exterior was crusted with the same deposit.

The dark red sand (the Red Sand) overlying the Gray Sand is almost indistinguishable from the sand that forms the border of the draw. Initially, this similarity led those studying the geology of the site to conclude that the Gray Sand preceded all of the red sand in the vicinity of the site and was older than the Folsom materials found on the surface nearby on several of the wind-exposed surfaces of that red sand. This view was later rejected; instead, it was proposed that there were at least two dark red sands in the vicinity of the site, one of which was older than even the White Sand, and that the Red Sand overlying the Gray Sand was moved to its present position by slumping or other mass-movement processes.

A few fossil bones were found in the Red Sand in the bottom of the blowout. These included horse, antelope, large and small *Capromeryx* (or *Mazama*), deer, and turtle. Over the Red Sand were two units of tan-colored sand, both of which contained only modern fauna.

Since the original stratigraphic position of the human remains could not be firmly established because of the surface context of the human bones, microchemical analyses were used to determine the original sediment in which the bones had been buried and whether the human bones had been in that deposit for the same period as the extinct fauna. The most informative were the fluorine and nitrogen analyses. The results showed that the animal bones in each of the stratigraphic units had different chemical contents, as would be expected if it is assumed that bones in the same deposit for a similar period of time will contain similar chemical constituents in similar amounts, and, conversely, bones in different deposits or in the same deposit for different periods of time will have different chemical proportions. The results of the analyses of the human bones were closely similar to those of a horse bone found in the Gray Sand, and the bones, therefore, are probably the same age.. The analysis of the human remains also indicated that they were younger than the faunal remains found in the White Sand and older than those in the overlying Red Sand and both the two units of the Tan Sand.

The age of the Midland occupation in Bed B of the Gray Sand has been controversial. In addition to the two ^{14}C dates from the White Sand previously noted, unburned bone fragments from the Gray Sand were dated to 5150 B.C. ± 1000 (7100 years B.P.), a date that has been rejected because it is too recent for the fauna; while an oily residue from a burned caliche rock from the Gray Sand yielded a ^{14}C of 18,450 B.C. ± 900 (20,400 years B.P.). The latter date has been rejected as too old. Uranium-isotope dating was in an early phase of its development in the mid-1950s, and human bone dated by that technique in 1956 yielded an average age of 18,050 B.C. ± 2000 (20,000 years B.P.). These original analyses were recalculated using a formula that is now regarded as more accurate, and this recalculation gave an age of 9550 B.C. (11,500 years B.P.). At the same time, a mastoid process from the human skull was also analyzed, and this gave an age of 9650 B.C. ± 800 (11,600 years B.P.). Both of these recent U-series dates are in the general range for the probable age of extinction for the Pleistocene horse and the *Capromeryx* antelope.

It has also been suggested that the Gray Sand may be correlated with a highly calcare-

ous sandy loam draw-margin facies that is widespread on the Llano Estacado. It is believed that this sandy loam on the southern Llano Estacado is younger than 8050 B.C. (10,000 years B.P.). However, this may be too recent for the horse in the Gray Sand. At other localities on the High Plains, Midland points have been found stratigraphically both below Folsom (Blackwater Draw) and above Folsom (Hell Gap). An age contemporary with Folsom, dated to 9050–8050 B.C. (11,000–10,000 years B.P.), or even slightly younger, may be indicated for the Midland occupation and the human remains.

Fred Wendorf

Further Readings

Holiday, V.T., and D.J. Meltzer. 1993. Geoarchaeology of the Midland (Paleoindian) Site and the Age of the Midland Skull. *Current Research in the Pleistocene* 10:41–43.

Wendorf, F., and A.D. Krieger. 1959. New Light on the Midland Discovery. *American Antiquity* 25:66–78.

Wendorf, F., A.D. Krieger, and C.C. Albritton. 1955. *The Midland Discovery: A Report on the Pleistocene Human Remains From Midland, Texas* (with a description of the skull by T.D. Stewart). University of Texas Press, Austin.

Schmitt Chert Mine

Multidisciplinary investigation of the late Middle Prehistoric (Late Plains Archaic) Schmitt chert mine (24BW559) was initiated in 1972 by Montana State University and pursued annually through 1989. The Three Waters Quarries, which consists of a mine, open-pit quarries, and extensive workshops and camps, occupies a 105-ha (260-acre) area on the north margin of the semiarid Three Forks Basin at an elevation of 1,345 m (4,415 feet). The chert mine is in the Horseshoe Hills of Broadwater County, Montana. It is 1.6 km (1 mile) downstream from the point where the Gallatin, Madison, and Jefferson rivers join to form the Upper Missouri River, across the river west from Trident, and 8 km (5 miles) north of Three Forks in Gallatin County. The quarried landscape consists of rugged ridges and steep-walled canyons dominated by barren limestone outcrops.

Peoples of the Pelican Lake phase (1200 B.C.–A.D. 350, or 3150–1600 years B.P.) extracted quantities of chert from solution cavities in the

Excavations underway at the Late Prehistoric Schmitt Chert Mine at the Three Waters Quarries, Upper Missouri River drainage. (Courtesy of Museum of the Rockies/Montana State University-Bozeman)

form of nodules, lentils, and incompletely silicified nodules and casts. Substantial amounts of hematite and free manganese oxide, associated with chert formation by replacement of calcium carbonate, may also have been quarried from localized deposits within the limestone. Mined cavities and galleries within the Mission Canyon or Lodgepole Member (chert-bearing layers) extended 4.5 m (14.8 feet) below the weathered, gently westward-dipping bedrock surface of the Madison Limestone Formation. Flaked-stone artifacts recovered by excavation from mine fill included corner-notched projectile points, unhafted and hafted knives, end and side scrapers, perforators, and discoids. Numerous cobble and grooved hammerstones used to fragment bedrock were found. Large numbers of well-preserved bone and antler prys, cylinders, wedges, shaft straighteners, and knapping tools, as well as metapodial awls recycled from the campsite, were distributed throughout the mine backfill.

Species principally utilized as food and toolmaking raw material were bison (*Bison bi-*

son bison), mountain sheep (*Ovis canadensis*), pronghorn antelope (*Antilocapra americana*), white-tailed (*Odocoileus virginianus*) and mule (*O. hemionus*) deer, and wapiti (*Cervus elaphus*). Abundant bones, dentitions, and shells from utilized striped skunk (*Mephitis mephitis*), hawk (*Buteo* sp.), painted turtle (*Chrysemys picta*), cottontail rabbit (*Sylvilagus nuttalii*), white-tailed jackrabbit (*Lepus townsendii*), Canada beaver (*Castor canadensis*), river mussel (*Margaritifera margaritifera*), and fat mucket (*Lampsilis siliquoidea radiata*) derive from subsistence and industrial activities. A dentary and a femur of an adult and the neonatal skull and partial skeleton of dogs (*Canis familiaris*) found in the mine fill may reflect food-residue disposal practices or the use by dogs of underground cavities as dens.

Four identically sized, perforated, and polished marine snails (*Olivella* sp.) suggest exchange networks or wide-ranging territoriality, as do quantities of obsidian, basalt, porcelanite, Knife River flint, argillite, and exotic chert artifacts and debitage distributed within the mine fill. The Schmitt mine, except for two small-scale prospects in the vicinity, is the smallest in scale of the three quarried limestone exposures at the Three Waters Quarries. The two northern quarries, which were excavated into sidehill exposures, are undisturbed. Chert from all three quarries was processed in the main upland workshop/campsite north of the mine. Four tipi rings surround the mine and other tipi rings accompany the habitation/workshop site below the bluff on the fan slope that leads to the Missouri River terrace.

Leslie B. Davis

Further Readings

Davis, L.B. 1982. Archaeology and Geology of the Schmitt Chert Mine, Missouri Headwaters. *Guidebook for Field Trip.* Presented at the Thirty-Fifth Annual Meeting of the Geological Society of America, Montana State University, Bozeman.

———. 1983. The Schmitt Chert Mine Investigations. In *Headwaters Heritage History*, pp. 10–12. Diamond Jubilee Edition. Three Forks Area Historical Society, Artcraft Printers, Butte.

———. 1987. Quarriers of Stone. *Montana Outdoors* 18(4):27–31.

Younger, J. 1986. *Functional Interpretation of Microwear Patterns on Bone Awls From the Schmitt Chert Mine,*

24BW559, Montana. Unpublished Master's thesis. Department of Anthropology, University of Denver, Denver.

Scott County Pueblo

Scott County pueblo is a distinctive site complex made up of the ruins of a small seven-room pueblo and nearby irrigation ditches in the Ladder Creek Valley of west-central Kansas. Originally investigated in 1898 by naturalists S.W. Williston and H.T. Martin from the University of Kansas (Williston and Martin 1900), the associated artifacts are typical of Late Plains Indian chipped-stone tools and pottery. A few Southwestern pueblo artifacts also were found as well as some iron pieces of European origin. On the basis of the artifacts, the pueblos, irrigation ditches, and a post-European contact date, Williston identified the site as the location

Top: El Cuartelejo pueblo as it may have appeared when occupied. (Prepared by T. A. Witty, Jr.) Bottom: Pueblo ruins in Scott County, Kansas, investigated in 1899 by Professor H. T. Martin and recognized as El Cuartelejo. (From the photographic collections of the Museum of Anthropology, University of Kansas, Lawrence, Kansas)

of El Cuartelejo. Spanish documents relate a scenario of two Puebloan groups, first Taos, ca. A.D. 1650, then Picuris, A.D. 1698, that fled into the Plains to escape Spanish rule and live with a band of Plains Apaches. Both groups were later returned to their pueblos by the Spanish in separate expeditions. The place and area became known as El Cuartelejo, and the Apaches the Cuartelejo band. Historian Alfred B. Thomas (1935) and others, using Spanish documents, argued that El Cuartelejo was in the vicinity of Pueblo, Colorado, but no archaeological evidence supports this interpretation.

In 1939, Waldo R. Wedel of the Smithsonian Institution excavated a midden area north of the pueblo and, on the basis of the recovered material, assigned it to the Dismal River aspect (Wedel 1959). In 1965, James Gunnerson also excavated two Dismal River house floors a few hundred meters (yards) north of the pueblo (Gunnerson 1968). In 1970, Thomas A. Witty, Jr., reexcavated the pueblo and three adjacent borrow areas as part of an interpretative development plan (Witty 1983). In 1965, the pueblo was designated a National Historic Landmark. As a result of the later archaeological work and reinterpretation of documents, the site is considered to be affiliated with El Cuartelejo and the Cuartelejo Apache. The pueblo is the northwesternmost such structure from the traditional pueblo area.

Thomas A. Witty, Jr.

Further Readings

Gunnerson, J.H. 1968. Plains Apache Archaeology: A Review. *Plains Anthropologist* 13(41):167–189.

Thomas, A.B. 1935. *After Coronado: Spanish Exploration Northeast of New Mexico, 1696–1727.* University of Oklahoma Press, Norman.

Wedel, W.R. 1959. *An Introduction to Kansas Archeology.* Bulletin no. 174. Bureau of American Ethnology, Smithsonian Institution, Washington, D.C.

Williston, S.W., and H.T. Martin. 1900. *Some Pueblo Ruins in Scott County, Kansas.* Transactions, Kansas State Historical Society, Topeka.

Witty, T.A., Jr. 1983. *An Archeological Review of the Scott County Pueblo.* Bulletin, vol. 2. Oklahoma Anthropological Society, Norman.

See also DISMAL RIVER ASPECT

Scraper

A chipped-stone scraper, as perceived by most North American prehistorians, is a morpho-technological type and is defined primarily on the basis of form and the location of secondary modification. Scraper form is variable but is usually round, oblong, or teardrop-shaped, and length varies from ca. 2 to 15 cm (0.8–5.8 inches). This substantial formal and metric variability dilutes the functional integrity of the type; that is, many scrapers were prehistorically not used to scrape. For this reason, the more prudent lithic analysts have regarded the scraper as a morphological and not a functional entity, except where demonstrated otherwise.

Retouch on scrapers is most frequently abrupt, particularly on one end or side, and is typically noninvasive; that is, it does not extend very far across the surface of the piece. Scrapers that do exhibit invasive retouch have often been transformed from a bifacial projectile point by blunting and rounding the previously pointed end. Research on European Middle Paleolithic scrapers has demonstrated that resharpening scraper bits can change the entire typological assessment of the piece and thereby affect its interpretation (Dibble 1987). The same phenomenon may have occurred in North American assemblages. George C. Frison (1968) has established that, in the Plains, scrapers were frequently sharpened and that their sharpening flakes can provide information on the location

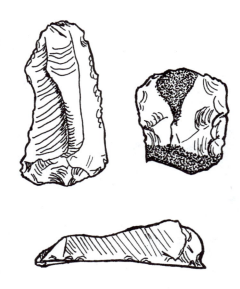

Scraper. (*Courtesy of the Wilford Archaeology Laboratory, University of Minnesota*)

of the refurbishing activity and the original nature of the task.

Several approaches have been taken to the analysis of scrapers. Edwin N. Wilmsen (1968) tried to show a correspondence between the edge angle of a scraper bit and the substances worked by it, but his methodology was so seriously flawed that the approach was never pursued. Hallam L. Movius, Jr., and others (1968), using an "attribute analysis" approach, also measured edge angles as well as several other dimensions of scrapers and other European Upper Paleolithic tools. By performing multiple measurements and judiciously recombining these measurements, they were able to characterize and even reconstruct the form of each scraper studied. The problem was that the method was time consuming and few researchers could use this information to answer pertinent human behavioral questions; therefore, this approach, too, has languished.

The most fruitful analytical approach to scrapers has been the study of use-wear. Among the several analyses of this formal class, probably the most thorough experimentally based one was performed by John W. Brink (1978). Experimenting with wood, antler, bone, and hide, Brink concluded that the wear formed by working each of these materials is sufficiently distinct to be able to distinguish the type of material worked from the wear alone. Among other published analyses using this technique, one of the most noteworthy is a study of scraper planes from southern California that demonstrated that they were probably used to pulp fibers from the leaves of the agave plant (Salls 1985).

George H. Odell

Further Readings

Brink, J.W. 1978. *An Experimental Study of Microwear Formation on Endscrapers.* Mercury Series Paper no. 83. Archaeological Survey of Canada, National Museum of Man, Ottawa.

Dibble, H.L. 1987. The Interpretation of Middle Paleolithic Scraper Morphology. *American Antiquity* 52:109–117.

Frison, G.C. 1968. A Functional Analysis of Certain Chipped Stone Tools. *American Antiquity* 33:149–155.

Movius, H.L., Jr., N.C. David, H.M. Bricker, and R.B. Clay. 1968. *The Analysis of Certain Major Classes of Upper Paleolithic Tools.* Bulletin no. 26. American School of Prehistoric Research, Peabody Museum of American Archaeology and Ethnology, Harvard University, Cambridge.

Salls, R.A. 1985. The Scraper Plane: A Functional Interpretation. *Journal of Field Archaeology* 12:99–106.

Wilmsen, E.N. 1968. Functional Analysis of Flaked Stone Artifacts. *American Antiquity* 33:156–161.

Seip

The Seip (33RO40) group is located within a sharp bend of Paint Creek ca. 15 km (9.3 miles) southwest of the Hopewell site on the North Fork of Paint Creek in southern Ohio. Seip contained ca. 3 km (2 miles) of walls enclosing ca. 49 ha (121 acres), a separate small enclosure, the second-largest Ohio Hopewell mound (Seip-Pricer), more than 20 smaller mounds, and other features, including isolated burials, pits, small middens, and bladelet-making localities. Among the mounded features are essentially empty prepared floors, simple burials, single wooden structures without burials, and two separate multiroomed great houses containing a variety of ceremonial/ritual remains, including tombs. The vast majority of in situ remains lay at the base of the mounds. The main enclosure walls were shaped into a basic circle-and-square configuration that is closely repeated at Baum, 9 km (9.6 miles) downstream. The square enclosure-wall segments were only 1.2–1.5 m (4–5 feet) high and composed of subsurface red clays apparently chosen for the purpose. The largest circular portion was built using adjacent or close borrow pits. Considerable cultural debris from earlier Hopewellian use of these areas was thus incorporated into the walls. The second major construction phase of Seip-Pricer Mound (ca. 4 m, or 13 feet, of the final 9.5-m, or 31-foot, height) also contained cultural debris from nearby surface soils. There is little other stratigraphic evidence that is helpful in constructing an intrasite chronology. The few radiocarbon dates are consistent with site use through much of Ohio Hopewell times (ca. 100 B.C.–A.D. 450, or 2050–1500 years B.P.). The construction of the major enclosure was probably not concurrent with major mound construction. The use of the Seip-Pricer great house possibly occurred ca. A.D. 300 (1650 years B.P.). Studies of the burial patterns and demography at Seip indicate that semiautonomous social units, each composed of one or more lineages, shared the use of the great houses. Site use overlapped with that of other regional sites, but again, the details do not have absolute dates attached. The architectural designs of both great houses and the pair of major conjoined enclosures (Seip and Baum) indicate strong cultural ties with groups who constructed Edwin Harness Mound and the Liberty and Works East enclosure in the main Scioto Valley ca. 30 km (18.5 miles) to the east. The structure of major artifact deposits and some burial practices at the Seip-Pricer great house suggest cultural ties to Mound 25 at the Hopewell site. A few Connestee sherds and radiocarbon dates from a locality immediately outside the major enclosure suggest contacts with areas of the Appalachian Plateau during the fourth century A.D. The quantities of mica and the occurrence of steatite artifacts in other areas of the site add time depths to such contacts. Copper and marine objects from diverse site features complete the most common Ohio Hopewell exotic trio. Other rare materials occur, but in more limited provenance.

N'omi B. Greber

Further Readings

Baby, R.S., and S.M. Langlois. 1979. Seip Mound State Memorial: Nonmortuary Aspects of Hopewell. In *Hopewell Archaeology: The Chillicothe Conference,* edited by D.S. Brose and N. Greber, pp. 16–18. Kent State University Press, Kent.

Greber, N. 1979. Variation in Social Structure Among Classic Ohio Hopewell Peoples. *Midcontinental Journal of Archaeology* 3(3):35–78.

———. 1984. Geophysical Remote Sensing at Archaeological Sites in Ohio: A Case History. Paper presented at a special session, "Archaeology and Geophysics," at the Annual Meeting of the Society of Exploration Geophysics, Atlanta. Published in volume of the proceedings.

———. 1994. Two Geometric Enclosures in Paint Creek Valley: An Estimate of Possible Changes in Community Patterns Through Time. In *Ohio Hopewell Community Organization,* edited by W. Dancy. Kent State University Press, Kent, in press.

Konigsberg, L.W. 1985. Demography and Mortuary Practices at Seip Mound One.
Midcontinental Journal of Archaeology 10(1):123–148.

Mills, W.C. 1909. Explorations of the Seip Mound. *Ohio Archaeological and Historical Quarterly* 18:269–321.

Shetrone, H.C., and E.F. Greenman. 1931. Explorations of the Seip Group of Prehistoric Earthworks. *Ohio Archaeological and Historical Quarterly* 40:343–509.

See also OHIO HOPEWELL

Selkirk

Selkirk has been referred to as a culture, a complex, and a composite, but in most respects it is similar to Blackduck, the major difference being strikingly different pottery assemblages. Selkirk and Blackduck pottery are found together on sites within the Blackduck distribution in Ontario and central Manitoba. Pure Selkirk sites occur farther north in Ontario, Manitoba, and Saskatchewan, penetrate into the Lichen Woodland forests (a forest type that occurs north of the Boreal Forest and south of the Tundra), and reach westward along the Churchill River drainage to Alberta.

Sites have been dated from A.D. 900 (1050 years B.P.) to European contact in the seventeenth century and are attributed to the Cree. The historically documented close relationship between the Cree and the Ojibwa in the western portion of the Canadian Shield is the most parsimonious explanation for the intermingling of Selkirk and Blackduck pottery in the region intermediate between the two distributions. Regional variants of the Selkirk pottery assemblage, as with Blackduck, probably reflect some of the regionally distinct band clusters identified by European observers. Also, with some qualifications, it is generally agreed that Selkirk, like Blackduck, developed out of a Laurel-culture base and specifically in central Manitoba. The stone and bone industries of Selkirk and Blackduck are very similar, as are settlement and subsistence patterns and traits, such as the initial appearance of stone and pottery smoking pipes. Unlike a portion of the Blackduck people, however, Selkirk hunters appear to have been excluded from the parklands of Saskatchewan by contemporary Plains people, although Plains influences are apparent in both the stone and the pottery technology.

Much of the rock art throughout the Selkirk

distribution probably relates to Cree shamanic practices or, in the regions of Selkirk-Blackduck overlap, to Cree-Ojibwa ceremonialism. Little is known of burial practices other than the presence at a site on the Red River south of Lake Winnipeg of flexed and bundle pit burials that were occasionally capped with stone slabs and provided with grave offerings, including dogs.

The archaeology of Selkirk reflects the highly mobile hunters and fishers described by early fur traders. Attempts to draw sharp cultural boundaries or define homogeneous archaeological constructs are likely to be frustrated. The exceptional degree of mobility and freedom of personal choice, noted historically for the Algonquian-speaking peoples of the Canadian Shield, is also apparent in their technology.

J.V. Wright

Further Readings

Dickson, G.A. 1980. *The Kame Hills Site*. Papers in Manitoba Archaeology, Final Report no. 9. Department of Cultural Affairs and Historical Resources, Historic Resource Branch, Province of Manitoba, Winnipeg.

Meyer, D., and D. Russell. 1987. The Selkirk Composite of Central Canada: A Reconsideration. *Arctic Anthropology* 24(2): 1–31.

Rajnovich, G. 1983. *The Spruce Point Site: A Comparative Study of Selkirk Components in the Boreal Forest*. Conservation Archaeology Report no. 1. Northwest Region, Ministry of Citizenship and Culture, Toronto.

Selkirk Composite

The Selkirk composite, consisting of four to five regional complexes, is one of two major composites spread across the western Boreal Forest and adjacent parkland of central Canada during the Late Woodland period. Although there is some variation in the age ranges of the complexes, which may reflect different sample sizes of dates, most dates tend to fall in the A.D. 1200–1700 (750–250 years B.P.) range. The complexes are considered to be the precontact record of Algonquian-speaking Cree groups. Selkirk materials were first defined by Richard S. MacNeish (1958). Regional variability was later recognized by Walter M. Hlady (1971), but it was not until the 1980s that E. Leigh

Syms's concept of the composite was applied to define a systematic set of interrelated complexes (Syms 1980; Rajnovich 1983; Meyer and Russell 1987; Lenius and Olinyk 1990). The complexes are distinguished primarily by variation in vessel form, such as neck shape and vessel contour, vessel decoration, and differences in the diversity of ceramic shapes (e.g., the limited distribution of ceramic lamps). Although there is general agreement that the four northern complexes—Pehonan, Clearwater Lake, Kisis, and Kame Hills—fall within the Selkirk composite, Brian J. Lenius and Dave M. Olinyk have presented compelling arguments that the Winnipeg River complex should be transferred to the Rainy River composite (Lenius and Olinyk 1990).

E. Leigh Syms

Further Readings

Hlady, W.M. 1971. *An Introduction to the Archaeology of the Woodland Area of Northern Manitoba*. Manitoba Archaeological Newsletter, vol. 8, nos. 2–3.

Lenius, B.J., and D.M. Olinyk. 1990. The Rainy River Composite: Revisions to Late Woodland Taxonomy. In *The Woodland Tradition in the Western Great Lakes: Papers Presented to Elden Johnson*, edited by G.E. Gibbon, pp. 77–112. Publications in Anthropology no. 4. University of Minnesota Press, Minneapolis.

MacNeish, R.S. 1958. *An Introduction to the Archaeology of Southeastern Manitoba*. Bulletin no. 157. National Museum of Canada, Ottawa.

Meyer, D., and D. Russell. 1987. The Selkirk Composite of Central Canada: A Reconsideration. *Arctic Anthropology* 24(2):1–31.

Rajnovich, G. 1983. *The Spruce Point Site: A Comparative Study of Selkirk Components in the Boreal Forest*. Conservation Archaeology Report no. 1. Northwest Region, Ministry of Citizenship and Culture, Toronto.

Syms, E.L. 1980. The Co-Influence Sphere Model: A New Paradigm for Plains Developments and Plains-Parkland-Woodland Processual Interrelationships. In *Directions in Manitoba Prehistory*, edited by L.F. Pettipas, pp. 111–140. Manitoba Archaeological Society, Winnipeg.

Serpent Mound, Great

The Great Serpent Mound (33AD01) of Adams County, Ohio, is the finest example of a prehistoric animal effigy mound in North America and, possibly, the world. It is a clay embankment shaped like a snake more than 396 m (1,300 feet) long; a smaller, oval embankment at the northwest end has been interpreted as part of the head or an object at the snake's open mouth (see Figure 1). The effigy, in its present restored state, averages 1.2–1.5 m (4–5 feet) in height along the body and tapers gradually to less than 0.3 m (1 foot) near the tail. Its width is generally from 6 to 7.6 m (20–25 feet). The Serpent Mound is located in a wedge-shaped portion of south-central Ohio that is a northern extension of the Lexington Plain of Kentucky. The typically rolling-hill-and-river-valley terrain is interrupted in the vicinity of Serpent Mound by the remnants of a cryptoexplosion crater ca. 8 km (5 miles) in diameter (Riedel 1972).

Figure 1. (top) Great Serpent mound, Adams County, Ohio. (Illustration by R. V. Fletcher and T. L. Cameron) Figure 2. (bottom) Comparison of Great Serpent mound and Late Prehistoric iconography: a. conventionalized rattlesnake eye, Mississippian period, Tennessee; b. Great Serpent Mound, Adams County, Ohio. (Illustration by R. V. Fletcher and T. L. Cameron)

Serpent Mound has puzzled researchers since the mid-nineteenth century. E.G. Squier and E.H. Davis published the first map of Serpent Mound in 1848. They suggested parallels between the "serpent-and-oval" configuration (as they saw it then) and serpent-and-circle/egg/world symbolic parallels in Hindu, Greek, Egyptian, and Chinese mythologies. The next significant map was produced by J.P. McLean in 1885. His version defined the embankment more accurately than Squier and Davis's, and he questioned their Old World interpretation of Serpent Mound. W.H. Holmes (1886) followed with an even more accurate map and suggested that the "egg" represented the eye of the serpent (Putnam 1890). This latter view is supported by modern iconographic comparisons with Mississippian rattlesnake eye motifs (see Figure 2; Fletcher et al. 1994). The most comprehensive discussion of early Serpent Mound maps is in C.C. Willoughby (1919).

F.W. Putnam of Harvard University's Peabody Museum of American Archaeology and Ethnology ensured the preservation of this remarkable earthwork. In 1883, during his first visit to Serpent Mound, he took photographs and measurements of its dimensions. He returned in 1886 and, seeing that the effigy would soon be destroyed, obtained an option on the property before returning to Boston in search of funds. The money was raised by subscription. The property was operated by the Peabody Museum as a public park for 16 years before being deeded to the Ohio Historical Society in 1900 (Randall 1905).

No diagnostic artifacts were found in the Serpent Mound embankment during Putnam's first excavations in 1887 (Putnam 1890). However, he did recover artifact assemblages from burial mounds, graves, and a multicomponent occupation site in the vicinity of the effigy. Later investigators attributed most of the artifacts to the Early Woodland period (Greenman 1935), and J.B. Griffin (1943) tentatively assigned the embankment itself to the Adena culture, although he identified both Adena and Fort Ancient (Baum focus) components in the occupation site. Griffin's Adena-origin theory has been generally accepted because of the close proximity of the mound to definite Adena burials and artifacts (Webb and Snow 1945; Webb and Baby 1957).

In 1991, a team of avocational and professional archaeologists excavated a trench through a section of the Serpent Mound (Fletcher et al. 1994). Two carbon samples recovered from basket-loaded mound fill produced identical AMS (accelerator mass spectrometry) dates of A.D. 1030 ± 70 (920 years B.P.), which fall within the Early Fort Ancient (Baum focus, ca. A.D. 950–1200, or 1000–750 years B.P.), or Late Prehistoric, time period. The possibility that Serpent Mound is a Fort Ancient rather than an Adena manifestation—and that the serpent is a rattlesnake in Mississippian iconography—remains tentative. More subsurface investigations are needed to resolve the issue.

Robert V. Fletcher
Terry L. Cameron

Further Readings

Fletcher, R.V., T.L. Cameron, B.T. Lepper, D.A. Wymer, and W. Pickard. 1994. *Serpent Mound Project*. Ohio Historical Society, Columbus.

Greenman, E.F. 1935. *Guide to Serpent Mound*. Ohio State Archaeological and Historical Society, Columbus.

Griffin, J.B. 1943. *The Fort Ancient Aspect*. University of Michigan Press, Ann Arbor.

Holmes, W.H. 1886. A Sketch of the Great Serpent Mound. *Science* 8(204):624–628.

McLean, J.P. 1885. The Great Serpent Mound. *American Antiquarian* 7:44–47.

Putnam, F.W. 1890. The Serpent Mound of Ohio. *Century Magazine* 39:871–888.

Randall, E.O. 1905. *The Serpent Mound*. Ohio State Archaeological and Historical Society, Columbus.

Reidel, S.O. 1972. *Geology of the Serpent Mound Cryptoexplosion*. Unpublished Master's thesis. Department of Geology, University of Cincinnati, Cincinnati.

Squier, E.G., and E.H. Davis. 1848. *Ancient Monuments of the Mississippi Valley*. Contributions to Knowledge no. 1. Smithsonian Institution, Washington, D.C.

Webb, W.S., and R.S. Baby. 1957. *The Adena People no. 2*. Ohio Historical Society, Columbus.

Webb, W.S., and C.E. Snow. 1945. *The Adena People*. Reports in Anthropology and Archaeology, vol. 6. University of Kentucky, Lexington.

Willoughby, C.C. 1919. The Serpent Mound of Adams County. *American Anthropologist* 21:153–164.

See also ADENA; FORT ANCIENT CULTURE

Shell Middens

Shell middens are a distinct type of archaeological site characterized by large accumulations of mollusk shells discarded by humans as food-processing debris. The shells of bivalves (oysters, clams, or mussels) are the principal constituents in most shell middens, along with variable quantities of other refuse such as animal bones and lithic debris. The timing, location, and intensity of molluscan use as a dietary resource were tied to regional patterns of food procurement, human population density, and the stabilization of sea levels and drainage systems following the Pleistocene. Evidence shows that persistent utilization of mollusks in America began ca. 4000 B.C. (5950 years B.P.). The long-term harvest of shellfish at a single location often resulted in large, elevated middens covering ca. 1 ha (2.5 acres) that are sometimes referred to as "shell mounds." In some cases, the less active portions of these large middens were used by native peoples as habitation or burial areas. Extensive marine-shell middens are found along the Atlantic and Pacific coasts of North America. Interior waters supported freshwater mussels that were commonly used as a food resource, with the largest midden sites found adjacent to rivers in the southeastern United States and along the Upper Mississippi River. Interest in American shell middens was stimulated by pioneer interdisciplinary archaeological work in the mid-nineteenth century at the Danish *kjoekkenmoeddinger,* or kitchen midden, sites composed of marine shell. An English-language summary of this work (Lubbock 1872) led to the systematic excavations of American shell middens that helped dispel the popular concept that they were of nonhuman origins. Interpretations drawn from early shell-midden excavations were important to the development of American archaeology in illustrating a number of methodological and theoretical concepts.

James L. Theler

Further Readings

Lubbock, J. 1872. *Pre-Historic Times.* D. Appleton, New York.

Theler, J.L. 1987. *Woodland Tradition Economic Strategies: Animal Resource Utilization in Southwestern Wisconsin and Northeastern Iowa.* Report no. 17. Office of the State Archaeologist, University of Iowa, Iowa City.

Trigger, B.G. (editor). 1986. *Native Shell Mounds of North America: Early Studies.* Garland, New York.

Waselkov, G.A. 1987. Shellfish Gathering and

Stratified Woodland tradition (ca. A.D. 100–500) shell midden along the Mississippi River at site 47CR186 in southwestern Wisconsin. (1980 photograph by J. L. Theler).

Shell Midden Archaeology. In *Advances in Archaeological Method and Theory*, vol. 10, edited by M.B. Schiffer, pp. 93–210. Academic Press, San Diego.

Webb, W.S. 1984. *Indian Knoll*. University of Tennessee Press, Knoxville.

Shell Money (California)

In late prehistory, California societies developed systems of money for use in exchange and rituals. The common currency was a string of shell beads, with beads of clamshell the most typical form. Clamshells occurred along many sections of California coast. Local peoples would collect shells, break them into pieces 2–4 cm (1–1.5 inches) in width, and drill holes through each piece. Pieces would be strung together, and their edges ground on coarse stone slabs until smooth-edged disks resulted. Early disk beads were often up to 2 cm (1 inch) in diameter, while later ones were smaller as a rule, often less than 1 cm (0.5 inches). Uniform string lengths and bead counts were not used, but ethnographic data show that a standard string was the length of the distance between an adult's nose tip and outstretched fingertip: ca. 80–90 cm (31–35 inches) long and containing 150 or more beads.

In central and northern California, additional types of shells were used for money strings. *Olivella* shells, either whole with their tips ground off to allow stringing or broken so that pieces of the side walls could be made into flat disk beads, were common. In northwestern California, the *Dentalium* shell was also used. Not native to California, *Dentalium* shells were collected in Puget Sound and traded south overland to reach their users in California. These horn-shaped shells were strung in groups of the same length—the longer the shell, the fewer that would be required for a string, and the more valuable the resulting string. A single string of large *Dentalium* shells was worth many times more than a string of smaller shells or clamshells. Northwestern California also had an even more highly prized form of bead money, one made of small cylindrical beads of baked magnesite.

The shell-money system possessed many attributes found in modern currencies. Shell money had a widely recognized intrinsic value. It could also be converted into a variety of commodities and services, used in ritual activities, such as making offerings during ceremonies or making contributions to burial offerings, and used for more purely economic transactions. Although it was manufactured continuously by coastal populations, shell money was not subject to serious inflation. Through such devices as burning strings of beads during rituals and burying beads with the deceased, beads were taken out of circulation in more or less the same proportion that new money was created. The existence of regional exchange networks helped distribute shell money around the state on a regular basis. Shell money also helped California exchange systems evolve from purely kin-based reciprocity to more fully economic trading systems. It is, therefore, a significant element of the cultural complexity achieved by Late Prehistoric California societies.

Joseph L. Chartkoff

Further Readings

Chagnon, N.A. 1970. Ecological and Adaptive Aspects of California Shell Money. *Archaeological Survey Annual Report* 12:1–26. University of California, Los Angeles.

Shetrone, Henry Clyde (1876–1954)

A newspaperman in Columbus, Ohio, H.C. Shetrone became interested in archaeology while preparing articles on William C. Mills's excavations (which began in 1898 and spanned 30 years) of the Adena, Gartner, Edwin Harness, and Seip mounds for the Ohio State Museum. He became Mills's assistant at the museum in 1913 and collaborated with him on many projects, including excavations in Ohio at Tremper in 1915, the Fuert mound and village site in 1917, and the Mound City group in 1921 and 1922 and the compilation of Mills's *Archaeological Atlas of Ohio* (1914), which recorded the location by county of hundreds of mounds, earthworks, and villages. When Mills was made director of the Ohio State Archaeological and Historical Society in 1921, Shetrone was appointed curator of archaeology, and when Mills died in 1928, he was appointed director of the museum and the society, which prevented him from continuing active fieldwork. As a fieldworker, however, he directed and published the results of excavations at the Campbell Island village site, the Hine mound and village site, the Wright mounds, the Ginther mound, the Miesse mound, the Hopewell earthworks, and Seip Mound 1, all in Ohio. His article "The Culture Problem in Ohio Archae-

Henry C. Shetrone. (Reprinted with permission from American Antiquity *21[3]:296)*

ology" (1920) was an early recognition of the necessity of organizing the Ohio archaeological record into complexes within a cultural-historical, space-time framework, and his book *The Mound-Builders* (1930) was an early synthesis of the prehistoric cultures of the eastern United States. Shetrone remained active in North American archaeology after he became director of the museum and society, although his contributions were now mainly administrative and synthetic. For example, he surveyed point collections in the state in a study of "The Folsom Phenomena As Seen From Ohio" (1936), established a lithic laboratory for the eastern United States in 1938, wrote a synopsis of West Virginia archaeology, and produced a survey of aboriginal art in the eastern United States. Although Shetrone retired in 1946, he remained actively associated with the museum until his death in 1954.

Guy Gibbon

Further Readings

Setzler, F.M. 1956. Henry Clyde Shetrone—1876–1954. *American Antiquity* 21:296–299.

Shetrone, H.C. 1920. The Culture Problem in Ohio Archaeology. *American Anthropologist* 22:144–172.

———. 1930. *The Mound-Builders.* Appleton-Century, New York.

———. 1936. The Folsom Phenomena As Seen From Ohio. *Ohio State Archaeological and Historical Quarterly* 46: 240–526.

Shield Culture

Shield-culture people (formerly, Shield Archaic) occupied the southern half of the Canadian Shield, a physiographic region involving 4.6 million km² (1.8 million square miles). Characterized by exposed rock, muskeg, and interconnected waterways and covered mainly by the Boreal Forest and Lichen Woodland vegetation provinces with Great Lakes–St. Lawrence forest along its southern margin, it was a region that placed severe constraints upon human occupation. Mobility (canoe, toboggan, snowshoe) was essential to survival, as food resources were dispersed and frequently subject to cyclical fluctuations. Endemic forest fires also altered the abundance and nature of resources over large areas.

Shield culture developed out of Plano culture in the western periphery of the Canadian Shield ca. 7000 B.C. (8950 years B.P.). It then spread eastward as plants, followed by animals, occupied lands released by glacial ice and associated bodies of water. This gradual colonizing movement ended on the coast of the Labrador Sea at 1000 B.C. (2950 years B.P.). Continuities in technology, settlement patterns, and, inferentially, subsistence suggest that Shield-culture people were the ancestors of the Cree, Ojibwa, Algonkin, and Montagnais peoples encountered by Europeans in the seventeenth century. Indeed, the lifeway of the northern Algonquian-speaking peoples appears to have been essentially the same as their Shield-culture predecessors.

Chipped-stone projectile points, knives, and scrapers dominated the archaeological toolkit. Acid soils have dissolved all bone so nothing is known of the bone-tool technology. For the same reason, inferences on subsistence must be extrapolated from settlement-pattern evidence, such as sites located at caribou or moose water crossings and base camps at fish-spawning locales. Fish and big game appear to have been subsistence mainstays. The basic settlement strategy was to locate in areas containing a range of resources and alternative routes for water travel to avoid being stranded by unfavorable winds. Most archaeological sites represent warm-weather camps. Dispersal of small family groups in the winter was the likely norm unless a caribou pound was particularly productive. A major problem for archaeologists is locating these winter camps in the dense forests of the Canadian Shield.

Rare features containing some of the finest native-copper tools and ornaments known from North America have been interpreted as graves in which all bone has disappeared. Chipped-stone tools are also common in these features and include many manufactured from a distinctive North Dakota chalcedony that was traded as far east as 2,000 km (1,240 miles) from the geological source. In addition to this evidence of trade with contemporary peoples on the Plains, there were contacts with populations in the lower Great Lakes–St. Lawrence region and the Gulf of St. Lawrence. It has been proposed (Wright 1995) that ca. 1500 B.C. (3450 years B.P.), Shield-culture people obtained bow-and-arrow technology from early Paleoeskimo people along the Labrador coast and then introduced the new weapon system into the interior of the continent.

Like the situation at the time of early European contact, Shield-culture societies would have consisted of small regional bands, related through marriage, within which there was considerable individual freedom of movement and decision. Archaeologists speculate that women were more likely to move from one band to another than men, a pattern that has been noted historically by northern ethnologists. The archaeology of the Canadian Shield reflects a basic continuity of a way of life that first appeared 9,000 years ago.

J.V. Wright

Further Readings

Wright, J.V. 1972. *The Shield Archaic*. Publications in Archaeology no. 3. National Museum of Man, National Museums of Canada, Ottawa.

———. 1981. Prehistory of the Canadian Shield. In *Subarctic*, edited by J. Helm, pp. 86–96. Handbook of North American Indians, vol. 6, W.C. Sturtevant, general editor. Smithsonian Institution, Washington, D.C.

———. 1995. *A History of the Native People of Canada: 1. 10,000–1,000 B.C.* Mercury Series Paper no. 152. Archaeological Survey of Canada, Canadian Museum of Civilization, Hull.

Shoop Site

The Shoop site (36Da20) is located in the ridge and valley section of central Pennsylvania. One of the largest Paleoindian sites in the eastern United States, it has had a significant effect on Paleoindian research in this part of North America since the 1950s. Shoop was discovered in the 1930s by amateur archaeologists. The first extensive research was conducted by Dr. John Witthoft, who published a classic article (1952) based on a surface collection of more than 8 ha (20 acres) and an analysis of ca. 2,000 artifacts, including more than 1,500 pieces of debitage, 400 tools, and 53 projectile points. Although many of his ideas have been revised, they played a significant role in interpretations of the Paleoindian period for more than 30 years.

Shoop is situated ca. 9.6 km (6 miles) east of the Susquehanna River on a ridge overlooking Armstrong Creek. The site, which covers an area of 16.2 ha (40 acres), consists of at least 15 concentrations of artifacts, each of which ranges from 15.2 m (50 feet) to more than 91.4 m (300 feet) in diameter. All of the artifacts lie in the plow zone, and to date (1996) very little systematic excavation has taken place. Although artifact densities are relatively low, Shoop has been heavily collected since the 1930s. There are currently more than 5,000 artifacts available for analysis at the Pennsylvania State Museum, the Smithsonian Institution, and in several amateur collections.

Since Witthoft's work, Edwin N. Wilmsen (1970), Steve L. Cox (1986), Gary L. Fogelman (1986), and Kurt W. Carr (1989) have conducted major analyses of the site material, which suggest that (1) a blade-core technology was not used, as was once thought; (2) Witthoft's Enterline Chert tradition does not differ from other fluted-point production strategies; and (3) the site was not pre-Clovis but was more or less contemporary with other eastern Clovis sites. Approximately 145 fluted points have been recovered from the Shoop site. In contrast to other fluted-point sites in the Northeast, most of which are rejects that were broken during production, all those at Shoop were discarded as finished tools. Although many of the Shoop points are relatively narrow because of heavy reworking, they seem to be essentially Clovis in style and probably date to the early part of the Paleoindian period. The fact that ca. 35 percent of all artifacts are heat spalled suggests that prehistoric fires were common and that charcoal may be present for a much-needed radiocarbon date.

The proportion of tools (15–45 percent) to debitage in each concentration is very high; the dominant tool type is the end scraper, more than 700 of which have been collected from the site. End scrapers represent at least 37 percent of all tools and 10 percent of the entire assemblage. Other tool types, in order of their frequency, include utilized flakes, side scrapers, late-stage bifaces, projectile points, wedges, drills, concavities (spokeshaves), awls, gravers, and perforators.

Witthoft's most controversial observations about Shoop concern the interpretation of the hilltop ecological setting and the lithic-utilization pattern that was practiced; the debate about these continues. At least 75 percent of all sites in the state are in, or adjacent to, floodplains. Shoop is in a very different ecological setting. Various explanations have been offered to account for this difference, including the location of Shoop near a caribou migration route, but no consensus has been achieved. The caribou-migration hypothesis is supported by the identification of cervid (deer, elk, moose, or caribou) blood on one tool in an examination of a limited number of tools for blood residue (Hyland et al. 1990).

According to Witthoft, well more than 95 percent of the artifacts are made on Onondaga chert, whose source is 402 km (250 miles) to the north in western New York State. Paleoindian research in the 1970s by William M. Gardner (1979) and others concluded that, south of the glaciated region, Paleoindians were not traveling long distances. Instead, they were tied to local quarries and lithic sources and exploiting locally available food resources. By contrast, Shoop resembles sites, such as Vail in Maine and Debert in Nova Scotia, that are in what David J. Meltzer (1984) has termed the "glaci-ated region" of northeastern North America. The site seems to be the most southern extension of a cultural adaptation that involved long-distance travel and the exploitation of migratory animals.

Kurt W. Carr

Further Readings

Carr, K.W. 1989. The Shoop Site: Thirty-Five Years After. In *New Approaches to Other Pasts,* edited by W.F. Kinsey and R.W. Moeller, pp. 5–28. Archaeological Services, Bethlehem.

Cox, S.L. 1986. A Re-Analysis of the Shoop Site. *Archaeology of Eastern North America* 14:101–170.

Fogelman, G.L. 1986. *Shoop: Pennsylvania's Famous Paleo Site: A Popular Version.* Fogelman, Turbotville.

Gardner, W.M. 1979. Paleoindian Settlement Pattern and Site Distribution in the Middle Atlantic. Paper presented at the Middle Atlantic Archaeological Conference, Rehoboth Beach.

Hyland, D.C., J.M. Tersak, J.M. Adovasio, and M.I. Seigel. 1990. Identification of the Species of Origin of Residual Blood on Lithic Material. *American Antiquity* 55:104–112.

Meltzer, D.J. 1984. On Stone Procurement and Settlement Mobility in Eastern Fluted Point Groups. *North American Archaeologist* 6(1):1–24.

Wilmsen, E.N. 1970. *Lithic Analysis and Cultural Inference: A Paleo-Indian Case.* University of Arizona Press, Tucson.

Witthoft, J. 1952. A Paleo-Indian Site in Eastern Pennsylvania: An Early Hunting Culture. *Proceedings of the American Philosophical Society* 96(4):464–495.

Sierra Nevada and Cascade Ranges

California's greatest mountain ranges, the Sierra Nevada and the southern Cascades, provide much of the state's ecological and topographic diversity in a relatively confined area. For prehistoric cultures, they formed a barrier or limiting factor to interaction between cultures of interior California and those of the Great Basin. At the same time, they provided many resources in close proximity because their great elevation allowed biomes to change with altitude. The slopes of the ranges were used seasonally by cultures from both California and the

Great Basin. Distinctive archaeological complexes of varying ages have been found in the ranges. The extent to which they reflect seasonal use by cultures based at the foot of the mountains, and to what extent they reflect distinct mountain populations, is unclear, debated, and probably variable at different times and places. In terms of distinctive archaeological patterns, however, these ranges can be usefully studied as a province of their own.

The Sierra Nevada consists of a great tilt-block formation of mid- to later-Cenozoic age. Its rocks originated as much older marine deposits. Tectonic activity metamorphosed the original sediments and thrust the block upward with a steep eastern face and a much more gradual western slope. The uplifted escarpments were subsequently further affected by erosion, Pleistocene glaciation, and volcanic activity. The Mammoth Ski Basin, for example, is a volcanic caldera 25 km (15.5 miles) in diameter. Thermal springs and obsidian deposits are common along the eastern base of the Sierras for the same reason (Bateman and Wahrhaftig 1966; Alt and Hyndman 1975).

The Sierras parallel the Central Valley for more than 650 km (403 miles). They run in a NNW-SSE direction. The tallest Sierran peak, Mt. Whitney (elev. 4,418 m, or 14,496 feet) is the highest in the contiguous 48 states. Dozens of peaks exceed 4,000 m (13,122 feet) in elevation. The eastern base of the range generally lies only 15–25 km (9.3–15.5 miles) east of the crest, while the western slope averages a gradient of only about 2 percent with a base lying 120 km (74 miles) or more west of the crest (Hill 1975; Moratto and Goldberg 1982).

Before the 1849 Gold Rush, the Sierras were occupied by speakers of five major languages with a dozen or more distinct dialects. Much of the southern Sierras was held by Shoshonean- (Uto-Aztecan) speaking peoples, such as the Kawaiisu, Tubatulabal, and Monache. The western foothills of the southern Sierras were controlled by Yokuts-speaking peoples of the Penutian language stock, which incorporated ca. 15 small tribes that included the Poso Creek, Tule-Kaweah, King's River, and Northern Hill dialects. The central Sierras were largely occupied by speakers of another Penutian language, Miwok. A third Penutian language, Maidu, was spoken by peoples in the northern Sierras. Hokan-speaking Washo people lived around Lake Tahoe and along adjacent parts of the Sierra crest (Kroeber 1925;

Levy 1978; Spier 1978; Wilson and Towne 1978; Moratto 1984; Moratto et al. 1988).

The Cascades form a separate geological province from the Sierra Nevada. During the Mesozoic, ca. 140 million years ago, tectonic activity broke apart the blocks from which the Sierras and the Klamath mountains developed. The Klamath base block was rotated more to an east-west direction and shifted west 100 km (62 miles). The gap created was eventually filled by the foundations of the Cascade Range.

While the Sierras form a vast granitic batholith, the Cascades are a volcanic range. They do not form a great mountain wall like the Sierras but are composed of volcanic highlands resulting from old lava flows and uplifts, which, in turn, are punctuated by more recent cindercones. California's last major volcanic eruption took place in the years 1914–1921 at Mt. Lassen. Snowcapped Mt. Shasta, north of the Sacramento River Valley, can be seen from mountaintops all the way to the Pacific Coast.

Like the Sierras, the Cascades also exhibited a great deal of cultural and linguistic diversity. Penutian-speaking Maidu and Konkow people held the southern margins of the Cascades. Hokan-speaking Atsugewi people lived to the north of the Maidu, and the Hokan-speaking Yana and Yahi lived north of the Konkow. The Atsugewi, like their northern neighbors, the Achomawi, were Hokan-speaking relatives of the Shasta, as were the Okwanuchu, who lived on the southern side of Mt. Shasta. The Penutian-speaking Wintu were expanding into territories occupied by Hokan-speaking groups at the end of prehistory. North of the Achomawi, on the Modoc Plateau, lived the Modoc people, linguistic relatives of the Klamath people of Oregon (Garth 1978; Olmstead and Stewart 1978; Riddell 1978; Silver 1978; Moratto 1984).

The Sierras and the Cascades were among the last parts of California to be studied archaeologically. Systematic studies did not begin until after World War II, when proposals for reservoir construction led to 40 years of field research, mainly in the valleys of the larger streams on the lower slopes of the western Sierras and southern Cascades. Most substantial of them all has been the New Melones Archaeological Project in the central Sierras (e.g., Moratto et al. 1988). In the higher regions, the 1952 survey by R.F. Heizer and A.B. Elsasser (1953) produced the first regional culture sequence. The Yosemite National Park area has seen sustained research because of support from the National Park Service (Fitzwater 1962, 1968a, 1968b).

The southern Sierra sequence is best known from studies done in the building of the Buchanan Reservoir (Moratto 1968, 1970, 1972). E.W. Ritter (1970), working at the Oroville Reservoir, has defined the most widely used sequence for the northern Sierras. M.A. Baumhoff (1955, 1957) pioneered archaeology in the Yana area of the southern Cascades, while F.A. Riddell's work (1956) at Tommy Tucker Cave was important to Cascades, as well as Great Basin, archaeology. Because of the influence of reservoir archaeology, the Cascades region is especially characterized by a plethora of local sequences with little systematic integration. M.J. Moratto (1984:334–338) and Moratto et al. (1988) provide useful summaries. This review summarizes the region's patterns and relates them to the general J.L. Chartkoff and K.K. Chartkoff model (1984).

Paleoindian archaeology in the mountains is even more meager than in most other parts of California. No definitive fluted-point occupation sites are known, although the discovery of an isolated fluted point is occasionally reported. In the nineteenth century, a number of reports of human remains in pre-Holocene deposits, such as the Calaveras skull (Ayres 1882), Gold Springs (Sinclair 1908), Tuolumne Table Mountain (Becker 1891), and Clay Hill (Whitney 1880), were made, but all have proved insupportable. Claims of association between human remains and the bones of extinct Pleistocene animals, at Tranquillity (Heizer and Cook 1952) and at Potter Creek Cave (Sinclair 1904), have also proved mistaken (Berger et al. 1971).

Probably the best candidate for early age comes from the Farmington region in the central Sierran foothills. There, an extensive industry of large crude flake and core tools, such as heavy bifaces and coarse-edged scrapers, has been found in the midst of unmodified stream gravels at more than 40 sites. As has happened so often with Paleoindian archaeology in North America, the crudeness of these tools and the absence of more refined, typologically distinct tools have been taken as evidence of great age. In this case, recent geological assessments suggest that the artifacts may predate gravel deposits that were laid down in the period 10,050–5050 B.C. (12,000–7000 years B.P.) (Ritter et al. 1976). If so, the Farmington materials may be associated with Early and Middle Archaic oc-

cupation of the lower Sierran foothills, possibly as early as the end of the Paleoindian period (9050 B.C., or 11,000 years B.P.; Chartkoff and Chartkoff 1984), but they are more likely equivalent to the San Dieguito or Western Pluvial Lakes traditions (Moratto 1984).

As of the mid-1990s, the Farmington materials represent the most significant example of Sierran archaeology older than the Middle Archaic (6050 B.C., or 8000 years B.P.). Undoubtedly the effects of the end of glaciation made much of the higher mountains unusable for a longer period of time than any other part of the state. For the Middle Archaic (6050–4050 B.C., or 8000–6000 years B.P.), materials are known for a few areas. The Clarks Flat locality at New Melones Reservoir (Moratto et al. 1988:508–509) is among the best-studied examples. There, small occupations were found at several sites along an oxbow of the Stanislaus River at an elevation of ca. 600 m (1,968 feet). The occupations appeared to be temporary campsites characterized by a wide variety, but a modest number, of tools: backed scrapers, scraper-planes, backed bladelets, choppers, hammerstones, and some projectile points and milling tools. The variety of tools suggests that various subsistence activities were practiced there, involving both plants and animals of many species. Although the river was used for water plants and waterfowl, fish seem not to have been exploited. Tool materials show good use of locally available chert but also reliance on obsidian and basalt, which had to be acquired from elsewhere.

By Late Archaic times (4050–2050 B.C., or 6000–4000 years B.P.), occupations were present in more areas of the mountains. In New Melones, the Texas Charley phase (4050–2650 B.C., or 6000–4600 years B.P.) is followed by the Calaveras phase (2650–1050 B.C., or 4600–3000 years B.P.). Around Lake Tahoe, the Spooner phase (4050–2050 B.C., or 6000–4000 years B.P.) represents the start of that region's continuous sequence (Elston et al. 1976). In the southern Sierras, the Lamont phase extends from 4050 to 1250 B.C. (6000–3200 years B.P.) (McGuire and Garfinkel 1980). The Lamont materials give a useful picture of life at that time in the higher elevations. Campsites were small and temporary, probably occupied in summers by people from the east side of the mountains, as suggested by the occurrence of Pinto-style projectile points. Chipped-stone scraping and cutting tools are present, along with some ground-stone tools thought to be associated with processing piñon nuts. Basalt is the material used to make the great majority of these tools. The scarcity of obsidian and shell suggests that trade routes were not very active.

The region's archaeological record blossoms during the subsequent Pacific period (2050 B.C.–A.D. 1750, or 4000–200 years B.P.), with most of the known sequences having their start during the early Pacific period (2050–550 B.C., or 4000–2500 years B.P.). The Martis complex near Lake Tahoe (Heizer and Elsasser 1953), first stage of the first sequence to be discovered for the Sierras, starts ca. 2050 B.C. (4000 years B.P.). At Oroville, Ritter's (1970) sequence starts with the Mesilla complex (ca. 1050 B.C., or 3000 years B.P.). At Yosemite, the Crane Flat phase begins that area's sequence (Fitzwater 1962, 1968a, 1968b). These sequences allow summaries of how cultures changed through the early, middle, late, and final Pacific periods.

In the early Pacific period, substantial populations appear for the first time in the mountains. They appear to be organized in small communities that live in base camps at low elevations and move into the mountains seasonally, mainly in summer. Their homes and other structures are temporary. Food economies are diversified, with emphasis on the use of hard seeds ground on millingstones and the hunting of varied game, especially deer, using spears and spear throwers. *Olivella* shell beads from the coast and obsidian from east of the Sierras or Clear Lake in the North Coast Range indicate some degree of long-distance exchange.

The middle Pacific period (550 B.C.–A.D. 450, or 2500–1500 years B.P.) is represented by such phases as late Mesilla and early Bidwell at Oroville (Ritter 1970), Chowchilla at Buchanan Reservoir (Moratto 1972), late Martis at Tahoe (Heizer and Elsasser 1953), Sierra at New Melones (Moratto et al. 1988), and Canebreak at the Chowchilla River (McGuire and Garfinkel 1980). This era sees the beginning of more substantial winter base camps at lower elevations. Millingstones become more important, and some storage facilities appear, suggesting a growing focus on surplus harvesting of hard seeds. House construction becomes more substantial, and archaeologists have found many well-packed floors in some sites. The spear and spear thrower are still the major hunting weapons, indicating the importance of deer and other larger mammals, but fishing gear also appears, as do mortars and pestles, showing that salmon

and acorns are starting to be used significantly. Village sites develop cemeteries, in which the common burial style is extended, with substantial amounts of grave goods. The amount of obsidian and coastal shells such as *Olivella* and *Haliotis* is greater than before. Greater varieties and quantities of beads suggest a growing degree of social differentiation.

The late Pacific period (A.D. 450–1450, or 1500–500 years B.P.) is present in such phases as Sweetwater at Oroville (Ritter 1970), the early King's Beach period at Tahoe (Heizer and Elsasser 1953), the Redbud phase at New Melones (Moratto et al. 1988), the Tamarack phase at Yosemite (Fitzwater 1962), the Raymond phase on the Chowchilla River (Moratto 1972), and the Sawtooth phase on the Upper Kern River (McGuire and Garfinkel 1980). In general, the late Pacific seems to have been a time of cultural regression in the mountains. The size of populations, the number of village sites, and the amount of regional exchange all are lower than before. Nevertheless, significant developments are reflected in the data that do exist. During this period, the bow and arrow replaces the spear and spear thrower, resulting in a dramatic shrinkage in projectile-point sizes and changes in point styles. While millingstones and manos remain well used, mortars and pestles become more abundant, showing the growing importance of acorn and pine-nut harvests. The bedrock mortar and the cobble pestle are especially notable at this time. Burial customs change, with loosely and tightly flexed burials becoming more common than extended burials. Numbers of grave goods decline. Burials show, though, an apparent increase in violent deaths, suggesting growing conflict among communities. At the same time, mortuary caves in the lower foothills come into use for the deposition of many deceased.

The final Pacific period (A.D. 1450–1800, or 500–150 years B.P.) is represented in all sequences. Good examples come from the Oroville phase at Oroville Reservoir (Ritter 1970), the late King's Beach material at Tahoe (Heizer and Elsasser 1953), the Horseshoe Bend phase at New Melones (Moratto et al. 1988), the Mariposa phase at Yosemite (Fitzwater 1962), the Madera phase at Buchanan Reservoir (Moratto 1972), and the Chimney phase on the Upper Kern River (McGuire and Garfinkel 1980). In each case, these phases represent the archaeology of the historically known peoples of the area, such as the Konkow at Oroville, the

S

Washo at Lake Tahoe, the Miwok at New Melones and Yosemite, the Yokuts on the Chowchilla River, and the Tubatulabal on the Kern River.

The final Pacific period is the most florescent in the mountain sequence. Populations grow to greater numbers than ever before, communities increase in number and size, and architecture becomes more substantial and varied. Regional exchange is aided by the use of shell bead money, mushrooms. Although the variety of species taken in hunting and gathering remains great, more emphasis is placed on acorns, salmon, and deer. Burials start to shift more toward cremations, and grave goods once again become abundant, indicating even greater social differentiation than in previous times. Some burials are made beneath house floors. The Eastgate and the Rose Spring projectile points characteristic of the late Pacific are replaced by Desert Side-Notched and Cottonwood points in the final Pacific. Milling tools, both the mano and millingstone and the bedrock mortar with cobble pestle, remain abundant, and bird-bone tube beads and steatite ornaments become so. Rock art is being produced at this time, and probably earlier as well. The Kern River Canyon and Grinding Rock State Park near Jackson are two of the more important rock-art localities in the mountains.

The archaeology of the mountains shows trends similar to those of surrounding regions, even though some of the specific manifestations differ. The mountains have less early archaeology than most parts of the state, but once occupation becomes established, it is possible to see such trends as the development of increasingly diversified foraging economies followed by selective intensification of the use of key species. Population growth generally follows the improvement of adaptive efficiency. Mountain archaeology reflects interaction with surrounding areas in most periods, as well as the growth of social differentiation, though perhaps less extreme than in some other areas. California's mountains have been not only important zones for exploitation but also significant elements in the larger picture of the prehistoric evolution of complex societies and relationships in the state.

Joseph L. Chartkoff

Further Readings

Alt, D.D., and D.W. Hyndman. 1975. *Roadside Geology of Northern California.* Mountain Press, Missoula.

Ayres, W.O. 1882. The Ancient Man of Calaveras. *American Naturalist* 16:845–854.

Bateman, P.C., and C. Wahrhaftig. 1966. Geology of the Sierra Nevada. *Bulletin of the California Division of Mines and Geology* 190:107–172.

Baumhoff, M.A. 1955. Excavation of Site Teh-1 (Kingsley Cave). *University of California Archaeological Survey Reports* 30:40–73.

———. 1957. *An Introduction to Yana Archaeology.* Archaeological Survey Reports no. 40. University of California Press, Berkeley.

Becker, G.F. 1891. Antiquities From Under Tuolumne Table Mountain in California. *Bulletin of the Geological Society of America* 2:189–200.

Berger, R., R. Protsch, R. Reynolds, C. Rozaire, and J.R. Sackett. 1971. New Radiocarbon Dates Based on Bone Collagen of California Paleoindians. *Contributions of the University of California Archaeological Research Facility* 12:43–49.

Chartkoff, J.L., and K.K. Chartkoff. 1984. *The Archaeology of California.* Stanford University Press, Stanford.

Elston, R., J.O. Davis, A. Leventhal, and C. Covington. 1977. The Archaeology of the Tahoe Reach of the Truckee River. Ms. on file, Tahoe-Truckee Sanitation Agency, Reno.

Fitzwater, R.J. 1962. Final Report on Two Seasons' Excavations at El Portal, Mariposa County, California. *Archaeological Survey Annual Report* 4:234–285. University of California, Los Angeles.

———. 1968a. Excavations at Crane Flat, Yosemite National Park. *Archaeological Survey Annual Report* 10:276–302. University of California, Los Angeles.

———. 1968b. Excavations at the Hodgdon Ranch Site (Tuo-236). *Archaeological Survey Annual Report* 10:303–314. University of California, Los Angeles.

Garth, T.R. 1978. Atsugewi. In *California,* edited by R.F. Heizer, pp. 236–248. Handbook of North American Indians, vol. 8, W.C. Sturtevant, general editor. Smithsonian Institution, Washington, D.C.

Heizer, R.F., and S.F. Cook. 1952. Fluorine and Other Chemical Tests of Some

North American Human and Fossil Bones. *American Journal of Physical Anthropology* 10(3):289–303.

Heizer, R.F., and A.B. Elsasser. 1953. *Some Archaeological Sites and Cultures of the Central Sierra Nevada.* Archaeological Survey Reports no. 12. University of California Press, Berkeley.

Hill, M. 1975. *Geology of the Sierra Nevada.* University of California Press, Berkeley.

Kroeber, A.L. 1925. *Handbook of the Indians of California.* Bulletin no. 78. Bureau of American Ethnology, Smithsonian Institution, Washington, D.C.

Levy, R. 1978. Eastern Miwok. In *California,* edited by R.F. Heizer, pp. 398–413. Handbook of North American Indians, vol. 8, W.C. Sturtevant, general editor. Smithsonian Institution, Washington, D.C.

McGuire, K.R., and A.P. Garfinkel. 1980. *Archaeological Investigations in the Southern Sierra Nevada: The Bear Mountain Segment of the Pacific Crest Trail.* Cultural Resources Publications, Archaeology. Bureau of Land Management, Bakersfield.

Moratto, M.J. 1968. *A Survey of the Archaeological Resources of the Buchanan Reservoir Area, Madera County, California.* Occasional Papers in Anthropology, vol. 4, no. 1. San Francisco State University, San Francisco.

———. 1970. *Buchanan Archaeological Project: Report of 1969 Excavations.* Papers, vol. 7. Treganza Anthropology Museum, California State University, Sacramento.

———. 1972. *A Study of Prehistory in the Southern Sierra Nevada Foothills, California.* Unpublished Ph.D. dissertation, Department of Anthropology, University of Oregon, Eugene.

———. (editor). 1984. *California Archaeology.* Academic Press, New York.

Moratto, M.J., and S.K. Goldberg. 1982. *New Melones Archaeological Project, California: Natural History.* Coyote Press, Salinas.

Moratto, M.J., J.D. Tordoff, and L.H. Shoup. 1988. *Culture Change in the Central Sierra Nevada; 8000 B.C.–A.D. 1950.* Final Report of the Melones Archaeological Project, vol. 9. Infotec, Fresno.

Olmstead, D.L., and O.C. Stewart. 1978. Achumawi. In *California,* edited by R.F.

Heizer, pp. 225–235. Handbook of North American Indians, vol. 8, W.C. Sturtevant, general editor. Smithsonian Institution, Washington, D.C.

Riddell, F.A. 1956. *Final Report on the Archaeology of Tommy Tucker Cave.* Archaeological Survey Reports no. 35. University of California Press, Berkeley.

———. 1978. Maidu and Konkow. In *California,* edited by R.F. Heizer, pp. 370–386. Handbook of North American Indians, vol. 8, W.C. Sturtevant, general editor. Smithsonian Institution, Washington, D.C.

Ritter, E.W. 1970. Northern Sierra Foothill Archaeology: Culture History and Culture Process. *Center for Archaeological Research at Davis Publications* 2:171–184. University of California, Davis.

Ritter, E.W., B.W. Hatoff, and L.A. Payen. 1976. Chronology of the Farmington Complex. *American Antiquity* 41:334–341.

Silver, S. 1978. Shastan Peoples. In *California,* edited by R.F. Heizer, pp. 211–224. Handbook of North American Indians, vol. 8, W.C. Sturtevant, general editor. Smithsonian Institution, Washington, D.C.

Sinclair, W.J. 1904. The Exploration of Potter Creek Cave. *University of California Publications in American Archaeology and Ethnology* 2(1):1–27.

———. 1908. Recent Investigations Bearing on the Question of the Occurrence of Neocene Man in the Auriferous Gravels of the Sierra Nevada. *University of California Publications in American Archaeology and Ethnology* 7(2):107–131.

Spier, R.F.G. 1978. Foothill Yokuts. In *California,* edited by R.F. Heizer, pp. 471–484. Handbook of North American Indians, vol. 8, W.C. Sturtevant, general editor. Smithsonian Institution, Washington, D.C.

Whitney, J.D. 1880. *The Auriferous Gravels of the Sierra Nevada in California.* Memoirs, vol. 3, no. 1. Museum of Comparative Zoology, Harvard College, Cambridge.

Wilson, N.L., and A.H. Towne. 1978. Nisenan. In *California,* edited by R.F. Heizer, pp. 387–397. Handbook of North American Indians, vol. 8, W.C. Sturtevant, general editor. Smithsonian Institution, Washington, D.C.

S

Signal Butte

Rising 45.7 m (150 feet) above the Kiowa Creek Valley floor in the Nebraska Panhandle's North Platte Valley, Signal Butte (25SF1) is an isolated remnant of the Wildcat Hills escarpment. Stratified Middle and Late Prehistoric archaeological deposits are contained within the 2.4-m (8-foot) -thick cap of loess that mantles the butte. Primary excavations were undertaken in 1931 and 1932 under the direction of William Duncan Strong (1935), then affiliated with the University of Nebraska, Lincoln, and the Smithsonian Institution, Washington, D.C. Additional work was carried out in the 1950s (Bliss 1950). Excavation depth reached ca. 2.4 m (8 feet) and revealed three distinct cultural horizons.

Signal Butte I, the oldest component, was deposited by Middle Archaic McKean-complex groups, who inhabited the butte between 2500 and 2000 B.C. (4450–3950 years B.P.). Signal Butte is the southernmost McKean-complex type site, although some components are documented in northeast Colorado. It is also one of only a handful of McKean butte-top components and the richest component attributed to the complex. Signal Butte II produced a variety of corner-notched projectiles similar to those discovered at Plains Late Archaic sites. Some forms are also commonly associated with Plains Woodland components, although Woodland ceramics are absent in the Signal Butte II collection. The component probably dates between 2000 B.C. and A.D. 500 (3950–1450 years B.P.). Signal Butte III represents occupation by Plains Village–pattern populations, the most intensive by Central Plains–tradition (A.D. 900–1400, or 1050–550 years B.P.) and Dismal River–phase (A.D. 1700–1750, or 250–200 years B.P.) people.

Along with Ash Hollow Cave, Signal Butte served to establish the fundamental stratigraphic sequence of central Great Plains Middle and Late Prehistoric cultures. In addition, Signal Butte is relatively rich in artifacts, features, and animal bone; the richness of these data has been particularly useful in reconstructing settlement patterns and resource use in the prehistoric North Platte Valley. Finally, major sites on isolated high buttes are rare phenomena on the Plains, so Signal Butte provides a chronicle of this unique form of adaptation. Reasons offered for this type of settlement revolve largely around defense and an ability to watch game from afar. Signal Butte was designated a National Historic Landmark in 1966.

John R. Bozell
John Ludwickson

Further Readings

Bliss, W.L. 1950. Early and Late Lithic Horizons in the Plains. In *Proceedings of the Sixth Plains Archaeological Conference, University of Utah Anthropological Papers* 11:108–116.

Forbis, R.G. 1985. The McKean Complex As Seen From Signal Butte. In *McKean/Middle Plains Archaic: Current Research*, edited by M. Kornfeld and L.C. Todd. Occasional Papers on Wyoming

Signal Butte site, Nebraska. (Photograph by J. R. Bozell and L. Ludwickson)

Archaeology no. 4. Office of Wyoming State Archaeologist, Laramie.

Mulloy, W. 1958. A Preliminary Historical Outline for the Northwestern Plains. *University of Wyoming Publications* 22(1):1–235.

Strong, W.D. 1935. *An Introduction to Nebraska Archeology.* Miscellaneous Collections, vol. 93, no. 10. Smithsonian Institution, Washington D.C.

Silver Mound

Silver Mound (47JA21) is a prehistoric quarry located in west-central Wisconsin near the small town of Hixton in Jackson County. The site is a bedrock outlier near the northernmost extension of Wisconsin's unglaciated "driftless area." Silver Mound contains a localized outcrop of a distinct, high-quality orthoquartzite known as Hixton silicified sandstone (HSS), often referred to as Hixton quartzite. Silver Mound was exploited by many prehistoric cultures throughout the Upper Midwest for the production of stone tools. Some locales at Silver Mound were damaged during highway and railroad construction earlier in the twentieth century. Additionally, in early historic times, Euro-Americans in fruitless search of silver ore expanded some prehistoric quarry pits with dynamite, hence the name Silver Mound. Despite these modifications, Silver Mound is still pocked with hundreds of pristine aboriginal quarry pits. Several small rock shelters that appear to have functioned as quarry/workshop and habitation sites are also present. Adjacent cultivated fields are littered with artifacts and lithic debitage that document nearly 11,500 years (ca. 9500 B.C.–A.D. 1750, or 11,450–200 years B.P.) of continuous quarrying, flintknapping, hunting, hide processing, and other activities.

Paleoindians (ca. 9500–7000 B.C., or 11,450–8950 years B.P.) appear to have exploited the Silver Mound quarries more heavily than later groups. Paleoindian flintknappers are known for selecting the highest-quality and most aesthetically pleasing raw materials available for production of stone tools, especially projectile points. Hixton silicified sandstone possesses these essential qualities. Numerous temporally diagnostic Paleoindian projectile points manufactured from HSS and exotic lithic materials have been recovered at the Silver Mound locale. Point types reminiscent of Clovis, Gainey, Folsom, Plainview, Agate Basin,

Hell Gap, and Cody indicate periodic visits to the site by people associated with these complexes. Paleoindian projectile-point types manufactured from HSS have been reported at sites throughout the Midwest and Ontario. HSS Clovis points have been found in Kentucky, Ohio, Indiana, Illinois, and Missouri sites up to ca. 900 km (559 miles) away. Later Paleoindian (ca. 8500–7000 B.C., or 10,450–6950 years B.P.) specimens manufactured from HSS have been recovered at sites in Michigan, Iowa, Minnesota, and Thunder Bay, Ontario. Similarly, Paleoindian points manufactured from exotic lithic materials such as Knife River flint (western North Dakota), obsidian (northwestern Wyoming), and Moline chert (northwestern Illinois) have been recovered at Silver Mound. How "exotics" such as these are incorporated into a site assemblage is a problem many Paleoindian archaeologists working in the Eastern Woodlands are attempting to resolve.

Production of points for retooling was probably an important activity at Silver Mound. Many of the Paleoindian specimens recovered at the site have a short, blunt, and sometimes asymmetrical configuration, a morphology characteristic of projectile points that have been heavily resharpened. No longer functional, they were discarded at Silver Mound when new specimens were subsequently manufactured. Exhausted HSS specimens at Silver Mound suggest that Paleoindian groups periodically returned to the site. Points manufactured from exotic materials may indicate interaction with other groups or utilization of quarries beyond the "driftless area."

Little is known about Wisconsin's Paleoindian inhabitants. Continued investigation at Silver Mound and other site types throughout the state will undoubtedly provide important data about these people. Such data may aid in understanding temporal, spatial, and economic relationships with other Paleoindian groups in the Eastern Woodlands and the Plains.

Matthew Glenn Hill

Further Readings

Behm, J.A. 1984. Comments on Brown's Research at Silver Mound. *Wisconsin Archeologist* 65(2):169–173.

Ellis, C.J., and J.C. Lothrop (editors). 1989. *Eastern Paleo-Indian Lithic Resource Use.* Westview Press, Boulder.

Gramly, R.M. 1980. Raw Materials Source Areas and "Curated" Tool Assemblages.

American Antiquity 45:823–833.

Hill, M.G. 1994. Paleoindian Projecticle Points From the Vicinity of Silver Mound (47JA21), Jackson County, Wisconsin. *Midcontinental Journal of Archaeology* 19(2):223–259.

Tankersley, K.B., and B.L. Isaac (editors). 1990. *Paleo-Indian Economies of Eastern North America*. JAI Press, Greenwich.

Sinagua Tradition

"Sinagua" is the term given by Harold S. Colton in 1939 to the prehistoric tradition of the Flagstaff and Verde Valley regions. Spanish for "without water," it was the term applied to the San Francisco Peaks by early Spanish explorers. Two geographic divisions have been recognized: the Northern Sinagua, in the region around Flagstaff, Arizona, and the Southern Sinagua, in the Verde Valley in central Arizona. More specifically, the territory of the Northern Sinagua is bounded on the north by the Little Colorado River, on the south by the ponderosa-pine forest along the Mogollon Rim, on the west by the San Francisco Peaks, and on the east by East Clear Creek. The territory of the Southern Sinagua comprises the Verde Valley, which is bounded on the north by Chino Valley, on the south by the confluence of the East Verde River with the Verde River, on the west by the Black Hills, and on the east by the Mogollon Rim.

The Sinagua tradition is as "real" an archaeological entity as any other of our cultural constructs. Characteristics of the tradition include paddle-and-anvil-produced plain ware and smudged red ware ceramics, the lack of formalized decorated ceramics, extended inhumation burials, rectangular kivas with benches, larger structures than those of neighboring groups (average room or pithouse size is 4 x 5 m, or 13 x 16.4 feet), unusually large community rooms in sites believed to be community centers, lambdoidal cranial deformation, and highly active exchange relationships with neighboring groups. Although both the Flagstaff and the Verde Valley areas provide evidence of use in the Archaic period, the Sinagua tradition does not appear to have developed from this Archaic base. Rather, it appears on the scene ca. A.D. 650 (1300 years B.P.) as a fully formed cultural expression that probably originated in the Mogollon tradition of east-central Arizona.

Separate phase systems have been developed for the Flagstaff and the Verde Valley areas. Although the dating of these phases is a topic of investigation, the A.D. dates listed here are generally used.

SINAGUA PHASE SYSTEMS

Northern Sinagua		Southern Sinagua	
Cinder Park	650–700	Hackberry	650–800
Sunset	700–900	Cloverleaf	800–900
Rio de Flag	900–1066	Camp Verde	900–1150
Angell-Winona	1066–1100		
Padre	1100–1150		
Elden	1150–1250	Honanki	1150–1300
Turkey Hill	1250–1300		
Clear Creek	1300–1400	Tyzigoot	1300–1400

The pattern of cultural development within the tradition is similar to that found in many other parts of the Southwest. Early populations were agricultural and lived in extended-family pithouse communities. Some sites were larger than others and are thought to have been community centers, for they contain a very large structure called a "community room." Through time, populations increased and there was a trend toward aggregation, especially after A.D. 1150 (800 years B.P.), that is typified by sites such as Honanki, Palatki, Elden Pueblo, and Wupatki. Central places developed by A.D. 1100 (850 years B.P.), perhaps in response to increased trade relationships and increased social complexity. A few sites can be identified as major centers on the basis of their highly patterned layout in elevated situations, their association with likely trade routes, and the presence of a ballcourt, walled courtyards, and a community room. One such site, Ridge Ruin, is particularly important in that the Burial of the Magician found there proves the existence of Hopilike societies in the Flagstaff area by A.D. 1200 (750 years B.P.). Population increase and aggregation culminated after A.D. 1300 (650 years B.P.) in the great pueblos of Anderson Mesa, such as Kinnikinick, the Pollock site, Nuvakwewtaga in Chavez Pass, and the famous sites of the Verde Valley, such as Tuzigoot, Montezuma Castle, Sacred Mountain, and the Clear Creek ruins.

A major focus of early research was the nature of the Sinagua tradition. Some considered it an environmental variant of the Anazazi. Others contended that its presence was the result of multicultural colonial migrations to the Flagstaff area, migrations intent on taking advantage of the improved agricultural conditions that resulted from the cinder fall from Sunset Crater in A.D. 1064 and 1066. Other problems that occupied early researchers were dating, boundaries, the influences of Sunset Crater, and the "frontier phenomenon." The geographic location of the Sinagua is directly adjacent to several other prehistoric groups, many of whom were thought to have occupied the same sites and even the same structures, as Sinagua. To some degree, these arguments continue today.

The traditional, or "Black Sand," model of Sinagua prehistory as formulated by Colton views the Sinagua as a peripheral agricultural group that was outside the mainstream of prehistoric cultural developments until Sunset Crater erupted in A.D. 1064 and 1066. The cinder fall from these eruptions served to retard moisture evaporation from the soil, thus creating more than 1,287 km² (800 square miles) of new farmland that had not previously been available due to a lack of moisture. News of this new farmland spread throughout the Southwest, causing a prehistoric land rush by at least eight different cultures and a considerable population increase in the area. Interaction between the immigrants and the local Sinagua formed a new cultural expression that lasted until the cinder cover blew away, ca. A.D. 1125, and people began to move to the Verde Valley, Anderson Mesa, and Phoenix areas, where they introduced new cultural traits. Continued environmental degradation also led to the abandonment of these areas, with the remnants of the Sinagua eventually joining proto-Hopi groups in the Little Colorado River Valley and Hopi Mesa country.

New interpretations suggest that the influence of Sunset Crater and migrations on cultural developments in this region has been considerably overrated. Environmental change, increasing participation in pan-Southwestern exchange systems, population aggregation, and changing agricultural technologies and intensification are now viewed as major factors in the region's cultural development. Paleomagnetic dating of lava flows from Sunset Crater suggests that there were episodic eruptions for more than two centuries. Excavations at a number of sites, particularly at Elden Pueblo, have found evidence of this long-term eruptive sequence, including the initial eruptions and other major ones in ca. A.D. 1180 and 1250. Climate change, some population shifts, and changing agricultural strategies are now also seen as alternatives to the hypothesis of population increases. In-creased trade and social responses to this process are suggested as major factors in cultural development and increasing sophistication. Repetitive distance spacing between pueblos in the Verde Valley suggests interconnected communities specializing in procurement of wild plants and animals for food in the uplands and intensive agricultural production in the riparian lowlands. Other spacing factors suggest connectivity between the late pueblos of the Verde Valley and those in the Flagstaff, Tonto Basin, and White Mountain areas. Deteriorating environmental conditions caused by the Great Drought of A.D. 1276–1299 are no longer seen as major factors in population shifts in the Verde Valley, since a number of late sites have been located in uplands away from riverine environments.

Modern investigations in the Sinagua area continue to deal with some of the older research problems, but more emphasis is placed on questions concerning cultural complexity, social organization, settlement patterns, community boundaries, exchange relationships, and land-use patterns. Rather than view Sinagua as a peripheral result of the influence of more "dominant" cultures, modern archaeologists tend to examine the tradition as an independent entity that was responding to a changing environment and shifting social interactions with other prehistoric groups.

Peter J. Pilles, Jr.

Further Readings

Colton, H.S. 1939. *Prehistoric Culture Units and Their Relationships in Northern Arizona.* Bulletin no. 17. Museum of Northern Arizona, Flagstaff.

———. 1946. *The Sinagua: A Summary of the Archaeology of the Region of Flagstaff, Arizona.* Bulletin no. 22. Museum of Northern Arizona, Flagstaff.

———. 1960. *Black Sand: Prehistory in Northern Arizona.* University of New Mexico Press, Albuquerque.

Downum, C.E. 1988. *"One Grand History": A Critical Review of Flagstaff Archaeology, 1851 to 1988.* Unpublished Ph.D. dissertation, Department of Anthropology, University of Arizona, Tucson.

———. 1992. The Sinagua: Prehistoric People of the San Francisco Mountains. *Plateau* 63(1).

Kamp, K.A., and J.C. Whittaker. 1990. Lizard Man Village: A Small Site Perspective on

Northern Sinagua Social Organization. *Kiva* 55(2):99–125.

Pilles, P.J., Jr. 1987. The Sinagua: Ancient People of the Flagstaff Region. In *Wupatki and Walnut Canyon: New Perspectives on History, Prehistory, Rock Art,* edited by D.G. Noble, pp. 1–12. School of American Research Press, Santa Fe.

Sullivan, A.P. 1986. The Interpretation of Prehistoric Political Complexity in the Central and Northern Southwest: Toward a Mending of the Models. *Journal of Field Archaeology* 13:233–238.

Wilson, J.P. 1969. *The Sinagua and Their Neighbors.* Unpublished Ph.D. dissertation, Department of Anthropology, Harvard University, Cambridge.

Site

A site is a spatial clustering of artifacts, features, structures, or nonartifactual remains, such as animal and plant remains, that were manufactured, modified, or used by humans.

Guy Gibbon

Smith, Harlan Ingersoll (1872–1940)

Harlan I. Smith excavated extensively throughout portions of eastern and northern North America in the 1890s and the early twentieth century. While he was a University of Michigan student, he began fieldwork in 1891 when he was employed by F.W. Putnam of the Peabody Museum of American Archaeology and Ethnology at Harvard University to assist Charles Metz in the exploration of the Madisonville village site in Ohio. While curator of the anthropological collections of the University of Michigan from 1891 to 1893, he visited other sites in Ohio in 1892 and explored mounds near Madison, Wisconsin, in 1893. In 1894, as an explorer for the Archaeological Institute of America, he investigated possible garden beds near Kalamazoo, Michigan. In 1895, Smith joined the staff of the American Museum of Natural History in New York, where he was placed in charge of excavations at the Fox farm site in Kentucky that same year. He was in charge of nearly all archaeological explorations on the American Museum's Jesup North Pacific Expedition (1897–1903) directed by Franz Boas, the first major archaeological explorations in the Pacific Northwest. He investigated areas of British Columbia between 1897 and 1899, worked in 1903 in the Yakima Valley in Washington State, and explored areas of Wyoming, Alaska, and British Columbia from 1907 to 1909. Smith was assistant curator at the American Museum from 1900 to 1910 and associate curator in 1911. In 1911, he was appointed archaeologist in the newly created Division of Anthropology of the Geological Survey of Canada, and he eventually became chief archaeologist of the National Museum of Canada, a position he retained until his retirement in 1937. While there, he conducted extensive archaeological and ethnographic investigations across Canada, including some of the earliest professional archaeology in Nova Scotia. He was also a founder of the American Anthropological Association.

Although he was an indifferent fieldworker, Smith was a prolific writer, and his publications remained the only reported excavations in much of British Columbia, Nova Scotia, and Washington for many years. He is mainly remembered in Canada for amassing a vast amount of scattered information in the archaeological files of the Division of Anthropology and for his organization of archaeology in that country. His report on his excavations at the Fox farm site in *The Prehistoric Ethnology of a Kentucky Site* (Smith 1910b) is an example of the early-twentieth-century functionalist movement in the United States. In that report, he sought to reconstruct the lifeways of the site's inhabitants by viewing individual artifacts from a series of functional perspectives, including "securing food," "tools used by women," and "resources in animal and plant materials."

Guy Gibbon

Further Readings

Smith, H.I. 1910a. *Archaeology of the Yakima Valley.* Anthropological Papers, vol. 6. no. 1. American Museum of Natural History, New York.

———. 1910b. *The Prehistoric Ethnology of a Kentucky Site.* Anthropological Papers, vol. 6, pt. 2. American Museum of Natural History, New York.

———. 1929. *The Archaeology of Merigomish Harbour, Nova Scotia.* Bulletin no. 47. Anthropology Series no. 9, pp. 6–104. National Museum of Canada, Department of Mines, Ottawa.

Smith, H.I., and W.J. Wintemberg. 1929. *Some Shell-Heaps in Nova Scotia.* Bulletin no. 47. National Museum of Canada, Ottawa.

Wintemberg, W.J. 1940. Harlan Ingersoll Smith. *American Antiquity* 1:63–64.

Smoky Hill Phase

One of five recognized taxa of the Late Prehistoric Central Plains tradition, the Smoky Hill phase occurs in the Lower Kansas River and Republican River basins in Kansas in an area characterized by abundant gray Permian chert, a key attraction for early settlement. Sites also occur throughout the Upper Big and Little Blue River basins and on Salt Creek in the Platte River Basin and Table Rock on the Big Nemaha River in Nebraska. Smoky Hill emerged ca. A.D. 1000 (950 years B.P.), perhaps from early Upper Republican–phase expressions. Expansion northeast from north-central Kansas resulted in a "new" manifestation, the Nebraska phase, near the mouth of the Platte River in Nebraska ca. A.D. 1000 (950 years B.P.); that is, at virtually the same time as the emergence of Smoky Hill in its "home" territory. The Smoky Hill phase terminated ca. A.D. 1350–1400 (600–550 years B.P.).

Smoky Hill ceramics are "conservative," with a high frequency of grog-tempered, globular jars with undecorated collared rims and unthickened rims both plain and bearing lip decoration. Interaction with Mississippian immigrants brought profound changes in the Smoky Hill phase, adding crushed-shell-tempered pottery and low rolled-rim oval-mouthed jars; handles and other appendages also increased. Sites in the far southwest corner of Nebraska have Smoky Hill–like assemblages, sites in the Loup River Basin in central Nebraska have Smoky Hill similarities, and the Uncas site is an outlying, heavily "Mississippianized" Smoky Hill component in northern Oklahoma. The significance of Smoky Hill expansion is unclear, as is its relationship with expressions such as the Pomona aspect.

Smoky Hill houses are generally, large (83.6–167.2 m^2, or 900–1,800 square feet), square, surface-built wattle-and-daub structures with four central roof supports, a central fire basin, and an extended entry. Some are smaller (9.3–74.3 m^2, or 100–800 square feet), more rounded, and built in shallow basins. Houses contain several cylindrical or bell-shaped storage-refuse pits. Smoky Hill sites include solitary houses, hamlets, and small villages. Lithics are dominated by gray, often banded, Permian "Florence" chert, which was crucial to Smoky Hill emergence and subsequent history. Typical Central Plains–tradition stone tools of all categories are found. Bone- and antler-tool assemblages are not well known due to poor preservation, but in addition to bison-scapula tools, split deer/pronghorn proximal metapodial awls, and other items, there are also a few bison-tibia digging-stick tips suggesting southern Plains influences.

John Ludwickson
John R. Bozell

Further Readings

Brown, M. 1972. *Cultural Behavior As Reflected in the Vertebrate Faunal Assemblages of Three Smoky Hill Sites*. Unpublished Master's thesis. Department of Anthropology, University of Kansas, Lawrence.

Hill, A.T., and P.L. Cooper. 1937. The Schrader, Champe, and Fremont 1 Sites. *Nebraska History Magazine* 14(4):223–252.

Johnson, A.E. 1973. Archaeological Investigations at the Budenbender Site, Tuttle Creek Reservoir, North-Central Kansas, 1957. *Plains Anthropologist* 18(62/1–2):271–299.

Steinacher, T.L. 1976. *The Smoky Hill Phase and its Role in the Central Plains Tradition*. Unpublished Master's thesis. Department of Anthropology, University of Nebraska, Lincoln.

Vehik, S.C., and P. Flynn. 1982. Archaeological Excavations at the Early Plains Village Uncas Site (erKA172). *Bulletin of the Oklahoma Anthropological Society* 31:3–70.

Snaketown

Snaketown, AZ U:13:1 (ASM), is a large Hohokam site located along the Gila River in Arizona between Phoenix and Tucson. One of the largest Hohokam sites, Snaketown was occupied from ca. A.D. 300 to 1100 (1650–850 years B.P.). At its greatest extent, after A.D. 900 (1050 years B.P.), Snaketown encompassed an estimated 400 houses, 60 mounds, two ballcourts, canals, wells, and a cremation area.

Archaeologists worked at Snaketown in three separate expeditions. The first, which was conducted from 1934 to 1935 and led by Harold S. Gladwin of the private Gila Pueblo Foundation, uncovered 40 prehistoric houses and one-half of a ballcourt and tested four trash mounds (Gladwin et al. 1937). The material uncovered during this initial foray was critical in establishing a chronology for the Hohokam. Unlike other portions of the southwestern United States, the Hohokam area lacks trees suitable for tree-ring dating. Dating Hohokam remains depends largely on less precise chronometric techniques (particularly radiocarbon dating and archaeomagnetic dating), stratigraphy, and ceramic seriation. These dating methods are open to varied interpretations, and the chronology established at Snaketown in the 1930s led to considerable debate among Southwestern archaeologists.

The argument eventually prompted Emil W. Haury, who was instrumental in working out the initial chronology, to return to Snaketown in 1964–1965. Working through the University of Arizona, Tucson, Haury concentrated on addressing three questions in this second expedition (Haury 1976). First, he reevaluated the chronology by excavating test trenches through deeply stratified trash mounds and by utilizing innovative chronometric techniques. Second, he attempted to answer the question of whether the sedentary, farming Hohokam developed out of an indigenous Archaic population or migrated from Mesoamerica and displaced the local Archaic groups. Finally, he explored the issue of continuing Mesoamerican influence on Hohokam developments. The second Snaketown excavations unearthed 166 structures and 29 mounds, in addition to large portions of outdoor-activity areas. Haury concluded that the initial Snaketown chronology was largely correct. He argued that the presence of canals and a well-developed ceramic technology in the earliest levels at Snaketown indicated that the Hohokam must have migrated to the area as a sedentary, farming culture and not developed in the area from local Archaic populations. He also traced the continuing influence from Mesoamerica on Hohokam culture, but he argued that this was largely in the form of ideas rather than migrations or political connections.

A third expedition was sponsored by the National Park Service for a proposed National Monument at Snaketown. David Wilcox, with the Arizona State Museum, Tucson, directed a survey of the northern portion of Snaketown in 1980–1981 before the survey was halted because of objections from Native American landowners. Although unable to complete the field project, Wilcox and his collaborators reanalyzed the structure of Snaketown based on data from the earlier excavations (Wilcox et al. 1981). This study provides one of the most detailed examinations of a large pre-Classic Hohokam site. The conclusions altered existing views of Hohokam household and site layout and formed an important foundation for subsequent work in the area.

Patricia L. Crown

Further Readings

Galdwin, H.S., E.W. Haury, E.B. Sayles, and N. Gladwin. 1937. *Excavations at Snaketown, Material Culture.* Medallion Paper no. 25. Gila Pueblo, Globe.

Haury, E. 1976. *The Hohokam: Desert Farmers and Craftsmen.* University of Arizona Press, Tucson.

Noble, D.G. 1991. *The Hohokam: Ancient People of the Desert.* School of American Research Press, Santa Fe.

Wilcox, D.R., T.R. McGuire, and C. Sternberg. 1981. *Snaketown Revisted.* Archaeological Series no. 155. Arizona State Museum, University of Arizona, Tucson.

See also BALLCOURT; HOHOKAM CULTURE AREA; PLATFORM MOUNDS (SOUTHWEST)

Sonota Burial Complex

The Sonota Burial complex is a Plains Middle Woodland burial pattern defined by Robert W. Neuman (1975) from burial mounds along the Missouri River in northern South Dakota and southern North Dakota and along the Sheyenne River in southeastern North Dakota. Mounds combine Hopewell-like and Plains traits (Johnson 1977) and date between A.D. 1 and 450 (1950–1500 years B.P.). The circular mounds have a central rectangular subfloor tomb that was roofed over and then covered with the earthen mound. Roofing timbers may be burned. Burials are usually secondary, with multiple individuals in a group in the subfloor tomb and sometimes in the mound fill; large sections of bison are sometimes present in the mound fill. Human bones and artifacts may have hematite staining. There is evidence that the bodies were sometimes dismembered. Burial goods include imitation and real bear-canine pendants; modified human facial and jaw bones; bone beads; pieces of antler and antler pins; bone awls; shells of *Dentalium*, *Olivella*, and conch; pottery; and chipped-stone tools, including Besant projectile points. The pottery is typically cord roughened, but a reconstructed vessel from the Arpan mound was smoothed. Ceramic decoration includes a row of punctates below the lip. Stone tools are frequently made from Knife River flint.

Since the late 1970s, some archaeologists have expanded the complex to include occupation sites with Besant points even when the burial-complex traits and specialized artifacts are not present. This approach appears to gloss over critical cultural differences and to homogenize the Plains Middle Woodland period.

Ann M. Johnson

Further Readings

Johnson, A.M. 1977. Review of *The Sonota Complex and Associated Sites on the Northern Great Plains,* by R.W. Neuman, Published in Nebraska State Historical Society, Publications in Anthropology 6. *American Antiquity* 42:139–140.

Neuman, R.W. 1975. *The Sonota Complex and Associated Sites on the Northern Great Plains.* Publications in Anthropology no. 6. Nebraska State Historical Society, Lincoln.

South Appalachian Tradition

The term "South Appalachian tradition" is used to refer to evidence for cultural continuity of appreciable antiquity in the eastern part of the lower Southeast, in an area centered on Georgia and South Carolina. Initially based on ceramic technology, specifically the occurrence of carved-paddle stamping on pottery, continuity is also indicated in the local projectile-point sequence, which is sometimes also called the Piedmont tradition (Oliver 1985). Traditions are defined as, among other things, "persistent configurations in simple technologies" (Willey and Phillips 1958:37). Continuity in projectile point and ceramic manufacturing behavior characterizes the South Appalachian tradition to the point that many archaeologists view it as defining a loosely knit culture area with roots well back into the Archaic, and perhaps to the Paleoindian period.

The concept was originally proposed by William Henry Holmes in a 1903 paper in the *Twentieth Annual Report of the Bureau of American Ethnology* entitled "Aboriginal Pottery of the Eastern United States," his monumental synthesis of ceramic artifacts recovered from throughout the Eastern Woodlands by the excavations of the bureau's Mound Division. Holmes noted that the ceramics from the general Georgia–South Carolina area, or what he called the "South Appalachian" area, were characterized by a distinctive, stamped exterior finish, which suggested a common background:

> . . . a culture of somewhat greater marked characteristics comprises the states of Georgia, South Carolina, and contiguous portions of Alabama, Florida, North Carolina, and Tennessee. . . . [T]he ceramic phenomena of this province include one great group of products to which has been given the name South Appalachian stamped ware. . . . [T]his stamped pottery is obtained from mounds, graves of several classes, village sites, and shell heaps. . . . [T]he remarkable style of decoration, more than other features, characterizes this pottery. Elaborately figured stamps were rarely used elsewhere (Holmes 1903:130–133).

The existence of a South Appalachian cultural province characterized by a distinctive ceramic tradition and covering the area described by Holmes is now universally accepted. A South Appalachian geographic variant of Mississippian has been proposed (Griffin 1967:185) and has been subject to extensive analysis and synthesis (e.g., Ferguson 1971; Hally 1994).

Widespread use of carved wooden paddles to finish pottery first occurred in the Early Woodland period, shortly after 1000 B.C. (2950 years B.P.), with the appearance of dentate-, check-, and simple-stamped ceramics variously classified in the Refuge, Deptford, and Cartersville series. Some continuity is indicated with earlier, Late Archaic Stallings and Thom's Creek ceramics, which were occasionally simple stamped; check and dentate stamping (some of the latter are clearly applied with a paddle) may also be an attempt to imitate earlier drag-and-jab and separate punctated decorations. Complicated stamping, the application of elaborate curvilinear and rectilinear designs, appears ca. 100 B.C. (2050 years B.P.) or shortly thereafter with the Santa Rosa–Swift Creek series and continues unabated through the historic period; major later series include Napier, Etowah, Savannah/Wilbanks, Lamar, and Qualla. Some of the most elaborate design motifs, including representations of animals and cosmological themes, occur early on Swift Creek ceramics.

Subsequent designs are typically less complex geometric arrangements, variations on circles, ovals, triangles, and spirals. Throughout the Woodland and Mississippian periods, similar motifs tend to occur almost contemporaneously across the South Appalachian area, indicating an appreciable degree of interaction among the local societies.

Clear morphological continuity is also indicated in projectile points in this area, from side-notched Late Paleoindian Hardaway and Taylor forms, through corner-notched Early Archaic Palmer and Kirk types, to a series of stemmed types, including Kirk, Stanly, Savannah River, Small Savannah River, Gypsy, and Swannanoa (Oliver 1985). The appearance of large triangular points in the Early Woodland marks the end of this stemmed manufacturing tradition. While gradually reduced in size, triangular forms continue through the historic period over much of the area and are considered a local tradition. The only other apparent discontinuity in projectile-point manufacture occurs during the Middle Archaic, when the contracting- and straight-stemmed Morrow Mountain and Guilford types appear, types that are thought by some to represent intrusive traditions. While other ceramic and projectile-point types and technologies are also present in the area, particularly at the geographic margins, and with greater or lesser incidence over time, the persistence of the South Appalachian culture area is recognizable throughout much of prehistory.

David G. Anderson

Further Readings

Ferguson, L.G. 1971. *South Appalachian Mississippian.* Ph.D. dissertation, Department of Anthropology, University of North Carolina, Chapel Hill. University Microfilms, Ann Arbor.

Griffin, J.B. 1967. Eastern North American Archaeology: A Summary. *Science* 156:175–191.

Hally, D.J. 1994. An Overview of Lamar Culture. In *Ocmulgee Archaeology 1936–1986,* edited by D.J. Hally, pp. 144–174. University of Georgia Press, Athens.

Holmes, W.H. 1903. Aboriginal Pottery of the Eastern United States. *Annual Report of the Bureau of American Ethnology* 20:1–237.

Oliver, B.L. 1985. Tradition and Typology: Basic Elements of the Carolina Projectile Point Sequence. In *Structure and Process in Southeastern Archaeology,* edited by R.S. Dickens and H.T. Ward, pp. 195–211. University of Alabama Press, Tuscaloosa.

Willey, G.R., and P. Phillips. 1958. *Method and Theory in American Archaeology.* University of Chicago Press, Chicago.

South Platte Phase

The South Platte phase of the Colorado Plains Woodland regional variant in the western Plains subarea of the Plains Woodland pattern was proposed by W.B. Butler (1986) to resolve taxonomic problems caused by conflicts between definitions for the Parker and Graneros foci of A.M. Withers (1954), the early Ceramic period of J.J. Wood (1967), and the Hog Back phase of C.E. Nelson (1971), none of which was found to be a valid construct.

Although some superficial resemblances exist, the Colorado Plains Woodland is not part of the "classic" Woodland of the east. Pottery and the bow and arrow are present, but horticulture does not appear to have been an important element in the economy in northeastern Colorado. Elaborate burial practices are absent, and only a few accompaniments occur in a grave. Small corner-notched arrow and dart points, small triangular side-notched and tri-notched arrow points, cord-marked ceramics with straight to slightly inverted rims and a conoidal base, and expanding-based drills are recognized as definitive cultural markers for Colorado Plains Woodland occupations. Settlement is associated with permanent water, with a preference for locations with a south-facing exposure or on high points of land. Data on architecture are almost nonexistent. The best that can be said is that shelter may have been constructed on a pragmatic basis. The Colorado Plains Woodland peoples represented by the South Platte phase were hunters and gatherers well adapted to the plains of northeastern Colorado, southeastern Wyoming, western Nebraska, and western Kansas during the later third of the Sub-Boreal, the Scandic, and the Neo-Atlantic climatic episodes (ca. A.D. 100–1150, or 1850–800 years B.P.).

William B. Butler

Further Readings

Butler, W.B. 1986. *Taxonomy in Northeastern Colorado Prehistory.* Unpublished Ph.D. dissertation, Department of Anthropology, University of Missouri, Columbia.

———. 1988. The Woodland Period in Northeastern Colorado. *Plains Anthropologist* 33(122):449–466.

Butler, W.B., S.A. Chomko, and J.M. Hoffman. 1986. The Red Creek Burial, El Paso County, Colorado. *Southwestern Lore* 52(2):6–27.

Nelson, C.E. 1971. The George W. Lindsay Ranch Site, 5JF11. *Southwestern Lore* 37(1):1–14.

Withers, A.M. 1954. Reports of Archaeological Fieldwork in Colorado, Wyoming, New Mexico, Arizona and Utah in 1952 and 1953: University of Denver Archaeological Field Work. *Southwestern Lore* 19(4):1–3.

Wood, J.J. 1967. Archaeological Investigations in Northeastern Colorado. Unpublished Ph.D. dissertation, Department of Anthropology, University of Colorado, Boulder.

See also ARKANSAS PHASE

Southeast Alaskan Sequence

Southeast Alaska encompasses the Alexander Archipelago and the adjacent mainland of Alaska's Panhandle, which extends from Yakutat Bay in the north to the Canadian border in the east and south. The region's culture history is not well defined because few sites have produced sizable artifact assemblages, a result of limited sampling and relatively low artifact densities. Most of the region's ca. 1,000 recorded sites are known from Tlingit and Haida ethnohistory and have yet to be tested for prehistoric components. The region's cool, rainy climate is not conducive to preservation of the organic artifacts for which the ethnographic groups are famous.

Early Period. Most coastal areas were deglaciated by at least 9050–8050 B.C. (11,000–10,000 years B.P.). The Early, or Paleomarine, period, which began in 7550 B.C. (9500 years B.P.), has been defined from materials at the Ground Hog Bay 2 and Hidden Falls sites. Ground Hog Bay 2 is located on an elevated marine terrace on the mainland; its lower components (7250–2050 B.C., or 9200–4000 years B.P.) contain microblade cores, microblades, macroblade and flake cores, hammerstones, a few broken bifaces, choppers, scrapers, and utilized flakes. Sourced obsidian originated on Mount Edziza in the Upper Stikine region. The 7550–6650 B.C. (9500–8600 years B.P.) component at Hidden Falls, which is on Baranof Island, lies between glacial deposits and includes

Stone trap complex in Warm Chuck Inlet, Heceta Island. (June 1995 photograph by M. Moss)

Wood stake weir, Chaik Bay, Admiralty Island. (July 1991 photograph by M. Moss)

a microblade industry, split cobble and pebble tools, scrapers, gravers, burinized flakes, and a biface tip. Obsidian artifacts were traced to Mount Edziza and Suemez Island. The oldest direct evidence for a marine-oriented economy comes from a 6250 B.C. (8200 years B.P.) shell midden at Chuck Lake on Heceta Island, where bottomfish and shellfish dominate the faunal assemblage. The site is ca. 15 m (49 feet) above sea level and 800 m (2,625 feet) from saltwater; what is now Chuck Lake probably was the upper end of an estuary. A microblade industry was found, along with a unilaterally barbed, bone-point fragment. The location of Early period sites shows local variation in sea-level histories across the region. Microblade industries are diagnostic, representing a tradition that appears to have lasted for 5,000 years. The presence of Mount Edziza and Suemez Island obsidian in Early sites indicates long-distance travel or trade.

Middle Period. Few sites dating to 5050–3550 B.C. (7000–5500 years B.P.) are known, but ground stone appears after this gap, and bone tools increase in frequency. This parallels transitions between Ocean Bay I and Ocean Bay II on Kodiak Island and between the Moresby and Graham traditions on the Queen Charlottes. Whether there was a gradual transformation or a replacement of technological traditions is

unknown, but by 3050 B.C. (5000 years B.P.) the Middle period was underway. It lasted until A.D. 450 (1500 years B.P.). Some scholars have divided the post-3550 B.C. (5500 years B.P.) period into early, middle, and late developmental stages, but the southeast Alaskan sequence is too poorly known to warrant division between an early and middle stage at this time. The 2650–1250 B.C. (4600–3200 years B.P.) component from Hidden Falls contains ground-slate points, polished adzes, chipped stone, a few unilaterally barbed bone points, labrets, stone beads, an incised flake, and a segmented stone. In the 350 B.C.–A.D. 650 (2300–1300 years B.P.) component, bone artifacts increase in frequency with barbed and unbarbed points, harpoon valves, and bone slats resembling plate armor. Also present are shell and teeth ornaments, ground and pecked mauls, beaver-incisor chisels, and bird-bone tubes. A unilaterally barbed-bone harpoon head with offset linehole (2200–1850 B.C., or 4150–3800 years B.P.) was found at Rosie's Rockshelter on Heceta Island. The 2150 B.C.–A.D. 550 (4100–1400 years B.P.) bone-artifact assemblage from Coffman Cove on Prince of Wales Island includes unilaterally and bilaterally barbed harpoon points, a bipoint, a weapon socket, and a flaker.

During the Middle period, artifact types appear that resemble ethnographic types, hence the "developmental stage" designation. Sites are more numerous, larger, and tend to be located along modern beaches, which indicates landscape stabilization. Seasonal variation in site use has been detected. For instance, faunal remains from the 350 B.C.–A.D. 650 (2300–1300 years B.P.) component at Hidden Falls suggest a late winter–early spring occupation. A 3,000-year-old fish weir at Favorite Bay, Admiralty Island, indicates mass salmon harvest, a definite precursor to ethnographic lifeways.

Late Period. After A.D. 450 (1500 years B.P.), cultural patterns more closely resemble those of ethnographic groups. The Late period is best known from Frederica de Laguna's excavations at Old Town, Yakutat, which was associated with the Eyak, and at Daxatkanada, Admiralty Island, which was associated with the Tlingit. Assemblages from these and other sites indicate cultural continuity with the Middle period, with the addition of splitting adzes, stone lamps or mortars, incised stones, and small amounts of iron, copper, and amber. Some of these traits are shared with Pacific Eskimo groups and probably reflect increased interaction across the north Pacific coupled with Protohistoric influences. After A.D. 950 (1000 years B.P.), there is a marked increase in the number of defensive sites, suggesting increased contact or territorial circumscription.

Madonna Moss

Further Readings

Ackerman, R.E., T.D. Hamilton, and R. Stuckenrath. 1979. Early Culture Complexes on the Northern Northwest Coast. *Canadian Journal of Archaeology* 3:195–209.

Ackerman, R.E., K.C. Reid, J.D. Gallison, and M.E. Roe. 1985. *Archaeology of Heceta Island: A Survey of 16 Timber Units in the Tongass National Forest, Southeastern Alaska.* Project Report no. 3. Center for Northwest Anthropology, Washington State University, Pullman.

Arndt, K., R.H. Sackett, and J.A. Katz. 1987. *A Cultural Resources Overview of the Tongass National Forest, Alaska: 1. Overview.* GDM, Fairbanks. Submitted to the U.S. Forest Service, Tongass National Forest, Juneau. Contract no. 53–0109–6–00203.

Davis, S.D. 1990. Prehistory of Southeastern Alaska. In *Northwest Coast*, edited by W. Suttles, pp. 192–202. Handbook of North American Indians, vol. 7, W.C. Sturtevant, general editor. Smithsonian Institution, Washington, D.C.

———. (editor). 1989. *The Hidden Falls Site, Baranof Island, Alaska.* Aurora Monograph Series no. 5. Alaska Anthropological Association.

Laguna, F. de. 1960. *The Story of a Tlingit Community: A Problem in the Relationship Between Archeological, Ethnological and Historical Methods.* Bulletin no. 172. Bureau of American Ethnology, Smithsonian Institution, Washington, D.C.

Laguna, F. de., F.A. Riddell, D.F. McGeein, K.S. Lane, and J.A. Freed. 1964. *Archeology of the Yakutat Bay Area, Alaska.* Bulletin no. 192. Bureau of American Ethnology, Smithsonian Institution, Washington, D.C.

Moss, M.L., and J.M. Erlandson. 1992. Forts, Refuge Rocks, and Defensive Sites: The Antiquity of Warfare Along the North Pacific Coast of North America. *Arctic Anthropology* 29(2):73–90.

Moss, M.L., J.M. Erlandson, and R. Stuckenrath. 1989. The Antiquity of Tlingit Settlement on Admiralty Island, Southeast Alaska. *American Antiquity* 54:534–543.

———. 1990. Wood Stake Weirs and Salmon Fishing on the Northwest Coast: Evidence From Southeast Alaska. *Canadian Journal of Archaeology* 14:143–158.

Southeastern Ceremonial Complex

Southeastern Ceremonial complex (SECC) is the name for a set of distinctive ritual paraphernalia and associated symbols and iconographic themes that are widely, although sparsely, present at Mississippian-period sites, together with the belief systems that gave rise to these material expressions. Major iconic themes consist of the warrior (either decapitated or victorious), the birdman (centered on an anthropomorphized hawk), the chunkey player, the piasa (a bird-snake-cat combination), and more generalized serpent imagery. Images of monsters that combine different animals and humans with animals are ever present. Distinctive motifs are the bellows-shaped apron, the bi-lobed arrow, the forked-eye surround, the looped square, the ogee, the cross-in-circle, and many others. Major artifacts include columella pendants, copper-plate headdresses, engraved-shell

S

cups, engraved shell gorgets, long-nosed god maskettes, maces, and monolithic axes.

Although grave furnishings have been the principal source of archaeological material, these objects were not made solely for mortuary use. Wear and tear on many of these objects show that they had long histories of use before final interment. Not only are certain objects, mainly copper plates, old by the time they were buried, but many were widely traded. Objects bearing distinctively regional styles are sometimes found together, and look-alike pieces have been recovered 1,620 km (1,000 miles) apart. The concentration of SECC objects at Etowah, Moundville, and Spiro is probably due in large part to a combination of geographical factors and political domination.

As the archaeological contexts for this body of material have become better known, considerable change over time can be documented in the kind of artifacts and expressive imagery given prominence at specific times. The mortuary contexts from which these objects have come has changed as well, while the ritual systems appear to have remained stable and very conservative. A large area of the Southeast, the Midwest, and the eastern Plains were once linked in the production and exchange of these and other more utilitarian items. A broad series of rocks, minerals, and marine shells was brought into this network of exchange in the subcontinent of the eastern Woodlands. Not all of these precious objects were converted into items recognized in the SECC, such as pearl beads or mica flakes, but they appear in the same contexts as the elaborately crafted and decorated objects that are so recognized. Broad as this network was, the use and display of SECC items was socially restricted and probably heavily overlain with religious sanctions; hence, the relative rarity of these objects and their overwhelming association with ritual deposits and the graves of the elite.

The use and display of these material manifestations of ritual were governed by social conventions of three basic kinds: communal cults associated with community-wide rites of intensification; kin-group cults with control over esoteric knowledge and cultic paraphernalia that confer mastery over the supernatural; and priestly cults in which a small number of individuals control the rites and paraphernalia of highly sanctified institutions (Knight, Jr. 1986). The objects, emblems, and iconography associated with the SECC belong mainly to the sec-

ond category, the clan or lineage cults. Vernon J. Knight, Jr. (1986) called this the warfare/cosmogony complex. One of the principal images of the SECC, the birdman, is connected with a complex symbolism that associates the prowess of the hawk in hunting to success in war. The hawk is connected with ancestral cults of the elite and the sacred fire of the community.

The initial period in which the SECC emerged as a distinctive material expression has been labeled the developmental period and can be placed between A.D. 1150 and 1250 (800–700 years B.P.). Distinctive elements of this period are the Long Nosed God maskettes, hypertrophic axe heads of greenstone, chipped-stone maces, and engraved-shell cups. In the subsequent classic expression, associated with the Late Wilbanks of Etowah and the Moundville II and Spiro III periods at these sites (A.D. 1250–1350, or 700–600 years B.P.), monolithic axes, perforated axe heads, repoussé copper headdresses, and engraved-shell gorgets rise to prominence instead. The final period, which extends to European contact, is associated with the Moundville III period and with Dallas and Lamar cultures. It witnessed a decline in craftsmanship and a widespread proliferation of established forms in new social settings.

The Southeastern Ceremonial complex was originally defined by A.J. Waring, Jr., and Preston Holder (1945) on the basis of the high degree of similarity in exotic artifacts and imagery found associated with the elite dead at three widely separated sites in the Southeast: Etowah, Moundville, and Spiro. Many of their original thoughts on timing and source have been replaced as our knowledge of the archaeological contexts and chronology of the SECC has increased. The compressed time scale they attributed to the SECC led them and other archaeologists to place the SECC near the time of the expedition of Spanish explorer Hernando de Soto, and the age-area historical conceptions likewise in vogue back then dictated that this complex represent a single cult spreading rapidly from a single center. None of these expectations has been borne out. Furthermore, the Mesoamerican connections, though implicit in the original definition, are now regarded as more complicated than a single-source model implies. For instance, major themes such as the birdman are found represented in the Late Woodland period, and many motifs have analogues in the Middle Woodland period.

Knight (1986) regards the customary list of

material markers as simply the warfare/cosmogony complex of a much more comprehensive set of cultic institutions that underwent development throughout the entire period. James A. Brown and Knight have called attention to a wide range of cultic connections having to do with success in warfare, ritual adoption of foreigners, widespread beliefs in the procreative powers of various spirits, and the power concentrated in ancestor shrines.

James A. Brown

Further Readings

Brose, D.S., J.A. Brown, and D.W. Penney. 1985. *Ancient Art of the American Woodland Indians.* Abrams, New York.

Brown, J.A. 1976. The Southern Cult Reconsidered. *Midcontinental Journal of Archaeology* 2:115–135.

Brown, J.A., R.A. Kerber, and H.D. Winters. 1990. Trade and the Evolution of Exchange Relations at the Beginning of the Mississippian Period Before A.D. 1200. In *Mississippian Emergence: The Evolution of Ranked Agricultural Societies in Eastern North America*, edited by B.D. Smith, pp. 251–280. Smithsonian Institution Press, Washington, D.C.

Galloway, P. (editor). 1989. *Southern Ceremonial Complex, Artifacts and Analysis: The Cottonlandia Conference.* University of Nebraska Press, Lincoln.

Knight, V.J., Jr. 1986. The Institutional Organization of Mississippi Religion. *American Antiquity* 51:675–87.

Phillips, P., and J.A. Brown. 1978. *Pre-Columbian Shell Engravings From the Craig Mound at Spiro, Oklahoma*, pt. 1. Peabody Museum of American Archaeology and Ethnology, Harvard University, Cambridge.

Waring, A.J., Jr., and P. Holder. 1945. A Prehistoric Ceremonial Complex in the Southeastern United States. *American Anthropologist* 47:1–34.

Williams, S. (editor). 1968. *The Waring Papers: The Collected Works of Antonio J. Waring, Jr.* Papers no. 58. Peabody Museum of American Archaeology and Ethnology, Harvard University, Cambridge.

Southeastern Paleoindian

Paleoindian assemblages in the Southeast are commonly, if somewhat arbitrarily, placed into Early, Middle, and Late subperiods, with estimated temporal ranges of ca. 10,550–8950 B.C. (12,500–10,900 years B.P.), 8950–8550 B.C. (10,900–10,500 years B.P.), and 8550–8050 B.C. (10,500–10,000 years B.P.), respectively (Anderson 1990; all dates refer to uncorrected radiocarbon years before the present). These three subperiods correspond to the occurrence of (Early) lanceolate fluted points resembling western Clovis forms; (Middle) fluted and unfluted forms with broad blades and constricted hafts like the Cumberland, Suwannee, Simpson, Quad, and Beaver Lake types; and (Late) resharpened lanceolate corner- and side-notched forms like Dalton, San Patrice, Bolen, and Big Sandy. The dating for the first two of these subperiods relies primarily on the cross-dating of the diagnostic bifaces with morphologically similar forms. Early Paleoindian Clovis points are securely dated to ca. 9250–8950 B.C. (11,200–10,900 years B.P.) in the Southwest and Lower Plains, while fluted forms with deeply indented bases have been dated somewhat later, to ca. 8650 B.C. (10,600 years B.P.), at sites in the Northeast. Stratigraphic evidence exists supporting all or parts of this relative sequence from several locations in the Southeast, most notably Hester in Mississippi, Dust Cave in Alabama, and Silver Springs in Florida. Only Late Paleoindian Dalton and early side-notched Bolen/Big Sandy assemblages are reasonably well dated, at Dust Cave, Page-Ladson in Florida, and Rodgers Shelter in Missouri.

Large numbers of fluted points occur in the Southeast, particularly along the major drainages of the Midsouth. Until the 1980s, few large, diversified Clovis-site assemblages had been found or recognized, which led to the widespread view that the southeastern Early Paleoindian archaeological record consisted primarily of isolated point finds or light artifact scatters, the remains of small foraging groups characterized by a high residential mobility (Meltzer 1988). Major sites with extensive and diverse assemblages dating to the Early and immediately following Middle Paleoindian subperiods do occur in some parts of the region, however, particularly along the Tennessee and Cumberland river valleys, in northern Florida, and in Virginia. At some of these sites, of which Carson-Conn-Short in Tennessee is a good example, dozens, and in a few cases hundreds, of points and formal unifacial tools have been found, as well as large blades and blade cores

S

that rival, if not exceed, the blade technology found on some classic western Clovis sites.

In almost every state, individuals are compiling information about Paleoindian sites and artifacts, most typically locational and measurement data on fluted points. In 1994, locational and/or metric data were compiled for ca. 5,000 fluted points from the Southeast and more than 8,000 fluted points from eastern North America as a whole (Faught et al. 1994). Dense concentrations of artifacts occur in the major river valleys of the interior Southeast and Lower Midwest. These may represent places where initial extended settlement occurred, staging areas from which the exploration and eventual occupation of the larger region may have proceeded. The numbers of fluted points from the eastern United States so vastly exceed the numbers reported to date from the western half of the continent that if initial human entry was through the ice-free corridor onto the Great Plains, or else along the Pacific rim, it is possible that these original immigrants did not have Clovis technology when they arrived or, alternatively, that it was not until these populations reached the East that they really took off. Where Clovis technology arose and how it spread is unknown, and while an origin somewhere in the East is not altogether implausible, there is no chronological support for it yet.

The existence of dense concentrations of fluted points in some parts of the Southeast while other areas are nearly devoid of these artifacts indicates a highly selective use of the landscape rather than a pattern of near-continuous mobility. Large areas of the Gulf and Atlantic Coastal Plain appear to have seen only minimal utilization, while dense concentrations of sites and artifacts occur along portions of major interior drainages like the Tennessee, Cumberland, and Ohio rivers. If these concentrations reflect areas of initial settlement, their irregular distribution also suggests that colonization likely proceeded in a leap-frog fashion rather than a continuous wave of advance.

The directions and extent to which Early Paleoindian populations moved over the landscape in the Southeast are being explored through detailed lithic source identification analyses that document the distances raw materials used for artifacts moved from quarry areas. In some parts of the region, movement of raw materials up to 200–300 km (124–186 miles) has been demonstrated, particularly in the Kentucky-Indiana-Ohio area and in North and South Carolina, while in other areas, notably southern Virginia, materials typically moved over much shorter distances. These patterns appear to be related to raw-material availability, with more long-distance movement of material in areas where sources of replacement stone were few and far between. Direct procurement of lithic raw material is indicated, as there is little evidence for the extensive and specialized reduction/manufacturing activity of large numbers of bifaces or cores characteristic of production for exchange. An excellent examination of Paleoindian mobility is J.A. McAvoy's (1992) analysis of assemblage and raw-material data from Williamson and many other sites in southern Virginia in the reconstruction of band territories, annual ranges, and settlement organization.

If the southeastern Clovislike forms are contemporaneous with their western counterparts, an occurrence between ca. 9250 and 8950 B.C. (11,200–10,900 years B.P.) is likely. Unfortunately, there are few early radiocarbon dates in secure contexts from the region. At the Johnson-Hawkins site near Nashville, Tennessee, a deeply buried hearth with associated fluted preforms yielded a date of 9750 B.C. ± 980 (11,700 years B.P.). Two sites from Florida provide fairly strong evidence for the existence of considerably older, possibly pre-Clovis, occupations in the region. They date to 10,550–10,050 B.C. (12,500–12,000 years B.P.). At Page-Ladson, five dates bracketing this interval have been obtained from a level containing a mastodon tusk with cut marks on it, and at Little Salt Springs, a wooden spear associated with a giant tortoise was dated to 10,080 B.C. ± 200 (12,030 years B.P.). No other firm evidence supporting pre-Clovis occupations has been found in the Southeast, in spite of the extensive research- and cultural-resource-management-based survey and excavation activity that has taken place. Lithic-reduction analyses conducted over the past two decades have, in fact, led to the dismissal of home-grown pre-Clovis candidates like the Lively pebble-tool complex from Alabama, formed in actuality of cores from initial-stage lithic reduction by Archaic populations. Recent accelerator mass spectrometry dating of the Natchez human pelvis, found with late Pleistocene megafaunal remains, gave a determination of 3630 B.C. ± 80 (5580 years B.P.). Many more dates with small sigmas and plenty of associated artifacts are needed before there is widespread acceptance among professional archaeologiists that human occupation in the region predates ca. 9250 B.C. (11,200 years B.P.), or even that fluting technology could be earlier in the Southeast than in the western half of the continent.

Direct associations between human and now-extinct terminal Pleistocene fauna have been found in Florida, including the remains of a giant tortoise at Little Salt Spring and the discovery in the Wacissa River of a *Bison bison antiquus* skull with a projectile point embedded in its forehead. In addition, a number of tools carved from green proboscidean ivory and other modified megafaunal bone have been found in Florida's rivers and sinks. Indisputable associations of humans and mastodon have also been found at Kimmswick in southern Missouri and possibly at the Coates-Hindes site in western Tennessee. It is thus probable that southeastern Paleoindians hunted now-extinct Pleistocene fauna and megafauna at least some of the time. But because direct associations between Paleoindians and megafauna have been rare in the East, at least when compared to their occurrence in the western part of the continent, and because megafaunal extinctions are assumed to have been over fairly early, by ca. 8850 B.C. (10,800 years B.P.), some archaeologists have argued that the subsistence strategies of eastern Paleoindian groups were directed primarily to modern species, with Pleistocene megafauna only a small and infrequent part of the diet (e.g., Meltzer and Smith 1986). What the minimal subsistence data from this time period in the Southeast indicate is that extinct, rather than modern, fauna were the prey of choice. Accordingly, modern fauna, such as deer and smaller mammalian species like rabbits, raccoons, and opossums, may have been second-line resources, taken only when megafauna were not readily available.

Five sites with stratified deposits spanning the Middle Paleoindian through Early Archaic periods, a time that marks both the extinction of Pleistocene fauna and the forced adoption of modern game species, as well as the onset of Holocene climatic conditions and resource structure/vegetational patterns, have been examined and reported in detail. These include Hester in Mississippi, an open-air site; the Haw River floodplain open-air sites in North Carolina; the Hardaway mountaintop workshop/base camp in North Carolina, which was the subject of extensive additional excavations in the 1970s and 1980s, and the assemblage of

which was used to help formulate the Archaic cultural sequence for the lower Southeast; the Page-Ladson site in Florida, a now-submerged and partly filled-in sinkhole in the Aucilla River bottom; and Dust Cave in Alabama, a deeply stratified rock shelter. Preservation of floral and faunal remains at the latter two sites, Page-Ladson and Dust Cave, is remarkable, with worked bone common, including bone needles and fishhooks, at Dust Cave. These same two sites have produced large numbers of logically ordered radiocarbon dates, demonstrating, among other things, that side-notched point forms (locally described as Big Sandy, Bolen, or Early Side-Notched) first appeared ca. 8250 B.C. (10,200 years B.P.), somewhat earlier than previously thought.

Other major later Paleoindian excavations and analyses include the extensive work with the Suwannee assemblages from the Harney Flats base camp site near Tampa Bay, Florida, and at two Dalton sites in northeast Arkansas, the Sloan cemetery and the Brand campsite. Dalton settlement systems have been explored in both the central Mississippi Valley and the Georgia Piedmont, and the close affinities evident between Clovis and Dalton technology suggest that Dalton evolved directly from Clovis in the central Mississippi Valley, perhaps as early as 8850 B.C. (10,800 years B.P.). Finally, the examination of early human occupations on now-submerged portions of the continental shelf has resulted in the discovery of a number of sites in submerged contexts, some an appreciable distance into the Gulf of Mexico (see Anderson and Sassaman 1996 for summaries of Paleoindian and Early Archaic research in the Southeast).

David G. Anderson

Further Readings

Anderson, D.G. 1990. The Paleoindian Colonization of Eastern North America: A View From the Southeastern United States. In *Early Paleoindian Economies of Eastern North America,* edited by K.B. Tankersley and B.L. Isaac, pp. 163–216. Research in Economic Anthropology, Supplement no. 5. JAI Press, Greenwich.

Anderson, D.G., and K.E. Sassaman. 1996. *The Paleoindian and Early Archaic Southeast.* University of Alabama Press, Tuscaloosa.

Faught, M.K., D.G. Anderson, and A. Gisiger. 1994. North American

Paleoindian Database: An Update. *Current Research in the Pleistocene* 11:32–35.

McAvoy, J.M. 1992. *Nottoway River Survey Part I Clovis Settlement Patterns: The 30 Year Study of a Late Ice Age Hunting Culture on the Southern Interior Coastal Plain of Virginia.* Special Publication no. 28. Archaeological Society of Virginia, Richmond.

Meltzer, D.J. 1988. Late Pleistocene Human Adaptations in Eastern North America. *Journal of World Prehistory* 2:1–53.

Meltzer, D.J., and B.D. Smith. 1986. Paleo-Indian and Early Archaic Subsistence Strategies in Eastern North America. In *Foraging, Collecting, and Harvesting: Archaic Period Subsistence and Settlement in the Eastern Woodlands,* edited by S. Neusius, pp. 1–30. Center for Archaeological Investigations, Southern Illinois University, Carbondale.

See also AUCILLA RIVER SITES; DALTON; DUST CAVE; HARDAWAY SITE; KIMMSWICK; RODGERS SHELTER

Southern California Coast

The coastal region of southern California extends from Morro Bay, 150 km (93 miles) upcoast from Santa Barbara, to the Mexican border. It includes more than 400 km (248 miles) of shoreline and extends as much as 100 km (62 miles) inland. Culturally, it may continue south into Baja California for another 200 km (124 miles) or more. Also included are the major coastal islands of this zone, especially the northern Channel Islands of Santa Cruz, Santa Rosa, and San Miguel, and the more southerly islands of Santa Catalina, San Clemente, and San Nicolas. This area saw the development of a long, rich cultural tradition that culminated in some of the most elaborate hunter-gatherer societies known.

Coastal southern California has been studied archaeologically since the nineteenth century. Multiple local-culture sequences have been proposed for each coastal county—San Luis Obispo, Santa Barbara, Ventura, Los Angeles, Orange, and San Diego—as well as for the northern and southern Channel Islands. Influential models have been offered by D.B. Rogers (1929), M.J. Rogers (1929, 1938, 1958), A.E. Treganza and A. Bierman (1958), P.C. Orr (1943), and W.J. Wallace (1955), among others.

The most comprehensive regional models in use are C.N. Warren's (1968) and C. D. King's (1981, 1990), which are summarized here and linked with the more general J.L. Chartkoff and K.K. Chartkoff (1984) framework.

A Paleoindian presence along the southern California coast has long been asserted, but all evidence remains controversial. Orr (1968) and R. Berger (Orr and Berger 1966) have noted the occurrence of dwarf mammoths on Santa Rosa Island and the discovery of carbon materials dating to more than 18,050 B.C. (20,000 years B.P.), but most authorities remain unconvinced that either the bones or the carbon can be directly connected with human traces. On the mainland, coastal southern California has seen several claims for Pleistocene-age human remains, but the method used to calculate their ages, aspartic acid racemization, has been generally discredited for that purpose. Similar claims for early cultural sites at Texas Street, Del Mar, Calico, and elsewhere have met with similar disproofs. As of the mid-1990s, a sound basis is lacking for accepting human presence in the area before the end of the Wisconsin glaciation ca. 10,050 B.C. (12,000 years B.P.). Recent discoveries of fluted points along the southern California coast (Erlandson and Colton 1991:4), however, establish human presence there as early 10,050–9050 B.C. (12,000–11,000 years B.P.). This early presence has been called "Paleo-Coastal" by M.J. Moratto (1984). He sees it as analogous to the Western Pluvial Lakes tradition, the final Paleoindian stage of the interior deserts, which extends into the Early Archaic (9050–6050 B.C., or 11,000–8000 years B.P.) and incorporates the San Dieguito tradition of Warren's model.

The San Dieguito tradition (9050–6050 B.C., or 11000–8000 years B.P.; Warren 1967a), described below, is by far the best-established and documented Early Archaic tradition of the southern California coast. The Middle Archaic is represented in Warren's model by the Encinitas tradition, which ends in the Santa Barbara–Los Angeles area by 3050 B.C. (5000 years B.P.) but continues in the San Diego area until A.D. 750 (1200 years B.P.). The Encinitas tradition does not reflect the more general transition from Middle Archaic (6050–4050 B.C., or 8000–6000 years B.P.) to Late Archaic (4050–2050 B.C., or 6000–4000 years B.P.) to early Pacific (2050–550 B.C., or 4000–2500 years B.P.) in the Chartkoff and Chartkoff model.

King's (1981) model is more specific to the

Chumash ethnographic area, which is centered in Santa Barbara and Ventura counties and the Northern Channel Islands. His sequence begins with an Early period (4050–450 B.C., or 6000–2400 years B.P.), which ignores the Paleo-Coastal materials and coincides with Chartkoff and Chartkoff's Middle and Late Archaic. King's Early period, with three subdivisions, is followed by a Middle period with five subdivisions (450 B.C.–A.D. 1100, or 2400–850 years B.P.) and a Late period with three subdivisions (A.D. 1100–1750, or 850–200 years B.P.). His model is heavily oriented toward the emergence of Late Prehistoric–complex cultures and so has only moderate bearing on the region's Archaic and earlier archaeology.

In Warren's (1968) more comprehensive scheme, the successor to the Encinitas tradition north of San Diego County is the Campbell tradition (3050 B.C.–A.D. 450, or 5000–1500 years B.P.). The cultural developments of the Campbell tradition reflect the patterns of the early and middle Pacific periods of Chartkoff and Chartkoff, even though the Campbell tradition starts somewhat earlier. For the Santa Barbara area, Warren defines the time from A.D. 450 to 1782 (1500–168 years B.P.) as the Chumash tradition, reflecting D.B. Rogers's (1929) use of Canalino. Rogers's term should be seen as more general than the ethnographic Chumash culture's boundaries, since it is meant to refer to the Protohistoric predecessors of all of the ethnic groups along the coast. This includes the Shoshonean-speaking Gabrielino and Fernandeno peoples of Los Angeles and Orange counties, who are understood to have migrated into the area around that time. Warren's Chumash tradition coincides with Chartkoff and Chartkoff's late (A.D. 450–1450, or 1500–500 years B.P.) and final (A.D. 1450–1750, or 500–200 years B.P.) Pacific periods. King's Late period also is generally equivalent to the late and final Pacific periods in terms of time and implications for development.

The Historic period commenced when non-Indian settlement began to impact on traditional cultures. In each area, the onset of historic settlement began when a local mission was founded: 1769 in San Diego and 1782 in Santa Barbara, for example. Chartkoff and Chartkoff used the 1769 San Diego date as the general boundary for their Historic period (Moratto 1984:125; Erlandson and Colton 1991:2).

Because there are no widely accepted Paleoindian sites along the southern California coast to date (1996), the area's established archaeological-site sequence starts with the San Dieguito material. Examples of that tradition are found throughout the southern California coast. The earliest Channel Island sites resemble some late San Dieguito mainland sites. M.J. Rogers (1945) defined the San Dieguito pattern at the C.W. Harris site in San Diego County. Malaga Cove Phase I near Redondo Beach, Los Angeles County, is a well-reported example (Wallace 1955). The Diablo Creek site in San Luis Obispo County has a basal occupation that appears to be San Dieguito. Perhaps the best-studied coastal San Dieguito occupation is the Great Western site A occupation near Batequitos Lagoon in northern San Diego County (Kaldenberg 1976). E.L. Davis (Davis et al. 1969) and Moratto (1984:104) prefer the term "Paleo-Coastal" tradition to San Dieguito, because it emphasizes a cultural adaptation and the relationship of the tradition to contemporary materials in the interior deserts: the Western Pluvial Lakes tradition. Warren (1967a), by contrast, uses San Dieguito to refer to both the coastal and the desert cultures of the Early Archaic.

The San Dieguito form of culture reflects minor, but significant, changes from inland Paleoindian materials. The tool assemblage is modest in variety and fairly similar throughout its distribution regardless of local environmental differences. Gone are distinctive Paleoindian elements, such as fluted or other large, well-made, projectile points, or any association with Pleistocene large game. San Dieguito sites reflect little hunting, have few faunal remains, few, if any, projectile points (any present are inevitably crudely chipped, large-stemmed or corner-notched varieties), nor any small scraper industries. Also absent are tools associated with intensive seed or other plant harvesting, such as milling tools or bone awls for making basketry. Typical tools include hammerstones, heavy choppers, heavy scrapers, and heavy knifelike bifacial pieces. Sites have minimal amounts of ash or fire-cracked rocks. They lack cemeteries or ornamental artifacts. Some rock alignments are thought to represent windbreaks or other shelter features. A few late San Dieguito sites show some collection of coastal shellfish, which indicates a possible transition toward a more diversified and locally based economy.

The following Encinitas tradition is better represented in the region's archaeological record. In San Diego County, M.J. Rogers's

(1945) La Jolla complex reflects this era. In the Los Angeles and Ventura county areas, the Topanga complex, especially Phase II, largely reflects this pattern (Treganza and Bierman 1958) and has been integrated into the more widely distributed model of Wallace's (1955) Millingstone horizon. Millingstone-horizon sites, in addition to the Topanga Canyon examples at LAn-1 and LAn-2, are also found at Malaga Cove (Wallace 1955), Zuma Creek (Peck 1955), Little Sycamore Canyon (Wallace et al. 1956) in Ventura County, and the Glen Annie site in Santa Barbara County, among many other places. Most of the early horizons on the Channel Islands belong to this period, as does D.B. Rogers's (1929) Oak Grove culture in Santa Barbara.

Warren's Encinitas tradition displays several key changes in adaptation. Most diagnostic is the appearance of millingstones and manos, which indicates the systematic exploitation of hard seeds. Abundant core tools, especially scraper planes, indicate processing of vegetal matter. Faunal remains include land mammals, such as rabbits and deer, sea mammals, such as seals and sea lions, up to 20 or more species of shellfish in some sites, fish remains from near-shore species, and waterfowl. Projectile points are much more common than in San Dieguito assemblages. Also diagnostic are cogged stones and discoidals. Even inland sites, such as Century Ranch (King et al. 1968), yield significant amounts of ocean fauna remains.

Encinitas sites are often large and indicate occupation for extended parts of the year. This is the first era in regional prehistory in which numbers of burials occur in sites. The distinctive Millingstone-horizon practice of having extended burials beneath cairns of millingstones is part of this pattern. Santa Barbara sites have remains of semisubterranean pithouses at this time. Community size is still modest, but economies are much more diversified than in earlier times. A greater adaptive efficiency allowed Encinitas communities to develop greater degrees of sedentism than ever before. Some evidence for regional exchange of obsidian, steatite, and other distinctive materials also is known for Encinitas sites (Chartkoff 1989). Population increased greatly from the earlier San Dieguito times. Since the size of individual communities did not become markedly greater, it is likely that many more individual communities were formed and that the average size of territories shrank accordingly.

The Campbell tradition evolved from Encinitas foundations. Some subsistence elements were added, but the economy tended to concentrate on selected resources. Campbell sites yield more evidence of exotic raw materials than do Encinitas assemblages, which indicates greater levels of exchange. Campbell assemblages are richer in ornamental artifacts, such as beads and pendants, than their predecessors. The abundance of mortars and pestles shows the development of acorn processing as a major focus. Campbell burials are usually flexed rather than extended and are often accompanied by red ocher or abalone (*Haliotis*) shells. They have more grave goods than Encinitas burials, with more variation among grave lots, but not enough to demonstrate marked contrasts in social standing.

Campbell sites are more numerous per unit of time than Encinitas sites in the same habitat, which is taken to mean that population growth was continuing, and more strongly associated with shoreside locations. In the Santa Barbara area, Campbell sites reflect a strong emphasis on the hunting of land and sea mammals. From the Los Angeles area southward, they show less focus on hunting and more on plant processing, especially acorns and hard seeds. Compared to later times, mortars and pestles are not well finished, but some notable elaborations of ornamental pieces occur. Moratto (1984:161) illustrates a bone tube from Mescalitan Island's Campbell phase that has hundreds of tiny disc shell beads cemented to its exterior with asphaltum. The Little Harbor site on Santa Catalina Island (Meighan 1959) illustrates one of the many island examples of Campbell occupations.

Warren's (1968) Chumash tradition, starting ca. A.D. 500 (1450 years B.P.), represents the maturing of the Protohistoric cultures of the region. It follows D.B. Rogers's (1929) definition of the Canalino period and is generally coordinate with Chartkoff and Chartkoff's (1984) late and final Pacific periods and King's (1990) Late period. Some groups, such as the Chumash (Ventura, Santa Barbara, and San Luis Obispo counties and the northern Channel Islands) and the Tipay and Ipay of San Diego County, are understood to have developed locally out of Campbell-tradition ancestors. Others, particularly the Shoshonean-speaking communities of Los Angeles and Orange counties and the southern islands (Gabrielino, Luiseno, and Fernandeno), are understood to represent a migration of proto-Shoshonean speakers from the interior deserts to the coast ca. 50 B.C.–A.D. 450 (2000–1500 years B.P.).

The Chumashian areas in particular represent the region's climax of development. The economy in those areas was based on intensive maritime exploitation supplemented by acorns and hard seeds on the mainland. Oceangoing plank canoes fostered a dynamic regional exchange network. Elaborate and finely wrought craftwork developed in stone, bone, shell, and other media. Beads became enormously abundant, apparently changing in significance from ornaments to economic symbols (King 1981). Finely crafted mortars, pestles, stone bowls, figurines, tubes, charmstones, beads, awls, shell fishhooks, whistles, hairpins, and small projectile points were made. Villages were larger than ever, some reaching populations estimated at 1,000–1,500. Permanent villages featured extensive architecture and cemeteries and socially complex communities. Whereas earlier sites show evidence of more confined shell midden mounds, Chumash-tradition sites, such as Malibu, Rincon, and Mikiw, sprawl along the shore and up the creek banks for 0.5–1.0 km (0.3–0.6 miles). Developments elsewhere along the southern California coast were nearly as dramatic (Glassow 1977, 1980).

Chumash-tradition cultures were at their developmental peaks when Spanish and other European outsiders began to make contact, starting with Juan Cabrillo's expedition of 1542–1543. Archaeology has yet to shed much light on the impact of these intermittent contacts on local cultures, much less on the efforts made by Indians to cope with permanent Spanish settlement starting in 1769. In the following 30 years, Spain established a series of missions, military posts, villages, and ranches between San Luis Obispo and San Diego and, in the process, impressed virtually all local Indians into slavery. Between enslavement and epidemics, native cultures and populations were decimated quickly. Although some individuals were able to survive the mission era, and although survivors managed to preserve some aspects of their traditional cultures, the onset of missionization brought to an abrupt end the autonomous development of culture and society along the southern California coast.

Joseph L. Chartkoff

Further Readings

Chartkoff, J.L. 1989. Exchange Systems in the Archaic of Coastal Southern California. *Proceedings of the Society for California Archaeology* 2:167–186.

Chartkoff, J.L., and K.K. Chartkoff. 1984. *The Archaeology of California*. Stanford University Press, Stanford.

Davis, E.L., C.W. Brott, and D.L. Weide. 1969. *The Western Lithic Co-Tradition*. Papers, vol. 6. San Diego Museum of Man, San Diego.

Erlandson, J., and R. Colton. 1991. *Hunter-Gatherers of Early Holocene Coastal California*. Perspectives in California Archaeology, vol. 1. Institute of Archaeology, University of California, Los Angeles.

Glassow, M.A. 1977. An Archaeological Overview of the Northern Channel Islands, California. Ms. on file, Western Archaeological Center, National Park Service, Tucson.

———. 1980. Recent Developments in the Archaeology of the Channel Islands. In *The California Islands: Proceedings of a Multidisciplinary Symposium*, edited by D.M. Power, pp. 79–102. Santa Barbara Museum of Natural History, Santa Barbara.

Greenwood, R.S. 1972. *9,000 Years of Prehistory at Diablo Canyon, San Luis Obispo County, California*. Occasional Papers no. 7. San Luis Obispo County Archaeological Society, San Luis Obispo.

Harrison, W.M. 1965. Mikiwi: A Coastal Chumash Village. *Archaeological Survey Annual Report* 7:91–178. University of California, Los Angeles.

Kaldenberg, R.L. 1976. *Paleo-Technical Change at Rancho Park North, San Diego County, California*. Unpublished Master's thesis. Department of Anthropology, San Diego State University, San Diego.

Kaldenberg, R.L., and P.H. Ezell. 1974. Results of the Archaeological Mitigation of Great Western Sites A and C, Located on the Proposed Rancho Park North Development. Ms. on file, Department of Anthropology, California State University, San Diego.

King, C.D. 1981. *The Evolution of Chumash Society: A Comparative Analysis of Artifacts Used in Social System Maintenance in the Santa Barbara Channel Region Before A.D. 1804*. Unpublished Ph.D. dissertation, Department of Anthropology, University of California, Davis.

———. 1990. *Evolution of Chumash Society.* Garland, New York.

King, C.D., T. Blackburn, and E. Chandonet. 1968. The Archaeological Investigation of Three Sites on the Century Ranch, Western Los Angeles County, California. *Archaeological Survey Annual Report* 10:12–161. University of California, Los Angeles.

Meighan, C.W. 1959. The Little Harbor Site, Catalina Island: An Example of Ecological Interpretation in Archaeology. *American Antiquity* 24:383–405.

Moratto, M.J. (editor). 1984. *California Archaeology.* Academic Press, Orlando.

Orr, P.C. 1943. Archaeology of Mescalitan Island and Customs of the Canaliño. *Santa Barbara Museum of Natural History Occasional Papers* 5:1–61.

———. 1968. *Prehistory of Santa Rosa Island.* Santa Barbara Museum of Natural History, Santa Barbara.

Orr, P.C., and R. Berger. 1966. The Fire Areas on Santa Rosa Island, California. *Proceedings of the National Academy of Sciences* 56(5):1049–1416.

Peck, S.L. 1955. *An Archaeological Report on the Excavation of a Prehistoric Site at Zuma Creek, Los Angeles County, California.* Papers no. 2. Archaeological Survey Association of Southern California, Los Angeles.

Rogers, D.B. 1929. *Prehistoric Man of the Santa Barbara Coast.* Santa Barbara Museum of Natural History, Santa Barbara.

Rogers, M.J. 1929. The Stone Art of the San Dieguito Plateau. *American Anthropologist* 31(3):454–467.

———. 1938. Archaeological and Geological Investigations in an Old Channel of the San Dieguito Valley. *Carnegie Institution of Washington Yearbook* 37:344–345.

———. 1945. An Outline of Yuman Prehistory. *Southwestern Journal of Anthropology* 1:167–198.

———. 1958. San Dieguito Implements From the Terraces of the Rincon-Patano and Rillito Drainage System. *Kiva* 24(1):1–23.

Treganza, A.E., and A. Bierman. 1958. The Topanga Culture: Final Report on Excavations, 1948. *University of California Anthropological Records* 20(2):45–86.

True, D.L. 1958. An Early Complex in San Diego County, California. *American Antiquity* 23:255–263.

———. 1980. The Pauma Complex in Northern San Diego County: 1978. *Journal of New World Archaeology* 3(4):1–39.

True, D.L., C.W. Meighan, and H. Crew. 1974. *Archaeological Investigations at Molpa, San Diego County, California.* Publications in Anthropology no. 11. University of California Press, Berkeley.

Wallace, W.J. 1954. The Little Sycamore Site and Early Milling Stone Cultures in Southern California. *American Antiquity* 20:112–123.

———. 1955. A Suggested Chronology for Southern California Coastal Archaeology. *Southwestern Journal of Anthropology* 11:214–230.

Wallace, W.J., E.S. Taylor, R.J. Desautals, H.R. Hammond, H. Gonzales, J. Bogart, and J.P. Redwine. 1956. *The Little Sycamore Shellmound, Ventura County, California.* Contributions to California Archaeology no. 2. Archaeological Research Associates, Los Angeles.

Warren, C.N. 1967a. The San Dieguito Complex: A Review and Hypothesis. *American Antiquity* 32:168–185.

———. 1967b. The Southern California Milling Stone Horizon: Some Comments. *American Antiquity* 32:233–236.

———. 1968. Cultural Tradition and Ecological Adaptation on the Southern California Coast. In *Archaic Prehistory in the Western United States,* edited by C. Irwin-Williams, pp. 1–14. Contributions in Anthropology, vol. 1, no. 3. Eastern New Mexico University, Portales.

Warren, C.N., and D.L. True. 1961. The San Dieguito Complex and Its Place in California Prehistory. *Archaeological Survey Annual Report* 3:246–338. University of California, Los Angeles.

Southern (Columbia) Plateau

The Southern (Columbia) Plateau is the interior, intermontane region of the northwestern United States. It includes eastern Washington State, northern and central Idaho, western Montana, and northern Oregon. At contact in the early eighteenth century A.D., most of the region's people spoke one or another Penutian language (Nez Perce, Cayuse, and Sahaptin), though Interior Salish speakers occupied the very northern portions of the region, and Paiute and

Shoshonean speakers lived on the southern edges of the Plateau.

The Columbia Plateau's western boundary is the eastern flanks of the Cascade Mountain Range; its eastern boundaries are the northern Rocky Mountains. The Okanagan Highlands of northern Washington State and southern British Columbia form its northern boundary, while the southern boundary merges with the Great Basin in the High Basin and Range country of central Oregon. The Columbia Basin, located in central Washington State, is the region's dominating physiographic feature. It is low in elevation and was produced by the extrusion of Columbia River basalts during the Miocene, giving it its distinctive flat topography. Its eastern portions are mantled by Pleistocene loess. The Columbia Plateau is drained by the Columbia River and its principle tributary, the Snake River, which meet at the western edge of the basin. Except in the lowest portions of the basin, these rivers and their tributaries flow through steep-walled canyons, sometimes several thousand feet deep.

The Columbia Plateau is in the rain shadow of the Cascades. The dry western portions receive as little as 25 cm (10 inches) of rain annually. Rainfall increases to the east, as elevation rises. The dominant vegetation at low elevations is a cold, steppe grassland with sage brush (*Artemisia*). The deeply dissected eastern portions of the Plateau are environmentally diverse, with dry steppes in very low regions and seasonally wet meadows, prairies, and extensive forests at higher elevations. Forest cover ranges from low-elevation ponderosa-pine forests to subalpine forests dominated by alpine fir and aspen.

Native economies and settlement patterns were significantly altered, particularly in the southeastern plateau, by the introduction of the horse in the early eighteenth century. Some groups, such as the Nez Perce, began to spend long periods of time on the High Plains of central Montana, hunting bison. However, major portions of the earliest economic and settlement patterns persisted. People usually spent the winter months in villages in canyon bottoms subsisting on dried fish, primarily salmon, meat, and vegetable foods, particularly dried roots. In spring, people dispersed out of the canyons to resource habitats scattered across higher elevations. Very large aggregations of people formed around camas (*Camassia quamash*) harvesting grounds in mid to late summer. Camas roots were a major food resource that was processed, consumed, and widely traded.

Archaeological research in the Columbia Plateau was initiated in the very late nineteenth century when Harlan I. Smith of the American Museum of Natural History, New York, traveled through the region and investigated a site in the Yakima River drainage. Systematic research did not begin until after World War II, when dam construction on the Columbia River and its tributaries led to surveys and excavations within the potential dam reservoirs. While the dam-building period has ended, archaeological work in the region has intensified since the early 1960s, as a result of other development and construction.

The Columbia Plateau is divided into a series of regions, based on drainages, and particular stretches of rivers. These divisions reflect research history as well as topography. In this encyclopedia, the middle Columbia River includes the stretch of the Columbia River from the international boundary to the eastern end of the Columbia River Gorge, where the river flows through the Cascades. The Lower Snake River region includes the drainage of the Snake River from the upper end of Hell's Canyon to the river's confluence with the Columbia River. It also includes the lower reaches of the Clearwater River and the Salmon River.

Kenneth M. Ames

Further Readings

Ames, K.M. 1991. Sedentism: A Temporal Shift or a Transitional Change in Hunter-Gatherer Mobility Patterns? In *Between Bands and States*, edited by S. Gregg, pp. 108–134. Occasional Paper no. 9. Center for Archaeological Investigations, Southern Illinois University, Carbondale.

Campbell, S.K. (editor). 1985. *Summary of Results, Chief Joseph Dan Cultural Resources Project, Washington.* Office of Public Archaeology, Institute of Environmental Studies, University of Washington, Seattle.

Galm, J.R., G.D. Hartmann, R.A. Masten, and G.O. Stephenson. 1981. *A Cultural Resources Overview of Bonneville Power Administration's Mid-Columbia Project, Central Washington.* Eastern Washington University Reports in Archaeology and History no. 100–16. Archaeological and Historical Services, Cheney.

S

Schalk, R.F., and G.C. Cleveland. 1983. A Chronological Perspective on Hunter-Gatherer Land Use Strategies in the Columbia Plateau. In *Cultural Resource Investigations for the Lyons Ferry Fish Hatchery Project, Near Lyons Ferry, Washington,* edited by R.F. Schalk, pp. 11–56. Project Report no. 8. Laboratory of Archaeology and History, Washington State University, Pullman.

Southern Great Basin Late Prehistoric Period

Southern Paiute, Western Shoshone, and Kawaiisu peoples occupied the southern Great Basin, which includes southern Nevada and the adjacent part of the California desert, when Euro-American explorers first reached the area. The Late Prehistoric archaeological record—that is, the record for the A.D. 1150–1750 (800–200 years B.P.) period, is presumably theirs, as is the ethnohistoric record. Today, their descendants live in scattered reservations and settlements in the region. Their languages are part of the Numic division of the Uto-Aztecan linguistic family. Historical linguistics indicate that the Numic languages had their origin in the southwestern Great Basin in the vicinity of Death Valley. By ca. 50 B.C. (2000 years B.P.), they had begun to differentiate and spread to the northeast. This reconstruction has important implications for the archaeological record of the southern Great Basin, for it places the Numic homeland within it and implies that Numic speakers, or at least the Numic languages, replaced earlier peoples or languages in relatively recent times. Such a replacement scenario is at odds, however, with Native American traditional history.

The traditional lifeways of the southern Great Basin people are best known from the work of ethnographers, such as Julian H. Steward, Isabel T. Kelly, and Catherine S. Fowler (Steward 1938; Kelly and Fowler 1986). They depict an annual cycle in which groups moved to a variety of resource areas for hunting and foraging. Although this is an arid area, it offered several staples to its human inhabitants: pine nuts in the higher mountains, agave at intermediate elevations, and mesquite along drainages on the valley floors. Deer and desert bighorn were large game, but small game, especially rabbits and desert tortoise, were perhaps equally important. Late in the Late Prehistoric period, Southern Paiute groups adopted native agriculture when they occupied areas along the courses of the Virgin and Muddy rivers in southern Nevada, southwestern Utah, and northwestern Arizona that had been vacated by the Virgin Anasazi. They grew some maize, squash, and winter wheat. Late Prehistoric people made a variety of perishable items, including burden baskets, winnowing trays, seed beaters, and pitch-coated jugs for water. They also made cradle boards, capes woven of strips of rabbit or other fur, and nets for catching small game.

Archaeologists identify Late Prehistoric components by the presence of brown-ware pottery and small arrow points known as Desert Side-Notched. The pottery was built by coiling. It was then thinned by several methods, including finger scraping and the paddle-and-anvil technique. These artifacts are found on the kinds of sites that one would expect from ethnographic descriptions of early historic lifeways. The people made use of caves and rock shelters, which are sometimes associated with roasting pits in which agave and other foods were cooked. Otherwise, they built temporary shelters, usually of brush, that leave no traces in the archaeological record. They camped at various places, including at springs or along drainages, in mesquite groves, and in piñon groves. Since both earlier and later people also used these kinds of places, the components from different time periods have been disturbed and mixed. As a result, and given the temporary nature of these occupations, archaeologists find the study of the material remains of the Late Prehistoric period extremely difficult.

Margaret M. Lyneis

Further Readings
Fowler, D.D., and D.B. Madsen. 1986. Prehistory of the Southeastern Area. In *Great Basin,* edited by W.L. D'Azevedo, pp. 173–182. Handbook of North American Indians, vol. 11, W.C. Sturtevant, general editor. Smithsonian Institution, Washington, D.C.

Kelly, I.T., and C.S. Fowler. 1986. Southern Paiute. In *Great Basin,* edited by W.L. D'Azevedo, pp. 368–411. Handbook of North American Indians, vol. 11, W.C. Sturtevant, general editor. Smithsonian Institution, Washington, D.C.

Steward, J.H. 1938. *Basin-Plateau Aboriginal Sociopolitical Groups.* Bulletin no. 120. Bureau of American Ethnology, Smithsonian Institution, Washington, D.C.

Warren, C.N., and R.H. Crabtree. 1986.
Prehistory of the Southwestern Area. In
Great Basin, edited by W.L. D'Azevedo,
pp. 183–205. Handbook of North
American Indians, vol. 11, W.C. Sturtevant, general editor. Smithsonian Institution, Washington, D.C.

Southern Northwest Coast

Little is known about the earliest inhabitants of
the southern Northwest Coast, the portion of
the ethnographic Northwest Coast culture extending from Point Grenville on the southern
Washington coast to Cape Mendocino on the
northern California coast. Isolated finds of

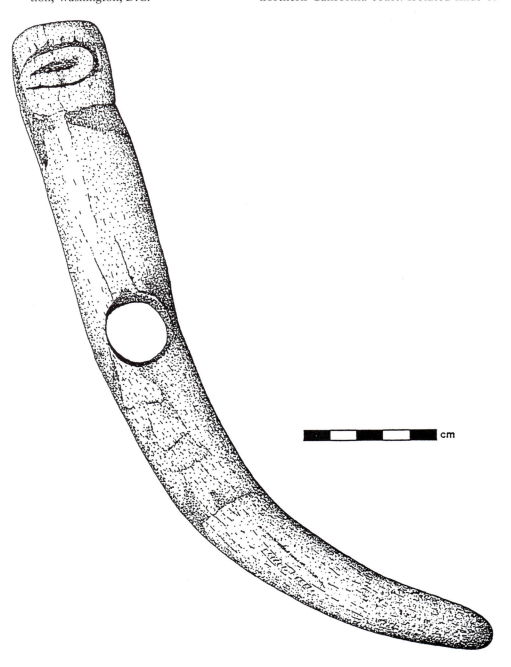

Digging stick handle with classic Northwest Coast eye motif. (Prepared by R. Minor)

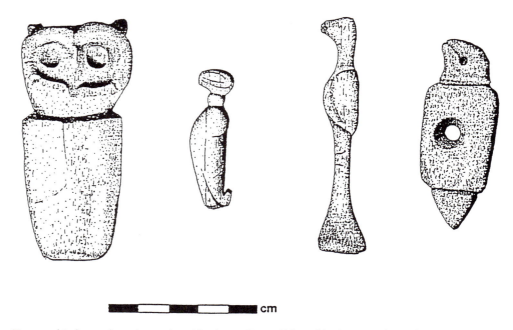

Zoomorphic figures from the southern Northwest Coast. (Adapted by R. Minor from Thomas 1992)

fluted points in the interior indicate that native peoples were in western Oregon and Washington by 9950–8050 B.C. (11,500–10,000 years B.P.), but any evidence of occupation along the immediate coastal margin during this largely hypothetical pre-Archaic period has been inundated by the postglacial rise in sea level.

The earliest evidence for people on the southern Northwest Coast is assigned to the Early Archaic period (8050–3550 B.C., or 10,000–5500 years B.P.). It has been suggested that the earliest inhabitants were "premarine" or "prelittoral" cultures (Ross 1990:554–555; Lyman 1991:79–80). Such lifeways may be represented by the Youngs River complex near the mouth of the Columbia River, estimated on the basis of projectile-point comparisons to date between 8050 and 4050 B.C. (10,000–6000 years B.P.). This complex exhibits obvious similarities to the Old Cordilleran and Olcott complexes of the Puget Sound region, which are generally interpreted as antedating the emergence of marine-oriented cultures in that region. Lithic sites found primarily along the southern Oregon coast have also been cited as evidence of premarine or prelittoral cultures. Marine molluscan remains are absent at these localities, leading to the presumption that the subsistence practices of their occupants were focused primarily on terrestrial resources. Projectile-point

comparisons suggest a possible age range of 8050–1050 B.C. (10,000–3000 years B.P.). However, with the exception of one questionable radiocarbon date of 6360 B.C. ± 110 (8310 years B.P.) from the Neptune site on the central Oregon coast, as of the mid-1990s all other radiocarbon dates indicate that lithic sites are not older than nearby shell middens.

The earliest direct evidence of the exploitation of marine resources has been found at Tahkenitch Landing on the south-central Oregon coast. Faunal and geomorphic evidence indicates that an estuary was once present in today's freshwater Tahkenitch Lake. The Tahkenitch I component, represented by cultural materials underlying a shell midden, contained charcoal that yielded radiocarbon dates of 6010 B.C. ± 90 (7960 years B.P.) and 4730 B.C. ± 80 (6680 years B.P.). While some fragments of marine shell are present, the primary subsistence focus was on fishing for marine species, with hunting of marine birds, harbor seal, and mule deer also indicated. This evidence suggests that exploitation of marine resources, though without intensive use of mollusks, has considerable time depth on the southern Northwest Coast.

The Middle Archaic period (3550–1050 B.C., or 5500–3000 years B.P.) is characterized by the earliest evidence of more broadly based marine-oriented subsistence activities as reflected by sites with substantial shell-midden deposits. The earliest intensive exploitation of molluscan resources occurred in the Tahkenitch II component associated with a charcoal-based radiocarbon date of 3150 B.C. ± 70 (5100 years B.P.). At Yaquina Head on the north-central Oregon coast, the initial occupation was associated with nonshell cultural deposits, charcoal from which produced radiocarbon dates of 2150 B.C. ± 60 (4100 years B.P.) and 2100 B.C. ± 60 (4050 years B.P.). Charcoal recovered from the earliest shell deposits on the headland yielded radiocarbon dates of 1720 B.C. ± 70 (3670 years B.P.) and 1320 B.C. ± 70 (3270 years B.P.). With three charcoal-based radiocarbon dates of 3440 B.C. ± 100, 3330 B.C. ± 80, and 3190 B.C. ± 90 (5390, 5280, 5140 years B.P., respectively), the Cape Blanco lithic site on the southern Oregon coast is the earliest well-dated example of this site type.

By the Late Archaic period (1050 B.C.–A.D. 450, or 3000–1500 years B.P.), sites containing evidence of intensive marine-oriented economies were present all along the southern Northwest Coast. A number of these sites appear to represent villages. The Palmrose site, just south of the Columbia River on the northern Oregon coast, contains the earliest evidence of the emergence of complex cultures similar to those of the ethnographic period. A rectangular semisubterranean plank house, apparently identical to the ethnographic house form, has been radiocarbon dated to 615 B.C. ± 70 (2565 years B.P.). This site has produced a large number of sculpted bone and antler artifacts with anthropomorphic and zoomorphic designs in the Northwest Coast art style. These artifacts and designs indicate strong ties with cultures to the north in the Strait of Georgia–Strait of Juan de Fuca region between 750 B.C. and A.D. 250 (2700–1700 years B.P.).

The Formative period (A.D. 450–1750, or 1500–200 years B.P.) reflects the full emergence of ethnographic culture patterns characterized by large villages, ranked societies, and artistic elaboration. Among the sites most representative of this period are Minard on the southern Washington coast; Ti-1, Seal Rock, Umpqua/Eden, and Lone Ranch Creek on the Oregon coast; and Point St. George and Gunther Island on the northern California coast. During the Protohistoric era, a late subdivision of the Formative period, Asian ceramics, beeswax, and other nonnative artifacts were introduced along the northern Oregon coast, apparently from shipwrecks of Spanish Manila galleons between A.D. 1550 and 1650 (400–300 years B.P.). The introduction of epidemic diseases in Protohistoric times led to rapid decline in the native population. As a result, the complexity of southern Northwest Coast societies is almost certainly underestimated in the limited ethnographic record.

Rick Minor

Further Readings

Connolly, T.J. 1992. *Human Responses to Change in Coastal Geomorphology and Fauna on the Southern Northwest Coast: Archaeological Investigations at Seaside, Oregon.* Anthropological Papers no. 45. Department of Anthropology, University of Oregon, Eugene.

Lyman, R.L. 1991. *Prehistory of the Oregon Coast: The Effects of Excavation Strategies and Assemblage Size on Archaeological Inquiry.* Academic Press, San Diego.

Minor, R. 1990. *Yacina Head: A Middle Archaic Settlement on the North-Central Oregon Coast.* Report no. 100. Heritage Research Associates, Reno. Reprinted 1991 as Culture Resource Series no. 6. Bureau of Land Management, Portland.

Minor, R., and K.A. Toepel. 1986. *The Archaeology of the Tahkenitch Landing Site: Early Occupation on the Oregon Coast.* Report no. 46. Heritage Research Associates, Eugene.

Ross, R.E. 1990. Prehistory of the Oregon Coast. In *Northwest Coast,* edited by W. Suttles, pp. 554–559. Handbook of North American Indians, vol. 7, W.C. Sturtevant, general editor. Smithsonian Institution, Washington, D.C.

Woodward, J.A. 1986. Prehistoric Shipwrecks on the Oregon Coast? Archaeological Evidence. In *Contributions to the Archaeology of Oregon, 1983–1986,* edited by K.M. Ames, pp. 219–264. Occasional Papers no. 3. Association of Oregon Archaeologists, Portland.

Southern Rocky Mountain Early Archaic Regional Variant

This regional variant was proposed in 1986 by William B. Butler to designate occupations that date between the Paleoindian and Middle Archaic periods in the southern Rocky Mountains of Colorado (ca. 5550–3050 B.C., or 7500–

5000 years B.P.). Artifacts in variant components include Pryor Stemmed, Lovell Constricted, and James Allen projectile points; side and end scrapers; beveled and unbeveled blades; spokeshaves; and bone awls. The projectile points and tool complexes reflect a primarily mountain-oriented cultural adaptation. It has been suggested that Pryor Stemmed and Lovell Constricted in Wyoming represent a transition toward hunting and gathering as the environment became increasingly dry with the approach of the Altithermal (Husted and Edgar 1968). The Altithermal was a period of decreased winter/spring precipitation with a generally warm and dry climate, ca. 5150–3550 B.C. (7100–5500 years B.P.) (Husted and Edgar 1968; Benedict and Olson 1978; Benedict 1979). The Pryor/Lovell complexes are best known from the mountains of Montana and Wyoming. Their topographic settings and associated tools in Colorado sites (Fourth of July Valley, Dead of Winter, Hungry Whisler, Albion Boardinghouse) generally conform to those of Pryor Stemmed complexes in Wyoming (Frison and Grey 1980). The taxon was presented as a regional variant rather than a phase because its precise relationships with Paleoindian- and Archaic-period complexes have yet to be firmly demonstrated. Its association with the Archaic is favored due to the absence of Pleistocene megafauna in associated assemblages. To date (1996), this regional variant is restricted to the mountains of Colorado.

William B. Butler

Further Readings

Benedict, J.B. 1979. Getting Away From It All: A Study of Man, Mountains, and the Two-Drought Altithermal. *Southwestern Lore* 45(3):1–12.

———. 1981. *The Fourth of July Valley: Glacial Geology and Archeology of the Timberline Ecotone.* Research Report no. 2. Center for Mountain Archeology, Ward.

Benedict, J.B., and B.L. Olson. 1978. *The Mount Albion Complex: A Study of Prehistoric Man and the Altithermal.* Research Report no. 1. Center for Mountain Archeology, Ward.

Butler, W.B. 1986. *Taxonomy in Northeastern Colorado Prehistory.* Unpublished Ph.D. dissertation, Department of Anthropology, University of Missouri, Columbia.

Frison, G.C., and D.C. Grey. 1980. Pryor Stemmed: A Specialized Paleo-Indian Ecological Adaptation. *Plains Anthropologist* 25(87):27–46.

Husted, W.M., and R. Edgar. 1968. The Archaeology of Mummy Cave: An Introduction to Shoshonean Prehistory. Ms. on file, Department of Anthropology, University of Wyoming, Laramie.

See also ALBION BOARDINGHOUSE PHASE

Southwest Culture Area

According to a phrase coined by Erik Reed, the Southwest extends "from Durango, Colorado, to Durango, Mexico, and from Las Vegas, New Mexico, to Las Vegas, Nevada." This vast reach of North America was a single natural and cultural region until the United States seized half of it from Mexico. From that time, political division has warped our knowledge of the land, including its prehistory. The U.S. half of the region is the best-known archaeological area on the continent; the Mexican half, the least known. Exploitation of the Sonora-Sinaloa coast is for the most part a missing piece of the archaeological puzzle. Major prehistoric cultures of the region include Paleoindian, Southwestern Archaic, Anasazi, Casas Grandes, Hohokam, Mogollon, Patayan, Salado, and Sinagua, and the less-known Trincheras, Rio Sonora, Huatabampo, and Loma San Gabriel cultures of Mexico. Other names for the region include Ralph L. Beals's "Greater Southwest," and Paul Kirchoff's "Arid America" and "Oasis America." From a Mexican perspective, the same region is "Northwest Mexico" or "Northern Mexico."

The area is varied but shares a single theme: aridity. Lowland areas include the Sonoran, Chihuahuan, and Mojave deserts. They are blistering hot in summer months but are punctuated by life-giving streams—the Colorado, Gila, Altar, Sonora, Bravo (Grande), and Conchos—and isolated mountain ranges. (To the south in Sonora, desert gives way to subtropical thorn forest, where the Fuerte, Mayo, and Yaqui flow.) In the lowlands, life focused on the waterways, with their biotic wealth, fertile soil, and water. Other parts of the desert supported human populations, but at lower densities. In contrast, large mountain masses, such as the Sierra Madre Occidental, the Mogollon highlands, and the southern Rockies, are marked by heavy rain and snow, as well as forests of pine, fir, and spruce. However, the growing season was often

Formative cultures and areas of the prehistoric Southwest. Boundaries indicate the approximate extent of specific cultures or areas; they do not imply territorial limits in the modern sense. (Drawn by D. A. Phillips, Jr.)

too short for prehistoric cultigens. Upland prehistoric life prospered, therefore, in intermediate elevations, such as the flanks of the Sierra Madre and Rockies or the Colorado Plateau, where increased rainfall coincides with a longer growing season.

Early Paleoindian hunters (the Clovis culture) roamed from one end of the region to the other, but later Paleoindian remains are concentrated near the High Plains. Throughout the region, Paleoindians gave way to Archaic for-

agers and hunters. Formative lifeways, with mixed farming-foraging economies, pottery making, and small villages, were common by A.D. 500 (1450 years B.P.). Several small-scale regional networks emerged over the next millennium but most collapsed, leading to abandonment, reorganization, or reversion to less sedentary patterns. Aboriginal groups were disrupted by the arrival of Europeans and their diseases in the 1500s, but many native cultures persisted and today are thriving.

Traditional definitions of the Southwest as a culture area have depended on trait lists. As L.S. Cordell (1984) has remarked, the region is known by what was present (crops such as maize, beans, squash, and cotton; an array of farming methods, including canal irrigation; plain, textured, and painted pottery; villages; and small-scale but specialized structures for social or ceremonial functions) and what was absent (urban states like those of southern Mexico). But there is a limitation to the trait-list approach: No single culture or period within the Southwest displays all of these features.

The basic Southwest-culture pattern was derived from existing cultures in southern Mexico, but did Mesoamerica intervene in the Southwest or was the contribution made indirectly through diffusion of traits? The question has engendered a long and noisy debate. A.V. Kidder, for example, argued that Mesoamerica provided little more than the "germs" of Southwestern culture; 50 years later, Di Peso described the entire prehistory of the Southwest as a response to specific events in Mesoamerica. Today, most Southwesternists follow Kidder's decades-old formula; a few, led by J. Charles Kelley, argue for a moderate degree of direct interaction.

To move beyond such debates, one must eschew the trait-list approach and perceive the Southwest in terms of cultural-evolutionary processes at the continental level. Prior to 1000 B.C. (2950 years B.P.), all of arid North America was occupied by Archaic foragers, who moved seasonally to exploit wild plant and animal foods; in the next 20 centuries, some of these foragers transformed themselves by adopting farming in increasingly intensive forms, by settling in permanent villages, and by creating social networks focused on small-scale regional centers. In the same broad span of years, other cultures became involved only marginally or temporarily in the same processes, and still others never gave up their dependence on nomadic foraging.

From this perspective, it is not the cultural unity of the region that matters, but its diversity, the unevenness with which basic "traits" were adopted or maintained. The goal of Southwest archaeology is to describe and explain this diversity. Viewed in terms of prehistoric processes, the Southwest ceases to be a bounded area of independent cultures with shared attributes. It becomes a single complicated interplay of cultural and natural history on the vast stage of arid North America. In this sense,

the study of Southwest archaeology is just beginning.

David A. Phillips, Jr.

Further Readings

Cordell, L.S. 1984. *Prehistory of the Southwest.* Academic Press, San Diego.

Cordell, L.S., and G.J. Gumerman. 1992. *Dynamics of Southwest Prehistory.* Smithsonian Institution Press, Washington, D.C.

Phillips, D.A., Jr. 1989. Prehistory of Chihuahua and Sonora, Mexico. *Journal of World Prehistory* 3:373–401.

Wilcox, D.R. 1986. A Historical Analysis of the Problems of Southwest-Mesoamerican Connections. In *Ripples in the Chichimec Sea: New Considerations of Southwest-Mesoamerican Interactions*, edited by F.J. Mathien and R.H. McGuire, pp. 9–44. Southern Illinois University Press, Carbondale.

Woodbury, R.B. 1979. Prehistory: Introduction. In *Southwest*, edited by A. Ortiz, pp. 22–30. Handbook of North American Indians, vol. 9, W.C. Sturtevant, general editor. Smithsonian Institution, Washington, D.C.

Southwestern Archaic

Despite the fact that it constitutes ca. 75 percent of the known span of human occupation in the Southwest, the Archaic period remains the least understood portion of the archaeological record for most of the region. Limited research has resulted in problems in definition, cultural taxonomy, terminology, and chronometry. There is general agreement about what constitutes the material and temporal core of the Archaic period, but continuing disagreement about how to differentiate it from the preceding Paleoindian period (ca. 9550–6550 B.C., or 11,500–8500 years B.P.) and how to mark its termination. In the broadest sense, the Archaic is that period of time when the Southwest was inhabited by small, highly mobile social groups that moved through different biotic communities in an annual cycle to take advantage of seasonally available plant and animal resources. It postdates the extinction of the late Pleistocene (ca. 9050–8050 B.C., or 11,000–10,000 years B.P.) megafauna, except for bison, and, depending upon the source, terminates with the appearance of either agriculture or ceramics. Ground-stone seed-milling equipment (manos and metates) and small atlatl-dart projectile points are hallmarks of the period. If one employs these criteria, the temporal limits of the Archaic vary subregionally across the Southwest. In general, however, ground-stone seed-milling tools are present by 6550–6050 B.C. (8500–8000 years B.P.), and perhaps as much as 2,000 years earlier. The period ends in most areas of the Southwest at ca. A.D. 150–450 (1800–1500 years B.P.), if the arrival of pottery is used to define its termination, or at ca. 1250–550 B.C. (3200–2500 years B.P.), if the arrival of agriculture is used.

History of Research

Recognition of the existence of preceramic Southwestern cultures dates to the late nineteenth and early twentieth centuries, when burials and large storage cists containing basketry, maize and other cultigens, atlatls, spear points, wooden tools, and other nonceramic artifacts were discovered stratigraphically below Puebloan deposits in the rock shelters of southeastern Utah and northeastern Arizona. By 1927, these remains were formally recognized as Basketmaker II. On theoretical grounds alone, Basketmaker I, anticipated to be an earlier, preagricultural, hunting-gathering manifestation, was named but not defined. Also in 1927, artifacts found in association or apparent association with late Pleistocene megafauna at Folsom in northeastern New Mexico and at Double Adobe in southeastern Arizona demonstrated a potential several-thousand-year time depth for the preceramic period of Southwestern prehistory.

Subregional Archaic Complexes. The decades between 1930 and 1970 witnessed the discovery of numerous surficial, buried, and stratified preceramic sites in all parts of the Southwest and surrounding regions. Surface collection was the investigative technique for many of these sites, but some excavation was done in rock shelters and at sites buried in alluvial or aeolian deposits. Relative chronologies were constructed from stratified sites, and, in some cases, the associated fauna or depositional contexts could provide rough temporal estimates. With the advent of radiocarbon dating in the 1950s, more precise dating became possible. In the absence of pottery, variability in projectile-point morphology (and, to a lesser degree, other stone implements) came to be used for diagnosing cultural and temporal affinity. Among the first to be recognized

in the 1930s and 1940s were the Pinto, San Jose, Gypsum, and Amargosa complexes; each was characterized by a diagnostic point style. Because the work was done at a subregional level and because there was little comparative information or chronometry available, a bewildering array of "cultures" and "complexes" had been identified by 1960. Encompassing considerable variation in geographic and temporal scale, many of these complexes have been subsumed by later, more inclusive cultural taxonomies. Principal among the latter was the Cochise culture, defined in southern Arizona but employed over much of the southern and central Southwest, including northern Sonora (Sayles and Antevs 1941; Sayles 1983). In the northern Southwest, Cynthia Irwin-Williams (1973) proposed the Oshara tradition to designate the post-Paleoindian, pre-Anasazi cultural manifestation. The Chihuahua tradition has been defined recently (MacNeish 1993) to describe Archaic materials in southeastern New Mexico and northern Chihuahua. The degree to which any of these subregional cultures or traditions can be distinguished from one another, or where the boundaries for a given tradition may lie, continue to be problematic.

A Regional View of the Archaic. Beginning in the late 1960s, perspectives began to shift toward a broader, regional assessment of similarities that united many of these preceramic manifestations. In fact, use of the term "Archaic" began in the Southwest only in the 1960s (Irwin-Williams 1968). The Picosa concept (Irwin-Williams 1967) was the first attempt to view the region as a whole, and as distinct from the pan-Western Desert culture, and was based on perceived similarities in projectile-point styles and other attributes across much of the Southwestern region beginning at ca. 3050 B.C. (5000 years B.P.) and lasting until 1050 B.C. (3000 years B.P.). More recently, "Southwestern Archaic" has been proposed as a loose organizing concept to attempt to integrate what appear to be approximately synchronous assemblages of artifacts and changes in subsistence-related technologies over most of the Southwest. At least four schemes for temporal division of the Southwestern Archaic have been proposed (Irwin-Williams 1979; Huckell 1984; Berry and Berry 1986; Matson 1991). Nevertheless, subregional cultural entities, such as the Cochise culture and the Oshara tradition, continue to be used in different parts of the Southwest. Today, Southwest archaeologists recognize regional similarities among Archaic artifact assemblages, even as many continue to define and employ subregional "cultures" of far more limited areal extent. (For related illustrative materials see section entitled "Entries by Culture Area and Topical Category" starting on page xxix of the front matter of this encyclopedia.) The following sections briefly sketch what is known of the Southwestern Archaic, using a three-part Early, Middle, Late division.

The Early Archaic Period

Without question, the Early Archaic period is the least-known portion of the Southwestern Archaic. Confusion over what is Early Archaic has developed from different usage of the term by workers in various parts of the Southwest.

In the southern portion of the Southwest, the Sulphur Spring stage of the Cochise culture represents the Early Archaic. It was first identified from deeply buried alluvial sites in southeastern Arizona that yielded simple slab metates and oval cobble manos, along with simple unifacial and bifacial flaked implements. Radiocarbon dates place its inception between ca. 7050 and 6050 B.C. (9000–8000 years B.P.), and perhaps as early as 8550 B.C. (10,500 years B.P.). Early claims for the association of this cultural manifestation with extinct Pleistocene fauna have not been substantiated. No convincing projectile points have been found in securely dated sites, although a long, tapering-stemmed point similar to the Lake Mohave, Jay, or Great Basin Stemmed series may be expected. A slightly younger Cazador stage with projectile points was proposed (Sayles 1983) but has been rejected on geoarchaeological grounds (Waters 1986).

In the northern Southwest, the Jay phase of the Oshara tradition begins at least 6050–5550 B.C. (8000–7500 years B.P.) in northeastern New Mexico and part or all of northeastern Arizona. It is characterized by a long, tapering-stemmed point and a variety of unifacial and bifacial retouched tools. Simple ground-stone milling equipment appears to be present.

Recent work (Matson 1991) in the eastern Great Basin and northern Colorado Plateau has suggested that the Early Archaic there may be represented by Pinto points, Elko Side-Notched points, and Elko Corner-Notched points. Points of these types, along with ground-stone milling

equipment, have been found in rock shelters in eastern Utah associated with radiocarbon dates in the 6050–4050 B.C. (8000–6000 years B.P.) range.

In southeastern New Mexico and northwestern Chihuahua, the Early Archaic period may be represented by the Gardner Springs phase of the Chihuahua tradition. Dated between 6050 and 4050 B.C. (8000–6000 years B.P.), this phase contains stemmed points as well as ground-stone milling equipment. An industry apparently lacking ground-stone implements, San Dieguito, has been defined in southern California, western Arizona, and northwestern Sonora (Warren 1984). Large unifaces, scrapers, and bifaces are typical implements, and long, tapering-stemmed points of the Western Pluvial Lakes tradition of the Great Basin may also be included. It is often considered Paleoindian, but persists until perhaps 5050 B.C. (7000 years B.P.), well into what is the Archaic period for the rest of the Southwest.

Early Holocene climate was cooler and wetter than today, with greater winter precipitation. After ca. 7050 B.C. (9000 years B.P.), the climate shifted toward hotter summers and increasing summer precipitation. Southwestern plant communities of the time differed markedly from those of today and doubtless so did Early Archaic patterns of subsistence. Little is known of Early Archaic–period adaptive strategies or patterns of seasonal movement. A diversified hunting-gathering subsistence base seems probable, and Early Archaic point styles have been recovered from a broad range of elevations encompassing different environmental zones. This suggests seasonal population movements to exploit plant and animal resources occurring in distinctive communities along elevational and physiographic gradients. Geographic scales of mobility, group size and organization, and other aspects of Early Archaic life remain poorly known.

The Middle Archaic Period

The inception of the Middle Archaic period has been placed by different workers as early as 4850 B.C. (6800 years B.P.) or as late as 2850 B.C. (4800 years B.P.). Assignment of dates is dependent upon which stages or phases of which cultural traditions are included in a given definition. As shown, the period between 5050 B.C. and 1550 B.C. (7000 and 3500 years B.P.) does contain several distinctive projectile-point styles that may serve as diagnostic markers.

In the southern Southwest, the Chiricahua stage of the Cochise culture represents some or all of this period. A side-notched, concave-base point style (Chiricahua) was thought typical, but it is now known that straight-stemmed Pinto; slightly flaring-stemmed San Jose points; short, contracting-stemmed Gypsum points; and lanceolate or triangular concave-based Humboldt or Cortaro points are also present. Basin metates appear for the first time during the Chiricahua stage.

In the northern Southwest, the Bajada, San Jose, and part of the Armijo phases of the Oshara tradition represent the Middle Archaic period. Associated projectile-point styles are generally the same forms as those listed for the southern Southwest, although the side-notched, concave-base, and short, contracting-stemmed forms may be less frequent. Again, the northern Colorado Plateau may differ from the Oshara tradition, with points of the Elko series and side-notched, concave-base styles being more common.

It is noteworthy that Pinto, San Jose, and various side-notched points occur throughout the Southwestern region during this period. Recognition of this distribution led to the definition of the "Picosa" (an acronym of *Pi*nto, *Co*chise, and *Sa*n Jose) culture concept, a "continuum of closely related cultures" found across the Southwest after 3050 B.C. (5000 years B.P.) and continuing until perhaps 1050 B.C. (3000 years B.P.) (Irwin-Williams 1967).

The Middle Archaic period encompasses much of the climatically dynamic middle Holocene, including the Altithermal period between ca. 5550 B.C. (7500 years B.P.) and the onset of essentially modern climatic conditions after 2050 B.C. (4000 years B.P.). Altithermal climate may have varied from extremes of hot, dry to hot, wet summers, with cold, comparatively dry winters. Middle Holocene plant communities may have been compositionally similar to modern ones, but different in their elevational and spatial distributions. It is probably useful to conceive of the Middle Archaic period as encompassing a considerable range of land-use strategies that changed, perhaps frequently, with middle Holocene environmental conditions. Some areas of the Southwest may have been abandoned during parts of the period, and boundaries of foraging ranges between different cultural groups (as marked by point styles) may have shifted with environmental changes within and outside the Southwestern region. The variety of point styles found during this period may document such movements. It is during the Middle Archaic period that simple pole-and-brush and wattle-and-daub structures first appear in several parts of the region, suggesting greater settlement permanence, at least on a seasonal basis. Judging from projectile-point distributions and data from obsidian sourcing studies, the scale of mobility and/or interaction between subregions was great. It was formerly believed that agriculture appeared in the Southwest during the later part of this period, but recent work has not supported this idea (Wills 1988).

The Late Archaic Period

The Late Archaic period begins ca. 1550–1050 B.C. (3500–3000 years B.P.), after the establishment of essentially modern climatic and biotic conditions. Problems of definition also cloud the Late Archaic picture. In the northern Southwest, this period includes the earliest phase of the Anasazi culture, Basketmaker II, which, although preceramic, is not classified as Archaic by most workers. However, in the southern Southwest, the San Pedro stage of the Cochise culture is considered Late Archaic, although it is largely coeval with Basketmaker II. Further complicating the problem is the fact that agriculture appears to have arrived in the Southwest ca. 1250–850 B.C. (3200–2800 years B.P.), and apparently rapidly became an important aspect of the subsistence strategy over much, but not all, of the region. Thus, the question remains whether the Archaic period should end with the adoption of agriculture, or the adoption of ceramics, or when continuity can be recognized with the later ceramic-producing tradition of a particular subregion.

The San Pedro stage of the Cochise culture and Basketmaker II represent a similar cultural pattern over much of the Southwest and share a basic side- to corner-notched point style. Basin metates are common, as are manos shaped to a circular form. However, in one scheme for the northern Colorado Plateau, short, contracting-stemmed Gypsum points are viewed as Late Archaic, and, in the Oshara tradition, the later part of the Armijo phase, with its stemmed, serrated points, falls into the Late Archaic (Matson 1991). In southeastern

New Mexico, the Late Archaic includes the later portions of the Fresnal phase of the Chihuahua tradition, which has points similar to both of the above, along with corner-notched points. The subsequent Hueco phase of this tradition also falls within the Late Archaic.

As noted above, agriculture is incorporated into the subsistence strategy to varying degrees, and at different times, in different portions of the Southwest. In both the southern and the northern Southwest, San Pedro and Basketmaker II communities with pithouses, large bell-shaped storage pits, burials, and well-developed cultural deposits with high artifact densities are known by 850–450 B.C. (2800–2400 years B.P.). Such communities bespeak greatly reduced residential mobility in comparison to the Middle Archaic, and they are often located close to high-quality arable land. Hunting and gathering remained an important part of Late Archaic subsistence, and it is possible that some form of seasonal mobility to obtain plant and animal resources continued to be a primary economic pattern. Agriculture did not become important in the area of the Chihuahua tradition, despite the fact that it apparently was adopted very early there, nor did it appear in the eastern third of New Mexico and western third of Arizona until the early centuries A.D. This compounds the definitional problems discussed above, for it is probable that, in these areas, the "Archaic" period (in the sense of a hunting-gathering adaptation) persists long after A.D. 450 (1500 years B.P.).

Bruce B. Huckell

Further Readings

Berry, M., and C.S. Berry. 1986. Chronological and Conceptual Models of the Southwestern Archaic. In *Anthropology of the Desert West: Essays in Honor of Jesse D. Jennings,* edited by C.J. Condie and D.D. Fowler, pp. 253–327. Anthropological Papers no. 11. University of Utah Press, Salt Lake City.

Bryan, K., and J.H. Toulouse, Jr. 1943. The San Jose Non-Ceramic Culture and Its Relation to a Puebloan Culture in New Mexico. *American Antiquity* 8:269–280.

Campbell, E.W.C., and W.H. Campbell. 1935. *The Pinto Basin Site*. Papers no. 9. Southwest Museum, Los Angeles.

Campbell, J.M., and F.H. Ellis. 1952. The Atrisco Sites: Cochise Manifestations in the Middle Rio Grande Valley. *American Antiquity* 17:211–221.

Fay, G.E. 1967. *An Archaeological Study of the Peralta Complex in Sonora, Mexico.* Occasional Papers in Anthropology, Archaeology Series no. 1. Museum of Anthropology, Colorado State College, Greeley.

Harrington, M.R. 1933. *Gypsum Cave, Nevada*. Papers no. 8. Southwest Museum, Los Angeles.

Huckell, B.B. 1984. *The Archaic Occupation of the Rosemont Area, Northern Santa Rita Mountains, Southeastern Arizona.* Archaeological Series no. 147, vol. 1. Arizona State Museum, University of Arizona, Tucson.

Hunt, A.P., and D. Tanner. 1960. Early Man Sites Near Moab, Utah. *American Antiquity* 26:110–117.

Irwin-Williams, C. 1967. Picosa: The Elementary Southwestern Culture. *American Antiquity* 32:441–457.

———. 1968. The Reconstruction of Archaic Culture in the Southwestern United States. In *Early Man in Western North America,* edited by C. Irwin-Williams, pp. 48–54. Contributions in Anthropology, vol. 5, no. 1. Eastern New Mexico University, Portales.

———. 1973. *The Oshara Tradition: Origins of Anasazi Culture.* Contributions in Anthropology, vol. 5, no. 1. Eastern New Mexico University Paleo Indian Institute, Portales.

———. 1979. Post-Pleistocene Archeology, 7000–2000 B.C. In *Southwest,* edited by A. Ortiz. Handbook of North American Indians, vol. 9, W.C. Sturtevant, general editor. Smithsonian Institution, Washington, D.C.

Jennings, J.D. 1957. *Danger Cave.* Anthropological Papers no. 27. University of Utah Press, Salt Lake City.

MacNeish, R.S. 1989. *Defining the Archaic Chihuahua Tradition.* Annual Report of the Andover Foundation for Archaeological Research, Andover.

———. (editor). 1993. *Preliminary Investigations of the Archaic in the Region of Las Cruces, New Mexico.* Historic and Natural Resources Report no. 9. Cultural Resources Management Program, Directorate of the Environment, U.S. Army Air Defense Artillery Center, Fort Bliss.

Matson, R.G. 1991. *The Origins of South-*

western *Agriculture*. University of Arizona Press, Tucson.

Renaud, E.B. 1942. *Reconnaissance in the Upper Rio Grande Valley of Colorado and Northern New Mexico*. Publications in Anthropology for 1942. University of Denver, Denver.

Rogers, M.J. 1939. *Early Lithic Industries of the Lower Basin of the Colorado River and Adjacent Desert Areas*. Papers no. 3. San Diego Museum of Man, San Diego.

———. 1966. *Ancient Hunters of the Far West*. Union-Tribune Publishing, San Diego.

Sample, L.L., and A. Mohr. 1960. Some Preceramic Sites Near Farmington, New Mexico. *Masterkey* 34:138–146.

Sayles, E.B. 1983. *The Cochise Cultural Sequence in Southeastern Arizona*. Anthropological Papers no. 42. University of Arizona Press, Tucson.

Sayles, E.B., and E. Antevs. 1941. *The Cochise Culture*. Medallion Paper no. 29. Gila Pueblo, Globe.

Warren, C.N. 1984. The Desert Region. In *California Archaeology*, edited by M.J. Morrato, pp. 339–430. Academic Press, San Diego.

Waters, M.R. 1986. *The Geoarchaeology of Whitewater Draw, Arizona*. Anthropological Papers no. 45. University of Arizona Press, Tucson.

Wendorf, F., and T.H. Thomas. 1951. Early Man Sites Near Concho, Arizona. *American Antiquity* 17:107–114.

Wills, W.H. 1988. *Early Prehistoric Agriculture in the American Southwest*. School of American Research Press, Santa Fe.

Spence River Phase

Spence River is a Late Prehistoric cultural phase embracing the upper and middle Mackenzie River Valley in the western Subarctic zone of the Canadian Northwest Territories, an area that historically, and at present, was the home of Dene speakers of the Slavey-Hare language (or dialect continuum). It is likely that the Spence River phase represents the culture of their precontact ancestors. Material remains are usually sparse and unremarkable, a characteristic of Subarctic archaeology in general. Stratigraphically, the Spence River phase is found above the White River volcanic ash, which is dated to ca. A.D. 700 (1250 years B.P.), and persisted until the end of the precontact period at ca. A.D. 1800 (150 years B.P.). By this time, microblades appear to have gone out of use in the Mackenzie Valley. Most sites include lithic projectile points strongly reminiscent of contemporaneous points from the northern Plains. The relative narrowness of the hafting element on these points suggests the diffusion of bow-and-arrow technology from the south at this time.

David Morrison

Further Readings

Morrison, D. 1984. The Late Prehistoric Period in the Mackenzie Valley. *Arctic* 37:195–209.

Spier, Leslie (1893–1961)

Leslie Spier was a student of Franz Boas at Columbia University; Spier's two major contributions to archaeology occurred early in his career in the 1910s and involved the application of statistical methods. One of those (Spier 1918) applied probability theory to intradeposit distributions of paleoliths in Trenton, New Jersey, gravels to demonstrate that they were deposited by geologic processes and, therefore, a previously reported "argillite culture" did not exist. His other, now better-known, contribution (Spier 1917) was the testing and refinement of a frequency seriation approach to chronological ordering initiated in the Southwest by A.L. Kroeber in 1915. Kroeber (1916) had collected pottery sherds from the surface of a site in the Zuni region, then divided them into types and compared type frequencies to develop a historical sequence. The method is based on the assumption that cultural objects closer together in a temporal series will be more similar than more widely separated objects in the series. Spier tested the validity of this relative dating method by seriating collections of pottery he had gathered from the surface of a large number of Zuni sites and then comparing the sequence with one he had constructed through stratigraphic excavations. His analysis, which was presented in the form of tables and frequency graphs, demonstrated that seriation and stratigraphy produced comparable results, a conclusion that greatly influenced the practice of culture history. He may have been the first American archaeologist to use the term "seriation." Spier soon turned from archaeology to other anthropological pursuits, perhaps, as W.W. Taylor (1963) suggested, because he became disenchanted with culture-historical reconstruction as practiced at the time.

Guy Gibbon

Further Readings

Kroeber, A.L. 1916. Zuñi Potsherds. *Anthropological Papers of the American Museum of Natural History* 18(1):7–37.

Spier, L. 1917. *An Outline for a Chronology of Zuñi Ruins.* Anthropological Papers, vol. 18, no. 3. American Museum of Natural History, New York.

———. 1918. The Trenton Argillite Culture. *Anthropological Papers of the American Museum of Natural History* 22(4):167–226.

———. 1931. N.C. Nelson's Stratigraphic Technique in the Reconstruction of Prehistoric Sequences in Southwestern America. In *Methods in Social Science,* edited by S.A. Rice, pp. 275–283. University of Chicago Press, Chicago.

Taylor, W.W. 1963. Leslie Spier, 1893–1961. *American Antiquity* 28:379–381.

See also ABBOTT, CHARLES C.; PALEOLITH

Spiro

Spiro (34LS46) is the premier Late Prehistoric Caddoan Area Mississippian civic-ceremonial center. Located in LeFlore County in eastern Oklahoma and dating to ca. A.D. 1000–1350/1400 (950–600/550 years B.P.), Spiro consists of two sections, a village site covering ca. 10 ha (25 acres) of a terrace in the Arkansas River Valley and a bordering upland mound "enclosure" that covers ca. 20 ha (50 acres). A number of components are present, but the most prominent are associated with the Caddoan Harlan (ca. A.D. 1000–1200/1250, or 950–750/700 years B.P.) and Spiro (ca. A.D. 1200/1250–1350/1400, or 750/700–600/550 years B.P.) phases. During the Harlan phase, a circular arrangement of low conical mounds and two platform mounds, the largest of which is called the Brown Mound, were constructed on the upland section of the site. The examined conical mounds covered the foundations of what have been interpreted as mortuary facilities for processing and storing the dead before final interment. It seems likely that the largely empty central "enclosure" formed by the mounds was used for ceremonial purposes. The village was occupied at this time on the terrace below.

During the subsequent Spiro phase, the site became the premier Caddoan center when a new mound type was constructed in the Spiro village area. Called the Craig Mound, this new mortuary-structure complex, which combined aspects of both mortuary and platform mounds, may have served as the ancestral shrine of the regional elite. The mound actually grew in stages, with its first phases consisting of a simple conical accretional burial mound in which burials were placed between large sheets of cedar bark. This Great Mortuary contained one of the richest and best preserved assemblages of material from the Southeastern Ceremonial complex known. Several phases of pyramidal mound construction followed, with the last combining features of mortuary and platform mounds.

The location of Spiro in the middle of the most productive and environmentally stable portion of the agricultural landscape in the region further attests to its singular significance within the Caddoan system.

Guy Gibbon

Further Readings

Brown, J.A. 1966. *Spiro Studies: 1. Description of the Mound Group.* University of Oklahoma Research Institute, Norman.

———. 1971a. The Dimensions of Status in the Burials at Spiro. In *Approaches to the Social Dimensions of Mortuary Practices,* edited by J.A. Brown, pp. 92–112. Memoir no. 25. Society for American Archaeology, Washington, D.C.

———. 1971b. *Spiro Studies: 3. Pottery Vessels.* University of Oklahoma Research Institute, Norman.

———. 1975. Spiro Art and Its Mortuary Contexts. In *Death and the Afterlife in Pre-Columbian America,* edited by E.P. Benson, pp. 1–32. Dumbarton Oaks Research Library and Collections, Washington, D.C.

———. 1976. *Spiro Studies: 4. The Artifacts.* Stovall Museum of Science and History, Norman.

Brown, J.A., R.E. Bell, and D.G. Wyckoff. 1978. Caddoan Settlement Patterns in the Arkansas River Drainage. In *Mississippian Settlement Patterns,* edited by B.D. Smith, pp. 169–200. Academic Press, New York.

Hamilton, H.W., J.T. Hamilton, and E.F. Chapman. 1974. *Spiro Mound Copper.*

Missouri Archaeological Society, Columbia.

Orr, K.G. 1946. The Archaeological Situation at Spiro, Oklahoma: A Preliminary Report. *American Antiquity* 11:228–256.

Phillips, P., and J.A. Brown, with E. McFadden, B.C. Page, and J.P. Brain. 1975–1982. *Pre-Columbian Shell Engravings: From the Craig Mound at Spiro, Oklahoma.* Peabody Museum of American Archaeology and Ethnology, Harvard University, Cambridge.

See also CADDOAN AREA MISSISSIPPIAN; SOUTHEASTERN CEREMONIAL COMPLEX

Spud

The spud, or "spatulate celt," is a large object with a long stem that expands or flares out at one end. That end can be bulbous, shovel shaped, or occasionally barbed. Spuds are always ground and polished. They were made from a variety of rocks, including igneous stones, cannel coal, slate, and chert. They have been found most frequently in burial contexts. Because of their lack of use-wear, they have been considered ritual objects, most specifically war clubs. The distribution of the spud includes the American Southeast and the southern Midwest. This distribution centers on the Tennessee-Cumberland valleys, a region that provided suitable stone and within which a large number of spuds have been unearthed. They have been discovered at large centers such as Cahokia in Illinois and Spiro in Oklahoma. Spuds are found exclusively in a Late Prehistoric context, estimated at A.D. 1100–1350 (850–600 years B.P.).

George H. Odell

Further Readings

Moorehead, W.K. 1910. *The Stone Age in North America.* Houghton Mifflin, Boston.

Pauketat, T.R. 1983. A Long-Stemmed Spud From the American Bottom. *Midcontinental Journal of Archaeology* 8:1–15.

Squash

Squash are the fleshy fruit of various species of cultivated *Cucurbita* (family Cucurbitaceae) eaten as a vegetable; the term is derived from the Narragansett word *askutasquash*. Other related terms include summer squash (fruit eaten while immature), winter squash (fruit eaten mature and easily stored whole or sliced and dried), pumpkin (large, orange, coarse-textured squash used when mature), marrow (large, elongate, smooth-skinned summer squash such as zucchini), and gourds (taxa with inedible hard-shelled fruits). In addition to the fruit, the flowers and the seeds may also be eaten, including those of gourds with bitter, inedible flesh. The seeds have often been used as a vermifuge. The fruit of gourds and hard-shelled edible squash can be used as containers such as water bottles, rattles, and fishnet floats.

The genus *Cucurbita* is native to the New World and includes about 20 species. Of these, five species were domesticated prehistorically and, along with bottle gourd, are among the oldest cultivated plants of the New World. Most of the domesticated species involve complexes of domesticated and feral forms and wild populations. The antiquity of these forms and the sometimes contradictory nature of archaeological, morphological, and chemical data often make it difficult to precisely reconstruct areas of either origin or ancestry. Three of the five domesticated species occurred prehistorically in North America. The most familiar of these in the United States is *Cucurbita pepo* L., a diverse species that includes the forms known as scallop or patty-pan, acorn, pumpkin, zucchini, yellow crookneck and yellow straightneck, and yellow-flowered or egg gourds. Of these, pumpkins and some forms of yellow-flowered gourds evolved in Mexico, while other gourds and squash were apparently developed through selection by the prehistoric inhabitants of what is now the United States. *C. pepo* remains have been recovered from Mexican sites dating to more than 8050 B.C. (10,000 years B.P.) and demonstrate that this was one of the first plants domesticated in Mexico. Although the earliest archaeological record of *C. pepo* from the United States may be that of *Cucurbita* rind dating to only 5050 B.C. (7000 years B.P.), *pepo* seeds have also been recovered from precultural deposits in a Florida sinkhole site dating to 12,050–8050 B.C. (14,000–10,000 years B.P.). Potential wild ancestors include *C. texana* of the southern United States and *C. fraterna* of Mexico.

The cushaw squash (*C. argyrosperma* Huber, formerly *C. mixta* Pang.) was apparently derived from wild *C. sororia* L.H. Bailey of Mexico and Central America. It first appears ca. 5250 B.C. (7200 years B.P.) in sites in the Tehuacan Valley of Mexico and gave rise to several distinctive varieties. One of these, the "green striped cushaw" (var. *callicarpa*), spread into northwestern Mexico and the southwestern United States by ca. A.D. 330 (1620 years B.P.). Cushaws reached the southeastern United States at least 100–200 years prior to European contact in ca. A.D. 1500 (450 years B.P.). The butternut squash and Kentucky field pumpkin represent a species (*C. moschata* Poir.) now commonly grown in the West Indies and in lowland Central and lowland tropical South America. This species was cultivated in Peru ca. 3050 B.C. (5000 years B.P.) and reached Mexico ca. 1450 B.C. (3400 years B.P.). It was cultivated on a limited basis in the American Southwest by ca. 1050 B.C. (900 years B.P.). The bottle gourd (*Lagenaria siceraria* [Mol.] Standl.) is another ancient domesticated cucurbit. It was present in Peru by 11,050 B.C. (13,000 years B.P.), in Mexico by 7050 B.C. (9000 years B.P.), and in Florida by 5340 B.C. (7290 years B.P.). The bottle gourd is thought to be indigenous to Africa, and there has been considerable speculation about whether the Peruvian material represents natural or human dispersal to South America. The okeechobee gourd (*Cucurbita okeechobeensis* L.H. Bailey) has a limited distribution in the Lake Okeechobee, Florida, region. Recently, it has been shown to be virtually identical to *C. martinezii* L.H. Bailey from the east coast of Mexico, suggesting a historic or prehistoric introduction into Florida for which there is currently no archaeological evidence. The buffalo gourd (*C. foetidissima* HBK) is common in archaeological contexts in the American Southwest, where the seeds and root may have been used for food.

Frances B. King

Further Readings

Bates, D.M., R.W. Robinson, and C. Jeffrey (editors). 1990. *Biology and Utilization of the Cucurbitaceae.* Cornell University Press, Ithaca.

Decker-Walters, D.S. 1990. Evidence for Multiple Domestications of *Cucurbita pepo*. In *Biology and Utilization of the Cucurbitaceae,* edited by D.M. Bates, R.W. Robinson, and C. Jeffrey, pp. 96–101. Cornell University Press, Ithaca.

Doran, G.H., D.N. Dickel, and L.A. Newsom. 1990. A 7,290-Year-Old Bottle Gourd From the Windover Site, Florida. *American Antiquity* 55:354–360.

Fritz, G. 1986. *Prehistoric Ozark Agriculture: The University of Arkansas Rockshelter Collections.* Unpublished Ph.D. dissertation, Department of Anthropology, University of North Carolina, Chapel Hill.

Heiser, C.B., Jr. 1979. *The Gourd Book.* University of Oklahoma Press, Norman.

———. 1989. Domestication of Cucurbitaceae: *Cucurbita* and *Lagenaria.* In *Foraging and Farming: The Evolution of Plant Exploitation,* edited by D.R. Harris and G.C. Hillman, pp. 471–480. Unwin Hyman, London.

Merrick, L.C. 1990. Systematics and Evolution of a Domesticated Squash, *Cucurbita argyrosperma,* and Its Wild and Weedy Relatives. In *Biology and Utilization of the Cucurbitaceae,* edited by D.M. Bates, R.W. Robinson, and C. Jeffrey, pp. 77–95. Cornell University Press, Ithaca.

Smith, B. 1987. The Independent Domestication of Indigenous Seed-Bearing Plants in Eastern North America. In *Emergent Horticultural Economies of the Eastern Woodlands,* edited by W.F. Keegan. Occasional Paper no. 7. Center for Archaeological Investigations, Southern Illinois University, Carbondale.

Squier, Ephraim G. (1821–1888)

A Chillicothe newspaper editor, E.G. Squier was commissioned by the American Ethnological Society in 1845 to report on the earthworks in Ohio. With E.H. Davis, he opened more than 200 mounds and surveyed many more in a two-year period. Their joint report (Squier and Davis 1848) was one of the first scientific monographs of the newly founded Smithsonian Institution and an early exemplar of scientific, descriptive archaeology. They accurately mapped a large number of mounds, organized the earthworks they examined into general functional classes, measured and described stratigraphic levels within the mounds they excavated, and synthesized the survey data of other investigators. They proposed explicit hypotheses concerning the uses of earthworks and lines of investigation to test these hypotheses, recognized intrusive burials, and organized artifacts for description by type of material, among other accomplishments. The overall scientific tone of the manuscript was due, however, to heavy editing by Joseph Henry, secretary of the Smithsonian, for Squier and Davis supported the "Mound Builder myth," believing that American Indians and their ancestors were incapable of erecting the mounds. They thought the mounds of southern Ohio indicated the presence of a high civilization whose members had probably migrated to Mexico. Squier defended unilineal evolutionism and the doctrine of psychic unity. He also explored mounds in western New York (1849) because he wanted to learn more about the Mound Builders. Squier later became a diplomat, exploring the archaeological record in Nicaragua and Peru, as he traveled widely throughout Latin America.

Guy Gibbon

Further Readings

Squier, E.G. 1849. *Aboriginal Monuments of New York*. Contributions to Knowledge no. 2. Smithsonian Institution, Washington, D.C. Revised 1851 as *Antiquities of the State of New York*. G.H. Derby, Buffalo.

Squier, E.G., and E.H. Davis. 1848. *Ancient Monuments of the Mississippi Valley*. Contributions to Knowledge no. 1. Smithsonian Institution, Washington, D.C.

Willey, G.R., and J.A. Sabloff. 1980. *A History of American Archaeology*. 2nd ed. W.H. Freeman, San Francisco.

See also DAVIS, EDWIN H.; MOUND BUILDER MYTH

St. Helena Phase

The St. Helena phase (A.D. 1100–1400, or 850–550 years B.P.) is one of the five recognized taxa of the Late Prehistoric Central Plains tradition and may stretch from Dakota County along the Missouri River bluffs to Knox County, Nebraska. Isolated finds also occur on the South Dakota side. St. Helena ceramics and other artifacts from Dakota and Dixon counties are more similar to those in the Nebraska phase than to those in St. Helena type sites in Cedar County, although some northern Nebraska-phase sites closely resemble Cedar County sites. Taxonomic reconsideration of these issues is clearly warranted.

St. Helena houses are small; 70 percent are 27.9–74.3 m² (300–800 square feet) in size. The houses had wattle-and-daub walls and were erected in nearly square housepits dug up to 1 m (3.3 feet) into sterile soil. An entry passage sloped to ground surface from the middle of one wall. Most houses had four roof-support posts arranged around a central fire hearth. Two houses had gabled roofs supported on a midline

ridge pole; fire basins in the latter houses were slightly offset toward the front of the floor as in Middle Missouri–tradition houses.

St. Helena pottery vessels are globular jars with cord-roughened surfaces. Only one "bottle" is known, and bowls occur rarely. Clay pipes and ceramic anthropomorphic and zoomorphic effigies are found. Jars have either collared rims, usually bearing incised decoration; decorated and plain unthickened rims; or a diagnostic "broad-beveled lip" form similar to unthickened rims in cross section but for the exaggerated lip that is treated like a collar for decoration. Chipped-stone tools include side-notched and multiple side-and-base-notched arrow points, unnotched triangular point preforms or knives, drills, narrow and broad ovate and alternately beveled knives, large bifacial chipped celts or quarry blanks, end scrapers, gravers, side scrapers, sandstone and scoria ("clinker") abraders, ground and polished celts, limestone "pebble" and other pipes, red pipestone stemmed pipes, limestone and calcite beads, and hammerstones. Three limestone disk-shaped earspool fragments were originally identified as platform pipes. Two cobble "mauls," one with evidence of a groove, were found at one site. Bone tools include bison-scapula digging and hoeing tools, cleavers and other knives, split proximal deer/pronghorn metapodial awls, ulna awls, eyed needles, deer-mandible corn shellers, shaft wrenches, and bone fishhooks. Antler tools include cylinders, flaking tools, shaft wrenches, bracelets, and bowguards. Mussel-shell beads, pendants, zoomorphic effigy figures, and scrapers occur. A bison-metatarsal flesher with tarsal bones attached and two bison-frontal-bone and horn-core scoops are Middle Missouri–tradition tools, suggesting external contacts. St. Helena–phase subsistence focused on bison, deer, and gardening.

The St. Helena phase, though entirely within the Central Plains tradition, had contact with Middle Missouri–tradition peoples. St. Helena is similar to the Itskari phase and the Initial Coalescent. Some St. Helena peoples were remnants of Itskari-phase populations that had migrated to South Dakota, were defeated and expelled in the fourteenth century, and recolonized in northeast Nebraska. Dixon and Dakota County sites, however, are outgrowths of the Nebraska phase and are largely unrelated to events in Cedar County.

John Ludwickson

Further Readings

Barker, A.W. 1988. *Stylistic Variation and St. Helena Phase Systematics.* Unpublished Master's thesis. Department of Anthropology, Wichita State University, Wichita.

Blakeslee, D.J. (editor). 1988. *St. Helena Archaeology: New Data, Fresh Interpretations.* J and L Reprint, Lincoln.

Cooper, P.L. 1936. Archaeology of Certain Sites in Cedar County, Nebraska. In *Chapters in Nebraska Archaeology,* vol. 1, no. 1, edited by E.H. Bell, pp. 11–145. University of Nebraska, Lincoln.

Frantz, W.F. 1963. *Four Aksarben Sites in Dakota County, Nebraska.* Unpublished Master's thesis. Department of Anthropology, University of Nebraska, Lincoln.

See also CENTRAL PLAINS TRADITION; INITIAL COALESCENT (CAMPBELL CREEK AND/OR ARZBERGER PHASE); NEBRASKA PHASE

St. Johns Tradition

St. Johns tradition is the archaeological name given to the post-Archaic prehistoric and early historic aboriginal way of life in northeast Florida, lasting from ca. 550 B.C. (2500 years B.P.) to the late sixteenth century. The tradition was defined and analyzed by John Goggin, who characterized it as "a pottery using, mound building, semi-sedentary complex probably with agriculture . . . notable neither for its technology and material culture nor for its ceremonial aspects" (1952:68). People of the St. Johns tradition relied heavily on the aquatic resources of the St. Johns River as well as the Atlantic Coast lagoons and estuaries.

The Protohistoric sixteenth-century tribes of the St. Johns tradition, especially the Eastern Timucua, are widely known for their portrayal by the Huguenot artist Jacques LeMoyne, after whose paintings Theodore deBry engraved the famous plates in Volume 2 of his *America* (Lorant 1965). These illustrations of Timucua ceremonies and daily activities, accompanied by LeMoyne's narrative, presented the first European descriptions of North American natives and present a rich, though European, view of the Timucan people before the onset of disease and decline (Swanton 1922).

People of the St. Johns tradition participated in the broad patterns of cultural development evident throughout the eastern United States, but were, at the same time, unusually conservative in maintaining their own distinctive way of life. There is clear evidence of inter-

Historic "borrowing" of shell mounds in northeast Florida, St. Johns River culture area. Many of the roads, especially along the coast, in this part of the state are paved with shell from such mounds. (Courtesy of Division of Historical Resources, Florida Department of State)

Another view of borrowing from northeast Florida shell mounds. (Courtesy of Division of Historical Resources, Florida Department of State)

action with other traditions, especially along the Gulf of Mexico Coast, represented by foreign ceramics and such status goods as platform smoking pipes, ground-stone celts, copper masks, galena, and mica, and traits like burial mounds and temple mounds. Nonetheless, the St. Johns tradition from ca. 550 B.C. (2500 years B.P.) is persistent in its archaeological expressions of subsistence, settlement, technology, and artifact styles for 2,000 years and even continues the basic patterns established as early as the beginning of the fiber-tempered Orange period ca. 2050 B.C. (4000 years B.P.).

Goggin's temporal divisions and chronological markers for the St. Johns tradition have been modified only slightly (Milanich 1994), but his original subareas are no longer much used. Within the 2,000 years of St. Johns–tradition occupation in northeast Florida, Goggin defined two major periods, St. Johns I and St. Johns II, beginning ca. 500 B.C. and A.D. 800 (2550 and 1150 years B.P.), respectively. On the basis of foreign ceramics from other parts of the southeastern United States, the periods were subdivided into St. Johns Ia, early; St. Johns Ia, late; St. Johns Ib; St. Johns IIa, St. Johns IIb, and St. Johns IIc, the latter representing the time of European contact. Assignment of sites to vari-

ous subperiods depends upon rather specific distinctions based on the presence or absence of various pottery types, most of which are quite rare and unlikely to be adequately represented in small collections. Moreover, it is not clear that environmental conditions or adaptations differed significantly from one subperiod to the next.

Throughout the St. Johns I and II periods, reliance on the St. Johns River system for food resources and transportation remains central to the adaptation. People continue to occupy the same kinds of riverbank locations, and the presence of larger and more numerous shell-midden sites attests to the continuing use of freshwater snails, mainly *Viviparous georgianus,* for food. There is no doubt that agriculture was practiced; Spanish and French documents of the mid-sixteenth century recount the reliance of Indians, as well as Europeans, on the annual corn crop. However, direct archaeological evidence of maize agriculture is lacking. Cultivation of domestic plants was likely introduced at the beginning of the St. Johns I period, along with a variety of cultural traits that constitute an associated complex of technology, social organization, and ideology evident throughout the Southeast. During the early part of the St.

Johns I period, this use of plants is characterized as limited horticulture; by the time of European contact, it is recognized as agriculture, but the degree of reliance on agriculture remains unclear (Milanich 1994:268–269). Comparison of the site-distribution patterns of the St. Johns I and II periods shows that the total number of sites is greater in the later period, and that, while riverine and coastal locales remain important, the number of sites in inland environments increases, reflecting the growing importance of crops and possibly a corresponding increase in population (Miller 1991).

The archaeological evidence for social organization during the St. Johns I and II periods— that is, before the time of European accounts— is not direct. Complex social stratification among Eastern Timucua chiefdoms is well documented by European observers in the sixteenth century. In archaeological contexts, it is clear that certain individuals received preferential treatment in terms of burial offerings, and it is assumed that this was a reflection of status. In the earliest part of the St. Johns I period, grave offerings are rare in burial mounds, and it would appear that all people were buried in mounds. After ca. A.D. 100 (1850 years B.P.), the distinctive Hopewellian complex of burial artifacts appears in mounds. For the first time in the archaeological record of the St. Johns region, such foreign materials as galena, mica, copper, quartz, cut animal jaws, earspools, animal effigies, and plummets appear in burial-mound contexts (Milanich and Fairbanks 1980:160–162).

At the beginning of St. Johns II times, ca. A.D. 800 (1150 years B.P.), foreign ceramics of nonutilitarian design are common in burial mounds; mounds become larger; and it appears that only a few individuals are accorded the privilege of mound burial. By St. Johns IIb times, beginning ca. A.D. 1300 (650 years B.P.), the St. Johns tradition incorporates elements of Mississippian culture so common at that time throughout the southeastern United States, although its effect may not have been so pronounced as among Fort Walton people, for example, where reliance on agriculture was more thorough and the accompanying social and ideological elements would have had more adaptive value. This is the cultural manifestation encountered, recorded to some extent, and largely decimated by Europeans in the sixteenth century in Florida. It is represented in northeast Florida by the major ceremonial centers of Shields Mound in Duval County, Mount Royal

in Putnam County, and Thursby Mound in Volusia County, among others. All of the major Mississippian-period mounds in northeast Florida are along the St. Johns River and consist, at least in part, of freshwater shells.

The decline of St. Johns people was rapid. Presuming that the culture recorded by the French and the Spaniards in the 1560s was intact (and not all scholars accept this view), its total collapse took little more than a few generations. In 1579, Governor Marquez of St. Augustine, Florida, reported to the Spanish king his success at reducing the Indian threat by burning villages, food stores, and other supplies (Connor 1930:225). Epidemics began at least with British admiral Sir Francis Drake's raid of St. Augustine in 1586, if not earlier, and in a well-documented example, 50 percent of the recorded Christian population of 16,000 Indians died in the plague of 1613–1617 (Dobyns 1983). By 1650, the Eastern Timucua were severely decimated (Deagan 1978), and the successful adaptation of the St. Johns tradition to the rich lands of northeast Florida had virtually disappeared.

James J. Miller

Further Readings

Connor, J.T. 1930. *Colonial Records of Spanish Florida: 2. 1577–1580.* Publication no. 5. Florida State Historical Society, Deland.

Deagan, K.A. 1978. Cultures in Transition: Fusion and Assimilation Among the Eastern Timucua. In *Tacachale—Essays on the Indians of Florida and Southeast Georgia*, edited by J.T. Milanich and S. Proctor, pp. 89–119. University Presses of Florida, Gainesville.

Dobyns, H.F. 1983. *Their Numbers Become Thinned: Native Population Dynamics in Eastern North America.* University of Tennessee Press, Knoxville.

Goggin, J.M. 1952. *Space and Time Perspective in Northern St. Johns Archeology, Florida.* Publications in Anthropology no. 47. Yale University Press, New Haven.

Lorant, S. 1965. *The New World: The First Pictures of America.* rev. ed. Edited and annotated by S. Lorant. Duell, Sloan, and Pearce, New York.

Milanich, J.T. 1994. *Archaeology of Precolumbian Florida.* University Press of Florida, Gainesville.

Milanich, J.T., and C.H. Fairbanks. 1980. *Florida Archaeology.* Academic Press, New York.

Miller, J.J. 1991. *The Fairest, Frutefullest and Pleasantest of All the World: An Environmental History of the Northeast Part of Florida.* Unpublished Ph.D. dissertation, Graduate Group in City and Regional Planning, University of Pennsylvania, Philadelphia.

Swanton, J.R. 1922. *Early History of the Creek Indians and Their Neighbors.* Bulletin no. 73. Bureau of American Ethnology, Smithsonian Institution, Washington, D.C.

St. Lawrence Island Sites

In 1928, Henry B. Collins of the Smithsonian Institution, Washington, D.C., began archaeological investigations in the St. Lawrence Island area of Alaska in the hope of finding additional artifacts of the Old Bering Sea culture. The culture had been discovered by Diamond Jenness (1928) in 1926 on Little Diomede Island in the Bering Strait. Excavations were initiated east of St. Lawrence Island in a midden site at the southern tip of the northernmost island in the Punuk Island chain. The deep midden contained artifacts incised with straight lines, dots, and circles in an art form that Collins called the Punuk style. It proved to be intermediate between Late Prehistoric and modern artifact types; that is, between Old Bering Sea and St. Lawrence Island Eskimo. Only three Old Bering Sea–style artifacts were recovered from the bottom of the excavation. In the hope of finding a better expression of the Old Bering Sea culture, Collins spent the remainder of the 1928 season and the whole 1929 season at the large midden site of Kiagelak on the southeast tip of St. Lawrence Island. Again, only a few Old Bering Sea artifacts were recovered at the very lowest levels. In 1928 and 1929, he also stopped briefly at the modern village of Gambell on the northwestern tip of the island to determine the area's site potential.

The village of Gambell is located on a forward beach of a gravel spit that extends westward from the rocky headland of Cape Chibukak. A series of beach strands with associated old village sites lay between the village and the cape. In 1927, Otto Geist of the Alaska Agricultural College and School of Mines (now the University of Alaska) had made preliminary excavations at the site of Seklowaghyaget, which was adjacent to the modern village of Gambell; at Ievogiyoq, which was intermediate between Gambell and the cape; and at Miyowagh, an old village at the foot of the cape. At Miyowagh, Punuk-style artifacts were found in the upper levels, and Old Bering Sea–style artifacts with graceful, curvilinear lines were found in the lower levels. Geist returned in 1928 to continue excavations in the vicinity of Gambell and to conduct surveys along the coast. He spent the winter of 1928–1929 at Gambell and, during the following summer, continued testing sites in the area. Initial testing was also begun at the large mound at Kukulik, which was 8 km (5 miles) east of the village of Savoonga along the north shore of the island. Geist concluded that the huge Kukulik mound, while probably containing a full sequence from Old Bering Sea to modern times, would be too expensive to excavate and planned to return to Gambell. He was not able to obtain further research funds until 1931. Meanwhile, Collins had also reached the conclusion that Gambell was the best area to investigate the St. Lawrence Island chronological sequence through beach-ridge dating. Convinced that Geist had decided to work at Kukulik, he began excavating the Gambell sites during the summer of 1930. He concluded his investigations after the field season of 1931.

The Miyowagh site is close to the foot of Cape Chibukak on the most ancient beach, which contained Old Bering Sea and early Punuk (ca. 50 B.C.–A.D. 750, or 2000–1200 years B.P.) artifacts. Still lower was the Ievogiyoq site, which was occupied during the main phase of the Punuk culture. Finally, the site of Seklowaghyaget, which was occupied during the final phases of the Punuk culture and the transition into the Late Prehistoric phase (A.D. 1350–1450, or 600–500 years B.P.) prior to Euro-American contact, was on more recent beaches next to the village of Gambell.

While the sequence determined by the location of sites on beach strands and the changes in harpoon forms and art styles was corroborated, Collins remained unsatisfied with the amount of evidence he had found for the Old Bering Sea culture. He noted that the Miyowagh site had both Punuk and Old Bering Sea artifacts and wondered if the later Punuk people might have disturbed the earlier Old Bering Sea deposits while excavating their houses. In the talus slope back of the Miyowagh site, he uncovered artifacts and two house foundations (the Hillside site) that he judged to belong to a pure phase of the Old Bering Sea culture. The art style was more geometric, with straight lines as opposed to the more curvilinear elements of Old Bering Sea styles 2 and 3 found at the Miyowagh site.

Collin's typology of harpoon types and art styles based upon his investigations of the Gambell sites has provided the framework for the chronological ordering in this region of Eskimo sites dating to 50 B.C.–A.D. 1750 (2000–200 years B.P.). Later radiocarbon dating has verified the temporal sequence. Further refinements came with the discovery of the Okvik site by Geist in 1931 and its excavation in 1934 (the report was published by Rainey in 1941), and by additional excavations at the Hillside site by J.L. Giddings (Rainey 1941; Giddings 1960). The Okvik and Hillside sites were then regarded as cultural expressions of an earlier phase that preceded the Old Bering Sea culture within the Bering Sea prehistoric sequence. Later radiocarbon dates from St. Lawrence Island (Rainey and Ralph 1959; Ralph and Ackerman 1961) and research by Russian archaeologists at prehistoric Eskimo cemeteries on the Chukchi Peninsula (Arutiunov et al. 1964) have suggested that Okvik and the Old Bering Sea cultures were contemporaneous.

Robert E. Ackerman

Further Readings

Ackerman, R.E. 1984. Prehistory of the Asian Eskimo Zone. In *Arctic,* edited by D. Damas, pp. 106–118. Handbook of North American Indians, vol. 5, W.C. Sturtevant, general editor. Smithsonian Institution, Washington, D.C.

Arutiunov, S.A., M.G. Levin, and D.A. Sergeev. 1964. Ancient Cemeteries of the Chukchi Peninsula. *Arctic Anthropology* 2(1): 143–154.

Collins, H.B. 1937. *The Archeology of St. Lawrence Island.* Miscellaneous Collections, vol. 96, no. 1. Smithsonian Institution, Washington, D.C.

Geist, O., and F.G. Rainey. 1936. *Archaeological Excavations at Kukulik, St. Lawrence Island, Alaska.* Miscellaneous Publications of the University of Alaska, vol. 2. GPO, Washington, D.C.

Giddings, J.L. 1960. The Archaeology of Bering Strait. *Current Anthropology* 1(2):121–138.

Jenness, D. 1928. Archaeological Investigations in Bering Strait. *Bulletin* 50:71–80. Annual Report of the National Museum of Canada, 1926. Ottawa.

Rainey, F.G. 1941. Eskimo Prehistory: The Okvik Site on the Punuk Islands. *Anthropological Papers of the American Museum of Natural History* 37(4):413–569.

Rainey, F., and E. Ralph. 1959. Radiocarbon Dating in the Arctic. *American Antiquity* 24(4):365–374.

Ralph, E., and R. Ackerman. 1961. University of Pennsylvania Radiocarbon Dates IV. *Radiocarbon* 3(4):4–14.

Stage

A stage is a segment along a developmental or sometimes an evolutionary trajectory—as compared to a unit of time or period—that can crosscut archaeological cultures, traditions, geographic areas, and time periods. Generally, "stage" denotes a level of technological achievement or sociocultural integration, such as Archaic and chiefdom. Familiar stage schemes are G.R. Willey and P. Phillips's (1958) five developmental stages for the New World (Lithic, Archaic, Formative, Classic, Post-Classic) and E. Service's (1971) band, tribe, chiefdom, state sequence. The concept has the disadvantage of suggesting bounded and discontinuous segments in what often may be smoothly continuous developments.

Guy Gibbon

Further Readings

Service, E. 1971. *Primitive Social Organization: An Evolutionary Perspective.* 2nd ed. Random House, New York.

Willey, G.R., and P. Phillips. 1958. *Method and Theory in American Archaeology.* University of Chicago Press, Chicago.

Stallings Culture

Centered on the Savannah River Valley in South Carolina and Georgia, the Late Archaic Stallings culture was among several southeastern hunter-gatherer societies to experience relatively high levels of cultural complexity. As part of the Shell Mound Archaic, Stallings populations accumulated shellfish remains at sites in the middle Savannah Valley and along the Georgia-Carolina coasts (see Figure). Combined with other evidence for subsistence expansion, technological innovations, and redundant land-use patterns, the sometimes enormous heaps of shell and other refuse at locations such as the type site, Stallings Island (9CB1) (Claflin 1931), indicate a degree of settlement permanence and economic intensity usually reserved for food-producing societies. Processes contributing to the rise and fall of Stallings culture remain shrouded in mystery, but they assuredly involved extralocal influences and a history deeply rooted in the preceding Middle Archaic period.

Depending on how one wishes to define Stallings culture, its duration can be anywhere from 1,000 to 2,000 years. The chief diagnostic trait is Stallings fiber-tempered pottery, the oldest well-documented pottery in North America. Appearing as early as 2550 B.C. (4500 years B.P.) in the Lower Savannah River Valley (Stoltman 1966, 1974), Stallings pottery was joined by Thom's Creek sand-tempered ware several centuries later (Trinkley 1980), and both persisted to ca. 1050 B.C. (3000 years B.P.), the close of the Late Archaic period. As for diagnostic lithic artifacts, large stemmed bifaces, such as Savannah River Stemmed (Coe 1964), appeared at the onset of the Late Archaic period (3050 B.C., or 5000 years B.P.) and continued in a variety of forms throughout the period. Finally, if viewed as a way of life, Stallings culture had a long period of development, a florescence, and a seemingly rapid decline with considerable diversity throughout, making it difficult to delimit temporal boundaries on the basis of a few material traits.

As with the timing of Stallings culture, its geographical expanse is bound by the traits one

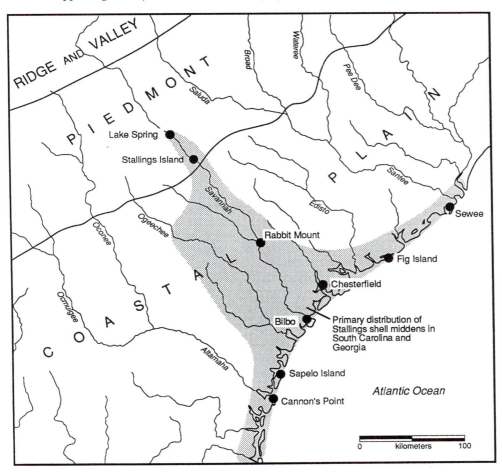

Primary distribution of Late Archaic Stallings shell middens in South Carolina and Georgia and locations of select sites. (Drawn by K. E. Sassaman)

wishes to emphasize. Typical Stallings fiber-tempered pottery, with its repertoire of punctated and incised decorations, is more or less restricted to the area depicted in Figure, although reports of Stallings pottery elsewhere are not unusual. Based on subtle differences in decoration and pottery technology, ethnic distinctions between interior riverine and coastal populations probably existed. Those distinctions are underscored by the use of type names other than Stallings for Georgia coastal assemblages (e.g., St. Simons ware; DePratter 1979), and by the prevalence of Thom's Creek pottery in assemblages from coastal South Carolina. While the significance of these material differences is debatable, less ambiguous are the regional distributions of shell-midden sites. Shell middens are not known from the Piedmont-draining river valleys adjacent to the Savannah Valley. Thus, although certain diagnostic traits are pervasive, the distribution of shell middens may circumscribe one local subset of a variegated culture of macroregional proportions.

Recent work at sites lacking shellfish remains, including remote upland locations, shows that Stallings settlement involved a variety of site types and configurations. Large riverine camps lacking shellfish often contain scores of pits and hearths, at least some of which are associated with architectural evidence (Elliott et al. 1994). Upland sites likewise contain pit features and indirect traces of structures, with one recently excavated upland site containing a small pithouse with an earth oven (Ledbetter 1991). Taken together, the range of site types and locational variation suggests a seasonal settlement system involving a dispersed upland pattern in the fall and winter, with warm-season aggregation at riverine sites. A similar suite of site types is observed on the coast, where large shell rings are accompanied by smaller, amorphous shell middens and nonshell sites. Shell-ring functions are not fully understood, although one study clearly demonstrated that rings were occupied for domestic purposes (Trinkley 1985); postulated, but never verified, are ceremonial functions for rings.

Stallings subsistence was based on the seasonal exploitation of wild plants and animals. A conspicuous component of Stallings middens is white-tailed deer, the bones and antlers of which were used for a variety of tools, including awls, projectiles, hafts, and fishhooks. Aquatic turtles were a significant summer resource, as were varieties of fish. Direct evidence for anadromous fish is lacking, but there are lines of circumstantial evidence to suggest that spring fish runs were important to the river-based communities. Knowledge of plant use is especially limited apart from the routine observation of hickory nutshell and occasionally acorn; evidence for early domesticates, such as cucurbits (squash), has never been observed.

Other knowledge about Stallings economy comes from analyses of subsistence technology. Innovations are legion to the Stallings material inventory. Besides the pottery already noted, innovations included perforated soapstone cooking stones, items well suited to indirect "stone boiling" because of soapstone's resistance to thermal shock. Grooved axes and spear-thrower weights (bannerstones) became prevalent and diversified during the Stallings era. Each of these innovations, like pottery, has been viewed as a response to increased settlement permanence and concomitant economic intensification. Soapstone, axes, and bannerstones were also apparently traded among individuals and thus assumed importance beyond utilitarian function. In fact, alliances involving the exchange of soapstone appear to have been an impediment to the adoption of fiber-tempered pottery, or at least caused many participants to use early pottery in traditional ways, namely, as containers for stone boiling (Sassaman 1993).

The role of alliance and exchange in contributing to the development of Stallings culture is a topic in need of further study. Although evidence for long-distance exchange is weak, the extraction and exportation of soapstone from sites in the western Piedmont of Georgia as part of the Poverty Point exchange network may have indirectly involved Stallings individuals. Some limited evidence for craft specialization or surplus production has been observed at Stallings sites. Involvement in surplus production or long-distance exchange likely contributed to the ability of individuals to exert influence locally, perhaps even to the point of driving production beyond the immediate needs of households. However, what few skeletal data there are for Stallings sites reveal no apparent status differences, and no other lines of evidence for differentiation are seen in local data. Instead, the answers to issues of social complexity may require larger scales of analysis to examine the effects of extralocal processes. Such thinking was commonplace in the archaeology of yesteryear (e.g., Waring 1968) but has since gone out of vogue. Considering the trends of mid-South populations toward economic intensification, interpersonal strife, and long-distance exchange, it is probable that cultures such as Stallings, albeit geographically remote, owed their existence to such large-scale connections.

The collapse of Stallings culture came with little fanfare. After 1550 B.C. (3500 years B.P.)., large shell-midden sites in the Savannah Valley were abandoned, as were other large riverine sites. Dispersed upland settlement became the strategy of choice as groups seem to have opted for less integration and conformity. Coastal shell middens continued to form but were generally smaller in size and more widely dispersed. By 1050 B.C. (3000 years B.P.), the material inventory of Stallings culture was replaced by elements of the emerging Woodland traditions. Both local and extralocal processes are implicated in these changes, as are environmental factors, such as floodplain development and sea-level fluctuations. Sites of the Stallings culture now exist as targets of looting and destruction, as archaeologists continue to salvage what they can to address persistent questions about the timing, organization, and history of this hunter-gatherer society.

Kenneth E. Sassaman

Further Readings

Claflin, W.H., Jr. 1931. *The Stalling's Island Mound, Columbia County, Georgia.* Papers, vol. 14, no. 1. Peabody Museum of American Archaeology and Ethnology, Harvard University, Cambridge.

Coe, J.L. 1964. *The Formative Cultures of the Carolina Piedmont.* Transactions, vol. 54, no. 5. American Philosophical Society, Philadelphia.

DePratter, C.B. 1979. Ceramics. In *The Anthropology of St. Catherine's Island: The Refuge-Deptford Mortuary Complex,* edited by D.H. Thomas and C.S. Larsen, pp. 109–132. Anthropological Papers, vol. 56, pt. 1. American Museum of Natural History, New York.

Elliott, D.T., R.J. Ledbetter, and E.A. Gordon. 1994. *Data Recovery at Lovers Lane, Phinizy Swamp and the Old Dike Sites, Bobby Jones Expressway Extension Corridor Augusta, Georgia.* Occasional Papers in Cultural Resource Management no. 7. Georgia Department of Transportation, Atlanta.

Ledbetter, R.J. 1991. Late Archaic/Early Woodland Structures From the Mill Branch Sites, Warren County, Georgia. *Early Georgia* 19(2):34–46.

Sassaman, K.E. 1993. *Early Pottery in the Southeast: Tradition and Innovation in Cooking Technology.* University of Alabama Press, Tuscaloosa.

Stoltman, J.B. 1966. New Radiocarbon Dates for Southeastern Fiber-Tempered Pottery. *American Antiquity* 31:872–874.

———. 1974. *Groton Plantation: An Archaeological Study of a South Carolina Locality.* Monograph no. 1. Peabody Museum of American Archaeology and Ethnology, Harvard University, Cambridge.

Trinkley, M.B. 1980. A Typology of Thom's Creek Pottery for the South Carolina Coast. *South Carolina Antiquities* 12:1–35.

———. 1985. The Form and Function of South Carolina's Early Woodland Shell Rings. In *Structure and Process in Southeastern Archaeology,* edited by R.S. Dickens and H.T. Ward, pp. 102–118. University of Alabama Press, Tuscaloosa.

Waring, A.J., Jr. 1968. The Bilbo Site, Chatham County, Georgia. In *The Waring Papers: The Collected Works of Antonio J. Waring, Jr.,* edited by S. Williams, pp. 152–197. Papers, vol. 58. Peabody Museum of Archaeology and Ethnology, Harvard University, Cambridge.

Steatite

Steatite is a metamorphic rock composed of compacted talc with serpentine. Since its surface texture is somewhat soaplike, its popular name is "soapstone." It was formed from the metamorphosis of the igneous rock peridottite. Despite its metamorphic genesis, it is extremely soft for a rock and is easily carved. As a result, it was a popular material for prehistoric stoneworking. It was widely used by California cultures, especially in the last years of prehistory (2050 B.C.–A.D. 1769, or 4,000–181 years B.P.). Its softness largely restricted its use to ornaments, such as effigies, figurines, beads, tubes, and pipes, and certain utilitarian objects in which softness was not a problem, such as stone bowls and frying griddles. When exposed to fire, however, steatite can harden markedly; steatite griddles and cooking bowls can gain considerable hardness with use. Steatite occurs in a number of mountain locations in California,

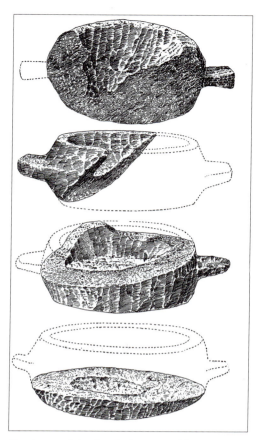

Steatite vessels broken during quarry/shaping work, Rose Hill Quarry, Connecticut. (Reprinted from Smithsonian Institution, Bureau of American Ethnology, Bulletin 60, Figure 104)

but by far the most important source was Santa Catalina Island off the southern California coast. There, steatite quarrying began at least by 6050 B.C. (8000 years B.P.) and continued throughout prehistory. The manufacture and export of steatite objects were the most important economic activities of the islanders. Canoes took cargoes to the mainland, where the artifacts were exchanged or traded as far inland as the Southwest.

Steatite was also used extensively in different contexts and for a variety of purposes in other areas of North America. In the eastern Arctic, it was carved into human and Arctic animal shapes in the widespread and long-lasting Dorset art tradition (550 B.C.–A.D. 1000, or 2500–950 years B.P.) and by later (after A.D. 1000, or 950 years B.P.) Thule people. Rather than "pure art," these carvings probably had ideological significance within Dorset and Thule

cosmologies. Soapstone vessels replaced ceramic vessels in some regions of the eastern Arctic, and crescent-shaped lamps of the material were preferred to pottery lamps in some regions.

Heavy, carved-soapstone bowls were present in New England by ca. 1500–1200 B.C. (3450–3150 years B.P.), where they were probably used by terminal Archaic (ca. 1650–700 B.C., or 3600–2650 years B.P.) Susquehana-tradition populations as cooking vessels. Found mainly in larger base camps, they were manufactured until supplanted by ceramic vessels ca. 700 B.C. (2650 years B.P.). Even after that date, crushed soapstone was used as a temper in some early ceramics. The raw material for these bowls, which had oval-to-rectangular shapes, flat bottoms, and lug handles on each long end, was obtained through long-distance trade from sources in southern New England and central Pennsylvania, and perhaps to the south. These durable bowls seem to have been widely traded and invested with special social significance, for "killed" pots are found in Orient-phase cemeteries on eastern Long Island. Some archaeologists have suggested that regional soapstone bowls were copies of wooden prototypes and models, in turn, for early ceramic shapes.

Soapstone was used even more extensively in the Eastern Woodlands in the Mid-Atlantic region and the Southeast. As in the Northeast, cultural soapstone is nearly exclusively associated in these regions with Late Archaic complexes. In the Southeast, although it was carved into atlatl weights, net sinkers, ornaments, and some other items, it was used mainly to manufacture perforated slabs and large, heavy containers, both of which were important components in the region's preceramic cooking technology. Bowls of material from sources in the Piedmont of western Georgia and southern Alabama were popular items in the Poverty Point trade network and in other southeastern trade networks. Because some predate local fiber-tempered ceramic vessels and resemble them in shape, a few archaeologists have suggested that they were prototypes for the first southeastern clay containers, too. Kenneth E. Sassaman (1993) has proposed a social model for the role of soapstone bowls in southeastern exchange alliances and has raised the possibility that their role in regulating and maintaining intersocietal relations impeded the adoption of ceramic vessels in some parts of this subarea.

Joseph L. Chartkoff
Guy Gibbon

Further Readings

Elliott, D.T. 1981. *Soapstone Use in the Wallace Reservoir: A Tool for Interpreting Prehistory*. Wallace Reservoir Project Contribution no. 5. Department of Anthropology, University of Georgia, Athens.

Ferguson, T. 1980. *Prehistoric Soapstone Procurement in Northwestern South Carolina*. Unpublished Master's thesis. Department of Anthropology, University of Tennessee, Knoxville.

Gifford, E.E. 1932. The Northfork Mono. *University of California Publications in American Archaeology and Ethnology* 31:15–65.

Holmes, W.H. 1912. Steatite. In *Handbook of American Indians North of Mexico*, edited by F.W. Hodge. *Bulletin of the Bureau of American Ethnology* 30:635–636.

Hudson, T., and T.C. Blackburn. 1983. *Food Preparation and Shelter*. The Material Culture of the Chumash Interaction Sphere, vol. 2, T.C. Blackburn, general editor. Anthropological Papers no. 27. Ballena Press, Menlo Park.

Maxwell, M.S. 1985. *Prehistory of the Eastern Arctic*. Academic Press, New York.

Sassaman, K.E. 1993. *Early Pottery in the Southeast: Tradition and Innovation in Cooking Technology*. University of Alabama Press, Tuscaloosa.

Smith, B.W. 1981. The Late Archaic-Poverty Point Steatite Trade Network in the Lower Mississippi Valley: Some Preliminary Observations. *Florida Anthropologist* 34:120–125.

Snow, D. 1980. *The Archaeology of New England*. Academic Press, New York.

Steed-Kisker Phase

Sites of the Steed-Kisker phase (A.D. 1000–1300, or 950–650 years B.P.) are situated along both sides of the Missouri River and nearby hinterlands, from Kansas City north to the vicinity of St. Joseph, Missouri. Settlements consist of clusters of two to three dwellings, associated outbuildings, and storage facilities dispersed over the countryside around a mounded burial facility. Houses are rectangular earthlodges comparable to those of the contemporaneous Central Plains tradition or, on occasion, post-trench wall structures similar to Mississippian houses to the east. Burials in the mounded features are either extended or flexed inhumations or bundle burials. Males, females, and children are all represented in the mounds.

Subsistence was based on agriculture, especially corn, beans, and squash. These crops were supplemented by hunting and gathering a wide range of plants and animals available in the gallery forests and prairie lands along the Missouri. The bow and arrow tipped with small triangular side-notched points was the principal hunting implement. Most Steed-Kisher pottery is plain surfaced and shell tempered, although some cord-marked sand-tempered pottery is present at most sites. A small proportion of the shell-tempered pottery may represent trade with Mississippian populations to the east, a form of interaction also indicated by occasional finds of chipped-stone hoe blades and effigy pipes. Other components of the artifact assemblage, including tools of chipped stone and bone, show close parallels with assemblages from the Central Plains tradition to the west.

Occasionally interpreted as a western Mississippian complex or an eastern Central Plains manifestation, the taxonomic status of Steed-Kisker remains enigmatic. Frontier relationships with Nebraska-culture peoples to the north and Pomona peoples to the south and west are also topics of research.

Alfred E. Johnson

Further Readings

Logan, B. (editor). 1990. *Archaeological Investigations in the Plains Village Frontier, Northeastern Kansas*. Project Report Series no. 70. Museum of Anthropology, University of Kansas, Lawrence.

O'Brien, P.J. 1978. Steed-Kisker: A Western Mississippian Settlement System. In *Mississippian Settlement Patterns*, edited by B.D. Smith, pp. 1–20. Academic Press, New York.

Shippee, J.M. 1972. *Archaeological Remains in the Area of Kansas City: The Mississippian Period*. Research Series no. 9. Missouri Archaeological Society, Columbia.

Wedel, W.R. 1943. *Archaeological Investigations in Platte and Clay Counties, Missouri*. Bulletin no. 183. U.S. National Museum, Washington, D.C.

Stemmed Point Tradition

The term "Stemmed Point tradition" is used in two overlapping ways in the archaeology of western North America. A.L. Bryan (1980) employs it as the name of a *technological tradition* that unites similar-appearing early stemmed points from the Columbia-Fraser Plateau, the Great Basin, and the Plano tradition of the Plains. R.L. Carlson (1983) uses it as an all-embracing *cultural tradition* in the intermontane Far West. Among regional expressions of the cultural tradition are the Lake Mojave complex of California and Nevada, the Western Pluvial Lakes tradition of eastern Oregon, the early Hatwai assemblages from Idaho, the Windust phase and Lind Coulee components from eastern Washington, and less well-known assemblages from the Oregon coast and the headwaters of the Columbia River in British Columbia and adjacent Alberta. The cultural tradition probably evolved from the Fluted Point tradition in the intermontane west, with the Plano tradition evolving under similar influences on the Plains. In its core area, it is identifiable artifactually by the co-occurrence of crescents and long-stemmed points that are either rounded or concave at the end of the stem in archaeological contexts dating to 8550–6550 B.C. (10,500–8500 years B.P.). Earlier dates at two sites, Smith Creek Cave in Nevada and Fort Rock Cave in Oregon, are generally discounted. Bison remains and bones of other mammals, as well as numerous scrapers and projectile points, indicate that this was primarily a hunting tradition. Atlatl spurs are found in some components. In the Columbia-Snake drainage, it falls in the time period before the pursuit of salmon became the primary subsistence activity.

The distribution of the intermontane Stemmed Point tradition has been correlated with the distribution of aboriginal languages of the Penutian phylum: Chinookan, Sahaptian, Klamath-Modoc, and California Penutian. It is possible that this tradition marks the spread of the ancestors of native peoples speaking these languages throughout much of the Far West.

Roy L. Carlson

Further Readings

Bryan, A.L. 1980. The Stemmed Point Tradition: An Early Technological Tradition in Western North America. In *Anthropological Papers in Memory of Earl H. Swanson, Jr.,* edited by L. Harten, C. Warren, and D. Tuohy, pp. 77–107. Special Publication. Idaho Museum of Natural History, Pocatello.

Carlson, R.L. 1983. The Far West. In *Early Man in the New World,* edited by R. Shutler, Jr., pp. 73–96. Sage, Beverly Hills.

———. 1991. Clovis From the Perspective of the Ice-Free Corridor. In *Clovis: Origins and Adaptations,* edited by R. Bonnichsen and K. Turnmire, pp. 81–90. Center for the Study of the First Americans, Oregon State University, Corvallis.

Carlson, R.L., and L. Dalla Bona (editors). 1996. *Early Human Occupation in British Columbia.* University of British Columbia Press, Vancouver.

Willig, J.A., C.M. Aikens, and J.L. Fagan (editors). 1988. *Early Human Occupation in Far Western North America: The Clovis-Archaic Interface.* Nevada State Museum, Carson City.

Sterns Creek Variant

Although detailed information is available from only the Walker Gilmore site 13 km (8 miles) south of Plattsmouth, Nebraska, the Sterns Creek variant of the Plains Woodland pattern seemingly represents a distinct complex with an extensive range along the Missouri River and its tributaries in eastern Nebraska and western Iowa.

The stratigraphy at Walker Gilmore is complex, involving a series of human occupation zones interbedded in the alluvial sequence of two terrace remnants. While earlier investigations (Sterns 1915; Strong 1935; Champe 1946) recognized three of the occupation zones as Sterns Creek Woodland, more recent excavations (Hass 1982) were able to identify five. Basic continuities in artifact styles demonstrate reoccupation by the same or closely related social groups. A Nebraska-culture occupation overlies the uppermost Woodland level. Best represented in occupation levels 2, 3, and 4, Sterns Creek features include hearths, storage pits, middens, and structural remains. The latter suggest elliptical shelters with double or triple walls of light, flexible post construction that vary in size from 4.6–6.1 m (15–20 feet) by 0.3–1.2 m (1–4 feet). Some burned daubing clay has been recovered, as well as preserved reeds and bark segments that were probably wall- and roof-covering materials. Their small size and lack of internal features suggest that the structures were not domiciles but storage or food-preparation areas.

Burial features associated with the variant

may include White Swan mound in south-central South Dakota and the Whitten site in southeastern Nebraska. White Swan mound covered a rectangular pit, although the only burials found were secondary examples from the fill and at the base of the mound. Accompanying the burials were two small, vertically elongated pots, shell ornaments, perforated canine teeth, and projectile points. At Whitten, despite the fact that burial mounds had reportedly been leveled by cultivation, excavations (Hill and Cooper 1937:338–345) succeeded in disclosing two concentrations of human remains. Flexed and extended primary burials were present, as were secondary interments. In addition to ceramic associations that suggest a Sterns Creek affiliation, burial accompaniments included bone armlets and shell beads.

The subsistence strategy of the Sterns Creek people was broadly based and included hunting, gathering, and at least limited horticulture. Larger mammalian forms hunted included deer, bison, elk, and antelope. Smaller forms, including birds, were taken as well. Small, triangular, notched and unnotched projectile points indicate the use of the bow and arrow as the principal hunting weapon. Freshwater mollusks were obtained from nearby watercourses. The gathering of wild-vegetable foods is indicated by handstones and by black walnuts, hickory nuts, hazel nuts, ground nuts, and wild beans. Squash and bottle-gourd seeds demonstrate the practice of horticulture. Sterns Creek pottery vessels were elongated, with conoidal bases and slightly outflaring rims. Cord marked, brushed, plain, and simple-stamped surface finishes have all been identified. Decoration, limited to the rim area, consists of finger impressions, punctates, or incisions immediately below or across the lip.

Prior to D.R. Haas's 1982 analysis of Holder's 1968 excavations at Walker Gilmore, several Sterns Creek–variant characteristics, such as ceramic styles and the absence of maize horticulture, were believed compatible with an early Late Woodland assignment (Tiffany 1978:Table 1) and radiocarbon dates of A.D. 525 ± 110 (1425 years B.P.) from White Swan mound (Trautman 1978:Table 1) and A.D. 920 ± 150 (1030 years B.P.) from Walker Gilmore (Crane and Griffin 1962:193). The most acceptable date range for Walker Gilmore, A.D. 1116–1255 (834–695 years B.P.), seems surprisingly late. Contemporaneity of the Sterns Creek variant of the Late Plains Woodland pattern and the

Nebraska variant of the Central Plains tradition is suggested.

Alfred E. Johnson

Further Readings

Champe, J.L. 1946. *Ash Hollow Cave.* University of Nebraska Studies, n.s., no. 1. University of Nebraska, Lincoln.

Crane, H.R., and J.B. Griffin. 1962. University of Michigan Radiocarbon Dates, VII. *Radiocarbon* 4:183–203.

Haas, D.R. 1982. *Walker Gilmore: A Stratified Woodland Period Occupation in Eastern Nebraska.* Technical Report no. 8022. Division of Archaeological Research, Department of Anthropology, University of Nebraska, Lincoln.

Hill, A.T., and P. Cooper. 1937. The Archaeological Campaign of 1937. *Nebraska History Magazine* 18(4):241–359.

Sterns, F.H. 1915. A Stratification of Cultures in Eastern Nebraska. *American Anthropologist* 17(1):135–137.

Strong, W.D. 1935. *An Introduction to Nebraska Archaeology.* Miscellaneous Collections, vol. 93, no. 10. Smithsonian Institution, Washington, D.C.

Tiffany, J.A. 1977. Artifacts From the Sharp's Site: A Sterns Creek Component in Southwestern Iowa. *Journal of the Iowa Archaeological Society* 24:85–124.

Trautman, M.A. 1963. Isotopes, Inc. Radiocarbon Measurements III. *Radiocarbon* 5:62–79.

Steward, Julian H. (1902–1972)

Educated as an anthropologist at the University of California, Berkeley, Julian Haynes Steward is usually considered an ethnologist. However, like A.L. Kroeber, a mentor at Berkeley, he made substantive and theoretical contributions to archaeology and is considered a seminal figure in the development of modern American archaeology. Of 184 entries in the bibliography accompanying his *American Anthropologist* obituary (Manners 1973), more than one-quarter are concerned at least in part with archaeology. Although Steward's interests were numerous and varied, his contributions to North American archaeology can be divided into three categories: field investigations, the concept of "cultural ecology," and the concept of "multilinear evolution."

Steward, unlike most ethnologists in the

1930s critical of archaeological practice, conducted considerable archaeological research. His most intensive involvement was between 1930 and 1933 when he was a professor at the University of Utah, but he continued to write reviews of Far West monographs in archaeology throughout his career.

Although Steward's concepts of, and research programs for, the investigation of cultural ecology and cultural evolution are intimately intertwined, they are discussed separately here for purposes of explication. In contrast to prevailing archaeological practice, which stressed the construction of taxonomies and the use of migration and diffusion as causative principles, he argued that human behavior was determined by its context within an ecosystem and that cultures must be understood as adaptations to these kinds of natural systems. His research program was rooted in a materialist base–superstructure formulation in which the base, the "cultural core," consisted of those technological, economic, and other practices of a culture most closely related to subsistence activities and, thus, of major adaptive significance. Lower components of the superstructure, such as social and political organization, were configured to make base practices as efficient as possible, and the ideological component, the peak of the superstructure, sanctified the system as a whole. An analysis of a culture, then, whether ethnological or archaeological, would proceed by first establishing the role played by ecological factors in determining the base, and then by discerning what the components of the superstructure were and how they were functional adjustments to the base.

Many elements of Steward's theoretical perspective are encapsulated in his processual approach to cultural ecology. Among these are: (1) a constant and intense interest in cause-and-effect relations in cultural phenomena; (2) a functional interpretation of culture; (3) a focus on the identification of culture types, as opposed to a focus on culture areas; (4) a strong emphasis on technological determinism; (5) a focal stress on the role played by ecological factors in shaping sociocultural systems; and (6) a commitment to empirical validation and the role of science in anthropology. Because he thought that it was easier to discover causes in simpler societies, he initiated his program in the mid-1930s in a now-classic study of the Shoshoneans of the Great Basin (Steward 1938). This and other investigations led him to believe that

people in similar environments at the same level of sociocultural integration will have a similar type of culture. Steward's search for "causes" is often misunderstood. Rather than the focus of his program, it was only a means to understanding the processes responsible for specific cultural-ecological orientations and, ultimately, to the generation of deductive statements or theory, a sequence he regarded as the essence of science.

At a different level of analysis, Steward was interested in understanding culture change and in discovering cross-cultural processual regularities in the transformation of societies. The latter interest was in part a reaction against the orientations of contemporary historical particularists and cultural historians, which ignored "abstraction" and the search for regularities, and in part an extension of his earlier training in zoology and geology. These components of his theoretical perspective stressed that, while ever-shifting external factors operate to change societies, studies of cultural causality should focus on internal adjustments made in response to these factors, and that sequences of culture change are more likely to be similar among societies at the same level of sociocultural integration in similar environments; that is, that culture evolution is multilinear rather than unilinear.

Other Steward contributions concern settlement-pattern research, the direct-historical approach, the culture-stage concept, the practical use of archaeology, and the use of ethnographic analogy in archaeological interpretation. Although Steward had already developed many aspects of his research programs by the late 1930s, they did not become widely integrated into North American archaeology until the publication in 1955 of *Theory of Culture Change: The Methodology of Multilinear Evolution*, a synthesis of many of his most important positions. While amended in significant ways, they have remained an important component of research by both "new" and "traditional" archaeologists, perhaps because their key variables, such as technology, settlement patterns, and the environmental context of cultures, are empirical and relatively accessible to archaeological study. Yet, Steward has still not received the credit he is due as a significant intellectual contributor to the New Archaeology and to much of archaeological practice in general in North America since the mid-1950s. His explicitly materialist view of culture, emphasis on empirical data and science, adaptation, and processual explanations, and his cultural-ecological and

-evolutionary orientations are much more substantial contributions than those, for example, of Walter W. Taylor and Joseph R. Caldwell, often cited as the forebears of the New Archaeology. On the debit side, these same widely accepted contributions have played a role in the discipline's growing isolation within anthropology by detracting from the interpretive research programs that dominate contemporary sociocultural anthropology.

Guy Gibbon

Further Readings

Manners, R.A. 1973. Julian Haynes Steward, 1902–1972. *American Anthropologist* 75:886–903.

Steward, J.H. 1933. *Archaeological Problems of the Northern Periphery of the Southwest.* Bulletin no. 5. Museum of Northern Arizona, Flagstaff.

———. 1937a. *Ancient Caves of the Great Salt Lake Region.* Bulletin no. 116. Bureau of American Ethnology, Smithsonian Institution, Washington, D.C.

———. 1937b. Ecological Aspects of Southwestern Society. *Anthropos* 32:87–104.

———. 1938. *Basin-Plateau Aboriginal Sociopolitical Groups.* Bulletin no. 120. Bureau of American Ethnology, Smithsonian Institution, Washington, D.C.

———. 1942. The Direct Historical Approach to Archaeology. *American Antiquity* 7:337–343.

———. 1955. *Theory of Culture Change: The Methodology of Multilinear Evolution.* University of Illinois Press, Urbana.

Steward, J.H., and F.M. Setzler. 1938. Function and Configuration in Archaeology. *American Antiquity* 4:4–10.

Stillwater Marsh

Stillwater Marsh is a 14,165-ha (35,000-acre) wetland in the Carson Sink near the town of Fallon in western Nevada. A 1980–1981 surface survey of the Carson Sink and Stillwater Range found very few sites in the marsh itself (Kelly 1985). However, flooding from 1982 to 1986 and subsequent near-desiccation of the marsh revealed dozens of archaeological sites and human burials. Archaeological sites in the marsh date to 1050 B.C.–A.D. 1250 (3000–700 years B.P.); the majority may date to A.D. 650–1250 (1300–700 years B.P.). No later sites have been found, although they occur west of the marsh; earlier sites may be buried more deeply. The marsh has a complex hydrology due to shifting stream channels, variable stream discharge, and seismic activity. Site distribution may reflect changes in marsh location or deposition rates only, rather than intensity of use.

Sites consist of extensive middens, the most salient features of which are a few to several dozen circular pits per site. There are postholes, storage pits 1–2 m (3.3–6.6 feet) in diameter, and houses up to 5–6 m (16.4–19.7 feet) in diameter and 50 cm (19.7 inches) deep. Few sites have been excavated, but data current to the mid-1990s indicate a hunting-and-gathering economy focused on marsh resources, especially bulrush seeds, freshwater mollusks, minnows, and waterfowl, as well as small rodents and mammals; some bighorn sheep remains are also present. There is little evidence of bifacial-tool manufacture in the sites; instead, tools were expedient flakes derived from heavily reduced cores.

Burials from the marsh form the largest skeletal series known in the Great Basin (Brooks et al. 1988; Larsen and Kelly 1995). There are slightly more males than females represented. Six ^{14}C dates range from 930 B.C. to A.D. 1750 (2880–200 years B.P.), but four cluster in the A.D. 650–1250 (1300–700 years B.P.) range. Most individuals were buried in the fetal position with few grave goods. Analyses indicate a healthy population that underwent periodic stress, although not as severe as that of some other foragers. The robusticity of limb bones and heavy eburnation of joints indicate great physical demands, and males apparently did more walking than females. Bone chemistry reflects a diet that may not have included much piñon. At the request of the Fallon Paiute–Shoshone tribe, the remains were reburied in a subterranean crypt.

Robert L. Kelly

Further Readings

Brooks, S.T., M.B. Haldeman, and R.B. Brooks. 1988. *Osteological Analyses of the Stillwater Skeletal Series, Stillwater Marsh, Churchill County, Nevada.* Cultural Resource Series no. 2. Region 1, U.S. Fish and Wildlife Service, Portland.

Janetski, J.C., and D.B. Madsen (editors). 1990. *Wetland Adaptations in the Great Basin.* Occasional Papers no. 1. Museum of Peoples and Cultures, Brigham Young University, Provo.

S

Kelly, R.L. 1985. *Hunter-Gatherer Mobility and Sedentism: A Great Basin Study.* Unpublished Ph.D. dissertation, Department of Anthropology, University of Michigan, Ann Arbor.

———. 1988. The Three Sides of a Biface. *American Antiquity* 53:717–734.

Larsen, C.S., and R.L. Kelly. 1995. *The Bioarchaeology of Stillwater Marsh, Western Nevada.* Anthropological Paper no. 77. American Museum of Natural History, New York.

Raven, C., and R.G. Elston. 1988. *Preliminary Investigations in Stillwater Marsh: Human Prehistory and Geoarchaeology.* Cultural Resource Series no. 1. 2 vols. Region 1, U.S. Fish and Wildlife Service, Portland.

———. 1989. *Prehistoric Human Geography in the Carson Desert: A Predictive Model of Land-Use in the Stillwater Wildlife Management Area.* Cultural Resource Series nos. 3–4. Region 1, U.S. Fish and Wildlife Service, Portland.

See also HIDDEN CAVE; WESTERN AND CENTRAL BASIN WETLAND AND LAKESIDE ADAPTATIONS

Stone Disks (California)

Prehistoric cultures in coastal southern California produced a variety of ground-stone disk artifacts whose ages are known but whose uses remain problematic. Discoidals are round-to-ovoid disks that are generally 7–15 cm (3–6 inches) in diameter and 4–7 cm (1.5–3 inches) thick. They have flat-to-slightly-convex faces and edge profiles. Cogged stones are similar in size and shape, but they have deep or wide grooves cut into the rims to give the piece a gearlike appearance. Grooves may range in number from one to 20; most cogged stones have eight to 12. Perforated stones, or doughnut stones, are also similar in size, but they are less finely made and, instead of grooves at the rim, have a single large hole drilled through the center.

Discoidals and cogged stones tend to occur together in the same deposits. They are known along the coast, on some Channel Islands from the Santa Barbara to the San Diego areas, and as far inland as the San Bernardino region. Most examples date between 4050 and 1050 B.C. (6000–3000 years B.P.). Between Santa Barbara and Los Angeles, these forms occur in associa-

tion with hard-seed–processing campsites in the chaparral zone. Closer to San Diego, the types have rarely been found in association with functional tool sets, but a number have been found in apparent caches or pits below living surfaces—in one case, seven were found stacked one on top of the other in a pit. Although discoidals and cogged stones have been studied stylistically, no direct evidence of their function has been found. For the most part, they stopped being produced ca. 1050 B.C. (3000 years B.P.), when cultural patterns previously known for the interior deserts began to appear along coastal southern California. No ethnographic counterparts are known.

Perforated stones occur separately from cogged stones and discoidals in southern California. They are known mainly from the period after 1050 B.C. (3000 years B.P.) and are often described as digging-stick weights. Digging sticks are historically known wooden tools made of poles that are sharpened at one end. Used for turning over soil to expose roots, bulbs, and tubers, they were made in most parts of California. A definitive or exclusive link between perforated stones and digging sticks has not been established. The fact that most California ethnographic groups made digging sticks but not perforated stones may suggest other uses. The occurrence of perforated stones along the coast in Late Prehistoric fishing cultures may indicate that at least some were used as net weights.

Joseph L. Chartkoff

Further Readings
Moratto, M.J. (editor). 1984. *California Archaeology.* Academic Press, New York.

Peck, S.L. 1955. *An Archaeological Report on the Excavation of a Prehistoric Site at Zuma Creek, Los Angeles County, California.* Papers no. 2. Archaeological Survey Association of Southern California, Los Angeles.

Treganza, A.E., and A. Bierman. 1958. The Topanga Culture: Final Report on Excavations, 1948. *University of California Archaeological Records* 20(2):45–86.

Wallace, W.J. 1955. A Suggested Chronology for Southern California Coastal Archaeology. *Southwestern Journal of Anthropology* 11:214–230.

Warren, C.N. 1968. Cultural Tradition and Ecological Adaptation on the Southern California Coast. In *Archaic Prehistory in the Western United States,* edited by

C. Irwin-Williams, pp. 1–14. Contributions in Anthropology, vol. 1, no. 3. Eastern New Mexico University, Portales.

Strong, William Duncan (1899–1962)

Known primarily for his contributions to Plains archaeology in the late 1930s, William Duncan Strong also was the first professional archaeologist to excavate in northern Labrador (Strong 1930), to establish a cultural sequence for the Buena Vista Lake region of the San Joaquin Valley in California (while directing Civil Works Administration excavations in the years 1933–1934), and to produce, with W.E. Schenck and Julian H. Steward, the first comprehensive site survey and excavation report in the Pacific Northwest (Strong et al. 1930). The latter set a precedent in the region for careful and detailed work. As a graduate student of A.L. Kroeber at the University of California, Berkeley, in the 1920s, Strong developed the use of statistical coefficients of correlation in the seriation of ceramic styles. Strong, who adopted Kroeber's view that "archaeology is anthropology," was one of the first North American archaeologists, in his "Anthropological Theory and Archaeological Fact" (1936), to express dissatisfaction with the limited goals of chronological ordering that dominated the discipline at the time.

Strong earned his Ph.D. in anthropology from Berkeley in 1926. While a professor at the University of Nebraska (1929–1931), he began illustrating these principles by applying the direct-historical approach to Nebraskan prehistory, excavating historic Pawnee sites, contact-period sites, and precontact sites to establish a cultural sequence for the central Plains. His 1935 monograph, *An Introduction to Nebraska Archaeology,* became an exemplar for this kind of work, stimulating interest in the direct-historical approach, the ethnic identification of archaeological complexes, and a "newer functional archaeology" in which a more sophisticated application of ethnographic analogy was made in the contextual and functional interpretation of archaeological data. While at the University of Nebraska, Strong was the director for the Smithsonian Institution of the Nebraska-Plains area, and he established the university as the major center of development for Plains archaeology and helped build a firm foundation for Plains archaeology itself. He was appointed senior anthropologist in the Bureau of American Ethnology at the Smithsonian Institution in Washington, D.C., in 1931, and in 1933 he was sent as a representative of the bureau to British Honduras on an archaeological expedition. The remainder of his successful career focused on Central and South American archaeology.

Guy Gibbon

Further Readings

Strong, W.D. 1930. A Stone Culture From Northern Labrador and Its Relation to the Eskimo-Like Cultures of the Northeast. *American Anthropology* 32:126–144.

———. 1935. *An Introduction to Nebraska Archaeology.* Miscellaneous Collections, vol. 93, no. 10. Smithsonian Institution, Washington, D.C.

———. 1936. Anthropological Theory and Archaeological Fact. In *Essays in Anthropology Presented to A.L. Kroeber,* edited by R.H. Lowie, pp. 359–370. University of California Press, Berkeley.

———. 1940. From History to Prehistory in the Northern Great Plains. *Smithsonian Miscellaneous Collections* 100:353–394.

Strong, W.D., W.E. Schenck, and J.H. Steward. 1930. *Archaeology of the Dalles-Deschutes Region.* University of California Publications in American Archaeology and Ethnology, vol. 24, no. 1. University of California Press, Berkeley.

Willey, G.R. 1988. *Portraits in American Archaeology.* University of New Mexico Press, Albuquerque.

Sumpweed

Sumpweed, or marshelder (*Iva annua* var. *macrocarpa*), is, like sunflower (*Helianthus annuus* var. *macrocarpus*), a member of the aster family that was domesticated in eastern North America before the introduction of corn. Unlike sunflower, domesticated sumpweed did not survive into modern times; therefore, its status and economic potential are less frequently appreciated. Because the wild plant does not produce showy flowers and usually grows in narrow, linear bands along floodplains, most people today are unfamiliar with it. Nevertheless, the archaeological record indicates that sumpweed was a significant food source for some midwestern hunter-gatherers before 1000 B.C. (2950 years B.P.) and that it persisted as an economic plant until the arrival of Europeans. Its use probably declined, however, after A.D. 1200 (750 years B.P.). We have no written descriptions of its cultivation or preparation as a food.

The realization that sumpweed was once a domesticate began with excavations of dry rock-shelter sites in the Ozarks and in Kentucky during the 1920s and 1930s. Ethnobotanist M.R. Gilmore noted in 1931 that sumpweed fruits (the fruit is an achene, a kernel inside a brittle pericarp) from stored deposits in Ozark rock shelters were much larger than those produced by wild plants. He inferred that they were cultivated, but he thought that prehistoric people probably used them for perfume or medicine rather than for food. An abundance of sumpweed seeds in paleofeces from Newt Kash Hollow Shelter, reported by Volney Jones in 1936, furnished proof of their consumption. Jones submitted samples of archaeological sumpweed achenes from six sites to botanist S.F. Blake, who formally designated them as a distinct variety. Blake (1939:84) regarded the new variety as "an ancient cultivated strain obtained by selection, and now extinct," which is the view accepted today. Wild-sumpweed achenes are usually less than 3 mm (0.1 inches) long and are rarely longer than 4 mm (0.2 inches). Archaeological specimens range up to nearly 10 mm (0.4 inches); the average length for some samples is greater than 7 mm (0.3 inches).

An AMS (accelerator mass spectrometry) radiocarbon date on carbonized sumpweed from the Napoleon Hollow site in Illinois documents that size increase resulting from domestication had occurred by 2000 B.C. (3950 years B.P.). A seed cache from Marble Bluff in Arkansas shows that, by 1000 B.C. (2950 years B.P.), even larger achenes were being stored in bags along with sunflower, squash (*Cucurbita pepo* ssp. *ovifera*), and chenopod (*Chenopodium berlandieri* ssp. *jonesianum*) seeds, all probably intended for planting. Cultigen-sumpweed fruits are ubiquitous in storage pits and paleofeces deposited in caves and rock shelters during the first millennium B.C., and they are frequently recovered from features at open-air sites dating to the first millennium A.D. Several of the native eastern crops, especially sunflower, remained popular after the intensification of corn agriculture at ca. A.D. 1000 (950 years B.P.), but sumpweed production declined. It did not cease altogether, however, as demonstrated by samples from two Ozark rock shelters dating to ca. A.D. 1400–1650 (550–300 years B.P.), and by specimens from a Protohistoric site in North Carolina.

Harvesting experiments using wild stands show that sumpweed holds considerable economic potential. The oily seeds are a concentrated energy source, high in fat and low in

Wild (left) and domesticated (center and right) Iva annua *(var.* macrocarpa) *achenes. The wild sumpweed fruits are modern. The large achenes in the center come from Alum Cave, an Ozark rockshelter, and are undated. The specimens on the right come from feature 71 at Cloudsplitter Rockshelter in eastern Kentucky, and date to the first millennium B.C. The archaeological remains in this photograph are curated by the Museum of Anthropology, University of Michigan, Ann Arbor. (Photograph by G. Fritz)*

moisture content. They are nutritious, with high levels of protein, calcium, iron, phosphorus, potassium, thiamine, and niacin. Sumpweed fell out of the eastern North American crop inventory due to some unknown combination of factors. For millennia, however, it nourished prehistoric farmers whose ancestors brought it into cultivation.

Gayle Fritz

Further Readings

Asch, D.L., and N.B. Asch. 1978. The Economic Potential of *Iva annua* and Its Prehistoric Importance in the Lower Illinois Valley. In *The Nature and Status of Ethnobotany,* edited by R.I. Ford, pp. 301–341. Anthropological Papers no. 67. Museum of Anthropology, University of Michigan, Ann Arbor.

Blake, S.F 1939. A New Variety of *Iva ciliata* From Indian Rock Shelters in the South Central United States. *Rhodora* 41:81–86.

Gilmore, M.R. 1931. Vegetal Remains of the Ozark Bluff-Dweller Culture. *Papers of the Michigan Academy of Science, Arts, and Letters* 14:83–102.

Jones, V. 1936. The Vegetal Remains of Newt Kash Hollow Shelter. In *Rock-Shelters in Menifee County, Kentucky,* edited by W.S. Webb and W.D. Funkhouser, pp. 147–165. Reports in Anthropology and Archaeology, vol. 3, no. 4. Department of Anthropology, University of Kentucky, Lawrence.

Yarnell, R.A. 1978. Domestication of Sunflower and Sumpweed in Eastern North America. In *The Nature and Status of Ethnobotany,* edited by R.I. Ford, pp. 289–299. Anthropological Papers no. 67. Museum of Anthropology, University of Michigan, Ann Arbor.

Sunflower

Producers and consumers of large sunflower (*Helianthus annuus* var. *macrocarpus*) seeds and oil can thank prehistoric agriculturalists in eastern North America for domesticating this crop. Although independent series of sunflower domestication may also have occurred in Mexico and the Southwest, only in the Eastern Woodlands is there a documented sequence of increase in seed size and entrenchment into the native cropping system that began thousands of years ago, flourished at European contact, and

persisted long after. Wild sunflowers are not native to the midwestern region where domestication occurred. Weedy plants growing today in eastern North America spread as colonizers, probably the result of both ancient and recent land modifications. The ancestor of cultigen sunflower migrated or was transported from the West, and the domestication process probably involved wild and weedy plants in the mid-continent.

Such sunflowers seldom, if ever, produce achenes (kernel plus shell) longer than 7 mm (0.3 inches) in length, but prehistoric archaeological specimens are as long as 17 mm (0.7 inches). An early stage of domestication is reflected by slightly larger than weedy-sized seeds (5.7–7.4 mm, or 0.2–0.3 inches, long) from the Hayes site in Tennessee, one of which yielded an AMS (accelerator mass spectrometry) radiocarbon date of 2315 B.C. ± 60 (4265 years B.P.). By 1000 B.C. (2950 years B.P.), achenes stored at Marble Bluff in Arkansas averaged ca. 9 mm (0.4 inches) in length. The next 2,500 years witnessed selection for larger seeds, breeding of strains with different seed colors, and widening of the range across which sunflower was grown. The combined archaeological and ethnographic records show that, by early historic times, native farmers from Texas, Mississippi, and North Carolina north to Quebec and west to the Great Plains grew sunflowers.

Early European travelers in the Southeast noted the use of sunflower seeds in bread and broth. In the Northeast, sunflower oil was used for food and cosmetic purposes. In the Southwest, where it may not have been grown before European contact, sunflowers with black seeds were grown primarily for making purple dye and body paint.

Buffalo Bird Woman, the nineteenth-century Hidatsa farmer raised at Like-a-Fishhook Village in North Dakota, described methods of cultivation, harvesting, processing, and storage. The Hidatsa sunflower plant was not monocephalic but bore both large and small heads, as may have been the case for prehistoric plants, judging by specimens found in Ozark and Kentucky rock shelters. Large seed disks were cut and dried first, but small seeds from the "baby" heads were sometimes beaten into a basket. The small seeds were preferred because they were oilier, but only the large seeds were planted. After cleaning, parching, and pounding the seeds, the people cooked the oily meal in a mixed-vegetable dish, made into a high-energy

Domesticated sunflower achenes in a clump to-gether with squash seeds from the Marble Bluff site (3SE1), Searcy County, Arkansas. Three radiocarbon dates from this burned cache of stored seeds indicate that these specimens are ca. 3000–3200 years old. The seed clump is accessioned as 32–23–345 in the University Museum, University of Arkansas, Fayetteville. (Photograph by G. Fritz)

ball carried by warriors and hunters, or mixed with corn flour. Buffalo Bird Woman's family usually stored two or three sacks of sunflower seeds for winter use.

Sunflower may never have been a staple food for Indian people, but seeds remain economically important today as a source of protein, fat, and concentrated energy, and the flowering plants add beauty to fields and gardens far beyond their North American homeland.

Gayle Fritz

Further Readings

Crites, G.B. 1993. Domesticated Sunflower in Fifth Millennium B.P. Temporal Context: New Evidence From Middle Tennessee. *American Antiquity* 58:146–148.

Heiser, C.B. 1976. *The Sunflower.* University of Oklahoma Press, Norman.

Wilson, G.L. 1987. *Buffalo Bird Woman's Garden.* Minnesota Historical Society, St. Paul.

Yarnell, R.A. 1978. Domestication of Sunflower and Sumpweed in Eastern North America. In *The Nature and Status of Ethnobotany,* edited by R.I. Ford, pp. 289–299. Anthropological Papers no. 67. Museum of Anthropology, University of Michigan, Ann Arbor.

Swift Creek

Swift Creek is a Middle Woodland–period (ca. 200 B.C.–A.D. 400, or 2150–1550 years B.P.) archaeological culture located in Georgia, northern Florida, and small portions of adjoining states; it was named after the type site, a single platform mound and associated village area, excavated near Macon, Georgia, during the WPA era (Kelly and Smith 1975). Swift Creek components are identified by elaborate curvilinear, complicated-stamped ceramics that often exhibit animal or cosmological motifs. Swift Creek populations participated in the panregional Hopewellian interaction and religious complex, with its emphasis on widespread exchange of extralocal raw materials and finished products, elaborate mortuary ritual, and a highly individualistic and egalitarian animal-centered hunting/guardian spirit–based ceremonialism and ritual (Brose 1985; Penny 1985).

Swift Creek and other contemporaneous South Appalachian–area ceramic-design motifs are found at sites as far removed as Pinson in western Tennessee, Mann in southern Indiana, and Rutherford in southern Illinois, and at a number of the major mound centers in Ohio, including Hopewell, Harness, McGraw, Mound City, Tremper, Turner, and Seip. Besides pottery, other presumably locally derived materials, such as mica and galena, saw widespread distribution throughout the East (Goad 1979); it is also possible that perishables, such as feathers, carved masks or other objects, or unusual foods, were moving. The preeminent product coming from the Swift Creek–culture area, at least in terms of archaeological visibility, was conch or whelk shell. Probable source areas for this shell were the northern and western Gulf Coast of Florida and, to a lesser extent, the lower Atlantic seaboard.

The distribution of Swift Creek sites and centers appears to have been shaped by the panregional demand for shell and by regional physiographic conditions that constrained the routes through which this commodity could pass into the interior. A number of major sites are located in coastal areas, including Bernath and Block-Sterns in western Florida, near presumed sources of shell (Bense 1993). The major Middle Woodland settlements along or near the Chattahoochee River at Mandeville and Kolomoki in south Georgia, and in the northwestern part of the state at Shaw and Tunacunnhee, likely were way stations along a north-south trade axis leading from the Gulf Coast to the Tennessee River and from there downstream and overland into the heart of the Midwest, perhaps via sites like Pinson and Mann. These communication routes closely correspond to the location of major historic Indian trails, which likely had considerable antiquity (Goad 1979:244–245). While elaborate burials characterized by classic Hopewellian grave goods, such as copper panpipes and earspools, prismatic blades, galena, cut mica, and platform pipes, are found at many Swift Creek centers, these materials occurred within otherwise purely local Woodland assemblages. At Mandeville, dated from A.D. 100 to 450 (1850–1500 years B.P.), for example, the period of greatest Hopewellian influence was also the period with the most pronounced occurrence of Santa Rosa/Swift Creek materials; at Tunacunnhee, ceramics from the Cartersville, Connestee, and Candy Creek series were found at a nearby habitation site assumed to be contemporaneous.

Swift Creek complicated-stamped ceramics represent a continuation of the South Appalachian carved-paddle decorative tradition. They replaced the plain, check-, and simple-stamped ceramics of the Deptford and Cartersville series in northern Florida and southern Georgia in the first decades of the first millennium A.D. and were replaced, in turn, by Weeden Island ceramics and culture ca. A.D. 400 (1550 years B.P.). In central and northern Georgia, Swift Creek ceramics appeared about the same time but continued in use as late as A.D. 750 (1200 years B.P.), when they were replaced by the Late Woodland Napier series. At many sites in this area, they co-occur with Connestee-like, Deptford, and Cartersville ceramics. Early Swift Creek designs are usually of simple curvilinear design based on concentric circles and ovals. Rims are typically notched or scalloped, and tetrapods are common. Late Swift Creek assemblages, postdating ca. A.D. 500 (1450 years B.P.), are characterized by an increase in the incidence of plain pottery and folded rims, a decline in the incidence of notched and scalloped rims, and (usually) more complex complicated-stamped designs with some zoned stamping. Some design motifs and rim treatments have proven to be highly sensitive temporal markers, and some appear to come from specific sites. A fine-lined variant of Swift Creek, called B-Complex to differentiate it from classic south and central Georgia materials, is found in the northern and eastern Georgia Piedmont and appears to be transitional between Swift Creek and Napier. Middle Woodland sites in extreme eastern Georgia and South Carolina are largely dominated by Deptford and Cartersville ceramics and are almost completely devoid of Swift Creek influence, although occasional sherds are found; a similar situation occurs in western North Carolina, where assemblages are dominated by Connestee-like ceramics. During the period when Swift Creek ceramics were manufactured in central and northern Georgia, small square-stemmed projectile points were largely replaced by triangular forms, while to the south, primarily stemmed forms are found.

Swift Creek complicated-stamped pottery, which is characterized by elaborate and richly symbolic design motifs, offers an almost unparalleled opportunity to explore questions of Middle Woodland worldview and cosmology. Both animal motifs and cosmological themes occur (Snow and Stephenson 1993). Some of these motifs may have served as individual or lineage/community guardian spirits or representations of more general forces of the cosmos, such as the sky and the underworld (Penny 1985:184–189). Hopewellian avian images, for example, often include raptors and ducks, which are thought to reflect a dichotomy between the separate domains of the sky and the watery underworld. These representations, fairly common on classic Ohio, Havana, and Marksville vessels, are less commonly seen among Swift Creek designs, suggesting that the latter may reflect a less ordered or more casual and diversified view of the natural world and the cosmos.

Swift Creek populations in some areas built platform as well as burial mounds that were likely important arenas where competition between individuals and lineages occurred. Evidence for summit structures has been found at some; at others, hearths suggesting communal ritual or feasting are present; at still others, little or no evidence has been discovered for how the mounds functioned. Swift Creek sites with platform mounds, besides the type site itself, include Mandeville, Kolomoki, Annewakee Creek, and Cold Springs in Georgia, Garden Creek in western North Carolina, a Connestee occupation but with some associated Swift Creek sherds, and McKeithan in northeast Florida (Jefferies 1994). At some coastal sites like Bernath in northwest Florida, ring middens appear to be an equivalent to the mound- and plaza-based centers found in the interior. The extent of monumental construction at Swift Creek sites appears to be closely tied to proximity to regional trading and communications routes. Major mound centers or sites with impressive mortuary remains in the Swift Creek area, such as Mandeville, Kolomoki, or Tunacunnhee, typically occur along or near these routes. Mound construction is less extensive or absent in areas farther away from them, as is evidence for elaborate Hopewell-related mortuary ritual. A number of small Swift Creek mound centers have been documented in northern Georgia that may have been shrines where relatively uncomplicated communal ritual occurred.

Swift Creek centers evolved over time. They experienced major periods of growth, inter- or intraregional interaction, and decline and abandonment, organizational fluctuations that also appear to have characterized the use of major Ohio Hopewell centers. Disruptions at any point in the distribution network may have had ripple effects over much larger areas, and interaction may have been much greater at some times than at others. There is some evidence that interaction between the Southeast and the Midwest increased in the centuries immediately after A.D. 150 (1800 years B.P.) (Brose 1985:76–77). While panregional interaction declined markedly after A.D. 400 (1550 years B.P.) or so, Swift Creek culture itself either continued or transformed itself locally, with no evidence for a break in continuity. The reasons for the decline in the larger Hopewellian interaction network and ritual may be tied to the appearance of the bow and arrow, which apparently took place about the end of the Middle Woodland period in many parts of the East. The introduction of this technology, when coupled with increasing regional population, may have brought about conditions in which raiding or warfare became more prevalent than trade and ritual as a means of achieving social objectives.

David G. Anderson

Further Readings

Bense, J.A. 1993. Santa Rosa-Swift Creek in Northwest Florida. *Proceedings of the Ocmulgee National Monument, Macon, Georgia, Swift Creek Conference, May 28–29, 1993.* Lamar Institute, Watkinsville.

Brose, D.S. 1985. The Woodland Period. In *Ancient Art of the American Woodland Indians,* edited by D.S. Brose, J.A. Brown, and D.W. Penny, pp. 42–91. Abrams, New York.

Goad, S.I. 1979. Middle Woodland Exchange in the Prehistoric Southeastern United States. In *Hopewell Archaeology: The Chillicothe Conference,* edited by D.S. Brose and N. Greber, pp. 239–246. Kent State University Press, Kent.

Jefferies, R.W. 1976. *The Tunacunnhee Site: Evidence of Hopewell Interaction in Northwest Georgia.* Anthropological Papers no. 1. University of Georgia Press, Athens.

———. 1994. The Swift Creek Site and Woodland Platform Mounds in the Southeast. In *Ocmulgee Archaeology 1936–1986,* edited by D.J. Hally, pp. 71–83. University of Georgia Press, Athens.

Kelly, A.R., and B.A. Smith. 1975. *The Swift Creek Site, 9-Bi-3, Macon, Georgia.* Prepared by the Southeastern Archaeology Center, University of Georgia, Athens. Contract no. 500041720. Copies available from the Department of Anthropology, University of Georgia, Athens.

Penny, D.W. 1985. Continuities of Imagery and Symbolism in the Art of the Woodlands. In *Ancient Art of the American Woodland Indians,* edited by D.S. Brose, J.A. Brown, and D.W. Penny, pp. 147–198. Abrams, New York.

Snow, F., and K. Stephenson. 1993. Swift Creek Designs: A Tool for Monitoring Interaction. *Proceedings of the Ocmulgee National Monument, Macon, Georgia, Swift Creek Conference, May 28–29, 1993.* Lamar Institute, Watkinsville.

See also GARDEN CREEK SITE; HOPEWELL INTERACTION SPHERE; KOLOMOKI; MANDEVILLE; MANN SITE; MCKEITHEN SITE; PINSON MOUNDS SITE

T

Taltheilei Tradition

The Taltheilei tradition encompasses the later prehistory of the Subarctic Northwest Territories and adjacent northern prairie provinces east of the Mackenzie Valley. It is divided into five phases, all centering on the range of the modern Beverly caribou herd both north and south of the tree line. Most Taltheilei-tradition sites have poor organic preservation, so knowledge of the tool inventory is largely limited to lithic artifacts. Lithic projectile points seem to provide the most consistent yardstick for measuring stylistic change over time. Thick, narrow, parallel-tanged points characterize the earliest, or pioneering, phase (ca. 650–500 B.C., or 2600–2450 years B.P.), while thinner points with wider shoulders denote the following Early phase (500–100 B.C., or 2450–2050 years B.P.). The Middle phase (ca. 100 B.C.–500 A.D., or 2050–1450 years B.P.) has tapered-stem points, while the Late phase (500 A.D. to contact) is characterized by side- and corner-notched points, apparently diffused from the northern Plains. The Taltheilei tradition appears to lead directly to the postcontact culture of the historic Dene (formally called the Chipewyan and Yellowknife). Throughout, the way of life appears to have focused on caribou hunting at tundra water crossings and forest corrals.

Sequential radiocarbon dates and site dispersion in both forest and tundra suggest that the Taltheilei tradition entered the Beverly-herd range from the Lake Athabasca area to the south during a post-600 B.C. (2550 years B.P.) warming trend that followed the Pre-Dorset occupation of the area. The earliest sites are consistently absent in the Bathurst and Kaminuriak caribou ranges to the west and east, although these areas were occupied by latter Taltheilei peoples. A possible origin in northwestern British Columbia has been suggested, but that is unproven (Gordon 1977a). Despite apparent direct cultural continuity between Taltheilei and historic Dene culture, the earliest acceptable radiocarbon dates are six centuries older than glottochronological estimates for the dispersion of Athabaskan languages east of the Mackenzie River.

Taltheilei takes its name from Taltheilei Narrows ("fast water"), the narrow channel between the East Arm of Great Slave Lake and the lake proper. First used archaeologically as a complex by Richard S. MacNeish in 1951, it became a phrase and tradition in the Taltheilei Shale tradition of William Noble in 1971.

Bryan C. Gordon

Further Readings

Gordon, B.C. 1977a. Chipewyan Prehistory. In *Prehistory of the North American Sub-Arctic: The Athapascan Question*, edited by J.W. Helmer, S. Van Dyke, and F.J. Kense, pp. 72–76. Chacmool: Archaeological Association, University of Canada, Calgary.

———. 1977b. Prehistoric Chipewyan Manipulation of a Barrenland Caribou Water-Crossing. *Western Canadian Journal of Anthropology* 7(1):69–83.

MacNeish, R.S. 1951. An Archaeological Reconnaissance in the Northwest Territories. *Bulletin* 123:24–41. National Museum of Canada, Ottawa.

Noble, W.C. 1971. Archaeological Surveys and Sequences in the Central District of Mackenzie, NWT. *Arctic Anthropology* 3:102–135.

Tangle Lakes District

The Tangle Lakes Archaeological District in Alaska contains one of the largest concentrations of archaeological sites in the American Subarctic and perhaps the highest density of early sites anywhere in North America. Occupation spans ca. 11,000 years, from the final Pleistocene to almost living memory. The archaeological record is discontinuous, however, which reflects the reality of great resource variability in an ecosystem undergoing vast long-term changes and short-term fluctuations. These changes and fluctuations would have had a profound impact upon the hunters of interior Alaska, who were following a way of life established in its essentials by their earliest American ancestors.

Forming a rectangle ca. 24 x 7 km (15 x 4 miles), the Tangle Lakes (near 63° north latitude, 146° west latitude) consist of a chain of lakes in, and just south of, the Amphitheater Mountains of the central Alaska Range. They are the headwaters of the Delta River, which flows north of the Tanana and connects eventually with the Bering Sea. However, the archaeological district itself takes in much more territory than the Tangle Lakes. The first sites were found in 1956, and an intensive survey was begun 10 years later. Recent surveys have been carried out by federal agencies.

More than 300 sites have been cataloged. Although the majority are surficial, a significant number are in situ and provide uniquely valuable evidence on Alaskan prehistory. In addition to well-represented and well-characterized late Pleistocene–early Holocene Denali-complex sites, there are stratified, dated sites of Northern Archaic (ca. 2250 B.C., or 4200 years B.P.) and subsequent cultures that are intermediate to sparse late Athabascan sites. A chert quarry in the district is the only one of its kind in Alaska. Of particular interest are the Phipps site (cataloged as Mt. Hayes 111; Denali; 8200 B.C., or 10,150 years B.P.); Whitmore Ridge (Mt. Hayes 72; Denali; 8320 B.C., or 10,270 years B.P.); Sparks Point (Mt. Hayes 149; Denali; 7190 B.C., or 9140 years B.P.); two Northern Archaic sites, Hamilton (Mt. Hayes 35; 2500 B.C., or 4450 years B.P.) and Reger (Mt. Hayes 166; 2150 B.C., or 4100 years B.P.); and the Portage site (Mt. Hayes 121; 75 B.C., or 2025 years B.P.).

Frederick Hadleigh West

Taphonomy

Since the 1970s, taphonomy has become central to the study of animal remains from archaeological sites. The literal definition of taphonomy as "the laws of death and burial" only mini-

Tangle Lakes. A significant number of Late Pleistocene–Early Holocene sites of the Beringian tradition have been found in this region. (Photograph by F. H. West)

mally describes the nature of contemporary taphonomic analysis. In the broadest sense of the term, taphonomy's realm includes the study of all the biological, physical, and chemical processes operating from the moment of an animal's death until bones are recovered and studied as fossil or subfossil specimens. Such processes can include, but are not restricted to, decay and decomposition, carnivore consumption/modification, butchery and processing by humans, insect burrowing, transport or rearrangement by flowing water, gnawing by rodents, weathering, crushing, trampling, burning, and mode of burial. Burial is not, however, the end point for the consideration of processes of modification. Burrowing rodents, etching by plant roots, chemical alteration, carbonate accumulation, compaction and warping, and reexposure and reburial can all continue to alter assemblage properties. Finally, a significant factor in the formation of archaeological faunal assemblages is the actions of archaeologists themselves. Decisions about excavation, documentation, collection, and curation are often a predominant factor in the "creation" of faunal patterns. Taphonomy is a major form of middle-range research that investigates the linkages between observations in the archaeological record and interpretation of the range of processes that produced the record.

The introduction of a taphonomic perspective has had several major influences on archaeological research. First, it is clear that patterning in animal remains from archaeological sites can no longer be interpreted directly in terms of human actions. Broken bones alone are not sufficient evidence to assert that humans were removing marrow. Disarticulated and scattered bones do not imply that humans had dismembered animal carcasses. Differences in body-part frequencies are not necessarily providing information about human selection and transport decisions. The growing awareness that there is a vast difference between pattern recognition and behavioral interpretation has led to an increasingly more sophisticated battery of analytic techniques that seek to understand the full range of processes behind the observed patterning. As a direct consequence of such investigations, it is clear that taphonomic studies play a fundamental role in all aspects of understanding human paleoecology. As initially discussed in archaeology, taphonomic analyses were considered solely an evaluation of the amount of behavioral information loss. How-

ever, for many researchers, it is now common to view such processes as adding information about the more comprehensive paleoecology of a deposit. Finally, acknowledgment of the role taphonomic factors have played in archaeological-record formation and recognition that an understanding of those processes is of fundamental importance to the interpretation of human paleoecology are beginning to restructure the organization of archaeological projects. While once considered a specialized pursuit that could be undertaken as a later, postexcavation component of investigation, it is now understood that, to meet its full integrative potential, taphonomic analysis must be incorporated into all phases of archaeological research.

Lawrence C. Todd

Further Readings

Behrensmeyer, A.K. 1991. Terrestrial Vertebrate Accumulations. In *Taphonomy: Releasing the Data Locked in the Fossil Record*, edited by P.A. Allison and D.E.G. Briggs, pp. 291–335. Plenum Press, New York.

Binford, L.R. 1981. *Bones: Ancient Men and Modern Myths*. Academic Press, New York.

Bunn, H.T. 1991. A Taphonomic Perspective on the Archaeology of Human Origins. *Annual Review of Anthropology* 20:433–467.

Gifford, D.P. 1981. Taphonomy and Paleoecology: A Critical Review of Archaeology's Sister Disciplines. In *Advances in Archaeological Method and Theory*, vol. 4, edited by M.B. Schiffer, pp. 365–438. Academic Press, New York.

Todd, L.C. 1987. Analysis of Kill-Butchery Bonebeds and Interpretation of Paleoindian Hunting. In *The Evolution of Human Hunting*, edited by M.H. Nitecki and D.V. Nitecki, pp. 225–266. Plenum Press, New York.

Taylor, Walter W. (1913–1997)

A controversial figure in the history of American archaeology, Walter W. Taylor, in his polemical *Study of Archeology* (1948), accused the leading American archaeologists of the day, including Alfred V. Kidder, William S. Webb, Emil W. Haury, Frank H.H. Roberts, Jr., James B. Griffin, and William A. Ritchie, of limiting their research to narrow, anthropologically sterile objectives. While claiming that their goals were the reconstruction and explanation of prehistoric ways of life, most archaeologists, according to Taylor, actually produced descriptive comparisons of "diagnostic" artifacts and explanations of changes that relied on external factors, especially diffusion and migration. In this view, these limited goals had a stultifying effect on investigations of the archaeological record: Floral and faunal remains tended to be ignored, details of artifact provenance were generally omitted, and insufficient quantitative data were presented. In general, the cultural-historical goals of the period failed to generate culturally relevant data.

Besides providing a critique of the current cultural-historical approach, *A Study of Archeology* offered a historical perspective on the development of the discipline and Taylor's own programmatic outline of what an anthropologically relevant archaeology should be. His research program, called the conjunctive approach, was contextual and functional. Viewing the site as the primary unit of analysis, he proposed that detailed "contextual" intrasite studies be added to already common chronological and intersite studies. Attention was to be given to all artifacts and features, to quantitative, spatial, and temporal interrelationships, to the paleoenvironmental context of the site, and to any related ethnographic data. The goal was to recover as much information from the site as possible. This mass of data was then to be used to reconstruct everything possible about the functionally integrated pattern of life at the site and to account for how new ways of life at the site came about. The ultimate goal of the conjunctive approach was the same as the principal goal of anthropology: a general understanding of how and why people behave as they do.

A Study of Archeology was frequently cited by New Archaeologists of the 1960s as a seminal influence on their own research program. Among the shared assumptions of the two programs were a view of cultures as functionally integrated systems with economic, social, and ideological components; the belief that cultures must be studied holistically and from the "inside"; an emphasis on the use of ethnographic analogy in the interpretation of site materials and their interrelationships; and an interest in reconstructing how people lived at sites. There were also fundamental differences between the two programs. For instance, in contrast to the New Archeologists, Taylor embraced an idealist view of culture and an inductive model of science; his work also lacked a concept of cultures as ecologically adaptive systems, a cultural-evolutionary point of view, and a developed sense of process.

Taylor's *Study of Archeology*, the first monographic critique of American archaeology, was an expression, along with papers by William D. Strong, Clyde Kluckhohn, and Julian H. Steward and Frank M. Setzler, of a late-1930s critique of the dominant taxonomic and cultural-historical goals of American archaeology. The manuscript was a revision of Taylor's Harvard University doctoral thesis, which he began in the late 1930s under the influence of Kluckhohn and completed in 1942. The nature and magnitude of Taylor's contribution to the development of American archaeology remain topics of contention. Taylor failed in his own lack of fieldwork and subsequent publications to develop his approach, and most of his field studies in the American Southwest and Coahuilo, Mexico, were never published. At the very least, *A Study of Archeology* helped pave the way for the acceptance of approaches in archaeology, like New Archeology, that stress detailed, holistic, and functional interpretations in the reconstruction of prehistoric patterns of life.

Guy Gibbon

Further Readings

Kluckhohn, C. 1940. The Conceptual Structure in Middle American Studies. In *The Maya and Their Neighbors*, edited by C.L. Hay et al., pp. 41–51. Appleton-Century, New York.

Steward, J.H., and F.M. Setzler. 1938. Function and Configuration in Archaeology. *American Antiquity* 4(1):4–10.

Strong, W.D. 1936. Anthropological Theory and Archaeological Fact. In *Essays in Anthropology*, edited by R.H. Lowie, pp. 359–368. University of California Press, Berkeley.

Taylor, W.W. 1948. *A Study of Archeology*. Memoir no. 69. American Anthropological Association, Menasha.

———. 1954. Southwestern Archaeology: Its History and Theory. *American Anthropologist* 56:561–575.

Trigger, B.G. 1989. *A History of Archaeological Thought*. Cambridge University Press, Cambridge.

Willey, G.R., and J.A. Sabloff. 1993. *A History of American Archaeology*. 3rd ed.

W.H. Freeman, San Francisco.

Woodbury, R.B. 1954. Review of *A Study of Archeology,* by W.W. Taylor. *American Antiquity* 19:292–296.

Tchefuncte Culture

Tchefuncte is an Early Woodland culture of the Lower Mississippi Valley. It dates to the Tchula period between the terminal Archaic Poverty Point and Middle Woodland Marksville periods, or to ca. 850–150 B.C. (2800–2100 years B.P.). It is contemporary, in whole or part, with Marion, Adena, Alexander, Deptford, Refuge, and other cultures in the Eastern Woodlands. Geographically, it extends throughout the Mississippi alluvial valley from a northerly point just below the junction of the Mississippi and Arkansas rivers to the Gulf of Mexico and from valley wall to wall, an area ca. 650 km (400 miles) long and between 80 and 200 km (50–125 miles) wide.

Tchefuncte is the first Lower Mississippi culture to have abundant pottery. Tchefuncte decorations first appear on ceramics at the Poverty Point site ca. 1250 B.C. (3200 years B.P.) and possibly a century or so earlier. This early or proto-Tchefuncte pottery is stratigraphically lower than fiber-tempered ware, which is the earliest ceramic throughout most of the southeastern United States. Late Tchefuncte pottery incorporates some classic Marksville decorations, and Tchefuncte and Marksville wares are often found together in midden and mound contexts, dating to ca. 100 B.C. (2050 years B.P.).

Tchefuncte pottery is unique. Fabric is soft, untempered, and typically foliated. Legged vessels are common. Decoration includes simple and drag-and-jab incising, smooth and dentate rocker-stamping, simple stamping, unzoned fingernail and tool punctating, and zoned punctating.

Other ceramic artifacts include a few biconical clay cooking objects and tubular clay pipes.

Stone, bone, antler, and shell tools round out Tchefuncte assemblages. They form diverse sets, depending on location and function. Small Pontchartrain, Gary, Palmillas, Maçon, Elam, Ellis, and other hafted bifaces characterize lithic assemblages everywhere, but other bifacially chipped-stone tools are limited to drills, celts and adzes, and battered-edge scaled pieces. Rare flake tools include edge-chipped (nibbled, denticulated, retouched, and backed) pieces, notches, and gravers. Ground- and polished-stone tools include abraders, sandstone saws, pitted stones, boatstones, bar weights, celts, and grooved plummets. Bone and antler were fashioned into socketed-, harpoon-, and splinter-type projectile points, atlatl hooks, perforators, flakers, fishhooks, and jaw- and penis-bone ornaments; shell was used to make gouges, chisels, and containers. Bone, antler, and shell artifacts tend to dominate near the coast; stone artifacts, inland.

Tchefuncte sites are usually small, but some long-used shell middens on the coast, such as Big Oak Island and Morton Shell Mound, cover more than 1 ha (2.5 acres). Inland sites, such as Lafayette Mounds, Coulee Crow, Russell Landing, Bayou Louis, Boothe Landing, and Beau Mire, tend to be larger, sometimes covering 2–3 ha (5–7.5 acres), and may have one to five associated earth mounds. Mounds are conical affairs, ranging from 1 to 5 m (3.3–16.5 feet) in height and from 20 to 35 m (65.5–115 feet) in diameter. They were used for burial and primarily contain disarticulated individuals of both sexes and all ages that were interred without grave furniture. One studied skeletal sample from sites around Lake Pontchartrain reveals that these people were long headed, of average height, and apparently healthy, except for some cases of osteoporosis.

Tchefuncte culture is a culture of the floodplain and coastal marshes and, in some quarters, is the first to wean itself of upland ties. Big Oak and Little Oak islands furnish a good example of marsh adaptation on the eastern side of the Mississippi Valley. After first serving as a residential location, Big Oak Island became a fishing and rangia-shucking camp, probably for people from nearby Little Oak Island. It was finally turned into a burying ground, probably for Little Oak peoples. The focus of the Oak islands subsistence was the rangia clam-freshwater drum prey-predator niche in the brackish marsh. The people of Morton Shell Mound, located on a salt dome on the opposite side of the Mississippi Valley, got their meat primarily from deer and other mammals, alligators, birds, and fish, and their plant foods from various nuts, fruits, and seeds. Squash and bottle gourd are present in minor amounts, insufficient to alter our view of Morton subsistence, as well as Tchefuncte subsistence in general, as being based on logistical hunting and gathering. People at inland sites took advantage of whatever their particular catchments offered, primarily nuts, acorns, fish, and upland and aquatic game. Such adaptability to varying foods and seasonal peculiarities of diverse environments is a hallmark of Tchefuncte culture.

Tchefuncte exchange pales in comparison with Poverty Point. Small amounts of novaculite and quartz crystal went down valley from Hot Springs, Arkansas, probably in ad hoc transactions.

Socioculturally, Tchefuncte culture was made up of many diverse groups, whose common bond was pottery decoration and not genealogy or ethnicity. These groups were probably organized on a tribal level, some more rigidly than others. Tchefuncte culture was expansive, pushing into new areas and environments. This push may have been precipitated by population growth or economic opportunity, or both, or it may simply reflect shifting population; whatever the case, it took some peoples away from the valley walls, where they had clung tenaciously for millennia.

Tchefuncte culture seems simplistic when compared with preceding Poverty Point and following Marksville cultures, but appearances are misleading. Take away the large Poverty Point site, and there is not much that distinguishes the organizational rudiments of Tchefuncte and Poverty Point cultures. Take away ca. 3 kg (6.6 lbs) of exotic grave goods from the excavated Marksville mounds and some pottery designs, and there is not much that distinguishes Tchefuncte and Marksville. Tchefuncte culture was one that quite literally was on the move, one that ushered in the container revolution, and one that set the pace for future developments out in the Mississippi floodplain.

Jon L. Gibson

Further Readings

Byrd, K.M. 1994. Tchefuncte Subsistence Practices at the Morton Shell Mound, Iberia Parish, Louisiana. *Louisiana Archaeology* 16 (for 1989):1–146.

Dye, D.H., and R.C. Brister (editors). 1986. *The Tchula Period in the Mid-South and Lower Mississippi Valley*. Archaeological Report no. 17. Mississippi Department of Archives and History, Jackson.

Ford, J.A., and G.I. Quimby. 1945. *The Tchefuncte Culture: An Early Occupation of the Lower Mississippi Valley*. Memoir no. 2. American Anthropological Association, Menasha.

Gibson, J.L. 1975. The Tchefuncte Culture in the Bayou Vermilion Basin, South Central Louisiana. *Bulletin of the Texas Archeological Society* 45:67–95.

Jenkins, N.J., D.H. Dye, and J.A. Walthall. 1986. Early Ceramic Development in the Gulf Coastal Plain. In *Early Woodland Archeology*, edited by K.B. Farnsworth and T.E. Emerson, pp. 546–563. Kampsville Seminars in Archeology, vol. 2. Center for American Archeology Press, Kampsville.

Neuman, R.W. 1984. *An Introduction to Louisiana Archaeology*. Louisiana State University Press, Baton Rouge.

Shenkel, J.R. 1974. Big Oak and Little Oak Islands: Excavations and Interpretations. *Louisiana Archaeology* 1:37–65.

———. 1981. Pontchartrain Tchefuncte Site Differentiation. *Louisiana Archaeology* 8:21–36.

Weinstein, R.A. 1986. Tchefuncte Occupation in the Lower Mississippi Delta and Adjacent Coastal Zone. In *The Tchula Period in the Mid-South and Lower Mississippi Valley*, edited by D.H. Dye and R.C. Brister, pp. 102–127. Archaeological Report no. 17. Mississippi Department of Archives and History, Jackson.

Weinstein, R.A., and P.G. Rivet. 1978. *Beau Mire: A Late Tchula Period Site of the Tchefuncte Culture, Ascension Parish, Louisiana*. Anthropological Report no. 1. Louisiana Archaeological Survey and Antiquities Commission, Baton Rouge.

Tellico Archaic

From 1967 to 1981, the University of Tennessee, Department of Anthropology, under contract to the Tennessee Valley Authority and the National Park Service, conducted archaeological investigations in the last 48 km (30 miles) of the Little Tennessee River Valley in eastern Tennessee in mitigation of the impact of the Tellico Reservoir. The discovery of buried, stratified Early, Middle, and Late Archaic deposits preserved in T1 alluvial sediments led to excavations at eight sites and the location of 60 others through backhoe testing. Almost 250,000 lithic artifacts were recovered from undisturbed Archaic contexts along with 22 kg (59 lbs) of archaeobotanical remains; recorded features exceeded 1,000. The database, especially for the Early Archaic, is among the best in the eastern United States; the investigations confirmed typological sequences reported earlier (e.g., the St. Albans site) and expanded our knowledge of assemblage content. Of importance are the Kirk Corner-Notched cluster and the Bifurcate tradition.

Important Early Archaic sites include Rose Island, Icehouse Bottom, Calloway Island, and Bacon Farm; Middle Archaic sites: Icehouse Bottom and Howard; Late Archaic sites: Iddins. With some overlap, radiocarbon dates established the following chronology of phases/temporal units:

Early Archaic: Lower Kirk (8000–7300 B.C., or 9950–9250 years B.P.), Upper Kirk (7400–6800 B.C., or 9350–8750 years B.P.), St. Albans (6900–6500 B.C., or 8850–8450 years B.P.), LeCroy (6500–5800 B.C., or 8450–7750 years B.P.), and Kanawha (6100–5800 B.C., or 8050–7750 years B.P.).

Middle Archaic: Kirk Stemmed (6000–5800 B.C., or 7950–7750 years B.P.), Stanly (5800–5500 B.C., or 7750–7450 years B.P.), Morrow Mountain (5500–5000 B.C., or 7450–6950 years B.P.); isolated finds of Guilford and Sykes points suggest only a light and sporadic late Middle Archaic (5000–3000 B.C., or 6950–4950 years B.P.) occupation.

Late Archaic: Savannah River (3000–1800 B.C., or 4950–3750 years B.P.) and Iddins (1800–1200 B.C., or 3750–3150 years B.P.).

Jefferson Chapman

Further Readings

Chapman, J. 1975. *The Rose Island Site and the Bifurcate Point Tradition.* Report of Investigations no. 14. Department of Anthropology, University of Tennessee, Knoxville.

———. 1977. *Archaic Period Research in the Lower Little Tennessee River Valley–1975: Icehouse Bottom, Harrison Branch, Thirty Acre Island, Calloway Island.* Report of Investigations no. 18. Department of Anthropology, University of Tennessee, Knoxville.

———. 1978. *The Bacon Farm Site and a Buried Site Reconnaissance.* Report of Investigations no. 23. Department of Anthropology, University of Tennessee, Knoxville.

———. 1979. *Archaeological Investigations at the Howard (40MR66) and Calloway Island (40MR41) Sites.* Report of Investigations no. 27. Department of Anthropology, University of Tennessee, Knoxville.

———. 1981. *The Bacon Bend and Iddins Sites: The Late Archaic Period in the Lower Little Tennessee River Valley.* Report of Investigations no. 31. Department of Anthropology, University of Tennessee, Knoxville.

———. 1985a. Archaeology and the Archaic Period in the Southern Ridge-and-Valley Province. In *Structure and Process in Southeastern Archaeology,* edited by R.S. Dickens, Jr., and H.T. Ward, pp. 137–153. University of Alabama Press, Tuscaloosa.

———. 1985b. *Tellico Archaeology: 12,000 Years of Native American History.* Report of Investigations no. 43. Department of Anthropology, University of Tennessee, Knoxville.

Chapman, J., and A.B. Shea. 1981. The Archaeobotanical Record: Early Archaic Period to Contact in the Lower Little Tennessee River Valley. *Tennessee Anthropologist* 6:61–84.

Thedford II

Thedford II (AgHk-6) is an Early Paleoindian site typologically dated to ca. 8750 B.C. (10,700 years B.P.); it covers 700 m² (837 square yards) in a cultivated field in Ontario 15 km (9 miles) from the modern Lake Huron shore. At the time of occupation, it was close to the shore of Lake Algonquin, a late glacial high water level in the Huron Basin, and was apparently situated in a spruce parkland.

Investigations at the site yielded 159 stone tools and preforms, 1,010 pieces of flaking debris, and several plow-disturbed feature remnants, among which was a cache containing as many as 13 fluted bifaces. The stone-artifact assemblage, both tools and debris, is largely (more than 80 percent) on Fossil Hill formation chert from outcrops 170 km (105 miles) northeast of the site. The stone material is believed to have been obtained by the Paleoindian occupants during the course of their normal annual settlement movements. The dominance of this chert at at least six other sites in the Thedford II vicinity suggests the habitual use of certain settlement ranges over an extended period of time. The remainder of the Thedford II assemblage consists of small amounts of materials from other distant bedrock sources, such as Bayport chert from a source in Michigan 150 km (95 miles) northwest of the site. These other cherts were probably obtained by exchange and other forms of social interaction with other

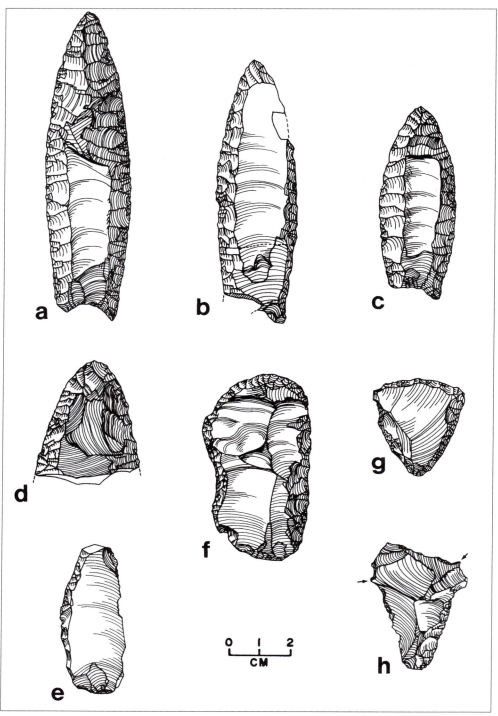

Flaked stone artifacts from the Thedford II site, Ontario (a-c. fluted points and preforms; d. tip of biface knife resharpened by unifacial edge beveling; e. side scraper; f. end and concave side scraper on large "blade-flake"; g. trianguloid end scraper on flake from large biface core; h. multi-spurred graver or micropiercer on end biface thinning flake, with arrows showing spur locations). (From Deller and Ellis 1992. Reproduced courtesy of the Museum of Anthropology, University of Michigan)

bands that were exploiting different geographic areas rather than as a product of normal settlement moves.

The blanks used for tools were consistently derived from standardized core forms, including large biface cores and roughly conical cores, used to produce "blade-flakes." Reduction of these cores apparently occurred near the stone source, as the debris from Thedford II and other sites in the area exclusively represents the final stages of tool manufacture and edge resharpening, such as channel flakes and uniface retouch flakes. The tools recovered include many typical Paleoindian tool forms like trianguloid end scrapers and gravers (see Figure); artifacts often considered typical of northeastern Paleoindian sites, such as fluted drills and *pièces esquillées,* are notable by their absence. Also, the site produced several not widely recognized tool types of potential diagnostic value, such as large ovate bifaces resharpened at the tip by unifacial edge beveling.

Spatial analyses revealed that the site included six discrete clusters of debris arranged in a highly patterned layout, suggesting contemporaneous use. Five of these clusters were arranged in a semicircle around the northern site margin. These areas were of a consistent size (ca. 100 m², or 120 square yards) and yielded similar numbers (19–25) and kinds of tools and debris. Each also had a wide variety of tools, suggesting they were not specialized-activity locations. Each of these areas may represent the work area of a small social unit, such as a family, for different raw-material profiles in each area suggest that they were made by different individuals, and there are consistent but minute differences in projectile-point form and manufacture between areas. The final area was centrally located, covered ca. 200 m² (717 square yards), and had a broad tool inventory. It may have been a communal work area used by all site occupants.

Christopher Ellis

Further Readings

Deller, D.B., and C.J. Ellis 1992a. The Early Paleo-Indian Parkhill Phase in Southwestern Ontario. *Man in the Northeast* 44:15–54.

———. 1992b. *Thedford II: A Paleo-Indian Site in the Ausable River Watershed of Southwestern Ontario.* Memoir no. 24. Museum of Anthropology, University of Michigan, Ann Arbor.

Thomas, Cyrus (1825–1910)

An entomologist from Illinois, Cyrus Thomas was selected by John Wesley Powell in 1882 to head the Division of Mound Exploration of the Bureau of American Ethnology. His main task was to explore the Mound Builder problem; that is, to determine who built the earthworks scattered throughout the Eastern Woodlands. Utilizing a combination of extensive survey and limited test-excavation at important sites, small crews under his direction investigated more than 2,000 mounds between 1882 and 1886. Although a believer at first in a separate Mound Builder race, Thomas quickly realized that the mounds had been constructed by the ancestors of a variety of different Native American tribes and nations. His *Report of the Mound Explorations of the Bureau of Ethnology* (1894), which organized mounds by culture areas, disproved the then popular "lost Mound Builder race" hypothesis. The report describes in detail many of the mounds and burials explored and makes use of an early form of the direct-historical approach in its attack on the Mound Builder problem. Most sites are treated, however, as if they were culturally homogeneous, and evidence of local cultural change is largely ignored,

Cyrus Thomas (Courtesy of the National Anthropological Archives, Smithsonian Institution, Photograph No. 67–A)

even though stratigraphic methods were employed in their excavation. These latter views are reflections of Thomas's assumption that Native Americans continued to live in the same regions with minimal change once they had settled the continent. The same assumption is evident in his attempt to demonstrate that the level of complexity of past Indian communities was no greater than that of their seventeenth- and eighteenth-century descendants. Thomas also summarized North American archaeology in a text in 1898; attacked, with William Henry Holmes, claims of the discovery of "paleolithic" tools in very ancient geological contexts; and made significant contributions to Meso-american archaeology.

Guy Gibbon

Further Readings

Thomas, C. 1885. Who Were the Mound-builders? *American Antiquarian and Oriental Journal* 2:65–74.
———. 1894. Report of the Mound Explorations of the Bureau of Ethnology. *Bureau of American Ethnology Annual Report* 12:3–742.
———. 1898. *Introduction to the Study of North American Archaeology*. Robert Clarke, Cincinnati.

See also MOUND BUILDER MYTH; POWELL, JOHN WESLEY

Thomas Riggs Phase

Villages of the Thomas Riggs phase, a Late Prehistoric Middle Missouri–tradition Extended-variant phase, are found in central South Dakota along the Missouri River, principally along the lower reaches of the Oahe Reservoir. Although radiocarbon dates do not precisely date the phase, they do indicate that it probably dates to the early part of the A.D. 1100–1500 (850–450 years B.P.) time span, which is consistent with present ideas of local prehistory. The Fort Yates phase is a closely related and contemporaneous phase that occupied the Missouri Valley farther upriver in modern-day south-central North Dakota. Most communities are relatively small and unfortified, although at least one of them—Thomas Riggs, the type site—was surrounded on three sides by a ditch. The long rectangular houses that typify the phase have vertical side walls and a central ridgepole. A covered entry faces southwest. The houses were not usually placed in any particular order, though some are roughly arranged in rows.

The ceramics consist of moderately sized jars whose exterior surfaces were either smoothed or stamped with a grooved paddle. Rims are either straight or collared (an angular S-rim), with the more elaborate decoration on rims of the latter variety. Vessels have distinctive designs incised on the shoulder, and incised or cord-impressed patterns embellishing the rims. Small triangular chipped-stone arrow points, drills, end scrapers, and a variety of large and small bifaces are common. Ground-stone tools included grooved mauls, axes, celts, and a variety of grinding stones. Bison-scapula hoes are the most conspicuous objects of worked bone, but a wide variety of tools are of this material. Lesser numbers of objects were made of antler or shell. The temporal and cultural relations of this phase with the Fort Yates phase remain unclear. However, both were significant predecessors of the Huff phase that, in turn, was the ancestral base of the historic Mandan Indians.

W. Raymond Wood

Further Readings

Hurt, W.R., Jr. 1953. *Report of the Investigation of the Thomas Riggs Site, 39HU1, Hughes County, South Dakota*. Archaeological Studies Circular no. 5. South Dakota Archaeological Commission, Pierre.
Johnston, R.B. 1967. The Thomas Riggs Site (39HU1) Revisited, Hughes County, South Dakota. *American Antiquity* 32:393–395.

See also FORT YATES PHASE; MIDDLE MISSOURI TRADITION

Thule Culture

As an organized, scientific discipline, archaeology in the North American Arctic can be said to have begun with Therkel Mathiassen's identification of the prehistoric Thule culture in the Canadian Arctic. Working at several locations on Baffin Island and around the northwest coast of Hudson Bay in the early 1920s, Mathiassen found abundant evidence of an early "Eskimo" culture that he named "Thule" after previous finds from the Thule district of northwest Greenland. Although comparative archaeological data were almost nonexistent, Mathiassen suggested an Alaskan origin for Thule culture and an age of ca. A.D. 950 (1000 years B.P.).

Subsequent archaeological work has confirmed and amplified Mathiassen's original interpretations. It is now clear that Thule culture has a pan-Arctic distribution from the Bering Strait to Greenland, that it arose in northwestern Alaska from the preceding Birnirk culture, and that it is the culture immediately underlying the various regional cultures of the historic Inuit. There is little doubt that the bearers of Thule culture were ethnically Inuit and that they spoke a language ancestral to the Inuit language—Inuktitut or Inupiaq—now spoken across the North American Arctic. The linguistic and other cultural similarities uniting all modern Inuit are the products of a common Thule legacy.

The transition between the preceding Birnirk culture and Thule in northwestern Alaska seems to date to ca. A.D. 900–1000 (1050–950 years B.P.). The distinction between the two is based on minor stylistic changes in the Alaskan sequence and especially on the fact that, at about this time, Thule culture began to expand rapidly eastward. This expansion was based on a migration or a series of migrations that everywhere replaced the earlier Dorset-culture inhabitants of the eastern Arctic with Thule Inuit newcomers. The Dorset/Thule transition in Canada and Greenland is abrupt and complete, with little if any evidence of Dorset cultural or biological survival.

Reasons for this dramatic expansion are far from clear, but they may relate in part to slightly warmer climatic conditions at this time. Thule people were superb hunters, able to tackle even the gigantic bowhead whale. Warmer climatic conditions ca. A.D. 950 (1000 years B.P.) seem to have expanded the range of the Pacific bowhead population east into the Canadian Arctic islands, where it briefly overlapped with the range of the Atlantic bowhead. This may have helped attract Thule hunters east. It is certain that many Canadian Thule groups depended heavily on bowhead-whale hunting, even framing their sod winter houses with whale rib and jaw bones. But Thule people also early occupied areas where whales seem to have been unknown. Certainly, Thule hunters were adept at more than whale hunting and successfully exploited the whole range of Arctic animal life, particularly caribou, ringed seal, and, where available, walrus.

As reflected in their archaeological remains, Thule people enjoyed a highly developed and classic Eskimo culture. They had kayaks and umiaks for water transportation, dogsleds, lamps and cooking pots of soapstone or clay, composite sinew-backed bows, a number of harpoon types for hunting different types of sea mammals, and a complex range of other tools for hunting, fish, sewing, and tool manufacture. They lived in heavy sod houses in the winter and skin tents during the brief Arctic summer. Climatic deterioration in much of the central Arctic during the Little Ice Age (ca. A.D. 1550–1850, or 400–100 years B.P.) may have been fundamental in the transition between Thule culture and the various regional Inuit cultures of the historic period. Perhaps the most basic change was a widespread trend away from the summertime open-water hunting of sea mammals, including whales, toward the wintertime sea-ice hunting of a much more restricted range of species, principally ringed seal. Related changes include the abandonment of the heavy sod "whalebone" house in favor of the much more flexible snow house, and the abandonment in some regions of both the large skin umiak and the oceangoing version of the kayak. Outside of the central Arctic, less rigorous environmental conditions meant that the ancestral Thule way of life persisted into the historic period.

David Morrison

Further Readings

Mathiassen, T. 1927. *Archaeology of the Central Eskimos: The Thule Culture and Its Position Within the Eskimo Culture.* Report of the Fifth Thule Expedition 1921–1924, vol. 4, nos. 1–2. Glydenclalski Boghandel, Nordisk Forlag, Copenhagen.

McCartney, A. (editor). 1979. *Thule Eskimo Culture: An Anthropological Retrospective.* Mercury Series Paper no. 88. Archaeological Survey of Canada, National Museum of Man, Ottawa.

Morrison, D. 1989. Radiocarbon Dating Thule Culture. *Arctic Anthropology* 26(2):48–77.

See also THULE TRADITION

Thule Tradition

The Thule tradition is a "lumper's" category that includes many Arctic cultures, especially Thule culture and its immediate ancestors and close relatives—Birnirk, Punuk, and Old Bering Sea—along with all "Eskimo" cultural manifestations in the Bering Sea area dating since ca. A.D. 1000 (950 years B.P.). It thus embraces the later prehistory of all Eskimos, both Yupik and Inupiat/Inuit, living north of the Alaska Peninsula. Even in the Pacific Eskimo area, the Thule-tradition influence is generally seen in the adoption of such "Thule" traits as pottery.

While perhaps useful as a descriptive device, the Thule tradition is not a unified entity. From its northwest Alaskan homeland, Thule culture (in the strict sense) spread into Canada and Greenland via migration, but south of Bering Strait any cultural expansion was more a matter of diffusion, with the local Norton-culture population remaining largely in place. This difference in process probably underlies, at least in part, the linguistic distinction between Yupik and Inupiak/Inuktituut-speaking Eskimos, with the former tracing linguistic continuity from the Norton culture, and the latter from the Birnirk and Thule cultures. It might be better to limit the Thule tradition to the Thule culture and its immediate relatives (Old Bering Sea, Birnirk, and Punuk) and to use the more general term "Neoeskimo" to signify all recent Eskimo cultures.

David Morrison

Further Readings

Dumond, D. 1987. *The Eskimos and Aleuts.* 2nd ed. Thames and Hudson, New York.

See also THULE CULTURE

Thunderbird Site

The Thunderbird site (44WR11) is a stratified Paleoindian through Early Archaic quarry-related base camp located on the south bank of the South Fork of the Shenandoah River in Warren County, Virginia. It measures ca. 70 x 1,300 m (76.6 x 1,422 yards) and slopes slightly, with one-third of the site within a plow zone and the lower two-thirds buried by up to 1.1 m (3.6 feet) of sediment. Three Paleoindian levels have been identified: Eastern Clovis, Mid-Paleo, and Dalton. Continuity with the succeeding Early Archaic (sequentially, Palmer and Kirk Corner Notched, Big Sandy I, and Kirk Stemmed) is evident in many areas of technology.

An oval postmold structure, ca. 6 x 12 m (20 x 39.5 feet), is associated with either the Clovis or the Mid-Paleo level. Interior post-molds may represent structural features, rebuilding efforts, or multiple structures. Intrasite variation shows a linked activity area that extended along a spring stream from the structure to the old river bank. The presence of generalized processing activities that utilized scrapers of varying kinds, wedges, and other prepared and expedient bifacial and unifacial tools dominates the structure area. Biface reduction and toolmaking, especially projectile-point manufacture, took place closer to the riverbank, where discrete knapping clusters are common. The size and structure of these clusters vary. At one extreme is a U-shaped cluster, ca. 1 m^2 (1.2 square yards) in size, that was the result of the reduction of a single core. The absence of artifacts within the U has been interpreted as a knee "shadow" where the knapper knelt to work. At the other extreme are debitage clusters up to 3 x 4 m (10 x 13 feet) that contain only later reduction stage flakes and bifaces. Tools are rare in the knapping areas, although expedient utilized flakes and scrapers do occur.

Several integrated-activity locations are indicated by pockets of artifact clusters still discernible in the plowed portion of the site. Presumably, these represent different social aggregates, some of which probably occupied the site at the same time. Based on the overall size of this area of integrated-activity locations, which is comparable to, if more compact than, the size of known hunting camps in the area, such an aggregate probably represents the basic long-term socioeconomic unit.

While the site's technological function was the replenishment of the toolkit, as indicated by the discard of extensively curated projectile points and scrapers, most of which are of material other than jasper and virtually the only nonjasper at the site, the Thunderbird base camp is also thought to have had a strong social-intercourse function. The jasper, being a fixed and desired resource in a rapidly changing environment, is seen as a draw both for its technological utility and for its predictable location for otherwise dispersed social aggregates. The site's desirable environmental setting also served to enhance this social element.

The Thunderbird site was only one component in the larger Flint Run–complex of sites that includes a quarry, a reduction station, and a satellite support camp. No charcoal has been recovered that can be used to date the Paleoindian levels, though they are earlier than the 7980 B.C. (9930 years B.P.) radiocarbon assay associated with a Palmer Corner Notched level.

William M. Gardner

Further Readings

Gardner, W.M. (editor). 1974. *The Flint Run Paleo-Indian Complex: A Preliminary Report, 1971–73 Seasons*. Occasional Publication no. 1. Archeology Laboratory, Department of Anthropology, Catholic University of America, Washington, D.C.

See also FLINT RUN COMPLEX

Tierra Blanca Complex

Tierra Blanca–complex sites are in the northern Llano Estacado region of the Texas Panhandle and likely date to A.D. 1450–1650 (500–300 years B.P.). While there has been some limited excavation along with surveys, very little had been published as of the mid-1990s. Origins of the complex are uncertain. Although Tierra Blanca occupies the area that once belonged to people of the Antelope Creek phase, it is likely intrusive into the area. Sites include large villages that have stone foundations for jacal-like structures. There are also small campsites, some of which have tipi rings. Subsistence strategies are uncertain, especially strategies for obtaining plant foods. Some researchers think that they farmed; others think that they may have traded for maize. They definitely engaged in bison hunting. Ceramics were small, squat, globular vessels with faintly striated surfaces and fine-sand temper that share similarities with Southwestern utility wares. Bone tools are not described. Stone tools include small triangular side-notched and unnotched points; alternately beveled, diamond-shaped knives; end scrapers; and drills. Trade materials include Puebloan ceramics, obsidian, turquoise, and *Olivella* shell. The Tierra Blanca complex is most likely the archaeological reflection of the Querechos (Plains Apaches) encountered by the Spanish explorer Francisco Vásques de Coronado in 1541 and the Vaquero Apache encountered by Juan de Oñate in 1601.

Susan C. Vehik

Further Readings

Habicht-Mauche, J.A. 1987. Southwestern-Style Culinary Ceramics on the Southern Plains: A Case Study of Technological Innovation and Cross-Cultural Interaction. *Plains Anthropologist* 32:175–189.
———. 1992. Coronado's Querechos and Teyas in the Archaeological Record of the Texas Panhandle. *Plains Anthropologist* 37:247–259.
Hughes, J.T. 1991. Prehistoric Cultural Developments on the Texas High Plains. *Bulletin of the Texas Archeological Society* 60:1–55.

Tipi Ring, Stone

Circular arrangements of unmodified stones, tipi rings are probably the most common site and feature type found in the northern Plains. Stone tipi rings are found less commonly throughout the central and southern Plains and also occur infrequently in neighboring areas of the Southwest, the Plateau, and the Great Basin. Stone tipi rings have been found in association with cultural complexes dating from ca. 3050/2550 B.C. into the nineteenth century A.D. (5000/4500–100 years B.P.). Extensive archaeological and ethnographic evidence indicates that the stones served to hold down or secure the cover of the pole-framed, skin-covered tipi characteristic of Plains Indian groups. Ethnographic accounts indicate that wooden pegs were also

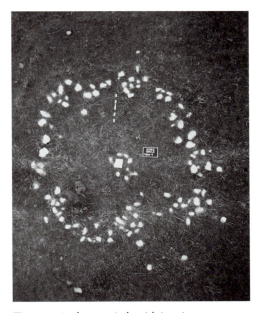

Tipi ring-sized stone circle with interior stone hearth from a site in north-central Montana. Square tile marks define the ring center. The 1 m scale in the north half of the ring is aligned north-south. (Illustration by J. Brumley)

frequently used to secure the tipi cover. Stone tipi rings may have been used when natural stone for their construction was available and/or when the ground was too hard to drive wooden stakes into it.

Stone-circle sites are predominantly found along prairie edges bordering coulees, streams, or river valleys or atop ridges and high hills. Their presence in such prominent locations may reflect cultural selection factors and/or simply depositional environments in which the rings have not become buried. Site size varies from single rings to several hundred ring features. Rings generally range from 2.5 to 8.5 m (8.2–27.9 feet) in inside diameter with a mean diameter of 4.6 m (15 feet). Other types of stone circles are also found on the Plains, but they are generally larger or smaller than tipi rings and, in some instances, form part of a feature such as a medicine wheel.

Although the "classic" tipi ring consists of a simple circle of stone, in reality stone tipi rings vary widely in form. Partial tipi rings consist of arcs of stone that do not form complete circles. Suggested explanations for partial rings are that stones forming the arc were placed only in the direction of prevailing winds and that later groups removed the stones from one side of an existing ring to use the stones for other purposes. The width of tipi-ring walls can vary from one stone to a heavy band of stones up to 0.5 m (1.6 feet) in width. Sometimes a break or gap is present in the ring wall, suggesting the location of a doorway. Small well-defined stone rings or simple scattered clusters of stone reflecting hearth locations may or may not be associated with tipi rings. Where present, such hearths can be situated either inside or just outside the ring.

John Brumley

Further Readings

Davis, L.B. (editor). 1983. *From Microcosm to Macrocosm: Advances in Tipi Ring Investigations and Interpretation.* Memoir. No. 19. Plains Anthropologist, Lincoln.

Quigg, J.M., and J.H. Brumley. 1984. *Stone Circles: A Review Appraisal and Future Directions.* Division of Archaeology and Historic Preservation, State Historical Society of North Dakota, Bismarck.

Tobacco

Tobacco (*Nicotiana* spp.) is an addictive narco-stimulant widely used for magico-religious and medicinal purposes. It has been smoked, snuffed, chewed, licked, drunk, and applied as a juice or poultice. It has served as an offering to, or mediator with, the spirit world. The genus *Nicotiana* includes ca. 60 species, mostly from tropical America. Six species were used by groups in North America: *N. rustica* L., *N. tabacum* L., *N. attenuata* Torr., *N. trigonophylla* Dunal, *N. clevelandii* Gray, and subspecies or varieties of *N. quadrivalvis* Pursh or *N. bigelovii* (Torr.) Watson (terminology disputed). Archaeologically and historically, tobacco was one of the most widely gathered and grown plants in North America. The presence of pipes does not necessarily point to tobacco use, since more than 60 other plants were smoked.

The genus may be identified archaeologically by its seeds, capsules, distinctive hairs (trichomes), and pollen and by chemical analysis of residues. As of the mid-1990s, distinctive phytoliths had not been identified. It may be possible to identify tobacco use by examination of human tissue. Most archaeological identifications rest upon seeds. Across species, seeds range from 0.4 to 1.3 mm (0.02–0.05 inches) in length; within species, seeds may be highly polymorphic. Paleoethnobotanists disagree on whether certain species may be positively identified by their seeds alone, and many species identifications in the literature are based on correlation with historic distributions of species rather than on strict morphological comparisons. The tobacco seeds so far recovered from more than 100 sites in eastern North America alone generally are low in ubiquity, account for less than 1 percent of all identified seeds, and are recovered from domestic rather than special contexts.

The earliest tobacco reported dates to the Middle Woodland (ca. 100 B.C.–A.D. 320, or 2050–1630 years B.P.), at four sites near the confluence of the Mississippi and Illinois rivers. The earliest tobacco in the Plains has been recovered from A.D. 450–660 (1500–1290 years B.P.) Late Woodland contexts at sites in Iowa; in the Southwest, from A.D. 621–660 (1329–1290 years B.P.) Basketmaker III sites in northeastern Arizona; and in southern Ontario, from an A.D. 700–800 (1250–1150 years B.P.) Princess Point component. Tobacco seeds are unlikely to be recovered without the use of flotation; thus, gaps in their archaeological distribution probably relate more to deficiency of flotation recovery than to lack of prehistoric use. Tobacco is noticeably underrepresented from archaeological contexts in the Northeast, the eastern seaboard, the Southeast, the South, California, and Texas.

Although many archaeologists believe that tobacco most likely spread from South America to North America through Mexico, others suggest a possible introduction through the Gulf or Caribbean. Gaps in the archaeological record do not allow either scenario to be tested, but the evidence does point to the importance of the Missouri and Mississippi river valleys as avenues of transmission.

Gail E. Wagner

Further Readings

Goodspeed, T.H. 1954. *The Genus* Nicotiana: *Origins, Relationships, and Evolution of Its Species in the Light of Their Distribution, Morphology, and Cytogenetics.* Chronica Botanica, vol. 16. Waltham.

Haberman, T.W. 1984. Evidence for Aboriginal Tobaccos in Eastern North America. *American Antiquity* 49:269–287.

Toltec Mounds Site

One of the largest sites in the Lower Mississippi Valley, Toltec Mounds (3LN42) was a major ceremonial center of the Plum Bayou culture (A.D. 700–950, or 1250–1000 years B.P.). Located 24 km (15 miles) southeast of Little Rock,

Arkansas, it is on an abandoned channel of the Arkansas River on the west edge of the Mississippi Alluvial Plain. The name "Toltec" is a misnomer, as it was not occupied or built by Toltecs from Mexico. First reported in 1876 as the Knapp mound group, it is now a National Historic Landmark and is preserved as an Arkansas state park with interpretive programs for the general public.

Long-term research plans were developed by the Arkansas Archeological Survey in 1976 for the site that include excavation and other continuing investigations. The only prior scientific excavations were a brief test of one mound in 1966 by the University of Arkansas Museum and the testing of several mounds in 1883 by Edward Palmer for the Bureau of Ethnology at the Smithsonian Institution, Washington, D.C., where the artifacts are stored.

Toltec Mounds, which is on a lake bank, includes 18 known mounds surrounded on three sides by a ditch and an embankment that encompass 40 ha (99 acres). Mound construction began ca. A.D. 650 (1300 years B.P.), although the occupation began by A.D. 550 (1400 years B.P.). Of the 18 mounds, six have been partly excavated and disclose a variety of uses. One was a burial mound enlarged by accretion; another, a multiple-stage platform 11.5 m (38 feet) high for a temple or priest's house. A third was a small, low platform used for religious

Mound B at the Toltec Mounds site. At 11.5 m high, it is the second highest mound at the site. (Illustration by M. A. Rolingson)

activities, including feasts, and the remaining three were low multiple-stage platforms (less than 1.5 m, or 5 feet, high) with residences on them. Preconstruction design concepts are evident in their distribution, which is around one or possibly two rectangular plazas or squares. Several of the mounds were aligned with solstice and equinox solar positions. A standard unit of measurement, 47.5 m (156 feet), was used to establish distances between mounds, and the lengths of the plaza, embankment, and ditch. Toltec Mounds was not inhabited by large numbers of people but was instead the ceremonial center of a dispersed population that lived in small multiple-household sites in the area.

Archaeologists have assumed that the construction of earthworks is indirect evidence of an agricultural economy and that maize agriculture was important at the site by ca. A.D. 900 (1050 years B.P.). Analysis of floral samples from the site indicates, however, that the intensified production of indigenous seed crops was more important than maize agriculture. These probable domesticates include little barley, maygrass, chenopod, erect knotweed, and an unidentified seed type that was the most common charred form. Acorn and hickory nuts were also important foods. Analysis of the fauna indicates a reliance on white-tailed deer, turkey, and raccoon, although birds, fish, and other mammals were used as well. This subsistence pattern shows closer links with the central than with the Lower Mississippi Valley.

The artifact assemblage generally conforms to Late Woodland assemblages rather than to Mississippian. Ceramics were clay tempered with simple decoration, although minor amounts of shell-tempered pottery were also produced. Local lithics were used for a variety of tools; one diagnostic trait is the use of quartz crystal for utilitarian tools.

Martha Ann Rolingson

Toqua

The Toqua site (40MR6) is located on the lower Little Tennessee River near its confluence with Toque Creek in Monroe County, eastern Tennessee. The name "Toqua" or "Toco" refers to the eighteenth-century A.D. Cherokee settlement found there. James Mooney (1900) translates the town name as "place of a mythic great fish." Duke Phillipe of France visited Toqua in 1797 and wrote one of the most detailed descriptions ever made of a Cherokee council house. His brother's drawing of the site is the only contemporary image known to exist of an eighteenth-century Cherokee town.

The site consists of the remains of the Cherokee village and of a large, late Mississippian-period (ca. A.D. 1300–1600, or 650–350 years B.P.) Dallas-phase palisaded town with a platform mound. Archaeological studies at Toqua were conducted by John W. Emmert under the direction of Cyrus Thomas of the Smithsonian Institution, Washington, D.C., in the 1880s. George D. Barnes, a local relic collector, conducted extensive excavations at the site in the 1930s. The University of Tennessee carried out major excavations at Toqua from 1975 to 1977, before the site was flooded by the Tellico Reservoir in 1979. Completely excavated were the primary Dallas mound, Mound A, which stood ca. 8 m (26 feet) high, and the secondary mound, Mound B, which stood ca. 1 m (3.3 feet) high. Mound A consisted of 16 major construction phases. Buildings placed on the mound summit were identified with 12 construction phases. On the west mound summit are pairs of rectangular structures, with one about twice the floor area of the other (91 m², or 109 square yards, and 41 m², or 49 square yards). The larger building probably was used for community rituals, while the smaller structure served as a residence for a high-status individual. Associated structures on the east mound summit were arbors or porches. Toward the end of the occupation, high-status individuals were buried on the east mound summit. On the north side of Mound A, the successive building of as many as 12 structures was synchronized with the construction activities on the east and west summits. Across the village plaza ca. 70 m (230 feet) south-southeast of Mound A was Mound B. It contained three construction stages, several structures, and numerous burials. North of Mound B and north-northeast of Mound A stood a charnel house.

Ca. 4.4 ha (11 acres) of the Dallas and Cherokee village areas were surface collected, and 1.3 ha (3 acres) were excavated and mapped. In the Dallas-village area, 57 domestic dwellings and more than 450 burial and 1,400 other features were investigated. The plaza area on the east side of Mound A had been enlarged in some areas with small pebbles; midden deposits, nearly 1 m (3.3 feet) thick, and numerous structure replacements were present adjacent to the plaza. At different times, three distinctive palisades enclosed successively smaller areas of

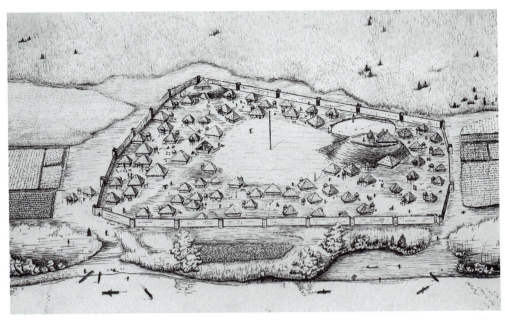

Artist reconstruction of the Mississippian occupation at Toqua. (Drawing by Tom Whyte, courtesy of the Frank H. McClung Museum, University of Tennessee)

the Dallas village, reducing its size from ca. 3.9 to 1.7 ha (9.6–4.2 acres). The primary Cherokee occupation is located outside the Dallas village to the east. Two council houses, each measuring ca. 16 m (52.5 feet) in diameter, 10 domestic dwellings, and small numbers of burials and pit features represent this component.

Gerald F. Schroedl

Further Readings

Mooney, J.M. 1900. Myths of the Cherokees. *Annual Report of the Bureau of American Ethnology* 19:3–576.

Polhemus, R. 1987. *The Toqua Site: A Late Mississippian Dallas Phase Town.* 2 vols. Report of Investigations no. 41. Department of Anthropology, University of Tennessee, Knoxville.

Schroedl, G.F. 1978. Louis-Phillipe's Journal and Archaeological Investigations at the Overhill Cherokee Town of Toqua. *Journal of Cherokee Studies* 3(4):206–220.

Town Creek Site

The Town Creek mound and village site (31MG2, 31MG3) is located in Montgomery County, North Carolina, on the west bank of the Little River near its confluence with Town Fork Creek. This location places it in the Sand-

hills region of the southern North Carolina Piedmont. Excavations began at Town Creek in 1937 as part of a Works Progress Administration (WPA) project and continued until 1984. The culture that was responsible for Town Creek has been named "Pee Dee," after the Pee Dee River that drains south-central North Carolina and northeastern South Carolina.

The Town Creek site is unique in several respects. It represents the easternmost expression of Mississippian culture in North Carolina, and it is the only temple-mound site known in the state outside the Appalachian Summit region. Town Creek has also been designated a State Historic Site and is the only state park dedicated to North Carolina's native population. Perhaps the most interesting facet of Town Creek's uniqueness is that, from 1937 until 1984, the excavations were under the direction of a single individual, Joffre L. Coe.

Ca. 9,290 ha (22,956 acres) have been excavated at Town Creek. The mound itself, though not large by Mississippian standards, was the most striking feature. It stood at the western end of a plaza area that was flanked by several mortuary structures. Another temple building was located opposite the mound on the eastern edge of the plaza. Four different palisades surrounded the complex at various times. Although the mound was totally excavated, it has been rebuilt and the final temple building has been reconstructed on its top. The "minor temple," or "priest's house," on the opposite side of the plaza also has been reconstructed, as has the smaller of the four palisades.

Although earlier and later peoples lived at Town Creek, it reached its heyday as a ceremonial center during the fourteenth century A.D. when it was occupied by people of the Pee Dee culture. It has been said that the cultural expression represents one of the best examples of a movement of people in the southeastern United States. The nature and extent of this migration into the southern North Carolina Piedmont probably will never be known, but there is little doubt that the cultural traditions reflected at Town Creek had their origins elsewhere. Many of the distinctive Pee Dee ceramic styles show close affinities to other well-known temple-mound sites to the south, including the Irene site near Savannah, Georgia; the Hollywood site on the Savannah River in Richmond County, Georgia; the Mulberry site near Camden, South Carolina; and the Fort Watson Mound in Clarendon County, South Carolina.

H. Trawick Ward

Further Readings

Coe, J.L. 1952. The Cultural Sequence of the North Carolina Piedmont. In *Archaeology of the Eastern United States,* edited by J.B. Griffin, pp. 301–311. University of Chicago Press, Chicago.

———. 1995. *Town Creek Indian Mound: A Native American Legacy.* University of North Carolina Press, Chapel Hill.

Reid, J.J. 1965. A Comparative Statement of Ceramics From the Hollywood and Town Creek Mounds. *Southern Indian Studies* 17:13–25.

South, S.A. 1972. *Indians in North Carolina.* North Carolina Division of Archives and History, Department of Cultural Resources, Raleigh.

———. 1976. The Temple at Town Creek State Historic Site, North Carolina. *Notebook of the Institute of Archaeology and Anthropology,* vol. 5, no. 5. University of South Carolina, Columbia.

Tradition

"Tradition" is a concept that refers to artifact forms, art styles, assemblages of tools, subsistence practices, architectural styles, or other technological or cultural patterns at different levels of abstraction that persist for appreciable periods of time within delimited, but often large, geographic areas. Examples are the Arctic Small Tool tradition of Alaska and the Woodland tradition of the Eastern Woodlands. In G.R. Willey and P. Phillips's (1958) cultural-historical synthesis of New World prehistory, traditions are major cultural groupings characterized by continuity of a complex of subsistence practices, technology, and ecological adaptation even though shifts in cultural adaptation may have taken place. They are not culture types, such as "hunter-gatherer" or "tribal"; they emphasize persistence and continuity through time rather than culture change; and they last much longer than single phases or horizons.

Guy Gibbon

Further Readings

Willey, G.R., and P. Phillips. 1958. *Method and Theory in American Archaeology.* University of Chicago Press, Chicago.

Transitional Complex

The Transitional complex is best conceived as a distinctive lithic assemblage found on the Queen Charlotte Islands of the northern coast of British Columbia. In some cases, the assemblages occur in Graham-tradition shell middens dating later than 3050–2550 B.C. (5000–4500 years B.P.); in other cases, they occur by themselves in non-shell-midden contexts dating in the same age range. The Transitional complex includes a variety of simple unifacially retouched, convex-edged basalt flakes and a system of bipolar core reduction. The end products of that bipolar industry were sometimes small elongated microbladelike *pièce-esquillée* spalls, suggesting relationships with the preceding microblade-dominated Moresby tradition. The Transitional complex occurs in a number of Queen Charlotte sites, including Graham-tradition shell middens like Blue Jackets Creek near Masset, where it is found mixed with a wide range of Developmental-stage artifacts and also occasionally as discrete lithic assemblages in non-shell-midden contexts. The best example of the latter is Zone II of the Skoglund's Landing site, also near Masset, where a large Transitional-complex collection dominated by unifacially retouched flakes and products of bipolar percussion is associated with radiocarbon age estimates of 2215 B.C. ±

80 (4165 years B.P.) and 560 B.C. ± 85 (2510 years B.P.).

Knut R. Fladmark

Further Readings

Fladmark, K. 1989. The Native Culture History of the Queen Charlotte Islands. In *The Outer Shores: Proceedings of the Queen Charlotte Islands First International Scientific Symposium, University of British Columbia*, edited by G.G.E. Scudder and N. Gessler, pp. 199–221. Queen Charlotte Islands Museum, Skidegate.

Treganza, Adán (1916–1968)

Adán Eduardo Treganza belonged to that generation of archaeologists trained at the University of California, Berkeley, in the 1940s who filled the first faculty positions for California archaeologists at many of the state's colleges and universities. Treganza taught at California State University, San Francisco, for his entire career. He conducted excavations in several parts of the state and became one of California's most prolific and influential researchers. While still a student, he produced with Professor Robert F. Heizer the first major study of prehistoric mining and quarrying for the state (Heizer and Treganza 1944). They later worked at Topanga Canyon near Los Angeles, where Treganza defined the first Archaic sequence for that region (Treganza 1950; Treganza and Malamud 1950; Treganza and Bierman 1958). The archaeological field schools around San Francisco Bay led by Treganza for 18 years provided much of the primary data for the region's chronology and cultural reconstructions (Treganza 1955, 1958a, 1959a, 1966a, 1966b; Davis and Treganza 1959; Treganza and King 1968). Treganza produced some of the most important work on Paleoindian and Early Archaic cultures of the Sierra Nevada (Treganza 1952). Probably his most significant work took place in foothill reservoirs from the San Joaquin Valley (Treganza 1960) to Mt. Shasta (Treganza 1953; 1955, 1958b 1959b; Treganza and Heicksen 1960, 1969). Using funding opportunities provided by reservoir salvage archaeology in the South Coast ranges, North Coast ranges, Sierra Nevada, Southern Cascades, and Klamath Mountains, he did much of the pioneering research in little-studied regions while training later archaeologists.

Joseph L. Chartkoff

Further Readings

Davis, J.T., and A.E. Treganza. 1959. The Patterson Mound: A Comparative Analysis of the Archaeology of Site Ala-328. *University of California Archaeological Survey Reports* 47:1–92.

Heizer, R.F., and A.E. Treganza. 1944. Mines and Quarries of the Indians of California. *California Journal of Mines and Geology* 40(3):291–359.

Treganza, A.E. 1950. *The Topanga Culture and Southern California Prehistory.* Unpublished Ph.D. dissertation, Department of Anthropology, University of California, Berkeley.

———. 1952. Archaeological Investigations in the Farmington Reservoir Area, Stanislaus County, California. *University of California Archaeological Survey Reports* 14:1–37.

———. 1953. The Archaeological Resources of Seven Reservoir Areas in Central and Northern California. Ms. on file, National Park Service, San Francisco.

———. 1954. Salvage Archaeology in the Nimbus and Redbank Reservoir Areas, Central California. *University of California Archaeological Survey Reports* 26:1–39.

———. 1955. Salvage Archaeology at Sites Nap-74 and Nap-93 in the Monticello Reservoir Area, California. Ms. on file, National Park Service, San Francisco.

———. 1958a. The Examination of Indian Shellmounds Within San Francisco Bay With Reference to the Possible 1579 Landfall of Sir Francis Drake, Second Season. Ms. on file, Department of Anthropology, California State University, San Francisco.

———. 1958b. Salvage Archaeology in the Trinity Reservoir Area, Northern California. *University of California Archaeological Survey Reports* 43:1–38.

———. 1959a. The Examination of Indian Shellmounds in the Tomales and Drakes Bay Areas With References to Sixteenth Century Historic Contacts. Ms. on file, California Department of Parks and Recreation, Sacramento.

———. 1959b. Salvage Archaeology in the Trinity Reservoir Area—Field Season 1958. *University of California Archaeological Survey Reports* 46:1–32.

———. 1960. Archaeological Investigations

in the San Luis Reservoir Area, Merced County, California. Ms. on file, California Department of Parks and Recreation, Sacramento.

———. 1966a. Archaeological Investigations in the Bolinas Bay Area With Reference to the 1579 Landfall of Francis Drake. Ms. on file, Department of Anthropology, California State University, San Francisco.

———. 1966b. Archaeological Observations at Angel Island State Park. Ms. on file, California Department of Parks and Recreation, Sacramento.

Treganza, A.E., and A. Bierman. 1958. The Topanga Culture: Final Report on Excavations. *University of California Anthropological Records* 20(2): 45–86.

Treganza, A.E., and M.H. Heicksen. 1960. *Salvage Archaeology in the Whiskeytown Reservoir Area and the Wintu Pumping Plant, Shasta County, California.* Occasional Papers in Anthropology no. 1. Department of Anthropology, San Francisco State College, San Francisco.

———. 1969. *Salvage Archaeology in the Black Butte Area, Glenn County, California.* Occasional Papers in Anthropology no. 2. San Francisco State College, San Francisco.

Treganza, A.E., and T.F. King. 1968. Archaeological Studies in Point Reyes National Seashore, 1959–1968. Ms. on file, National Park Service, San Francisco.

Treganza, A.E., and C.G. Malamud. 1950. The Topanga Culture: First Season's Excavation of the Tank Site, 1947. *University of California Anthropological Records* 12(4):129–157.

Trempealeau Locality

The Trempealeau locality, situated in the Upper Mississippi River Valley at the mouth of the Trempealeau River in western Wisconsin, contains significant habitation and mound sites from all prehistoric time periods. Isolated bedrock bluffs rising from the valley floor on the Wisconsin side of the Mississippi River visually mark the locality for dozens of kilometers upriver and downriver. The floodplain and adjacent landforms provided plentiful subsistence resources, arable land, and transportation routes. Trempealeau served as a habitation and interaction center for thousands of years (ca. 8050 B.C.–A.D. 1650, or 10,000–300 years B.P.). Fluted points indicate Paleoindian use of high terraces. Stratified Archaic sites are located on the margins of floodplain lakes or old river channels. Early investigators found more than 1,000 Woodland mounds on terraces and bluff tops throughout the locality. Large Oneota villages from ca. A.D. 1300 (650 years B.P.) are the most recent of Trempealeau's major prehistoric occupations. However, Trempealeau is best known for its Hopewell (Middle Woodland) and Mississippian sites.

W.C. McKern's 1928 and 1930 excavations in the locality defined the type sites of the "Trempealeau Focus," a Hopewell complex (McKern 1931). Burials placed in rectangular bark-covered central tombs contained exotic artifacts of copper, Knife River flint, and obsidian. J. Freeman's 1966 excavations produced further evidence of Hopewell interaction during Middle Woodland times, ca. A.D. 100 (1850 years B.P.) (Freeman 1968). The Hopewell-related occupations of western Wisconsin are now known as the Trempealeau phase (Stoltman 1979). The Mississippian presence at Trempealeau is best known from the Little Bluff platform mound and nearby Squier Garden site. Trempealeau was the location of a Cahokia outpost and the setting for the earliest substantial Mississippian contact or influence in the Upper Mississippi Valley, ca. A.D. 950–1000 (1000–950 years B.P.). A group of immigrants from the Cahokia area in Illinois probably built or directed the building of an earthen mound on the summit of Little Bluff, a ridge overlooking the Upper Mississippi Valley. The mound consists of two adjoining platforms, one 16 x 18 m (52.5 x 59 feet) and the other 11 x 15 m (36 x 49 feet), connected to a smaller platform by a ramp 22 m (72 feet) long and 4 m (13 feet) wide. Although only 2.6 m (8.5 feet) high, the structure may have been modeled after Monks Mound, the largest structure at Cahokia. At the foot of Little Bluff, the Squier Garden site contains Cahokialike pottery diagnostic of the Emergent and Early Mississippian periods. After A.D. 1050 (900 years B.P.), Mississippian contact or influence in the region shifted from Trempealeau to the Red Wing area ca. 120 km (75 miles) to the northwest, where a Mississippian presence continued until ca. A.D. 1150 (800 years B.P.).

William Green

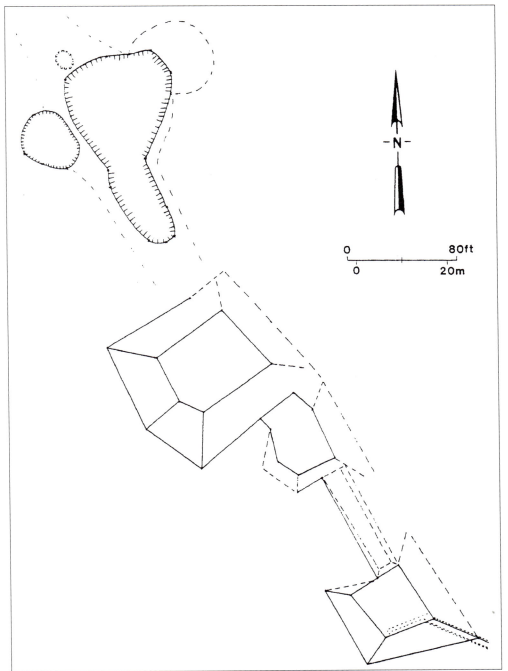

Trempealeau site. (Illustration by W. Green)

Further Readings

Freeman, J. 1968. Hopewell Indians. *Wisconsin Academy Review* 15(1):5–7.

Green, W. 1986. Hopewell Artifacts From Shrake Mound 39, Trempealeau County, Wisconsin. *Midcontinental Journal of Archaeology* 11:3–10.

Green, W., and R.L. Rodell.1994. The Mississippian Presence and Cahokia Interaction at Trempealeau, Wisconsin. *Ameri-*

can Antiquity 59:334–359.

McKern, W.C. 1931. A Wisconsin Variant of the Hopewell Culture. *Bulletin of the Public Museum of the City of Milwaukee* 10:185–328.

Stoltman, J.B. 1979. Middle Woodland Stage Communities of Southwestern Wisconsin. In *Hopewell Archaeology: The Chillicothe Conference*, edited by D. Brose and N. Greber, pp. 122–139. Kent State University Press, Kent.

Tularosa Cave

Tularosa Cave (LA 4427) is a small rock shelter overlooking the Tularosa River, an upland tributary to the San Francisco River in the Mogollon Mountains of west-central New Mexico. Excavations by the Field Museum of Natural History, Chicago, in 1950 recorded a complex stratigraphy that included an extensive preceramic (Archaic-period) horizon in which were found several thousand desiccated maize cobs. Two radiocarbon dates at ca. 350 B.C. (2300 years B.P.) were obtained on maize from the preceramic levels, making the site one of the earliest known agricultural locations in North America at the time. The extraordinarily large collection of perishable material found in Tularosa Cave, especially basketry, cordage,

skin bags, and cotton textiles, has provided an exceptional picture of prehistoric technology. Most of these remains postdate the preceramic occupation and are assigned to the Mogollon cultural tradition.

In addition to the evidence for preceramic maize, the Field Museum investigations at Tularosa Cave made two other major contributions. First, according to the excavators (Martin et al. 1952), the distribution of temporal diagnostics, particularly ceramic types, from the earlier (lower) portions of the cave deposits to the younger (upper) levels supported chronological models built on excavations at numerous nearby open-air habitation sites. In other words, the single temporal sequence at Tularosa Cave conformed to a general chronology complied from several noncontemporaneous settlements. Second, during one chronological phase named "Georgetown," estimated at ca. A.D. 500–700 (1450–1250 years B.P.), a decline in the amount of cultivated plant material was interpreted as evidence for a shift away from agriculture to increased dependence on hunting and gathering. Both of these conclusions have been challenged. William R. Bullard (1962) made an extensive review of the criteria used to assign individual excavation levels to different chronological units and demonstrated that inconsistencies made the published results unjustifiable.

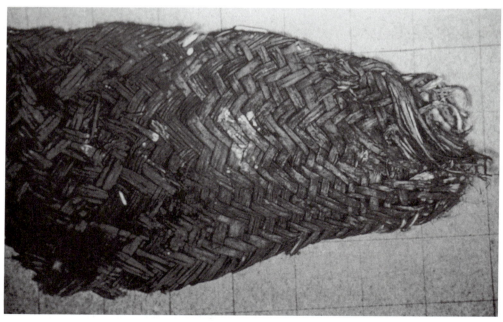

Plaited sandal made of wide elements, from Tularosa Cave. The background is divided into one inch squares. (Courtesy of the Wilford Archaeology Laboratory, University of Minnesota)

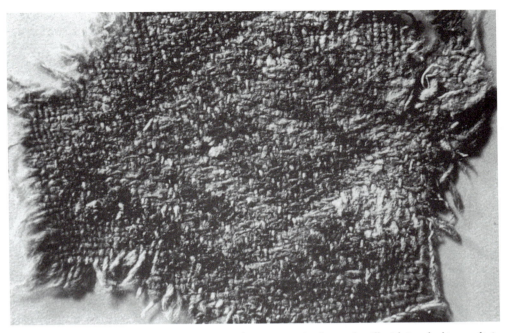

Fragment of woven cotton textile with geometric design woven in diamond twill with interlocking wefts in three colors, from Tularosa Cave. Length is 8.7 cm. (Courtesy of the Wilford Archaeology Laboratory, University of Minnesota)

Other researchers found similar problems in the methods used to track changes through time in the amounts of cultivated versus wild-plant remains. Consequently, more recent discussions of Tularosa Cave tend to focus on the preceramic horizon, where the integrity of the deposits is generally accepted, rather than on later material.

Archaeologists often assume mistakenly that the Field Museum excavations were the first investigations at Tularosa Cave. In fact, the site was originally excavated by W. Hough in 1905 as part of the 2nd Museum Gates-Expedition. Hough's investigations reached bedrock and recorded a variety of stratigraphic patterns, including the use of the shelter as a turkey pen and the existence of Pueblo rooms that once sealed the entrance. When the Field Museum initiated studies at Tularosa Cave, the site was already widely regarded as important due to the copious quantities of perishable objects and food remains found there, which included bottle gourd (*Lagenaria* sp.), a domesticate imported from Mesoamerica. It seems likely that the impetus for the 1950 excavations at Tularosa Cave by Field Museum researchers was at least partly the result of the discovery of preceramic maize at nearby Bat Cave in 1947.

Some cultigens from Tularosa Cave that were collected by the Field Museum have recently been dated by radiocarbon methods. These new dates for maize, beans (*Phaseolus vulgaris*), and squash (*Cucurbita pepo*) at ca. 450 B.C. (2400 years B.P.) substantiate the earlier dates run by the Field Museum. Additional information on the Late Archaic use of the shelter may be difficult to recover given existing problems in the Field Museum documentation and the fact that deposits remaining in the shelter after the 1950 excavations have apparently been destroyed by vandals.

W.H. Wills

Further Readings

Bullard, W.R. 1962. *The Cerro Colorado Site and Pithouse Architecture in the Southwestern United States Prior to A.D. 900.* Papers, vol. 74, no. 2. Peabody Museum of American Archaeology and Ethnology, Harvard University, Cambridge.

Haury, E. 1962. The Greater American Southwest. In *Courses Toward Urban Life: Some Archaeological Considerations of Cultural Alternates,* edited by R.J. Braidwood and G.R. Willey, pp. 106–131. Publications in Anthropology no. 32. Viking Fund, New York.

Hough, W. 1907. *Antiquities of the Upper Gila and Salt River Valleys in Arizona and New Mexico.* Bulletin no. 35. Smithsonian Institution, Washington, D.C.

Martin, P.S., J.B. Rinaldo, E. Bluhm, H. Cutler, and R. Grange. 1952. *Mogollon Cultural Continuity and Change: The Stratigraphic Analysis of Tularosa and Cordova Caves.* Fieldiana: Anthropology, vol. 40. Field Museum of Natural History, Chicago.

Wills, W.H. 1988. *Early Prehistoric Agriculture in the American Southwest.* School of American Research Press, Santa Fe.

Tule Springs

The paleontological/archaeological site of Tule Springs (26CK244-248, 250) is located ca. 16 km (10 miles) north of Las Vegas, Nevada. This area is within the northern boundary of the Mojave Desert, with its characteristic flora and fauna. During paleontological excavations at the site in 1933, Fenley Hunter and his colleagues found an obsidian flake in possible association with apparent charcoal and ashes, as well as the bones of late Pleistocene forms of camel, bison, and horse. A block of earth containing the obsidian flake and the remains of the presumably split and burned extinct mammals was sent to G.G. Simpson, a paleontologist at the American Museum of Natural History in New York. He described the material in an article that discussed the flake and its apparent relationship to late Pleistocene faunal remains (Simpson 1933). At the time of this discovery in the early 1930s, many American archaeologists did not accept a New World association of Pleistocene extinct mammals with human artifacts, a reaction in part to the earlier Folsom point find.

Mark Harrington at the Southwest Museum in Los Angeles, California, was among the first to appreciate the significance of the Pleistocene fauna and the possible obsidian flake association. The museum made three expeditions to the Tule Springs locality (1933, 1955, and 1956), with crews staying a total of eight weeks and three days (Harrington and R.D. Simpson 1961). In 1955, more significance was added to Harrington's and G.G. Simpson's interpretation of the data from the Tule Springs locality when a sample of the "charcoal" produced a ^{14}C date older than 21,850 B.C. (23,800 years B.P.), making Tule Springs one of the old-

est archaeological sites in North America.

In 1962–1963, the Nevada State Museum in Carson City conducted a major excavation at Tule Springs with Richard Shutler in charge. The field project, which lasted four months, was funded by a grant from the National Science Foundation and from a private source, H.C. Smith, who was a builder by vocation and an archaeologist by avocation. This was a multidisciplinary approach utilizing the combined efforts of archaeologists, geologists, paleontologists, a botanist, a radiocarbon specialist, and many auxillary investigators. In the Tule Springs–site area, which was 183 x 670.6 m (600 x 2,200 feet), a total of 200,000 tons of earth were moved by trowel, dental tool, whisk broom, and large earthmoving equipment. More than 2,134 m (7,000 feet) of bulldozed trenches, averaging 4.6 m (15 feet) in depth, were cut to give stratigraphic cross sections of the geology of Las Vegas wash and adjacent areas, the first application of this technique in paleontology/archaeology. The problems faced in 1962 were whether humans and Pleistocene fauna were contemporaneous at Tule Springs and, if so, at what time level. The geological research at Tule Springs had three objectives: "1) To determine the stratigraphic relationships of its artifacts and fossils; 2) to determine the relation of the Tule Springs site geology to that of the surrounding region; and 3) to place the Tule Springs data in proper perspective with late Pleistocene events in North America" (Shutler 1967:22).

During the Tule Springs–site excavation, five main localities were tested for stratigraphic evidence of human artifacts associated in a cultural context with extinct mammals. The main questions asked were whether the apparent hearth areas indicated a human presence and whether the hearths were associated with the bones of Pleistocene mammals. The analysis of the "charcoal" in this Tule Springs exploration proved it was carbonized plant material. It had accumulated in the bottom of spring chambers located within different areas of the site and dated to 30,000–40,000 years ago.

Data from the 1962–1963 research indicated that Locality 1 had a stratigraphic sequence that included extinct camel, mammoth, horse, and other animals. Five utilized human-made flakes were radiocarbon dated to 10,050–6050 B.C. (12,000–8000 years B.P.). At Locality 2, numerous bones, including those of bison, horse, and mammoth, were found in the spring chamber. Two possible bone tools were recov-

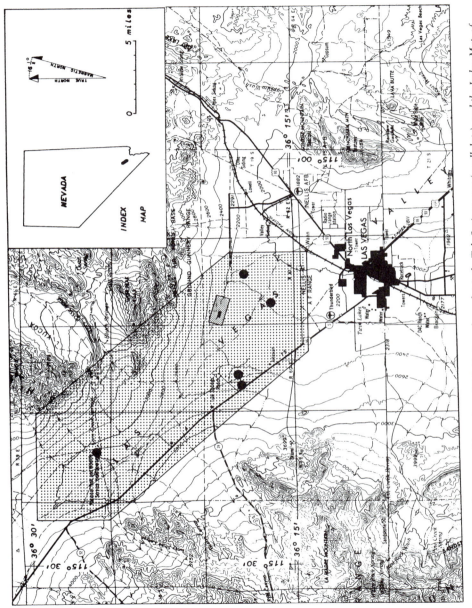

Location map showing the topographic setting of Tule Springs (large dots), the Tule Springs area (small dots), and the Index Map of Nevada (inset). (Drawn by R. H. Brooks and D. R. Tuohy)

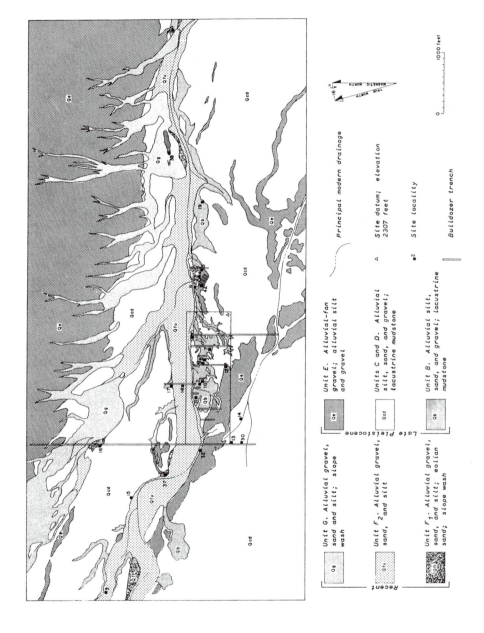

Geologic map of the Tule Springs area, showing the sites and bulldozer trenches. (Drawn by R. H. Brooks and D. R. Tuohy)

ered from upper levels and are problematically dated at more than 9050 B.C. (11,000 years B.P.). Extinct camel bone was found in Locality 3. The 1962–1963 excavation of this locality exposed a probable bone tool and a caliche bead that were radiocarbon dated to 9050–5050 B.C. (11,000–7000 years B.P.). Locality 4a is a deep trench cut near the Finley Hunter site. A subsequent excavation by hand exposed a well-made quartzite scraper dated to 9050–8050 B.C. (11,000–10,000 years B.P.). Locality 5 had a good faunal deposit of mammoth, camel, horse, and an extinct giant condor. A bipointed bone tool was exposed and may represent a time period between 11,050 and 10,050 B.C. (13,000–12,000 years B.P.).

Research at the Tule Springs site resulted in extensive data on the geology, paleontology, and palynology of the site, which led to a reevaluation of the southern Great Basin's paleoenvironment during the late Pleistocene and early Holocene. In none of the five localities were human tools found in association with fossil animal remains. Nor was there evidence substantiating a human presence at Tule Springs prior to 11,050 B.C. (13,000 years B.P.).

Richard H. Brooks
Donald R. Tuohy

Further Readings

Harrington, M.R., and R.D. Simpson. 1961. *Tule Springs, Nevada, With Other Evidences of Pleistocene Man in North America*. Papers no. 18. Southwest Museum, Los Angeles.

Shutler, R. 1967. Introduction. In *Pleistocene Studies in Southern Nevada*, edited by H.M. Wormington and D. Ellis, pp. 21–23. Anthropological Papers no. 13. Nevada State Museum, Carson City.

Simpson, G.G. 1933. *A Nevada Fauna of Pleistocene Type and Its Probable Association With Man*. Novitates no. 667. American Museum of Natural History, New York.

Wormington, H.M., and D. Ellis (editors). 1967. *Pleistocene Studies in Southern Nevada*. Anthropological Papers no. 13. Nevada State Museum, Carson City.

Turner Site

Located in Hamilton County, Ohio, on the Little Miami River, the Turner site (33HA41) provides the largest body of archaeological data for the Hopewell complex in the Miami River drainage. Frederick Ward Putnam excavated Turner from 1882 to 1911 for the Peabody Museum of American Archaeology and Ethnology of Harvard University. All prehistoric remains have since been destroyed by a gravel pit.

The earthworks at Turner consisted of a large, oval, earthen enclosure on the second river terrace that was connected to an earthen circle on the terrace above by a ramp or graded way. A long narrow enclosure was nearby. Smaller circles lay within the large enclosure, and mounds were built both within the earthworks and outside the elevated circle to the west. A series of seven connected mounds within the oval enclosure evidently covered the main ceremonial precinct at the site, which contained numerous clay basins and burnt areas. Two of these basins in particular, in Mounds 3 and 4, contained a great number and variety of artifacts, including copper and mica cutouts; other copper ornaments; beads of pearl, copper, and shell; engraved bone; bear canines; meteoric iron; and copper nuggets. A group of terra-cotta figurines of men and women was found in Mound 4. Intriguing structures under the floor of Mound 3, which consisted of fire pits with flues extending under a burned floor, may have provided a means of creating a forced draft to raise the temperature in open fires. Mound 12 in the elevated circle contained a central basin that had been covered with a small primary mound and surrounded by a stone wall. Upon and outside this wall were several burials. Likewise, one of the Marriott mounds west of the circle contained a basin and burials. Excavation of sections of the walls of the large enclosure disclosed hearths, basins, postmolds, and some burials, indicating that ceremonial activities had also occurred in these areas before the earthen banks had been constructed.

Many of the graves at Turner were clustered together on a ridge in the large enclosure that, before cultivation, may have been another mound. Most of the graves, both cremations and inhumations, were lined with stone slabs. Orientation of the body and the nature of grave goods have been examined by N.B. Greber (1979), who concluded that they probably indicated the group membership and status of individuals. Although some amount of domestic refuse was encountered, as at other Hopewell ceremonial centers, evidence of the daily life of the people is lacking. Due to the early date of the site's excavation, no absolute chronological data are available. Based upon ceramic evidence and stylistic studies of other artifact types, Turner is a relatively late (ca. A.D. 350, or 1600 years B.P.) Hopewell site.

Katharine C. Ruhl

Further Readings

Greber, N.B. 1979. Variations in Social Structure of Ohio Hopewell Peoples. *Midcontinental Journal of Archaeology* 4:35–78

Putnam, F.W. 1886. Explorations in Ohio: The Marriott Mound, No. 1, and Its Contents. *Eighteenth and Nineteenth Annual Reports* 3:449–466. Peabody Museum of American Archaeology and Ethnology, Harvard University, Cambridge.

Willoughby, C.C., and E.A. Hooten. 1922. *The Turner Group of Earthworks, Hamilton County, Ohio.* Papers, vol. 8, no. 3. Peabody Museum of American Archaeology and Ethnology, Harvard University, Cambridge.

U

Uhle, Max (1856–1944)

A German-born and -trained archaeologist influenced by Flinders Petrie, a famous English archaeologist who had devised a technique of seriation, or "sequence dating," in his work in Upper Egypt, Max Uhle is best known for his pioneering chronological studies in South America, most notably in Peru and Bolivia. However, he also pioneered seriational and stratigraphic studies in North America in his excavations at the Emeryville shell mound in the San Francisco Bay area of California (Uhle 1907). Besides excavating parts of the mound "stratum by stratum," he provided a table summarizing changes in numbers of implements in the 10 principal strata, recognized continuity from stratum to stratum, noted changes in burial pattern and shellfish species between lower and upper layers, argued that the mound was formed over a considerable period of time, distinguished three different cultural expressions or stages in the mound, and compared the mound to others in the United States and Europe. Although his analysis of cultural microchange in the mound was a revolutionary breakthrough at the time, his work was harshly criticized by A.L. Kroeber, the administrator of the Hearst funds that supported the excavations. Kroeber (1909:16) argued that "the recent civilization is still so simple . . . in central California . . . [that] any radically simpler culture than the recent one . . . must have been so extremely rude as to make its existence a short time ago seem more than questionable to anyone impressed with the evident historical antiquity of a fairly well developed civilization elsewhere in America." The dispute is a reflection of the assumptions at the time that change had been minimal in North America in prehistoric times and that any significant cultural changes had to involve major shifts in technology and subsistence, as in the Paleolithic-to-Neolithic transition in Europe.

Guy Gibbon

Further Readings

Kroeber, A.L. 1909. The Archaeology of California. In *Putnam Anniversary Volume*, edited by F. Boas, pp. 1–42. Stechert, New York.

Rowe, J.H. 1954. *Max Uhle, 1856–1944: A Memoir of the Father of Peruvian Archaeology*. Publications in American Archaeology and Ethnology, vol. 46, no. 1. University of California Press, Berkeley.

Uhle, M. 1907. *The Emeryville Shellmound*. Publications in American Archaeology and Ethnology, vol. 7, no. 1. University of California Press, Berkeley.

Willey, G.R., and J.A. Sabloff. 1993. *A History of American Archaeology*. 3rd ed. W.H. Freeman, San Francisco.

Uncas Complex

The Uncas complex is known from one excavated site with four houses and from occasional surface finds in north-central Oklahoma along the Arkansas River and its tributaries. Radiocarbon and archaeomagnetic assays suggest a fourteenth-century A.D. date. Its origins are uncertain, but Uncas is most likely derived from earlier Plains Village–tradition occupations of the area, even though the ceramics strongly resemble some types associated with the Smoky Hill variant. It is uncertain what became of the Uncas complex. It may have been ancestral to the Lower Walnut focus.

The Uncas settlement has small semipermanent-to-permanent hamlets consisting of several semisubterranean houses that are square in outline with rounded corners and four center support posts. Construction involves wattle-and-daub walls with a grass roof. Even though direct evidence of horticulture is missing, it was likely part of the subsistence base. Although faunal materials were poorly preserved, deer and bison remains occur in nearly the same frequencies. Turkey and turtle remains have also been identified. Part of a bison-scapula hoe was recovered. Ceramics are globular with rounded bottoms and shell or fossil-shell temper. Surfaces are plain or cord marked and then smoothed over. Incised designs on some vessels involved opposed diagonal lines within triangles. Stone tools found include small triangular side-notched points; end scrapers; and alternately beveled, diamond-shaped, and ovate knives. Grinding implements, including some covered heavily with red pigment, are common. Ground-stone shaft smoothers are also present. Wood tools were represented by the charred remains of a fire drill hearth. Alibates agatized dolomite from the Texas Panhandle was obtained through trade. All of the Alibates was recovered from one house, where it occurred as finely made projectile points and alternately beveled, diamond-shaped knives.

Susan C. Vehik

Further Readings

Galm, J.R. 1979. *The Uncas Site: A Late Prehistoric Manifestation in the Southern Plains.* Research Series no. 5. Archaeological Research and Management Center, University of Oklahoma, Norman.

Vehik, S.C., and P. Flynn. 1982. Archaeological Excavations at the Early Plains Village Uncas Site (34Ka172). *Bulletin of the Oklahoma Anthropological Society* 31:5–70.

Uniface

"Uniface" is a common generic term for a stone artifact that exhibits secondary modification on only one of its surfaces. Employed in this way, the term includes all nature of modification of that surface, from edge-restricted to invasive. Some researchers have found it advantageous to subdivide unifacially modified objects, using the term "retouched piece" for artifacts whose retouch is limited to the margin, and "uniface" for tools whose retouch is invasive or occupies a relatively large portion of their interior. The invasively modified uniface type is ubiquitous in the North American mid-continent but not present in large numbers in most lithic industries. For instance, the type was present in both the Early and Middle Archaic assemblages of the Campbell Hollow site in west-central Illinois, but it made up only moderately more than 1 percent of the type collections (Odell 1985).

George H. Odell

Further Readings

Odell, G.H. 1985. Lithic Assemblage. In *The Campbell Hollow Archaic Occupation*, edited by C.R. Stafford, pp. 37–52. Research Series, vol. 4. Center for American Archeology, Kampsville.

University Indian Ruin

Byron Cummings, who was director of the Arizona State Museum and chairman of the University of Arizona Department of Anthropology, initiated a field school at University Indian Ruin (AZ B:9:33) in Tucson, Arizona, in 1930 after 2.4 ha (6 acres) of the site were donated to the University of Arizona (the preserved area of the site is now 5.3 ha [13 acres]). For most of the 1930s, Cummings and his successor, Emil W. Haury, used the site as a field school. The major work was directed by Julian D. Hayden, who supervised Civilian Conservation Corps (CCC) workers in large-scale excavations for three months at the beginning of 1940. Hayden completed a manuscript on the site by October of 1942, but the report was not published until 1957.

The work at University Ruin by Hayden is important for its detailed reporting of Classic-period (A.D. 1150–1450, or 800–500 years B.P.) architecture. Hayden documented Classic-period pithouses and variability in surface rooms with post-reinforced and solid adobe walls. The adobe rooms were built on top of the surface of this artificial mound, which was enclosed by a compound wall. He also partly excavated an artificially filled platform mound. The quality and detail of Hayden's architectural recordings, and his profiles that documented erosional and construction sequences, are exemplary. He also provided detailed data on ceramics, flaked and ground stone, and other artifacts. Alan Ferg (1985) has reported on bird bones from the site.

While Hayden presented a well-informed discussion at the time of artificially filled mounds in the Hohokam area, platform mounds are now known to be present at large villages in the eastern portion of the Papagueria, in the Tucson Basin, along the San Pedro River, in the Tonto Basin, and most abundantly in the Salt and Gila river areas of the Phoenix Basin. Such mounds appear to have developed earliest in the Phoenix Basin, but the temporal and spatial patterns of their spread to outlying areas are still being explored. Regional variability is likely, but a general trend toward aggregation of population soon after A.D. 1300 appears to be broadly indicated. Hayden viewed mounds as defensive features. This interpretation is also an element of some recent models, but there is increasing evidence of a ceremonial function for mounds; archaeologists also often see them as evidence of increased social complexity.

The issue of the abandonment of the University Indian Ruin, like most other late Classic sites, is highly uncertain. Jeddito Black-on-yellow, which is generally a late intrusive type in the Hohokam area, is not reported from the University Indian Ruin. It is found at several nearby sites, however, which might indicate continued occupation of the general vicinity. A most intriguing report is Hayden's recounting of Ben Wetherill's excavation in a portion of University Indian Ruin in 1932–1933, in which he purportedly recovered a restorable Spanish maiolica ware bowl. Though it was reported to have been taken back to the Arizona State Museum, it could not be found even in 1940.

Hayden also presented an excellent synthesis of regional prehistory. Although he largely disavowed the "Salado" model that formed his interpretive framework in the 1940s, nearly all of the issues that he identified, including population movement, cultural identity, warfare, and trade relations, remain topics of active debate.

William H. Doelle

Further Readings

Ferg, A. 1985. Avifauna of the University Indian Ruin. *Kiva* 50:111–128.

Fish, S.K., P.R. Fish, and J.H. Madsen (editors). 1992. *The Marana Community in the Hohokam World.* Anthropological Papers no. 56. University of Arizona Press, Tucson.

Hayden, J.D. 1957. *Excavations, 1940, at University Indian Ruin, Tucson, Arizona.* Technical Series no. 5. Southwestern Monuments Association, Gila Pueblo, Globe.

Kelly, W.H. 1936. University Indian Ruin. *Kiva* 1(8):1–4.

Wallace, H.D., and J.P. Holmlund. 1984. The Classic Period in the Tucson Basin. *Kiva* 49:167–194.

Upper Canark Regional Variant

The Upper Canark regional variant was defined by C.R. Lintz in 1986. The variant concept has not been widely employed on the southern Plains, with Canark the first and, so far, only one to be proposed. Canark is considered part of the Plains Village tradition and dates to A.D. 1250–1500 (700–450 years B.P.). However, there are enough differences that a distinct Southern Plains Village tradition is sometimes recognized. Upper Canark is geographically restricted to the area along and between the Upper Canadian River and the southern tributaries of the Upper Arkansas River. This area includes the High Plains of the Texas and Oklahoma panhandles and adjacent portions of southeastern Colorado and northeastern New Mexico.

There are at present (1996) two members of the Upper Canark variant: the Apishapa and the Antelope Creek phases. The distinguishing characteristic of these phases is architecture. Unlike those of most members of the Plains Village tradition, houses of Upper Canark members have foundations composed of vertical rows of stone slabs. Roofs or superstructures were of more perishable materials. House sites can vary from single-room structures to contiguous multiroom ones. Other aspects of the cultural assemblage of Upper Canark share similarities with the Plains Village tradition, including globular shaped, cord-marked pottery; small triangular side-notched projectile points; snub-nosed end scrapers; flanged drills; and slab metates and one-handed manos. Subsistence involved a mix of bison hunting, gathering, and horticulture. It is possible that the importance of bison hunting increased through time. External trade relations involve the Southwest for Puebloan pottery, turquoise, and obsidian. Marine shell could have come from the Atlantic, the Pacific, or the Gulf, though the Pacific is most often mentioned. Smoky Hill jasper from northwestern Kansas is the most obvious Plains resource.

Susan C. Vehik

Further Readings

Lintz, C.R. 1986. *Architecture and Community Variability Within the Antelope Creek Phase of the Texas Panhandle.* Studies in Oklahoma's Past no. 14. Oklahoma Archeological Survey, Norman.

See also ANTELOPE CREEK PHASE; APISHAPA PHASE; PLAINS VILLAGE TRADITION

Upper Mississippian Culture

"Upper Mississippian culture" is a taxonomic term in the Midwestern Taxonomic system that was popular from the late 1930s to the early 1950s. It grouped Late Prehistoric horticultural societies along the northern part of the Eastern Woodlands that were considered Mississippian-culture derivatives. Examples are supposed Woodland-Mississippian blends, such as Fort Ancient in the Ohio Valley and Owasco-Iroquois of central New York, and "attenuated" Mississippianlike cultures, such as Oneota. The term is seldom used anymore because the derivative relationships with Mississippian culture proved unfounded or have not been demonstrated in a processual, as compared to a taxonomic, sense.

Guy Gibbon

Further Readings

McKern, W.C. 1939. The Midwestern Taxonomic Method As an Aid to Archaeological Culture Study. *American Antiquity* 4:301–313.
———. 1945. Preliminary Report on the Upper Mississippi Phase in Wisconsin. *Bulletin of the Public Museum of the City of Milwaukee* 16:109–285.
Wilford, W.A. 1955. A Revised Classification of the Prehistoric Cultures of Minnesota. *American Antiquity* 21:130–142.

See also FORT ANCIENT CULTURE; ONEOTA

Upper Purgatoire Complex

The Upper Purgatoire complex is composed of the remains of people who lived in the foothills of the Upper Purgatoire River Valley in south-central Colorado near the turn of the first millennium A.D. They had a hunting-and-gathering economy but grew some plants, including maize, beans, and squash. The complex of materials has been divided by Caryl E. Wood and Gerald A. Bair (1980) into three subphases of a Sopris phase, a concept defined by Herbert W. Dick in 1963. Galen R. Baker (1964) suggested adding the St. Thomas phase to this taxon, but that was rejected by Stephen K. Ireland (1971).

Characteristics of the Initial Sopris subphase (ca. A.D. 1000–1100, or 950–850 years B.P.) include semisubterranean pithouses and jacal structures, Taos Gray and Sopris Plain ceramics, a preponderance of basin metates over slab and trough metates, and greater numbers of corner-notched projectile points compared to side-notched and stemmed forms. Elbow pipes were present throughout the phase. During the Early Sopris subphase (ca. A.D. 1100–1150, or 850–800 years B.P.), architectural materials shifted from jacal to a predominant use of adobe, and trough metates replaced basin types as the most common form. Taos Gray and Sopris Plain remained the dominant ceramic types, but incised wares from the northern Rio Grande, some cord-marked types, polished and corrugated wares, and occasional Taos Black-on-White and Red Mesa Black-on-White were present, too; so were small shell and stone disk beads. In the Late Sopris subphase (ca. A.D. 1150–1225, or 800–725 years B.P.), grooved mauls appeared; slab metates replaced trough metates; and unfaced, horizontally dry-laid sandstone-slab masonry replaced adobe as the preferred building material, although adobe and jacal continued to be used. Taos Gray Incised was the predominant ceramic ware, but Taos Gray and Sopris Plain were also abundant. Red Mesa Black-on-White pottery decreased in quantity, cord-marked and polished wares declined in importance, and Taos Black-on-White increased in quantity.

The Sopris phase may be more closely related to Anasazi occupations in Michael L. Glassow's (1972) Cimarron district in northeastern New Mexico, and/or to the Upper Rio Grande Valley, than to Plains cultures. Since most sites of the Upper Purgatoire complex are now under Trinidad Lake, future studies of the complex must be accomplished through reanalysis of recovered materials.

William B. Butler

Further Readings

Baker, G.R. 1964. The Archaeology of the Park Plateau in Southeastern Colorado. *Southwestern Lore* 30(1):1–18.
Dick, H.W. 1963. *Preliminary Report: Trinidad Reservoir, Las Animas County,*

Colorado. Contract report to the National Park Service. Midwest Archaeological Center, Lincoln.

Glassow, M.L. 1972. *The Evolution of Early Agricultural Facilities Systems in the Northern Southwest.* Unpublished Ph.D. dissertation, Department of Anthropology, University of California, Los Angeles.

Ireland, S.K. 1971. The Upper Purgatoire Complex: A Reappraisal. *Southwestern Lore* 37(2):37–51.

Wood, C.E., and G.A. Bair. 1980. *Trinidad Lake Cultural Resource Study Part II: The Prehistoric Occupation of the Upper Purgatoire Valley, Southeastern Colorado.* Contract report to the National Park Service. Interagency Archaeological Services, Denver.

Upper Republican Phase

The Upper Republican phase is one of five recognized taxa of the Late Prehistoric Central Plains tradition and is sometimes used erroneously as a synonym for any Central Plains–tradition expression west of the Nebraska phase. Upper Republican occurs in the middle reaches of the Republican, Solomon, and other western Nebraska and Kansas rivers. Emerging ca. A.D. 1000 (950 years B.P.), the Upper Republican phase radiated throughout these river basins and disappeared ca. A.D. 1350 (600 years B.P.). "Upper Republican" was used by R.A. Krause (1969) to designate a regional variant composed of the Solomon River, Classic Republican, and Loup River phases. Loup River (the Itskari phase) is now considered a distinct taxon, while the Upper Republican phase is subdivided into Upper Republican I (A.D. 1000–1100, or 950–850 years B.P.), Upper Republican II (A.D. 1100–1250, or 850–700 years B.P.), and Upper Republican III (A.D. 1250–1350, or 700–600 years B.P.) subphases. These reflect the appearance and radiation of Upper Republican during the favorable Neo-Atlantic climatic episode and its contraction and disappearance during the succeeding Pacific episode.

Upper Republican houses are nearly square wattle-and-daub structures built on the surface without an excavated housepit. They have four (rarely, six) central roof supports around a central fire basin and an extended entry passage emerging from one wall. Seventy-five percent of the houses are from 46.5 to 102 m² (500–1,100 square feet) in area. Several subfloor cylindrical or bell-shaped storage/refuse pits are usually present. Settlement types include solitary houses, hamlets, and small villages of up to a dozen houses with work/storage areas and subsistence-extraction camps. The dead were buried in communal ossuaries with few or no grave goods.

Upper Republican emerged in a region of abundant brown Republican River or Smoky Hill jasper and green Bijou Hills or Bloomington quartzite. Extensive use of these for making triangular side-notched arrow points, bifaces, drills, and end scrapers is diagnostic of Upper Republican. Large, thick almond-shaped bifacial "quarry blanks" are common. Sand-tempered, cord-roughened globular pottery jars with unthickened and, more typically, collared rims are another trait. Handles or other appendages do not occur. A diagnostic decoration is an incised horizontal-parallel-line pattern on collar faces, though other motifs also occur. Late Upper Republican sites continue this motif but on narrower beveled lips of unthickened rims. Abraders of gray Oglala and red Dakota sandstone, pebble hammerstones, pebble pipes, and other stone-pipe forms occur. Digging and cutting tools made of bison scapula, awls of split (quartered) deer/pronghorn proximal metapodials, and other bone and antler tools and ornaments, such as tubular beads, occur. Upper Republican people gathered wild plants, tended gardens, fished, and hunted a wide range of vertebrates, including bison.

Beyond the periphery of Upper Republican domiciliary distribution in northeast Colorado, western Nebraska, and southeast Wyoming are Central Plains–tradition camps lacking architecture. These are not Upper Republican but appear to be a separate phenomenon that requires phase-level designation.

John Ludwickson
John R. Bozell

Further Readings
Bozell, J.R. 1991. Fauna From the Hulme Site and Comments on Central Plains Tradition Subsistence Variability. *Plains Anthropologist* 36(136):229–253.

Krause, R.A. 1969. Correlation of Phases in Central Plains Prehistory. *Plains Anthropologist* 14(44), pt. 2:82–96.

Ludwickson, J. n.d. The Shipman Site: An Upper Republican Phase Settlement in the Guide Rock Locality. Ms. in possession of author.

U

Roper, D.R. 1990. Artifact Assemblage Composition and the Hunting Camp Interpretation of High Plains Upper Republican Sites. *Southwestern Lore* 56(4).

Wedel, W.R. 1986. *Central Plains Prehistory: Holocene Environment and Culture Change in the Republican River Basin.* University of Nebraska Press, Lincoln.

Wood, W.R. (editor). 1969. *Two House Sites on the Central Plains.* Memoir no. 6. Plains Anthropologist, Lincoln.

Upper Sonoran Agricultural Complex

The Upper Sonoran Agricultural complex is one of seven clusters of crop plants thought to be important because each has a different sort of history and archaeological significance. This complex is composed of maize, or corn (*Zea mays*), a suite of varieties of squashes and pumpkins (*Cucurbita pepo*), common beans (*Phaseolus vulgaris*), and bottle gourd (*Legenaria siceraria*). Corn, squash, and beans were domesticated from wild relatives in the highlands of central Mexico. When and where bottle gourd was originally domesticated remains unknown, but it also is thought to have become integrated into the complex in Mexico.

The Upper Sonoran Archaeological complex was central to agricultural economies throughout North and Middle America as well as Andean South America when Europeans arrived in the sixteenth and seventeenth centuries A.D. By 1960, archaeological remains had provided clear evidence that the complex also had formed the economic basis of prehistoric Andean and Mesoamerican civilizations, prehistoric Puebloan and Mississippian cultures, and Late Woodland and Protohistoric cultures in the Plains and Eastern Woodland regions of the United States. It seemed obvious that additional knowledge of the complex would be crucial for understanding the history and evolution of New World agriculture.

During the next 20 years, successful searches were conducted to identify the timing and place of origin of these crop plants, new investigations were carried out to reassess their early economic significance, and new archaeological information was provided by technological developments in the recovery and study of macroscopic botanical remains, pollen grains, and opal phytoliths. This work clarified a great deal of the history and cultural significance of the elements of the complex and the complex itself. Richard I. Ford's 1981 review recognized that the practice of corn and squash cultivation diffused to the American Southwest from Mexico before beans and bottle gourd were introduced ca. 500–300 B.C. (2450–2250 years B.P.). Though the earliest apparent dates for maize pollen and macrofossils in the Southwest were debatable, Ford speculated that corn may have been grown during preceramic times in this culture area for perhaps 1,000 years before it became a staple. This new evidence demonstrated that, in both Mexico and the Southwest, knowledge and production of these crops, especially corn, did not stimulate rapid establishment of agricultural economies or village settlement patterns.

A link between sedentism, widespread trade, and corn-beans-squash agriculture in the prehistory of the Eastern Woodlands region was generally assumed in the mid-1960s (Griffin 1967). Deconstruction of that theory was begun when Richard A. Yarnell (1964) proposed that squash and gourd husbandry was established in the Eastern Woodlands earlier than the cultivation of maize and beans. By 1980, it was clear that though corn had diffused from the Southwest to the Eastern Woodlands before 300 B.C. (2250 years B.P.), it did not become a significant feature of subsistence patterns in the region until after A.D. 800 (1150 years B.P.), when common beans and field agriculture, in contrast to garden agriculture, rapidly became widely established.

The historical and archaeological value of the Upper Sonoran Agricultural–complex concept was significantly modified by these results, although, as of 1985, Ford still considered it a useful concept, and introductory textbooks continued to suggest that maize farming was the economic base of Early and Middle Woodland–period sedentary groups (Wenke 1984:424). However, the following half decade offered further developments that have worked to undermine the utility and relevance of the concept. Researchers applying the technology of molecular biology identified the specific ancestor of corn (Doebley 1990), and they were able to separate the Mexican ancestor of the squash first cultivated in the Southwest from the prairie ancestor of the squash first cultivated in the Eastern Woodlands (Decker 1988). Direct AMS (accelerator mass spectrometry) radiocarbon dating also documented the occurrence of early Southwestern maize in the 2000–1500 B.C. (3950–3450 years B.P.) range (as previously suggested by palynological data) (Wills 1988) and the use in the Eastern Woodlands of bottle gourds and squash by 5000 B.C. (6950 years B.P.). These developments have led to new views of the economic significance and cultural evolutionary implications of systematic farming by populations that practiced hunting-and-gathering economies and to a wider acceptance of David Rindos's (1984) view of early mutualistic relationships between potential crop plants and people.

In the 1990s, the concept of the Upper Sonoran Agricultural complex remains a useful way to identify the suite of crop plants most significant to the economies of the great majority of agricultural native societies of late prehistory and colonial times in the New World. Further analyses of the histories of maize and beans continue to yield insights into the archaeological expression of the process of diffusion. However, the concept has been essentially ignored in recent treatments of prehistoric agriculture by Richard S. MacNeish (1991), Patty Jo Watson (1989, 1992), W.H. Wills (1988), Gayle J. Fritz (1990), and others, and has almost completely lost the value it long held for the study of the history and evolution of agricultural economies and of sedentary settlement systems beyond the borders of Mesoamerica.

James Schoenwetter

Further Readings

Decker, D.S. 1988. Origin(s), Evolution and Systematics of *Cucurbita pepo* (Cucurbitaceae). *Economic Botany* 42(1):4–15.

Doebley, J. 1990. Molecular Evidence and the Evolution of Maize. *Economic Botany* 44(3):S6–S27.

Doran, G.H., D.N. Dickel, and L.A. Newsom. 1990. A 7,290-Year-Old Bottle Gourd From the Windover Site, Florida. *American Antiquity* 55:354–360.

Ford, R.I. 1981. Gardening and Farming Before A.D. 1000: Patterns of Prehistoric Cultivation North of Mexico. *Journal of Ethnobiology* 1:6–27.

———. 1985. Patterns of Prehistoric Food Production in North America. In *Prehistoric Food Production in North America*, edited by R.I. Ford, pp. 341–364. Anthropological Paper no. 75. Museum of Anthropology, University of Michigan, Ann Arbor.

Fritz, G.J. 1990. Multiple Pathways to Farming in Precontact Eastern North America. *Journal of World Prehistory* 4(4):387–435.

Gepts, P., K. Kmieck, P. Pereira, and F.A. Bliss. 1988. Dissemination Pathways of Common Bean (*Phaseolus vulgaris*, Fabaceae) Deduced From Phaseolin Electrophoretic Variability: 1. The Americas. *Economic Botany* 42(1):73–85.

Griffin, J.B. 1967. Eastern North American Archaeology: A Summary. *Science* 156(3772):175–191.

MacNeish, R.S. 1991. *The Origins of Agriculture and Settled Life*. University of Oklahoma Press, Norman.

Rindos, D. 1984. *The Origins of Agriculture: An Evolutionary Perspective*. Academic Press, New York.

Smiley, F.E. 1985. *The Chronometrics of Early Agriculture Sites in Northeastern Arizona*. Unpublished Ph.D. dissertation, Department of Anthropology, University of Michigan, Ann Arbor.

Watson, P.J. 1989. Early Plant Cultivation in the Eastern Woodlands of North America. In *Foraging and Farming: The Evolution of Plant Exploitation*, edited by D. Harris and G. Hillman, pp. 555–571. Unwin Hyman, London.

———. 1992. *The Origins of Agriculture in International Perspective*. Smithsonian Institution Press, Washington, D.C.

Wenke, R.J. 1984. *Patterns in Prehistory*. 2nd ed. Oxford University Press, New York.

Wills, W.H. 1988. Early Agriculture and Sedentism in the American Southwest: Evidence and Interpretations. *Journal of World Prehistory* 2:445–488.

Yarnell, R.A. 1964. *Aboriginal Relationships Between Culture and Plant Life in the Upper Great Lakes Region*. Anthropological Paper no. 23. Museum of Anthropology, University of Michigan, Ann Arbor.

See also EASTERN AGRICULTURAL COMPLEX; LOWER SONORAN AGRICULTURAL COMPLEX

U

V

Vail Site

The Vail site (MSM 81.1) is one of eight Early Paleoindian sites within a 16-m (10-mile) -long stretch of the Magalloway River Valley, Oxford County, northwestern Maine. This complex, perhaps representing just a few human generations during the initial settlement of northeastern North America, is characterized by a suite of distinctive flaked-stone tools. Moderately to deeply concave fluted points, fluted drills, spurred triangular scrapers, wedges (*pièces esquillées*), combination side scrapers and utilized flakes, and various delicate engraving and cutting tools are abundant. The former presence of large biface cores ("platterlike bifaces") and broad fluted knives is indicated by fragments and resharpening flakes. Presumed sources of raw material for these flaked tools lie at considerable distances (100–300 km, or 62–186 miles) from the Magalloway Valley as well as close at hand. It is evident that the earliest occupants of the river valley had a highly mobile lifestyle that carried them across northern New England and ultimately eastward to the Atlantic Ocean shore. Although no food bone or other dietary remains were preserved at the Magalloway sites, it is surmised that inhabitants were intent upon ambushing caribou or some other migratory herd animal (Gramly 1982, 1984). In support of this hypothesis is the fact that sites are located on the windswept side of the valley near natural constrictions of the valley walls. The argument also is strengthened by the remarkable discovery in 1980 at Vail of five broken projectile points, thought to have tipped handheld spears or lances, which were restored from fragments from widely separated locations. At only one other Early Paleoindian site in North American (Murray Springs in Arizona) has it

been possible to conjoin spear points found at widely separated task areas.

The Vail site is an open encampment covering ca. 0.4 ha (1 acre). Despite heavy erosion caused by waves from human-made Aziscohos Lake, eight artifact scatters (or loci) remained for excavators. The loci are thought to mark tent sites and associated work spots. No structural remains were noted. Loci separated by as much as 100 m (328 feet) are linked by conjoined fluted twist drills and fluted projectile points. Tool and meat sharing between households is thought to have occurred. At least two dwellings stood at the Vail site during each episode of occupation. Judging by the quantity of stone artifacts and their stylistic uniformity, the Vail site may have been reinhabited 18–20 times, perhaps in successive years.

The Vail encampment has three satellite sites, which are located upwind on the opposite shore of an ancient channel of the Magalloway River. Two of these sites yielded only fluted projectile points and are interpreted as ambushing places, or "kill sites." The third locality produced only large cutting tools, such as utilized flakes, backed bifaces, and biface cores. These finds likely mark an abattoir, or butchering site. Five fluted point tips, which were excavated from one of the kill sites, were refitted to basal sections from the Vail habitation site.

Only two archaeological features survived at the Vail site, a hearth or cooking pit and a storage chamber or cachepit. Wood charcoal from their fill provided a series of radiocarbon ages spanning the interval 9170–8350 B.C. (11,120–10,300 years B.P.). Dating was done both by conventional means and by tandem linear accelerator mass spectrometry. Only one other site of the Magalloway Valley complex yielded features: the Adkins encampment, which lies 1–2 km (0.6–1.2 miles) downriver of Vail. There an impressive boulder-rimmed storage pit was discovered near a single tent site and associated Early Paleoindian flaked-stone tools.

Richard Michael Gramly

Further Readings

Gramly, R.M. 1982. *The Vail Site: A Palaeo-Indian Encampment in Maine.* Bulletin no. 30. Buffalo Society of Natural Sciences, Buffalo.

———. 1984. Kill Sites, Killing Ground and Fluted Points at the Vail Site. *Archaeology of Eastern North America* 12:110–121.

———. 1985. Recherches archelogiques au site paleoindian de Vail dans le nord-ouest du Maine, 1980–1983. *Recherches Amérindiennes au Québec* 15(1–2):57–118.

———. 1988. *The Adkins Site: A Palaeo-Indian Habitation and Associated Stone Structure.* Persimmon Press, Buffalo.

Valley Variant

Valley-variant sites are concentrated in an area from western Iowa across the Missouri River and along the Platte River and its northern tributaries to the eastern edge of the High Plains in western Nebraska. They occur in both the eastern prairies and the prairie-plains border zones. Valley Cord Roughened ceramics are found over a much larger range, as indicated by the discovery of sherds in Yuma County, Colorado, northwestern North Dakota, and central Wyoming. A limited number of radiocarbon dates from Valley-variant components suggests a Middle Plains Woodland temporal placement of A.D. 1–500 (1950–1450 years B.P.).

Settlement-pattern data are limited, although excavations at the Schultz site on the northern side of Mira Creek, a tributary of the North Loup River in central Nebraska, disclosed a village site covering ca. 2,787 m² (30,000 square feet) and an occupation zone varying from 40.6 to 101.6 cm (16–40 inches) in depth, which suggests an extensive period of occupation or a sequence of reoccupations over a long period of time. Features consisted of nine probable houses, one borrow pit or house, and six storage pits. Valley-variant burial practices include inhumations in village sites, ossuaries, and burial mounds.

Data on the Valley-variant subsistence base suggest a generalized hunting-and-gathering pattern. Hunting involved the taking of bison, deer, small mammals, rodents, turtles, and birds. Freshwater mussel shells and fish bones indicate some reliance on aquatic resources. A lack of grinding tools for the preparation of vegetable foods is notable in Valley-variant artifact assemblages, although the presence of wild-plant-food gathering is suggested by several wild seed types and corn (*Zea mays*) at the Rainbow site in Iowa.

Alfred E. Johnson

Further Readings

Benn, D.W. 1990. *Woodland Cultures on the Western Prairies: The Rainbow Site.* Report no. 18. Office of the State Archaeologist, University of Iowa, Iowa City.

Hill, A.T., and M.F. Kivett. 1940. *Woodland-Like Manifestations in Nebraska.* Nebraska History, vol. 21, no. 3. Lincoln.

O'Brien, P.J. 1971. Valley Focus Mortuary Practices. *Plains Anthropologist* 16(53):165–182.

Ventana Cave

Ventana Cave (AZ Z:12:5 ASM) is 120 km (75 miles) west of Tucson, Arizona, on the Tohono O'odham (formerly Papago) Indian Reservation. This 55-m (180-foot) -long, 6–20-m (20–66-foot) -deep rock shelter lies at the foot of a vertical rock face ca. 150 m (492 feet) above the surrounding paloverde–saguaro cactus desert scrub. It was formed by the seepage of water along a contact between volcanic agglomerate and an overlying basalt; a spring inside the cave still yields water. Ventana Cave was completely excavated in 1941–1942 under the direction of Emil W. Haury of the University of Arizona and yielded a stratified record of Paleoindian, Archaic, Hohokam, and Tohono O'odham occupations. The Paleoindian occupation occurred in the volcanic-debris layer, a carbonate- and silica-cemented silty sand consisting of volcanic ash with rock fragments of basalt, agglomerate, and rhyolite. Primarily fluvial, it included significant contributions of aeolian, tuffaceous dust. It extended over the lowest, central portion of the cave, covered an area ca. 20 m (66 feet) long by 9 m (29.5 feet) wide and up to 0.5 m (1.7 feet) thick, and was erosionally truncated.

Scattered through the volcanic-debris layer were flaked-stone implements, charcoal, animal bone, and fragments of marine shell. No discrete hearths, pits, or other features were present. Ninety stone artifacts were recovered; debitage was also present but was not collected. The assemblage of stone artifacts was named the Ventana complex and included two projectile points, 11 unifacial-flake knives, 63 scrapers, three gravers, three choppers, six planes, a hammerstone, and a mano. One of the two points bore morphological similarities to Folsom points; it was not fluted, however, but manufactured by marginal-pressure retouching of a thin flake of black basalt. The other point was a small leaf-shaped specimen of clear quartz that is not easily compared with any known type. The scrapers were morphologically diverse but predominantly classified as side and oval or discoidal forms. A large, circular, carefully shaped, bifacial mano of rhyolite, carefully pecked to shape on both its faces and edges, was an unexpected discovery. Forty-seven fragments of *Laevicardium* shell, available from the Gulf of California ca. 145 km (233 miles) southwest of Ventana Cave, were found. These large cockleshells may have served as containers. Bones of extinct animals were also found, including horse, tapir, sloth, four-pronged antelope, bison, and lion or jaguar. Horse far outnumbered all other taxa, accounting for 39 percent of the extinct fauna. Extant taxa were also present, including jackrabbit, prairie dog, badger, and mule deer.

Haury (1950) concluded that the Ventana complex was distinct from, but related to, the Folsom and San Dieguito complexes. Geologic data and the presence of extinct animals suggested that it was at least 10,000 years old and probably a hunting culture. In 1975, Haury and Julian D. Hayden reported a radiocarbon date on charcoal from the volcanic debris layer of 9350 B.C. ± 1200 (11,300 years B.P.). They suggested that the basalt "Folsomoid" point was a "local imitation of a Clovis point" and that the leaf-shaped quartz point was also Clovis related by "material and technology." In their view, the Ventana complex was basically San Dieguito with some Clovis influence. Bruce B. Huckell and C. Vance Haynes, Jr. (1995) recently reported 10 radiocarbon dates from the volcanic-debris layer; all but one were in the early Holocene, ranging from ca. 8650 to 6850 B.C. (10,600–8800 years B.P.). The assemblage is thus post-Clovis and probably more closely related to early Holocene industries of the arid West than to Plains Paleoindian manifestations.

Bruce B. Huckell

Further Readings

Colbert, E.H. 1973. Further Evidence Concerning the Presence of Horse at Ventana Cave. *Kiva* 39:25–33.

Haury, E.W. 1950. *The Stratigraphy and Archaeology of Ventana Cave*. University of Arizona Press, Tucson; University of New Mexico Press, Albuquerque.

Haury, E.W., and J.D. Hayden. 1975. Preface. In *The Archaeology and Stratigraphy of Ventana Cave,* pp. v–vi. 2nd ed. University of Arizona Press, Tucson.

Huckell, B.B., and C.V. Haynes, Jr. 1995. The Ventana Complex: New Dates and New Ideas on Its Place in Early Holocene Western Prehistory. Paper presented at the Sixtieth Annual Meeting of the Society for American Archaeology, Minneapolis.

Vickers Focus

The Vickers focus is thought to represent a small-scale horticultural practice in the central parklands of Manitoba. Radiocarbon dating places the focus at ca. A.D. 1450 (500 years B.P.). Sites are typically located on high ground north of major riverine channels, and their inhabitants appear to have relied upon potholes for a water source. At these latitudes (49°–50°north), low areas such as floodplains are subject to late spring and early fall frosts. Although drier, high ground is better suited to horticultural crops. The Vickers focus is understood to be a transitional society composed of dispersed band/village aggregations that spread over the landscape to take advantage of carefully selected locations suitable to a lifeway based on limited horticulture and diverse hunting and gathering. The presence of catlinite, grey soapstone, Knife River flint, and Tongue River silicified sediment in sites indicates a widespread trade network.

Vickers-focus sites share markedly similar ceramics, including an unusual decorative feature of finger-pinched nodes as exterior lip decoration. Twisted-cord or tool impressions on the interior and exterior of lips are common, and rim profiles vary from flared, through straight, to S–cross sections. Grog and mussel shell, as well as sand and grit, were used for temper. Exterior finish ranges from smoothed through obliterated fabric, to clearly defined cord/fabric marking, to small amounts of check stamping. Exterior brushing is present as a minor element. In large part, these ceramics re-

Vickers focus pottery sherds. (Photograph by B. Nicholson)

semble plain wares common in Mississippian sites to the south and materials of the Scattered Village complex in North Dakota.

Vickers-focus sites contain stone and/or scapula hoes and crude grinding paraphernalia. Recovery of catlinite pipes and tablets and vessels with effigy tabs is restricted to the Lowton site. The wide range of variation in materials suggests a prehistoric analogue to the poly-ethnic coresidence or fused ethnicity associated with the historic Cree–Assiniboine Young Dog band. The Vickers-focus people were drawn from diverse origins, but they were assimilated by similar subsistence practices and a tribal social organization.

Bev Nicholson

Further Readings

Nicholson, B.A. 1991. Modeling a Horticul-tural Focus in South-Central Manitoba During the Late Prehistoric Period—The Vickers Focus. *Midcontinental Journal of Archaeology* 16(2):163–188.

———. 1992. Variables Affecting Site Selec-tion by Late Prehistoric Groups Follow-ing a Hunting/Horticultural Lifeway in South-Central Manitoba. Paper pre-sented at the Twenty-Fourth Annual Chacmool Conference, Calgary.

Virgin Anasazi

The Anasazi of the Virgin region are the farthest west of the prehistoric Anasazi. Their region straddles two physiographic provinces: part of the Colorado Plateau north of the western Grand Canyon, and the southeastern edge of the Great Basin. On the plateaus of southern Utah and northern Arizona, they occupied parklands of grass and sage that mingled with stands of piñon and juniper at elevations of 1,524–2,134 m (5,000–7,000 feet). In the lower elevations of the St. George Basin of southwest-ern Utah and the riverine valleys of southern Nevada, they were in desert environments where creosote bush was common. There, their sites hugged the margins of permanent streams, the Virgin River and its tributaries, the St. Clara River and the Muddy River.

Early investigations in the region include those of Neil M. Judd (1926) near Kanab, Utah, J.L. Nusbaum's (1922) at Cave DuPont, west of Kanab, and M.R. Harrington's (1925, 1937) in southern Nevada.

The earliest Virgin Anasazi sites date prior to A.D. 500 (1450 years B.P.) and are similar to Basketmaker II in other Anasazi areas. Residen-tial sites include pithouses. Food and seeds were stored in pits or in slab-lined cists in rock shel-ters. Over the course of ca. 1,000 years of de-velopment, their storage facilities changed to rows of store rooms built on, or just below, the surface. They were constructed of masonry where tabular rock such as sandstone was avail-able; otherwise, of adobe or jacal. Pit structures continued to be used as residences at some sites into the A.D. 1100s (850–750 years B.P.), but at other sites surface rooms served as residences.

The requirements of their crops seem to have determined site locations. On the plateaus, they were situated for dry-farming of deep soils or in areas where local runoff was concentrated and could be diverted onto their gardens. At lower elevations, they apparently used small-scale irrigation. They grew maize, beans, and squash. In southern Nevada, they also grew cotton and, perhaps, amaranth. Like other Anasazi, they gathered wild foods and hunted. In southern Nevada, rabbits and desert tortoise were common meats; they were supplemented with bighorn sheep taken in the adjacent moun-tains. On the plateau, where ungulates were more available, they hunted bighorn sheep, pronghorn, and deer, but they also consumed rabbit in some quantity. By ca. A.D. 1100 (850 years B.P.), domestic turkeys were present, too.

Sites are generally small. They provided living and storage rooms for a few families. Along the Muddy River in southern Nevada, such sites are numerous and close to one an-other. Compact villages seem to be absent. The kiva seems to have been lacking for most of their history, but its use spread into the eastern part of their area ca. A.D. 1100 (850 years B.P.). Without a common ceremonial structure, households apparently maintained informal links with one another. They exchanged pottery and shell beads and probably foods and other perishables.

An exchange network linked lowland sites with those of the Colorado Plateau. Distinctive pottery with olivine inclusions, made on the Uinkaret Plateau, is plentiful in southern Ne-vada sites. From farther east, the southern Ne-vada communities received red-ware pottery from the Kayenta and Mesa Verde people. Shell ornaments from the coast of California and the Gulf of California reached the southern Nevada households. Salt was mined from deposits now flooded by Lake Mead in southern Nevada, as was low-grade turquoise from a locality near Boulder City, Nevada.

The Virgin Anasazi occupation seems to have been much attenuated by ca. A.D. 1200 (750 years B.P.), although there is evidence of occupation, or reoccupation, of some sites during the 1200s (750–650 years B.P.). A period of undependable rainfall ca. A.D. 1120–1150 (830–800 years B.P.) may have destabilized their food-production systems, but it did not immediately lead to full abandonment of the region. There is little or no evidence of cultural continuity between the Virgin Anasazi and the Southern Paiutes, who seem to have replaced them.

Margaret M. Lyneis

Further Readings

Aikens, C.M. 1965. *Excavations in Southwest Utah.* Anthropological Papers no. 76. University of Utah Press, Salt Lake City.

Dalley, G.F., and D.A. McFadden. 1988. *The Little Man Sites: Excavations on the Virgin River Near Hurricane, Utah.* Cultural Resource Series no. 17. Utah State Office, Bureau of Land Management, Salt Lake City.

Harrington, M.R. 1925. The "Lost City" of Nevada. *Scientific American* 133:14–25.

———. 1937. Excavation of Pueblo Grande de Nevada. *Bulletin of the Texas Archaeological and Paleontological Society* 9:130–145.

Judd, N.M. 1926. *Archaeological Observations North of the Rio Colorado.* Bulletin no. 82. Bureau of American Ethnology, Smithsonian Institution, Washington, D.C.

Larson, D.O., and J. Michaelsen. 1990. Impacts of Climatic Variability and Population Growth on Virgin Branch Anasazi Cultural Developments. *American Antiquity* 55:227–249.

Lyneis, M.M. 1992. *The Main Ridge Community at Lost City: Virgin Anasazi Architecture, Ceramics, and Burials.* Anthropological Papers no. 117. University of Utah Press, Salt Lake City.

Nickens, P.R., and K.L. Kvamme. 1981. Archaeological Excavations at the Kanab Site. In *Excavation of Two Anasazi Sites in Southern Nevada,* assembled by R.E. Fike and D.B. Madsen. Cultural Resource Series no. 9. Utah State Office, Bureau of Land Management, Salt Lake City.

Nusbaum, J.L. 1922. *A Basket-Maker Cave in Kane County, Utah; With Notes by A.V. Kidder and S.J. Guernsey.* Indian Notes and Monographs no. 29. Museum of the American Indian-Heye Foundation, New York.

Shutler, R., Jr. 1961. *Lost City: Pueblo Grande de Nevada.* Anthropological Papers no. 5. Nevada State Museum, Carson City.

Westfall, D.A. 1986. Life in the Land of Little Water: The Prehistory of the Arizona Strip. The Arizona Strip: Splendid Isolation. *Plateau* 57(2):18–21.

———. 1987. The Pinenut Site: Virgin Anasazi Archaeology on the Kanab Plateau of Northwestern Arizona. Cultural Resource Series Monographs no. 4. Arizona State Office, Bureau of Land Management, Phoenix.

Walker Road Site

Walker Road (HEA-130) is a stratified prehistoric site in central Alaska that contains an occupation level assigned to the Early Paleoindian Nenana complex. The site is located in the northern foothills of the Alaska Range near the town of Healy (63°53' north, 149°02' west) and occupies a south-facing promontory on an unnamed creek in the Nenana Valley (ca. 430 m, or 1,411 feet, above sea level). Walker Road was discovered by J.F. Hoffecker in 1980 and subsequently investigated by Hoffecker, W.R. Powers, and T. Goebel during the period 1984–1990; an area of ca. 200 m² (239 square yards) had been excavated as of 1996 (Powers and Hoffecker 1989; Powers et al. 1990; Goebel et al. 1991).

Two occupation horizons are buried in deposits of loess and aeolian sand that unconformably overlie a stream terrace composed of possible late Middle Pleistocene glaciofluvial outwash. Radiometric dates and stratigraphic correlation with other localities in the Nenana Valley indicate that the aeolian deposits, which are ca. 1 m (3.3 feet) in total depth, date from 10,050 B.C. (12,000 years B.P.) to the present. The lower occupation layer occurs near the base of these deposits in silt loam (loess); conventional and AMS (accelerator mass spectrometry) radiocarbon dates on wood charcoal from former hearths in this layer range from 9870 B.C. ± 200 to 9060 B.C. ± 230 (11,820–11,010 years B.P.). An overlying buried soil horizon yielded a date of 6770 B.C. ± 250 (8720 years B.P.). The upper occupation layer occurs near the modern ground surface and dates to the late Holocene (less than 1550 B.C., or 3,500 years B.P.); an underlying buried soil horizon yielded an age range of 2465–1866 B.C. (4415–3816 years B.P.) (Powers et al. 1990; Goebel et al. 1991).

Ca. 4,500 lithic artifacts were recovered from the lower occupation level. A variety of raw materials, including brown and tan chert, chalcedony, quartzite, rhyolite, and basalt, are represented in the assemblage. Most artifacts were found in large debris concentrations, two of which are associated with former hearths. Tools comprise 184 items (4.1 percent of all lithic artifacts recovered) and include small teardrop-shaped bifacial points (Chindadn points), end scrapers, side scrapers, wedges (*pièces esquillées*), perforators, and planes (Goebel et al. 1991). Wedge-shaped microcores and microblades, which are found in many early Alaskan sites, are completely absent. On the basis of the technological and typological character of the artifacts, the assemblage is assigned to the Nenana complex, which is, in turn, widely regarded as part of the Paleoindian tradition (Powers and Hoffecker 1989; Goebel et al. 1991). Although faunal remains from Walker Road are confined to small unidentifiable fragments, data from other Nenana-complex sites suggest that their occupants hunted a variety of medium and large mammals, including extinct late Pleistocene forms such as steppe bison (*Bison priscus*) (Powers and Hoffecker 1989). The upper occupation level contains a small number of isolated lithic artifacts without diagnostic forms; the cultural affiliation of this assemblage is undetermined.

John F. Hoffecker

Further Readings
Goebel, T., R. Powers, and N. Bigelow. 1991. The Nenana Complex of Alaska and Clovis Origins. In *Clovis: Origins and*

Adaptations, edited by R. Bonnichsen and K. Turnmire, pp. 49–79. Center for the Study of the First Americans, Oregon State University, Corvallis.

Powers, W.R., and J.F. Hoffecker. 1989. Late Pleistocene Settlement in the Nenana Valley, Central Alaska. *American Antiquity* 54:263–287.

Powers, W.R., F.E. Goebel, and N.H. Bigelow. 1990. Late Pleistocene Occupation at Walker Road: New Data on the Central Alaskan Nenana Complex. *Current Research in the Pleistocene* 7:40–43.

See also NENANA COMPLEX

Wall-Trench Structures

The use of wall-trench structures is a characteristic Mississippian-tradition (ca. A.D. 900–1600, or 1050–350 years B.P.) building-construction technique in the Eastern Woodlands. Long narrow (ca. 20–30 cm, or 8–12 inches) trenches were dug ca. 25–40 cm (10–16 inches) deep, and small posts were set within them to form relatively substantial walls and interior partitions. Individual trenches usually have U-shaped cross sections with vertical sides and rounded ends that do not intersect the trenches of perpendicular walls. The posts, set vertically or at a slight inward slant into the trenches, were apparently bent together at the top to form an arched roof. Wattle-and-daub sheathing covered the walls, and thatch covered the roof.

Most wall-trench structures were square-to-rectangular semisubterranean buildings used for a variety of purposes, including enclosed work areas, public facilities, temples on platform mounds, large storage facilities, and domestic dwellings. Typical wall lengths were ca. 3–5 m (10–16 feet). Most structures had wall trenches along all four walls, but various combinations with post-constructed walls have been encountered; a common pattern is a structure with three wall-trenched walls and a post-constructed or partial wall-trench wall along the fourth side. Entrances were normally at the corners of the buildings. The remains of interior benches, roof supports, fireplaces, processing racks, storage pits, and other features are often found in building interiors, which were occasionally partitioned with internal wall trenches. Double or extra wall trenches are fairly common, with many the result of rebuilding. Square-to-rectangular structures vary considerably in size and shape, with the trend toward larger, more nearly square buildings. Small circular wall-trench structures that are thought to have been used as sweat lodges or above-ground storage facilities are not unusual. In some situations, wall trenches were used only for a subsidiary section of a building, such as an extended entranceway.

Mississippian wall-trench houses were usually components of spatially distinct household clusters that consisted of a grouping of one or two wall-trench houses, storage and processing pits and structures, and other specialized features. Household clusters like these are considered the minimal Mississippian community unit and are thought to be associated with individual corporate groups, such as a nuclear family, an extended family, or some other functional group organized around economic, political, or religious activities.

Guy Gibbon

Further Readings

Milner, G.R. 1984. *The Julien Site.* American Bottom Archaeology, FAI-270 Site Reports, vol. 7. Published for the Illinois Department of Transportation by the University of Illinois Press, Urbana.

———. 1990. The Late Prehistoric Cahokia Cultural System of the Mississippi River Valley: Foundations, Florescence, and Fragmentation. *Journal of World Prehistory* 4(1):1–43.

Milner, G.R., T.E. Emerson, M.W. Mehrer, J.A. Williams, and D. Esarey. 1984. Mississippian and Oneota Period. In *American Bottom Archaeology,* edited by C.J. Bareis and J.W. Porter, pp. 158–186. University of Illinois Press, Urbana.

Smith, B.D. (editor). 1978. *Mississippian Settlement Patterns.* Academic Press, New York.

See also MISSISSIPPIAN CULTURE

Wallace, William J. (1915–)

William J. Wallace was among those archaeologists trained at the University of California, Berkeley, in the 1940s who developed the major programs of academically based California archaeological research at the state's other colleges and universities. Wallace joined the faculty at the University of Southern California in 1952 and served more than 25 years. He worked throughout the state, from the Oregon border (Wallace and Taylor 1952) to the Mexican border (Wallace and Taylor 1958), and from the coast (Wallace 1954) to the mountains (Wallace 1951) and on into the desert (Wallace 1962b). He played a key role in helping define the Millingstone horizon for coastal southern California (Wallace 1954, 1955b, 1966; Wallace, et al. 1956). His most enduring work has proved to be his desert studies, especially in Death Valley (Wallace 1955a, 1977; Wallace and Wallace 1978) and the western Colorado desert (Wallace and Taylor 1958; Wallace and Desautels 1960; Wallace 1962a).

Joseph L. Chartkoff

Further Readings

Wallace, W.J. 1951. *The Archaeological Deposits in Moaning Cave, Calaveras County, California.* Archaeological Survey Reports no. 12. University of California, Berkeley.

———. 1954. The Little Sycamore Site and Early Milling Stone Cultures in Southern California. *American Antiquity* 20:112–123.

———. 1955a. Early Man in Death Valley. *Archaeology* 8(2):88–92.

———. 1955b. A Suggested Chronology for Southern California Coastal Archaeology. *Southwestern Journal of Anthropology* 11:214–230.

———. 1958. Archaeological Investigations in Death Valley National Monument. *Archaeological Survey Reports* 42:7–22. University of California, Berkeley.

———. 1962a. *Archaeological Explorations in the Southern Section of Anza-Borrego Desert State Park.* Archaeological Reports no. 5. California Department of Parks and Recreation, Sacramento.

———. 1962b. Prehistoric Cultural Development in the Southern California Deserts. *American Antiquity* 28:172–180.

———. 1966. Hollywood Riviera: An Early Milling Stone Horizon Site in Los Angeles County, California. *American Antiquity* 31:422–427.

———. 1977. A Half-Century of Death Valley Archaeology. *Journal of California Archaeology* 4(2):249–258.

Wallace, W.J., and R.J. Desautels. 1960. *An Excavation at Deep Tank-Squaw Tank Site, Joshua Tree National Monument, California.* Contributions to California

Archaeology, vol. 3, no. 1. Archaeological Research Associates, Los Angeles.

Wallace, W.J., and E. Taylor. 1952. *Excavation of Sis-13: A Rock Shelter in Siskiyou County, California.* Archaeological Survey Reports no. 15. University of California, Berkeley.

———. 1955. Archaeology of Wildrose Canyon, Death Valley National Monument. *American Antiquity* 20:355–367.

———. 1958. An Archaeological Reconnaissance in Bow Willow Canyon, Anza-Borrego Desert State Park. *Masterkey* 32(5):155–166.

Wallace, W.J., and E. Wallace. 1978. Ancient Peoples and Cultures of Death Valley National Monument. Acoma Books, Ramona.

Wallace, W.J., E.S. Taylor, R.J. Desautls, H.R. Hammond, H. Gonzales, J. Bogart, and J.P. Redwine. 1956. *The Little Sycamore Shellmound, Ventura County, California.* Contributions to California Archaeology, no. 2. Archaeological Research Associates, Los Angeles.

Warren Wilson Site

The Warren Wilson site (31 BN29) is located on the Swannanoa River in Buncombe County, North Carolina. This location places it in the Appalachian Summit region, the ancestral home of the Cherokee Indians. Excavations at Warren Wilson began in 1965 as part of the University of North Carolina's Cherokee Archaeological Project, which was designed to trace the origins of Cherokee culture. Work continued at the site, on a seasonal basis, until 1984. As of mid-1996, approximately one-third of the 1.2-ha (3-acre) village had been excavated.

Warren Wilson is a stratified, multicomponent site, with its main occupation dating to the Pisgah phase (A.D. 1100–1400, or 850–550 years B.P.) of the South Appalachian Mississippian tradition. A total of 14 house structures have been identified within a series of multiple palisade lines. Although the site may have been expanding and contracting through time, there is also evidence that the interior of the village was enclosed by palisades for ceremonial reasons, whereas the outer palisades were used simultaneously for defensive purposes.

The houses are square to rectangular in outline and average a little less than 6 m (20 feet) on a side. Most contain evidence of a cen--

tral clay hearth, consisting of a shallow basin surrounded by a clay collar. One of the distinguishing characteristics of Pisgah houses is parallel entry trenches. These trenches held two rows of saplings that formed the framework for a low tunnel-like entryway. Wall posts were set in closely spaced individual holes, and four large interior posts were placed equidistant from the walls as roof supports. The absence of fired-clay plaster or "daub" suggests that the walls of Warren Wilson houses were covered with cane mats or bark. Straw thatch or bark probably served as the roofing material.

Often, burials were placed inside the houses, sometimes beneath the hearths. Three types of burial pits have been identified at Warren Wilson: simple pits and two varieties of shaft-and-chamber pits. The former consist of oval-shaped graves with straight sides and flat bottoms. Central chamber pits were created by excavating a smaller pit in the floor of the burial shaft. The resulting shelves were used to support the ends of logs placed over the chamber to cover the body. In some cases, the burial chamber was tunneled into the wall of the central shaft at the bottom of the pit, creating a side chamber. These chambers were also covered with logs or, occasionally, large stones. Bodies are usually tightly flexed and lack grave offerings. However, one adult male was found accompanied by a large number of tools and ornaments made of bone, shell, and mica.

Subsistence remains reflect a mixed economy relying equally on agricultural production and hunting and gathering wild-food resources. The fertile bottoms surrounding the Warren Wilson site were ideal for agricultural pursuits, and the hardwood forests of the surrounding uplands offered a cornucopia of wild plants and animals for food.

H. Trawick Ward

Further Readings

Dickens, R.S., Jr. 1976. *Cherokee Prehistory: The Pisgah Phase in the Appalachian Summit Region.* University of Tennessee Press, Knoxville.

Keel, B.C. 1976. *Cherokee Archaeology: A Study of the Appalachian Summit.* University of Tennessee Press, Knoxville.

Purrington, B.L. 1983. Ancient Mountaineers: An Overview of the Prehistoric Archaeology of North Carolina's Western Mountain Region. In *The Prehistory of North Carolina: An Archaeological Symposium,* edited by M.A. Mathis and J.J. Crow, pp. 83–160. North Carolina Division of Archives and History, Department of Cultural Resources, Raleigh.

Wascana Ware

Wascana-ware pottery appears on the Saskatchewan plains after A.D. 1300 (650 years B.P.) in sites containing Plains Side-Notched projectile points. While its geographic distribution is subject to debate, most sites with similar pottery are located in the central part of the province in an area that extends north of the Qu'Appelle Valley into the parkland belt north of Saskatoon. Prehistorians affiliate Mortlach with either the Assiniboin, a Siouan group, or the Atsina, an Algonkin group.

Wascana ware was originally described by Alice Kehoe in 1959. It is difficult to define because of the variety of vessel forms, exterior surface treatments, and decorations present. Although many pottery assemblages are highly fragmented, usually 80 percent of the vessels have either straight rim, angled rim, or S-profiles. The globular vessels, probably formed using the paddle-and-anvil technique, have thin walls and a compact paste lightly tempered with sand or finely crushed granite. Exterior surfaces are either smoothed plain or carry impressions produced by cord- or fabric-wrapped paddles. A wide variety of decorations appears on the exterior surface of this kind of pottery; cord-wrapped-tool impressions and punctates appear most frequently. Decoration appears on the lips of 90 percent of the pots; other areas, from the upper part of the rim to the shoulder angle, may also be decorated. Horizontal, vertical, or oblique lines; various tool or finger-made impressions; and single rows or clusters of punctates may appear alone or in elaborate combination.

Large sites containing Wascana ware are found in coulees and river valleys; these probably represent winter camps. Smaller sites have been identified in the parkland, usually near aspen groves. The people appear to have followed a mobile plant-gathering and bison-hunting economy. It is extremely difficult to establish the positions of various indigenous Plains peoples about the time of European contact at the turn of the eighteenth century. The records of European travelers show that both Atsina and Assiniboin groups were known to occupy the area where Wascana-ware assemblages are found.

Mary Malainey

Further Readings

Kehoe, A. 1959. Ceramic Affiliations in the Northwestern Plains. *American Antiquity* 25:237–246.

Malainey, M. 1991. *Internal and External Relationships of Saskatchewan Plains Pottery Assemblages: Circa A.D. 1300 to Contact.* Unpublished Master's thesis. Department of Anthropology and Archaeology, University of Saskatchewan, Saskatoon.

Wettlaufer, B. 1955. *The Mortlach Site in the Besant Valley of Central Saskatchewan.* Anthropological Series no. 1. Saskatchewan Museum of Natural History, Regina.

Washington Ocean Coast Sequence

The outer coast of Washington State is a rugged, wild, and largely undeveloped area. Much of it cannot be reached by road, and it has been the subject of only limited archaeological research. While the first studies to be undertaken anywhere on the Washington coast were conducted during the first decade of the twentieth century, the era of modern archaeological fieldwork did not begin until several relatively large-scale site surveys were conducted in the late 1940s and 1950s. The majority of the known prehistoric-site inventory was recorded during this period. The excavation of prehistoric sites began in the late 1950s, but most of the available data come from excavations undertaken since 1970. Most of these have been relatively small-scale studies; a notable exception has been the work at the Ozette village site.

Erosion of the bank at Ozette during the winter of 1970 resulted in the discovery of a waterlogged portion of this site with well-preserved organic cultural materials. The exposed strata contained the remains of at least five large Late Prehistoric split-cedar plank longhouses and their contents. Among the latter were large numbers of perishable wooden and woven-plant-fiber artifacts without precedent from Washington-coast sites. While the represented interval has not been well dated, these preserved organic materials are believed to date within the ca. A.D. 1550–1750 (400–200 years B.P.) period. Eleven years of work in the "wet" portion of Ozette resulted in the excavation of three complete longhouses, a portion of a fourth, and much of the contemporaneous exterior deposits around them; the recovered collection includes ca. 60,000 artifacts and more than 1 million faunal remains. As such, it is something of an understatement to suggest that the findings from Ozette dominate our perceptions of the late prehistory of the Washington coast.

Archaeological site surveys and excavations to the mid-1990s have produced an inventory of 125 prehistoric archaeological sites, and at least limited excavation data are available for 17 of them. Reflecting the relative recency of the excavation efforts, 15 of these 17 sampled sites are represented by at least one radiocarbon date. Six other Washington-coast sites are also represented by at least one radiocarbon date, though they have not been excavated.

The work on Washington-coast sites exhibits a number of biases and other inherent limitations that restrict its research value. Such limitations include implicit or nonexistent research designs, small sample sizes of artifacts, incomplete and inaccurate reporting of data, and ambiguous use of analytical and conceptual terms. All of the sampled sites are relatively recent occupations and all are shell-midden deposits. Additionally, the database is marked by a strong geographic bias; 13 of the sampled sites are located along a 60-km (37-mile) stretch on the northernmost portion of the coast; the remaining ca. 300 km (186 miles) of the Washington coastline are represented by only four excavated sites.

Environmental and cultural conditions on the Washington coast strongly suggest that the northern and southern portions of this area may have culture histories that differ significantly. In this regard, the geographic bias in the available archaeological data figures prominently. The vast majority of available data pertain only to the northern coast; the southern coast is much more poorly known. Potential limitations imposed by this situation are at least partly mitigated by the observation that the data from the southern Washington coast suggests that this area's culture history probably shares much with that of the somewhat better documented Columbia River mouth immediately to the south.

There are no proposed cultural chronologies that directly address the southern Washington coast. The oldest dated materials are associated with a date of A.D. 90 ± 100 (1860 years B.P.) at the Martin site. Both the bone- and the pecked- and ground-stone-tool assemblages from this site are much like those reported to the north and to the south in northwestern

Oregon. The only readily apparent difference is that the ground-slate knives found to the north do not occur at the Martin site. However, the chipped-stone assemblage from Martin is clearly distinct from those in northern Washington-coast sites. Chipped stone is well represented at the Martin site: The most common objects are small triangular and narrow-necked stemmed projectile points. The collection exhibits many similarities with the Late Prehistoric (50 B.C.–A.D. 1750, or 2000–200 years B.P.) Ilwaco phase of the nearby Columbia River mouth. Later prehistoric materials from the southern Washington coast are much like those from the Martin site and, thus, maintain the apparently strong similarity with the Ilwaco phase. As described, the latter represents essentially a prehistoric Chinookan cultural pattern focusing on riverine and estuarine fishing and near-shore terrestrial hunting.

A chronology proposed for the Olympic Peninsula of Washington in 1983 by E.O. Bergland spans 12,000 years, but dated materials from the ocean coast represent only the last 4,000 years or so. The oldest dated materials fall within his Middle Prehistoric period (4050–1050 B.C., or 6000–3000 years B.P.) and are associated with a date of 1860 B.C. ± 60 (3810 years B.P.) at the Waatch village site. The deposit contains an assemblage of bone and pecked-, ground-, and simple chipped-stone tools much like those reported from the west coast of Vancouver Island. Later Early Maritime–period (1050 B.C.–A.D. 950, or 3000–1000 years B.P.) assemblages appear to be similar in content. The most recent Prehistoric Northwest Coast period, which is best represented by the Ozette collection, maintains a strong continuity with earlier assemblages, with one notable exception: Stone chipping virtually disappears. All northern Washington-coast assemblages reflect clear indications of a sophisticated economy of offshore sea-mammal hunting and hook-and-line fishing, much like that noted for the historic Makah and Quileute peoples.

The available data from the Washington coast indicate that two relatively distinct Late Prehistoric regional patterns were present: a southern pattern related to that of the Columbia River mouth and northwestern Oregon, and a northern pattern related to that of the west coast of Vancouver Island. While differing in their economic orientations, both appear to have been collector-type settlement-and-subsistence systems already in place by ca. 1050–50

B.C. (3000–2000 years B.P.). Moreover, each pattern exhibits strong continuities with the early historic Native American cultures of its region. What that strongly suggests is that the ethnographic groups of the Washington coast are the descendants of cultural traditions that have long temporal duration in this region.

Gary C. Wessen

Further Readings

Bergland, E.O. 1983. *Summary Prehistory and Ethnography of the Olympic National Park, Washington.* Cultural Resources Division, National Park Service, Pacific Northwest Region, Seattle.

Roll, T.E. 1974. *The Archaeology of Minard: A Case Study of a Late Prehistoric Northwest Coast Procurement System.* Unpublished Ph.D. dissertation, Department of Anthropology, Washington State University, Pullman.

Samuels, S.R. (editor). 1991. *Ozette Archaeological Project Research Reports: 1. House Structure and Floor Midden.* Reports of Investigation no. 63. Department of Anthropology, Washington State University, Pullman.

Wessen, G.C. 1990. Prehistory of the Ocean Coast of Washington. In *Northwest Coast,* edited by W.P. Suttles, pp. 412–421. Handbook of North American Indians, vol. 7, W.C. Sturtevant, general editor. Smithsonian Institution, Washington, D.C.

Washita River Phase

The Washita River phase was originally called the Grant focus and then the Washita River focus. The phase dates between A.D. 1250 and 1450 (700–500 years B.P.). Most sites occur on the middle reaches of the Washita River in central to west-central Oklahoma. Within the phase, there were probably eastern and western divisions as well as temporal differences. Washita River–phase origins lie in the Custer phase (A.D. 950–1250, or 1000–700 years B.P.) in the same area and probably in other related cultures that are still poorly known.

Settlements consist of villages, rock shelters, and special-purpose sites. Villages are larger than in the Custer phase and include from five to 20 houses that are square to rectangular in outline. Center support posts are usually present but can be variable in number, ranging from two to six. Extended entryways are also sometimes present. Construction was of wattle and daub with a thatched grass roof. Cemeteries can be found adjacent to villages. Washita River–phase burials have been interpreted to reflect an egalitarian society with some limited evidence for the inheritance of sociopolitical status (Bell 1984).

Subsistence was based on hunting, gathering, and horticulture. Bison was more important than during the Custer phase and became increasingly so the more westerly and recent the sites. Pronghorn, elk, and a variety of small mammals were hunted. Turtles, fish, mussels, and birds were also eaten, and diverse fruits, nuts, and seeds were collected. Horticulture was more important than during the Custer phase, especially toward the east. Corn, beans, and squash have all been identified at Washita River–phase sites.

Ceramics were globular to vase shaped with round-to-flat bases. Tempering material included shell, limestone, and caliche. While peoples in western sites retained pottery styles more common in the Custer phase, those at eastern sites made greater use of shell tempering, plain surfaces, and flat bases. Plain surfaces in general were more common than during the Custer phase. Decoration was rare but included punctates, incising, and appliqué. Bone tools included bison-tibia digging-stick tips; bison-scapula, bone, and horn-core hoes; awls of a variety of types; fishhooks; deer-jaw sickles; and deer-bone shaft wrenches. Stone tools included small triangular points, with side-notched forms more common than unnotched forms; end scrapers; several types of drills; and alternately beveled, diamond-shaped knives. Ground-stone pipes, celts, shaft abraders, manos, and metates were common.

Evidence for trade is greater than in the Custer phase. Materials acquired included steatite; selenite (possibly from the Great Salt plains); Frisco chert (central Oklahoma); Florence-A chert (north-central Oklahoma); Alibates agatized dolomite (Texas Panhandle); conch and *Olivella* shell, earspools, and Caddoan and Tennessee-Cumberland river area ceramics (probably from the Arkansas River Valley Caddo); piñon nuts (western Oklahoma Panhandle); and obsidian (New Mexico and Idaho). Some Caddoan vessels may be local copies; Frisco chert may have been directly procured by people in eastern Washita River–phase settlements; and Alibates occurs in nearby river gravels.

The fate of Washita River–phase people is a matter of debate. Traditionally, they were thought to have moved to central Kansas, where they became known as the Little River focus of the Great Bend aspect. More recently (Baugh 1982), it has been suggested that they developed in situ into the Wheeler phase.

Susan C. Vehik

Further Readings

Baugh, T.G. 1982. *Edwards I (34BK2): Southern Plains Adaptations in the Protohistoric Period.* Studies in Oklahoma's Past no. 8. Oklahoma Archeological Survey, Norman.

Bell, R.E. 1984. The Plains Villagers: The Washita River. In *Prehistory of Oklahoma,* edited by R.E. Bell, pp. 307–324. Academic Press, Orlando.

Brooks, R.L. 1987. *The Arthur Site: Settlement and Subsistence Structure at a Washita River Phase Village.* Studies in Oklahoma's Past no. 15. Oklahoma Archeological Survey, Norman.

Drass, R.R., and P. Flynn. 1990. Temporal and Geographic Variations in Subsistence Practices for Plains Villagers in the Southern Plains. *Plains Anthropologist* 35:175–190.

Drass, R.R., and F.E. Swenson. 1986. Variation in the Washita River Phase of Central and Western Oklahoma. *Plains Anthropologist* 31:35–49.

Watercraft (California)

Watercraft played significant roles in prehistoric economies over much of California. Occupation of the Channel Islands began as early as 8050 B.C. (10,000 years B.P.). Water gaps of at least 32 km (20 miles) were crossed, though the forms of the earliest watercraft are unknown. Evidence of watercraft from effigies, rock art, and, occasionally, physical remains is available in some areas as far back as 50 B.C. (2000 years B.P.). In coastal southern California, oceangoing canoes were built of wood planks sewn together and caulked with asphaltum. In northwestern California, dugout canoes made of cedar and other large-trunked trees were used both on major rivers and along the coast. The deltas, rivers, and lakes of central California were navigated using reed boats built of bundles of tule tied together. Watercraft were used for fishing, hunting, plant harvests, shipping, and transportation.

Joseph L. Chartkoff

Further Readings

Chartkoff, J.L., and K.K. Chartkoff. 1984. *The Archaeology of California.* Stanford University Press, Stanford.

Heizer, R.F. (editor). 1978. *California.* Handbook of North American Indians, vol. 8, W.C. Sturtevant, general editor. Smithsonian Institution, Washington, D.C.

Webb, William Snyder (1882–1964)

A physicist by training and profession, William Snyder Webb became interested in Native Americans when he was a federal employee among the Seminoles in Indian Territory (now Oklahoma) in the years 1904–1907. He joined the Physics Department of the University of Kentucky in 1907 and, by the early 1920s, had begun surveying and excavating sites in the state in his spare time with W.D. Funkhouser, a zoologist. Their *Ancient Life in Kentucky* (1928) was a major popular survey that provided functional interpretations of the lifeways of Native Americans in the past, a widespread endeavor in the early twentieth century. Influenced later by the Midwestern Taxonomic Method, Webb ceased to study the behavior of prehistoric peoples and concentrated on the elaboration of trait lists. While head of the Physics Department, he was also appointed head of a new Department of Anthropology and Archaeology in 1926, mainly to legally accept the gift of a truck for archaeological research from the National Research Council. Between 1929 and 1952, he authored or coauthored at least 30 numbers in *University of Kentucky Reports in Anthropology and Archaeology,* all of which dealt with fieldwork in the state during which he pioneered detailed stratigraphic procedures. Appointed supervising archaeologist for all TVA (Tennessee Valley Authority) archaeology projects in 1934, he became the most prolific publisher of the federally funded project era, seeing four monumental reports through to publication between 1938 and 1951 (Webb 1938, 1939; Webb and DeJarnette 1942; Webb and Wilder 1951).

Guy Gibbon

William S. Webb. (Reprinted with permission from American Antiquity 30[4]:470)

Further Readings

Funkhouser, W.D., and W.S. Webb. 1928. *Ancient Life in Kentucky.* Geologic Reports, ser. 6, no. 34. Kentucky Geological Survey, Frankfort.

Haag, W.G. 1965. William Snyder Webb, 1882–1964. *American Antiquity* 30:470–473.

Schwartz, D.W. 1967. *Conceptions of Kentucky Prehistory.* University of Kentucky Press, Lexington.

Webb, W.S. 1938. *An Archaeological Survey of the Norris Basin in Eastern Tennessee.* Bulletin no. 118. Bureau of American Ethnology, Smithsonian Institution, Washington, D.C.

———. 1939. *An Archaeological Survey of the Wheeler Basin on the Tennessee River in Northern Alabama.* Bulletin no. 122. Bureau of American Ethnology, Smithsonian Institution, Washington, D.C.

———. 1946. *Indian Knoll, Site Oh 2, Ohio County, Kentucky.* Reports in Anthropology and Archaeology, vol. 4, no. 3, pt. 1. University of Kentucky, Lexington.

Webb, W.S., and D.L. De Jarnette. 1942. *An Archaeological Survey of Pickwick Basin in the Adjacent Portions of the States of Alabama, Mississippi, and Tennessee.* Bulletin no. 129. Bureau of American Ethnology, Smithsonian Institution, Washington, D.C.

Webb, W.S., and C.E. Snow. 1945. *The Adena People.* Reports in Anthropology

and Archaeology, vol. 6. University of
Kentucky, Lexington.
Webb, W.S., and C.G. Wilder. 1951. *An Ar-
chaeological Survey of Guntersville Ba-
sin on the Tennessee River in Northern
Alabama.* University of Kentucky Press,
Lexington.

Wedel, Waldo R. (1908–1996)

Waldo Rudolph Wedel was born in Newton,
Kansas. He received anthropology degrees from
the University of Arizona, the University of
Nebraska (1931), and the University of California, Berkeley (a Ph.D. in 1936). Influenced by
William Duncan Strong and geographer Carl
Sauer, Wedel applied multidisciplinary approaches to anthropological archaeology on the
Plains, especially the relationship between humans and the environment, with a strong hu-
manist emphasis. He adapted and utilized the
direct-historical approach to the archaeology of
the Caddoan (Pawnee and Wichita), Kansa, and
Apache peoples. Wedel joined the Smithsonian
Institution, Washington, D.C., in 1936. From
1946 to 1949, he organized its River Basin Surveys, Missouri Basin Project, in Lincoln, Nebraska. Wedel has worked in the Plains from
Texas to the Dakotas and at sites from Paleoindian to historic in age, though with an emphasis on sixteenth-to-seventeenth-century Protohistoric Plains Village–pattern sites. Renowned
as a superb writer, Wedel periodically produced
authoritative syntheses of Plains archaeology.
He retired in 1976, though he remained active
in research until his death.

John Ludwickson

Further Readings

Gunnerson, J.H. 1982. Waldo R. Wedel,
    Archeologist: Perspectives That Grew
    in the Plains. In *Plains Indian Studies:
    A Collection of Essays in Honor of John
    C. Ewers and Waldo R. Wedel,* edited by
    D.H. Ubelaker and H.J. Viola, pp. 18–
    24. Contributions to Anthropology no.
    30. Smithsonian Institution, Washington,
    D.C. (A list of Wedel's writings to 1981
    is on pp. 33–39.)
Wedel, W.R. 1961. *Prehistoric Man on the
    Great Plains.* University of Oklahoma
    Press, Norman.
———. 1977. The Education of a Plains Ar-
    cheologist. *Plains Anthropologist* 22(75):
    1–12.

———. 1986. *Central Plains Prehistory:
    Holocene Environments and Culture
    Change in the Republican River Basin.*
    University of Nebraska Press, Lincoln.

Weeden Island Culture

The Late Woodland Weeden Island culture was
located on the Gulf Coastal Plain in Florida,
Alabama, and Georgia ca. A.D. 300–1200
(1650–750 years B.P.). Due to early and continued interest in its burial mounds, in which
elaborate grave goods were placed, it is one of
the best-known Late Woodland cultures in the
Southeast.

The beginning of the Weeden Island culture is identified by archaeologists by a transition in pottery from pots stamped with small
paddles with carved designs (called complicated
stamping) to ones with incised and punctated
decorations. During the first half of the A.D.
300–1200 (1650–750 years B.P.) period, pottery
was decorated with combinations of complicated stamping, punctating, incising, and rocker
stamping. Better-made special pottery, often
shaped into animal, human, composite, and
other forms, was placed in burial mounds.
Weeden Island mortuary pottery was the best
prehistoric Indian ceramic ever made in eastern
North America.

Coastal Weeden Island societies subsisted
mainly on marine resources, especially fish and
shellfish. Inland groups focused on wetland and
other interior food sources, such as deer and
nuts. Their main settlements were large base
camps that were occupied for most, if not all,
of the year by at least part of the population.
These settlements were usually located near rich
forest hammocks that had easy access to permanent fresh water and a diversity of environments. Some people living in base camps along
the northern Gulf Coast organized their refuse
deposits into shapes, such as donuts and rectangles. They kept the interiors of these shapes
clear of debris. It is now thought that these
"ring midden" settlements were special locations at which rituals and activities were conducted. There were also small special-purpose
sites.

Ca. A.D. 800 (1150 years B.P.), there was a
burst of new Weeden Island settlement in the
interior at the head of small streams and along
the shoreline of the upper bays. This was likely
a spillover of excess population from the coastal
strip and lower bays, where population had

grown beyond what those environments could support.

Weeden Island mortuary customs included the burial of elite people in mounds. A single mound was often built adjacent to larger settlements, although some settlements had several mounds. Burial mounds were usually dome shaped and constructed of several layers of earth. While the mounds varied in detail, in most instances they consisted of a primary mound built over a log-lined burial pit, some of which had stone caps. A cache that contained special mortuary vessels, and often human cremations and skulls, was placed on the surface of the east side of the primary mound. The mound might then be burned and covered with a cap of stones. A second layer of earth, which could contain bones from previously deceased people (secondary burials), was then placed over the primary mound. Some mounds were reused, with new tombs or burial pits placed in earlier layers. Platform mounds were also constructed. These mounds supported special residences or mortuary houses, where mortuary activities such as body processing were conducted. Two important Weeden Island mound centers have been investigated: McKeithen in north Florida and Kolomoki in southwest Georgia. The story they tell is especially revealing about the inner workings of the Weeden Island culture.

The McKeithen site was a horseshoe-shaped ring midden with a clean interior plaza. Three mounds were built on the ring midden, one on each end and one at the center of the horseshoe. The mounds covered platforms that were constructed to elevate a mortuary, or charnel house, and a residence. The mortuary mound, which was screened from the village, had several pits in which bodies presumably were buried and allowed to decompose. The skeletons were then exhumed, and the bones cleaned for storage. Several large posts, some ca. 1.2 m (4 feet) in diameter, had been raised on this platform. The residential mound supported a rectangular building. The third mound supported a special building called a charnel house, where processed human remains consisting primarily of bundles of bones were stored.

The archaeologist who excavated McKeithen, Jerald T. Milanich (1994), thinks that a local leader, called a "Big Man," lived on the residential mound and that the presence of the mounds was directly related to the emergence and death of this local leader, who lived in the fifth century A.D. The "Big Man" was able to command special treatment, the building of the mounds, and special mortuary rituals for his kin group. During his heyday, the settlement was probably the center of local sociopolitical events. Studies indicate that he used special pottery containers and ate special food. Members of his family who died before him were prepared for reburial in the mortuary mound by a specialist. When the "Big Man" died ca. A.D. 475 (1475 years B.P.), he was buried in the floor of his residence on the mound, and the stored remains of his deceased family members were removed from the charnel house and buried in the mound. All buildings on the mounds were then burned. The remains of at least 36 people were placed at ca. 1.5-m (5-foot) intervals around the edge of the platform of the mortuary mound, and a cache of at least 18 pottery vessels was placed on its southeast edge. Rocks were then placed on the southwest edge of the platform before it and the other mounds were capped with a layer of sand. Settlement continued at McKeithen after the mounds were capped, but no more mounds were built. The population that continued to live at McKeithen appears to have been smaller than the one there when the "Big Man" was alive.

Kolomoki, the largest-known Weeden Island–period mound center, is ca. 322 km (200 miles) northwest of McKeithen. While it, too, had a horseshoe-shaped village, the horseshoe enclosed four mounds, and four more mounds were outside it. The main period of occupation and mound building at Kolomoki was ca. A.D. 300–500 (1650–1450 years B.P.), the same time as the florescence at McKeithen. The largest-known Weeden Island mound yet discovered is at Kolomoki. It is a rectangular platform mound 17 m (56 feet) tall and 99 x 61 m (325 x 200 feet) at the base with a red-clay cap that covers an earlier white-clay cap.

Two dome-shaped mounds that covered platforms of white or yellow clay have been investigated at Kolomoki. They contained the remains of 86 people who had been buried with the highest-status individual. One mound contained four log and stone tombs in the floor of a building that had been burned and buried. The other platform was covered with rocks prior to the interment of skeletons. Some of the people buried in the mounds are thought to have been killed in a special mass-burial event. Personal ornaments, such as shell beads and copper-covered earspools, were the main grave goods. Elaborate mortuary pottery vessels were cached on the eastern side of both burial mounds. Human skulls were placed in one vessel cache.

Because of the size and the number of mounds, Kolomoki was likely the sociopolitical center of a more powerful leader than the one at McKeithen or anywhere else in the region at the time. As at McKeithen, when the leader died, the buildings on the mounds were apparently burned, and the cremated and bundled remains of his kinsmen who had died before him were placed on the platforms and covered with earth.

After ca. A.D. 800 (1150 years B.P.), construction of Weeden Island mound centers and elaborate burials generally ceased, although the Weeden Island culture continued for several centuries. During the latter time, small amounts of ornamental mortuary pottery were placed in small burial mounds, which appear to have been used as community cemeteries rather than as tombs restricted to the elite.

Judith A. Bense

Further Readings

Bense, J.A. 1994. *Archaeology of the Southeastern United States.* Academic Press, San Diego.

Milanich, J.T. 1994. *Archaeology of Precolumbian Florida.* University of Florida Press, Gainesville.

Milanich, J.T., J. Chapman, A.S. Cordell, S. Hale, V.J. Knight, and B. Sigler-Lavalle. 1984. *McKeithen Weeden Island: The Culture of North Florida, A.D. 200–900.* Academic Press, San Diego.

See also KOLOMOKI; MCKEITHEN SITE

West Coast Culture Type

The rugged west coast of Vancouver Island, from Cape Cook south to Point No Point, was the historic homeland of the Nuu-chah-nulth people, formerly known as the Nootka. The West Coast culture type represents the material remnants of their prehistoric ancestors.

The West Coast culture type is defined on the basis of excavation at a relatively small number of sites. Much of our information comes from Yuquot, a large village site at the entrance to Nootka Sound that has an archaeological record extending back to ca. 2350 B.C. (4300 years B.P.). At the head of the sound is the

village of Kupti, where limited test excavation revealed deposits covering the last 1,100 years of prehistory (ca. A.D. 750–1850). To the south, in Hesquiat Harbour, excavations at a number of sites have provided evidence for the last 1,800 years of prehistory (ca. A.D. 50–1850). In western Barkley Sound, farther to the south, recent research at the large village of T'ukw'aa revealed an archaeological record of ca. 1,200 years, and test excavation at nearby Ch'uumat'a extends our knowledge back to ca. 1850 B.C. (3800 years B.P.). While artifacts recovered from Nootka Sound and Hesquiat Harbour are similar, some differences exist with the Barkley Sound sites. Nevertheless, all can be encompassed within the culture type (see Figure).

Artifacts of bone and antler dominate the assemblages from all sites. Most common are bone points of a variety of types, presumed to be parts of composite fishing gear (such as barbs on fishhooks, arming points of toggling harpoon heads, and teeth of herring rakes). Slender bone bipoints, assumed to be fish gorges, are also common. Other typical tools include bone fishhook shanks, toggling harpoon valves, awls and needles, unilaterally barbed points, and both unilaterally and bilaterally barbed nontoggling harpoon heads. Decorative items such as combs and pendants are rare. Whalebone implements include bark shredders, bark beaters, and harpoon foreshafts.

Artifacts of shell and tooth are important, although much less common. The large mussel shell of the outer coast was an important raw material for knives and small celts. Beaver teeth were used for small woodworking tools. Decorative items include pendants made of seal and bear canine teeth, perforated or ringed at the root end for suspension. *Dentalia* shell beads are rare.

At all sites, the stone artifacts consist primarily of abrasive stones. The ubiquity of this tool type indicates its utility in shaping other implements of wood, bone, shell, and stone. Stone fishhook shanks, hand mauls, celts with rounded polls, and ground-stone points (rare) are also found.

The scarcity of chipped-stone artifacts is one of the defining characteristics of the West Coast culture type. Except for chipped-stone pebbles (possibly wedges) from both Yuquot and Kupti, chipped stone is absent from the Nootka Sound sites previously mentioned and from T'ukw'aa. However, very small amounts of chipped-stone artifacts, including bifaces,

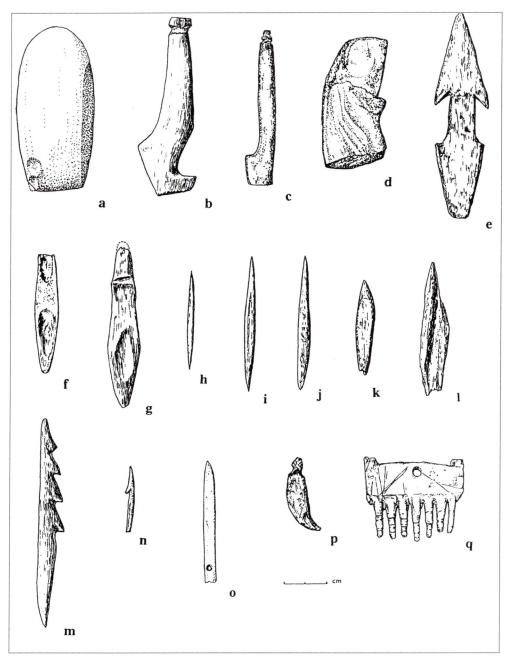

Artifacts of the West Coast culture type: a) round-polled stone celt (Yuquot); b) stone fishhook shank (Yuquot); c) bone fishhook shank (Ch'uumat'a); d) mussel shell celt (T'ukw'aa); e) bilaterally barbed harpoon head (Ch'uumat'a); f) channeled valve for composite harpoon head (T'ukw'aa); g) slotted valve for composite harpoon head (Yuquot); h, i) bone bipoints (T'ukw'aa); j) bone point, probably a fishhook barb (T'ukw'aa); k) bone point, probably an arming point on a composite toggling harpoon head (T'ukw'aa); l) bone splinter awl (T'ukw'aa); m) barbed bone point, possibly an arrow point (Yuquot); n) small barbed point, probably a fishhook barb (T'ukw'aa); q) bone comb (T'ukw'aa). Length of a) is 7.6 cm, with the rest drawn to the same scale. (Drawn by A. D. McMillan, Yuquot artifacts are redrawn from Dewhirst 1980)

have been found on some beach surfaces in Nootka Sound and have been excavated at Hesquiat Harbour and Ch'uumat'a. Nevertheless, they make up only a small part of the total artifact inventory of the excavated sites.

In all cases, the artifact list gives only an impoverished glimpse into the past culture. Most implements would have been of wood, bark, root, and other perishable materials. The overwhelming dominance of such raw materials in the culture is evident from ethnographic descriptions and from excavations at other sites with greater preservation. At the Ozette site, among the closely related Makah of the Olympic Peninsula, water-saturated soils hold the nearly complete material culture of a Late Prehistoric house, where objects of bone, antler, shell, and stone form only a minor portion of the total.

Two excavated sites in modern Nuu-chah-nulth territory reveal a somewhat different picture. At Shoemaker Bay in the Alberni Valley at the end of a long inlet that extends from Barkley Sound, excavation revealed evidence of at least two components between ca. 1000 B.C. and A.D. 1850 (2950–100 years B.P.). Artifacts throughout the sequence more closely resemble those of contemporary cultures in the Strait of Georgia and are quite dissimilar from those described here as the West Coast culture type. This fits with ethnographic indications that the original occupants had been Salish-speakers and that the Nuu-chah-nulth had seized the Alberni Valley only in relatively recent times, perhaps at the beginning of the historic period. Somewhat similar material has come from the Little Beach site at Ucluelet, on western Barkley Sound. Burials, some under low rock cairns, were found in shell-midden deposits dating between 2050 and 1050 B.C. (4000–3000 years B.P.). A large chipped-stone point and a stone labret suggest differences from the West Coast culture type, but the artifact total is too small to make conclusive statements.

A number of large Nuu-chah-nulth village sites are associated with defensive or refuge areas—usually on top of a steep-sided bluff or islet immediately adjacent to the village. Only the defensive site at T'ukw'aa has had substantial excavation. Radiocarbon dates indicate that this retreat was used for at least 800 years. Artifacts and other recovered remains belong to the West Coast culture type and are essentially the same as those recovered from the village area.

Burial caves and rock shelters form another common category of sites in Nuu-chah-nulth territory. Individuals were placed in such sheltered locations in boxes or, occasionally, in historic trunks. A large burial cave in Hesquiat Harbour contained nearly 7,000 glass beads and numerous cedar boxes and fragments; cedar-bark robes, mats, and baskets; and cordage of cedar bark, cedar withe, and kelp. All such sites, however, may belong to the historic period.

The people who left the remains of the West Coast culture type had an economy that was strongly oriented to maritime resources. A thorough study of the faunal remains is available only for the Hesquiat Harbour sites. There, fish dominated the nonshellfish resources; rock fishes were most common, followed by salmon, herring, and dogfish. Sea mammals, including whales, seals, and porpoises, were also common. Coast deer and a variety of birds were encountered less frequently in the faunal assemblages. A similar open-ocean orientation is evident in the Barkley Sound sites, where fish, ranging in size from herring to tuna, clearly dominate the nonshellfish fauna, and sea mammals of a variety of species are also well represented. A somewhat different pattern would be expected from more inner-coast sites, given their access to important salmon-spawning rivers. At all sites, shellfish would have made up a significant portion of the diet.

Artifacts of the West Coast culture type closely resemble those used by the Nuu-chah-nulth people ethnographically. Although some culture change is evident during the more than 4,000 years represented by this culture type, even from the earliest levels at Yuquot the basic pattern of Nuu-chah-nulth life is discernible.

Alan D. McMillan

Further Readings

Dewhirst, J. 1980. *The Indigenous Archaeology of Yuquot, a Nootkan Outside Village.* National Historic Parks and Sites Branch, Parks Canada, Ottawa.

Western and Central Basin Wetland and Lakeside Adaptations

Wetlands in Nevada are at Walker, Pyramid, and Winnemucca lakes, in the Carson (Stillwater Marsh) and Humboldt sinks, and at the Ruby Valley Marsh; in Oregon, they are in the Fort Rock Basin and the Warner Valley, at nearby Lake Abert, and in the Harney Basin; in northeastern California, they are in Surprise Valley. Wetlands in these areas vary in terms of their size, productivity, salinity, seasonal variability, the presence of marshes, and the productivity of the surrounding landscape. Some are lakes without marshes; others are predominantly marshes with little open water. Shifting stream channels affect their productivity. For example, the Walker River, which feeds Walker Lake, periodically changes its course and runs into the Carson River. As a result, Walker Lake becomes desiccated and the Carson Sink wetter. Highly variable precipitation makes desert wetlands highly variable in size and productivity from year to year. All of these factors produce different archaeological records in each wetland.

The history of Pleistocene lakes, such as Lake Lahonton in western Nevada, has long been a central focus of basin study, even before I. Russell's 1895 monograph, "Present and Extinct Lakes of Nevada." While these large lakes were dry by ca. 8050 B.C. (10,000 years B.P.), research by R. Morrison, J. Davis, R. Thompson, and L. Benson has revealed their complex late Pleistocene and Holocene histories.

In the early twentieth century, a number of ethnographers collected "memory culture" from wetland groups that has proven useful in archaeological interpretation. Ethnographic data were collected by W. Park (Fowler 1989) on the Northern Paiute, and I. Kelly (1932) on the Surprise Valley Piaute. These data show a wide variety of wetland lifeways: from sedentary occupation of large, deep pithouses in the Klamath region, to seasonal (winter) occupation of villages with summer nomadism in the Walker and Pyramid Lake areas, to perhaps an even more mobile lifestyle around the Carson sink. Fish were taken with spears, hooks, nets, poisons, and traps and, once dried, were an important winter food resource. Waterfowl were driven into nets or hunted from tule-reed boats with bunt-tipped arrows and decoys. The people collected a variety of seeds and roots and stored them for the winter. In some places, women gathered summer seeds in the uplands while men remained at the wetlands to fish and hunt waterfowl, periodically supplying the women's summer camps with food. It must be noted that anthropologists collected these data long after Euro-American settlement, which began in earnest ca. 1850, had substantially altered aboriginal lives; hence,

they cannot provide direct analogies for precontact lifeways.

Some of the earliest archaeological research in the Great Basin focused on lake or marsh sites. L. Loud excavated Lovelock Cave in 1912 and, with M. Harrington, in 1924 (Loud and Harrington 1929). They found caches of duck decoys, nets, dried fish, and fishhooks along with basketry, sandals, and burials. L. Cressman (1942) conducted surveys of pluvial-lake basins in the northwestern Great Basin, J. O'Connell (1975) surveyed Surprise Valley, and M. Weide (1968) studied Warner Valley. Caches containing dried fish, trolling lines, bipointed and composite hooks, and barbed spearheads in Pyramid Lake cave sites enhanced our knowledge of fishing technology (Tuohy 1993). These research developments offered an alternative to Jennings's (1957) "Desert culture" concept, which emphasized seasonal mobility and the use of a diversity of food resources. The alternative was expressed most explicitly by R. Heizer in the 1960s. Heizer, who had worked in the Humboldt Sink from the 1930s through the 1970s, coined the term "limnosedentism" to describe a sedentary or semisedentary lifeway with focal use of wetland resources. This interpretation was based on the archaeologically rich sites found on the shores of Humboldt Marsh, some of which contained shallow house depressions; on the artifacts recovered from Lovelock and nearby Humboldt Cave; and on analyses of coprolites from Lovelock Cave, which showed the use of minnows, bulrush, and cattail.

While some ethnographic and archaeological data suggest reduced residential mobility for groups using wetland resources, other sources indicated significant mobility. Cave sites around the Humboldt and Carson sinks, including Lovelock, Hidden, and Humboldt, were used predominantly for caches, suggesting that the sinks were periodically or seasonally abandoned. (Caches also appear in cave sites near Pyramid Lake and Lake Abert; unfortunately, many of these sites, as well as those in the Carson and Humboldt sinks, were damaged by looters decades ago.) This led D. Thomas (1985) to propose a "limnomobile" model in which wetlands served as settlement anchors but did not provide all food resources.

Finally, in the 1980s, in the Carson and Humboldt sinks, as well as in the Harney Basin and the Warner Valley, and, to the east, the Great Salt Lake area, flooding exposed dozens of sites containing pits and houses, as well as burials. As a result of these discoveries and a changing emphasis in research from culture-historical to ecological approaches, the 1980s and 1990s saw a new round of research into the use of wetlands. This research has revealed a complex pattern of wetland-resource utilization. Evidence for the use of fish dates to ca. 7550 B.C. (9500 years B.P.) in the Pyramid Lake area, and wetland resources have undoubtedly been utilized throughout the period of human occupation of the Great Basin. Semisubterranean pithouses in Surprise Valley date earlier than 3050 B.C. (5000 years B.P.). In many areas, however, a wetlands-oriented economy appears not to have been established until 2050 B.C. (4000 years B.P.). This may be related to the onset of the Neoglacial, when slightly cooler and wetter conditions might have made lake basins more attractive places than during the warmer and drier early Holocene (ca. 8050–5050 B.C., or 10,000–7000 years B.P., in the Basin). Pithouse villages appear near Lake Abert by at least 2050 B.C. (4000 years B.P.). They grew in size and abundance ca. 50 B.C. (2000 years B.P.), but may not have been used after A.D. 1650 (300 years B.P.). In Harney Basin, evidence for fishing appears by 2050 B.C. (4000 years B.P.) and for pithouses by 1250 B.C. (3200 years B.P.), although both could have appeared earlier. In Warner Valley, pithouse villages, some of which may be more than 4,000 years old, occur near the wetlands, but they also appear in surrounding upland areas where camas, yampa, bitterroot, and wild onion could have been gathered. This suggests either seasonal mobility or periodic abandonment of the wetlands for upland areas. As in Harney Basin, there is less evidence for a Late Prehistoric occupation in the Warner Valley; perhaps it was occupied by a more mobile or transient population. In the Carson Sink, villages may date primarily to A.D. 650–1350 (1300–600 years B.P.). They tend to contain relatively shallow pithouses, although some may be as deep as those found in the northwestern Great Basin. Archaeological and human-bone-chemistry studies suggest that piñon may have figured less prominently in the diet here than elsewhere in the Great Basin (Larsen and Kelly 1995). Late Prehistoric archaeology reflects a more mobile or transient population, perhaps evidence of immigration into the area of Numic speakers with a different settlement-subsistence strategy. Finally, while Ruby Valley has not been well studied, it appears that occupation there

spanned the same time frame as elsewhere; however, there is no evidence yet of pithouse villages. Pottery may have been introduced to this region slightly earlier than elsewhere in the central Great Basin, where it dates to ca. 1250 (700 years B.P.).

Differences in regional prehistories are partly a function of the different availability of wetland and upland resources. Fish were important everywhere, but some basins, such as the Carson Sink, may have had only minnows, while others, such as Pyramid and Walker lakes and some of the northwestern basins, supported substantial fisheries of larger species, such as trout, suckers, and redsides. A variety of plants were utilized, including bulrush, cattail, pondweed, camas, and pickleweed, and a variety of water birds, especially coots and other ducks. Moreover, the basins differ in the availability of upland resources; some areas, for example, contain nearby stands of piñon pine, whose seeds were dietary staples in many areas of the Great Basin, while others do not. Experimental research by, for example, K. Jones and D. Madsen (1989) and S. Simms (1987), shows some resources are collected and/or transported more efficiently than others.

Research in the 1990s into the prehistoric use of the Great Basin wetlands focuses on how the distributions of different kinds of resources between the wetlands and the surrounding environmental matrix might have favored the adoption of different kinds of settlement strategies.

Robert L. Kelly

Further Readings

Cressman, L.S. 1942. *Archaeological Researches in the Northern Great Basin of South-Central Oregon.* Publication no. 538. Carnegie Institution of Washington, Washington, D.C.

Fowler, G.S. 1989. *Willard Z. Park's Ethnographic Notes on the Northern Paiute of Western Nevada, 1933–1940,* vol. 1. Anthropological Papers no. 114. University of Utah Press, Salt Lake City.

———. 1993. *In the Shadow of Fox Peak: An Ethnography of the Cattail-Eater Northern Paiute People of Stillwater Marsh.* Cultural Resource Series no. 5. Region 1, U.S. Fish and Wildlife Service, Portland.

Heizer, R.F., and L.K. Napton. 1970. *Archaeology and the Prehistoric Lacustrine*

Subsistence Regime As Seen From Lovelock Cave, Nevada. Archaeological Research Facility Contributions no. 10. University of California, Berkeley.

Janetski, J.C., and D.B. Madsen (editors). 1990. *Wetland Adaptations in the Great Basin.* Occasional Papers no. 1. Museum of Peoples and Cultures, Brigham Young University, Provo.

Jennings, J.D. 1957. *Danger Cave.* Anthropological Papers no. 27. University of Utah Press, Salt Lake City.

Jones, K.T., and D.B. Madsen. 1989. Calculating the Cost of Resource Transport: A Great Basin Example. *Current Anthropology* 30:529–534.

Kelly, I.T. 1932. Ethnography of the Sunrise Valley Paiute. *University of California Publications in American Archaeology and Ethnology* 31(3):67–210.

Larsen, C.S., and R.L. Kelly. 1995. *The Bioarchaeology of Stillwater Marsh, Western Nevada.* Anthropological Papers no. 77. American Museum of Natural History, New York.

Loud, L.L., and M. Harrington. 1929. Lovelock Cave. *University of California Publications in American Archaeology and Ethnology* 25(1):1–183.

O'Connell, J.F. 1975. *The Prehistory of Surprise Valley.* Anthropological Papers no. 4. Ballena Press, Los Altos.

Russell, I. 1895. Present and Extinct Lakes of Nevada. *National Geographic Monographs* 4(1):101–132.

Simms, S. 1987. *Behavioral Ecology and Hunter-Gatherer Foraging: An Example From the Great Basin.* BAR International Series no. 381. British Archaeological Reports, London.

Thomas, D.H. 1985. *The Archaeology of Hidden Cave, Nevada.* Anthropological Papers, vol. 61, pt. 1. American Museum of Natural History, New York.

Tuohy, D.R. 1993. *Pyramid Lake Prehistory: Part One.* Anthropological Papers no. 24. Nevada State Museum, Carson City.

Weide, M.L. 1968. *Cultural Ecology of Lakeside Adaptations in the Western Great Basin.* Unpublished Ph.D. dissertation, Department of Anthropology, University of California, Los Angeles.

See also HIDDEN CAVE; LOVELOCK CAVE; STILLWATER MARSH

Western Plains Early Archaic Regional Variant

Defined by William B. Butler (1986) as a taxon for Plains and mountain occupations during the Early Archaic period, this regional variant originally consisted of three phases: Magic Mountain (ca. 3050–2550 B.C., or 5000–4500 years B.P.), Mount Albion (ca. 4050–3050 B.C., or 6000–5000 years B.P.), and Albion Boardinghouse (ca. 5650–4050 B.C., or 7600–6000 years B.P.). Recent research suggests that only the Magic Mountain phase is closely affiliated with Plains occupations. The Mount Albion and Albion Boardinghouse phases, in this view, have a mountain orientation in the Southern Rocky Mountain Early Archaic regional variant (Butler 1986).

William B. Butler

Further Readings

Butler, W.B. 1986. *Taxonomy in Northeastern Colorado Prehistory.* Unpublished Ph.D. dissertation, Department of Anthropology, University of Missouri, Columbia.

See also ALBION BOARDINGHOUSE PHASE; MAGIC MOUNTAIN PHASE; MOUNT ALBION PHASE; SOUTHERN ROCKY MOUNTAIN EARLY ARCHAIC REGIONAL VARIANT

Western Plains Late Archaic Regional Variant

Defined by William B. Butler (1986) as a taxon, this variant includes the Late Archaic–period Front Range phase (ca. 810 B.C.–A.D. 100, or 2760–1850 years B.P.) in the Plains area of eastern Colorado.

William B. Butler

Further Readings

Butler, W.B. 1986. *Taxonomy in Northeastern Colorado Prehistory.* Unpublished Ph.D. dissertation, Department of Anthropology, University of Missouri, Columbia.

See also FRONT RANGE PHASE

Western Plains Middle Archaic Regional Variant

Defined by William B. Butler (1986) as a taxon, the variant includes the Middle Archaic–period Apex phase (ca. 2550–810 B.C., or 4500–2760 years B.P.) in the Plains area of eastern Colorado.

The variant is similar in many respects to the McKean period of the High Plains and interior basins of Wyoming.

William B. Butler

Further Readings

Butler, W.B. 1986. *Taxonomy in Northeastern Colorado Prehistory.* Unpublished Ph.D. dissertation, Department of Anthropology, University of Missouri, Columbia.

See also APEX PHASE; MCKEAN

Western Red Cedar

The western red cedar tree (*Thuja plicata* Donn) was the most widely used plant species in northwestern North America. One of the majestic conifers of the coast, it towers to 70 m (230 feet) above the moist rain-forest floor with flexible swooping branches clad in pungent scaly leaves. The natural range today extends from the Alaskan Panhandle through British Columbia to northwest California and inland along the moist west side of the Rocky Mountains and adjacent systems of southeast British Columbia, Idaho, and Montana. In prehistoric times, western red cedar was much less abundant, becoming widespread when cool and moist climates developed between 3050 and 550 B.C. (5000–2500 years B.P.), the same time the first signs of massive woodworking technology began to appear.

The long, straight-grained, rot-resistant trunk supplied exceptionally resilient but easy-to-work wood. Coastal peoples fashioned dugout canoes, house posts, crest, and mortuary poles. Planks were split from living trees with stone mauls and wooden wedges and finished with stone or shell adzes. On the coast and in the interior, smaller pieces of wood were manufactured into storage and cooking boxes; everyday tools, weapons, or utensils, including harpoon shafts, dishes, and canoe paddles; and ceremonial items such as rattles and masks.

Strips of fibrous inner bark of young red cedars were split and beaten out into strands that were woven into baskets, capes, mats, and blankets. In the spring, the whiplike branches and pliable roots were harvested and softened into raw material for rope—useful in binding and also in the making of nets and lines. Skilled women of the Plateau culture area made watertight baskets from the roots. Even the fresh green leafy boughs provided aromatic bedding for the home.

Richard Hebda

Further Readings

Hebda, R.J., and R.W. Mathewes. 1984. Holocene History of Cedar and Native Indian Cultures of the North American Pacific Coast. *Science* 225:711–713.

Stewart, H. 1984. *Coast Indians.* Douglas and McIntyre, Vancouver.

Western Stemmed Tradition

Prior to the emergence of Desert Archaic adaptive patterns ca. 6050–5050 B.C. (8000–7000 years B.P.), Great Basin populations are believed to have followed a lifestyle focused largely on marsh, lake, and riverine resources. These early people, designated the Western Stemmed tradition because of the characteristic large stemmed projectile points they used, were living during a time of considerable environmental change: from moist, cool conditions of the late Pleistocene to warmer and drier conditions in the early Holocene. During the Pleistocene, most valleys in the Great Basin contained large pluvial lakes. They began to shrink during the latter part of this period and ultimately disappeared during the early Holocene. It was once believed that, because of the association of their sites with the old shores and beaches of these now-extinct pluvial lakes, Western Stemmed–tradition people focused their subsistence exclusively around these lakes. Sites representative of the Western Stemmed tradition are now known to occur in many environmental contexts, including lakeside, marsh, riverine, even upland; thus, ideas concerning their lifestyle have changed.

Although subsistence data from this period are rare, these early people are believed to have been highly mobile hunter-gatherers, who ranged over large areas within a single year. In addition to large stemmed projectile points, their toolkits contained items such as crescents, large bifaces, dome-shaped scrapers, gravers, and choppers; conspicuously absent are the grinding stones so prevalent in later, Archaic assemblages. The nature of this toolkit has led some researchers to the conclusion that the people of the Western Stemmed tradition hunted now-extinct megafauna, such as mammoth, mastodon, and camel; there is, however, no direct evidence demonstrating this focus. Given the distribution of these early sites across many different environmental contexts, a generalized focus including both hunting and gathering is more likely. Data suggest that population density was low during this early period but began to increase sometime during the Early Archaic (Elston 1982). With the changing environment came changing adaptations. By the end of the early Holocene (5550 B.C., or 7500 years B.P.), the lifestyle of the Western Stemmed tradition appears to have given way to that of the Desert Archaic.

Charlotte Beck
George T. Jones

Further Readings

Aikens, C.M. 1982. Archaeology of the Northern Great Basin: An Overview. In *Man and Environment in the Great Basin,* edited by D.B. Madsen and J.F. O'Connell, pp. 139–155. SAA Papers no. 2. Society for American Archaeology, Washington, D.C.

Beck, C., and G.T. Jones. 1990. The Late Pleistocene/Early Holocene Archaeology of Butte Valley, Nevada: Three Seasons' Work. *Journal of California and Great Basin Anthropology* 12:231–261.

Elston, R.G. 1982. Good Times, Hard Times: Prehistoric Culture Change in the Western Great Basin. In *Man and Environment in the Great Basin,* edited by D.B. Madsen and J.F. O'Connell, pp. 186–206. SAA Papers no. 2. Society for American Archaeology, Washington, D.C.

Price, B.A., and S.E. Johnston. 1988. A Model of Late Pleistocene and Early Holocene Adaptation in Eastern Nevada. In *Early Human Occupation in Far Western North America: The Clovis-Archaic Interface,* edited by J.A. Willig, C.M. Aikens, and J.L. Fagan, pp. 231–250. Anthropological Papers no. 21. Nevada State Museum, Carson City.

Willig, J.A., and C.M. Aikens. 1988. The Clovis-Archaic Interface in Far Western North America. In *Early Human Occupation in Far Western North America: The Clovis-Archaic Interface,* edited by J.A. Willig, C.M. Aikens, and J.L. Fagan, pp. 1–40. Anthropological Papers no. 21. Nevada State Museum, Carson City.

White Rock/Glen Elder "Phase"

The White Rock phase was a distinctive archaeological expression occurring on the Lower Republican and Solomon rivers in the central Plains ca. A.D. 1500–1600/1650 (450–350/300 years B.P.). The White Rock phase is significant in that it was one of the earliest manifestations of organized, seasonal bison-hunting camps away from the semipermanent horticulture-oriented village sites.

The most diagnostic artifact is a sand-tempered, simple-stamped, and/or smoothed pottery ware characterized by globular and flat-shouldered jars with unthickened rims, tool decoration on the lip or rim interior, and incised or trailed geometric decoration on the shoulder. In virtually all respects except for tempering material, the ware resembles Oneota pottery.

Villages occur along the Solomon River and on White Rock Creek, a Republican River tributary, in northern Kansas. At site 14JW1, two plow-disrupted houses with four central roof-support posts arranged around a central fire hearth were discovered; house shape was not determinable. Several "bell-shaped," cylindrical, or basin-shaped pits were found. Corn kernels and bison-scapula hoes were found at the villages. Projectile points occur in a ratio of 9:1 for unnotched versus side-notched forms. Small triangular bifacial knives, ovate knives, and alternately beveled four-edged knives are found, as are end scrapers, chipped celts (quarry blanks), and retouched flakes. Awls, flakers, worked ribs, and cancellous-tissue abraders are among the few bone tools reported. Sandstone abraders, grinding/anvil stones, grooved cobble mauls, hammerstones, and rare red pipestone (catlinite?) smoking pipes have been found.

Seasonal bison-hunting camps have been excavated on Prairie Dog Creek in southern Nebraska. Small, cylindrical or basin-shaped storage pits and outside hearths were found, but no "bell-shaped" pits or houses. Evidence for gardening was absent at hunting camps. Approximately the same assemblage of chipped-stone tools occurred at these camps as at the villages, but bone tools were almost absent (though food-scrap bone was preserved), and only a few hammerstones and sandstone abraders were found. Almost all faunal remains were bison.

Villages reflect stone procurement from Permian sources to the east and the south and Niobrara jasper from the north and the west. The hunting camps in Nebraska are dominated by tools made of local Niobrara jasper and indicate that stone procurement was another task carried out there.

John Ludwickson

Further Readings

Marshall, J.O. 1967. *The Glen Elder Focus.* Unpublished Master's thesis. Department of Anthropology, University of Nebraska, Lincoln.

Neuman, R.W. 1963. *Archeological Salvage Investigations in the Lovewell Reservoir Area, Kansas.* Bulletin no. 185. River Basin Surveys Paper no. 32. Bureau of American Ethnology, Smithsonian Institution, Washington, D.C.

Rusco, M.K. 1960. *The White Rock Aspect.* Notebook Series no. 4. Laboratory of Anthropology, University of Nebraska, Lincoln.

Wickliffe Site

The Wickliffe site (15BA4) is located in Ballard County, Kentucky, on the bluffs of the Mississippi River ca. 5 km (3 miles) south of the mouth of the Ohio River. Radiocarbon dates assign the occupation to ca. A.D. 1100–1350 (850–600 years B.P.), with additional mortuary activity until ca. A.D. 1400 (550 years B.P.). The site contains a central plaza with two platform mounds; the plaza is surrounded by a rich midden deposit and several smaller, round or conical mounds of uncertain significance.

The Wickliffe site was first recorded in a Kentucky geographical survey in 1888. In 1932, the property was purchased by Fain W. King, a businessman from Paducah, Kentucky, with the intent of creating a tourist attraction, much like Dickson Mounds in Illinois. King funded his own excavations to 1939. Until 1983, the facility was operated for tourism under the name "Ancient Buried City," or sometimes the "King Mounds." An open-burial display of ca. 150 sets of human remains, ostensibly in situ, was the centerpiece of the exhibits. King excavated in six areas of the site, which were designated Mounds A through F. Although he and his wife, Blanche Busey King, published several articles about their excavations and interpretations of the Wickliffe site, no systematic analysis was ever conducted. Sketchy field notes of only the first month of King's excavations are known to exist. The site, and its collections and tourism facilities, were donated to Murray State University (MSU) in 1983. MSU's Wickliffe Mounds Research Center began a long-term project to upgrade the public-education programs and exhibits, to catalog and analyze the extant collections, and to renew research on the site.

That research has established a three-period, intrasite chronology: early Wickliffe (A.D. 1100–1200, or 850–750 years B.P.); middle Wickliffe (A.D. 1200–1250, or 750–700 years B.P.); and late Wickliffe (A.D. 1250–1350, or 700–600 years B.P.). The Wickliffe-site cemetery appears to be intrusive into Mound C and is provisionally assigned to an unnamed post-Wickliffe period that dates to ca. 1350–1400 (600–550 years B.P.). Characteristic ceramic handle and plate rim forms relate the Wickliffe periods to regional horizon markers in the Lower Ohio Valley. Early Wickliffe deposits cluster around the central plaza, which suggests that the site was founded as a compact settlement without mounds. Middle Wickliffe domestic deposits expanded areally, in part due to displacement by platform Mounds A and B on the west and north sides of the plaza, respectively. Mound A was a ceremonial mound, while the buried summits of Mound B support middens that indicate a residential function. During the late Wickliffe period, the domestic occupation, which by now crowded the edges of the bluff, achieved its greatest area; the final stages of the mounds were also constructed. The village evidently was abandoned ca. 1350 (600 years B.P.). The cemetery, which is in the northeast sector of the site, appears to intrude onto late Wickliffe midden deposits, suggesting that a dispersed population lingered in the Wickliffe region and utilized the Wickliffe site as a center for ceremonial and mortuary activities.

Kit W. Wesler

Further Readings

Drooker, P.B. 1992. *Mississippian Village Textiles at Wickliffe.* University of Alabama Press, Tuscaloosa.

Wesler, K.W. 1991. Ceramics, Chronology, and Horizon Markers at Wickliffe Mounds. *American Antiquity* 56:278–290.

Willamette Valley Sequence

The Willamette Valley of western Oregon is the only interior province within the ethnographic Northwest Coast culture area. Historically, the greater part of the floor of the Willamette Valley was occupied by Kalapuyan peoples, while the mountains of the Cascade Range on the valley's east side were inhabited by the Molala. The small portion of the valley below

Willamette Falls was occupied by Chinookan peoples of the Lower Columbia Valley. Willamette Falls posed a substantial barrier to the upstream migration of anadromous fish, and the archaeological record indicates that the Willamette Valley's prehistoric inhabitants depended more heavily on hunting and gathering than on fishing.

The earliest evidence of occupation, which has been assigned to a largely hypothetical Paleoindian period (9550–8050 B.C., or 11,500–10,000 years B.P.), occurs in the form of isolated finds of Clovis and Folsom fluted projectile points. Although not directly dated, these finds are assumed to be roughly the same age as fluted points found elsewhere in North America. Finds of other stylistically early projectile points, including some in alleged association with extinct megafauna, were reported in the 1940s, but the validity of these claims has never been conclusively established.

The Early Archaic period (8050–4050 B.C., or 10,000–6000 years B.P.) is characterized by leaf-shaped projectile points. The earliest radiocarbon-dated evidence of occupation was found at sites along the Long Tom River, where charcoal recovered as deep as 2.5 m (8.2 feet) below the surface produced five radiocarbon dates ranging from 8010 B.C. ± 140 to 5740 B.C. ± 80 (9960–7690 years B.P.). While no diagnostic artifacts were found, charred hazelnut fragments, sandstone pebbles, and obsidian flakes were associated with the charcoal. At the nearby Hannavan Creek site, a rock oven containing hundreds of well-preserved camas bulbs produced radiocarbon dates of 5800 B.C. ± 90 and 4880 B.C. ± 100 (7750 and 6830 years B.P.), although no diagnostic artifacts were associated with this feature either. Early Archaic sites in the Cascades include Cascadia Cave, whose initial occupation was radiocarbon dated at 5960 B.C. ± 280 (7910 years B.P.), and Baby Rock Shelter, where artifacts were found below 4895 B.C. (6845 years B.P.) volcanic ash from the eruption of Mount Mazama at present-day Crater Lake.

The Middle Archaic (4050–50 B.C., or 6000–2000 years B.P.) is characterized by stemmed, broad-necked projectile points that are assumed to have been used with the atlatl and dart. The more common occurrence of mortars and pestles and the increased frequency of rock ovens associated with camas preparation suggest an expansion in the importance of vegetal resources in native subsistence. Charred camas bulbs and associated ovens produced radiocar-

bon dates of 1280 B.C. ± 150 (3230 years B.P.) at the Flanagan site, 370 B.C. ± 80 (2320 years B.P.) at the Benjamin site, and 95 B.C. ± 120 (2045 years B.P.) at the Lingo site. The earliest use of acorns, recovered from a hearth on the Luckiamute River, is radiocarbon dated at 3300 B.C. ± 270 (5250 years B.P.) The only example of a prehistoric house so far reported in Willamette Valley, a pithouse with associated postholes and central hearth discovered at the Hurd site, yielded radiocarbon dates of 850 B.C. ± 110 and 870 B.C. ± 230 (2800 and 2820 years B.P.). Five flexed burials found at the Lingo site represent the earliest evidence of mortuary practices in the valley.

The Late Archaic period (50 B.C.–A.D. 1750, or 2000–200 years B.P.), which is characterized by the appearance of small narrow-necked projectile points assumed to have been used with the bow and arrow, is represented at scores of floodplain sites, suggesting an increasingly dense population by Late Prehistoric times. Marine-shell artifacts, mostly beads and pendants indicative of interactions with coastal peoples, have been recovered at a few sites, notably the Lingo site and the Fuller, Fanning, and Spurland mounds. Waisted obsidian blades, suggesting contacts with northwestern California, were found at the Fuller and Shedd mounds. Flexed burials continued as the primary mortuary pattern. Head flattening, a custom among the ethnographic Kalapuyans, is represented by a single skeleton recovered from Fanning mound.

The Historic period (A.D. 1750–1855) began with the introduction of items of Euro-American manufacture and extended to the removal of native groups to reservations. Diagnostic artifacts include such items as copper ornaments and bracelets, glass trade beads, and iron knives. Ridgon's Horse Pasture Cave is noteworthy for containing a record of the Late Archaic–Historic period transition in the Cascades. Overall, however, relatively few sites are known to have been occupied during this interval, apparently due to the rapid decimation of the native population as a result of the introduction of European diseases.

Information available as of the mid-1990s suggests that the prehistoric inhabitants of the Willamette Valley had little contact with coastal peoples until the Late Archaic period and that sustained contacts may have begun only within the last few hundred years before European contact. Although certain aspects of Formative-stage cultures, notably social ranking, are attributed to the ethnographic Kalapuyans, these developments apparently occurred so late as to be almost absent in the archaeological record. The cultural sequence clearly indicates the interior, as opposed to coastal, nature of Willamette Valley's prehistoric inhabitants, whose lifeways appear to have had more in common with Plateau cultures than with those of the Northwest Coast.

Kathryn Anne Toepel
Rick Minor

Further Readings

Aikens, C.M. (editor). 1988. *Archaeological Studies in the Willamette Valley, Oregon.* Anthropological Papers no. 8. Department of Anthropology, University of Oregon, Eugene.

Cheatham, R.D. 1988. *Late Archaic Settlement Pattern in the Long Tom Sub-Basin, Upper Willamette Valley, Oregon.* Anthropological Papers no. 39. Department of Anthropology, University of Oregon, Eugene.

Minor, R., and K.A. Toepel. 1981. Archaeological Overview. In *Prehistory and History of BLM Lands in West-Central Oregon: A Culture Resource Overview,* edited by S.D. Beckham, R. Minor, and K.A. Toepel, pp. 117–183. Anthropological Papers no. 25. Department of Anthropology, University of Oregon, Eugene.

Pettigrew, R.M. 1990. Prehistory of the Lower Columbia and Willamette Valley. In *Northwest Coast,* edited by W.B. Suttles, pp. 518–529. Handbook of North American Indians, vol. 7, W.C. Sturtevant, general editor. Smithsonian Institution, Washington, D.C.

Toepel, K.A. 1986. *The Flanagan Site: 6,000 Years of Occupation in the Upper Willamette Valley, Oregon.* Unpublished Ph.D. dissertation, Department of Anthropology, University of Oregon, Eugene.

Willey, Gordon R. (1913–)

Gordon R. Willey is one of the preeminent figures in modern American archaeology. His pioneering surveys in the Viru Valley on the northern Peruvian coast helped launch settlement-pattern research as an integral part of archaeological methodology, and his 1953 publication *Prehistoric Settlement Patterns in the Viru Valley, Peru* has become a classic work in the field. Willey is renowned for both the breadth of his fieldwork (in the southeastern United States, Peru, lower Central America, and southern Mesoamerica) and his landmark syntheses of American archaeology and its development.

In relation to North American archaeology, Willey worked in the Southeast, especially in Georgia, Louisiana, and Florida, during the late 1930s and early 1940s. His field research and laboratory analyses resulted in a number of important publications, including *Crooks Mound: A Marksville Period Site in LaSalle Parish, Louisiana* (Willey and Ford 1940), *Archaeology of the Florida Gulf Coast* (1949), and an influential synthetic article, "An Interpretation of the Prehistory of the Eastern United States" (Willey and Ford 1941). The first volume of Willey's two-volume *Introduction to American Archaeology,* which focused on North America and appeared in 1966, provided a highly useful and widely read overview of the culture history of the area. In the 1950s, Willey

Gordon R. Willey. Belize River valley excavations ca. mid-1950s. (Reprinted with permission from American Antiquity 45[2]:229)

turned his attention to the Maya area, directing projects at Barton Ramie, Altar de Sacrificios, Seibal, and Copan, with special attention to settlement history. He is highly regarded for his interpretations of the growth of Maya civilization (Willey 1987).

Willey worked at the Smithsonian Institution in the 1940s; in 1950, he became Bowditch Professor of Mexican and Central American Archaeology and Ethnology at Harvard University and curator of Middle and South American archaeology at the Peabody Museum of American Archaeology and Ethnology at Harvard, where he has remained. In 1987, he was named Bowditch Professor Emeritus. He has received numerous awards in recognition of his research and writings and has served as president of both the American Anthropological Association (1961) and the Society for American Archaeology (1967–1968).

Jeremy A. Sabloff

Further Readings

Willey, G.R. 1949. *Archaeology of the Florida Gulf Coast.* Miscellaneous Collections, vol. 113. Smithsonian Institution, Washington, D.C.

———. 1953. *Prehistoric Settlement Patterns in the Viru Valley, Peru.* Bulletin no. 155. Bureau of American Ethnology, Smithsonian Institution, Washington, D.C.

———. 1966–1971. *An Introduction to American Archaeology.* 2 vols. Prentice-Hall, Englewood Cliffs.

———. 1987. *Essays in Maya Archaeology.* University of New Mexico Press, Albuquerque.

———. 1988. *Portraits in American Archaeology: Remembrances of Some Distinguished Americanists.* University of New Mexico Press, Albuquerque.

———. 1990. *New World Archaeology and Culture History: Collected Essays and Articles.* University of New Mexico Press, Albuquerque.

Willey, G.R., and J.A. Ford. 1940. *Crooks Mound: A Marksville Period Site in LaSalle Parish, Louisiana.* Anthropological Study no. 3. Louisiana Department of Conservation, Baton Rouge.

———. 1941. An Interpretation of the Prehistory of the Eastern United States. *American Anthropology* 43:325–363.

Willey, G.R., and P. Phillips. 1958. *Method and Theory in American Archaeology.*

University of Chicago Press, Chicago.

Willey, G.R., and J.A. Sabloff. 1993. *A History of American Archaeology.* 3rd ed. W.H. Freeman, New York.

Williams Complex

The Williams complex is located in the Souris River Basin on the northeastern Plains (Syms 1972, 1992). It dates to the A.D. 1500s–1600s (450–250 years B.P.) and is one of several regional complexes that overlie the earlier Woodland-focused Rainy River composite (Lenius and Olinyk 1990; Syms 1992). Although understanding of the culture dynamics of the northeastern Plains is still in its infancy (Syms 1992), the complex appears to share a few attributes with the Wascana ware of east-central Saskatchewan (Malainey 1990).

Materials from the type site, the Brockinton site on the Souris River of southwestern Manitoba, indicate a typical nomadic Plains subsistence based primarily on bison (Syms 1972, 1985). It is characterized by shallow side-notched points and distinctive ceramics. Most of the vessels are medium-sized bowls. Several bowls with shallow rims are decorated with cord-impressed patterns along the lip. Decoration also occurs on the rim as borders of triangular spaces filled with small hollow-tool punctates, perhaps produced by feathers or very small rodent limb bones, and as a main pattern with a rainbow design on the exterior surface. Cord-wrapped-tool impressions are also a common attribute.

E. Leigh Syms

Further Readings

Lenius, B.J., and D.M. Olinyk. 1990. The Rainy River Composite: Revisions to Late Woodland Taxonomy. In *The Woodland Tradition in the Western Great Lakes: Papers Presented to Elden Johnson,* edited by G.E. Gibbon, pp. 77–112. Publications in Anthropology no. 4. Department of Anthropology, University of Minnesota, Minneapolis.

Malainey, M. 1990. *Internal and External Relationships of Saskatchewan Plains Pottery Assemblages: Circa A.D. 1300 to Contact.* Unpublished Master's thesis. Department of Anthropology and Archaeology, University of Saskatchewan, Saskatoon.

Syms, E.L. 1972. The 1971 Field Season in

the Southwestern Manitoba Research Area. Ms. on file, Manitoba Museum of Man and Nature, Winnipeg.

————. 1985. Brockinton. In *The Canadian Encyclopedia,* p. 230. Hurtig, Edmonton.

————. 1992. Ceramics on the N.E. Plains Outside of the Middle Missouri Trench: Increasing Diversity and Regionalism. Plains Village Cultural Developments in the Northeastern Plains, session of the Fiftieth Plains Anthropological Conference, Lincoln. Ms. on file, Manitoba Museum of Man and Nature, Winnipeg.

Williamson

Anyone who visits the Williamson Paleoindian site (44DW1) in southeastern Virginia and entertains hopes of finding a beautiful Clovis fluted projectile point is doomed to bitter disappointment. The very most that one can hope to find is unfinished rejects or a tool used by the fluted-point makers—and, after years of intensive search since the first confirmed discovery of the site in 1947, these are becoming scarce indeed. This great site, the most extensive Paleoindian site yet found in North America, covers ca. 405 ha (1,000 acres) of land. Untold hundreds of tons of chipping debris, waste flakes and spalls, exhausted blade cores, and rejected lithic material litter the creek bottoms, hills, and slopes for at least 1.6 km (1 mile) on both sides of the fall-line zone of Little Cattail Creek in Dinwiddie County, Virginia. At least 80 percent of this area are woodlands and pasture, and the remaining 20 percent cultivated fields. The Williamson site has produced more than 200 fluted points and bases; more than 3,000 end scrapers; 2,000 side scrapers; 500 drills, gravers, and special tools; and 500 preforms plus tips and bases. Unknown amounts of hammerstones, wedges, and splitters are also present.

Certain areas of the site could be designated camp or habitation areas, for there are artifact concentrations that contain completed fluted projectile points, core blades, various types of scrapers, and other tools, and special tools in both local lithics and exotic cryptocrystalline lithics from faraway sources of silicious material acquired in the travels of the flint-knappers during their seasonal rounds. Seldom does one find finished points or tools and quantities of pressure flakes outside these habitation areas, which are located on hilltops, presumably to escape the biting flies that lurk in the vicinity of animal herds in summer. The various herd animals of the late Pleistocene and the early Holocene periods congregated at or near the fall line of creeks and rivers during spring and fall migrations to summer and winter pastures. They congregated there for the simple reason that they could ford the rocky rapids and shallows of the streams without having to swim, which was very tiring and made them vulnerable to predators, both animal and human. The migrating animals of the period were mammoth, mastodon, bison, caribou, musk-ox, elk, and possibly horse and camel.

The sources of the fluted-point-maker's lithic material, called Cattail Creek chalcedony, were boulders and possibly logs of replaced wood (petrified wood) found in the creek bottom and eroding out of the hillsides and hilltops of the area. One log or boulder of this chalcedony might contain silicious material of a rainbow of colors: red-brown, yellow, blue, black, gray, and white and translucent agate. It is jasper, moss agate, carnelian, chert, and flint all in one matrix. Light blue and blue-gray are the dominant colors and seem to have been preferred. Most of the wastage of material on the site is due to flaws, geodes, and seams or bands of softer or harder stone, which were discarded by the knappers in their search for workable lithic material.

Fine-quality silicious material, such as Cattail Creek chalcedony, is rarely found in southeastern Virginia and the northeastern North Carolina Piedmont and coastal plain. The early hunters valued it highly and traveled great distances to procure it. The great quantity of lithic debris scattered over the site and the variations in fluted-point styles and tools suggest that they returned to this lithic source for many, many generations, perhaps from 9050 to 7050 B.C. (11,000–9000 years B.P.) and later. It is believed that this Cattail Creek lithic complex is the oldest fluted-point complex found in eastern North America, far older than the Thunderbird complex of the northern Shenandoah Valley and the Bullbrook site in Massachusetts, the Debert site in Nova Scotia, or the Vail site in Maine. All exhibit characteristics of later fluted points, such as deep concave bases and thinner point blades.

Judging from fluted points and chipping debris from an ever-widening array of sites containing Cattail Creek chalcedony and from the exotic lithics recovered at the Williamson site, it appears that the sphere of activity of people associated with the site was to the south. Only two or three instances of Cattail Creek lithics have been found at any distance north, northwest, or northeast of the quarry site on Cattail Creek. It appears that the hunters of the Cattail Creek lithic complex followed herd animals southeastward to the southern cape of Chesapeake Bay and then out on the Continental Shelf between Norfolk Canyon as it cuts down through the shelf to the next canyon to the south, which formerly drained Albemarle Sound from near Oregon Inlet to Cape Hatteras. They then moved along the northern shore of Albemarle Sound and west to central North Carolina south of Greensboro before turning north to Danville, Virginia, and northeastward to the Williamson site for a new supply of lithic material. In all, their movements covered a southern radius of 274 km (170 miles).

Floyd Painter

Further Readings

Haynes, C.V. 1972. Stratigraphic Investigations at the Williamson Site, 1972 Dinwiddie County, Virginia. *Chesopiean: A Journal of North American Archaeology* 10(4):107–114.

Johnson, G.H. 1978. *An Analysis of Lithic Material From the Williamson Site.* Quarterly Bulletin, vol. 33, no. 2. Archaeological Society of Virginia, Richmond.

McAvoy, J.M. 1992. *Nottaway River Survey: 1. Clovis Settlement Patterns.* Special Publication no. 28. Archaeological Society of Virginia, Richmond.

McCary, B.C. 1951. A Workshop Site of Early Man in Dinwiddie County, Virginia. *American Antiquity* 17:9–71.

McCary, B.C.J., C. Smith, and C.E. Gilliam. 1949. *A Folsom Workshop on the Williamson Farm, Dinwiddie County, Virginia.* Quarterly Bulletin, vol. 4, no. 2. Archaeological Society of Virginia, Richmond.

Painter, F. 1970. *The Cattail Creek Fluting Tradition and Its Complex—Determining Lithic Debris.* Bulletin no. 13. Southeastern Archaeological Conference, Norfolk, Virginia.

Peck, R.M. 1985. *The Williamson Site, Dinwiddie County, Virginia.* Edited and published by the author.

Windust Complex

The Windust complex or, as it is better known to regional scholars, the Windust phase, includes the earliest well-dated archaeological assemblages in the northwestern United States. Windust is best represented at a number of sites along or near the Snake River in the Columbia Plateau of Washington State, and in north-central Idaho, and north-central and northeastern Oregon. Marmes Rock Shelter, located near the confluence of the Palouse River and the Snake River, is the major Windust site. It yields not only a large Windust component, but human cremations as well. Lind Coulee is the major stratified open site with Windust materials. Located near a fossil lake in the Columbia Basin north of the Snake River, it dates to ca. 6750 B.C. (8700 years B.P.). The largest assemblage of Windust artifacts was recovered at the Hatwai site on the Clearwater River in northern Idaho. The Windust phase spans the 8850–6550 B.C. (10,800–8500 years B.P.) period. The earliest dates on Windust materials, which just postdate Clovis, cluster between 8850 and 8650 B.C. (10,800–10,600 years B.P.). A date of 8870 B.C. ± 140 (10,820 years B.P.) from the Hatwai site is the earliest radiocarbon date based on wood charcoal firmly associated with Windust materials. Contemporary dates from the Marmes Rock Shelter on the Palouse River in south-central Washington State are based on freshwater mussel shell, as is a date of 12,050 B.C. ± 1160 (14,000 years B.P.) from the Granite Point site, which is on the Snake River in southeastern Washington.

Artifact assemblages include a variety of large stemmed projectile points, as well as some lanceolate forms. Most assemblages contain utilized and worked flakes, cobble tools, scrapers, knives, and bifaces. Less common are well-made bone tools, which include bone points and needles, edge-ground cobbles, antler wedges, abraders, and millingstones. The utilized and worked flakes are the most common forms. The stemmed projectile points typically have broad straight-to-contracting stems relative to their overall size. Shoulders are of varying size and shape. The blades of the points vary considerably, since many were reworked and resharpened before finally being discarded. The edges of the stems are heavily ground. One site, Pilcher Creek in the Blue Mountains of northeastern Oregon, produced soapstone figurines. The site appears to have been located near the soapstone quarry. Such figurines have not been recovered in any other Windust site.

Windust appears to be the northern variant of a widespread technological tradition in western North America that followed Clovis. Windust projectile points are morphologically and technologically similar to points found in southern British Columbia and to the south in the Great Basin and California. They are particularly similar to materials of the Western Pluvial Lakes tradition of south-central Oregon and Nevada, where stemmed projectile points are associated with radiocarbon dates as old as 9250 B.C. (11,200 years B.P.), which makes them contemporary with Clovis. While Clovis artifacts do occur in the Intermontane Plateau, none have been recovered in a dated context. Elsewhere, Clovis's age has been established at ca. 9550–9250 B.C. (11,500–11,200 years B.P.). The historical and technological links, if any, between Clovis and Windust are unknown. Both are characterized by well-made bone tools, particularly small needles, but they are otherwise different.

At 8850 B.C. (10,800 years B.P.), the climate of the Columbia Plateau was much colder than now. The dominant vegetation covering the cold steppe was *Artemesia* (sage). By 8550 B.C. (10,500 years B.P.), protected areas began to be reforested. Windust sites are concentrated in places that would have been wetter than surrounding areas during this period. They are found along rivers, as well as at higher elevations. The evidence indicates that Windust subsistence practices included hunting, gathering, and fishing. Wapiti (American elk), deer, pronghorn antelope, and bison, as well as rabbits, hares, and beaver were hunted. There is no direct evidence of the collection and processing of plants for food, though the location of some sites near major root-producing meadows and the occasional presence of grinding and milling-stones indicate that plants were exploited. Freshwater mollusks were also collected. Exploited fish include anadromous salmon and trout, large minnows, and suckers. Salmon and bison may have been heavily exploited at certain favored locations, but there is no evidence that Windust people focused heavily on any particular resource. Rather, they seem to have exploited food resources as they were available in the environment.

Population levels appear to have been quite low. There is no evidence for storage or structures of any kind. In fact, aside from Marmes Rock Shelter, there are few features of any kind

associated with Windust materials. A well-stratified open site with hearths and other features would make a significant contribution to our knowledge of Windust.

By 6050 B.C. (8000 years B.P.), Windust-style projectile points were replaced by laurel-leaf-shaped lanceolate points known as Cascade points. Other than the shift in projectile-point style, and a possible shift in settlement pattern, there is strong technological, economic, and cultural continuity between Windust and succeeding archaeological manifestations at least as late as 5050 B.C. (7000 years B.P.).

Kenneth M. Ames

Further Readings

Ames, K.M. 1988. Early Holocene Forager Mobility Strategies on the Southern Columbia Plateau. In *Early Human Occupation in Far Western North America: The Clovis-Archaic Interface,* edited by J.A. Willig, C.M. Aikens, and J. Fagan, pp. 325–360. Anthropological Papers no. 21. Nevada State Museum, Carson City.

Leonhardy, F.C., and D.G. Rice. 1970. A Proposed Culture Typology for the Lower Snake River Region, Southeastern Washington. *Northwest Anthropological Research Notes* 4(1):1–29.

Rice, D.G. 1972. *The Windust Phase in Lower Snake River Prehistory.* Report of Investigations no. 50. Laboratory of Anthropology, Washington State University, Pullman.

Wintemberg, William J. (1876–1941)

An early professionally trained Canadian archaeologist, William John Wintemberg worked extensively throughout Canada in the first half of the twentieth century. He made especially significant contributions to the study of the Late Prehistoric occupation of southern Ontario in numerous articles and in standardized reports of the Uren (1928), Roebuck (1936), Lawson (1939), Middleport (1948), and Sidney-MacKay (1946) village sites.

A protégé of Dr. David Boyle, the first archaeological curator of the Ontario Provincial Museum, Wintemberg maintained close ties with that institution until he began his 30 years of service for the National Museum of Canada in Ottawa in 1911; there, his professional career developed under the supervision of Harlan Ingersoll Smith. Wintemberg excavated various shell heaps in 1913–1914 on Nova Scotia's southeastern coast and, in the late 1920s, was one of the earliest trained archaeologists to work in Newfoundland, Saskatchewan, and Alberta. In Newfoundland, he continued Diamond Jenness's work on the Beothuck problem, which refers to the fate of the now-extinct Beothuck Indians, and on the Dorset culture, which had been tentatively isolated as a culture by Jenness in 1923. His discovery of pure Dorset sites along the northwestern coast of New Foundland in 1927 and 1929 helped validate the concept of a Dorset culture. A posthumous paper in 1942 traced the distribution of aboriginal pottery in Canada.

A craftsman by training, he became interested in the function of the artifacts that he was recovering from Iroquoian sites in southern Ontario and conducted many experiments to determine how they had been manufactured and used. He analyzed and described archaeological materials in terms of functional categories and used these categories to reconstruct the lifeways of the inhabitants of these sites. This early functional approach was being developed and systematized at the time by A.C. Parker, Harlan Smith, William S. Webb, and others. The approach, whose roots extend back to the early nineteenth century in Europe, was temporally eclipsed by the Midwestern Taxonomic Method in the 1930s. Wintemberg's (1928, 1936, 1939) attempts to link village sites with historic Iroquoian tribes are early examples of the direct-historical approach.

Guy Gibbon

Further Readings

Trigger, B.G. 1978. William J. Wintemberg: Iroquoian Archaeologist. In *Essays in Northeastern Anthropology in Memory of Marian E. White*, edited by W.E. Engelbrecht and D.K. Grayson, pp. 5–21. Occasional Publications in Northeastern Anthropology no. 5. Department of Anthropology, Franklin Pierce College, Rindge.

Wintemberg, W.J. 1928. *Uren Prehistoric Village Site, Oxford County, Ontario.* Bulletin no. 51. National Museum of Canada, Ottawa.

———. 1936. *Roebuck Prehistoric Village Site, Grenville County, Ontario.* Bulletin no. 83. National Museum of Canada, Ottawa.

———. 1939. *Lawson Prehistoric Village Site, Middlesex County, Ontario.* Bulletin no. 94. National Museum of Canada, Ottawa.

———. 1939–1940. Eskimo Sites of the Dorset Culture in Newfoundland: Parts I–II. *American Antiquity* 5(1):83–102, 5(4):309–333.

———. 1942. The Geographical Distribution of Aboriginal Pottery in Canada. *American Antiquity* 8:129–141.

———. 1946. The Sidey-MacKay Prehistoric Village Site. *American Antiquity* 11:154–182.

———. 1948. *The Middleport Prehistoric Village Site.* Bulletin no. 109. National Museum of Canada, Ottawa.

World-Systems Approach

The world-systems approach is a framework for understanding cultural evolution in North America based upon the idea that the proper unit of analysis for cultural evolutionary theory is a world-system defined in terms of an economic interdependence (division of labor), and not a unit defined in terms of judicial, political, cultural, geographical, or other criteria. The basic premise of the world-systems approach is that economic interdependence continuously forms and reforms the social and political relations that express cultural patterns and organizational structures. This approach envisions both a geographic (core/periphery) differentiation between localized populations, through which particular populations come to play particular roles in a world-system as their economic, political, and social institutions change to better fit the demands of their specialization, and a continuous competition between differentiated areas (cores and peripheries). In this way, the world-systems approach sees cultural evolution in North America stemming from the interplay of two overlapping processes: competition between geographically localized populations; and differentiation, division of labor, and interdependence between these same populations.

North American archaeologists who employ a world-systems approach find it particularly useful in developing cultural-evolutionary theory, for three primary reasons. First, it is inherently spatial, focusing attention on geographical relations between cores and peripheries, including access to resources, transportation, population, and the like. Second, it is multilevel, so that as an economic interdependence creates a world-system within a given region, it also extends outward to interregional relationships and inward to intragroup ones. Third, because the world-systems approach allows one to predict a given population's social and political organization based upon its position of specialization in a world-system, it also allows for the prediction of how social and political organization will change given specific alterations in the economic interdependence that creates the world-system.

Peter Peregrine

Further Readings

Chase-Dunn, C., and T. Hall. 1991. *Core/Periphery Relations in Precapitalist Worlds.* Westview Press, Boulder.

McGuire, R.H. 1989. The Greater Southwest As a Periphery of Mesoamerica. In *Centre and Periphery,* edited by T. Champion, pp. 40–66. Unwin Hyman, London.

Peregrine, P.N., and G.M. Feinman. 1996. *Pre-Columbian World-Systems.* Prehistory Press, Madison.

Whitecotton, J., and R. Pailes. 1986. New World Precolumbian World Systems. In *Ripples in the Chichimec Sea,* edited by F.J. Mathien and R.H. McGuire, pp. 181–204. Southern Illinois University Press, Carbondale.

Y

Yellow Jacket Ruin

Yellow Jacket ruin (5MT5) is one of the largest recorded multicomponent Anasazi sites in the Mesa Verde region of southwestern Colorado. It was one of the first Anasazi ruins described by explorers in the McComb Military Expedition of 1859, who referred to it as Surouaro, from the Ute term meaning "desolation." Jesse Walter Fewkes (1919) also described Surouaro as one of the largest sites in the Montezuma Valley.

The site is an aggregation of nearly two dozen rubble mounds covering 20 ha (49.4 acres) of a mesa spur at the head of Yellow Jacket Canyon near Pleasant View, Colorado. Each contains the ruins of numerous contiguous rooms. Some of the roomblocks probably reached two to three stories in height. The linear roomblocks are separated by long, open plazas, with a central "avenue" running roughly north-south through the ruin. Based upon the large blocky masonry and the presence of multiple kivas in each roomblock, the primary occupation at the site dates to the twelfth and thirteenth centuries A.D. Estimates of the number of rooms and kivas at Yellow Jacket vary. Arthur Rohn (1989) believes that the site contains 1,800 rooms and more than 160 kivas; he estimates that, during the height of its occupation, it may have housed 2,500 people. A more conservative appraisal made by Frederick Lange and others (Lange et al. 1986) estimates that 124 kivas and several hundred rooms may be present at the site, which also contains the remains of a large reservoir.

Early ceramics on the site surface indicate that the masonry roomblocks probably overlie pithouse settlements dating to A.D. 500 (1450 years B.P.). The temporal depth of occupation at Yellow Jacket ruin is borne out by research undertaken by the University of Colorado on nearby habitation sites. Excavations at Porter pueblo, the Stevenson site, and 5MT3, all located across the canyon from the main ruin, have uncovered occupations dating to ca. A.D. 500–1300 (1450–650 years B.P.).

It is likely that the main ruin at Yellow Jacket represents the thirteenth-century aggregation of a large Anasazi community. Excavations and surface-survey data from other large sites in the Montezuma Valley, including Sand Canyon pueblo, indicate that, prior to the major aggregations of the twelfth and thirteenth centuries, the Anasazi generally occupied relatively small, dispersed settlements. Occupants of these settlements were integrated into local communities, and community members constructed great kivas and Chaco-style great houses to foster the social integration of their dispersed community. The presence of at least one great kiva and a probable Chaco-style great house in the northern portion of Yellow Jacket ruin indicates that the ruin was probably an integrative center serving a dispersed community before it became a major residential aggregation site during the twelfth and thirteenth centuries.

Yellow Jacket ruin remains largely unexcavated. C.T. Hurst and V.F. Lotrich (1932) excavated portions of Yellow Jacket ruin in the 1930s, and Western State College in Gunnison, Colorado, also worked on a small part of the ruin in the 1950s. There has been a long history of unsystematic digging at the site. Unprovenanced artifacts looted from Yellow Jacket ruin are in private collections donated to the Anasazi Heritage Center in Dolores, Colorado, and to Fort Lewis College in Durango, Colorado. Two-thirds of the ruin is owned by the

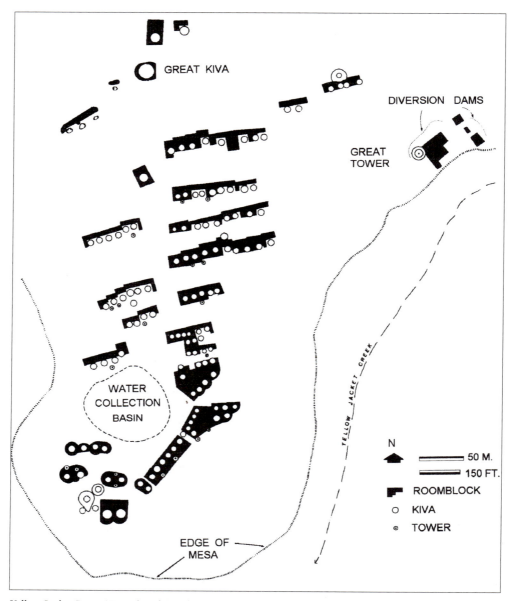

Yellow Jacket Ruin, SW Colorado. (Adapted by M. A. Adler from Lange et al. 1986)

Archaeological Conservancy; the remaining third is privately owned.

Michael A. Adler

Further Readings

Fewkes, J.W. 1919. *Prehistoric Villages, Castles, and Towers of Southwestern Colorado.* Bulletin no. 70. Bureau of American Ethnology, Smithsonian Institution, Washington, D.C.

Hurst, C.T., and V.F. Lotrich. 1932. An Un- usual Mug From Yellowjacket Canyon. *El Palacio* 33(21–22):195–198.

Lange, F., N. Mahaney, J.B. Wheat, and M. Chenault. 1986. *Yellow Jacket: A Four Corners Anasazi Ceremonial Center.* Johnson Books, Boulder.

Rohn, A. 1989. Northern San Juan Prehistory. In *Dynamics of Southwest Prehistory,* edited by L.S. Cordell and G.J. Gumerman, pp. 149–177. Smithsonian Institution Press, Washington, D.C.

Wheat, J.B. 1980. Yellow Jacket Canyon Archaeology. In *Insights Into the Ancient Ones,* edited by J. Berger and E. Berger, pp. 60–66. Mesa Verde Press, Cortez.

Yonkee

The Powers-Yonkee site (24PR5) in Wyoming and a small set of related sites figure prominently in northwestern Plains prehistory. Well-documented Yonkee components cluster in the Powder and Tongue river basins within 100 km (62 miles) of the Wyoming-Montana border. Lesser sites are in west-central and north-central Montana and northwestern Wyoming.

Most radiocarbon dates on Yonkee components are in the 1050–550 B.C. (3000–2500 years B.P.) range. A series of unfortunate coincidences from the original 1961 excavation at Powers-Yonkee suggested an age 1,500–2,000 years older. A radiocarbon date of 2500 B.C. ± 125 (4450 years B.P.). for a single large skull intermediate between *Bison bison* and *Bison antiquus* and classification of projectile points as a "variant" of the then newly defined McKean type appeared to corroborate the relative antiquity of the site. It now appears that (1) the radiocarbon date was in error, possibly from sample contamination or inadequate association; (2) the bison was misidentified or did not come from the Yonkee bonebed; and (3) the attribution of the projectile points as a McKean variety has little foundation.

The distinctive Yonkee projectile point provides the principal identifying criterion of this taxon. Point size and weight fall within the limits (near the low end) of atlatl dart points (ca. 4 g, or 0.13 ounces). Length typically exceeds twice the width, giving the impression of a long, slender projectile point. Blade shape tends toward excurvate with a pronounced tendency to show an incurvate profile on the distal third, which produces a sharp tip. Relatively shallow, open notches low on the lateral edges create the impression of corner notching or corner removal. The position and size of the notch typically produces a base about nine-tenths the width of the blade. Rounding of the basal corners and a characteristic shallow basal indentation or notch on most specimens leave the base with a "mouse-eared" appearance. Within the primary area of Yonkee distribution, locally available porcelainite dominates the lithic-material choice.

Until about 1988, bison kills provided the sole context for Yonkee components. All of the Yonkee bison bone appears to be from bison of modern configuration. None of the kill sites display evidence of extensive carcass processing, such as smashed and calcined bone or fire-cracked rock. Most carcasses exhibit straightforward disarticulation, with many major elements remaining in anatomical position. The extent of disarticulation is consistent with stripping the carcass for removal of major muscle groups. Seasonality of the kills shows substantial intersite variation.

Early reports on Yonkee bison kills interpreted them as arroyo traps. As such, those sites have figured prominently in thinking about the evolution of communal bison killing. J.P. Albanese (1978) argued that, at the time of the kill, the arroyo at Buffalo Creek (previously known as the Mavrakis-Bentzen-Roberts site)

Yonkee points. (Illustration by T. E. Roll)

had a sinuous rather than a straight course and a broad flat bottom at least three times as wide and a third as deep as the modern arroyo. He also called attention to substantial similarity in the paleotopography of Powers-Yonkee and Buffalo Creek. Work in 1985 at Powers-Yonkee demonstrated the presence of an ancient arroyo much broader and shallower than the modern setting. This evidence, along with the discovery of posts and postmolds at Buffalo Creek (Bentzen 1962), provides reason to question the original interpretation of these kills as arroyo traps. While the topography of a broad, shallow arroyo undoubtedly contributed to the efficiency of the kill, the possibility of more elaborate structures, perhaps a true pound or corral, cannot be discounted. Excavations at Kobold added jumping to the repertoire of Yonkee communal bison-killing techniques (Frison 1970).

Tom E. Roll

Further Readings

Albanese, J.P. 1978. Paleotopography and Bison Traps. In *Bison Procurement and Utilization: A Symposium,* edited by L.B. Davis and M. Wilson, pp. 185–193. Memoir no. 14. Plains Anthropologist, Lincoln.

Bentzen, R. 1961. *The Powers-Yonkee Bison Trap, 24PR5.* Report of the Sheridan Chapter, Wyoming Archaeological Society, Sheridan.

———. 1962. *The Mavrakis-Bentzen-Roberts Bison Trap, 485H311.* Report of the Sheridan Chapter, Wyoming Archaeological Society, Sheridan.

Frison, G.C. 1970. The Kobold Site, 148H406: A Post-Altithermal Record of Buffalo-Jumping for the Northwestern Plains. *Plains Anthropologist* 15(47):1–35.

———. 1991. *Prehistoric Hunters of the High Plains.* 2nd ed. Academic Press, San Diego.

Miller, M.E. 1985. Interassemblage Variability Among Five Middle Plains Archaic Bison Kills. In *McKean/Middle Plains Archaic: Current Research,* edited by M. Kornfeld and L.C. Todd, pp. 147–153. Occasional Papers on Wyoming Archaeology no. 4. Sheridan.

Z

Zuni Pueblo

Zuni Pueblo is located in west-central New Mexico on the New Mexico–Arizona border. It is the home of members of the Zuni tribe (population 8,500). T.J. Ferguson and E. Richard Hart (1985) note that, according to Zuni tradition, after creation in the first and innermost womb of the world, the Zuni people (who refer to themselves as Ashiwi) were led through many struggles by their immortal gods to the surface of the Earth Mother and into the light of the Sun Father. After a long journey searching for the middle place, the place where they were destined to make their home, K'yan'asdebi, the water spider, assisted them in finding the exact center point, Halona:ltiwana, the place today called Zuni Pueblo.

When the Spanish arrived in the American Southwest in the sixteenth century A.D., the Zuni occupied six or seven villages along the Zuni River, including Hawikku, Kwa'kin'a, Halona:wa (Zuni Pueblo), Mats's:kya, Kechiba:wa, and possibly Chalo:wa. The villages constitute the legendary Seven Cities of Cibola that were sought by Francisco Vásquez de Coronado in A.D. 1540. These ancestral villages, which, with the exception of Zuni Pueblo, have long been abandoned, are some of the most interesting and important archaeological sites in the American Southwest. While the details of abandonment are unknown, after the Pueblo Revolt of 1680 the Zuni people coalesced into Zuni Pueblo. Despite the fact that Coronado found neither riches nor cities of gold, the name "Cibola" is still used to refer to these sites, as well as to the region in general.

The architecture of Zuni Pueblo has long fascinated visitors. Ferguson and Barbara Mills (1987) in their extensive study of the architec-ture of the pueblo note that the major occupation of the site probably began by A.D. 1425 (525 years B.P.), although ceramics dating to earlier periods are also found in the lowermost excavated deposits. Historic photographs dating to the late 1800s show the pueblo as a series of four-to-five-story-tall, largely windowless apartmentlike buildings, with access restricted by ladders to rooftop entries. Rooftops were clearly public spaces, and the arrangement of the pueblo clearly reflected the need for protection from raiders. Victor Mindeleff's map of the pueblo shows seven large roomblocks separated by a number of plazas and streets. Construction materials were primarily sandstone blocks plastered with adobe, although a number of more recently constructed buildings were of adobe bricks. In 1630 or 1631, a Catholic mission was established on the outskirts of the pueblo, although the more recent building construction has given the mission a more central position. Important architectural features include the use of north-south and east-west coordinate axes important in Zuni conceptions of space, rooftop terraces that maximize passive solar heating, and an orientation that offers protection from cold winter and spring winds. The roomblocks are oriented inward and offer terraces that oversee plazas used for religious purposes. Although many of the architectural elements remain visible today, the cessation of raiding has resulted in the reduction in the height of the pueblo, the addition of ground-level entries, and a general expansion of the pueblo at ground level. Open space within the pueblo has also increased, according to Ferguson and Mills.

Zuni Pueblo and its people have offered generations of hospitality to anthropologists, notably Adolph F. Bandelier, Ruth Bunzel, Frank H. Cushing, Jesse W. Fewkes, F.W. Hodge, A.L. Kroeber, Elsie Clews Parsons, Frank H.H. Roberts, Jr., Leslie Spier, and Matilda Coxe Stevenson, among many others. Given this hospitality, and the ancestral link to, and knowledge of, the people who created the archaeological record in the area, the people of Zuni Pueblo have helped shape contemporary archaeology and anthropology.

Robert D. Leonard

Further Readings

Ferguson, T.J., and E.R. Hart. 1985. *A Zuni Atlas.* University of Oklahoma Press, Norman.

Ferguson, T.J., and B.J. Mills. 1987. Settlement and Growth of Zuni Pueblo: An Architectural History. *Kiva* 52(4):243–266.

The Zuni People. 1972. *The Zunis: Self Portrayals.* Mentor, New York.

See also CIBOLA BRANCH

Index

(**boldface** indicates a major discussion of the topic; *italic* indicates illustrative material)

ceramics *(continued)*:
    Anasazi culture:
        general features, 14, 15
        Kayenta branch, 408, *409, 410*
        Mesa Verde, 513
    Anderson phase, Middle Missouri, 17
    angel site/phase, Middle Mississippi, 18
    Antelope Creek phase, Plains Village tradition, 20
    Bear Village, Mogollon, 57
    Belle Glade culture, Florida, 61
    Broken K Pueblo, Arizona, 94
    C.W. Harris site, 192
    Caborn-Welborn phase, Mississippi, 99
    Cambria, Middle Missouri, 113–114, *114*
    Chauga, 144
    Chucalissa site, 152
    Cibola branch, Anasazi, 153, 155
    Crab Orchard tradition, 180–181
    Custer phase, 191
    Dallas culture, 193
    Far Northeast, 135–138
    Fort Ancient, 288
    Gila Polychrome, 532, 729, 731
    Grasshopper pueblo, 323
    Great Basin, 249
    Gulf Tradition, 342–343
    Havana complex, 343
    Henrietta focus, Southern Plains village, 359
    Hohokam, Southwest, 622
    Hopewell culture:
        Mandeville, 490
        Mann, Middle Woodland, 491
    Hudson Bay Lowlands, 379
    Intermountain tradition, 390
    Killarney focus, 417, *418*
    Little Colorado branch, Anasazi, *463*, 465
    Lower Loup phase, Central Plains, 476
    Madisonville site, Fort Ancient, 487
    Markville complex, 343, 496–497
    McGraw, Hopewell culture, Middle Woodland, 504
    Miller culture, Middle Woodland, 527, *528*
    Nebraska phase, Central Plains, 557
    Norton, Alaska, 590, 591
    Numic style, 593
    Oneota culture, Mississippi, 613
    paddle and anvil technique, **620**, 629, 630, 790
    Patayan cultural area, Southwest, 629–630
    Plains Village, 334–335
    Plaquemine culture, 657
    Porter complex, 343
    Poverty Point culture, 342
    Pratt complex, 681
    Red Wing locality, *709, 710*
    Rio Grande branch, Anasazi, 717–718
    Salado polychrome, 729, 731–732
    San Simon branch, Mogollon, 741
    Sandy Lake tradition, 746, *746*
    Smoky Hill tradition, 773
    South Appalachian tradition, 775

    Swift Creek, 824, 825
    Thomas Riggs phase, Middle Missouri, 836
    Tierra Blanca complex, 839
    Uncas Complex, Southern Plains, 856
    Valley-variant sites, Plains, 864
    Vickers focus, Manitoba, 865–867, *866*
    Washita River phase, Southern Plains, 875
    Weeden Island, 343
    Wickliffe site, 887
    Williams complex, Northeast Plains, 890.
    See also pottery
ceremonial centers:
    Caddoan Area, Mississippi, 101
    Goforth-Saindon sites, 316–317
    Mann, Hopewell culture, Middle Woodland, 491
    Pinson Mounds, 647
    Spiro, 802
    Town Creek site, 842–843
ceremonial culture:
    Native American, SECC, 779–780
    Northwest Coast, 578
cerros de trincheras, 622
Chaco branch, Anasazi, 15, 16, **138–139**, 155
Chaddoan sites, George C. Davis site, 312–313
Chagas disease, 351
chalcedony, 200
    Cattail Creek, 891
Champe, John Leland, **140**, *140*
"channel flake," 280
Chapman, Carl Haley, **140–141**, *141*
Charles culture, Fraser River Canyon, 296–297
Charles/St. Mungo culture, Northwest, 141–143
charmstones, **143**, *588, 697, 787*
Chauga site, South Carolina, **143–144**
Chenopodium, 144, **144–145**, 181, 237, 239, 822
Cherokee sites/tradition:
    ancestral home of, 871
    Chief Oconastota, burial site of, 152
    Chota-Tanasee, 150–152, *151*
    Sewer site, **145–146**, *145*, 469
chert, 23, **146**, 219, 307, *308*, 309–310, 354, 426, 435, 460, 522–524, *523*, 537 626, 632, 698, 707, 750, 762, 773, 833
    debitage sites, 147, 307, 309–310.
    See also flint
Cheyenne culture, Biesterfeldt site, North Dakota, 66
chi thos (scraping tool), 574. *See also* tools
Chickamauga Reservoir, Hiwassee Island site, 361
Chihuahua tradition, Southwest Archaic, 798
Chilcotin Plateau area, Canada, **146–149**, *147*
Chiliwist phase, Okanagan Valley, 604–605
Chinese porcelains, Pacific period, California, 129
Chinookan people, Willamette Valley, 888
Chiricahua stage, Cochise culture, 799
Chocise Culture, The, 167
chopper, **149**, *149*
Choris culture, Arctic, **149–150**, 268–269, 591
Chota-Tanasee sites, **150–152**, *151*
choupichoul, 145

lithic debitage *(continued)*:
    Aucilla River sites, Paleoindian, Florida 37
    Clovis cultural complex, 162
    Miller complex, 525, 769
lithic technology, 200–201, 319–320, 346, 387, 401, 439, 472, 600, 632, 653, 827, 844, 891
    Debert/Belmont Complex, 199–200
    Early Coast Microblade, 227
    Paleoindian, 4, **460–461**.
    See also tools
little barley *(Hordeum pusillum)*, 238
Little Colorado branch, Anasazi, **461–446**, *462, 463, 464*
Little Ice Age, 10, 247, 327, 392, 433, **466–467**, 837
Little River focus, Great Bend aspect, 467. *See also* Lower Walnut focus
Locarno Beach culture, Northwest Coast, 468–469
Lochnore phase, Plateau pithouse tradition (PPT), 663
Lockhart site, Paleoindian site, 278–279
log crib tombs, Adena culture, Woodland, 6
Logan Creek complex, Early Plains Archaic, 469–470
Logan Creek site, 469
loghouses:
    Draper site, 220
    Hochelaga culture, 362
    Iroquoian culture, 393, 394
    Plateau, 470
"logistical-collector," foraging strategy, Plateau pithouse tradition (PPT), 663
longhouses, Clearwater River, 734–735, *735*
Loseke Creek variant, Late Plains Woodland, 470–471
Lost Race theory, 471–472
Lost Terrace site, Northwest Plains, **472–473**, *472*
Lost Tribe theory, 473
Louisiana Purchase, 430
Loup River phase. *See* Itskari phase, Central Plains
Lovell Constricted projectile points, *688*, **688–689**, *794*
Lovelock Cave, 380, **473–474**, *882*
Lowder's Ferry, corner-notched tradition, 178. *See also* tools
Lower Columbia River Valley, **474–476**, *475*
Lower Loup phase, Pawnees, Central Plains, 476–477
Lower River focus, Great Bend aspect, 333, **467**
Lower Snake River, sequences of, 477–479
Lower Sonora Argricultural complex, 479–480
Lower Walnut focus, Great Bend aspect, 333, **480–481**. *See also* Little River focus
Lubbock Lake, High Plains, **481–483**, *482*, 655
Lubbock Lake National Historic and State Archeological Landmark, 481
Luna, Tristán de, 420
Luna Village, Pine Lawn branch, Mogollon, 645
Lusk cultural complex, Hell Gap site, 483

M

MacCorkle stemmed projectile points, bifurcate, 68
MacDonald painted corrugated pottery, 286
mace, **485**, *485*
MacHaffie site, Paleoindian, 278, **485–486**, *486*
Mackenzie Corridor, Alaska, 63
Mackenzie River Valley, Subarctic, 801
Macon Plateau site, Ocmulgee, 600–601
Madeline Dunes phase, Eastern California, 241
"Madisonville focus," 486
"Madisonville horizon," 288–289, 487
Madisonville site, Fort Ancient, 486–487
Magic Mountain phase, Plains Archaic, 303, **487–488**, 550, 884
magnesite cylinders, Pacific period, California, 130
Main Shelter, Modoc Rock Shelter, 535–536
maize:
    Anderson phase, Middle Missouri, South Dakota, 17
    Aztalan, Middle Mississippi, Wisconsin, 41
    cobs:
        Bat Cave, evolution of, 53–55
        Tularosa Cave, 53, 848
    Colorado Plains Woodland variant, 32
    Fremont culture, 299, 300
    Mississippi culture, Eastern Woodlands, 533
    Oneota culture, Mississippi, 612
    recovery of, Pratt complex, 681
    Redbird phase, Plains Village, 713
    ridged-field agriculture, 716
    San Simon branch, Mogollon, Southwest, 740
    Southwest, 614
    Sunwatch Village, Fort Ancient, 385
    Toltec Mounds, 842
    Upper Sonoran Agricultural complex, 860.
    See also corn
malaria, European induced, 351
mammoth (Elephantidae *Mammuthus*), **488–490**, *489*
    disappearance of, 500
    Eastern California, 240
    hunting, Domebo site, 214–215
    skeleton of, 457–458, *457*
Mandan culture, 164–165, 352–353, 428, 429. *See also* Coalescent tradition
Mandan Indians, Anderson phase, Middle Missouri, 17
Mandeville site, Hopewell, 490–491
Mann site, Hopewell, 491–49**2**
manos, 492–493, 528, **529–530**, 587
maple sugaring, 493–494
Marginella shells, Hopewell culture, 519
Maritime Archaic tradition, 267, **494–496**, *495*, 698, 706
    Eastern Woodlands, 256
Marksville ceramic complex, Hopewell, 496–497
Marpole culture type, British Columbia, **497–499**, *498*
Martin, Paul Sidney, 499–500
Martin site, Northwest Coast, 873–874

salt, uses of, 736
salt mining, Anasazi, Virgin region, 867
salt pans, Great Basin, 326
salt production, site of, 336
San Carlos Apache Indian Reservation, 75
San Diego, establishment of, 109, 110, 111
San Dieguito phase, C.W. Harris site, 191, 240
San Dieguito tradition, California coast, 784, 785
San Francisco phase, Pine Lawn branch, Mogollon, 645
San Francisco red pottery, 286
San Jose phase, Oshara tradition, Picosa, 613
San Pedro stage, Cochise culture, 799–800
San Pedro Valley, Clovis sites, 737–740
San Simon branch, Mogollon, 740–741
Sand Canyon pueblo, Mesa Verde, *742*, 897
Sand Lake Onesta, ridged-field agriculture, 716, *716*
Sand Lake site, Oneota culture, **742–744**, *743*
Sandia Cave, Las Huertas Canyon, *744*, **744–746**, *745*
Sandia Cave: A Study in Controversy, 745
Sandia point knives, 745
sandstone, 557
Sandy Lake, Late Woodland, *746*, **746–747**
Santa Cruz site, 126
"Santa Theresa complex," 127
Santander, Fray Diego de, Gran Quivira, 321
Saqqaq site/tradition, Arctic, 28, 29, 268, 684–685, **747**
Saratoga Springs pattern, California, 108
Saratoga Springs period/culture, 242
Savanah River stemmed projectile point, Stallings culture, 811
Saxidomus, shells, 55
Scharbauer site, Monahans Draw, Texas, 747–749
Schmitt chert mines, Late Plains, **749–751**, *750*
Scott County Pueblo, Late Plains, *751*, **751–752**
Scottsbluff projectile points, 169, 170, 275, 375, 455
scraper, *752*, **752–753**
"searcher," adaptive strategy, California, 588
seashells, use of, 55. *See also* shells
"Sedalia diggers," Phillips Spring site, 639
Sedentary period, Papagueria, Hohokam, 622
Seip site, Ohio Hopewell, 753–754
Seip-Pricer mound, 753
Selkirk ceramics, 78, 125, **754–755**
Selkirk culture, Shield culture, Canada, 451, **754–755**
Serpent mounds, Rice Lake, Canada, 714
Seven Cities of Cibola, 153, 155, 901
Sevier Lake, 246, 247
sewing tradition, Koniag culture, Kodiak Island, 432
shaman kits:
    charmstones, 143, 697
    Pacific period, California, 128
    quartz, 697
shaman pole, Jones-Miller, Hell Gap, 401
shamanistic activities:
    Besant phase, Plains Archaic, Canada, 63
    California, 724

Fraser River Stone Scupltural Complex, 298
"Shell Heap People, the," 388
shell money system, California, 343, **759**, 766
shells:
    Archaic period, California, 108, 126, 127
    Pacific period, California, 110, 130, 587.
    See also dentalium; glycymeri; marginella; olivella; saxidomus; and tivola shells
Shetrone, Henry Clyde, 373, **759–760**, *760*
Shield culture, Eastern Woodlands, 256, 267, 268
    people, 760–761
ship wrecks, 110, 793
Shonitkwu period, Pacific Northwest, **411**, 433
Shoop site, Paleoindian, Pennsylvania, 761–762
Shoshone ceramics, Great Basin, 249
Shoshone Ware, Intermountain tradition, 390
Shoup phase, Salmon River, 733
Shuswap Horizon, Plateau pithouse tradition (PPT), 663
Shwayip period, Kettle Falls, Pacific Northwest, 412
Sierra Nevada range, 762–767
Signal Butte site, Plains, *768*, **768–769**
Silicates. *See* chert, flint
Silver Mound, Paleoindian, 769–770
Silvernale phase, Red Wing locality, **709**, 710, 711
Sinagua cultural area, 629, 631
Sinagua tradition, Southwest, 770–772
Sinaikst period, Kettle Falls, Pacific Northwest, 412
Siouan language group, Eastern Woodlands culture, 253
site, archeological term, 772
"site formation process," 455
Skamel culture sequence, Fraser River Canyon, 297
Skeena phase, Kitselas Cayon, 423
Skitak period, Kettle Falls, Pacific Northwest, 412
Slavey-Hare language group, 801
Slawmtehus period, Kettle Falls, Pacific Northwest, 411
Slocan phase, Arrow/Slocan, Plateau, 33
Slocan Valley, Plateau, sequences of, 33–34
small pox:
    Bad River, 45
    Chilcotin Plateau area, 146
    European induced, 351, 394
    Knife River, 428, 429, 430
smelts, 265
Smith, Harlan Ingersoll, 772–773
Smith site, Blackduck pottery, 77
Smithsonian, role of, 271
Smoky Hill phase, Central Plains tradition, 131, **773**
Smoky Hills jasper, 455, 495, 859
Snails, river, **720–721**, 807
Snaketown site, Hohokam, 622, **773–774**
    rancheria at, 701
Snowflake pottery, 286

tools, sites/traditions (continued):

turkey (continued):
    Frontenac Island, 304
    Grasshopper pueblo, 323
    Kansas City Hopewell, 407
    pen, Tularosa Cave, 849
    Point of Pines Ruin, Mogollon, 671
    Sunwatch Village, Fort Ancient, 385
    Uncas Complex, Southern Plains, 856
    Woodland tradition, Early, 229
Turkey Foot Ridge, Pine Lawn branch, Mogollon, 645
Turner Farm site, Red Paint culture, 706, 707
Turner site, Ohio Hopewell, 853–854
turquoise:
    Casas Grandes, 122
    Pratt complex, 681
Tuscon Basin Red-on-buff pottery, 622
Tutchone Athapaskans, ancestors of, 10
Tuwiuca phase. See Pueblo III stage, Little Colorado
Tyuonyi, Frijoles Canyon, Anasazi, 48, 49

U

Uhle, Max, 855
Uncas complex, Southern Plains, 855–856
Under Mount St. Elias, 439
UNESCO World Heritage Site, Head-Smashed-In Buffalo Jump (HSI), 351
ungulates, Plateau fauna, 666–667
uniface, 856
unit houses, Anasazi culture, 425, 444
University Indian Ruin, 856–857
University of Kentucky Reports in Anthropology and Archaeology, 876
Upper Canark, Plains Village, 20, 857–858
Upper Mississippi culture, 858
Upper Purgatoire complex, 858–859
Upper Republican phase, Central Plains, 131, 859–860
Upper Sonoran Agricultural complex, 860–861
Utah Lake, 246, 247, 249
Utz site, 647
uxorilocal residence groups, Broken K Pueblo, 94

V

Vail site, Maine, 863–864
Valley-variant sites, High Plains, 864
Vallican phase, Arrow/Slocan, British Columbia, 33
Ventana Cave, Southwest, 622, 864–865
Vesterbygd settlement, Inugsuk culture, 391
Vickers focus, Canada, 865–867, 866
Village of the Great Kivas, Zuni Pueblo, 155
"Vinette I," type, 136
Virgin region, Anasazi, 867–868
vision pits, Blackduck culture, 77–78
Vulcan phase, Onesta, American Bottom, 703

W

Wakashan language group, 633

Walker Road site, Alaska, 206, 559, 560, 869–870
Wallace, William J., 870–871
Walling site, Copena complex, 175
Walls Engraved ceramics, Chucalissa site, 152
wall-trench structures, Eastern Woodland, 870. See also fortifications
Wanikan (wild-rice gatherer), Sandy Lake, 746
"war arrows," Punuk culture, 694
warfare, Pacific period, California, 108
Warren Wilson site, Appalachia, 871–872
Wasatch Range, Great Basin, 326
Wascana ware, 872–873
Washington state, Ocean Coast sequence, 873–874
Washita River phase, Southern Plains, 874–875
water control system, Chaco branch, Anasazi, 139
watercraft:
    Brand site, Dalton period, Arkansas, 92
    California, 875–876
      Northwestern, 588
    Dorset culture, 216
    Lake Forest Archaic, 441
    Lamoka Lake site, Mast Forest, 442
    Locarno Beach, 468
    Navy Board Inlet, 594
    Northern Plano culture, 574
    Northwest Coast cultural area, 575, 578
    Okanagan Valley, 605
    Old Bering Sea/Okvik culture, 605
    Punuk culture, 694
    Santa Barbara region, 726
    Saqqaq site/tradition, Arctic, 747
waterfowl, Great Basin, 246
water-leaching technique, acorns, 5
wattle-and-daub:
    Caborn-Welborn phase, Mississippi, 99
    Central Plains tradition, 131
    Custer phase, 191
    Dallas culture, 193
    Nebraska phase, Central Plains, 556–557
    St. Helena phase, Central Plains, 805
    Sunwatch Village, Fort Ancient, 385
    Uncas Complex, Southern Plains, 856
    Upper Republican phase, Central Plains, 859
    Washita River phase, Southern Plains, 875
Webb, William Snyder, 876, 876–877
Wedel, Waldo R., 877
Weeden Island culture:
    Gulf Coastal Plain, 877–879
    McKeithen, Gulf Coastal Plain, 507, 878
weirs. See fish weirs
West Coast, cultural type, Canada, 879, 880, 881
West Shelter, Modoc Rock Shelter, 535
Western Fluted point tradition:
    Canadian Plateau, Early period, 227, 228
    Eastern California, 240
Western Great Basin, Archaic, 328–330
Western Plains:
    Archaic:
      Albion phases, 11–12, 550, 884
      Front Range phase, 303–304, 884
    Early Archaic regional variant, 550, 884